ECCLESIASTICAL LAW

ECCLESIASTICAL LAW

THIRD EDITION

MARK HILL

Of the Middle Temple, Barrister
Honorary Professor of Law and Fellow of the Centre for
Law and Religion, Cardiff University
Chancellor of the Diocese of Chichester and the Diocese in Europe
One of Her Majesty's Recorders assigned to the Midland Circuit
Sometime Senior Visitor, Emmanuel College, Cambridge

OXFORD
UNIVERSITY PRESS

Great Clarendon Street, Oxford OX2 6DP

Oxford University Press is a department of the University of Oxford.
It furthers the University's objective of excellence in research, scholarship,
and education by publishing worldwide in

Oxford New York

Auckland Cape Town Dar es Salaam Hong Kong Karachi
Kuala Lumpur Madrid Melbourne Mexico City Nairobi
New Delhi Shanghai Taipei Toronto

With offices in

Argentina Austria Brazil Chile Czech Republic France Greece
Guatemala Hungary Italy Japan Poland Portugal Singapore
South Korea Switzerland Thailand Turkey Ukraine Vietnam

Oxford is a registered trade mark of Oxford University Press
in the UK and in certain other countries

Published in the United States
by Oxford University Press Inc., New York

© Mark Hill, 2007

The moral rights of the author have been asserted

Crown copyright material is reproduced under Class Licence
Number C01P0000148 with the permission of OPSI
and the Queen's Printer for Scotland

Database right Oxford University Press (maker)

First published 2007

All rights reserved. No part of this publication may be reproduced,
stored in a retrieval system, or transmitted, in any form or by any means,
without the prior permission in writing of Oxford University Press,
or as expressly permitted by law, or under terms agreed with the appropriate
reprographics rights organization. Enquiries concerning reproduction
outside the scope of the above should be sent to the Rights Department,
Oxford University Press, at the address above

You must not circulate this book in any other binding or cover
and you must impose the same condition on any acquirer

British Library Cataloguing in Publication Data

Data available

Library of Congress Cataloging in Publication Data

Hill, Mark, 1965-
  Ecclesiastical law / Mark Hill. -- 3rd ed.
    p. cm.
  Includes bibliographical references and index.
  ISBN-13: 978-0-19-921712-0 (alk. paper) 1. Ecclesiastical law--Great Britain.
2. Church and state--Great Britain. 3. Church of England--Government. 4. Canon law. I.
Title.
  KD8642.H55 2007
  262.9'8342--dc22
                                                                          2007028540

Typeset by Cepha Imaging Private Ltd., Bangalore, India
Printed in Great Britain
on acid-free paper by
Biddles Ltd., King's Lynn, Norfolk

ISBN 978–0–19–921712–0

1 3 5 7 9 10 8 6 4 2

PREFACE

'The Church of England is not itself a legal entity'.[1]

Few anticipated that the juridical status of the established church in England would occupy the time of the Judicial Committee of the House of Lords in the opening years of the twenty-first century just as the Human Rights Act 1998 was beginning to take effect and as the Law Lords were preparing to vacate the Palace of Westminster in favour of a Supreme Court to be carved out of Middlesex Guildhall on the unfashionable side of Parliament Square. But so said the late, and much missed, Lord Hobhouse of Woodborough in his speech in the case of *Aston Cantlow PCC v Wallbank*. He continued by clarifying that the 'legal entities' are the various office-holders and bodies which form part of the Church of England's component structures. It is with the law which both establishes and regulates those individuals and institutions that this text is concerned, now matured into the adulthood of a third edition after the infancy and adolescence, respectively, of those which preceded it.

Much has happened in the seven years since the second edition was written. The Churchwardens Measure 2001, anticipated in the materials and presaged in the text, did indeed receive royal assent and has duly effected changes to the method of appointment of churchwardens and their length of service. The Synodical Government (Amendment) Measure 2003 which came into force on 1 January 2004, brought into effect certain recommendations of the Bridge Report, 'Synodical Government in the Church of England'. In consequence, the General Synod convened in 2005 in a slimmed-down form, the better to transact both its deliberative and its legislative business. As ever, the Church Representation Rules have been subject to a number of amendments. The bedding down of the recently created Archbishops' Council has continued with some minor changes being effected by the National Institutions of the Church of England (Transfer of Functions) Order 2007.

Readers familiar with the second edition of this work should find it easy to navigate its composition and layout, which are largely unchanged. However, in recognition of the major changes wrought by the Clergy Discipline Measure 2003,

---

[1] *Aston Cantlow and Wilmcote with Billesley Parochial Church Council v Wallbank* [2004] 1 AC 546, [2003] 3 All ER 1213 HL, per Lord Hobhouse of Woodborough at para 84.

which introduced an entirely new procedure for the discipline of clergy, Chapter 6 has been retitled and written afresh.[2] The Measure created new offices—the President and Deputy President of Tribunals, Registrars of Tribunals, and a Designated Officer—together with an over-arching Clergy Discipline Commission serving both the Northern and Southern Provinces. Henceforward, proceedings concerning clerical misconduct will be adjudicated not in the consistory court but before a disciplinary tribunal, constituted for the diocese in question from personnel drawn from a provincial panel. These new provisions do not apply, however, to offences of doctrine, ritual or ceremonial, and the commentary on the law concerning these matters which remains applicable has been retained.

With the notable exception of the Clergy Discipline Measure 2003, most of the General Synod's legislative output has been in the form of amending measures making a series of modest—though significant—changes to the law of the Church. The Care of Cathedrals (Amendment) Measure 2005 has occasioned rewriting to Chapter 8 and it is anticipated that its provisions will progressively have been brought into force by the time this volume is published. Other changes in the text have resulted from the Church of England (Pensions) Measure 2003, Stipends (Cessation of Special Payments) Measure 2005,[3] Church of England (Miscellaneous Provisions) Measures of 2005 and 2006 respectively, and Pastoral (Amendment) Measure 2006. The latter will now permit the creation of a lease of part of a church, thereby enabling more imaginative use to be made of church buildings as advocated in various quarters including the Report of the Church Heritage Forum, *Building Faith in Our Future* (2004).

Changes to the practice and processes for the appointment of bishops, including those contained in the Vacancy in See (Amendment) Regulations 2003, are reflected in Chapter 4. Although the prospect of the consecration of women bishops has animated discussion and debate, it has yet to produce any change in the law. The ten-year period during which money was payable to priests and deacons leaving the Church of England under the Ordination of Women (Financial Provisions) Measure 1993 has now expired and the Episcopal Ministry Act of Synod, which provides for alternative episcopal oversight during the current period of reception, remains in force despite a degree of lobbying for its rescission.

New secular legislation since the last edition includes the Census (Amendment) Act 2000, which permitted the inclusion in the national census of a question

---

[2] The Measure is supplemented by the Clergy Discipline Rules 2005, the Clergy Discipline (Appeal) Rules 2005, and by a Code of Practice (2005) and written guidance on sentencing.
[3] This had the effect of removing the legal obstacle preventing the appointment of a non-stipendiary minister to a benefice for which a guaranteed annuity was payable under s 1 of the Endowments and Glebe Measure 1976.

Preface

concerning religious affiliation and yielded a surprisingly high level of Christian allegiance. The House of Commons (Removal of Clergy Disqualification) Act 2001 enabled clergy to stand for election to Parliament, whilst the Criminal Justice Act 2003 took away their exemption from jury service by amending the Juries Act 1974. The Civil Partnership Act 2004, and its inter-relationship with both sacramental and secular marriage, is not without controversy, although the House of Bishops in its *Pastoral Statement on Civil Partnerships* (2005) declared entering into a civil partnership as not intrinsically incompatible with holy orders.

The long-awaited *Legal Opinions Concerning the Church of England* saw the light of day in the Spring of 2007 and recourse has been had to this body of learning, produced by the General Synod's Legal Advisory Commission, wherever possible, adopting the abbreviated reference *Legal Opinions* in the text and footnotes for the sake of convenience.

Perhaps unsurprisingly in an increasingly litigious age, the body of case law being produced by the ecclesiastical courts continues to expand. The Ecclesiastical Law Collection at the Middle Temple Library in London maintains a comprehensive series of Consistory and Commissary Court Cases, the majority of which are otherwise unreported. The judgments are also available on a CD-ROM which can be purchased from the Ecclesiastical Law Society.[4] Many of the cases concern exhumation, but the breadth of the subject matter is apparent from the length of Chapter 7, which has been substantially revised in this edition. The selection of cases for inclusion in the Materials section has not been easy. Space is limited and views will differ upon what is of greatest significance. Emphasis has been placed upon the recent and mainstream, with older and peripheral cases being dropped. Three recent judgments of the Court of Arches have been reproduced in full,[5] since they are of wider application both in relation to substantive law and procedure. As was the case in the previous edition of this work, the transcripts of certain unreported decisions have been included[6] where a fuller report may be of interest to practitioners and scholars. Readers may wish to retain the second edition to refer to the transcripts of judgments which have not been reproduced in the Materials for this edition due to the limitations of space.[7]

---

[4] www.ecclawsoc.org.uk/newshop/shop.shtml.

[5] *Re Blagdon Cemetery* [2002] Fam 299; *Re Emmanuel Church Bentley* [2006] Fam 239; *Re Welford Road Cemetery, Leicester* [2007] 2 WLR 506.

[6] *Blake v Associated Newspapers Limited* (July 2003), Gray J, concerning whether issues of doctrine were justiciable in the secular courts, and *Parochial Church Council of Aston Cantlow and Wilmcote with Billesley v Wallbank* (February 2007), Lewison J, on the assessment of quantum in cases concerning chancel repair liability.

[7] Note particularly *Harries v Church Commissioners* (ethical investment); *Brown v Runcie*, *R v Ecclesiastical Committee of Both Houses of Parliament, ex parte the Church Society* and *R v Archbishops of Canterbury and York, ex parte Williamson* (each concerning the status of canons and measures); *Diocese of Southwark v Coker* (employment of clergy); *Gill v Davies* (injunction to

Preface

The rapid evolution of ecclesiastical law has not come to a halt. More change is afoot, but I have fought shy of including a discussion of such changes when the timescale for their implementation is yet to be ascertained and their full effect is somewhat uncertain. Three matters, however, merit mention by way of prefatory comment. The Dioceses, Pastoral and Mission Measure was approved by the General Synod at its February 2007 group of sessions. It is expected to have a smooth passage through the Ecclesiastical Committee and receive the royal assent during 2007. Since it is likely to effect significant changes to the Pastoral Measure 1983 during the lifetime of this edition, the text of the 1983 Measure has not been included in the Materials where the available space is extremely limited. Readers must refer to the second edition of this work for the current text, and for the text of other statutes, measures and statutory instruments, which have not been altered since the second edition but for which room regrettably cannot be found in this volume. However, section 56 of the Pastoral Measure 1983 is reproduced in splendid isolation in its amended form following the Pastoral (Amendment) Measure 2006. This provision is likely to prove important in the community use of churches in the twenty-first century.

The raft of legislative material on clergy conditions of service received widespread approval at the February 2007 group of sessions of the General Synod and at the time of writing stands referred to a revision committee. What is currently proposed in the draft Ecclesiastical Offices (Terms of Service) Measure and related Regulations will have an effect upon the performance of and expectations for clergy. This may also need to be considered in the light of the possible revisiting of the nature of clerical office holders hinted at in a recent House of Lords' decision.[8] The employment status of clergy is beyond the scope of this book and reference should be made to specialists labour law texts for a full treatment of this emerging area of law.

At the same group of sessions a less encouraging fate befell the draft Marriage Measure. This was to make provision for broadening the categories of persons entitled to marry in their parish church. For a variety of reasons the General Synod did not feel able to approve the revised draft and accordingly took the unusual step of referring it to a further revision committee. Whether, and if so in what form, this legislation will come into force is a matter for speculation.

---

prevent irregular ordination); *Cheesman v Church Commissioners* (reason for pastoral reorganisation); *R v Bishop of Stafford ex parte Owen* (renewal of licence for team rector); *Re St Luke the Evangelist, Maidstone* and *Re St Mary the Virgin, Sherborne* (both dealing with changes to listed church buildings).

[8] *Percy v Church of Scotland National Board of Mission* [2006] 2 AC 28. See also the decision of the Employment Appeal Tribunal in *New Testament Church of God v Stewart* [2007] IRLR 178.

Broad matters of religious liberty and human rights have occupied the secular courts since the coming into force of the Human Rights Act 1998. These have included religious dress,[9] the chastising of children,[10] forced marriage,[11] religious observance in the workplace,[12] and the exemption of religious organizations from anti-discrimination legislation.[13] These matters are discussed briefly in the text where they arise, but readers must look elsewhere for a full treatment of the growing body of case law under Article 9 of the European Convention on Human Rights.[14]

The updating of an authoritative text such as this can be lonely, tedious and time-consuming. It has been rendered more pleasurable by two factors. First and foremost has been the generous provision of accommodation and research facilities at Emmanuel College, Cambridge. I am grateful to the Governing Body for electing me as Senior Visitor for the Lent term of 2007 and for welcoming me so warmly into the corporate life of both college and chapel during my stay. I am particularly grateful to the Dean, the Reverend Jeremy Caddick; the Master, Lord Wilson of Dinton; and the other Fellows for their support and encouragement. High table dining has increased my knowledge and understanding of cabinet government, eighteenth-century number theory and Puccini's lesser known opera scores, but little of this newly acquired learning has found its way into the text which follows.

Secondly, I am grateful to a number of friends, associates and colleagues who have commented upon various drafts of the manuscript or the compilation of materials. I want, in particular, to thank John Baker, Christine Barnett, Gerald Bray, Rupert Bursell, Sheila Cameron, Frank Cranmer, Norman Doe, Judith Egar, Richard Helmholz, Adrian Iles, Corinne Iten, Sue Jones, Christopher Lowson, Robert Ombres, John Rees, Russell Sandberg, Stephen Slack, Ingrid Slaughter and Robert Wellen. Peter Moore, once again, has applied his critical mind to the entire manuscript, checking references, eliminating infelicities and inconsistencies, and compiling the tables and index. His contribution has been

---

[9] *R (on the application of Begum) v Headteacher and Governors of Denbigh High School* [2006] 2 WLR 719.
[10] *R v Secretary of State for Education and Employment and others ex parte Williamson* [2005] 2 AC 246, HL.
[11] *R (Baiai) v Secretary of State for the Home Department* [2007] 1 WLR 693, Silber J, affirmed by the Court of Appeal on 23 May 2007, [2007] EWCA Civ 478, Waller, Buxton and Lloyd LJJ.
[12] *Copsey v WWB Devon Clays Ltd* [2005] ICR 1789, CA.
[13] *R (on the application of Amicus) v Secretary of State for Trade and Industry* [2004] EWHC 860, Richards J.
[14] M Hill (ed), *Religious Liberty and Human Rights* (Cardiff: University of Wales Press, 2002); R Ahdar and I Leigh, *Religious Freedom in the Liberal State* (Oxford: Oxford University Press 2005); S Knights, *Freedom of Religion, Minorities and the Law* (Oxford: Oxford University Press, 2007); M Hill, 'The Permissible Scope of Legal Limitations on the Freedom of Religion or Belief in the United Kingdom' (2005) 19(2) Emory International Law Review 1129; and M Hill and R Sandberg, 'Is Nothing Sacred? Clashing Symbols in a Secular World' (2007) *Public Law* 488.

immeasurable, as has been the input and enthusiastic support of James Mannion, to whom I am greatly indebted. I should also like to thank Oxford University Press for its professional commitment to this text and to express my gratitude to Benjamin Roberts, Sandra Sinden and Roxanne Selby in particular.

For such errors and omissions as remain I alone am responsible, although I propose taking all reasonable steps to pass the buck whenever possible.

The law is stated as at 1 May 2007.

NMH
3 Pump Court
Temple
London EC4

Feast of St Philip and St James, 2007

ACKNOWLEDGEMENTS

Copyright in the Canons of the Church of England vests in the Archbishops' Council. They are reproduced with permission and are available online at www.cofe.anglican.org/about/churchlawlegis/canons/whole.pdf.

Copyright in the judgments in the following cases vests in the Incorporated Society of Law Reporting for England and Wales. The extracts are reproduced with permission.

> *Re Blagdon Cemetery* [2002] Fam 299;
> *Re Emmanuel Church Bentley* [2006] Fam 239;
> *Re Welford Road Cemetery, Leicester* [2007] 2 WLR 506.

All other extracts from judgments are taken from official transcripts and are Crown copyright. The judgments are unapproved.

The collation of the Acts of Parliament, Measures and Statutory Instruments was facilitated from the statutory database of LEXIS NEXIS Butterworths (a division of Reed Elsevier (UK) Limited).

The *Legal Opinions Concerning the Church of England* (8th edn, Church House Publishing, London, 2007) were published in their updated form in the Spring of 2007. They are produced by the Legal Advisory Commission of the Church of England, established by the General Synod of the Church of England through the Archbishops' Council. For convenience they are referred to in the text and footnotes by the abbreviated reference *Legal Opinions*.

CONTENTS—SUMMARY

Table of Cases	xxv
Table of Canons	xxxv
Table of Statutes and Measures	xxxix
Table of Rules, Regulations and Other Instruments	lvii
1. The Nature and Sources of Ecclesiastical Law	1
2. The Constitution of the Church of England	33
3. The Parish	63
4. Clergy	115
5. Services and Worship	151
6. Clergy Discipline	181
7. Faculty Jurisdiction	219
8. Cathedrals	281
Materials	
The Canons of the Church of England	311
Statutes and Measures	373
Statutory Instruments	543
Church Representation Rules	617
Cases	657
Index	707

CONTENTS

Table of Cases   xxv
Table of Canons   xxxv
Table of Statutes and Measures   xxxix
Table of Rules, Regulations and Other Instruments   lvii

1. The Nature and Sources of Ecclesiastical Law

Introduction	1.01
Purpose	1.03
Historical development	1.06
The early Church	1.07
Medieval Church law	1.08
The Reformation	1.12
Post-Reformation	1.16
Establishment	1.19
Acts, Measures and Canons	1.22
Acts of Parliament	1.23
Measures	1.25
The Human Rights Act 1998	1.26
Canons	1.28
Questioning the *vires* of draft Measures and of Canons	1.30
Secondary legislation	1.32
Other sources of ecclesiastical law	1.33
Case law and precedent	1.33
Quasi-legislation	1.35
Jus divinum	1.36
Custom	1.38
Jus liturgicum and dispensation	1.40
Religious freedom in secular law	1.42

2. The Constitution of the Church of England

Introduction	2.01
Towards autonomy	2.04

Synodical government	2.10
The Archbishops' Council	2.11
Composition	2.12
Purpose and function	2.13
General Synod	2.15
Composition	2.15
Purpose and function	2.21
Diocesan synods	2.26
Composition	2.26
Purpose and function	2.27
Deanery synods	2.33
Composition	2.34
Purpose and function	2.35
The Church Commissioners	2.38
Church courts and tribunals	2.46
Chancellors	2.47
Vicars-General	2.52
Registrars	2.53
Archdeacons	2.57
Consistory courts	2.58
Appellate courts	2.59
The Court of Faculties	2.61
Judicial review	2.62

3. The Parish

Parish structure	3.01
The electoral roll	3.03
Annual parochial church meeting	3.07
Parochial church councils	3.11
Composition	3.12
District church councils	3.16
Joint parochial church councils	3.18
Team councils	3.19
Group councils	3.20
Functions of the PCC	3.21
Churchwardens	3.32
Qualifications	3.33
Choosing churchwardens	3.35

Admission and term of office	3.40
Resignation and vacation of office	3.42
Custom	3.44
Episcopal powers	3.46
Misconduct	3.47
Powers and duties	3.48
Deputy churchwardens	3.57
Other lay officers	3.59
Sidesmen	3.60
Parish clerks and sextons	3.61
Treasurers	3.63
PCC secretaries	3.64
Organists	3.65
Readers	3.67
Deaconesses	3.71
Lay workers	3.72
Religious communities	3.75
Parochial property	3.76
Chancel repair	3.78
Quinquennial inspection	3.82
Parochial finance	3.84
Pastoral schemes and orders	3.86
Sharing of church buildings	3.95
Ecumenical relations	3.99
Non-parochial units	3.103
Peculiars	3.104
Private chapels	3.105
Other chapels	3.106
Guild churches	3.108

4. Clergy

Introduction	4.01
Selection and training	4.04
Ordination	4.06
Functions and duties	4.11
Deacons	4.11
Priests	4.13
Beneficed clergy	4.17
Patronage	4.18

Suspension of presentation	4.23
Institution, collation and induction	4.27
Unbeneficed clergy	4.29
Assistant curates	4.30
Priests-in-charge	4.32
Revocation of licences	4.33
Permission to officiate	4.36
Visitations	4.37
Retirement and removal	4.38
Vacation of benefices	4.43
Group and team ministries	4.47
Other appointments	4.52
Rural deans	4.53
Archdeacons	4.54
Diocesan bishops	4.56
Suffragan bishops	4.65
Archbishops	4.66

5. Services and Worship

Introduction	5.01
Liturgy	5.02
Regular services	5.09
Baptism	5.12
Confirmation	5.16
Holy communion	5.18
Reservation of the sacrament	5.27
Holy matrimony	5.31
Preliminaries	5.32
Marriage by banns	5.36
Marriage by licence	5.40
Registrar's certificate	5.43
Solemnisation of marriage	5.44
Marriages in chapels	5.48
Further marriage of divorced persons	5.49
Burials and funerals	5.51
Other services	5.57
Daily offices	5.57
Visitation of the sick	5.58

Exorcism	5.59
Special services	5.60
Confession	5.61

6. Clergy Discipline

Introduction	6.01
Institutions and personnel	6.04
Clergy Discipline Commission	6.04
President of tribunals	6.06
Registrar of tribunals	6.07
Provincial panels	6.08
Disciplinary tribunals	6.09
Vicar-General's court	6.10
Designated officer	6.11
Jurisdiction	6.12
Misconduct	6.13
Time limits	6.16
Complainants	6.17
Procedure	6.22
Preliminary scrutiny	6.23
No further action	6.28
Conditional deferment	6.29
Conciliation	6.31
Penalty by consent	6.33
Formal investigation	6.35
Suspension during proceedings	6.37
Conduct of disciplinary tribunals	6.39
Penalties	6.47
Proceedings in secular courts	6.54
Nullification, removal of prohibition and pardon	6.55
Appeals	6.58
Costs and legal aid	6.67
The Archbishops' List	6.69
Offences involving doctrine, ritual or ceremonial	6.73
Investigation	6.74
Hearing and appeals	6.76
Censures	6.77

7. Faculty Jurisdiction

Introduction	7.01
Minor works	7.03
Overriding duty	7.04
The ecclesiastical exemption	7.05
Care of places of worship	7.08
The role of the archdeacon	7.09
Temporary reordering	7.13
Matters of urgency	7.14
Visitations	7.15
Diocesan advisory committees	7.16
National amenity societies	7.18
Formulating proposals	7.19
Seeking advice	7.22
Preliminary advice	7.22
Listed churches	7.23
Formal advice	7.25
DAC certificate	7.32
The petition	7.34
Public notice	7.37
Archdeacon's jurisdiction	7.43
Chancellor's jurisdiction	7.47
Special notice	7.47
Consultation with the Council for the Care of Churches	7.51
Objections	7.53
Unopposed petitions	7.56
Contested proceedings	7.57
Answer to particulars of objection	7.57
Disposal by written representations	7.58
Directions	7.60
Hearing	7.63
Evidence	7.64
Grant of planning permission	7.66
Service of documents	7.67
Burden and standard of proof	7.68
Judgments and orders	7.73
Contempt of court	7.76
Appeals	7.77

Costs	7.79
Emergency and remedial powers	7.83
Particular cases	7.90
Altars	7.91
Churchyards	7.92
Demolition	7.97
Disability Discrimination Act 1995	7.102
Disposal of church property	7.103
Exhumation	7.104
Fonts	7.112
Graves	7.113
Right of burial	7.113
Reservation of gravespace	7.114
Erection of headstone	7.115
Inscriptions	7.116
Libraries	7.117
Licences and leases	7.118
Memorials	7.121
Movables and ornaments	7.123
Pews	7.125
Reordering	7.126
Trees	7.128
Care of places of worship	7.130

8. Cathedrals

Introduction	8.01
Cathedral bodies and personnel	8.05
The Council	8.06
The Chapter	8.09
The College of Canons	8.13
The bishop	8.15
The dean	8.17
Residentiary canons	8.20
Non-residentiary canons	8.25
Other staff	8.26
Cathedral community	8.28
Property and finance	8.29
Ministry	8.32

Care and maintenance	8.35
Fabric advisory committee	8.37
Cathedrals Fabric Commission	8.39
Procedure	8.41
Enforcement	8.49

MATERIALS

The Canons of the Church of England

A. The Church of England	311
B. Divine Service and the Administration of the Sacraments	312
C. Ministers, their Ordination, Function and Charge	335
D. The Order of Deaconesses	349
E. The Lay Officers of the Church	352
F. Things Appertaining to Churches	357
G. The Ecclesiastical Courts	360
H. The Synods of the Church	363
Supplementary Material	369
Proviso to Canon 113 of the Code of 1603	369
Admission of Baptised Children to Holy Communion Regulations 2006	369

Statutes and Measures

Church of England Assembly (Powers) Act 1919	373
Inspection of Churches Measure 1955	375
Parochial Church Councils (Powers) Measure 1956	378
Ecclesiastical Jurisdiction Measure 1963	382
Faculty Jurisdiction Measure 1964	402
Matrimonial Causes Act 1965	405
Synodical Government Measure 1969	405
Sharing of Church Buildings Act 1969	412
Repair of Benefice Buildings Measure 1972	420
Church of England (Worship and Doctrine) Measure 1974	429
Incumbents (Vacation of Benefices) Measure 1977	431

Pastoral Measure 1983	444
Patronage (Benefices) Measure 1986	447
Care of Cathedrals Measure 1990	461
Care of Churches and Ecclesiastical Jurisdiction Measure 1991	477
Priests (Ordination of Women) Measure 1993	493
Care of Cathedrals (Supplementary Provisions) Measure 1994	496
National Institutions Measure 1998	500
Cathedrals Measure 1999	506
Churchwardens Measure 2001	518
Clergy Discipline Measure 2003	524

Statutory Instruments

Patronage (Benefices) Rules 1987	543
Faculty Jurisdiction (Injunctions and Restoration Orders) Rules 1992	546
Faculty Jurisdiction (Appeals) Rules 1998	549
Faculty Jurisdiction Rules 2000	559
Clergy Discipline Rules 2005	577
Clergy Discipline (Appeal) Rules 2005	607

Church Representation Rules

Part I: Church Electoral Roll	617
Part II: Parochial Church Meetings and Councils	620
Part III: Deanery Synods	631
Part IV: Diocesan Synods	634
Part V: House of Laity of General Synod	638
Part VI: Appeals and Disqualifications	643
Part VII: Supplementary and Interpretation	647
Appendix II: General Provisions Relating to Parochial Church Councils	652

Cases

Re Blagdon Cemetery	657
Blake v Associated Newspapers Limited	665
Re Emmanuel Church, Bentley	672
Re Welford Road Cemetery, Leicester	686
Aston Cantlow and Wilmcote with Billesley Parochial Church Council v Wallbank	702

Index   707

TABLE OF CASES

References are to paragraphs in the text, or to page numbers in the Materials.
Cases with bold page numbers are reported in the Materials.
To avoid confusion, —'s in the dedication of a church is omitted, save where the context requires it.

Abdulaziz Cabales and Balkandali v United Kingdom (1985) 7 EHRR 471 .... p 697
All Saints, Beckley, Re (2006) 9 Ecc LJ 241, Chichester Cons Ct 7.107
All Saints, Bradley, Re (1997) 4 Ecc LJ 770, Winchester Cons Ct 7.121
All Saints, Burbage, Re (2007) 14 February (unreported), Salisbury Cons Ct 7.23, 7.126
All Saints, Crondall, Re (2002) 6 Ecc LJ 420, Guildford Cons Ct 7.71
All Saints, Featherstone, Re (1999) 5 Ecc LJ 391, Wakefield Cons Ct 1.34, 7.118
All Saints, Harborough Magna, Re [1992] 1 WLR 1235, [1992] 4 All ER 948,
    Coventry Cons Ct .... 1.34, 7.118; p 673
All Saints, Hordle, Re (2002) 7 Eccd LJ 238, Winchester Cons Ct 7.66
All Saints, Leamington Priors, Re [1963] 2 All ER 1062, [1963] 1 WLR 206,
    Coventry Cons Ct .... p 702
All Saints, Melbourn, Re [1990] 1 WLR 833, [1992] 2 All ER 786,
    Ct of Arches 7.10, 7.68, 7.70, 7.72
All Saints, North Street, Re (1999) 5 Ecc LJ 486, York Cons Ct...................... 7.80
All Saints, Small Heath, Re (1998) 5 Ecc LJ 211, Birmingham Cons Ct. 7.80
Allason v Haines (1995) Times, 25 July, Owen J .... p 671
Allwood (minors), deceased, Re (1999) 5 Ecc LJ 389, Southwark Cons Ct 7.107
Anisminic Ltd v Foreign Compensation Commission [1969] 2 AC 147, [1969]
    1 All ER 208, HL 1.25
Argar v Holdsworth (1758) 2 Lee 515. .... 5.34
Argyll, Duchess of, v Duke of Argyll [1967] Ch 302, [1965] 1 All ER 611 .... 5.62
Aston Cantlow and Wilmcote with Billesley, Warwickshire, PCC v Wallbank
    (2000) 81 P & CR 14, [2000] 2 EGLR 149, (2000) 5 Ecc LJ 494 .... 3.78; p 702
Aston Cantlow and Wilmcote with Billesley, Warwickshire, PCC v Wallbank
    [2001] EWCA Civ 713, [2002] Ch 51, [2001] 3 All ER 393, (2001)
    6 Ecc LJ 172, CA .... 1.19, 3.78, 3.79; p 702
Aston Cantlow and Wilmcote with Billesley, Warwickshire, PCC v Wallbank [2003]
    UKHL 37, [2004] 1 AC 546, [2003] 3 All ER 1213, (2003)
    7 Ecc LJ 364, HL 1.01, 1.19, 1.47, 2.38, 3.01, 3.11, 3.21–3.23,
                                              3.78, 3.81, 5.50, 8.30; p 702
Aston Cantlow and Wilmcote with Billesley, Warwickshire, PCC v Wallbank (2007)
    Times, 21 February. .... 3.80, 8.30; p **702**
Atkins, Re. *See* Church Norton Churchyard, Re
Attorney-General ex rel Bedfordshire County Council v Howard United Reformed
    Church Trustees, Bedford [1976] AC 363, [1975] 2 All ER 337, HL. 7.05
Attorney-General v Dean and Chapter of Ripon Cathedral [1945] 1 Ch 239,
    [1945] 1 All ER 479 .... 1.02
Attorney-General v Wiltshire United Dairies (1921) 37 TLR 884, CA 3.85
Ayuntamiento de Mula v Spain, Reports of Judgments and Decisions 2001-I, 531 .... 3.22
Azmi v Kirklees Metropolitan Council, ET, Case 1801450/06 (6 October 2006),
    affd EAT, Appeal No UKEAT/0009/07/MAA (30 March 2007) 1.50

Banister v Thompson [1908] P 362, Ct of Arches 5.34
Barthorpe v Exeter Diocesan Board of Finance [1979] ICR 900, EAT 3.70
Beamish v Beamish (1861) 9 HL Cas 274 .... 5.44
Bideford Parish, Re [1900] P 314, Ct of Arches 7.94
Bishop of Exeter v Marshall (1868) LR 3 HL 17 .... 1.39
Bishopwearmouth, Rector and Churchwardens of v Adey. *See* St Michael and All Angels, Bishopwearmouth, Re
Blackburn v Attorney-General [1971] 1 WLR 1037, [1971] 2 All ER 1380, CA 1.36
Blagdon Cemetery, Re [2002] Fam 299, [2002] 4 All ER 482, (2002) 6 Ecc LJ 420,
  Ct of Arches .... 1.03, 1.33, 1.34, 3.76, 5.01, 7.106, 7.107; p **657**, 688
Blake v Associated Newspapers Ltd [2003] EWHC 1960, (2003)
  7 Ecc LJ 369, Gray J .... 1.43, 5.01; p **665**
Blake v Director of Public Prosecutions [1993] Crim LR 586, DC 1.37
Bland v Archdeacon of Cheltenham [1972] Fam 157, [1972] 1 All ER 1012,
  Ct of Arches 1.35, 5.01, 5.12, 6.13, 6.15, 6.77
Bow Spring (Owners) v Manzanillo II (Owners) (Practice Note) [2005] 1 WLR 144 ...... p 685
Brightlingsea Churchyard, Re (2004) 8 Ecc LJ 233, Chelmsford Cons Ct 5.51, 7.95
Brown v Bishop of Carlisle (2003) 7 Ecc LJ 239, Archbishop of York 4.34
Brown v Cotterill (1934) 51 TLR 21 .... p 692
Brown v Runcie (1990) Times, 26 June 1.31, 2.24, 2.25, 5.04
Brown v Runcie (1991) Times, 20 February, CA 1.28, 1.29, 1.31, 2.24, 2.25, 5.01, 5.04
Burridge v Tyler [1992] 1 All ER 437, Ct of Arches 6.09
Buttes Gas and Oil Co v Hammer [1982] AC 888, [1983] 3 All ER 616, HL .... p 671
Byron Memorial, St Mary Magdalene, Hucknall, Re (1996) 4 Ecc LJ 767,
  Southwell Cons Ct 7.116

Caister-on-Sea Parish, Re [1958] 1 WLR 309, *sub nom* Norfolk County Council v
  Knights and Caister-on-Sea Joint Burial Committee [1958] 1 All ER 394,
  Norwich Cons Ct 7.92
Calvert v Gardiner [2002] EWHC 1394 (QB), (2002) 7 Ecc LJ 99 .... 1.29, 3.51, 4.35, 4.49
Capel St Mary, Suffolk, Rector and Churchwardens v Packard [1927] P 289,
  Ct of Arches .... 5.61; p 678
Cheesman v Church Comrs [2000] 1 AC 19, [1999] 3 WLR 630, (1999) Times,
  18 March, 5 Ecc LJ 305, PC 3.86, 3.88, 3.92, 4.46
Chipchase v Chipchase [1939] P 391, [1939] 3 All ER 895 .... 5.38
Christ Church, Alsager, Re [1999] Fam 142, [1999] 1 All ER 117,
  Ch Ct of York .... 1.03, 1.34, 7.78, 7.105, 7.107; pp 659–663
Christ Church, Chislehurst, Re [1973] 1 WLR 1317, [1974] 1 All ER 146,
  Rochester Cons Ct .... 7.68; p 678
Christ Church, Timperley, Re (2004) 7 Ecc LJ 496, Chester Cons Ct 7.115
Christ Church, Waltham Cross, Re (2001) 6 Ecc LJ 290, St Albans Cons Ct 7.124
Christ Church, Weelock, Re (1999) 5 Ecc LJ 388, Chester Cons Ct 7.96
Christchurch, Sparkbook, Re (2005) 8 Ecc LJ 493, Birmingham Cons Ct 7.101
Christchurch, Wheelock, Re (1996) 4 Ecc LJ 766, Chester Cons Ct 7.115
Church Norton Churchyard, Re [1989] Fam 37, *sub nom* Re Atkins [1989]
  1 All ER 14, Chichester Cons Ct .... p 661
Clifton v Ridsdale (1876) 1 PD 316, Ct of Arches 1.39
Coekin v Bishop of Southwark (2006) 9 Ecc LJ 145, Archbishop of Canterbury 4.09, 4.34
Coleford Cemetery, Re [1984] 1 WLR 1369, Bath and Wells Cons Ct 7.118
Collard's Will Trusts, Re [1961] Ch 293, [1961] 1 All ER 821 .... 3.04
Cooper v Dodd (1850) 7 Notes of Cases 514 .... 1.17
Crawley Green Road Cemetery, Luton, Re [2001] Fam 308, (2000) 6 Ecc LJ 168,
  St Albans Cons Ct .... 2.62, 7.111; p 663

Davies v Presbyterian Church of Wales [1986] ICR 280, [1986] 1 All ER 705, HL 1.44
Dilhorne Churchyard, Re (2000) 6 Ecc LJ 53, Lichfield Cons Ct 7.114
Dilworth v Lovat Highland Estates Ltd and Trustees for St Benedict's Abbey (1999) 1.44
Diocese of Southwark Election Appeal (December 1995) 2.18
Diocese of Southwark Election Appeal (February 1996) 2.18
Diocese of Southwark v Coker [1998] ICR 140, CA 4.31, 4.42
Dodleston Churchyard, Re. *See* St Mary, Dodleston Churchyard, Re
Dödsbo v Sweden (Application 61564/00), 17 January 2006 (2006)
    8 Ecc LJ 496, E Ct HR 2.62, 7.111
Dorchester Abbey, Re (2002) 7 Ecc LJ 105, Oxford Cons Ct. 7.71, 7.102
Douglas v Hello! Ltd [2001] QB 967, [2001] 2 All ER 289, CA 1.47
Dupuis v Parishioners of Ogbourne St George [1941] P 119, Ct of Arches. 7.121
Durrington Cemetery, Re [2001] Fam 33, (2000) 6 Ecc LJ 80, Chichester
    Cons Ct . . . . 2.62, 7.107, 7.111; p 663

Elphick v Church Commissioners [1974] AC 562, PC 3.92
Emmanuel Church, Bentley, Re [2006] Fam 39, Ct of Arches 7.36, 7.37, 7.55,
                                                                                                                                        7.58, 7.119; p **672**
Emmanuel, Northwood, Re (1998) 5 Ecc LJ 213, London Cons Ct 7.20
Escot Church, Re [1979] Fam 125, Exeter Cons Ct. 7.83
Exeter (Bishop of) v Marshall. *See* Bishop of Exeter v Marshall

Forbes v Eden (1867) LR 1 Sc & Div 568, HL 1.44

Gardiner, Re Jean, deceased (2003) 7 Ecc LJ 493, Carlisle Cons Ct 7.107
Gateshead Metropolitan Borough Council v Secretary of State for the Environment
    [1994] 1 PLR 85, CA . . . . p 682
General Assembly of the Free Church of Scotland v Lord Overtoun, Macalister v
    Young [1904] AC 515, 7 F (HL) 1, 12 SLT 297, HL. . . . . p 668
Gill v Davies (1997) 5 Ecc LJ 131 . . . . 1.44, 4.09, 5.62
Gilmour v Coats [1949] AC 426, [1949] 1 All ER 848, HL. 1.43
Gorham v Bishop of Exeter (1850) 7 Notes of Cases 413, (1850) Moore's Special
    Report 462, PC 5.01
Grosvenor Chapel, South Audley Street, Re (1913) 29 TLR 286, London Cons Ct 1.33

H, Re (Child's Name: First Name) [2002] 1 FLR 973, CA 5.17
H, Re (Minors) (Sexual Abuse: Standard of Proof) [1966] AC 563, [1966]
    1 All ER 1, HL. 6.45
Hadmor Productions Ltd v Hamilton [1983] 1 AC 191, [1982] 1 All ER 1042, HL . . . . . . p 695
Hamilton and Greer v Hencke (1995) 21 July (unreported), May J . . . . p 671
Hargreaves v Church Commissioners [1983] 2 AC 457, [1983] 3 All ER 17, PC. 3.92
Harries v Bishop of Chester (2005) 9 Ecc LJ 141, Archbishop of York 4.34
Harries v Church Commissioners for England [1992] 1 WLR 1241, [1993]
    2 All ER 300. . . . . 1.36, 2.45
Holy Cross, Greenford Magna, Re (2005) 8 Ecc LJ 378, London Cons Ct. 7.115
Holy Cross, Pershore, Re [2002] Fam 1, (2001) 6 Ecc LJ 86,
    Worcester Cons Ct 7.17, 7.71
Holy Monasteries v Greece (1995) 20 EHRR 1. . . . . 3.22
Holy Trinity, Bosham, Re [2004] Fam 125, [2004] 2 All ER 820, (2003)
    7 Ecc LJ 494, Chichester Cons Ct. 7.10, 7.81, 7.108, 7.110
Holy Trinity Church, Idle, Re (2006) 9 Ecc LJ 245, Bradford Cons Ct 7.119
Holy Trinity Churchyard, Freckleton, Re [1994] 1 WLR 1588, Blackburn Cons Ct 7.116
Holy Trinity, Eckington, Re (1999) 5 Ecc LJ 489, Worcester Cons Ct 7.112
Holy Trinity, Freckleton, Re (No 2) (1995) 3 Ecc LJ 429, Blackburn Cons Ct 7.116

Holy Trinity, Seghill, Re (2000) 6 Ecc LJ 85, Newcastle Cons Ct 7.116
Hutchins v Denziloe and Loveland (1792) 1 Hag Con 170 . . . . 3.52

Ivory v Dean and Chapter of St Paul's Cathedral (1995) 6 November,
    Industrial Trib (unreported) 3.62

J, Re (Specific Issue Orders: Muslim Upbringing and Circumcision) [1999]
    2 FLR 678 . . . . 5.12

Kemp v Wickes (1809) 3 Phillim 264 . . . . 1.22, 5.13
Keynsham Cemetery, Re [2003] 1 WLR 66, (2002) 7 Ecc LJ 103, Bath and
    Wells Cons Ct . . . . 7.95; p 689, 691, 692, 694, 698, 699
Keynsham Cemetery, Re (No 2) (2003) 7 Ecc LJ 492, Bath and Wells Cons Ct 7.95
Kingston Cemetery, Re (2000) 19 CCCC No 24, Southwark Cons Ct . . . . p 661

Lambeth Cemetery, Re, Re Streatham Park Cemetery (2002) 7 Ecc LJ 237, Southwark
    Cons Ct 7.107
Lapford (Devon) Parish Church, Re [1955] P 205, [1954] 3 All ER 484,
    CA 1.34, 1.41, 5.07, 5.27, 5.28
Lee, Re Edwards Charles, deceased (1995) 4 Ecc LJ 763, Sodor and Man Cons Ct 7.116
Locabail (UK) Ltd v Bayfield Properties Ltd [2000] QB 451, [2000]
    1 All ER 65, CA 4.45
Locock, deceased, Re. See St Nicholas, Sevenoaks, Re
Lydbrook Parochial Church Council v Forest of Dean District Council (2003)
    7 Ecc LJ 494, County Ct. 7.95

Mackonochie v Lord Penzance (1881) 6 App Cas 424, HL 1.15
Macmanaway, Re, [1951] AC 161, PC 4.14
Mandla v Dowell Lee [1983] 2 AC 548, [1983] 1 All ER 1062, HL. . . . . p 697
Mangotsfield Cemetery, Re (2005), Times, 26 April, (2005) 8 Ecc LJ 237,
    Bristol Cons Ct. 7.107
Manoussakis v Greece (1997) 23 EHRR 387 . . . . 1.46; p 670
Marshall v Graham [1907] 2 KB 112, DC 1.19
Metropolitan Church of Bessarabia v Moldova (2002) 35 EHRR 306 . . . . 1.46
Middleton v Crofts (1736) 2 Atk 650 . . . . 5.40
Millar and Simes v Palmer and Killby (1837) 1 Curt 540. . . . . 3.77
Miresse deceased, Re (2003) 7 Ecc LJ 368, Southwark Cons Ct 7.107
Morley Borough Council v St Mary the Virgin, Woodkirk (Vicar and
    Church-wardens). See St Mary the Virgin, Woodkirk, Re
Moysey v Hillcoat (1828) 2 Hag Ecc 30, Ct of Arches 3.55

Neary v Dean of Westminster (1998) 5 Ecc LJ 303 . . . . 3.65
New Testament Church of God v Stewart [2007] IRLR 178, (2006)
    9 Ecc LJ 239, EAT 4.42
Newport Borough Council v Secretary of State for Wales [1998] Env LR 178 . . . . p 682
Nickalls v Briscoe [1892] P 269, Ct of Arches . . . . p 682
Norfolk County Council v Knights and Caister-on-Sea Joint Burial Committee.
    See Caister-on-Sea Parish, Re
North Wingfield, Re (2002) 7 Ecc LJ 238, Derby Cons Ct 7.115
Northwaite v Bennett (1834) 2 Cr & M 316. . . . . 3.77

Oppenheimer v Cattermole [1976] AC 249, [1975] 1 All ER 538, HL 1.36
Otto-Preminger-Institut v Austria (1995) 19 EHRR 34, E Com HR. . . . . p 670

P, Re (Section 91(14) Guidelines) (Residence and Religious Heritage) [1999]
   2 FLR 573 .... 5.12
Peek v Trower (1881) 7 PD 21, Ct of Arches .... p 674
Pell v Addison (1860) 2 F & F 291 .... 3.80; p 704
Percy (AP) v Board of National Mission of the Church of Scotland [2006]
   2 AC 28, [2006] 4 All ER 1354, HL 4.42
Plaxtol Churchyard, Re (1999) 5 Ecc LJ 306, Rochester Cons Ct 7.116
Prebble v Television New Zealand Ltd [1995] 1 AC 321, [1994]
   3 All ER 407, PC .... p 669, 671
Prussner v Germany (1986) 8 EHRR 79 .... 5.12

R v Archbishop of Canterbury [1902] 2 KB 503 .... 1.14
R v Archbishop of Canterbury, ex parte Williamson (Porvoo Declaration) (1996)
   15 March (unreported) 1.30
R v Archbishops of Canterbury and York, ex parte Williamson (1994) Times,
   9 March, CA .... 1.25, 2.05; p 668
R v Bishop of Bristol, ex parte Williamson (1994) 25 March (unreported) 3.50, 4.08, 5.45
R v Bishop of Sarum [1916] 1 KB 466 .... 3.47
R v Bishop of Southwark, ex parte the PCC and Churchwardens of St Luke,
   Kingston (1995) 13 November (unreported) 4.23
R v Bishop of Stafford, ex parte Owen (2000) 6 Ecc LJ 83, CA 1.35, 4.39, 4.49
R v Bishopwearmouth Burial Board (1879) 5 QBD 67 .... 7.95
R v Chancellor of the Chichester Consistory Court, ex parte News Group
   Newspapers [1992] COD 48 .... 2.62
R v Chancellor of St Edmundsbury and Ipswich Diocese, ex parte White [1948]
   1 KB 195, [1947] 2 All ER 170, CA 2.62
R v Chief Rabbi of the United Hebrew Congregations of Great Britain and the
   Commonwealth, ex parte Wachmann [1992] 1 WLR 1036, [1993]
   2 All ER 249 .... 1.43; p 668
R v Dibdin [1910] P 57, CA 5.26
R v Ecclesiastical Committee of Both Houses of Parliament, ex parte
   The Church Society (1993) 22 October, CA 5.01
R v Ecclesiastical Committee of Both Houses of Parliament, ex parte
   The Church Society (1994) 6 Admin LR 670, (1993) Times,
   4 November, CA 1.25, 1.30, 1.44, 2.02, 2.05
R v Editor, Printers and Publishers of the Daily Herald, ex parte Bishop
   of Norwich [1932] 2 KB 402 .... 7.76
R v Exeter Consistory Court, ex parte Cornish (1998) 5 Ecc LJ 212, CA 2.62
R v H M Treasury, ex parte Smedley [1985] QB 657, [1985] 1 All ER 589, CA 1.30
R v Imam of Bury Park Jame Masjid, Luton, ex parte Sulaiman Ali [1992] COD 132,
   Independent 13 September 1991 .... p 668
R v Imam of Bury Park Jame Masjid, Luton, ex parte Sulaiman Ali [1994]
   COD 142, Times, 12 May 1993, CA .... p 668
R v Legislative Committee of the Church Assembly, ex parte Haynes Smith
   [1928] 1 KB 411, DC 1.25
R v Provincial Court of the Church in Wales, ex parte Williams (1998)
   5 Ecc LJ 217 .... 1.43, 2.50, 2.62
R v Rice (1697) 1 Ld Raym 138 .... 3.47
R v Secretary of State for the Home Department, ex parte Bentley [1994] QB 349,
   [1993] 4 All ER 442, DC 6.80
R v Secretary of State for Transport, ex parte Factortame Ltd (No 2) [1991] 1 AC 603,
   [1991] 1 All ER 70, ECJ and HL 1.25
R v Sharpe (1857) Dears & B 160 .... 7.104

R (Begum) v Headteacher and Governors of Denbigh High School [2004] EWHC
    1389 (Admin), [2004] All ER (D) 108, (2004) 8 Ecc LJ 113, Admin Ct 1.49
R (Begum) v Headteacher and Governors of Denbigh High School [2005] EWCA
    Civ 199, [2005] 2 All ER 396, (2005) 8 Ecc LJ 239, CA 1.49
R (Begum) v Headteacher and Governors of Denbigh High School [2007] 1 AC 100,
    [2006] 2 All ER 487, HL 1.49
R (Gibbs) v Bishop of Manchester [2007] EWHC 480, [2007] All ER (D) 256,
    Admin Ct. 3.74, 4.35
R (London Borough of Hackney) v Rottenberg [2007] EWHC 166 (Admin) 3.51
R (Williamson) v Secretary of State for Education and Employment [2002]
    1 FLR 493 . . . . 1.48
R (Williamson) v Secretary of State for Education and Employment [2003]
    QB 1300, [2003] 1 All ER 385, CA 1.48
R (Williamson) v Secretary of State for Education and Employment [2005]
    2 AC 246, [2005] 2 All ER 1, HL 1.48, 1.50
Representative Body of the Church in Wales v Tithe Redemption Commission
    [1944] AC 228, [1944] 1 All ER 710, HL. 3.81
Ridsdale v Clifton. *See* Clifton v Ridsdale

St Agnes, Toxteth Park, Re [1985] 1 WLR 641, Liverpool Cons Ct 7.01
St Andrew, Heddington, Re [1978] Fam 121, Salisbury Cons Ct. 7.63
St Andrew, North Weald Bassett, Re [1987] 1 WLR 1503, Chelmsford Cons Ct 7.118
St Andrew (Old Church), Hove, Re (2005) 8 Ecc LJ 377, Chichester Cons Ct. 7.107
St Andrew, Thornhaugh, Re [1976] Fam 230, [1976] 1 All ER 154, Peterborough
    Cons Ct 7.96
St Ann, Kew, Re [1977] Fam 12, [1976] 1 All ER 461, Southwark Cons Ct. 7.93
St Augustine, Scissett, Re (2003) 7 Ecc LJ 495, Wakefield Cons Ct 7.126
St Barbara, Earlsdon, Re (2002) 7 Ecc LJ 490, Coventry Cons Ct 7.91
St Barnabas, Dulwich, Re [1994] Fam 124, Southwark Cons Ct 7.97
St Barnabas, Heaton, Re (2004) 8 Ecc LJ 232, Bradford Cons Ct 7.119
St Barnabas, Kensington, Re [1991] Fam 1, [1990] 1 All ER 169, London Cons Ct. . . . 7.112
St Botolph without Aldgate (Vicar and One Churchwarden) v Parishioners of
    St Botolph without Aldgate [1892] P 161, London Cons Ct 7.118
St Catherine, Littleton, Re (2005) 8 Ecc LJ 376, Winchester Cons Ct 7.91
St Christopher, Church Cove, Re (2000) 5 Ecc LJ 492, Guildford Cons Ct. 7.101
St Clement, Leigh-on-Sea, Re [1988] 1 WLR 720, Chelmsford Cons Ct. 7.94
St Dunstan, Cheam, Re (2007) 22 January (unreported), Southwark Cons Ct. 7.111
St Edburga, Abberton, Re [1962] P 10, [1961] 2 All ER 429, Ct of Arches . . . . p 685
St Edward the Confessor, Mottingham, Re [1983] 1 WLR 364, Southwark Cons Ct. . . . 7.123
St George, Deal, Re [1991] Fam 6, Canterbury Commissary Ct 7.112
St George, Oakdale, Re [1976] Fam 210, [1975] 2 All ER 870, Salisbury Cons Ct. 7.02
St George the Martyr, Holborn, Re (1997) 5 Ecc LJ 67, London Cons Ct 7.21
St Giles, Horstead Keynes, Re (2002) 7 Ecc LJ 102, Chichester Cons Ct 7.124
St Gregory, Offchurch, Re [2000] 4 All ER 378, [2000] 1 WLR 2471, (2000)
    6 Ecc LJ 82, Coventry Cons Ct. 7.71
St Gregory, Tredington, Re [1972] Fam 236, [1971] 3 All ER 269,
    Ct of Arches 7.10, 7.103
St Helen, Bishopsgate, Re (1993) 3 Ecc LJ 256, London Cons Ct 1.34, 7.70, 7.72
St Hugh, Bermondsey, Re (1999) 5 Ecc LJ 390, Southwark Cons Ct 1.35, 5.01
St James, Birdham, Re (2006) 20 November (unreported), Chichester Cons Ct. 7.103
St James, Braithwell, Churchyard, Re (2002) 7 Ecc LJ 239, Sheffield Cons Ct 7.115
St James, Pokesdown, Re (2000) 9 August (unreported), Winchester Cons Ct 7.93
St James, Shirley, Re [1994] Fam 134, Winchester Cons Ct. 1.35, 5.14, 7.112

Table of Cases

St James, Stalmine, Re (2000) 6 Ecc LJ 81, Blackburn Cons Ct 7.66
St James, New Malden, Re [1994] Fam 44, [1994] 1 All ER 85,
  Southwark Cons Ct 7.58, 7.69
St James' Chapel, Callow End, Re [2001] 1 WLR 835, (2000) 5 Ecc LJ 495,
  Worcester Cons Ct 7.97
St James' Churchyard, Hampton Hill (1982) 4 CCCC No 25, London Cons Ct ..... p 664
St John, Bishop's Hatfield, Re [1967] P 113, [1966] 2 All ER 403, St Albans Cons Ct 7.02
St John, Chelsea, Re [1962] 1 WLR 706, [1962] 2 All ER 850, London
  Cons Ct ..... 3.76, 7.02, 7.92, 7.93, 7.118; p 688, 701
St John the Baptist, Bishop's Castle, Re (1999) 5 Ecc LJ 487, Hereford Cons Ct 7.116
St John the Baptist, Halifax, Re (2000) 6 Ecc LJ 167, Wakefield Cons Ct 7.103
St John the Evangelist, Blackheath, Re (1998) 5 Ecc LJ 217, Southwark Cons Ct 7.72, 7.81
St John the Evangelist, Brierley, Re [1989] Fam 60, [1989] 3 All ER 214,
  Bradford Cons Ct 5.07, 5.27
St John the Evangelist, Chopwell, Re [1995] Fam 254, Durham Cons Ct 5.30, 7.124
St John the Evangelist, Dudley Wood, Re (2005) 8 Ecc LJ 493, Worcester Cons Ct 7.102
St Kenelm, Upton Snodsbury, Re (2001) 6 Ecc LJ 293, Worcester Cons Ct 7.66
St Laurence, Alvechurch, Re (2003) TLR 508, (2003) 7 Ecc LJ 367,
  Worcester Cons Ct 7.66
St Leonard, Beoley, Re (1998) 5 Ecc LJ 216, Worcester Cons Ct 7.114
St Luke, Chelsea, Re [1976] Fam 295, [1976] 1 All ER 609, London Cons Ct 7.68
St Luke, Holbeach Hurn, Re [1991] 1 WLR 16, [1990] 2 All ER 749,
  Lincoln Cons Ct 7.114
St Luke the Evangelist, Maidstone, Re [1995] Fam 1, [1995] 1 All ER 321,
  Ct of Arches ..... 1.33, 1.34, 7.04, 7.70, 7.71, 7.127; p 674, 682
St Margaret, Brightside, Re (1996) 4 Ecc LJ 765, Sheffield Cons Ct 7.112
St Margaret, Eartham, Re [1981] 1 WLR 1129, Ct of Arches 7.121
St Margaret, Hawes, Re, Re Holy Trinity, Knaresborough [2004] 1 All ER 71, (2003)
  7 Ecc LJ 364, Ripon and Leeds Cons Ct ..... 7.119; p 673, 681, 683
St Mark, Haydock, Re (No 2) [1981] 1 WLR 1167, Liverpool
  Cons Ct ..... 7.81, 7.115; p 702
St Mark, Marske-in-Cleveland, Re (2000) 5 Ecc LJ 491, York Cons Ct 7.119
St Mark, Rusthall, Biggin Hill (1992) 13 May (unreported), Rochester Cons Ct 1.34
St Mark, Worsley, Re (2006) 9 Ecc LJ 147, Manchester Cons Ct 7.107
St Martin le Grand, York, Re [1990] Fam 63, [1989] 2 All ER 711,
  York Cons Ct 1.34, 7.93, 7.94
St Mary, Aldermary, Re [1985] Fam 101, [1985] 2 All ER 445,
  London Cons Ct 1.33, 7.118
St Mary, Balham, Re [1978] 1 All ER 993, Southwark Cons Ct ..... 7.03; p 699
St Mary, Banbury, Re [1986] Fam 24, [1985] 2 All ER 611, Oxford Cons Ct 7.68, 7.125
St Mary, Banbury, Re [1987] Fam 136, [1987] 1 All ER 247,
  Ct of Arches 7.70, 7.125, 7.126
St Mary, Barnes, Re [1982] 1 WLR 531, [1982] 1 All ER 456,
  Southwark Cons Ct 2.50, 2.51
St Mary, Barton-on-Humber, Re [1987] Fam 41, [1987] 2 All ER 861,
  Lincoln Cons Ct 7.81, 7.103
St Mary, Dodleston Churchyard, Re [1996] 1 WLR 451, Cons Ct 7.114
St Mary, Fawkham, Re [1981] 1 WLR 1171, Ct of Arches 7.115
St Mary, Kings Worthy, Re (1998) 5 Ecc LJ 133, Winchester Cons Ct 7.66
St Mary, Kingswinford, Re [2001] 1 WLR 927, (2000) 5 Ecc LJ 492,
  Worcester Cons Ct 7.115
St Mary, Longstock, Re [2006] 1 WLR 259, (2005) 8 Ecc LJ 494,
  Winchester Cons Ct 7.71, 7.122

St Mary, Luton, Re [1967] P 151, [1966] 3 All ER 638, St Albans Cons Ct 7.93
St Mary, Luton, Re [1968] P 47, [1966] 3 All ER 638 at 648, Ct of Arches . . . . 7.93; p 702
St Mary, Oldswinford, Re (1998) 5 Ecc LJ 302, Worcester Cons Ct. 7.116
St Mary, Shortlands, Re (2003) 7 Ecc LJ 363, Rochester Cons Ct 7.112
St Mary, Slaugham, Re (No 2) (2006) January (unreported), Chichester Cons Ct 7.102
St Mary, Sledmere, Re (2007) (unreported), York Cons Ct 7.110
St Mary, Tyne Dock, Re [1954] P 369, [1954] 2 All ER 339, Durham
    Cons Ct 1.41, 5.07, 7.124
St Mary, Tyne Dock, Re (No 2) [1958] P 156, [1958] 1 All ER 1, Durham
    Cons Ct 1.34, 7.124
St Mary, Warwick, Re [1981] Fam 170, Coventry Cons Ct 7.117
St Mary, Westwell, Re [1968] 1 WLR 513, [1968] 1 All ER 631, Canterbury
    Commissary Ct 1.39
St Mary and All Saints, Trentham, Re (2004) 8 Ecc LJ 115, Lichfield Cons Ct. 7.01
St Mary le Bow, Re [1984] 1 WLR 1363, London Cons Ct 7.103
St Mary Magdalene, Lyminster, Re (1990) 9 CCCC No 1, (1990) 2 Ecc LJ 127,
    Chichester Cons Ct . . . . p 661, 663
St Mary Magdalene, Paddington, Re [1980] Fam 99, [1980] 1 All ER 279,
    London Cons Ct 7.02
St Mary Magdalene and St Denys, Midhurst, Re (2002) 7 Ecc LJ 104,
    Chichester Cons Ct 7.22
St Mary the Virgin, Bathwick, Re (2005) 1 June (unreported), Bath and
    Wells Cons Ct 7.53
St Mary the Virgin, Horsham, Re (1999) 5 Ecc LJ 388, Chichester Cons Ct 7.121
St Mary the Virgin, Hurley, Re [2001] 1 WLR 831, (2000) 6 Ecc LJ 166,
    Oxford Cons Ct 7.107
St Mary the Virgin, Sherborne, Re [1996] Fam 63, [1996] 3 All ER 769,
    Ct of Arches . . . . 1.33, 7.21, 7.71, 7.72, 7.78, 7.79; p 701, 702
St Mary the Virgin, West Moors, Re [1963] P 390, [1962] 3 All ER 722,
    Salisbury Cons Ct. 7.124
St Mary the Virgin, Woodkirk, Re [1969] 1 WLR 1867, *sub nom* Morley Borough
    Council v St Mary the Virgin, Woodkirk (Vicar and Churchwardens)
    [1969] 3 All ER 952, Ch Ct of York 7.02, 7.93
St Matthew, Hutton Buscel, Re (2000) 5 Ecc LJ 486, York Cons Ct. 7.103
St Matthew, Wimbledon, Re [1985] 3 All ER 670, Southwark Cons Ct. 5.27, 7.81
St Michael, Aveley, Re (1997) 4 Ecc LJ 770, Chelmsford Cons Ct 1.35, 7.80, 7.118
St Michael and All Angels, Bishopwearmouth, Re [1958] 1 WLR 1183, *sub nom* Rector
    and Churchwardens of Bishopwearmouth v Adey [1958] 3 All ER 441,
    Durham Cons Ct 1.34, 1.41, 5.07, 5.27
St Michael and All Angels, Great Torrington, Re [1985] Fam 81, [1985]
    1 All ER 993, Ct of Eccl Causes Res 7.10, 7.68, 7.123
St Nicholas, Arundel, Re (2001) 6 Ecc LJ 290, Chichester Cons Ct. 5.30, 7.124
St Nicholas, Baddesley Ensor, Re [1983] Fam 1, [1982] 2 All ER 351,
    Birmingham Cons Ct. 7.113, 7.114
St Nicholas, Bookham, Re (2003) 8 Ecc LJ 112, Guildford Cons Ct 7.124
St Nicholas, Gosforth, Re (1988) 1(5) Ecc LJ 4, Newcastle Cons Ct 7.112
St Nicholas, Pevensey, Re (2002) 7 Ecc LJ 236, Chichester Cons Ct 7.107
St Nicholas, Plumstead, Re Rector and Churchwardens of [1961] 1 WLR 916,
    [1961] 1 All ER 298, Southwark Cons Ct. 1.34, 1.41, 5.07, 5.27
St Nicholas, Remenham, Re (2006) 9 Ecc LJ 238, Oxford Cons Ct. 7.115
St Nicholas, Sevenoaks, Re, Re Locock deceased [2005] 1 WLR 1011, (2004)
    8 Ecc LJ 232, Ct of Arches 7.109
St Nicholas, Swayfield, Re (2002) 7 Ecc LJ 235, Lincoln Cons Ct 7.96

Table of Cases

St Oswald King and Martyr, Oswestry, Re (2000) 6 Ecc LJ 78, Lichfield Cons Ct 7.124
St Paul, Covent Garden, Re [1974] Fam 1, London Cons Ct..................... 1.33, 7.118
St Paul, Drightlington, Re (2006) 9 Ecc LJ 239, Wakefield Cons Ct 7.115
St Peter, Bushey Heath, Re [1971] 1 WLR 357, [1971] 2 All ER 704,
    St Albans Cons Ct 7.94, 7.118
St Peter, Oundle, Re (1996) 4 Ecc LJ 764, Peterborough Cons Ct 7.80, 7.122
St Peter, Racton, Re (2001) 6 Ecc LJ 291, Chichester Cons Ct..................... 7.12
St Peter, Roydon, Re [1969] 1 WLR 1849, [1969] 2 All ER 1233,
    Chelmsford Cons Ct... 3.25, 3.26
St Peter, Walworth, Re (2002) 7 Ecc LJ 103, Southwark Cons Ct 7.71
St Peter, St Helier, Merton, Re [1992] 1 WLR 343, Southwark Cons Ct 7.75
St Peter, St Helier, Morden, Re [1951] P 303, [1951] 2 All ER 53,
    Southwark Cons Ct 7.124
St Peter and St Paul, Leckhampton, Re [1968] P 495, [1967] 3 All ER 1057,
    Gloucester Cons Ct 1.41, 5.07, 5.27
St Peter and St Paul, Scrayingham, Re [1992] 1 WLR 87, [1991] 4 All ER 411,
    York Cons Ct 7.81
St Peter and St Paul, Upper Teddington, Re [1993] 1 WLR 852, London Cons Ct........ 7.66
St Peter and St Paul, Wantage, Re (No 2) (1999) 5 Ecc LJ 387, Oxford Cons Ct 7.80
St Philip, Alderley Edge, Re (1996) 4 Ecc LJ 765, Chester Cons Ct 7.119
St Stephen, Walbrook, Re [1987] Fam 146, [1987] 2 All ER 578, Ct of Eccl
    Causes Res 1.34, 5.01, 7.68, 7.70, 7.81, 7.91, 7.123, 7.126
St Thomas, Kimberworth, Re (1998) 5 Ecc LJ 302, Sheffield Cons Ct................. 7.116
St Thomas, Lymington, Re [1980] Fam 89, Winchester Cons Ct..................... 7.93
St Thomas, Pennywell, Re [1995] Fam 50, [1995] 4 All ER 167,
    Durham Cons Ct 5.02, 5.07, 5.27–5.30, 7.124
St Thomas, Stourbridge, Parish, Re (2001) 20 CCCC No 39, Worcester Cons Ct 7.71
St Thomas à Becket, Framfield, Re [1989] 1 WLR 689, [1989] 1 All ER 170,
    Chichester Cons Ct 7.03, 7.81
Sahin v Turkey (2005) 41 EHRR 8.. 1.46
Serif v Greece (2001) 31 EHRR 561, E Ct HR .... 1.46, p 670
Sinyanki, Re (1864) 12 WR 825... 4.34
Small, deceased, Re (2005) 9 Ecc LJ 238, Manchester Cons Ct 7.115
South London Crematorium, Re, Petition of Ruby Harding (1999) 27 September
    (unreported), Southwark Cons Ct.. p 662
Southwark, Diocese of v Coker. See Diocese of Southwark v Coker
Stephens v Avery [1988] Ch 449, [1988] 2 All ER 477 .... 5.62
Stocks, Re John, deceased (1995) Times, 5 September, 4 Ecc LJ 527,
    Sheffield Cons Ct... 1.34, 7.105
Stourbridge St Thomas Parish, Re (2001) 20 CCCC No 39, Worcester Cons Ct 7.71
Stuart v Haughley Parochial Church Council [1'936] Ch 32, CA 3.06
Swaden, deceased, Re (2005) 8 Ecc LJ 238, Southwark Cons Ct 7.107

Talbot, Re [1901] P 1, London Cons Ct .... 7.107; p 658, 662
Thompson v Dibdin [1912] AC 533, HL.................................. 5.26, 5.34
Tonbridge School Chapel, Re [1993] 1 WLR 1138, [1993] 2 All ER 350,
    Rochester Cons Ct 7.02, 7.08
Tonbridge School Chapel, Re (No 2) [1993] Fam 281, [1993] 2 All ER 338,
    Rochester Cons Ct 7.118
Tyler v United Kingdom, Application 21283/93, 5 April 1994 (unreported),
    E Com HR.. 2.50

Varsani v Jesani [1999] Ch 219, [1998] 3 All ER 273, CA....................... 1.43, 1.44

Table of Cases

Wadsley Parish Church, Re (2001) 6 Ecc LJ 172, Sheffield Cons Ct 7.71
Welford Road Cemetery, Leicester, Re [2007] 1 All ER 426, [2007] 2 WLR 506,
    (2006) 9 Ecc LJ 243, Ct of Arches. 2.62, 3.76, 7.02, 7.79, 7.84,
  7.86, 7.88, 7.89, 7.92, 7.95; p **686**
West Midlands Probation Committee v Secretary of State for the Environment
    (1997) 76 P & CR 589. . . . . p 682
West Norwood Cemetery, Re [1994] Fam 210, [1995] 1 All ER 387,
    Southwark Cons Ct . . . . 7.02, 7.84, 7.92; p 688, 692, 696, 699
West Norwood Cemetery, Re (No 2) [1998] Fam 84, [1998] 1 All ER 606,
    Southwark Cons Ct 4.55
West Norwood Cemetery, Re (2000) 6 July (unreported), Southwark Cons Ct . . . . p 663
West Pennard Churchyard, Re [1992] 1 WLR 32, [1991] 4 All ER 124, Bath and
    Wells Cons Ct 5.51, 7.114
Westwell Bridleway, Re (FP5/U3100/7/19) 5 March 2005 (unreported). 3.76
Whixall Old Burial Ground, Re (2000) 5 Ecc LJ 495, Lichfield Cons Ct. 1.35
Wickhambrook Parochial Church Council v Croxford [1935]
    2 KB 417, CA. . . . . 3.80, 3.81; p 703
Williams v Bishop of Bangor (1999) 5 Ecc LJ 304, Provincial Ct in Wales 4.38, 6.80
Williamson v Archbishop of Canterbury (1994) Times, 25 November. 2.40
Williamson v Archbishops of Canterbury and York (1996) 5 September
    (unreported). 1.25, 1.28–1.30, 2.05, 4.08
Williamson v Dow (1994) 16 April (unreported) 4.08, 5.45
Wise v Metcalfe (1829) 10 B & C 299 . . . . 3.80; p 703, 704
Woldingham Churchyard, Re [1957] 1 WLR 811, [1957] 2 All ER 323,
    Southwark Cons Ct . . . . 7.03, 7.81, 7.115; p 701
Wraxall Churchyard, Re (2004) 7 Ecc LJ 497, Bath and Wells Cons Ct 7.114
Wright and Advertiser Newspapers Ltd v Lewis (1990) 53 SASR 416,
    S Australia S C . . . . p 669
Wyndham v Cole (1875) 1 PD 130, Ct of Arches 3.66

X deceased, Re (2001) 6 Ecc LJ 413, Liverpool Cons Ct 7.107
X v Denmark (7374/76) DR5, 147, E Ct HR. 5.12

TABLE OF CANONS

References are to paragraphs in the text or to page numbers in the Materials.
Canons with bold page numbers are set out in the Materials.

Amending Canon 23 . . . . .4.16; p 354	
para 2 . . . . 4.64	
Amending Canon 25, 26 . . . . 2.15	
Amending Canon 29 (draft) 4.40, 4.42	
39 Articles of Religion 4,04, 5.27	
art 25 . . . . 5.15, 5.27	
27 . . . . 5.12	
28 . . . . 5.19, 5.21, 5.27	
37 . . . . 1.20	
Canons Ecclesiastical 1603 . . . . 1.16	
canon 73 . . . . 5.59	
113 proviso . . . . 1.16, 5.62, p 324, **369**	
127 . . . . 2.47	
Revised Canons Ecclesiastical (1969) 1.16	
Canon A 1 – A 3 . . . . p **311**	
A 4 . . . . 4.06; p **311**	
A 5, A 6 . . . . p **312**	
A 7 . . . . 1.20; p **312**	
A 8 . . . . p **312**	
B 1 . . . . 4.06, 5.03, 5.06–5.08; p **312**	
para 1 . . . . 5.07	
(a) 1.40	
2 . . . . 5.06, 5.08	
B 2 . . . . 5.07, 5.08, 5.29, 5.52; p **313**	
para 1, 2 . . . . 5.04	
2A(1) 5.02, 5.07	
(6), (7) 5.02	
B 3 . . . . 5.07; p **314**	
para 1 . . . . 3.29, 5.05	
2 . . . . 3.29, 5.05, 5.07	
4 . . . . 5.05, 5.07	
5 . . . . 5.05	
B 4 . . . . 5.08, 5.60; p **315**	
para 1, 2 . . . . 5.07, 5.08	
3 . . . . 1.40, 5.07, 5.08	
B 5 . . . . p **316**	
para 1 . . . . 5.06–5.08, 5.29	
2, 3 . . . . 5.07, 5.08	
4 . . . . 5.08	
B 5A . . . . 5.04, 5.07, p **316**	
B 6 . . . . p **316**	
B 7 . . . . p **317**	
B 8 . . . . p **317**	
para 2 . . . . 3.29	
proviso 3.29	
3 . . . . 5.22	
B 9 . . . . p **317**	
para 1, 2 . . . . 5.11	
B 10 . . . . 5.09, 8.32; p **317**	
B 11 . . . . 4.12, 4.13; p **255**	
B 11 . . . . 4.15, 4.16; p **317**	
para 1, 2 . . . . 5.09, 5.57	
3 . . . . 5.10	
B 12 . . . . p **318**	
para 1 . . . . 5.22	
2 . . . . 5.24	
3 . . . . 1.41, 5.22	
4 . . . . 5.22	
B 13 . . . . p **318**	
para 1 . . . . 5.09, 8.32	
2 . . . . 8.32	
B 14 . . . . p **318**	
para 1 . . . . 5.09	
2 . . . . 5.10	
B 14A . . . . 4.15, 4.16, 5.10, 5.57; p **319**	
para 1 . . . . 1.41	
(a), (b) 5.10	
(i), (ii) 5.10	
2 . . . . 5.10	
B 15 . . . . 5.24; p **319**	
para 1, 2 . . . . 5.24	
B 15A . . . . 5.18; p **319**	
para 1(a), (b) 5.18	
(c), (d) . . . . . . 5.18; p 369	
3 . . . . 5.18

Revised Canons Ecclesiastical (1969) (*cont.*)
 B 16 . . . . 5.25, 5.26; p **320**
  para 1 . . . . 5.26
 B 17 . . . . p **320**
  para 1 . . . . 3.53, 5.23
  2, 3 . . . . 5.23
 B 17A . . . . 5.23; p **320**
 B 18 . . . . p **320**
  para 1 . . . . 1.41, 5.11
  2, 3 . . . . 5.11
 B 19 . . . . p **321**
 B 20 . . . . 3.29, 3.66; p **321**
  para 1 . . . . 3.65
  3 . . . . 3.66
 B 21 . . . . 5.13; p **322**
 B 22 . . . . p **322**
  para 2 . . . . 5.12
  4 . . . . 5.12, 6.15
  5, 6 . . . . 5.12
 B 23 . . . . p **322**
  para 1, 2, 4 . . . . 5.13
 B 24 . . . . 5.12; p **323**
  para 3 . . . . 5.16
 B 25 . . . . 5.14; p **323**
 B 26 . . . . p **323**
  para 1, 2 . . . . 5.15
 B 27 . . . . p **323**
  para 1–5 . . . . 5.16
  6 . . . . 5.17
 B 28 . . . . p **324**
 B 29 . . . . 5.61; p **324**
  para 2, 3 . . . . 5.61
  4 . . . . 3.30, 5.61
 B 30 . . . . p **325**
  para 1 . . . . 5.49
  3 . . . . 5.33
 B 31 . . . . p **325**
  para 1, 2 . . . . 5.32
 B 32 . . . . 5.32; p **326**
 B 33 . . . . 5.33; p **326**
 B 34 . . . . p **326**
  para 2, 3 . . . . 1.41, 5.41
 B 35 . . . . p **326**
  para 2 . . . . 5.32, 5.38
  3, 4 . . . . 5.44
  5 . . . . 3.66, 5.44
 B 36 . . . . p **327**
 B 37 . . . . p **327**
  para 1 . . . . 5.58
  2 . . . . 5.23, 5.58
 B 38 . . . . p **327**
  para 2 . . . . 5.07, 5.51,
  5.52, 7.113
  proviso 5.52

 3 . . . . 5.55
 4(a), (b) 5.56
 5 . . . . 5.51
 6 . . . . 5.52
 7 . . . . 5.56
 B 39 . . . . p **328**
  para 1 . . . . 5.54
  2 . . . . 5.16
 B 40 . . . . 5.23; p **328**
 B 41 . . . . p **328**
  para 1 . . . . 3.105, 5.23
  2 . . . . 3.106, 5.23
  3 . . . . 5.23
 B 42 . . . . p **329**
  para 2 . . . . 1.41
  3(1)–(3) 5.03
 B 43 . . . . 1.28, 3.97, 3.99,
  5.23, 8.33; p **330**
  para 1–7 . . . . 3.99
  9 . . . . 3.100
  10 . . . . 3.96, 8.33
  11 . . . . 3.100
 B 44 . . . . 1.28, 3.97, 3.99,
  3.101, 5.23; p **332**
  para 1(1), (3) 3.101
  2(1), (3) 3.102
  3(1) 3.102
  4 . . . . 3.102
  (1) 3.102
  5 . . . . 3.102
  6 . . . . 3.101,
  3.102, 8.33
  7 . . . . 3.101, 3.102
  8 . . . . 3.102
 C 1 . . . . 4.27, 5.22; p **335**
  para 1 . . . . 4.01
  2 . . . . 4.38
  3 . . . . 4.37
 C 2 . . . . p **336**
  para 1, 2 . . . . 4.59
  3, 4 . . . . 4.56
 C 3 . . . . p **336**
  para 1, 2 . . . . 4.06
  3, 4 . . . . 4.07
  4A, 5, 6, 8 . . . . 4.06
 C 4 . . . . 4.04; p **336**
  para 1 . . . . 4.04
  2, 3 . . . . 4.05
  3A 1.41, 4.04, 4.05
  4 . . . . 4.05
 C 4A . . . . 1.28, 4.01; p **337**
 C 4B . . . . 1.28, 4.01; p **338**
 C 5 . . . . p **338**
  para 1 . . . . 4.47

Revised Canons Ecclesiastical (1969) (cont.)
  C 5 (cont.)
        2 . . . . 4.47
          (e) 3.75
          proviso 4.07
        4, 5 . . . . 4.09
  C 6 . . . . p 338
    para 1(a), (b) 4.07
        2(a), (b) 4.07
  C 7 . . . . 4.04, 4.55; p 338
  C 8 . . . . 4.53; p 339
    para 3 . . . . 4.36
        4 . . . . 4.17
        5 . . . . 4.10
  C 9 . . . . p 340
  C 10 . . . . p 340
    para 1, 2 . . . . 4.27
        3 . . . . 4.22
        4–7 . . . . 4.27
        8 . . . . 4.22
  C 11 . . . . p 341
    para 1–3 . . . . 4.38
  C 12 . . . . 4.36; p 341
    para 1, 2 . . . . 4.30
        5 . . . . . . 4.33–4.36, 4.67
        6 . . . . 4.35, 4.49
  C 13 . . . . p 342
    para 1 . . . . 4.07, 4.28
        2 . . . . 1.41, 4.07
        3 . . . . 4.07
  C 14 . . . . p 343
    para 3 . . . . . . 4.07, 4.28, 4.32
  C 15 . . . . 5.06;
                        p 343, 673
    para 1(1) 4.07, 4.28
        (4) 4.07
        (5) 4.28
        (6) 4.32
        4 . . . . 4.07, 4.32
  C 17 . . . . p 345
    para 2–4 . . . . 4.66
  C 18 . . . . 4.56; p 345
    para 1 . . . . 4.56
        2 . . . . 4.60
        3 . . . . 2.52, 4.60
        4 . . . . 4.37, 4.60–4.62
        5 . . . . 4.61
        6 . . . . 4.60, 4.62
        7 . . . . 4.60
        8 . . . . 4.61
  C 19 . . . . 4.64
  C 20 . . . . p 346
    para 1, 2 . . . . 4.65
        3 . . . . 1.41, 4.65

C 21 . . . . 8.18,
                                8.22; p 346
    para 1 . . . . 8.18, 8.20
        1A 8.20
        2, 3 . . . . 8.22
        4 . . . . 8.22, 8.27
C 22 . . . . 4.54; p 347
    para 1 . . . . 4.54
        2, 3 . . . . 4.55
        4 . . . . 4.37, 4.55
        5 . . . . 4.55, 7.15
C 23 . . . . 4.53; p 347
    para 1 . . . . 4.53
        2 . . . . 3.05, 4.53
        3, 4 . . . . 4.53
C 24 . . . . 4.16, 5.09; p 348
    para 4 . . . . 4.16
C 25 . . . . p 348
    para 1 . . . . 4.16
        2 . . . . 1.41, 4.16
        3, 4 . . . . 4.16
C 26 . . . . 6.13; p 349
    para 1 . . . . 4.15, 5.06
        2 . . . . 4.13, 4.15
C 27 . . . . 4.15, 6.13; p 349
C 28 . . . . 6.13; p 349
    para 1 . . . . 4.13
        2 . . . . 1.41, 4.13
        3 . . . . 4.13
D 1 . . . . 3.71; p 349
    para 3(b) 5.22
        4(c) 5.53
D 2 . . . . 3.71; p 350
    para 2A 3.71
D 3 . . . . 3.71; p 351
E 1 . . . . p 352
    para 4 . . . . 3.48, 7.63
        5 . . . . 3.48, 3.53,
                         3.54, 3.82
E 2 . . . . 3.10; p 352
    para 1 . . . . 3.60
        2 . . . . 3.10, 3.40, 3.60
        3 . . . . 3.51, 3.60
E 3 . . . . 3.61, 3.62; p 353
E 4 . . . . p 353
    para 1 . . . . 3.68
        2 (a) 3.70
          (b) 3.70, 5.37
          (c) 3.70, 5.22
        2A 5.53
        3 . . . . 3.68, 3.70
E 5 . . . . p 353
    para 1–3 . . . . 3.67
        4–6 . . . . 3.68

Revised Canons Ecclesiastical (1969) (*cont.*)

E 6 . . . . p **353**
    para 1 . . . . 3.68
        2 . . . . 3.68, 3.74
        3 . . . . 3.69, 4.67
        4 . . . . 3.70
E 7 . . . . 3.72; p **355**
    para 1(a)–(c) 3.72
        2–4 . . . . 3.73
        5(a), (b) 3.73
        (c) 3.73, 5.37, 5.53
        (d) 3.73
E 8 . . . . 3.72, 3.74; p **356**
    para 5 . . . . 4.67
F 1 . . . . 3.29, 3.48,
                    7.123; p **357**
    para 1 . . . . 5.14, 7.112
        2 . . . . 1.35, 1.38,
                    5.14, 7.112
        3 . . . . 5.14
F 2 . . . . 3.29, 3.48,
                    7.123; p **357**
    para 1 . . . . 7.91
F 3 . . . . 3.29, 3.48; p **357**
F 4, F 5 . . . . 3.29, 3.48; p **358**
F 6 . . . . 3.29, 3.48,
                    7.123; p **358**
F 7 . . . . 3.29, 3.48,
                    7.123; p **358**
    para 1, 2 . . . . 3.50, 7.125
F 8 . . . . 3.29, 3.48, 7.123; p **358**
F 9 . . . . 3.29, 3.48; p **358**
F 10 . . . . 3.28, 3.29, 3.48,
                    7.123; p **358**

F 11 . . . . 3.29, 3.48, 5.46; p **359**
    para 1 . . . . 5.37
F 12 . . . . 3.29, 3.48; p **359**
F 13 . . . . 3.29, 3.48; p **359**
    para 3 . . . . 3.55, 7.01, 7.02
        4 . . . . 3.54
F 14 . . . . .3.29, 3.48, 3.53,
             3.82, 5.37, 7.123; p **359**
F 15 . . . . p **359**
    para 1, 2 . . . . 3.51
        3 . . . . 3.52
F 16 . . . . p **360**, 674
F 17, F 18 . . . . p **360**
G 1 . . . . p **360**
G 2 . . . . p **361**
    para 2 . . . . 2.47
        3 . . . . 2.48
G 3 . . . . p **362**
G 4 . . . . p **362**
    para 2 . . . . 2.47, 2.53
        3 . . . . 2.54
G 5 . . . . 4.62, p **363**
    para 1 . . . . 4.37
G 6 . . . . 3.49; p **363**
    para 1 . . . . 4.37
H 1 . . . . p **363**
    para 2 . . . . 1.28
H 2 . . . . 2.16; p **364**
    para 1(d), (dd), (e) 2.16
H 3 . . . . p **368**
    para 1 . . . . 2.15
        (b), (bb), (d) 2.15
        2 . . . . 2.15

TABLE OF STATUTES AND MEASURES

References are to paragraphs in the text, or to page numbers in the Materials.
Provisions with bold page numbers are set out in the Materials.

Accession Declaration Act 1910 (10 Edw
    7 & 1 Geo 5, c 29) 1.20
Act of Settlement 1700 (12 & 13 Will
    3, c 2)—
    s 3 . . . . 1.20
Act of Uniformity 1548 (2 & 3
    Edw 6, c 1)—
    s 1 . . . . 5.02
Act of Uniformity 1662 (14 Cha 2,
    c 4) 1.04, 1.40, 5.02
    s 10 . . . . 1.04, 4.53, 8.20
    15 . . . . 1.04
    Schedule 5.02
Ancient Monuments Consolidation
    and Amendment Act 1913
    (3 & 4 Geo 5, c 32)—
    s 22 . . . . 7.05
Appellate Jurisdiction Act 1876
    (39 & 40 Vict, c 59)—
    s 25 . . . . 2.47
Appointment of Bishops Act 1533
    (25 Hen 8, c 20) 8.14
    s 3 . . . . 4.58
    4, 5 . . . . 4.59

Baptismal Fees Abolition Act 1872
    (35 & 36 Vict, c 36)—
    s 1 . . . . 5.12
Benefices Act 1898 (61 & 62 Vict,
    c 48) 4.22
    s 2(1)(b) 4.22
    3(2) 4.22
Benefices (Exercise of Rights of
    Presentation) Measure 1931
    (21 & 22 Geo 5, no 3)—
    s 1–3 . . . . 3.29
Benefices Measure 1972 (no 3) 4.22
    s 1 (1), (2) 4.22
Benefices (Transfer of Rights of
    Patronage) Measure 1930
    (21 & 22 Geo 5, no 8)—
    s 2, 4 . . . . 3.29

Bill of Rights 1688 (1 Will & Mar,
    sess 2, c 2) 1.20
    s 1 . . . . 1.20
Births and Deaths Registration Act 1926
    (16 & 17 Geo 5, c 48)—
    s 3(1) 5.54
Bishops (Retirement) Measure 1986
    (no 1)—
    s 1(1) 4.64
    3(1), (2), (5) 4.64
    4 . . . . 4.67
    6(1), (2), (4), (5) 4.67
Brawling Act 1553 (1 Mar,
    sess 2, c 3) 5.28
Burial Act 1853 (16 & 17 Vict,
    c 134) 7.95
Burial Act 1857 (21 & 22 Vict,
    c 81) . . . . p 658
    s 25 . . . . 5.54, 7.104;
                                      p 659, 688
Burial Laws Amendment Act 1880
    (43 & 44 Vict, c 41)—
    s 1, 6 . . . . 5.53
    13 . . . . 5.52
    Sch A 5.53

Canon Law Act 1543 (35 Hen 8,
    c 16) 1.13
Care of Cathedrals (Amendment)
    Measure 2005 (no 2) 8.03, 8.39
    s 16 . . . . 8.03
Care of Cathedrals Measure 1990
    (no 2) 2.52, 8.03, 8.36,
                        8.39, 8.41, 8.49, 8.50
    s 1 . . . . 8.37, 8.40; p **461**
    2 . . . . 8.41, 8.42, 8.50–8.54; p **461**
    (1) 8.41
    (a) 8.36
    (b) 8.36, 8.39
    (bb), (c) 8.36
    (2) (a)–(c) 8.36
    (3) 8.36

Care of Cathedrals Measure 1990
    (no 2) (cont.)
    3 . . . . p 462
        (2) (a), (aa), (b)–(e) 8.39
        (2A) 8.39
        (3) 8.40
    4 . . . . p 463
        (1) 8.37
        (2)(a), (b) 8.37
        (3) 8.38
    5 . . . . p 463
        (1)(a), (b) 8.41
        (2) 8.41
    6 . . . . p 463
        (1) 8.42
            (a) (i)–(iii) 8.42
            (iv) 8.42, 8.44
            (b) 8.42
        (2), (2A)–(2D), (3) 8.42
        (3A) 8.42, 8.54
    6A . . . . 8.36, 8.42; p 464
    7 . . . . p 465
        (1) 8.43
            (a), (b) 8.43
        (2), (3) 8.43
    8 . . . . p 466
        (1), (1A), (2), (2A),
            (2B), (3) 8.44
    9 . . . . p 466
        (1) 8.43
        (2) 8.43, 8.45
        (3), (4) 8.43
    10 . . . . p 467
        (1), (2) 8.45
        (3)(a)–(c) 8.45
        (4), (7) 8.45
    10A . . . . p 468
        (1), (2) 8.47
    10B . . . . 8,47; p 468
    10C . . . . 8.45; p 468
    11 . . . . p 469
        (1) 8.39
    11A . . . . 8.37, 8.40; p 469
        (a)–(e) 8.46
    12 . . . . p 469
        (1), (2) 8.35
    13 . . . . p 469
        (1), (1B), (2) 8.35
        (3), (4) 8.31
    14 . . . . p 470
        (1), (5), (6) 8.35
    14A . . . . p 471
        (1), (2) 8.35
    14B . . . . 8.35; p 471
    15 . . . . 8.48; p 472
    18 . . . . 8.03
    Sch 1 . . . . p 473
        para 1, 3, 3A, 4, 14, 14A 8.40
            16A 8.43
    Sch 2 . . . . p 475
        para 1 . . . . 8.38
            (a), (b) 8.38
            2–5, 7, 8, 12 . . . . 8.38
Care of Cathedrals (Supplementary
    Pro-visions) Measure 1994
    (no 2) 2.52, 8.15, 8.49
    s 1 . . . . 8.50; p 496
    2 . . . . p 497
        (1) 8.50
        (2)(a)–(c) 8.50
        (3) 8.50
    3 . . . . 8.51; p 497
        (1), (2) 8.51
        (3)(a)–(c) 8.51
        (4), (5) 8.51
    4 . . . . 8.54; p 498
        (1), (2) 8.52
    5 . . . . p 498
        (1)–(3) 8.52
    6 . . . . p 498
        (1), (3) 8.52
        (4)–(7) 8.53
        (9), (10) 8.54
    7(4) 8.42, 8.54
    8 . . . . 7.82, 8.54
    9 . . . . 8.51
    10 . . . . p 499
    Schedule—
        para 2 . . . . 8.54
            4 . . . . 7.82
Care of Churches and Ecclesiastical
    Jurisdiction Measure 1991
    (no 1) 7.04, 7.128
    s 1 . . . . 1.03, 7.04; p 477, 681
    2 . . . . 2.32; p 477
        (1) 7.16
        (2) 7.09, 7.16
        (5) 3.82, 7.17
    4 . . . . p 478
        (1)(a), (b) 3.54
        (2)–(4) 3.54
    5 . . . . 3.08; p 478
        (1) 3.54
        (3) 3.08, 3.54
        (4), (5) 3.54
    6 . . . . p 478
        (1) 3.82, 7.128
        (2)–(4) 7.128

Table of Statutes and Measures

Care of Churches and Ecclesiastical
    Jurisdiction Measure 1991
    (no 1) (*cont.*)
7 . . . . p **479**
8(1) 1.34, 7.76, 7.82, 8.54
9 . . . . 2.53
11 . . . . p **479**
  (1) 3.104, 7.02, 7.128
  (2)–(4) 7.02
  (8) 7.03
12 . . . . 7.84; p **480**, 696
  (1) 7.74
    (a) 7.09, 7.74
    (b) 7.74
  (2) 7.74, 7.83
13 . . . . p **480**
  (1), (2) 7.83
  (4) 7.84
  (5) 7.02, 7.03, 7.84;
                            p 695, 696
  (6) . . . . 7.09, 7.88; p 695
  (7) 7.83
  (8) 7.86
  (9) 7.83, 7.86
  (10) 7.86
  (11) . . . . 7.89; p 695
14 . . . . 2.57; p **481**
  (1) 7.09
  (2) 7.13
  (5)(a) 7.79
  (6) 7.13
15 . . . . p **482**
  (1), (2) 7.25
  (3) 7.17
16 . . . . p **482**
  (1)(a) 7.09, 7.10, 7.34
    (b), (c) 7.10, 7.34
  (2) 7.09, 7.34
  (4) 7.10, 7.81
17 . . . . 7.50, 7.97; p **482**
  (2) 7.97, 7.98
  (3)(a) 7.98
  (4) 7.100
    (a)(ii) 7.50, 7.98
    (b) 7.50, 7.98
    (d) 7.58
      (ii) 7.99
  (5) 7.100
    (a) 7.50, 7.98
18 . . . . 7.97; p **484**
  (1)(a), (b) 7.101
  (2)(a), (b) 7.101
  (3) 7.101
19 . . . . p **484**
20 . . . . 7.11; p **484**
21 . . . . p **485**
  (1), (2), (5)–(7) 7.12
22 . . . . 7.02; p **485**
23, 25 . . . . p **486**
26 . . . . p **487**
  (1) (a), (e) 1.32
27 . . . . p **488**
28 . . . . p **489**
29 . . . . 8.51; p **489**
30 . . . . p **489**
31 . . . . p **489**
  (1) 7.18, 7.128
Sch 1 . . . . 7.16; p **491**
  para 1 . . . . 7.16
    2 . . . . 7.09, 7.16
    3 . . . . 7.16
    4(a) 7.16
    (b) 7.16, 7.18
    5(a)–(d) 7.16
    12–14 . . . . 7.16
Sch 2 . . . . 7.17; p **492**
  para 1(a)–(g) 7.17
    2(a)–(h) 7.17
Sch 3—
  para 2–4 . . . . 3.82
Sch 4—
  para 2(a) 2.47
    (c), (d) 2.48
    4(b) 2.49
    8 . . . . 1.34
    9 . . . . 7.82
    11 . . . . 7.76, 8.54
Sch 5—
  para 2(a) 2.53
    3 . . . . 2.54
Care of Places of Worship Measure
    1999 (no 2) 3.103, 7.08, 7.130
s 1(1), (2) 7.08
  3 (1) 7.08
    (2) 7.08, 7.130
    (4) 7.130
  5 . . . . 1.32
Cathedral Dignitaries (Retirement)
    Measure 1949 (no 1) 8.2 4
Cathedrals Measure 1963 (no 1) 8.01
Cathedrals Measure 1976 (no 1) 8.01
Cathedrals Measure 1999
  (no 1) 8.01, 8.05, 8.26
Pt I (ss 1–27) 8.05
s 1 . . . . 8.04, 8.05, 8.07,
                8.11, 8.14, 8.17, 8.26, 8.31,
                          8.37, 8.40; p **506**
  2 . . . . 8.05; p **506**

Cathedrals Measure 1999 (no 1) (cont.)
3 . . . . p 506
    (1), (2) 8.06
    (3) 8.06
        (a), (b) 8.06
    (4)(a)–(f) 8.06
    (5) 8.06
    (6) 8.07
        (a), (b) 8.07
        (c) 8.07, 8.12
        (d), (e) 8.07
    (7)(a)–(c) 8.07
    (8) 8.06
4 . . . . p 507
    (1)–(5) 8.09
    (6) 8.09
        (a) 8.17
    (7) 8.09
    (8)(a)–(e) 8.11
        (f) 8.08, 8.11
        (g), (h) 8.11
    (9) 8.11, 8.29
    (10) 8.11
    (12) 8.09, 8.11
5 . . . . p 508
    (1) 8.13
    (2)(a)–(c) 8.13
        (d) 8.13, 8.25
        (e) 8.13
    (3) 8.14
    (4)(a) 8.12, 8.14
        (b), (c) 8.14
6 . . . . 8.04, 8.15; p 508
    (1), (2) 8.15
    (3)–(7) 8.16
    (8), (9) 8.15
7 . . . . p 509
    (1) 8.17, 8.18
    (2)(a)–(e) 8.17
    (3)(a)–(c) 8.10
        proviso 8.10
    (4) 8.19
8 . . . . p 509
    (1) 8.21
    (2) 8.21
        proviso 8.21
    (3) 8.21
9 . . . . 8.35; p 510
    (1)(a) 8.05, 8.29
        (b) 8.20
        (c) 8.25, 8.26
        (d) 8.21, 8.25
        (e) 8.26
        (f) 8.26, 8.35
        (g) 8.26
        (h) 8.09, 8.26
    (2)(a), (b) 8.18
    (3) 8.28
10 . . . . 8.09; p 510
    (1) 8.28
        (a) 8.28
11 . . . . p 511
    (a) 8.21
    (b) 8.09
12 . . . . p 511
    (2), (3) 8.02, 8.09
    (4), (5) 8.02, 8.10
13 . . . . 8.29; p 512
14 . . . . p 512
    (1) 8.29
15 . . . . p 512
    (1) 8.29
        (a), (b) 8.29
16 . . . . p 513
    (1)(a)–(d) 8.30
    (2)–(4) 8.30
17, 18 . . . . 8.30; p 513
19 . . . . 8.31; p 513
20 . . . . 8.35; p 513
    (1), (2) 8.31
21 . . . . p 514
    (1), (2) 8.17, 8.21
22 . . . . 8.17, 8.21; p 514
23 . . . . p 514
    (a), (b) 8.27
24 . . . . 8.29; p 514
25 . . . . 8.30; p 514
    (1) 8.27
26 . . . . 8.30; **5.14**
    proviso 8.30
27 . . . . p 514
    (1)–(3) 8.12
Pt II (ss 28–32) 8.05
s 28 . . . . p 515
    (1)–(3) 8.08
29 . . . . p 515
    (1)–(3) 8.08
30 . . . . 8.08; p 515
31 . . . . 8.08; p 516
    (2) 8.08
32–34 . . . . p 516
35 . . . . p 516
    (1) 8.05, 8.06, 8.13,
                                      8.25, 8.28
    (3)–(5) 8.29
    (6) 8.05
36 . . . . 8.05, p 517
    (1) 8.33

Table of Statutes and Measures

Cathedrals Measure 1999 (no 1) (cont.)
  36 (cont.)
    (1A) 8.32
    (4) 8.18
  37 . . . . 8.01; p **518**
  38(1), (2) 8.05
  39 . . . . 8.05
    (1) 2.34, 8.28
  Sch 1 . . . . 8.05
    para 1, 5 . . . . 8.05
  Sch 2—
    para 8 . . . . 2.34, 8.28
Cemeteries Clauses Act 1847 (10 &
  11 Vict, c 65) . . . . p 687, 688
  s 23 . . . . p 687
Chancel Repairs Act 1932 (22 & 23
  Geo 5, c 20) . . . . 1.19, 3.80; p 702
  s 2 . . . . 3.78, 3.80; p 702
    (1)–(3) . . . . .3.80; p 704
Channel Islands (Church Legislation)
  Measure 1931 (21 & 22 Geo 5,
  no 4) 2.09
Channel Islands (Representation)
  Measure 1931 (21 & 22 Geo 5,
  no 5) 2.18, 2.19
Charities Act 1993 (c 10)—
  s 43 . . . . 8.12
    (2) 3.10
    (3)(a) 3.10
  72 . . . . 8.09
    (1) 3.10, 3.34
Charities Act 2006 (c 50) 1.23, 3.08
Children Act 1975 (c 72)—
  s 108(1)(a) 5.32
  Sch 3—
    para 8 . . . . 5.32
Children and Young Persons Act 1933
  (23 & 24 Geo 5, c 12)—
  Sch 1 . . . . 3.34
Church Commissioners (Loans for
  Theological Colleges and Training
  Houses) Measure 1964 (no 1) 2.40
Church Commissioners Measure 1947
  (10 & 11 Geo 6, no 2) 2.38
  s 1(1) 2.38
    (2) 2.39
  2 . . . . 2.38, 3.83
  3 . . . . 2.43
  4 . . . . 2.41
    (1) 2.39
  5(1)–(3) 2.41
  6 . . . . 2.43
    (3)(a) 2.43
    (3B) 2.43

  7(2)(a) 2.41
  10(5), (6) 2.44
    (6) . . . .
  Sch 1—
    para 1, 2 . . . . 2.39
Church Commissioners Measure
  1964 (no 8)—
  s 1 . . . . 2.43
  2 . . . . 2.43
    (3) 2.41
Church Commissioners Measure
  1970 (no 3)—
  s 1 . . . . 2.43
Church Dignitaries (Retirement)
  Measure 1949 (12, 13 & 14 Geo 6,
  no 1) 4.54, 8.23
  s 1(1) 8.23
    (2) 8.24
    (3) 8.24
      proviso 8.24
    (4) 8.24
  2(1) 8.24
  12 . . . . 8.23
  13(5) 8.23
  14(1), (2) 8.24
  15 . . . . 8.24
Church of England Assembly (Powers)
  Act 1919 (9 & 10 Geo 5,
  c 76) 1.44, 204, 303
  s 1 . . . . p **373**
  2 . . . . p 374
    (2) 2.07
  3 . . . . p 374
    (1), (2), (3), (5) 2.07
    (6) 1.25, 2.05
      proviso 2.05
  4 . . . . 1.25, 2.05, 2.08; p 374
    proviso 2.05, 2.07
  Appendix—
    para 15 . . . . 2.21
Church of England Convocations
  Act 1966 (c 2) 1.23
  s 1(1) 1.38
Church of England (Ecumenical Relations)
  Measure 1988 (no 3) 1.28, 3.99
Church of England (Legal Aid and
  Miscellaneous Provisions)
  Measure 1988 (no 1)—
  s 5 . . . . 3.02, 3.106
  7 (2)(a) 4.31
  11 . . . . 3.86
  14(1) 7.82
  Sch 2—
    para 1 . . . . 7.82

Table of Statutes and Measures

Church of England (Legal Aid)
  Measure 1994 (no 3)............6.67
  s 2(1) 3.69
  4..............................1.32
  7(2) 7.82
  Sch 1
    para 5.......................3.69
  Sch 2—
    para 1.......................7.82
Church of England Marriage Measure
  (proposed) 5.36, 5.40
  cl 1(1), (5)–(7)..................5.36
Church of England (Miscellaneous
  Provisions) Measure 1976 (no 3)—
  s 1(3) 1.28
  6(1) 5.51, 7.113
  (2) 7.113, 7.114
Church of England (Miscellaneous
  Provisions) Measure 1978
  (no 3)—
  s 1 ....2.25
Church of England (Miscellaneous
  Provisions) Measure 1983
  (no 2)—
  s 8(1)–(3), (5)...................4.64
Church of England (Miscellaneous
  Provisions) Measure 1992 (no 1)—
  s 1(1) 3.56, 4.26
  2(1) 5.52
  (2) 4.17, 5.55
  (3) 4.17, 5.52
  (4) 5.52
  3 ....5.56
  (1) 5.51, 7.113
    proviso....................5.51
  (2) 5.51
  13 ....2.55
  14 .... 4.01, 4.53
  15 .... 4.01, 8.20
  16 ....4.01
  17(1) 4.24
  Sch 3—
    para 21.....................4.24
Church of England (Miscellaneous
  Provisions) Measure 1995 (no 2)—
  s 5 ....8.18
Church of England (Miscellaneous
  Provisions) Measure 2000 (no 1)—
  s 4 ....2.44
  12(1), (2).....................4.53
  (4)................... 2.33, 4.53
  17 ....4.18
  Sch 2—
    para 1......................2.44

Church of England (Miscellaneous
  Provisons) Measure 2006
  (no 1).........................2.40
  s 2 ....2.39
  7(2) 2.47
  (3) 2.48
  (5) 2.49
  8 ....2.22
  Sch 2.........................2.39
Church of England (Pensions)
  Measure 2003 (no 2)............2.04
Church of England (Worship and
  Doctrine) Measure 1974
  (no 3)............. 1.28, 5.02, 5.07
  s 1 ....2.04; p 429
  (1) 1.04, 1.28, 5.02, 5.04
  (3) 3.29
  (5) 5.08
  (6) 5.04
  2 ....p **430**
  3 .... 1.28, 2.25; p **430**
  4 .... 1.28; p **430**
  (1) 5.01
  (2) 5.01, 5.04
  5 ....p **431**
  6 ....p **431**
  (1) 1.28
  (2) 5.52
  (3) 1.04, 1.40, 5.02, 5.07
  Sch 1—
    para 2.......................5.52
  Sch 2 ....1.04, 1.40, 5.02, 5.07
Churchwardens (Appointment and
  Resigna-tion) Measure 1964
  (no 3)............ 11.38, 3.32, 3.44
  s 12(2) 1.38
  13 ....1.38
  15(3) 1.38, 3.44
Churchwardens Measure 2001
  (No 1) 1.38, 2.04, 3.32, 3.34,
                3.44, 3.46, 3.47, 3.57, 3.108
  s 1 ....p **518**
  (1) 3.35
  (2)(a), (b).....................3.35
  (3)(a)–(d).....................3.33
  (4)............1.41, 3.33, 3.35, 3.48
  (5) 3.35
  2 ....p **519**
  (1)–(3)............... 3.34, 3.40, 3.43
  3 .... 3.34; p **520**
    proviso....................3.34
  4 ....p **520**
  (1)–(3).......................3.35
  (4)(a), (b).....................3.35

Churchwardens Measure 2001
(No 1) (cont.)
  4 (cont.)
    (5) 3.36
    (6)(a) 3.35
      (b) 3.36
    (7), (8) 3.39
  5 . . . . p 520
    (1) 3.37
    (2)–(4) 3.35, 3.37
    (5)–(8) 3.38
  6 . . . . p 521
    (1) 3.40, 3.41
    (2) 3.41
      (a), (b) 3.41
    (3), (4) 3.41
  7 . . . . p 522
    (1)–(3) 3.42
  8 . . . . 3.41; p 522
    (1)(a), (b) 3.43
      (c) 3.43, 3.47
    (2) 3.41, 3.43
  9 . . . . 3.44; p 522
  10 . . . . p 522
    (1)(a)–(e) 3.46
    (2) 33.46
  11 . . . . p 523
    (1) 3.44
    (2) 1.38, 3.44
      proviso 3.44
  12 . . . . 1.38, 3.44, 3.108; p 523
    (1), (2) 3.45
    (3) 1.38, 3.45
  13 . . . . p 523
    (1) 3.44
  14 . . . . 3.34
  15(1) 3.38
    (2) 3.32
  Sch 1—
    para 1 . . . . 3.34
  Sch 2 . . . . 3.38
  Sch 3 . . . . 3.32
City of London (Guild Churches)
  Act 1952 (15 & 16 Geo 6 &
  1 Eliz 2, c xxxviii) 3.108
Civil Liability (Contribution)
  Act 1978 (c 47) 7.95
Civil Partnership Act 2004
  (c 33) 1.24, 2.06, 5.49
  s 255, 259 . . . . 1.24, 2.06
Clandestine Marriages Act 1753
  (26 Geo 2, c 33) 5.34
Clergy Discipline Measure 2003
  (no 3) 2.46, 2.52, 2.56, 2.58,
        2.60, 3.106, 4.10, 4.19, 4.33, 4.35,
        4.36, 4.64, 6.01, 6.07, 6.11,
        613–615, 6.26, 6.39, 6.46, 6.51,
        6.67, 6.69, 6.73, 6.77, 6.80
  s 1 . . . . 1.03, 6.01; p 524
  2 . . . . 6.09; p 524
  3 . . . . 2.46; p 524
    (1) 6.04
      (a), (b) 6.04
    (2) 6.04
    (3)(a)–(c) 6.05
  4 . . . . p 524
    (1)–(3) 6.06
  5 . . . . p 525
    (1), (2), (6), (7) 2.56, 6.07
  6 . . . . p 525
    (1)(a), (b) 6.12
    (2)(a)–(c) 6.12
    (3)–(5) 6.12
  7 . . . . p 526
    (2) 4.33
  8 . . . . p 526
    (1) 4.33, 6.54
      (a)–(d) 6.13
    (2) 4.33, 4.35, 4.36, 6.12
    (3) 4.14, 6.15
  9 . . . . 6.16; p 526
  first and second
    provisos 6.16
  10 . . . . 6.16; p 526
    (1)(a)(i) 6.17
      (ii) 3.49, 6.17
      (iii) 6.17
    (b)(i), (ii) 6.19
    (2)(a)–(c) 6.20
    (3) 6.20
  11 . . . . p 527
    (1) 6.23
      (a), (b) 6.23
    (2) 6.24
      proviso 6.24
    (3)–(5) 6.24
    (6) 6.23
  12 . . . . p 528
    (1) 6.25, 6.37
      (a), (b) 6.27, 6.32
      (c) 6.27
      (d) 6.27, 6.29, 6.32
      (e) 6.27, 6.29, 6.32, 6.34
    (2) 6.25
  13 . . . . p 528
    (2), (3) 6.28
  14 . . . . p 528
    (1)–(4) 6.29

Clergy Discipline Measure 2003
(no 3) (cont.)
- 15 .... 6.39; p **529**
  - (1)–(3) 6.31
  - (4) 6.32
    - (a)–(c) 6.32
  - (5)(a), (b) 6.32
- 16 .... 6.51; p **529**
  - (1), (2) 6.33
  - (3) 6.34
  - (4) 6.33
- 17 .... p **529**
  - (1) 6.35
  - (2)–(5) 6.36
- 18 .... p **530**
  - (1) 6.39
  - (2)(a) 6.36, 6.39
  - (b) 6.39
  - (3)(a), (b) 6.45
  - (c) 6.43
- 19 .... p **530**
  - (1)(a)–(c) 6.47
  - (2) 6.47
    - proviso 6.47
- 20 .... p **531**
  - (1), (2) 2.60, 6.58
- 21 .... p **531**
  - (1) 6.08
  - (2)(a), (b) 6.08
    - (c) 6.08, 6.09
  - (3), (4) 6.08
  - (5) 6.08
    - proviso 6.08
  - (6)–(8) 6.08
- 22 .... 2.46, 6.09; p **532**
  - (1)(a)–(c) 6.09
  - (2) 6.09
- 23 .... p **532**
  - (1)(a)–(c) 6.10
  - (2)(a)–(c) 6.10
  - (3) 6.10
- 24 .... 4.38, 6.33,
                          6.64; p **533**
  - (1)(a), (b) 6.48
    - (c) 6.33, 6.48
    - (d)–(f) 6.48
  - (2) 6.48
- 25 .... p **533**
  - (1)–(4) 6.49
- 26 .... 4.38; p **533**
  - (1)(a), (b) 6.55
  - (2), (3) 6.55
- 27 .... 6.56; p **534**
- 28 .... 6.57; p **534**
- 29 .... 6.14; p **534**
- 30 .... p **534**
  - (1)(a), (b) 6.54
  - (2)–(5), (7) 6.54
- 31 .... 6.54; p **535**
- 32 .... 6.54; p **536**
- 33, 34 .... 6.14, 6.54; p **536**
- 35 .... p **536**
- 36 .... 6.62; p **537**
  - (1) 6.14, 6.37
    - proviso 6.37
  - (2)–(4) 6.38
  - (5) 6.14
  - (6) 6.37
- 37 .... 6.37, 6.62; p **537**
- 38 .... 6.30; p **538**
  - (1)(a)–(e) 6.69
  - (2) 6.70
  - (3) 6.71
  - (4) 6.72
    - proviso 6.72
- 39 .... 6.02; p **539**
  - (1), (3), (4) 6.05
- 40 .... p **539**
  - (1), (2) 6.54
- 41 .... 6.66; p **539**
- 42 .... p **539**
  - (2)(a), (b) 6.17
  - (3) 6.17
  - (4)(a), (b) 6.17
  - (5)(a), (b) 6.17
  - (6)(a), (b) 6.17
- 43 .... 6.48; p **540**
  - (1) 6.11, 6.12
- 45 .... 6.36
- Sch 1—
  - para 3 .... 6.58

Clergy Ordination Act 1804
  (44 Geo 3, c 43)—
  s 1 .... 4.06

Clergy (Ordination and Miscellaneous
  Provisions) Measure 1964
  (no 6) 4.36
  s 1(1) 4.04
  2 .... 4.06
  8 .... 4.56
  9 .... 4.04, 4.05

Clergy (Ordination) Measure 1990
  (no 1)
  s 1 .... 4.04, 4.05

Clerical Disabilities Act 1870
  (33 & 34 Vict, c 91) 6.69

Table of Statutes and Measures

Clerical Disabilities Act 1870
(Amendment) Measure 1934
(24 & 25 Geo 5, no 1) 4.38
  s 1(1) 4.38
    (i)–(iii) 4.38
    (2), (3) 4.38
  2(1) 4.38
Clerical Subscription Act 1865
(28 & 29 Vict, c 122)—
  s 1 . . . . 5.07
  4 . . . . 4.07
Compulsory Church Rate Abolition
Act 1868 (31 & 32 Vict, c 109) 3.28
Coronation Oath Act 1688 (1 Will
& Mar c 6) 1.20
Court of Probate Act 1857 (20 & 21
Vict, c 77) 1.33, 2.46
Courts Act 1971 (c 23)—
  s 17(1) 2.48
Courts and Legal Services
Act 1990 (c 41) 6.07
  s 7(2) 2.47
  71 . . . . 2.47, 2.53, 6.08
  Sch 10—
    para 17 . . . . 2.47
Criminal Damage Act 1971 (c 48) 7.03
Criminal Justice Act 1925 (15 &
16 Geo 5, c 86)—
  s 41 . . . . 7.63
Criminal Justice Act 2003 (c 44)—
  Sch 33 . . . . 4.14
Criminal Law Act 1967 (c 58) 5.28

Data Protection Act 1984 (c 35) 1.23
Data Protection Act 1998 (c 29) 1.23
Deaconesses and Lay Ministry
Measure 1972 (no 4)—
  s 1 . . . . 3.72
Deacons (Ordination of Women) Measure
1986 (no 4) 1.28, 3.71, 4.01
  s 1 . . . . 3.71
  2(1) 3.71
Diocesan Boards of Education
Measure 1991 (no 2)—
  s 1 . . . . 2.32
    (2) 2.26
  2 . . . . 2.32
  Schedule—
    Pt I—
      para 4 . . . . 2.26
Diocesan Boards of Finance Measure
1925 (15 & 16 Geo 5, no 3) 2.29
  s 3 . . . . 2.29

Diocesan Stipends Funds Measure
1953 (1 & 2 Eliz 2, no 2)—
  s 1 . . . . 2.04
Diocese in Europe Measure 1980
(no 2) 2.09, 2.10
Dioceses, Pastoral and Mission
Measure (proposed) 3.02, 3.86
  cl 54 . . . . 7.51
  Sch 5—
    para 12 . . . . 4.24
Dioceses Measure 1978 (no 1)
  s 10 . . . . 4.61, 4.65
  11 . . . . 4.61, 4.65
    (7) 4.61
  17 . . . . 2.26
Disability Discrimination Act 1995
(c 50) 7.102
  s 25 . . . . 7.102
  Sch 3—
    Pt II 7.102
Disused Burial Grounds Act 1884
(47 & 48 Vict, c 72)—
  s 3 . . . . 7.93

Ecclesiastical Canons Act 1535
(27 Hen 8, c 15) 1.13
Ecclesiastical Commissioners Act 1836
(6 & 7 Will 4, c 77) 2.38
Ecclesiastical Commissioners Act 1840
(3 & 4 Vict, c 113) 2.42
  s 27 . . . . 8.18, 8.20
Ecclesiastical Commissioners Act 1850
(13 & 14 Vict, c 94)—
  s 1 . . . . 2.19
Ecclesiastical Courts Act 1855 (18 &
19 Vict, c 41) 2.46
Ecclesiastical Courts Jurisdiction Act
1860 (23 & 24 Vict, c 32) 3.52
  s 2, 3 . . . . 3.52
Ecclesiastical Dilapidations Measure
1923 (14 & 15 Geo 5, no 3)—
  s 52 . . . . 3.78, 3.81
Ecclesiastical Fees Measure 1986
(no 2) 3.56, 7.79, 7.82
  s 2 . . . . 3.84
Ecclesiastical Judges and Legal Officers
Measure 1976 (no 2)—
  s 1(1) 2.48
  2 . . . . 2.48
  3(1)–(4), (4A), (4B), (4C) 2.53
  4(1)–(4), (5A), (5C) 2.54
  5(3), (6) 2.54
  7(1), (2) 2.55

Ecclesiastical Jurisdiction Act 1847
   (10 & 11 Vict, c 98)—
  s 5 . . . . 5.40
Ecclesiastical Jurisdiction Measure 1963
   (no 1) 2.46, 2.47, 2.52, 2.58,
       3.104, 4.10, 4.19, 4.38, 4.64, 5.08,
       6.01, 6.09, 6.13–6.15, 6.46, 6.69,
       6.73, 6.74, 6.77, 6.79
  s 1 . . . . p 382
    (1) 2.47
   2 . . . . p 382
    (1), (1A), (2) 2.47
    (4) 2.48
      (c) 2.48
    (4A), (5) 2.48
   2A . . . . 2.48; p 383
    (1), (2) 2.48
   3 . . . . p 383
    (2)(a) 1.34, 2.59, 2.60, 6.58
      (b), (c) 2.60, 6.58
   4 . . . . p 384
    (1), (1A), (2) 2.49
   5 . . . . 2.59, 6.76,
                       7.77; p 385
   6 . . . . 2.47; p 385
    (1)(b) 2.58, 704
      (bb), (c)–(e) 2.58
   7 . . . . p 386
    (1A) 8.54
    (2) 7.78
   8 . . . . p 386
   10 . . . . p 387
    (1) 2.59, 7.77
    (3)–(5) 7.77
   11 . . . . p 388
    (2)(a) 6.76
    (4) 6.76
   12 . . . . 2.48; p 388
   13 . . . . p 388
    (2) 2.47
   14 . . . . p 388
    (1) (a), (b) 6.13
   15–20 . . . . p 389
   21 . . . . p 390
   23(1) 6.74
   38 . . . . p 391
   39 . . . . p 391
    (1) 6.74
   40 . . . . 6.74; p 391
   41 . . . . 6.74; p 392
   42 . . . . 6.75; p 392
    (7) 6.75
   43 . . . . 6.75; p 393
   44 . . . . p 393

   45 . . . . p 393
    (1)(g) 6.76
    (2), (3) 6.76
   46 . . . . p 394
    (1) 2.51
      proviso 4.60
   47 . . . . p 394
    (1)(b) 1.34, 2.59, 7.77
   48 . . . . 1.34; p 394
    (5) 1.34
   49 . . . . p 395
    (1)(a)–(e) 6.77
    (2) 6.78
    (3) 6.76
    (4)–(6) 6.78
   50 . . . . 6.79; p 395
      proviso 6.79
   51 . . . . 6.79; p 396
      proviso 6.79
   52 . . . . p 396
   53 . . . . 6.80; p 396
   54 . . . . 6.79
   58 . . . . p 396
   60 . . . . 7.82; p 397
    (1) 7.79
    (2) 8.54
    (3)(b) 7.82
   61 . . . . p 397
    (1), (2) 7.82
   62, 63 . . . . p 398
   66 . . . . p 398
    (3), (4) 3.104
   67, 69–71 . . . . p 399
   72–74 . . . . p 400
   75, 76, 78 . . . . p 401
   80 . . . . 7.63, 8.52; p 401
   81 . . . . p 401
    (1) 8.52
    (2), (3) 7.76, 8.54
   82(2)(c) 3.47, 3.50
   83 . . . . p 402
    (2)(d) 2.52
  Sch 1—
    Pt I 2.48
Ecclesiastical Licences Act 1533
   (25 Hen 8, c 21) 1.20, 2.61
  s 3 . . . . 4.66, 5.41
  4–10 . . . . 5.40
  11, 12 . . . . 5.40, 5.41
Ecclesiastical Offices (Age Limit)
   Measure 1975 (no 2)—
  s 1(3) 4.19, 4.39, 4.54, 4.64,
                      4.67, 8.19, 8.22
    (4)(d) 4.64

Ecclesiastical Offices (Age Limit)
 Measure 1975 (no 2)— (cont.)
 2 .... 4.67
 3(1)(a) 4.64
  (b)....................... 4.54
  (2) 3.29, 4.39
 7(4) 4.64
 Schedule..............4.19, 4.39, 4.54,
  4.64, 4.67, 8.19, 8.22
Ecclesiastical Offices (Terms of Service)
 Measure (proposed) 4.40, 4.42
Education Act 1996 (c 56) 1.23, 1.48
Enabling Act. *See* Church of England
 Assembly (Powers) Act 1919
Endowments and Glebe Measure
 1976 (no 4) 4.26
 s 15 .... 3.84
Environmental Protection Act
 1990 (c 43).................... 3.51
Equality Act 2006 (c 3)............. p 697
Extra-Parochial Ministry Measure
 1967 (no 2) 3.02, 4.36
 s 1 .... 3.02, 4.17
 2 (1)............... 3.02, 3.106, 5.23
  (1A).......................3.106
  (2) 3.02, 4.17, 5.23
  (3) 3.106
  (4) 3.106, 4.36

Faculty Jurisdiction Measure
 1964 (no 5)—
 s 1 .... p 402
 3 .... 7.96; p 403
  (2), (3) 7.96
  (4) 3.76, 7.96, 7.121
 4 ....p 403
 5 ....p 696
 6 ....p 404
 7 ....p 404
  (1) 7.02, 7.92
 8 ....p 404
 11 .... 7.82; p 404
 12 ....7.13
 15 ....p 404
Family Law Reform Act 1969 (c 46)—
 s 2(1)(c) 5.32
 33(1) 5.32
 Sch 2—
  para 9, 10..................... 5.32

Gender Recognition Act 2004
 (c 7) 5.16, 5.35
 s 11, 22....................... 5.35
 Sch 4 .... 5.35

House of Commons (Clergy
 Disqualification) Act 1801
 (41 Geo 3, c 63) 4.14
House of Commons (Removal of
 Clergy Disqualification)
 Act 2001 (c 13)................ 4.13
 s 1(1) 4.12
Human Rights Act 1998 (c 42)....... 1.19,
  1.29, 1.30, 1.32, 1.42, 1.43, 1.45,
  1.47, 2.05, 2.62, 3.01, 3.21, 3.22,
  3.81, 4.15, 4.45, 5.50, 5.62;
  p 663, 697, 703
 s 1(3) 3.52
 2(1)(a)–(d)..................... 1.27
 3(1) 1.26, 1.29
  (2)(a) 1.26
 4(2), (5) 1.27
 6(1) 2.62, 5.50
  (3)(a) 2.62
 10(2), (6) 1.27
 12(4) .... p 670
 13 .... 1.27, 1.47
  (1) ....3.52; p 670
 21(1) 1.26, 1.29, 1.30
 Sch 1 .... 1.26
  Art 6, 8....................... 1.26
  9, 10............... 1.26, 3.52
  11, 12................ 1.26
 First Protocol—
  Art 2........................ 1.26

Incumbents (Vacation of Benefices)
 (Amendment) Measure 1993
 (no 1).................. 3.26, 4.43
 s 5, 6......................... 4.40
 7 .... 3.26
 8 .... 4.41
Incumbents (Vacation of Benefices)
 Measure 1977 (no 1)........ 2.46, 3.26,
  3.47, 3.88, 4.26, 4.43, 4.46,
  4.54, 8.24
 s 1 .... p 431
 1A ....p 432
  (1), (1A), (2), (6), (7) 4.43
 2 ....p 433
  (1), (5) 4.44
 3 ....p 433
  (1) 4.44
  (d) 4.44
  (1A) 4.44
 4 ....p 434
  (1) 4.45
 5 .... 4.45; p 434
 6 .... 4.40; p 434

Table of Statutes and Measures

Incumbents (Vacation of
 Benefices) Measure 1977
 (no 1) (*cont.*)
  7 . . . . 4.45; p **435**
    (4), (5) .4.45
  7A . . . . 4.40; p **435**
    (1), (2) .4.45
  8 . . . . p **436**
  9 . . . . p **436**
    (1), (2), (4), (5). 4.45
  9A . . . . p **436**
    (1) 4.45
      (a). 4.40
    (2) 4.45
    (3) 4.40
  10 . . . . .p **437**
    (2), (5) 4.46
    (6) 3.10, 3.26,
                         3.34, 4.45, 4.46
    (7), (9) 4.46
  11 . . . . .p **438**
    (2)(a)–(d) 4.41
    (3), (6), (7) 4.41
  12 . . . . .p **439**
  13 . . . . 4.41; p **439**
    (1)(a) 4.45
  14 . . . . .p **439**
  16, 17. . . . . .p **440**
  18 . . . . .p **440**
    (2) 1.32
  19 . . . . .p **441**
  19A . . . . 4.43; p **441**
  20(1) 8.24
  Sch 1 . . . . p **441**
    para 1 . . . . .4.45
      proviso 4.45
      3(1), (2), (4)–(6) 4.45
  Sch 2 . . . . p **443**
Inspection of Churches Measure
  1955 (3 & 4 Eliz 2, no1) 3.82,
                                4.55, 7.130
  s 1 . . . . 3.08, 3.54; p **375**
    (1) 2.30
    (2)(c) 3.82, 7.17
      (d) 3.82, 7.130
    1A . . . . 3.82; p **375**
    1B . . . . p **376**
    2 . . . . p **376**
      (1) 7.130
    3, 4. . . . . p **376**
    5, 6. . . . . p **377**

Juries Act 1974 (c 23) 4.14

Land Registration Act 1925 (15 &
  16 Geo 5, c 21)—
  s 70(1)(c) 3.79
Land Registration Act 2002 (c 9) 3.79
  s 11(4)(a) 3.79
    12(2)(b) 3.79
    29(2)(a)(i) 3.79
    30(2)(a)(i) 3.79
    117(2) 3.79
  Sch 1—
    para 16. .3.79
  Sch 3—
    para 16. .3.79
Lecturers and Parish Clerks Act 1844
  (7 & 8 Vict, c 59)—
  s 2, 4. . . . . .3.61
Local Government Act 1972 (c 70)—
  s 80 . . . . .4.14
    215(1), (2) 7.95
  Sch 4—
    para 14(a). . . . . p **688**
Lord Hardwicke's Marriage Act 1753. *See*
  Clandestine Marriages Act 1753

Marriage Act 1949 (12, 13 & 14
  Geo 6, c 76) 1.23, 5.32, 5.40
  s 1(1) 5.32
    2 . . . . .5.32
    3(1), (3) 5.32
    4 . . . . .5.44
    5 . . . . .5.40
    5A 5.35
    5B(1), (2). 5.35
    6(1), (2) 5.36, 5.46
      (3), (4) .5.36
    7(1), (2) 5.38
      (3) 5.37
    8 . . . . .5.37
    9 . . . . 3.70, 3.73
      (1) 5.37
      (2)(a), (b) 5.37
    11 . . . . .5.38
    12(1) 5.36
      (2) 5.38
    13 . . . . .5.39
    14(1) 5.39
    15(1) 5.36, 5.40
    16(1)(a)–(c) 5.42
      (1A), (1B), (2), (2A),
        (2B), (3) 5.42
    17 . . . . .5.43
    22 . . . . .5.44
    25(a) 5.40

Table of Statutes and Measures

Land Registration Act 1925 (15 & 16 Geo 5, c 21)— *(cont.)*
  27(4) 5.43
  31(4) 5.43
  35(3) 5.36
  53(a) 5.46
  55(1)–(3) 5.46
  57(1) 5.47
  59, 60, 62, 63 . . . . 5.47
  68(2), (3) 5.48
  69(1), (4) 5.48
  72(1) 5.36
  75(1)(a) 5.44
    (b) 5.32
    (c) 5.40
  76(1) 547
  78(1) 532
  Sch 1—
    Pt I 5.32
Marriage Act 1994 (c 34) 5.40
Marriage of British Subjects (Facilities) Act 1915 (5 & 6 Geo 5, c 40)—
  s 1(a) 5.39
Marriage (Prohibited Degrees of Relation-ship) Act 1986 (c 16) 5.35
  s 1(4) 5.42
    (6) 5.32
  3 . . . . 5.35
  Sch 1—
    para 4 . . . . 5.42
    8 . . . . 5.32
Matrimonial Causes Act 1857 (21 & 22 Vict, c 85) 2.46
Matrimonial Causes Act 1965 (c 72) 5.35
  s 8 . . . . p 405
    (2)(a), (b) 5.35, 5.50
Matrimonial Causes Act 1973 (c 18) 5.31
Mental Health Act 1983 (c 20)—
  s 94 . . . . 4.18
  96(5) 4.18

National Institutions Measure 1998 (no 1) 2.11, 2.38
  s 1 . . . . p 500
    (1) 2.11, 2.13
    (3) 2.12
  2 . . . . 2.40; p 500
    (1)–(3) 2.42
  3 . . . . p 501
    (2) 2.13

4 . . . . p 500
  (1)–(3) 2.13
5 . . . . p 501
  (1)(c) 2.20
6 . . . . p 502
7(1) 2.39
9 . . . . p 503
  (b) 2.11
10, 11 . . . . p 503
12 . . . . p 504
13(1) 2.19, 3.08
Sch 1 . . . . p 504
  para 1(1)–(3) 2.12
  2 . . . . 2.12
  16 . . . . 2.13
Sch 4—
  para 2, 3 . . . . 2.41
  4 . . . .
  6 . . . . 2.43
  8 . . . . 2.39
Sch 5—
  para 2(b) 2.19
    (e) 3.08
National Service Act 1948 (11 & 12 Geo 6, c 64)—
  s 1 . . . . 4.14
  Sch 1 . . . . 4.14

Occupiers' Liability Act 1957 (5 & 6 Eliz 2, c 31) 7.95
Open Spaces Act 1887 (50 & 51 Vict, c 32)—
  s 4 . . . . 7.93
Open Spaces Act 1906 (6 Edw 7, c 25)
  s 6 . . . . 7.94
Overseas and Other Clergy (Ministry and Ordination) Measure 1967 (no 3)
  s 1(1)–(3), (6) 4.10
  5 . . . . 4.09
    (1)–(3) 4.09

Parochial Church Councils (Powers) Measure 1956 (4 & 5 Eliz 2, no 3) 3.03, 3.11, 3.21, 3.26, 3.28, 8.02
  s 1 . . . . p 378
  2 . . . . p 378
    (1) 3.21
    (2)(a) 3.21
    (b) 3.21, 5.01
    (c), (d) 3.24
    (3) 3.09, 3.24
  3 . . . . 3.27, 8.10; p 378

Parochial Church Councils (Powers)
Measure 1956 (4 & 5 Eliz 2,
no 3) (cont.)
- 4 .... 3.27; p **378**
  - (1)(ii)(a) 3.84
  - (b) 3.82
  - (c) 7.96, 7.128
- 5 .... 3.27; p **379**
  - (1) 8.10
- 6 .... 3.27, 8.10; p **380**
  - (1), (3) 3.82
- 7 .... p **381**
  - (i), (ii) 3.28
  - (iii) 3.28, 3.61, 8.10
  - (iv) 3.28, 5.23, 8.10
  - (v) 3.28
- 8 .... 3.08, 3.29, 8.10; p **381**
- 9 .... 8.10; p **381**
  - (1) 3.28
  - (3) 3.26, 3.61

Parochial Libraries Act 1708
(7 Anne, c 14)................ 7.117

Parochial Registers and Records
Measure 1978 (no 2)............ 5.14
- s 2 .... 5.14
- 3(1), (4) 5.54
- 6(2) 3.56

Parsonages Measure 1938 (1 & 2 Geo 6,
no 3)—
- s 1(1), (3) 3.83
- 3(1) 3.29

Pastoral (Amendment) Measure 1982
(no 1)......................... 3.86

Pastoral (Amendment) Measure 1994
(no 1)—
- s 13 .... 3.90

Pastoral (Amendment) Measure 2006
(no 2)—
- s 1(b) 7.120

Pastoral Measure 1968
(no 1)................. 2.32, 3.86

Pastoral Measure 1983 (no 1) 1.38,
3.86, 3.88, 3.98, 4.46, 7.02, 7.120,
8.02, 1.38, 3.86, 3.88,
- Pt I (s 1–16) 3.16, 3.18
- s 1 .... 2.32
  - (1), (2) 3.86
- 2 .... 2.32
  - (1), (2) 3.86
  - (3)(a) 3.86
  - (b) 1.38, 3.86
  - (4) 3.86
- 2A 3.02
- 3(1) 3.86

- (2)(a), (b) 3.86
- (c) 3.29, 3.86
- (d)–(f) 3.86
- (3), (5)–(8) 3.86
- (9), (10) 3.87
- 4(1) 3.87
- (2)(a), (b) 3.87
- 5(1)–(3) 3.90
- (4) 3.90
- proviso 3.90
- 6(1), (2) 3.91
- (3) 3.91
- (a), (b) 3.91
- (4) 3.91
- 7(1), (2) 3.91
- 8(1) 3.92
- (2)–(4) 3.93
- 9(1), (2), (6) 3.92
- 13 .... 3.86
- 16(2) 3.86
- 17 .... 8.02
- (1)(a)–(d) 3.88
- (5) 3.88
- 18 .... 4.48
- (2) 3.18
- (4) 3.88, 4.48
- 20 .... 4.49
- (1) 4.49
- (a) 4.49
- (2), (3) 4.17, 4.49
- (6) 4.49
- (7), (8) 4.17, 4.49
- (10) 4.51
- 21 .... 4.50
- (1)(a), (b) 4.50
- proviso 4.50
- (2) 4.50
- (4) 4.51
- 23(5) 4.17
- 25 .... 3.94, 6.66
- 26 .... 3.94
- 29 .... 3.98
- (2) 3.35
- 32 .... 4.18
- 37(1)(a)–(f) 3.89
- 40 .... 3.58, 4.48
- 42 .... 2.32
- 56 .... 7.02, 7.120; p **445**
- (2) 7.118
- (2A) 7.120
- (2F)(b) 7.120
- (3)(a) 7.118
- 67(1) 4.23, 4.24
- (a)–(c) 4.23

Table of Statutes and Measures

Pastoral Measure 1983 (no 1) (*cont.*)
  67(1) (*cont.*)
    (2), (4)–(7) 4.24
    (5A) 6.24
  68(3), (4) 4.32
  69 . . . . 4.19, 4.25
    (1)(a)–(d) 4.25
  70 . . . . 4.19
  82 . . . . 4.18
  85(2)–(4) 8.20
  Sch 1 . . . . 3.86
    para 3 . . . . 4.65
  Sch 3—
    para 4(2)(d) 3.58
      13(a) 4.48
  Sch 4 . . . . 3.94, 4.45, 6.66
  Sch 5—
    para 5–12 . . . . 2.32
Patronage (Benefices) Measure
  1986 (no 3) 8.18
  s 1 . . . . p 447
    (1), (2) 4.18
  2 . . . . 4.18; p 447
  3 . . . . p 447
    (1)–(5), (7), (8) 4.18
  4, 5 . . . . p 448
  Pt II (s 7–24) 3.16
  s 7 . . . . p 449
    (1)–(5) 4.19
  8 . . . . p 449
    (1)(a), (b) 4.19
    (2) 4.18, 4.19
    (3)–(7) 4.19
  9 . . . . p 450
    (1) 4.19
  10 . . . . p 451
  11 . . . . p 451
    (1)(a)–(e) 4.20
      (f) 3.30, 4.20
  12 . . . . p 452
    (5), (8), (9) 4.20
  13 . . . . p 453
    (1)(a), (b) 4.21
    (2)–(6) 4.21
  14, 15 . . . . 4.21; p 454
  16 . . . . p 454
    (1) 4.22
      (a), (b) 4.21
  17 . . . . p 455
  18(1) 4.22
  19 . . . . p 455
  20 . . . . p 456
  21 . . . . 4.18; p 456
  22 . . . . p 456

  23 . . . . 3.18, 3.19,
                                   4.18; p 456
  24, 25 . . . . p 457
  26–28 . . . . 2.32; p 458
  29 . . . . p 458
  33 . . . . 4.19
  37, 38 . . . . p 458
  39 . . . . p 460
  41 . . . . 4.18, 4.24
  Sch 2—
    para 20 . . . . 3.18, 3.19
  Sch 3 . . . . 2.32
  Sch 4—
    para 18 . . . . 4.24
      20 . . . . 4.25
  Sch 5 . . . . 4.18
Pensions Measure 1997 (no 1)—
  s 10(1) 2.44
  Sch 1—
    para 3 . . . . 2.44
Planning (Listed Buildings and
  Conservation Areas)
  Act 1990 (c 9)—
  s 60(1), (3), (4) 7.05
    (5) 7.06
Pluralities Act 1838 (1 & 2 Vict,
  c 106) 4.13
  s 28–30 . . . . 4.13
    32–51 . . . . 4.16
    95 . . . . 4.31
      proviso 4.31
    97 . . . . 4.31
    102 . . . . 4.36
    114 . . . . 4.16
Pluralities Acts Amendment
  Act 1885 (48 & 49 Vict, c 54)—
  s 12 . . . . 4.16
Police and Criminal Evidence
  Act 1984 (c 60)—
  s 26(1) 3.52
    76, 78 . . . . 5.62
    82(3) 5.62
    119(2) 3.52
  Sch 7—
    Pt I 3.52
Prayer Book (Alternative and
  other Services) Measure
  1965 (no 1) 5.02
Prayer Book (Further Provisions)
  Measure 1968 (no 2)—
  s 5 . . . . 5.52
Prayer Book (Versions of the Bible)
  Measure 1965 (no 4)
  s 1 proviso 3.29

Table of Statutes and Measures

Priests (Ordination of Women) Measure
  1993 (no 2) 1.28, 1.35, 3.30,
        4.01, 4.20, 4.63, 8.34
 s 1 .... p **493**
  (1) 1.28
  (2) 4.02
 2 .... p **493**
  (1), (2) 4.63
 3 .... 3.16, 3.18; p **494**
  (1) 3.30, 4.50
  (2)–(5) 3.30
  (7) 3.30, 4.20
 4 .... p **494**
  (1)–(3), (5) 8.34
 5 .... p **495**
  (c) 8.34
 6 .... 6.25
 7, 8. .... p **495**
 9 .... p **496**
 10 .... 4.16, 4.50
 11 .... p **496**
 Sch 1 .... 3.30; p **496**
 Sch 2 .... 8.34; p **496**
 Sch 3—
  para 1 .... 4.16
  7 .... 4.50
Prison Act 1952 (15 & 16 Geo 6
  & 1 Eliz 2, c 52)—
 s 7(1) 3.02
Protection of Children
  Act 1999 (c 14) 1.23

Queen Anne's Bounty Act 1703
  (2 & 3 Ann, c 20) 2.38

Repair of Benefice Buildings Measure
  1972 (no 2) 2.30
 s 1 .... 2.32; p **420**
  (1) 2.30, 2.32
 2, 3. .... p **421**
 4 .... p **422**
 5 .... 3.83; p **423**
 8, 9. .... p **423**
 10 .... 2.30; p **423**
 11–13 .... p **424**
 14 .... p **425**
 15 .... 2.30; p **425**
 16, 17. .... p **426**
 19 .... 2.30
 20 .... 2.30, 7.128; p **426**
 21, 23. .... p **427**
 29 .... 3.83; p **428**
 30, 31. .... p **428**
 31 ....

Representation of the People
  Act 1983 (c 2)—
 s 1 .... 4.14

Sacrament Act 1547 (1 Edw 6, c 1)—
 s 8 .... 5.20, 5.25
School Standards and Framework
  Act 1998 (c 31) 1.23
 s 131 .... 1.48
Sex Discrimination Act 1975 (c 65) 2.05
 s 77 .... 4.42
Sharing of Church Buildings
  Act 1969 (c 38). 1.23, 3.95, 7.08
 s 1 .... p **412**
  (1), (2) 3.96
  (3)(a) 3.29, 3.96
  (b) 3.96
  (4), (8)–(10) 3.96
 2 .... 3.97; p **413**
 3 .... p **414**
  (1) 3.97
 4 .... p **415**
  (1)–(3) 3.97
 5 .... 3.96; p **415**
  (1)–(3) 3.98
  (4)(a), (b) 3.98
 6 .... 3.98; p **415**
 7, 8. .... p **416**
 9 .... 3.98; p **415**
 10 .... p **417**
  (1) 3.96
 11 .... p **417**
  (1) 3.95
 12 .... p **418**
  (1) 3.96
 Sch 2 .... 3.95; p **419**
Sharing of Church Buildings
  Measure 1970 (no 2) 3.95
Submission of the Clergy Act 1533
  (25 Hen 8, c 19) 1.12, 1.13,
          1.28, 1.29
 s 1 .... 1.28
 3 .... 1.28, 1.39
Suffragan Bishops Act 1534
  (26 Hen 8, c 14)—
 s 1, 2, 6. .... 4.65
Synodical Government Measure
  1969 (no 2) 1.29, 2.04, 2.33, 3.03
 s 1 .... 2.04; p **405**
  (1) 1.28
  (2) 1.28, 1.29
  (3) 1.28
  (b) 1.39
  (5) 1.28

Table of Statutes and Measures

Synodical Government Measure
    1969 (no 2) (*cont.*)
    2 .... p 406
        (1) 1.25, 2.15, 2.22, 2.25
        (2) 1.25
    3 .... p 406
    4 .... p 406
        (2)(a)–(e) 2.27
            proviso 2.28, 5.01
        (3)–(5) 2.28
        (7) 2.26
    5 .... p 407
        (2) 2.33
        (3) 2.35
            (a)–(e) 2.35
            proviso 2.35, 5.01
        (4) 2.29, 2.35, 5.01
    6 .... 3.09, 3.21, 3.24, 5.01
    7 .... p 408
        (1) proviso 2.25
    9(2) 2.23
    Sch 1—
        para 1 .... 1.28
    Sch 2 .... 1.31, 2.21, 2.22; p 408
        art 1 .... 2.15
            2 .... 2.15, 2.16, 2.18
            3(1) 2.22
            4(1) 2.20
                (2) 2.22
            5(1) 2.23
                proviso 2.23
                (2) 2.23
                proviso 2.23
            6 .... 2.21
                (a) 2.24
                    (i) 1.25

                    (ii) 1.28
                    (iv) 1.35
        7(1), (2), (5) 2.24
            (6) 1.31, 2.24
        8 .... 2.27
            (1), (1C), (2) 2.25
        10(2) 2.20
        11(1), (3) 2.22
        12(2) 2.20
    Sch 3 .... 2.18, 3.03
    (*see also* Church Representation
        Rules *in Table of Rules and
        Regulations*)

Team and Group Ministries Measure
    1995 (no 1) 3.86, 4.29
    s 1 .... 4.49
        5(3) 3.89
        12 .... 3.96
    Sch 1 .... 4.49
Tithe Act 1936 (26 Geo 5 &
    1 Edw 8, c 43) 3.78
    s 1 .... 3.84
Town and Country Planning
    Act 1990 (c 8)
    Pt VIII, ch I (s 197–214D) 7.128
Treasure Act 1996 (c 24) 8.36, 8.42
Trustee Act 2000 (c 29) 8.30

United Reformed Church
    Act 1972 (c xvii)—
    s 24(1) 3.95

TABLE OF RULES, REGULATIONS AND OTHER INSTRUMENTS

References are to paragraphs in the text or to page numbers in the Materials.
Provisions with bold page numbers are set out in the Materials.

Admission of Baptised Infants to Holy
    Communion Regulations 2006.... 5.18
    para 5, 9 .... 5.18

Care of Cathedrals Rules 1990,
    SI 1990/2335 .... 8.03
Care of Cathedrals Rules 2006,
    SI 2006/1941 .... 8.03
    r 8 .... 8.43
Church Accounting Regulations 2006
    (GS 1624) 3.08
Church of England (Legal Aid) Rules
    1995, SI 1995/2034 .... 1.32, 6.67
Church Representation Rules (Synodical
    Government Measure 1969,
    Sch 3) 2.15, 2.18, 2.26,
                    2.31, 3.03, 3.11, 8.10
    r 1 .... 3.43; p **617**
        (1) 3.04
        (2) 3.04
            proviso 3.04
        (4) 3.04
        (7), (8) 3.05
        (9) 3.04, 3.05
        (10) 3.05
    2 .... p **618**
        (1) 3.06
        (4) 3.06, 3.43
    3–5 .... p **620**
    6 .... p **620**
        (1)–(5) 3.07
    7 .... 3.07; p **621**
        (3) 3.07
    8 .... p **621**
        (1), (3) 3.07
    9 .... p **622**
        (1)(a)–(e) 3.08
        (3) 3.08
            (b), (c) 3.09
        (4) 3.08, 3.09

        (5) 3.10, 3.60
            (a), (b) 3.10
            (c) 3.10, 3.60
            (d) 3.10, 3.63
        (7) 3.09
        (8), (9) 3.07
    10 .... p **623**
        (1) 3.10
        (2) 3.60
        (3) 3.10
            (a), (b) 3.10
    11 .... 3.10, 3.38; p **623**
        (8)(a) 3.38
    12 .... 3.10, 3.12, 3.38; p **624**
    13 .... p **624**
        (1) 3.38
    14 .... p **624**
        (1)(a) 3.12
            (aa) 3.12, 3.15
            (b) 3.12, 3.68, 3.74
            (c) 3.12
            (d) 3.12, 3.48
            (e) 3.12, 3.68
            (f) 3.04, 3.12
            (g), (h) 3.12
        (2) 3.13, 3.48
        (3) 3.14
    15 .... 3.15, 3.63; p **626**
    16 .... p **626**
        (1), (3), (4) 3.13
    17 .... 3.13; p **626**
    18 .... 3.13; p **626**
        (1)(b) 3.16, 3.57
        (2), (3) 3.16
        (4) 3.12, 3.16, 3.57
        (5) 3.17
            (a)–(c) 3.17
        (5A) 3.17
        (6) 3.16
        (7)–(9) 3.17

Church Representation Rules (Synodical
  Government Measure 1969,
  Sch 3) (cont.)
  19 .... 3.13; p **628**
    (1) 3.18
      (a)................. 3.18, 3.48
      (b), (c) 3.18
      (3), (4), (6)–(8)...............3.18
  20 .... 3.13; p **629**
    (1)(a) 3.19
      (i)–(iv) 3.19
      proviso 3.19
    (2)–(4)................ 3.19, 3.20
    (5) 3.20
    (6), (7) 3.19, 3.20
  21 .... 3.13; p **630**
    (1)(a), (c) 3.20
    (3) 3.20
  22, 23................... 3.09; p **630**
  24 .... 2.34; p **631**
    (6)(b) 3.04
  25 .... 2.34; p **632**
  26 .... 2.30, 2.34; p **633**
  27 .... 2.34, 8.28; p **633**
  28 .... 2.30, 2.37; p **633**
  29 ....p **634**
  30 .... 2.26; p **634**
    (2) 4.65
    (4)(a)(ii)....................8.18
  31 .... 2.26, 2.36; p **635**
    (1) 2.26
  32 .... 2.26, 3.36; p **636**
  33 .... 2.26; p **637**
  34 ....p **637**
    (1)(e), (g), (i), (j)..............2.31
      (k) 2.28
  35 ....p **638**
    (1) 2.36
      (a)–(c) 2.19
    (3) 2.18, 2.36
    (4) 2.18
  36 ....p **639**
    (1) 2.18, 2.19
    (2) 2.18
  37 ....p **640**
  38 .... 2.18, 2.30; p **640**
  39 .... 2.18; p **640**
    (5)(b) 2.18
  40 .... 2.18; p **642**
  41 ....p **642**
  42 ....p **642**
    (1)(a)–(g) 2.19
    (2) 2.19

43 .... 2.18; p **643**
  (1)(a) 3.04, 3.06
  (5) 3.06
44 .... 2.18; p **643**
45 .... 2.18; p **645**
46 ....p 646
46A .... 3.10, 3.14; p **647**
47, 48.......................p 647
49 .... 3.14; p **649**
50–52 ....p **649**
53 ....p **650**
  (5) 3.05
  (6) 4.67
54 ....p **651**
  (1) 3.10, 6.08
  (8) 3.08
Appendix I......................3.04
Appendix II .... 3.15; p **652**
  para 1(d)(i)–(iii)...............3.64
    (e)(i) 3.15, 3.63
    (ii)...................3.63
  2, 3........................3.15
  5(b) 3.12, 3.15
  6, 10–12..................3.15
  14(a), (b) 3.15
  15..........................3.15
  18................... 3.15, 3.26
Church Representation Rules
  (Amendment) Resolution 1998,
  SI 1998/319..................3.17
Church Representation Rules
  (Amendment) Resolution 2004,
  SI 2004/1889.................3.03
Civil Partnership Act 2004 (Overseas
  Relationships and Consequential
  etc Amendments) Order
  (proposed) 2.06
Civil Partnership (Judicial Pensions and
  Church Pensions etc) Order 2005,
  SI 2005/3129..................2.06
  art 4(3).......................4.16
  Sch 3—
    para 1(1), (2) 4.16
Clergy Discipline Appeal Rules 2005,
  SI 2005/3201............ 6.02, 6.59
  r 1 .... 6.59; p **607**
  2 ....p **607**
    (1), (2) 6.59
  3 ....p **607**
  4 .... 6.58; p **607**
  5 ....p **607**
    (1) 6.60
    (2)(a)–(g) 6.60

Table of Rules, Regulations and Other Instruments

Clergy Discipline Appeal Rules 2005,
   SI 2005/3201 (*cont.*)
  6, 7 . . . . 6.60; p **608**
  8 . . . . p **608**
    (1), (2) 6.61
  9 . . . . p **608**
    (2)–(6) 6.61
    (7)(a)–(c) 6.61
    (8), (9) 6.61
  10 . . . . p **609**
    (1)–(3) 6.62
  11, 12 . . . . 6.62; p **609**
  13, 14 . . . . 6.62; p **610**
  15 . . . . p **610**
  16 . . . . 6.62; p **610**
  17, 18 . . . . 6.62; p **611**
  19 . . . . 6.63; p **611**
  20 . . . . p **611**
  21–24 . . . . p **612**
  25 . . . . 6.63; p **612**
  26 . . . . p **612**
    (a)–(c) 6.63
  27 . . . . p **612**
    (a)–(e) 6.64
  28 . . . . 6.64; p **612**
    (4) 6.65
  29–31 . . . . 6.65; p **613**
  32, 33 . . . . p **613**
  34 . . . . p **613**
    (1), (2) 6.68
  35 . . . . p **614**
  36, 37 . . . . 6.64; p **614**
  38–41 . . . . p **614**
  42–44 . . . . p **615**
  Schedule—
  Form A1, A2 . . . . 6.60
    A3 . . . . 6.61
Clergy Discipline Code of Practice
  (GS 1585) 6.02, 6.18
  para 1, 2, 4 . . . . 6.02
    9 . . . . 6.13
    12 . . . . 6.17
    22 . . . . 6.12
    26, 28, 30 . . . . 6.13
    32 . . . . 6.17
    38–40, 42 . . . . 6.18
    55 . . . . 6.16
    70, 75, 76 . . . . 6.23
    106 . . . . 6.24, 6.28
    112 . . . . 6.25
    126 . . . . 6.29
    140–156 . . . . 6.32, 6.33
    158–170 . . . . 6.54

    175 . . . . 6.36
    184–192 . . . . 6.42
    213 . . . . 6.38
Clergy Discipline Commission Guidance
  on Penalties (2006) 6.50
  para 1 . . . . 6.54
    2(a)–(e) 6.51
    3(a)–(f) 6.52
    4–7 . . . . 6.53
Clergy Discipline Rules 2005, SI 2005/
  2022 . . . . 6.02, 6.03, 6.11, 6.41
  r 1 . . . . 6.03; p **577**
    (a)–(d) 6.03
  2 . . . . p **577**
    (1), (2) 6.03
  3 . . . . p **577**
  4 . . . . p **577**
    (1) 6.18
    (2)(a) 6.18
      (vii) 6.20
    (b) 6.17
    (c) 6.18
    (d) 6.18, 6.20
  5 . . . . p **578**
  6 . . . . p **578**
    (1), (2) 6.20
  7 . . . . p **578**
    (2), (3) 6.20
  8 . . . . p **578**
    (1)–(5) 6.16
  9 . . . . p **579**
    (1) 6.23
      (a) 6.16
    (2) 6.23
  10 . . . . 6.23; p **579**
    (2)–(4) 6.23
  11 . . . . 6.23; p **580**
  12 . . . . p **580**
    (1) 6.24
  13 . . . . p **580**
    (1) 6.24
  14 . . . . 6.24; p **580**
  15 . . . . p 580
    (1) 6.24
  16 . . . . p **581**
    (1), (2), (4) 6.24
  17 . . . . p **581**
    (1) 6.25
      (c), (d) 6.25
    (2) 6.25
      (a)–(f) 6.25
    (3)–(6) 6.25
    (7) 6.27

Table of Rules, Regulations and Other Instruments

Clergy Discipline Rules 2005,
SI 2005/2022 (*cont.*)
- 18 . . . . 6.25; p 582
- 19 . . . . p 582
  - (1) 6.26
    - (a)–(d) 6.26
- 20 . . . . 6.28; p 582
  - (b) 6.28
- 21 . . . . p 582
  - (1)–(4) 6.28
- 22 . . . . 6.28; p 583
- 23, 24. . . . . 6.29; p 583
- 25 . . . . p 583
  - (1)(a) 6.29
    - (b), (c) 6.30
  - (2) 6.30
- 26 . . . . 6.31; p 583
- 27 . . . . p 584
  - (2)–(7) 6.33
  - (8) 6.34
- 28 . . . . p 585
  - (1)–(4) 6.35
  - (5) 6.36
- 29 . . . . p 585
  - (1)–(3) 6.36
- Pt VI (r 30–34) 6.35
- r 30 . . . . p 586
  - (1)(a), (b) 6.40
  - (2)–(7) 6.40
- 31 . . . . 6.40; p 586
- 32 . . . . 6.40; p 587
- 33 . . . . p 587
  - (1)(a)–(l) 6.40
- 34 . . . . 6.40; p 587
- Pt VII (r 35, 36) 6.35
- r 35 . . . . 6.41; p 588
- 36 . . . . 6.41; p 589
- Pt VIII (r 37–53) 6.35
- 37 . . . . p 589
  - (1), (2) 6.09
- 38 . . . . 6.42; p 589
- 39 . . . . p 590
  - (a), (b) 6.42
- 40 . . . . 6.43; p 590
- 41, 42. . . . . 6.42; p 590
- 43 . . . . 6.44; p 590
- 44 . . . . p 590
- 45 . . . . 6.42; p 590
- 46 . . . . 6.41; p 590
- 47 . . . . p 590
  - (a)–(f) 6.43
- 48 . . . . 6.43; p 591
- 49 . . . . p 591
  - (a)–(e) 6.43
- 50 . . . . p 591
  - (1), (3) 6.45
- 51 . . . . p 591
  - (a), (b) 6.47
- 52 . . . . p 591
  - (1)–(3) 6.47
- 53 . . . . p 591
  - (1)–(3) 6.49
- 54 . . . . 6.46; p 592
- 55 . . . . 5.92
- 56, 57. . . . . 6.17; p 592
- 58 . . . . 6.39; p 592
  - (1), (2) 6.39
- 59 . . . . p 593
  - (1)–(3) 6.21
  - (4) 6.21, 6.36
- 60 . . . . 6.37; p 593
- 61 . . . . 6.37; p 593
  - (2) 6.37
- 62 . . . . 6.37; p 593
- 63 . . . . 6.37, 6.38; p 594
- 64, 65. . . . . 6.38; p 594
- 66 . . . . p 595
  - (1), (2), (5) 6.37
- 67–70 . . . . 6.54; p 595
- 71 . . . . 6.54; p 596
- 72 . . . . p 596
  - (1), (2) 6.54
- 73 . . . . p 596
- 74 . . . . p 596
  - (1)–(3) 6.69
- 75 . . . . p 596
  - (1)–(5) 6.70
- 76 . . . . p 597
  - (1), (2), (4)–(7) 6.71
- 77 . . . . 6.73; p 597
- 78–80 . . . . 6.73; p 598
- 81 . . . . p 598
- 82 . . . . 6.19; p 598
- 83 . . . . 6.29; p 599
- 84 . . . . p 599
- 85–87 . . . . 6.37; p 599
- 88 . . . . 6.37; p 600
- 89–91 . . . . p 600
- 92 . . . . 6.17; p 600
- 93, 94. . . . . 6.17; p 601
- 95 . . . . 6.17; p 602
- 96 . . . . 6.17; p 603
- 97 . . . . p 604
  - (1)(a)–(c) 6.55
  - (2)–(4) 6.55
- 98 . . . . 6.56; p 604
- 99 . . . . p 604
- 100 . . . . p 605

Table of Rules, Regulations and Other Instruments

Clergy Discipline Rules 2005,
    SI 2005/2022 (*cont.*)
    101 . . . . p 605
        (1) 6.45
    102 . . . . p 605
        (1) 6.46
    103 . . . . 6.46; p 605
    104 . . . . p 606
    105 . . . . p 606
        (1), (2) 6.46
    106 . . . . 6.11, 6.23, 6.35, 6.39,
                      6.40, 6.43; p 606
    Schedule—
        Form 1a 6.18
             1b 6.19
             1c 6.16
             2 . . . . 6.25
             3 . . . . 6.20
             7 . . . . 6.33
             8, 9 . . . . 6.40
             12a, 13a 6.37
Convention for the Protection of Human
    Rights and Fundamental Freedoms
    ('The European Convention on
    Human Rights') (1950) 2.05
    Art 6 . . . . 2.50, 2.62, 4.45
        8 . . . . 2.62, 4.15, 4.45,
                          5.62, 7.111
        9 . . . . 1.45–1.50, 2.62,
                          4.05, 7.111
            para 1 . . . . 1.45, 1.46, 1.49
               2 . . . . 1.45, 1.46, 1.48, 1.50
        10, 11 . . . . 2.62
        12 . . . . 5.50
    First Protocol—
        Art 1 . . . . 3.78, 3.81

Diocesan Chancellorship Regulations
    1993, SI 1993/1841—
    reg 3 . . . . 2.48
Disability Discrimination Act 1995:
    Code of Practice: Goods, Facilities,
    Service and Premises (2002) 7.102

Ecclesiastical Exemption (Listed
    Buildings and Conservation Areas)
    Order 1994, SI 1994/1771—
    art 2(1) 8.03
        4(a) 7.06–7.08
        (b) 7.06, 8.03
        (c)–(g) 7.06
        5(1)(a)–(d) 7.07
        (2)(a) 8.30
        (3) 7.07

        6(1) 7.08
        (2)(a)–(c), (e) 7.08
Ecclesiastical Jurisdiction (Care of
    Places of Worship) Rules 2000,
    SI 2000/2048 . . . . 1.32
Ecclesiastical Offices (Terms of Service)
    Regulations (proposed) 4.40, 4.42
Employment Equality (Age) Regulations
    2006, SI 2006/1031 . . . . 4.39
Episcopal Ministry Act of Synod
    1993 . . . . 1.35, 3.31, 4.63
    para 7 . . . . 3.31, 4.63
        8(1) 3.31
        9, 10 . . . . 3.31
European Convention on Human
    Rights. *See* Convention for the
    Protection of Human Rights and
    Fundamental Freedoms

Faculty Jurisdiction (Appeals) Rules
    1998, SI 1998/1713 . . . . 7.77, 7.78
    r 3 . . . . p 549
      4, 5 . . . . p 550
      6 . . . . p 551
      7 . . . . p 552
      8 . . . . 7.79; p 553
      9–11 . . . . p 553
      12 . . . . 7.78; p 554
      13, 14 . . . . p 554
      15–17 . . . . p 555
      18, 19 . . . . p 556
      20 . . . . p 557
      21–26 . . . . p 558
Faculty Jurisdiction (Care of Places of
    Worship) Rules 2000,
    SI 2000/2048 . . . . 7.08, 7.131
    r 3(a), (b) 7.131
      7(3)(b) 7.131
      16(1) 7.131
      (2)(a)–(d) 7.131
      37 . . . . 7.132
Faculty Jurisdiction (Injunctions and
    Restoration Orders) Rules 1992,
    SI 1992/2884 . . . . 7.84, 7.86, 7.132
    r 1 . . . . p 546
      2 . . . . p 546
        (1) 7.85
      3 . . . . 7.85; p 547
      4 . . . . p 547
        (1)–(3) 7.85
      5 . . . . p 547
        (1)(a)(i)–(iii) 7.85
        (b) 7.85
        (2), (3) 7.85

lxi

Faculty Jurisdiction (Injunctions and
    Restoration Orders) Rules 1992,
    SI 1992/2884 (*cont.*)
  6 .... p **547**
    (1), (2) 7.86
  7 .... p **548**
    (1) 7.86
    (2)(a)–(c) 7.86
    (3) 7.86
  8 .... p **548**
    (1) 7.87
      (a)–(c) 7.87
    (2) 7.88
  9 .... 7.88; p **548**
  10 .... p **549**
    (1) 7.85
    (2), (3) 7.89
  11 .... 7.89; p **549**
  Appendix—
    Form 1 .... 7.85
         2, 3 .... 7.86
         4 .... 7.87
         5, 6 .... 7.88
Faculty Jurisdiction Rules 2000,
    SI 2000/2047 .... 1.32, 7.06,
                   7.22, 7.25, 7.43, 7.44
  r 1 .... p **559**
  2 .... p **559**
    (1) 7.26
  3 .... p **560**
    (1) 7.25, 7.104
    (2) 7.25, 7.31
    (3)(a) 7.26
       (b) 7.18, 7.27
    (4) 7.25, 7.129
    (5), (6) 7.31, 7.32
    (7) 7.33, 7.51
  4 .... p **560**
    (1) 7.35
      (a), (b) 7.35
    (2) 7.36
    (3) 7.129
    (4) 7.35
  5 .... 7.35; p **561**
  6 .... p **561**
    (1) 7.34, 7.104
    (2) 7.37
    (3)(a)–(c) 7.37
    (4) 7.38
      (a) (ii) 7.38
      (b)(i), (ii) 7.38
      (d) 7.38
    (5)(a)–(d) 7.39
    (6) 7.42

  7 .... p **562**
    (1) 7.43
    (2) 7.44
    (4), (5) 7.46
  8 .... p **563**
    (1)(a), (b) 7.46
    (2) 7.46
    (3) 7.14, 7.46
      (c) 7.79
  9 .... p **563**
    (1) 7.13
      (a)–(c) 7.13
    (2)–(5) 7.13
  10 .... p **564**
    (1)(a)–(g) 7.45
  11 .... p **564**
  12 .... p **564**
    (2) 7.56
  13 .... p **564**
    (1), (2) 7.47
    (3) 7.47, 7.48
      (a)–(c) 7.47
    (4) 7.49
    (5) 7.47, 7.48
    (6) 7.47, 7.48, 7.54
    (7) 7.47
      (a), (b) 7.50, 7.98
    (8) 7.37, 7.40, 7.104
    (9) (a), (b) 7.40, 7.104
    (10) 7.41
  14 .... 7.25, 7.41; p **566**
  15 .... p **566**
    (1)(a)–(c) 7.51
    (2) 7.51
    (3)–(5) 7.52
    (6) 7.51
  16 .... p **567**
    (1) 7.53, 7.54
    (2)(a) 7.53
      (b) 7.09, 7.53
      (c), (d) 7.53
      (e) 7.18, 7.53
      (f), (g) 7.53
    (3)(a), (b) 7.54
    (4)(i)–(iv) 7.55
    (5) 7.52, 7.54
    (6) 7.54
  17 .... 7.56; p **568**
  18 .... 7.57; p **568**
  19 .... p **568**
    (1) 7.60
    (2)(i)–(v) 7.60
    (3)(a)–(e) 7.61
    (4) 7.62

Table of Rules, Regulations and Other Instruments

Faculty Jurisdiction Rules 2000,
   SI 2000/2047 (*cont.*)
  20 .... p 569
    (1), (2) 7.63
  21 .... p 569
    (1)(a), (b) 7.64
    (2), (3) 7.64
  22 .... p 569
    (a)–(c) 7.99
  23, 24 .... 7.65; p 570
  25 .... p 570
    (1)–(3) 7.65
  26 .... 7.58; p 570
    (2)(a)–(c) 7.58
    (3), (4) 7.58
    (5)–(8) 7.59
  27 .... 7.73; p 571
  28 .... p 571
    (1), (2) 7.10
  29 .... 7.12; p 571
  30 .... 7.63; p 571
  31 .... p 572
    (1)(a)–(e) 7.67
    (2), (4) 7.67
  32 .... p 572
  33 .... p 573
    (1), (2) 7.44
  34 .... 7.62; p 573
  35 .... 7.63; p 573
  36 .... p 573
    (1) 7.35, 7.56
  Appendix A .... 7.43, 7.45; p 573
  Appendix B .... 7.24; p 575
    para 1 .... 7.18, 7.27
      2.1(ii) 7.28
      3 .... 7.29
      3.1, 3.2 .... 7.29
      4 .... 7.30
      4.1 .... 7.30
      5 .... 7.29, 7.30
      6 .... 7.31
        (a) 7.31
      6.1 .... 7.31
      7, 8 .... 7.31
  Appendix C—
    Form 1 .... 7.32
       2 .... 7.35
       3 .... 7.37, 7.42, 7.47
       4 .... 7.48, 7.54, 7.55, 7.98
       5, 6 .... 7.46, 7.56, 7.73
       7 .... 7.13
       9 .... 7.51
      10 .... 7.65, 7.99
      11 .... 7.99
      12 .... 7.10
      13, 15 .... 7.12
      16 .... 7.129

Gender Recognition (Disclosure of
   Information) (England, Wales and
   Northern Ireland) (No 2) Order
   2005, SI 2005/916 .... 5.35

Incumbents (Vacation of Benefices) Rules
   1994, SI 1994/703 .... 1.32, 4.45
  r 10 .... 4.45

Land Registration Act 2002
   (Transitional Provisions) (No 2)
   Order 2003, SI 2003/2431 .... 3.79
Lord Chancellor (Transfer of Functions
   and Supplementary Provisions)
   (No 3) Order 2006,
   SI 2006/1640—
    art 3 .... 2.39
    Sch 1—
      para 2 .... 2.39

Patronage (Benefices) Rules 1987,
   SI 1987/773—
    r 1–3 .... p 543
    4–7 .... p 544
    8–14 .... p 545
    15–17 .... p 546

Regulations Concerning Marriage and
   Divorce 1957 .... 5.49
   para 1 .... 5.49
Regulations on the Administration
   of Holy Communion 1969 .... 5.22
Royal Proclamation (Order of the
   Communion), March 1548 ...... 5.20

Synodical Government (Channel
   Islands) Order 1970,
   SI 1970/1117 .... 2.09

Vacancy in See Committees
   (Amendment) Regulations
   2003 .... 4.57
Vacancy in See Committees
   Regulations 1993—
   reg 1, 5 .... 4.57

1

THE NATURE AND SOURCES OF ECCLESIASTICAL LAW

Introduction	1.01	Canons	1.28
Purpose	1.03	Questioning the *vires* of draft	
Historical development	1.06	Measures and of Canons	1.30
The early Church	1.07	Secondary legislation	1.32
Medieval Church law	1.08	**Other sources of ecclesiastical law**	1.33
The Reformation	1.12	Case law and precedent	1.33
Post-Reformation	1.16	Quasi-legislation	1.35
Establishment	1.19	*Jus divinum*	1.36
Acts, Measures and Canons	1.22	Custom	1.38
Acts of Parliament	1.23	*Jus liturgicum* and dispensation	1.40
Measures	1.25	**Religious freedom in secular law**	1.42
The Human Rights Act 1998	1.26		

Introduction

The legal regulation of the Church of England in the twenty-first century reflects its historic origins and its subsequent evolution in social, political and ecumenical contexts. 'The Church of England as a whole has no legal status or personality. There is no Act of Parliament that purports to establish it as the Church of England,' said Lord Hope of Craighead in a recent case heard in the House of Lords,[1] 'the relationship which the state has with the Church of England is one of recognition, not of the devolution to it of any of the powers or functions of government'.[2] Lord Hobhouse of Woodborough, delivering a concurring opinion, stated, 'the Church of England is not itself a legal entity. The legal entities are

1.01

---

[1] *Aston Cantlow and Wilmcote with Billesley Parochial Church Council v Wallbank* [2004] 1 AC 546, [2003] 3 All ER 1213 HL at para 61.
[2] Ibid para 61, per Lord Hope of Craighead.

the various office-holders and various bodies set up within that structure'.³ Ecclesiastical law exists to facilitate and animate these various persons and bodies.

1.02 The Church of England as a whole, and each of its component institutions, are subject to a variety of laws, rules, and norms, some imposed by the State, some made by the Church with the concurrence of the State, and others created internally by the Church itself at national, provincial, or diocesan level. The laws applicable to the Church of England are to be found in Acts of Parliament; in Measures and Canons; in a variety of rules and regulations; in the common law of England as revealed in the judgments of ecclesiastical and temporal courts; in custom; and in divine or natural law. Each of these sources is discussed more fully below. The law of the Church of England is part of the law of the land. As Uthwatt J stated in *Attorney-General v Dean and Chapter of Ripon Cathedral*: 'The law is one, but jurisdiction as to its enforcement is divided between the ecclesiastical courts and the temporal courts'.⁴ Throughout this text, the term 'ecclesiastical law' is used to denote the law of the Church of England, howsoever created, and, save where the context indicates otherwise,⁵ the expression 'canon law' is used restrictively to mean the Canons of the Church of England.⁶

Purpose

1.03 The purpose of the law of and for the Church is much the same today as it was in the days of the early Church. It is to regulate the functioning of the Church and the conduct of its component members by a combination of commands, prohibitions and permissions. Such purpose is realised in a number of ways: by God through revelation (*jus divinum*); by the Church through its internal mechanisms of government and by the State through secular legislation (*jus humanum*). Superficially, the law is concerned only with order and discipline, but a closer analysis reveals that it touches upon spiritual, theological, pastoral and evangelistic concerns at the heart of the Christian faith.⁷

---

³ Ibid para 84, per Lord Hobhouse of Woodborough.
⁴ *Attorney-General v Dean and Chapter of Ripon Cathedral* [1945] Ch 239 at 245, [1945] 1 All ER 479 at 483.
⁵ For example, in relation to canons of the Catholic Church.
⁶ For a discussion of the terminological problems posed by expressions such as 'canon law' and 'ecclesiastical law', see N Doe, *The Legal Framework of the Church of England* (Oxford: Clarendon Press, 1996) 12–16.
⁷ For recent examples, see the Care of Churches and Ecclesiastical Jurisdiction Measure 1991, s 1, which gives statutory articulation to the role of the parish church 'as a local centre of worship and mission'; and the Clergy Discipline Measure 2003, s 1, which declares that 'any body or person on whom functions in connection with the discipline of persons in Holy Orders are conferred by this Measure shall, in exercising those functions, have due regard to the role in that connection of the bishop or archbishop who, by virtue of his office and consecration, is required to administer

1.04 The law ought not to be seen as a negative and oppressive instrument. Ombres[8] contrasts morality, religion and law, each of which, to a greater or lesser extent, is part of an individual's life experience. Contrary to the perception that law is an alien concept in the relationship between God and man, he indicates that law, as applied ecclesiology, contributes to sustaining and expressing the freedom of the children of God. The life of the Church is structured in its institutions and organizations as is thought pastorally appropriate in its sacramental making present of Christ's life, death and resurrection.[9] Being both utilitarian and pastoral, the law of the Church seeks actively to assist members of the Church following in the way of Christ and to prevent anything which may impede either the Church itself or any of its members in their faith. The law in many instances provides the liturgical framework within which an expression of faith may take place. The *Book of Common Prayer*, for example, originally derived its legal authority from its annexation to the Act of Uniformity 1662.[10] The functions of law in general have been categorized as follows: to aid a society to achieve its goals; to afford stability; to protect personal rights; and to assist in the education of society.[11] With particular reference to the laws of the Roman Catholic Church, Coriden asserts that 'the canons also help to create and maintain the metaphors and symbols which influence the faithful subtly but strongly'.[12]

1.05 It may seem incongruous that an individual professing the Christian faith, which is, by its nature, the expression of a personal spiritual belief, should fall to be governed by man-made laws and regulations. However, the integrity of any Church, or indeed any secular institution, depends upon certain beliefs and behaviour being common to all its members. Proper internal governance needs greater

---

discipline'. Note also the discussion of the theology of burial in cases such as *Re Christ Church, Alsager* [1999] Fam 142, [1999] 1 All ER 117, Ch Ct of York, and *Re Blagdon Cemetery* [2002] Fam 299, [2002] 4 All ER 482, Ct of Arches.

[8] R Ombres, 'Why then the law?' [1974] New Blackfriars 296.

[9] Ombres, 'Why then the law?' (n 8 above) 302. Attempts at an Anglican articulation of the interface between canon law and theology are to be found in N Doe, 'Towards a Critique of the Role of Theology in English Ecclesiastical and Canon Law' (1992) 2 Ecc LJ 328; M Hill, 'Gospel and Order' (1997) 4 Ecc LJ 659; and D Hope, 'The Letter Killeth, but the Spirit Giveth Life' (1997) 4 Ecc LJ 694.

[10] All but ss 10 and 15 of the Act of Uniformity 1662 was repealed by the Church of England (Worship and Doctrine) Measure 1974, s 6(3), Sch 2, which provided in s 1(1) that 'forms of service contained in the Book of Common Prayer [shall] continue to be available for use in the Church of England'.

[11] JA Coriden, *An Introduction to Canon Law* (London: Burns & Oates, 1991) 5–6. By analogy, writes Coriden, canonical rules fulfil these functions within the Church.

[12] Coriden, *An Introduction to Canon Law* (n 11 above) 6: 'For example,' he says, 'the canons call marriage a covenant rather than a contract, and a parish is described as a community of the faithful rather than a territorial part of a diocese. The effects of these characterisations, over time, are profound'. See also E Corecco, *The Theology of Canon Law: A Methodological Question* (Pittsburgh: Duquesne University Press, 1992).

sophistication if a Church has many members and is evangelical in nature.[13] Further, it was Christ himself who instructed his apostles to 'bind' and to 'loose', thereby commissioning them to make provision for what was acceptable and what was not.[14] Accordingly, the apostles and elders individually and collectively began a process of law-making for the Christian Church.[15]

Historical development

1.06 In relation to the Church of England, a thorough review of the historical development of the law of the Church is to be found in the Report of the Archbishops' Commission on Canon Law published in 1947.[16] It is dealt with here in summary form only.[17]

The early Church

1.07 As the Christian Church expanded, local customs grew up and synods began to regulate the practices of the Church within their area. The only laws common to the whole Church were to be found in Holy Scripture. In the fourth century, written enactments began to appear following provincial councils of bishops including the first General Council of the whole Church at Nicaea in 325.[18] These were styled 'canons', meaning 'yardsticks' or standards by which matters were to be judged.[19] They dealt in the main with everyday church life. The Council of Nicaea created three major sees, or patriarchates, to which local churches could

---

[13] For a discussion of the theology of canon law, see R Ombres, 'Faith, Doctrine and Roman Catholic Canon Law' (1989) 1 Ecc LJ 33.

[14] See Matt 16:19; 18:18; 19:28; Luke 22:28–30; 10:16.

[15] See by way of example the rules relating to the conduct of worship prescribed by St Paul in his first epistle to the Corinthians, particularly chs 11 and 14. Note also the synod of Jerusalem, probably held in AD 48, and referred to in Acts 15.

[16] *The Canon Law of the Church of England* being the Report of the Archbishops' Commission on Canon Law (London: SPCK, 1947). See also E Kemp, 'The Spirit of the Canon Law and its Application in England' (1987–88) 1 (1, 2) Ecc LJ 5, and G Bray (ed), *The Anglican Canons 1529–1947* (Woodbridge: Boydell Press, 1998) xxi–cxii.

[17] For a more detailed treatment, see JH Baker, *An Introduction to English Legal History* (4th edn, London: Butterworths, 2002) 126–132; JH Baker *Oxford History of the Laws of England 1483–1558*, Vol VI (Oxford: Oxford University Press, 2003) 233–275; and RH Helmholz, *The Canon Law and Ecclesiastical Jurisdiction from 597 to the 1640s*, Oxford History of the Laws of England, Vol I (Oxford: Oxford University Press, 2004).

[18] The primary purpose of the Council of Nicaea was to define widely applicable norms to protect and foster church unity in order to provide identity, co-ordination and social regulation to a rapidly expanding church. See J Alesandro, 'General Introduction' in J Coriden, T Green and D Heintschel, *The Code of Canon Law—A Text and Commentary* (New York: Paulist Press, 1985) 1.

[19] See W Bright, *The Canons of the First Four General Councils, with Notes* (2nd edn, Oxford: Clarendon Press, 1882) 2–5.

appeal for definitive judicial rulings. These were Rome, Alexandria and Antioch, to which Constantinople and Jerusalem were added in 381. An early example of such an appeal is found in a letter dated 385 from Bishop Siricius of Rome to Himerius, Bishop of Tarragona, on the subject of ordinations, baptisms, and penances. Siricius' reply came to be known as a decretal, and in time a substantial collection of these built up. Although these decretals were issued in order to resolve particular disputed questions, the principles which they enunciated became of wider application. General Councils of the Church were summoned by the Roman Emperor and their decisions were enacted as state legislation. The emperors did not hesitate to enact laws for the church, and Justinian's Digest contains a substantial amount of ecclesiastical law. However, when an imperial council held in Constantinople in 691–2 (the council *in Trullo*) issued a code of canons, the Roman church refused to accept it, thereby creating an independent Western canonical tradition.

Medieval Church law

The Church law which thus developed was somewhat ad hoc, being neither comprehensive nor universal. During the sixth century, attempts were made to produce collections of canons and decretals. The first known collection is the *Dionysiana*,[20] which was of limited practical use, since it was arranged chronologically and not thematically. This, or a similar work referred to as the *Liber Canonum*, formed the basis for ten canons adopted at the Council of Hertford in 673. Certain Anglo-Saxon secular laws passed by the *witenagemot* (comprising the king, bishops and chief laity) dealt with the protection of the clergy and church property and imposed penalties for breaches of Church law. In addition, books known as *penitentials* began to appear. These concerned aspects of moral theology and listed penances for particular sins.[21]

1.08

By the eleventh century, the collections of canons and decretals were becoming more sophisticated, partly in response to a reform movement which centralized control of the Western Church in the Roman papacy. Burchard of Worms and Bishop Ivo of Chartres each produced collections, but the major work of the time is generally accepted to have been Gratian's *Concordance of Discordant Canons*, completed in about 1140 and known generally as the *Decretum*.[22] It took the form

1.09

---

[20] It was compiled by Dionysius Exiguus, a Scythian, probably in the fifth or first half of the sixth century. See C Gallagher, *Church Law and Church Order in Rome and Byzantium* (Aldershot: Ashgate Variorum, 2002).
[21] See *The Canon Law of the Church of England* (n 16 above) ch II.
[22] Long tradition identified Gratian as a Camaldolese monk who taught in Bologna during the twelfth century. See RH Helmholz, *The Spirit of Classical Canon Law* (Georgia: University

of a casebook of canon law and a reconciliation or harmonization of existing inconsistencies. Brundage regarded these events as something of a jurisprudential revolution:

> Up to the time of [Gratian's *Decretum*] there had been no clear line of demarcation between theology and canon law. Hitherto those who had studied and taught theology had treated the canons as moral prescriptions and dealt with them as a kind of applied theology that furnished guidance to confessors, church administrators, and other authorities in dealing with practical situations.[23]

Gratian's work in turn became the first part of a number of canon law collections which came to be known as the *jus commune*.[24] The very act of codification led to the work becoming obsolete, and successive popes through necessity created further legislation.[25] The compilations of papal decretals which emerged were published under five separate headings, a format which remained standard until the Reformation.[26] In 1500 they were all published together, along with Gratian's *Decretum*, and given the collective title *corpus juris canonici*, by which they are usually known today.

1.10 The English Church was governed by this emerging body of laws, which was applied in Church courts from the eleventh or twelfth century until the Reformation.[27] As ZN Brooke observed, 'The English Church recognized the same law as the rest of the Church. It possessed and used the same collections of church law that were employed in the rest of the Church'.[28] However, it remained the case that the local custom and usage of the Church in England was effective to

---

of Georgia Press, 1996) 7–8, and A Winroth, *The Making of Gratian's Decretum* (Cambridge: Cambridge University Press, 2000).

[23] JA Brundage, *Law, Sex and Christian Society in Medieval Europe* (Chicago: University of Chicago Press, 1987) 233. See also C Duggan, *Canon Law in Medieval England* (London: Variorum, 1982), and JA Brundage, *Medieval Canon Law* (London: Longman, 1995). For a broader discussion, see RH Helmholz, *The Spirit of Classical Canon Law* (Georgia: University of Georgia Press, 1996) passim, and RH Helmholz, *The Canon Law and Ecclesiastical Jurisdiction from 597 to the 1940s*, Oxford History of the Laws of England, Vol I, (Oxford: Oxford University Press, 2004) 67–106.

[24] The *Decretals* or *Liber Extra* of Gregory IX (1234) compiled by Raymond of Peñafort; the *Sext* of Boniface VIII (1298); the *Clementines* of Clement V (1317); the *Extravagantes* of John XXII (1325); and the *Extravagantes Communes* (by 1484).

[25] See *The Canon Law of the Church of England* (n 16 above) ch III. For a more recent treatment, see RH Helmholz, *The Canon Law and Ecclesiastical Jurisdiction from 597 to the 1940s*, Oxford History of the Laws of England, Vol I, (Oxford: Oxford University Press, 2004) 11–40.

[26] These headings were: judge (ecclesiastical officials), judgment (court procedures), clergy, matrimony, and crime (church discipline).

[27] See, by way of illustration, G Evans, 'Lanfranc, Anselm and a New Consciousness of Canon Law in England' in N Doe, M Hill and R Ombres (eds), *English Canon Law* (Cardiff: University of Wales Press, 1998) 1–12.

[28] ZN Brooke, *The English Church and the Papacy* (Cambridge: Cambridge University Press, 1931, 2nd edn, re-issued 1989) 113.

modify the *jus commune*.²⁹ This was recognized by William Lyndwood in his *Provinciale*, which he completed in 1430 and which arranged in five books the constitutions of the province of Canterbury in line with the papal codes, giving to those codes the highest regard, subject only to local modifications.³⁰

English canonists prior to the Reformation applied law which, according to Stubbs, came from one of three sources. These were the canon law of Rome, the common law of England and the provincial law of the Church of England.³¹ Stubbs' analysis was accepted by Maitland,³² but the two jurists differed as to the respective status of the sources.³³ In essence, whereas Stubbs maintained that the canon law of Rome was authoritative only if ratified in national or provincial Church councils, Maitland asserted that the vast majority, if not all, of Roman canon law was regarded as absolutely binding of itself. In a detailed comparative critique by Helmholz of the theses of Stubbs and Maitland, it is suggested that medieval canonists were less concerned with rules of recognition and legislative sovereignty than with the continuity and effectiveness of spiritual courts by the application of existing law.³⁴

1.11

The Reformation

With the declaration of Henry VIII as Supreme Head of the Church in England, a jurisprudential revolution was inevitable, but it came about gradually and not systematically.³⁵ Legislation in 1533³⁶ provided for the appointment of a Commission of 32 persons to examine the existing canon law and provincial constitutions. The Commission, whose powers were only exercisable with the royal assent, was enjoined to abolish such of the canon law and constitutions of which it disapproved, but was given no power to draw up new canons.

1.12

---

²⁹ See *The Canon Law of the Church of England* (n 16 above) 37–38 for such issues as tithing, the rector's responsibility for the upkeep merely of the chancel and not the entire church, and the use of the Sarum rite.
³⁰ For a detailed treatment, see BE Ferme, *Canon Law in Late Medieval England—A Study of William Lyndwood's Provinciale with Particular Reference to Testamentary Law* (Rome, 1996).
³¹ See W Stubbs, 'Historical Appendix', *Report of the Commissioners into the Constitution and Working of the Ecclesiastical Courts* (London, 1883) Vol I.
³² FW Maitland, *Roman Canon Law in the Church of England* (London: Methuen, 1898).
³³ See generally EW Kemp, *An Introduction to Canon Law in the Church of England* (London: Hodder & Stoughton, 1957) 11–32.
³⁴ RH Helmholz, *Roman Canon Law in Reformation England* (Cambridge: Cambridge University Press, 1990) 4–12. This involves a departure from a twentieth-century positivist analysis.
³⁵ See generally D MacCulloch, 'The Birth of Anglicanism' (2004) 7 Ecc LJ 418.
³⁶ Submission of the Clergy Act 1533 (25 Hen 8, c 19).

1.13 Attempts to create a new code were made during the lifetime of Henry VIII and under Edward VI,[37] but without success.[38] However, the consequence of this legislative impotence was not a jurisprudential vacuum, nor widespread lawlessness within the church and state, since it was prescribed in the final section of the Submission of the Clergy Act 1533 that until the Commission to be established under the Act had completed its work, all canons, constitutions, Ordinances and Synodals Provincial being already made, 'which were not contrariant or repugnant to the law, statutes and customs of this realm, nor to the damage or hurt of the King's prerogative' were to continue in force.[39]

1.14 Accordingly, the canon law as it stood in 1535, to the extent that it was not contrary to common law or prerogative, remained in force, not by dint of any papal or other Church authority, but by virtue of statute.[40] This body of pre-Reformation law remains in force today as part of the ecclesiastical common law to the extent that it has not been abrogated by any later legislative enactment or contrary custom.[41] The abolition of the canon law faculties at Oxford and Cambridge in 1535[42] meant that future canon lawyers would be trained in English common law first, and would then have to learn the procedures of canon law on their own. Standards were upheld by Doctors' Commons, a society of ecclesiastical lawyers based in London,[43] but the influence of common law on the church courts increased considerably after the Reformation.

1.15 As a matter of interpretation, the delineation between those parts of the *corpus juris canonici* as were contrary to common law and prerogative and those which

---

[37] Under the Submission of the Clergy Act 1533 (25 Hen 8, c 19), the Ecclesiastical Canons Act 1535 (27 Hen, c 15), and the Canon Law Act 1543 (35 Hen 8, c 16), the latter including a power to make new Canons. See G Bray (ed), *Tudor Church Reform: The Henrician Canons of 1535 and the Reformatio Legum Ecclesiasticarum* (Woodbridge: Boydell Press, 2000).

[38] A new code was published by John Foxe in 1571. See G Bray, 'Loose Canons—The Strange Afterlife of the *Reformatio Legum Ecclesiasticarum*' in N Doe, M Hill and R Ombres (eds), *English Canon Law* (Cardiff: University of Wales Press, 1998) 36–47.

[39] The Canon Law Act 1543 (35 Hen 8, c 16) added to those matters which were to continue in force, 'other ecclesiastical laws or jurisdictions spiritual as be yet accustomed and used here in the Church of England'.

[40] The practical effect of this is illustrated in E Duffy, 'The Shock of Change: Continuity and Discontinuity in the Elizabethan Church of England' (2004) 7 Ecc LJ 428; and E Duffy, *The Stripping of the Altars: Traditional Religion in England c1480–c1580* (New Haven: Yale University Press, 1992). The analogy might be made with the status of European law in the United Kingdom today, which has direct applicability by virtue of a domestic statute, the European Communities Act 1972.

[41] See generally *R v Archbishop of Canterbury* [1902] 2 KB 503 at 543 and 564.

[42] See CNL Brooke (ed), *The History of the University of Cambridge* Vol 1 to 1546 (Cambridge: Cambridge University Press, 1988) 332–333, and P Hughes, *The Reformation in England* (3rd edn, London: Burns & Oates, 1963) 239.

[43] See P Barber, 'England's Last Bachelors and Doctors of Canon Law' (2005) 8 Ecc LJ 80.

were not is a fine line to draw.⁴⁴ It was discussed in detail in the House of Lords in *Mackonochie v Lord Penzance*.⁴⁵ Included within the laws applied in ecclesiastical courts were elements of the secular law (the *corpus juris civilis*), particularly in relation to testamentary and matrimonial cases. In addition, the courts applied unwritten church and state laws (the *lex non scripta*) derived from immemorial usage.⁴⁶

Post-Reformation

Despite the establishment of the Commissions referred to in the foregoing passage and the drafting and approval by the Canterbury Convocation of a number of canons, it was not until 1603 that a definitive collection of canons was produced. It was the work of Richard Bancroft, then Bishop of London and later Archbishop of Canterbury, together with a number of leading ecclesiastical lawyers. The canons were passed by the Convocation of Canterbury⁴⁷ and were confirmed the following year in letters patent by James I, who ordered that they be observed in the province of York. Anxious that no precedent be established whereby the self-governance of the northern province be usurped, the York Convocation protested. The King relented and issued it a licence to enact the canons separately. It duly ratified them on 5 March 1606.⁴⁸ 1.16

The 1603 collection comprised 141 canons, of which 97 were adaptations of previous canons, orders and injunctions. Most of the new jurisprudence related to procedure in the ecclesiastical courts. Although many of the draft canons which had been prepared subsequently to the break with Rome were included, most of the actual law is that of the Middle Ages, adapted and refined as appropriate.⁴⁹ The 1603 canons remained unchanged until 1865, after which a few additions and modifications were made from time to time. The canons of 1603, as subsequently amended, were not comprehensive nor were they intended to be. In 1640, seventeen further canons were enacted by the Convocation of 1.17

---

44 See *The Canon Law of the Church of England* being the Report of the Archbishops' Commission on Canon Law (London: SPCK, 1947) ch IV.
45 *Mackonochie v Lord Penzance* (1881) 6 App Cas 424, HL.
46 Contrary to contemporary jurisprudence, pre-Reformation canon law permitted local custom to abrogate canon law. See RH Helmholz, 'The Canons of 1603: The Contemporary Understanding' in N Doe, M Hill and R Ombres (eds), *English Canon Law* (Cardiff: University of Wales Press, 1998) 23–35.
47 See JV Bullard, *Constitutions and Canons Ecclesiastical 1604* (London: Faith Press, 1934).
48 See generally G Bray, *The Anglican Canons 1529–1947* (Woodbridge: Boydell Press, 1998) liv–lxi.
49 RH Helmholz, 'The Canons of 1603: The Contemporary Understanding' in Doe, Hill and Ombres (eds), *English Canon Law* (n 46 above). See also Bray, *The Anglican Canons 1529–1947* (n 48 above) lx, and T Briden and B Hanson, *Moore's Introduction to English Canon Law* (3rd edn, London: Mowbray, 1992) 5–6.

Canterbury under the royal licence and confirmed by letters patent. However, since Parliament had by this time been dissolved, it was doubted whether legally the Convocation could sit. At the restoration in 1660, they were passed over in silence and their authority remained doubtful. High churchmen occasionally appealed to them for support, but as far as is known, such appeals were invariably rejected.[50]

1.18 By 1865, it was clear that the 1603 canons were out of date and the newly revived Convocations tried to revise them. The attempt failed, and for many years canon law was virtually ignored in the Church of England, and occasionally ridiculed for its evident anachronisms. Revival began in 1939 with the appointment of a commission to study the question in detail. The commission reported in 1947, after which canon law reform began in earnest. After extensive revision, and the last-minute retention of Canon 113 from 1603, which could not be adequately adjusted to fit modern legal requirements, an entirely new set of canons came into force in 1964 and 1969.[51] These have been amended with some regularity and, indicative of the ephemeral nature of its canon law today, the Canons of the Church of England are now published in looseleaf form, subject to periodic updates.[52]

Establishment

1.19 The meaning, effect and future of establishment is a complex matter of history, ecclesiology, sociology and politics which is beyond the scope of this book.[53] However, the fact that the Church of England is the established Church in England informs an understanding of its legal relationship with the State and the manner of its self-regulation. The abolition of papal authority at the time of

---

[50] See *Cooper v Dodd* (1850) 7 Notes of Cases 514 at 516.

[51] See *The Canon Law of the Church of England* being the Report of the Archbishops' Commission on Canon Law (London: SPCK, 1947). See also P Boulton, 'Twentieth Century Revision of Canon Law in the Church of England' (2000) 5 Ecc LJ 353.

[52] The Canons of the Church of England, in their present form, are reproduced in their entirety in the Materials. They are also available online at www.cofe.anglican.org/about/churchlawlegis/canons/whole.pdf.

[53] For analysis and commentary, see F Cranmer, 'Church-State Relations in the United Kingdom: A Westminster View' (2001) 6 Ecc LJ 111; and D McClean, 'The Changing Legal Framework of Establishment' (2004) 7 Ecc LJ 292. For fuller coverage, see P Cornwell, *Church and Nation* (Oxford: Blackwell, 1983), S Lamont, *Church and State: Uneasy Alliances* (London: Bodley Head, 1989), C Buchanan, *Cut the Connection—Disestablishment and the Church of England* (London: Darton, Longman and Todd, 1994), J Moses, *A Broad and Living Way—Church and State, a Continuing Establishment* (Norwich: Canterbury Press, 1995), M Furlong, *C of E—The State It's In* (London: Hodder and Stoughton, 2000), P Avis, *Church, State and Establishment* (London: SPCK, 2001) and T Hobson, *Against Establishment—An Anglican Polemic* (London: Darton, Longman and Todd, 2003).

the Reformation and the recognition of the Sovereign as Supreme Governor of the Church of England created a discernible unity between the Church and the State, the results of which are evident today. In the context of a recent appeal on an obscure point of law under the Chancel Repairs Act 1932, the judicial committee of the House of Lords enjoyed a rare opportunity to consider the constitutional status of the Church of England in contemporary jurisprudence.[54] Lord Nicholls of Birkenhead observed:

> Historically the Church of England has discharged an important and influential role in the life of this country. As the established church it still has special links with central government. But the Church of England remains essentially a religious organisation. This is so even though some of the emanations of the church discharge functions which may qualify as governmental. Church schools and the conduct of marriage services are two instances. The legislative powers of the General Synod of the Church of England are another. This should not be regarded as infecting the Church of England as a whole, or its emanations in general, with the character of a governmental organisation.[55]

Having cited passages from the second edition of this work,[56] Lord Hope of Craighead stated that the Church of England as a whole has no legal status or personality.[57] Whilst acknowledging that the Church of England had regulatory functions within its own sphere of activity, he concluded that it could not be considered to be a part of government, observing that the State has not surrendered or delegated any of its functions or powers to the Church: 'The relationship which the state has with the Church of England is one of recognition, not of the devolution to it of any of the powers or functions of government.'[58] Lord Rodger of Earlsferry, in a concurring speech, observed that 'the juridical nature of the Church [of England] is, notoriously, somewhat amorphous'.[59] He concluded,

---

[54] See *Aston Cantlow and Wilmcote with Billesley Parochial Church Council v Wallbank* [2004] 1 AC 546; [2003] 3 All ER 1213, HL.

[55] Ibid per Lord Nicholls of Birkenhead at para 13.

[56] Ibid at para 58 referring to M Hill, *Ecclesiastical Law* (2nd edn, Oxford: Oxford University Press, 2001), paras 3.11 and 3.74.

[57] *Aston Cantlow* (see n 54) at para 61 per Lord Hope of Craighead. He continued, 'There is no Act of Parliament that purports to establish it as the Church of England: *Sir Lewis Dibdin, Establishment in England: Essays on Church and State* (Macmillan, 1932), p 111. What establishment in law means is that the state has incorporated its law into the law of the realm as a branch of its general law. In *Marshall v Graham* [1907] 2 KB 112, 126 Philimore J said: 'A Church which is established is not thereby made a department of state. The process of establishment means that the state has accepted the Church as the religious body in its opinion truly teaching the Christian faith, and given to it a certain legal position, and to its decrees, if rendered under certain legal conditions, certain civil sanctions.' The Church of England is identified with the state in other ways, the monarch being the head of each.'

[58] *Aston Cantlow* (n 54 above) at para 61 per Lord Hope of Craighead.

[59] Ibid at para 154 per Lord Rodger of Earlsferry.

The mission of the Church is a *religious* mission, distinct from the secular mission of government, whether central or local. Founding on scriptural and other recognised authority, the Church seeks to serve the purposes of God, not those of the government carried on by the modern equivalents of Caesar and his proconsuls. This is true even though the Church of England has certain important links with the state. Those links, which do not include any funding of the Church by the government, give the Church a unique position but they do not make it a department of state: *Marshall v Graham* [1907] 2 KB 112, 126, per Phillimore J. In so far as the ties are intended to assist the Church, it is to accomplish the Church's own mission, not the aims and objectives of the Government of the United Kingdom.[60]

These assertions may seem both obvious and self-evident, but the Court of Appeal had previously reached the opposite conclusion on the specific question of whether a parochial church council is a public authority for the purposes of the Human Rights Act 1998.[61] The Court of Appeal regarded the established nature of the Church of England as imbuing its component institutions with a governmental function sufficient to render them public authorities. The analysis of the House of Lords is much to be preferred, being more cogent and more soundly argued. The consequent reversal of the Court of Appeal's ruling accorded with widespread academic opinion.[62]

1.20 The Sovereign acting according to the laws of the realm is the highest power under God in the kingdom[63] and, since the Act of Settlement 1701, must be in communion with the Church of England.[64] The Sovereign is not a minister of the word of God nor of the sacraments,[65] but is supreme Ordinary and visitor and exercises certain powers formerly vested in the Pope such as the granting of licences and dispensations under the Ecclesiastical Licences Act 1533.[66] Significant rights of patronage vest in the Sovereign, including the appointment

---

[60] Ibid at para 156 per Lord Rodger of Earlsferry.
[61] *Aston Cantlow and Wilmcote with Billesley Parochial Church Council v Wallbank* [2002] Ch 51, [2001] 3 All ER 393, CA, Sir Andrew Morritt V-C, Robert Walker and Sedley LJJ.
[62] See D Oliver, 'Chancel Repairs and the Human Rights' [2002] Public Law 651; I Leigh, 'Freedom of religion: public/private, rights/wrongs' in M Hill (ed), *Religious Liberty and Human Rights* (Cardiff: University of Wales Press, 2002) 128–158; I Dawson and A Dunn, 'Seeking the principle: chancels, choices and human rights' (2002) 22 Journal of Legal Studies 238; S Whale, 'Pawnbokers and parishes: the protection of property under the Human Rights Act' [2002] EHRLR 67 at 78–79; and M Hill's case note and editorial in the *Ecclesiastical Law Journal* at (2001) 6 Ecc LJ 173 and (2004) 7 Ecc LJ 246–249 respectively. Note, however, the partial dissent of Lord Scott of Foscote in the House of Lords on the public authority issue: *Aston Cantlow* (n 54 above) paras 130–132.
[63] Canon A 7.
[64] See generally the Bill of Rights 1688 (1 Will & Mar sess 2, c 2), the Coronation Oath Act 1688 (1 Will & Mar, c 6), the Act of Settlement 1700 (12 & 13 Will 3, c 2) 53, and Accession Declaration Act 1910 (10 Edw 7 & 1 Geo 5, c 29).
[65] The Thirty-Nine Articles of Religion, art 37.
[66] The Sovereign does not have a general power to dispense from the laws ecclesiastical: Bill of Rights Act 1688, s 1.

of all bishops and archbishops,[67] and the role of the appellate function of the Privy Council is an important regulatory process within the Church of England.[68]

The Lords Spiritual[69] are a significant presence in the House of Lords, and it was thought likely that the Church of England would maintain a representation, albeit more limited, in any reformed Upper Chamber, supplemented by representatives of other Christian and non-Christian Churches.[70] The Second Church Estates Commissioner is, by convention, a member of the House of Commons taking the government whip. There are significant burdens attached to establishment such as the duty to baptise, marry and bury parishioners irrespective of their religion[71] and the obligation to maintain thousands of listed church buildings. In addition, as discussed below, Measures and Canons require parliamentary and royal approval respectively.

1.21

Acts, Measures and Canons

Though written in 1809, the following definition of the sources of ecclesiastical law remains relevant today, and is a useful starting point for an examination of contemporary sources of ecclesiastical law:

1.22

> The law of the Church of England, and its history, are to be deduced from the ancient general Canon Law; from the particular constitutions made in this country to regulate the English Church; from our own Canons; from the Rubric [of the *Book of Common Prayer*], and from any Acts of Parliament that may have been passed upon the subject; and this whole may be illustrated, also, by the writings of eminent persons.[72]

What follows is a brief discussion of each of the various sources.[73]

---

[67] See Chapter 4.
[68] See Chapters 3, 4 and 6.
[69] Namely the Archbishops of Canterbury and York together with the 24 senior diocesan bishops.
[70] See *A House for the Future*, the Report of the Royal Commission on Reform of the House of Lords (Cmnd 4534, January 2000) which recommended that the representation of the Church of England remain, though cut from 26 bishops to 16 representatives, chosen however the Church itself decides and not necessarily bishops. Alongside these would be five Church representatives from other parts of the United Kingdom, five from other Christian Churches within England, and five from other faiths. This was superseded, inter alia, by a White Paper, *The House of Lords: Reform* (Cmnd 7027, February 2007), published shortly before the House of Commons expressed a preference for an entirely elected second chamber (on 7 March 2007) and the House of Lords for one that was wholly appointed (on 14 March 2007). It is therefore not currently possible to predict the likely outcome of the current proposals for reform.
[71] Discussed in Chapter 5.
[72] Per Sir John Nicholl in *Kemp v Wickes* (1809) 3 Phillim 264 at 276, Ct of Arches.
[73] Note also AT Denning, 'The Meaning of Ecclesiastical Law' (1944) 60 LQR 235 and Q Edwards, 'The Canon Law of the Church of England: Its Implications for Unity' (1988) 1 Ecc LJ 18.

Acts of Parliament

1.23 Since the Church of England remains the established Church in England, the inextricable link between Church and State permits the State to legislate for the Church and its religious affairs, either directly or by implication. Examples of this in more recent times include the Marriage Act 1949, the Church of England Convocations Act 1966, the Sharing of Church Buildings Act 1969, the Education Act 1996, and the School Standards and Framework Act 1998. Of less direct though no less important application is the Charities Act 2006[74] and certain provisions of the Data Protection Acts of 1984 and 1998 and the Protection of Children Act 1999.[75]

1.24 More recently, two obscure provisions of the Civil Partnership Act 2004 have had the effect of giving to government ministers unprecedented power to legislate for the Church of England. Section 255 deals generally with pensions but section 259 goes further and states that a Minister of the Crown may by order make such further provision as he considers appropriate for the general purposes, or any particular purpose, of the Civil Partnership Act, or for giving full effect to the Act or any provision of it. Such an order may amend, repeal or revoke any Church legislation. The precise scope of this novel ministerial intervention is discussed in Chapter 2, at paragraph 2.06.

Measures

1.25 The General Synod of the Church of England has the power to legislate by Measure[76] which formerly vested in the Church Assembly. A Measure has the full force and effect of an Act of Parliament[77] and may relate to any matter concerning the Church of England.[78] The status and effect of Measures have been the subject of judicial comment in a number of cases. In *R v Ecclesiastical Committee of Both Houses of Parliament, ex parte The Church Society*,[79] it was held that section 3(6) of the Church of England Assembly (Powers) Act 1919 was not to be construed narrowly so as to preclude the passing of a Measure which permitted a change in doctrine.

---

[74] See generally, M Rodríguez Blanco, 'Religion and the Law of Charities' (2006) 8 Ecc LJ 246.
[75] For the more recent of these, see D McClean, 'Recent Legislation' (2000) 5 Ecc LJ 477.
[76] Synodical Government Measure 1969, s 2(1), Sch 2, art 6(a)(i).
[77] Church of England Assembly (Powers) Act 1919, s 4. The extent to which parliamentary sovereignty may have been eroded by the direct application of European legislation in the light of *R v Secretary of State for Transport, ex parte Factortame Ltd (No 2)* [1991] 1 AC 603, [1991] 1 All ER 70, ECJ and HL, is considered in Doe, *The Legal Framework of the Church of England* (Oxford: Clarendon Press, 1996) 58 n 13 and 66.
[78] Church of England Assembly (Powers) Act 1919, s 3(6), applied by the Synodical Government Measure 1969, s 2(2).
[79] *R v Ecclesiastical Committee of Both Houses of Parliament, ex parte The Church Society* (1994) 6 Admin LR 670, *The Times*, 4 November 1993, CA.

This interpretation was affirmed by the Court of Appeal in *R v Archbishops of Canterbury and York, ex parte Williamson*[80] and the Master of the Rolls further stated that once a Measure 'has been duly enacted by the Houses of Parliament, and has received the Royal Assent, it enjoys the invulnerability of an Act of Parliament and it is not open to the courts to question *vires* or the procedure by which it was passed, or to do anything other than interpret it'.[81] In *Williamson v Archbishops of Canterbury and York*,[82] Morritt LJ observed 'the Church of England is and at all material times has been the established church. As such its doctrines and government were and are susceptible to change by the due processes of law'. The argument advanced by Mr Williamson to the effect that the Queen was in breach of her coronation oath when granting the Royal Assent to the Priests (Ordination of Women) Measure 1993 was roundly rejected.

The Human Rights Act 1998

Measures must be read and given effect in a way which is compatible with the European Convention on Human Rights.[83] This applies regardless of when the Measure was enacted.[84] In interpreting a Measure, a court must strive to find a reading which is compatible with Convention rights, and be less concerned with an enquiry into the intention of the draftsman.[85] The same principle applies for all primary and delegated legislation.[86]

1.26

---

[80] *R v Archbishops of Canterbury and York, ex parte Williamson*, The Times, 9 March 1994, CA. Note also the earlier decision of *R v Legislative Committee of the Church Assembly, ex parte Haynes Smith* [1928] 1 KB 411, DC.

[81] The point had been left undecided in the *Church Society* case (n 79 above). The argument that a Measure was a form of delegated legislation, the *vires* of which could be questioned as had been the case in *Anisminic Ltd v Foreign Compensation Commission* [1969] 2 AC 147, [1969] 1 All ER 208, HL, was rejected. This decision was approved and followed by a differently constituted Court of Appeal in the consolidated appeals of *Williamson v Archbishops of Canterbury and York*, 5 September 1996, CA (unreported).

[82] *Williamson v Archbishops of Canterbury and York* (n 81 above), in which the Court of Appeal dealt with the appeal in action LTA 96/524/D together with renewed applications for leave to move for judicial review in FC3/94/5724D, FC3/94/6163D, FC3/96/7211D and FC3/96/5805D.

[83] Human Rights Act 1998, s 3(1). The Act was brought into effect in England on 2 October 2000. Measures of the Church Assembly and General Synod are expressly classified as 'primary legislation' in s 21(1).

[84] Ibid s 3(2)(a).

[85] The rights are set out in the Human Rights Act 1998, Sch 1. Of particular relevance are Articles 6 (fair trial); 8 (respect for private and family life); 9 (freedom of thought, conscience and religion); 10 (freedom of expression); 11 (freedom of assembly and association); 12 (right to marry); and Article 2 of the First Protocol (right to education).

[86] For a general discussion, see M Hill, 'A New Dawn for Freedom of Religion: Grounding the Debate' in M Hill (ed), *Religious Liberty and Human Rights* (Cardiff: University of Wales Press, 2002) 1–13.

1.27 In determining any question which may arise in connection with a Convention right, a court or tribunal must take into account judgments and decisions of the European Court of Human Rights in Strasbourg.[87] However, if a court's determination of any question arising under the Act might affect the exercise by a religious organization of the right to freedom of religion, it must have 'particular regard' to the importance of that right.[88] If a court is satisfied that a provision in a Measure is incompatible with a Convention right it may make a declaration of incompatibility.[89] Although provision exists for remedial action by a government minister to remove an incompatibility following a declaration regarding a piece of legislation,[90] this does not apply in relation to Measures.[91]

Canons

1.28 The power to legislate by canon now vests in the General Synod.[92] Before 1970, it was exercised on a provincial basis by each of the Convocations of Canterbury and York.[93] The Royal Assent and licence is required for the making, executing and promulging of any canon, and no canon may be made which is contrary or repugnant to the royal prerogative, or the customs, laws or statutes of the realm.[94] However, this prohibition does not apply in the case of canons made under the Church of England (Worship and Doctrine) Measure 1974.[95] This encompasses the approval, amendment, continuance and discontinuance of forms of service and the making of provision for any matter to which any of the rubrics of the *Book of Common Prayer* relate.[96] Equally a parent Measure may render lawful

---

[87] Human Rights Act 1998, s 2(1)(a). Opinions of the Commission and decisions of the Committee of Ministers must also be taken into account (s 2(1)(b)–(d)), although these bodies ceased to produce such opinions and decisions on 1 November 1998.

[88] Ibid s 13.

[89] Ibid s 4(2). For these purposes 'court' means the House of Lords, Privy Council, Court of Appeal and High Court: ibid s 4(5). It does not include the consistory court, although there is nothing to stop a consistory court from asserting that a statute is incompatible with a Convention right whilst nonetheless applying it.

[90] Ibid s 10(2). The minister is not obliged to do so.

[91] Ibid s 10(6).

[92] Synodical Government Measure 1969, s 1(1), (3), (5); Sch 1, para 1; Sch 2, art 6(a)(ii).

[93] Ibid s 1(2). Canon H 1, para 2, preserves the right of the Convocations to meet separately for the purpose of considering matters concerning the Church of England and making provision for such matters by appropriate instrument.

[94] Submission of the Clergy Act 1533 (25 Hen 8, c 19), ss 1, 3, applied by the Synodical Government Measure 1969, s 1(3).

[95] Church of England (Worship and Doctrine) Measure 1974, s 6(1).

[96] Ibid s 1(1). Special voting provisions apply under this Measure. See ibid ss 3, 4.

the making of particular provision by canon.[97] This 'convenient practice', to borrow from the judgment of Dillon LJ in *Brown v Runcie*,[98] effectively precludes any challenge to the lawfulness of the canon, since the parent Measure is declaratory of the law of the realm.[99] Examples of this practice include the Deacons (Ordination of Women) Measure 1986, which permitted the promulging of what became Canon C 4A; the Priests (Ordination of Women) Measure 1993, which did likewise for Canon C 4B; and the Church of England (Ecumenical Relations) Measure 1988, which paved the way for Canons B 43 and B 44, the so-called ecumenical canons.

To the extent that canons are classified as 'subordinate legislation'[100] under the Human Rights Act 1998, then they, like Measures, will fall to be read and given effect in a way which is compatible with Convention rights.[101] The Act includes within the definition of 'subordinate legislation' any 'other instrument made under primary legislation'.[102] This is sufficiently broad to cover canons made pursuant to powers given to Synod under the Synodical Government Measure 1969.[103] However, some canons promulged prior to the 1969 Measure coming into force were arguably not made under primary legislation[104] and, if so, the provisions of the Human Rights Act 1998 will not apply to them.[105]

1.29

---

[97] In *Williamson v Archbishops of Canterbury and York*, 5 September 1996, CA (unreported), Morritt LJ stated 'the effect of the Measure is *pro tanto* to override the Submission of the Clergy Act 1533 to the extent necessary to permit the ordination of women in accordance with the Canon specifically authorized by the Measure'.

[98] *Brown v Runcie*, The Times, 20 February 1991, CA.

[99] A more cumbersome process was utilized in the Church of England (Miscellaneous Provisions) Measure 1976, s 1(3) of which expressly ousted the restriction otherwise imposed by the Submission of the Clergy Act 1533, s 3.

[100] It was maintained by counsel for the respondents in *Brown v Runcie* (n 98 above) that canons and measures are both primary legislation. Such a submission was not ruled on in the case or in the *Williamson* litigation (n 81 above) which followed. It is respectfully suggested that the better view is that measures are primary legislation and canons secondary or subordinate. The previous sentence (in the second edition of this work) was cited and approved by Burton J in *Calvert v Gardiner and others* [2002] EWHC 1394 (QB), 10 May 2002, unreported.

[101] Human Rights Act 1998, s 3(1).

[102] Ibid s 21(1).

[103] Synodical Government Measure 1969, s 1(2), which is classified as 'primary legislation' under the Human Rights Act 1998, s 21(1).

[104] Unless one takes a very generous reading of the Submission of the Clergy Act 1533.

[105] The piecemeal amendment of the Canons of the Church of England since 1969 will pose a number of problems of interpretation in that certain parts of certain canons may be subject to scrutiny under the Act whilst others are not.

Questioning the *vires* of draft Measures and of Canons

1.30 Measures are properly regarded as primary, not subordinate, legislation, despite the apparent exercise of powers delegated by Parliament initially to the Church Assembly and thereafter to General Synod.[106] As explained above, once a measure has received the Royal Assent, its *vires* cannot be questioned by a court. A question which remains unanswered, however, is whether the secular courts have jurisdiction to review the *vires* of a draft measure prior to it receiving the Royal Assent.[107] When giving leave to move for judicial review in the *Church Society* case, Simon Brown LJ considered it arguable that the court did have such a jurisdiction.[108] At the full hearing less than a week later, the Divisional Court dismissed the application on its merits and did not address the issue of jurisdiction which McCowan LJ described as 'plainly a weighty and difficult matter'.[109] When the Court of Appeal considered the *Williamson* case, the particular measure then in question had received the Royal Assent and the question was therefore academic. Sedley J had considered the argument 'theoretically available'.[110] It remains to be seen whether this matter will be further argued.

1.31 As to canons, these are in a slightly different category. In proceedings to challenge the validity of a canon not yet promulged, Hoffmann J summarized the objections of the joint presidents of Synod as follows:

> First ... that the question of whether this canon required a special majority had been the subject of a ruling by the Archbishop of York as chairman during the passage of the canon through the General Synod and that since the General Synod was exercising legislative powers this court has no jurisdiction to enquire into whether that ruling was right or wrong, any more than it would have jurisdiction to enquire into proceedings in Parliament. Secondly ... that if the court did have such jurisdiction it could be invoked only by proceedings for judicial review and not by an ordinary writ claiming a declaration.[111]

---

[106] See para 1.25 above. For the purposes of the Human Rights Act 1998, Measures of the Church Assembly and Synod are classified as 'primary legislation': s 21(1). Curiously, in the Report from the Joint Committee on Delegated Legislation (1971–72 HL, 184; HC, 475), x, Synodical Measures appear as the first example of forms of delegated, as opposed to primary, legislation.

[107] A full discussion appears in Doe, *The Legal Framework of the Church of England* (Oxford: Clarendon Press, 1996) 60–62.

[108] Reliance was placed upon *R v HM Treasury, ex parte Smedley* [1985] QB 657, [1985] 1 All ER 589, CA.

[109] *R v Ecclesiastical Committee of Both Houses of Parliament, ex parte The Church Society* (1994) 6 Admin LR 670, The Times, 4 November 1993, CA.

[110] *R v Archbishop of Canterbury, ex parte Williamson (Porvoo Declaration)*, 15 March 1996 (unreported). An application for leave, renewed following the refusal from Sedley J, was dismissed by the Court of Appeal together with other applications in *Williamson v Archbishops of Canterbury and York* (n 81 above).

[111] *Brown v Runcie*, The Times, 26 June 1990, Hoffmann J. Reliance would doubtless have been placed on the conclusive determination clauses in the Synodical Government Measure 1969, Sch 2, particularly para 7(6).

However, Hoffmann J considered it unnecessary to express any opinion on these constitutional matters, since he rejected the challenge on its merits. Similarly in the Court of Appeal the issues, though raised by way of a respondents' notice, did not form the basis of argument.[112] Whether the validity of a canon or a draft Measure may be challenged in the secular courts remains a moot constitutional point.

Secondary legislation

In addition to Acts of Parliament and Measures, which are primary legislation in its strict sense, various types of secondary or subordinate legislation have an impact on the operation of the Church of England. These include matters such as the Incumbents (Vacation of Benefices) Rules 1994,[113] the Church of England (Legal Aid) Rules 1995,[114] the Ecclesiastical Jurisdiction (Care of Places of Worship) Rules 2000[115] and the Faculty Jurisdiction Rules 2000.[116] They are each in the form of statutory instruments made pursuant to primary legislation. As such, the provisions of the Human Rights Act 1998, discussed above,[117] apply to them. They must therefore be read and given effect in a manner compatible with the rights set out in the European Convention on Human Rights.

1.32

Other sources of ecclesiastical law

Case law and precedent

There is a substantial body of ecclesiastical and secular common law which has been built up by judicial decisions over centuries. The doctrine of *stare decisis* which is well developed in secular jurisprudence[118] seeks to ensure consistency and predictability in judicial decision-making. Although the strict theoretical canonist would see no place for precedent in canon law, it being a doctrine of the

1.33

---

112 *Brown v Runcie*, The Times, 20 February 1991, CA.
113 SI 1994/703, made pursuant to the Incumbents (Vacation of Benefices) Measure 1977, s 18(2).
114 SI 1995/2034, made pursuant to the Church of England (Legal Aid) Measure 1994, s 4.
115 SI 2000/2048, made pursuant to the Care of Churches and Ecclesiastical Jurisdiction Measure 1991, s 26(1)(e) as amended by the Care of Places of Worship Measure 1999, s 5.
116 SI 2000/2047, made pursuant to the Care of Churches and Ecclesiastical Jurisdiction Measure 1991, s 26(1)(a).
117 See para 1.26 above.
118 See generally R Cross and JW Harris, *Precedent in English Law* (4th edn, Oxford: Clarendon Press, 1991).

common lawyer,[119] the decisions of ecclesiastical courts are today generally considered to be binding on the particular court making the decision and on courts of inferior jurisdiction.[120] Guidelines enunciated in the course of judgments, whilst not determinative and immutable statements of law, are highly persuasive, particularly when they have been adopted or applied in subsequent cases.[121]

1.34 The decision of a consistory court of one diocese does not formally bind that of another,[122] nor are decisions of the Court of Arches and those of the Chancery Court of York strictly binding on one another, they being of co-ordinate jurisdiction.[123] In recent years, however, the strict rules of precedent have been tempered by an increasing pragmatism in producing homogeneity in judicial decisions both at first instance and in the two appeal courts.[124] A number of factors have led to this: first the increase in the reporting of decisions;[125] secondly the borrowing of reasoning and the application of guidelines enunciated in consistory courts of other dioceses;[126] thirdly the adoption and approval by appeal

---

[119] See Halsbury's Laws of England (London, 1975) vol 14, para 1271. The introduction of the doctrine is traced to the nineteenth century and, amongst other things, the dissolution of Doctors' Commons under the Court of Probate Act 1857.

[120] Examples of this in the consistory court include *Re Grosvenor Chapel, South Audley Street* (1913) 29 TLR 286, London Cons Ct; *Re St Paul, Covent Garden* [1974] Fam 1, London Cons Ct; and *Re St Mary, Aldermary* [1985] Fam 101, [1985] 2 All ER 445, London Cons Ct.

[121] See by way of example *Re St Luke the Evangelist, Maidstone* [1995] Fam 1, [1995] 1 All ER 321, Ct of Arches (alterations to the fabric of a listed church); *Re St Mary the Virgin, Sherborne* [1996] Fam 63 at 68–69, [1996] 3 All ER 769 at 774, Ct of Arches (the award of costs); and *Re Blagdon Cemetery* [2002] Fam 299, [2002] 4 All ER 482, Ct of Arches (exhumation).

[122] *Re St Michael and All Angels, Bishopwearmouth* [1958] 1 WLR 1183 at 1189, *sub nom Rector and Churchwardens of Bishopwearmouth v Adey* [1958] 3 All ER 441 at 445, 446, Durham Cons Ct; and *Re Rector and Churchwardens of St Nicholas, Plumstead* [1961] 1 WLR 916 at 918, [1961] 1 All ER 298 at 299, Southwark Cons Ct. See also *Re St Martin le Grand, York* [1990] Fam 63 at 71–72, [1989] 2 All ER 711 at 720, York Cons Ct. However, such decisions are frequently considered and afforded considerable weight in the development of an ecclesiastical common law.

[123] *Re St Mary, Tyne Dock (No 2)* [1958] P 156 at 159, [1968] 1 All ER 1 at 8–9, Durham Cons Ct. Likewise, the Court of Arches is not strictly bound by decisions of the Court of Ecclesiastical Causes Reserved nor vice versa: see *Re St Stephen, Wallbrook* [1987] Fam 146 at 197G–198B, [1987] 2 All ER 578 at 604B–F, Ct of Eccl Causes Res, per Sir Ralph Gibson.

[124] Doe in *The Legal Framework of the Church of England* (Oxford: Clarendon Press, 1996) 157 refers to 'the benign form of the precedent doctrine' which he classifies as a doctrine of adoption whereby courts follow earlier decisions though not strictly obliged to do so. For a more detailed discussion, see N Doe, 'Canonical Doctrines of Judicial Precedent: A Comparative Study' (1994) 54 The Jurist 205.

[125] See, for example, the case notes which have appeared in the *Ecclesiastical Law Journal* since 1987.

[126] In *Re All Saints, Harborough Magna* [1991] 1 WLR 1235, [1992] 4 All ER 948, the Coventry Consistory Court adopted and accepted the reasoning of an unreported decision from that of Rochester, *Re St Mark, Rusthall, Biggin Hill*, 13 May 1992. Harborough Magna has duly been followed in *Re All Saints, Featherstone* (1999) 5 Ecc LJ 391, Wakefield Cons Ct.

courts of first instance decisions;[127] fourthly the change in the composition of the Court of Arches in faculty appeals into a body comprising the Dean of the Arches together with two diocesan chancellors;[128] and fifthly the *de facto* elision of the Court of Arches and Chancery Court of York into what is effectively a single court of appeal for both provinces.[129] It has been suggested that some latitude might be allowable for the Court of Arches to depart from an earlier decision but that strong reason would be needed.[130] Specific statutory provision is made in respect of decisions of the Privy Council and Commission of Review.[131] Most significantly, a Commission of Review is not bound by any decision of the Privy Council in relation to any matter of doctrine, ritual or ceremonial.[132]

Quasi-legislation

When considering written sources of ecclesiastical law, regard must be had to what is styled 'quasi-legislation', which is a burgeoning source of governance and regulation in the Church of England.[133] It comprises policy documents, regulations, directions, codes of practice, circulars, guidance and guidelines. Some are issued nationally, some at the provincial level and others by individual dioceses. Some are technically delegated legislation; others have uncertain provenance and authority. They are interstitial in their nature, filling legislative lacunae,

1.35

---

[127] In *Re St Luke the Evangelist, Maidstone* [1995] Fam 1, [1995] 1 All ER 321, the Court of Arches adopted and approved an approach to certain faculty matters in the form of three questions identified by Chancellor Cameron in *Re St Helen's, Bishopsgate* (1993) 3 Ecc LJ 256, London Cons Ct. See also *Re Christ Church, Alsager* [1999] Fam 142, [1999] 1 All ER 117, in which the Chancery Court of York adopted with minor modifications the guidelines set out by Chancellor McClean in *Re John Stocks, deceased* (1995) 4 Ecc LJ 527, Sheffield Cons Ct. However, the approach in *Alsager* was revisited in the subsequent case of *Re Blagdon Cemetery* [2002] Fam 299, [2002] 4 All ER 482, Ct of Arches.

[128] In the first judgment of the Court of Arches as newly constituted, the Dean stated that the court would continue, so far as may be proper, to give guidance when deciding specific appeals. 'The value of that general guidance will be greatly increased by the wider composition of the court … It will be the intention for the norm to be one judgment with which all three judges can agree': *Re St Luke the Evangelist, Maidstone* [1995] Fam 1 at 4, [1995] 1 All ER 321 at 323, Ct of Arches. This practice has been consistently followed in subsequent cases.

[129] It was stated in *Re St Mary, Tyne Dock (No 2)* [1958] P 156 at 159, [1958] 1 All ER 1 at 8–9, Durham Cons Ct, that a judgment of the Arches Court of Canterbury was not a binding authority in the province of York but was naturally to be treated with the greatest respect, in particular because the judge in each of the provincial courts was required by statute to be the same person: Ecclesiastical Jurisdiction Measure 1963, s 3(2)(a). Now that in faculty appeals the Dean and Auditor sits also with two chancellors (ibid s 47(1)(b) substituted by the Care of Churches and Ecclesiastical Jurisdiction Measure 1991, s 8(1), Sch 4 para 8), the level of respect is likely to be still greater.

[130] See *Re Lapford (Devon) Parish Church* [1955] P 205, [1954] 3 All ER 484, CA.

[131] Ecclesiastical Jurisdiction Measure 1963, s 48.

[132] Ibid s 48(5).

[133] See N Doe, 'Ecclesiastical Quasi-Legislation' in N Doe, M Hill and R Ombres (eds), *English Canon Law* (Cardiff: University of Wales Press, 1998) at 93–103.

supplementing, clarifying and interpreting formal law. Of particular interest are Acts of Convocation and Statements by the House of Bishops.[134] Such pronouncements are not law per se, nor do they have the force of a statute, but they have 'great moral force as the considered judgment of the highest and ancient synod of the province'.[135] It is not uncommon for the consistory court to place reliance on quasi-legislation.[136] More generally, quasi-legislation has ramifications in the field of judicial review. It may create rights and duties and foster legitimate expectation whereby disregard of its content might give rise to redress by way of a public law remedy in the Administrative Court.[137] There is as yet no refined or coherent jurisprudence on ecclesiastical quasi-legislation.[138]

Jus divinum

1.36 The secular courts have developed a theory and model of natural law. This is instanced in the Nuremberg war trials, where crimes against humanity were formulated and enforced, and in decisions in civil cases which refused to recognise as law certain property legislation passed by the Nazi government.[139] So abhorrent was the legislation to certain fundamental freedoms that the English courts refused to cloak it with the dignity of law or to enforce it.[140] Arguably, natural law is the *jus divinum* of the non-believer and accordingly it will be given credence in Church courts. Although not expressed as such, the arguments advanced on behalf

---

[134] The Episcopal Ministry Act of Synod 1993, which concerns continuing episcopal oversight consequent upon the implementation of the Priests (Ordination of Women) Measure 1993, is a recent example. It has been suggested that Acts of Synod are a species of delegated legislation, made under the authority of the Synodical Government Measure 1969, Sch 2 art 6(a)(iv), but this is questionable.

[135] This quotation is lifted from the judgment in *Bland v Archdeacon of Cheltenham* [1972] Fam 157 at 166, [1972] 1 All ER 1012 at 1018, Ct of Arches, and relates to an Act of Convocation although the principle is of general application.

[136] See by way of example, *Re St James, Shirley* [1994] Fam 134, Winchester Cons Ct, where effect was given to a *Response by the House of Bishops to Questions Raised by Diocesan Chancellors* dated June 1992 even though the Response did not sit easily with Canon F 1, para 2. See also *Re St Michael, Aveley* (1997) 4 Ecc LJ 770, Chelmsford Cons Ct, where the chancellor placed weight on the Report of the Archbishops' Commission on Rural Areas, *Faith in the Countryside* (1990). This was also done in *Re Whixall Old Burial Ground* (2000) 5 Ecc LJ 495, Lichfield Cons Ct. Further, in *Re St Hugh, Bermondsey* (1999) 5 Ecc LJ 390, Southwark Cons Ct, Chancellor George in considering issues of religious pluralism noted the Board of Mission's publication *Communities and Buildings, Church of England Premises and Other Faiths* (1996).

[137] See *R v Bishop of Stafford, ex parte Owen* (2000) 6 Ecc LJ 83 CA.

[138] See Doe, 'Ecclesiastical Quasi-Legislation' in Doe, Hill and Ombres (eds), *English Canon Law* in N Doe, M Hill and R Ombres (eds), *English Canon Law* (Cardiff: University of Wales Press, 1998) 93–103.

[139] *Oppenheimer v Cattermole* [1976] AC 249, [1975] 1 All ER 538, HL. Cf *Blackburn v Attorney-General* [1971] 1 WLR 1037, [1971] 2 All ER 1380, CA.

[140] For a general discussion see N Doe, 'The Problem of Abhorrent Law and the Judicial Idea of Legislative Supremacy' (1988) Liverpool Law Review 113.

of the Bishop of Oxford and his co-plaintiffs in their challenge to the investment policy of the Church Commissioners clearly embodied the assertion that the disregarding of factors such as the morality of investing in armaments, gambling, alcohol or tobacco was contrary to Christian principles. The case, however, was determined on principles of the law of trusts, and the Christian or ethical issues formed only a minor part of the judgment.[141]

1.37 In the case of *Blake v Director of Public Prosecutions*,[142] an Anglican priest accused of an offence of criminal damage sought to argue that his conviction was wrongly obtained since, inter alia, he was acting in accordance with instructions from God. His appeal was unsuccessful, the court refusing to entertain any challenge to the wording of a statute whose meaning was plain on its face.

Custom

1.38 The place of custom in the Church of England raises a number of issues upon which differing opinions are held. Custom, to the legal historian, connotes a local usage. In this sense it has received a degree of statutory recognition. For example, the Churchwardens (Appointment and Resignation) Measure 1964 (since repealed) provided at section 12(2): 'In the case of any parish where there is an existing custom which regulates the number of churchwardens or the manner in which [they] are chosen, nothing in this Measure shall affect that custom'. Existing custom was defined in section 13 as 'a custom existing at the commencement of this Measure which has continued for a period including the last forty years before its commencement'.[143] The Churchwardens Measure 2001 preserves existing custom[144] but empowers the meeting of parishioners to abolish it.[145] By statute, the monarch may determine when the Convocations of Canterbury and York may be called together and dissolved, 'notwithstanding any custom or rule of law to the contrary'.[146] Equally, though in less clear language, the Pastoral Measure 1983 gave to the pastoral committee of each diocese the duty to 'have regard also to the traditions ... of individual parishes' when making schemes.[147] One canon permits of the existence of custom negating what would otherwise

---

[141] *Harries v Church Commissioners for England* [1992] 1 WLR 1241, [1993] 2 All ER 300, Sir Donald Nicholls V-C.
[142] *Blake v Director of Public Prosecutions* [1993] Crim LR 586, DC.
[143] The Churchwardens (Appointment and Resignation) Measure 1964 came into force on 1 January 1965: ibid s 15(3).
[144] See the Churchwardens Measure 2001, s 11(2).
[145] Ibid s 12. The consent of any person involved other than the minister is required: s 12(3).
[146] Church of England Convocations Act 1966, s 1(1).
[147] Pastoral Measure 1983, s 2(3)(b). Tradition may bear a broader meaning than churchmanship.

be a canonical duty. It reads, 'the font shall stand as near to the principal entrance as conveniently may be, *except there be a custom to the contrary*'.[148]

1.39 As to customary law in a more general sense, pre-Reformation canon law continues to operate in the Church of England by means of incorporation into the common law on condition that it is not repugnant to the royal prerogative or the customs, laws or statutes of the realm.[149] For such custom still to be operative, it must have continued and been uniformly recognised and acted upon by the bishops of the Anglican Church since the Reformation.[150] No usage is to be considered as binding 'unless pleaded and proved to have been recognised, continued and acted upon in England since the Reformation'.[151] There is some debate as to whether custom may prevail over positive law[152] or whether its role is secondary or even obsolete.[153] Secular jurisprudence precludes a custom from abrogating any statute. With regard to the Church, the Privy Council has stated, 'usage, for a long series of years, in ecclesiastical customs especially, is entitled to the greatest respect; it has every presumption in its favour; but it cannot prevail against positive law, though where doubt exists, it might turn the balance'.[154] The better view is that the customary rule of recognition which existed at the time of the Reformation permitting custom to override positive law (*contra legem*) became obsolete. The Church of England became a national church and progressively legislated for itself. The concept of local custom mitigating the rules of a universal Church was of no application. Custom cannot override statute. However, the Church today acknowledges custom as a source of primary law where formal law is otherwise silent (*praeter legem*) and as an interpretative or facilitative means of implementing formal law (*secundum legem*).[155]

---

[148] Canon F 1, para 2 (emphasis added).
[149] Submission of the Clergy Act 1533, s 3, applied by the Synodical Government Measure 1969, s 1(3)(b).
[150] *Bishop of Exeter v Marshall* (1868) LR 3 HL 17 at 53–56.
[151] *Re St Mary, Westwell* [1968] 1 WLR 513, [1968] 1 All ER 631, Commissary Ct. It has been suggested that this reformulation of the rule of recognition means that custom may arise without episcopal consent. See Doe, *The Legal Framework of the Church of England* (Oxford: Clarendon Press, 1996) 86–87.
[152] See *The Canon Law of the Church of England*, being the Report of the Archbishops' Commission on Canon Law (London: SPCK, 1947) 66–69, and RH Helmholz, 'The Canons of 1603: The Contemporary Understanding' in N Doe, M Hill and R Ombres (eds), *English Canon Law* (Cardiff: University of Wales Press, 1998) 23–25.
[153] See R Bursell, 'What is the Place of Custom in English Canon Law? A Report of the Ecclesiastical Law Society Working Party' (1989) 1Ecc LJ 12.
[154] *Clifton v Ridsdale* (1876) 1 PD 316 at 331.
[155] See Doe, *The Legal Framework of the Church of England* (Oxford: Clarendon Press, 1996) 86–87.

Jus liturgicum and dispensation

Allied to custom is the *jus liturgicum*: the right of the bishop to authorize forms of service and deviations therefrom.[156] It has been of limited application since the advent of the *Book of Common Prayer* which created a uniformity of liturgy.[157] However, in relation to services for which no provision was made in the *Book of Common Prayer* the *jus liturgicum* survived.[158] The 1928 Prayer Book, despite being rejected by Parliament, was widely used. This expression of the *consensus fidelium*, reflecting the approval given by the Church Assembly, represented the pragmatic and practical (though probably unlawful) operation of the *jus liturgicum*.[159] The legality of services of consecration of church buildings, for example, may be justified by an appeal to the *jus liturgicum*.[160] Formal recognition has been given to this limited form of *jus liturgicum* in Canon B 4 para 3, thus making redundant much of the historical debate.[161]

1.40

Finally, mention should be made of the relaxation of canon law through dispensation.[162] Though well developed in Roman Catholic canon law, no explicit doctrine of equity is discernible in the laws of the Church of England. The reservation of the sacrament, considered for some time strictly illegal, received approval in a number of cases by an appeal to the doctrine of necessity.[163] More generally,

1.41

---

[156] See J Gainer, 'The *Jus Liturgicum* of the Bishop and the Church in Wales' in N Doe (ed), *Essays in Canon Law* (Cardiff, 1992) 111–132.

[157] The relevant parts of the Act of Uniformity 1662 have been repealed by the Church of England (Worship and Doctrine) Measure 1974, s 6(3), Sch 2. The forms of service contained in the *Book of Common Prayer* remain authorized for use in the Church of England under Canon B 1, para 1(a).

[158] A contrary view is expounded by R Bursell in *Liturgy, Order and the Law* (Oxford: Clarendon Press, 1996) 27, and, more mellowly, in 'Consecration, *Jus Liturgicum* and the Canons' in N Doe, M Hill and R Ombres (eds), *English Canon Law* (Cardiff: University of Wales Press, 1998) 71–81.

[159] The status of the *Book of Common Prayer* under the Act of Uniformity 1662 precluded the purported declaration in 1929 by the House of Bishops that the 1928 Prayer Book may be used. Note the Acts of the Convocations of Canterbury and York (London: SPCK, 1961) 61 at 63.

[160] See HW Cripps, *A Practical Treatise on the Law Relating to Church and Clergy* (8th edn, London: Sweet and Maxwell, 1937) 198.

[161] See Chapter 5. See also 'Lawful Authority', a memorandum by Vaisey J to *The Canon Law of the Church of England*, being the Report of the Archbishops' Commission on Canon Law (London: SPCK, 1947), discussed in Doe, *The Legal Framework of the Church of England* (Oxford: Clarendon Press, 1996) 300–302, and R Bursell, *Liturgy, Order and the Law* (n 158 above) 271–279.

[162] Doe, *The Legal Framework of the Church of England* (Oxford: Clarendon Press, 1996) 48–52.

[163] See *Re St Mary, Tyne Dock* [1954] P 369, [1954] 2 All ER 339, Durham Cons Ct; *Re Lapford (Devon) Parish Church* [1955] P 205, [1954] 3 All ER 484, CA; *Re St Michael and All Angels, Bishopwearmouth v Adey* [1958] 1 WLR 1183, *sub nom Rector and Churchwardens of Bishopwearmouth v Adey* [1958] 3 All ER 441, Durham Cons Ct; *Re Rector and Churchwardens of St Nicholas, Plumstead* [1961] 1 WLR 916, [1961] 1 All ER 298, Southwark Cons Ct; and *Re St Peter and St Paul, Leckhampton* [1968] P 495, [1967] 3 All ER 1057, Gloucester Cons Ct.

specific powers are given to archbishops,[164] bishops[165] and ministers[166] to dispense from what would otherwise be duties. It has application also to the laity.[167] Whilst there has been some measured call for a revival or extension of the practice of dispensation[168] it is not generally regarded as having any broad application beyond those occasions where specific provision is made.

Religious freedom in secular law

1.42 As has already been stated, the ecclesiastical law by which the Church of England is governed is part of the law of the land and its courts are courts of the realm. Mention has been made of various Acts of Parliament which touch upon the operation of religious organizations generally and the Church of England in particular. Among the most important of these is the Human Rights Act 1998, the nature and effect of which has been given detailed treatment earlier in this chapter.

1.43 The principle of religious liberty has long been recognized at common law, albeit it has never previously been guaranteed as is now the case under the Human Rights Act 1998. A self-denying principle of non-interference by which the judiciary decline to enter into questions concerning the internal affairs of religious organizations is now well acknowledged. Lord Reid explained it as follows: 'No temporal court of law can determine the truth of any religious belief: it is not competent to investigate any such matter and it ought not to attempt to do so.[169]

---

[164] For example Canon B 34, paras 2, 3, dispensing with banns, and Canon C 4, para 3A, concerning removal of the impediment of remarriage on admission to holy orders.

[165] For example Canon B 12, para 3, dispensing with the prohibition that no person shall distribute the sacrament unless ordained; Canon B 18, para 1, approval of a reasonable cause why a sermon is not preached each Sunday; Canon B 34, para 3, dispensing with banns; Canon B 42, para 2, permitting Latin services; Canon C 13, para 2, dispensing from oath of allegiance for overseas ministry; Canons C 20, para 3, and C 25, para 2, permitting alternative residence for suffragan bishops and beneficed priests respectively; and Canon C 28, para 2, permitting ministers to engage in other occupations.

[166] For example Canon B 14A, para 1, dispensing with morning and evening prayer and celebration of holy communion jointly with the PCC (if occasional) and authorized by the bishop (if regular).

[167] A bishop, in exceptional circumstances, may permit an individual to hold office as a churchwarden even notwithstanding the statutory requirements not being met: Churchwardens Measure 2001, s 1(4).

[168] See the report *Dispensation in Practice and Theory with Special Reference to Anglican Churches* (London, 1942) 159.

[169] *Gilmour v Coats* [1949] AC 426, [1949] 1 All ER 848, HL. See also, *R v Chief Rabbi of the United Hebrew Congregations of Great Britain and the Commonwealth, ex parte Wachmann* [1992] 1 WLR 1036, [1993] 2 All ER 249, Simon Brown J; *R v Provincial Court of the Church in Wales, ex parte Williams* (1998) 5 Ecc LJ 217, Latham J; *Varsani v Jesani* [1999] Ch 219, [1998] 3 All ER 273, CA.

Note, by way of example, the decision of Gray J in *Blake v Associated Newspapers Ltd*,[170] in which a defamation action was stayed on the basis that the doctrinal validity or otherwise of an alleged consecration was declared to be non-justiciable.[171]

1.44 The courts have repeatedly expressed their unwillingness to trespass into matters of doctrine but their preparedness to do so where necessary. Lord Colonsay stated in *Forbes v Eden* that, 'a Court of Law will not interfere with the rules of a voluntary association unless to protect some civil right or interest which is said to be infringed by their operation. Least of all will it enter into questions of disputed doctrine, when not necessary to do so in reference to civil interests'.[172] These are generally of a financial nature or in relation to property.[173] The position in the Church of England is a little different because its governing instruments are part of the law of the land, directly applicable in the courts, as opposed to the internal rules and regulations of other religious organizations. In the *Church Society* case, consideration was given as to who would be the arbiter of 'fundamental' were it to be the case that the Church of England Assembly (Powers) Act 1919 did not permit a Measure to deal with such a matter. McCowan LJ stated, 'I have every confidence that if this task were thrust upon the courts they would find it possible to form a view on what was fundamental, though with very great reluctance, particularly in the area of doctrine'.[174] In *Gill v Davies*,[175] an injunction was granted in the High Court to prevent an ordination taking

---

170 *Blake v Associated Newspapers Ltd* (2003) 7 Ecc LJ 369, Gray J. The judgment is reproduced in the Materials.
171 Gray J held that the matter was non-justiciable since 'many of the issues [fell] within the territory which the courts, by self-denying ordinance, will not enter' and answering such questions 'would involve a detailed and painstaking examination of questions of doctrine, theology and ecclesiology combining an assessment of history and a full understanding of contemporary and emergent theology and ecumenism'.
172 *Forbes v Eden* (1867) LR 1 Sc & Div 568, HL. Lord Cranworth, in his speech, dealt with the matter simply: 'If funds are settled to be disposed of amongst members of a voluntary association according to their rules and regulations, the Court must necessarily take cognizance of those rules and regulations for the purpose of satisfying itself as to who is entitled to the funds'.
173 *Forbes v Eden* (1867) LR 1 Sc & Div 568, HL; *Davies v Presbyterian Church of Wales* [1986] 1 ICR 280, [1986] 1 All ER 705, HL; *Varsani v Jesani* [1999] Ch 219, [1998] 3 All ER 273, CA; and the Scottish case of *Dilworth v Lovat Highland Estates Ltd and Trustees for St Benedict's Abbey* (1999) (www.scotscourts.gov.uk): 'It is well established that the Court will take no concern with the internal resolutions or agreement of voluntary associations … In the absence of any suggestion that the pursuer has suffered or will suffer patrimonial loss or loss to his reputation, the question as to whether the Trustees have acted contrary to the statutes of the Congregation is not a matter of which this Court can take cognisance', per Lord Philip.
174 *R v Ecclesiastical Committee of Both Houses of Parliament, ex parte The Church Society* (1994) 6 Admin LR 670, The Times, 4 November 1993, CA.
175 *Gill v Davies* (1997) 5 Ecc LJ 131, Smith J.

place which did not have the sanction of the acting bishop.[176] A fuller discussion of this subject is beyond the scope of this work.[177]

1.45 A number of cases have been determined by the English courts dealing with freedom of religion under Article 9 of the European Convention on Human Rights. Judicial approaches have varied, but it is possible to divine broad principles which have emerged since 2 October 2000 when the Human Rights Act 1998 came into force.[178] Article 9 provides as follows:

1. Everyone has the right to freedom of thought, conscience and religion; this right includes freedom to change his religion or belief, and freedom, either alone or in community with others and in public or private, to manifest his religion or belief, in worship, teaching, practice and observance.

2. Freedom to manifest one's religion or beliefs shall be subject only to such limitations as are prescribed by law and are necessary in a democratic society in the interests of public safety, for the protection of public order, health or morals, or the protection of the rights and freedoms of others.

1.46 In line with other international human rights instruments on religious liberty, Article 9 provides a positive right to both the freedom of thought, conscience and religion and to the manifestation of that freedom. The right to freedom of thought, conscience and religion is absolute. This includes the right to hold a religion or belief and to change it and the right not to allow the State to determine whether one's religion or belief is legitimate.[179] In contrast, the right to manifest one's religion or belief is qualified by Article 9(1) in that the manifestation must be 'in worship, teaching, practice and observance' and by the limitations in

---

[176] The injunction was granted with great reluctance and sought to preserve the status quo for a very short period pending the arrival in the diocese of the newly appointed bishop. The reasoning, in one respect, is unsatisfactory in that the judge recognized that were she not to grant the injunction, then the Revd Kenneth Moulder, the parish priest of the church where the ordination was to take place, would commit a disciplinary offence under ecclesiastical law. Nonetheless, she declined to injunct him on this ground because 'he is an adult and intelligent man and it is for him, as it seems to me, to decide how to behave in accordance with his own conscience'.

[177] A detailed consideration may be found in M Hill, 'Judicial Review of Ecclesiastical Courts' in N Doe, M Hill and R Ombres (eds), *English Canon Law* (Cardiff: University of Wales Press, 1998) 104–114; M Hill, 'Church Autonomy in the United Kingdom' in G Robbers (ed), *Church Autonomy: A Comparative Study* (Frankfurt: Peter Lang, 2001) 267–283; M Hill, 'Judicial Approaches to Religious Disputes' in R O'Dair and A Lewis (eds), *Law and Religion*, Current Legal Issues IV (Oxford: Oxford University Press, 2001) 409–420.

[178] See M Hill, 'A New Dawn for Freedom of Religion: Grounding the Debate' in M Hill (ed) *Religious Liberty and Human Rights* (Cardiff: University of Wales Press, 2002) 1–13; M Hill, 'The Permissible Scope of Legal Limitations on the Freedom of Religion in the United Kingdom' (2005) 19(2) *Emory International Law Review* 1129–1186.

[179] *Manoussakis v Greece* (1997) 23 EHRR 387; *Metropolitan Church of Bessarabia v Moldova* (2002) 35 EHRR 306.

Article 9(2) which permit the State to interfere with the individual right:

(a) if that interference is prescribed by law in that it has some basis in domestic law, is accessible and its effects foreseeable;[180]
(b) if it meets one of the legitimate aims outlined in the Article;[181] and
(c) if the interference is necessary in a democratic society in that the interference corresponds to a pressing social need and is proportionate to the legitimate aim pursued.[182]

1.47 Mention must be made of section 13 of the Human Rights Act 1998 which provides:

> If a court's determination of any question arising under this Act might affect the exercise by a religious organisation (itself or its members collectively) of the Convention right to freedom of thought, conscience and religion, it must have particular regard to the importance of that right.

The section was a result of lobbying by religious groups concerned, amongst other things, that they might be classified as public authorities under the Act.[183] Its effect and significance remain unclear. Certain cases on a parallel provision on freedom of expression have hinted that the courts might afford considerable weight (though not presumptive priority) to the right.[184] Whether the section is a symbolic political statement designed to placate religious opponents,[185] or at best an articulation and codification of the pre-existing position prior to the Human Rights Act 1998[186] is a matter of subjective opinion.[187]

1.48 The House of Lords has had occasion to consider Article 9 in relation to the chastisement of children and the wearing of Islamic dress. In *R (Williamson) v Secretary of State for Education and Employment*,[188] the headmaster, teachers

---

180 *Sahin v Turkey* (2005) 41 EHRR 8 (Grand Chamber decision).
181 Namely 'public safety, for the protection of public order, health or morals, or for the protection of the rights and freedoms of others'.
182 *Serif v Greece* (2001) 31 EHRR 561, E Ct HR.
183 When the House of Lords was invited to rule upon the status of a parochial church council, it concluded that it was not a public authority for the purposes of the Human Rights Act 1998. Lord Nicholls of Birkenhead drew attention to the irony that, were component institutions of the Church of England to be classified as public authorities, they would, by definition, lose their status of 'victim' and with it any right of action in respect of a violation of Convention rights, including that of freedom of religion: see *Aston Cantlow and Wilmcote with Billesley Parochial Church Council v Wallbank* [2004] 1 AC 546, [2003] 3 All ER 1213, HL, at para 15.
184 *Douglas v Hello! Ltd* [2001] QB 967, [2001] 2 All ER 289, CA, per Sedley LJ.
185 See P Cumper, 'The Protection of Religious Rights under Section 13 of the Human Rights Act 1998' [2000] Public Law 265.
186 M Hill, 'Judicial Approaches to Religious Disputes' in R O'Dair and A Lewis (eds), *Law and Religion*, Current Legal Issues IV (Oxford: Oxford University Press, 2001) 419.
187 Section 13 hardly features in higher court judgments concerning freedom of religion under Article 9.
188 [2005] 2 AC 246 HL, [2005] UKHL 15.

and parents of children at an independent school claimed that corporal punishment was a doctrinal necessity of their faith, required to instil a 'godly character'. They alleged that the extended ban on corporal punishment under section 548 of the Education Act 1996[189] was incompatible with their right to manifest their religion in practice under Article 9. They lost at first instance,[190] and in the Court of Appeal.[191] Unsurprisingly they lost again in the House of Lords, but on significantly different grounds. Whereas the majority in the Court of Appeal had found that the infliction of corporal punishment was not a manifestation of religious beliefs, and thus Article 9 had no application, the House of Lords was less restrictive. Their Lordships accepted that the applicants' beliefs were engaged, and that corporal punishment was a manifestation of those beliefs.[192] They acknowledged that section 548 constituted an interference with the manifestation of those beliefs but one which was justified under Article 9(2).[193] The interference was prescribed by law, aimed at protecting children and promoting their well-being, and was not a disproportionate restriction on parental rights: 'Parliament was entitled to decide that ... a universal ban was preferable to a selective ban which exempts schools where the parents and teachers have an ideological belief in the efficacy and desirability of a mild degree of carefully-controlled corporal punishment'.[194]

1.49 The House of Lords returned to the subject of Article 9 in a case concerning religious dress, *R (Begum) v Headteacher and Governors of Denbigh High School*.[195] A Muslim girl ceased attending school because the school refused to allow her to wear the jilbab. At first instance, Bennett J held that although her refusal to respect the school uniform policy was motivated by religious belief, there had been no interference with her Article 9(1) right since her exclusion from school

---

[189] Introduced by section 131 of the School Standards and Framework Act 1998.

[190] *R (Williamson) v Secretary of State for Education and Employment* [2002] 1 FLR 493, Elias J.

[191] *R (Williamson) v Secretary of State for Education and Employment* [2003] QB 1300, [2003] 1 All ER 385, CA, per Buxton, Rix and Arden LJJ.

[192] The House of Lords evinced a willingness to give a more generous interpretation of 'manifestation' than that afforded by the European Court of Human Rights in Strasbourg. Lord Nicholls of Birkenhead observed, at paragraph 32, 'I do not read the examples of acts of worship and devotion given by the European Commission ... as exhaustive of the scope of manifestation of a belief in practice'. It is submitted that the adoption of this more generous approach in the domestic courts is to be preferred.

[193] For a discussion see S Langlaude, 'Flogging Children With Religion: A Comment on the House of Lords' Decision in *Williamson*' (2006) 8 Ecc LJ 339.

[194] *R (Williamson) v Secretary of State for Education and Employment* [2005] 2 AC 246, [2005] 2 All ER 1, HL, per Lord Nicholls of Birkenhead at para 51. He continued, 'Parliament was entitled to take this course because this issue is one of broad social policy'. In contrast, the speech of Baroness Hale, though concurring in the result, was based upon an evaluation of the development of children's rights and did not address Article 9 jurisprudence.

[195] *R (Begum) v Headteacher and Governors of Denbigh High School* [2007] 1 AC 100, [2006] 2 All ER 487, HL.

was based simply upon her disobedience to the uniform policy.[196] This approach was ill-founded and contrary to Strasbourg jurisprudence, and the Court of Appeal reversed the decision.[197] Brooke LJ, giving the judgment of the court, held that Article 9(1) was engaged but that flaws in the school's process in drawing up its uniform policy meant that the school could not justify its interference with the Convention right.[198]

1.50 The House of Lords allowed the further appeal, rejecting the Court of Appeal's overly formulaic interpretation of Article 9(2), and held that there was no breach of Article 9. Lords Bingham of Cornhill, Hoffmann and Scott of Foscote asserted that a school was a 'specific situation' where, under Strasbourg jurisprudence, limitations on the exercise of the right were permissible.[199] Lord Nicholls of Birkenhead recognized that the pupil's Article 9 right had been engaged but concluded that the interference was justified under Article 9(2). It is submitted that Lord Nicholls' approach, consistent with that in *Williamson*,[200] ought to be adopted in resolving Article 9 claims in the future.[201] More detailed treatment of the emergent jurisprudence concerning religious liberty under Article 9 of the European Convention on Human Rights is beyond the scope of this work.[202]

---

196 *R (Begum) v Headteacher and Governors of Denbigh High School* [2004] EWHC 1389 (Admin), [2004] All ER (D) 108, Admin Ct, Bennett J.

197 *R (Begum) v Headteacher and Governors of Denbigh High School* [2005] EWCA Civ 199, [2005] 2 All ER 396, CA, per Brooke, Mummery and Scott Baker LJJ. Note the criticism of the Court of Appeal's judgment in T Poole, 'Of Headscarves and Heresies: The Denbigh High School Case and Public Authority Decision Making under the Human Rights Act' [2005] *Public Law* 685.

198 Paras 75–76. The inadequacies in the reasoning in the Court of Appeal are addressed in M Hill and R Sandberg, 'Muslim Dress in English Law: Lifting the Veil on Human Rights' (2006) Vol 1 *Derecho y Religión* 302–328.

199 This approach is flawed. The 'specific situation' analogy is not applicable in a state secondary school since the voluntary contractual feature present in the workplace or university is missing. See the criticism of the reasoning (though not the conclusion) in M Hill and R Sandberg, 'Is Nothing Sacred? Clashing Symbols in a Secular World' (2007) *Public Law* 488.

200 *R (Williamson) v Secretary of State for Education and Employment* [2005] 2 AC 246, [2005] 2 All ER 1, HL.

201 Regrettably, there are already indications that the overly narrow approach of Lord Bingham may be being adopted uncritically in lower courts and tribunals. See *Azmi v Kirklees Metropolitan Council* ET, Case No 1801450/06 (6 October 2006), affirmed in the Employment Appeal Tribunal, Appeal No UKEAT/0009/07/MAA (30 March 2007).

202 For a detailed treatment, see R Ahdar and I Leigh, *Religious Freedom in the Liberal State* (Oxford: Oxford University Press, 2005), and S Knights, *Freedom of Religion, Minorities and the Law* (Oxford, 2007). See also M Hill, 'A New Dawn for Freedom of Religion: Grounding the Debate' in M Hill (ed) *Religious Liberty and Human Rights* (Cardiff: University of Wales Press, 2002) 1–13; M Hill, 'The Permissible Scope of Legal Limitations on the Freedom of Religion in the United Kingdom' (2005) 19(2) *Emory International Law Review* 1129–1186.

2

THE CONSTITUTION OF THE CHURCH OF ENGLAND

Introduction	2.01	Purpose and function	2.35
Towards autonomy	2.04	The Church Commissioners	2.38
Synodical government	2.10	Church Courts and Tribunals	2.46
The Archbishops' Council	2.11	Chancellors	2.47
Composition	2.12	Vicars-General	2.52
Purpose and function	2.13	Registrars	2.53
General Synod	2.15	Archdeacons	2.57
Composition	2.15	Consistory courts	2.58
Purpose and function	2.21	Appellate courts	2.59
Diocesan synods	2.26	The Court of Faculties	2.61
Composition	2.26	Judicial Review	2.62
Purpose and function	2.27		
Deanery synods	2.33		
Composition	2.34		

Introduction

The Church of England comprises the provinces of Canterbury[1] and York and is but one part of the Church of God on Earth. It belongs to, and is occasionally confused with, the worldwide Anglican Communion. The Anglican Communion comprises a number of autonomous national and regional churches.[2] Each is self-governing but they remain in communion one with another by dint of their

2.01

---

[1] The Diocese of Gibraltar in Europe deems itself to be within the Province of Canterbury and subject to the metropolitan jurisdiction of the Archbishop of Canterbury: Constitution of the Diocese in Europe (1995), para 2.

[2] For a detailed consideration of the ecclesiastical legal systems of the various provinces, see N Doe, *Canon Law in the Anglican Communion—A Worldwide Perspective* (Oxford: Oxford University Press, 1998).

common inheritance and beliefs.³ The Lambeth Conference provides a forum through which each of the Churches may meet and exchange opinions.⁴ Examples of other Churches within the Anglican Communion are the Church in Wales, the Church of Ireland, the Scottish Episcopal Church, the Episcopal Church in the United States of America, the Anglican Church of Australia, the Anglican Church of Canada, the Church of the Province of Central Africa and the Holy Catholic Church in Japan.⁵

2.02 The Church of England is the established Church in England and, historically, its governance was by public general Acts of Parliament. However, the twentieth century witnessed increasing self-determination afforded to the Church of England. The catalyst for change was the Report of the Archbishops' Committee on Church and State of 1916, which asserted:

> The main defect of the present situation ... is that, whereas no considerable reform can be achieved without Parliamentary action, Parliament has neither the leisure, fitness or inclination to perform efficiently the function of an ecclesiastical legislature. The remedy which recommends itself to [this] committee is to give to the Church the right to legislate and, at the same time, to provide a means by which full powers of scrutiny, criticism and veto are reserved to the State.⁶

2.03 The solution sought was one which would release valuable parliamentary time for secular business, leave the Church of England free to determine its own requirements, safeguard individual rights and freedoms, and preserve the historic relationship of Church and State.

---

³ For treatment of legal matters concerning the functioning of the Anglican Communion, see N Doe, 'Canon Law and Communion' (2002) 6 Ecc LJ 241; N Doe, 'The Common Law of the Anglican Communion' (2003) 7 Ecc LJ 4; and N Doe, 'The Anglican Covenant Proposed by the Lambeth Commission' (2005) 8 Ecc LJ 147.

⁴ The Archbishop of Canterbury acts as a focus of unity for the Communion, together with the Primates Meeting, the Anglican Consultative Council and the Lambeth Conference. In April 2002, the Primates Meeting 'recognised that the unwritten law common to the Churches of the Communion and expressed as shared principles of canon law may be understood to constitute a fifth instrument of unity. ... Given that law may be understood to provide a basic framework to sustain the minimal conditions which allow the Churches of the Communion to live in harmony and unity, the observances of the ministry of Word and Sacrament call us all to live by a maximal degree of Communion through grace'. In September 2002, the Anglican Consultative Council approved the establishment of an Anglican Communion Legal Advisers Network, and commissioned it to produce a statement of the principles of canon law common to the Churches.

⁵ For an exhaustive list of all churches and provinces of the Anglican Communion and for a commentary on the Lambeth Conference, see the *Church of England Yearbook* published annually by Church House Publishing.

⁶ The 'mischief' as outlined by the Report (at page 39) was discussed in *R v Ecclesiastical Committee of Both Houses of Parliament, ex parte The Church Society* (1994) 6 Admin LR 670, The Times, 4 November 1993, CA, per McCowan LJ.

Towards autonomy

The year 1919 saw the passage of what is usually referred to as the Enabling Act.[7] This gave to the National Assembly of the Church of England (or 'Church Assembly' as it was more commonly known)[8] the power to legislate by Measure.[9] As a result of the Synodical Government Measure 1969, the Church Assembly was reconstituted and renamed the General Synod of the Church of England[10] and Synod additionally empowered to legislate by canon, a power which had hitherto vested in the Convocations of Canterbury and York.[11] The formation of the Church Assembly marked a significant reduction in the legislative role of Parliament over the affairs of the Church of England. However, as the passage of the draft Churchwardens Measure in 1999 served to illustrate, the residuary powers retained by Parliament are far from being a dead letter.[12]

2.04

Measures have the full force and effect of Acts of Parliament and can amend or repeal Acts of Parliament.[13] Once a Measure has received the Royal Assent, its *vires* may not be challenged in the courts.[14] A Measure may relate to 'any matter concerning the Church of England'.[15] This expression carries its ordinary meaning and is not to be narrowly construed so as to prevent Synod passing a Measure concerning a fundamental change in doctrine.[16] However, a Measure may not make any alteration in the composition or powers or duties of the Ecclesiastical Committee of Parliament or in the parliamentary procedures

2.05

---

[7] Namely the Church of England Assembly (Powers) Act 1919, a statute allowing the laity (other than members of Parliament) to participate in Church government for the first time.

[8] It was created by the conflation of the Convocations of Canterbury and of York.

[9] See W McKay, *Erskine May's Treatise on the Laws, Privileges, Proceedings and Usage of Parliament* (23rd edn, London: LexisNexis, 2004) 701–705. The legal status of a Measure is considered in Chapter 1 paras 1.25 and 1.30.

[10] Hereafter 'Synod'.

[11] Synodical Government Measure 1969, s 1; Canon H 1. Note also the Church of England (Worship and Doctrine) Measure 1974, s 1, which makes particular provision for canons concerning worship.

[12] See B Hanson, 'Report on the General Synod of the Church of England, July and November Sessions, 1999', (2000) 5 Ecc LJ 382. Note also amendments to the proposed Church of England (Pensions) Measure 2003 made at the behest of the Ecclesiastical Committee of Parliament, noted in S Slack, 'Report on the General Synod of the Church of England, July Session, 2002' (2003) 7 Ecc LJ 78.

[13] Church of England Assembly (Powers) Act 1919, s 4. See, for example, the Priests (Ordination of Women) Measure 1993, s 6, which ousted the provisions of the Sex Discrimination Act 1975.

[14] *R v Archbishops of Canterbury and York, ex parte Williamson*, The Times, 9 March 1994, CA.

[15] Church of England Assembly (Powers) Act 1919, s 3(6).

[16] *R v Ecclesiastical Committee of Both Houses of Parliament, ex parte The Church Society* (n 6 above); *R v Archbishops of Canterbury and York, ex parte Williamson* (n 14 above); *Williamson v Archbishops of Canterbury and York*, 5 September 1996, CA (unreported).

prescribed under section 4 of the 1919 Act.[17] The Human Rights Act 1998, which came into effect in England on 2 October 2000, requires all Measures, whenever passed, to be read and given effect in a way which is compatible with the rights contained in the European Convention on Human Rights.[18]

2.06 Two sections of the Civil Partnership Act 2004 sit somewhat uncomfortably with this process of autonomy.[19] They provide that a Minister of the Crown may by order amend, repeal or revoke Church legislation, a term defined so as to include Measures of the Church Assembly or General Synod and any orders, regulations or other instruments made by virtue of such Measures.[20] This amounts to a curtailment of autonomy on the part of the Church of England, albeit partial, with a specificity of purpose, and reliant upon benign and consensual exercise by the Government.[21] The words of the statute are clear and unambiguous, and the absence of any express provision for seeking the concurrence of General Synod gives considerable power to the Executive, rather than to Parliament as a whole, in theory if not also in practice, to legislate for the Church of England.[22]

2.07 If Synod desires a Measure to be passed into law, the draft Measure is dealt with in Synod in a similar fashion to a Bill in Parliament and is then referred to

---

[17] Church of England Assembly (Powers) Act 1919, s 3(6) proviso.
[18] See Chapter 1, paras 1.26–1.27.
[19] See M Hill, 'Uncivil partnership with the state?' Church Times, 2 February 2007, and 'Editorial' (2007) 9 Ecc LJ 1, and, for a contrary view by way of response, see S Slack, 'Church Autonomy and the Civil Partnership Act: A Rejoinder' (2007) 9 Ecc LJ 206.
[20] Section 255 of the Civil Partnership Act 2004 is anodyne enough, limiting this new form of ministerial intervention to amendments, repeals or revocations in any Church legislation relating to pensions, allowances or gratuities with respect to surviving civil partners or their dependants. However, section 259 goes further and is much more widely drafted. It empowers a Minister by order to make 'such further provision as he considers appropriate for the general purposes, or any particular purpose, of the Civil Partnership Act, or for giving full effect to the Act or any provision of it'.
[21] In the course of parliamentary debate on 19 July 2005 concerning the proposed Civil Partnership Act 2004 (Overseas Relationships and Consequential, etc Amendments) Order, Lord Sainsbury of Turville, the Under-Secretary of State in the Department for Trade and Industry, stated, 'by convention the Government do not legislate for the Church of England without its consent. I stress that the provisions in the order amending Church legislation have been drafted by Church lawyers, consulted on internally within the Church, and finally have been approved by the Archbishops' Council and the House of Bishops. The Church has asked that we include the amendments in the order, which we are content to do'. (Grand Chamber, 19 July 2005, GC192–193). This was confirmed in debate by the Bishop of Worcester and there was a similar exchange on the Civil Partnership (Judicial Pensions and Church Pensions, etc) Order in which Lord Evans of Temple Guiting spoke for the Government and the Bishop of St Albans for the Church of England (30 November 2005, Column 293–295).
[22] The Parliamentary debates in the above instances referred to consent being forthcoming from the Archbishops' Council and the House of Bishops. No reference is made to the General Synod, which is the legislative body of the Church of England.

Synod's Legislative Committee, which submits it to the Ecclesiastical Committee of Parliament.[23] The Ecclesiastical Committee, which comprises members of all major parties in both Houses,[24] then drafts a report on the nature and effect of the proposed Measure, having particular regard to the constitutional rights of all Her Majesty's subjects.[25] Once the report is prepared, it is communicated to the Legislative Committee of Synod, which has the option of withdrawing the proposed Measure. This course would be adopted were the report to be unfavourable, since there is no provision for varying a Measure after it has been presented for consideration by the Ecclesiastical Committee.[26] There is, however, power to divide a proposed Measure into two or more separate Measures if the Chairman of Committees of the House of Lords and the Chairman of Ways and Means in the House of Commons are of the opinion that it deals with separate subjects. Thereafter, each of the divided parts is treated as a separate Measure.[27]

If the option of withdrawal is not taken, the proposed Measure and the report of the Ecclesiastical Committee are laid before both Houses of Parliament. Upon a resolution being passed by each House that the proposed Measure be presented to the Queen, it is so presented and has the same force and effect as an Act of Parliament upon the Royal Assent being signified in like manner.[28] Parliament has no power to amend or vary a proposed Measure; it merely resolves whether or not to present it to the Queen in the form in which it is drafted. **2.08**

Certain parts of the Church of England fall outside the foregoing procedures. The Channel Islands, for example, are annexed to the Diocese of Winchester but have their own systems of law, both secular and ecclesiastical. Provision is made under the Channel Islands (Church Legislation) Measure 1931 and the Synodical Government (Channel Islands) Order 1970[29] for Measures to be brought into effect in the Channel Islands subject to necessary modifications.[30] Equally, there are certain anomalies regarding the Diocese of Sodor and Man.[31] **2.09**

---

[23] Church of England Assembly (Powers) Act 1919, s 3(1).
[24] Ibid s 2(2).
[25] Ibid s 3(3). In the course of its consideration, a joint conference of the Ecclesiastical Committee and the Legislative Committee may be held at the instance of either committee: see s 3(2).
[26] Ibid s 3(5). An indication that a report is likely to be unfavourable affords Synod the opportunity of amending the proposed Measure and then re-presenting it in a form which would produce a more positive report.
[27] Ibid s 4 proviso.
[28] Ibid s 4.
[29] SI 1970/1117.
[30] A full discussion is beyond the scope of this book, but see G Phillips, 'Canon and Ecclesiastical Law in the Channel Islands', LLM dissertation (Cardiff, University of Wales, 1996).
[31] See A Pearce, 'The Offshore Establishment of Religion: Church and Nation on the Isle of Man' (2003) 7 Ecc LJ 62; K Gumbley, 'Church Legislation in the Isle of Man' (1994) 4 Ecc LJ 240.

The Diocese in Europe, being a creature of statute,[32] is a jurisprudential anomaly, consideration of which is beyond the scope of this work.[33]

Synodical government

2.10 It is frequently said that the Church of England is episcopally led and synodically governed, but this trite truism belies a sophisticated internal governance through a pyramid structure of dispersed authority with General Synod at its top and parochial church councils at the 'grass roots' level. Between these lie diocesan synods and deanery synods. The composition of each body includes clergy and laity (either elected or *ex officio*) in prescribed proportions.[34] The powers and responsibilities of parochial church councils are discussed in Chapter 3. Each parish is part of a deanery, which is part of an archdeaconry, which, save where the whole diocese constitutes a single archdeaconry, is part of a diocese, which, in turn, is part of a province. Just as each of the two provinces of the Church of England is presided over by an archbishop,[35] so is each diocese under the charge of a bishop. There are 30 dioceses in the province of Canterbury[36] and 14 in that of York.

The Archbishops' Council

2.11 The Archbishops' Council is a creature of statute established on 1 January 1999.[37] The Council was the product of a major restructuring of the national organs of administration of the Church of England.[38] The National Institutions Measure 1998, which brought the Council into being, defines the Council's purpose

---

[32] Diocese in Europe Measure 1980.
[33] Its governing instrument is a constitution, paragraph 2 of which declares that the diocese 'shall be deemed to be within the Province of Canterbury'. Paragraph 22(a) makes provision for the canons and ecclesiastical law of the Church of England to apply in the diocese 'so far as the local law of any state or country shall permit' and 'with such modifications or exceptions as … are deemed appropriate by the Archbishop of Canterbury acting with the concurrence of the vicar general of the Province … '.
[34] See below.
[35] The Archbishop of Canterbury is styled Primate of All England and that of York, Primate of England. In addition to their provincial functions each has his own diocesan responsibilities.
[36] This includes the Diocese in Europe, which was founded pursuant to the Diocese in Europe Measure 1980. For the purposes of synodical elections, as to which see below, the Diocese in Europe is treated as being part of the province of Canterbury. See the *Church of England Yearbook*.
[37] National Institutions Measure 1998.
[38] See *Working as One Body*, the Report of the Archbishops' Commission on the Organisation of the Church of England (GS 1178, 1995).

as being 'to co-ordinate, promote, aid and further the work and mission of the Church of England'.[39] The Council for the first time brought together at a national level executive policy and resource decision-making in a single body. The Council is accountable to Synod but not subordinate to it, and acts as a national executive of the Church of England.[40]

Composition

The Archbishops' Council comprises the following: 2.12

(a) the Archbishops of Canterbury and York;
(b) the Prolocutors of the Convocations of Canterbury and York;
(c) the chairman and vice-chairman of the House of Laity;
(d) two bishops elected by the House of Bishops from among its members;
(e) two clerks in Holy Orders elected by the House of Clergy from among its members;
(f) two lay persons elected by the House of Laity from among its members;
(g) up to six persons appointed by the Archbishops of Canterbury and York acting jointly;[41]
(h) one of the Church Estates Commissioners appointed by the Archbishops of Canterbury and York acting jointly.[42]

The Archbishops of Canterbury and York are the joint presidents.[43]

Purpose and function

The objects of the Archbishops' Council are 'to co-ordinate, promote, aid and further the work and mission of the Church of England'.[44] It must cause a report of its work and proceedings during the year in question, including any decisions taken as to its future work, to be laid before Synod before the end of June in the following year, and at each group of sessions cause an account of the matters discussed and the decisions taken by it at its meetings held since the previous 2.13

---

[39] National Institutions Measure 1998, s 1(1).
[40] Synod must be given the opportunity at each group of sessions to consider any report or budget laid before it by the Council, to consider such other matters as may be referred to it by the Council and to question representatives of the Council in connection with any such report, budget or other matter: National Institutions Measure 1998, s 9(b).
[41] This is subject to the approval of Synod. In considering the making of any such appointment the Archbishops of Canterbury and York must consult the Archbishops' Council and the Appointments Committee of the Church of England: National Institutions Measure 1998, s 1(3), Sch 1 para 1(3).
[42] Ibid Sch 1 para 1(1), (2).
[43] Ibid Sch 1 para 2.
[44] Ibid s 1(1).

group of sessions to be laid before Synod for its approval.[45] It is funded partly through the Church Commissioners and partly through apportionment on the dioceses and is required to frame an annual budget.[46] The Council has taken over certain of the functions of the Church Commissioners such as distribution of clergy stipends and administration of parochial fees. The accounts of the Council are subject to an independent audit each year.[47] The Council has a chief executive known as the Secretary General.[48]

2.14 The Council has a support structure which comprises a number of divisions, boards and councils each with responsibility for specific areas of work. They may broadly be classified under the following general heads: education, cathedrals and church buildings, ministry, mission and public affairs, central secretariat, legal, communications and human resources.[49]

General Synod

Composition

2.15 The General Synod of the Church of England comprises three houses and recently underwent a reduction in its overall membership, effective from the quinquennium inaugurated in November 2005. The House of Bishops is made up of the Archbishops of Canterbury and York, all diocesan bishops,[50] the Bishop of Dover,[51] other persons in episcopal orders residing in either province who are members of the Archbishops' Council,[52] and seven representatives elected by and from among the suffragan bishops (other than the Bishop of Dover)[53] of

---

[45] Ibid s 4(1), (2).
[46] Ibid s 4(3).
[47] National Institutions Measure 1998, s 3(2).
[48] Ibid Sch 1 para 16.
[49] This list does not purport to be exhaustive. Reference may usefully be made to the *Church of England Yearbook* published annually by Church House Publishing which sets out all commissions, committees and other bodies together with details of membership and contact addresses. In 2005, the Council launched an independent service review in three phases over two to three years of the work of all the Council's staff.
[50] Canon H 3 para 1 (for the province of Canterbury) and para 2 (for that of York).
[51] Canon H 3 para 1(b), as amended by Amending Canon 25 promulged in July 2000. The Bishop of Dover is a suffragan bishop in the Diocese of Canterbury, who discharges significant episcopal functions in the diocese which the Archbishop of Canterbury is unable to undertake due to his provincial, national and international roles.
[52] It also includes the Bishop to the Forces, if chosen as a representative by the Forces Synodical Council: Canon H 3 para 1(bb).
[53] Suffragan bishop in this context also includes other persons in episcopal orders working in a diocese in the province who are members of the house of bishops of that diocese: Canon H 3 para 1(d) (as renumbered by amendment).

each province (four from Canterbury and three from York).[54] It is the fusion of the Upper Houses of the Convocations of Canterbury and York.[55]

2.16 Similarly, the House of Clergy comprises the fused Lower Houses of the two Convocations.[56] That of Canterbury comprises:

(a) three persons elected by and from among the deans of all the cathedral churches;
(b) either the Dean of Jersey or the Dean of Guernsey;
(c) three or four clergy elected or chosen from among the chaplains of the armed forces;[57]
(d) the Chaplain General of Prisons;[58]
(e) proctors of the clergy (being no more than 128 for the dioceses and four for the universities);[59]
(f) not more than two persons chosen by and from the priests and deacons who are members of religious communities;
(g) the Dean of Arches and Auditor, the Vicar-General of the province, the third Church Estates Commissioner, the chairman of the Church of England Pensions Board, and any member of the Archbishops' Council beneficed, licensed or resident in the province; and
(h) up to three clergy duly co-opted.

2.17 The Lower House of the Convocation of York is made up of:

(a) two persons from among the deans;
(b) proctors of the clergy (being no more than 54 for the dioceses and two for the universities);
(c) not more that two persons chosen by and from among the priests and deacons who are members of religious communities;
(d) the Vicar-General and any member of the Archbishops' Council beneficed, licensed or resident in the province; and
(e) up to two clergy duly co-opted.

---

[54] The number for the Province of Canterbury had previously been six. The change was effected by Amending Canon 26. See Convocations (Election to Upper House) Rules (Amendment) Resolution 2005.
[55] Synodical Government Measure 1969, s 2(1), Sch 2 arts 1, 2; Canon H 3 (as amended). See also the Clergy Representation Rules.
[56] Synodical Government Measure 1969, Sch 2 art 2. Canon H 2 sets out representation of the clergy in the Lower House of Convocation.
[57] The total number of representatives of the forces, whether episcopal, clerical or lay may not exceed seven: Canon H 2 para 1(d).
[58] Or where the holder is not in holy orders, such prison chaplain as may be nominated by the Archbishop of Canterbury: Canon H 2 para 1(dd).
[59] Not more than one archdeacon may be elected for each diocese, or for each electoral area if a diocese is so divided: Canon H 2 para 1(e).

2.18 The House of Laity is made up of laity elected as diocesan representatives in accordance with the Church Representation Rules.[60] The number of representatives returned by each diocese reflects the total number of persons on the electoral rolls of parishes within the diocese and is fixed by resolution of Synod prior to the election.[61] Directly elected members are supplemented by those specially elected and by *ex officio* members. The total number of members directly or specially elected[62] may not exceed 136 for the province of Canterbury or 59 for that of York; and no diocese is to have fewer than three members, save for the Diocese in Europe, which has two, and that of Sodor and Man, which has one.[63] The diocesan electors consist of the members of the houses of laity of all the deanery synods in the diocese other than co-opted members.[64] Detailed provisions are made for the conduct of elections and for appeals.[65] The presiding officer must, within seven days of a written request, supply free of charge to all duly nominated candidates a copy of the names and addresses of the qualified electors.[66] There is no obligation under the Church Representation Rules or otherwise to hold hustings.[67]

2.19 Thus the House of Laity comprises:

(a) directly elected members as discussed above;[68]
(b) two lay members chosen by and from the members of religious communities who have their mother house in either province;[69]
(c) one representative from Jersey and one from Guernsey and its dependencies elected in accordance with the Channel Islands (Representation) Measure 1931;[70]

---

[60] Synodical Government Measure 1969, Sch 2 Art 2. The Church Representation Rules, which have been substantially amended and renumbered, appear as Sch 3 to the Measure. For the sake of convenience they are reproduced in their current form as a separate section in the Materials.

[61] Church Representation Rules, r 36(2).

[62] The only specially elected members are currently those for the Channel Islands, which are under the jurisdiction of the Bishop of Winchester: see ibid r 36(1) and the Channel Islands (Representation) Measure 1931.

[63] Church Representation Rules, r 36(1). The apportionment between the provinces of Canterbury and York is required to be as nearly as possible in a proportion of 70 to 30: r 36(2).

[64] Ibid r 35(3), save for the Diocese in Europe in which the diocesan electors are specifically elected by the annual meetings of chaplaincies: r 35(4), and to be eligible for election as a diocesan elector, an individual must be aged 18 or over, an actual communicant, and included on the electoral roll of the chaplaincy.

[65] Ibid rr 38–40, 43–45.

[66] Church Representation Rules, r 39(5)(b). Although there is no requirement to provide address labels, it is important that any diocesan policy in this regard is strictly followed since the provision of labels to one or some but not all of the candidates may give rise to an impression of unfairness leading to the election being declared void: *Diocese of Southwark Election Appeal* (December 1995).

[67] *Diocese of Southwark Election Appeal* (February 1996).

[68] Church Representation Rules, r 35(1)(a).

[69] Ibid r 35(1)(b).

[70] Ibid r 36(1).

(d) the Dean of Arches; the Vicars-General of each province; the three Church Estates Commissioners; the Chairman of the Central Board of Finance; and the Chairman of the Church of England Pensions Board provided they are not in Holy Orders;[71]

(e) the lay members of the Archbishops' Council who are actual communicants;[72]

(f) up to five actual lay communicants of eighteen years or upwards duly co-opted.[73]

The Archbishops of Canterbury and York are joint presidents, and any question concerning the interpretation of the Constitution of General Synod must be referred to them for determination.[74] Synod must appoint a Legislative Committee (whose role has already been discussed) and may make provision for a Standing Committee and such other committees, commissions and bodies as it deems expedient.[75]

2.20

Purpose and function

General Synod is both a legislative and a deliberative body.[76] By its constitution it is empowered to exercise two functions.[77] First, it is to consider matters concerning the Church of England and make provision for them by measure, canon, order[78] or act of synod and, secondly, it is to consider and express its opinion on any other matters of religious or public interest. It has no judicial function. Equally, although the Synodical Government Measure 1969 is silent, Synod lacks any executive function, the Archbishops' Council now undertaking the functions formerly discharged by its Standing Committee.[79]

2.21

---

[71] Ibid rr 35(1)(c), 42(1)(a)–(f). The Ecclesiastical Commissioners Act 1850, s 1 provides that the First and Second Commissioners must be lay members of the Church of England; accordingly the conditional element refers only to the Third.

[72] Church Representation Rules, r 42(1)(g); National Institutions Measure 1998, s 13(1), Sch 5 para 2(b).

[73] Church Representation Rules, r 42(2).

[74] Synodical Government Measure 1969, s 2(1), Sch 2 arts 4(1), 12(2).

[75] Ibid Sch 2 art 10(2). The Archbishops of Canterbury and York acting jointly were empowered, after consultation with any body significantly affected, to transfer to the Archbishops' Council any function previously exercised by the Standing Committee of General Synod or any of its sub-committees: National Institutions Measure 1998, s 5(1)(c).

[76] For a general discussion, see P Moore (ed), *The Synod of Westminster: Do We Need It?* (London: SPCK, 1986).

[77] Synodical Government Measure 1969, Sch 2 art 6.

[78] This includes a regulation or other subordinate instrument as may be authorized by Measure or Canon.

[79] Note that paragraph 15 of the Appendix to the Church of England Assembly (Powers) Act 1919 had expressly debarred the Church Assembly from exercising any power or performing any functions distinctively belonging to the bishops in right of their episcopal office. There is no equivalent to this provision in Sch 2 to the Synodical Government Measure 1969.

2.22 General Synod is required to meet on at least two occasions each year.[80] It usually now meets each year in February at Church House, Westminster and in July at the University of York.[81] Synod's procedure is governed by its constitution[82] and its standing orders.[83] Its business and procedure at any meeting is regulated by the chairman at the time,[84] who is one of a panel appointed by the presidents from any of the Houses.[85]

2.23 A motion for the final approval of a Measure or Canon is not deemed to be carried unless, on a division by Houses, it receives the assent of the majority of the members of each House present and voting.[86] All other motions are normally to be determined by a simple majority of the members of the Synod present and voting, by way of a show of hands or a division.[87]

2.24 Provision of the type mentioned in Article 6(a) of the Synod's constitution[88] concerning doctrinal formulae or the services or ceremonies of the Church of England or the administration of its sacraments or sacred rites must be referred to the House of Bishops and may only be presented for the approval of Synod in the form approved by the House.[89] At the request of either of the Convocations of Canterbury or York, or of the House of Laity, such a provision must be referred to the two Convocations, sitting separately for their provinces, and to the House of Laity. The provision may not be submitted to Synod for final approval unless it has been approved by each House of the two Convocations and by the House of Laity.[90] If such a provision fails to secure the necessary support in any of the Houses, it may not be proposed again in the same or a similar form until a new Synod is elected. Questions relating to compliance with these provisions

---

[80] Synodical Government Measure 1969, s 2(1), Sch 2 art 3(1).
[81] A further session may be convened in November in Church House, Westminster should there be sufficient business to require it.
[82] To be found in the Synodical Measure 1969, Sch 2 (as amended).
[83] Ibid s 2(1), Sch 2 art 11(1).
[84] Ibid Sch 2 art 11(3).
[85] Ibid Sch 2 art 4(2). The former limit on the size of the panel was removed by the Church of England (Miscellaneous Provisions) Measure 2006, s 8, which effected an amendment to the Synodical Government Measure 1969, Sch 2 art 4(2).
[86] Ibid Sch 2 art 5(1). This requirement may, however, be dispensed with by permission of the chairman and with the leave of Synod given in accordance with the standing orders: Sch 2 art 5(1) proviso.
[87] Ibid Sch 2 art 5(2). On a motion other than one relating to the course of business or procedure, any 25 members present may demand a division by houses. It is not deemed to be carried unless it receives a majority in each house: Sch 2 art 5(2) proviso.
[88] Ibid Sch 2 art 6(a): Measures, Canons, Orders, Regulations or other subordinate instrument, and Acts of Synod.
[89] Ibid Sch 2 art 7(1).
[90] Ibid Sch 2 art 7(2). In the case of objection by one House of one of the Convocations, a second reference may be made and, upon a second objection by one House only, provision may be made for reference to the Houses of Bishops and Clergy of Synod for approval by a two-thirds majority vote in substitution for approval by the four Houses separately: see Sch 2 art 7(5).

are to be determined conclusively by the Presidents and Prolocutors of the Houses of the Convocations and the Prolocutor and Pro-Prolocutors of the House of Laity.[91]

2.25 A motion for the final approval of a measure or canon providing for permanent changes in the services of baptism, holy communion or in the Ordinal is not deemed to be carried unless it receives the assent of a majority in each House of Synod of not less than two-thirds of those present and voting.[92] A Canon which concerns worship or doctrine may not be submitted for Royal Assent unless it has received final approval in Synod with a majority in each House of not less than two-thirds of those present and voting.[93] Any amendment to the Church Representation Rules requires a two-thirds majority in each House.[94] Changes to the baptism or communion services or to the Ordinal may not be finally approved by Synod unless the Measure or Canon or its substance has been approved by a majority of the dioceses at diocesan synods.[95]

Diocesan synods

Composition

2.26 A diocesan synod comprises a house of bishops, a house of clergy, and a house of laity.[96] It performs the functions of the former diocesan conference.[97] Membership is governed by the Church Representation Rules.[98] Diocesan synod comprises *ex officio* members and others, clergy and laity, elected by deanery

---

[91] Ibid Sch 2 art 7(6). Whether such a determination, deemed conclusive by statute, precludes any subsequent legal challenge was a matter upon which Hoffmann J considered it unnecessary to express any opinion at first instance and which did not fall to be determined in the Court of Appeal in *Brown v Runcie*, The Times, 26 June 1990, Hoffmann J; The Times, 20 February 1991, CA. See also Chapter 1, paras 1.30–1.31.

[92] Synodical Government Measure 1969, Sch 2 art 8(1C) (added by the Church of England (Miscellaneous Provisions) Measure 1978, s 1). Any question as to whether article 8 applies or whether its provisions are complied with is to be conclusively determined by the presidents, the Prolocutors of the Lower Houses of the Convocations and the Prolocutor and Pro-Prolocutor of the House of Laity of Synod: Synodical Government Measure 1969, Sch 2 art 8(2).

[93] Church of England (Worship and Doctrine) Measure 1974, s 3. See also *Brown v Runcie*, The Times, 26 June 1990, per Hoffmann J at first instance, and *Brown v Runcie*, The Times, 20 February 1991, CA, on appeal.

[94] Synodical Government Measure 1969, s 7(1) proviso.

[95] Ibid s 2(1), Sch 2 art 8(1). The same applies to schemes affecting a constitutional union or a change in the relationship between the Church of England and another Christian body in the Church of England.

[96] Church Representation Rules, r 30.

[97] These were dissolved in 1970 pursuant to the Synodical Government Measure 1969, s 4(7).

[98] Church Representation Rules, rr 30–33.

synods or co-opted.[99] Elections take place every three years.[100] Individual dioceses may implement schemes varying these procedures to meet the special circumstances of the diocese,[101] and provision may also be made for area synods for any episcopal area constituted within a diocese.[102]

Purpose and function

2.27 The purpose of the diocesan synod is to consider matters concerning the Church of England, to make provision for such matters in relation to its diocese and to consider and express its opinion on matters of religious or public interest.[103] In addition, it advises the bishop on any matters on which he may consult the synod and considers and expresses its opinion on any matters referred to it by the General Synod, and in particular the approval or disapproval of provisions relating to forms of Christian worship or union with other Christian bodies.[104] Two further functions which must now be discharged[105] are to consider the proposals for the annual budget for the diocese and to approve or disapprove them, and to consider the annual accounts of the diocesan board of finance.[106]

2.28 The function of advising the bishop[107] may be discharged on behalf of the diocesan synod by the bishop's council and the standing committee.[108] The diocesan synod may not, however, issue any statement purporting to declare the doctrine of the Church on any question.[109] It must keep the deanery synods informed of the policies and problems of the diocese and of the business to come before it. Through deanery synods, it must keep itself informed of events and opinion in the parishes and provide opportunities for discussion in its meetings of matters raised by deanery synods and parochial church councils.[110]

---

[99] Note also that in the event that the bishop declines to chair the Diocesan Board of Education, the person otherwise appointed is to be an *ex officio* member of diocesan synod: Diocesan Boards of Education Measure 1991, s 1(2), Schedule Part I para 4.
[100] Church Representation Rules, r 31(1).
[101] Ibid r 33.
[102] Dioceses Measure 1978, s 17.
[103] Synodical Government Measure 1969, s 4(2)(a).
[104] Ibid s 4(2)(b), (c), Sch 2 art 8.
[105] Introduced by the Synodical Government (Amendment) Measure 2003, s 1.
[106] Synodical Government Measure 1969, s 4(2)(d) and (e) (as amended) respectively.
[107] In respect of this the bishop has a corresponding duty of consultation under ibid s 4(3).
[108] Ibid s 4(4). There is a mandatory requirement that a bishop make provision for a bishop's council and a standing committee: Church Representation Rules, r 34(1)(k), under which the membership is provided for by standing orders and its functions are those exercisable under the Synodical Government Measure 1969, s 4(4), and such other functions as may be provided for by standing orders, by the Church Representation Rules, or by any Measure or Canon.
[109] Synodical Government Measure 1969, s 4(2) proviso.
[110] Ibid s 4(5).

Diocesan synods

Each diocese must have a diocesan board of finance, which is a company for the purposes of English company law and which holds property for purposes connected with the Church of England and transacts business in relation thereto.[111] Its composition is regulated by Measure, as are its functions, which are to deal with matters concerning Church land and money in accordance with the instructions of the diocesan synod.[112] The collection of the diocesan quota is administered in accordance with diocesan norms, although there is provision for the diocesan synod to delegate to deanery synods functions including the determination of parochial shares.[113]

2.29

Other functions fall to be dealt with by the diocesan synod. These include prescribing and regulating the composition and procedure of deanery synods.[114] The diocesan synod may subdivide the diocese into areas for the purpose of elections to General Synod.[115] It is responsible for establishing procedures for the inspection and repair of buildings, including a scheme for the inspection of churches by architects at least once every five years.[116] It also has certain responsibilities for clergy houses under the auspices of the diocesan parsonages board.[117]

2.30

Procedure is governed by the Church Representation Rules and is further set out by way of standing orders. All three component houses of the diocesan synod (bishops, clergy and laity) must assent to a decision if it is to be deemed to have the assent of synod. Generally, such assent is presumed by the majority vote of all members of synod present and voting unless the bishop (if present) or any ten members present demand that a separate vote be taken of each of the houses of clergy and laity.[118] In the event of an equal division of votes in the house of bishops, the diocesan bishop has a second or casting vote[119] and he also has a right to require that his opinion on any question be recorded in the minutes.[120]

2.31

In addition to the bishop's council, the standing committee and the diocesan board of finance which have already been mentioned, other boards and

2.32

---

[111] Diocesan Boards of Finance Measure 1925.
[112] Ibid s 3.
[113] Synodical Government Measure 1969, s 5(4). For a consideration of the quota system more generally see Chapter 3, and N Doe, *The Legal Framework of the Church of England* (Oxford: Clarendon Press, 1996) 478–482.
[114] Church Representation Rules, r 28. This includes a power to vary the rules as to membership: ibid r 26.
[115] Ibid r 38.
[116] Inspection of Churches Measure 1955, s 1(1).
[117] Repair of Benefice Buildings Measure 1972. See eg, ibid ss 1(1), 10, 15, 19, 20.
[118] Church Representation Rules, r 34(1)(e), (g).
[119] Ibid r 34(1)(i).
[120] Ibid r 34(1)(j).

committees exist within the diocese, each with varying responsibilities. They include:

(a) the diocesan parsonages board, a body corporate responsible for matters relating to property owned by the Church;[121]
(b) the diocesan pastoral committee, responsible for reviewing the arrangements for pastoral supervision in the diocese and making recommendations in relation thereto;[122]
(c) the diocesan board of education, responsible for promoting education consistent with the faith and practice of the Church of England and co-operation with other religious bodies and local education authorities;[123]
(d) the diocesan advisory committee, to advise on matters arising under the faculty jurisdiction;[124]
(e) the diocesan board of patronage, responsible for certain appointments to benefices;[125] and
(f) the diocesan redundant churches uses committee, charged with finding alternative uses for redundant churches.[126]

Deanery synods

2.33 The Synodical Government Measure 1969 defines 'deanery' as meaning rural deanery,[127] although in urban areas the epithet 'rural' is frequently omitted. A deanery is a collection of neighbouring parishes. To each deanery the bishop appoints a rural dean. The bishop may, by order, declare that the office be called that of area dean.[128] Deanery synods, of which the rural dean is joint chairman, were established in 1970 in succession to ruri-decanal conferences (where they existed), which were dissolved.[129]

---

[121] Repair of Benefice Buildings Measure 1972, s 1. The diocese may determine that the diocesan board of finance is to constitute the diocesan parsonages board, in which case the latter's functions must be undertaken through a special committee: s 1(1).
[122] Pastoral Measure 1983, ss 1, 2. This Measure replaced the Pastoral Measure 1968.
[123] Diocesan Boards of Education Measure 1991, ss 1, 2.
[124] Care of Churches and Ecclesiastical Jurisdiction Measure 1991, s 2. The role and function of the DAC is considered in Chapter 7.
[125] Patronage (Benefices) Measure 1986, ss 26–28, Sch 3.
[126] Pastoral Measure 1983, s 42, Sch 5 paras 5–12.
[127] Synodical Government Measure 1969, s 9(2).
[128] Church of England (Miscellaneous Provisions) Measure 2000, s 12(4).
[129] Synodical Government Measure 1969, s 5(2).

Composition

A deanery synod comprises a house of clergy and a house of laity. All parish clergy in the deanery (beneficed and licensed) are members, and every three years each parish elects lay representatives at its annual parochial church meeting. Provision is made for certain *ex officio* members, including members of diocesan synod and General Synod, and for co-option. Somewhat complex provisions enable the diocesan synod to prescribe the number of representatives to be elected by each parish with the intention of obtaining a deanery synod numbering no more than 150 and no fewer than 50 persons. The maximum figure may be exceeded for the purpose of securing that the house of laity is not fewer in number than the house of clergy.[130] It is open to the diocesan synod to make a scheme for varying the rules relating to the composition of deanery synods in order to meet the special circumstances of the diocese or the deaneries or to secure better representation of clergy or laity or both.[131] There is also provision to secure representation of cathedral clergy and laity as appropriate.[132]

2.34

Purpose and function

The functions of a deanery synod are prescribed by Measure.[133] They are to consider matters concerning the Church of England and to make provision for such matters in relation to the deanery. A deanery synod is to consider and express its opinion on any matters of religious or public interest, and to discuss and formulate common policies on problems concerning parishes in the deanery. In addition, it is to foster a sense of community and interdependence among the parishes and promote the whole mission of the Church, pastoral, evangelistic, social and ecumenical. It must consider the business of the diocesan synod, particularly any matters referred to it by General Synod, and, where appropriate, sound out parochial opinion. It must make known and give effect to any provision made by the diocesan synod and, of its own volition, may raise matters with the diocesan synod.[134] Like the diocesan synod, the deanery synod is precluded from issuing any statement purporting to declare the doctrine of the Church on any question.[135] Note also that if the diocesan synod delegates to the deanery synods functions in relation to the parishes of their deaneries and in particular

2.35

---

130 Church Representation Rules, rr 24, 25.
131 Ibid r 26.
132 Ibid r 27; Cathedrals Measure 1999, s 39(1), Sch 2 para 8.
133 Synodical Government Measure 1969, s 5(3).
134 Ibid s 5(3)(a)–(e).
135 Ibid s 5(3) proviso.

the determination of parish shares in quotas allocated to the deaneries, the deanery synods must exercise those functions.[136]

2.36 In addition to the collective powers exercised by the deanery synod, its members have considerable power and influence, in that they form the electoral college for superior synods. The house of clergy and house of laity of the deanery synod elect members to the corresponding houses of the diocesan synod and the members of the house of laity of the deanery synod vote for representatives from the diocese to be members of the House of Laity of General Synod.[137]

2.37 The rural dean and a member of the house of laity are the joint chairmen, and a secretary must be appointed. A specified minimum number of meetings must be held each year, a report of the proceedings prepared and circulated to all parochial church councils in the deanery, and a standing committee constituted. Subject to rules prescribed by the diocesan synod, the deanery synod regulates its own procedure.[138]

The Church Commissioners

2.38 'The Church of England as a whole has no legal status or personality',[139] but, through its constituent institutional and corporate parts, is a substantial owner of land and investments, much of which is in the hands of the Church Commissioners. In 1948, the Church Commissioners were established as a body corporate[140] in place of two bodies of some antiquity, namely the Governors of the Bounty of Queen Anne for the Augmentation of the Poor Clergy, established under the Queen Anne's Bounty Act 1703; and the Ecclesiastical Commissioners, which were created under the Ecclesiastical Commissioners Act 1836. All functions, rights and privileges of the two bodies vested in the Church Commissioners, and all property held by or in trust for either body thenceforward was held by or in trust for the Church Commissioners.[141] It was the opinion of the Lambeth Group, having reviewed the operation of the Church Commissioners following a much publicized decrease in the value of their assets, that 'many of the problems

---

[136] Synodical Government Measure 1969, s 5(4). 'Quota' is defined as meaning an amount to be subscribed to the expenditure authorized by diocesan synods. Surprisingly, this is the only reference to quota in any Act, Measure or Canon.
[137] Church Representation Rules, rr 31, 32, 35(1), (3).
[138] Ibid r 28.
[139] *Aston Cantlow and Wilmcote with Billesley Parochial Church Council v Wallbank* [2004] 1 AC 546, [2003] 3 All ER 1213, HL, per Lord Hope of Craighead at para 61. Note also Lord Rodger of Earlsferry at para 154: 'The juridical nature of the Church [of England] is, notoriously, somewhat amorphous'.
[140] Church Commissioners Measure 1947, s 1(1).
[141] Ibid s 2.

The Church Commissioners

which have been encountered stem from the structure of the Commissioners' organization which was not well suited to present-day requirements'.[142] Significant changes to the Church Commissioners Measure 1947 were introduced by the National Institutions Measure 1998 which came into effect on 1 January 1999. These changes affect both the composition of the Commissioners and the way in which their money is distributed.

The Church Commissioners now comprise: 2.39

(a) the First Lord of the Treasury;
(b) the Lord President of the Council;
(c) the Home Secretary;
(d) the Speaker of the House of Commons;
(e) the Speaker of the House of Lords;[143]
(f) the Secretary of State for the Department of Culture, Media and Sport;
(g) the Archbishops of Canterbury and York;
(h) the three Church Estates Commissioners;[144]
(i) four bishops elected by and from among the House of Bishops;
(j) two deans elected by and from among the cathedral deans;[145]
(k) three other clergy elected by those members of the House of Clergy who are not deans;
(l) four persons elected by the House of Laity;
(m) three persons nominated by Her Majesty;
(n) three persons nominated by the Archbishops of Canterbury and York acting jointly;
(o) three persons nominated by the Archbishops of Canterbury and York acting jointly after consultation with the Lord Mayors of the Cities of London and York, the Vice-Chancellors of the Universities of Oxford and Cambridge and such other persons as appear to the Archbishops to be appropriate.[146]

---

[142] Report to the Archbishop of Canterbury by the Lambeth Group and Coopers and Lybrand (19 July 1993) page 4 para 7.

[143] The reference to the Speaker of the House of Lords was inserted in substitution for the Lord Chancellor by the Lord Chancellor (Transfer of Functions and Supplementary Provisions) (No 3) Order 2006, SI 2006/1640, Art 3, Sch 1, para 2.

[144] The First and Second Church Estates Commissioners are appointed by the Crown, the third by the Archbishop of Canterbury. The First and Second must be laymen, the Third need not. They hold office during the pleasure of the Crown or Archbishop as appropriate. The First and Third are salaried and the Second, by convention, is always a member of the House of Commons who takes the government whip.

[145] References to provosts were removed from the 1947 Measure by the Church of England (Miscellaneous Provisions) Measure 2006, s 2, Sch 2.

[146] Church Commissioners Measure 1947, s 1(2), Sch 1 para 1 (substituted by the National Institutions Measure 1998, s 7(1), Sch 4 para 8). At least one of the nine nominees under the last three categories must be or have been Queen's Counsel.

Elected commissioners hold office for five years and nominated commissioners for such period as the person nominating may determine.[147] The Archbishop of Canterbury is chairman of the Commissioners.[148]

2.40 The functions of the Church Commissioners are varied and not susceptible to simple exposition. They include:

(a) holding and administering endowments formerly vested in Queen Anne's Bounty and the Ecclesiastical Commissioners and carrying them into their general fund;

(b) the support of diocesan bishops;

(c) applying their general fund in the making of grants for stipends[149] and parsonage houses, clergy pensions, church building and loans to theological colleges;[150]

(d) the approval of some dealings with glebe and parsonage houses and with chapter property; and

(e) the preparation of schemes and orders in relation to pastoral reorganization and redundant churches.

2.41 So broad is the ambit of responsibility of the Church Commissioners, and so diverse their composition, that they transact their business through an executive body known as the Board of Governors.[151] The Board comprises all of the Commissioners save the officers of state listed in (a)–(f) of paragraph 2.39 above.[152] The Board is chaired by the Archbishop of Canterbury or, in his absence, such member as the Board may elect.[153] In every financial year, the Church Commissioners must hold an annual general meeting to consider the annual report and accounts and to consider the recommendations of the Board as to the allocation of such money as the Board may report to be available.[154] The Commissioners are free to regulate their own procedure.[155]

---

[147] Church Commissioners Measure 1947, Sch 1 para 2 (as so substituted).
[148] Ibid s 4(1).
[149] There is nothing objectionable in the application of accumulated funds to compensate those clergy opposed to the ordination of women; nor to the payment of stipends to women priests: *Williamson v Archbishop of Canterbury*, The Times, 25 November 1994, Lightman J.
[150] Church Commissioners (Loans for Theological Colleges and Training Houses) Measure 1964. Some of this support is now distributed by the Archbishops' Council under the National Institutions Measure 1998, s 2, although the payment of clergy pensions (for pre-1998 service only) remains an obligation of the Commissioners. The holding of benefice capital is to be transferred to dioceses by the Church of England (Miscellaneous Provisions) Measure 2006, coincidentally with amendments to the Parsonages Measure Rules.
[151] Church Commissioners Measure 1947, s 5(3).
[152] Ibid s 5(1) (substituted by the National Institutions Measure 1998, Sch 4 para 3).
[153] Church Commissioners Measure 1947, s 5(2).
[154] Ibid s 4, amended by the Church Commissioners Measure 1964, s 2(3), and the National Institutions Measure 1998, Sch 4 para 2.
[155] Church Commissioners Measure 1947, s 7(2)(a).

2.42 The Church Commissioners must determine the amount of income from their assets which is to be made available to the Archbishops' Council for application or distribution for any of the purposes for which it could have been applied by the Commissioners themselves at the end of 1998 and pay that amount to the Council in equal monthly instalments.[156] Before determining the amount, the Commissioners must consult the Council and have regard to any proposals made by the Council.[157] In applying or distributing the Commissioners' money, the Council is required to pay particular regard to the requirements of section 67 of the Ecclesiastical Commissioners Act 1840 relating to the making of additional provision for the cure of souls in parishes where such assistance is most required.[158]

2.43 In addition to the Board there are statutory Assets and Audit Committees.[159] The Assets Committee acts in the name of the Commissioners in the management of their assets.[160] It is empowered and obliged to act on behalf of the Commissioners in all matters relating to the management of their assets and may sell, purchase, exchange or let land and make, realize and change investments.[161] The Audit Committee, as its name suggests, reviews the Commissioners' accounting policies and practices and keeps under review the effectiveness of their internal control system.[162] Additionally, it has a duty to report to the officers of state listed in (a)–(f) at paragraph 2.39 above on any matter relating to the functions and business of the Commissioners which causes the Committee grave concern and about which the Board of Governors has been unable to satisfy the Committee.

2.44 The Church Commissioners must keep a general fund into which must go all income received from property and funds held by them and from which must be discharged all commitments to which that income is subject and all expenses and obligations falling upon the Commissioners in the execution of their functions.[163] Any balance from time to time remaining is available for any purpose, for which

---

[156] National Institutions Measure 1998, s 2(1).
[157] Ibid s 2(2).
[158] Ibid s 2(3).
[159] Church Commissioners Measure 1947, ss 3, 6. See also the Church Commissioners Measure 1964, ss 1, 2; and the Church Commissioners Measure 1970, s 1; National Institutions Measure 1998, Sch 4 para 6.
[160] Church Commissioners Measure 1947, s 6(3)(a).
[161] Ibid s 6(3)(a).
[162] Ibid s 6(3B), added by the National Institutions Measure 1998, Sch 4 para 4.
[163] Church Commissioners Measure 1947, s 10(6) (amended by the Pensions Measure 1997, s 10(1), Sch 1 para 3). This does not apply to separate funds or trusts maintained by the constituent authorities (ie Queen Anne's Bounty and the Ecclesiastical Commissioners) prior to their amalgamation, which continue to be separately administered: Church Commissioners Measure 1947, s 10(5).

the surplus of the common fund of the Ecclesiastical Commissioners or of the corporate fund of Queen Anne's Bounty would have been available.[164] The Commissioners no longer keep the capital and income accounts for the diocesan stipends fund, this responsibility having been transferred to the diocesan board of finance for each diocese.[165]

2.45 The extent to which the Church Commissioners should and do utilize moral or Christian principles in their extensive powers of investment was considered by the High Court in 1991 at the behest of the Bishop of Oxford and others.[166] Sir Donald Nicholls, the Vice-Chancellor, considered affidavit evidence dealing with the manner in which the Commissioners formulated and implemented their investment policy. He heard objections relating to the Commissioners' significant investment in South African companies and their failure to build low cost accommodation for young people in rural areas. The Vice-Chancellor concluded that the primary object of the Commissioners, as trustees, was the generation of money. The Commissioners' stated investment policy (quoted verbatim from their annual report for 1989), included 'ethical' considerations[167] but not such as to be financially disadvantageous. For the Commissioners to go further in implementing an ethical policy to the financial detriment of their asset portfolio would involve a departure from their legal obligations. Accordingly the relief sought was refused.[168]

Church courts and tribunals

2.46 The number and variety of courts and tribunals within the Church of England continues to grow.[169] Tribunals and courts exist to deal with the discipline of deacons, priests, bishops and archbishops;[170] the consistory court is concerned with Church land, buildings and contents;[171] and pastoral breakdown is dealt

---

[164] Ibid s 10(6).
[165] Diocesan Stipends Fund Measure 1953, s 1, as amended by the Church of England (Miscellaneous Provisions) Measure 2000, s 4, Sch 2 para 1.
[166] *Harries v Church Commissioners for England* [1992] 1 WLR 1241, [1993] 2 All ER 300.
[167] These include a refusal to invest in companies whose main business is in armaments, gambling, alcohol or tobacco. Newspapers, though included on the 'prohibited list' at the time of the judgment, were removed in 2006.
[168] Different considerations may apply if an investment of a particular type would conflict with the purposes of a trust or would alienate some of those who support a charity financially.
[169] Since the last edition of this work, the Clergy Discipline Commission has been brought into existence and with it Bishop's Disciplinary Tribunals: Clergy Discipline Measure 2003, ss 3, 22.
[170] See Chapter 6.
[171] See Chapter 7.

with in a provincial tribunal.[172] The origins of the various courts owe much to the historical nature of the Church of England as the established Church of the realm.[173] The Ecclesiastical Jurisdiction Measure 1963 simplified a system which had become both moribund and cumbersome, and this in turn has been revisited in several material particulars in the Clergy Discipline Measure 2003.

Chancellors

The Ecclesiastical Jurisdiction Measure 1963 provides that for each diocese there is to be a court of the bishop thereof.[174] It is styled the consistory court, save in the diocese of Canterbury, where it is known as the commissary court.[175] Each court is presided over by a chancellor[176] (or commissary-general in that of the diocese of Canterbury),[177] who must be at least 30 years of age and either a person who has a seven year general qualification within the meaning of section 71 of the Courts and Legal Services Act 1990[178] or a person who holds or has held high judicial office, or the office of circuit judge.[179] The chancellor may be ordained or a layman, but if he is a layman, the bishop must satisfy himself that he is a communicant.[180] There is no express requirement that the person to be appointed chancellor have any experience of or expertise in the laws of the Church.[181] He is appointed by the bishop, who is obliged to consult the Lord Chancellor and the Dean of the Arches before making any such appointment.[182]

2.47

---

172 See the Incumbents (Vacation of Benefices) Measure 1977, discussed in Chapter 4.
173 The jurisdiction of church courts in matters of probate, matrimonial affairs and defamation were transferred to the secular courts by the Court of Probate Act 1857, the Matrimonial Causes Act 1857 and the Ecclesiastical Courts Act 1855 respectively.
174 Ecclesiastical Jurisdiction Measure 1963, s 1(1).
175 Ibid s 1(1). Hereafter, save where the context otherwise provides, the expression 'consistory court' includes commissary court.
176 Ibid s 2(1). By virtue of his office, the chancellor is also the official principal of the bishop: ibid s 13(2). This is, at best, a vestigial office, since the majority of the powers formerly exercised by the official principal now vest in the chancellor: see ibid s 6. Note also the role of vicar-general discussed below.
177 Ibid s 2(1).
178 Ecclesiastical Jurisdiction Measure 1963, s 2(2) (amended by the Courts and Legal Services Act 1990, s 7(2), Sch 10 para 17). See also Canon G 2 para 2.
179 Ecclesiastical Jurisdiction Measure 1963, s 2(2) (amended by the Church of England (Miscellaneous Provisions) Measure 2006, s 7(2)); Canon G 2 para 2. The expression 'high judicial office' is defined as meaning that of Lord Chancellor or Judge of the High Court or Court of Appeal: s 66(1), applying the Appellate Jurisdiction Act 1876, s 25.
180 Ecclesiastical Jurisdiction Measure 1963, s 2(2); Canon G 2 para 2.
181 Formerly there was such a requirement under Canon 127 of the 1603 Canons (now revoked). Compare Canon G 4 para 2, which requires registrars to be 'learned in the ecclesiastical laws and the laws of the realm'.
182 Ecclesiastical Jurisdiction Measure 1963, s 2(1A), (added by the Care of Churches and Ecclesiastical Jurisdiction Measure 1991, Sch 4 para 2(a)).

2.48 An individual may not hold more than two chancellorships.[183] A vacancy in see does not terminate the appointment of a chancellor.[184] However, a chancellor's appointment ceases[185] upon his attaining the age at which a circuit judge is obliged to vacate office, currently 70,[186] or upon his resignation or dismissal by the bishop consequent upon a resolution by the Upper House of Convocation that the chancellor is incapable of acting or unfit to act. The chancellor is required to take and subscribe the oath of allegiance and the judicial oath and, if he is a layman, a declaration of assent.[187]

2.49 A deputy chancellor may be appointed in one of two ways. A bishop may appoint a fit and proper person to act as deputy chancellor where for any reason the chancellor is unable to act as such or the office is vacant.[188] The chancellor may himself, with the bishop's consent, appoint a person as his deputy.[189] In either case, the person so appointed has all the powers and performs all the duties of the office of chancellor.[190] The person appointed deputy chancellor must have the qualifications required to be a chancellor[191] and must be 'a fit and proper person'.[192] A deputy chancellor is required to take and subscribe the same oaths as would a chancellor.[193] The appointment of a deputy chancellor under the new provisions continues for so long as the chancellor who appointed him remains in office and thereafter for a period of three months.[194]

---

[183] Diocesan Chancellorship Regulations 1993, SI 1993/1841, reg 3, made pursuant to the Ecclesiastical Jurisdiction Measure 1963, s 2A, added by the Ecclesiastical Judges and Legal Officers Measure 1976, s 2. The provision is not retrospective. By an amendment to ss 2A(1) and (2) of the 1963 Measure, effected by the Church of England (Miscellaneous Provisions) Measure 2006, s 7(3), regulations may also be made to limit the number of deputy chancellorships held by individuals. As at the date of writing, this power has not been exercised.

[184] Ecclesiastical Jurisdiction Measure 1963, s 12.

[185] Although the appointment ceases, the chancellor may continue to act in any proceedings of which the court was already seized: ibid s 2(4)(c), added by the Ecclesiastical Judges and Legal Officers Measure 1976, s 1(1).

[186] Ecclesiastical Jurisdiction Measure 1963, s 2(4), amended by the Care of Churches and Ecclesiastical Jurisdiction Measure 1991, Sch 4 para 2(c), read with the Courts Act 1971, s 17(1). The bishop has a discretion to authorize a chancellor's continuance in office beyond the compulsory age for retirement if he considers it desirable in the interests of the diocese. This may be done any number of times up to the age when a puisne judge of the High Court is obliged to vacate his office: Ecclesiastical Jurisdiction Measure 1963, s 2(4A), added by the 1991 Measure, Sch 4 para 2(d).

[187] Ecclesiastical Jurisdiction Measure 1963, s 2(5), Sch 1 Pt I; Canon G 2 para 3.

[188] Ecclesiastical Jurisdiction Measure 1963, s 4(1).

[189] Ibid s 4(1B), added by the Church of England (Miscellaneous Provisions) Measure 2006, s 7(5).

[190] Ecclesiastical Jurisdiction Measure 1963, s 4(1).

[191] Ibid s 4(2).

[192] Ibid s 4(1), (1A), added by the Care of Churches and Ecclesiastical Jurisdiction Measure 1991, Sch 4 para 4(b).

[193] Ecclesiastical Jurisdiction Measure 1963, s 4(2).

[194] Ibid s 4(1C). Or until the deputy chancellor reaches compulsory retirement age. He may be removed by the chancellor, after consultation with the bishop, if the chancellor considers that the deputy is incapable of acting or unfit to act: s 4(1B)(b).

2.50 Though appointed by the bishop and adjudicating matters in the bishop's court, the chancellor (and, *ex hypothesi*, his deputy) are independent of the bishop.[195] This position reflects the separation of powers between the executive and the judiciary in the secular sphere although, as with many constitutional models, the analogy is far from perfect. In a characteristically robust judgment of Garth Moore Ch in *Re St Mary, Barnes*, it was stated:

> the then petitioners [in an earlier matter, now seeking a further faculty] were foolish enough, for reasons best known to themselves, to crave the then bishop's judgment, and the then bishop ... purported to deal with the case himself. Whether or not he was, by reason of this unusual patent [of the chancellor in the Diocese of Southwark] ever legally seised of the case, it was, on constitutional grounds, highly undesirable that he should try to deal with it, for to do so involved a breach of the constitutional principle of the separation of the functions of the legislature, the executive and the judiciary, and a return to the absolutism of the Middle Ages condemned in this country since at least the middle of the seventeenth century. He was, moreover, even if legally seised of the matter, simply not capable of the task of dealing with it, as the sequel clearly shows.[196]

2.51 It is, however, possible for bishops to hear faculty cases,[197] either alone or with the chancellor, if provision is so made in the letters patent appointing the chancellor.[198] This was regarded by Moore Ch as 'antiquated and regrettable'[199] and is criticized by Newsom.[200]

Vicars-General

2.52 The office of vicar-general (both provincial and diocesan) is a venerable one[201] and is unaffected by the provisions of the Ecclesiastical Jurisdiction Measure 1963.[202] It is usual for a chancellor also to be constituted vicar-general in his letters patent. His powers and duties, *qua* vicar-general, are largely undefined, the

---

[195] See *Tyler v United Kingdom* (Application 21283/93), 5 April 1994, E Com HR (unreported), in which the Commission declared inadmissible an application claiming that the consistory court breached Article 6 of the European Convention on Human Rights. The text of the decision is reproduced in the Materials to the second edition of this work: M Hill, *Ecclesiastical Law* (Oxford: Oxford University Press, 2001). See also, by analogy, *R v Provincial Court of the Church in Wales, ex parte Williams* (1998) 5 Ecc LJ 217, Latham J.

[196] *Re St Mary, Barnes* [1982] 1 WLR 531 at 532G–H, [1982] 1 All ER 456 at 457, Southwark Cons Ct.

[197] But no other matters.

[198] Ecclesiastical Jurisdiction Measure 1963, s 46(1).

[199] *Re St Mary Barnes* [1982] 1 WLR 531 at 532, [1982] 1 All ER 456 at 457.

[200] GH and GL Newsom, *The Faculty Jurisdiction of the Church of England* (2nd edn, London: Sweet and Maxwell, 1993) 17.

[201] See A Pearce, 'The Roles of the Vicar General and Surrogate in the Granting of Marriage Licences' (1990) 2 Ecc LJ 28; T Coningsby, 'Chancellor, Vicar General, Official Principal—A Bundle of Offices' (1990) 2 Ecc LJ 273; and Pearce's letter in response (1990) 2 Ecc LJ 383.

[202] Ecclesiastical Jurisdiction Measure 1963, s 83(2)(d).

position being in the nature of a roving representative of the bishop.[203] It is as vicar-general that the chancellor grants marriage licences. A new jurisdiction falls to be exercised under the Care of Cathedrals (Supplementary Provisions) Measure 1994, under which the vicars-general of the provinces of Canterbury and York are empowered to grant injunctions and restoration orders in relation to acts done or threatened to be done in contravention of the provisions of the Care of Cathedrals Measure 1990. These emergency powers are exercised subject to an appeal to the Court of the Arches or the Chancery Court of York, as appropriate.[204] The Clergy Discipline Measure 2003 now gives to the vicar-general's court of each province a first instance jurisdiction in the trial of bishops and of the archbishop of the other province.[205]

Registrars

2.53 Although a provincial or diocesan registrar has no judicial powers,[206] his role is central to the smooth and effective running of the provincial and consistory courts. Each of the provinces of Canterbury and York is required to have a registrar, who performs specified statutory and other functions as provincial registrar and registrar of the provincial court in addition to those previously performed by the archbishop's legal secretary.[207] He is appointed by the archbishop of the province[208] and also acts as the archbishop's legal advisor.[209] He must have a general qualification within the meaning of section 71 of the Courts and Legal Services Act 1990, and must be learned in the ecclesiastical laws and the laws of the realm and be a communicant.[210] A deputy provincial registrar may be appointed by the provincial registrar, with the consent of the archbishop, or by the archbishop.[211]

2.54 Furthermore, each diocese is required to have a registrar to perform the functions imposed by statute and canon law on him or on the registrar of the consistory

---

[203] See generally Canon C 18 para 3.
[204] See Chapter 8.
[205] See Chapter 6.
[206] Save as may be delegated to him by the chancellor for the purposes of giving directions or holding a pre-trial review.
[207] Ecclesiastical Judges and Legal Officers Measure 1976, s 3(1), (2). The office may be held by two persons jointly: ibid s 3(4).
[208] Ibid s 3(3).
[209] Ibid s 3(1).
[210] Canon G 4 para 2.
[211] Ecclesiastical Judges and Legal Officers Measure 1976, s 3(4A), (4B), (4C), added by the Care of Churches and Ecclesiastical Jurisdiction Measure 1991, s 9, Sch 5 para 2(a).

court and the functions previously performed by the bishop's legal secretary.[212] The diocesan registrar is appointed by the bishop but, prior to making any such appointment, the bishop must consult the bishop's council and standing committee of the diocesan synod.[213] The appointee also acts as legal advisor to the bishop.[214] He takes the same oaths as the chancellor.[215] A registrar is required to resign at the age of seventy,[216] and his appointment may be terminated upon 12 months' written notice from the bishop.[217] A deputy diocesan registrar may be appointed by the registrar in the same way as a chancellor might appoint a deputy[218] and, if the bishop is of the opinion that the registrar is unable or unlikely to perform his duties or it would be inappropriate for him to perform them, he may request the provincial registrar to appoint a fit and proper person to perform those duties.[219]

2.55 It is the responsibility of the registrar to ensure that the diocesan and provincial courts are convened as and when required, that the requisite notices are complied with and that the necessary fees are paid. Many registrars tender advice and assistance on an informal basis concerning practice and procedure to litigants, who are frequently unfamiliar with the workings of church courts. The diocesan registrar carries out the responsibilities formerly undertaken by the archdeacon's registrar[220] but is not required to attend archdeacon's visitations.[221]

2.56 Under the Clergy Discipline Measure 2003, the archbishops of Canterbury and York, after consultation with the president of tribunals, each appoint for their province a registrar of tribunals,[222] whose responsibilities comprise directing and supervising the general administration of disciplinary tribunals in the province and exercising functions conferred under the Measure.[223] The provincial

---

212 Ecclesiastical Judges and Legal Officers Measure 1976, s 4(1), (2). This office may also be held by two persons acting jointly: ibid s 4(4).
213 Ibid s 4(3).
214 Ibid s 4(1).
215 Canon G 4 para 3.
216 Ecclesiastical Judges and Legal Officers Measure 1976, s 5(3).
217 Ibid s 5(6). This may only be done with the consent of the archbishop. Newsom suggests that it would be good practice to enter into a contract of employment to which the diocesan board of finance should be a party providing for a shorter notice period: GH and GL Newsom, *The Faculty Jurisdiction of the Church of England* (2nd edn, London: Sweet and Maxwell, 1993) 20.
218 Ecclesiastical Judges and Legal Officers Measure 1976, s 4(5A) (added by the Care of Churches and Ecclesiastical Jurisdiction Measure 1991, Sch 5 para 3). See para 2.49 above.
219 Ecclesiastical Judges and Legal Officers Measure 1976, s 4(5C), as so added. This presupposes that no deputy registrar has been appointed.
220 Ibid s 7(1), (2).
221 Church of England (Miscellaneous Provisions) Measure 1992, s 13.
222 Clergy Discipline Measure 2003, s 5(1), (2).
223 Ibid, s 5(6). In the case of any inability or unwillingness to act, the registrar of the other province is empowered to act in his stead: s 5(7).

Archdeacons

2.57 Brief mention ought to be made of the archdeacon's court, which fell into desuetude in the course of the nineteenth century, largely because its jurisdiction was nearly coterminous with that of the consistory court, thus rendering it otiose. A quasi-judicial function falls to be exercised by way of the archdeacon's visitation, and this is discussed in Chapter 3. It should be noted that the restructuring of the faculty jurisdiction has to some extent revived the archdeacon's judicial function, since it vests in the archdeacon the delegated power to determine certain faculty matters.[224]

Consistory courts

2.58 The consistory court no longer has a criminal jurisdiction under the Ecclesiastical Jurisdiction Measure 1963 for offences of misconduct concerning priests or deacons. With effect from 1 January 2006, these matters are the subject of an entirely new procedure under the Clergy Discipline Measure 2003, which is dealt with in detail in Chapter 6. The consistory court has retained its first instance faculty jurisdiction,[225] which is the subject matter of Chapter 7.

Appellate courts

2.59 Appeals from the consistory court generally lie to the provincial court of appeal. In the province of Canterbury, this is the Court of the Arches; in that of York, the Chancery Court of York. The former is presided over by the Dean of the Arches and the latter by the Auditor.[226] Both offices are required to be held by the same person.[227] In a faculty case, appeals are heard by the Court of Arches,[228] unless they concern doctrine, ritual or ceremonial (styled reserved matters), in which case the appeal is to the Court of Ecclesiastical Causes Reserved.[229]

---

[224] Care of Churches and Ecclesiastical Jurisdiction Measure 1991, s 14. See Chapter 7.
[225] Ecclesiastical Jurisdiction Measure 1963, s 6(1)(b). Other areas of jurisdiction are set out in ibid s 6(1)(bb)–(e), but these are so rarely used as not to merit separate consideration.
[226] Ecclesiastical Jurisdiction Measure 1963, s 3(2)(a).
[227] The Dean of the Arches and Auditor is appointed by the Archbishops of Canterbury and York jointly, with the approval of the monarch: ibid s 3(2)(a).
[228] Comprising, in this instance, the Dean of the Arches sitting with two diocesan chancellors designated by the Dean: Ecclesiastical Jurisdiction Measure 1963, s 47(1)(b).
[229] Ibid s 10(1). The composition of the court is given at ibid s 5. As for determining to which tribunal the appeal lies and the appropriate procedure, see Chapter 7.

Under the Clergy Discipline Measure 2003, an appeal lies to the Court of Arches[230] **2.60**
from a determination of a disciplinary tribunal in a case of clerical misconduct.[231]
When exercising this jurisdiction, the Dean[232] sits with a further four judges; two
are in holy orders and are appointed by the Prolocutor of the Lower House of the
relevant province, and two are communicant laymen, appointed by the Chairman
of the House of Laity after consultation with the Lord Chancellor, and possessing
such judicial experience as the Lord Chancellor thinks appropriate.[233]

The Court of Faculties

Contrary to what its title may suggest, the Court of Faculties is not judicial in **2.61**
nature. It is the court of the Archbishop of Canterbury and has a vestigial jurisdiction in the exercise of legatine powers which belonged to the Archbishop at the
time of the Reformation. Power to grant dispensations, inter alia, was vested in the
Archbishop by virtue of the Ecclesiastical Licences Act 1533. The present-day
work of the Court of Faculties is largely confined to the granting of special marriage licences, the registration and regulation of notaries public and the issuing of
Lambeth degrees.

Judicial review

By dint of its anomalous position as the established Church in England, the **2.62**
courts of the Church of England are subject to judicial review when acting ultra
vires or in breach of natural justice.[234] The precise extent of the powers of the
Administrative Court to review decisions of the consistory court is unclear.[235]
The Provincial Court of the Church in Wales is not so liable.[236] Under the Human

---

[230] Or the Chancery Court of York as appropriate.
[231] Clergy Discipline Measure 2003, s 20(1). Likewise appeals lie to the appropriate provincial court from the Vicar General's court in misconduct cases concerning bishops or archbishops: ibid s 20(1).
[232] Or auditor, as appropriate.
[233] Clergy Discipline Measure 2003, s 20(2), incorporating by reference the Ecclesiastical Jurisdiction Measure 1963, s 3(2)(a)–(c).
[234] See *R v Chancellor of St Edmundsbury and Ipswich Diocese, ex parte White* [1948] 1 KB 195, [1947] 2 All ER 170, CA; *R v Chancellor of the Chichester Consistory Court, ex parte News Group Newspapers* [1992] COD 48; and *R v Exeter Consistory Court, ex parte Cornish* (1998) 5 Ecc LJ 212, CA.
[235] See M Hill, 'Judicial Review of Ecclesiastical Courts' in N Doe, M Hill and R Ombres (eds), *English Canon Law* (Cardiff: University of Wales Press, 1998) 104–114. Note also J Laws 'A Judicial Perspective on the Sacred in Society' (2004) 7 Ecc LJ 317 at 323.
[236] See *R v Provincial Court of the Church in Wales, ex parte Williams* (1998) 5 Ecc LJ 217.

Rights Act 1998, all courts and tribunals are included as public authorities,[237] and thus it is unlawful for them to act in a way which is incompatible with a Convention right.[238] This includes not merely the right to a fair trial under Article 6 but also, for example, the right to respect for private and family life under Article 8, freedom of thought, conscience and religion under Article 9, freedom of expression under Article 10, and freedom of assembly and association under Article 11, all of which (and others besides) are justiciable in the court or tribunal.[239]

---

[237] Human Rights Act 1998, s 6(3)(a).
[238] Ibid s 6(1).
[239] See M Hill, 'The Impact for the Church of England of the Human Rights Act 1998' (2000) 5 Ecc LJ 431; and M Hill, 'A New Dawn for Freedom of Religion' in M Hill (ed), *Religious Liberty and Human Rights* (Cardiff: University of Wales Press, 2002) 1–13. Convention rights have been the subject of judicial comment in *Re Durrington Cemetery* [2001] Fam 333, [2000] 3 WLR 1322, Chichester Cons Ct, Hill Ch; and *Re Crawley Green Road Cemetery* [2001] Fam 308, St Albans Cons Ct, Bursell Ch, both of which are discussed in R Sandberg, 'Human Rights and Human Remains: The Impact of *Dödsbo v Sweden*' (2006) 8 Ecc LJ 453. Note also *Re Welford Road Cemetery, Leicester* [2007] 1 WLR 506, [2007] 2 All ER 426, Ct of Arches.

3

THE PARISH

Parish structure	3.01	Parish clerks and sextons	3.61
The electoral roll	3.03	Treasurers	3.63
Annual parochial church meeting	3.07	PCC secretaries	3.64
Parochial church councils	3.11	Organists	3.65
Composition	3.12	Readers	3.67
District church councils	3.16	Deaconesses	3.71
Joint parochial church councils	3.18	Lay workers	3.72
Team councils	3.19	Religious communities	3.75
Group councils	3.20	**Parochial property**	3.76
Functions of the PCC	3.21	Chancel repair	3.78
Churchwardens	3.32	Quinquennial inspection	3.82
Qualifications	3.33	**Parochial finance**	3.84
Choosing churchwardens	3.35	**Pastoral schemes and orders**	3.86
Admission and term of office	3.40	**Sharing of church buildings**	3.95
Resignation and vacation of office	3.42	**Ecumenical relations**	3.99
Custom	3.44	**Non-parochial units**	3.103
Episcopal powers	3.46	Peculiars	3.104
Misconduct	3.47	Private chapels	3.105
Powers and duties	3.48	Other chapels	3.106
Deputy churchwardens	3.57	Guild churches	3.108
Other lay officers	3.59		
Sidesmen	3.60		

Parish structure

The most visible symbol of the existence of the Church of England is its parish **3.01** churches, which dominate both the urban and, more particularly, the rural landscape. It is at their parish church that the majority of the Church of England worships (if only occasionally), and it is in the parish church that residents of the parish are baptised, married and, if there be room in the churchyard, buried. The parish is also the most localized of the organs of government of the Church. It is in the forum provided at annual parochial church meetings and parochial church council (PCC) meetings that the voices of the people in the pews may be heard.[1] Furthermore, the joint exercise by priest and people of their local ministry is a significant element of contemporary Christian outreach. This chapter examines in some detail the nature of the parish, the respective roles of priest and people within the parish, and the rights and duties of the PCC, churchwardens and others.

3.02 A parish[2] is a geographical area within which pastoral ministry, often known as the cure of souls, is provided in a diocese.[3] The cure of souls is shared with the bishop of the diocese. The parochial system grew out of the practice of bishops sending priests from the cathedral to more distant places in order to preach and administer the sacraments. With the passing of time, churches were built and endowed, and priests were appointed to serve in them.[4] These historic parishes have been altered and modified to take account of social and population changes over the centuries. A parish is not always identical in extent to the benefice of which it may form part. The benefice is often now a larger area, comprising several parishes, and historically it provided the 'living' for the incumbent who served in it. The incumbent is appointed by the patron and may be assisted in the cure of souls in the parishes of the benefice by other ministers.[5] Patronage and the appointment of clergy are discussed in Chapter 4.

---

[1] The legal status of a PCC was considered by the House of Lords in *Aston Cantlow and Wilmcote with Billesley Parochial Church Council v Wallbank* [2004] 1 AC 546, [2003] 3 All ER 1213, HL. The Court of Appeal had determined that a PCC was a public authority for the purposes of the Human Rights Act 1998, basing its conclusion largely on the fact that the Church of England was by law established. The House of Lords rejected both the reasoning and the conclusion of the Court of Appeal. With reference to PCCs, Lord Nicholls of Birkenhead said at para 14: 'their constitution and functions lend no support to the view that they should be characterised as governmental organisations, or, more precisely, in the language of the statute, public authorities'.

[2] An amorphous creature exists in the nature of a putative parish and is known as a 'conventional district'. They are areas placed with the consent of the incumbent and the bishop under a curate-in-charge who has responsibility for the cure of souls within the district. It has its own churchwardens, electoral roll and PCC and has to be renewed with every change of incumbency of the parish within which it lies. There is now a statutory requirement for the diocesan pastoral committee to review the arrangements for pastoral supervision in conventional districts at least once every five years: Pastoral Measure 1983, s 2A, as inserted by the Synodical Government (Amendment) Measure 2003, s 2(2).

[3] Note the provisions in the proposed Dioceses, Pastoral and Mission Measure which was approved by the General Synod in February 2007 and which prescribe for Bishop's Mission Orders. See also the various contributions in S Croft (ed), *The Future of the Parish: Shaping the Church of England in the Twenty-First Century* (London: Church House Publishing, 2007).

[4] Such endowments led to the system of patronage and the right to present clergy to benefices.

[5] There is statutory provision for other clergy to be permitted to exercise a particular ministry within another's benefice in particular circumstances. Under the Extra-Parochial Ministry Measure 1967, a bishop may license a clergyman to officiate (save for marriages of housebound or detained persons) at a named institution, such as a hospital, university or school, free from the control of the incumbent of the parish within which the institution is situated: ibid s 2(1), (2), amended by the Church of England (Legal Aid and Miscellaneous Provisions) Measure 1988, s 5. The same freedom is also granted to enable a priest to minister at the home of a person on the electoral roll

The electoral roll

For many years the wider involvement of the laity in the affairs of the Church was extremely limited, since all decision-making powers lay in the hands of the incumbent and churchwardens. The Church of England Assembly (Powers) Act 1919 sought for the first time to introduce lay involvement into the democratic process of the church.[6] Following a number of statutory enactments, the present position is regulated by the Synodical Government Measure 1969 and, in particular, the Church Representation Rules, which form Schedule 3 to the Measure.[7] In addition, there is the Parochial Church Councils (Powers) Measure 1956 and several other statutes, Measures and Canons which give to the PCC specific powers and duties.

3.03

At the heart of the democratic process, however, lies the electoral roll which every parish is obliged to maintain and make available for inspection by *bona fide* inquirers.[8] A lay person is entitled to have his name entered on the roll of the parish if that person:

3.04

(a) is baptised; and
(b) is aged at least 16; and
(c) has signed the application form in Appendix I of the Church Representation Rules and declared himself to be either:
  (i) a member of the Church of England or of a Church in communion therewith resident in the parish; or
  (ii) such a member and, not being resident in the parish, to have habitually attended public worship in the parish during a period of six months prior to enrolment;[9] or
  (iii) a member in good standing of a Church which subscribes to the doctrine of the Holy Trinity (not being a Church in communion with the Church

---

of his parish but resident in another: Extra-Parochial Ministry Measure 1967, s 1. Note also the position of prison chaplains under the Prison Act 1952, s 7(1).

[6] See Chapter 1. A number of church councils existed prior to the passing of the 1919 Act but they did so at the will of the incumbent and exercised only such power and authority as he chose to delegate.

[7] A number of modest, but significant, changes were effected to the 1969 Measure by the Synodical Government (Amendment) Measure 2003 which came into force on 1 January 2004. See also the Church Representation Rules (Amendment) Resolution 2004, SI 2004/1889. The changes are dealt with individually in the text as they arise.

[8] Church Representation Rules, r 1(1). This should not be confused with the electoral register maintained by local authorities. The criteria for enrolment are considered in D Lamming, 'The Church Electoral Roll: Some Vagaries of the Church Representation Rules' (2006) 8 Ecc LJ 438.

[9] For problems of definition of 'habitual' attendance, see Lamming, 'The Church Electoral Roll' (n 8 above).

of England) and also prepared to declare himself to be a member of the Church of England having habitually attended public worship in the parish during a period of six months prior to enrolment.[10]

The difficulty with the foregoing categorization is that 'membership' is nowhere defined.[11] Baptism is self-evidently not the test, nor is habitual worship, as these terms appear elsewhere in the rule. Mere residence in the parish confers rights to baptism, marriage and burial, but something more than that is envisaged. The inference is that 'membership' requires something more than the exercise of such rights, although what that may be is difficult to express.[12] It would appear to be a self-defining concept.[13] Whilst an individual may, subject to the qualification provisions, be on the electoral roll of more than one parish, he must choose one of them for the purpose of the qualification for election to a deanery or diocesan synod, or to the General Synod.[14]

3.05 A church electoral roll officer must be appointed by the PCC whose duty it is to keep the roll up to date[15] and to report additions and removals to the next meeting of the PCC and publish notice of them.[16] A person's name must be removed from the roll if that person:

---

[10] Church Representation Rules, r 1(2). An exception to the age limit under head (b) is where an individual's sixteenth birthday falls between the date upon which the new roll is prepared and the date of the next annual parochial church meeting, in which case enrolment takes effect from the date of the birthday: ibid r 1(2) proviso.

[11] For a comparative analysis, see P Colton, 'The Pursuit of a Canonical Definition of Membership in the Church of Ireland' (2008) 10 Ecc LJ (forthcoming).

[12] For a discussion, see N Doe, *The Legal Framework of the Church of England* (Oxford: Clarendon Press, 1996) 222–224.

[13] It has been argued that if a person completes and signs a from of application for enrolment, he or she is entitled to have his or her name entered on the electoral roll by dint of the self-certification, and the electoral roll officer is under a duty to add the person's name to the roll without further enquiry. See, Lamming, 'The Church Electoral Roll' (n 8 above). A literal reading of r 1(2) leads to this conclusion, despite the obviously nonsensical result of an electoral roll officer being duty bound to act upon a document which he knows to be false or does not believe to be true. The right of appeal under r 43(1)(a) against a refusal (discussed below) would be nugatory if the duty were absolute, particularly, if the name could be immediately removed under r 1(9). The better course would be for the electoral roll officer to decline to add the name, thereby leaving the applicant, if he feels aggrieved, to appeal the matter. As was said in another context, 'the court will not insist on circuity of action if the same result as can legitimately be achieved by circuitous action can be achieved by direct action'. See *Re Collard's Will Trusts* [1961] Ch 293, [1961] 1 All ER 821, 823 per Buckley J.

[14] Church Representation Rules, r 1(4). Likewise an individual must choose one such parish for the exercise of *ex officio* membership (i) of a PCC in consequence of lay membership of a deanery or diocesan synod or of the General Synod (r 14(1)(f)), or (ii) of a deanery synod in consequence of lay membership of a diocesan or area synod or of the General Synod (r 24(6)(b)).

[15] Ibid r 1(7). For a discussion see, D Lamming, 'The Church Electoral Roll' (n 8 above).

[16] Church Representation Rules, r 1(8). In so doing he acts under the direction of the PCC: r 1(7). Canon C 23 para 2 states that in the case of any omission in any parish to prepare and maintain an electoral roll, the rural dean on such omission being brought to his notice must ascertain and report to the bishop the cause thereof. This canonical duty is replicated in the Church Representation Rules, r 53(5).

(a) dies; or
(b) becomes a clerk in holy orders; or
(c) signifies in writing a desire that his name be removed; or
(d) ceases to reside in the parish unless after so ceasing he continues in any period of six months habitually to attend public worship there; or
(e) is not resident in the parish and has not habitually attended public worship in the parish during the preceding six months;[17] or
(f) was not entitled to have his name on the roll in the first place.[18]

Removal of a name from the roll does not preclude it being entered again should an individual subsequently acquire the right to have it entered.[19]

3.06 The roll must be revised annually by or under the direction of the PCC.[20] Every parish was required to compile a completely new roll prior to the annual parochial church meeting[21] in 2007, and must do so again every succeeding sixth year.[22] A right of appeal exists in relation to enrolment or refusal of enrolment; and to removal and refusal to remove.[23]

Annual parochial church meeting

3.07 Every parish is required to hold an annual parochial church meeting (APCM)[24] no later than 30 April each year.[25] Every lay person whose name appears on the electoral roll is entitled to attend and take part in the proceedings.[26] Additionally, a clerk in holy orders is entitled to attend and take part if he is resident in the parish or a habitual worshipper at a church in the parish or if he is a co-opted

---

[17] Whether or not the electoral roll officer must accept without question the self-certified status of an applicant as to habitual attendance (discussed above) removal is predicated upon the subjective determination of the electoral roll officer as to that individual's continuing status: see, Lamming, 'The Church Electoral Roll' (n 8 above).

[18] Ibid r 1(9). Note that there is an exception in relation to attendance at public worship if an individual is prevented from so doing by 'illness or other sufficient cause'.

[19] Ibid r 1(10).

[20] Ibid r 2(1). Mandatory notification provisions must be followed.

[21] See below.

[22] Ibid r 2(4).

[23] Ibid r 43(1)(a). The appeal is determined by three or more appointed lay members of the bishop's council: r 43(5). Note the declaratory relief sought in the Chancery Division in the unusual case of *Stuart v Haughley Parochial Church Council* [1936] Ch 32, CA, discussed in Lamming, 'The Church Electoral Roll' (n 8 above) at 446–451. Any challenge to a decision of an appeal panel would now be by way of judicial review on the basis of bad faith or *Wednesbury* unreasonableness.

[24] This meeting should be distinguished from a PCC meeting and from the annual meeting of parishioners when churchwardens are chosen, as to which see below.

[25] Church Representation Rules, r 6(1).

[26] Ibid r 6(2). No other lay person is so entitled.

member of the PCC.[27] The APCM is convened in accordance with the Church Representation Rules,[28] and is chaired by the minister, if present, the vice-chairman of the PCC or a chairman chosen at the meeting.[29] The chairman may exercise a casting vote if there is an equal division of votes.[30] The secretary of the PCC or another person appointed by the APCM must act as clerk to the meeting and record the minutes thereof.[31] The meeting has power to adjourn and to determine its own rules of procedure.[32]

3.08 The business of the APCM is largely administrative. It receives from the PCC and is free to discuss:

(a) a report on changes to the electoral roll;
(b) an annual report of the proceedings of the PCC and the activities of the parish generally;
(c) the financial statements of the PCC for the previous year to 31 December, independently examined or audited;[33]
(d) a report upon the fabric, goods and ornaments of the church or churches in the parish;[34]
(e) a report on the proceedings of the deanery synod.[35]

3.09 The financial statements[36] must have been considered and, if thought fit, approved by the PCC and signed by the chairman.[37] Any person entitled to attend the

---

[27] See ibid r 6(3), the provisions of which are somewhat detailed. Note also the provision in relation to team and group ministries: r 6(4), (5).

[28] See ibid r 7. Provision is made in the case of a vacancy of the benefice or when the minister is absent or incapacitated: r 7(3).

[29] Ibid r 8(1).

[30] Ibid r 8(3). No clerical chairman may vote in the election of parochial representatives of the laity: r 8(3).

[31] Ibid r 9(9).

[32] Ibid r 9(8).

[33] Provision is made for the form of the accounts and their public display: see ibid rr 9(3), (4), 54(8); National Institutions Measure 1998, s 13(1), Sch 5 para 2(e). Note also the provisions of the Parochial Church Councils (Powers) Measure 1956, s 8, and the Church Accounting Regulations 2006 (GS 1624) which came into force on 1 August 2006. It is anticipated that once the relevant parts of the Charities Act 2006 have been brought into force (currently expected in 2008), PCCs with incomes of £100,000 per annum or more will be required to register with the Charity Commission.

[34] ie under the Care of Churches and Ecclesiastical Jurisdiction Measure 1991, s 5. This report, styled the Annual Fabric Report, must be prepared by the churchwardens and first delivered by them to the PCC at its meeting immediately before the APCM, thereby permitting the PCC to make any amendments: s 5(3). It should deal, in particular, with action taken or proposed in relation to the implementation of any recommendation contained in the quinquennial report under the Inspection of Churches Measure 1955, s 1.

[35] Church Representation Rules, r 9(1)(a)–(e).

[36] These are required to be displayed on a notice board at the church for a continuous period of at least seven days before the APCM: ibid r 9(3)(c).

[37] Ibid r 9(3)(b). Following the meeting the financial statements, together with the PCC report, must be published and displayed and copies sent to the secretary of the diocesan board of finance: r 9(4).

APCM may ask any question about parochial church matters, or bring about a discussion of any matter of parochial or general Church interest, by moving a general resolution or by moving to give any particular recommendation to the PCC in relation to its duties.[38] In the exercise of its functions the PCC is obliged to take into consideration any expression of opinion by the APCM, or indeed any parochial church meeting.[39]

In addition, the APCM is required to perform the following:[40]

3.10

(a) in every third year, to elect parochial representatives of the laity to deanery synod;[41]
(b) to elect parochial representatives of the laity to the PCC;[42]
(c) to appoint sidesmen;[43]
(d) to appoint an independent examiner or auditor to the PCC for the following year.[44]

A person qualified to be elected as a lay representative must be on the electoral roll of the parish, an actual communicant,[45] and aged at least 16 (for the PCC) or 18 (for deanery synod).[46] No person may be nominated unless he has signified his consent to serve or in the opinion of the APCM there is evidence of his willingness to serve.[47] A person may not serve on a PCC if he has been disqualified under rule 46A of the Church Representation Rules.[48] To be appointed sidesman, one's name must be on the electoral roll of the parish.[49]

---

[38] Ibid r 9(7).
[39] Parochial Church Councils (Powers) Measure 1956, s 2(3), substituted by the Synodical Government Measure 1969, s 6. Provision exists for the convening of special and extraordinary parochial church meetings: Church Representation Rules, rr 22, 23.
[40] It must do so in this order: ibid r 9(5).
[41] Ibid r 9(5)(a). The conduct of these elections and those of the lay representatives is set out in r 11 subject to a power to vary in r 12.
[42] Ibid r 9(5)(b).
[43] Ibid r 9(5)(c). Both this provision and Canon E 2 are couched in mandatory language but it is nowhere stated how many sidesmen there should be, nor what sanction exists for a failure to appoint.
[44] Church Representation Rules, r 9(5)(d). The meaning of 'auditor' and 'independent examiner' is identical to that in the Charities Act 1993, ss 43(2) and 43(3)(a) respectively: Church Representation Rules, r 54(1). They may not be members of the PCC: ibid r 9(5)(d).
[45] 'Actual communicant' is defined in ibid r 54(1).
[46] Ibid r 10(1). Unless the individual is under 18 years of age at the date of the election, his name must have been entered on the electoral register for at least the previous six months: ibid r 10(1)(a), as amended by Synodical Government (Amendment) Measure 2003, Schedule para 2.
[47] Church Representation Rules, r 10(3)(a).
[48] Ibid r 10(3)(b). This covers disqualification under the Charities Act 1993, s 72(1), from being a charity trustee, and disqualification from holding office under the Incumbents (Vacation of Benefices) Measure 1977, s 10(6). The former also applies in relation to the deanery synod.
[49] Church Representation Rules, r 10(3); Canon E 2 para 2.

Parochial church councils

3.11 The parochial church council (PCC) is the central forum for decision-making and discussion in relation to parish affairs. Its composition is regulated by the Church Representation Rules and its powers and duties are to be found in those rules, in the Parochial Church Councils (Powers) Measure 1956, and elsewhere in other Statutes, Measures and Canons.[50]

Composition

3.12 The PCC consists of:

(a) all clerks in holy orders beneficed in or licensed to the parish;[51]
(b) if part of a team, all clerical members of the team;
(c) any deaconesses or lay workers licensed to the parish;
(d) the churchwardens,[52] being actual communicants whose names are on the church electoral roll;
(e) such readers as the APCM may determine;[53]
(f) lay members of General, diocesan and deanery synods whose names are on the church electoral roll;
(g) elected lay representatives;[54] and
(h) co-opted members (if the PCC so decides) not exceeding one-fifth of the elected lay representatives or two persons, whichever be greater.[55]

---

[50] The legal status of a PCC was the subject of an appeal to the House of Lords in *Aston Cantlow and Wilmcote with Billesley Parochial Church Council v Wallbank* [2004] 1 AC 546, [2003] 3 All ER 1213, HL.

[51] This includes a cleric duly authorized to act as chairman of PCC meetings in accordance with para 5(b) of Appendix II: Church Representation Rules, r 14(1)(aa). This provision is particularly useful in some large multi-parish benefices where clergy other than the minister might have pastoral care of particular parishes.

[52] And any deputy churchwardens: see ibid, r 18(4).

[53] The readers must be licensed to the parish or an area including the parish and have their names on the church electoral roll: ibid r 14(1)(e).

[54] Absent a resolution to the contrary, each parish has six representatives of the laity when there are not more than 50 on the electoral roll, nine when there are not more than 100, and a further three for every additional 100 or part thereof up to a maximum of 15: Church Representation Rules, r 14(1)(g) as amended by Synodical Government (Amendment) Measure 2003, Schedule para 3. Any or all of the foregoing numbers may be altered by resolution of the APCM, such altered representation being effective from the following APCM: Church Representation Rules r 14(1)(g). The APCM may, by resolution, provide for election by single transferable vote and make provision for postal votes, each resolution taking effect at the following APCM: ibid r 12.

[55] Ibid r 14(1)(a)–(h). Such co-opted members may be either clerks in holy orders or actual lay communicants aged 16 or more: r 14(1)(h).

3.13 The recently established norm is for elected lay representatives to hold office for three years from the APCM with one-third retiring each year.[56] However, the APCM may resolve to adopt a practice which departs from this norm, such practice taking effect as from the following APCM.[57] Any such variation must be reviewed at least once every six years.[58] Qualifying churchwardens become members of the PCC from the date they are chosen rather than the later date when they are admitted to office.[59] The APCM may decide to limit the number of years during which a lay representative may continuously hold office, and may specify a minimum interval after which a person may stand again for election.[60] Special provisions exist for parishes with more than one place of worship,[61] and for team and group ministries, for the creation, inter alia, of schemes for joint PCCs[62] and for team or group councils.[63] These are discussed in more detail below.

3.14 Any elected member of the PCC may resign upon signed notice in writing to the secretary.[64] Membership of the PCC ceases if the name of an elected representative is removed from the church electoral roll or not included in a new roll,[65] or if such representative becomes disqualified from serving.[66]

3.15 General provisions relating to PCCs are to be found in Appendix II to the Church Representation Rules, although, with the consent of the diocesan synod, any PCC may vary them in so far as they relate to that council.[67] They provide for the minister of the parish to be the chairman and for the election of a lay person as vice-chairman.[68] In addition, they allow for the appointment of a secretary, a treasurer[69]

---

[56] Ibid r 16(1) as amended by the Synodical Government (Amendment) Measure 2003, Schedule para 4.
[57] Church Representation Rules, r 16(3) as amended.
[58] Ibid r 16(4) as amended.
[59] Ibid r 14(2).
[60] Ibid r 17.
[61] Ibid r 18.
[62] Ibid r 19.
[63] Ibid rr 20 and 21 respectively.
[64] Ibid r 49.
[65] The criteria for removal are set out in para 3.05 above. In appropriate circumstances, the PCC may consider the co-option of the individual concerned.
[66] Church Representation Rules, r 14(3), 46A. The causes of disqualification are set out at n 48 above.
[67] Ibid r 15. Any question on the interpretation of Appendix II is to be referred to the bishop and any decision given by him or a person appointed by him is final: App II para 18.
[68] In the case of a multi-parish benefice, a priest or deacon, licensed or with a permission to officiate in the parish, may be authorized by the bishop to be chairman of PCC meetings, following a joint application by the minister of the parish and the PCC and with the agreement of the cleric concerned: para 5(b) of Appendix II. Such person thereby becomes a member of the PCC: Church Representation Rules, r 14(1)(aa).
[69] In the absence of a treasurer, the responsibilities fall to be discharged by the churchwardens: ibid App II para 1(e)(i). It is considered undesirable for the same person to be both treasurer and secretary: *Legal Opinions* 132.

and an electoral roll officer. At least four meetings per year must be held.[70] If the chairman refuses or neglects to convene a meeting within seven days of receiving a written request signed by at least one-third of the members of the PCC, those members may themselves convene a meeting.[71] The meeting is not quorate unless at least one-third of the members are present, and no business which is not specified on the agenda may be transacted, save with the consent of three-quarters of the members present.[72] Business is decided by a simple majority vote,[73] with the chairman having a casting vote.[74] Minutes must be kept.[75] The PCC must have a standing committee, comprising not fewer than five persons,[76] which has power to transact the business of the PCC between meetings, subject to any directions which the PCC may give.[77] Other committees may be appointed by the PCC and may include persons who are not members of the PCC, but the minister must be an *ex officio* member of all such committees.[78]

District church councils

3.16 Where there are two or more districts within one benefice, the APCM has power to make a scheme for the election of a district church council (DCC).[79] The scheme must provide for the election of lay representatives, for *ex officio* members and for chairmanship.[80] The scheme may also provide for the delegation by the PCC to a DCC of such functions as the scheme may specify, and for the election of deputy churchwardens and delegation of functions to them.[81] It may not, however, file separate annual accounts.[82]

---

[70] Church Representation Rules, App II para 2.
[71] Ibid App II para 3.
[72] Ibid App II para 6.
[73] Ibid App II para 10.
[74] Ibid App II para 11.
[75] These should record the persons present and, if one-fifth of the members present and voting on any resolution so require, the minutes must record the names of the members voting for and against that resolution: ibid App II para 12, which also provides for access to the minutes.
[76] Ibid App II para 14(a). The minister and churchwardens are *ex officio* members.
[77] Ibid App II para 14(b).
[78] Ibid App II para 15.
[79] Ibid r 18(1)(b). A special parochial church meeting has the same powers: ibid r 18(6).
[80] Ibid r 18(2). It must contain such other provisions as to membership and procedure as the APCM considers appropriate: ibid r 18(2).
[81] Ibid r 18(3), (4). Certain functions may not be delegated: that of an interested party under the Pastoral Measure 1983, Part I (ss 1–16 (pastoral schemes)); functions under the Patronage (Benefices) Measure 1986, Part II (ss 7–24 (exercise of rights of presentation)); and those under the Priests (Ordination of Women) Measure 1993, s 3 (passing of resolutions as to the ministry of women priests).
[82] A power to this effect, deeming a DCC to be a separate parish for the purpose of producing financial statements for presentation to the APCM, failed to find favour with the Charity Commission who took exception to a body, which is not a separate legal entity and which exercises merely a delegated authority, filing charity accounts. Accordingly the provisions briefly contained in

The scheme requires the approval of at least two-thirds of those present and voting **3.17**
at the APCM, and may not come into force until such time as the bishop's council
and standing committee may determine, being not later than the next APCM.[83]
The bishop's council and standing committee must determine whether or not the
scheme may come into operation, with or without amendment.[84] A scheme may
be amended or revoked by a subsequent scheme, passed in accordance with the
rules.[85] No scheme to establish a DCC may come into operation when provision
has been made under an existing pastoral scheme or instrument of the bishop and
such provision remains extant.[86] Every member of a team ministry has the right to
attend the meetings of a DCC within the benefice.[87]

Joint parochial church councils

Where there are two or more parishes in a single benefice, or where two or more **3.18**
benefices are held in plurality, the APCMs of all or some of the parishes may make
a scheme to establish a joint PCC.[88] It will comprise all the ministers of the parishes and such representatives of the parishes elected by and from among
the other PCCs as the scheme may specify.[89] The scheme must make provision
for chairmanship, meetings and procedure and for the delegation by the PCCs
of such of their functions as it may specify.[90] As with a scheme for a DCC, the
bishop's council and standing committee must determine whether or not it is to
come into operation.[91] The joint council must meet from time to time for the
purpose of consulting together on matters of common concern.[92] The functions
of the PCC in respect of the selection of a new incumbent are exercised by
the joint council.[93] A scheme may be amended or revoked by a subsequent

---

r 18(5A) of the Church Representation Rules (having been introduced by the Church Representation Rules (Amendment) Resolution 1998, SI 1998/319) were repealed by the Synodical Government (Amendment) Measure 2003 with effect from 1 January 2004, thereby restoring the mild inconvenience of the pre-1999 position.

[83] Church Representation Rules, r 18(5).

[84] Ibid r 18(5)(a)–(c). Any amendments must be approved at a special parochial church meeting by at least two-thirds of those present and voting: ibid r 18(5)(c).

[85] Ibid r 18(8).
[86] Ibid r 18(7).
[87] Ibid r 18(9).
[88] Ibid r 19(1).
[89] Ibid r 19(1)(a).

[90] Ibid r 19(1)(b), (c). Certain functions are non-delegable: those of an interested party under the Pastoral Measure 1983, Part I, and under the Priests (Ordination of Women) Measure 1993, s 3 (see n 81 above).

[91] Church Representation rules, r 19(4). Nor may a scheme be brought into effect when provision has been made under a pastoral scheme or instrument of the bishop establishing a joint PCC and such provision remains extant: r 19(6).

[92] Ibid r 19(3).
[93] Patronage (Benefices) Measure 1986, s 23, Sch 2 para 20.

scheme,[94] and ceases to have effect if the holding of the benefices in plurality is terminated.[95]

Team councils

3.19 Where a team ministry is established for a benefice which comprises more than one parish, the APCMs of the parish may make a joint scheme establishing a team council.[96] The council will comprise the team rector, the other members of the team, assistant curates, deaconesses and lay workers licensed to a parish but not members of the team, and lay representatives elected by and from among the lay representatives of the PCCs.[97] The delegation of PCC functions mirrors that for joint PCCs.[98] As with a scheme for a joint council, the bishop's council and standing committee must determine whether or not it is to come into operation.[99] The team council must meet from time to time for the purpose of consulting together on matters of common concern.[100] The scheme may be amended or revoked by a subsequent scheme.[101] The functions of the PCC in respect of the selection of a new incumbent are exercised by the joint council.[102]

Group councils

3.20 Where a pastoral scheme establishes a group ministry, the APCMs of the parishes in the area may make a joint scheme establishing a group council comprising all the members of the group ministry, every assistant curate, deaconess and lay worker licensed to any such parish, and such lay representatives elected by and from among the lay members of the PCC of each parish as may be specified.[103] The delegation of PCC functions is provided for.[104] Like provisions apply to a group council as to a team council.[105]

---

[94] Church Representation Rules, r 19(8).
[95] Ibid r 19(7). See the Pastoral Measure 1983, s 18(2).
[96] Church Representation Rules, r 20(1)(a).
[97] Ibid r 20(1)(a)(i)–(iv). Provision is to be made by self-selection to limit the clerical members and lay workers to no more than one-third of the team council: r 20(1) proviso.
[98] Ibid r 20(2).
[99] Ibid r 20(4). Nor may a scheme be brought into effect when provision has been made under a pastoral scheme establishing a team ministry or instrument of the bishop establishing a team ministry and such provision remains extant: r 20(6).
[100] Ibid r 20(3).
[101] Ibid r 20(7).
[102] Patronage (Benefices) Measure 1986, s 23, Sch 2 para 20.
[103] Church Representation Rules, r 21(1)(a).
[104] Ibid r 21(1)(c).
[105] Ibid r 21(3), applying, with modifications, r 20(2)–(7).

Functions of the PCC

3.21 Whilst examples of the traditional autocratic style of parish governance remain, the contemporary model of the relationship between a minister and the PCC is one of mutual co-operation and support, combining joint decision-making and a cross-fertilization of ideas and initiatives. The keynotes are interaction and consensus in what is often styled a collaborative ministry. The Parochial Church Councils (Powers) Measure 1956 provides that 'it shall be the duty of the minister and the parochial church council to consult together on matters of general concern and importance to the parish'.[106] The role of the PCC is significantly more extensive than merely controlling expenditure and maintaining the fabric of the church, although both these tasks are important. The functions of the PCC include co-operation with the minister in promoting in the parish the whole mission of the Church, pastoral, evangelistic, social and ecumenical, and the consideration and discussions of matters concerning the Church of England, or any other matters of religious or public interest.[107] The House of Lords, in the seminal case of *Aston Cantlow and Wilmcote with Billesley Parochial Church Council v Wallbank*,[108] was recently called upon to consider the role and functions of PCCs. It has been very rare in recent years for a case concerning the constitutional status of the Church of England to reach the House of Lords, and the opinions of the Lords of Appeal in Ordinary (Law Lords), albeit differently articulated and nuanced, merit detailed consideration. Lord Nicholls of Birkenhead concluded:

> [PCCs] are established as corporate bodies under a church measure, now the Parochial Church Council (Powers) Measure 1956 ... But the essential role of a [PCC] is to provide a formal means, prescribed by the Church of England, whereby *ex officio* and elected members of the local church promote the mission of the Church and discharge financial responsibilities in respect of their own parish church, including responsibilities regarding maintenance of the fabric of the building. This smacks of a church body engaged in self-governance and promotion of its affairs.[109]

---

[106] Parochial Church Councils (Powers) Measure 1956, s 2(1), substituted by the Synodical Government Measure 1969, s 6. Prior to the substitution, this had read, 'It shall be the primary duty of the council in every parish to co-operate with the minister in the initiation, conduct and development of church work both within the parish and outside'.

[107] Parochial Church Councils (Powers) Measure 1956, s 2(2)(a), (b) (as so substituted). Note, however, that the PCC may not declare the doctrine of the Church on any question: s 2(2)(b). Other specific powers and duties of the PCC are set out below.

[108] *Aston Cantlow and Wilmcote with Billesley Parochial Church Council v Wallbank* [2004] 1 AC 546, [2003] 3 All ER 1213, HL.

[109] *Aston Cantlow* (n 108 above), per Lord Nicholls of Birkenhead at para 14. He rejected the respondents' contention that the PCC, being a creature of statute and exercising statutory functions, was a public authority for the purposes of the Human Rights Act 1998.

3.22 Lord Hope of Craighead indicated that the Court of Appeal had left out of account Strasbourg jurisprudence as to the meaning to be given to the expression 'non-governmental organization'.[110] Citing a passage from the second edition of this work,[111] he stated that a PCC

> plainly has nothing whatever to do with the process of either central or local government. It is not accountable to the general public for what it does. It receives no public funding, apart from occasional grants from English Heritage for the preservation of its historic buildings. In that respect it is in a position which is no different from that of any private individual.[112]

He concluded that a PCC was not a 'core' public authority for the purposes of the Human Rights Act 1998.[113] So did the late Lord Hobhouse of Woodborough, who described the PCC as follows:

> Its functions, as identified … from the relevant statutory provisions, clearly include matters which are concerned only with the pastoral and organizational concerns of the diocese and the congregation of believers in the parish. It acts in the sectional not the public interest… But the PCC itself does not have such public responsibilities nor are its functions public; it is essentially a domestic religious body.[114]

3.23 Lord Scott of Foscote agreed with Lord Hope of Craighead and Lord Rodger of Earlsferry in holding that a PCC is not a public authority.[115] Lord Rodger put it as follows:

> The key to the role of the PCC lies in the first of its general functions: co-operation with the minister in promoting in the parish the whole mission of the church. Its other more particular functions are to be seen as ways of carrying out this general function. The mission of the church is a *religious* mission, distinct from the secular

---

[110] *Aston Cantlow* (n 108 above), per Lord Hope of Craighead at paras 47–52 referring to *Rothenthurm Commune v Switzerland* (1988) 59 DR 251, *Ayuntamiento de Mula v Spain*, Reports of Judgments and Decisions 2001-I, 531, *Holy Monasteries v Greece* (1995) 20 EHRR 1.
[111] M Hill, *Ecclesiastical Law* (2nd edn, Oxford: Oxford University Press, 2001) paras 3.11 and 3.74.
[112] *Aston Cantlow* (n 108 above), per Lord Hope of Craighead at para 59.
[113] Ibid at para 63, nor is the function of enforcing chancel repair liability a public as opposed to a private act which would be relevant in the case of a 'hybrid' public authority: paras 63–64. He stated 'the liability of the lay rector to repair the chancel is a burden which arises as a mater of private law from the ownership of glebe land' (para 63) and that the PCC 'is seeking to enforce a civil debt. The function which it is performing has nothing to do with the responsibilities which are owed to the public by the State' (para 64).
[114] Ibid, per Lord Hobhouse of Woodborough at para 86. He also concluded that chancel repair liability was private in nature and not public: 'it is something which [the lay rectors] had personally assumed voluntarily by a voluntary act of acquisition which at the time they apparently thought was advantageous to them'. See para 90.
[115] Ibid, per Lord Scott of Foscott at para 129. However, dissenting from the opinion of the other four Law Lords on this point, he considered that the enforcement of chancel repair liability was a function of a public nature: para 130. He nonetheless concurred in the unanimous opinion of the House of Lords that its enforcement was not incompatible with rights under the European Convention on Human Rights.

mission of government, whether central or local. Founding on scriptural and other recognised authority, the Church seeks to serve the purposes of God, not those of the government carried out by the modern equivalents of Caesar and his proconsuls. This is true even though the Church of England has certain important links with the state. Those links, which do not include any funding of the Church by the government, give the Church a unique position but they do not mean that it is a department of state. ... In so far as the ties are intended to assist the Church, it is to accomplish the Church's own mission, not the aims and objectives of the Government of the United Kingdom. The PCC exists to carry forward the Church's mission at the local level.[116]

3.24 In addition to its other functions, the PCC must make known and put into effect any provision made by the deanery or diocesan synod.[117] It may raise matters with either synod and furnish advice to them.[118] In exercising these functions, the PCC must take into consideration any expression of opinion by any parochial church meeting.[119]

3.25 Despite the enjoinder to co-operate, there remains the possibility of a disagreement between minister and PCC and the question of how any such impasse is to be resolved. In many cases, the group dynamic will settle the matter in favour of the stronger willed or more forceful. Commenting on the responsibilities of the PCC, Chancellor Forbes stated in *Re St Peter, Roydon*,[120] that:

> in carrying out any particular duty with which they are entrusted they must pay proper regard to the wishes and suggestions of the minister if the discharge of the duty impinges on church work in respect of which the minister has expressed a wish or suggestion; but having done that they must be free to differ from him if in their view the honest discharge of the particular duty requires them to do so.[121]

Chancellor Forbes further remarked that: 'In the true spirit of charity a clash between an incumbent and a council becomes unthinkable',[122] although he emphasized that the requirement for agreement between minister and PCC must signify a genuine and informed consent, else the statutory requirement is no more than a 'solemn farce'.[123]

3.26 However as the facts of *St Peter, Roydon*, combined with other anecdotal evidence suggest, clashes can and do occur. The Parochial Church Councils (Powers)

---

[116] Ibid, per Lord Rodger of Earlsferry at para 156 (emphasis in the original).
[117] Parochial Church Councils (Powers) Measure 1956, s 2(2)(c), substituted by the Synodical Government Measure 1969, s 6. This is without prejudice to the PCC's powers on any particular matter.
[118] Parochial Church Councils (Powers) Measure 1956, s 2(2)(d) (as so substituted).
[119] Ibid s 2(3) (as so substituted). The most likely source of such expressions of opinion is the APCM.
[120] *Re St Peter, Roydon* [1969] 1 WLR 1849, [1969] 2 All ER 1233, Chelmsford Cons Ct.
[121] [1969] 1 WLR at 1852F; [1969] 2 All ER at 1235B. Note that this comment was in the context of the former statutory wording which is reproduced in n 106 above.
[122] [1969] 1 WLR at 1853C; [1969] 2 All ER at 1235G.
[123] [1969] 1 WLR at 1852H; [1969] 2 All ER at 1235D.

Measure 1956 therefore provides that, in the event of the minister and the PCC being unable to agree as to any matter in which their agreement or joint action is required under the Measure, such matter is to be dealt with or determined in such manner as the bishop may direct.[124] This might, for example, take the form of mediation, arbitration or conciliation involving the bishop himself or someone nominated by him.[125] If the disagreement is serious, amounting to a pastoral breakdown, then the provisions of the Incumbents (Vacation of Benefices) Measure 1977 may become relevant. These are fully set out in Chapter 4.[126]

3.27 The PCC is a body corporate with perpetual succession, and any act made by it may be signified by an instrument executed pursuant to a PCC resolution by the chairman and two other members.[127] The PCC has powers which were formerly exercised by the vestry of the parish or the churchwardens.[128] These include control of the financial affairs of the church and the care, maintenance, preservation and insurance of the fabric of the church and all goods and ornaments, and the care and maintenance of the churchyard, whether open or closed. The PCC has power to acquire, hold, administer and dispose of property (real and personal) for any ecclesiastical purpose, or in connection with educational schemes for the provision of facilities for the spiritual, moral and physical training of persons living in or near the parish.[129]

3.28 The Parochial Church Councils (Powers) Measure 1956 sets out certain specific powers of the PCC, some of which are also articulated in the canons, namely:

(a) to frame an annual budget of money required for the maintenance of the work of the Church in the parish and to take steps to raise, collect and allocate such money;[130]

---

[124] Parochial Church Councils (Powers) Measure 1956, s 9(3). Note also that any question arising on the interpretation of the general provisions relating to PCCs are to be referred to the bishop and any decision given by him or by any person appointed by him on his behalf is final. See the Church Representation Rules, App II para 18.

[125] It could also take the form of an *ex cathedra* pronouncement, but this would be neither sensitive nor pastoral.

[126] Under provisions introduced into the 1977 Measure by the Incumbents (Vacation of Benefices) (Amendment) Measure 1993, the bishop has power to rebuke parishioners if, in the opinion of the provincial tribunal, any serious pastoral breakdown of the relationship between the incumbent concerned and the parishioners is one to which the parishioners' conduct has contributed over a substantial period, and he may, if he thinks fit, disqualify such of them as he thinks fit from being a churchwarden or member or officer of the PCC in question or of others within the diocese for a specified period not exceeding five years: see s 10(6) of the 1977 Measure as amended by s 7 of the 1993 Measure.

[127] Parochial Church Councils (Powers) Measure 1956, s 3.

[128] See ibid s 4.

[129] Ibid ss 5, 6.

[130] Ibid s 7(i).

(b) to raise a voluntary church rate;[131]
(c) to appoint and dismiss the parish clerk and sexton and to regulate the terms of their employment;[132]
(d) to determine the objects to which all money collected in church is to be allocated;[133] and
(e) to make representations to the bishop with regard to any matter affecting the welfare of the Church in the parish.[134]

The bishop has power to make rules for the carrying into effect of the Parochial Church Council (Powers) Measure 1956 within his diocese.[135]

3.29 The PCC is under a duty to furnish to the APCM the financial statements of the PCC.[136] It also enjoys:

(a) a right to be consulted under the Pastoral Measure 1983 in relation to a proposed pastoral scheme affecting the parish;[137]
(b) a right to object to the sale or pulling down of a residence belonging to the benefice or the erection of a new one;[138]
(c) a right to be heard on certain issues arising during the vacancy in the benefice or the proposed transfer of the right to patronage;[139]
(d) a voice in decisions as to the forms of service to be used in the church;[140] the version of scripture to be used in prayer book services;[141] the appointment and dismissal of the organist;[142] and the vesture to be worn by a minister at divine service.[143]

---

[131] Ibid s 7(ii). Save for certain exceptional cases, compulsory church rates were abolished by the Compulsory Church Rate Abolition Act 1868.
[132] Parochial Church Councils (Powers) Measure 1956, s 7(iii). This is exercisable jointly with the minister. Canon E 3 deals with the appointment by the minister and PCC of a parish clerk, sexton, verger or other officer.
[133] Parochial Church Councils (Powers) Measure 1956, s 7(iv); Canon F 10. This power is also exercised jointly by the minister and the PCC; and the Canon provides for determination by the Ordinary of any disagreement between them.
[134] Parochial Church Councils (Powers) Measure 1956, s 7(v).
[135] Ibid s 9(1).
[136] Ibid s 8. See para 3.07ff above.
[137] The PCC is an 'interested person' by virtue of the Pastoral Measure 1983, s 3(2)(c).
[138] Parsonages Measure 1938, s 3(1), which gives the PCC the right to be notified of a proposed transaction and to voice its objections.
[139] Benefices (Transfer of Rights of Patronage) Measure 1930, ss 2, 4; Benefices (Exercise of Rights of Presentation) Measure 1931, ss 1–3. See Chapter 4.
[140] Church of England (Worship and Doctrine) Measure 1974, s 1(3); Canon B 3 paras 1, 2. See Chapter 5.
[141] Prayer Book (Versions of the Bible) Measure 1965, s 1 proviso.
[142] Canon B 20, discussed further in paras 3.65 and 3.66 below.
[143] Canon B 8 para 2. In the event of disagreement between the minister and the PCC, the minister must refer the matter to the bishop whose direction must be obeyed: Canon B 8 para 2 proviso.

The PCC must be a party to any church-sharing arrangement.[144] Its consent is necessary for the extension of the tenure of office of a minister beyond the normal retiring age of 70.[145] The requirements under Canons F 1 to F 13 relating, inter alia, to the provision of church requisites are to be discharged by the PCC.[146]

3.30 A power of the PCC of more recent origin relates to its collective view concerning the ordination of women to the priesthood. A PCC is entitled to pass either or both of two resolutions under the Priests (Ordination of Women) Measure 1993.[147] Resolution A is that the PCC would not accept a woman as the minister who presides at or celebrates the holy communion or pronounces absolution in the parish.[148] Resolution B is that the PCC would not accept a woman as the incumbent or priest-in-charge of the benefice or as team vicar for the benefice. The PCC is not required to decide whether to pass either resolution except when a vacancy in the benefice arises.[149] Neither resolution may be passed unless the PCC secretary has given to the members at least four weeks' notice of the time and place of the meeting at which the matter is to be considered and the meeting is attended by at least half of the members of the PCC entitled to attend.[150] A copy of any resolution must be served on the bishop and other named persons.[151] Any resolution remains in force until it is rescinded.[152]

3.31 Where either resolution is in force, the PCC may petition the bishop requesting that appropriate episcopal duties in the parish should be carried out in accordance with the Episcopal Ministry Act of Synod 1993.[153] Upon receipt of the petition, the diocesan bishop is required to consult with the minister and the PCC and,

---

[144] Sharing of Church Buildings Act 1969, s 1(3)(a). See paras 3.95ff below.
[145] Ecclesiastical Offices (Age Limit) Measure 1975, s 3(2).
[146] Canon F 14. These provisions relate to the font, altar, communion plate, communion linen, minister's surplices, reading desks and pulpit, seats in church, bells, Bible, *Book of Common Prayer*, alms box, register books for baptisms, confirmations, banns, marriages and burials, a register book of services and the care and repair of churches and chapels.
[147] See the Priests (Ordination of Women) Measure 1993, s 3(1), Sch 1.
[148] This may not be considered by a PCC if the incumbent, priest-in-charge, team vicar or assistant curate in the benefice is a woman: ibid s 3(3). It is questionable whether Resolution A is sufficient to oust the canonical right of a priest under Canon B 29 para 4 to exercise the ministry of absolution, without the permission of the minister having the cure of souls, in respect of any person who is in danger of death or if there is some urgent or weighty cause.
[149] Patronage (Benefices) Measure 1986, s 11(1)(f) (added by the Priests (Ordination of Women) Measure 1993, s 3(7)). The matter is now an additional requirement of the statutory meeting of the PCC whenever there is a vacancy.
[150] Ibid s 3(4).
[151] Ibid s 3(5). The other persons are the rural dean, lay chairman of deanery synod, diocesan registrar, designated officer of the diocese, and registered patron.
[152] Ibid s 3(2). The same notice and attendance provisions apply to a meeting of the PCC convened to consider a resolution to rescind: ibid s 3(4).
[153] Episcopal Ministry Act of Synod 1993, para 7. This is commonly styled 'resolution C'.

having done so, to make appropriate arrangements.[154] The bishop is not obliged to make such arrangements unless he is satisfied that the notice and attendance provisions were complied with, that at least two-thirds of the PCC present and voting were in favour of the resolution in question and that the minister was in favour of the resolution, whether or not he was present and voted.[155] Subject to the requirements of the Act of Synod, a petition may be withdrawn at any time and, in any event, the workings of any arrangements must be reviewed at least once every five years.[156]

Churchwardens

3.32 The present role of the churchwarden is very different from that of bygone years, when he was actively involved in local administration, largely of a secular nature. It is no longer the legal duty of any eligible householder to serve as churchwarden if appointed. The Churchwardens Measure 2001 came into force on 1 January 2002.[157]

Qualifications

3.33 Churchwardens are chosen from persons who have been baptised and:

(a) whose names are on the electoral roll;
(b) who are actual communicants;
(c) who are aged at least 21;
(d) who are not disqualified.[158]

Where a person is not qualified under (a), (b) or (c), the bishop may permit that person to hold office, if it appears to the bishop that there are exceptional circumstances which justify a departure from the requirements.[159]

3.34 Disqualification arises in a number of instances: first, 'general disqualifications' arising from:

(a) a disqualification from being a charity trustee under section 72(1) of the Charities Act 1993;

---

154 Ibid, para 8(1). Such arrangements provide for episcopal duties to be carried out by a bishop other than the diocesan bishop, namely a diocesan bishop of another diocese, a suffragan or assistant bishop in the relevant region or a provincial episcopal visitor ('flying bishop') appointed by the archbishop.
155 Ibid, para 10.
156 Ibid para 9.
157 It repealed in its entirety the Churchwardens (Appointment and Resignation) Measure 1964: Churchwardens Measure 2001, s 15(2), Sch 3.
158 Churchwardens Measure 2001, s 1(3)(a)–(d).
159 Ibid s 1(4).

(b) a conviction of an offence mentioned in Schedule 1 to the Children and Young Persons Act 1933; and

(c) disqualification from being chosen for the office of churchwarden under section 10(6) of the Incumbents (Vacation of Benefices) Measure 1977.[160]

Secondly, there is a disqualification once an individual has served six successive periods of office as churchwarden.[161] It is, however, open to a meeting of the parishioners to pass a resolution that the six-year maximum is not to apply in the parish.[162] No account is taken of any period of office prior to the Churchwardens Measure 2001 coming into force.[163]

Choosing churchwardens

3.35 There are to be two churchwardens for each parish.[164] A person may not be chosen unless he has signified his consent to serve and not signified consent to serve for the same period in another parish.[165] The churchwardens are chosen annually, not later than 30 April each year,[166] by a meeting of the parishioners.[167] Candidates must be nominated and seconded in writing by persons entitled to attend the meeting, and each nomination paper must include a statement, signed by the person nominated, that he is willing to serve as a churchwarden and is not disqualified under one of the three general disqualifications.[168] The nomination paper is only valid if received by the minister of the parish before the commencement of the meeting.[169]

---

[160] Churchwardens Measure 2001, s 2(1)–(3).
[161] Ibid s 3. The disqualification lasts for two years before such a person may be chosen again.
[162] Ibid s 3 proviso. Any resolution may be revoked by a subsequent meeting of parishioners.
[163] Ibid s 14, Sch 1 para 1.
[164] Ibid s 1(1). As to existing customs, see para 3.44 below. Where by a pastoral scheme or otherwise a parish has more than one parish church, each is to have two churchwardens: ibid s 1(2)(a). A parish centre of worship (designated under Pastoral Measure 1983, s 29(2)) is deemed to be a parish church: Churchwardens Measure 2001, s 1(2)(b).
[165] Ibid s 1(5). This need not be in writing, but see ibid s 4(3), discussed below. Exceptions exist in the case of related parishes and where the election in the other parish has already taken place and the person concerned was not elected.
[166] Ibid s 4(1).
[167] Ibid s 4(2). The composition of this meeting is discussed in para 3.37 below. The meeting is convened by the minister (or the churchwardens during a vacancy) signing a notice (r 5(2)) stating the place, date and hour when it is to be held (r 5(3)); to be affixed on or near the principal door of the parish church for a period including the last two Sundays before the meeting (r 5(4)).
[168] Ibid s 4(3). The overlap between this and the provisions of ibid s 1(5) is a little unfortunate. Equally, it is curious that no provision is made for disqualification based upon six continuous years in office. It is perhaps assumed that the parish will have constructive notice of this.
[169] Ibid s 4(4)(a). Where the bishop's dispensation is required under ibid s 1(4) (see para 3.33 above), such permission must be given before the nomination paper is received: ibid s 4(4)(b). During a period when there is no minister the paper is to be received by the churchwarden who signed the notice convening the meeting: ibid s 4(6)(a).

3.36 If the minister considers that the election of any particular person nominated might give rise to serious difficulties between the minister and that person in the carrying out of their respective functions, the minister may, before the election is conducted, make a statement to the effect that only one churchwarden is to be elected by the meeting of the parishioners.[170] If such a statement is made, one churchwarden is appointed by the minister from among the persons nominated, and the other is elected by the meeting.[171]

3.37 The meeting of parishioners is deemed to be a joint meeting of those whose names are on the electoral roll of the parish and those resident in the parish whose names are on the local government register of electors.[172] It is convened by the minister or, when there is no minister or when the minister is unable or unwilling to do so, by the churchwardens.[173] A notice, signed by the minister or a churchwarden, must be affixed on or near to the principal door of the parish church and every other building licensed for public worship in the parish for a period including the last two Sundays before the meeting.[174] It must state the place, date and time at which the meeting will be held.[175]

3.38 The minister or, if he is not present, a chairman chosen by the meeting presides,[176] and a person appointed by the meeting acts as clerk and records the minutes.[177] The meeting has power to adjourn and to determine its own rules of procedure.[178] In the case of an equal division of votes on any question (other than the election of a churchwarden) the chairman does not have a casting vote and the motion is treated as lost.[179] The election of churchwardens, however, is carried out in accordance with rule 11 of the Church Representation Rules,[180] which provides that where there is an equality of votes, the decision between the persons for whom an equal number of votes have been cast is to be taken by lot.[181]

---

[170] Ibid s 4(5), which does not apply during any period when there is no minister: ibid s 4(6)(b).
[171] Ibid s 4(5). The name of the person appointed by the minister is required to be announced before the election is conducted.
[172] Ibid s 5(1). The common practice of convening this meeting immediately before the APCM will doubtless continue.
[173] Ibid s 5(2).
[174] Ibid s 5(4).
[175] Ibid s 5(3).
[176] Ibid s 5(5).
[177] Ibid s 5(8).
[178] Ibid s 5(7).
[179] Ibid s 5(6).
[180] See the Church Representation Rules, r 13(1); Churchwardens Measure 2001, s 15(1), Sch 2.
[181] Church Representation Rules, r 11(8)(a). The option to vary the method of election by scheme under r 12 would not appear to be available in the case of churchwardens.

3.39 A person may be chosen to fill a casual vacancy among the churchwardens at any time.[182] Such person is chosen in the same manner as the churchwarden whose place he is to fill.[183]

Admission and term of office

3.40 A person chosen by the meeting does not become churchwarden until admitted to office.[184] This takes place at a time and place appointed by the bishop annually, being no later than 31 July each year.[185] The person chosen appears before the bishop or his substitute (generally the archdeacon) and makes a declaration that he will faithfully and diligently perform the duties of his office[186] and that he is not disqualified under any of the three general disqualifications.[187]

3.41 The length of a churchwarden's term of office depends upon whether he is chosen again as churchwarden at the next meeting of parishioners. If he is so chosen and duly admitted to office before 31 July, his original term expires on the date of admission, but if he is not admitted before 31 July, his term expires on that date.[188] If, however, he is not chosen again at the next meeting, and (i) his successor is admitted to office prior to 31 July, his term ends on the date of his successor's admission, but if (ii) his successor is not so admitted, the term ends on 31 July.[189] Where a term of office expires without a successor having been admitted, a casual vacancy is deemed to have arisen.[190] A person chosen to fill a casual vacancy, however arising, is to be admitted within three months after he is chosen or before the date of the next annual meeting of parishioners, whichever be earlier.[191]

---

[182] Churchwardens Measure 2001, s 4(7).
[183] Ibid s 4(8), save that where the previous churchwarden was appointed by the minister and the minister has ceased to hold office, the replacement is to be elected by a meeting of the parishioners.
[184] Ibid s 6(1).
[185] Ibid s 6(1).
[186] This is a restatement of Canon E 1, para 2.
[187] Churchwardens Measure 2001, s 6(1). The three disqualifications are those under s 2(1)–(3), for which see para 3.34 above. Again, no provision is made for the declaration to deal with disqualification based upon six continuous years in office.
[188] Ibid s 6(2)(a).
[189] Ibid s 6(2)(b). If there is doubt as to which of the new churchwardens is an individual's successor, the bishop may designate one for this purpose: s 6(2). This is a poorly worded sub-section. If the successor is not admitted by 31 July, then by virtue of s 6(1) he has not become a churchwarden and cannot therefore be designated by the bishop. The contrary deeming provision under s 8(2) is expressly limited to s 8. The sub-section can only be read qualifying new churchwardens with 'or persons chosen for the office of churchwarden', alternatively by restricting the final sentence to the application of paragraph (b)(i) alone.
[190] Ibid s 6(3).
[191] Ibid s 6(4).

Resignation and vacation of office

3.42 A person may resign the office of churchwarden by written notice of intention to resign served on the bishop by post.[192] Resignation is effective at the end of two months following service of the notice or on such earlier date as may be determined by the bishop after consultation with the minister and any other churchwarden of the parish.[193]

3.43 The office of churchwarden is vacated if:

(a) the churchwarden's name is removed from the electoral roll under rule 1 of the Church Representation Rules;[194] or
(b) his name is not on a new roll prepared under rule 2(4); or
(c) he becomes disqualified under one of the three general disqualifications.[195]

For the purposes of this provision, a person who has been chosen but not admitted to office is deemed to be a churchwarden.[196]

Custom

3.44 The Churchwardens Measure 2001 does not affect local Acts or schemes which make contrary provision affecting churchwardens,[197] nor does it affect any existing custom which regulates the number of churchwardens or the manner in which they are chosen.[198] However, where prior to 1 January 1965[199] a custom existed for any churchwardens to be chosen by the vestry jointly with any other person or persons, the meeting of parishioners is substituted for the vestry.[200] The provisions of the Measure do not apply to Guild Churches save that all churchwardens must now be actual communicant members of the Church of England unless the bishop permits otherwise.[201]

---

[192] Ibid s 7(1), (2).
[193] Ibid s 7(3).
[194] The grounds for removal from the roll include death, ordination, written request, non-residence, or wrongful inclusion. It does not include illness or other incapacity.
[195] Churchwardens Measure 2001, s 8(1)(a)–(c). The disqualifications are set out in s 2(1)–(3): see para 3.34 above.
[196] Ibid s 8(2).
[197] Ibid s 11(1).
[198] Ibid s 11(2). See also s 12 and para 3.45 below. An existing custom is one existing on the coming into force of the Measure which has continued for a period commencing before 1 January 1925: ibid s 13(1).
[199] This was the date upon which the Churchwardens (Appointment and Resignation) Measure 1964 came into force: ibid s 15(3).
[200] Churchwardens Measure 2001, s 11(2) proviso.
[201] Ibid s 9.

3.45 A meeting of parishioners may pass a resolution abolishing an existing custom which regulates the number of churchwardens or the manner in which they are chosen.[202] The resolution takes effect from the date of the next meeting of parishioners by which churchwardens are to be elected.[203] A custom which involves a person other than the minister in the choice of churchwardens may not be abolished without the written consent of that person.[204]

Episcopal powers

3.46 In carrying out the provisions of the Churchwardens Measure 2001, the bishop has power to make provision for any matter not provided for; to appoint a person to do any act in respect of which there has been neglect or default on the part of a person or body charged with any duty; to extend or alter certain time limits or modify procedure; to direct a fresh choice where there has been no valid choice; and to give directions for removing any difficulty which might have arisen.[205] He is not, however, empowered to validate anything which was invalid at the time it was done.[206]

Misconduct

3.47 Save for the compulsory vacation of office upon a churchwarden becoming disqualified,[207] there is no power to remove or suspend a churchwarden for misconduct.[208] It is doubtful whether the removal of a churchwarden could be effected by any alternative procedure, such as the exercise of visitatorial powers,[209] or by a resolution of an extraordinary meeting of parishioners.[210] If a churchwarden has been properly chosen *intra vires* the bishop or archdeacon cannot refuse to admit him to office, no matter what view he may take as to the person's suitability.[211]

---

[202] Ibid s 12(1).
[203] Ibid s 12(2).
[204] Ibid s 12(3).
[205] Ibid s 10(1)(a)–(e).
[206] Ibid s 10(2).
[207] Ibid s 8(1)(c), discussed in para 3.43 above. The procedure under the Incumbents (Vacation of Benefices) Measure 1977 is dealt with in Chapter 4.
[208] The jurisdiction of consistory courts to hear and determine proceedings against lay officers was abolished by the Ecclesiastical Jurisdiction Measure 1963, s 82(2)(c).
[209] A proposed power in an earlier draft of the Measure, which would have enabled the bishop to suspend a churchwarden, failed to find favour with the Ecclesiastical Committee of both Houses of Parliament, and was removed by the General Synod from the final version of Churchwardens Measure 2001 when it was duly submitted for approval by the Committee.
[210] See R Phillimore, *The Ecclesiastical Law of the Church of England* (2nd edn, London: Sweet & Maxwell, 1895) vol II 1489.
[211] *R v Bishop of Sarum* [1916] 1 KB 466. The case concerned the use by the churchwarden near the chancel steps of 'filthy and indecent language to the rector and in the presence of the rector's wife'.

In *R v Rice*[212] it was held that the Archdeacon of St Asaph had wrongly declined to admit a churchwarden duly elected by the parish. The objection was that he was 'a dairyman in poor circumstances'. However reasonable the objection, the bishop's task is ministerial and his view on the merits is irrelevant.[213]

Powers and duties

Many of the churchwarden's historic duties have devolved onto the PCC. These include the responsibility for the provision of requisites for divine service, such as books, linen, plate and furniture.[214] In law, churchwardens rank as quasi-corporations for holding the goods of the church in perpetuity.[215] They are *ex officio* members of the PCC,[216] and their membership thereof runs from the date of their election or appointment and not that of their admission to office.[217] **3.48**

The responsibilities of churchwardens are set out in Canon E 1. They are required to discharge such duties as are by law and by custom assigned to them, to be foremost in representing the laity and in co-operating with the incumbent, and to maintain order and decency in the church and churchyard, especially during the time of divine service.[218] In addition to these practical and bureaucratic tasks, it is often forgotten that churchwardens are charged with active participation in the Church's mission since, in the words of the canon, 'they shall use their best endeavours by example and precept to encourage the parishioners in the practice of true religion and to promote unity and peace among them'.[219] The Ordinary may make inquiries of them at any time, and the churchwardens may inform the Ordinary of any matters in their parish requiring his intervention.[220] In addition, **3.49**

---

212 *R v Rice* (1697) 1 Ld Raym 138.
213 He may, however, seek to mitigate the effects of an indolent or defaulting churchwarden by invoking the powers discussed at 3.46 above.
214 See Canons F 1–F 14.
215 See *Blackstone's Commentaries on the Laws of England* (14th edn, 1803) 394. Churchwardens must sue and be sued in their individual names and not in any corporate capacity. As to the passing of church property to a successor, see Canon E 1 para 5.
216 Church Representation Rules, r 14(1)(d), if they are actual communicants whose names are on the church electoral roll. Only if the bishop had dispensed with either or both of these requirements under the Churchwardens Measure 2001, s 1(4), would a churchwarden not automatically be a member of the PCC.
217 Church Representation Rules, r 14(2). A churchwarden remains a member of the PCC until he ceases to be qualified: ibid r 14(2). It follows that there will be a period when both incoming and outgoing churchwardens are members of the PCC.
218 Canon E 1 para 4. They are also empowered to institute a complaint against a priest or deacon in the parish: Clergy Discipline Measure 2003, s 10(1)(a)(ii).
219 Canon E 1 para 4.
220 *Legal Opinions* 126–127.

Chapter 3: The Parish

they must reply to the archdeacon's articles of inquiry for the purposes of his annual visitation.[221]

3.50 As officers of the Ordinary, and subject to his direction, the churchwardens must allocate seats among parishioners and others in such manner as the service of God may be best celebrated, subject to such rights to seats as may have been conferred by faculty, prescription or statutory authority and to the minister's right to allocate seats within the chancel.[222] Churchwardens may not prevent a parishioner from entering for want of space, nor may they prevent a parishioner from standing if there be insufficient seats, so long as there is no interference with the conduct of the service. They may remove a person in a seat allocated for someone else, provided it may be done without unnecessary force and without causing public scandal or disturbing divine service.[223]

3.51 In maintaining order and decency in the church and churchyard, churchwardens may be assisted by sidesmen.[224] They must not allow the occurrence of secular meetings inconsistent with the sanctity of the place,[225] nor the bells to be rung at any time contrary to the minister's direction.[226] In addition, they must prevent any person behaving in the church, porch or churchyard during divine service so as to create a disturbance and must take care that nothing is done there contrary to church or civil law.[227]

3.52 If any person is guilty of riotous, violent or indecent behaviour in any church, chapel or churchyard (whether or not during a service) or of disturbing, vexing,

---

[221] Canon G 6.

[222] Canon F 7 para 2. There is a mandatory requirement for seats to be provided for the use of parishioners and others who attend divine service: Canon F 7 para 1. In *R v Bishop of Bristol, ex parte Williamson*, 25 March 1994 (unreported, CO/764/94), objection was taken that the applicant had been told that admission to a service at the cathedral to be held on 12 March 1994 for the ordination of women to the priesthood was by ticket only. This was rejected by MacPherson J on the basis that there was no evidence that the applicant had sought and been refused admission and, in any event, he had known that the event was to have been ticket-only sufficiently far in advance to have obtained pre-emptive relief from the court, but he declined to do so. See *Legal Opinions* 305.

[223] The jurisdiction of the consistory court in suits of perturbation of seats has been abolished: Ecclesiastical Jurisdiction Measure 1963, s 82(2)(c).

[224] Canons E 2 para 3, and F 15 para 1.

[225] Canon F 15 para 1.

[226] Canon F 15 para 1. See also Canon F 8 para 2. Whether the ringing of church bells may amount to a public nuisance under the Environmental Protection Act 1990 or at common law has provoked a degree of academic discussion. See RH Bloor, 'Clocks, Bells and Cockerells' (1995) 3 Ecc LJ 393; T Watkin, 'A Happy Noise to Hear? Church Bells and the Law of Nuisance' (1996) 4 Ecc LJ 545; and S Thomas and T Watkin, 'Oh Noisy Bells Be Dumb' (1995) JPL 1097. See also *Calvert v Gardiner and others* [2002] EWHC 1394 (QB), Burton J. For a consideration of the interplay between freedom of religion and statutory nuisance in the context of worship in a synagogue, see the decision of the Divisional Court in *R (on the application of London Borough of Hackney) v Rottenberg* [2007] EWHC 166 (Admin).

[227] Canon F 15 para 2. See also P Barber, 'Outrageous Behaviour' (1996) 4 Ecc LJ 584.

troubling or misusing any minister officiating there, the churchwardens or their assistants must take care to restrain the offender and, if necessary, proceed against him according to law.[228] A delicate balance needs to be maintained now that the right to freedom of expression under the European Convention on Human Rights has a place in English domestic law.[229] A churchwarden cannot interfere with the conduct of a service by the minister on the ground of any impropriety in its performance unless the minister's behaviour is riotous, violent or indecent, in which case the powers outlined above would apply. The proper course is to raise the matter with the Ordinary.[230]

3.53 The churchwardens must, with the advice and direction of the minister, provide sufficient bread and wine for holy communion.[231] The plate, ornaments and other movable goods of the church are in the legal ownership of the churchwardens as a quasi-corporation.[232]

3.54 The churchwardens must, in consultation with the minister, compile and maintain a full terrier of all lands, and an inventory of all articles appertaining to their church or churches; and must insert in a log book a note of all works of alterations, additions, repairs to, and other events affecting the church, lands and articles.[233] A copy of the inventory must be sent to such person as the bishop may designate.[234] The churchwardens must inspect (or cause an inspection to be made of) the fabric of the church and all articles appertaining to the church at least once

---

[228] Canon F 15 para 3. See also the Ecclesiastical Courts Jurisdiction Act 1860, which creates an offence of riotous, violent or indecent behaviour in a place of worship (whether during a service or not) (ibid s 2), and gives to churchwardens a power of arrest (ibid s 3, amended by the Police and Criminal Evidence Act 1984, ss 26(1), 119(2), Sch 7 Pt I). It was under these provisions that Peter Tatchell was arrested, charged and convicted for disrupting a sermon delivered by the Archbishop of Canterbury at a service of Holy Communion in Canterbury Cathedral on Easter Day 1998.

[229] Human Rights Act 1998, s 1(3), Sch 1 Art 10. Note the inter-relationship with freedom of thought, conscience and religion in Art 9, the importance of the exercise of which by any religious organization must be given particular regard by the courts: Human Rights Act 1998, s 13(1).

[230] See *Hutchins v Denziloe and Loveland* (1792) 1 Hag Con 170.

[231] Canon B 17 para 1. The cost of the elements falls on the PCC: Canon F 14.

[232] Canon E 1 para 5. Both the goods and an inventory duly maintained are to be passed on to their successors: Canon E 1 para 5.

[233] Care of Churches and Ecclesiastical Jurisdiction Measure 1991, s 4(1)(a), (b), (2). In so doing they act in consultation with the recommendations of the Council for the Care of Churches as to the form of the terrier, inventory and log book: ibid s 4(3). The log book must include a note of the location of the relevant documents: ibid s 4(1)(b). Canon E 1 para 5 also deals with the keeping of an inventory. Note also the duty under Canon F 13 para 4 to keep a record of all alterations, additions, removals or repairs. It is not specified upon whom this duty falls although the context suggests it is the churchwardens.

[234] Care of Churches and Ecclesiastical Jurisdiction Measure 1991, s 4(4). The designated person must be informed of any alterations at such intervals as the bishop may direct from time to time: ibid s 4(4).

a year.[235] As soon as practicable at the beginning of each calendar year, the churchwardens must produce to the PCC the terrier, inventory, and the log book relating to events occurring in the previous year, together with such other records as they consider likely to assist the PCC in discharging its functions in relation to the fabric of the church and articles appertaining to it.[236] The terrier, inventory and log book so produced must be accompanied by a statement signed by the churchwardens to the effect that the contents thereof are accurate.[237] The churchwardens must deliver the Annual Fabric Report to the PCC at its meeting next before the APCM and, with such amendments as the PCC may make, to the ensuing APCM.[238]

3.55 It is the duty of the churchwardens to obtain a faculty if any alterations, additions, removals or repairs are proposed to be made in the fabric, ornaments or furniture of the church.[239] Care, maintenance and insurance is, however, a matter for the PCC, and contracts relating to such matters ought to be made by and in the name of the PCC rather than the churchwardens or, indeed, the incumbent. Although the freehold of the church is vested in the incumbent, who is the custodian of the keys of the church, the churchwardens have the right of free access to the church for the performance of their duties.[240]

3.56 During a vacancy in the benefice, the churchwardens and the rural dean automatically become the sequestrators of the benefice.[241] The income receivable by the sequestrators is now generally confined to marriage, burial and other fees.[242] The churchwardens have the custody of the church register books during a vacancy in the benefice.[243]

Deputy churchwardens

3.57 Where a parish has two or more churches or places of worship, the APCM may make a scheme providing for the election of a district church council for the district

---

[235] Ibid s 5(1). This is in addition to the quinquennial inspection by the parish architect pursuant to a scheme made under the Inspection of Churches Measure 1955, s 1. The Annual Fabric Report is discussed at n 34 above.
[236] Care of Churches and Ecclesiastical Jurisdiction Measure 1991, s 5(4).
[237] Ibid s 5(5).
[238] Ibid s 5(3). See para 3.08 above.
[239] Canon F 13 para 3. There is a like duty on the minister.
[240] See *Moysey v Hillcoat* (1828) 2 Hag Ecc 30, Ct of Arches.
[241] Church of England (Miscellaneous Provisions) Measure 1992, s 1(1). One additional person may be appointed by the bishop if he considers it desirable: ibid s 1(1). A writ of sequestration is no longer necessary.
[242] See generally the Ecclesiastical Fees Measure 1986 and annual Parochial Fees Orders made thereunder.
[243] Parochial Registers and Records Measure 1978, s 6(2).

in the parish in which one such church or place of worship is situated.[244] The scheme may provide for the election or choice of one or two deputy churchwardens and the delegation to them of such functions of the churchwardens relating to any church or place as the scheme may specify, and the churchwardens may, subject to the scheme, delegate to them such of their functions as they think fit.[245] The scheme may also provide for the deputy churchwardens to be *ex officio* members of the PCC.[246]

Alternatively, a pastoral scheme may establish a team ministry for a parish in which there are two or more churches or places of worship. The scheme may similarly make provision for the election or choice of one or two deputy churchwardens for such church or place of worship and for the functions of the churchwardens to be delegated to such deputy churchwardens.[247] **3.58**

Other lay officers

In addition to the individual and collective contributions of churchwardens and PCCs, the Church of England is served by the laity in a variety of different ways. Some are salaried but the majority are not. This depends upon the nature and extent of their responsibilities and the resources of each parish. **3.59**

Sidesmen

Sidesmen are appointed by the APCM or, if the need arises between APCMs, by the PCC.[248] Any number may be appointed, so long as each is on the electoral roll of the parish.[249] The mandatory language of rule 9(5) of the Church Representation Rules indicates that there is a legal obligation to appoint sidesmen, but the manner of their appointment is not specified. A sidesman's duty is to promote the cause of true religion in the parish and to assist the churchwardens in the discharge of their duties in maintaining order and decency in the church and churchyard, especially during the time of divine service.[250] **3.60**

---

[244] Church Representation Rules, r 18(1)(b).
[245] Ibid r 18(4). The Churchwardens Measure 2001 is silent as to the method of choice or election of deputy churchwardens, nor does it extend the disqualification provisions to apply to them.
[246] Church Representation Rules, r 18(4).
[247] Pastoral Measure 1983, s 40, Sch 3 para 4(2)(d).
[248] Church Representation Rules, r 9(5)(c); Canon E 2 para 1.
[249] Church Representation Rules, r 10(2); Canon E 2 para 2.
[250] Canon E 2 para 3.

Parish clerks and sextons

3.61 Parish clerks[251] and sextons are to be appointed by the PCC and the incumbent acting jointly, who must determine their salaries and the conditions of their employment.[252] An appointee must be a 'fit and proper person' who must perform such services upon such terms and conditions as the PCC and the incumbent may think fit.[253] It is good practice to ensure that a written contract of employment is drawn up, terminable on notice by either party. It is also prudent to take out a proper policy of insurance to indemnify the PCC against any claims brought relating to accidents arising in the course of his employment.

3.62 Canon E 3 includes a reference to a verger or other officer and it would seem that similar provisions to those listed above would apply to these and to cleaners and other paid or voluntary staff. All such persons, if remunerated, are employees who enjoy certain rights justiciable in the employment tribunal.[254] In *Ivory v Dean and Chapter of St Paul's Cathedral*,[255] the tribunal determined that the applicant, a virger at St Paul's Cathedral, had been unfairly dismissed but her complaint of sex discrimination was dismissed. The respondent cathedral failed to undertake any consultation in relation to the reorganization of its staffing and there were no objective criteria used to select the applicant for redundancy. She was found to have been constructively dismissed.

Treasurers

3.63 Since the giving of alms and their collection is an integral part of many services, and since by the nature of the diocesan structure a heavy financial responsibility falls on each parish to contribute towards the work of the Church nationally as well as meeting its own immediate requirements, every PCC should appoint one or more of its members as treasurer through whom proper stewardship of the church's resources can be exercised.[256] In the absence of the appointment of a treasurer, the functions of the office are to be performed by such of the

---

[251] If a person in holy orders is appointed parish clerk, he is licensed by the bishop in the same manner as a stipendiary curate and treated in like fashion: Lecturers and Parish Clerks Act 1844, ss 2, 4.

[252] Parochial Church Councils (Powers) Measure 1956, s 7(iii); Canon E 3. In the event of the PCC and the incumbent being unable to agree, the matter shall be dealt with or determined in such manner as the bishop may direct: Parochial Church Council (Powers) Measure 1956, s 9(3).

[253] Canon E 3.

[254] This was formerly styled the industrial tribunal.

[255] *Ivory v Dean and Chapter of St Paul's Cathedral*, 6 November 1995 (unreported), Stratford Industrial Tribunal (10316/93/S).

[256] Church Representation Rules, r 15, App II para 1(e)(i).

churchwardens as are members of the PCC or by some other fit person.[257] In addition, the APCM must appoint an independent examiner or auditor for a term of office ending at the next meeting.[258]

PCC secretaries

3.64 The PCC must appoint one of its number to act as secretary, failing which the office of secretary must be discharged by some other fit person who does not become a member of the PCC unless co-opted.[259] Where a person other than a member of the PCC is appointed to act as secretary, that person may be paid such remuneration as the PCC deems appropriate.[260] The secretary has charge of all documents, save the church electoral roll, is responsible for keeping the minutes and recording all resolutions passed by the PCC and must keep the secretary of the deanery and diocesan synods informed as to his name and address.[261]

Organists

3.65 The appointment of an organist, choirmaster or director of music and the termination of such employment is exercisable by the minister with the agreement of the PCC.[262] The archdeacon may direct that the agreement of the PCC be dispensed with in the case of termination of employment if he considers the circumstances so require.[263] The much publicized dismissal of the organist of Westminster Abbey has important lessons for organists and their employers.[264] The lack of openness by the organist in financial matters and the deriving of secret profits were, in the words of Lord Jauncey of Tullichettle, 'such as fatally undermined the relationship of trust and confidence which should have subsisted between [the organist] and the abbey'.[265] He had previously held that 'the character of the institutional employer, the role played by the employee in that institution and the degree of trust required of the employee vis-à-vis the employer must all

---

[257] Ibid App II para 1(e)(i), which provides that such other person does not thereby become a member of the PCC, though he may be co-opted. A person (other than a PCC member) who is appointed treasurer may be paid such remuneration as the PCC deems appropriate, but he is then ineligible to be a PCC member: App II para 1(e)(ii).
[258] Ibid r 9(5)(d).
[259] Ibid App II para 1(d)(i).
[260] Ibid App II para 1(d)(ii). A secretary in receipt of remuneration is ineligible to be a member of the PCC.
[261] Ibid App II para 1(d)(iii).
[262] Canon B 20 para 1.
[263] Canon B 20 para 1.
[264] See *Neary v Dean of Westminster* (1998) 5 Ecc LJ 303.
[265] Transcript at 50.

be considered in determining the extent of the duty and the seriousness of any breach thereof'.[266]

3.66 As with the other offices, it is generally prudent to have a written agreement drawn up and signed. Such contract should incorporate by reference the provisions of Canon B 20, which places upon the minister the duty to ensure that only such chants, hymns, anthems and other settings are chosen as are appropriate to the solemn act of worship and prayer in the house of God.[267] However, the minister must pay heed to the advice and assistance of the organist or choirmaster in the choosing of chants, hymns, anthems and other settings and in the ordering of the music of the church.[268] The final responsibility and decision in these matters rests with the minister.[269] However, if the incumbent arbitrarily forbids his playing, the organist may appeal to the Ordinary.[270]

Readers

3.67 Readers fall into a different category from other lay officers, since they are not elected or employed but admitted and licensed by the bishop to perform ministry in the church.[271] A candidate for the office of reader in a parish is nominated to the bishop by the minister of that parish or by the rural dean or archdeacon if he is to serve in a wider area.[272] It is for the nominator (usually the minister of the parish) to satisfy the bishop that the candidate is of good life, sound in faith, a regular communicant and well fitted for the work of reader.[273] The candidate may not be admitted except it be found on examination by the bishop (or a competent person appointed by him) that he possesses a sufficient knowledge of Holy Scripture and of the doctrine and worship of the Church of England, that he is

---

[266] Transcript at 11.
[267] See generally *Legal Opinions* 106–109 and the model agreements drawn up by the Royal School of Church Music, one a contract of employment and the other a contract for services.
[268] Canon B 20 para 3.
[269] Whether 'minister' in this regard means the incumbent or the minister taking any particular service is not clear. Compare, eg, Canon B 35 para 5, which provides 'When matrimony is to be solemnised in any church, it belongs to the minister of the parish to decide what music shall be played [and] what hymns or anthems shall be sung … for the occasion'. See also HW Cripps, *A Practical Treatise on the Law Relating to Church and Clergy* (8th edn, London: Sweet and Maxwell, 1937) 514, which refers to the 'officiating minister'.
[270] See *Wyndham v Cole* (1875) 1 PD 130, per Sir Robert Phillimore. Pending a determination by the Ordinary, the organist must obey the minister's direction. Cf R Bursell, *Liturgy, Order and the Law* (Oxford: Clarendon Press, 1996) 80.
[271] See generally the *Bishops' Regulations for Reader Ministry* (Advisory Board of Ministry Policy Paper No 2, 1991). Many dioceses supplement these regulations with diocesan guidance or practice. Admission and licensing follows rigorous selection and training.
[272] Canon E 5 para 1.
[273] Canon E 5 para 2.

Other lay officers

able to read the services of the Church plainly, distinctly, audibly and reverently, and that he is capable both of teaching and preaching.[274]

3.68 The reader is admitted to the office by the bishop[275] and licensed by him to perform any duties which may be performed by a reader under Canon E 4 para 2, or as may be determined by Act of Synod.[276] The bishop of each diocese must keep a register book of all persons he has admitted as reader or licensed to exercise that office in any place.[277] Should a reader move to another diocese, admission to the office is not repeated.[278] A reader who is licensed to a parish and on its electoral roll may be a member of the PCC if the APCM so determines.[279] The Bishops' Regulations exhort the execution of a written agreement between the minister and the reader setting out the reader's duties, rights and obligations and the submission of an annual report to the Warden of Readers or an appointed delegate, at which time conditions of service ought also to be reviewed.[280]

3.69 A reader's licence may be revoked summarily by notice in writing at any time for any cause which appears to the bishop to be good and reasonable, after having given the reader sufficient opportunity of showing cause to the contrary.[281] The notice must include a statement that the reader may within twenty-eight days appeal to the archbishop of the province.[282] It would appear that legal aid is not generally available to readers in this process.[283]

3.70 A reader may visit the sick, read and pray with them, teach in Sunday school or elsewhere and undertake such pastoral and educational work and give such assistance to the minister as the bishop may direct.[284] He may read morning and

---

[274] Canon E 5 para 3.

[275] Admission takes the form of the delivery of the New Testament, but there is no imposition of hands: Canon E 5 para 5. At the time of admission, a reader is obliged to make the declaration set out in Canon E 5 para 4 in the presence of the bishop or his commissary. A certificate of admission is given to the newly admitted reader: Canon E 5 para 6.

[276] Canon E 4 para 1. An admitted reader may not exercise his office until he has been licensed save on a temporary basis with the written permission of the bishop: Canon E 6 para 1. The form of licensing is set out in Canon E 6 para 2.

[277] Canon E 4 para 3.

[278] Canon E 5 para 6. Licensing takes place in the ordinary way.

[279] Church Representation Rules, r 14(1)(e). This is in contrast with lay workers and deaconesses who are automatically members: ibid r 14(1)(b).

[280] *Bishops' Regulations for Reader Ministry* para 5:1–3. Diocesan norms generally provide for these matters.

[281] Canon E 6 para 3.

[282] Canon E 6 para 3. The archbishop may hear the appeal himself or appoint a diocesan or suffragan bishop to do so in his place. The archbishop may confirm, vary or cancel the revocation of the licence as he considers just and proper. There is no appeal from the decision of the archbishop although it may be amenable to judicial review.

[283] The Church of England (Legal Aid) Measure 1994, s 2(1), Sch 1 para 5, refers to the revocation of a licence granted to a 'minister, deaconess, lay worker or *stipendiary* reader' (emphasis added).

[284] Canon E 4 para 2(a).

evening prayer (save for the absolution), publish banns of marriage, read the word of God, preach, catechize children and receive and present the offerings of the people.[285] He may also distribute the holy sacrament to the people.[286] He may bury the dead or read the burial service before, at or after a cremation, but only with the goodwill of the person responsible and at the invitation of the minister.[287] Readers who are voluntary and unpaid should not accept a fee for their services.[288]

Deaconesses

3.71 The order of deaconesses was, at one time, the only order of ministry in the Church of England to which women were admitted by prayer and the laying on of hands.[289] However, it ceased to be possible to admit women to the order of deaconess on 16 February 1987 when the Deacons (Ordination of Women) Measure 1986 came into force.[290] Since women may now be admitted to the orders of deacon and priest (which are discussed in Chapter 4), further discussion of the order of deaconesses is unnecessary.[291]

Lay workers

3.72 Canons E 7 and E 8 deal with lay workers.[292] It should be remembered, however, that the admission of certain persons as lay workers does not obviate the responsibility which rests on others of the laity as a whole to support the mission of the Church.[293] The canons are largely self-explanatory. To be admitted as a lay worker, a man or woman must satisfy the bishop that he or she is baptised,

---

[285] Canon E 4 para 2(b). As to when lay persons may read banns, see the Marriage Age 1949, s 9.
[286] Canon E 4 para 2(c).
[287] Canon E 4 para 3.
[288] *Bishops' Regulations for Reader Ministry* para 6. Whilst almost all readers are voluntary and not salaried, there is provision for stipendiary appointments to be made, in which case prior to any licensing the bishop must satisfy himself that adequate provision has been made for the reader's stipend, for his insurance against sickness or accident and for a pension: Canon E 6, para 4. It would appear that there is no legal obstacle to stipendiary readers being regarded as employees, although there may be ambiguity as to the identity of the employer: see *Barthorpe v Exeter Diocesan Board of Finance* [1979] ICR 900, EAT, remitted to the industrial tribunal but settled before the hearing without the issue being determined.
[289] Canon D 1. Any deaconess licensed to a parish is a member of the PCC: Church Representation Rules, r 14(1)(b).
[290] Canon D 2 para 2A; Deacons (Ordination of Women) Measure 1986, s 2(1). A person accepted for training prior to that date remained entitled to be admitted.
[291] Provisions relating to their admission, licensing and functions are fully set out in Canons D 1–D 3 and the Deaconesses and Lay Ministry Measure 1972, s 1.
[292] The canons were promulged pursuant to the Deaconesses and Lay Ministry Measure 1972, s 1.
[293] Note particularly the duties imposed upon churchwardens and the PCC as discussed above.

confirmed and a regular communicant of the Church of England; has had the proper training; and possesses the other necessary qualifications.[294]

In the place where he is licensed to serve and under the discretion of the minister, a lay worker may lead the people in public worship, exercise pastoral care, evangelize,[295] instruct the people in the Christian faith and prepare them for the reception of the sacraments.[296] He may also say morning and evening prayer (save for the absolution), distribute the holy sacrament of the Lord's Supper and read the epistle and the gospel.[297] At the invitation of the minister, the bishop may authorize a lay worker to preach; to church women; with the goodwill of the person responsible to bury the dead or read the burial service before, at or after a cremation; and to publish banns of marriage.[298] **3.73**

The procedure for the admission and licensing of lay workers and for the revocation of such licences is set out in Canon E 8.[299] It broadly mirrors the provision for readers, including the maintaining of a register and the provision, where appropriate, of stipends and pensions. No declaration as to conduct is made by the lay worker.[300] Any lay worker licensed to a parish is a member of the PCC.[301] **3.74**

Religious communities

Members of religious communities, unless they be in orders, are not subject to ecclesiastical jurisdiction save that of the Ordinary of the order.[302] A bishop may admit into holy orders any person living under vows in the house of any religious order or community which is within his diocese.[303] Members of religious communities comprise a separate constituency for representation at General Synod.[304] **3.75**

---

[294] Canon E 7 para 1(a), (b) and (c) respectively. No definition is given in the canon of the terms 'proper training' or 'other necessary qualifications', leaving it therefore to episcopal discretion at diocesan level.

[295] A person admitted to the office of evangelist is thereby admitted as a lay worker of the church: Canon E 7 para 2.

[296] Canon E 7 para 3.

[297] Canon E 7 para 4.

[298] Canon E 7 para 5(a)–(d). As to the latter, see the Marriage Act 1949, s 9.

[299] For a consideration of the revocation of a licence on notice see *R (on the application of Gibbs) v Bishop of Manchester* [2007] All ER (D) 256, [2007] EWHC 480, Admin Ct, Munby J.

[300] Compare this with the declaration required of a reader by Canon E 6 para 2.

[301] Church Representation Rules, r 14(1)(b).

[302] See generally *A Directory of Religious Life* (Church of England Advisory Council on the Relations of Bishops and Religious Communities).

[303] Canon C 5 para 2(e).

[304] One member from each province who is a priest or deacon sits in the House of Clergy and two lay members from the Province of Canterbury and one from that of York sit in the House of Laity. See Chapter 2.

Parochial property

3.76 Parochial property comprises land (including buildings) and movable goods or chattels. The former category is divided into consecrated land and unconsecrated land.[305] This raises concepts which are alien to the secular law of property and are discussed in Chapter 7. Theoretically, the freehold of the parish church and its churchyard vests in the incumbent. However, the nature of his interest in the land is curtailed by virtue of the faculty jurisdiction, which may prevent him dealing with it as he may wish and which may compel him to suffer third party interference contrary to his wishes. The latter may include the exercise of rights of way,[306] the reservation of grave spaces, or the erection of tombstones. Although the incumbent may be the legal owner of the churchyard, he does not own the tombstones or monuments therein, which vest in the persons who erected them during their lifetime and thereafter in the heir at law of the person in whose memory the monument was erected.[307]

3.77 However, the liabilities of the incumbent in respect of the church and churchyard are limited to reflect the emasculation of his rights of ownership. The responsibility for maintaining the church building and the churchyard falls upon the PCC to the extent that it has funds at its disposal to do so.[308]

Chancel repair

3.78 The personal liability of the rector for repairs to the chancel no longer exists,[309] although the obligations of a lay rector still subsist,[310] and are better known in consequence of recent much publicized litigation.[311] A Law Commission Report

---

[305] 'The effect of the consecration of land by a bishop has always been to give the land a sacred character': *Re Welford Road Cemetery* [2007] 2 WLR 506, Ct of Arches at para 9, per Cameron (Dean), Turner and Hill Chs, applying *Re St John, Chelsea* [1962] 1 WLR 706; [1962] 2 All ER 850, London Cons Ct; and *Re Blagdon Cemetery* [2002] Fam 299, [2002] 4 All ER 482, Ct of Arches.

[306] For a consideration of the dedication of a right of way in a churchyard, see *Re Westwell Bridleway* (FPS/U3100/7/19, 5 March 2005, unreported), being the decision of an inspector appointed by the Secretary of State for the Environment, particularly paras 11–14. Note para 109: 'Bearing in mind canon law, I agree it could be inappropriate for a bridleway to cross consecrated ground. However, that would not, by itself, necessarily prevent the possibility of dedication'.

[307] Faculty Jurisdiction Measure 1964, s 3(4).

[308] *Northwaite v Bennett* (1834) 2 Cr & M 316; *Millar and Simes v Palmer and Killby* (1837) 1 Curt 540.

[309] Ecclesiastical Dilapidations Measure 1923, s 52.

[310] Chancel Repairs Act 1932, s 2.

[311] *Aston Cantlow and Wilmcote with Billesley Parochial Church Council v Wallbank* (2001) 81 P&CR 14, [2000] 2 EGLR 149, Ferris J; [2002] Ch 51, [2001] 3 All ER 393, CA, Sir Andrew Morritt V-C, Robert Walker and Sedley LJJ; [2004] 1 AC 546, [2003] 3 All ER 1213, HL, Lord Nicholls of Birkenhead, Lord Hope of Craighead, Lord Hobhouse of Woodborough, Lord Scott

in 1985, with a view to simplifying conveyancing, had recommended that chancel repair liability arising from the ownership of land, or from the ownership of corn rents or the rent charges not redeemed by the Tithe Act 1936, should be abolished after ten years.[312] The liability has been the subject of academic criticism,[313] to which the judiciary has added its voice.[314]

Historically, chancel repair liability was an overriding interest,[315] binding on owners of land even without notice. The Land Registration Act 2002 was enacted following the decision of the Court of Appeal in *Aston Cantlow*,[316] which declared the liability to be unenforceable. When the decision was reversed in the House of Lords, the Land Registration Act 2002 (Transitional Provisions) (No 2) (Order) 2003[317] was made. This introduced provisions into the 2002 Act under which chancel repair liability continues to be an overriding interest for ten years from the coming into force of the Act on 13 October 2003.[318] An application may be made prior to 13 October 2013 for registration of a caution or notice.[319] This will then give priority to the PCC over the interest of a first registered proprietor or anyone taking from him, or anyone taking from a registered proprietor.[320] If it is not registered, it is still enforceable after the ten-year period against the owner of rectorial land until he disposes of it, for it is only a successor in title who takes the land freed from liability.[321] **3.79**

The Chancel Repairs Act 1932 provides that where a chancel is in need of repair, the PCC may serve upon any person, who appears to be liable to repair the chancel, a notice in the prescribed form stating in general terms the grounds on which that **3.80**

---

of Foscote and Lord Rodger of Earlsferry. For the subsequent assessment of damages see The Times, 21 February 2007, Lewison J.

[312] *Liability for Chancel Repairs*, Law Com No 152, November 1985. On 18 February 1982, General Synod had supported a motion approving the phasing out of the liability over a period of 20 years. For a full discussion, see E Nugee, 'The Consequences of *Aston Cantlow*' (2004) 7 Ecc LJ 452. The phasing out did not proceed because expropriation without compensation would have run foul of Article 1 of the First Protocol to the European Convention on Human Rights.

[313] J Baker, 'Lay Rectors and Chancel Repairs' (1984) 100 LQR 181. The Law Commission Report (see n 312 above) referred to 'this relic from the past' as 'no longer acceptable'.

[314] Lord Nicholls spoke of 'the anachronistic, even capricious, nature of this ancient liability' (para 2). Ferris J, who dealt with the matter at first instance, recognized that the law relating to chancel repairs is capable of operating arbitrarily, harshly and unfairly (para 18).

[315] Land Registration Act 1925, s 70(1)(c).

[316] *Aston Cantlow and Wilmcote with Billesley Parochial Church Council v Wallbank* [2002] Ch 51 [2001] 3 All ER 393, CA.

[317] Land Registration Act 2002 (Transitional Provisions) (No 2) (Order) 2003, SI 2003/2431.

[318] Land Registration Act 2002, sch 1 para 16, and sch 3 para 16.

[319] Ibid, s 117(2): caution against first registration of unregistered land, or notice in the register in the case of registered land. No fee is chargeable.

[320] Ibid, ss 11(4)(a), 12(2)(b); and 29(2)(a)(i), 30(2)(a)(i).

[321] E Nugee, 'The Consequences of *Aston Cantlow*' (n 312 above). The failure to register, therefore, does not lead to the immediate extinction of the liability at the end of ten years, but it does eliminate the conveyancing trap for the benefit of purchasers.

person is alleged to be liable, and the extent of the disrepair, and calling on him to put the chancel in proper repair.[322] If the chancel is not put in proper repair within a month, the PCC may bring proceedings against the person on whom the notice was served to recover the sum required to put the chancel in proper repair.[323] If the court finds that the defendant would have been liable to be admonished to repair the chancel by the appropriate ecclesiastical court,[324] it must give judgment for the PCC for such sum as appears to the court to represent the cost of putting the chancel in proper repair.[325] The extent of the obligation was recently considered by Lewison J who declared his task was:

> to determine the sum that appears to me to represent the costs of putting the chancel in proper repair. Proper repair, in my judgment, necessarily means more than simply wind and watertight and must be assessed in accordance with the tests laid down in *Wise v Metcalfe* and *Pell v Addison*.[326]

3.81 The liability is personal and several and, in the event that the land in question is subdivided, the chancel repair liability attaches to the owners of each parcel of the divided property.[327] Further, the liability is not limited to the profits received from the rectorial property.[328] There is provision under section 52 of the Ecclesiastical

---

[322] Chancel Repairs Act 1932, s 2(1).
[323] Ibid s 2(2).
[324] The legal test for the court is whether the lay rector would have been liable to be admonished, and not whether the ecclesiastical court would in fact have admonished him in the particular case: *Wickhambrook Parochial Church Council v Croxford* [1935] 2 KB 417, CA, at 440 per Romer LJ. Lord Scott of Foscote (albeit in a passage of his opinion in which none of his fellow Law Lords concurred) indicated that section 2 of the Chancel Repairs Act 1932 imposes a power and not a mandatory duty, and suggested that a PCC might decide not to enforce the chancel repair liability. 'Trustees are not always obliged to be Scrooge' he remarked at para 137. But in the absence of some compelling justification, neglecting to recover the cost of repair is a breach of duty on the part of a charity trustee for which liability may attach.
[325] Ibid s 2(3). Prior to the 1932 Act, enforcement was dealt with in the ecclesiastical courts. An individual admonished to repair the chancel who did not do so could be made the subject of a decree of excommunication, or following transfer of proceedings from the consistory court to the High Court, proceedings for committal for contempt of court.
[326] *Aston Cantlow and Wilmcote with Billesley Parochial Church Council v Wallbank*, The Times, 21 February 2007, per Lewison J, applying *Wise v Metcalfe* (1829) 10 B&C 299, Bayley J; and *Pell v Addison* (1860) 2 F& F 291, Willes J, the latter using the expression 'substantial repair without ornament' at 292. The respondent's argument, based on an assertion contained in a website, that the liability extended merely to keep the chancel wind and weathertight, was expressly rejected by Lewison J.
[327] *Wickhambrook Parochial Church Council v Croxford* [1935] 2 KB 417, CA. An individual held liable would have a right of contribution against co-rectors. See also *Chivers & Sons Ltd v Air Ministry* [1955] Ch 585, [1955] 2 All ER 607, Wynn-Parry J.
[328] *Wickhambrook Parochial Church Council v Croxford* [1935] 2 KB 417, CA, per Romer LJ. In his speech in *Aston Cantlow and Wilmcote with Billesley Parochial Church Council v Wallbank* [2004] 1 AC 546, [2003] 3 All ER 1213, HL, Lord Scott of Foscote queried, at paras 105–109, whether *Wickhambrook* might be wrongly decided. As the point was not argued before him (nor were submissions invited on the matter), his remarks are of questionable authority and carry very little weight. See the speech of Lord Nicholls at para 3 and, more trenchantly, Lord Hobhouse at para 82. Viscount Simon LC left the question open in *Representative Body of the Church in Wales v*

Dilapidations Measure 1923 for a lay rector to compound his liability and thereby obtain a release from it.[329] In the unanimous opinion of the House of Lords in *Aston Cantlow*, chancel repair liability is compatible with convention rights under the Human Rights Act 1998.[330]

Quinquennial inspection

Each parish is required to appoint and retain an architect or chartered building surveyor approved by the Diocesan Advisory Committee (DAC) to inspect the church and report on it once every five years.[331] The inspection should extend to certain designated movables and ruins of particular interest or value and to all trees subject to local authority tree preservation orders.[332] The fees are paid from a fund established by diocesan synod and the report is sent to the incumbent, the archdeacon and the secretary of the DAC.[333] Although the churchwardens are the legal owners of the ornaments and furnishings of the church,[334] the responsibility for their maintenance rests with the PCC.[335] A PCC may not acquire any interest in land or in any personal property save with the consent of

3.82

Tithe Redemption Commission [1944] AC 228, [1944] 1 All ER 710, HL at 239 and 713 respectively. Lord Scott concluded 'whether the *Wickhambrook* case was rightly decided is open to debate at least in this House': para 122.

[329] Ecclesiastical Dilapidations Measure 1923, s 52. The procedure is cumbersome and the amount payable to compound the liability often proves prohibitive: see E Nugee, 'The Consequences of *Aston Cantlow*' (n 310 above).

[330] The argument was that enforcement of the liability amounted to a violation of Article 1 of the First Protocol to European Convention on Human Rights which provides for the peaceful enjoyment of possessions and declares that no one may be deprived of his possessions except in the public interest and subject to conditions provided by law. The Law Lords in *Aston Cantlow* were all of the opinion that there was no deprivation of possessions. Lord Hope stated at para 72, 'the liability is simply an incident of ownership of the land which gives rise to it'; Lord Hobhouse, having noted at para 91 that there is no Convention right to be relieved from the consequences of a bargain, albeit one made by a predecessor in title some two hundred years earlier, concluded at para 92 that the liability 'arises from the failure to perform a civil private law obligation which [the respondents] had voluntarily assumed'; and Lord Scott, at para 134, opined that the respondents acquired the rectorial property with full knowledge of the potential liability, and that he could see no incompatibility with the Convention right. Chancel repair liability was not considered by any of the Law Lords to be in the nature of a tax.

[331] Inspection of Churches Measure 1955. See ss 1(2)(c), 2(1), amended by the Care of Churches and Ecclesiastical Jurisdiction Measure 1991, s 2(5), Sch 3 paras 2, 4.

[332] For a list of all such items, see the Inspection of Churches Measure 1955, s 1A, added by the Care of Churches and Ecclesiastical Jurisdiction Measure 1991, Sch 3 para 3.

[333] Inspection of Churches Measure 1955, s 1(2)(d), amended by the Care of Churches and Ecclesiastical Jurisdiction Measure 1991, Sch 3 para 2.

[334] Canon E 1 para 5.

[335] Parochial Church Councils (Powers) Measure 1956, s 4(1)(ii)(b); Care of Churches and Ecclesiastical Jurisdiction Measure 1991, s 6(1); Canon F 14.

the diocesan board of finance, whose consent is also required for any disposition of such property.[336]

3.83 As to the parsonage houses, ownership vests in the incumbent. He cannot part with possession of the house, save with the consent of the Parsonages Board of the diocese, the bishop and the Church Commissioners, and the proceeds of sale must be retained as capital of the benefice.[337] Liability for the upkeep of parsonage houses rests with the diocese.[338]

Parochial finance

3.84 The Church remains heavily dependent upon the generous gifts of its members, both present and past. Recent years have seen a more centralized approach to finance, with resources being handled on a national or diocesan level rather than by individual parishes. All glebe land is now vested in and managed by the diocese,[339] and the practice of paying a tithe on land has effectively been abolished.[340] Fees for special services such as marriage and burial are now regulated by statutory instrument.[341] Many incumbents now opt to assign to the diocesan board of finance all fees receivable by them. The same principle applies in respect of the Easter offering which previously constituted a significant supplement to a clergy stipend. The PCC remains responsible for the incumbent's expenses of office. This may be met from collections in church.[342]

3.85 The diocese raises funds by way of voluntary taxation known variously as the diocesan quota or parish share.[343] Each parish is asked to contribute towards diocesan expenditure in accordance with that parish's needs and ability. In like fashion, each diocese is asked to contribute to the expenditure incurred by the Archbishops' Council through the Central Board of Finance. The payment of the quota is probably not a legally enforceable obligation, since it lacks the qualities of a binding contract. Indeed, the levying of the quota which is in the nature of a

---

[336] Parochial Church Councils (Powers) Measure 1956, s 6(1), (3).
[337] Parsonages Measure 1938, s 1(1), (3); Church Commissioners Measure 1947, s 2; Repair of Benefice Buildings Measure 1972, s 29.
[338] Repair of Benefice Buildings Measure 1972, s 5.
[339] Endowments and Glebe Measure 1976, s 15.
[340] Tithe Act 1936, s 1.
[341] Ecclesiastical Fees Measure 1986, s 2, which provides for Parochial Fees Orders to be made. They are generally made annually.
[342] Parochial Church Councils (Powers) Measure 1956, s 4(1)(ii)(a).
[343] The only reference to the quota in any Act or Measure is to be found in the Synodical Government Measure 1969, s 5(4). For a detailed discussion, see N Doe, *The Legal Framework of the Church of England* (Oxford: Clarendon Press, 1996) 478–482.

quasi-tax may be unlawful, since it is not done under the authority of Parliament.[344] Only a parish confident of being and remaining self-financing is in a position to take the bold step of not paying its quota.[345]

Pastoral schemes and orders

The Pastoral Measure 1983[346] provides for the establishment in each diocese of a pastoral committee.[347] Such committees must[348] review the arrangements for pastoral supervision in the diocese and, where it is considered desirable, make recommendations to the bishop.[349] Particular regard must be had to making provision for the cure of souls in the diocese as a whole.[350] Regard must be had to the traditions, needs and characteristics of individual parishes[351] and to any matters of diocesan policy indicated to the committee by the diocesan synod.[352] Before deciding to make any recommendation to the bishop the pastoral committee must ascertain the views of interested parties.[353] These comprise incumbents, patrons, PCCs, priests-in-charge of conventional districts, archdeacons and rural

3.86

---

[344] *Attorney-General v Wiltshire United Dairies* (1921) 37 TLR 884, CA.

[345] A full consideration of the complex inter-relationship between parish and diocese involving the various rights and duties of priest, diocese, churchwarden and PCC is beyond the scope of this work.

[346] This is a lengthy and complex piece of legislation, being a consolidation of the Pastoral Measure 1968 and the Pastoral (Amendment) Measure 1982. It was substantially amended as a consequence of the Team and Group Ministries Measure 1995. The Measure is supplemented by the *Pastoral Measure 1983: Code of Recommended Practice* (1999), a voluminous document which replaced the Code of 1983, but which provides guidance only and has no statutory force. Note also that the Pastoral Measure 1983 will be further amended by the proposed Dioceses, Pastoral and Mission Measure which was approved by the General Synod in February 2007. This will make significant changes to the process of re-configuring parishes, benefices and dioceses.

[347] Pastoral Measure 1983, s 1(1). Its constitution and rules of procedure are contained in ibid Sch 1: s 1(2).

[348] The mandatory nature of the committee's function was emphasized in *Cheesman v Church Commissioners* [2000] 1 AC 19 at 25F, (1999) 5 Ecc LJ 305, PC.

[349] Pastoral Measure 1983, s 2(1). The committee may act at the direction of the bishop or on its own initiative, in the latter case consulting the bishop and giving him particulars of the matters it proposes to consider and of the benefices which will be affected: ibid s 2(2).

[350] Ibid s 2(3)(a). This includes the provision of appropriate spheres of work and conditions of service for all persons engaged in the cure of souls and the provision of reasonable remuneration for such persons: s 2(3)(a). Consideration may be given to the qualities of individual incumbents and interpersonal difficulties with parishioners since to postulate an 'average' clergyman is to introduce artificiality into the process: see *Cheesman v Church Commissioners* [2000] 1 AC 19 at 27G–28A, PC. Note, however, the dissenting opinion of Lord Lloyd of Berwick at 33–44.

[351] Pastoral Measure 1983, s 2(3)(b). Compare 'regard' in this sub-section and 'particular regard' in the preceding one.

[352] Ibid s 2(4). Again, 'regard' only.

[353] Ibid s 3(1).

deans and the local planning authority.³⁵⁴ Provision is made for incumbents, team vicars and representatives of the PCC to have a meeting with the pastoral committee or a sub-committee.³⁵⁵ Before deciding to make a recommendation that a declaration of redundancy be made, the committee must ascertain the views of the local planning authority and obtain a report from the Council for the Care of Churches.³⁵⁶ The committee has wide powers to hold consultations and interviews and to make inquiries.³⁵⁷ Matters which straddle diocesan boundaries are dealt with by a joint pastoral committee upon which the Dioceses Commission is represented.³⁵⁸

3.87 When the pastoral committee has decided to make any recommendations, it formulates them in draft proposals and submits them to the bishop who may, with the agreement of the committee, make such amendments as he considers desirable.³⁵⁹ If the bishop approves the draft proposals (with or without amendments), he submits them to the Church Commissioners.³⁶⁰ The diocesan pastoral committee then sends a copy of the proposals as approved to every interested person, together with a notice of their right to make representations if the Church Commissioners prepare a draft scheme or order to give effect to the proposal.³⁶¹

3.88 A pastoral scheme may provide for the creation, whether by union or otherwise, of new benefices or parishes;³⁶² the dissolution of existing benefices or parishes; the alteration of the areas of existing benefices or parishes (including the transfer of a parish from one benefice to another) or the definition of their boundaries;³⁶³

---

354 Ibid s 3(2)(a)–(f). Different criteria apply in relation to schemes merely affecting archdeaconries or deaneries: ibid s 3(3), amended by the Church of England (Legal Aid and Miscellaneous Provisions) Measure 1988, s 11.
355 Pastoral Measure 1983, s 3(5) and (6) respectively.
356 Ibid s 3(7). The report must address the historic interest and architectural quality of each church; the historic interest and aesthetic qualities of their contents; and any special features of the churchyard: s 3(8).
357 Ibid s 16(2).
358 Ibid s 13.
359 Ibid s 3(9). To the draft proposals must be annexed a statement of the views of the interested parties and, in cases of redundancy, the report of the Council for the Care of Churches: s 3(10).
360 Ibid s 4(1). As to the importance of procedural fairness and legitimate expectation in the process under the Measure, see the Report of the Church Commissioners regarding a proposed pastoral scheme concerning the benefices of the Candover Valley and Wield in the diocese of Winchester, 3 April 2003, (2007) 9 Ecc LJ 346.
361 Pastoral Measure 1983, s 4(2)(a). They should also be informed that any interested person, other than a PCC, may by notice in writing relinquish his right to receive a copy from the Church Commissioners of the draft scheme or order: ibid s 4(2)(b).
362 This may be done notwithstanding that the parish thereby created will have no parish church when the provision comes into operation: ibid s 17(4).
363 Providing the criteria under the Pastoral Measure 1983 are carried out, it is immaterial that separate proceedings under the Incumbents (Vacation of Benefices) Measure 1977 have previously been initiated. The statutory regimes are separate and not interdependent: see *Cheesman v Church*

the creation of new extra-parochial places, the incorporation in parishes of existing extra-parochial places, or the alteration or definition of the boundaries of existing extra-parochial places; and the making of sharing agreements in respect of a church or parsonage house which will be in the joint ownership of the Church of England and another Church.[364]

3.89 The powers exercisable by pastoral order, however, are very fully stated in section 37 of the Pastoral Measure 1983, the more common of which are the power to alter the areas of benefices or parishes or to define their boundaries but not so as to transfer from a benefice or parish any church used for public worship; the power to alter the name of any benefice or parish; the power to provide for the holding in plurality of any two or more benefices; the power to provide for the creating, altering or dissolving, for designating, and for naming or altering the name of an archdeaconry or deanery; the power to assign a special cure of soul or other responsibilities to vicars in team ministries, to specify a term of years for members of a team, and otherwise to alter team or group ministries; and the power to provide for the designation or selection of incumbents of benefices held in plurality.[365] Team and group ministries are the subject of detailed treatment in Chapter 4.

3.90 The Church Commissioners consider the proposals submitted to them, and the bishop, in consultation with the diocesan pastoral committee, considers any comments the Commissioners make.[366] The Commissioners, with the agreement of the bishop given after consultation with the diocesan pastoral committee, may make such amendments to the proposals as they consider desirable.[367] The Commissioners then prepare a draft pastoral scheme or a draft pastoral order.[368]

3.91 Copies of a draft scheme or order must be served by the Commissioners on each of the interested parties together with a notice stating that written representations may be made to the Commissioners by a specified date.[369] The Commissioners

---

Commissioners [2000] 1 AC 19 at 25F–26H, PC (Lord Lloyd of Berwick dissenting). The 1983 Measure, however, cannot be invoked as a device when the real purpose is to deprive the incumbent of his benefice or to punish him or to remedy a breakdown in pastoral relations: [2000] 1 AC 19 at 33.

[364] Pastoral Measure 1983, s 17(1)(a)–(d), (5).

[365] Ibid s 37(1)(a)–(f), amended by the Team and Group Ministries Measure 1995, s 5(3).

[366] Pastoral Measure 1983, s 5(1). In cases of redundancy involving demolition, structural change, or for care and maintenance to pass to the Churches Conservation Trust (formerly the Redundant Churches Fund), then the Advisory Board for Redundant Churches must be consulted: ibid s 5(2), amended by the Pastoral (Amendment) Measure 1994, s 13.

[367] Pastoral Measure 1983, s 5(3).

[368] Ibid s 5(4). With the agreement of the bishop after consultation with the diocesan pastoral committee, the scheme or order may relate to some but not all of the proposals: ibid s 5(4) proviso.

[369] Ibid s 6(1). At least 28 days must be afforded for such representations. Note that an interested party may relinquish his right to a copy of the draft: ibid s 6(2).

must also send a notice concerning any draft scheme to the secretary of the PCC of any affected parish to be affixed on or near the principal door of the church.[370] There are additional requirements in relation to draft schemes providing for declarations of redundancy.[371] A draft scheme or order may be amended by the Commissioners as a result of such representations either at the request of or with the agreement of the bishop after consultation with the pastoral committee.[372]

3.92 Where the Commissioners, having considered the representations, are of opinion that the draft scheme should be made, they must submit it to the bishop for his consent and, once that consent is obtained, seal a copy and submit it for confirmation by Order in Council.[373] Any person who has made written representations with respect to the draft scheme may, within a specified period of not less than 28 days, appeal to the Privy Council against the scheme or any provisions thereof.[374] The appeal lies only with the leave of the Privy Council.[375] It may be made on the merits, in addition to any procedural irregularity, since the ambit of the appeal is much wider than a mere judicial review.[376] The Privy Council may allow the appeal, dismiss it and confirm the pastoral order, or return the scheme to the Commissioners for reconsideration.[377] The burden of proof is on the appellant and the civil standard applies, namely the balance of probabilities.[378]

3.93 In the case of a draft pastoral order, as opposed to a scheme, no confirmation by Order in Council is required and, accordingly, no appeal lies to the Privy Council. Unless, as a result of representations received, the Commissioners decide that the order should not be made or that the draft should be amended or further amended, they seal a copy of the order and send it to the bishop,[379] who may by applying his seal thereto make the order.[380] Proposals concerning the creation, dissolution or union of benefices or parishes, transferring any church from a benefice or parish, or making a church redundant, can only be achieved by a scheme.

---

[370] Ibid s 6(4). At least 28 days must be given for persons to respond to the notice: ibid s 6(4).
[371] See ibid s 6(3). A copy must be served on the Advisory Board for Redundant Churches, the Commonwealth War Graves Commission and, if applicable, the Churches Conservation Trust: ibid s 6(3)(a), as amended (see n 328 above). There must also be newspaper advertisement: ibid 6(3)(b).
[372] Ibid s 7(1). Like notice must be given of any amended scheme or order: ibid s 7(2).
[373] Ibid s 8(1).
[374] Ibid s 9(1).
[375] Ibid s 9(2).
[376] *Hargreaves v Church Commissioners* [1983] 2 AC 457, [1983] 3 All ER 17, PC. See also *Cheesman v Church Commissioners* [2000] 1 AC 19.
[377] Pastoral Measure 1983, s 9(6).
[378] *Elphick v Church Commissioners* [1974] AC 562, PC.
[379] Pastoral Measure 1983, s 8(3). Where no representations with regard to a draft order have been made, the Commissioners seal a copy and submit it to the bishop: s 8(2).
[380] Ibid s 8(4).

The incumbent of a benefice dissolved by a pastoral scheme or deemed to be **3.94** vacated; the archdeacon of an archdeaconry dissolved by a pastoral scheme; and a vicar in a team ministry whose office is abolished by or as a result of a pastoral scheme or order, is entitled to be paid compensation for any consequential loss.[381]

Sharing of church buildings

For the strengthening of ecumenical relations, combined with less esoteric con- **3.95** siderations of logistics and economy, a number of church buildings are shared by members of different denominations. Where there are joint services, this is generally under the auspices of a local ecumenical project, which is dealt with in the following section. Where the building is used at different times by different denominations, it is done by way of a sharing agreement, pursuant to the Sharing of Church Buildings Act 1969.[382] In addition to the Church of England, the denominations to which the Act applies are Baptist, Congregational, Methodist, United Reformed, Roman Catholic, Church in Wales, the Association of Churches of Christ in Great Britain and Ireland, and certain other Churches whose application to be included has been published in the *London Gazette*.[383]

The church building[384] may be owned by one, some or all of the participant **3.96** churches.[385] For the Church of England, the diocesan board of finance, the incumbent and the PCC of the parish where the building is or will be situated, and any team vicar or member of a team ministry, must each be a party to a sharing agreement.[386] For other Churches, the parties must be such person or persons as may be determined by the appropriate authority of that Church.[387] Before a sharing agreement can be made, the consent of the bishop and the pastoral

---

[381] See ibid ss 25, 26, Sch 4.
[382] See also the Sharing of Church Buildings Measure 1970; and the British Council of Churches, *Guidelines to the Sharing of Church Buildings Act 1969*.
[383] Sharing of Church Buildings Act 1969, s 11(1), Sch 2, amended by the United Reformed Church Act 1972, s 24(1).
[384] 'Church building' includes one to be used as a place of worship, as a church hall or centre, as a youth club, centre or hostel or as a residence for ministers or lay workers, but schools are expressly excluded: Sharing of Church Buildings Act 1969, s 12(1). Cathedrals, peculiars, extra-parochial and extra-diocesan places are also excluded: ibid s 10(1). Inter-denominational worship may nonetheless take place in a cathedral under Canon B 43 para 10.
[385] Sharing of Church Buildings Act 1969, s 1(2). However, a sharing agreement may not be made in relation to an existing consecrated church of the Church of England unless the church remains in the sole ownership of the Church of England or pursuant to a pastoral scheme: ibid s 5.
[386] Ibid s 1(3)(a), amended by the Team and Group Ministry Measure 1995, s 12.
[387] Sharing of Church Buildings Act 1969, s 1(3)(b).

committee of the diocese must be obtained.[388] The agreement is required to be under seal and registered.[389] It may be amended subject to the agreement of the parties and the statutory consents.[390]

3.97 Provision is made for safeguarding the purposes of a sharing agreement by way of trusts and for ensuring that such purposes are exclusively charitable.[391] The agreement must provide for the financial and other obligations of the parties for the provision, improvement and management of the building.[392] In the case of a building used for public worship, the agreement must make provision for determining the extent to which it is to be available for worship in accordance with the forms of service and practice of the sharing Churches respectively, and may provide for the holding of joint services.[393] Ministers, readers and lay preachers may participate, by invitation, in the worship of another sharing Church.[394] However, the participation in each other's worship is governed by the practices and disciplines of each Church in like manner as if the worship were in separate buildings.[395] This is governed by Canons B 43 and B 44, the 'ecumenical canons', discussed below.

3.98 A sharing agreement may not be made in relation to an existing consecrated church of the Church of England unless the church remains in the sole ownership of the Church of England or authority to make the agreement is given by a pastoral scheme.[396] An unconsecrated church which is the subject of a sharing agreement may not be consecrated unless, under the agreement, it is in the sole ownership of the Church of England.[397] The faculty jurisdiction applies to all consecrated buildings, including those subject to a sharing agreement, but the jurisdiction does not extend to movables required for the worship of any sharing Church other than the Church of England.[398] A church subject to a sharing agreement may become or remain a parish church if it is in the sole ownership of the Church of England,[399] otherwise it may be designated as a parish centre of worship.[400]

---

[388] Ibid s 1(4). A sharing agreement is an agreement made by two or more Churches for the sharing by them of church buildings: ibid s 1(1).
[389] Ibid s 1(8). For the Church of England, registration is to be in the registries of the diocese and province concerned: ibid s 1(8). It binds the successors to the parties: ibid s 1(9).
[390] Ibid s 1(10).
[391] Ibid s 2.
[392] Ibid s 3(1).
[393] Ibid s 4(1). The agreement may also dispense with the requirement to hold certain Church of England services on Sundays and other days: ibid s 4(1).
[394] Ibid s 4(2).
[395] Ibid s 4(3).
[396] Ibid s 5(1). For pastoral schemes, see the Pastoral Measure 1983.
[397] Sharing of Church Buildings Act 1969, s 5(2).
[398] Ibid s 5(3).
[399] Ibid s 5(4)(a).
[400] Ibid s 5(4)(b). As to parish centres of worship, see the Pastoral Measure 1983, s 29.

Provision is made for the solemnization of marriage in shared church buildings in accordance with the rites of the participating Churches.[401] The sharing agreement must contain provision for terminating the sharing of a church building or buildings including statutory consents.[402]

Ecumenical relations

3.99 On 30 January 1989, Canons B 43 and B 44 (the so-called 'ecumenical canons') were promulged pursuant to the Church of England (Ecumenical Relations) Measure 1988. They deal with relations between the Church of England and other Churches. Canon B 43 makes provision for ministers and lay persons who are baptised and in good standing in their own Church to be invited to perform certain duties within Church of England services as they may be authorized to perform in their own Church.[403] Such invitation may only be given by the incumbent, and is subject to certain conditions whereby the approval of the bishop and/or the PCC is first to be obtained, depending on the nature of the duty to be performed and whether it is to be done on a regular basis.[404] The canon also provides for bishops, priests, deacons, deaconesses, lay workers and readers of the Church of England to participate in services of other denominations, subject to certain approvals and restrictions.[405] There must be special circumstances to justify acceptance of an invitation to preside at holy communion and the rite and the elements used may not be contrary to the doctrine of the Church of England.[406] At an ordination or consecration, a bishop or priest may not do any act which is a sign of the conferring of holy orders unless that Church be an episcopal Church with which the Church of England has established intercommunion.[407] In the case of an incumbent withholding approval for a priest, deacon or lay person to participate in a service to be held within his parish, the applicant may appeal to the bishop.[408]

3.100 With the approval of the PCC and the bishop,[409] the incumbent of a parish may invite members of another Church to take part in joint worship with the

---

[401] See the Sharing of Church Buildings Act 1970, s 6.
[402] Ibid s 9.
[403] Canon B 43 para 1.
[404] Canon B 43 para 2. It applies, subject to certain variations, to cathedrals: Canon B 43 para 4.
[405] Canon B 43 paras 3, 6.
[406] Canon B 43 para 4.
[407] Canon B 43 para 5.
[408] Canon B 43 para 7.
[409] The approval of the bishop is to be in writing: Canon B 43 para 11.

Chapter 3: The Parish

Church of England, or to use a church building in the parish for worship in accordance with the other's forms of service and practice.[410]

3.101 A more formalized commonality of worship and ministry may be implemented by the establishment of a local ecumenical project (LEP) under Canon B 44. An LEP is created by an agreement entered into between a bishop and the appropriate authority of each participating Church in respect of any parish or part of a parish in his diocese.[411] The bishop may not enter into the agreement unless participation by the Church of England in the LEP has been approved by each of the following:

(a) the incumbent;
(b) 75 per cent of those present and voting at the PCC;
(c) either the annual parochial church meeting or a special parochial church meeting; and
(d) the diocesan pastoral committee after consultation with the deanery synod concerned or its standing committee.[412]

A cathedral church may be comprised in an LEP,[413] as may a non-parochial institution,[414] but in each case the approval conditions are varied.

3.102 The agreement creating the LEP may last for a specified period not exceeding seven years, but the period may be extended by agreement in writing made by the bishop.[415] No extension or amendment may be granted unless the bishop first obtains the consent of each incumbent and PCC concerned as well as the diocesan pastoral committee.[416] A scheme may be revoked by a bishop at any time after consultation with the appropriate authority of each participating Church, each PCC concerned and the diocesan pastoral committee.[417] A bishop who has given his agreement to participation in an LEP may by an instrument in writing made after consultation with the PCC of each parish concerned make provision for its operation, staffing and worship.[418] Detailed provisions designed to preserve the sacramental integrity of the participating Churches deal with what may be permitted and the extent of consultation first required.[419]

---

[410] Canon B 43 para 9.
[411] Canon B 44 para 1(1).
[412] Canon B 44 para 1(3).
[413] See Canon B 44 para 6.
[414] See Canon B 44 para 7.
[415] Canon B 44 para 2(1). Any number of extensions may be granted, but none may exceed seven years: Canon B 44 para 2(1).
[416] Canon B 44 para 2(3).
[417] Canon B 44 para 3(1).
[418] Canon B 44 para 4(1).
[419] See Canon B 44 paras 4–8.

Non-parochial units

3.103 A 'non-parochial unit', though not the most elegant of expressions, is any place of worship which falls outside the parish structure. The most common are cathedrals, which are discussed in Chapter 7. The more significant of the others are addressed in turn below. They merit particular attention in the light of the Care of Places of Worship Measure 1999, which has ended the anomaly of their having the benefit of the ecclesiastical exemption without the corresponding control of the faculty jurisdiction.[420]

Peculiars

3.104 Peculiar jurisdictions are those of which the diocesan bishop is not the Ordinary. The term 'peculiar' is generally taken to refer to a place which, although surrounded by a diocese, is not under the control of the bishop, nor is it visitable by him. Westminster Abbey and St George's Chapel, Windsor, are examples of what are styled royal peculiars.[421] The dean and chapter of each is the Ordinary and they are visitable only by the Crown. Other peculiar jurisdictions include royal residences, the Temple, the Universities of Oxford and Cambridge and certain colleges therein. The clerical staff of peculiars are appointed without reference to the bishop, who has no jurisdiction over them. Were a bishop to purport to license a priest to a peculiar, such licence would be of no effect. For the purposes of the Ecclesiastical Jurisdiction Measure 1963, extra-diocesan places, including peculiars (but not royal peculiars), are deemed to be situate within the diocese by which they are surrounded,[422] but they are not automatically within the jurisdiction of the consistory court.[423] It has more recently been declared that the jurisdiction of the consistory court applies to all parish churches within the diocese.[424] Peculiars were given the opportunity of applying to be included on the list maintained by the Council for the Care of Churches and thus become subject to the faculty jurisdiction.[425]

---

[420] See Chapter 7.
[421] See the historical discussion and recommendations contained in *The Royal Peculiars,* the Report of the Review Group set up by Her Majesty The Queen (London, 2001). Note also P Barber 'What is a Peculiar?' (1995) 3 Ecc LJ 299.
[422] Ecclesiastical Jurisdiction Measure 1963, s 66(3).
[423] Ibid ss 6(2), 66(4).
[424] Care of Churches and Ecclesiastical Jurisdiction Measure 1991, s 11(1).
[425] See Chapter 7.

Private chapels

3.105 A number of private chapels exist, many of which are served by their own chaplains. The chaplain, like any priest, requires a licence or written permission to officiate from the bishop, whose discretion in this regard is unfettered.[426] In addition, the consent is required of the incumbent in whose parish the chapel is situated. The celebration of holy communion on Sundays and greater feast days in private chapels is discouraged, in order that the residents might attend the parish church instead.[427]

Other chapels

3.106 The bishop may license a minister to perform such offices and services[428] as may be specified in the licence within any college, school, hospital or public or charitable institution, whether or not it possesses a chapel.[429] In contrast with the practice for private chapels, the performance of offices and services in accordance with such a licence is not dependent upon the consent of the incumbent of the parish in which the institution is situated. Money collected in the exercise of such licences is disposed of as the minister performing the service may determine, subject to the direction of the bishop.[430]

3.107 Particular provisions apply in relation to chapels of the armed forces which derive from the royal prerogative and not under statute.[431] Church of England chaplains to the forces are licensed by and under the jurisdiction of the Archbishop of Canterbury's Episcopal Representative to Her Majesty's Armed Forces.[432] Chief chaplains are designated archdeacon.[433]

---

[426] Save, perhaps, by judicial review in the Administrative Court were he to act unreasonably or fail to give reasons.
[427] Canon B 41 para 1.
[428] This does not extend to the solemnisation of marriage, save as provided for under the Extra-Parochial Ministry Measure 1967, s 2(1A), added by the Church of England (Legal Aid and Miscellaneous Provisions) Measure 1988, s 5 (marriage of housebound or detained person).
[429] Canon B 41 para 2; Extra-Parochial Ministry Measure 1967, s 2(1). A licence may be revoked by the bishop at any time: ibid s 2(4), but not on the ground of 'misconduct' within the meaning of the Clergy Discipline Measure 2003, in the case of which proceedings must be brought under that Measure.
[430] Extra-Parochial Ministry Measure 1967, s 2(3).
[431] See the Queen's Regulations for each of the services and also the Army Chaplains Act 1868.
[432] See generally D Bailey, 'Legal Regulation of the Appointment, Ministry and Episcopal Oversight of Army Chaplains', LLM dissertation (Cardiff: University of Wales, 1999).
[433] The Chaplain of the Fleet, Chaplain-General to the Forces and Chaplain-in-Chief for the navy, army and air force respectively.

Guild churches

Some 16 churches within the City of London, known as guild churches, have a particular status under the City of London (Guild Churches) Act 1952. They have no parish of their own, their former territory being subsumed into neighbouring parishes, but have their own incumbent, styled 'guild vicar', who is independent of the incumbent of the enlarged parish within whose boundary the guild church lies. The incumbent is presented by the patron to the bishop and is appointed for a term of years. Each guild church has its own guild clerk, churchwardens and electoral roll. The Churchwardens Measure 2001 does not apply to guild churches save that all churchwardens must now be actual communicant members of the Church of England unless the bishop permits otherwise.[434] Guild churches seek to make special provision for the spiritual needs of weekday workers in the City.[435]

3.108

---

[434] Churchwardens Measure 2001, s 12.
[435] For a full treatment, see 14 *Halsbury's Laws of England* (4th edn, London: Butterworths, 1982), paras 597–609.

4

CLERGY

Introduction	4.01	Revocation of licences	4.33
Selection and training	4.04	Permission to officiate	4.36
Ordination	4.06	**Visitations**	4.37
Functions and duties	4.11	**Retirement and removal**	4.38
Deacons	4.11	**Vacation of benefices**	4.43
Priests	4.13	**Group and team ministries**	4.47
Beneficed clergy	4.17	**Other appointments**	4.52
Patronage	4.18	Rural deans	4.53
Suspension of presentation	4.23	Archdeacons	4.54
Institution, collation and induction	4.27	Diocesan bishops	4.56
Unbeneficed clergy	4.29	Suffragan bishops	4.65
Assistant curates	4.30	Archbishops	4.66
Priests-in-charge	4.32		

Introduction

In its strict sense, the *laos*, or people of God, embraces all those who have been admitted to the Church through baptism, whether ordained or not. Popular usage makes a distinction between the ordained clergy on the one hand and the laity on the other.[1] There exist three holy orders in the Church of England: bishops, priests and deacons,[2] and no one may take such orders 'except he be called, tried, examined, and admitted thereunto'.[3] Until 1989, all three orders were open to men alone. Since February 1989, it has been lawful for women to be ordained to the office of deacon by virtue of Canon C 4A, promulged pursuant to the Deacons

4.01

---

[1] Throughout this book the modern usage is adopted and the term 'laity' is used to denote those members of the Church of England who are not ordained.
[2] Canon C 1 para 1.
[3] Canon C 1 para 1. See also the *Book of Common Prayer*, 'The Form and Manner of Making, Ordaining and Consecrating of Bishops, Priests and Deacons' (commonly called the Ordinal) and in particular the preface thereto.

(Ordination of Women) Measure 1986.[4] Since 22 February 1994, it has been lawful for women to be ordained priests by virtue of Canon C 4B, promulged pursuant to the Priests (Ordination of Women) Measure 1993.

4.02 Although there have been episcopal ordinations of women in other provinces of the Anglican Communion, the order of bishops currently remains an exclusively male preserve in the Church of England.[5] In July 2005 the General Synod resolved that the process for removing the obstacles to the consecration of women to the episcopate should be set in train.[6] It had the opportunity in February 2006 to consider the assessment of the various options for achieving that end made by a group chaired by the Bishop of Guildford on behalf of the House of Bishops.[7] That most favoured was 'transferred episcopal arrangements' (TEA), under which provincial regional bishops would exercise pastoral and sacramental functions (on behalf of the archbishop of the province) in relation to parishes opposed to women priests and women bishops, which would otherwise remain part of the geographical diocese in which they were situated. The Synod agreed that TEA merited further exploration and asked the House of Bishops to produce for the July 2006 group of sessions a statement of the theological, ecumenical and canonical implications of such an approach.[8]

4.03 In the July 2006 group of sessions, General Synod resolved to welcome and affirm the view of the majority of the House of Bishops that admitting women to the episcopate 'is consonant with the faith of the Church of England as the Church of England has received it and would be a proper development in proclaiming afresh in this generation the grace and truth of Christ'. Further, it agreed to a process which would allow continuing dialogue and discernment over the best way forward by setting up a drafting group to prepare a range of legislative options for consideration by the House of Bishops and the Synod in advance of the formal introduction of draft legislation.[9] Whether, and if so in what form, such legislation is enacted remains to be seen.

---

[4] A deacon may be appointed rural dean or non-residentiary canon in any cathedral church: Church of England (Miscellaneous Provisions) Measure 1992, ss 14 and 16 respectively. A deacon may also be appointed residentiary canon if ordained for more than six years: s 15.

[5] The Priests (Ordination of Women) Measure 1993, s 1(2) states 'nothing in this Measure shall make it lawful for a woman to be consecrated to the office of bishop'.

[6] The matter had been the subject of *Women Bishops in the Church of England? A Report of the House of Bishops' Working Party on Women in the Episcopate* (the Rochester Report) (GS 1557, 2004).

[7] *House of Bishops' Women Bishops Group Report* (the Guildford Report) (GS 1605, January 2006).

[8] *Women in the Episcopate*, a Report to the House of Bishops from the Bishops of Guildford and Gloucester (GS Misc 826, May 2006).

[9] See generally: S Slack, 'Synod Report 2006' (2007) 9 Ecc LJ 105 at 107–108.

Selection and training

The qualities required of persons to be ordained deacons and priests are set out **4.04**
in Canon C 4.[10] Providing the canonial requirements are met, a bishop has an
absolute discretion as to whom he ordains;[11] the effect of secular discrimination
legislation on this principle being, as yet, untested by legal challenge. However, a
person to be admitted to holy orders must be baptised and confirmed, be sufficiently instructed in holy scripture and in the doctrine, discipline and worship
of the Church of England and be of virtuous conversation and good repute and
such as to be a wholesome example and pattern to the flock of Christ.[12] Whether
or not these qualities are possessed is to be established by careful and diligent
examination, in relation to which there is a mandatory requirement that the
bishop call to his assistance the archdeacons and other ministers appointed for
the purpose.[13] The Ministry Division of the Archbishops' Council, and particularly the Vocation, Recruitment and Selection Committee, advises the Council
and the House of Bishops on a strategy for the development of vocation to ministry and on a policy for the selection of candidates for the accredited ministry.[14]

No person is to be admitted into holy orders if he is suffering or has suffered **4.05**
from some physical or mental infirmity which will prevent him ministering
the word and sacraments or from performing his other duties.[15] Illegitimacy is no
longer a bar to ordination or to consecration as a bishop.[16] A person who is divorced
and remarried or who is married to a divorcee (whose former spouse, in either
case, is living) may not be admitted to holy orders save with a faculty granted
by the archbishop for the removal of the impediment.[17] The House of Bishops
'does not regard entering into a civil partnership as intrinsically incompatible with
holy orders, provided the person concerned is willing to give assurances to his

---

10 See also the Clergy (Ordination and Miscellaneous Provisions) Measure 1964, s 9 (substituted by the Clergy (Ordination) Measure 1990, s 1), and Archbishops' Directions made pursuant to Canon C 4 para 3A.
11 See R Burn, *Ecclesiastical Law* (7th edn, London: Strahan, 1809) vol III 48–49.
12 Canon C 4 para 1. This is done on the basis of the bishop's knowledge or by 'sufficient testimony'. See also the Clergy (Ordination and Miscellaneous Provisions) Measure 1964, s 1(1); the preface to the Ordinal; and Canon C 7. Express reference is made to the Thirty-nine Articles of Religion, the *Book of Common Prayer* and the Ordinal.
13 Clergy (Ordination and Miscellaneous Provisions) Measure 1964, s 1(1); Canon C 7.
14 See the *Church of England Yearbook*.
15 Canon C 4 para 2.
16 Canon C 2 para 4.
17 Canon C 4 paras 3, 3A, and the Archbishops' Directions made thereunder; Clergy (Ordination and Miscellaneous Provisions) Measure 1964, s 9, substituted by the Clergy (Ordination) Measure 1990, s 1. Since the grant or refusal of such a faculty is discretionary, it is not open for a diocese to have an immutable policy not to consider such individuals for ordination since this would amount to an unlawful fettering of discretion.

or her bishop that the relationship is consistent with the standards for the clergy set out in *Issues in Human Sexuality*.[18]

Ordination

4.06 A deacon must be at least 23 years of age and a priest 24 before he may be ordained.[19] A deacon may not be ordained to the priesthood for at least one year, so that trial may be made of his behaviour in the office of deacon.[20] The Ordinal is the lawful form of ordaining both priests and deacons.[21] The proper times for such ordinations are the Sundays immediately following the Ember Weeks; or upon St Peter's Day, Michaelmas Day or St Thomas' Day (or within one week immediately following each such day); or upon such other day, being a Sunday, a holy day or one of the Ember Days, as the bishop of the diocese on urgent occasion appoints.[22] The service must be held in the cathedral church of the diocese or other church or chapel at the discretion of the bishop[23] after morning prayer is ended[24] and any form of holy communion authorized under Canon B 1 may be used.[25]

4.07 A person to be admitted into holy orders must first exhibit to the bishop of the diocese a certificate that he is provided of some ecclesiastical office within the diocese wherein he may attend the cure of souls and execute his ministry.[26] In addition, a bishop may ordain university fellows, schoolmasters, university or school chaplains, staff members of theological colleges and persons living under

---

[18] House of Bishops' *Pastoral Statement on Civil Partnerships* (July, 2005) para 19. For differing views on the nature of a civil partnership see J Humphreys, 'The Civil Partnership Act, Same-Sex Marriage and the Church of England' (2006) 8 Ecc LJ 289; M Scott-Joynt, 'Civil Partnership Act 2004: Dishonest Law?' (2007) 9 Ecc LJ 91; and Lord Falconer of Thoroton, 'Church, State and Civil Partners' (2007) 9 Ecc LJ 5. Whether seeking an assurance of the type envisaged by the *Pastoral Statement* might engage the principles of Article 8 of the European Convention on Human Rights, concerning respect for private and family life, is yet to be considered judicially: the balancing of this right with the Article 9 right to freedom of religion being notoriously controversial.

[19] Clergy Ordination Act 1804, s 1, amended by the Clergy (Ordination and Miscellaneous Provisions) Measure 1964, s 2; Canon C 3 paras 5 and 6 respectively. There is a dispensing provision in the Canon allowing for persons under the relevant age limit to be ordained if a faculty is obtained from the Archbishop of Canterbury, although the archbishop may not grant a faculty for the ordination of a priest below the age of 23.

[20] Canon C 3 para 8, which applies 'unless the bishop shall find good cause for the contrary'.
[21] Canon A 4.
[22] Canon C 3 para 1.
[23] Canon C 3 para 2.
[24] See the rubric at the commencement of the Ordinal in the *Book of Common Prayer*.
[25] Canon C 3 para 4A.
[26] Canon C 5 para 1. 'Ecclesiastical office' is not defined, nor is any form prescribed for the certificate.

vows in the house of any religious order or community.[27] Every person who is to be made a deacon must exhibit to the bishop a birth certificate and testimony of his former good life and behaviour from persons specified by the bishop.[28] Every person who is to be ordained priest must exhibit to the bishop his letters of orders and like testimony.[29] Prior to ordination, in the presence of the bishop, every person about to be ordained priest or deacon must take and subscribe the oath of allegiance,[30] make and subscribe the declaration of assent,[31] and take the oath of canonical obedience to the bishop.[32] Each person to be ordained is presented by one of the archdeacons,[33] and the priests taking part in the ordination, together with the bishop, lay their hands upon the head of every person who receives the order of priesthood.[34]

4.08 The Ordinal provides for the ordaining bishop to enquire of the congregation whether any person present 'knoweth any impediment or notable crime' in anyone to be admitted to the order of priesthood. Although no procedure is laid down for dealing with such objections as may be made, the proper course would be to entertain the objection and adjourn the service should legitimate investigation be necessary.[35] It would be wrong for a bishop to fetter his discretion by indicating in advance of the service that he would not hear any objection,[36] but the objection must relate to character and qualities of individual candidates for ordination and not to matters of law and general principle such as the validity of the ordination of women to the priesthood.[37]

4.09 No person may be admitted into holy orders by any bishop other than that of the diocese in which he is to exercise his ministry except if he brings with him letters dimissory from the bishop of such diocese.[38] A bishop within the province

---

27 Canon C 5 para 2. The relevant institution must be within the diocese: Canon C 5 para 2 proviso.
28 Canon C 6 para 1(a), (b).
29 Canon C 6 para 2(a), (b). Letters of orders are issued under the bishop's seal after ordination to record the event.
30 Clerical Subscription Act 1865, s 4; Canon C 13 para 1. The requirement may be dispensed with in relation to ministry overseas: Canon C 13 para 2. Instead of an oath, a solemn affirmation may be made: Canon C 13 para 3.
31 Canon C 15 para 1(4). The text of the declaration is in Canon C 15 para 1(1).
32 Canon C 14 para 3. This too may be by solemn affirmation instead: Canon C 15 para 4.
33 Canon C 3 para 3, or by his deputy or some such other persons as by ancient custom have the right so to do.
34 Canon C 3 para 4.
35 The analogy is well made with objections which might be raised during the marriage service.
36 See *Williamson v Dow*, 16 April 1994 (unreported), Arden J.
37 See *R v Bishop of Bristol, ex parte Williamson*, 25 March 1994, CO/764/94 (unreported), MacPherson of Cluny J, affirmed in a conjoined appeal *Williamson v Archbishops of Canterbury and York*, 5 September 1996, LTA 96/5284/D, CA (unreported), Simon Brown, Morritt and Phillips LJJ.
38 Canon C 5 para 4. The ancient privilege of any fellow of the University of Oxford or of Cambridge to be admitted into holy orders without letters dimissory by any bishop willing to ordain

of Canterbury or of York may ordain a person to exercise his ministry overseas, providing it is done at the request of the bishop of the diocese where the person is to work.[39] A person so ordained may exercise his ministry for a limited period in the province of Canterbury or of York before proceeding overseas, provided that a temporary permission is granted by the appropriate archbishop.[40]

4.10 The Archbishop of either province may grant permission for a priest or deacon ordained overseas to officiate in the province.[41] Such a cleric thereupon possesses all rights and advantages, and is subject to all duties and liabilities, as would be the case had he been ordained by the bishop of a diocese in the province.[42] This includes susceptibility to disciplinary process.[43] The discretion on whether or not to grant permission falls to be determined on the suitability of the candidate, the validity of his orders being determined by the ecclesiastical law applicable in the province where the ordination took place.[44]

---

him is unimpaired: Canon C 5 para 5. The carrying out of any ordination without the authority of the diocesan bishop is unlawful and may be restrained by an injunction in the civil courts: *Gill v Davies* (1997) 5 Ecc LJ 131, Smith J, where an interlocutory injunction lasting three months was granted to preserve the status quo pending the arrival in the diocese of the newly appointed diocesan bishop. The *ex tempore* judgment, however, is somewhat unsatisfactory in its reasoning. The text may be found in the Materials section of the second edition of this work: M Hill, *Ecclesiastical Law* (2nd edn, Oxford: Oxford University Press, 2001) 707–712. As to the consequences in terms of clergy discipline for those involved in irregular ordinations, see *Coekin v Bishop of Southwark* (2006) 9 Ecc LJ 145.

[39] Overseas and Other Clergy (Ministry and Ordination) Measure 1967, s 5(1); Canon C 5 para 4. The letters of orders must be endorsed to indicate that the person was ordained under section 5 of the Measure in pursuance of the request of the overseas bishop concerned. If the person to be ordained is not a United Kingdom citizen, the oath of allegiance may be dispensed with: s 5(2). Note that the Diocese in Europe, being deemed to be part of the Province of Canterbury, is not 'overseas' for the purposes of this Measure.

[40] Ibid s 5(3).

[41] Ibid s 1(1), (2); Canon C 8 para 5. An application in writing must be made by the individual concerned. Such permission may be either without limitation of time or for a limited period specified in the permission. A further permission may be granted: s 1(3).

[42] Ibid s 1(2).

[43] Ibid s 1(6), states that it is an offence against the laws ecclesiastical for an overseas cleric to officiate without permission under the 1967 Measure and for any cleric knowingly to allow such an offence to be committed in any church in his charge. However the subsection includes the words 'for which proceedings may be taken under the Ecclesiastical Jurisdiction Measure 1963'. It is submitted that this provision sensibly requires an amendment substituting, in the case of misconduct (but not for matters of doctrine, ritual and ceremonial) a reference to the Clergy Discipline Measure 2003. The general provisions of Interpretation Act concerning successor legislation are arguably insufficient to cure the specificity of this anomaly.

[44] For example if the minister of ordination was a woman bishop in a province where such practice was lawful: see *Legal Opinions* 71–81.

Functions and duties

Deacons

4.11 A deacon's function may be gleaned from the following statement from the *Book of Common Prayer* which is made by the bishop as part of the Ordering of Deacons if that form of service is used:

> It appertaineth to the office of a deacon, in the church where he shall be appointed, to serve, assist the priest in divine service, and specially when he ministereth the holy communion, and to help him in the distribution thereof, and to read holy scriptures and homilies in the church; and to instruct the youth in the catechism; in the absence of the priest to baptize infants; and to preach, if he be admitted thereto by the bishop. And furthermore, it is his office, where provision is so made, to search for the sick, poor, and impotent people of the parish, to intimate their estates, names, and places where they dwell, unto the curate, that by his exhortation they may be relieved with the alms of the parishioners, or others.[45]

4.12 A deacon may perform the burial service and, although he may lawfully solemnise marriage, it is canonically irregular, since the ceremony includes the giving of a blessing.[46] The rubric in the Ordinal at the conclusion of the Ordering of Deacons requires a deacon to continue in his office for a whole year (unless 'for reasonable causes it shall otherwise seem good to the bishop') in order that 'he may be perfect and well expert in the things pertaining to the ecclesiastical administration' and 'if he be found faithful and diligent he may be admitted by his diocesan to the order of priesthood'.

Priests

4.13 The function of a priest is to preach the Word of God and to administer the holy sacraments.[47] Central to the exercise of a vocation by a priest or deacon is an undertaking to devote one's life to the service of God and to no other inconsistent purpose.[48] The Pluralities Act 1838 forbids persons holding any cathedral preferment or benefice, curacy or lectureship, or licensed or allowed to perform any

---

[45] See the Ordinal in the *Book of Common Prayer*.
[46] See R Bursell, *Liturgy, Order and the Law* (Oxford: Clarendon Press, 1996) 176 n 209. See also K Stevenson, *Nuptial Blessing: A Study of Christian Marriage Rites* (London: Alcuin Club, 1982).
[47] In the Ordinal, the words spoken by the bishop after the laying on of hands and delivery of the Bible are 'Take thou authority to preach the Word of God, and to minister the Holy Sacraments in the congregation where thou shalt be lawfully appointed thereunto'.
[48] In the Ordinal, the bishop is required to address the ordinands as follows: 'Ye ought to forsake and set aside (as much as you may) all worldly cares and studies. We have good hope ... that you have clearly determined ... to give yourselves wholly to this office ... so that, as much as lieth in you, you will apply yourselves wholly to this one thing, and draw all your cares and studies this way'.

ecclesiastical office, from farming more than 80 acres of land without the permission of the bishop, or from engaging in trade, save for teaching, the buying and selling of household goods and certain other matters.[49] Furthermore, ministers may not engage in occupations and recreations such as do not befit their sacred calling, may be detrimental to the performance of their duties or may cause offence to others.[50] A minister may not engage in any trade or other occupation in such a manner as to affect the performance of the duties of his office, save as authorized by statutory enactment or by licence granted by the bishop.[51] Such licence may only be granted after consultation with the relevant PCC.[52] Should the bishop refuse to grant the licence, the minister may appeal to the archbishop.[53]

4.14 A clergyman who is a peer may sit in the House of Lords. There is no longer any bar upon a cleric being elected to the House of Commons;[54] there has never been any such restriction in relation to local government.[55] Clergy may vote at general and local government elections.[56] No disciplinary proceedings may be taken against a clergyman in respect of his political opinions or activities.[57] The clergy are no longer exempt from jury service,[58] but were traditionally immune from conscription to the armed forces.[59] They are privileged from arrest on civil process (though not criminal) when going to and from Convocation (if they be members) or when going to and from an episcopal visitation. They are specially protected by the criminal law while in a place of worship or officiating at a burial,[60] and beneficed property is exempt from sequestration, save by the bishop.[61]

4.15 Every bishop, priest and deacon is obliged by canon law to say daily the morning and evening prayer, either privately or openly, and to celebrate the holy communion

---

[49] Pluralities Act 1838, ss 28–30.
[50] Canon C 26 para 2.
[51] Canon C 28 para 1. This would be particularly relevant in the case of non-stipendiary ministry. As to the appointment of non-stipendiary ministers as incumbents, see *Legal Opinions* 54–56.
[52] Canon C 28 para 2.
[53] Canon C 28 para 3. The archbishop may confirm or overrule the refusal.
[54] House of Commons (Removal of Clergy Disqualification) Act 2001, repealing the House of Commons (Clergy Disqualification) Act 1801. The 2001 Act simply declares that 'a person is not disqualified from being or being elected as a member of the House of Commons merely because he has been ordained or is a minister of any religious denomination': s 1(1). On the extent of the former law, see *Re Macmanaway* [1951] AC 161, PC.
[55] The Local Government Act 1972, s 80, omits clergy from those disqualified.
[56] They are not disqualified under the Representation of the People Act 1983, s 1.
[57] Clergy Discipline Measure 2003, s 8(3), in relation to matters of 'misconduct', as defined in the Measure. See Chapter 6 for a fuller treatment of clergy discipline.
[58] Criminal Justice Act 2003, Sch 33, amending the Juries Act 1974.
[59] See, eg, the National Service Act 1948, s 1, Sch 1 (repealed).
[60] 14 *Halsbury's Laws of England* (4th edn, London: Butterworths, 1982) paras 1048–1050.
[61] Ibid paras 676 and 894.

(or be present thereat) on all Sundays and other principal feast days.[62] In addition, he must be diligent in daily prayer and intercession, in examination of his conscience and in his studies.[63] A minister at all times must be diligent to frame and fashion his life and that of his family according to the doctrine of Christ, and to make himself and them, as much as in him lies, wholesome examples and patterns to the flock of Christ.[64] The apparel of a bishop, priest and deacon must be suitable to his office and such as to be a sign and mark of his holy calling and ministry.[65]

4.16 It is the duty of an incumbent to reside within his benefice (or one of them if he holds more) and in the residence provided.[66] He may not be absent for an aggregate of more than three months in any one year unless he is legally exempt from residence or granted a licence by the bishop.[67] A failure to reside on the benefice will result in the forfeiture of part or all of the emoluments of the benefice, depending upon the period of absence.[68] An incumbent who is non-resident with the bishop's licence may not, without the bishop's permission, resume the duties of his benefice before the expiration of the period stated in the licence.[69] An incumbent's widow, widower or civil partner may continue to reside in the house of residence for a period of up to two months following the incumbent's death.[70] Specific mandatory duties are placed upon priests having a cure of souls. They are set out in Canon C 24 and, in brief summation, comprise:

(a) the saying of morning and evening prayer;
(b) the celebration of holy communion;

---

[62] Canon C 26 para 1. There is a dispensing provision in case of sickness or some other urgent cause. However, the dispensing powers in Canon B 14A apply to public worship under Canon B 11 and not the private obligation of the minister under Canon C 26 para 1.

[63] Canon C 26 para 1. This embraces 'the study of the holy Scriptures and such other studies as pertain to his ministerial duties'.

[64] Canon C 26 para 2. This provision, placing a responsibility upon a cleric for the conduct of family members, may fall foul of the Human Rights Act 1998, particularly the right to respect for private and family life under Article 8 of the European Convention on Human Rights. Note also that only the second limb is qualified by 'as much as in him lies'.

[65] Canon C 27.

[66] Pluralities Act 1838, ss 32–51; Canon C 25 para 1. If there is no fit house, the bishop may license the incumbent to reside in some fit and convenient house not belonging to the benefice so long as it is within three miles of the church, or two if in any city, borough town or market town. Canon C 25 para 4.

[67] Canon C 25 para 2. Where both partners to a marriage are incumbents, it is usual for one to be permitted to reside otherwise than within the benefice concerned. In the event of a refusal by the bishop to grant a licence, the incumbent may appeal to the archbishop who must confirm the refusal or direct the bishop to grant a licence as he deems right and proper: Canon C 25 para 3.

[68] Pluralities Act 1838, s 32. Recovery of forfeit emoluments is a matter for the consistory court: s 114.

[69] Pluralities Acts Amendment Act 1885, s 12.

[70] Pluralities Act 1838, s 36, as amended by the Priests (Ordination of Women) Measure 1993, s 10, Sch 3 para 1 and the Civil Partnership (Judicial Pensions and Church Pensions, etc) Order 2005, SI 2005/3129, Art 4(3), Sch 3 para 1(1), (2).

(c) preaching each Sunday;
(d) instructing parishioners;[71]
(e) teaching or visiting in schools;
(f) preparing candidates for confirmation;
(g) visiting the sick;
(h) consulting with the PCC; and
(i) making proper provision for his absences.

There is something of a dissonance between the duties placed on clergy in Canon C 24 and the provisions of Canon B 14A which came into effect in February 1994 but apply only to those services required under Canon B 11 and not those which a minister must provide to be said under Canon C 24.

Beneficed clergy

4.17 Parochial clergy fall into two categories: beneficed and unbeneficed. A benefice is a freehold office, the holder of which is known as 'the incumbent', but may also be styled 'rector' or 'vicar'. The incumbent is a corporation sole[72] and has a freehold interest in the emoluments of the benefice until retirement or vacation of the benefice.[73] The incumbent has the exclusive cure of souls within the parish, which he shares with the bishop. No clergyman may officiate within a parish without the incumbent's consent. To this general rule are certain limited exceptions:

(a) a minister of a parish may perform offices and services at the homes of persons on the church electoral roll of that parish but resident in another;[74]
(b) a minister of a parish may perform a funeral service in any crematorium or cemetery situated in another parish if the deceased dies in the minister's parish or was resident in or on the electoral roll of that parish prior to his death;[75]
(c) a minister licensed to perform offices and services at certain institutions does not require consent so to do from the minister of the parish in which the institution is situated;[76]

---

[71] See Amending Canon 23 which, with effect from February 2000, substituted 'parishioners of the benefice' for 'children', in relation to whom the duty to instruct had previously been limited by Canon C 24 para 4.
[72] See *Coke on Littleton, Institutes* (4th edn, London, 1639) vol 1 250a.
[73] The same status attaches to a rector or vicar of a new benefice created by pastoral scheme (Pastoral Measure 1983, s 23(5)), for a team rector (s 20(2)), and for a team vicar (s 20(3)), although a team vicar is not a corporation sole and each holds office for a term of years and not the traditional freehold.
[74] Extra-Parochial Ministry Measure 1967, s 1; Canon C 8 para 4.
[75] Church of England (Miscellaneous Provisions) Measure 1992, s 2(2).
[76] Extra-Parochial Ministry Measure 1967, s 2(2); Canon C 8 para 4. The institutions comprise universities, colleges, schools, hospitals, and public or charitable institutions.

(d) a minister licensed to perform funeral services on premises forming part of any such institution may perform a funeral service in any crematorium or cemetery if the deceased was resident in, employed by or enrolled as a student in that institution at the time of his death;[77]
(e) a team ministry rector's general responsibility for the cure of souls in the area of the benefice[78] may be subject to any special cure assigned to any vicar by the scheme itself or by the bishop's licence in respect of part of the area; a vicar's special responsibility for a particular pastoral function independent of the rector's general responsibility; or a vicar's general responsibility being shared with the rector in the area as a whole.[79]

Patronage

4.18 By virtue of the Patronage (Benefices) Measure 1986, which came into force on 1 January 1989, the position with regard to the law of patronage and advowsons was greatly simplified and much of the old law and practice is now only of interest to the historian. Patronage is the right to appoint or present a cleric to a benefice and is in itself a form of property which may be transferred from one person to another,[80] although it may not be sold.[81] A register of the patrons of every benefice is maintained in each diocesan registry where every transfer of a right of patronage is registered.[82] Notice must be given of any intended transfer and the bishop's consent is required, which may not be given until the PCC has been afforded one month within which to make representations.[83] Rights of patronage may also be transferred by pastoral scheme or order.[84] A transfer has no effect at law unless an application for registration is made within 12 months of the execution of the instrument of transfer.[85] The previous restriction, whereby no transfer may take

---

77 Church of England (Miscellaneous Provisions) Measure 1992, s 2(3).
78 Pastoral Measure 1983, s 20(7).
79 Ibid s 20(8). Team and group ministries are discussed in more detail in paras 4.47ff below.
80 Persons include offices (Patronage (Benefices) Measure 1986, s 2) and corporate or unincorporated bodies (s 8(2)). Children act by trustees as the property vests in them: see 14 *Halsbury's Laws of England* (4th edn, London: Butterworths, 1982) para 781. See also the Pastoral Measure 1983, s 82 in relation to patrons who are minors. The deceased act by personal representatives if the transfer of the right to present has not been registered when the vacancy occurs: Patronage (Benefices) Measure 1986, s 21. The Lord Chancellor exercises the right of presentation on behalf of mental patients: Mental Health Act 1983, ss 94, 96(5).
81 Patronage (Benefices) Measure 1986, s 3(1).
82 Ibid s 1(1). Any patron who failed to register within the registration period of 15 months of the coming into force of the Measure lost his entitlement to exercise the functions of patron of a benefice: s 1(2).
83 Ibid s 3(2)–(5).
84 Pastoral Measure 1983, s 32, amended by the Patronage (Benefices) Measure 1986, ss 23, 41, Sch 5.
85 Patronage (Benefices) Measure 1986, s 3(7).

effect during a vacancy in the benefice,[86] has now been ameliorated so as to permit such a transfer where the right to presentation has been suspended under the Pastoral Measure 1983 and a priest-in-charge has been duly appointed.[87]

4.19 It is for the patron to present his nominee to the bishop, so that he may be put in possession of the cure of souls (a process known as institution),[88] and the right arises when any benefice becomes vacant.[89] This may occur through the death of the incumbent, by his resignation, by cession,[90] by removal from office or deprivation[91] or by compulsory retirement.[92] When the bishop becomes aware of a vacancy or that a benefice is shortly to become vacant, he must give notice of that fact to the designated officer of the diocese.[93] As soon as practicable thereafter, the designated officer must send notice of the vacancy to the registered patron and the secretary of the PCC.[94] If the patron is an individual[95] and not a clerk in holy orders, he must make a declaration that he is an actual communicant member of the Church of England or appoint someone in his place who is a clerk in holy orders or, being a layman, is able to make the declaration of membership.[96] This must be done within two months of being notified of the vacancy.[97]

4.20 Within four weeks of the PCC, through its secretary, being notified of the vacancy, it must meet, on one or more occasions, for the purpose of preparing a statement describing the conditions, needs and traditions of the parish; appointing two lay members of the PCC to act as its representatives in the selection process; deciding whether to request the patron to consider advertising the vacancy;

---

[86] Ibid s 3(8).

[87] Patronage (Benefices) Measure 1986, s 3(8), amended by the Church of England (Miscellaneous Provisions) Measure 2000, s.17.

[88] When the bishop is himself the patron there is no presentation and the process is called 'collation'.

[89] Unless presentation is suspended under the Pastoral Measure 1983, ss 69, 70, discussed below.

[90] ie when the incumbent is created a diocesan bishop or appointed to another preferment which cannot be held with the benefice.

[91] The former under the Clergy Discipline Measure 2003, and the latter through simony or by censure of deprivation under Ecclesiastical Jurisdiction Measure 1963.

[92] Ecclesiastical Offices (Age Limit) Measure 1975, s 1(3), Schedule, discussed in paras 4.23ff below.

[93] Patronage (Benefices) Measure 1986, s 7(1), (2). Notice must also be given to the registrar: s 7(3). The designated officer is such person as the bishop, after consulting the bishop's council, designates or, failing designation, is the secretary of the pastoral committee: s 7(5).

[94] Ibid s 7(4).

[95] Certain restrictions upon Roman Catholics and Jews which prevented them from acting as patron have been removed: ibid s 33.

[96] Ibid s 8(1)(a), (b). Corporate and unincorporated bodies must appoint a person who is able and willing to make the declaration or is a clerk in holy orders: s 8(2). An individual patron who is qualified may nonetheless appoint a representative (s 8(3)); as may a non-ecclesiastical office holder if unable to make the declaration (s 8(4)) or the donee of a power of attorney (s 8(5)). Specified ecclesiastical bodies must appoint a clerk in holy orders or a representative: s 8(6), (7).

[97] Ibid s 9(1).

deciding whether to request a joint meeting of the PCC, the incumbent and the patron; deciding whether to request a statement in writing from the bishop describing in relation to the benefice the needs of the diocese and the wider interests of the Church; and deciding whether to pass either or both of resolutions A and B under the Priests (Ordination of Women) Measure 1993.[98] The joint meeting must be held within six weeks of the request from the PCC or the patron.[99]

There is no legal requirement regarding the method of selecting the presentee, although guidance is to be found in the Code of Practice.[100] The patron may not offer to present to the vacant benefice until the making of such offer has been approved by the parish representatives and the bishop.[101] A refusal by either the parish representatives or the bishop to approve the proposed offer must be communicated to the patron in writing, stating the grounds upon which the refusal is made.[102] If approval is refused, the patron may request the archbishop to review the matter.[103] Where a priest accepts an offer, the patron must send the bishop a notice presenting the priest for admission to the benefice.[104] Certain default powers and procedures are provided for.[105] Where after nine months of the benefice becoming vacant no notice of presentation has been received by the bishop, the right to present becomes exercisable by the archbishop.[106]

4.21

A bishop may refuse to institute a presentee in the following circumstances:

4.22

(a) if not more than three years have passed since the presentee was made deacon;
(b) if the presentee is unfit through physical or mental infirmity or incapacity, serious pecuniary embarrassment or scandal concerning his moral character;
(c) if the presentee has knowingly been a party to a transaction related to the presentation which is invalid;

---

[98] Patronage (Benefices) Measure 1986, s 11(1)(a)–(f), amended by the Priests (Ordination of Women) Measure 1993, s 3(7).
[99] Patronage (Benefices) Measure 1986, s 12(5). Fourteen days' notice must be given. The bishop and the patron may each appoint someone to attend on their behalf if they are themselves unable so to do: s 12(8). Unless the patron and bishop (or their appointees) are present together with at least one-third of the PCC, the meeting will not be treated as having been held: s 12(8). The secretary of the PCC must invite the rural dean and the lay chairman of the deanery synod to the meeting: s 12(9).
[100] *Patronage (Benefices) Measure 1986 Code of Practice: The Exercise of Rights of Presentation.*
[101] Patronage (Benefices) Measure 1986, s 13(1)(b). In addition, if a request for a joint meeting has been made, that meeting must have taken place or six weeks must have elapsed from the date of the request: ibid s 13(1)(a).
[102] Ibid s 13(4). If, after four weeks in the case of the bishop and two in the case of the PCC, no notice of refusal to approve has been received, approval will be deemed: s 13(2), (3).
[103] Ibid s 13(5). If the archbishop authorizes the patron to make the offer, the patron may then do so: s 13(5).
[104] Ibid s 13(6).
[105] Ibid ss 14, 15.
[106] Ibid s 16(1)(a). The same applies in the case of the bishop not receiving an acceptance of any offer made by him to collate a priest to the benefice: s 16(1)(b).

(d) if the presentee has had less than three years' experience as a full-time parochial minister.[107]

There is a right of appeal against a refusal by the bishop to institute and this right may be exercised within a month by either the patron or the presentee.[108] If no presentation is made within nine months of the vacancy, the right of presentation passes to the archbishop of the province.[109]

Suspension of presentation

4.23 If a benefice is vacant or shortly to become vacant, the bishop may give notice that the patron is not to exercise his right of presentation without the consent of the bishop and the pastoral committee although such notice of suspension may only be made with the consent of the pastoral committee and after consultation with the patron, the PCC and the chairmen of the deanery synod.[110] When making such consultations, the bishop must inform the consultees why he is considering whether he should exercise the power to suspend.[111] This would suggest that some proper reason must exist, in the absence of which the bishop's action would be amenable to judicial review.[112] An immutable policy of suspending presentation to all benefices amounting to a fettering of episcopal discretion would be unlawful.

4.24 The power to suspend may be exercised at any time within three months before the benefice is due to become vacant or at any time during the vacancy.[113]

---

[107] Benefices Act 1898, s 2(1)(b), in relation to the first three grounds; Benefices Measure 1972, s 1(1), in relation to the last. Canon C 10 para 3 reflects, but does not replicate, these requirements.

[108] Benefices Act 1898, s 3(2) (amended by the Patronage (Benefices) Measure 1986, s 18(1)); Benefices Measure 1972, s 1(2). Canon C 10 para 8 recognizes the right to appeal. Note that the manner of the appeal under each Measure is different. Under the 1898 Measure, the appellate tribunal comprises the archbishop of the province and the Dean of the Arches or Auditor, whereas under the 1972 Measure the archbishop sits alone. It would appear that both determine the matter *de novo* and there is no further appeal.

[109] Patronage (Benefices) Measure 1986, s 16(1).

[110] Pastoral Measure 1983, s 67(1)(a)–(c).

[111] Ibid s 67(1).

[112] In *R v Bishop of Southwark, ex parte the PCC and Churchwardens of St Luke, Kingston*, 13 November 1995 (unreported) (CO/2119/95), leave to petition for judicial review was granted by Brooke J, but the parties came to terms thereby obviating the need for a full hearing.

[113] Pastoral Measure 1983, s 67(2). The *Code of Recommended Practice to the Pastoral Measure 1983*, on its re-issue in May 2005 included the following revised text at paragraph 9.23: 'Suspension may also be renewed for a further period or periods … but only before the expiry of the suspension period. If a suspension period is not renewed before its expiry, no further suspension of presentation to a benefice is allowed during the relevant vacancy.' This restriction will be removed by the introduction of a new sub-section to the Pastoral Measure 1983 (to be numbered 67(5A)). See the proposed Dioceses, Pastoral and Mission Measure, Sch 5, para 12, approved by the General Synod in its February 2007 sessions. This subsection will make express provision for a new suspension period to be declared after the expiration of a previous suspension period subject to like notice being given.

The suspension period must be specified in the notice and may not exceed five years,[114] although it may be extended for further periods of no more than five years each subject to the same consents and consultations providing each further notice is given prior to the expiration of the subsisting suspension period.[115] Notice of suspension must be given to specified bodies and individuals and affixed at or near the door of the parish church or principal place of worship.[116] The suspension period may be brought to an end by expiry of the notice of suspension, by notice of termination, by consent to the exercise of the right to presentation, or by express operation of a pastoral scheme or order.[117]

4.25 A separate disentitlement to exercise the right of presentation exists where proposals have been submitted to the Church Commissioners relating to the making of a pastoral scheme or order.[118] In such circumstances, a patron may only present to a benefice with the consent of the diocesan pastoral committee and the bishop. This disentitlement lasts until the proposals are implemented, withdrawn or omitted or the expiry of three years from notification of the vacancy, whichever first occurs.[119]

4.26 During a period when the right to present is suspended, and during any other avoidance of the benefice,[120] the churchwardens and the rural dean are the sequestrators of the benefice.[121] They are required to receive the income of the benefice, principally fees for marriages and burials.[122]

Institution, collation and induction

4.27 The presentee must have been ordained priest by episcopal ordination in accordance with the provisions of Canon C 1.[123] If such ordination was by another bishop, then the presentee must first show the bishop his letters of orders or other

---

[114] Pastoral Measure 1983, s 67(1).
[115] Ibid s 67(5). But see n 113 for amending legislation.
[116] Ibid s 67(6), (7), amended by the Patronage (Benefices) Measure 1986, s 41, Sch 4 para 18, and the Church of England (Miscellaneous Provisions) Measure 1992, s 17(1), Sch 3 para 21. The persons and bodies comprise the diocesan pastoral committee, the patron, both chairmen of the deanery synod, the churchwardens and any sequestrators who may have been appointed.
[117] Pastoral Measure 1983, s 67(4).
[118] Ibid s 69, amended by the Patronage (Benefices) Measure 1986, Sch 4 para 20.
[119] Pastoral Measure 1983, s 69(1)(a)–(d).
[120] ie when the incumbent ceases to have the cure of souls whether through death, resignation, exchange of benefices, cession, deprivation, retirement or pursuant to a declaration under the Incumbents (Vacation of Benefices) Measure 1977.
[121] Church of England (Miscellaneous Provisions) Measure 1992, s 1(1). The bishop, if he considers it desirable, may appoint another person as an additional sequestrator.
[122] By virtue of the Endowments and Glebe Measure 1976, passim, other income is paid directly to the diocese.
[123] Canon C 10 para 1.

sufficient evidence of ordination.[124] No bishop may institute a priest until the expiry of three weeks from the service upon the secretary of the PCC of a notice stating his intention so to do.[125] Once that period is passed, the institution or collation should take place as soon as possible and, preferably, it should be held in the parish church of the benefice.[126] The bishop reads the words of institution with the presentee kneeling before him holding the seal appended thereto in his hand.[127] Provision is made for a commissary to give institution on behalf of the bishop if, for some grave and urgent cause, the bishop is unable to give it himself.[128]

4.28 Institution into the spiritualities is followed by induction by the archdeacon or his deputy[129] into possession of the temporalities of the benefice.[130] Generally, a single service in the parish church embraces institution and induction. Before admission, the presentee must make the declaration of assent[131] and take the oath of allegiance to the Queen[132] and of canonical obedience to the bishop.[133]

Unbeneficed clergy

4.29 Unbeneficed clergy comprise all those who have no freehold office: priests-in-charge of parishes, rectors[134] and vicars in team ministries, assistant curates, chaplains, lecturers and preachers, ministers of chapels and retired clergy. In order to be able to officiate, they require the licence or permission of the bishop of the diocese and, subject to the matters discussed above, the consent of the incumbent, if there be one, of the relevant parish.

Assistant curates

4.30 Assistant curates are licensed by the bishop on the nomination of the incumbent of the benefice concerned. In common with all licensed clergy, a priest from

---

[124] Canon C 10 para 2. The presentee may also be required to prove his former good life and behaviour.
[125] Canon C 10 para 4.
[126] Canon C 10 para 5.
[127] Canon C 10 para 6.
[128] Canon C 10 para 7.
[129] This is usually the rural dean: see Canon C 11 para 3.
[130] Canon C 11 para 1. This is usually done by the placing of the priest's hand on the key of the church door or some other part of the building: Canon C 11 para 2. A public notification of induction is often made by the tolling of the bell.
[131] Canon C 15 para 1(5). For the declaration, see Canon C 15 para 1(1).
[132] Canon C 13 para 1.
[133] Canon C 14 para 3.
[134] Prior to the passing of the Team and Group Ministries Measure 1995, it had been possible to be appointed to a freehold office of team rector.

another diocese must first satisfy the bishop that he is ordained and bring him testimony from the bishop of the diocese whence he came of his honesty, ability and conformity to the doctrine, discipline and worship of the Church of England.[135] A licence may be either general or for some particular office and may specify the term of years for which it will have effect.[136]

An assistant curate's licence may be revoked at any time.[137] An assistant curate is **4.31** not an employee and may not institute proceedings in the employment tribunal.[138] The incumbent has power to determine the appointment of an assistant curate on six months' notice, but only with the consent of the bishop.[139] If the bishop refuses his consent, the incumbent may appeal to the archbishop, who may confirm the refusal or grant such permission as he considers just and proper.[140] The assistant curate may resign on giving three months' notice to the incumbent and the bishop, although the latter may waive the requirement of notice.[141]

Priests-in-charge

A priest-in-charge may be appointed for a benefice to which a suspension period **4.32** applies.[142] The priest-in-charge must take the oath of canonical obedience[143] and the declaration of assent.[144] He has many of the same powers, rights, and duties as an incumbent, particularly in relation to the PCC,[145] and may be required to reside in the parsonage house.[146]

Revocation of licences

A minister's licence may not be terminated by reason of that person's miscon- **4.33** duct otherwise than by proceedings under the Clergy Discipline Measure 2003.[147]

---

[135] Canon C 12 para 2.
[136] Canon C 12 para 1.
[137] As to summary revocation, see below.
[138] *Diocese of Southwark v Coker* [1998] ICR 140, CA.
[139] Pluralities Act 1838, s 95.
[140] Ibid s 95 proviso.
[141] Ibid s 97, amended by the Church of England (Legal Aid and Miscellaneous Provisions) Measure 1988, s 7(2)(a).
[142] Pastoral Measure 1983, s 68(3). Before doing so the bishop must consult the PCC and, so far as reasonably practical, the patron.
[143] Canon C 14 para 3.
[144] Canon C 15 para 1(6). They also make the declaration of assent publicly and openly in the presence of the congregation of the first Sunday on which they officiate: Canon C 15 para 4.
[145] The expression 'minister' which appears in many canons and statutory provisions embraces a priest-in-charge.
[146] Pastoral Measure 1983, s 68(4).
[147] Clergy Discipline Measure 2003, s 8(2). The substantive provisions of the 2003 Measure came into force on 1 January 2006 and are the subject of detailed treatment in Chapter 6.

Misconduct has a particular statutory meaning in this regard,[148] which does not include matters of doctrine, ritual or ceremonial, which are expressly excluded from the operation of the 2003 Measure.[149] A bishop still has the power summarily to revoke a minister's licence,[150] provided the ground for so doing is not encompassed within the definition of misconduct for the purposes of the 2003 Measure.[151]

4.34 The notice of revocation must be in writing and 'for any cause which appears to the bishop to be good and reasonable'. It may not be served unless and until the proposed recipient has been given sufficient opportunity of showing reason to the contrary.[152] The recipient of the notice has 28 days from receipt to appeal to the archbishop of the province.[153] The appeal may be heard either by the archbishop of the province or by an appointee, being a diocesan or suffragan bishop in the province.[154] The archbishop (after hearing the appeal or receiving the report of his appointee) may confirm, vary or cancel the revocation of the licence as he considers just and proper.[155] The appeal is conducted in accordance with rules approved by the Archbishops of Canterbury and York, which may provide for the appointment of one or more persons to advise on any question of law arising in the course of the appeal.[156] There is no appeal from the decision of the archbishop.[157]

---

[148] Clergy Discipline Measure 2003, s 8(1). It comprises (a) doing an act in contravention of ecclesiastical law, (b) failing to do an act required by ecclesiastical law, (c) neglect or inefficiency in the performance of the duties of office, (d) conduct unbecoming a cleric. See Chapter 6.

[149] Clergy Discipline Measure 2003, s 7(2). Accordingly, a bishop still has power to revoke a licence summarily for a doctrinal offence.

[150] Canon C 12 para 5. See also *Legal Opinions* 68–70. Revocation on notice (as opposed to summary revocation) is discussed at para 4.35 below.

[151] Such circumstances are difficult to imagine and it is anticipated that the future use of the procedure for the summary revocation of a cleric's licence will be rare. An expressed aim of the Clergy Discipline Measure 2003 was to put beneficed and unbeneficed clergy on an equal footing in terms of disciplinary proceedings.

[152] Canon C 12 para 5.

[153] This right must be set out in the notice of revocation: Canon C 12 para 5.

[154] Canon C 12 para 5. The appointee may not be from the diocese concerned and, when the see of the archbishop is vacant, the function is that of the archbishop of the other province: Canon C 12 para 5.

[155] See *Re Sinyanki* (1864) 12 WR 825 which suggests that a decision upholding revocation ought to be based on the same grounds as that of the bishop. In *Coekin v Bishop of Southwark* (2006) 9 Ecc LJ 145, it was stated that the questions to be answered on a appeal are: (i) did the process undertaken by the bishop comply with the requirements of Canon C 12(5)? (ii) were the reasons given by the bishop for revoking the cleric's licence (a) factually correct, and (b) valid as a matter of law? The same approach was adopted by the Archbishop of York in *Brown v Bishop of Carlisle* (2003) 7 Ecc LJ 239, and is discussed in D Hope, 'Doctrine and Discipline' (2005) 8 Ecc LJ 32 at 36–39.

[156] For recent examples of successful appeals, see *Coekin v Bishop of Southwark* (2007) 9 Ecc LJ 145; and *Harries v Bishop of Chester* (2007) 9 Ecc LJ 141. In the latter case the Archbishop of Canterbury (exercising jurisdiction during the vacancy in see in York) declined to follow the recommendation of the Bishop of Durham (his appointee who heard the appeal). His jurisdiction to do so, and the grounds upon which he purported to act, might be considered to be questionable as noted at 9 Ecc LJ 142.

[157] Canon C 12 para 5.

Where revocation is made on notice, as opposed to summarily, the bishop is **4.35** not required to demonstrate grounds.[158] However, as with summary revocation, a licence may not be revoked on notice by reason of a cleric's misconduct otherwise than by way of proceedings under the Clergy Discipline Measure 2003.[159] What constitutes reasonable notice will depend upon the circumstances of the case including the period for which the licence has been held. An unduly short notice period would be deemed to amount to summary revocation, thereby activating the provisions of Canon C 12 para 5.[160] Where a minister has been granted a licence for a term of years, the bishop may revoke it prior to the expiration of that term; however such revocation is treated as one made under Canon C 12 para 5 importing the like right of appeal.[161]

Permission to officiate

The appointment of priests to officiate at particular places or institutions is generally effected by licence under the hand and seal of the bishop, or by giving written permission to officiate.[162] Their authority to officiate is governed by the Extra-Parochial Ministry Measure 1967. This Measure, unlike the Clergy (Ordination and Miscellaneous Provisions) Measure 1964, makes no specific provision for any appeal against the summary revocation of a licence to officiate at any university, college, school, hospital or public or charitable institution.[163] The provisions of Canon C 12 are sufficiently broad, however, to apply to 'any licence granted to any minister within [the] diocese'.[164] Likewise the wording of the Clergy Discipline Measure 2003 is such that no licence from the bishop may be terminated by reason of misconduct otherwise than by way of proceedings under the Measure.[165] A register must be kept in each diocesan registry of all licences granted.[166] **4.36**

---

[158] See *R (on the application of Gibbs) v Bishop of Manchester* [2007] All ER (D) 256, [2007] EWHC 480, Admin Ct, Munby J, concerning a bishop's licence granted to layman appointed to the office of Church Army captain, in which a passage to this effect from the second edition of this work was cited with approval.
[159] Clergy Discipline Measure 2003, s 8(2), discussed in para 4.33 above.
[160] See *Legal Opinions* 68.
[161] Canon C 12 para 6. The procedure for the appeal is set out at para 4.34 above. This provision does not to apply to team vicars. See *Calvert v Gardiner and others* [2002] EWHC 1394 (QB), Burton J, at para 36.
[162] Canon C 8 para 3.
[163] Extra-Parochial Ministry Measure 1967, s 2(4).
[164] Canon C 12 para 5.
[165] Clergy Discipline Measure 2003, s 8(2).
[166] Pluralities Act 1838, s 102.

Visitations

4.37 Priests and deacons who have received authority to minister in any diocese owe canonical obedience to the bishop of the diocese, and the bishop, in turn, owes due allegiance to the archbishop as his metropolitan.[167] It has been said that a bishop 'is first and foremost a pastor rather than a judge'.[168] The discipline of the Church is maintained, inter alia, by means of the visitation.[169] The purpose of a visitation is that the bishop may 'get some good knowledge of the state, sufficiency, and ability of the clergy and other persons whom he is to visit'[170] and the bishop has the right to perform acts for 'the edifying and well-governing of Christ's flock' and for supplying things which are lacking and correcting things which are amiss.[171] When a visitation is summoned, the bishop first delivers articles of inquiry to the minister and churchwardens upon which they are required to ground their presentments,[172] which may relate to the conduct of an incumbent or other priest. The archdeacon also has a role in ensuring that those who hold ecclesiastical office carry out their duties with diligence; he is required to bring to the bishop's attention matters which require correction or praise.[173]

Retirement and removal

4.38 Holy orders are, by their nature, indelible and no person who has been admitted to the order of bishop, priest or deacon can ever be divested of the character of that order.[174] A minister may, however, voluntarily relinquish the exercise of those orders, or be prohibited from their exercise.[175] Relinquishment is facilitated by deed, which relieves the person executing the deed from all disabilities, deprives him of all privileges and restores him, in practical terms, to the status

---

[167] Canon C 1 para 3.
[168] *Report of the Archbishops' Commission on Ecclesiastical Courts* (London, 1954) 51.
[169] See generally P Smith, 'Points of Law and Practice Concerning Ecclesiastical Visitations' (1991) 2 Ecc LJ 189.
[170] Canon C 18 para 4.
[171] Canon G 5 para 1.
[172] Canon G 6 para 1.
[173] Canon C 22 para 4.
[174] Canon C 1 para 2.
[175] Canon C 1 para 2. Prohibition may be for life or a limited period: Clergy Discipline Measure 2003, s 24. Deprivation and deposition remain available as sanctions for offences concerning doctrine, ritual or ceremonial under the provisions of the Ecclesiastical Jurisdiction Measure 1963. A censure of deposition passed under the 1963 Measure continues, although application may now be made for it to be nullified in certain limited circumstances. See Clergy Discipline Measure 2003, s 26, discussed at para 6.55.

of a layperson.[176] However, in reality the person's ordained status is merely suspended and liable to be revived (without any further ordination) upon the enrolment and record of the deed being vacated.[177] Following the vacation of the enrolment, there is a two-year moratorium, during which the priest concerned may not hold any benefice or other preferment but may only officiate as a minister in a diocese under the permission of the bishop.[178]

4.39 An incumbent or vicar in a team ministry is obliged to retire upon reaching 70 years of age.[179] However, where the bishop considers that the pastoral needs of the parish make it desirable that he should continue in office,[180] he may, with the consent of the PCC, authorize the incumbent's continuance in office for one or more periods not exceeding two years in total.[181]

4.40 Where a bishop is satisfied that it is proper to do so, he may instruct the secretary of the diocesan synod to institute an inquiry to consider whether an incumbent is unable, by reason of age or infirmity of mind or body, to discharge his duties adequately and, if so, whether it is desirable that he should resign his benefice or be given assistance in discharging those duties.[182] The incumbent may be ordered to undergo a medical examination, and inferences may be drawn from his refusal.[183] The bishop has power to inhibit the incumbent from exercising

---

[176] For a consideration of the nature of orders in a deposition appeal in the Church in Wales, see *Williams v Bishop of Bangor* (1999) 5 Ecc LJ 304, Provincial Ct in Wales.

[177] The procedure to effect vacation of enrolment is contained in the Clerical Disabilities Act 1870 (Amendment) Measure 1934. The person concerned petitions in writing the archbishop of the province within which is the diocesan registry where the relevant deed is recorded: s 1(1). The petition must specify why the deed was first executed, what work the applicant has been engaged in since and why he now wishes to resume the position of officiating minister, and must be verified by statutory declaration: s 1(1)(i)–(iii), (2). The archbishop must consult with the bishop of the relevant diocese and communicate his decision after 'such other inquiry and consultation as he shall deem necessary': s 1(3). If the archbishop thinks fit, he may, either forthwith or after an interval, by writing under his hand and archiepiscopal seal, request the vacation of the enrolment of the deed: s 1(3).

[178] Ibid s 2(1).

[179] Ecclesiastical Offices (Age Limit) Measure 1975, s 1(3), Schedule. In the case of fixed term, or time limited posts or offices with the prospect of renewal, to which the 1975 Measure does not apply, consideration will need to be given to the Employment Equality (Age) Regulations 2006 (SI 2006/1031) and for the need for a clear objective justification which would require a cleric to retire at a younger age than others doing similar work.

[180] For a judicial consideration of renewal of licences in a team ministry, see *R v Bishop of Stafford, ex parte Owen* (2000) 6 Ecc LJ 83, CA.

[181] Ecclesiastical Offices (Age Limit) Measure 1975, s 3(2).

[182] Incumbents (Vacation of Benefices) Measure 1977, s 6, the procedure in relation to which is set out below. It may be that the cumbersome process under the Measure might be avoided following the introduction of a capability procedure under the Ecclesiastical Offices (Terms of Service) Measure, the Ecclesiastical Offices (Terms of Service) Regulations and Amending Canon 29, all of which are in draft form at the time of writing.

[183] Incumbents (Vacation of Benefices) Measure 1977, s 7A, added by the Incumbents (Vacation of Benefices) (Amendment) Measure 1993, s 5.

his clerical duties whilst the inquiry is in train and, in certain circumstances, after it has reported.[184]

4.41 Where the tribunal has reported that, in its opinion, the incumbent is unable, by reason of age or infirmity of mind or body, to discharge adequately the duties attaching to his benefice, the bishop may notify the incumbent that it is desirable that he should resign his benefice.[185] If the incumbent refuses or fails to resign within one month, the bishop executes a declaration of avoidance declaring the benefice vacant.[186] Alternatively, the bishop may, with the consent of the incumbent, appoint and license an assistant curate to assist him, give to the incumbent up to two years' leave of absence or make other temporary provision for the discharge of his duties.[187] Provisions are made for financial compensation to be paid to an incumbent for loss suffered in consequence of the vacation of his benefice.[188]

4.42 Clerical discipline has been the subject of wholesale revision since the last edition of this work and receives a full treatment in Chapter 6. However the employment status of clergy merits brief mention in the light of certain recent developments. Traditionally clergy, as office holders, have not been regarded as having the status of employees and, accordingly, have been ineligible to claim a raft of labour law rights enforceable in the employment tribunal.[189] The House of Lords, considering the status of a minister in the Church of Scotland,[190] accepted that there were instances when an individual could be both an office holder and an employee under a contract of service. The majority concluded on the evidence that the Kirk had entered into a contract of employment with the minister,[191] and that as a matter of law it was not possible to contract out of the provisions of sex discrimination legislation.[192] How the House of Lords decision will play out in relation to

---

[184] Incumbents (Vacation of Benefices) Measure 1977, s 9A(1)(a), (3), added by the Incumbents (Vacation of Benefices) (Amendment) Measure 1993, s 6.
[185] Incumbents (Vacation of Benefices) Measure 1977, s 11(2)(a). The bishop may only do so if the provincial tribunal so recommended: s 11(3).
[186] Ibid s 11(6). The declaration takes effect from a date specified being no less than three nor more than six months thereafter.
[187] Ibid s 11(2)(b)–(d). If the incumbent refuses his consent to the appointment of an assistant after the expiration of one month, then the bishop may execute a like declaration of avoidance: s 11(7).
[188] Ibid s 13, amended by the Incumbents (Vacation of Benefices) (Amendment) Measure 1993, s 8.
[189] Note *Diocese of Southwark v Coker* [1998] ICR 140, CA, concerning an assistant curate.
[190] *Percy (AP) v Board of National Mission of the Church of Scotland* [2006] 2 AC 28, [2006] 4 All ER 1354, HL.
[191] *Percy* (above), para 41 per Lord Nicholls of Birkenhead.
[192] *Percy* (above), para 106 per Lord Hope of Craighead, citing the Sex Discrimination Act 1975, s 77. Note also the decision in *New Testament Church of God v Stewart* [2007] IRLR 178, (2006) 9 Ecc LJ 239, EAT.

Vacation of benefices

The Incumbents (Vacation of Benefices) Measure 1977[194] is concerned with occasions where there may have been a serious breakdown in the pastoral relationship between the incumbent and the parishioners, caused by the conduct of one or the other or both, over a substantial period.[195] This breakdown is described as 'a situation where the relationship between an incumbent and the parishioners ... is such as to impede the promotion in the parish of the whole mission of the Church of England, pastoral, evangelistic, social and ecumenical'.[196] The Measure allows for an inquiry to be made at the request of the incumbent, the archdeacon or two-thirds of the lay members of the PCC.[197] However, no inquiry may take place until the persons concerned have had the opportunity to resolve the pastoral situation in the parish. Accordingly, a request for an inquiry may only be made after a notice of intention to make a request has been served on the bishop and a period of at least six and no more than twelve months has elapsed.[198] The notice of intention and the request itself must be in writing and the request must particularize the facts relied on. They must be sent to the bishop and the secretary of the diocesan synod.[199] The latter must notify the incumbent, archdeacon and PCC as appropriate.[200] There is provision to withdraw a request, whereupon no further steps are taken under the Measure.[201]

4.43

---

[193] Consideration will also need to be given to the effect of the draft Ecclesiastical Offices (Terms of Service) Measure, the draft Ecclesiastical Offices (Terms of Service) Regulations, and draft Amending Canon No 29, each of which are currently before the General Synod and affect clergy conditions of service.

[194] This Measure was substantially amended by the Incumbents (Vacation of Benefices) (Amendment) Measure 1993. The legislative history of individual sections is not given in the following paragraphs.

[195] As has already been discussed, the Measure also deals with the physical or mental incapacity of the incumbent.

[196] Incumbents (Vacation of Benefices) Measure 1977, s 19A.

[197] Ibid s 1A(1). If the incumbent is himself the archdeacon, a majority of the bishop's council and standing committee of the diocesan synod may make the request.

[198] Ibid s 1A(1A).

[199] Ibid s 1A(2).

[200] Ibid s 1A(6).

[201] Ibid s 1A(7).

Chapter 4: Clergy

Procedure under the Incumbents (Vacation of Benefices) Measure 1977 (as amended) in cases of serious pastoral breakdown

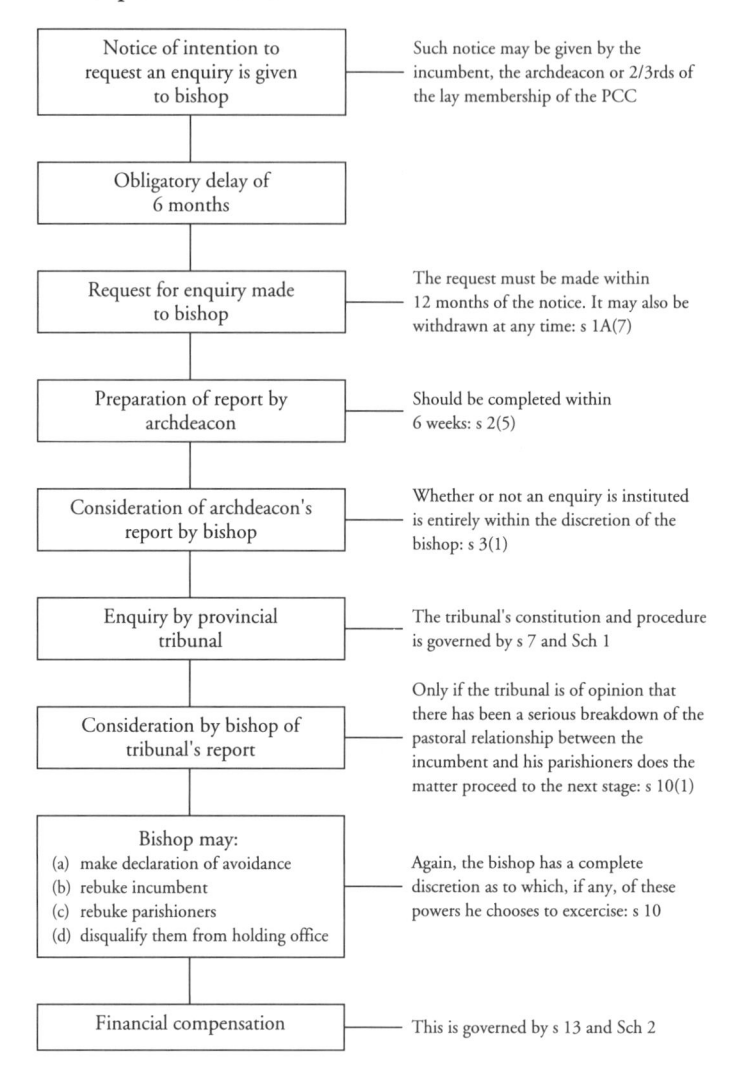

```
┌─────────────────────────────┐
│   Notice of intention to    │      Such notice may be given by the
│ request an enquiry is given │──── incumbent, the archdeacon or 2/3rds of
│          to bishop          │      the lay membership of the PCC
└─────────────┬───────────────┘
              │
┌─────────────┴───────────────┐
│     Obligatory delay of     │
│           6 months          │
└─────────────┬───────────────┘
              │
┌─────────────┴───────────────┐      The request must be made within
│  Request for enquiry made   │──── 12 months of the notice. It may also be
│          to bishop          │      withdrawn at any time: s 1A(7)
└─────────────┬───────────────┘
              │
┌─────────────┴───────────────┐
│    Preparation of report by │      Should be completed within
│          archdeacon         │──── 6 weeks: s 2(5)
└─────────────┬───────────────┘
              │
┌─────────────┴───────────────┐      Whether or not an enquiry is instituted
│ Consideration of archdeacon's│──── is entirely within the discretion of the
│       report by bishop      │      bishop: s 3(1)
└─────────────┬───────────────┘
              │
┌─────────────┴───────────────┐      The tribunal's constitution and procedure
│    Enquiry by provincial    │──── is governed by s 7 and Sch 1
│           tribunal          │
└─────────────┬───────────────┘
              │                      Only if the tribunal is of opinion that
┌─────────────┴───────────────┐      there has been a serious breakdown of the
│  Consideration by bishop of │──── pastoral relationship between the
│       tribunal's report     │      incumbent and his parishioners does the
└─────────────┬───────────────┘      matter proceed to the next stage: s 10(1)
              │
┌─────────────┴───────────────────┐
│ Bishop may:                     │
│ (a)  make declaration of avoidance│   Again, the bishop has a complete
│ (b)  rebuke incumbent           │── discretion as to which, if any, of these
│ (c)  rebuke parishioners        │   powers he chooses to excercise: s 10
│ (d)  disqualify them from holding office│
└─────────────┬───────────────────┘
              │
┌─────────────┴───────────────┐
│    Financial compensation   │──── This is governed by s 13 and Sch 2
└─────────────────────────────┘
```

4.44 Upon receipt of a request, the bishop directs the archdeacon (or in certain circumstances another archdeacon within the diocese) to report.[202] Within six weeks, the archdeacon must report to the bishop whether he considers that an inquiry would be in the best interests of the incumbent and the parishioners.[203] If the archdeacon considers that it would, the bishop then has a discretion and may, if he thinks fit, direct the secretary of the diocesan synod to institute an inquiry.[204] If no decision is made by the bishop within six months, a direction is deemed to have been given.[205] If the archdeacon reports that an inquiry should not be instituted, the incumbent and the PCC may within six months of the report inform the bishop that one is nevertheless required and the bishop has a discretion whether or not to institute one.[206]

4.45 The inquiry is conducted by a provincial tribunal consisting of five persons appointed by the vicar-general of the province.[207] The parties may each be represented by a barrister or solicitor.[208] The procedure is governed by the Incumbents (Vacation of Benefices) Rules 1994.[209] Hearings must normally be in private but at the request of the incumbent or if the tribunal so directs in the interests of justice or for any other good reason, they are in public.[210] The tribunal may order the incumbent to undergo a medical examination and may draw inferences from

---

[202] Ibid s 2(1). Where it is the archdeacon himself who makes the request for an inquiry, this six-week moratorium is unnecessary.

[203] Ibid s 2(5). In doing so he must have regard to the extent to which the Code of Practice promulgated by the House of Bishops has been complied with.

[204] Ibid s 3(1).

[205] Ibid s 3(1A).

[206] Ibid s 3(1)(d). Again, if the bishop makes no decision within six months, he is deemed to have given the requisite direction.

[207] Ibid ss 5, 7. Of the five, one must be a chancellor or Queen's Counsel, two priests and two lay persons appointed from panels established under the Pastoral Measure 1983, Sch 4: Incumbents (Vacation of Benefices) Measure 1977, Sch 1 para 1. They should have no connection with the diocese: Sch 1 para 1 proviso. The incumbent has a right of objection to members of the tribunal, such objection being determined by the vicar-general of the other province: Sch 1 para 3(1), (2). If the vicar-general upholds the objection, he then appoints someone else from the panel (Sch 1 para 1(4)) to whom the incumbent may also object: Sch 1 para 1(5). It is respectfully suggested that the provision in Sch 1 para 1(6) disentitling the incumbent to object when the effect of a successful objection would mean that the tribunal could not be constituted, the available panel being exhausted, is contrary to the Human Rights Act 1998. Article 6 of the European Convention on Human Rights provides for a right to a fair trial and this means one before an independent tribunal. See *Locabail (UK) Ltd v Bayfield Properties Ltd* [2000] QB 451, [2000] 1 All ER 65, CA.

[208] Incumbents (Vacation of Benefices) Measure 1977, s 7(5). For these purposes, unless the incumbent is also an archdeacon, the parties comprise the incumbent, the archdeacon, the PCC or representatives thereof. In addition, the incumbent may be assisted or represented by any person, whether professionally qualified or not: s 7(4).

[209] Incumbents (Vacation of Benefices) Rules 1994, SI 1994/703.

[210] Ibid r 10. Since disqualifications from office may be visited upon parishioners under the Incumbents (Vacation of Benefices) Measure 1977, s 10(6), it is arguable that were a request from a parishioner for the matter to be heard in public to be refused, this would be contrary to the Human Rights Act 1998, being a denial of a fair trial under Article 6 of the Convention. Indeed it may be

his failure to co-operate.[211] The tribunal reports to the bishop whether in its opinion there has been a serious breakdown of the pastoral relationship between the incumbent and the parishioners and whether such breakdown is one to which the conduct of either or both has contributed over a substantial period,[212] and it must include in its report recommendations of the action to be taken by the bishop.[213] Where the tribunal has reported to the bishop and the tribunal is of the stated opinion that the incumbent is unable, by reason of infirmity of mind or body, to discharge adequately the duties attaching to his benefice, the bishop may inhibit the incumbent from performing such duties if it appears to him desirable in the interests of the Church of England.[214] The inquiry process may be avoided if, following a request for one to be made, the incumbent requests the bishop to accept his resignation of his benefice.[215]

4.46 If, but only if, the tribunal so recommends, the bishop may execute a declaration of avoidance declaring the benefice vacant as from a specified date between three and six months thereafter.[216] Where the tribunal concludes that the pastoral breakdown was contributed to by the conduct of the incumbent over a substantial period, the bishop may rebuke him and may disqualify him from executing or performing rights and duties of his office for such a period as he may specify.[217] Where the conduct of the parishioners over a substantial period contributed to the breakdown, the bishop may rebuke such of them as he thinks fit and may disqualify them from being a churchwarden or member or officer of the PCC for such period as he may specify, not exceeding five years.[218] A disqualification imposed upon an incumbent or parishioner may be revoked by the bishop at any time.[219] The bishop may also give such pastoral advice and guidance to the incumbent and the parishioners as he considers appropriate.[220] Were an inquiry to be abandoned or, presumably, not to make a finding of serious pastoral breakdown,

---

open to criticism that one or more parishioners, who were not even parties to the proceedings, may yet be subject to disqualification.

[211] Incumbents (Vacation of Benefices) Measure 1977, s 7A(1), (2). Note that there may be an issue under the Human Rights Act 1998 concerning the right to privacy under Article 8 of the Convention.

[212] Incumbents (Vacation of Benefices) Measure 1977, s 9(1). Where it considers that the incumbent is unable to perform his duties by reason of age or infirmity of mind or body, it may so report instead of addressing the matter of pastoral breakdown: s 9(2).

[213] Ibid s 9(4). At least four members of the tribunal must be agreed before it may recommend that the bishop execute a declaration of avoidance: s 9(5).

[214] Ibid s 9A(1), (2).

[215] Ibid s 4(1). The incumbent remains entitled to compensation: s 13(1)(a).

[216] Ibid s 10(2). The bishop has a complete discretion and may decline to execute a declaration even if the tribunal so recommends.

[217] Ibid s 10(5).

[218] Ibid s 10(6).

[219] Ibid s 10(9).

[220] Ibid s 10(7).

it is nonetheless open for the diocesan pastoral committee to propose a scheme or order under the Pastoral Measure 1983 which affects the same benefice, provided the criteria under the latter Measure were met.[221]

Group and team ministries

Both in this chapter and the preceding one, mention is made of particular provisions applying in the case of group and team ministries. This section seeks to make certain points of general application in respect of parishes which are linked in various such ways. **4.47**

One example of parish clustering which falls short of a group or team ministry is the holding of two or more benefices in plurality.[222] Each parish may continue to function independently, although there is provision for a joint PCC to be established.[223] Save with the leave of the bishop, an incumbent may not resign one benefice without resigning them all.[224] **4.48**

A team ministry is created by a scheme which provides for the sharing of the cure of souls within a benefice.[225] The team rector is the incumbent of the benefice, although the cure of souls is shared with one or more other ministers, styled vicars, who are afforded a status equivalent to that of an incumbent.[226] The scheme makes provision for the sharing of the cure of souls for the benefice between the team rector and vicars.[227] The office of rector in a team ministry is for a term of years,[228] as is that of team vicar.[229] Such terms may be extended by licence under seal of the bishop for a further term or terms, not exceeding, in any extension, the **4.49**

---

[221] *Cheesman v Church Commissioners* [2000] 1 AC 19, PC. Lord Lloyd of Berwick, in his dissenting opinion, would have allowed the appeal, considering that the pastoral scheme in question was nothing other than a way round the Incumbents (Vacation of Benefices) Measure 1977.

[222] Pastoral Measure 1983, s 18.

[223] Ibid s 40, Sch 3 para 13(a). The same may be achieved by a resolution of the APCM of each parish: Church Representation Rules, r 19(1)(a).

[224] Pastoral Measure 1983, s 18(4).

[225] Ibid s 20(1). Section 20 was heavily amended by the Team and Group Ministries Measure 1995, s 1, and is set out in amended form in Sch 1.

[226] Pastoral Measure 1983, s 20(1)(a), (3). By virtue of having the same security of tenure as an incumbent, team vicars are not susceptible to the summary revocation of their licence under Canon C 12 para 6.

[227] Ibid s 20(7), (8).

[228] Ibid s 20(2). Prior to the passing of the Team and Group Ministries Measure 1995, it had been possible to hold the position of team rector as a freehold office.

[229] Pastoral Measure 1983, s 20(3). See the discussion of the legal status of a team vicar in *Calvert v Gardiner and others* [2002] EWHC 1394 (QB) Burton J, at paras 26ff.

original term.[230] A Code of Practice[231] seeks to regulate the renewal of tenure within a team ministry, and it would appear that non-compliance with the code may be subject to judicial review in the secular courts.[232]

4.50 Group ministries are associations of incumbents whose benefices collectively comprise the group.[233] Each incumbent has authority to perform throughout the area all such offices as he may perform within his own benefice but he must do so (otherwise than within his own benefice) only in accordance with the directions of the relevant incumbent.[234] A woman who is the incumbent of a benefice may not preside at or celebrate holy communion or pronounce absolution in a parish which has passed resolutions A or B.[235] An incumbent may not withdraw from the rights and duties of the group ministry without resigning his benefice.[236]

4.51 Provision is made in both team and group ministries for members to meet as a team for the purposes of discussing and reaching a common mind on all matters of general concern and special interest.[237]

Other appointments

4.52 The Church of England, like any other major institution, arranges its human resources with a distinct and recognizable hierarchy. This distribution reflects its synodical structure, outlined in Chapter 2. Save for cathedral clergy, who are discussed in Chapter 8, other church appointments are discussed below.

Rural deans

4.53 Each deanery has a rural dean, whose role and functions are prescribed in Canon C 23.[238] A deacon may be appointed rural dean.[239] It is now possible for

---

[230] Ibid s 20(6).
[231] *Team and Group Ministries: Code of Recommended Practice* (1996). As the Introduction makes plain, 'applying the principles of good practice set out in this Code could make the difference between a negative and a positive experience of collaborative ministry': para A1.
[232] See *R v Bishop of Stafford, ex parte Owen* (2000) 6 Ecc LJ 83, CA. The text of the judgment may be found in the Materials section of the second edition of this work: M Hill, *Ecclesiastical Law* (2nd edn, Oxford: Oxford University Press, 2001) 723–739.
[233] Pastoral Measure 1983, s 21.
[234] Ibid s 21(1)(a), (b).
[235] Ibid s 21(1) proviso, added by the Priests (Ordination of Women) Measure 1993, s 10, Sch 3 para 7. For the resolutions, see ibid s 3(1).
[236] Pastoral Measure 1983, s 21(2).
[237] Ibid ss 20(10) and 21(4) respectively.
[238] For a general discussion, see R Ravenscroft, 'The Role of the Rural Dean' (1998) 5 Ecc LJ 42.
[239] Church of England (Miscellaneous Provisions) Measure 1992, s 14. The declaration of lawfulness is expressed to be for the avoidance of doubt and notwithstanding anything in the Act of Uniformity 1662, s 10.

the bishop, by order, to declare that the office of rural dean, in any deanery in the diocese, is to be called the office of area dean.[240] The rural dean acts as a conduit for information between the parishes of the deanery and the bishop. He is under a duty to report to the bishop matters which it may be necessary or useful for the bishop to know, particularly serious illness or other distress among the clergy, vacancies and ministration during interregna, and ministers from other dioceses officiating otherwise than as permitted under Canon C 8.[241] In the case of an omission to prepare and maintain an electoral roll, or to form and maintain a PCC or hold an APCM, the rural dean, on such matters being brought to his attention, must ascertain the cause and report to the bishop.[242] If at any time the rural dean has reason to believe that there is any serious defect in the fabric, ornaments or furniture of any church or disrepair in any building of the benefice, he must report the matter to the archdeacon.[243] The rural dean is chairman of the deanery synod, jointly with a member of the house of laity.[244] Where a rural deanery is vacant or a rural dean is unable by reason of illness or absence to carry out any or all of his functions, the bishop may appoint another person to perform any or all of his functions for such period as is specified in the instrument of appointment.[245]

Archdeacons

The position of archdeacon, which is a freehold office, is pastoral, administrative, disciplinary and quasi-judicial.[246] A person may not be appointed archdeacon until completion of six years in holy orders, and the appointee must be in priest's orders at the time of appointment.[247] His appointment is within the gift of the diocesan bishop, although there is generally widespread consultation, which varies in its formality and extent from one diocese to another.[248] He is required to

4.54

---

[240] Church of England (Miscellaneous Provisions) Measure 2000, s 12(4). All references in enactments, canons and other instruments to a rural dean are to be construed as including an area dean.
[241] Canon C 23 para 1.
[242] Canon C 23 para 2.
[243] Canon C 23 para 3.
[244] Canon C 23 para 4.
[245] Church of England (Miscellaneous Provisions) Measure 2000, s 12(1). The bishop has power to appoint two or more persons and divide among them, whether territorially or otherwise, the functions to be performed: s 12(2).
[246] See Canon C 22. For a general discussion, see H Jones, '*Omnis Gallia* or the Role of the Archdeacon' (1991) 2 Ecc LJ 236; and R Ravenscroft, 'The Role of the Archdeacon Today' (1995) 3 Ecc LJ 379.
[247] Canon C 22 para 1.
[248] See *Senior Church Appointments, A Review of the Methods of Appointment of Area and Suffragan Bishops, Deans, Provosts, Archdeacons and Residentiary Canons* (GS 1019, 1992), App II paras 39–40. Consultation should embrace those within the diocese, eg representatives of the deaneries in the archdeaconry and the bishop's council, but also the archbishops' secretary for appointments and the Prime Minister's appointments secretary.

retire at the age of seventy.[249] He may be removed for mental or physical incapacity pursuant to the provisions of the Church Dignitaries (Retirement) Measure 1949,[250] or, if he is also an incumbent, under the Incumbents (Vacation of Benefices) Measure 1977.[251]

4.55 The archdeacon has a particular function in relation to the faculty jurisdiction, which is examined in detail in Chapter 7.[252] Within his archdeaconry, he exercises an Ordinary jurisdiction,[253] which he may either perform in person or through an official or commissory.[254] He assists the bishop in his pastoral care and office, ensures that all the duties of ecclesiastical offices are diligently performed and brings to the bishop's attention what calls for correction or merits praise.[255] He is required to assist the bishop in the examination of ordinands.[256] He must carry out an annual visitation, survey all church property, perform duties under the Inspection of Churches Measure 1955 and induct priests.[257]

Diocesan bishops

4.56 A bishop must be at least 30 years of age at the time of his consecration,[258] and may not be refused ordination on the ground of his illegitimacy.[259] He must be 'a godly and well learned man'.[260] Canon C 18 sets out his role as 'chief pastor' of all within the diocese and describes the nature of the office, 'to teach and to uphold sound and wholesome doctrine, and to banish and drive away all erroneous and strange opinions'. He is also to 'maintain quietness, love, and peace among all men'.[261]

---

[249] Ecclesiastical Offices (Age Limit) Measure 1975, s 1(3), Schedule. However, the bishop may extend his tenure for up to a further 12 months if he considers there are special circumstances rendering it desirable: s 3(1)(b).
[250] Discussed in Chapter 8.
[251] Discussed above, paras 4.43 ff.
[252] See Chapter 7.
[253] Canon C 22 para 2.
[254] Canon C 22 para 3. See, by way of example, *Re West Norwood Cemetery (No 2)* [1998] Fam 84, [1998] 1 All ER 606, Southwark Cons Ct, in which the archdeacon appointed an official in relation to a scheme of management for the consecrated part of a municipal cemetery.
[255] Canon C 22 para 4.
[256] Canon C 7.
[257] Canon C 22 para 5. He must, whether in person or by a deputy, survey all churches, chancels and churchyards and give directions for the amendment of all defects in the walls, fabric, ornaments and furniture: Canon C 22 para 5.
[258] Canon C 2 para 3.
[259] Clergy (Ordination and Miscellaneous Provisions) Measure 1964, s 8; Canon C 2 para 4.
[260] See 'The Form of Ordaining or Consecrating of an Archbishop or Bishop' in the *Book of Common Prayer*. See also Canon C 18 para 1.
[261] Canon C 18 para 1.

Other appointments

4.57 A bishop is appointed by the Crown upon the advice of the Prime Minister.[262] The manner of appointment reflects the delicate balance between the established nature of the Church of England and its autonomous self-governance.[263] Each diocese is required to establish and maintain a Vacancy in See Committee.[264] When a vacancy arises, it meets and after consultations prepares a Description of the Diocese and a Statement of Needs.[265] On the basis of their own consultations,[266] the appointments secretaries of the archbishops and the prime minister produce a Memorandum outlining their views on the requirements of the diocese and on the desired profile of the new bishop.[267] The Crown Nominations Commission[268] meets on two occasions,[269] on the second of which it votes on the shortlisted names to produce two for submission to the Crown.[270] The Archbishop of the Province then writes to the Prime Minister, submitting the two names and informing him of the number of members who supported each in the final ballot.[271]

---

[262] See a written parliamentary answer given by the Prime Minister on 8 June 1976 reproduced in *Senior Church Appointments* (n 248 above) App V. For a proposed change to this system, see the government Green Paper, *The Governance of Britain* (Cmnd 7170, 2007).

[263] See *Working With the Spirit: Choosing Diocesan Bishops*, A Review of the Operation of the Crown Appointments Commission and Related Matters (GS 1405, 2001). It reflects the fact that the role of a bishop is multi-faceted, being diocesan, national and to a degree international as well.

[264] Vacancy in See Committees Regulation 1993, reg 1, (as amended by the Vacancy in See Committees (Amendment) Regulation 2003). The committee comprises *ex officio* and elected representatives. The procedure to be adopted when a vacancy arises is summarized in the *Guidance Notes and Code of Practice* (January, 2004) issued under the amended regulations, and also in a *Briefing for Members of Vacancy in See Committees*.

[265] Vacancy in See Committees Regulation 1993, reg 5.

[266] Which latterly have included on an experimental basis the convening of an open meeting at which anyone may express views.

[267] The outgoing bishop is invited to give his views either orally or in writing. The Archbishops prepare a statement setting out the needs of the Church of England as a whole with particular regard to the range of skills, perspectives, and experience of existing members of the House of Bishops.

[268] The Crown Nominations Commission consists of the two Archbishops (as Chairman and Vice-Chairman), six members of the General Synod (three clergy, three lay), six members elected by the diocesan Vacancy in See Committee (at least three of them lay), and the two Appointments Secretaries (as non-voting members): see Crown Nominations Commission Standing Order, SO 122. The Archbishop of the Province concerned presides, although he may delegate presidency of all or part of a meeting to the other Archbishop. When a vacancy in the See of Canterbury or the See of York is considered, the membership is slightly different and a lay person presides.

[269] Following recommendations contained in *Working with the Spirit* (n 263 above) greater information on possible candidates is made available for the Crown Nominations Commission, including revised Register of Ministers forms, personal statements from candidates, and references: see *Choosing Diocesan Bishops* (GS Misc 770, January 2005).

[270] Each of the names submitted must have received the support of two-thirds of the members, voting in a secret ballot. When the two names have been identified, a further vote is taken, again by secret ballot, in order to allow the Commission's members to express a preference between them.

[271] The Prime Minister then has a choice in considering whom to commend to the Queen. He may select the first of the two names put to him (assuming that the Commission has expressed a preference between the two names put forward); or he may select the second; or he may ask the Commission to re-consider and submit further names (in which case the Commission is required to meet again).

4.58 Once the prime minister has reached his decision he invites the candidate concerned to accept the nomination. The Crown then grants to the College of Canons a licence (congé d'elire) to proceed to elect a bishop and a letter missive naming the person to be elected.[272] The fact of the election is communicated to the archbishop, who duly confirms the election by formal legal process.

4.59 Unless already in episcopal orders, the bishop elect is consecrated by the archbishop of the relevant province or a bishop appointed to act on his behalf, together with at least two other bishops.[273] Upon translation, the transfer of a bishop from one see to another, there is no consecration. The bishop elect is duly installed in the bishopric or enthroned.[274] On being made a bishop, all his other preferments are vacated.

4.60 The bishop's jurisdiction is that of the Ordinary, which he may exercise by himself or through a vicar-general or other commissary.[275] He has the right to correct and punish the 'unquiet, disobedient, or criminous'.[276] In addition, he may celebrate the rites of ordination and confirmation, consecrate new churches, institute to all vacant benefices and admit by licence to other offices.[277] His right of ordering, controlling and authorizing all services in churches, chapels, churchyards and consecrated burial grounds has been largely sublimated into a corporate responsibility exercised by the House of Bishops and by General Synod.[278] The granting of faculties is now exercised by the diocesan chancellor.[279]

4.61 A bishop has power temporarily to delegate any of his functions to a suffragan bishop.[280] For the more efficient running of a diocese, it may be divided into episcopal areas and one or more bishops designated to have episcopal oversight for such areas whether alone or jointly with the diocesan bishop.[281] The bishop presides over the diocesan synod[282] and is required to reside within his own diocese.[283]

---

[272] Appointment of Bishops Act 1533, s 3; Cathedrals Measure 1999, s 5(3).
[273] Canon C 2 para 1. The service should take place on a Sunday or some other holy day unless the archbishop for urgent and weighty cause appoints some other day: Canon C 2 para 2.
[274] Appointment of Bishops Act 1533, ss 4, 5.
[275] Canon C 18 paras 2, 3.
[276] Canon C 18 para 7. It has been said that this right also embraces lay discipline. See N Doe, *The Legal Framework of the Church of England* (Oxford: Clarendon Press, 1996) 232–233.
[277] Canon C 18 paras 4, 6.
[278] This is discussed in Chapter 5.
[279] Ecclesiastical Jurisdiction Measure 1963, s 46(1) proviso. See generally Chapter 7.
[280] Dioceses Measure 1978, s 10.
[281] Ibid s 11. Any such scheme does not divest the diocesan bishop of his functions: s 11(7).
[282] Canon C 18 para 4. He is required by the Synodical Government Measure 1969, s 4(3) to consult with the diocesan synod on matters of general concern and importance to the diocese. Where his assent is required to a resolution of diocesan synod, it should not lightly nor without grave cause be withheld: Canon C 18 para 5.
[283] Canon C 18 para 8. An exception to this requirement is when the bishop is resident in London during his attendance on Parliament or on the Court.

Other appointments

The Archbishops of Canterbury and York and the Bishops of London, Durham and Winchester sit in the House of Lords, together with twenty-one other bishops in order of seniority of appointment.[284]

4.62 The bishop may hold visitations in order 'to get some knowledge of the state, sufficiency, and ability of the clergy and other persons'.[285] There is a mandatory requirement to ensure that there are sufficient priests to minister the word and sacraments to the people in all parts of the diocese.[286]

4.63 The bishop must make provision for extended episcopal oversight of those which have petitioned the bishop accordingly.[287] Such oversight may be on a diocesan, regional or provincial basis.[288] If the latter, recourse is had to a provincial episcopal visitor (PEV), colloquially styled 'flying bishop'. Although strictly suffragan bishops, their responsibilities are provincial in nature rather than diocesan. Their existence stems from the Episcopal Ministry Act of Synod 1993 made at the time of the passing into law of the Priests (Ordination of Women) Measure 1993.[289] It provides for the establishment of two sees in the diocese of Canterbury (Ebbsfleet and Richborough) and one in that of York (Beverley). Each PEV must perform in any parish such duties as may be requested of him by the diocesan bishop concerned in extending pastoral care and providing sacramental ministry. This is commonly known as alternative or extended episcopal oversight.

4.64 A bishopric becomes vacant by death, prohibition or deprivation,[290] translation, resignation[291] or retirement. A bishop is required to retire at the age of 70.[292]

---

[284] Note however, *A House for the Future*, the Report of the Royal Commission on Reform of the House of Lords (Cmnd 4514, January 2000), which recommended that this be reduced to 16 representatives chosen by the Church of England and not necessarily bishops. Were an all-elected second chamber to be introduced, there would no longer be a place for the bishops.

[285] Canon C 18 para 4; Canon G 5. See also P Smith, 'Points of Law and Practice Concerning Ecclesiastical Visitations' (1991) 2 Ecc LJ 189; and the Report of the Ecclesiastical Law Society's Working Party on Ecclesiastical Visitations (1992) 2 Ecc LJ 347.

[286] Canon C 18 para 6. The expression 'as much as in him lies' presumably includes financial constraints.

[287] Episcopal Ministry Act of Synod 1993, para 7. Any bishop in office as at February 1994 had the right to make a written declaration prohibiting the ordination within the diocese of women as priests or their holding or exercising priestly office therein: Priests (Ordination of Women) Measure 1993, s 2(1), (2). None did so.

[288] For an assessment of the practical arrangements made for extended episcopal oversight during the five years since the Act of Synod was introduced, see *Episcopal Ministry Act of Synod—Report of a Working Party of the House of Bishops* (GS 1395, June 2000).

[289] Note also the *Code of Practice* issued by the House of Bishops on 12 January 1994.

[290] The respective procedures under the Clergy Discipline Measure 2003 and the Ecclesiastical Jurisdiction Measure 1963 are discussed in Chapter 6.

[291] Bishops (Retirement) Measure 1986, s 1(1).

[292] Ecclesiastical Offices (Age Limit) Measure 1975, s 1(3), Schedule. The provision does not apply to a diocesan bishop who was already in such office as at 1 January 1976, when the Measure came into force: ss 1(4)(d), 7(4). The archbishop may authorize a diocesan bishop to remain in

Where it appears to the archbishop that a bishop is incapacitated, by physical or mental disability, from the due performance of his episcopal duties, the archbishop may request the bishop to tender his resignation.[293] If the bishop refuses, fails or is prevented by infirmity from tendering his resignation within two months of receipt of the request to do so, the archbishop may by written instrument declare the bishopric vacant as from a specified future date.[294] The guardianship of the spiritualities during a vacancy no longer vests in the dean and chapter of the cathedral church.[295] If a bishop has executed an irreversible deed of resignation or he considers that he will be unable to discharge any or all of his functions by reason of illness or absence from the diocese, he may delegate to a person in episcopal orders such functions as may be specified in the instrument. Where a see is vacant, or not all episcopal functions[296] have been delegated by such an instrument, the power to make such an instrument vests in the archbishop of the province.[297] The role of acting bishop thus created may be exercised during a vacancy by two or more persons with the functions divided between them territorially or otherwise.[298]

Suffragan bishops

4.65 A suffragan bishop is one appointed by the bishop to assist him in his diocese.[299] Two names are presented by the prime minister whose advice, invariably to select the first-named, the sovereign follows.[300] A suffragan bishop is required to endeavour

---

office beyond retirement age for up to one year if he considers that there are special circumstances for so doing: s 3 (1)(a).

[293] Bishops (Retirement) Measure 1986, s 3(1). The request may only be made with the concurrence of the two senior diocesan bishops of the province and may not be made unless the archbishop has first sent to the bishop a notice of his intention to do so: s 3(1), (2). The bishop has 15 days from receipt of such notice to request a medical report whereupon any action under the Measure is stayed until such report has been obtained and considered: s 3(2).

[294] Ibid s 3(5).

[295] In February 2000, Amending Canon 23 para 2 revoked Canon C 19.

[296] Church of England (Miscellaneous Provisions) Measure 1983, s 8(1). Certain limitations are set out in the Measure. Although the consent of the diocesan synod is not required, there ought to be consultation with the bishop's council and the standing committee. The period of delegation may not exceed six months although such period may be extended by the archbishop of the province: s 8(2).

[297] Ibid s 8(3).

[298] Ibid s 8(5).

[299] Suffragan Bishops Act 1534, s 1. Note the particular responsibilities of provincial episcopal visitors discussed at para 4.63 above.

[300] See *Senior Church Appointments* (n 248 above), para 5.4; App II, paras 2–20. A recommendation that the method of selection be formalized by having a representative 'appointing group' whenever a vacancy occurs (paras 6.2–6.9 and 6.24–6.39) has not been implemented. The choice remains that of the bishop but the general practice is to consult both within and outside the diocese: see the *Code of Practice for Senior Church Appointments* (GS Misc 455, 1995).

faithfully to execute such things pertaining to the episcopal office as the bishop may delegate to him,[301] in accordance with the jurisdiction or power afforded him by the bishop.[302] A scheme may provide for the diocese to be divided into areas, each under the pastoral care of an area bishop to whom specific functions are delegated.[303] A suffragan bishop must reside in the diocese unless the bishop permits otherwise.[304] He is not eligible to sit in the House of Lords. He is an *ex officio* member of the diocesan synod[305] and the diocesan pastoral committee.[306] The retirement provisions for a suffragan bishop are identical to those of a diocesan bishop.[307]

Archbishops

4.66 The Archbishops of the provinces of Canterbury and of York are appointed by the Crown. The qualifications for appointment are the same as for a bishop. Each has metropolitical jurisdiction throughout the province to correct the defects of other bishops and jurisdiction as Ordinary during his metropolitical visitation.[308] He has the right to confirm the election of bishops within his province, to be their chief consecrator, to hear appeals in his provincial court, to hold metropolitical visitations, to preside in Convocation and (jointly with the archbishop of the other province) to be President of General Synod.[309] The Archbishop of Canterbury has power to grant licences and dispensations throughout all of England and not merely the province of Canterbury,[310] a vestige of the legatine power at the time of the Reformation.

4.67 An archbishop may resign at any time[311] and is obliged to retire at the age of 70,[312] although the sovereign has a discretion to authorize his continuance in office for a specified period not exceeding one year.[313] Where it appears to the two senior bishops of the province that the archbishop is incapacitated, by physical or mental disability, from performing his duties, they may request him to tender

---

[301] Dioceses Measure 1978, ss 10, 11; Canon C 20 para 1.
[302] Suffragan Bishops Act 1534, s 2; Canon C 20 para 2.
[303] This is discussed more fully in Chapter 2.
[304] Suffragan Bishops Act 1534, s 6; Canon C 20 para 3.
[305] Church Representation Rules, r 30(2).
[306] Pastoral Measure 1983, Sch 1 para 3.
[307] See para 4.64 above.
[308] Canon C 17 para 2. He may exercise such jurisdiction himself or by a vicar-general, official or other commissory: Canon C 17 para 3.
[309] Canon C 17 para 4.
[310] Ecclesiastical Licences Act 1533, s 3.
[311] Bishops (Retirement) Measure 1986, s 4. Such resignation is tendered in writing to the monarch.
[312] Ecclesiastical Offices (Age Limit) Measure 1975, s 1(3), Schedule.
[313] Ibid s 2.

his resignation.[314] If he does not do so within two months, they may, with the concurrence of the archbishop of the other province, petition Her Majesty to declare the archbishopric vacant, and she may do so by Order in Council.[315] Where an archbishopric becomes vacant through death, translation, resignation or retirement, many of the functions of the archbishop are exercised by the archbishop of the other province.[316]

---

[314] Bishops (Retirement) Measure 1986, s 6(1). This may only be done with the concurrence of the archbishop of the other province, and the request may not be made unless the two senior bishops have first sent to the bishop a notice of their intention to do so. The archbishop has 15 days from receipt of such notice to request a medical report whereupon any action under the Measure is stayed until such report has been obtained and considered: s 6(2).
[315] Ibid s 6(4), (5).
[316] See, eg, the Church Representation Rules, r 53(6); Canon C 12 para 5; Canon E 6 para 3; and Canon E 8 para 5.

5

SERVICES AND WORSHIP

Introduction	5.01	Registrar's certificate	5.43
Liturgy	5.02	Solemnisation of marriage	5.44
Regular services	5.09	Marriages in chapels	5.48
Baptism	5.12	Further marriage of divorced persons	5.49
Confirmation	5.16	**Burials and funerals**	5.51
Holy communion	5.18	**Other services**	5.57
Reservation of the sacrament	5.27	Daily offices	5.57
Holy matrimony	5.31	Visitation of the sick	5.58
Preliminaries	5.32	Exorcism	5.59
Marriage by banns	5.36	Special services	5.60
Marriage by licence	5.40	**Confession**	5.61

Introduction

The doctrine of the Church of England is to be found in its articles and formularies. The final approval by the General Synod of any canon, regulation, form of service or amendment thereof conclusively determines that the Synod is of the opinion that it is neither contrary to, nor indicative of any departure from, the doctrine of the Church of England in any essential matter. A PCC may not issue any statement purporting to declare the doctrine of the Church,[1] nor may a diocesan[2] or deanery[3] synod.[4] Equally, it is not for the judiciary in the secular courts to

5.01

---

[1] Parochial Church Councils (Powers) Measure 1956, s 2(2)(b), substituted by the Synodical Government Measure 1969, s 6.
[2] Synodical Government Measure 1969, s 4(2) proviso.
[3] Ibid s 5(3) proviso.
[4] Church of England (Worship and Doctrine) Measure 1974, s 4(1), (2). See also *Brown v Runcie*, The Times, 20 February 1991, CA.

articulate the doctrines of the Church.⁵ In *Gorham v Bishop of Exeter*, the advice of the Privy Council was that:

> This court has no jurisdiction or authority to settle matters of faith or to determine what ought in any case to be the doctrine of the Church of England. Its duty extends only to a consideration of the articles and formularies.⁶

Further, as Simon Brown LJ stated when granting leave to move for judicial review in *ex parte The Church Society*:

> I would certainly deprecate any attempt on either side to put before the court essentially theological or doctrinal disputes ... As it seems to me, however, this challenge can perfectly well be determined without entering into so unsuitable an area of argument.⁷

More recently, Gray J ruled that the validity or otherwise of a consecration was non-justiciable, and in consequence he ordered a stay of a defamation action.⁸

Liturgy

5.02 Following the Reformation, uniformity of liturgy was achieved in a single prayer book which was imposed upon the Church of England.⁹ The *Book of Common Prayer* carried with it statutory authority, being a Schedule annexed to the Act of Uniformity 1662, although the relevant parts of the Act have since been repealed.¹⁰ By the twentieth century, it was felt by a sizeable part of the membership of the Church of England that the *Book of Common Prayer* could usefully be supplemented by alternative forms of liturgy. In the 1920s, a new prayer book found

---

⁵ The church courts have less reticence, particularly in disciplinary matters where doctrine is in issue, eg: *Bland v Archdeacon of Cheltenham* [1972] Fam 157, [1972] 1 All ER 1012, Ct of Arches (refusal to baptise). Note also *Re St Stephen, Wallbrook* [1987] Fam 146; [1987] 2 All ER 578, Ct of Eccl Causes Res (significance of altar); *Re St Hugh, Bermondsey* (1999) 5 Ecc LJ 390, Southwark Cons Ct (multi-faith paintings). In the latter case, George Ch referred to the duty of the consistory court to 'safeguard sound doctrine'. The Court of Arches sought expert evidence on the theology of Christian burial in *Re Blagdon Cemetery* [2002] Fam 299, [2002] 4 All ER 482, Ct of Arches.

⁶ *Gorham v Bishop of Exeter* (1850) 7 Notes of Cases 413; (1850) Moore's Special Report 462, PC.

⁷ *R v Ecclesiastical Committee of Both Houses of Parliament, ex parte The Church Society*, 22 October 1993, (leave hearing) Simon Brown LJ and Buckley J (unreported). For a general discussion, see M Hill, 'Judicial Approaches to Religious Disputes' in R O'Dair and A Lewis (eds), *Law and Religion*, Current Legal Issues 4 (Oxford: Oxford University Press, 2001) 409.

⁸ *Blake v Associated Newspapers Limited* (2003) 7 Ecc LJ 369, [2003] EWHC 1960 (QB), Gray J. See also C Hill, 'Episcopal Lineage: A Theological Reflection on *Blake v Associated Newspapers Limited*' (2004) 7 Ecc LJ 334.

⁹ Act of Uniformity 1548, s 1.

¹⁰ Church of England (Worship and Doctrine) Measure 1974, s 6(3), Sch 2. Since the repeal of the relevant parts of the Act of Uniformity 1662 by the Church of England (Worship and Doctrine) Measure 1974, the rubrics of the *Book of Common Prayer* carry less legal authority: *Re St Thomas, Pennywell* [1995] Fam 50 at 65D, [1995] 4 All ER 167 at 181j–182a, Durham Cons Ct.

favour with the Convocations but was rejected by Parliament in 1927 and 1928.[11] It was not until 1965 that it became possible for forms of service to be authorized as alternatives to those set out in the *Book of Common Prayer*.[12] An enabling Measure now gives to Synod power to authorize by canon new forms of service.[13]

5.03 Canon B 1 lists all those forms of service authorized for use in the Church of England. Synod has given its approval to *Common Worship*, a comprehensive set of liturgical texts, by way of alternatives to, and supplementary to, those in the *Book of Common Prayer*. Provision is also made for the use of approved translations of authorized forms of service including British Sign Language.[14]

5.04 Synod may approve, amend, continue or discontinue any form of service, provided that it is of the opinion that it does not represent a departure from the doctrine of the Church and that any such decision is finally approved with a majority in each House of not less than two-thirds of those present and voting.[15] Such other forms of worship are to be alternatives to those contained in the *Book of Common Prayer*, which must continue to be available for use in the Church of England.[16] Where a form of service has been prepared with a view to its approval by Synod, the archbishops may, after consultation with the House of Bishops, authorize its experimental use for a period specified by them on such terms and in such places or parishes as they may designate.[17]

5.05 At parochial level, the decision as to the form of liturgy to be used rests with the minister and the PCC jointly.[18] In the event of disagreement, the services contained in the *Book of Common Prayer* are to be used, unless other authorized forms of service were in regular use during at least two of the four years immediately

---

[11] It was nonetheless widely used despite its ostensible unlawfulness.

[12] Prayer Book (Alternative and Other Services) Measure 1965 (repealed).

[13] Church of England (Worship and Doctrine) Measure 1974, s 1(1). The authorization of the services in the *Alternative Service Book 1980* expired on 31 December 2000. It is, however, open for the bishop of a diocese to approve the continued use for a limited period of forms of service which have ceased to be approved by General Synod: Canon B 2 para 2A(1). See also *Canon B 2: Approval of Continued Use of Forms of Service Which Have Ceased to be Authorised*, Guidelines issued by the House of Bishops (January 2000). A request for continued use must be made within 12 months of the form of service ceasing to be approved, and the period of approval may not exceed three years in the first instance and may be extended on one occasion only by no more than two years: para 2A(6), (7).

[14] Canon B 42 para 3(1)–(3).

[15] Church of England (Worship and Doctrine) Measure 1974, s 1(1); Canon B 2 paras 1, 2. The final approval by Synod of any canon or regulation conclusively determines that Synod is of such opinion: 1974 Measure, s 4(2). Whether or not the provisions of the 1974 Measure apply is to be determined by the Presidents of Synod in accordance with its standing orders, and whether such determination is reviewable in the courts was expressly left undecided in *Brown v Runcie*, The Times, 26 June 1990, Hoffmann J affd, The Times, 20 February 1991, CA.

[16] Church of England (Worship and Doctrine) Measure 1974, s 1(1).

[17] Ibid s 1(6); Canon B 5A.

[18] Canon B 3 para 1. This does not apply to occasional services.

preceding the date when any disagreement arose and the PCC resolves that those other forms of service are to be used to the exclusion of or in addition to those contained in the *Book of Common Prayer*.[19] In the case of occasional offices, other than confirmation,[20] it is for the minister who is to conduct the service to decide which form to use.[21] However, if any of the persons concerned objects to the form selected by the minister and he and the minister cannot agree on which is to be used, the matter must be referred to the bishop for his decision.[22]

5.06 Even within the constraints indicated above, there is substantial room for variation in the liturgy. The declaration of assent made by a priest under canon C 15 that 'I will use only the forms of service which are authorized or allowed by canon' applies only to public prayer and the administration of the sacraments.[23] For private prayer not involving the administration of the sacraments, the clergy may determine the nature of their own devotions.[24]

5.07 Further, lawful authority may permit a departure from an authorized service.[25] Such authority may be either express, such as an Act of Parliament, Measure or Royal Proclamation, or implied, for example, by necessity of circumstance.[26]

---

[19] Canon B 3 para 2.
[20] In the case of confirmation, the decision rests with the bishop who is to conduct the service after consulting the minister of the church where the service is to be held: Canon B 3 para 5.
[21] Canon B 3 para 4.
[22] Canon B 3 para 4.
[23] See also Canon B 1, 'Of conformity of worship' listing by categories authorized forms of service. A full list as at 1 January 2005 appears in the Supplementary Material accompanying the Canons of the Church of England. Each rite is separate and distinct and an amalgam of different rites may not be used, save pursuant to the minister's discretion under Canon B 5 para 1 to make variations which are not of any substantial importance: see *Legal Opinions* 315–316.
[24] In the light of the declaration of assent, the enjoinder in Canon B 1 para 2 that 'every minister shall use only the forms of service authorized by this canon' would seem to apply also to the obligatory saying in private of morning and evening prayer as required by Canon C 26 para 1. See R Bursell, *Liturgy, Order and the Law* (Oxford: Clarendon Press, 1996) 10.
[25] The elusive meaning of 'lawful authority' has been addressed in a scholarly memorandum by Vaisey J to be found in *The Canon Law of the Church of England*, being the Report of the Archbishops' Commission on Canon Law (London: SPCK, 1947) 215–223. What remains of this principle in the light of the Church of England (Worship and Doctrine) Measure 1974 and Canon B 1 para 1 is open to question. The expression 'lawful authority' no longer appears in current legislation, its last appearance being in the Clerical Subscription Act 1865, s 1 which was repealed by the Church of England (Worship and Doctrine) Measure 1974, s 6(3), Sch 2.
[26] The doctrine of necessity exists to abate the harsher consequences of the law. Examples include administering the holy communion to a person unable to kneel as required in the rubric of the Prayer Book or the reservation of the sacrament for those unable to attend church: see *Re St Mary, Tyne Dock* [1954] P 369, [1954] 2 All ER 339, Durham Cons Ct; *Re Lapford (Devon) Parish Church* [1955] P 205, [1954] 3 All ER 484, CA; *Re St Michael and All Angels, Bishopwearmouth* [1958] 1 WLR 1183, *sub nom Bishopwearmouth Rector and Churchwardens v Adey* [1958] 3 All ER 441, Durham Cons Ct; *Re St Nicholas, Plumstead, Rector and Churchwardens* [1961] 1 WLR 916, [1961] 1 All ER 298, Southwark Cons Ct; *Re St Peter and St Paul, Leckhampton* [1968] P 495, [1967] 3 All ER 1057, Gloucester Cons Ct; and *Re St John the Evangelist, Brierley* [1989] Fam 60, [1989] 3 All

It has been argued that the *jus liturgicum* has been abrogated,[27] but in reality concepts of *jus liturgicum* and lawful authority are now differently articulated within a more comprehensive statutory and canonical framework.[28] Whilst the combined effect of the Church of England (Worship and Doctrine) Measure 1974 and Canon B 1 is to make more systematic provision for conformity of worship, legitimate deviation from such forms has also been put on a more secure footing. It is lawful for the bishop to approve the continued use for a limited period of any form of service which has ceased to be approved by General Synod.[29] Customary use is a determinative factor when resolving disagreements about which form of service is to be used.[30] The bishop is required to resolve disputes concerning the form to be used for occasional services.[31] The Convocations, the archbishops and any Ordinary all have power to approve forms of service not provided for in the *Book of Common Prayer* or under Canon B 3.[32] Even the minister is empowered to make variations if 'not of substantial importance' and to use forms of service for which provision is not otherwise made so long as they be 'reverent and seemly and ... neither contrary to, nor indicative of any departure from, the doctrine of the Church of England in any essential matter'.[33]

5.08 Canon B 4 permits the Convocations of Canterbury and York, archbishops and bishops to approve forms of service for which no provision is made in the *Book of Common Prayer* or by General Synod providing that, in their opinion, the service is 'reverent and seemly' and not indicative of any departure from the doctrine of the Church in any essential matter.[34] A minister who is to conduct any service may, in his discretion, make and use any variations which are not of substantial importance in any form of worship authorized by Canon B 1.[35] The minister having the cure of souls may use forms of service considered suitable by him on occasions for which no provision has been made in the *Book of Common Prayer*,

---

ER 214, Bradford Cons Ct. For a thorough review of these and other authorities, see *Re St Thomas, Pennywell* [1995] Fam 50, [1995] 4 All ER 167, Durham Cons Ct.

[27] R Bursell, *Liturgy, Order and the Law* (Oxford: Clarendon Press, 1996) 271–279.

[28] See N Doe, *The Legal Framework of the Church of England* (Oxford: Clarendon Press, 1996) 301, 308. See also Chapter 1 paras 1.40 ff.

[29] Canon B 2 para 2A(1).

[30] Canon B 3 para 2.

[31] Canon B 3 para 4.

[32] Canon B 4 paras 1–3. Note also the authorization of experimental liturgy under Canon B 5A. A form of service prescribed by the bishop for the burial of suicides may be preferred over that which may be approved by General Synod under Canon B 2 if the person having charge of the burial so requests: Canon B 38 para 2.

[33] Canon B 5 paras 1–3. The PCC has a right to comment upon the choice of options within any authorized form of service: *Legal Opinions* 315, para 3.

[34] Church of England (Worship and Doctrine) Measure 1974, s 1(5); Canon B 4 paras 1, 2 and 3 respectively.

[35] Canon B 5 para 1.

Chapter 5: Services and Worship

or under Canon B 2 or Canon B 4, and he may permit another minister to use them.[36] If any question is raised about the observance of Canon B 5, it should be referred to the bishop, who may give pastoral guidance, advice or directions as he thinks fit.[37]

Regular services

5.09 The performance of certain services is obligatory. In both cathedral and parish churches, holy communion is to be celebrated at least on all Sundays, principal feast days and on Ash Wednesday.[38] In cathedral churches, morning and evening prayer are to be said or sung daily, with the inclusion of the litany on the appointed days.[39] Morning and evening prayer are to be said or sung in every parish church on all Sundays and other principal feast days and also on Ash Wednesday and Good Friday.[40] On all other days, the minister must make provision for morning and evening prayer to be said or sung in either the parish church or, after consultation with the PCC, elsewhere as may best serve to sustain the corporate spiritual life of the parish and the pattern of life enjoined upon ministers.[41] The duties imposed upon priests having a cure of souls are not entirely consistent with the provisions discussed in this paragraph.[42]

5.10 Anecdotal evidence suggests that in many parish churches, the foregoing obligations are not infrequently overlooked in practice, although they may strictly only be dispensed with in accordance with the provisions of Canon B 14A,[43] under which, on an occasional basis, the reading of morning and evening prayer may be dispensed with as authorized by the minister and the PCC acting jointly.[44] On a regular basis, however, it must be as authorized by the bishop on the request of the minister and the PCC acting jointly.[45] In either case, those authorizing the dispensation must be satisfied that there is good reason for doing so and must

---

[36] Canon B 5 para 2. All variations must be reverent and seemly and neither contrary to nor indicative of any departure from the doctrine of the Church of England in any essential matter: Canon B 5 para 3. It is the minister's responsibility to have a good understanding of the forms of service used and to endeavour to ensure that the worship offered glorifies God and edifies the people: Canon B 1 para 2.
[37] Canon B 5 para 4. This is without prejudice to the matter being the subject of proceedings under the Ecclesiastical Jurisdiction Measure 1963.
[38] Canons B 13 para 1, and B 14 para 1 respectively. In parish churches (but not cathedral churches) holy communion must also be celebrated on Maundy Thursday: Canon B 14 para 1.
[39] Canon B 10.
[40] Canon B 11 para 1.
[41] Canon B 11 para 2.
[42] Canon C 24. This is discussed in Chapter 4.
[43] See Canon B 11 para 3; B 14 para 2.
[44] Canon B 14A para 1(a).
[45] Canon B 14A para 1(b).

have regard to the frequency of services in other parish churches or places of worship in the benefice and must ensure that no church ceases altogether to be used for public worship.[46] Where there is more than one parish church or place of worship in the benefice or where benefices are held in plurality, the bishop may authorize proposals from the minister and PCC acting jointly as to what services may be held in each such place, or in the absence of any such proposals may make such directions as he considers appropriate.[47]

Except for some reasonable cause approved by the bishop, a sermon must be preached at least once each Sunday in every parish church.[48] The preacher 'shall endeavour with care and sincerity to minister the word of truth, to the glory of God and to the edification of the people'.[49] Those present at divine worship are enjoined by canon law audibly with the minister to make the answers appointed and in due place join in such parts of the service as are appointed to be said or sung by all present.[50] In addition, they must give reverent attention during the service, give due reverence to the name of the Lord Jesus, stand at the creed, and at the reading of the gospel at holy communion, and otherwise stand, kneel or sit as the rubrics of the service and locally established custom direct.[51]

5.11

Baptism

Baptism deserves first consideration, since it constitutes the reception of a person into the Church of God. Baptism happens once and for all time and, by its very nature, cannot be repeated.[52] If, however, there is a doubt as to whether an individual has been baptised, a conditional baptism may take place.[53] Baptism may occur at any stage in a person's life, and different provisions apply to the baptism of infants from those styled 'of riper years' who are able to answer for themselves.[54]

5.12

---

[46] Canon B 14A para 1(i), (ii).
[47] Canon B 14A para 2.
[48] Canon B 18 para 1. It may be preached by a minister, deaconess, reader or lay worker duly authorized by canon law. Also, at the invitation of the minister having the cure of souls, any other person may preach with the permission of the bishop given either in relation to the particular occasion or in accordance with diocesan directions: Canon B 18 para 2.
[49] Canon B 18 para 3.
[50] Canon B 9 para 1.
[51] Canon B 9 para 2. There would appear to be no sanction for failing to comply with this enjoinder save a rebuke or, possibly in an extreme case, refusal of the sacrament or lesser excommunication.
[52] For a full discussion of the theology and practices of baptism, see D Stancliffe, 'Baptism and Fonts' (1993) 3 Ecc LJ 141.
[53] See R Ombres, *Infant Baptism: The 1983 Code of Canon Law and Church of England Law* (Rome: Pontifical University of St Thomas Aquinas, 1999) 134. Valid baptism is not to be reiterated.
[54] Canon B 24. The forms of service also differ.

The practice of the Church of England favours infant baptism.[55] If a minister refuses or unduly delays to baptise an infant, the parents or guardians may apply to the bishop, who must, after consultation with the minister, give such directions he thinks fit.[56] The minister is, however, entitled to delay baptising an infant for the purposes of preparing or instructing the parents or guardians or godparents,[57] although there is no discretion where the child is in danger of death, in which case the minister has a duty to baptise.[58] Difficulties may arise if one parent is desirous of baptism and the other not.[59] If the parents reside outside the parish and neither is on the electoral roll of that parish, the minister may not proceed to baptise the child without having sought the goodwill of the minister of the parish within which the parents reside.[60] It is an offence for a minister to demand a fee for baptising.[61]

5.13 It is desirable that the sacrament of baptism be administered on Sundays at public worship when the most number of people come together.[62] It is generally conducted by a priest, but may be performed by a deacon in the absence of a priest.[63] Baptism by a lay person, though irregular, is effectual.[64] For every child to be baptised, there must be at least three godparents,[65] who make affirmations

---

[55] Thirty-nine Articles of Religion, art 27, which reads 'the Baptism of young children is in any wise to be retained in the Church, as most agreeable with the institution of Christ'. Note also the rubric in the *Book of Common Prayer*, which urges baptism not later than the first or second Sunday after birth.

[56] Canon B 22 para 2. See generally *Bland v Archdeacon of Cheltenham* [1972] Fam 157, [1972] 1 All ER 1012, Ct of Arches.

[57] Canon B 22 para 4. Note also *X v Denmark* (7374/76) DR 5, 157 Eur Ct of HR; and *Prussner v Germany* (1986) 8 EHRR 79 regarding the duty to baptise in other European states and the imposition of conditions by the clergyman concerned.

[58] Canon B 22 para 6. Ombres suggests that to call this an absolute duty is too strong: Ombres, *Infant Baptism* (n 53 above) 132 and points to the need for the consent of parents and godparents (which he discusses at 150) and to *Legal Opinions* 333–337. However, the duty under the canon is predicated upon the immediacy of death where enquiry into consent will be impossible, and the canonical duty will prevail.

[59] See Ombres, *Infant Baptism* (n 53 above) 125–129, 153–155. Reference is made to the refusal of a Muslim father to consent to his child's baptism. The judicial approach to disputes of this nature may be seen from *Re P (Section 91(14) Guidelines) (Residence and Religious Heritage)* [1999] 2 FLR 573; *Re J (Specific Issues Orders: Muslim Upbringing and Circumcision)* [1999] 2 FLR 678. See also *Legal Opinions* 333–337 on the issue of parental consent to baptism.

[60] Canon B 22 para 5. The requirement only extends to seeking and not obtaining such goodwill.

[61] Baptismal Fees Abolition Act 1872, s 1. However, a fee is payable to the incumbent, under the relevant Parochial Fees Order, for a certificate of baptism and searches of the baptismal register: see *Legal Opinions* 319.

[62] Canon B 21.

[63] See the *Book of Common Prayer*, 'Form and Manner of Making of Deacons', 'It appertaineth to the office of a deacon ...'

[64] *Kemp v Wickes* (1809) 3 Phillim 264. See Ombres, *Infant Baptism* (n 53 above) 132–133.

[65] Canon B 23 para 1. At least two must be of the same sex as the child and at least one of the opposite sex. Where three cannot conveniently be had, one godfather and one godmother will suffice. Parents may be godparents to their own children so long as there is at least one other godparent.

of faith for the child. A godparent must be both baptised and confirmed, although the minister has power to dispense with the latter requirement.[66] Godparents must be persons 'who will faithfully fulfil their responsibilities both by their care for the child ... and by the example of their own godly living'.[67]

5.14 Every church at which baptism is to be administered must have a font, sited as close to the principal entrance as is possible, unless there is a custom to the contrary or the Ordinary otherwise directs, whose bowl may be used for no purpose other than that of baptism.[68] The *Book of Common Prayer* contemplates that at an infant baptism, the child be dipped in the water 'discreetly but warily', but states that, if the child is weak, 'it shall suffice to pour water upon it'. When baptism takes place in church, it is followed by the signing of the sign of the cross on the forehead of the person baptised, although this is no part of the sacrament,[69] but symbolic of the admission of the child into membership of the Church. Accordingly, where a person is baptised in private, as, for example, in the case of urgency, signing takes place not at the baptism but at a later occasion in church. All baptisms are to be registered as soon as possible after they have occurred.[70] The manner in which the register is to be maintained is set out fully in the Parochial Registers and Records Measure 1978.

5.15 Paragraph 1 of Canon B 26 provides for the instruction of the young in the doctrine, sacraments and discipline of Christ and especially in the catechism. This duty is imposed on the minister, who may discharge it himself or through some godly and competent person appointed by him. All parents and guardians must take care that their children receive such instruction.[71]

---

[66] Canon B 23 para 4. The godparents must be present at the baptism in order to make the required affirmations and promises. It is suggested that provided two are physically present, additional godparents may attend via a video link: *Legal Opinions* 340 para 7 but many would regard this as unsatisfactory and demeaning to the nature of the sacrament, only to be adopted in the most exceptional of circumstances.

[67] Canon B 23 para 2. See Ombres, *Infant Baptism* (n 53 above) 155. See also M Reardon, *Christian Initiation: Baptismal Policy* (GS Misc 365, 1991). There is no provision for the removal or replacement of godparents: *Legal Opinions* 342.

[68] Canon F 1, paras 1–3. The Ordinary in this instance will be chancellor exercising the jurisdiction of the diocesan bishop in the consistory court. As to the number and position of fonts, see Chapter 7 and *Re St James, Shirley* [1994] Fam 134, Winchester Cons Ct.

[69] Canon B 25.

[70] Parochial Registers and Records Measure 1978, s 2. In relation to surnames and illegitimate children, see *Legal Opinions* 319.

[71] Canon B 26 para 2.

Chapter 5: *Services and Worship*

Confirmation

5.16 There is no clear theological justification for confirmation as a rite separate from baptism.[72] It is most probably the bestowal of the Holy Spirit upon the candidate to confirm and strengthen him in his baptismal vows, which are reaffirmed as part of the service, and is best regarded as the completion of the rite of baptism. There is an obligation under canon law to confirm an adult who is baptised 'so soon after his baptism as conveniently may be'.[73] In the Church of England, confirmation is performed by the diocesan bishop or another bishop acting on his behalf.[74] It is performed by the laying on of hands, accompanied by such words as are prescribed by the *Book of Common Prayer* or by other authorized forms of service.[75] The obligation on the minister is to 'seek out' persons whom he shall think meet to be confirmed and use his best endeavours to instruct them in the Christian faith.[76] He is required to ensure that a candidate for confirmation has come to the age of discretion, can say the creed, the Lord's Prayer and the ten commandments and can also render an account of his faith according to the catechism.[77] He must also satisfy himself that the candidate is baptised and inform the bishop of the candidate's name, age and date of baptism.[78] If there is doubt as to whether a candidate has been baptised, the minister must conditionally baptise that person before presenting him to the bishop.[79] The minister must record and enter each confirmation in his register book of confirmations, together with any change of name.[80]

5.17 So far as a change of name is concerned, a bishop has lawful authority to confirm a person by a new Christian name if it is desired for sufficient reason that a Christian name be changed.[81] The new Christian name is to be thereafter deemed

---

[72] See G Dix, *The Theology of Confirmation in Relation to Baptism* (Westminster: Dacre Press, 1946); GWH Lampe, *The Seal of the Spirit* (London: Longmans, Green & Co, 1951). Confirmation is not counted as a sacrament of the Gospel for it lacks any visible sign or ceremony ordained of God: Thirty-Nine Articles of Religion, art 25. See also *Ecumenical Relations: Code of Practice* (London: General Synod, 1989).
[73] Canon B 24 para 3.
[74] Canon B 27 para 1.
[75] See generally, J Behrens, *Confirmation, Sacrament of Grace* (Leominster: Gracewing, 1995).
[76] Canon B 27 para 2.
[77] Canon B 27 para 3.
[78] Canon B 27 para 4.
[79] Canon B 27 para 5.
[80] Canon B 39 para 2. The provisions of the Gender Recognition Act 2004, concerning the right of transsexuals to live in their acquired gender, makes no reference to alterations being made to baptism certificates or registers.
[81] Canon B 27 para 6. See *Legal Opinions* 321–332: a Christian name given at baptism can only formally be altered by Act of Parliament, at confirmation and on adoption. A person may be known by some other name or nickname as long as it is not used to defraud or deliberately mislead.

the lawful Christian name of such person.[82] It is good practice to include the new Christian name not merely in the register of confirmations but also at the relevant entry for the person's baptism in the baptism register.

Holy communion

Central to the worship of the Church of England is the celebration of what is variously described as holy communion, eucharist, mass or the Lord's supper. It has not been discussed until now, since baptism and, usually, confirmation are conditions precedent to participation in the sacrament. Under Canon B 15A, the following may[83] be admitted to holy communion: **5.18**

(a) members of the Church of England who have been confirmed[84] or are desirous to be confirmed;[85]
(b) baptised persons who are communicant members of other Churches which subscribe to the doctrine of the Holy Trinity and who are in good standing in their own Church;
(c) any other baptised person authorized to be admitted under regulations of Synod;[86] and
(d) any baptised person in immediate danger of death.[87]

See *Re H (Child's Name: First Name)* [2002] 1 FLR 973, CA, per Thorpe LJ, distinguishing the relative importance of surnames and given names.

[82] Canon B 27 para 6.

[83] The Canon uses the word 'shall'. For a discussion of the right to be admitted to communion, see N Doe, *The Legal Framework of the Church of England* (Oxford: Clarendon Press, 1996) 343.

[84] Confirmation includes not merely that done pursuant to the rites of the Church of England but also those who have been otherwise episcopally confirmed with unction or with the laying on of hands: Canon B 15A para 1(a).

[85] See the Guidelines agreed by the House of Bishops, *Admission of Baptised Persons to Holy Communion Before Confirmation* (March 1997), relating to Canon B 15A para 1(a). These include a recommendation that a register be maintained of every person admitted to holy communion and, as a matter of best practice, for baptismal certificates to be endorsed accordingly.

[86] See the Admission of Baptised Children to Holy Communion Regulations 2006, which are regulations of the General Synod approved in February 2006, and which came into effect from 15 June 2006. The regulations allow a bishop, in his absolute discretion, to permit applications to be made by incumbents for permission that children may be admitted to holy communion. Such applications may only be made after a resolution of support has been passed by the PCC. The bishop must be satisfied that the parish concerned has made adequate provision for preparation and continued nurture in the Christian life and will encourage any child admitted to Holy Communion to be confirmed at the appropriate time: para 5. A register is to be maintained and, where practicable, the date and place of the child's first admission should be recorded on the baptismal certificate: para 9.

[87] Canon B 15A para 1(a)–(d). In the case of any doubt as to the application of the Canon, the minister must refer to the bishop and follow his guidance thereon: Canon B 15A para 3.

5.19 Some discussion of the theological considerations which lie behind the sacrament is necessary. The doctrine of transubstantiation as it was understood in the Roman Church at the time of the Reformation is incompatible with Article 28 of the Thirty-nine Articles of Religion, which reads:

> Transubstantiation (or the change of the substance of Bread and Wine) in the Supper of the Lord, cannot be proved by holy Writ; but is repugnant to the plain words of Scripture, overthroweth the nature of a Sacrament, and hath given occasion to many superstitions.

5.20 In addition, the administration of the communion in both kinds (bread and wine) was ordered by statute,[88] non-communicating masses were considered undesirable and a rubric at the end of the order for the administration of the Lord's supper in the *Book of Common Prayer* states:

> And there shall be no Celebration of the Lord's Supper, except there be a convenient number to communicate with the Priest, according to his discretion. And if there be not above twenty persons in the Parish of discretion to receive the Communion: yet there shall be no Communion, except four (or three at the least) communicate with the Priest.

5.21 What is important is the outward and visible sign of the consecrated bread and wine properly used conveying an inward and spiritual grace by which communicants are strengthened and refreshed. It is both sacrificial and commemorative. As Article 28 states:

> The Supper of the Lord is not only a sign of the love that Christians ought to have among themselves one to another; but rather is a Sacrament of our Redemption by Christ's death: insomuch that to such as rightly, worthily, and with faith, receive the same, the Bread which we break is a partaking of the Body of Christ; and likewise the Cup of Blessing is a partaking of the Blood of Christ.

5.22 No person may consecrate and administer the holy sacrament unless he has been ordained priest by episcopal ordination in accordance with the provisions of Canon C 1.[89] A deacon may assist in the distribution and the reading of the holy scriptures. Readers and deaconesses are authorized to distribute the sacrament.[90] A lay person may distribute the sacrament to the people, provided he has been so authorized by the bishop under the regulations made by Synod.[91] Subject to the direction of the bishop, the epistle, Gospel and prayer of intercession may, at

---

[88] Sacrament Act 1547, s 8: Royal Proclamation (Order of the Communion) dated March 1548.
[89] Canon B 12 para 1.
[90] Canon D 1 para 3(b), and Canon E 4 para 2(c) respectively.
[91] Canon B 12 para 3. Regulations on the Administration of Holy Communion were made by the Church Assembly in November 1969, and are still in force.

Holy communion

the invitation of the minister, be read by a lay person.[92] The celebrant is required by canon to wear either a surplice or alb with scarf or stole.[93]

5.23 It is the responsibility of the churchwardens, with the advice and direction of the minister, to provide a sufficient quantity of bread and wine for the number of communicants that are from time to time to receive the same.[94] The bread, whether leavened or unleavened, must be 'of the best and purest wheat flour that conveniently may be gotten, and the wine the fermented juice of the grape, good and wholesome'.[95] The offertory taken during holy communion forms part of the general funds of the PCC.[96] Without the permission of the bishop, holy communion may not be celebrated in private houses, except when ministering to the sick,[97] in which case three or at least two others are to communicate along with the sick person, save in the case of a contagious disease, in which case the minister alone may communicate with him.[98] The celebration of holy communion in private chapels on Sundays is particularly discouraged, in order that the residents of the house may attend their parish church.[99] A bishop may license a minister to celebrate holy communion in colleges, schools, hospitals and public or charitable institutions.[100]

5.24 The rubric of the *Book of Common Prayer* for the order for the administration of the Lord's supper commences: 'So many as intend to be partakers of the holy communion shall signify their names to the curate, at least some time the day before'. It is doubtful whether this practice is ever obeyed. The minister is required to receive the sacrament on every occasion that he celebrates.[101] The rubric which concludes the order for the administration of the Lord's supper states that in cathedrals, collegiate churches and colleges, where there are many priests and deacons, they must all receive the communion with the priest every Sunday at least until they have a reasonable cause to the contrary. Further, every parishioner

---

[92] Canon B 12 para 4.
[93] Canon B 8 para 3.
[94] Canon B 17 para 1. The expense is to be borne by the PCC.
[95] Canon B 17 para 2. The bread is to be brought to the communion table in a paten or convenient box and the wine in a convenient cruet or flagon: Canon B 17 para 3. The doctrine of necessity may justify a departure from the strict application of these provisions, and is commonly invoked in the case of a cœliac or person with wheat intolerance, or those with alcohol dependency.
[96] Canon B 17A. Such finds are disposed of in accordance with the provisions of the Parochial Church Councils (Powers) Measure 1956, s 7(iv).
[97] Canon B 40.
[98] See the rubric to 'The Communion of the Sick' in the *Book of Common Prayer*. See also Canon B 37 para 2.
[99] Canon B 41 para 1.
[100] Canon B 41 para 2; Extra-Parochial Ministry Measure 1967, s 2(1). Any celebration does not require the consent of the priest within whose parish the institution is situated: ibid s 2(2); Canon B 41 para 3. Note also the ecumenical canons, B 43 and B 44.
[101] Canon B 12 para 2.

Chapter 5: Services and Worship

must communicate at least three times a year, of which Easter must be one. Canon B 15 extends this requirement, stating that it is the duty of all who have been confirmed to receive holy communion regularly and especially at the festivals of Christmas, Easter and Whitsun or Pentecost.[102] The canon also requires the minister to teach the people that they come to the holy sacrament with such preparation as is required by the *Book of Common Prayer*.[103]

5.25 Canon B 16, in somewhat arcane language, makes provision for 'notorious offenders' not to be admitted to holy communion. This is a serious step and one not to be taken lightly, since not only is the refusal uncharitable and, if unjustified, possibly defamatory, but it may be contrary to section 8 of the Sacrament Act 1547, which states that the minister '… shall not without lawful cause deny the [holy communion] to any person that will devoutly and humbly desire it, any law statute or custom contrary thereunto in any wise notwithstanding'.

5.26 Under Canon B 16, the minister must be persuaded of 'malicious and open contention with [the would-be communicant's] neighbours, or other grave and open sin without repentance'.[104] If he is so persuaded, he must give an account to the bishop and obey the bishop's order or direction. Until this procedure has been followed and until he has warned the would-be communicant not to come to the Lord's table, the minister is not to refuse the sacrament, unless it be a case of grave and immediate scandal to the congregation, in which case he must give an account of the matter to the bishop within seven days.[105] What constitutes a 'grave and open sin' is not made plain, nor is there any definition given of 'grave and immediate scandal'. The former must be something greater than the sinfulness common to all in the Church, for which absolution is sought and given during the communion service and the latter something more serious still.[106] The withholding of the sacrament is sometimes referred to as the lesser excommunication.

Reservation of the sacrament

5.27 A perennial question addressed by ecclesiastical lawyers is the lawfulness or otherwise of the reservation of the sacrament. This is the practice of setting apart a portion of the consecrated elements for subsequent administration to persons other than those present at the service in which the consecration took place.

---

[102] Canon B 15 para 1.
[103] Canon B 15 para 2.
[104] Canon B 16 para 1.
[105] Canon B 16 para 1. See also the rubric prefatory to the 'Order for Holy Communion' in the *Book of Common Prayer*.
[106] See generally *R v Dibdin* [1910] P 57, CA; affirmed as *Thompson v Dibdin* [1912] AC 533, HL.

The reserved sacrament is subsequently administered to those who, by reason of illness or otherwise, were unable to attend the service, or it is retained to be used should any sudden emergency arise prior to the next celebration. The judgment in *Re St Thomas, Pennywell*[107] is an erudite and comprehensive review of a number of previous authorities, the consideration of which is now otiose.[108] Those who assert the illegality of the practice rely upon passages from the Thirty-nine Articles of Religion[109] and parts of the rubric of the *Book of Common Prayer*.[110]

However, the practice of reservation is not uncommon[111] and it is justified on the grounds that it is necessary in order, inter alia, that the Church may fully minister to the sick and the housebound, since constraints of time and other duties may prevent priests from making individual sick room celebrations. In many dioceses, the practice of reservation is authorized by the bishop by way of diocesan regulations or otherwise. The mischief which the rubric in the *Book of Common Prayer* was designed to prevent was the profane or superstitious usage of consecrated elements.[112] The ecclesiastical courts generally require the bishop's sanction before reservation is authorized, he being the person best placed to judge whether in any parish the sacrament, if reserved, is likely to be adored or profaned.[113]

5.28

---

[107] *Re St Thomas, Pennywell* [1995] Fam 50, [1995] 4 All ER 167, Durham Cons Ct.

[108] The most significant of the last century are *Re Lapford (Devon) Parish Church* [1955] P 205, [1954] 3 All ER 484, CA; *Re St Michael and All Angels, Bishopwearmouth* [1958] 1 WLR 1183, *sub nom Rector and Churchwardens of Bishopwearmouth v Adey* [1958] 3 All ER 441, Durham Cons Ct; *Re St Nicholas, Plumstead, Rector and Churchwardens* [1961] 1 WLR 916, [1961] 1 All ER 298, Southwark Cons Ct; *Re St Peter and St Paul, Leckhampton* [1968] P 495, [1967] 3 All ER 1057, Gloucester Cons Ct; *Re St Matthew, Wimbledon* [1985] 3 All ER 670, Southwark Cons Ct; and *Re St John the Evangelist, Brierley* [1989] Fam 60, [1989] 3 All ER 214, Bradford Cons Ct.

[109] Article 25 states: 'The Sacraments were not ordained of Christ to be gazed upon, or to be carried about, but that we should duly use them', and Article 28 supplements this as follows: 'The Sacrament of the Lord's Supper was not by Christ's ordinance reserved, carried about, lifted up, or worshipped'.

[110] This provides that if any consecrated bread and wine remains at the end of a celebration of holy communion, 'it shall not be carried out of the Church, but the Priest, and such other of the Communicants as he shall then call unto him, shall, immediately after the Blessing, reverently eat and drink the same'.

[111] It was approved by the Church Assembly and would have been lawful under the deposited Prayer Book of 1928, had it not been rejected by Parliament. The Prayer Book, however, was widely used based, doubtless, on an appeal to the *jus liturgicum*. See generally *Re Lapford (Devon) Parish Church* [1955] P 205 and R Bursell, *Liturgy, Order and the Law* (Oxford: Clarendon Press, 1996), Appendix 3, 271–279.

[112] Reliance is placed on the Brawling Act 1553 which, until its repeal by the Criminal Law Act 1967, provided protection for the sacrament and the receptacle housing it. Arguably this evidences parliamentary recognition and approval of the practice of reservation.

[113] *Re St Thomas, Pennywell* [1995] Fam 50 at 62C–E, [1995] 4 All ER 167 at 179, Durham Cons Ct; GH and GL Newsom, *Faculty Jurisdiction of the Church of England* (2nd edn, London, 1993) 140.

5.29 The argument against reservation based upon the rubric in the *Book of Common Prayer* was roundly rejected in *Re St Thomas, Pennywell*, on the basis that since other forms of service contained no such direction and since those other forms were lawfully approved under Canon B 2, then the direction could not be a matter of 'substantial importance' under Canon B 5 para 1.[114] Chancellor Bursell concluded 'it follows that reservation may occur whichever rite is used—a conclusion that accords both with common sense and practicality'.

5.30 Although strictly the decision in *Re St Thomas, Pennywell* is binding only in the Diocese of Durham, it is a strong persuasive authority, likely to be followed in the consistory courts of the dioceses of both provinces.[115] It follows that much of the controversy concerning the legality of articles and of ceremonies associated with the practice of reservation may now be laid to rest.[116]

Holy matrimony

5.31 Holy matrimony, whilst sacramental in nature, has its origins in principles of contract whereby a man and a woman voluntarily form a lifelong union recognized by God. The State, however, makes express provision for its termination by divorce.[117] The Church recognizes a civil ceremony of marriage, conducted at a registry office, and makes provision for a service of blessing following such event. The Church has sought to continue to uphold the principle of life-long marriage, whilst at the same time providing a pastoral ministry to divorced persons who seek a further marriage in church.[118]

Preliminaries

5.32 Certain legal requirements are necessary before persons may marry.[119] Each party must be at least 16 years of age[120] and if either party (not being a widow or widower)

---

[114] *Re St Thomas, Pennywell* (n 114 above).

[115] The decision has been adopted, for example, in *Re St Nicholas, Arundel* (2001) 6 Ecc LJ 290, Chichester Cons Ct.

[116] See R Bursell, *Liturgy, Order and the Law* (Oxford: Clarendon Press, 1996) 71–79; *Re St Thomas, Pennywell* (n 113 above); *Re St John the Evangelist, Chopwell* [1995] Fam 254, [1996] 1 All ER 275, Durham Cons Ct.

[117] Matrimonial Causes Act 1973. For practice and procedure, see specialist texts such as M Everall (*et al*, eds), *Rayden and Jackson on Divorce and Family Matters* (18th edn, London: Butterworths, 2005).

[118] The law concerning the further marriage of divorced persons is discussed at para 5.49ff below.

[119] For general information, see *Anglican Marriage in England and Wales—A Guide to the Law for Clergy* (1999 edn), issued by the Faculty Office of the Archbishop of Canterbury.

[120] Marriage Act 1949, s 2; Canon B 31 para 1.

is under the age of 18 an appropriate form of consent is required.[121] Canon B 32 states that no minister may solemnise a marriage involving a person under 18 otherwise than in accordance with the laws relating to consent. More draconian, however, is the Marriage Act 1949, which provides that if a minister knowingly and willingly solemnises a marriage without banns having been duly published, except on authority of a special or common licence or a superintendent registrar's certificate, he is guilty of an offence and liable to imprisonment for a term not exceeding 14 years.[122] Further, the couple must not fall within the prohibited degrees of kindred and affinity.[123]

5.33 It is the duty of the minister, when application is made to him for matrimony to be solemnised, to inquire whether there be any impediment to the marriage or its solemnisation.[124] It is also his duty to explain to the couple the Church's doctrine of marriage and the need of God's grace in order that they may discharge aright their obligations as married persons.[125]

5.34 Assuming the legal requirements set out above to be satisfied, it is generally understood that there is a right to be married in one's parish church.[126] The right derives from the minister's duty to solemnise marriage, which he may undertake personally or by securing or permitting another cleric to officiate. If he refuses so to do without just cause, he commits an ecclesiastical offence for which he is punishable in the ecclesiastical courts.[127]

---

[121] Marriage Act 1949, ss 3(1), (3), 78(1) ('child'); Family Law Reform Act 1969, s 2(1)(c), 33(1), Sch 2 paras 9, 10.

[122] Marriage Act 1949, s 75(1)(b); Canon B 35 para 2. Publication of banns is void if any of the persons whose consent is required declares his dissent to the intended marriage publicly and openly in the church where they are published: Marriage Act 1949, s 3(3).

[123] Ibid s 1(1), Sch 1 Pt I (amended by the Children Act 1975, s 108(1)(a), Sch 3 para 8; and the Marriage (Prohibited Degrees of Relationship) Act 1986, s 1(6), Sch 1 para 8; and the Civil Partnership Act 2004, s 261, Sch 27 para 17); Canon B 31 para 2. There is an element of mutual inconsistency between the two tables. That in the statute is likely to be considered more authoritative than that in the canon.

[124] Canon B 33.

[125] Canon B 30 para 3.

[126] Clandestine Marriages Act 1753 (Lord Hardwicke's Marriage Act); *Banister v Thompson* [1908] P 362; *Thompson v Dibdin* [1912] AC 533, HL. The existence of such right has been questioned by N Doe: see *Legal Framework of the Church of England* (Oxford, 1996) 358–362. Cogent and compelling as his argument is, his academic treatise is unlikely to abrogate the assumed right and corresponding duty which now form part of the ecclesiastical customary law of the Church of England, albeit, as Doe indicates, as a legal fiction: at 359. For an authoritative and revisionist view doubting the received understanding and approving Doe, see M Smith, 'An Interpretation of *Argar v Holdsworth*' (1998) 5 Ecc LJ 34, and for a spirited defence of the orthodox view, see J Humphreys, 'The Right to Marry in Church: A Rehabilitation of *Argar v Holdsworth*' (2004) 7 Ecc LJ 405.

[127] *Argar v Holdsworth* (1758) 2 Lee 515. The duty extends in respect of all persons within the parish, whether or not they are baptised or consider themselves members of the Church of England. See 14 *Halsbury's Laws of England* (4th edn, London: Butterworths, 1982) para 1005.

Chapter 5: Services and Worship

5.35 The duty on that part of a priest to marry those who present themselves is subject to a number of statutory exceptions. The first of these, often styled a 'conscience clause', is to be found in the Matrimonial Causes Act 1965 and applies to clergy in the Church of England[128] who cannot be compelled to solemnise the marriage of any person whose former marriage has been dissolved and whose former spouse is still living.[129] This permits them not only to refuse to solemnise the marriage but also to prohibit the use of the church or chapel of which they are minister for such a purpose.[130] The same model was adopted by the Marriage (Prohibited Degrees of Relationship) Act 1986, which permits the clergy to refuse to marry those related by affinity whose marriage would have been void but for that Act, and to prohibit the use of the church accordingly.[131] However, the more recent exception created under the Gender Recognition Act 2004 is more narrowly drawn.[132] A Church of England minister is not obliged to solemnise the marriage of a person if he reasonably believes the person's gender to be an acquired gender under the 2004 Act.[133] It should be noted that section 22 of the Gender Recognition Act 2004 creates a general offence of unauthorized disclosure of information relating to a person's 'gender history'.[134] Although this applies only to those who have gained the information in an official capacity, that concept is broad enough to include receipt of information in connection with a voluntary organization. The Gender Recognition (Disclosure of Information) (England, Wales and Northern Ireland) (No 2) Order 2005[135] makes provision for exceptions for certain legal, medical, financial and religious purposes. In respect of the religious purposes, disclosure is permitted to enable any person to make a decision whether to officiate at or permit the marriage of the person.[136]

---

[128] It also applies to clergy of the Church in Wales.
[129] Matrimonial Causes Act 1965, s 8(2)(a).
[130] Ibid, s 8(2)(b).
[131] Marriage Act 1949, s 5A (amended by the Marriage (Prohibited Degrees of Relationship) Act 1986, s 3).
[132] And they differ as between the Church of England and the Church in Wales.
[133] Marriage Act 1949, s 5B(1) (amended by the Gender Recognition Act 2004, s 11, Sch 4). A clerk in holy orders of the Church in Wales, however, is additionally not obliged to permit the marriage to be solemnised in his church or chapel: Marriage Act 1949 s 5B(2) (as so amended).
[134] This is punishable by a fine of up to £5,000.
[135] Gender Recognition (Disclosure of Information) (England, Wales and Northern Ireland) (No 2) Order 2005, SI 2005/916.
[136] It also includes whether to appoint the person as a minister, office-holder or to any employment for the purposes of the religion, whether to admit them to any religious order or to membership, or to determine 'whether the subject is eligible to receive or take part in any religious sacrament, ordinance or rite, or take part in any act of worship or prayer, according to the practices of an organised religion': ibid art 4. If a decision other than one relating to marriage is being made, the person making the disclosure must reasonably consider that that person may need the information in order to make a decision which complies with the doctrines of the religion in question or avoids conflicting with the strongly held religious convictions of a significant number of the religion's followers.

Marriage by banns

By far the commonest form of marriage is marriage by banns. In such a case, the marriage must be solemnised in the church or chapel or, as the case may be, one of the churches or chapels where the banns have been published.[137] Banns are published in the parish church of the parish in which each partner to the marriage resides,[138] or, if proposals currently before General Synod are enacted,[139] one with which they have a 'qualifying connection'.[140] It would be for the individual wishing to have his or her marriage solemnised in accordance with this proposed provision to provide such information, written or otherwise, as the minister of the parish may require to be satisfied that the person has a qualifying connection.[141] **5.36**

A minister is not obliged to publish banns of matrimony unless the persons to be married deliver to him, at least seven days before the intended first publication, a notice in writing stating the Christian name and surname and the place of residence of each of them and the period during which each has resided there.[142] All banns must be published from a register provided by the PCC[143] and after each publication the relevant entry in the book must be signed by the person publishing the banns or by someone under his direction.[144] Generally, a clergyman must publish the banns.[145] If a clergyman does not officiate on any Sunday at the service at which it is usual to publish banns, the publication may be made by **5.37**

---

[137] Marriage Act 1949, s 12(1). Certain exceptions to this general rule exist in the case of plurality of benefices, pastoral schemes and churches which are being rebuilt or repaired.

[138] Ibid s 6(1). If a person resides in an extra-parochial place, that is deemed to constitute the parish and the authorized chapel constitutes the parish church: s 6(2). If the parish has no church or chapel, then the adjoining parish church is substituted: s 6(3). As to the meaning of 'residence', see *Legal Opinions* 359–360. Banns may also be published in the ordinary place of worship of each person to be married, even if he or she is not resident in the relevant parish: Marriage Act 1949, s 6(4). To claim a place as one's ordinary place of residence, one must be on the church electoral roll: ibid ss 6(4), 15(1), 35(3), 72(1). The banns must also still be published in the parish or parishes of residence: ibid s 6(4).

[139] The proposed Church of England Marriage Measure was referred back to a revision committee by General Synod in the February 2007 group of sessions for further consideration.

[140] Proposed Church of England Marriage Measure, cl 1(1),(5). The banns would still have to be published in the parish or parishes of residence: ibid cl 1(6). For background to provisions contained in the proposed Measure, see *Just Cause or Impediment?*, Report of the Review of Aspects of Marriage Law Working Group (GS 1436, November 2001); *The Challenge to Change*, Working Group Report (GS 1448, June 2002); *Marriage Law Review*, Interim Report by the Marriage Law Working Group (GS 1543, June 2004). The definition and extent of the categories of 'qualifying connection' are to be considered further by a revision committee with the expectation of submitting a revised draft of the proposed Measure to General Synod for final approval.

[141] Proposed Church of England Marriage Measure, cl 1(7).

[142] Marriage Act 1949, s 8.

[143] Ibid s 7(3); Canon F 11 para 1; Canon F 14.

[144] Marriage Act 1949, s 7(3).

[145] Ibid s 9(1). Banns may also be published by readers (Canon E 4 para 2(b)) and lay workers (Canon E 7 para 5(c)).

a clergyman at another service on that day,[146] or by a layman during the authorized public reading of morning or evening prayer.[147] The foregoing does not apply to a naval wedding, where banns are published at sea.[148]

5.38 Banns are to be published in an audible manner and in the form of words prescribed by the rubric prefixed to the office of matrimony in the *Book of Common Prayer*[149] on three Sundays preceding the solemnisation of marriage during morning service or, if there be no morning service on a Sunday on which they are to be published, during evening service.[150] A person's true name is to be stated, along with that of his parish. A true name need not be a person's baptismal name, but merely that which he customarily uses. The inclusion of a wrong name in the banns will not invalidate a marriage in the absence of wilful concealment.[151] A minister may not solemnise a marriage without production of a certificate that the banns have been properly published in such additional church or churches as the foregoing provisions require.[152] If a marriage is not solemnised within three months after the completion of the publication of the banns, the publication is void and no clergyman may solemnise the marriage on the authority of those banns.[153]

5.39 Special provisions exist in respect of the publication of banns outside England and Wales[154] and for the publication by the chaplain or captain of one of Her Majesty's ships on which an officer, seaman or marine is serving.[155]

Marriage by licence

5.40 The Marriage Act 1949 did not affect the powers of ecclesiastical authorities to grant licences dispensing with certain requirements of the Act.[156] A marriage by common licence must be solemnised in the parish church of the parish in which one of the parties to the marriage has had his usual place of residence for 15 days immediately before the grant of the licence, or in a parish church which is the usual place of worship of either or both of the parties.[157] Legislation currently

---

[146] Marriage Act 1949, s 9(2)(a).
[147] Ibid, s 9(2)(b).
[148] See para 5.39 below.
[149] Marriage Act 1949, s 7(2); Canon B 35 para 2.
[150] Marriage Act 1949, s 7(1).
[151] *Chipchase v Chipchase* [1939] P 391, [1939] 3 All ER 895.
[152] Marriage Act 1949, s 11.
[153] Ibid s 12(2). This does not preclude the banns being republished subsequently.
[154] See ibid s 13; Marriage of British Subjects (Facilities) Act 1915, s 1(a).
[155] Marriage Act 1949, s 14(1).
[156] Ibid s 5. See also the Ecclesiastical Licences Act 1533, ss 4–12, and the Ecclesiastical Jurisdiction Act 1847, s 5.
[157] Marriage Act 1949, s 15(1).

in draft[158] would provide that a common licence could also be granted for the solemnisation of a marriage in any church or chapel with which one of the parties had a 'qualifying connection'.[159] Save in pursuance of a special licence, the solemnisation of a marriage in a private house or any place other than a church or chapel is an ecclesiastical offence.[160]

5.41 The archbishop of each province, the bishop of every diocese and certain ecclesiastical judges may grant a common licence for the solemnisation of marriage without the publication of banns at a lawful time and in a lawful place within their respective jurisdiction.[161] In addition, the Archbishop of Canterbury has power to grant a special licence throughout all England and not merely within the province of Canterbury.[162] A common licence may only be used for the parties for whom it was intended to be obtained, and its grant is wholly discretionary and not of right.[163]

5.42 Before a common licence may be granted, a sworn declaration must be made by one of the parties to the marriage stating that there is no impediment to the marriage, that for at least 15 days prior to the grant one of the parties has been resident in the parish of the church where the marriage is to be solemnised or that it has been his or her usual place of worship and that, if either be a minor, the provisions relating to consent have been complied with.[164] The grant of a licence may be opposed by the entering of a caveat stating the objection, and no licence may be granted until either the caveat is withdrawn or the judge out of whose office the licence is to issue has certified that he has examined the matter of the caveat and is satisfied that it ought not to obstruct the grant of the licence.[165] If the marriage is not solemnised within three months of the grant of the licence, it is void, and no clergyman may solemnise the marriage on its authority.[166]

---

[158] Proposed Church of England Marriage Measure. See nn 139–140 above.

[159] The meaning to be given to 'qualifying connection' is yet to be determined by General Synod: n 140 above.

[160] Marriage Act 1949, s 75(1)(c). The marriage is void: s 25(a). See also *Middleton v Crofts* (1736) 2 Atk 650. The conduct of weddings in a variety of places which are licensed for such purposes under the Marriage Act 1994 are civil ceremonies and not performed in accordance with the rites of the Church of England.

[161] Canon B 34 para 3. The Archbishop of Canterbury has power to grant a common licence throughout all of England: Canon B 34 para 3.

[162] Canon B 34 para 2; Ecclesiastical Licences Act 1533, s 3.

[163] Note, however, that an appeal lies to the Lord Chancellor who may, if it seems fit, enjoin him to grant it and, in the event of his refusal to do so, may commission two other bishops to grant it: Ecclesiastical Licences Act 1533, ss 11, 12.

[164] Marriage Act 1949, s 16(1)(a)–(c), (1A), (1B), amended by the Marriage (Prohibited Degrees of Relationship) Act 1986, s 1(4), Sch 1 para 4.

[165] Marriage Act 1949 s 16(2), (2A), (2B) (as so amended).

[166] Ibid s 16(3).

Registrar's certificate

5.43 A marriage according to the rites of the Church of England may be solemnised on the authority of a certificate of a superintendent registrar in any church or chapel in which banns of matrimony may be published.[167] The service must be conducted by a clergyman, and the consent of the minister of the church or chapel is required. The solemnisation must occur no less than 21 days and no more than three months after the notice was entered in the marriage notice book.[168]

Solemnisation of marriage

5.44 Marriage is properly solemnised by a priest. It is lawful, though canonically irregular (because it includes the giving of a blessing), for the service to be conducted by a deacon.[169] A clergyman may not solemnise his own marriage.[170] Unless it is by special licence, the solemnisation must take place between 8am and 6pm in conformity with the general requirements relating to marriage.[171] The ceremony must be witnessed by at least two persons other than the officiating minister.[172] It is for the minister of the parish to decide what music shall be played at the solemnisation and what hymns and anthems are to be sung or what furnishings or flowers are to be placed in or about the church for the occasion.[173]

5.45 The rubric in the *Book of Common Prayer* for the solemnisation of matrimony states what is to follow in the event of any impediment being raised. It reads:

> if any man do allege and declare any impediment, why they may not be coupled together in Matrimony, by God's law, or the laws of this Realm; and will be bound, and sufficient sureties with him, to the parties; or else put in a caution (to the full value of such charges as the persons to be married do thereby sustain) to prove his allegation: then the solemnization must be deferred, until such time as the truth be tried.

In the unlikely event of such impediment being declared, the minister has a considerable discretion as to how he handles the situation.[174]

---

[167] Ibid ss 17, 26.
[168] Ibid ss 27(4), 31(4).
[169] See *Solemnization of Marriage by Deacons*: Guidelines issued by the Archbishops of Canterbury and York in January 1992. See also R Bursell, *Liturgy, Order and the Law* (Oxford: Clarendon Press, 1996) 176.
[170] *Beamish v Beamish* (1861) 9 HL Cas 274.
[171] Marriage Act 1949, s 4; Canon B 35 para 3. A solemnisation occurring outside these hours will attract a penalty of up to fourteen years imprisonment for the priest concerned: Marriage Act 1949 s 75(1)(a).
[172] Ibid s 22; Canon 35 para 4.
[173] Canon B 35 para 5. Tickets may be issued for the service but no parishioner may be excluded from the church.
[174] See, by analogy, objection taken during an ordination service: *Williamson v Dow*, 16 April 1994 (unreported), Arden J; *R v Bishop of Bristol, ex parte Williamson*, 25 March 1994, CO/764/94

5.46 The marriage must be registered by the clergyman by whom it is solemnised[175] who, immediately after the ceremony, must register in duplicate in two of the marriage registers furnished by the Registrar-General for England and Wales the particulars relating to the marriage in the prescribed form, which must be signed by the clergyman, the parties and two witnesses.[176] Every entry must be in consecutive order and the same number of the entry must be used in each book.[177] Any bona fide errors may be corrected by marginal notes, so long as they are made within one month of the original entry and are duly witnessed and attested.[178]

5.47 Each January, April, July and October the incumbent of every church or chapel where marriages are solemnised must supply the Registrar-General with true copies of all entries of marriages made during the preceding quarter or, if no marriage has been entered, he must certify that fact.[179] The registers must be kept safely by the incumbent until filled[180] and, once filled, one copy is to be delivered to the Registrar-General and the other to remain in the custody of the incumbent, along with the registers of baptism and burials.[181] If a church or chapel ceases to be used for the solemnisation of marriages, the registers are to be delivered to the incumbent of the parish church in which the disused church is situated.[182] The incumbent must allow searches of the registers to be made at all reasonable hours and, upon payment of the appropriate fee, must give certified copies of any entry.[183]

Marriages in chapels

5.48 The bishop may authorize the publication of banns of marriage for qualifying persons[184] in naval, military and air force chapels upon application by the Admiralty or the Secretary of State, as appropriate.[185] One or more clergymen must be appointed for the purpose of registering marriages, and no marriage may be solemnised save in that person's presence.[186]

(unreported), MacPherson of Cluny J. On the question of dealing with objections to marriage, see R Bursell, *Liturgy, Order and the Law* (Oxford: Clarendon Press, 1996) 186–189.
[175] Marriage Act 1949, s 53(a).
[176] Ibid s 55(1), (2). For the provision of registers, see Canon F 11.
[177] Marriage Act 1949, s 55(3).
[178] Ibid s 6(1), (2).
[179] Ibid s 57(1).
[180] Ibid s 59. If he carelessly loses or injures one, the incumbent may be fined: ibid s 76(1).
[181] Ibid s 60.
[182] Ibid s 62.
[183] Ibid s 63.
[184] Broadly speaking these are serving members of the regular, reserve and auxiliary forces, daughters of such people and members of visiting forces and their daughters: ibid s 68(2), (3).
[185] Ibid ss 68(2), 69(1).
[186] Ibid s 69(4).

Further marriage of divorced persons

5.49 The teaching and the practice of the Church of England with respect to a further marriage by a divorced person whose spouse is still alive has been subject to review and rearticulation.[187] The canons still provide that 'marriage is in its nature a union permanent and lifelong' terminable by the death of one partner.[188] With the rescission of paragraph 1 of the 1957 Act of Convocation,[189] the term 'indissoluble save by death' was lost, as was the exhortation not to use the marriage service in the case of anyone who had a former partner still living,[190] but marriage should always be undertaken as 'a solemn, public and life-long covenant between a man and a woman'.[191]

5.50 A priest is relieved of his duty to marry those who are entitled by law to be married in his church if one or both of the intended parties has been divorced and his or her partner is still living.[192] He may also refuse to allow his church to be used for such a purpose.[193] The Act does not preclude the priest from conducting such a marriage; it merely creates a permissive right entitling him lawfully to decline if his conscience so dictates. A capricious refusal, not based upon a conscientious objection, might be actionable under the Human Rights Act 1998.[194] Equally, the

---

[187] See *An Honourable Estate* (London: Church House Publishing, 1988); *Marriage: A Teaching Document from the House of Bishops* (London: Church House Publishing, 1999); *Marriage in Church After Divorce*, the Winchester Report (GS 1361, 2000); *Marriage in Church After Divorce*, A Report from the House of Bishops (GS 1449, May 2002). The latter states, 'The Church of England has sought both to uphold the principle of life-long marriage and to provide a pastoral ministry to divorced persons who seek a further marriage in church': para 1.

[188] See Canon B 30 para 1. The unanimous advice of the legal officers of General Synod (appearing as annex 2 to *Marriage in Church After Divorce*, A Report from the House of Bishops (GS 1449, May 2002)) was that the further marriage of a divorced person was not necessarily incompatible with the Church's doctrine of marriage since the characteristic and normative nature of marriage as a lifelong union was unchanged.

[189] *Regulations Concerning Marriage and Divorce*, Canterbury Convocation passed in May 1957, and declared an Act of Convocation on 1 October 1957, affirming resolutions of 1938 common to both the Canterbury and York Convocations.

[190] Paragraph 1 of the Act of Convocation of 1 October 1957, and the resolutions of 1938, were rescinded by General Synod with effect from 14 November 2003.

[191] See the pastoral introduction to the *Common Worship* Marriage Service. As to the controversial question on whether the passing of the Civil Partnership Act 2004 undermines the institution of marriage, General Synod passed several resolutions in its February 2007 group of sessions including one which acknowledged 'the diversity of views within the Church of England on whether Parliament might better have addressed the injustices affecting persons of the same sex wishing to share a common life had it done so in a way that avoided creating a legal framework with many similarities to marriage'.

[192] Matrimonial Causes Act 1965, s 8(2)(a).

[193] Ibid, s 8(2)(b).

[194] The right to marry is set out in Article 12 of the European Convention on Human Rights, and it is suggested that a minister of the Church of England, in performing functions relating to the solemnisation of marriage is a public authority for the purposes of s 6(1) of the Human Rights Act 1998: see *Aston Cantlow and Wilmcote with Billesley Parochial Church Council v Wallbank*

right being personal to the priest and exercisable according to his conscience, it is not open to the bishop or archbishop to seek to fetter its exercise by mandatory direction.[195]

Burials and funerals

The burial of the dead is governed by both ecclesiastical and civil law.[196] Every parishioner and every person dying in the parish is entitled by law to be buried in the parish churchyard or burial ground if there is one, regardless of whether he is a member of the Church of England or even Christian.[197] Such right, which is said to crystallize on death,[198] is conditional upon there being sufficient space in the ground for burial.[199] There is no right to be buried in any particular spot in the churchyard[200] and, in the absence of a faculty, no tombstone may be erected, nor may a person be buried in the church itself.[201] The common law right of burial now extends to include the interment of cremated remains.[202] A bishop may consecrate ground for the sole purpose of the burial of cremated remains.[203] Where a body is to be buried in accordance with the rites of the Church of England in unconsecrated ground, the minister on coming to the grave must first bless it.[204]

5.51

[2004] 1 AC 546, [2003] 3 All ER 1213, HL, particularly (albeit obiter) per Lord Hobhouse of Woodborough at para 86, and Lord Rodger of Earlsferry at para 170.

[195] There is nothing objectionable to the issuing of guidelines, and these may be useful to ensure procedural consistency, but the priest's statutory discretion must not be eroded. *Advice to Clergy Concerning Marriage and the Divorced* was issued by the House of Bishops in November 2002, and is included in the supplementary material to the Canons of the Church of England.

[196] For a detailed exposition, see D Smale, *Davies' Law of Burial, Cremation and Exhumation* (6th edn, Shaw & Sons, 1993, revised 1994).

[197] This right is the corollary of the minister's duty under Canon B 38 para 2, and extends to those whose names are entered on the church electoral roll of a parish at the time of their death: Church of England (Miscellaneous Provisions) Measure 1976, s 6(1).

[198] *Re West Pennard Churchyard* [1992] 1 WLR 32, [1991] 4 All ER 124, Bath and Wells Cons Ct, per Newsom Ch at 33 and 126 respectively.

[199] The right is enforceable by the personal representatives. For an example of a dispute as to the availability of space see *Re Brightlingsea Churchyard* (2004) 8 Ecc LJ 233, Chelmsford Cons Ct.

[200] Save where a space has been lawfully reserved, as to which see Chapter 7. See also P Sparkes, 'Exclusive Burial Rights' (1991) 2 Ecc LJ 133.

[201] As to the grant of faculties and the authority delegated to ministers, see Chapter 7.

[202] Church of England (Miscellaneous Provisions) Measure 1992, s 3(1). This right does not extend to churchyards or burial grounds which have been closed by Order in Council, in which case a faculty is required; and a faculty may set aside an area there for the burial of cremated remains generally: s 3(1) proviso.

[203] Ibid s 3(2).

[204] Canon B 38 para 5.

5.52 The minister of the parish is obliged to conduct the funeral, subject to due notice being given, and to do so in accordance with an authorized rite of the Church of England.[205] The minister of a parish situated wholly or partly in an area which is chargeable with the expenses of a cemetery or for which a crematorium or cemetery has been designated by the bishop is obliged to perform or arrange the performance of funeral services at such places in respect of his parishioners, those who die in the parish and those on the church electoral roll.[206] There are certain exceptions to this general rule: first, where the relatives request otherwise,[207] and secondly, where the burial service is expressly not to be said, namely over the bodies of those who die unbaptised,[208] who have taken their own lives while of sound mind, or who die excommunicate for some grievous and notorious crime and no man to testify to their repentance.[209] In each of the three cases where the burial service may not be used, the minister may use such service as may be prescribed or approved by the bishop.[210] If a form of service for the burial of suicides is approved by Synod under Canon B 2, this is to be used instead of that prescribed or approved by the bishop unless the person having charge or being responsible for the burial requests otherwise.[211]

5.53 The minister is bound to permit the burial to be conducted by anyone whom the relatives wish, provided it is done in a seemly and Christian fashion and, again at the relatives' request, he is bound to allow the burial to take place without a service.[212] Unordained persons may conduct funeral services[213] but if the Church of England service is to be read, this must be authorized by the incumbent of the parish in which the burial ground is situated.[214] Deaconesses, readers and lay workers may be authorized by the bishop to read the service and bury the dead.[215]

---

[205] Canon B 38 para 2.
[206] Church of England (Miscellaneous Provisions) Measure 1992, s 2(4).
[207] Discussed below.
[208] It need not be a baptism according to the rites of the Church of England, provided it was performed with water and in the name of the Trinity.
[209] Canon B 38 para 2. In the case of any doubt as to whether the deceased may be buried in accordance with the rites of the Church of England, the minister must refer the matter to the bishop and obey his order and direction: Canon B 38 para 6.
[210] Canon B 38 para 2; Burial Laws Amendment Act 1880, s 13; Prayer Book (Further Provisions) Measure 1968, s 5; Church of England (Worship and Doctrine) Measure 1974, s 6(2), Sch 1 para 2.
[211] Canon B 38 para 2 proviso.
[212] Burial Laws Amendment Act 1880, ss 1, 6. The request should be by notice in writing in the form prescribed by Sch A.
[213] Ibid s 6.
[214] *Legal Opinions* 251.
[215] Canon D 1 para 4(c), Canon E 4 para 2A, and Canon E 7 para 5(c) respectively. The 'goodwill of the persons responsible' is a prerequisite.

No body may be disposed of until a registrar's certificate or coroner's order has been issued, and a minister is under a duty as soon as possible after the burial to register it in the prescribed manner.[216] A faculty is required for the exhumation of human remains for reburial elsewhere.[217]

5.54

Cremation of a dead body is lawful in connection with Christian burial.[218] The minister of a parish may perform a funeral service in any crematorium or cemetery situated in another parish, if the deceased died in the minister's parish or was resident therein or on its church electoral roll.[219] Save as aforesaid, a priest is not entitled to conduct funeral services at a cemetery or crematorium outside his benefice, save with the consent of the incumbent of the place in which it is situated. If the person who is to conduct the service is from a different diocese, the consent of the bishop in whose diocese the cemetery or crematorium lies is also required.

5.55

When a body is to be cremated, the burial service may precede, accompany or follow the cremation and may be held either in church or in the crematorium.[220] A funeral service at a crematorium or cemetery may be performed only in accordance with directions given by the bishop.[221] The ashes of a cremated body should be reverently disposed of by a minister in a churchyard or other burial ground.[222]

5.56

Other services

Daily offices

The term 'office' has its root in the Latin word for duty, and relates to the daily cycle of services used in monastic and other orders. From the time of the Reformation, the official formularies of the Church of England made provision merely for two daily offices, matins and evensong. Many Anglican religious communities persist

5.57

---

216 Parochial Registers and Records Measure 1978, s 3(1). This does not apply to burial in a cemetery: s 3(4). See also the Births and Deaths Registration Act 1926, s 3(1), which requires the incumbent to return a detachable portion of the registrar's certificate to the registrar within 96 hours of the burial. Compliance with the secular law is expressly enjoined by Canon B 39 para 1.

217 Burial Act 1857, s 25. Provided the reburial is to be in consecrated ground, no Home Office licence is required: s 25. For further detail, see Chapter 7.

218 Canon B 38 para 3.

219 Church of England (Miscellaneous Provisions) Measure 1992, s 2(2). The consent of the minister in whose parish the cemetery or crematorium is situated is not required: s 2(1). Similar provisions exist in respect of licensed clergy in relation to deceased residents, employees or students of the institutions to which a cleric is licensed: see s 2(3).

220 Canon B 38 para 4(a).

221 Canon B 38 para 7.

222 Canon B 38 para 4(b); Church of England (Miscellaneous Provisions) Measure 1992, s 3.

in using all the old orders,[223] but unlike matins and evensong, they have no official place in the worship of the Church of England. The services of morning and evening prayer are to be said or sung in every parish church at least on all Sundays and other principal feast days and on Ash Wednesday and Good Friday.[224] On all other days, the minister must make provision for morning and evening prayer to be said or sung in the parish church or elsewhere.[225] These requirements may only be dispensed with in accordance with the provisions of Canon B 14A.[226] The use on Sundays of so-called 'family services' comprising choruses, prayers, talks and readings has been expressly discouraged by the Standing Committee of General Synod, in that the congregation ceases to be familiar with the authorized services, but *Common Worship* now affords more latitude.[227]

Visitation of the sick

5.58 A priest is under a canonical duty to 'use his best endeavours to ensure that he be speedily informed when any person is sick or in danger of death' and 'as soon as possible resort unto [such person] to exhort, instruct and comfort him in his distress in such manner as he shall think most needful and convenient'.[228] The *Book of Common Prayer* contains a form of service for the visitation of the sick and another for the communion of the sick. *Common Worship* makes alternative provision. Paragraph 2 of Canon B 37 permits the administration of the sacrament to the sick 'at such place and time as may be convenient'. This embraces hospitals, hospices, private homes and the scene of any emergency.

Exorcism

5.59 There is no mention of exorcism in the *Book of Common Prayer* or the current canons, although in Canon 73 of the Canons Ecclesiastical of 1603 it was provided that ministers were not to attempt the practice of exorcism without first obtaining the licence and direction of the bishop. A previous Archbishop of Canterbury indicated that exorcism should be performed only by an experienced person, authorized by the diocesan bishop, and should be followed by continuing pastoral care.[229] Diocesan regulations or norms generally make appropriate provision.

---

[223] ie Matins, lauds, prime, terce, sext, none, vespers and compline.
[224] Canon B 11 para 1. Readers and lay persons may be authorized to say or sing the office.
[225] Canon B 11 para 2.
[226] This is discussed at paras 5.10ff.
[227] *Liturgical Texts for Local Use* (CBF, 1988).
[228] Canon B 37 para 1.
[229] Statement to General Synod, 30 June 1975.

Special services

Special occasions such as a coronation, a day of national thanksgiving or the enthronement of a bishop may be marked by special forms of service approved pursuant to the provisions of Canon B 4.[230]

5.60

Confession

Penance or the ministry of absolution is the subject matter of Canon B 29. In addition to general confessions and absolutions, provision is made for private confession in appropriate circumstances.[231] Private confession is not obligatory,[232] and no priest may exercise the ministry of absolution in any place without the permission of the minister having the cure of souls thereof except in respect of any person who is in danger of death or if there is some urgent or weighty cause.[233]

5.61

A priest is enjoined not to break the 'seal of the confessional' under pain of irregularity.[234] Although a priest would commit a canonical offence were he to disclose matters communicated to him in the course of a private confession, it is uncertain whether the secular courts would consider such communications privileged, thereby entitling the priest to refuse to answer questions relating thereto.[235] The Criminal Law Revision Committee declined to recommend that priest-penitent communications be privileged.[236] In criminal proceedings, it is likely that a trial judge would exclude evidence of a confession made to a priest.[237] The penitent, and arguably the Church in a representative capacity, might be entitled to seek a quia timet injunction to prevent a priest from communicating information imparted during a confession.[238] Such relief is more likely to be granted following the passing of the Human Rights Act 1998, because of the express right to respect

5.62

---

[230] For a discussion of services of consecration, see R Bursell, 'Consecration, *Jus Liturgicum* and the Canons' in N Doe, M Hill and R Ombres (eds), *English Canon Law* (Cardiff: University of Wales Press, 1998) 71–81.

[231] Canon B 29 paras 2, 3. Private confession and absolution is expressed to be for those who cannot quiet their conscience through general absolution and, in particular, the sick.

[232] *Rector and Churchwardens of Capel St Mary, Suffolk v Packard* [1927] P 289, Ct of Arches.

[233] Canon B 29 para 4.

[234] See the Canons Ecclesiastical 1603, Canon 113 proviso. This is the only part of the 1603 Canons not to have been repealed.

[235] See generally R Bursell, 'The Seal of the Confessional' (1990) 2 Ecc LJ 84; G Nokes, 'Professional Privilege' [1950] 66 LQR 88; E Badeley, *The Privilege of Religious Confessions in English Courts of Justice* (London, 1865); P Winckworth, *The Seal of the Confessional and the Law of Evidence* (1952).

[236] Criminal Law Revision Committee, 11th Report (1972) paras 273, 274.

[237] A discretion so to do arises under the Police and Criminal Evidence Act 1984, ss 76, 78, 82(3).

[238] As to confidentiality generally, see *Duchess of Argyll v Duke of Argyll* [1967] Ch 302, [1965] 1 All ER 611; and *Stephens v Avery* [1988] Ch 449, [1988] 2 All ER 477.

for one's private life under Article 8 of the European Convention on Human Rights and the emergent torts involving invasions of privacy and confidentiality.[239] An Anglican priest is in a different position from a priest of another denomination, since the duty of confidentiality which attaches to him is part of the law of the land.[240] In practical terms, however, it would be surprising if the secular courts differentiated between the evidential effects of the sacrament of penance purely on the basis of the priest's denomination.[241]

---

[239] See M Hill, 'The Impact on the Church of England of the Human Rights Act 1998' (2000) 5 Ecc LJ 431.

[240] For a consideration (albeit somewhat unsatisfactory) of injunctive relief to enforce threatened breaches of canon law in a different context see *Gill v Davies* (1997) 5 Ecc LJ 131, Smith J, the text of which was reproduced in the second edition of this work: M Hill, *Ecclesiastical Law* (2nd edn, Oxford: Oxford University Press, 2001) 707–712.

[241] In many foreign jurisdictions, the civil laws of evidence grant a privileged status to all communications with priests (and counsellors and therapists), whether or not as part of auricular confession.

6

CLERGY DISCIPLINE

Introduction	6.01	Penalty by consent	6.33
Institutions and personnel	6.04	Formal investigation	6.35
Clergy Discipline Commission	6.04	**Suspension during proceedings**	6.37
President of tribunals	6.06	**Conduct of disciplinary tribunals**	6.39
Registrar of tribunals	6.07	**Penalties**	6.47
Provincial panels	6.08	**Proceedings in secular courts**	6.54
Disciplinary tribunals	6.09	**Nullification, removal of**	
Vicar-General's court	6.10	prohibition and pardon	6.55
Designated officer	6.11	**Appeals**	6.58
Jurisdiction	6.12	**Costs and legal aid**	6.67
Misconduct	6.13	**The Archbishops' List**	6.69
Time limits	6.16	**Offences involving doctrine,**	
Complainants	6.17	ritual or ceremonial	6.73
Procedure	6.22	Investigation	6.74
Preliminary scrutiny	6.23	Hearing and appeals	6.76
No further action	6.28	Censures	6.77
Conditional deferment	6.29		
Conciliation	6.31		

Introduction

The most profound change to the law of the Church of England since the publication of the previous edition of this work has been the enactment of the Clergy Discipline Measure 2003. This has created an entirely new process for the discipline of clergy in relation to matters which do not concern doctrine.[1]

6.01

---

[1] Cases involving matters of doctrine, ritual or ceremonial continue to be governed by the Ecclesiastical Jurisdiction Measure 1963 and these are addressed separately at paras 6.73ff below. A proposal for reform along similar lines to those of the Clergy Discipline Measure 2003 failed to find favour with the General Synod when debated in July 2004.

Chapter 6: Clergy Discipline

The Measure has its origins in the report of 1996, *Under Authority*,[2] which emphasized the expense and complexity of proceedings brought under the Ecclesiastical Jurisdiction Measure 1963, and the need to adopt the model of the secular employment tribunal wherever possible. The key change is to move part of the process from within the diocese, where it was previously within the jurisdiction of the consistory court, to a national system, with tribunals drawn from provincial panels. The Clergy Discipline Measure 2003 commences with a statutory statement of principle. Section 1 of the Measure reads:

> Any body or person on whom functions in connection with the discipline of persons in Holy Orders are conferred by this Measure shall, in exercising those functions, have due regard to the role in that connection of the bishop or archbishop who, by virtue of his office and consecration, is required to administer discipline.[3]

6.02 The new system of clergy discipline came into force on 1 January 2006, the institutions to regulate and enforce it having been established in advance.[4] The Measure is supplemented by the Clergy Discipline Rules 2005,[5] and by a Code of Practice.[6] The Rules, being a species of delegated legislation, have the force of law. The Code does not, but compliance with its provisions will be assumed to be in accordance with best practice.[7] The Code speaks of the purpose of discipline in relation to the clergy as being the imposition of an appropriate penalty, pastoral support, encouraging repentance and forgiveness, whenever possible putting right that which is wrong, attempting reconciliation, and moving on constructively from the past.[8] It also emphasizes the wider picture in having regard to the interests of justice for all who may be affected by the faults, failings or shortcomings of the clergy and the need to ensure that the clergy continue to be worthy of the great trust that is put in them as ordained ministers.[9]

---

[2] The Report of the General Synod Working Party Reviewing Clergy Discipline and the Working of the Ecclesiastical Courts (GS 1217, 1996).

[3] Clergy Discipline Measure 2003, s 1. The bishop's role is discussed further in paragraphs 90–95 of the Code of Practice made under the Measure. However, the Code contains a warning that 'a diocesan bishop must avoid personal involvement in the giving of care and support where formal disciplinary proceedings have been commenced (unless the bishop's functions under the Measure have been delegated by the bishop to another person) in case the bishop's impartiality appears as a result to be compromised': para 97.

[4] For an overview of the system, see A Iles, 'The Clergy Discipline Measure 2003: A Canter Through its Provisions and Procedures' (2007) 9 Ecc LJ 10.

[5] Clergy Discipline Rules 2005, SI 2005/2022. See also the Clergy Discipline Appeal Rules 2005, SI 2005/3201, which make procedural provision for appeals.

[6] Code of Practice (London, 2005) GS 1585, formulated and promulgated pursuant to Clergy Discipline Measure 2003, s 39. Its purpose is 'to provide guidance to all who are concerned in formal clergy discipline procedures under the Measure': para 1.

[7] Code of Practice, para 2.

[8] Ibid para 4.

[9] Ibid para 4.

The Clergy Discipline Rules 2005 commence with an articulation of their over- **6.03**
riding objective, which is

> to enable formal disciplinary proceedings brought under the Measure to be dealt with justly, in a way that is both fair to all relevant interested parties and proportionate to the nature and seriousness of the issues raised.[10]

The rules are, so far as is reasonably practicable, to be applied in accordance with certain principles, namely treating the complainant and the respondent on an equal footing procedurally, and keeping them informed of the procedural progress of the complaint, whilst avoiding undue delay and expense.[11] There is a duty on all parties to co-operate with any person, tribunal or court exercising any function under the Measure and to further the overriding objective.[12]

Institutions and personnel

Clergy Discipline Commission

The newly formed Clergy Discipline Commission[13] comprises not more than **6.04**
12 persons appointed by the Appointments Committee of the Church of England, of whom at least two are from each of the houses of General Synod and at least two are legally qualified.[14] The chairman and deputy chairman, appointed by the Appointments Committee, after consultation with the Dean of the Arches and Auditor from amongst the membership, are each required to be similarly legally qualified.[15]

The functions of the Commission are: **6.05**

(a) to give general advice to disciplinary tribunals, the courts of the Vicars-General, bishops and archbishops as to the penalties which are appropriate in particular circumstances;
(b) to issue codes of practice and general policy guidance to persons exercising functions in connection with clergy discipline;[16]

---

[10] Clergy Discipline Rules 2005, r 1.
[11] Ibid r 1(a)-(d).
[12] Ibid r 2(1). Any failure to co-operate by a party may result in adverse inferences being made against that party at any stage of the proceedings: r 2(2).
[13] The Commission was set up under the Clergy Discipline Measure 2003, s 3(1).
[14] Ibid s 3(1)(a), (b). Those legally qualified must have either a seven years' general qualification within the meaning of the Courts and Legal Services Act 1990 or hold or have held high judicial office or the office of circuit judge.
[15] Clergy Discipline Measure 2003, s 3(2).
[16] There is a specific duty to formulate and, with the approval of the Dean of Arches, promulgate guidance in a Code of Practice: ibid s 39(1). Before coming into force, it must first be approved by General Synod: s 39(3), (4).

(c) to provide an annual report to the General Synod through the House of Bishops.[17]

President of tribunals

6.06 The chairman of the Commission is also the president of tribunals whose functions include the issuing of practice directions, acting as chairman of a disciplinary tribunal where, in his opinion, important points of law or principle are involved; and exercising such other functions as may be prescribed.[18] The deputy chairman of the Commission is the deputy president of tribunals who acts for the president when the latter is absent or unable or unwilling to act.[19]

Registrar of tribunals

6.07 The archbishops of Canterbury and York, after consultation with the president of tribunals, each appoint for their province a registrar of tribunals who is required to have a general qualification within the meaning of the Courts and Legal Services Act 1990.[20] The registrar's responsibilities comprise directing and supervising the general administration of disciplinary tribunals in the province and exercising functions conferred under the Clergy Discipline Measure 2003.[21] In the case of any inability or unwillingness to act, the registrar of tribunals for the other province is empowered to act in his stead.[22]

Provincial panels

6.08 The personnel for disciplinary tribunals and the Vicar-General's court are drawn from a list for each province of persons available for appointment which is compiled and maintained by the Commission and called the provincial panel.[23] Each provincial panel contains the names of two lay persons and two clergy from each diocese nominated by the bishop after consultation with the bishop's council,[24] and ten persons nominated by the archbishop of the relevant province

---

[17] Ibid s 3(3)(a)–(c).
[18] Ibid s 4(1), (2).
[19] Ibid s 4(1), (3).
[20] Clergy Discipline Measure 2003, s 5(1), (2).
[21] Ibid s 5(6).
[22] Ibid s 5(7).
[23] Ibid s 21(1).
[24] Ibid s 21(2)(a), (b). The lay people must be resident in the diocese and on the electoral roll of a parish in the diocese or on the community roll of the cathedral; the clergy must also be resident in the diocese and must have served at least seven years in Holy Orders.

who are legally qualified.[25] In addition the archbishop of each province may nominate up to five lay persons and five clergy to the panel.[26] All persons nominated to the panel must be actual communicants.[27] Persons nominated to serve on the panel do so for six years and, on retiring, are eligible to serve for not more than one further period of six years.[28]

Disciplinary tribunals

6.09 When a complaint is to be referred under the Measure to a disciplinary tribunal, then one will be constituted for the diocese in question.[29] A disciplinary tribunal consists of a chairman,[30] together with two lay persons and two clergy, appointed by the president from the respective class of the relevant provincial panel, other than nominees of the bishop of the diocese concerned.[31] The president may not appoint any person unless he is satisfied that there is no reason to question the impartiality of that person, and he must first afford to the respondent an opportunity to make representations as to the suitability of those to be appointed.[32]

Vicar-General's Court

6.10 The Vicar-General's court exercises jurisdiction in disciplinary proceedings under the Measure in two separate circumstances, and its composition differs accordingly.

---

[25] Ibid s 21(2)(c). The legal requirement is that each has a seven year general qualification within the meaning of section 71 of the Courts and Legal Services Act 1990 or who have held or are holding high judicial office or the office of circuit judge.

[26] Clergy Discipline Measure 2003, s 21(3). The same provisions for residence (but on a provincial basis) and time in Orders apply.

[27] Ibid s 21(4). See the Church Representation Rules, r 54(1).

[28] Clergy Discipline Measure 2003, s 21(5). A transitional provision requires for one half of each class of those nominated on the first occasion to retire after three years, such determination to be by lot: s 21(5) proviso. Provision is made for members to continue to adjudicate upon any matters of which they were seized when their period of service on the panel expired (s 21(6)) and for the filling of casual vacancies (s 21(7), (8)).

[29] Ibid ss 2, 22.

[30] The chairman will be the president of tribunals or someone appointed by him drawn from those nominated to the legally qualified class of the panel under ibid s 21(2)(c).

[31] Ibid s 22(1)(a)–(c).

[32] Ibid s 22(2). The respondent has 14 days within which to make written representations as to the suitability of any proposed members of the tribunal (Clergy Discipline Rules 2005, r 37(1)), and in the event that an alternative person is proposed, a further 14 days will be afforded for representations from the respondent as to suitability (r 37(2)). It is respectfully submitted that the designated officer ought also to be afforded the opportunity to make representations since he may be aware of factors concerning possible partiality which are unknown to the respondent or the president. See generally *Burridge v Tyler* [1992] 1 All ER 437, Ct of Arches, concerning the need for transparency in the fairness of proceedings under the system pertaining under the Ecclesiastical Jurisdiction Measure 1963 in circumstances where a respondent or a witness may be known personally to one of those comprising the tribunal of fact.

In proceedings against a bishop the court consists of five members, namely the Vicar-General[33] of the relevant province; two clergy (one of whom must be in episcopal orders) appointed by the president of tribunals; and two lay persons appointed by the president of tribunals from the relevant class of the provincial panel of the other province from that in which the bishop concerned serves.[34] In the case of disciplinary proceedings against an archbishop, the court again consists of five persons but made up as follows: the Vicar-General of the other province;[35] two clergy (one of whom shall be in episcopal orders) appointed by the president of tribunals; and two lay persons appointed by the president of tribunals from among the relevant class of the provincial panel of the other province.[36] In both instances, the president of tribunals may not appoint any person unless he is satisfied that there is no reason to question the impartiality of that person, and he must first afford to the respondent an opportunity to make representations as to the suitability of those to be appointed.[37]

Designated officer

6.11 The designated officer is an officer of the legal office of the National Institutions of the Church of England designated by the Archbishops' Council for the purposes of the Clergy Discipline Measure 2003.[38] A more expansive definition is to be found in the Clergy Discipline Rules 2005, which states that he 'conducts the case on behalf of the complainant when the complaint is referred to the tribunal or the Vicar-General's court, and … acts independently from the complainant, the respondent, the bishop, the archbishop, or any other person or body'.[39]

Jurisdiction

6.12 A disciplinary tribunal constituted for a diocese has jurisdiction to hear and determine disciplinary proceedings against a priest or deacon (a) who, when the misconduct was alleged to have taken place, held preferment[40] in the diocese or

---

[33] In the event that the Vicar-General declares himself to be personally acquainted with the complainant or the respondent, the president of tribunals appoints a chairman from the legally qualified class of the other provincial panel than that in which the bishop serves: Clergy Discipline Measure 2003, s 23(1)(a).
[34] Ibid s 23(1)(a)–(c).
[35] In the event that the Vicar-General declares himself to be personally acquainted with the complainant or the respondent, the president of tribunals appoints a chairman from the legally qualified class of the provincial panel of the other province: ibid s 23(2)(a).
[36] Ibid s 23(2)(a)–(c).
[37] Ibid s 23(3).
[38] Ibid s 43(1).
[39] Clergy Discipline Rules 2005, r 106.
[40] For the purposes of this section, 'preferment' includes an archbishopric, a bishopric, archdeaconry or office in a cathedral or collegiate church, and a benefice, and every curacy, lectureship, readership,

was resident therein; or (b) who is alleged to have officiated as a minister in the diocese without authority.[41] The Vicar-General's court of each province has jurisdiction to determine disciplinary proceedings (a) against any bishop who, when the misconduct was alleged to have taken place, held preferment in the province or was resident therein; (b) against any bishop who is alleged to have officiated as a minister in the province without authority; and (c) against the archbishop of the other province.[42] Slightly cumbersome provisions exist to ensure that proceedings cannot proceed in relation to the same incident but in different *fora*, one on the basis of preferment, and the other on the basis of residence.[43]

Misconduct

Central to the Clergy Discipline Measure 2003 is the concept of misconduct, allegations of which form the basis of disciplinary proceedings for bishops, priests and deacons alike.[44] It is given statutory articulation under the Measure and is broader in its scope that that which pertained under the Ecclesiastical Jurisdiction Measure 1963.[45] Proceedings may now be instituted alleging any of the following acts or omissions:[46]

6.13

(a) doing any act in contravention of the laws ecclesiastical;[47]
(b) failing to do any act required by the laws ecclesiastical;
(c) neglect or inefficiency in the performance of the duties of office;[48]

---

chaplaincy, office or place which requires discharge of any spiritual duty: Clergy Discipline Measure 2003, ss 6(5), 43(1). It should also be noted here that in the case of a minister licensed to serve in a diocese by the bishop thereof, the licence shall not be terminated by reason of misconduct otherwise than by way of disciplinary proceedings under the Measure: s 8(2).

[41] Ibid s 6(1)(a), (b). Disciplinary proceedings can be instituted or continued even if the respondent resigns his or her position: Code of Practice, para 22.

[42] Clergy Discipline Measure 2003, s 6(2)(a)–(c).

[43] Ibid s 6(3), (4).

[44] Paragraph 9 of the Code of Practice states that 'minor complaints should not be the subject matter of formal disciplinary proceedings' and includes the following quotation from *Under Authority* (London, 1996) GS 1217 at C.3: 'in the case of many minor complaints an apology or an informal rebuke may be all that is required and the full complaints process would not need to come into play'.

[45] See para 6.15 of the second edition of this work, referring to the Ecclesiastical Jurisdiction Measure 1963, s 14(1)(a),(b).

[46] Clergy Discipline Measure 2003, s 8(1)(a)–(d).

[47] The Code of Practice comments at para 26, 'reference has to be made to the many principles of ecclesiastical law, which can be found in Acts of Parliament, Measures and Canons of the Church of England, statutory instruments, custom, and case law'. No further definition is offered.

[48] The Code of Practice states at para 28, 'it is not practical to give detailed guidance on what amounts to misconduct here as the circumstances could be infinitely variable'. The Code recognizes that if sufficiently serious, a single instance of neglect may amount to neglect, but envisages that generally neglect or inefficiency will amount to misconduct only if they occur over a period of time: para 28. There may be a degree of overlap between neglect of duty and contravention of

(d) conduct unbecoming or inappropriate to the office and work of a clerk in Holy Orders.[49]

6.14 Certain other specific matters under the Clergy Discipline Measure 2003 are stated to amount to misconduct for the purposes of the Measure. Any person who performs in the Church of England any function which, under a penalty imposed under the Clergy Discipline Measure 2003 or a censure imposed under the Ecclesiastical Jurisdiction Measure 1963, he is not permitted to perform commits an act of misconduct.[50] The failure to disclose a conviction or arrest is categorized as misconduct under section 8(1), being a failure to do an act required by the laws ecclesiastical.[51] A priest or deacon subject to suspension pending trial[52] who interferes with any person performing the services of a church in pursuance of arrangements made by the bishop, acts in contravention of the laws ecclesiastical.[53]

6.15 No proceedings of unbecoming conduct may be taken in respect of the lawful political opinions or activities of any bishop, priest or deacon.[54] Proceedings in relation to matters involving doctrine, ritual and ceremonial continue to be conducted in accordance with the Ecclesiastical Jurisdiction Measure 1963.[55] The dividing line between a complaint of misconduct which is justiciable under the Clergy Discipline Measure 2003 and matters of doctrine which are not may be difficult to draw on occasions. A refusal to baptise, for instance, engages both the canonical duty under Canon B 22(4) and the doctrine of the church.[56]

---

the laws of ecclesiastical. The adjudication in *Bland v Archdeacon of Cheltenham* [1972] Fam 157, [1972] 1 All ER 1012, Ct of Arches, may be persuasive authority for a refusal to baptise an infant being charged not as neglect of duty but as an offence under ecclesiastical law. However, the irregularity in that instance did not lead to the proceedings being struck out, it being a matter of form not substance.

[49] Reference is made in the Code of Practice, para 30, to Canons C 26, C 27 and C 28.
[50] Clergy Discipline Measure 2003, s 29. In the case of a person deposed from Holy Orders, disciplinary proceedings may be instituted as if he had not been deposed: s 29.
[51] Ibid s 33. The same applies under s 34 in the case of the duty to disclose divorce and separation orders.
[52] Under ibid s 36(1).
[53] Ibid s 36(5).
[54] Ibid s 8(3).
[55] See paras 6.73ff below.
[56] See *Bland v Archdeacon of Cheltenham* [1972] Fam 157, [1972] 1 All ER 1012, Ct of Arches, a case decided under the Ecclesiastical Jurisdiction Measure 1963. For a discussion, see R Bursell, 'Turbulent Priests: Clerical Misconduct Under the Clergy Discipline Measure' (2007) 9 Ecc LJ 2003.

Time limits

Proceedings must be instituted within one year of the misconduct in question, or the last instance of it in the case of a series of acts or omissions.[57] There are two exceptions to this strict rule. First, in the case of misconduct which also amounts to a criminal offence. In this instance, if the person concerned is convicted either on indictment or summarily, proceedings may be instituted[58] within 12 months of the conviction becoming conclusive, notwithstanding that a year has elapsed since the act or omission complained of.[59] Secondly, the president of tribunals may give his written permission for proceedings to be instituted after the expiry of the period of one year if he considers that there was good reason why the complainant did not institute proceedings at an earlier date.[60] He must consult with the complainant and the respondent before so doing,[61] and if permission is given, the president must specify the time within which the complaint in writing is to be made.[62]

6.16

Complainants

Disciplinary proceedings may be instituted against a priest or deacon by way of a complaint in writing[63] by:

6.17

(a) a person nominated by the PCC of any parish which has a proper interest in making the complaint;[64] or

---

[57] Clergy Discipline Measure 2003, s 9. It will clearly be a matter of fact and degree whether two or more isolated acts or omissions amount to a 'series' for the purpose of this section.

[58] The Measure does not expressly define what constitutes institution of proceedings but it is clear from s 10 that it is the making of the original complaint in writing. This is clarified in the Clergy Discipline Rules 2005, r 9(1)(a), which states that the date the complaint was received is the date when proceedings were instituted.

[59] Clergy Discipline Measure 2003, s 9, first proviso.

[60] Any application to permit a complaint to be made out of time must be made in writing in Form 1c in the Schedule to the Clergy Discipline Rules 2005, or in a document which is substantially to the like effect containing the information required in the form and setting out the reasons why proceedings were not instituted within time: r 8(1). The Code of Practice ventures certain justifiable reasons which include lack of knowledge, physical or mental disability, manipulation or abuse: para 55.

[61] Clergy Discipline Measure 2003, s 9, second proviso. A detailed timetable is set out for this consultation process in the Clergy Discipline Rules 2005, r 8(2)-(4). Although there is considerable latitude as to what might constitute 'good reason', the discretion falls to be exercised judicially, and the burden of proof would appear to lie on the complainant.

[62] Ibid r 8(5).

[63] The form and content of the written complaint is discussed below.

[64] Not less than two-thirds of the lay members of the PCC must be present at a duly convened meeting and not less than two-thirds of the lay members present and voting must pass a resolution to the effect that proceedings be instituted: Clergy Discipline Measure 2003, s 10(1)(a)(i). A certified copy of this resolution must accompany the complaint: Clergy Discipline Rules 2005, r 4(2)(b).

(b) a churchwarden of any such parish; or
(c) any other person who has a proper interest in making the complaint.[65]

Slightly different provisions apply in respect of cathedral clergy,[66] chaplains in sector ministries,[67] chaplains in the armed forces[68] and certain ministers with provincial licences.[69]

6.18 The written complaint must be made in Form 1a in the Schedule to the Clergy Discipline Rules 2005, or in a document which is substantially to the like effect.[70] It must state the bishop to whom the complaint is made; the full name and contact address, including postcode, of the complainant; the name and the position held of the priest or deacon about whom the complaint is made; why the complainant claims to have a proper interest or is otherwise entitled to make the complaint; in summary form the nature and details of the acts and omissions alleged to constitute misconduct; the date or dates of the alleged misconduct; and the evidence in

---

For provisions relating to a substitute complainant in the case of death, serious illness or incapacity, see rr 55, 57.

[65] Clergy Discipline Measure 2003, s 10(1)(a)(i)–(iii). There is an element of subjectivity as to what constitutes a proper interest for this purpose. It is submitted that it should be broadly interpreted so as to exclude the prurient busybody but admit those genuinely concerned with the subject matter of the complaint. See the limited guidance in paragraph 32 of the Code of Practice. It may be appropriate for the archdeacon to act as complainant if he feels that the matter should be dealt with on a disciplinary level but no formal complaint is likely to be made by anyone else: Code of Practice, para 12. For provisions relating to a substitute complainant in the case of death, serious illness or incapacity, see Clergy Discipline Rules 2005, rr 56 and 57.

[66] In this case proceedings may only be instituted by a person nominated by the council of the cathedral church or any other person, if the diocesan bishop concerned determines that he has a proper interest in making the complaint: Clergy Discipline Measure 2003, s 42(2)(a), (b). For further adaptations of the procedures in relation to clergy serving in a cathedral church, see the Clergy Discipline Rules 2005, r 92.

[67] In the case of a chaplain of a prison, hospital, university, school or other institution, disciplinary proceedings may be instituted only by a person duly authorized by the diocesan bishop concerned to institute such proceedings: Clergy Discipline Measure 2003, s 42(3). For further adaptations of the procedures in relation to clergy serving in such places see Clergy Discipline Rules 2005, r 93.

[68] In the case of a chaplain of one of the armed forces, disciplinary proceedings may be instituted only if the Archbishop of Canterbury determines that the person concerned has a proper interest in making the complaint: Clergy Discipline Measure 2003, s 42(4)(a). The complaint must be laid before the Archbishop of Canterbury and reference to the diocesan bishop is to be construed as referring to him: s 42(4)(b). For further adaptations of the procedures in relation to clergy serving in the armed forces, see the Clergy Discipline Rules 2005, r 94.

[69] In the case of a minister who has a licence from the archbishop of the province, disciplinary proceedings may be instituted only by a person duly authorized by the archbishop (Clergy Discipline Measure 2003, s 42(5)(a)), and in the case of a minister who has a licence from the University of Oxford or Cambridge, disciplinary proceedings may be instituted only by a person duly authorized by the Archbishop of Canterbury (s 42(6)(a)). In each instance complaint must be laid before the archbishop and reference to the diocesan bishop is to be construed as referring to him: s 42(5)(b) and s 42(6)(b) respectively. For further adaptations of the procedures in relation to clergy serving with an archbishop's licence, see the Clergy Discipline Rules 2005, r 95, and with a licence from the University of Oxford or Cambridge, r 96.

[70] Ibid r 4(1).

support upon which the complainant relies, which must be in writing and signed and dated by the maker in each case.[71] The complaint must contain a declaration that the complainant believes the facts of the complaint to be true,[72] and must be signed and dated by the complainant.[73] The Code of Practice recognized that complainants may need help to make a written complaint and states that each diocese should designate a person to ensure that appropriate help is made available to any complainant who needs it.[74]

6.19 In the case of a complaint against a bishop, the complaint must be made in writing by:

(a) a person nominated by the bishop's council of the diocese concerned;[75] or
(b) any other person who has a proper interest in making the complaint.[76]

6.20 A complaint concerning a priest or deacon is to be laid before the diocesan bishop;[77] that concerning a bishop before the relevant archbishop concerned; and that concerning an archbishop, the other archbishop.[78] The written complaint must be accompanied by written particulars of the alleged misconduct.[79] Written evidence in support of the complaint must be sent to the bishop (or archbishop as the case may be) either with the complaint or at such later time as he may allow.[80]

6.21 Where a complainant wishes to withdraw a complaint at any time before the bishop determines which course to pursue, the bishop, after consulting the

---

[71] Ibid r 4(2)(a).
[72] Ibid r 4(2)(c). The Code of Practice makes plain that anonymous complaints will not be considered: para 42.
[73] Clergy Discipline Rules 2005, r 4(2)(d).
[74] Code of Practice, para 38. The help could take the form of listening to the complainant and then transcribing the complaint and the evidence in support: para 39. The individual must be entirely independent and not otherwise involved in the complaint: para 40.
[75] Not less than two-thirds of the members of the council must be present at a duly convened meeting and not less than two-thirds of members present and voting must pass a resolution to the effect that proceedings be instituted: Clergy Discipline Measure 2003, s 10(1)(b)(i). As to the form of complaint and the requirement to attach a certified copy of the relevant resolution, see the Clergy Discipline Rules 2005, r 82, Schedule, Form 1b.
[76] Clergy Discipline Measure 2003, s 10(1)(b)(i), (ii).
[77] It may be sent or delivered: Clergy Discipline Rules 2005, r 4(2)(d).
[78] Clergy Discipline Measure 2003, s 10(2)(a)–(c).
[79] Ibid s 10(3). This must be in writing and signed and dated by the maker of the statement in each case: Clergy Discipline Rules 2005, r 4(2)(a)(vii). It must be made in Form 3 in the Schedule, or in a document which is substantially to the like effect, and must contain a declaration that the maker of the statement believes the facts in it are true: r 6(2). It must also indicate what parts are within the maker's own knowledge and which are matters of information and belief, in which case identifying the source: r 6(1).
[80] Clergy Discipline Measure 2003, s 10(3). Any request for permission to send evidence in support after the date of the complaint must be in writing and state reasons: Clergy Discipline Rules 2005, r 7(2). A reasonable period may be allowed by the bishop but this should not exceed twenty-eight days: r 7(3).

respondent in writing, must direct either that the complaint be withdrawn, or that it proceed with a substituted complainant.[81]

Procedure

6.22 What follows is a description of the procedure to be followed in the case of complaints against priests and deacons, which will be by far the most common. Where the procedure varies in respect of complaints against bishops and archbishops, this is indicated where necessary in the text or accompanying footnotes.

Preliminary scrutiny

6.23 When a complaint in writing has been properly made,[82] it must be referred in the first instance to the diocesan registrar.[83] This must be done within seven days of receipt of the complaint and written evidence in support.[84] He must scrutinize the complaint to verify that the complainant has capacity to make the complaint and to form a view as to whether or not there is sufficient substance in the complaint to justify proceeding with it.[85] The registrar must notify the responden that the complaint has been referred to him,[86] and may only consult the complainant for the purposes of clarification.[87]

---

[81] Ibid r 59(1)-(3). Once the bishop has directed that the complaint be formally investigated, the matter falls to be determined by the president: r 59(4).

[82] See paragraph 6.18 above.

[83] Clergy Discipline Measure 2003, s 11(1), or provincial registrar in the case of a bishop or archbishop. The registrar may delegate any or all of his functions under s 11 to such person as he may designate: s 11(6). There is no requirement for the delegate to be legally qualified. The Code of Practice emphasizes that the registrar should not give legal advice in relation to a complaint to anyone except the bishop: para 70.

[84] Clergy Discipline Rules 2005, r 9(2). Note the requirement for the bishop to send an acknowledgment to the complainant containing certain specified information: r 9(1). Where the misconduct alleged might constitute a criminal offence, the acknowledgment must state that the resolution of the complaint under the Measure may be postponed to await the outcome of police or other investigations: r 9(1).

[85] Clergy Discipline Measure 2003, s 11(1)(a), (b).

[86] Ibid s 11(1); Clergy Discipline Rules 2005, r 10. This notification must include details as to the registrar's function. There is provision in exceptional circumstances to delay notifying the respondent by up to 42 days for the protection of the interests of a child: r 10(2). 'Child' means a person under 18: r 106. The registrar must supply the respondent with a copy of the complaint and the written evidence (or an edited transcript of the complaint and evidence, redacted as appropriate where r 10(2) applies): r 10(3), (4). The Code of Practice states that every diocese should identify an appropriate person to offer practical help and advice, as well as identify where the respondent may obtain legal advice: para 75, although for obvious reasons, legal advice cannot be sought from the registrar of the diocese concerned: para 76.

[87] Clergy Discipline Rules 2005, r 11. Such consultation should be in writing, but if oral it must be reduced into written memoranda and copied to the registrar and complainant: r 11.

6.24 Within 28 days of receipt of the complaint[88] the registrar must send a written report to the bishop setting out his views as to whether the complainant has a proper interest in the complaint and whether there is sufficient substance in it to justify proceeding with it under the Measure.[89] On receipt of the report, the bishop may dismiss the complaint and, if he does, he must give written notice of the dismissal to the complainant and the respondent together with a copy of the report.[90] The complainant has the right to request the president of tribunals to review the dismissal.[91] The president may either uphold the dismissal or if he considers it to be plainly wrong, he may reverse it and direct the bishop to proceed with the complaint.[92]

6.25 If the complaint is not dismissed by the bishop, or if the president of tribunals directs the bishop to proceed with the complaint, the bishop must determine which of several courses of action to pursue.[93] He must do so within 28 days of receipt of the registrar's report, or of the direction of the president of tribunals, or such longer period as he considers to be justified in the particular circumstances of the case.[94] He must first request a written answer from the respondent to

---

[88] Or such longer period as he considers to be justified in the particular circumstances of the case: Clergy Discipline Measure 2003, s 11(2). If the registrar proposes to extend the period of 28 days, he must consult the complainant and the respondent before so doing: s 11(5). See also the consultation requirements under the Clergy Discipline Rules 2005, r 13(1). The period of 28 days may not be extended more than once: Clergy Discipline Measure 2003, s 11(2) proviso.
[89] Ibid s 11(2); Clergy Discipline Rules 2005, r 12(1). In the case of multiple complaints, see r 14.
[90] Clergy Discipline Measure 2003, s 11(3); Clergy Discipline Rules 2005, r 15(1).
[91] This right must be explained in the bishop's written notice (ibid r 15(2)); and the request must be made within 14 days of the notice of dismissal (r 16(1)). It must be in writing in Form 4 in the Schedule to the Rules or in a document substantially to the like effect, and must set out the reasons for seeking a review of the bishop's decision and be accompanied by a copy of the complaint and the written evidence of support, the registrar's report and the bishop's notice of dismissal: r 16(1). No further evidence may be submitted: r 16(2).
[92] Clergy Discipline Measure 2003, s 11(4). The president must notify the complainant, the respondent and the bishop in writing of his decision within 28 days of receiving the request for a review: Clergy Discipline Rules 2005, r 16(4). The expression 'plainly wrong' is to be interpreted as 'not within the range of reasonable decisions': Code of Practice, para 106. The president should not lightly overrule the exercise of an episcopal discretion.
[93] Clergy Discipline Measure 2003, s 12(1). Where the complaint is not dismissed, the bishop is required to notify the complainant and the respondent in writing that the complaint has not been dismissed, to provide the complainant and the respondent with a copy of the registrar's written report, to send the respondent a copy of Form 2 in the Schedule to the Rules, and request the respondent to submit a written answer to the complaint within 21 days using the form: Clergy Discipline Rules 2005, r 17(1). The Code of Practice expressly enjoins the bishop not to engage in 'plea-bargaining' with the respondent: para 112.
[94] Clergy Discipline Measure 2003, s 12(1). Where the bishop proposes to extend the period of 28 days, then before doing so he must consult the complainant and the respondent: s 12(2). See also the Clergy Discipline Rules 2005, r 18, which permits of multiple extensions providing the consultation process is followed. It would seem that such an extension ought to be made as a matter of course in almost every case since the time allowed for the respondent to submit his written answer (which may take up to 21 days) and evidence in support (possibly a further seven days) may exhaust

the complaint.[95] The answer,[96] which must be supplied within 21 days,[97] must provide the full name, contact address, including postcode and telephone number, of the respondent; state which, if any, matters are admitted and which are contested, and be accompanied by any written evidence in support upon which the respondent wishes to rely.[98] If the respondent admits any misconduct, the form must give details of any matters relied upon by way of mitigation.[99] It must be signed and dated by the respondent and contain a declaration that the respondent believes the facts of the answer to be true.[100] The bishop must send the complainant a copy of the respondent's answer and the evidence in support.[101]

6.26 There may be occasion when in addition to a complaint under the Clergy Discipline Measure 2003, other disciplinary, criminal or matrimonial processes are contemplated or initiated. Provision is therefore made for the registrar to extend the period for the submission of his written report, or, if he does not do so, for the bishop to extend the period for determining which course to pursue, until 28 days after being notified of the final outcome of those proceedings.[102] The alternative processes to which these provisions apply are:

(a) disciplinary proceedings in respect of any alleged misconduct during the course of any employment;[103]

(b) military discipline in respect of alleged misconduct during service in the armed forces;

(c) criminal proceedings following arrest on suspicion of committing a criminal offence;

(d) proceedings for divorce or judicial separation alleging adultery, unreasonable behaviour, or desertion.[104]

---

the entire 28-day period. It would be inappropriate for the bishop to make his determination without hearing from the respondent. There is a dissonance between provisions of the Measure and the Rules, the former being silent on the submission of an answer by the respondent at this stage.

[95] Clergy Discipline Rules 2005, r 17(1)(c), (d).

[96] This should be in Form 2 in the Schedule to the Rules or in a document which is substantially to the like effect: ibid r 17(2).

[97] Ibid r 17(1)(d). The respondent may be granted by the bishop a further seven days within which to submit any evidence in support: r 17(5).

[98] Ibid r 17(2)(a)-(c). Statements in support must be made in Form 3 in the Schedule or in a document substantially to the like effect, and contain a declaration that the maker of the statement believes the facts in it are true: r 17(4). Matters of information and belief may be included provided the source is identified: r 17(3).

[99] Ibid r 17(2)(d).

[100] Ibid r 17(2)(f), (e).

[101] Ibid r 17(6).

[102] Or notification that such other proceedings will not be pursued: ibid, r 19(1).

[103] In the case, for example, of chaplains under contracts of employment with their employer institutions.

[104] Clergy Discipline Rules 2005, r 19(1)(a)–(d).

6.27 The courses of action open to the bishop at this stage are as follows:[105]

(a) he may take no further action;
(b) he may, if the respondent consents, direct that the matter remain on the file conditionally;
(c) he may direct that an attempt be made to bring about reconciliation;
(d) he may impose a penalty by consent;
(e) he may direct the complaint to be formally investigated.[106]

Each available course is discussed separately below.

No further action

6.28 If the bishop determines that there is to be no further action he reduces his determination into writing and gives a copy to the complainant and the respondent.[107] The complainant has the right to refer the complaint to the president of tribunals who, if he considers that the bishop's determination was plainly wrong, may direct the bishop to pursue such of the courses listed above at (b) to (e) as he considers appropriate and the bishop must proceed accordingly.[108]

Conditional deferment

6.29 Where the bishop, with the consent of the respondent, determines that the matter is to be recorded conditionally,[109] both the complaint and the bishop's determination are notified to the archbishop concerned and remain on a record maintained by the diocesan registrar for such period as the bishop may determine,

---

[105] He may proceed whether or not an answer has been received: ibid, r 17(7).
[106] Clergy Discipline Measure 2003, s 12(1)(a)–(e).
[107] Ibid, s 13(2). See also Clergy Discipline Rules 2005, r 20. The complainant and the respondent must be notified of the complainant's right to refer the complaint to the president: r 20(b). The reference to the president must be made by the complainant within 14 days of receiving the bishop's determination that there is to be no further action: r 21(1). The referral must be in writing in Form 5 in the Schedule or in a document which is substantially to the like effect. It must state the grounds for requesting the president to consider the bishop's determination and be accompanied by a copy of the complaint and the respondent's answer (with the written evidence in support of each), the registrar's report, and the bishop's determination: r 21(2). The president must notify the bishop and the respondent that the written referral has been received and send each of them a copy: r 21(3). No new or further evidence may be submitted: r 21(4).
[108] Clergy Discipline Measure 2003, s 13(3). The decision must be given in writing within twenty-eight days, must include reasons, and must be sent to the complainant, the respondent and the bishop: Clergy Discipline Rules 2003, r 22. The expression 'plainly wrong' is suggestive of a broad margin of discretion to be afforded to the bishop. See by analogy para 106 of the Code of Practice discussed in note 92 above.
[109] Clergy Discipline Measure 2003, s 14(1). This is the term used in the section, the consequence of which is deferral.

not exceeding five years.[110] If another complaint is made against the respondent and that complaint is dealt with by means of conciliation, penalty by consent, or formal investigation,[111] then the earlier recorded complaint may be dealt with together with the other complaint.[112] In the absence of any other such complaint within the period specified, then no further action is taken.[113] The bishop must reduce his determination to writing and give a copy to the complainant and the respondent, together with a statement explaining the effect of the sanction.[114] The complainant has no right of appeal and may not seek a review of this penalty by the president of tribunals.[115]

6.30 The bishop must send to the archbishop a copy of the written determination, the complaint, and the respondent's answer (if any), whereupon the provincial registrar notes the conditional deferment.[116] He must also send to the diocesan registrar a copy of his written determination, the complaint with evidence in support, and the respondent's answer (if any) with evidence in support, and the registrar must maintain a record of the conditional deferment for such period not exceeding five years as the bishop may determine.[117]

Conciliation

6.31 Where the bishop determines that an attempt should be made to bring about conciliation, he must afford the complainant and the respondent an opportunity to make representations and, if both agree to the appointment of a conciliator, the appointment of a conciliator shall be made by the bishop with the agreement of the complainant and the respondent.[118] A person may not be appointed conciliator unless the bishop is satisfied that there is no reason to question the impartiality of that person.[119]

---

[110] Ibid s 14(2). For specific procedural requirements concerning the conditional deferment of a complaint against a bishop or archbishop, see the Clergy Discipline Rules 2005, r 83.
[111] ie under the Clergy Discipline Measure 2003, s 12(1)(c), (d) or (e).
[112] Ibid, s 14(3).
[113] Ibid, s 14(2).
[114] Ibid, s 14(4); Clergy Discipline Rules 2005, e 25(1)(a). Detailed requirements as to the form and content of the respondent's written consent are set out in r 23; and of the bishop's written determination in r 24.
[115] See the Code of Practice, para 126.
[116] Clergy Discipline Rules 2005, r 25(1)(b). Presumably the note would be in part (a) of the archbishops' list maintained pursuant to s 38 of the Clergy Discipline Measure 2003. See para 6.69 below.
[117] Clergy Discipline Rules 2005, r 25(1)(c). The record is not open to public inspection but must be made available to diocesan bishops and registrars: r 25(2).
[118] Clergy Discipline Measure 2003, s 15(1), (2). Detailed provisions concerning the manner in which the conciliation is to be conducted and amplifying those in the Measure are set out in the Clergy Discipline Rules 2005, r 26.
[119] Clergy Discipline Measure 2003, s 15(3).

The role of the conciliator is to use his best endeavours to bring about a reconciliation between the complainant and the respondent.[120] If within three months of his appointment[121] a conciliation is brought about, the conciliator must submit a report on the case to the bishop together with such recommendation as he may wish to make.[122] If a conciliation is not brought about but the complainant and the respondent agree that another conciliator should be appointed, the bishop may appoint that other person as the conciliator.[123] If a conciliation is not brought about and the complainant and the respondent do not agree either to an extension of time or the appointment of another conciliator, then the matter must be referred back to the bishop.[124] Upon the matter being referred back to the bishop, he may take no further action, make a conditional deferment, impose a penalty by consent, or direct the matter to be formally investigated.[125]

6.32

Penalty by consent

Where the bishop considers that the imposition of a penalty by consent is appropriate, he must afford the complainant and the respondent an opportunity to make representations.[126] If the respondent consents to the imposition of a penalty by consent and he and the bishop agree as to the penalty to be imposed,[127] the bishop may proceed to impose that penalty.[128] The bishop must notify the

6.33

---

[120] Ibid s 15(4). For further guidance as to the conduct of a conciliation, see the Code of Practice, paras 127–139.
[121] Or such further period as the conciliator, with the agreement of the complainant and the respondent, may allow: Clergy Discipline Measure 2003, s 15(4)(a). There seems to be no long-stop limitation on the length of time the conciliation process may last, provided its continuance continues to have the agreement of the complainant and respondent.
[122] Ibid s 15(4)(a).
[123] Ibid s 15(4)(b).
[124] Ibid s 15(4)(c).
[125] Ibid s 15(5)(b), specifying the options available at s 12(1)(a), (b), (d) and (e). The same courses of action are available to the bishop in the event that the complainant and the respondent do not agree to the appointment of a conciliator or as to the person to be appointed: s 15(5)(a). General guidance may be found in the Code of Practice at paras 140–156.
[126] Clergy Discipline Measure 2003, s 16(1). This is the extent of the involvement of the complainant, who has no right to seek a review by the president of tribunals as to the nature of any penalty subsequently imposed by consent. There is a fourteen day time limit for this consultation: Clergy Discipline Rules 2005, r 27(3). Guidance on the general conditions relevant in a decision to impose a penalty by consent are to be found in the Code of Practice at paras 140–156.
[127] The respondent's consent must be given in writing in Form 7 in the Schedule to the Rules or in a document which is substantially to the like effect: Clergy Discipline Rules 2005, r 27(4). For a discussion of the available penalties, see paras 6.47ff below.
[128] Clergy Discipline Measure 2003, s 16(1). Where it is agreed that prohibition for life or resignation is the appropriate course, the respondent and the bishop may each withdraw their agreement within seven days, and the prohibition or resignation will not be implemented: s 16(2). Further procedural requirements are set out in the Clergy Discipline Rules 2005, r 27(5). It will be noticed that 'resignation' is not one of the types of penalty listed in the Clergy Discipline Measure 2003, s 24.

complainant of any action taken under this provision[129] and must notify the archbishop and the registrar of the diocese of any penalty agreed.[130]

6.34 If the consent of the respondent to the imposition of a penalty by consent is not obtained, or if he and the bishop are unable to reach agreement as to the nature of the penalty, then the bishop must direct that the complaint be formally investigated.[131]

Formal investigation

6.35 Where the bishop directs that the complaint is to be formally investigated, he must refer the matter to the designated officer whose duty it is to cause investigations to be made into the complaint.[132] The complainant and the respondent are under a duty to co-operate with the designated officer during the investigation, in particular by responding in writing to any questions for clarification within 14 days, or such extended period as he may allow.[133] New material information disclosed by or on behalf of the respondent or complainant must be passed by the designated officer to the other party for comment.[134]

6.36 After due inquiries have been made into the complaint[135] the designated officer refers the matter to the president of tribunals for the purpose of deciding whether there is a case to answer in respect of which a disciplinary tribunal[136] should be

---

Its closest equivalent is 'removal from office' in s 24(1)(c). Under the Clergy Discipline Rules 2005, r 27(2), resignation by consent seems to be treated as a separate penalty.

[129] Clergy Discipline Measure 2003, s 16(4). This must be done within 14 days: Clergy Discipline Rules 2005, r 27(6).

[130] Clergy Discipline Measure 2003, s 16(4). This must also be done within 14 days: Clergy Discipline Rules 2005, r 27(7).

[131] Clergy Discipline Measure 2003, s 16(3), specifying the option available at s 12(1)(e). See also the Clergy Discipline Rules 2005, r 27(8).

[132] Clergy Discipline Measure 2003, s 17(1). The bishop must supply the designated officer (as to whom see para 6.11 above) with a copy of the complaint and the respondent's answer together with all written evidence in support of each, and the registrar's report: Clergy Discipline Rules, r 28(1). The bishop must give written notice of the referral to the complainant and the respondent within fourteen days: r 28(2).

[133] Ibid r 28(3).

[134] Ibid r 28(4). Note the interpretation section of the Rules, which provides that 'party' and 'parties' refer to the complainant and the respondent, except in Parts VI, VII, and VIII (which collectively deal with proceedings before a disciplinary tribunal) where they refer to the designated officer and the respondent: r 106.

[135] This is required to be done within three months of the receipt of the primary documentation by the designated officer: ibid r 28(5). This period may be extended for such period as the president deems to be justified in the particular circumstances of the case. Any application for an extension of time must be made by the designated officer in writing to the president, but there is no requirement to consult the complainant or respondent: r 28(5).

[136] Or the Vicar-General's court in the case of a complaint against a bishop or archbishop.

requested to adjudicate.¹³⁷ The president must make his decision within 28 days of the receipt of the designated officer's report.¹³⁸ If the president decides that there is a case to answer, he declares his decision¹³⁹ and refers the matter to a disciplinary tribunal.¹⁴⁰ He must specify in the written decision which allegation or allegations of misconduct are to be determined.¹⁴¹ If the president decides that there is no case to answer, he must declare his decision and thereafter no further steps may be taken in relation thereto.¹⁴² The president must reduce his decision to writing and give¹⁴³ a copy of it to the complainant, the respondent, the bishop and the designated officer.¹⁴⁴ Where a complainant wishes to withdraw a complaint after the bishop has directed that it be formally investigated, the president, after consulting the respondent, the bishop and the designated officer, may direct that the complaint proceed and that a nominated person be substituted as complainant.¹⁴⁵

Suspension during proceedings

6.37 Where a complaint in writing has been made against a priest or deacon¹⁴⁶ holding preferment in a diocese or where such a person is arrested on suspicion of committing

---

¹³⁷ Clergy Discipline Measure 2003, s 17(2). The Code of Practice recommends that the report from the designated officer covers the following matters: the substance of the complaint; the substance of the respondent's answer to the complaint; a summary of the evidence submitted in the case; an analysis of any relevant legal issues, and any other matters which the designated officer wishes to bring to the attention of the president: para 175.
¹³⁸ Clergy Discipline Rules 2005, r 29(1). There is no specific provision for this period to be extended.
¹³⁹ Written copies of the president's decision must be sent to the complainant, the respondent, the bishop and the designated officer: ibid r 29(1).
¹⁴⁰ Clergy Discipline Measure 2003, s 17(3). The reference is to the Vicar-General's court in the case of a complaint against a bishop or archbishop.
¹⁴¹ Clergy Discipline Rules 2005, r 29(2).
¹⁴² Clergy Discipline Measure 2003, s 17(4). There is no provision for any review of the president's decision or any right of appeal. Any determination would be susceptible to judicial review in the Administrative Court, however, were it to be perverse, or *Wednesbury* unreasonable, in the sense that it was not a decision which could reasonably have been reached on the basis of the evidence which the president had before him.
¹⁴³ The Clergy Discipline Measure 2003 uses the word 'give' (s 17(5)) importing a element of personal service, whereas the Clergy Discipline Rules 2005 use the word 'send' (r 29(1), (3)) suggesting that postal service is sufficient. However impractical, the term used in the primary legislation prevails over that in the secondary legislation, since the Rules may not re-write the statute, merely 'make provision for carrying into effect the provisions of this Measure': Clergy Discipline Measure 2003, s 45.
¹⁴⁴ Ibid s 17(5).
¹⁴⁵ Clergy Discipline Rules 2005, r 59(4). There is no guidance in the Rules as to the manner in which this discretion is to be exercised, nor of the consequences of the president not making such a direction. Presumably the president would exercise his discretion under the Clergy Discipline Measure 2003, s 18(2)(a), and direct that the complaint be withdrawn, whereupon no further action is taken.
¹⁴⁶ Similar provisions exist in respect of a bishop or archbishop subject to procedural variations: ibid s 37. Note also the Clergy Discipline Rules 2005, rr 85–88.

a criminal offence,[147] the bishop of the diocese may, by notice in writing, suspend that person from exercising or performing without the leave of the bishop any right or duty of or incidental to his office.[148] However, in the case of a complaint, the power to suspend does not arise unless and until the preliminary scrutiny by the registrar has been completed and the bishop has decided not to dismiss the complaint.[149] There are detailed requirements as to the contents of the notice of suspension[150] and the persons to be notified.[151] A priest or deacon served with a notice of suspension may appeal to the president who may, within 28 days of the lodging of the appeal, either confirm or revoke the suspension.[152] There is no stay of the suspension pending the determination of the appeal.[153]

6.38 The bishop may revoke a notice of suspension at any time, by notice in writing.[154] The suspension continues in force for three months or until the disciplinary or criminal proceedings are concluded, whichever occurs first.[155] In the event that the proceedings are not concluded within three months, further suspensions may be made on the same terms.[156] During the course of any suspension, the bishop may, after consultation with the churchwardens and with the incumbent or priest in charge concerned, make such arrangements as he thinks fit for the ministrations of the church or churches concerned.[157] A respondent's right to a stipend and housing is unaffected during the currency of any suspension.[158]

---

[147] Note that Form 13a in the Schedule to the Clergy Discipline Rules 2005, or a form substantially to the like effect is to be used in this instance: r 61(2).
[148] Clergy Discipline Measure 2003, s 36(1). In the case of an arrest for a criminal offence, the power to suspend becomes immediately exercisable by the bishop. The notice must be served on the priest or deacon concerned. See also the Clergy Discipline Rules 2005, rr 60, 61, the notice of suspension being in Form 12a or Form 13a in the Schedule to the Rules.
[149] Clergy Discipline Measure 2003, s 36(1) proviso, s 12(1).
[150] Clergy Discipline Rules 2005, r 62.
[151] Ibid r 63.
[152] Clergy Discipline Measure 2003, s 36(6). See also the Clergy Discipline Rules 2005, r 66(1), (2), which require the appeal to be made in writing within 14 days of the notice of suspension, and require the written appeal to set out grounds, and for a copy also to be sent to the bishop. The bishop has 14 days from the lodging of the appeal to send or deliver to the president written comments in answer, with a copy to the appellant.
[153] Ibid r 66(5).
[154] Clergy Discipline Measure 2003, s 36(2). See also the Clergy Disciplinary Rules 2005, r 64, specifying those to whom notice of revocation must be sent.
[155] Clergy Discipline Measure 2003, s 36(3). Where a suspension expires and no further notice of suspension is given by the bishop, or where proceedings under the Measure or criminal proceedings are concluded without the imposition of any penalty of prohibition, removal from office, or revocation of licence, the bishop must notify the priest and the persons specified in the Clergy Discipline Rules 1965, r 63 that the suspension has ended: r 65.
[156] Clergy Discipline Measure 2003, s 36(3).
[157] Ibid s 36(4).
[158] Code of Practice, para 213.

Conduct of disciplinary tribunals

In disciplinary proceedings under the Clergy Discipline Measure 2003, it is the duty of the designated officer or a person duly authorized by him to conduct the case for the complainant.[159] It remains open to the president to direct that a complaint may be withdrawn[160] or that an attempt, or further attempt, be made to bring about conciliation.[161]

6.39

Once a complaint has been referred to a tribunal for adjudication, the registrar of tribunals may hold one or more preliminary hearings to identify the issues and give directions.[162] Directions may be given at a hearing, during a telephone hearing or in writing,[163] and provision is made for such maters as legal representation and written submissions.[164] The form for an application is dealt with under the Rules, as is a procedure for setting aside or varying directions made without a hearing.[165] Directions may deal with the exchange of witness statements, disclosure of documents, written questions to the other party, expert evidence, exclusion of evidence, written outline argument, preparation of bundles, and the attendance of witnesses.[166] In addition, an order may be made for two or more complaints against the same complainant to be heard together, for complaints against more than one respondent to be heard on the same occasion, or for any part of the proceedings to be dealt with separately.[167] The registrar may at any stage refer any matter of difficulty or dispute to the chairman of the tribunal constituted

6.40

---

[159] Clergy Discipline Measure 2003, s 18(1). The complainant has little, if any, input as to the manner in which proceedings are to be conducted, but can expect to be kept fully informed. The complainant is not categorized as a party for the purposes of proceedings before a disciplinary tribunal: Clergy Discipline Rules 2005, r 106.

[160] Clergy Discipline Measure 2003, s 18(2)(a), whereupon no further action may be taken in the proceedings. There is no requirement under the Measure for the complainant to be consulted if such course is contemplated, nor is there any right of appeal or review. See also the Clergy Discipline Rules 2005, r 58. The direction may be made on the president's own initiative or on application by the respondent or designated officer: r 58(1). The discretion, it is submitted, must be judicially exercised being amenable to judicial review if irrational or *Wednesbury* unreasonable. The direction must be in writing and a copy given to the complainant, the respondent, the designated officer, the bishop, the registrar of tribunals, and the diocesan registrar: r 58(2).

[161] Clergy Discipline Measure 2003, s 18(2)(b), in which case the procedure under s 15 applies, as discussed in para 6.31 above.

[162] Clergy Discipline Rules 2005, r 30(1)(a). He must give notice to the parties of such hearings. In this context, parties mean the designated officer and the respondent: see r 106.

[163] Ibid r 30(3).

[164] Ibid r 30(4)-(7).

[165] Ibid rr 31, 32. See Schedule, Forms 8, 9.

[166] Ibid r 33(1)(a)-(i). A specific procedure concerning a production appointment concerning specific documents is provided in r 34.

[167] Ibid r 33(1)(j), (k) and (l) respectively.

Chapter 6: Clergy Discipline

for the hearing of the complaint.[168] He must also give directions for the just disposal of the proceedings in accordance with the overriding objective.[169]

6.41 The Clergy Discipline Rules 2005 make provision for witness statements to be exchanged in advance of hearings before tribunals, and for the tendering of witnesses for cross-examination.[170] Provision is made for expert evidence which broadly replicates that in civil proceedings in secular courts.[171]

6.42 The date and place for the hearing of the complaint is fixed by the registrar of tribunals.[172] The tribunal must act in accordance with the overriding objective and conduct the hearing in the manner it considers most appropriate to the issues before it and to the just handling of the complaint generally.[173] This includes setting a timetable for the hearing.[174] The hearing may be adjourned from time to time if necessary.[175] The registrar or the chairman of the tribunal may proceed with a hearing notwithstanding the absence of the complainant or the respondent, provided he is satisfied that the absent person has had notice of the hearing.[176] Oral evidence must be given on oath or solemn affirmation and must be recorded.[177]

6.43 Hearings take place in private, although they must be in public if the tribunal is satisfied that it is in the interests of justice to do so, or if the respondent so requests.[178] During any part of proceedings heard in public, the tribunal has power to exclude such person or persons as it may determine.[179] The tribunal may order that the name and any other identifying details of any person involved

---

[168] Ibid r 30(2).
[169] Ibid r 30(1)(b). The overriding objective is discussed in para 6.03 above.
[170] Ibid r 35. For provisions relating to oral evidence, cross-examination and submissions on evidence, the law and on issues generally, see r 44; and for the tribunal's power to require the personal attendance of a witness or expert, see r 46.
[171] Ibid r 36.
[172] Ibid r 38. This is done in consultation with the chairman of the tribunal and with due regard to the convenience of the complainant, the respondent, the designated officer and the witnesses.
[173] Ibid r 39(a). See the discussion of the overriding objective in para 6.03 above. Note also the section in the Code of Practice dealing with the conduct of proceedings: paras 184–192.
[174] Clergy Discipline Rules 2005, r 39(b).
[175] Ibid r 41.
[176] Ibid r 42.
[177] Ibid r 45. A manuscript note will presumably suffice.
[178] Clergy Discipline Measure 2003, s 18(3)(c). See also the Clergy Discipline Rules 2005, r 40. When a hearing is held in private, the following may attend in addition to the members and staff of the tribunal: the complainant and the respondent; the legal representatives of the respondent; the designated officer, any supporting staff, and any person authorized by him to conduct the case for the complainant; the bishop; the relevant archdeacon; any other person with the tribunal's permission: r 47(a)–(f).
[179] Clergy Discipline Measure 2003, s 18(3)(c). The tribunal has power to exclude from the hearing any person who threatens to disrupt or has disrupted the hearing or has otherwise interfered with the administration of justice: Clergy Discipline Rules 2005, r 48.

Conduct of disciplinary tribunals

or referred in the proceedings shall not be published or otherwise made public if satisfied that such an order is desirable to protect the private life of any person or the interests of any child or is otherwise in the interests of the administration of justice.[180]

If after referral of the complaint, the respondent makes an admission before or at the hearing, the tribunal may make a finding of misconduct on the basis of that admission without considering any or any further evidence, and the tribunal may then proceed to impose a penalty.[181] **6.44**

In disciplinary proceedings, the standard of proof is the civil standard,[182] namely on the balance of probabilities.[183] Determinations of any matter before the tribunal are made by majority.[184] Such decisions are pronounced in public together with reasons therefor.[185] Provision is made for documents to be delivered by first class post, by leaving it at a person's address, via the document exchange, or in any other manner, including electronic means, as the president, registrar or chairman of a tribunal may direct.[186] **6.45**

Save where the Rules provide that the time for doing an act may be extended by another person, the president may extend any time limit specified under the Rules for doing an act even if the time so specified has expired, unless an extension would be inconsistent with any provision of the Clergy Discipline Measure 2003.[187] In addition there is a general power to exclude irregularities or errors of procedure.[188] Acts or omissions amounting to a contempt may be certified by the chairman of the tribunal and referred to the High Court under section 81(3) of the Ecclesiastical Jurisdiction Measure 1963.[189] Any disciplinary proceedings are automatically terminated on the death of the respondent.[190] **6.46**

---

[180] Ibid r 49(a)–(e). 'Child' means a person under 18: r 106.
[181] Ibid r 43.
[182] Clergy Discipline Measure 2003, s 18(3)(a). This is a departure from the previous system when proof beyond reasonable doubt was required.
[183] Note, however, that the civil standard is flexible and 'the more serious the complaint the stronger should be the evidence before the tribunal concludes that the complaint is established': *Re H (minors) (sexual abuse: standard of proof)* [1996] AC 563 at 586–587, [1996] 1 All ER 1 at 16–18, HL, per Lord Nichols of Birkenhead.
[184] Clergy Discipline Measure 2003, s 18(3)(b); Clergy Discipline Rules 2005, r 50(1).
[185] Clergy Discipline Measure 2003, s 18(3)(b). See also the Clergy Discipline Rules 2005, r 50(3), which requires the determination to be recorded in writing with reasons, setting out the opinion of the majority of its members together with the minority opinions if any, and signed by each member.
[186] Ibid r 101(1).
[187] Clergy Discipline Rules 2005, r 102(2).
[188] Ibid r 103.
[189] Clergy Discipline Rules 2005, r 105(1). Failure to comply with an order is not deemed to be a contempt unless the order includes a proper penal notice: r 105(2).
[190] Ibid, r 54.

Penalties

6.47 Upon a finding by a disciplinary tribunal that the respondent has committed the misconduct complained of, the tribunal may impose one or more penalties,[191] defer consideration of the penalty,[192] or impose no penalty.[193] Before imposing a penalty, the tribunal may invite the bishop of the diocese concerned[194] to express in writing his views as to the appropriate penalty, and the tribunal must have regard to these views in imposing the penalty, if any.[195] However, if the bishop has given evidence in the proceedings, he may not be consulted.[196] The chairman of the tribunal must pronounce in public the penalty or penalties imposed by the tribunal and may sit alone for this purpose.[197]

6.48 The tribunal may impose one or more of the following penalties on a respondent upon a finding that he has committed any misconduct:

(a) prohibition for life from exercising any of the functions of his Orders;
(b) limited prohibition for a specific time from exercising any such functions;
(c) removal from office;[198]
(d) revocation of licence;
(e) injunction;
(f) rebuke.[199]

---

[191] The types and nature of available penalties are discussed in paras 6.48 to 6.53 below.
[192] And adjourn the proceedings accordingly.
[193] Clergy Discipline Measure 2003, s 19(1)(a)–(c).
[194] When the respondent is a bishop, the Vicar-General's court may invite the archbishop in similar terms, and in the case of an archbishop, the invitation is to the archbishop of the other province.
[195] Clergy Discipline Measure 2003, s 19(2). This subsection requires the bishop's views, if any, to be conveyed in writing to the respondent. Under the Clergy Discipline Rules 2005, a copy of the bishop's views must be provided by the tribunal to the respondent and to the designated officer: r 51(b). The bishop is afforded 14 days to express his views: r 51(a).
[196] Clergy Discipline Measure 2003, s 19(2) proviso.
[197] Clergy Discipline Rules 2005, r 52(1). It may be on the same occasion as the pronouncement of the determination of the complaint or at a later date: r 52(2). The 'decision to impose a penalty or penalties' must be recorded in writing and a copy sent to the respondent, the designated officer, the bishop, the registrar, and the provincial registrar: r 52(3). This rule is infelicitously drafted, since it is the actual penalty imposed which ought properly to be recorded, as opposed merely to the decision to impose it.
[198] Namely from any preferment held by the respondent. A fuller definition appears in the Clergy Discipline Measure 2003, s 43, under which 'preferment' includes 'an archbishopric, a bishopric, archdeaconry, dignity or office in a cathedral or collegiate church, and a benefice, and every curacy, lectureship, readership, chaplaincy, office or place which requires the discharge of any spiritual duty'. No penalty of removal from office imposed on an archbishop, bishop or Crown appointment (other than a parochial benefice) has effect until the penalty is confirmed by Her Majesty by Order in Council: s 24(2).
[199] Ibid s 24(1)(a)–(f). A discussion of penalties may be found in the Code of Practice at paras 196–203. Note also the Guidance on Penalties published by the Clergy Discipline Commission

Upon a finding that the respondent has committed misconduct, it is open to the tribunal to impose a conditional discharge whereby the respondent is discharged subject to the condition that he commits no misconduct during such period not exceeding two years as may be specified.[200] The tribunal must first be satisfied that it is inexpedient to impose a penalty having regard to the circumstances including the nature of the misconduct and the character of the respondent.[201] Before making such an order, the tribunal must explain to the respondent in ordinary language that if he commits further misconduct during the period specified in the order, a penalty may be imposed for the original offence.[202] Where misconduct is found to have been committed during the period specified in a conditional discharge, the tribunal may deal with the original matter in any manner originally open to the tribunal.[203]

6.49

The Clergy Discipline Tribunal issued Guidance on Penalties in March 2006. The guidelines, whilst not detracting from the broad discretion given to those who bear the responsibility of imposing penalties, indicate the starting point for deliberations. They emphasize that any penalty should be in due proportion to the misconduct, having taken into account and given due weight to all material circumstances including the particular facts of the misconduct.

6.50

In relation to the range of penalties that the bishop may impose by consent at the earlier stage in the proceedings,[204] prohibition for life is the most serious and should be imposed only where there appears to be no realistic prospect of rehabilitating the respondent back into ministry because the misconduct is so grave.[205] Limited prohibition is suitable for serious cases where there is a realistic prospect that the respondent, with appropriate pastoral and other support, could in the future resume normal duties of ministry.[206] Resignation does not prevent the respondent from seeking to serve in holy orders elsewhere, but in serious cases may be combined with prohibition for life or limited prohibition.[207] An injunction might be appropriate where a respondent is generally capable of performing

6.51

---

in March 2006, to be found at www.cofe.anglican.org/about/churchlawlegis/clergydiscipline/penalties.rtf.

[200] Clergy Discipline Measure 2003, s 25(1). The provincial registrar must maintain a record of conditional discharges, which is not open to public inspection but made available to diocesan bishops and registrars: Clergy Discipline Rules 2005, r 53(1), (2). The conditional discharge must be removed from the record at the end of the period specified: r 53(3).

[201] Clergy Discipline Measure 2003, s 25(1).

[202] Ibid s 25(2).

[203] Ibid s 25(4). Upon such a penalty being imposed, the original conditional discharge ceases to have effect: s 25(3).

[204] Under the Clergy Discipline Measure 2003, s 16: see para 6.33 above.

[205] Clergy Discipline Commission Guidance on Penalties (March 2006) para 2(a).

[206] Ibid para 2(b).

[207] Ibid para 2(c).

his or her normal duties but ought to be stopped from dealing with a particular aspect of those duties.[208] The injunction must be worded with sufficient clarity so that the respondent may know what he is required to do or prohibited from doing, since a breach is an act of misconduct under the Clergy Discipline Measure 2003 and could result in further disciplinary proceedings. A rebuke is the least serious of the penalties and can be used for acts and omissions of a less serious nature.[209] Conditional deferment is most likely to be suitable where the respondent admits the misconduct, and where such misconduct is not serious and is out of character and unlikely to be repeated.

6.52 The range of penalties which a disciplinary tribunal may impose includes prohibition for life, limited prohibition, injunction and rebuke, but additionally removal from office and revocation of licence are available.[210] These latter penalties do not prevent the respondent from serving as a clerk in holy orders in another post but, in serious cases, may be combined with prohibition for life or limited prohibition.

6.53 The Guidance on Penalties indicates that stealing deserves removal from office and prohibition;[211] likewise sexual misconduct including indecent assault on children, adultery, and downloading or possessing child pornography.[212] Misconduct in ministry may permit of reconciliation.[213] Misconduct such as persistent rudeness to parishioners, lateness without good reason, or a failure to comply with formal requirements such as keeping the register book of services may all merit a rebuke, with or without an injunction to ensure that there is no repetition. Conditional deferments or discharges could also be appropriate. If the misconduct were to be repeated in defiance of an injunction, removal from office would be likely to follow.[214] Removal from office could be appropriate in serious cases of breach of confidence depending on the gravity of the circumstances and nature of the disclosures. No specific guidance is given as to misconduct in private life but alcohol-related matters receive particular mention:

> Drunkenness without any aggravating features should normally be met with a rebuke or a conditional deferment or discharge. But it may be a sign that the cleric has a

---

[208] Ibid para 2(d).
[209] Ibid para 2(e).
[210] Ibid para 3(a)–(f).
[211] Ibid para 4. Depending on the sum involved, prohibition for a period of up to four or five years could be appropriate. Where the theft is systematic or involves a breach of trust there may be little prospect of reintroducing the respondent back into ministry and prohibition for life should usually follow. Conversely, a single incident occasioning no financial loss to the church might be dealt with by way of a rebuke.
[212] Ibid para 5.
[213] Ibid para 6.
[214] Ibid.

particular problem for which help is needed; a bishop should be alert to this and take steps to provide appropriate pastoral support.[215]

Domestic violence merits removal from office and prohibition for a specific period of time or for life. Engaging without authorization in a trade, profession or other activity which adversely affects the performance of a cleric's duties of office is inconsistent with the responsibilities of ministry. An injunction to stop such conduct should normally be imposed, together with a rebuke.[216]

Proceedings in secular courts

If a priest or deacon[217] is convicted, whether in England or elsewhere, of an offence and a sentence of imprisonment is passed on him,[218] or if he has a decree of divorce[219] or an order of separation made against him following a finding of adultery, unreasonable behaviour, or desertion, he is liable without further proceedings to a penalty of removal from office or prohibition[220] or both.[221] A penalty may not be imposed more than two years after the sentence becomes conclusive[222] or the decree absolute or order of separation is made,[223] and there is a statutory procedure to be followed. Where the bishop[224] proposes to impose such a penalty he must, after consultation with the president of tribunals, inform the person concerned in writing of the proposal together with an invitation to

6.54

---

[215] Ibid, para 7. A cleric convicted of driving with excess alcohol may, depending on the circumstances, receive a penalty of removal from office and prohibition for one or two years.
[216] Ibid, para 7.
[217] Similar provisions exist in relation to a bishop or archbishop subject to procedural variations: Clergy Discipline Measure 2003, s 31.
[218] Including one which is not implemented immediately.
[219] Which has been made absolute.
[220] Whether for life or limited.
[221] Clergy Discipline Measure 2003, s 30(1)(a), (b). See also the discussion contained in the Code of Practice at paras 158–170. Note the Clergy Discipline Commission Guidance on Penalties (March 2006) which states 'where a sentence of imprisonment is imposed by a court of law in the United Kingdom a member of the clergy should normally expect to be removed from the office by the bishop and to receive an order of prohibition': para 1.
[222] For further elucidation of when a conviction is deemed to be conclusive, and a consideration of proof of such convictions, see the Clergy Discipline Measure 2003, s 40(1), (2). The bishop may not proceed until the relevant court has sent the bishop the certificate of conviction: Clergy Discipline Rules 2005, r 67.
[223] Clergy Discipline Measure 2003, s 30(3). There would appear to be no discretion to extend this period, even in the event of concealment on the part of the person concerned. However the failure to disclose a conviction or arrest is categorized as misconduct under s 8(1), ie as a failure to do an act required by the laws ecclesiastical: s 33. The same applies in the case of the duty to disclose divorce and separation orders: s 34.
[224] As to which bishop may exercise the power, this is determined by reference to the 'relevant diocese' defined as that in which the person held preferment at the time, failing which that in which he resided, failing which that in which he was ordained: ibid s 30(7).

send representations in writing to the bishop within 28 days.[225] On the expiry of that period the bishop must decide whether or not to impose the penalty and inform the person in writing of his decision.[226] If the decision is to impose the penalty, the person concerned may request the archbishop to review the decision.[227] The archbishop may uphold or reverse the decision after consideration of all the circumstances, including any representations made.[228] Before imposing a penalty, the bishop, if it is practical to do so, must require the diocesan registrar to give not less than 14 days' notice in writing of the time and place at which the penalty will be imposed.[229] A penalty imposed under this provision has the same consequences as one imposed following a finding of misconduct in a disciplinary tribunal.[230]

Nullification, removal of prohibition and pardon

6.55 Where a priest or deacon is prohibited for life or deposed, he may make an application to the archbishop for the prohibition or deposition[231] to be nullified on the grounds that new evidence has come to light affecting the facts upon which the penalty was based; or the proper legal procedure was not followed.[232] If the archbishop considers that the prohibition or deposition was not justified[233]

---

[225] Ibid, s 30(2); Clergy Discipline Rules 2005, r 68.

[226] Clergy Discipline Measure 2003, s 30(2); Clergy Discipline Rules 2005, r 69.

[227] Clergy Discipline Measure 2003, s 30(2); Clergy Discipline Rules 2005, r 70. The application must be sent or delivered in writing to the archbishop or the relevant province within 21 days and contain details of the facts and matters which the priest or deacon wishes the archbishop to consider in conducting the review. The archbishop must arrange for a copy to be sent to the bishop. The bishop has 21 days from receipt to send or deliver to the archbishop written comments in response to the application for review, together with copies of any documents taken into account by the archbishop. Copies of this material must also be sent to the priest or deacon concerned: r 71.

[228] Clergy Discipline Measure 2003, s 30(2). He may conduct the review with or without a hearing: Clergy Discipline Rules 2005, r 72(1). Where there is no hearing, the written decision must be sent or delivered within three months, and when there is a hearing, within 28 days of its conclusion: r 72(2).

[229] Clergy Discipline Measure 2003, s 30(4). If the priest or deacon appears at the time and place he is entitled to be present when the penalty is imposed. When the penalty is imposed, the bishop must be attended by his diocesan registrar: s 30(5). The penalty must be reduced to writing and a copy sent to the archbishop and the diocesan registrar: s 30(5).

[230] Ibid s 32.

[231] Deposition was previously irreversible, so this new power may be significant in relation to cases of some antiquity. For a discussion of the irreversibility of deposition and its paradoxical relationship with the indelibility of orders, see para 6.80 below.

[232] Clergy Discipline Measure 2003, s 26(1)(a), (b). The application must be in writing, set out the reasons upon which it is made, and be accompanied by any evidence upon which the applicant seeks to rely: Clergy Discipline Rules 2005, r 97(1)(a)–(c).

[233] The archbishop may invite any person involved in the proceedings leading to the prohibition or deposition to make written representations within twenty-one days of being invited to do so

he may, after consultation with the Dean of Arches, declare that it be nullified whereupon it will be treated for all purposes in law as never having been imposed.[234]

6.56 Where a priest or deacon[235] is prohibited from exercising functions for a specific time then he 'acting jointly with the bishop of the diocese concerned' may make an application to the Dean of Arches sitting with the two Vicars-General for the removal of the prohibition.[236] Once the prohibition is removed, the priest or deacon becomes eligible for any preferment.[237]

6.57 Where an archbishop, bishop, priest or deacon is prohibited from exercising functions or removed from office, his incapacities cease if he receives a free pardon from the Crown.[238]

Appeals

6.58 An appeal lies to the Court of Arches[239] on the part of the respondent on any penalty imposed; on the part of the respondent on a question of law or fact, and on the part of the designated officer on a question of law, against any finding of the tribunal.[240]

---

and a copy is to be sent to the applicant: ibid r 97(2). The archbishop has a discretion whether or not to have a hearing and, after consideration with the Dean of Arches, must declare in writing whether the prohibition for life or deposition was justified. The declaration must be made within three months of receiving the application or within twenty eight days of the hearing if one is held: r 97(3), (4).

[234] Clergy Discipline Measure 2003, s 26(2). Similar provisions exist in relation to bishops and archbishops subject to procedural variations: s 26(3).

[235] The same applies in relation to bishops and archbishops subject to minor variations: ibid s 27.

[236] Ibid s 27. The section states, 'on receiving such an application they may make an order removing the prohibition'. This is a discretionary power, but the section is silent as to the manner in which the discretion is to be exercised. Since it is a joint application, the Dean and Vicars-General would have to have serious misgivings to refuse the order sought. As to the form and content of the application and time limits for its determination, see the Clergy Discipline Rules 2005, r 98, which broadly replicates the provisions for removal of prohibition for life and deposition, summarized at nn 232, 233 above.

[237] Clergy Discipline Measure 2003, s 27.

[238] Ibid, s 28. The individual will be restored to any preferment he previously held if it has not been filled in the meantime.

[239] Or the Chancery Court of York in the case of the northern province. See also the Clergy Discipline Appeal Rules 2005, r 4.

[240] Clergy Discipline Measure 2003, s 20(1). Appeals from the Vicar-General's court also lie to the Court of Arches or Chancery Court of York as appropriate: s 20(1). For the purposes of any appeal, the court comprises the Dean of Arches and Auditor together with two persons in holy orders and two lay persons appointed by the president from the provincial panel: s 20(2), incorporating by reference the Ecclesiastical Jurisdiction Measure 1963, s 3(2)(a)-(c) (as amended by the Clergy Discipline Measure 2003, Sch 1 para 3).

6.59 Detailed provisions for the conduct of appeals are set out in the Clergy Discipline Appeal Rules 2005,[241] which have an overriding objective, namely, 'to enable appeals in disciplinary proceedings under the Measure to be dealt with justly, in a way that is both fair to all relevant interested persons and proportionate to the nature and seriousness of the issues raised'.[242] So far as reasonably practicable, the rules are to be applied in accordance with the principle that undue delay and undue expense are to be avoided.[243] The parties are obliged to co-operate with any person or court exercising any function in connection with an appeal,[244] and any failure by an appellant to co-operate may result in that party's appeal being struck out.[245]

6.60 A written notice of appeal by a respondent must be sent or delivered to the provincial registrar in Form A1 in the Schedule to the Appeal Rules or a document substantially to the like effect.[246] It must state the full name, contact address including postcode, and telephone number of the respondent, and the like information for his solicitor if legally represented.[247] It must identify the tribunal which heard the complaint, and state the reference number and the date of the pronouncement of the decision in public.[248] It must also identify whether the appeal is against findings of fact or law or both, and penalty, or penalty alone.[249] It must set out briefly any findings of the tribunal on matters of law or fact against which the respondent wishes to appeal, and in respect of those findings set out briefly the reasons for appealing.[250] The notice must be signed and dated by the respondent or his representative.[251] Similar provisions apply to a written notice of appeal by the designated officer.[252] To any notice of appeal must be attached a copy of the tribunal's decision and, if a penalty was imposed, of the written decision imposing the penalty.[253]

6.61 The notice of appeal must be received by the provincial registrar within 28 days of the date of the pronouncement in public of the tribunal's decision, or of any

---

[241] Clergy Discipline Appeal Rules 2005, SI 2005/3201.
[242] Ibid r 1.
[243] Ibid r 1.
[244] Ibid r 2(1).
[245] Ibid r 2(2).
[246] Ibid r 5(1).
[247] Ibid r 5(2)(a), (b).
[248] Ibid r 5(2)(c).
[249] Ibid r 5(2)(d).
[250] Ibid r 5(2)(e). If the respondent is appealing against a penalty, the notice must state what the penalty is, and set out the reasons for appealing: r 5(2)(f).
[251] Ibid r 5(2)(g).
[252] Ibid r 6. The notice must be in Form A2 in the Schedule, and may only relate to matters of law, not to facts or penalty. Note that the heading to this rule misleadingly speaks of an appeal 'from' the designated officer, although the text correctly states 'by'.
[253] Ibid r 7.

penalty imposed by the tribunal, whichever is the later to occur.[254] The respondent or the designated officer may apply for permission to appeal out of time,[255] and any such application must set out the reasons why the appeal was not made within time and contain a declaration that the party making the application believes the facts of the application to be true.[256] It must be accompanied by a completed draft notice of appeal.[257] The application is determined by the Dean without a hearing,[258] who may give permission to appeal out of time if satisfied that there was good reason why the party making the application did not appeal within the time allowed, that there would be a good arguable case on appeal, and the other party would not suffer significant prejudice as a result of the delay.[259]

6.62 Pending the disposal of an appeal the implementation of any sentence is postponed,[260] during which time a respondent may also be suspended.[261] No further steps may be taken to record a penalty in the archbishops' list until proceedings on an appeal have been disposed of.[262] Provision is made for interim directions to be issued by the registrar for the just disposal of the proceedings in accordance with the overriding objective.[263] The Dean or the appellate court may on application or on their own initiative strike out an appeal if satisfied that the appeal is not being pursued with due expedition.[264] The matter may proceed notwithstanding the absence of a party if the registrar, Dean or the appellate court is satisfied that the absent party has had notice of the hearing.[265] No witness who gave evidence before the tribunal may be called to give oral evidence to the appellate court without permission from the registrar, the Dean or the appellate court,[266]

---

[254] Ibid r 8(1). At the same time, a copy must be sent or delivered by the appellant to the designated officer or the respondent as the case may be: r 8(2).
[255] Using form A3 in the Schedule to the Clergy Discipline Appeal Rules 2005.
[256] Ibid r 9(2). The application must be signed and dated.
[257] Ibid r 9(3), together with a copy of the tribunal's decision and the written decision imposing the penalty, if there was one. The person applying must send the application and documents to the registrar, with copies to the designated officer or respondent as the case may be: r 9(4).
[258] Ibid r 9(5). Before determining the application the Dean must give the other party 14 days within which to make written representations in response to the application, such representations to be copied to the other party: r 9(6).
[259] Ibid r 9(7)(a)–(c). The determination must be put in writing and sent or delivered to the parties within 21 days of the expiry of the time allowed for written representations to the putative respondent to the appeal: r 9(8). The draft notice will then be treated as the notice of appeal: r 9(9).
[260] Ibid r 10(1).
[261] Ibid r 10(2) referring to the powers of suspension in the Clergy Discipline Measure 2003, ss 36, 37.
[262] Clergy Discipline Appeal Rules 2005, r 10(3).
[263] Ibid rr 11, 12. This may be by way of a hearing, a telephone hearing or in writing. As to the overriding objective, see para 6.57 above.
[264] Ibid r 13.
[265] Ibid r 14.
[266] Ibid r 16.

and no new evidence may be adduced without the permission of the Dean or the appellate court.[267]

6.63 The Dean or the appellate court may allow the appeal to be withdrawn or the notice of appeal to be amended at any time before or at the hearing on such terms as may be just, which may include adjourning or postponing the hearing.[268] The hearing of the appeal must be in public, but at any stage the appellate court may sit in private and may exclude any person or persons if satisfied that to do so is desirable to protect the private life of any person, or the interests of a child, or is otherwise in the interests of the administration of justice.[269] On the same grounds, the appellate court may order that the name and other identifying details of any person involved or referred to in the proceedings must not be published or otherwise made public.[270]

6.64 On any appeal the appellate court may confirm, reverse or vary any finding of the tribunal; refer a particular issue back to the tribunal for hearing and determination in accordance with the appellate court's direction; order the complaint to be reheard by the same or a differently constituted tribunal; confirm or set aside a penalty; or substitute a greater or lesser penalty.[271] When the appropriateness of a penalty is under consideration, the court may invite the bishop of the diocese concerned to express in writing his views as to the appropriate penalty and the appellate court must have regard to any such views.[272] An appeal will continue despite the death of the complainant.[273] The Dean may give permission for an appeal to be heard following the death of a respondent, if satisfied that a point of law of general importance is in issue, or it is in the interests of justice.[274]

6.65 The determination of the appeal is according to the majority of the members of the appellate court and must be recorded in writing.[275] The Dean must pronounce

---

[267] Ibid r 17. Detailed requirements for an application for new evidence to be admitted are contained in r 18.
[268] Ibid r 19. The power vests in the Dean prior to the hearing, and in the appellate court thereafter.
[269] Ibid r 25. Note also the power to exclude persons who threaten to disrupt the proceedings: r 24.
[270] Ibid r 26(a)–(c).
[271] Ibid r 27(a)–(d). It may also impose one or more of the penalties under the Clergy Discipline Measure 2003, s 24, where the tribunal has not imposed any penalty or when upholding an appeal on a question of law by the designated officer: Clergy Discipline Appeal Rules 2005, r 27(e).
[272] Ibid r 28. In the case of an appeal from the decision of the Vicar-General's court, the view sought will be that of the archbishop, in the case of a bishop, or of the archbishop of the other province, in the case of an archbishop.
[273] Ibid r 36.
[274] Ibid r 37. In this case the Dean appoints a representative to stand in the place of the deceased respondent for the purpose of the appeal.
[275] Ibid r 29. The appellate court may omit from the written determination the name and any other identifying details of any person if satisfied that such an order is desirable to protect the private life of that person, or the interests of any child; or is otherwise in the interests of the administration of justice: r 31.

in public the determination of the appeal either at the end of the hearing or at a later date;[276] and any penalty imposed by the appellate court must be pronounced in public by the Dean who may sit alone for this purpose.[277]

Where the penalty of removal from office or revocation or a licence is subsequently revoked on appeal, the person concerned is entitled to compensation.[278] **6.66**

Costs and legal aid

The costs of the Clergy Discipline Commission and the related institutions under the Clergy Discipline Measure 2003 are borne by the Central Board of Finance of the Church of England, as are the costs of the designated officer. Ecclesiastical legal aid may be available for a respondent.[279] It is administered by the Legal Aid Commission. Before deciding whether to grant any legal aid and, if so, to what extent, the Commission considers all the circumstances of the matter, including any other financial resources available to the respondent.[280] **6.67**

Where a respondent's conduct in the course of appeal proceedings has been unreasonable, the provincial registrar, the Dean, or the appellate court may make at any stage an order for the payment of costs by the respondent to the Central Board of Finance of the Church of England.[281] **6.68**

The Archbishops' List

The archbishops, acting jointly, are required to maintain a list[282] of all clerks in Holy Orders: **6.69**

(a) upon whom a penalty or censure (by consent or otherwise) has been imposed under the Clergy Discipline Measure 2003 or the Ecclesiastical Jurisdiction Measure 1963;

---

276 Ibid r 30.
277 Ibid r 28(4).
278 Clergy Discipline Measure 2003, s 41, incorporating by reference the Pastoral Measure 1983, s 25 and Sch 4. The person concerned is treated as if he were the incumbent of a benefice deemed to be vacated.
279 Church of England (Legal Aid) Measure 1994; Church of England (Legal Aid) Rules 1995, SI 1995/2034.
280 Clergy who are members of a trade union may be eligible for legal advice and representation.
281 Clergy Discipline Appeal Rules 2005, r 34(1). Such order may be in respect of costs paid, or authorized by the Legal Aid Commission to be paid, out of the Legal Aid Fund in respect of the respondent's legal costs incurred in the appeal proceedings, and costs incurred by the Central Board of Finance arising out of or in connection with the appeal proceedings: r 34(2).
282 The list is in the custody of the Archbishop of Canterbury with a copy in the custody of the Archbishop of York: Clergy Discipline Rules 2005, r 74(1), (2). It is not open to public inspection but must be made available to the president, diocesan bishops of the Church of England and registrars: r 74(3).

(b) who have been deposed from orders under the 1963 Measure;
(c) who have executed a deed of relinquishment under the Clerical Disabilities Act 1870;
(d) who have resigned preferment following the making of a complaint in writing under the 2003 Measure, or under the 1963 Measure; or
(e) who, in the opinion of the archbishops, have acted in a manner (not amounting to misconduct) which might affect their suitability for holding preferment.[283]

6.70 When one of the archbishops, with the agreement of the other, has included a person in the list under (a) to (d) above, he must take all reasonable steps to inform that person in writing that he has done so and of the particulars recorded in respect of that person.[284] That person may request the president to review the matter,[285] and upon such review, the president may direct that person's continuance on the list or removal therefrom.[286] In the event of continuance, he may also direct that the particulars related to that person be altered in such manner as may be specified.[287]

6.71 Where the archbishop proposes to include a person under (e) above, he must first inform that person in writing of the proposal and the particulars to be recorded together with an invitation to send comments or representations in writing to the archbishop within a period of 21 days.[288] On the expiry of this period, the archbishop must decide whether or not to do so, and inform that person of his decision.[289] If the decision is one of inclusion, the person concerned may request the president to review the decision.[290]

6.72 The archbishop must review the inclusion of a person in the list five years after the inclusion, and also if so requested to do so by the person concerned or the bishop.[291]

---

[283] Clergy Discipline Measure 2003, s 38(1)(a)–(e).
[284] Ibid s 38(2). This must be done within 21 days: Clergy Discipline Rules 2005, r 75(1).
[285] The request must be sent within 21 days with a copy sent to the archbishop: ibid r 75(2). The archbishop then has 21 days to make written representations to the president with a copy to the person requesting the review: r 75(3).
[286] Clergy Discipline Measure 2003, s 38(2). The direction must be made within 42 days of receipt of the request for review: Clergy Discipline Rules 2005, r 75(4). A copy of it must be sent to the person making the request and the archbishop: r 75(5).
[287] Clergy Discipline Measure 2003, s 38(2).
[288] Ibid s 38(3). See also the Clergy Discipline Rules 2005, r 76(1).
[289] The consent of the other archbishop is required: ibid r 76(2).
[290] Clergy Discipline Measure 2003, s 38(3). The person concerned has twenty-one days within which to request the review and must do so in writing giving reasons: Clergy Discipline Rules 2005, r 76(4). The president must send a copy to the archbishop, who has 21 days to make written representations to the president: r 76(5). The president's decision must be made in writing within 42 days of receipt of the request (r 76(6)) and sent to the person requesting the review and the archbishop (r 76(7)).
[291] Clergy Discipline Measure 2003, s 38(4). The person concerned may not make a request within five years of the inclusion, or within five years of any previous review: s 38(4) proviso. No such

Offences involving doctrine, ritual or ceremonial

The terms of reference for the review of clergy discipline which led ultimately to the enactment of the Clergy Discipline Measure 2003 limited its scope to conduct cases and expressly left out of account the separate procedure for dealing with matters of doctrine, ritual and ceremonial.[292] This was the subject of a separate process of review, which recommended a change to a procedure modelled on what is now the Clergy Discipline Measure 2003, adapted to take account of the doctrinal nature of the allegations. However, these recommendations did not find favour with General Synod and proceeded no further than a draft measure.[293] Accordingly, the provisions of the Ecclesiastical Jurisdiction Measure 1963 continue to apply in such cases. There may well be instances where an allegation could be both misconduct under the Clergy Discipline Measure 2003, as well as a matter of doctrine, ritual or ceremonial under the Ecclesiastical Jurisdiction Measure 1963.[294] This jurisdictional question will need to be determined as a preliminary issue.[295]

6.73

Investigation

The procedure for hearing cases involving matters of doctrine, ritual or ceremonial varies depending upon whether the accused[296] is a deacon, priest, bishop or archbishop. Where the accused is a deacon or priest, the bishop must consider any complaint, and decide either to take no action or to refer the complaint for inquiry.[297] Where the complaint is made against a bishop, the archbishop has the same powers and duties as a bishop has in relation to a priest or deacon,[298]

6.74

---

restriction attaches to a request from the bishop of a diocese. Different provisions apply depending on the category of the list in which the person is included and the reason for the review: Clergy Discipline Rules 2005, rr 77–80.

[292] *Under Authority*, the Report of the General Synod Working Party Reviewing Clergy Discipline and the Working of the Ecclesiastical Courts (GS 1217, 1996).

[293] A draft Clergy Discipline (Doctrine) Measure was rejected by the General Synod when the matter was debated in July 2004, and there is no immediate prospect of this matter being revisited.

[294] See para 6.15 above. See also R Bursell, 'Turbulent Priests: Clerical Misconduct Under the Clergy Discipline Measure' (2007) 9 Ecc LJ 250.

[295] For a discussion of how cases of coterminous jurisdiction might be resolved, see R Bursell, 'Turbulent Priests' (above).

[296] The Ecclesiastical Jurisdiction Measure 1963 adopts the terminology of the criminal courts, as opposed to that of the employment tribunal, adopted in the Clergy Discipline Measure 2003, hence 'accused' rather than 'respondent'.

[297] Ecclesiastical Jurisdiction Measure 1963, s 39(1). This section expressly makes provision for the bishop to see the accused and the complainant either separately or together in private.

[298] Ibid s 40.

and where it is made against an archbishop, there is no informal process and the matter is automatically referred for inquiry.[299]

6.75 The inquiry takes the form of a committee which decides, by majority, whether there is a case to answer. For a deacon or priest, the committee comprises a member of the Upper House of Convocation, two members of the Lower House and two chancellors, and, for a bishop or archbishop, an even number of persons appointed by the Upper House of Convocation and the Dean of the Arches or his deputy. The committee may decide there is no case to answer, or it may decide that there is, in which case it must specify the offence for trial by the Court of Ecclesiastical Causes Reserved.[300] The Upper House of Convocation then appoints a person to promote the complaint.[301] There is a third and somewhat anomalous course which the committee may take. It may decide there is a case to answer but nonetheless dismiss the complaint on one of three grounds, namely:

(a) that the complaint is too trivial to warrant further proceedings;
(b) that the offence was committed under extenuating circumstances; or
(c) that further proceedings would not be in the interests of the Church of England.[302]

Hearing and appeals

6.76 The Court of Ecclesiastical Causes Reserved is made up of five judges and three diocesan or former diocesan bishops.[303] In addition, when trying an accused, the court must sit with between three and five advisers who are eminent theologians or liturgiologists.[304] The court is not bound by previous decisions of the Privy Council in matters of doctrine, ritual or ceremonial.[305] If the accused is found guilty, the court decides what censure is warranted.[306] However, unless the accused has previously been admonished for an offence of the same or a substantially similar nature, the most severe censure which may be imposed is one of monition.[307] In all doctrine cases, regardless of the status of the accused, an appeal lies from the Court of Ecclesiastical Causes Reserved to a Commission of Review

---

[299] Ibid s 41.
[300] On procedure generally, see ibid s 42.
[301] Ibid s 43.
[302] Ibid s 42(7). The reason for so doing should be stated.
[303] Ibid, s 5. The judges, appointed by the Queen, must all be communicants and at least two of them must hold or have held high judicial office: ibid s 5.
[304] Ibid s 45(2). The advisers are selected by the Dean of the Arches from a panel maintained by the Upper Houses of the Convocations of Canterbury and York with the approval of the Lower Houses: ibid s 45(2).
[305] Ecclesiastical Jurisdiction Measure, s 45(3).
[306] Ibid s 45(1)(g).
[307] Ibid s 49(3).

constituted as aforesaid.³⁰⁸ This comprises five persons appointed by the Queen, of whom three are Lords of Appeal and two Lords Spiritual.³⁰⁹ There is no longer any further appeal to the Privy Council.

Censures

Whether the accused is a bishop, priest or deacon, any of the following censures may be imposed for offences involving doctrine, ritual or ceremonial heard under the Ecclesiastical Jurisdiction Measure 1963.³¹⁰ **6.77**

(a) deprivation, being the removal of a person from any preferment which he holds and disqualification from holding any future preferment;³¹¹
(b) inhibition, being disqualification from exercising the functions of his order for a specified time;
(c) suspension, being disqualification for a specified time from exercising or performing (without the leave of the bishop) any right or duty of or incidental to his preferment or from residing in the residence of his preferment;
(d) monition, being an order to do or refrain from doing a specified act; and,
(e) rebuke, which is a public reprimand.

Following a period of suspension or inhibition, the person may not be readmitted to his benefice or permitted to exercise the functions of his order until he satisfies the bishop of his good conduct during the term of his suspension or inhibition.³¹² Only one censure may be imposed for any one offence, save that where suspension is pronounced, inhibition may also be pronounced for the same period.³¹³ The Queen is required to confirm any censure of deprivation on a bishop or archbishop.³¹⁴ A person who is subject to a sentence of deprivation may be appointed by a bishop to a preferment providing both the archbishop of the province and (if he is a deacon or priest) the bishop of the diocese in which the proceedings were instituted give their consent.³¹⁵ **6.78**

---

308 Ibid s 11(2)(a).
309 Ibid s 11(4).
310 They are listed ibid s 49(1)(a)–(e), and, prior to the passing of the Clergy Discipline Measure 2003, the identical penalties applied in conduct cases. Note the restriction or penalty set out in para 6.76 above.
311 The sentence of deprivation ought not to be imposed in order to part an incumbent from his benefice, however desirable or pastoral such a course may be. The paramount consideration in selecting the appropriate sentence should be the gravity of the offence or the totality of the offences: *Bland v Archdeacon of Cheltenham* [1972] Fam 157 at 171, [1972] 1 All ER 1012 at 1021, Ct of Arches.
312 Ecclesiastical Jurisdiction Measure 1963, s 49(2). If the person suspended or inhibited is himself a bishop, then it is the Upper House of Convocation which must be satisfied as to his good conduct.
313 Ibid s 49(6).
314 Ibid s 49(4). This is done by Order in Council.
315 Ibid s 49(5). The archbishop may direct the deprivation to cease upon such appointment.

6.79 Where a censure of deprivation is pronounced on any priest or deacon, the bishop may depose him from holy orders,[316] an action known colloquially as 'unfrocking'. Before so doing, he must serve on the person concerned and on the provincial registrar a written notice of his intention so to do, whereupon the person concerned has one month within which to appeal to the archbishop, and he may not be deposed unless and until the appeal is determined and dismissed.[317] Where a censure of deprivation is pronounced on an archbishop or bishop, the Upper House of Convocation may, by resolution, depose him from holy orders.[318] Any person who performs any function which he is disqualified from performing pursuant to any censure commits an offence under the Ecclesiastical Jurisdiction Measure 1963.[319]

6.80 The question of the reversibility or otherwise of deposition has been the subject of ecclesiastical judicial process in the Church in Wales.[320] Though not forming part of the judgment, it was conceded in argument that deposition is reversible under the Constitution of the Church in Wales.[321] The position in England is regarded as being otherwise, deposition being irreversible.[322] A free pardon granted by the Crown affects both ecclesiastical censures and criminal penalties in the secular courts. A person granted such a pardon must be restored to any preferment he previously held if it has not been filled in the meantime.[323]

---

[316] Ibid s 50. The sentence of deposition must be recorded in the diocesan registry.

[317] Ibid s 50 proviso. If the diocesan be the archbishop, the appeal is to the archbishop of the other province.

[318] Ibid s 51. The person concerned must be given the opportunity to make written and oral representations before any motion for such a resolution is put: s 51 proviso.

[319] Ibid s 54.

[320] *Williams v Bishop of Bangor* (1999) 5 Ecc LJ 304, Prov Synod of Ch in Wales. The appeal was heard in chambers but the judgment was made public.

[321] Cf N Doe, *Canon Law in the Anglican Communion—A Worldwide Perspective* (Oxford: Oxford University Press, 1998) 91–92, where it is stated that only the laws of Australia, New Zealand, England, the West Indies and ECUSA would seem to suggest the reversibility of deposition.

[322] The theological and ecclesiological issues raised in the seeming paradox of irreversibility of deposition and indelibility of orders held in tension by a Church which preaches forgiveness is beyond the scope of this work. In relation to matters of misconduct justiciable under the Clergy Discipline Measure 2003, this anomaly in penalty does not apply. See para 6.55 above.

[323] Ecclesiastical Jurisdiction Measure 1963, s 53. In *R v Secretary of State for the Home Department, ex parte Bentley* [1994] QB 349, [1993] 4 All ER 442, DC, the concept of the conditional pardon was acknowledged for the first time in English law. It may thus be possible for a cleric to be pardoned because of the disproportionate severity of the censure instead of merely, as the traditional understanding had hitherto been, on the basis of his innocence. This jurisprudence appears to have influenced the nature of penalties under the Clergy Discipline Measure 2003. See paras 6.47ff above.

7

FACULTY JURISDICTION

Introduction	7.01	Hearing	7.63
Minor works	7.03	Evidence	7.64
Overriding duty	7.04	Grant of planning permission	7.66
The ecclesiastical exemption	7.05	Service of documents	7.67
Care of places of worship	7.08	Burden and standard of proof	7.68
The role of the archdeacon	7.09	Judgments and orders	7.73
Temporary reordering	7.13	Contempt of court	7.76
Matters of urgency	7.14	Appeals	7.77
Visitations	7.15	**Costs**	7.79
Diocesan advisory committees	7.16	**Emergency and remedial powers**	7.83
National amenity societies	7.18	**Particular cases**	7.90
Formulating proposals	7.19	Altars	7.91
Seeking advice	7.22	Churchyards	7.92
Preliminary advice	7.22	Demolition	7.97
Listed churches	7.23	Disability Discrimination Act 1995	7.102
Formal advice	7.25	Disposal of church property	7.103
DAC certificate	7.32	Exhumation	7.104
The petition	7.34	Fonts	7.112
Public notice	7.37	Graves	7.113
Archdeacon's jurisdiction	7.43	Right of burial	7.113
Chancellor's jurisdiction	7.47	Reservation of gravespace	7.114
Special notice	7.47	Erection of headstone	7.115
Consultation with the Council		Inscriptions	7.116
for the Care of Churches	7.51	Libraries	7.117
Objections	7.53	Licences and leases	7.118
Unopposed petitions	7.56	Memorials	7.121
Contested proceedings	7.57	Movables and ornaments	7.123
Answer to particulars of objection	7.57	Pews	7.125
Disposal by written representations	7.58	Reordering	7.126
Directions	7.60	Trees	7.128
		Care of places of worship	7.130

Introduction

7.01 A faculty is a permissive right to effect some alteration to a church building or its contents. It is the duty of the minister and the churchwardens to obtain a faculty before executing any alterations, additions, removals or repairs to the fabric, ornaments or furniture of the church.[1] Carrying out works in the absence of an appropriate faculty is illegal, even though the works may later be rendered legitimate by a confirmatory faculty.[2] The faculty jurisdiction is exercised in the consistory court by the chancellor of the diocese or, for certain specified matters, by the archdeacon.

7.02 The faculty jurisdiction extends to all consecrated churches and churchyards.[3] Consecration is not coterminous with dedication, even though both expressions import the hallowing of land for godly purposes. Dedication is, in law, merely a declaration of intent as to the purpose for which land is to be put. Consecration, however, is the setting aside of land solely for sacred use in perpetuity.[4] The outward sign of such setting aside is generally a religious ceremony performed by the bishop, but, as a matter of law, the land becomes consecrated by the bishop signing the sentence of consecration, which is then lodged in the diocesan registry. Once consecrated, the land and everything on it comes within the jurisdiction of the Ordinary, exercised by the chancellor in the consistory court. Those parts of municipal cemeteries which are consecrated are subject to the faculty

---

[1] Canon F 13 para 3.

[2] Note that a person who commissions the carrying out of works without the authority of a faculty is unable to seek an indemnity for his costs from the PCC if he is sued by a supplier or workman: *Re St Agnes, Toxteth Park* [1985] 1 WLR 641 at 643F–G, Liverpool Cons Ct. For a consideration of a petition for a confirmatory faculty for unauthorized works, see *Re St Mary and All Saints, Trentham* (2004) 8 Ecc LJ 115, Lichfield Cons Ct.

[3] Note the position with regard to peculiars and to chapels within institutions, discussed below, and the separate system of regulation for cathedrals discussed in Chapter 8. A peculiar which is also a parish church is subject to the faculty jurisdiction: Care of Churches and Ecclesiastical Jurisdiction Measure 1991, s 11(1).

[4] Such land may only be freed for secular purposes by Act of Parliament or Measure, by a direction given under the Pastoral Measure 1983, or by a faculty. Such faculties are granted only in exceptional cases. See, for example, *Re St John, Chelsea* [1962] 1 WLR 706 at 714, [1962] 2 All ER 850 at 857, London Cons Ct, and *Re St Mary the Virgin, Woodkirk* [1969] 1 WLR 1867 at 1873H, *sub nom Morley Borough Council v St Mary the Virgin, Woodkirk (Vicar and Churchwardens)* [1969] 3 All ER 952 at 957, Ch Ct of York; see also *Re Tonbridge School Chapel* [1993] 1 WLR 1138, [1993] 2 All ER 350, Rochester Cons Ct. As to the power of the bishop to remove the legal effects of consecration, see the Care of Churches and Ecclesiastical Jurisdiction Measure 1991, s 22. It is anticipated that the new provisions in s 56 of the Pastoral Measure 1983 (as amended), which permit the creation of a lease over consecrated land, will increase the number of instances of secular uses of churches, concurrently with sacred use. See *Building Faith in Our Future*, a statement on behalf of the Church of England by the Church Heritage Forum (Church House Publishing, London, 2004).

Introduction

jurisdiction, but the jurisdiction will be exercised sparingly.[5] Everything in or on the land is included within the jurisdiction, as are the fabric, ornaments and furniture of the church. The ecclesiastical jurisdiction also extends to unconsecrated land surrounding, or adjacent or ancillary to, a church,[6] and to certain buildings[7] which, though unconsecrated, are licensed by the bishop for public worship.[8]

Minor works

The chancellor must given written guidance to all PCCs, ministers and churchwardens as to those matters within the jurisdiction of the consistory court which he for the time being considers, after consultation with the DAC, to be of such a minor nature that they may be undertaken without a faculty.[9] The PCC, minister and churchwardens may seek informal advice from the archdeacon, the DAC or the registrar as to whether any proposed works are covered by the minor works provisions. Caution should always be exercised, since a person carrying out works without a faculty may be liable to a civil action for trespass to land or goods and a criminal prosecution under the Criminal Damage Act 1971.[10] Equally a PCC would be in breach of trust if it dissipated its funds on the cost of works not

7.03

---

[5] For example, the power to make a restoration order under section 13(5) of the Care of Churches and Ecclesiastical Jurisdiction Measure 1991 following unlawful acts in relation to a 'church or churchyard' does not extend to the consecrated parts of local authority cemeteries. See *Re Welford Road Cemetery, Leicester* [2007] 2 WLR 506, [2007] 1 All ER 426, Ct of Arches, paras 56–58, rejecting the contrary view which had earlier been expressed by Gray Ch in *Re West Norwood Cemetery* [1994] Fam 210, [1995] 1 All ER 387, Southwark Cons Ct.

[6] Faculty Jurisdiction Measure 1964, s 7(1).

[7] For a discussion of what constitutes a curtilage for the purposes of s 7, see *Re St John, Bishop's Hatfield* [1967] P 113, [1966] 2 All ER 403, St Albans Cons Ct. See also *Re St George, Oakdale* [1976] Fam 210 at 214, [1975] 2 All ER 870 at 878, Salisbury Cons Ct; and *Re St Mary Magdalene, Paddington* [1980] Fam 99, [1980] 1 All ER 279, London Cons Ct.

[8] Care of Churches and Ecclesiastical Jurisdiction Measure 1991, s 11(2). Where the bishop, after consultation with the DAC, considers that the building ought not to be subject to the faculty jurisdiction, he may direct that this provision is not to apply: s 11(3). Having so directed, if he considers, again after consultation with the DAC, that any article appertaining to the building should be subject to the faculty jurisdiction by reason of its being of outstanding architectural, artistic, historical or archaeological value, or significant monetary value, or at special risk of being stolen or damaged, he may direct that it be subject to the faculty jurisdiction: s 11(4).

[9] Ibid s 11(8). The Ecclesiastical Judges Association has sought to achieve a broad consistency of approach amongst chancellors as to the content of their written guidance. An unauthorized act purportedly performed under the minor works provisions may be undone by a restoration order: s 13(5).

[10] See *Re Woldingham Churchyard* [1957] 1 WLR 811, [1957] 2 All ER 323, Southwark Cons Ct; *Re St Mary, Balham* [1978] 1 All ER 993 at 997a, Southwark Cons Ct.

authorized by a faculty, and a minister might face disciplinary proceedings for breach of his oath of canonical obedience.[11]

Overriding duty

7.04 It is the duty of every person or body carrying out functions of care and conservation under the Care of Churches and Ecclesiastical Jurisdiction Measure 1991 or under any other enactment or rule of law relating to churches to have due regard to the role of the church as a local centre of worship and mission.[12] The duty certainly applies to the DAC and the Council for the Care of Churches. The spirit of the provision is applied in practice by English Heritage and 'in so far as the National Amenity Societies and conservation groups generally are prepared to adopt the same approach, it will undoubtedly be of assistance to the chancellor'.[13]

The ecclesiastical exemption

7.05 An ecclesiastical building which is, for the time being, used for ecclesiastical purposes is exempted from the need for listed building consent.[14] This should not be perceived as a privilege afforded to the Church of England, because it extends to other denominations and, further, because its continuance is predicated upon an alternative, and equally rigorous, system being maintained for the regulation of alterations to their historic church. Although 'ecclesiastical building' is not defined, clergy residences are expressly excluded.[15] Equally, there is no definition of 'ecclesiastical purposes', but it has been taken to denote use for corporate worship and might also extend to any purpose which the Church authorities

---

[11] See *Re St Thomas à Becket, Framfield* [1989] 1 WLR 689, [1989] 1 All ER 170, Chichester Cons Ct.

[12] Care of Churches and Ecclesiastical Jurisdiction Measure 1991, s 1. It has been held that this statutory duty does not apply to a chancellor, whose function is not one of care and conservation but judicial, namely, 'to hear and determine ... a cause of faculty': Ecclesiastical Jurisdiction Measure 1963, s 6(1)(b). Even had the chancellor been included in the scope of the general duty, it would have added nothing to his existing duty and practice: see *Re St Luke the Evangelist, Maidstone* [1995] Fam 1 at 7A–C, [1995] 1 All ER 321 at 326, Ct of Arches.

[13] *Re St Luke the Evangelist, Maidstone* [1995] Fam 1 at 7B–C, [1995] 1 All ER 321 at 326.

[14] Planning (Listed Buildings and Conservation Areas) Act 1990, s 60(1). See generally, C Mynors, *Listed Buildings, Conservation Areas and Monuments* (4th edn, London, 2006) paras 16.3.2, and *The Ecclesiastical Exemption: What It Is and How It Works* (Department of National Heritage and Cadw: Welsh Historic Monuments, September 1994). The origin of the ecclesiastical exemption is to be found in the Ancient Monuments Consolidation and Amendment Act 1913, s 22.

[15] Planning (Listed Buildings and Conservation Areas) Act 1990, s 60(3). The expression is broader than Anglican and includes the Roman Catholic Church and the Free Churches: *Attorney-General ex rel Bedfordshire County Council v Howard United Reformed Church Trustees, Bedford* [1976] AC 363, [1975] 2 All ER 337, HL.

Introduction

might think likely to foster Christian fellowship among the members of the congregation.[16] A building is deemed to be used for ecclesiastical purposes if it would be so used but for works currently taking place.[17] It therefore follows that listed building consent is not required for the alteration or extension of a listed ecclesiastical building of any denomination provided it is used for ecclesiastical purposes both before and after the works, nor is it required where such a building is to be partly demolished, provided ecclesiastical use continues in the part that remains.[18]

The Secretary of State may by order restrict or exclude from the 'ecclesiastical exemption' particular buildings or particular categories of building.[19] Accordingly, the 'exemption' now applies only to works to buildings owned by religious bodies which have in place satisfactory internal systems of control approved by the Secretary of State for Culture, Media and Sport.[20] These comprise the Church of England, the Church in Wales, the Roman Catholic Church, the Methodist Church, the Baptist Union and the United Reformed Church.[21] The operation of the 'ecclesiastical exemption' was reviewed in 1997,[22] and the content of that review helped shape the Faculty Jurisdiction Rules 2000. It has been subject to further consideration as part of the government's review on the future management of England's historic church buildings.[23] **7.06**

In relation to the Church of England,[24] the ecclesiastical exemption applies to: **7.07**

(a) any church building within the faculty jurisdiction;[25]

---

[16] See *Attorney-General ex rel Bedfordshire County Council v Howard United Reformed Church Trustees, Bedford* [1976] AC 363 at 377, [1975] 2 All ER 337 at 345, HL, per Lord Cross.
[17] Planning (Listed Buildings and Conservation Areas) Act 1990, s 60(4).
[18] See C Mynors, *Listed Buildings, Conservation Areas and Monuments* (n 14 above) para 16.3.1. Planning permission, however, would still be required.
[19] Planning (Listed Buildings and Conservation Areas) Act 1990, s 60(5).
[20] The criteria applied by the Secretary of State are to be found in PPG 15 at para 8.4. They include the need for independent, expert assessment, for notification to heritage bodies and amenity societies, for effective appeals, for regular inspections and records to be taken, and for enforcement procedures. See also *The Ecclesiastical Exemption* (n 14 above) para 6.0.
[21] Ecclesiastical Exemption (Listed Buildings and Conservation Areas) Order 1994, SI 1994/1771, art 4(a)–(g).
[22] See J Newman, *A Review of the Ecclesiastical Exemption from Listed Building Control conducted for the Department for Culture, Media and Sport and the Welsh Office* (September 1997).
[23] *The Ecclesiastical Exemption: The Way Forward*, Department for Culture, Media and Sport (July 2005). See the Third Report of the Select Committee on Culture, Media and Sport (July 2006), and, more recently, the government White Paper, *Heritage Protection for the Twenty-First Century* (March 2007, Cmnd 7057) which confirmed the continuance of the 'ecclesiastical exemption' for the Church of England and those other denominations to which it currently applies but not its further extension.
[24] The exemption, as it applies to cathedral churches of the Church of England, is separately considered in Chapter 8.
[25] Ecclesiastical Exemption (Listed Buildings and Conservation Areas) Order 1994, Arts 4(a), 5(1)(a).

(b) any object or structure within such a church building;[26]
(c) any object or structure fixed to the exterior of such a church building;[27] and
(d) any object or structure within the curtilage of such a church building which, although not fixed to the building, forms part of the land.[28]

However, the 'exemption' is not retained in respect of an object or structure under (c) or (d) above, if that object or structure is itself a separately listed building.[29]

Care of places of worship

7.08 In the Church of England, the 'exemption' is also retained for works to buildings[30] within a peculiar[31] or religious community;[32] to buildings used for worship within any university, college, school, hospital, Inn of Court or other public or charitable institution;[33] and to buildings subject to a church sharing agreement.[34] Provision was made in the Care of Places of Worship Measure 1999 for such places to apply for inclusion on a list compiled and maintained by the Council for the Care of Churches.[35] For so long as a building is included on the list, it is subject to the faculty jurisdiction, subject to certain modifications.[36] Time for applying for inclusion on the list has expired, and those ecclesiastical buildings which have not been included have now become subject to the system of control for listed buildings operated by local authorities.

---

[26] Ibid art 5(1)(b).
[27] Ibid art 5(1)(c).
[28] Ibid art 5(1)(d).
[29] Ibid art 5(3).
[30] The building concerned must be an ecclesiastical building used for ecclesiastical purposes in order to attract the exemption in the first place: see above. Residences and buildings in secular use do not have the benefit of the exemption even though they may be within a peculiar jurisdiction or part of a religious community.
[31] Ecclesiastical Exemption (Listed Buildings and Conservation Areas) Order 1994, art 6(1), (2)(a).
[32] Ibid art 6(2)(c).
[33] Ibid art 6(2)(b). Such places are generally not subject to the faculty jurisdiction. Note, however, *Re Tonbridge School Chapel* [1993] 1 WLR 1138, [1993] 2 All ER 350, Rochester Cons Ct.
[34] Ecclesiastical Exemption (Listed Buildings and Conservation Areas) Order 1994, art 6(2)(e). See the Sharing of Church Buildings Act 1969, and Chapter 3. The agreement must be made by one or more of the exempt denominations (see above) or any Church in membership with the Baptist Union of Great Britain or of Wales.
[35] Care of Places of Worship Measure 1999, s 1(1), (2).
[36] Ibid s 3(1), (2). See also the Faculty Jurisdiction (Care of Places of Worship) Rules 2000, SI 2000/2048. The operation of the faculty jurisdiction to this class of building is discussed below. Such buildings will automatically fall within the Ecclesiastical Exemption (Listed Buildings and Conservation Areas) Order 1994, art 4(a).

The role of the archdeacon

7.09 Works of alteration and repair vary from the trivial to the major. Some proposals may be highly controversial. The archdeacon is empowered to grant faculties in certain unopposed causes.[37] Not infrequently, faculties are granted subject to the works being supervised by the archdeacon.[38] He is a member of the DAC.[39] He may institute proceedings for obtaining a faculty in relation to any parish within his archdeaconry.[40] He is an 'interested person' for the purposes of entering an objection to a proposed faculty in any parish in his archdeaconry.[41] He may make an application for an injunction or a restoration order.[42]

7.10 When the archdeacon makes an appearance in faculty proceedings, it is generally at the request of the chancellor and in a role akin to that of *amicus curiae*. Archdeacons ought to be represented by counsel or a solicitor, so that professional cross-examination of witnesses may take place and the chancellor addressed fully on the facts and law.[43] The bishop may appoint another person to act in place of the archdeacon if:

(a) the archdeaconry is vacant; or
(b) the archdeacon is incapacitated by absence or illness from acting; or
(c) in the opinion of the bishop the archdeacon is for any other reason unable or unwilling to act or it would be inappropriate for him to act.[44]

The costs of an archdeacon or acting archdeacon are borne by the diocesan board of finance, provided his participation is approved by the bishop after consultation with the board.[45]

7.11 The archdeacon is entitled to convene an extraordinary meeting of the PCC or an extraordinary parochial church meeting if it appears to him that anything has been done in a parish in his archdeaconry which ought not to have been done

---

[37] Care of Churches and Ecclesiastical Jurisdiction Measure 1991, s 14(1), see para 7.43 below.
[38] Ibid s 12(1)(a).
[39] Ibid s 2(2), Sch 1 para 2.
[40] Ibid s 16(1)(a). He is deemed to have an interest in the proceedings: ibid s 16(2).
[41] Faculty Jurisdiction Rules 2000, SI 2000/2047, r 16(2)(b).
[42] Care of Churches and Ecclesiastical Jurisdiction Measure 1991, s 13(6), discussed further below.
[43] See *Re St Gregory, Tredington* [1972] Fam 236, [1971] 3 All ER 269, Ct of Arches; *Re St Michael and All Angels, Great Torrington* [1985] Fam 81, [1985] 1 All ER 993, Ct of Eccl Causes Res; *Re All Saints, Melbourn* [1990] 1 WLR 833, [1992] 2 All ER 786, Ct of Arches; and *Re Holy Trinity Bosham*, [2004] Fam 125, [2004] 2 All ER 820, Chichester Cons Ct.
[44] Care of Churches and Ecclesiastical Jurisdiction Measure 1991, s 16(3)(a)–(c). Note also the Faculty Jurisdiction Rules 2000, r 28(1). The instrument of appointment must be in Form No 12 in App C to the rules: r 28(2).
[45] Care of Churches and Ecclesiastical Jurisdiction Measure 1991, s 16(4).

without a faculty, or anything which ought to have been done in connection with the care of any church in his archdeaconry or any article appertaining to any such church has not been done.[46]

7.12 Further, if the archdeacon considers that an article of architectural, artistic, historical or archaeological value is exposed to danger of loss or damage and ought to be removed to a place of safety, he may order its removal accordingly.[47] If anyone on whom the archdeacon's order is served refuses to comply with it, the archdeacon may apply to the consistory court for a mandatory order compelling delivery up of the article.[48] When a place of safety order has been made by the archdeacon, he must within 28 days apply to the consistory court for a faculty authorizing the retention of the article in a place of safety.[49]

Temporary reordering

7.13 Archdeacons no longer have power to issue certificates for minor works.[50] Instead, they exercise in their own right a delegated power to grant faculties, which is discussed more fully below. In addition, the archdeacon has power to grant a licence in writing for a temporary period not exceeding 15 months for a scheme of minor reordering.[51] The scheme must not involve any interference with the fabric of the church, nor the fixing of any item to the fabric of the church, nor the disposal of any fixtures which, if not required for the scheme, are to be safeguarded and stored so that they may be easily reinstated.[52] The archdeacon may add such other conditions to the licence as may be considered necessary,[53] and must submit a copy of it to the registrar and the secretary of the DAC.[54] The 15-month period may not be extended by the archdeacon, although if a petition for a chancellor's faculty in

---

[46] Ibid s 20.
[47] Ibid s 21(1). 'Article' does not include certain records and registers: see s 21(7). Unless he is of the opinion that the article should be removed immediately, the archdeacon must notify the churchwardens, the PCC, the DAC and any person having custody of the article of the facts as they appear to him and afford such persons 28 days within which to make written representations to him: s 21(2). See also Faculty Jurisdiction Rules 2000, r 29 which provides for an order in App C, Form No 15 or, in a case of urgency, Form No 13.
[48] Care of Churches and Ecclesiastical Jurisdiction Measure 1991, s 21(5). See, by way of example, *Re St Peter, Racton* (2001) 6 Ecc LJ 291, Chichester Cons Ct.
[49] Care of Churches and Ecclesiastical Jurisdiction Measure 1991, s 21(6).
[50] An archdeacon's certificate issued under the Faculty Jurisdiction Measure 1964, s 12 (repealed) remains in force as if it were a faculty granted under the Care of Churches and Ecclesiastical Jurisdiction Measure 1991, s 14(2): s 14(6).
[51] Faculty Jurisdiction Rules 2000, r 9(1). For the form of licence, see App C, Form No 7. If he declines to grant a licence, the archdeacon must advise the minister to apply to the chancellor for an interim faculty authorizing the scheme: ibid r 9(5).
[52] Ibid r 9(1)(a)–(c).
[53] Ibid r 9(2).
[54] Ibid r 9(3).

respect of the scheme is submitted to the registry not later than two months before the expiry of the period, the scheme is deemed to be authorized until the determination of the petition by the chancellor.[55]

Matters of urgency

An archdeacon is under a mandatory duty to inform the registrar, who must immediately refer the matter to the chancellor, if he becomes aware of any matter for which a faculty is required (whether or not a petition has been submitted) and he considers: **7.14**

(a) that it needs to be dealt with urgently without reference to the DAC;
(b) that it may necessitate the issue of an injunction, the making of a restoration order or the grant of an interim faculty; or
(c) that it may give rise to any question as to the payment of costs and expenses.[56]

The chancellor may give such licence or other directions as are appropriate in the circumstances of the case.

Visitations

The archdeacon is required to hold yearly visitations and, in addition, to survey (in person or by a deputy) all churches, chancels and churchyards and give directions for the amendment of all defects in the walls, fabric, ornaments and furniture.[57] Only when these directions are ignored will it prove necessary for the archdeacon to invoke the statutory powers discussed at paragraph 7.81 and following below. **7.15**

Diocesan advisory committees

Every diocese must have an advisory committee for the care of churches.[58] The Diocesan Advisory Committee,[59] as it is known (DAC), comprises a chairman, the archdeacons of the diocese and not fewer than 12 other members.[60] The chairman **7.16**

---

[55] Ibid r 9(4).
[56] Ibid r 8(3).
[57] Canon C 22 para 5. Note also the powers conferred on the archdeacon by the Inspection of Churches Measure 1955.
[58] Care of Churches and Ecclesiastical Jurisdiction Measure 1991, s 2(1). It must have a written constitution containing the provisions in Sch 1 to the Measure: s 2(2).
[59] The committee is known as the '[name of diocese] Diocesan Advisory Committee': ibid Sch 1 para 1.
[60] Ibid Sch 1 para 2.

is appointed by the bishop after consultation with the bishop's council, the chancellor and the Council for the Care of Churches.[61] The other members comprise two persons appointed by the bishop's council from among the elected members of diocesan synod and at least ten other persons appointed by the bishop's council.[62] Of these ten, one is appointed after consultation with English Heritage,[63] one after consultation with the Local Government Association[64] and one after consultation with the national amenity societies.[65] The bishop's council must ensure that, between them, the members have knowledge of the history, development and use of church buildings; of Church of England liturgy and worship; and of architecture, archaeology, art and history; together with experience of the care of historic buildings and their contents.[66] With the consent of the bishop, the DAC may co-opt additional members.[67] The bishop may appoint suitably qualified persons to act as consultants if the DAC so requests him.[68] The secretary is appointed by the bishop after consultation with the chairman of the DAC and the chief administrative officer of the diocese.[69] The members of the DAC give their services free of charge, but the expenses of enabling the DAC to discharge its functions properly and effectively are required to be met by the diocesan board of finance.[70]

7.17 The functions of the DAC are set out in Schedule 2 to the Care of Churches and Ecclesiastical Jurisdiction Measure 1991. They are:

(a) to act as an advisory body on matters affecting places of worship in the diocese and, in particular, to give advice when requested to the bishop, chancellor, archdeacons, PCCs and intending applicants for faculties,[71] on

---

[61] Ibid Sch 1 para 3.
[62] Ibid Sch 1 para 4(a), (b).
[63] Its full title is The Historic Buildings and Monuments Commission for England.
[64] This association was formed by the merger of the Association of County Councils, the Association of District Councils and the Association of Metropolitan Authorities on 1 April 1997, and was designated for the purposes of the Care of Churches and Ecclesiastical Jurisdiction Measure 1991, Sch 1, by order of the Dean of the Arches dated 13 December 1998.
[65] Care of Churches and Ecclesiastical Jurisdiction Measure 1991, Sch 1 para 4(b). The identity and purposes of the national amenity societies are set out in paragraph 7.18.
[66] Ibid Sch 1 para 5(a)–(d).
[67] Ibid Sch 1 para 12. Co-opted members may not exceed one-third of the total number of other members.
[68] Ibid Sch 1 para 13.
[69] Ibid Sch 1 para 14.
[70] Ibid s 2(6). The expenses must be approved by the board before they are incurred: ibid s 2(6) proviso.
[71] Ibid s 2(5), Sch 2 para 2(a)–(e). Advice must also be given, if requested, to the diocesan pastoral committee, persons engaged in the planning, design or building of new places of worship in the diocese not within the jurisdiction of the consistory court, and such other persons as the DAC may consider appropriate: Sch 2 para 2(f)–(h).

matters relating to:
- (i) the grant of faculties;
- (ii) the architecture, archaeology, art and history of places of worship;
- (iii) the use, care, planning, design and redundancy of places of worship;
- (iv) the use and care of the contents of such places;
- (v) the use and care of churches and burial grounds;

(b) to review and assess the degree of risk to materials or of loss to archaeological or historic remains or records, arising from any proposals relating to the conservation, repair or alteration of places of worship, churchyards and burial grounds;

(c) to develop and maintain a repository of records relating to the conservation, repair and alteration of places of worship, churchyards and burial grounds;

(d) to issue guidance for the preparation and storage of such records;

(e) to make recommendations as to the circumstances when the preparation of such a record should be made a condition of a faculty;

(f) to take action to encourage the care and appreciation of places of worship, churchyards and burial grounds and the contents of such places, and for that purpose to publicize methods of conservation, repair, construction, adaptation and redevelopment;

(g) to perform such other functions as may be assigned to the DAC by any enactment or canon, by resolution of diocesan synod or as may be requested by the bishop or chancellor.[72]

The DAC is required to approve the appointment of a qualified person to inspect the churches in the diocese and report on every church inspected pursuant to schemes established by the diocesan synod.[73] The secretary to the DAC must compile and maintain a register of all petitions for a faculty referred to the DAC for advice and ensure that the register is available for inspection by the public by prior appointment.[74] Although the agenda for and minutes of DAC meetings ought to be promptly and effectively disseminated to those with an interest in their content, it is not considered that the applicants, would-be objectors or the general public should be afforded general access to those meetings.[75]

---

[72] Ibid Sch 2 para 1(a)–(g).
[73] Inspection of Churches Measure 1955, s 1(2)(c).
[74] Care of Churches and Ecclesiastical Jurisdiction Measure 1991, s 15(3).
[75] *Legal Opinions* 275, which suggest, correctly it is submitted, that *obiter dictum* to the contrary in *Re Holy Cross, Pershore* [2002] Fam 1, Worcester Cons Ct, paras 60–62 should be disregarded, since the analogy sought to be made with public access to meetings of democratically elected members of local authority committees and sub-committees is not appropriate.

National amenity societies

7.18 In addition to English Heritage, a number of other bodies exist which have an expertise and legitimate interest in church buildings and for whom provision is made within the faculty jurisdiction. Such bodies, referred to throughout the statutory provisions as the 'national amenity societies' comprise:

(a) the Ancient Monuments Society (before 1715);
(b) the Council for British Archaeology;
(c) the Georgian Group (1700–1840);
(d) the Society for the Protection of Ancient Buildings;
(e) the Victorian Society (1837–1914); and
(f) the Twentieth Century Society (1914 onwards).[76]

The functions of these bodies are threefold.[77] Collectively they are consulted upon the appointment of one person to the DAC of each diocese.[78] Individually they have a right of consultation where significant changes to a listed church are proposed,[79] and are classified as 'interested persons' for the purposes of objecting to a proposed faculty being granted.[80] The dates appearing after the names of certain of the National Amenity Societies above indicate the period of building[81] with which they are concerned and in relation to which consultation should take place when certain faculties are sought. The Ancient Monuments Society is particularly interested in sizeable extensions to churches of any date and proposals affecting features of importance by way of alteration or removal. The Council for British Archaeology will have a concern in operations that will affect the archaeology of the fabric of the church (or below the ground of the church) or in the churchyard.[82]

---

[76] Care of Churches and Ecclesiastical Jurisdiction Measure 1991, s 31(1). The dates given in brackets indicate the period in which the society has an interest.

[77] For further and more detailed information, see *The National Amenity Societies: Their Role in the Conservation of Anglican Churches* (Council for the Care of Churches, 1998).

[78] Care of Churches and Ecclesiastical Jurisdiction Measure 1991, Sch 1 para 4(b).

[79] Faculty Jurisdiction Rules 2000, r 3(3)(b), App B para 1.

[80] Ibid r 16(2)(e).

[81] It is not merely the date when the church was constructed which matters. Significant alterations, extensions or reorderings in later periods must also be considered.

[82] See generally, *Making Changes to a Listed Church*, Guidelines for Clergy, Churchwardens and Parochial Church Councils (January 1999) paras 7.1–7.7.

Formulating proposals

7.19 Alterations to church buildings can generate strong feelings in parishes. There may well be legitimate differences of opinion between and amongst the minister, the churchwardens and the PCC. The worshipping community may be divided, as may those in the locality who have little or no connection with the church. It is imperative, particularly when major works are contemplated, that the proposals are given wide publicity and that all opinions are given proper consideration.[83] If the impression is given that a small cabal is steering through a particular project, this may cause resentment which will have become entrenched by the time the matter is before the consistory court.

7.20 In *Re Emmanuel, Northwood*, Chancellor Cameron commended the practice of addressing at least three core questions: why? how? and when?

> Under why, the PCC should address the perceived problems and need for change and produce a written document identifying them. Under how, there should be a feasibility study with drawings and approximate costs based on a detailed brief, which tackles the identified problems and needs and offers alternatives, if any. Under when, consideration should be given to whether the changes could or should be introduced in stages, for cost or other reasons, and the extent to which experimentation would be appropriate or desirable.[84]

The chancellor stated that the congregation should be kept informed as each question is examined, through the parish magazine or an informatory leaflet, and that there should be an opportunity for the congregation to consider the results of each examination before any final decision is made by the PCC. She concluded:

> a petition for a faculty should not be presented until full consultation has taken place. This does not mean that the PCC has to secure unanimous support before a petition is presented, nor that it has to jeopardise parts of the scheme to try to meet objections if those parts are regarded by the minister and the PCC as important in promoting in the parish the whole mission of the Church. The matter has then to be put to the test in the consistory court.[85]

7.21 In addition to widespread consultation within the parish, it is also important that proposals which involve alteration to the fabric and furnishings of a listed church be properly prepared by an architect or surveyor so that all bodies which have a legitimate concern about them can see exactly what is involved. Such plans form the basis for a dialogue between an experienced church architect and surveyor and

---

[83] See generally S Cameron, 'Re-Ordering Historic Churches' (2001) 6 Ecc LJ 26.
[84] *Re Emmanuel, Northwood* (1998) 5 Ecc LJ 213, London Cons Ct. The case concerned a substantial reordering but the approach is equally appropriate when an extension or other major work is contemplated.
[85] *Re Emmanuel, Northwood* (1998) 5 Ecc LJ 213, London Cons Ct.

the bodies concerned with conservation which frequently can result in some variation being agreed which will meet the conservation objection whilst at the same time still preserving the substance of the proposed works.[86] As Chancellor Cameron has stated:

> For the benefit of other parishes in the future I make it quite clear that plans in support of a major scheme of alteration of a listed church will have to be prepared in sufficient detail to enable me, and the bodies concerned with conservation, to understand easily what the details of the work proposed are ... If a PCC has sufficient enthusiasm for a project to wish to obtain a faculty then the reasonable cost of professional advice and assistance must be allowed for in the overall cost of the scheme.[87]

Many of the matters with which the chancellor was concerned in each of these cases will now fall to be addressed in the course of drafting the Statement of Significance and Statement of Needs, which are discussed below. Further, the proper and prudent approach which should be followed by a PCC in estimating the overall costs of any proposed works is to add an allowance for the cost of obtaining a faculty, together with the cost of any likely archaeological monitoring.[88]

Seeking advice

Preliminary advice

7.22 It will be apparent from the foregoing that in the process of formulating proposals, particularly for major projects, parishes are well advised to seek advice from the DAC, one or more of the National Amenity Societies, and/or the local planning authority. Whilst provision is made for this in a formal manner in the Faculty Jurisdiction Rules 2000, discussed below, much may be gained from seeking informal advice at an early stage.[89]

---

[86] *Re St George the Martyr, Holborn* (1997) 5 Ecc LJ 67 at 68, London Cons Ct.
[87] *Re St George the Martyr, Holborn* (above). See also *Re St Peter, Oundle* (1996) 4 Ecc LJ 764, Peterborough Cons Ct.
[88] *Re St Mary the Virgin, Sherborne* [1996] Fam 63 at 69F, [1996] 3 All ER 769 at 774j–775a, Ct of Arches.
[89] For a discussion of the nature of consultation, and the weight to be afforded to sometimes conflicting opinions, see *Re St Mary Magdalene and St Denys, Midhurst* (2002) 7 Ecc LJ 104, Chichester Cons Ct. Hill Ch stated at para 5 of the judgment: 'Consultation must not be confused with subjugation. A parish should not feel obliged to take on board each and every comment from an amenity society or other consultee. It should, of course, give such comments the careful and considered weight which they deserve being the professional views expressed by persons with considerable expertise and experience. They should not, however, unquestioningly incorporate every aspect of sometimes mutually contradictory advice, since, in doing so, the essence of a valid project may be compromised'.

Listed churches

Timely advice is especially necessary in relation to a listed church. The Rule Committee established under the Care of Churches and Ecclesiastical Jurisdiction Measure 1991, has produced a booklet, *Making Changes to a Listed Church*[90] containing guidelines which, though having no statutory force, should (if followed) avoid delay and misunderstanding. Parishes are encouraged to establish the grade of their church's listing and to obtain a copy of the list description,[91] with the help of which they may prepare a Statement of Significance identifying the important features that make major contributions to the character of the church.[92] The minister, churchwardens and PCC should then prepare a Statement of Needs giving the reasons why they consider changes are necessary.[93] These two statements, the second in particular, are core documents for the parish architect or surveyor, the DAC, English Heritage, the National Amenity Societies and the local planning authority. They will also fall to be considered by the chancellor. They should therefore be compiled thoroughly and with care. A summary of alternative ways of making changes so as to meet identified needs is also recommended.

7.23

Upon this information, the architect can begin to prepare preliminary sketches and drawings. Once the PCC has considered these, consultation should then take place with the DAC,[94] English Heritage, such of the National Amenity Societies as may have an interest in the church,[95] and the local planning authority.[96] This wide consultation is recommended for changes which make a 'significant difference' to the interior or exterior of a church.[97] Together with the architect, the

7.24

---

[90] *Making Changes to a Listed Church*, Guidelines for Clergy, Churchwardens and Parochial Church Councils (January 1999).

[91] *Making Changes to a Listed Church* (n 90 above) para 3.1.

[92] *Making Changes to a Listed Church* (n 90 above) para 4.5. This document is of permanent value and may be updated from time to time as new information comes to light.

[93] *Making Changes to a Listed Church* (n 90 above) para 5.2. It is important to focus on the concept of necessity at an early stage because this is the first test which will fall to be applied by the chancellor when applying the *Bishopsgate* questions in determining the petition (see paras 7.70ff below). For an example of a proposed reordering failing to secure a faculty because necessity was not made out, see *Re All Saints, Burbage*, (14 February 2007, unreported) Salisbury Cons Ct.

[94] The secretary of the DAC may be able to point the parish towards other churches in the dioceses where similar needs have been addressed.

[95] As to these, see para 7.18 above.

[96] *Making Changes to a Listed Church* (n 90 above) para 7.1. Note also the benefit of consulting local amenity societies.

[97] *Making Changes to a Listed Church* (n 90 above) para 8.1. There is no simple definition of 'significant difference' but examples given include alterations to the fabric such as the creation or filling in of a window or doorway, the placing of a new wall between the nave and the tower, or the removal of a chancel screen or wall. Removal of pews or other furnishings may also qualify. Guidance may also be had from the Faculty Jurisdiction Rules 2000, App B, which is discussed in more detail below.

parish should take a common sense approach as to whether the change proposed will make the church significantly different from its condition and appearance beforehand.[98] The guidelines conclude:

> The fact that a scheme contains controversial elements does not mean that it has to be abandoned. The chancellor may allow it to proceed in whole (or in part) and grant a faculty accordingly. However, early consultation and a readiness to listen on all sides have the merit that they will nearly always reduce, if not eliminate, the areas of conflict. In terms of saving expense and delay it is a very worthwhile step in the process.[99]

Formal advice

7.25 The Faculty Jurisdiction Rules 2000 provide as a general rule in all cases that intending applicants for a faculty must seek the advice of the DAC prior to lodging a petition.[100] An intending applicant should submit to the DAC designs, plans, photographs and other documents giving particulars together with a summary list of the works or proposals.[101] This enables the DAC to carry out its function of furnishing advice in relation to any works or proposals.

7.26 In relation to a listed church, however, there are additional requirements to which the remainder of this section is devoted. Where significant changes to a listed church are proposed[102] the intending applicant should[103] also submit:

(a) a Statement of Significance, being 'a document which summarises the historical development of the church and identifies the important features that make major contributions to the character of the church'; and
(b) a Statement of Needs, being 'a document which sets out the reasons why it is considered that the needs of the parish cannot be met without making changes to the church building and the reasons why the changes are regarded as necessary to assist the church in its worship and mission'.[104]

---

[98] *Making Changes to a Listed Church* (n 90 above) para 8.2
[99] *Making Changes to a Listed Church* (n 90 above) para 9.2.
[100] Faculty Jurisdiction Rules 2000, r 3(1). The chancellor may not make a final determination in any faculty matter without first seeking the advice of the DAC, save in cases of exhumation or reservation of a gravespace or where he is satisfied that the matter is sufficiently urgent: r 14, repeating the Care of Churches and Ecclesiastical Jurisdiction Measure 1991, s 15(1). An archdeacon must seek the advice of the DAC before making a final determination in any cause of faculty unless the action proposed relates exclusively to exhumation or the reservation of a gravespace: Care of Churches and Ecclesiastical Jurisdiction Measure 1991, s 15(2).
[101] Faculty Jurisdiction Rules 2000, r 3(2). This does not apply in relation to works to trees: r 3(4), which is addressed at paragraphs 7.128, 7.129 below.
[102] As to which, see above.
[103] This is directory not mandatory but a failure to do so will almost inevitably delay the consideration of any subsequent petition.
[104] Faculty Jurisdiction Rules 2000, r 3(3)(a). The definitions are lifted directly from the interpretation provision at r 2(1).

These documents, which ought to have been drafted at an early stage as discussed above, are intended to inform the DAC and the chancellor about particular points of importance from a conservation point of view.

In addition, the intending applicant should consult English Heritage, such of the National Amenity Societies as appear likely to have an interest in the listed church or the works, and the local planning authority, if the works for which a faculty is to be sought: 7.27

(a) involve alteration to or extension of a listed church to such an extent as is likely to affect its character as a building of special architectural or historic interest; or
(b) are likely to affect the archaeological importance of the church or archaeological remains existing within the church or its curtilage; or
(c) involve demolition affecting the exterior of an unlisted church in a conservation area.[105]

Such consultation is qualified as being 'so far as provided by and in accordance with the criteria set out' in the remainder of Appendix B.[106]

The guidance in Appendix B is readily comprehensible in the context of the guidelines, *Making Changes to a Listed Church*, discussed above. In relation to English Heritage, all alterations affecting grade I or II* listed churches merit consultation, as do all works likely to affect the archaeological importance of the church under (b) above. Consultation in relation to grade II listed churches is limited to works under (a) which comprise the demolition or removal of all or a substantial part of the structure of the interior.[107] 7.28

The age of the church and the nature and effect of the works determine which one or more of the National Amenity Societies ought to be consulted in relation to works under categories (a), (b) and (c).[108] Whatever the grade of listing, consultation in relation to an alteration or extension under (a) above is required when the work comprises the demolition of a significant part of the structure of the interior, the removal of major internal fixtures such as fixed pews, a rood screen or an organ, or the addition of any significant new element such as the creation of a new space through subdivision.[109] 7.29

---

[105] Ibid r 3(3)(b), App B para 1.
[106] Ibid App B para 1.
[107] Ibid App B para 2.1(ii). This includes principal internal elements such as a staircase, gallery, load bearing wall, floor structure or roof structure and major internal fixtures such as fixed pews, a rood screen or organ.
[108] The period covered by each is set out in para 7.18 above.
[109] Faculty Jurisdiction Rules 2000, App B paras 3, 3.1, 3.2, noting the meaning given to alteration at para 5.

7.30 Any works under any of categories (a), (b) or (c), whatever grade the listing, require consultation with the local planning authority.[110] In relation to an extension, such consultation is otiose, since planning permission will be required in any event. In relation to category (a), the same meaning is given to alteration as for consultation with the National Amenity Societies.[111]

7.31 Where consultation is required, the intending applicant must submit to the relevant body designs, plans or other documents (including photographs) giving particulars of the works together with a summary list of the works, a Statement of Significance and a Statement of Needs.[112] The particulars should be sufficiently clear for a comparison to be made between the church in its existing state and in its future state so as to enable an assessment to be made of the likely impact of the works.[113] When submitting the particulars to any of the consultative bodies, the intending applicant should write to that body stating that its response will be taken into account provided it is received within 28 days from the date of the letter.[114] The intending applicant should inform the secretary of the DAC which bodies have been consulted and the date upon which the 28-day response period is due to expire.[115] On receipt of a response within the 28-day period, the intending applicant should provide a copy to the secretary of the DAC.[116] The DAC is not obliged to await a response which is not received within the 28-day period before reaching a decision and issuing a certificate under rule 3(5) or rule 3(6).[117]

DAC certificate

7.32 If the DAC decides to recommend the works or proposals or to raise no objection to them, its decision, together with any provisos, must be set out in a certificate and sent to the intending applicant along with the documents which

---

[110] Ibid App B para 4.
[111] Ibid App B paras 4, 4.1 and 5.
[112] Ibid App B para 6. Although the rule does not expressly so provide, common sense and administrative efficiency dictate that the same Statement of Significance and Statement of Needs ought to be submitted to these bodies as are submitted to the DAC. The other documents ought likewise to be the same. The wording in App B para 6(a) is similar but not identical to that in r 3(2).
[113] Ibid App B para 6.1.
[114] Ibid App B para 7. This is the same period as for consultation in relation to listed building consent.
[115] Ibid App B para 8.
[116] Ibid.
[117] Ibid.

had been submitted.[118] If the DAC decides not to recommend the works or proposals, it so informs the intending applicant.[119] In the latter case, the certificate should advise the intending applicant that he is entitled to petition the chancellor for a faculty if he so wishes, notwithstanding the decision of the DAC.[120]

7.33 In either of the above cases, where it appears to the DAC that the works:

(a) involve alteration to or extension of a listed church to such an extent as is likely to affect its character as a building of special architectural or historic interest;
(b) are likely to affect the archaeological importance of the church or archaeological remains existing within the church or its curtilage; or
(c) in the case of an unlisted church in a conservation area, will involve demolition affecting the exterior of the church,

the DAC certificate may include a recommendation to the intending applicant that he should consult English Heritage or the local planning authority, or one or more of the National Amenity Societies, or the Council for the Care of Churches or any other body or person or persons, if he has not already done so.[121]

The petition

7.34 Proceedings for a faculty may be instituted by the archdeacon of the archdeaconry where the parish is situated, by the minister and churchwardens of the parish, as is usually the case, or by any other person appearing to the court to have a sufficient interest in the matter.[122] A person on the electoral roll but not resident in the parish is deemed to have an interest as if he were a parishioner.[123] The question of sufficient interest is one of fact and degree, to be determined by the chancellor in each case.[124]

7.35 Once the DAC's certificate has been received, the applicant may submit a petition for a faculty to the diocesan registry.[125] It must be in the prescribed form.[126]

---

[118] Ibid r 3(5). Form No 1 in App C is used. It is also good practice to annex to the certificate some statement to the effect that the certificate does not amount to authorization for the works.
[119] Ibid r 3(6). Form No 1 in App C is again used.
[120] Ibid r 3(6).
[121] Ibid r 3(7). It is a mandatory requirement to consider making such a recommendation.
[122] Care of Churches and Ecclesiastical Jurisdiction Measure 1991, s 16(1)(a)–(c).
[123] Ibid s 16(2).
[124] See GH and GL Newsom, *The Faculty Jurisdiction of the Church of England* (2nd edn, London: Sweet and Maxwell, 1993) 51–56. There is no mechanism for the DAC to determine that an intending applicant lacks sufficient interest, although advice could be sought from the chancellor.
[125] Faculty Jurisdiction Rules 2000, r 4(1).
[126] Ibid r 4(1); App C Form No 2. No departure from this form is permitted under r 36(1).

It is possible to bypass the consultation and certification process,[127] but such instances are likely to be rare. The works or proposals must be fully and accurately stated in the petition and identical to those for which the DAC has supplied its certificate.[128] The DAC certificate and the documents submitted to the DAC must be submitted with the petition.[129] A petition for the demolition or partial demolition of a church must include all statements and information as are required by the prescribed form.[130]

7.36 Where significant changes to a church are proposed, a copy of the designs, plans, photographs and other documents submitted with the petition must be displayed in the church and remain on display until the petition has been determined.[131]

Public notice

7.37 As soon as a petitioner is ready to submit a petition for a faculty, he must fill in the public notice in the prescribed form,[132] describing the works or proposals in the same manner as they are described in the Schedule to the petition.[133] As soon as it has been filled in, the petitioner must immediately send a copy of it, together with the petition and accompanying documents, to the registry.[134] A copy must also be sent to English Heritage or any other grant-making body in accordance with the terms of any previous grant to the church.[135]

7.38 The public notice must then be displayed for a continuous period of not less than 28 days.[136] The display must be both inside the church on a notice board or in some other prominent position,[137] and outside on a notice board or in some

---

[127] Ibid r 4(4). Even in cases of extreme urgency, Form No 2 ought still to be used: r 4(4).
[128] Ibid r 4(1)(a).
[129] Ibid 4(1)(b).
[130] Ibid r 5. Again, App C Form No 2 is used.
[131] Ibid r 4(2). The importance of this statutory requirement was emphasized in *Re Emmanuel Church, Bentley* [2006] Fam 39, Ct of Arches.
[132] This was formerly styled the citation. For the public notice, see the Faculty Jurisdiction Rules 2000, App C Form No 3. The importance of this statutory requirement was also emphasized in *Re Emmanuel Church, Bentley* (n 131 above).
[133] Faculty Jurisdiction Rules 2000, r 6(1). This does not apply where the petitioner is not the minister or a churchwarden or where the petition relates to exhumation or reservation of a gravespace (ibid r 6(1)), in which case the public notice is to be sent to the registrar who gives directions about display: rr 6(2), (3)(b), 13(8).
[134] Ibid r 6(3)(a).
[135] Ibid r 6(3)(c).
[136] Ibid r 6(4). If the works relate to a place of worship which is not the parish church or to a churchyard or consecrated burial ground not belonging to a parish church, the public notice should also be displayed at the parish church: r 6(4)(a)(ii).
[137] Ibid r 6(4)(b)(i).

The petition

other prominent position, whether on the outside of the church door or elsewhere, so that it is readily visible to the public.[138]

The registrar may give directions to the petitioner if, on receipt of the petition and copy public notice, he considers: **7.39**

(a) that the works or proposals are not adequately described;
(b) that a copy of the public notice should be displayed inside or outside any other church or place of worship in the parish;
(c) that a copy should be displayed in some prominent position elsewhere in the parish, whether inside or outside a building, where it will be clearly visible to the public;
(d) that the public notice should be displayed for longer than 28 days.[139]

In relation to a petition for a faculty for exhumation, it is for the registrar to complete the public notice and to give directions for its display, subject to any directions from the chancellor.[140] If the chancellor is satisfied that any near relatives of the deceased still living and any other persons concerned are the petitioners or that they consent to the faculty being granted, the chancellor may dispense with the issue of a public notice and order the issue of a faculty immediately.[141] In any other case, he may dispense with public notice and direct that such persons be specially notified.[142] **7.40**

In cases of emergency which involve the interests of safety or health, or the preservation of a church or part of it, which are of sufficient urgency to justify the grant of a faculty without obtaining the advice of the DAC,[143] the chancellor may dispense with the display of a public notice and direct that a short period of notice be given to bodies which would otherwise be consulted.[144] **7.41**

Upon the expiry of 28 days, or such longer period as may have been directed, a copy of the public notice must be returned to the registrar with the certificate of publication duly completed by the petitioner.[145] **7.42**

---

[138] Ibid r 6(4)(b)(ii). When the petition concerns a churchyard or consecrated burial ground not belonging to the parish church, then the display at the parish church need only be outside: r 6(4)(d).
[139] Ibid r 6(5)(a)–(d).
[140] Ibid r 13(8).
[141] Ibid r 13(9)(a).
[142] Ibid r 13(9)(b).
[143] As to this, see ibid r 14.
[144] Ibid r 13(10). No emergency, it would seem, is sufficient to dispense entirely with the mandatory notices to those bodies which must be consulted.
[145] Ibid r 6(6). Form No 3 in App C is to be used.

Archdeacon's jurisdiction

7.43 The archdeacon has power to exercise the jurisdiction of the consistory court where:

(a) the works or proposals fall within the categories specified in Appendix A to the Faculty Jurisdiction Rules 2000;
(b) the petition is unopposed; and
(c) the DAC's certificate either recommends or raises no objection to them.[146]

Appendix A, in broad terms, embraces the following:

(a) minor alterations, repairs and decoration relating to the fabric;
(b) repairs to fixtures such as heating, lighting, organs, bells and clocks and certain new work of a similar nature;
(c) the introduction and repair of movables; and
(d) minor works affecting the churchyard.[147]

7.44 If the registrar is satisfied that the subject matter of the petition falls within the archdeacon's jurisdiction, he endorses it accordingly and sends it to the archdeacon for his consideration.[148] Although non-compliance with the Faculty Jurisdiction Rules 2000 does not render any proceedings void unless the chancellor so directs,[149] they may be set aside as irregular.[150]

7.45 Notwithstanding the jurisdiction of the archdeacon, the registrar must refer to the chancellor any petition:

(a) in which a confirmatory faculty is required;
(b) where the proposals raise a question of law or as to the doctrine, ritual or ceremonial of the Church of England or affect the legal rights of any person or body;
(c) when any person or body may need to be specially notified;
(d) where there is uncertainty whether the subject matter comes within Appendix A;
(e) where the DAC has not recommended the works;
(f) where the petition raises matters which may justify the issue of any injunction; or

---

[146] Ibid r 7(1).
[147] Ibid App A, which sets out in some detail the specific categories of work.
[148] Ibid r 7(2).
[149] Ibid r 33(1).
[150] Ibid r 33(2).

(g) where, for any other reason, it is desirable to refer the matter to the chancellor.[151]

7.46 An archdeacon must decline to exercise jurisdiction where he is the minister of the parish concerned or where he has been personally involved with the petitioner in relation to the subject matter of the petition, or otherwise to such an extent that the archdeacon deems it inappropriate so to do.[152] This is in addition to his general power to decline to exercise his jurisdiction 'for any reason' and to refer the matter to the chancellor for decision or advice.[153] If the archdeacon decides to grant a faculty, he endorses the petition accordingly and returns it to the registrar, who, on the expiry of the period for objection and provided it remains unopposed, issues a faculty and a certificate to be completed in accordance with the requirement in the faculty.[154] If an objection is received then the archdeacon's decision is of no effect and the petition is referred to be dealt with by the chancellor.[155]

Chancellor's jurisdiction

Special notice

7.47 If the chancellor directs or the law otherwise requires any person to be specially notified, the registrar must serve on that person a copy of the public notice.[156] The chancellor may also order that relevant details from the public notice be published in newspapers or other periodicals.[157] In particular, the chancellor must direct that English Heritage, the local planning authority and relevant National Amenity Societies must be specially notified if, on preliminary consideration, the chancellor considers that the works proposed:

(a) involve alteration to or extension of a listed church to such an extent as is likely to affect its character as a building of special architectural or historic interest;
(b) are likely to affect the archaeological importance of the church or archaeological remains existing within the church or its curtilage; or

---

[151] Ibid r 10(1)(a)–(g).
[152] Ibid r 8(1)(a), (b).
[153] Ibid r 8(2). Note also the duty of the archdeacon to inform the registrar of matters of urgency for referral to the chancellor: see r 8(3), discussed above.
[154] Ibid r 7(4). For the faculty, see App C Form No 5, and for the certificate, see App C Form No 6.
[155] Ibid r 7(5).
[156] Ibid r 13(1). For the public notice, see App C Form No 3.
[157] Ibid r 13(2).

(c) involve demolition affecting the exterior of an unlisted church in a conservation area.[158]

Such notification is not required if it appears to the chancellor from the available information that each of the bodies has been consulted about the works and has indicated that it has no objection or comment to make.[159] The chancellor must direct that the Commonwealth War Graves Commission be specially notified if he considers that the works or proposals will or may affect a grave or memorial which it maintains.[160]

7.48 In any case where a body has been specially notified, it has a period of 28 days from the service of the special notice to send to the registry and the petitioner a written notice of objection[161] or to send comments to the registrar in respect of the proposed works.[162]

7.49 The chancellor must direct that a notice stating the substance of the petition and giving a date by which any objection is to reach the registrar must be published by the petitioner in a newspaper circulating in the locality if:

(a) the proposals involve the alteration to or extension of a grade I or II* listed church or the exterior of a grade II listed church to such an extent as is likely to affect its character as a building of special architectural or historic interest; or

(b) the proposals involve demolition affecting the exterior of an unlisted church in a conservation area.[163]

7.50 In the case of demolition or partial demolition, particular provisions apply.[164] Notice is to be given to the Council for the Care of Churches and the DAC and, in certain circumstances, to the Secretary of State, the local planning authority, English Heritage and the National Amenity Societies.[165] Publication of an appropriate notice is also required in the *London Gazette* and such other newspapers as the chancellor may require.[166]

---

[158] Ibid r 13(3)(a)–(c). For the power to object or comment, see ibid r 13(6), discussed below.
[159] Ibid r 13(3). The previous consultation may have been by an intending applicant under r 3(3)(b) prior to DAC certification, or at the subsequent recommendation of the DAC under r 3(7), each of which is discussed below.
[160] Ibid r 13(5).
[161] The notice contains the information required by ibid App C Form No 4.
[162] Ibid r 13(6). This applies to bodies notified under r 13(3) or r 13(5).
[163] Ibid r 13(4).
[164] Care of Churches and Ecclesiastical Jurisdiction Measure 1991, s 17. These are discussed below.
[165] Ibid s 17(4)(b), (5)(a); Faculty Jurisdiction Rules 2000, r 13(7)(a).
[166] Care of Churches and Ecclesiastical Jurisdiction Measure 1991, s 17(4)(a)(ii); Faculty Jurisdiction Rules 2000, r 13(7)(b).

Consultation with the Council for the Care of Churches[167]

7.51 Unless the chancellor is satisfied that there has already been consultation with the Council for the Care of Churches in respect of the proposals, the chancellor must direct the registrar to serve on the Council notice in the prescribed form where a petition for a faculty:

(a) concerns an article[168] of particular historic, architectural, archaeological or artistic interest, and involves the introduction, conservation, alteration or disposal of that article;
(b) involves the alteration to or extension of a listed church or reordering of any church, which is likely in the opinion of the chancellor significantly to affect (when completed) the setting of any such article;
(c) involves the movement or removal of any such article, which in the opinion of the DAC may be adversely affected thereby unless specific precautions are taken.[169]

7.52 In any other case, the chancellor may direct the registrar to serve notice on the Council, where he considers that advice from the Council would be of assistance.[170] Whenever notice is given, the form must be accompanied by the petition and such of the documents as were submitted with it as the registrar considers appropriate.[171] The written advice of the Council must be sent to the registrar as soon as practicable but in any event not later than six weeks from the date of receipt of the notice.[172] If the advice is not received within that time or within such longer period as may be granted on the request of the Council, the chancellor may proceed to determine the petition without such advice.[173]

---

[167] Under clause 54 (as currently numbered) of the draft Dioceses, Pastoral and Mission Measure (approved by General Synod in February 2007) the Council for the Care of Churches will be replaced by the Church Buildings Council, whose functions will include the consideration of requests for advice from registrars, chancellors and DACs.

[168] 'Article' includes not only an ornament or moveable object, but also an object fixed to land or a building and a part of any such object: Faculty Jurisdiction Rules 2000, r 15(6).

[169] Ibid r 15(1)(a)–(c), (2). For the notice, see App C Form No 9. The DAC may recommend that intending applicants consult the Council for the Care of Churches: r 3(7). The criteria prescribed for the DAC in making the recommendation differ from those laid down for the chancellor.

[170] Ibid r 15(3).
[171] Ibid r 15(4).
[172] Ibid r 16(5).
[173] Ibid r 15(5).

Objections

7.53 Objection to the grant of a proposed faculty may be made by letter of objection by any interested person sent to the registrar and the petitioner.[174] The categories of interested persons comprise:

(a) any resident of the parish or person on its electoral roll;
(b) the archdeacon;
(c) the PCC;
(d) the local planning authority for the area within which the church is situated;
(e) any National Amenity Society;
(f) any other body designated by the chancellor for the purpose of the petition; and
(g) any other person or body appearing to the chancellor to have a sufficient interest in the subject matter of the petition.[175]

7.54 An interested person, or a body specially cited, has 28 days within which to send a written notice of objection to the registry and the petitioner.[176] Upon receipt of a letter of objection from an interested person, the registrar must, after the end of the period for public display, inform the objector in writing that he may leave the chancellor to take the letter of objection into account in reaching a decision or send to the registrar formal written particulars of objection in the prescribed form and thereby become a party to the proceedings.[177] If the former course is taken, the letter of objection is sent to the petitioners to allow them to comment on it before the chancellor reaches a decision.[178]

7.55 The registrar is obliged to supply the interested person with a copy of the form for written particulars of objection[179] and to inform him that if there is no response and no particulars of objection are received by the registrar within 21 days, he will be treated as having chosen for his letter of objection to stand.[180] The registrar must also inform the interested person of the consequences of the decision, namely

---

[174] Ibid r 16(1). There is no legal constraint preventing a member of a PCC, who disagrees with the majority in resolving to petition for a faculty, from making and pursuing an objection on his own behalf: *Re St Mary the Virgin, Bathwick*, (1 June 2005, unreported), Bath and Wells Cons Ct.
[175] Faculty Jurisdiction Rules 2000, r 16(2)(a)–(g).
[176] Ibid rr 13(6), 16(1). For an interested person the 28 days run from the display of the public notice. For a body specially cited they run from the service of the special notice.
[177] Ibid r 16(3)(a), (b). For the particulars of objection, see App C Form No 4.
[178] Ibid r 16(3)(a), (5). The petitioner has seven days within which to comment on the letter of objection. The chancellor must take into account any such letters and comments when reaching a decision on the merits or giving directions: r 16(6).
[179] Ibid r 16(4)(iii). For the particulars of objection, see App C Form No 4.
[180] Ibid r 16(4)(iv). The importance of complying with these provisions was stressed by the Court of Arches in *Re Emmanuel Church, Bentley* [2006] Fam 39, Ct of Arches.

unless he sends in formal written particulars he will not be entitled to be heard at any hearing in open court nor to make written representations, nor will he be a party for the purposes of any order for costs. He must also send a brief statement in terms approved by the chancellor as to the principles which apply to costs in the consistory court.[181]

Unopposed petitions

In the case of a petition which falls outside the archdeacon's jurisdiction in relation to which no letter of objection has been received or, if such letter has been received, no particulars of objection have been submitted within the time allowed, or where the chancellor is satisfied that all the parties concerned consent to the grant of a faculty, the chancellor may, subject to the production of any relevant evidence as he may require, grant the faculty.[182] Any faculty granted by the chancellor in unopposed proceedings must be in the prescribed form and is to be accompanied by a certificate in the prescribed form to be completed in accordance with the requirement in the faculty.[183]

7.56

Contested proceedings

Answer to particulars of objection

Where particulars of objection have been submitted to the registry, the petitioner may, and if ordered to do so must, submit to the registry a written answer thereto within 21 days of their submission.[184]

7.57

Disposal by written representations

If the chancellor considers it expedient to do so[185] and is satisfied that all the parties to the proceedings have agreed in writing,[186] he may order that the proceedings

7.58

---

181 Faculty Jurisdiction Rules 2000, r 16(4)(i), (ii). Costs are discussed separately below.
182 Ibid r 17.
183 Ibid r 12(2). For the faculty and the certificate, see App C Forms Nos 5 and 6. A form of like character with such variations as circumstances may require can be used: ibid r 36(1).
184 Ibid r 18. A copy must be served on all the other parties.
185 For a helpful illustrative list of criteria when a determination by written representations may be considered expedient, see *Re St James's, New Malden* [1994] Fam 44 at 47H–48A, [1994] 1 All ER 85 at 89, Southwark Cons Ct, per Gray Ch.
186 The importance of securing agreement in writing from any objector was emphasized by the Court of Arches in *Re Emmanuel Church, Bentley* [2006] Fam 39, Ct of Arches.

be determined upon consideration of written representations instead of by a hearing in open court.[187] When such an order has been made, the registrar must give notice requiring the petitioner to submit and serve a written statement of his case and supporting evidence within 21 days; for each of the other parties to submit and serve a written statement in reply and supporting evidence within 21 days thereafter; and for the petitioner to submit and serve a written statement in response within 14 days after that.[188] If any party does not comply with any such direction, the chancellor may declare him to be in default and proceed to dispose of the case without further reference to him.[189]

7.59 The chancellor may at any stage revoke an order that proceedings be determined on written representations, and direct instead that they be determined at an oral hearing.[190] Unless such an order is made, the chancellor determines the proceedings upon the pleadings and written statements and evidence duly submitted, and his decision is as valid and binding on all parties as if it had been made after an oral hearing.[191] The chancellor may inspect the church or any article or thing the subject of the petition or concerning which any question arises in the proceedings.[192] The chancellor or the registrar, if so authorized by the chancellor, may give such other directions as appear just and convenient for the expeditious dispatch of proceedings by way of written representations.[193]

Directions

7.60 In any faculty proceedings the chancellor may give directions in writing without a hearing or may hold a hearing for directions which the parties or their representatives, whether legally qualified or not, and such other persons as the chancellor deems fit, will be requested to attend.[194] The purposes of the giving of directions are to encourage the parties to co-operate with each other in the exchange of information and documents; to fix timetables or otherwise control the progress of proceedings; to identify the issues which will need to be resolved at a hearing; to deal with as many aspects of the matter as possible on the same occasion; and to

---

[187] Faculty Jurisdiction Rules 2000, r 26. Certain faculties for demolition or partial demolition may not be granted unless the chancellor has heard evidence in open court: Care of Churches and Ecclesiastical Jurisdiction Measure 1991, s 17(4)(d).
[188] Faculty Jurisdiction Rules 2000, r 26(2)(a)–(c).
[189] Ibid r 26(3). It is open to the party in default to apply for such declaration to be revoked, and the chancellor may revoke it on such terms as to costs or otherwise as may be just: ibid r 26(4).
[190] Ibid r 26(5). He must give directions for the future conduct of the proceedings.
[191] Ibid r 26(7).
[192] Ibid r 26(6).
[193] Ibid r 26(8).
[194] Ibid r 19(1). The chancellor or the registrar (if authorized by the chancellor) presides at any hearing for directions: r 19(1).

give directions to ensure that the petition is considered and determined as quickly and efficiently as possible.[195]

Having regard to the foregoing purposes, the chancellor must direct: **7.61**

(a) how any evidence may be presented, whether by written statement or report followed by oral evidence at the hearing, or otherwise;
(b) where there is a large number of objectors making a similar point or points in the written objections, that a specified number of them are to represent the interest of all those objectors at the hearing and may appear by themselves or by representatives, whether or not legally qualified;
(c) that there be an exchange of the reports of expert witnesses to be called by the parties and that they be requested to identify matters upon which they agree and disagree;
(d) that the number of expert witnesses be limited;
(e) that any reports provided by the DAC, the Council for the Care of Churches, English Heritage, any National Amenity Society or any local planning authority or other body be copied to the parties not less than 21 days before the date of the hearing.[196]

In deciding whether and how to give directions, the chancellor or registrar must **7.62** have regard to all the circumstances including the justice of the case, the desirability of minimizing dispute, saving unnecessary expense, avoiding delay, the number of objectors and the grounds of objection.[197]

Hearing

Within 28 days of the last date for complying with any directions which may **7.63** be given, the registrar must lay all the documents submitted to the registry before the chancellor, who must give directions as to a time and place for the hearing of the case.[198] In addition to notifying the parties, the registrar must give written notice of the time and place of the hearing to the archdeacon, the Council for the Care of Churches, the DAC and any body which has given advice to the chancellor.[199] A chancellor may exercise his powers at any place but, when a hearing is deemed appropriate, it should take place in a location convenient to the court, due regard being paid to the convenience of the parties and witnesses.[200]

---

[195] Ibid r 19(2)(i)–(v).
[196] Ibid r 19(3)(a)–(e).
[197] Ibid r 19(4). On any procedural question or issue, the chancellor is guided so far as practicable by the Civil Procedure Rules for the time being in force: r 34.
[198] Ibid r 20(1).
[199] Ibid r 20(2).
[200] Ecclesiastical Jurisdiction Measure 1963, s 80.

The chancellor may adjourn the hearing of any proceedings or application from time to time on such terms as he considers just.[201] Most chambers matters are held in the diocesan registry and the majority of open court hearings in the particular church concerned, where proper decorum may be maintained by the churchwardens.[202] If the chancellor is of the opinion that by reason of the fact that the registrar has acted for any of the parties or has otherwise been personally connected with the proceedings he ought not to sit as clerk of the court at the hearing, another practising solicitor or diocesan registrar must be appointed by the chancellor in his place.[203] Photographing or sketching the chancellor or witnesses in the court or its precincts is a contempt of court punishable by a fine.[204]

Evidence

7.64 The evidence at a hearing must be given orally, save that the chancellor may direct that all or any part be taken before an examiner or on affidavit,[205] or that a written statement may be given in evidence without the attendance of its maker.[206] In the latter case, on receipt of the statement, the chancellor may require the maker to attend for the purposes of cross-examination.[207] An application by a non-party to submit a written statement may be made provided a copy of the written statement is submitted to the registry and a copy delivered to the parties not less than 21 days before the date of the hearing.[208]

7.65 The chancellor may direct the attendance of a member of the DAC, the Council for the Care of Churches or any other person to give evidence at the hearing if it appears to him that such person may be able to give relevant evidence and is willing to give it.[209] The Council for the Care of Churches and English Heritage may apply to give evidence. Such application must be in the prescribed form, be accompanied by a statement of the evidence to be relied upon, and be made to the registry not less than 21 days before the hearing.[210] In any such case, the registrar must give the parties to the proceedings not less than 14 days' notice in writing that the

---

[201] Faculty Jurisdiction Rules 2000, r 35.
[202] See Canon E 1 para 4.
[203] Faculty Jurisdiction Rules 2000, r 30.
[204] Criminal Justice Act 1925, s 41. See *Re St Andrew, Heddington* [1978] Fam 121, Salisbury Cons Ct.
[205] Faculty Jurisdiction Rules 2000, r 21(1)(a).
[206] Ibid r 21(1)(b).
[207] Ibid r 21(3).
[208] Ibid r 21(2).
[209] Ibid r 25(1).
[210] Ibid rr 23 and 24 respectively. For the form of application, see App C Form No 10. Particular provisions apply in the case of demolition or partial demolition, discussed below.

evidence is to be given and of the name and address of the proposed witness.[211] The evidence given will be subject to cross-examination by the parties to the proceedings.[212]

Grant of planning permission

The 'ecclesiastical exemption' removes churches from the need for listed building consent but planning permission is still required in respect of operational development, namely the construction of a new church, or the extension of an existing one, or works which materially affect the exterior of the church or its environs.[213] The chancellor generally expects planning permission to have been granted, in outline at least,[214] prior to a petition being lodged for a faculty. It is considered that if issues are raised with the local planning authority by objectors, such as car parking, access, traffic flow and the effect of proposals on the views and the privacy of neighbouring landowners, and planning permission is nonetheless granted, those matters cannot be re-litigated in the consistory court in the absence of some sound and compelling reason.[215]

7.66

Service of documents

The service of any document may be effected by leaving it at the proper address of the person to be served; by sending it by post to that address or by leaving it

7.67

---

[211] Ibid r 25(2). In the case of a witness directed to attend by the chancellor (where no statement of the evidence will have been supplied), the registrar must state the nature of the evidence required of the witness: ibid r 25(2).

[212] Ibid r 25(3).

[213] Floodlighting and the repair of footpaths are instances where some local planning authorities require planning permission to be sought and others do not.

[214] Or a written declaration that planning permission is not required.

[215] See *Re St Peter and St Paul, Upper Teddington* [1993] 1 WLR 852, London Cons Ct; *Re St Mary, Kings Worthy* (1998) 5 Ecc LJ 155, Winchester Cons Ct; *Re St James, Stalmine* (2000) 6 Ecc LJ 81, Blackburn Cons Ct; *Re St Kenelm, Upton Snodsbury* (2001) 6 Ecc LJ 293, Worcester Cons Court; and *Re All Saints, Hordle* (2002) 7 Ecc LJ 238, Winchester Cons Court. In *Re St Laurence, Alvechurch* (2003) 7 Ecc LJ 367, Worcester Cons Court, Mynors Ch stated at paras 63–64: 'a consistory court should not reconsider matters such as the bulk, height and scale of an extension, or its architectural relationship to the listed building to which it is to be attached, since those matters must have been considered by the planning authority when it granted planning permission. Indeed the very fact that listed building consent is not required means that the authority would (or should) have been all the more likely to give thorough consideration to such matters, since it would not have a second chance to do so. Further, the result of allowing a consistory court to revisit these matters following an earlier decision by the planning authority to grant planning permission would in effect be to grant to those dissatisfied by that decision a right of appeal—a development that has been steadfastly resisted by Parliament in spite of much pressure in certain quarters'.

at a document exchange.[216] Service by fax is only permissible where the party acts by a solicitor.[217] The chancellor or registrar may direct that service be effected in any other manner, including electronic means.[218]

Burden and standard of proof

7.68 The burden of proof generally lies on the petitioner, who is normally proposing a change to the status quo. The desires of the parishioners are of considerable weight and, where there is unanimity, their wishes may determine a petition where the evidence is otherwise evenly balanced.[219] Where the parishioners are divided, the force of the majority view will be diminished. There is, however, no presumption that the views of the parishioners will invariably prevail, since such is to usurp the function of the chancellor and the discretion which he is obliged by statute to exercise. There is some difficulty in proving the views of the parishioners, since they may not necessarily be coterminous with the minuted decisions of the PCC. Petitions bearing numerous signatures are of little evidential value without proof of the representations which preceded the application of each signature.[220] An alternative course is for the churchwardens (*qua* officers of the bishop) to give evidence on oath as to the result of inquiries conducted by themselves concerning local opinion.[221]

7.69 As to the standard of proof, the civil standard is applied, so that a faculty will issue if the balance of evidence favours its grant rather than its refusal. It has been stated that the 'more apt' approach to the granting of any faculty is that 'the answer should be "yes" unless there are good reasons for saying "no"'.[222]

7.70 However, the position is different when a listed building is concerned. Various articulations of the appropriate test have been propounded over the years,[223] but

---

[216] Faculty Jurisdiction Rules 2000, r 31(1)(a)–(c). 'Proper address' is taken to be a person's usual or last known address, or the business address of the solicitor, if any, acting for him in the proceedings: r 31(2).
[217] Faculty Jurisdiction Rules 2000, r 31(1)(d), (4).
[218] Ibid r 31(1)(e).
[219] See *Re St Michael and All Angels, Great Torrington* [1985] Fam 81, [1985] 1 All ER 993, Ct of Eccl Causes Res; *Re St Mary, Banbury* [1986] Fam 24, [1985] 2 All ER 611, Oxford Cons Ct; *Re St Stephen, Walbrook* [1987] Fam 146, [1987] 2 All ER 578, Ct of Eccl Causes Res; *Re All Saints, Melbourne* [1990] 1 WLR 833, [1992] 2 All ER 786, Ct of Arches.
[220] See *Re Christ Church, Chislehurst* [1973] 1 WLR 1317 at 1321, [1974] 1 All ER 146 at 150, Rochester Cons Ct.
[221] *Re St Luke, Chelsea* [1976] Fam 295 at 317–318, [1976] 1 All ER 609 at 628, London Cons Ct.
[222] *Re St James, New Malden* [1994] Fam 44 at 48H, [1994] 1 All ER 85 at 90, Southwark Cons Ct.
[223] *Re St Mary, Banbury* [1987] Fam 136, [1987] 1 All ER 247, Ct of Arches, as developed in *Re All Saints, Melbourn* [1990] 1 WLR 833 at 844A, [1992] 2 All ER 786 at 796, Ct of Arches.

the Court of Arches, in its judgment in *Re St Luke the Evangelist, Maidstone*,[224] has declared that the correct approach is to adopt what are generally styled the '*Bishopsgate* Questions',[225] namely:

(a) Have the petitioners proved a necessity for some or all of the proposed works either because they are necessary for the pastoral well-being of [the parish] or for some other compelling reason?
(b) Will some or all of the works adversely affect the character of the church as a building of special architectural and historical interest?
(c) If the answer to (b) is yes, then is the necessity proved by the petitioners such that in the exercise of the court's discretion a faculty should be granted for some or all of the works?[226]

The consistory courts of both provinces have been 'loyally applying' this approach,[227] such that it is now regarded as having universal application.[228] The suggestion of one chancellor that a fourth question be added[229] has not gained currency.[230] However, contrary to the clear prescriptive guidance of the Court of Arches,[231] in a number of cases determined on their own particular facts, the

7.71

A different test had been propounded by the Court of Ecclesiastical Causes Reserved in *Re St Stephen, Walbrook* [1987] Fam 146 at 192, [1987] 2 All ER 578 at 600, Ct of Eccl Causes Res.
[224] *Re St Luke the Evangelist, Maidstone* [1995] Fam 1, [1995] 1 All ER 321, Ct of Arches.
[225] First posed by Chancellor Cameron in *Re St Helen, Bishopsgate*, 26 November 1993 (unreported), London Cons Ct, noted in (1993) 3 Ecc LJ 256.
[226] This passage was quoted and approved in *Re St Luke the Evangelist, Maidstone* [1995] Fam 1 at 8H–9B, [1995] 1 All ER 321 at 328, Ct of Arches.
[227] To quote from *Re Wadsley Parish Church* (2001) 6 Ecc LJ 172, Sheffield Cons Court, per McClean Ch.
[228] The *Bishopsgate* Questions were discussed and followed by the Court of Arches in *Re St Mary the Virgin, Sherborne* [1996] Fam 63, [1996] 3 All ER 769, Ct of Arches In *Re St Mary, Longstock*, [2006] 1 WLR 259, Winchester Cons Ct, Hill Dep Ch stated at para 11, 'there is a danger of descending into too sophisticated an analysis of the *Bishopsgate* questions. They derive from a first instance decision of the highly experienced Cameron Ch (as she then was); were readily adopted by the Court of Arches in *Re St Luke the Evangelist, Maidstone*; and have been consistently applied subsequently by the appellate court and consistory courts of both provinces. They have brought about a welcome consistency of approach. But ... they are not a catechism nor a mantra. I do not think it would be helpful for me to reformulate the questions. Nothing is gained by different chancellors articulating subtly nuanced variations of principles of general application'.
[229] Mynors Ch in *Re Holy Cross, Pershore* [2002] Fam 1, (2001) 6 Ecc LJ 86, Worcester Cons Ct, had proposed that 'there is a fourth question that should always be asked ... namely, what are likely to be the pastoral consequences, both short-term and looking further ahead, of making a proposed change?'.
[230] In *Re Wadsley Parish Church* (2001) 6 Ecc LJ 172, Sheffield Cons Court, McClean Ch stated 'I fear that I am not attracted by the notion of a "fourth *Bishopsgate* question" I believe that the *Bishopsgate* questions provide a framework which enables all relevant matters to be considered. What factors are relevant, and the weight each factor should be given, must depend on the particular constellation of facts: whether for example, the parish is divided or is faced only with opposition from without. I do not think it would be helpful to develop a *Bishopsgate* catechism and so impose an unduly prescriptive framework on the balancing process chancellors must perform'.
[231] *Re St Mary the Virgin, Sherborne* [1996] Fam 63, [1996] 3 All ER 769, Ct of Arches at pp 77–78, and p 782 respectively: ' ... by the questions and their order we wish to stress the fact that

order in which the first two questions are asked has been reversed by the chancellor, without the strong presumption against change being displaced.[232]

7.72 'Necessity' is a broad concept.[233] It embraces more than merely unavoidable repair work and includes works 'necessary for … pastoral well-being … or for some other compelling reason'.[234] In *Re St John the Evangelist, Blackheath*, Chancellor George ventured that 'necessity' and 'necessary' in the context of the *Bishopsgate* Questions mean 'something less than essential, but more than merely desirable or convenient; in other words something that is requisite or reasonably necessary'.[235] However the test is put, in the case of a listed building the burden of proof lies on those who advocate the alteration, and it is a burden which is not easily discharged.

Judgments and orders

7.73 The chancellor may either deliver an ex tempore judgment upon the conclusion of argument or a reserved judgment, which is normally in writing. Whichever be the case, he should allow the parties the opportunity to address him upon the terms of any proposed order, including the question of costs. If the chancellor decides to grant a faculty, following a hearing in open court or a determination on written representations, the registrar issues a faculty in the prescribed form adapted to meet the circumstances of the case, together with a certificate to be completed in accordance with the requirement in the faculty.[236] The certificate must be completed and returned to the registry within four weeks of completion of the works.

---

with listed buildings the presumption is so strongly in favour of no alteration that the first question which must be asked is: are the alterations necessary? The present order of questions emphasises that for listed buildings the presumption is heavily against change. To change the order of the questions would, we believe, cause confusion and might seem to some to indicate a relaxation of the requirements before change will be authorised. No such relaxation is intended or desired by this court'.

[232] *Re St Gregory, Offchurch* [2000] 1 WLR 2471, [2000] 4 All ER 378, Coventry Cons Ct, a case concerning a memorial window, which was followed in *Re St Mary, Longstock*, [2006] 1 WLR 259, Winchester Cons Ct. See also *Re St Peter, Walworth* (2002) 7 Ecc LJ 103, Southwark Cons Court; *Re Parish of Stourbridge, St Thomas* (2001) 20 CCCC No 39, Worcester Cons Court, *Re All Saints Church, Crondall* (2002) 6 Ecc LJ 420, Guildford Cons Court, and *Re Dorchester Abbey* (2002) 7 Ecc LJ 105, Oxford Cons Court. For an insightful discussion, see W Adam, 'Changing Approaches to the *Bishopsgate* Questions' in (2003) 7 Ecc LJ 215.
[233] See *Re St Mary the Virgin, Sherborne* [1996] Fam 63, [1996] 3 All ER 769, Ct of Arches.
[234] To borrow from the judgment of Cameron Ch (as she then was) in *Re St Helen, Bishopsgate* (1993) 3 Ecc LJ 256, a factor also to be found in *Re All Saints, Melbourn* [1990] 1 WLR 833, [1992] 2 All ER 786.
[235] *Re St John the Evangelist, Blackheath* (1998) 5 Ecc LJ 217, Southwark Cons Ct.
[236] Faculty Jurisdiction Rules 2000, r 27. For the form of faculty, see App C Form No 5, and for the form of certificate, see App C Form No 6.

7.74 Any number of conditions may be attached to a faculty,[237] and their status may be heightened by extracting an undertaking as to compliance. Such conditions may include a condition that the works are supervised by the archdeacon or another person,[238] such as an architect, or that a specified period of time is to elapse before an article may be disposed of.[239] Nearly all faculties include a time limit within which the authorized works must be completed. A faculty which authorizes works to be done may order that in the case of default by the person authorized to carry them out, the archdeacon should do so and the expenses he incurs be borne by that person.[240]

7.75 A chancellor has power to amend or set aside a faculty whenever he is satisfied that it is just and expedient to do so,[241] thus the inclusion in an order of the expressions 'until further order' or 'with liberty to apply', whilst they may be useful clarification and a reminder for the parties, are strictly unnecessary.

Contempt of court

7.76 If a person is in contempt of the consistory court, whether by act or omission, the chancellor may certify the act or omission to the High Court.[242] On receiving the certificate, the High Court may thereupon inquire into the alleged act or omission and, after hearing any witnesses who may be produced against or on behalf of the person who is the subject of the allegation, and after hearing any statement that may be offered in defence, may exercise the same jurisdiction and powers as if that person had been guilty of contempt of the High Court.[243]

Appeals

7.77 Appeals are governed by the Faculty Jurisdiction (Appeals) Rules 1998.[244] Faculty appeals are heard by the Court of Arches,[245] unless they concern a question of doctrine, ritual or ceremonial. In the latter, which are styled reserved matters, the

---

[237] Care of Churches and Ecclesiastical Jurisdiction Measure 1991, s 12(1).
[238] Ibid s 12(1)(a).
[239] Ibid s 12(1)(b).
[240] Ibid s 12(2).
[241] Faculty Jurisdiction Rules 2000, r 33(2). See also *Re St Peter, St Helier, Merton* [1992] 1 WLR 343, Southwark Cons Ct.
[242] Ecclesiastical Jurisdiction Measure 1963, s 81(2), substituted by the Care of Churches and Ecclesiastical Jurisdiction Measure 1991, s 8(1), Sch 4 para 11.
[243] Ecclesiastical Jurisdiction Measure 1963, s 81(3), as so substituted. This is done by motion. See also *R v Editor, Printers and Publishers of the Daily Herald, ex parte Bishop of Norwich* [1932] 2 KB 402.
[244] Faculty Jurisdiction (Appeals) Rules 1998, SI 1998/1713.
[245] In which the Dean of Arches sits together with two diocesan chancellors designated by the Dean: Ecclesiastical Jurisdiction Measure 1963, s 47(1)(b).

appeal is to the Court of Ecclesiastical Causes Reserved.[246] In determining to which court an appeal lies, the chancellor is required to certify upon the application of the party desiring to appeal whether or not a question of doctrine, ritual or ceremonial is involved.[247] Notwithstanding the certificate, the appellate courts each have jurisdiction to cross-refer the matter to the more appropriate tribunal.[248]

7.78 Leave is required before a faculty matter may be appealed to the Court of Arches. Such leave may be given by the consistory court or, if it is refused, by the Dean of Arches.[249] Leave will usually be given if there is an argument which may be presented with a reasonable chance of successfully reversing the decision of the consistory court.[250] Appeals are governed by the provisions of the Faculty Jurisdiction (Appeals) Rules 1998.[251] The Court of Arches may direct that an appeal be determined on written representations if it appears just so to do.[252] Further evidence may be adduced on appeal if the Court of Arches grants leave.[253]

Costs

7.79 An archdeacon has no power to award costs or expenses,[254] and is required to refer to the chancellor any petition for a faculty where he considers that the matter, 'gives rise to any question as to the payment of costs or expenses'.[255] The chancellor may at any stage of the proceedings order any party to give security for costs.[256] The Court of Arches has observed that the principles which apply within the faculty jurisdiction on the subject of costs do not appear to be well known or understood.[257] Two separate items of cost fall to be considered—first the court costs themselves, and secondly the legal fees, expenses and disbursements which

---

[246] Ibid s 10(1). The composition of the court is given at ibid s 5.
[247] Ibid s 10(3).
[248] Ibid s 10(4), (5).
[249] Ibid s 7(2).
[250] See the guidance in *Re St Mary the Virgin, Sherborne* [1996] Fam 63 at 66G–H, [1996] 3 All ER 769 at 772e, Ct of Arches.
[251] SI 1998/1713.
[252] *Re Christ Church, Alsager* [1999] Fam 142 at 145A–C, [1999] 1 All ER 117 at 119, Ch Ct of York.
[253] Faculty Jurisdiction (Appeals) Rules 1998, r 12.
[254] Care of Churches and Ecclesiastical Jurisdiction Measure 1991, s 14(5)(a).
[255] Faculty Jurisdiction Rules 2000, r 8(3)(c).
[256] Ecclesiastical Jurisdiction Measure 1963, s 60(1). The Court of Arches has power to order security for the costs of an appeal: Faculty Jurisdiction (Appeals) Rules 1998, SI 1998/1713, r 8.
[257] *Re St Mary the Virgin, Sherborne* [1996] Fam 63 at 69F, [1996] 3 All ER 769 at 774b, Ct of Arches.

may be incurred by the parties. Accordingly, the Court of Arches sought to set out the relevant principles which may be summarized as follows:

(a) Court fees:
  (i) When proposed works are unopposed and have the support of the DAC, the fees may be borne by the diocesan board of finance if such a diocesan arrangement is in place.
  (ii) If proposed works are opposed, fees become payable at rates fixed by Fees Orders made by the Fees Advisory Commission under the Ecclesiastical Fees Measure 1986 and such fees are payable by the petitioner even when an opposed petition is granted.
  (iii) An order for reimbursement by an objector to the petitioner of some or all of the court fees is unlikely to be made unless there is clear evidence of unreasonable behaviour which has unnecessarily added to the procedural costs prior to or at the hearing.
  (iv) Since appeals to the Court of Arches lie only with leave, the same principles will apply as in the consistory court on the question of court costs.
(b) Legal expenses of the parties
  (i) The practice in the consistory court is not to make an order for costs between the parties save where unreasonable behaviour has occurred.
  (ii) If a party appeals to the Court of Arches and is unsuccessful, then there is no reason why as a general rule that party should not pay the other party's costs of the appeal.[258]

The Ecclesiastical Judges Association has produced a booklet which gives further guidance on the manner in which issues of costs fall to be determined.[259] Objectors have been ordered to reimburse the petitioners in whole or in part in a number of instances. The determining factor is the extent to which any unreasonable conduct on their part has resulted in additional costs. In both *Re St Peter, Oundle*[260] and *Re All Saints, North Street*,[261] the non-acceptance by the opponents of uncontested expert evidence was considered unreasonable. In *Re All Saints, Small Heath*,[262] the lack of realism and common sense on the part of the Victorian Society was regarded as unreasonable. In another case, Chancellor Cameron ordered that certain objectors make a contribution to the costs of a matter determined on

7.80

---

[258] *Re St Mary the Virgin, Sherborne* [1996] Fam 63 at 68F–71A, [1996] 3 All ER 769 at 774c–775h, Ct of Arches. The Court of Arches departed from this principle in relation to a cross-appeal in *Re Welford Road Cemetery, Leicester* [2007] 1 All ER 426, [2007] 2 WLR 506, citing exceptional features peculiar to the particular case.
[259] *Guidance on the Award of Costs in Faculty Proceedings in the Consistory Court* (Ecclesiastical Judges Association, February 2000).
[260] *Re St Peter, Oundle* (1996) 4 Ecc LJ 764, Peterborough Cons Ct.
[261] *Re All Saints, North Street* (1999) 5 Ecc LJ 486, York Cons Ct.
[262] *Re All Saints, Small Heath* (1998) 5 Ecc LJ 211, Birmingham Cons Ct.

written representations. She remarked 'informed opposition within a democratic church is acceptable but an unwillingness to look at the matter objectively and on the basis of information is in my judgment unreasonable and unacceptable'.[263] In one case, however, an opponent who was held not to have behaved unreasonably, was ordered to pay a proportion of the court costs, representing the time taken up in considering the 'less weighty' grounds which he had advanced.[264]

7.81 It is also not unknown for stonemasons or others involved in carrying out works to be ordered to pay costs.[265] The expenses of an archdeacon[266] intervening in proceedings with the leave of the court will generally be treated as court costs unless a good reason is shown to the contrary.[267] They will therefore fall to be borne by the petitioner in the ordinary course of events. The rationale is that the archdeacon is not a party in the traditional adversarial sense arguing for a contrary result, but instead acts as *amicus curiae*, assisting the court in addressing matters of evidence and law. This approach is followed in the booklet emanating from the Ecclesiastical Judges Association.[268]

7.82 As to the amount of any costs, the court fees are fixed under Fees Orders made by the Fees Advisory Commission pursuant to the Ecclesiastical Fees Measure 1986. In broad terms, the fees are made up of a lodgment fee, a 'correspondence fee' covering the registrar's supervisory costs and hearing fees, including those for pre-trial reviews and directions, as well as for the time taken in preparing a judgment. Any legal costs of one party ordered to be paid by another are subject to taxation.[269] Alternatively, a specified gross sum in lieu of taxed costs may be specified.[270]

---

[263] *Re St Michael, Aveley* (1997) 4 Ecc LJ 770, Chelmsford Cons Ct.
[264] *Re St Peter and St Paul, Wantage (No 2)* (1999) 5 Ecc LJ 387, Oxford Cons Ct.
[265] *Re Woldingham Churchyard* [1957] 1 WLR 811, [1957] 2 All ER 323, Southwark Cons Ct; *Re St Mark, Haydock (No 2)* [1981] 1 WLR 1167, Liverpool Cons Ct. See also *Re St Thomas à Becket, Framfield* [1989] 1 WLR 689, [1989] 1 All ER 170, Chichester Cons Ct, in which an architect was criticized for supervising works for which no faculty had been obtained, and *Re St Peter and St Paul, Scrayingham* [1992] 1 WLR 87, [1991] 4 All ER 411, York Cons Ct.
[266] These are the responsibility of the diocesan board of finance: Care of Churches and Ecclesiastical Jurisdiction Measure 1991, s 16(4).
[267] *Re St John the Evangelist, Blackheath* (1998) 5 Ecc LJ 217, Southwark Cons Ct. Reliance was placed on *Re St Mary, Barton-on-Humber* [1987] Fam 41 at 57, [1987] 2 All ER 861 at 877, Lincoln Cons Ct; *Re St Stephen, Walbrook* [1987] Fam 146 at 158, [1987] 2 All ER 578 at 605, Ct of Eccl Causes Res; and *Re St Matthew, Wimbledon* [1985] 3 All ER 670 at 673, Southwark Cons Ct. The point was conceded by counsel in *Re Holy Trinity, Bosham* [2004] Fam 125, [2004] 2 All ER 820, Chichester Cons Ct.
[268] *Guidance on the Award of Costs in Faculty Proceedings* (n 259 above) para 13.
[269] See generally the Ecclesiastical Jurisdiction Measure 1963, s 60, amended by the Church of England (Legal Aid and Miscellaneous Provisions) Measure 1988, s 14(1), Sch 2 para 1; the Care of Churches and Ecclesiastical Jurisdiction Measure 1991, s 8(1), Sch 4 para 9; the Church of England (Legal Aid) Measure 1994, s 7(2), Sch 2 para 1; and the Care of Cathedrals (Supplementary Provisions) Measure 1994, s 8, Schedule para 4. The taxing officer is the registrar, subject to an appeal to the chancellor.
[270] Ecclesiastical Jurisdiction Measure 1963, s 60(3)(b).

Awards for the payment of costs may be recovered by proceedings in the county court for the district in which the award was made as if the sum was a contract debt payable by the person against whom it was made.[271] The registrar's certificate that the amount stated is due to be paid pursuant to an order of the consistory court is conclusive evidence of the facts certified.[272] Furthermore, any sum payable by virtue of an order of the consistory court in or consequent upon any proceeding for a faculty are, if the county court so orders, recoverable by execution issued from the county court or otherwise as if payable under an order of that court.[273]

Emergency and remedial powers

The consequences of works being carried out in the absence of a faculty were discussed at the beginning of this chapter. An application may be made for a confirmatory faculty, but one will not be granted as of right and, if granted, may be subject to conditions and also carry cost penalties. If an article is introduced without a faculty,[274] it will be necessary to seek a confirmatory faculty for its retention and, in the alternative, a faculty for its removal should the former not be granted. The archdeacon's default powers have already been discussed.[275] The chancellor has power to issue a special citation adding as a party to the proceedings a person alleged to be responsible, wholly or in part, for an act or default in consequence of which proceedings have been instituted.[276] Such person may be ordered to pay all or part of the costs of and consequential to the proceedings, including expenses incurred in carrying out the works authorized by the faculty.[277] Unless deliberate concealment can be shown, the foregoing powers may not be invoked more than six years after the act was committed.[278]

7.83

The consistory court has power to issue injunctions to prevent threatened illegal acts and restoration orders to restore the status quo following illegal acts.[279] The exercise of these powers is governed by the Faculty Jurisdiction (Injunctions and

7.84

---

[271] Ibid s 61(1).
[272] Ibid s 61(2).
[273] Faculty Jurisdiction Measure 1964, s 11.
[274] *Re Escot Church* [1979] P 125, Exeter Cons Ct. An object which is unlawfully introduced into a church may only be removed with the authority of a faculty.
[275] Care of Churches and Ecclesiastical Jurisdiction Measure 1991, s 12(2).
[276] Ibid s 13(2).
[277] Ibid s 13(1).
[278] Ibid s 13(7), (9).
[279] Ibid s 13(4), (5). A purported restoration order which amounts to improvement and goes beyond that which the court considers necessary 'for the purpose of restoring the position so far as possible to that which existed immediately before the act was committed' (s 13(5)) will be struck down: *Re Welford Road Cemetery, Leicester* [2007] 2 WLR 506, [2007] 1 All ER 426, Ct of Arches, para 55.

Restoration Orders) Rules 1992, and any order made in the absence of compliance with these rules is susceptible to being set aside on appeal.[280] The power to make a restoration order concerns the commission of unlawful acts 'in relation to a church or churchyard in the diocese'.[281] The Court of Arches has determined that, despite a first instance decision to the contrary,[282] the expression 'churchyard' in this instance bears its ordinary meaning,[283] and that the chancellor's enforcement powers under this provision do not extend to the consecrated part of local authority cemeteries.[284]

7.85 The Rules provide for the archdeacon, or any other person appearing to the registrar or chancellor to have a sufficient interest in the matter,[285] to make an appropriate application in writing supported by affidavit.[286] The application may not be served unless it contains details of a date of hearing provided by the registrar who issues the application.[287] Service must be effected upon the person against whom an order is sought at least two days before the date of the hearing and, if faculty proceedings are already in train in relation to the same matter, upon all parties to those proceedings.[288] A copy of the application must be sent by the applicant to the archdeacon and the minister.[289] The registrar must be satisfied that the relevant persons have been served before he lays the application before the chancellor.[290]

7.86 Any person served with an application may serve and lodge affidavit evidence by way of answer within 14 days or, subject to the directions of the chancellor,

---

[280] As was the case in *Re Welford Road Cemetery, Leicester* [2007] 2 WLR 506, [2007] 1 All ER 426, Ct of Arches, discussed further below.

[281] Care of Churches and Ecclesiastical Jurisdiction Measure 1991, s 13(5).

[282] *Re West Norwood Cemetery* [1994] Fam 210, [1995] 1 All ER 387, Southwark Cons Ct, at 230 and 404 respectively per Gray Ch in which he had held that a churchyard included a burial ground or a cemetery.

[283] Namely 'an enclosed ground on which a church stands, esp as used for burials' (*Shorter Oxford English Dictionary* (5th edn, Oxford: Oxford University Press, 2002), as adopted in *Re Welford Road Cemetery, Leicester* [2007] 2 WLR 506, [2007] 1 All ER 426, Ct of Arches, para 57.

[284] *Re Welford Road Cemetery, Leicester* [2007] 2 WLR 506, [2007] 1 All ER 426, Ct of Arches, para 58. However, the general power in the Care of Churches and Ecclesiastical Jurisdiction Measure 1991, s 12, 'is widely drawn and enables the court to require work to be done as a condition of a faculty': para 59. This will be a matter of fact and degree in each individual case.

[285] Faculty Jurisdiction (Injunctions and Restoration Orders) Rules 1992, SI 1992/2884, r 3.

[286] Ibid r 4(1), (2). Form 1 in the Appendix should be used.

[287] Ibid r 4(3).

[288] Ibid r 5(1)(a)(i), (ii), (b). Should service prove impracticable, leave may be obtained for such steps to be taken as the registrar directs to bring the application to the notice of the person to be served: r 5(1)(a)(iii). Although the rule refers to the court giving leave, it would appear that only the registrar has power to do so because he is prevented from laying an application before the chancellor until he is satisfied that service has been effective: r 5(3). For the purposes of these rules, 'court' includes the registrar: ibid r 2(1). As to the mode of service, see r 10(1).

[289] Ibid r 5(2).

[290] Ibid r 5(3). Proof of service may be by way of affidavit.

may give oral evidence at the hearing.[291] Evidence at the hearing is on affidavit, unless leave is given for evidence to be taken orally, and the deponents may be required to be cross-examined.[292] The chancellor may issue an injunction or make a restoration order on such terms as appear to him to be just.[293] There is a mandatory requirement that he sets out those terms in an order in the prescribed form, which must contain a notice stating that failure to comply without reasonable excuse with any requirement of the injunction is a contempt of court.[294] Any order requiring a person to do an act must state the time within which that act is to be done,[295] and the chancellor must give such directions as to service of the order as he considers appropriate.[296] The chancellor may on the hearing of the application, give such directions in relation to the institution of faculty proceedings as he considers appropriate.[297] No restoration order will be granted in respect of a wrong which occurred more than six years prior to the application, unless deliberate concealment can be shown.[298]

Where the urgency is so great that the applicant considers it necessary to apply to the chancellor without effecting service as outlined above, he may so inform the registrar, who must immediately refer the matter to the chancellor, and the chancellor may issue an injunction on such terms as may appear to him to be just by way of an order in the prescribed form.[299] However, he must require the applicant to serve an application immediately on the persons against whom the injunction is issued, order that the injunction is to continue in force for a specified time which, unless he otherwise directs, is not to be more than 14 days, and give directions for the hearing of the application.[300]   **7.87**

---

[291] Ibid r 6(1), (2).
[292] Ibid r 7(1).
[293] Ibid r 7(2)(a).
[294] Ibid r 7(2)(a) and Appendix, Forms 2, 3. The absence of a penal notice was one of the reasons for setting aside the so-called 'restoration order' made by the chancellor in *Re Welford Road Cemetery, Leicester* [2007] 2 WLR 506, [2007] 1 All ER 426. Further, there was no reference in the chancellor's judgment to the Faculty Jurisdiction (Injunctions and Restoration Orders) Rules 1992.
[295] Ibid r 7(2)(b).
[296] Ibid r 7(2)(c).
[297] Ibid r 7(3).
[298] Care of Churches and Ecclesiastical Jurisdiction Measure 1991, s 13(8), (9), (10). The six-year period runs from the time when the archdeacon discovered the concealment or could, with reasonable diligence, have discovered it: s 13(9).
[299] Faculty Jurisdiction (Injunctions and Restoration Orders) Rules 1992, s 8(1) and Appendix, Form 4.
[300] Ibid r 8(1)(a)–(c). Should it transpire that the injunction ought not to have been granted, an undertaking in damages is a normal prerequisite in civil litigation.

7.88 The chancellor has power to issue an injunction of his own motion.[301] In addition, the chancellor may make a restoration order of his own motion[302] but only after first considering the desirability of directing a special citation requiring a person's attendance before the court and giving that person an opportunity to be heard as to whether or not a restoration order should be made.[303] In *Re Welford Road Cemetery*, a so-called 'restoration order' was quashed on the basis that the chancellor 'was in error because procedural fairness demanded that the council should be forewarned and given a proper opportunity to address the court about such an order and its proposed extent, and this was not done'.[304]

7.89 The chancellor may vary, extend or discharge the order as he thinks fit[305] and give such directions as appear necessary to enable the proceedings to be expeditiously and justly determined, including adjourning them from time to time on such terms as he considers fit.[306] He may also make such order for costs as he considers just.[307] Failure to comply with an injunction or restoration order is a contempt of court.[308] It is particularly important, therefore, that injunctions and restoration orders state with precision what is required of the wrongdoer, in order that he may effect compliance.[309]

Particular cases

7.90 It is not the purpose of this work to examine each and all of the many particular instances where the faculty jurisdiction falls to be invoked.[310] However, what follows is a brief miscellany of the more common. For convenience, they are arranged alphabetically.

---

[301] Ibid r 8(2) and Appendix Form 5. See also the Care of Churches and Ecclesiastical Jurisdiction Measure 1991, s 13(6).
[302] Ibid s 13(6).
[303] Faculty Jurisdiction (Injunctions and Restoration Orders) Rules 1992, r 9 and Appendix Form 6.
[304] *Re Welford Road Cemetery, Leicester* [2007] 2 WLR 506, [2007] 1 All ER 426, Ct of Arches, para 52.
[305] Faculty Jurisdiction (Injunctions and Restoration Orders) Rules 1992, r 10(2).
[306] Ibid r 10(3).
[307] Ibid r 11.
[308] Care of Churches and Ecclesiastical Jurisdiction Measure 1991, s 13(11).
[309] *Re Welford Road Cemetery, Leicester* [2007] 2 WLR 506, [2007] 1 All ER 426, Ct of Arches, para 58.
[310] Reference may be made to the collection of judgments maintained at the Middle Temple Library, in its series of Consistory and Commissary Court Cases, which commence in 1891 and continue to the present day. The text of judgments for the period 1891–2004 is available on CD-ROM and may be purchased from the Ecclesiastical Law Society.

Altars

The Canons require that in every church a convenient table of wood, stone or other suitable material must be provided for the celebration of holy communion; and it must stand in the main body of the church or in the chancel.[311] What constitutes a table and the nature of eucharistic sacrifice are widely discussed in the three substantive judgments of the Court of Ecclesiastical Causes Reserved in *Re St Stephen, Walbrook*,[312] delivered respectively by the Rt Revd Eric Kemp, then Bishop of Chichester, Sir Ralph Gibson and Sir Anthony Lloyd.[313] **7.91**

Churchyards

Churchyards may be consecrated or unconsecrated. Those contiguous to church buildings are usually consecrated and fall within the jurisdiction of the consistory court.[314] As the late Chancellor Gray observed: **7.92**

> The effect of consecration is to subject the land consecrated to the Ordinary, who thenceforth has jurisdiction to see that in the consecrated ground the laws of the church are observed, and in particular to see that in consecrated places of burial all conditions which the laws of the church require in relation to the bodies or persons buried there are observed.[315]

Unconsecrated churchyards within the curtilage of the church are covered by the faculty jurisdiction.[316] Those parts of local authority cemeteries which are consecrated also come within the faculty jurisdiction, albeit there is no power to make a restoration order.[317]

So long as the churchyard remains 'open', ie it is possible in practical terms to carry out further burials,[318] nothing may be authorized in any part of it which will prevent that part being used for burials.[319] The role of the consistory court in relation **7.93**

---

[311] Canon F 2 para 1. Any dispute as to where it should stand must be determined by the Ordinary. See Canon F 2 para 1. This will be the chancellor exercising the jurisdiction of the bishop in the consistory court.

[312] *Re St Stephen, Walbrook* [1987] Fam 146, [1987] 2 All ER 578, Ct of Eccl Causes Res. For a more recent discussion, see *Re St Catherine, Littleton* (2005) 8 Ecc LJ 376, Winchester Cons Ct. For a dispute concerning moving an altar to allow westward facing eucharistic presidency, see *Re St Barbara, Earlsdon* (2002) 7 Ecc LJ 490, Coventry Cons Ct.

[313] The Bishop of Rochester and the Rt Revd KJ Woollcombe each concurred with all three.

[314] *Re Caister-on-Sea Parish* [1958] 1 WLR 309, *sub nom Norfolk County Council v Knights and Caister-on-Sea Joint Burial Committee* [1958] 1 All ER 394, Norwich Cons Ct; *Re St John, Chelsea* [1962] 1 WLR 706, [1962] 2 All ER 850, London Cons Ct.

[315] *Re West Norwood Cemetery* [1994] Fam 210 at 223E, Southwark Cons Ct.

[316] Faculty Jurisdiction Measure 1964, s 7(1).

[317] *Re Welford Road Cemetery, Leicester* [2007] 2 WLR 506, [2007] 1 All ER 426, Ct of Arches, para 58.

[318] The consequences of closure are discussed below.

[319] See *Re St Martin le Grand, York* [1990] Fam 63, [1989] 2 All ER 711, York Cons Ct.

to a consecrated burial ground was discussed in *Re St John, Chelsea*.[320] Save for the purpose of enlarging a church, chapel, meeting house or other place of worship,[321] no building may be erected upon a disused burial ground.[322] This prohibition includes any temporary or moveable building.[323]

7.94 There is a provision under the Open Spaces Act 1906 for the transfer, subject to the grant of a faculty, of a disused burial ground to a local authority so that it may be enjoyed by the public as an open space.[324] Easements such as rights of way or rights to light may be created over a churchyard.[325]

7.95 The closure of a burial ground by Order in Council under the Burial Act 1853 will only be ordered after a full investigation as to whether any parts of it already used for burial may be reused.[326] Once closed, the obligations for maintenance may be passed by the PCC to the local authority.[327] Following such a transfer, the element of control which is the necessary foundation of liability under the Occupiers' Liability Act 1957 passes from the PCC to the local authority. Even if in particular circumstances a PCC is found voluntarily to have retained some residual control over the churchyard, it is entitled to claim an indemnity or contribution

---

[320] *Re St John, Chelsea* [1962] 1 WLR 706, [1962] 2 All ER 850, London Cons Ct. See also *Re St Mary the Virgin, Woodkirk* [1969] 1 WLR 1867, *sub nom Morley Borough Council v St Mary the Virgin, Woodkirk (Vicar and Churchwardens)* [1969] 3 All ER 952, Ch Ct of York.

[321] What constitutes such an extension has been addressed in *Re St Mary, Luton* [1967] P 151, [1966] 3 All ER 638, St Albans Cons Ct, affd [1968] P 47, [1966] 3 All ER 638 at 648, Ct of Arches; *Re St Ann, Kew* [1977] Fam 12, [1976] 1 All ER 461, Southwark Cons Ct; and *Re St Thomas, Lymington* [1980] Fam 89, [1980] 2 All ER 84, Winchester Cons Ct.

[322] Disused Burial Grounds Act 1884, s 3. It is immaterial whether or not the burial ground has been partially or wholly closed for burials: Open Spaces Act 1887, s 4. What matters is whether it has ceased to be used for interments.

[323] Ibid s 4. A temporary building which enlarges a church may be permitted. See *Re St James, Pokesdown*, (9 August 2000, unreported), Winchester Cons Ct, per Hill Dep Ch, in which a portable classroom was permitted during the redevelopment of the neighbouring church school, such classroom being connected to the church and serving also for Sunday school and other church purposes.

[324] Open Spaces Act 1906, s 6.

[325] See *Re Bideford Parish* [1900] P 314, Ct of Arches; *Re St Clement, Leigh-on-Sea* [1988] 1 WLR 720, Chelmsford Cons Ct; *Re St Martin le Grand, York* [1990] Fam 63, [1989] 2 All ER 711, York Cons Ct. As to the creation of a legal easement over unconsecrated land, see *Re St Peter, Bushey Heath* [1971] 1 WLR 357, [1971] 2 All ER 704, St Albans Cons Ct and *Re Westwell Bridleway* (FPS/U3100/7/19, 5 March 2007, unreported).

[326] See, by way of example, *Re Brightlingsea Churchyard* (2004) 8 Ecc LJ 233, Chelmsford Cons Ct. Once the churchyard is closed, no faculty may be granted for the erection of any building upon it save for the enlargement of an existing church, as discussed above: Disused Burial Grounds Act 1884, s 3.

[327] Local Government Act 1972, s 215(1), (2). Where notice is properly served under section 215, it is not open for the local authority to agree with the PCC to limit its maintenance liability or to confine it to particular areas in the churchyard. The decision in *Lydbrook Parochial Church Council v Forest of Dean District Council* (2003) 7 Ecc LJ 494, Gloucester County Court, reinforces the legal position that the duty is one of substantive maintenance and not merely management of decline (see generally *R v Burial Board of Bishopwearmouth* (1879) 5 QBD 67 at 68) nor is it conditional on adequate funds being available.

from the local authority pursuant to the Civil Liability (Contribution) Act 1978 in the event that the authority's breach of duty occasions injury.[328] The primary responsibility for memorials lies with the legal owner, but there is a secondary liability in respect of public safety which arises from the legal responsibility for the maintenance of the burial ground.[329]

Unless and until the duty of maintenance is transferred to the local authority, it is for the PCC to manage and maintain the churchyard.[330] The reordering of churchyards allows for monuments and headstones to be relocated and for kerbstones to be removed.[331] This enables the churchyard to be more conveniently maintained and may permit further burials.[332] Useful guidance can be found in *The Churchyards Handbook*.[333] A petition for a faculty is made in the usual way, although specific directions may be given for advertisement and giving notice to, for example, the Commonwealth War Graves Commission. Since tombstones and other monuments are owned neither by the incumbent nor the PCC, permission should be obtained from the owner before they are moved.[334] However, where the owner withholds his consent or cannot be found, a faculty may nonetheless be granted in respect of the moving, demolition, alteration or execution of other work to it, notwithstanding that it was erected under an earlier faculty.[335] Such faculty may not be granted, however, if the owner satisfies the court that he is able and willing within a reasonable time to remove the monument and carry out such work as may be necessitated by such removal.[336]

7.96

---

[328] See 'The Maintenance of Memorials in Closed Churchyards', an opinion of the Legal Advisory Commission of the General Synod of the Church of England (January 2007).

[329] See *Re Welford Road Cemetery, Leicester* [2007] 2 WLR 506, [2007] 1 All ER 426, Ct of Arches, applying *Re Keynsham Cemetery* [2003] 1 WLR 66, (2002) 7 Ecc LJ 103, Bath and Wells Cons Ct, in which a faculty was granted approving a scheme for establishing the safety of memorials using a topple tester. This scheme was later varied to substitute a 35kg force in accordance with industry practice: (2004) 7 Ecc LJ 492.

[330] Parochial Church Councils (Powers) Measure 1956, s 4(1)(ii)(c).

[331] See, by way of example, *Re St Nicholas, Swayfield* (2003) 7 Ecc LJ 235, Lincoln Cons Ct.

[332] For an illustration of the consequences which might follow when a churchyard reordering is carried out without a faculty, see *Re Christ Church, Wheelock* (1999) 5 Ecc LJ 388, Chester Cons Ct.

[333] T Cocke (ed), *The Churchyards Handbook* (4th edn, London: Church House Publishing, 2001).

[334] See the Faculty Jurisdiction Measure 1964, s 3. 'Owner' means the person who erected the monument and, after his death, the heir or heirs at law of the person in whose memory the monument was erected: s 3(4).

[335] Ibid s 3(2). See also *Re St Andrew, Thornhaugh* [1976] Fam 230, [1976] 1 All ER 154, Peterborough Cons Ct.

[336] Faculty Jurisdiction Measure 1964, s 3(3).

Demolition

7.97 Save in the case of an emergency, no demolition or partial demolition of a church may take place without the grant of a faculty.[337] Such faculty may only be granted on limited grounds and subject to detailed provisions as to notice, representation and consent.[338] The court must be satisfied that another church or part thereof will be erected on the site to take the place of what is demolished.[339] A hearing in open court is a mandatory requirement when oral evidence must be received from, among others, the Council for the Care of Churches. The court must treat the petition with the same detailed consideration as an application for listed building consent.[340]

7.98 Where the petition relates to the demolition or partial demolition of a church,[341] the registrar must give notice to the Council for the Care of Churches and the DAC and, if the church is a listed building or in a conservation area, the Secretary of State, the local planning authority, English Heritage and the National Amenity Societies.[342] The bodies concerned have a period of 28 days within which to give advice or to send to the registry a written notice of objection in the prescribed form.[343] A notice stating the substance of the petition must be published in the *London Gazette* and in such other newspapers as the court may specify.[344]

7.99 A member of the Council for the Care of Churches[345] may apply to give evidence at the hearing and, where notice of a petition has been given to the Council, it may, within six weeks of being so notified, make an application in the prescribed form and submit it to the registry together with a statement of the evidence to be relied on.[346] Any other person may do likewise, using another prescribed form, within four weeks of the last publication of the notice in the *London Gazette* or other newspaper.[347]

---

[337] See the Care of Churches and Ecclesiastical Jurisdiction Measure 1991, s 18.
[338] See ibid s 17. For a discussion of what constitutes demolition for the purpose of ibid s 17, see *Re St James' Chapel, Callow End* [2001] 1 WLR 835, Worcester Cons Ct.
[339] Care of Churches and Ecclesiastical Jurisdiction Measure 1991, s 17(2).
[340] *Re St Barnabas, Dulwich* [1994] Fam 124 at 132F, Southwark Cons Ct.
[341] And falls within the Care of Churches and Ecclesiastical Jurisdiction Measure 1991, s 17(2) or (3)(a).
[342] Faculty Jurisdiction Rules 2000, r 13(7)(a). See also the Care of Churches and Ecclesiastical Jurisdiction Measure 1991, s 17(4)(b), (5)(a).
[343] Faculty Jurisdiction Rules 2000, r 13(7)(a). For the form of objection, see App C Form No 4.
[344] Care of Churches and Ecclesiastical Jurisdiction Measure 1991, s 17(4)(a)(ii); Faculty Jurisdiction Rules 2000, r 13(7)(b).
[345] Or a person authorized by the Council.
[346] Faculty Jurisdiction Rules 2000, r 22(a), (c). For the form of application, see App C Form No 10.
[347] Ibid r 22(b), (c). For the form of application, see App C Form No 11. The chancellor may decline to hear the evidence if the application or the evidence is frivolous or vexatious: Care of Churches and Ecclesiastical Jurisdiction Measure 1991, s 17(4)(d)(ii).

The court may not grant a faculty for the demolition or partial demolition of **7.100**
a church unless the petitioner has the written consent of the bishop to the proceedings being brought, the above notices have been given, the advice tendered by the DAC has been considered, and the chancellor has heard in open court the evidence from the Council for the Care of Churches and from any other person, unless in the opinion of the judge the application of such person or the evidence which he gives is frivolous or vexatious.[348] Further, if the church is a listed building or in a conservation area, before the court may grant a faculty it must have considered the advice of such of the bodies as tendered it, and permitted the Royal Commission on the Historical Monuments of England to have access for recording purposes.[349]

Separate provisions apply in cases of emergency.[350] Where the chancellor is satis- **7.101**
fied that demolition of the whole or part of a church is necessary in the interests of safety or health or for the preservation of the church, and, having regard to the urgency of the matter, there is insufficient time to obtain a faculty, he may by an instrument under his hand authorize the work.[351] If the church is a listed building or in a conservation area, he must further be satisfied that temporary support or shelter is impracticable and that the works are limited to the minimum measures immediately necessary.[352] The instrument must be sent to the Council for the Care of Churches and the local planning authority.[353] It may contain a provision requiring works for the subsequent restoration of the church to be carried out, subject to obtaining any faculty.[354]

Disability Discrimination Act 1995

The approach to reordering of churches and other alterations to their fabric must **7.102**
be informed by the provisions of the Disability Discrimination Act 1995.[355] A raft of provisions under the Act relating to the adaptation of buildings and

---

[348] Ibid s 17(4).
[349] Ibid s 17(5). In practice this task (if performed at all) is undertaken by English Heritage.
[350] See for example, *Re St Christopher, Church Cove* (2000) 5 Ecc LJ 492, Guildford Cons Ct. A more contentious decision is that of *Re Christchurch, Sparkbrook* (2005) 8 Ecc LJ 493, Birmingham Cons Ct.
[351] Care of Churches and Ecclesiastical Jurisdiction Measure 1991, s 18(1)(a).
[352] Ibid s 18(1)(b).
[353] Ibid s 18(3). In the case of a church which is a listed building or in a conservation area, the instrument must require the person to whom it is issued, as soon as practicable after the work is carried out, to give to the local planning authority notice in writing describing the works carried out: s 18(2)(b).
[354] Ibid s 18(2)(a).
[355] See *Re St John the Evangelist, Dudley Wood* (2005) 8 Ecc LJ 493, Worcester Cons Ct; *Re St Mary, Slaugham (No 2)*, (January 2006, unreported), Chichester Cons Ct. Note also *Re Dorchester Abbey* (2002) 7 Ecc LJ 105, Oxford Cons Ct.

their contents came into force on 1 October 2004.[356] A detailed discussion of the provisions of the Act is beyond the scope of this book,[357] but mention should be made of the need to carry out an 'access audit'.[358] Such audit could lead to altering procedures and providing auxiliary aids or to overcoming barriers created by physical features. A disabled person who claims to have been the subject of discrimination has a right of action to sue the provider in the county court and may seek damages, including compensation for injury to feelings.[359]

Disposal of church property

7.103 Often churches are minded to dispose of objects which belong to the church, either altruistically for the benefit of another church in this country or abroad, or to raise finance for some other purpose. The churchwardens, in whom legal title vests, may only sell such items if the PCC has given its consent and if a faculty has been granted.[360] The consistory court will be guided when considering petitions of this nature by the principles enunciated in *Re St Gregory, Tredington*, but each case will fall to be determined on its own facts.[361] Some special reason is required, being both good and sufficient, although it is not necessary to prove in every case that the goods are redundant or that there is a financial emergency in the parish.[362]

---

[356] Note also the Disability Discrimination Act 1995: Code of Practice: Goods, Facilities, Service and Premises, produced by the Disability Rights Commission (27 May 2002).

[357] See C Mynors, 'Accessibility: The New Legislation' (2003) 7 Ecc LJ 143; B Doyle, *Disability Discrimination: Law and Practice* (4th edn, Bristol: Jordans, 2003).

[358] See *Widening the Eye of a Needle: Access to Church Buildings for People with Disabilities* (2nd edn, London: Church House Publishing, 2002) and *Disability Discrimination Act 1995: Taking Account of Its Implications for the Fabric of Churches and Cathedrals: Advisory Note by the Council for the Care of Churches and the Cathedral Fabric Commission*.

[359] Disability Discrimination Act 1995, s 25, Sch 3 pt II.

[360] In the absence of such consent and of a faculty, title will not pass due to the doctrine *nemo dat quod non habet*. See *Re St Mary, Barton-Upon-Humber* [1987] Fam 41, [1987] 2 All ER 861, Lincoln Cons Ct. Note also, however, the six-year limitation period which applies in relation to the remedial powers of the consistory court, as discussed above. For a more recent example, where the parish purported to conclude a contract for the sale of an organ by eBay prior to the grant of, still less application for, a faculty, see *Re St James, Birdham* (20 November 2006, unreported) Chichester Cons Ct.

[361] *Re St Gregory, Tredington* [1972] Fam 236, [1971] 3 All ER 269, Ct of Arches. See also *Re St Mary le Bow* [1984] 1 WLR 1363, London Cons Ct. The suggestion in *Tredington* that there should always be a hearing in open court has lost its rationale now that provision exists for the determination of petitions on written representations. The current practice is generally not to convene a hearing unless the nature of the dispute requires one.

[362] Although a financial emergency was made out in *Re St Matthew, Hutton Buscel* (1999) 5 Ecc LJ 486, York Cons Ct, and such a consideration probably proved determinative in the *Tredington* case (n 361 above), it is suggested that it is unnecessary to demonstrate a dire monetary need before a faculty can issue. Support for this is to be found in *Re St John the Baptist, Halifax* (2000) 6 Ecc LJ 167, Wakefield Cons Ct; *Re St Giles, Lincoln* (2006) 9 Ecc LJ 143, Lincoln Cons Ct, and *Re St John the Baptist, Stainton-by-Langworth* (2006) 9 Ecc LJ 144, Lincoln Cons Ct.

Exhumation

To dig up a corpse unlawfully is an indictable offence.[363] A faculty is required and, if the reburial is not also to be in consecrated ground, so also is a Home Office licence.[364] It is unnecessary to seek the advice of the DAC before lodging a petition for a faculty for exhumation,[365] and the requirement of public notice is slightly modified.[366]

7.104

Mindful of increasing numbers of applications for exhumation, the Chancery Court of York, in giving judgment in *Re Christ Church, Alsager*,[367] sought to provide guidance to assist chancellors in determining such petitions.[368] This comprised a list of factors which argue for and against the grant of a faculty, but the general test was encapsulated in the question, 'is there a good and proper reason for exhumation, that reason being likely to be regarded as acceptable by right thinking members of the Church at large?'[369] However, the guidance proved difficult to apply in practice with any degree of consistency, and this was not assisted by the highly subjective element to the determinative question.[370]

7.105

The Court of Arches revisited the law of exhumation in *Re Blagdon Cemetery*,[371] and in doing so commissioned expert evidence on the theology of burial.[372] The court emphasized the distinction between burial in consecrated as opposed to unconsecrated ground. Consecration serves to set land apart for sacred use and brings it within the jurisdiction of the consistory court. Christian doctrine speaks of entrusting the person in peace to God for their ultimate destination in the heavenly Jerusalem. This does not sit easily with the concept of 'portable remains'. Thus 'the norm is permanence in relation to Christian burial'.[373] Rejecting the

7.106

---

363 *R v Sharpe* (1857) Dears & B 160.
364 Burial Act 1857, s 25.
365 Faculty Jurisdiction Rules 2000, r 3(1).
366 Ibid rr 6(1), 13(8). Near relatives and others may be specially cited if they are not petitioners. It may be dispensed with entirely if the chancellor is satisfied that all living near relatives or other persons concerned are petitioners or consent to the proposed faculty being granted: r 13(9)(a), (b).
367 *Re Christ Church, Alsager* [1999] Fam 142, [1999] 1 All ER 117, Ch Ct of York. See also R Bursell, 'Digging Up Exhumation' (1998) 5 Ecc LJ 18.
368 *Re Christ Church, Alsager* [1999] Fam 142 at 148G–149B, [1999] 1 All ER 117 at 121h–123b. The guidance was a slightly reformulated version of that given by Chancellor McClean in *Re John Stocks, deceased* (1995) 4 Ecc LJ 527, Sheffield Cons Ct.
369 *Re Christ Church, Alsager* [1999] Fam 142 at 149C, [1999] 1 All ER 117 at 122c.
370 See, by way of example, P Petchey, 'Exhumation Reconsidered' (2001) 6 Ecc LJ 122.
371 *Re Blagdon Cemetery* [2002] Fam 299, [2002] 4 All ER 482, Ct of Arches. The modern practice is to treat the Court of Arches and the Chancery Court of York as a single court, the decisions of each court being binding precedents in both the northern and southern province of the Church of England. See the discussion of precedent in Chapter 1.
372 This evidence was subsequently published, in an expanded form, in C Hill, 'A Note on the Theology of Burial in Relation to Some Contemporary Questions' (2004) 7 Ecc LJ 447.
373 *Re Blagdon Cemetery* [2002] Fam 299; [2002] 4 All ER 482, Ct of Arches, para 28. The Court offered the following advice: 'It is therefore very important that cemetery managers and funeral

formulation of the test in *Alsager*, the Court of Arches stated: 'we have concluded that there is much to be said for reverting to the straightforward principle that a faculty for exhumation will only be exceptionally granted'.[374] Recognizing the variety of wording used in judgments in articulating what is essentially a matter of discretion, the Court of Arches continued:

> We consider that it should always be made clear that it is for the petitioner to satisfy the consistory court that there are special circumstances in his/her case which justify the making of an exception from the norm that Christian burial (that is burial of a body or cremated remains in a consecrated churchyard or consecrated part of a local authority cemetery) is final. It will then be for the chancellor to decide whether the petitioner has so satisfied him/her.[375]

7.107 The Court of Arches proceeded to consider some relevant factors, many of which had been the subject of comment in *Alsager*, without detracting from the fact that each petition will fall to be considered on its own facts:[376]

(i) advancing years, deteriorating health, or change in place of residence which makes visiting a grave difficult or impossible[377] are insufficient to justify an exception to the norm, although a serious psychiatric or psychological condition linked to the location of the grave might;[378]

(ii) long delay with no credible explanation may tip the balance against the grant of a faculty, but lapse of time alone is not the test;[379]

---

directors give a simple explanation to the bereaved about the difference between consecrated land (to which the theology of burial has application) and unconsecrated land. Members of the public do have choices nowadays in relation to burial and cremation and places of disposal of the dead, and they need to be informed in making their choices': para 26.

[374] *Re Blagdon Cemetery* (n 373 above) para 33.

[375] *Re Blagdon Cemetery* (n 373 above) para 35.

[376] *Re Blagdon Cemetery* (n 373 above) para 35. The judgment is reproduced in full in the Materials.

[377] The fact that a burial ground was unkempt and attracted undesirable vagrants thereby deterring visiting by relatives was not regarded as a sufficient ground of exceptionality: *Re St Andrew (Old Church) Hove* (2005) 8 Ecc LJ 377, Chichester Cons Ct.

[378] For example in *Re Allwood (minors), deceased* (1999) 5 Ecc LJ 389, Southwark Cons Ct, the trauma of a highly publicized interment of octuplets rendered it too upsetting for the parents subsequently to visit their children's grave, and in *Re St Mark, Worsley* (2006) 9 Ecc LJ 147, Manchester Cons Ct, a widow secured the exhumation of her late husband's remains from the grave in which her parents and grandparents were buried, because she found it intolerable to visit the family grave having discovered after his death that her late husband had been conducting an extra-marital affair for almost their entire marriage. Note also *Re X* (2001) 6 Ecc LJ 413, Liverpool Cons Ct, in which an exhumation was authorized at the behest of a sibling in respect of the remains of her sister which were interred alongside those of her father who, it was later discovered, had sexually abused the deceased and another sister in their childhood.

[379] Exhumations have been permitted after substantial periods: 173 years in *Re St Mary the Virgin, Hurley* [2001] 1 WLR 831, Oxford Cons Ct, and 110 years in *Re Talbot* [1901] P 1, London Cons Ct.

(iii) mistake as to the location of a grave[380] may be a ground for exhumation, but a change of mind as to the place of burial on the part of relatives or others responsible for the burial should not be treated as an acceptable ground for authorizing exhumation;[381]
(iv) local support such as that of relatives, the incumbent or the PCC will not normally be relevant;[382]
(v) the desirability of equal treatment requires the court to consider any precedent which might be set;[383] and
(vi) burials of family members in double or triple depth graves are to be encouraged because 'they express family unity and they are environmentally friendly in demonstrating an economical use of land for burials'.[384]

A number of recent cases have dealt with applications for exhumation for the purposes of research. In *Re Holy Trinity, Bosham*,[385] a faculty was sought to carry out a detailed archaeological investigation of two grave sites in the nave of the church, involving the opening up of the putative coffin of the Saxon King Harold Godwinson for visual examination and the removal of a sample of bone from that coffin for destructive DNA testing. The chancellor offered some guiding principles for determining petitions of this type:

7.108

> As I read the authorities, the following approach would appear to be appropriate in cases such as these: (1) as a matter of Christian doctrine, burial in consecrated ground

---

[380] Other types of mistake may also give rise to an exceptional reason to exhume. See by way of example, *Re All Saints, Beckley* (2006) 9 Ecc LJ 241, Chichester Cons Ct.

[381] For a discussion of mistake, coupled with forgery, see *Re Swaden* (2005) 8 Ecc LJ 238, Southwark Cons Ct. See also *Re Lambeth Cemetery, Re Streatham Park Cemetery* (2002) 7 Ecc LJ 237, Southwark Cons Ct; *Re Jean Gardiner, deceased* (2003) 7 Ecc LJ 493, Carlisle Cons Ct; *Re Miresse, deceased* (2003) 7 Ecc LJ 368, Southwark Cons Ct; and *Re Mangotsfield Cemetery* (2005) 8 Ecc LJ 237, Bristol Cons Ct. Whether *Re Durrington Cemetery* [2001] Fam 33, Chichester Cons Ct, could have come within the doctrine of mistake (as the Court of Arches suggests in *Blagdon* at para 36(iii)) is a matter of debate: the Jewish relatives well knew the consequences of burial in consecrated ground and deferred to the deceased's widow's wishes at the time, but sought to revisit the matter after she had emigrated.

[382] This marks a departure from the view expressed by the Chancery Court of York in *Re Christ Church, Alsager* [1999] Fam 142 at 149G, [1999] 1 All ER 117 at 122. Where there was an absence of unanimity amongst the close relatives of the deceased, this was held to be a powerful factor which militated against the granting of a faculty: *Re St Nicholas, Pevensey* (2002) 7 Ecc LJ 236, Chichester Cons Ct.

[383] This is likewise a departure from *Alsager* in which the setting of a precedent had been considered as irrelevant.

[384] *Re Blagdon Cemetery* [2002] Fam 299, [2002] 4 All ER 482, Ct of Arches, para 36(iv). In allowing the appeal, the Court of Arches added: 'In doing so it should not be assumed that whenever the possibility of a family grave is raised a petition for a faculty for exhumation will automatically be granted': para 40.

[385] *Re Holy Trinity, Bosham* [2004] Fam 125, [2004] 2 All ER 820, Chichester Cons Ct. As to the conservation and archaeological issues involved, see, more recently, *Guidance for Best Practice for Treatment of Human Remains Excavated from Christian Burial Grounds in England* issued by English Heritage, the Cathedrals Fabric Commission for England and the Council for the Care of Churches (January 2005).

is final and permanent; (2) this general norm creates a presumption against exhumation; (3) exhumation in this context comprises any disturbance of human remains which have been interred; (4) departure from such presumption can only be justified if special circumstances can be shown for making an exception to the norm; (5) an applicant might be able to demonstrate a matter of great national, historic or other importance concerning human remains; (6) an applicant might also be able to demonstrate the value of some particular research or scientific experimentation; (7) only if the combined effect of evidence under (5) and (6) proves a cogent and compelling case for the legitimacy of the proposed research will special circumstances be made out such as to justify a departure from the presumption against exhumation.[386]

7.109 This approach was specifically approved by the Court of Arches in the case of in *Re St Nicholas, Sevenoaks*,[387] in which the appellant had been refused a faculty to exhume the remains of his great-grandfather to extract a sample of bone for DNA testing to establish whether there was scientific support for the long-held belief in the appellant's family that the deceased was the illegitimate son of a daughter of Queen Victoria. In each of these cases the petition failed on the basis that the evidence produced was insufficiently compelling to displace the presumption against exhumation.

7.110 More recently, in *St Mary, Sledmere*,[388] the foregoing approach was again approved and applied. The petitioner, a professor of virology, sought the exhumation of the body of Sir Mark Sykes who had died in Paris in 1919 as one of some 50 million casualties of a Spanish influenza epidemic. His body was returned to England and buried in sealed lead coffin such that it was believed that tissue material could be extracted and tested to assist in the clinical treatment of the avian H5N1 virus and the use of immunosuppressive drugs. The chancellor considered that, although the prospects of success were speculative, the potential public benefit arising from successful research would be significant in terms of an advance in the treatment of dangerous diseases.[389] That being so, this was an exceptional case in which the presumption against exhumation was displaced and a faculty was granted accordingly.[390]

7.111 There has been some limited consideration of the application of the Human Rights Act 1998 to cases of exhumation. In *Re Durrington Cemetery*,[391] exhumation was permitted so as to allow the deceased to be reburied in a Jewish cemetery in accordance with the law and customs of the Jewish faith, to which he had ascribed. As an additional ground, and therefore *obiter dictum*, account was taken

---

[386] *Re Holy Trinity, Bosham* (n 385 above) para 31, per Hill Ch.
[387] *Re St Nicholas, Sevenoaks* [2005] 1 WLR 1011.
[388] *Re St Mary, Sledmere* (2007, unreported) York Cons Ct.
[389] Not merely an increase in historic knowledge as in *Bosham* and *Sevenoaks*.
[390] *Re St Mary, Sledmere* (2007, unreported) York Cons Ct, para 21.
[391] *Re Durrington Cemetery* [2001] Fam 33, Chichester Cons Ct.

of the freedom of the surviving relatives to manifest their religion and belief in practice and observance as safeguarded under Article 9 of the European Convention on Human Rights.[392] A decision of the European Court of Human Rights held[393] that a ruling of the Swedish authorities not to permit the exhumation of human remains and their re-interment in a family grave did not amount to a violation of Article 8 of the Convention, the right to a private and family life.[394]

Fonts

Canon law provides that every church where baptism is to be administered must be provided with a decent font with a cover to keep it clean.[395] The font must stand as near to the principal entrance as conveniently may be, save where there is an established custom to the contrary or where the Ordinary otherwise directs.[396] The strict rigour of the canon may be regarded as slightly tempered by statements made by the House of Bishops regarding the liturgical appropriateness of the position of fonts.[397] Although the matter is not without controversy, there does not appear to be any canon or rule of law which prevents there being more than one font in a church, although one is normal.[398] Designs for fonts which allow for baptism to be administered in a number of ways are to be encouraged.[399]

7.112

---

[392] See also the approach adopted in respect of the burial of a humanist in consecrated ground in *Re Crawley Green Road Cemetery, Luton* [2001] Fam 308, St Albans Cons Ct.

[393] Albeit by a bare 4:3 majority of the judges.

[394] *Dödsbo v Sweden*, App No 61564/00 (2006) 8 Ecc LJ 496, E Ct HR. The court acknowledged that there was interference with the applicant's family life, but that it was in accordance with law and in pursuit of a legitimate aim. See R Sandberg, 'Human Rights and Human Remains: The Impact of *Dödsbo v Sweden*' (2006) 8 Ecc LJ 453. Counsel did not consider the Article 8 point to be arguable in *Blagdon* (n 384 above) and it was not pursued, and although the point was not raised in *Re St Dunstan, Cheam* (22 January 2007, unreported), Southwark Cons Ct, there is some discursive *obiter dictum* on the subject in the judgment of Petchey Dep Ch.

[395] Canon F 1 para 1.

[396] Canon F 1 para 2. In this instance the Ordinary is a reference to the chancellor exercising the bishop's jurisdiction in the consistory court. See, by way of example, *Re St Mary, Shortlands* (2003) 7 Ecc LJ 363, Rochester Cons Ct.

[397] See *Re St James, Shirley* [1994] Fam 134, Winchester Cons Ct. The judgment relied upon the *Response by the House of Bishops to Questions Raised by Diocesan Chancellors* (June 1992), particularly paras 2.6.3ff.

[398] *Re St Barnabas, Kensington* [1991] Fam 1, [1990] 1 All ER 169, London Cons Ct; *Re St George, Deal* [1991] Fam 6, Canterbury Commissary Ct. The contrary view, namely that there can be only one font, just as there is only one baptism, was asserted in *Re St Nicholas, Gosforth* (1998) 1 Ecc LJ 4, Newcastle Cons Ct. It is regarded as the liturgical norm in the *Response of the House of Bishops* (n 397 above). See also *Re St Margaret, Brightside* (1996) 4 Ecc LJ 765, Sheffield Cons Ct; *Re Holy Trinity, Eckington* (1999) 5 Ecc LJ 489, Worcester Cons Ct; and note D Stancliffe, 'Baptism and Fonts' (1993) 3 Ecc LJ 141.

[399] *Re St Margaret, Brightside* (1996) 4 Ecc LJ 765, Sheffield Cons Ct.

Graves

Right of burial

7.113 Every parishioner[400] has a right to be buried in the consecrated graveyard of the parish if there is one which remains open for burials.[401] Other persons may be buried only with the consent of the minister, the giving or withholding of which is to be exercised in accordance with general guidance given by the PCC.[402] The position within the churchyard for any burial to take place is a matter for the minister, save that he may not utilize a space already reserved by faculty. The same spot may be used more than once.

Reservation of gravespace

7.114 A faculty may be granted for the reservation of a particular gravespace for a parishioner or non-parishioner,[403] the matter being entirely within the discretion of the consistory court.[404] Once granted, the faculty precludes the incumbent from permitting a burial in the plot to which the faculty relates. The court will be more disposed to grant a faculty in respect of a person with a right to be buried in the churchyard than of one without such an entitlement.[405] The court will have to be satisfied that there is sufficient space in the churchyard so that the parishioners are not prejudiced.[406] It is imperative that churchyard plans be kept accurate and up to date,[407] and it is good practice for any reserved space to be physically marked on the ground.[408]

---

[400] The right extends to persons on the church electoral roll: Church of England (Miscellaneous Provisions) Measure 1976, s 6(1); and to anyone dying in the parish: Canon B 38 para 2.

[401] Canon B 38 para 2. The right extends to the interment of ashes: Church of England (Miscellaneous Provisions) Measure 1992, s 3(1); Canon B 38 para 2.

[402] Church of England (Miscellaneous Provisions) Measure 1976, s 6(2). The minister's refusal to consent may not be questioned in the consistory court: *Re St Nicholas, Baddesley Ensor* [1983] Fam 1 at 5, [1982] 2 All ER 351 at 352j–353a, Birmingham Cons Ct.

[403] Church of England (Miscellaneous Provisions) Measure 1976, s 6(2).

[404] See *Re West Pennard Churchyard* [1992] 1 WLR 32, [1991] 4 All ER 124, Bath and Wells Cons Ct. See also *Re Wraxall Churchyard* (2004) 7 Ecc LJ 497, Baths and Wells Cons Ct.

[405] The consistory court, however, will generally support a PCC's policy of non-reservation unless such policy reveals *mala fides* or is wholly unreasonable. See *Re Dilhorne Churchyard* (1997) 6 Ecc LJ 77, Lichfield Cons Ct. See also *Re St Mary, Dodleston, Churchyard* [1996] 1 WLR 451, Chester Cons Ct.

[406] See *Re St Nicholas, Baddesley Ensor* [1983] Fam 1, [1982] 2 All ER 351, Birmingham Cons Ct.

[407] See *Re St Luke, Holbeach Hurn* [1991] 1 WLR 16 at 27, [1990] 2 All ER 749 at 758, Lincoln Cons Ct.

[408] The judgment in *Re St Leonard, Beoley* (1998) 5 Ecc LJ 216, Worcester Cons Ct sets out guidelines for the diocese in relation to reservation of gravespaces.

Erection of headstone

Permission is required before any monument may be erected over a grave.[409] It is for the incumbent to ensure compliance with the chancellor's guidelines which delegate to him the authority to authorize the introduction of certain classes of monument.[410] Proposed monuments which fall outside the guidelines, or which the incumbent considers merit consideration by the chancellor, are dealt with by a faculty application in the normal way.[411] Churchyard regulations generally do not permit the inclusion of photographic images, and faculties are routinely refused for such proposals.[412] Any permission given by the incumbent for the erection of a memorial which falls outside the type specified in the instrument of delegation will be a nullity. The chancellor should ensure that a consistent approach is adopted within the diocese and, more particularly, within each churchyard to ensure that all bereaved relatives are treated fairly.[413] He may also have to balance the competing wishes of those who knew the deceased, such as spouses, former spouses and partners, be they heterosexual or homosexual.[414]

7.115

Inscriptions

Any inscription on a monument or headstone must be reverent and seemly.[415] It will be read by future generations that may know nothing of the person to whom it relates. The use of pet names, nicknames or other familiar terms

7.116

---

409 See *Re Woldingham Churchyard* [1957] 1 WLR 811, [1957] 2 All ER 323, Southwark Cons Ct. Items unlawfully introduced, such as kerb stones or chippings, may be made the subject of a faculty requiring their removal: *Re St Paul, Drighlington* (2006) 9 Ecc LJ 239, Wakefield Cons Ct. See also *Re North Wingfield* (2002) 7 Ecc LJ 238, Derby Cons Ct. In relation to an unlawful memorial concerning cremated remains, see *Re Holy Cross, Greenford Magna* (2005) 8 Ecc LJ 378, London Cons Ct.

410 They are enjoined not to accede to unsuitable requests from bereaved relatives out of justifiable motives of sympathy: *Re St Mary, Fawkham* [1981] 1 WLR 1171 at 1175G, Ct of Arches. A petition was refused for the introduction of a heart-shaped memorial which had been fabricated but was contrary to churchyard regulations, and had not been authorized: *Re Small, deceased* (2005) 9 Ecc LJ 238, Manchester Cons Ct.

411 See, eg, *Re St Mary, Kingswinford* [2001] 1 WLR 927, Worcester Cons Ct.

412 *Re Christ Church, Timperley* (2004) 7 Ecc LJ 496, Chester Cons Ct. A memorial which included a ceramic plaque with a black and white photograph of the deceased was ordered to be removed because it did not comply with the churchyard rules: *Re St Nicholas, Remenham* (2006) 9 Ecc LJ 238, Oxford Cons Ct. See also *Re St James, Braithwell* (2002) 7 Ecc LJ 239, Sheffield Cons Ct, refusing permission for a porcelain portrait, following *Re Christ Church, Harwood* [2002] 1 WLR 2055, Manchester Cons Ct.

413 See, eg, *Re Christchurch, Wheelock* (1996) 4 Ecc LJ 766, Chester Cons Ct.

414 See, eg, *Re St Mark, Haydock (No 2)* [1981] 1 WLR 1167, Liverpool Cons Ct.

415 As to concerns about the absence of any Christian content, see *Re Byron Memorial, St Mary Magdalene, Hucknall* (1996) 4 Ecc LJ 767, Southwell Cons Ct; and *Re Plaxtol Churchyard* (1999) 5 Ecc LJ 306, Rochester Cons Ct.

is widely discouraged.[416] However, Chancellor McClean has indicated 'provided there is nothing scandalous or open to theological objection, I take the view that the bereaved should express their love and respect for the deceased in the language which comes naturally to them'.[417] The content must be accurate and not such as to mislead.[418]

Libraries

7.117 Books owned by the church are treated in the same manner as any other goods. However, special provisions exist under the Parochial Libraries Act 1708 to protect parish libraries from 'embezzlement'. Formerly, the books were inalienable, save where there were duplicate copies and the Ordinary consented to the disposal of a spare copy. Now, the consistory court may grant a faculty authorizing a sale and directing that the proceeds be applied for specified ecclesiastical purposes of the parish.[419]

Licences and leases

7.118 It is often convenient and lucrative for a licence to be granted, allowing for the use of part of a church or churchyard for some secular purpose.[420] Whereas the freehold vests in the incumbent, control is a matter for the bishop, exercised by the chancellor in the consistory court.[421] It is unlawful to sell or otherwise dispose of a church or part of a church, including any consecrated land belonging or annexed to it.[422] A faculty may, however, permit the granting of a licence for a 'suitable use'.[423]

---

[416] *Re Holy Trinity Churchyard, Freckleton* [1994] 1 WLR 1588, Blackburn Cons Ct. Note, however, *Re Holy Trinity, Freckleton (No 2)* (1995) 3 Ecc LJ 429, Blackburn Cons Ct, in which a petition for exhumation was granted by Spafford Dep Ch so that the deceased might be reinterred in a municipal cemetery where a less restrictive approach was adopted.
[417] *Re St Thomas, Kimberworth* (1998) 5 Ecc LJ 302, Sheffield Cons Ct. See also *Re Holy Trinity, Seghill* (2000) 6 Ecc LJ 85, Newcastle Cons Ct, and *Re Edward Charles Lee, deceased* (1995) 4 Ecc LJ 763, Sodor and Man Cons Ct.
[418] See *Re St Mary, Oldswinford* (1998) 5 Ecc LJ 302, Worcester Cons Ct. See also *Re St John the Baptist, Bishop's Castle* (1999) 5 Ecc LJ 487, Hereford Cons Ct.
[419] See *Re St Mary, Warwick* [1981] Fam 170, Coventry Cons Ct.
[420] For example, the siting of scaffolding to permit work to neighbouring buildings or the swing of a crane through the airspace above a churchyard. Absent a licence pursuant to a faculty, these would amount to trespass.
[421] See *St Botolph without Aldgate (Vicar and One Churchwarden) v Parishioners of St Botolph without Aldgate* [1892] P 161 at 167, London Cons Ct, per Tristram Ch.
[422] Pastoral Measure 1983, s 56(2). Note, however, *Re Tonbridge School Chapel (No 2)* [1993] Fam 281, [1993] 2 All ER 338, Rochester Cons Ct, concerning the lease of a private chapel to a charity, and *Re St Peter, Bushey Heath* [1971] 1 WLR 357, [1971] 2 All ER 704, St Albans Cons Ct, concerning the creation of an easement over land which was unconsecrated.
[423] Pastoral Measure 1983, s 56(3)(a). See generally *Re St Paul, Covent Garden* [1974] Fam 1, London Cons Ct, and *Re St Mary, Aldermary* [1985] Fam 101, [1985] 2 All ER 445, London Cons Ct.

This may be the case even if the incumbent objects, although the court should give serious consideration to the nature of his objections.[424] The general principles regarding the secular use of premises was discussed in *Re St John, Chelsea*[425] and in *Re All Saints, Featherstone*.[426] In a number of cases, the court has had regard to Chapter 11 of *Faith in the Countryside*,[427] which emphasized that churches be seen as places which can properly be used for purposes other than worship. These matters were similarly articulated in *Building Faith in Our Future*.[428]

7.119 The licence should be granted by the incumbent under the authority of a faculty or, if more convenient, by the court itself, and it is prudent that the PCC be made both a party and the recipient of the licence fee. The precise terms of the licence ought to be set out in a separate agreement and, where it will last for a significant period, provision should be made for periodic reviews of the licence fee. It is a manifestation of proper Christian stewardship that an appropriate fee is obtained, and a faculty may be refused if the fee is inadequate.[429] The terms should ensure that the fabric of the church is protected and that the sacred use of the building is not compromised. Provision should also be made for public liability insurance and an indemnity against claims brought by visitors to the premises in the exercise of the licence. Many applications of this nature relate to telecommunications equipment where regard must be given to the effect on the health and safety of those frequenting the premises or resident nearby.[430]

7.120 The power to grant a lease is of more recent origin and is to be found in section 56 of the Pastoral Measure 1983, as amended by the Pastoral (Amendment) Measure 2006. Hitherto funding bodies have felt that a licence gives insufficient security of tenure for the purposes of collaborative ventures involving community

---

[424] *Re St Andrew, North Weald Bassett* [1987] 1 WLR 1503, Chelmsford Cons Ct.

[425] *Re St John, Chelsea* [1962] 1 WLR 706, [1962] 2 All ER 850, London Cons Ct. See *Re All Saints, Harborough Magna* [1991] 1 WLR 1235, [1992] 4 All ER 948, Coventry Cons Ct; and cf *Re Coleford Cemetery* [1984] 1 WLR 1369, Bath and Wells Cons Ct.

[426] *Re All Saints, Featherstone* (1999) 5 Ecc LJ 391, Wakefield Cons Ct, in which Collier Ch commented that secondary uses that are consistent with the mission and pastoral outreach of the Church should be permitted so long as they do not compromise the primary uses of the building for worship, pastoralia and mission or of the land for Christian burial.

[427] *Report of the Archbishops' Commission on Rural Areas* (1990). See also S Wiggs, 'The Community Use of Churches' (2000) 5 Ecc LJ 348. See for example *Re St Michael, Aveley* (1997) 4 Ecc LJ 770, Chelmsford Cons Ct.

[428] *Building Faith in Our Future*, a statement on behalf of the Church of England by the Church Heritage Forum (Church House Publishing, London, 2004).

[429] See *Re St Philip, Alderley Edge* (1996) 4 Ecc LJ 765, Chester Cons Ct.

[430] Such matters were fully considered in *Re St Mark, Marske-in-Cleveland* (2000) 5 Ecc LJ 491, York Cons Ct, *Re St Margaret, Hawes, Re Holy Trinity, Knaresborough* [2004] 1 All ER 71, (2003) 7 Ecc LJ 364, Ripon and Leeds Cons Ct; *Re St Barnabas, Heaton* (2004) 8 Ecc LJ 232, Bradford Cons Ct; and *Re Holy Trinity Church, Idle* (2006) 9 Ecc LJ 245, Bradford Cons Ct. As to the weight to be afforded to local feeling, see also *Re Emmanuel Church, Bentley* [2006] Fam 39, Ct of Arches.

use of church buildings.⁴³¹ Under this new power, a faculty may be granted subject to the qualification that, taken as a whole, the church building will continue to be used primarily as a place of worship, and that the additional use is not inconsistent with the use of the rest of the premises primarily as a place or worship.⁴³²

Memorials

7.121 No memorial may be erected in a church without a faculty, and such faculties should be 'sparingly conceded'.⁴³³ The Court of Arches has indicated that a case of 'exceptionality' must be made out in relation to the character or service of the person to be commemorated.⁴³⁴ A memorial once it is erected does not become part of the freehold of the church, nor does it vest in the churchwardens, but remains the property of those who erected it and, after their death, of the heir at law of the person in whose memory it was erected.⁴³⁵

7.122 Additions or adornments to the church, such as a stained glass window, fall to be considered on their individual merits, even though the item may be installed in memory of an individual and at the expense of a benefactor. It is unnecessary for the court to address the test of exceptionality.⁴³⁶ In *Re St Peter, Oundle*,⁴³⁷ the consistory court determined that there was no legal, theological or other objection to the erection within the church of carved likenesses of the incumbent and the former bishop as label stops on the arches in the nave.⁴³⁸

Movables and ornaments

7.123 Historically, the consistory court was frequently being asked to determine whether the presence within a church or the proposed introduction of certain objects was illegal. A major objection was that they were or might be used as objects

---

⁴³¹ Previously a lease of part of a church could only be granted after the making of a scheme for partial redundancy under the Pastoral Measure 1983. See *Wider Use of Part or Parts of a Church: a Guide to Section 56 of the Pastoral Measure 1983 (As Amended)* prepared by the Legal Office of the National Institutions of the Church of England (January 2007), and *Building Faith in Our Future* (n 428 above).

⁴³² Pastoral Measure 1983, s 56(2A) (as amended by the Pastoral (Amended) Measure 2006, s 1(b). No residential use will be permitted, except by a person who is required as a condition of his employment to reside on the premises: Pastoral Measure 1983, s 56(2F)(b).

⁴³³ *Dupuis v Parishioners of Ogbourne St George* [1941] P 119 at 121, Ct of Arches.

⁴³⁴ *Re St Margaret, Eartham* [1981] 1 WLR 1129, Ct of Arches. The exceptionality test falls to be applied in the individual circumstances of each case: compare *Re St Mary the Virgin, Horsham* (1999) 5 Ecc LJ 388, Chichester Cons Ct, with *Re All Saints, Bradley* (1997) 4 Ecc LJ 770, Winchester Cons Ct.

⁴³⁵ Faculty Jurisdiction Measure 1964, s 3(4).

⁴³⁶ *Re St Mary, Longstock* [2006] 1 WLR 259, Winchester Cons Ct.

⁴³⁷ *Re St Peter, Oundle* (1996) 4 Ecc LJ 764, Peterborough Cons Ct.

⁴³⁸ The chancellor accepted the proposition advanced by counsel for the petitioners that the carved likenesses were not memorials and the test of exceptionality did not apply.

of superstitious reverence. The PCC is obliged to provide and maintain a font, holy table, reading desks and a pulpit, seats for the congregation, church bell, and an alms box.[439] Whilst each and all of these items are legal per se and there is a mandatory duty to provide them, their nature and aesthetic quality is a matter to be determined by the consistory court in considering whether to grant a faculty for their introduction, alteration or removal.[440] In addition, as with any object introduced into the church, care must be taken to ensure the safeguarding of sound doctrine.[441]

7.124 Following the decisions in *Re St Thomas, Pennywell*[442] and *Re St John the Evangelist, Chopwell*,[443] many of the older decisions on illegality may now be disregarded.[444] The previous rigorist approach should no longer be followed and the rubrics in the *Book of Common Prayer* and elsewhere are now to be given the elasticity that in practice they require.[445] In addition to an aumbry, hanging pyx and sacrament house, a tabernacle may also now be regarded as legal.[446] Candles and their holders, acolytes' chairs, votive candle stands, thuribles and stands, sanctuary bells, holy water stoups and aspergills are regarded as legal objects.[447] Stations of the cross have

---

[439] See Canons F 1, F 2, F 6, F 7, F 8, F 10, and the duty at F 14.

[440] See *Re St Michael and All Angels, Great Torrington* [1985] Fam 81, [1985] 1 All ER 993, Ct of Eccl Causes Res; and *Re St Stephen's, Walbrook* [1987] Fam 146, [1987] 2 All ER 578, Ct of Eccl Causes Res.

[441] See, eg, *Re St Edward the Confessor, Mottingham* [1983] 1 WLR 364, Southwark Cons Ct, in which Moore Ch refused to grant a faculty for the introduction next to the font of a plaque depicting the washing of the infant Jesus on the grounds that it might suggest that Christ's baptism occurred in infancy and that it might equate the act of washing with the sacrament of baptism.

[442] *Re St Thomas, Pennywell* [1995] Fam 50, [1995] 4 All ER 167, Durham Cons Ct.

[443] *Re St John the Evangelist, Chopwell* [1995] Fam 254, [1996] 1 All ER 275, Durham Cons Ct.

[444] Save for *Re St Peter, St Helier, Morden* [1951] P 303, [1951] 2 All ER 53, Southwark Cons Ct; *Re St Mary, Tyne Dock* [1954] P 369, [1954] 2 All ER 339, Durham Cons Ct; *Re St Mary, Tyne Dock (No 2)* [1958] P 156, [1958] 1 All ER 1, Durham Cons Ct; and *Re St Mary the Virgin, West Moors* [1963] P 390, [1962] 3 All ER 722, Salisbury Cons Ct, there are no reported cases since 1950 of objects being declared illegal per se or tainted with illegality by superstitious reverence. For a discussion of the practice of reservation of the sacrament, see Chapter 5.

[445] R Bursell, *Liturgy, Order and the Law* (Oxford: Clarendon Press, 1996) 14–15.

[446] *Re St Thomas, Pennywell* [1995] Fam 50, [1954] 4 All ER 167, Durham Cons Ct. The chancellor is entitled to take into account the view of the democratically elected PCC as to the churchmanship of the parish where it had voted to support the incumbent's petition for the installation of an aumbry: *Re St Giles, Horsted Keynes* (2002) 7 Ecc LJ 102, Chichester Cons Ct.

[447] *Re St John the Evangelist, Chopwell* [1995] Fam 254, [1996] 1 All ER 275, Durham Cons Ct. Chancellor Bursell held, inter alia, that processions with or without lighted candles were doctrinally acceptable (at 260B); that items that assist private devotions may be admitted as long as they do not detract from the devotions of others nor from the services and ministrations within the church itself (at 261D); that the ceremonial use of incense is not contrary to Anglican doctrine and its use in liturgy is a variation not of substantial importance (at 262E, H); that the same is true of sanctuary bells (at 264C, E) and that the blessing and sprinkling of holy water is neither contrary to nor indicative of any departure from the doctrine of the Church of England in any essential matter (at 268D). In relation to the votive candle stands, the faculty was expressed to be 'until further notice' so that the court might retain control in the event that they fell into 'superstitious uses'. Note the

also been held to be lawful in a number of recent cases,[448] as has an icon from the eastern orthodox tradition.[449]

Pews

7.125 There is a mandatory requirement to provide seats in church for the use of parishioners and others who attend divine service.[450] Their allocation is the responsibility of the churchwardens.[451] Such right of allocation is subject to the rights of particular persons to seats which may be conferred by faculty, prescription or statutory authority.[452] This creates difficulties if the minister and PCC wish to remove pews or reorder the interior of the church. If pew or seat rights have been created which, on their proper construction, are perpetual, a faculty cannot be granted permitting the removal of the seats or pews in question unless the present owners of the rights consent.[453]

Reordering

7.126 Changing patterns of worship may dictate the relocation or removal of fixtures, fittings and ornaments in a church. A balance must be struck between the dynamic quest for change and the dogged retention of the present or the half-remembered past. The Church of England has been constantly evolving and will continue to do so. Accordingly, a guiding principle when addressing the reordering of the interior of a church is that any changes should be reversible.[454] The present generation is but the temporary custodian of the fabric and fixtures of the church. Each case will fall to be determined on its merits, but where the proposals relate to a listed church, then the *Bishopsgate* questions[455] will need to be addressed and the petitioners will need to make out a case of necessity.[456]

---

refusal to admit a votive candle stand in *Re St Oswald King and Martyr, Oswestry* (1998) 6 Ecc LJ 78, Lichfield Cons Ct.

[448] *Re Christ Church, Waltham Cross* (2001) 6 Ecc LJ 290, St Albans Cons Ct. Bursell Ch stated that a faculty will only be granted where there appears to be no danger of the stations becoming objects of 'superstitious reverence'. This decision was followed and applied in *Re St Nicholas, Arundel* (2001) 6 Ecc LJ 290, Chichester Cons Ct, paras 50–51.

[449] *Re St Nicholas, Bookham* (2003) 8 Ecc LJ 112, Guildford Cons Ct.

[450] Canon F 7 para 1.

[451] Canon F 7 para 2. The churchwardens are subject to the direction of the Ordinary and the minister retains the right to allocate seats in the chancel.

[452] Canon F 7 para 2. Pew rights are in the nature of quasi-easements.

[453] *Re St Mary, Banbury* [1986] Fam 24, [1985] 2 All ER 611, Oxford Cons Ct; and *Re St Mary, Banbury* [1987] Fam 136, [1987] 1 All ER 247, Ct of Arches.

[454] See *Re St Stephen, Walbrook* [1987] Fam 146, [1987] 2 All ER 578, Ct of Eccl Causes Res; and *Re St Mary, Banbury* [1987] Fam 136, [1987] 1 All ER 247, Ct of Arches.

[455] See para 7.70 above.

[456] See *Re St Augustine, Scissett* (2003) 7 Ecc LJ 495, Wakefield Cons Ct. An example of petitioners failing to discharge the burden of proof on the issue of necessity may be seen in *Re All Saints, Burbage*, (14 February 2007, unreported), Salisbury Cons Ct.

7.127 The archdeacon has power to grant a licence in writing for a scheme of reordering for a temporary period not exceeding 15 months.[457] Where there is a significant divergence of view within the parish, the more prudent course would be to seek an interim faculty from the chancellor, who could then address the different opinions by way of a hearing. For a consideration of the principles to be applied, see *Re St Luke the Evangelist, Maidstone*,[458] and, with particular reference to churches which are listed buildings, see the discussion of burden and standard of proof at para 7.68ff above.

Trees

7.128 Since the coming into force of the Care of Churches and Ecclesiastical Jurisdiction Measure 1991, the consistory court has exercised jurisdiction over trees, being articles affixed to land.[459] The chancellor, after consultation with the DAC, is required to give written guidance to all PCCs as to the planting, felling, lopping and topping of trees in churchyards.[460] Proceeds from the sale of timber are payable to the PCC to be applied in the maintenance of the churchyard or church.[461] There is no ecclesiastical exemption in relation to Part VIII, Chapter I (sections 197–214D) of the Town and Country Planning Act 1990, which deals with the protection of trees, and it would be prudent for the chancellor's guidance to remind PCCs of the provisions of the secular law in this regard.[462]

7.129 The procedures for obtaining a faculty are varied in cases when the intending applicant proposes to carry out works to a tree or trees or in a consecrated burial ground for which a faculty is required. The application form is completed and sent to the DAC at the time advice is sought.[463] Once the advice of the DAC has been received by way of certificate in the ordinary way, the form is sent to the registry.[464]

---

[457] Faculty Jurisdiction Rules 2000, r 9, which is discussed at para 7.13 above.
[458] *Re St Luke the Evangelist, Maidstone* [1995] Fam 1, [1995] 1 All ER 321, Ct of Arches.
[459] Care of Churches and Ecclesiastical Jurisdiction Measure 1991, ss 6(4), 11(1), 31(1). Section 6(4) provides that the Repair of Benefice Buildings Measure 1972, s 20, which conferred jurisdiction on the parsonages board or the diocesan board of finance, ceases to have effect in relation to trees.
[460] Care of Churches and Ecclesiastical Jurisdiction Measure 1991, s 6(3). The powers, duties and liabilities of the PCC with respect to the care and maintenance of the churchyard extend to trees therein: s 6(1). As to these powers etc, see the Parochial Church Councils (Powers) Measure 1956, s 4(1)(ii)(c).
[461] Care of Churches and Ecclesiastical Jurisdiction Measure 1991, s 6(2).
[462] This covers such matters as tree preservation orders and trees in conservation areas and is one of the few instances where there is dual control by both the secular and the ecclesiastical authorities.
[463] Faculty Jurisdiction Rules 2000, r 3(4). For the form, see App C, Form No 16.
[464] Ibid r 4(3).

Care of places of worship

7.130 As discussed above, church buildings which for the time being are on a list maintained by the Council for the Care of Churches under the Care of Places of Worship Measure 1999 are subject to the faculty jurisdiction of the consistory court of the diocese in which they are situated.[465] Such buildings, and any object or structure fixed to them, are subject to the Inspection of Churches Measure 1955, subject to minor modifications, the most significant of which being that the Council for the Care of Churches is substituted for the PCC.[466]

7.131 The Faculty Jurisdiction (Care of Places of Worship) Rules 2000 largely replicate the provisions of the Faculty Jurisdiction Rules 2000 and, accordingly they are not reproduced in the materials. The most significant modifications are:

(a) those entitled to petition for a faculty in relation to a building are the person or body who made the application for inclusion on the list or any other person whom the chancellor considers to have a sufficient interest;[467]
(b) petitioners are to seek the directions of the registrar in relation to the display of the public notice;[468] the same general provision requiring a public display both inside and outside the building for at least 28 days may thus be provided for having regard to the individual circumstances of each building, some of which, for example, may be on private property;
(c) any 'interested person' may object to a proposed faculty;[469] it is for the chancellor to determine whether a person or body of persons has a sufficient interest in the subject matter of the petition.[470]

7.132 The Faculty Jurisdiction (Injunctions and Restoration Orders) Rules 1992 apply with necessary modifications to buildings under the list maintained by the Council for the Care of Churches.[471]

---

[465] Care of Places of Worship Measure 1999, s 3(2). See para 7.08 above.
[466] Ibid s 3(4), amending the Inspection of Churches Measure 1955, ss 1(2)(d), 2(1).
[467] Faculty Jurisdiction (Care of Places of Worship) Rules 2000, SI 2000/2048, r 3(a), (b).
[468] Ibid r 7(3)(b).
[469] Ibid r 16(1).
[470] Ibid r 16(2)(a). Other interested persons are the archdeacon, the local planning authority, any National Amenity Society and any other body designated by the chancellor: r 16(2)(b)–(d).
[471] Faculty Jurisdiction (Care of Places of Worship) Rules 2000, r 37.

8

CATHEDRALS

Introduction	8.01	Other staff	8.26
Cathedral bodies and personnel	8.05	Cathedral community	8.28
		Property and finance	8.29
The Council	8.06	Ministry	8.32
The Chapter	8.09	Care and maintenance	8.35
The College of Canons	8.13	Fabric advisory committee	8.37
The bishop	8.15	Cathedrals Fabric Commission	8.39
The dean	8.17	Procedure	8.41
Residentiary canons	8.20	Enforcement	8.49
Non-residentiary canons	8.25		

Introduction

The latter part of the twentieth century saw a steady stream of legislation concerning cathedrals which had two broad aims: consistency of governance and protection of the nation's built heritage. The Cathedrals Measure 1963 provided a regime for revising the constitutions and statutes of cathedrals and providing for their management, funding and staffing.[1] The 1963 Measure was substantially repealed by the Cathedrals Measure 1999.[2] This provided a single broad framework of governance for cathedrals,[3] but one which was capable of flexible adaptation

8.01

---

[1] The Cathedrals Commission was established to prepare a scheme for each cathedral to bring its constitution and statutes into conformity with the provisions of the 1963 Measure, which rationalized the holding of property by automatically vesting land in the capitular body. Significant changes, including the substitution of the Cathedral Statutes Commission for the Cathedrals Commission, were effected by the Cathedrals Measure 1976.

[2] See generally *Heritage and Renewal*, The Report of the Archbishops' Commission on Cathedrals (Church House Publishing, 1994).

[3] Note that the Cathedrals Measure 1999, like its predecessors, does not apply to the Cathedral Church of Christ in Oxford (Christ Church), which remains *sui generis*: s 37. Since the Measure only extends to cathedral churches in England, those in the diocese of Sodor and Man and the diocese of Gibraltar in Europe are not affected.

to suit local circumstances. The 1999 Measure also made it possible for individual cathedrals to draw up their own governing instruments—the constitution and statutes—in terms that satisfied the requirements of the statutory framework, and to amend or replace these instruments as and when necessary.

8.02 The 1999 Measure ended, for almost all purposes, the distinction found in the earlier legislation between 'dean and chapter cathedrals'[4] and what the legislation termed 'parish church cathedrals'.[5] The latter were among the cathedrals for dioceses of more recent origin. However, the Measure did not terminate the parochial status of cathedrals where the parochial role was no longer central to the cathedral's life and work, as had been recommended by the Archbishops' Commission.[6] Thus all those cathedrals which were parish churches before the 1999 Measure or had a parish connected with them in some other way[7] retained that status.[8] In particular, under the 1999 Measure, the provisions of the Church Representation Rules relating to parishes and those of the Parochial Church Councils (Powers) Measure 1956 apply, although with substantial modifications and omissions,[9] in relation to the parishes of those cathedrals which previously had no corporate body known as the dean and chapter.

8.03 The carrying out of alterations to any cathedral is governed by the provisions of the Care of Cathedrals Measure 1990.[10] The Measure followed the Faculty Jurisdiction Commission's Report, *The Continuing Care of Churches and Cathedrals* (1984), and provides a statutory framework comparable to, but different from,

---

[4] Namely those which before the 1999 Measure had a corporate body known as the dean and chapter. These may be subdivided into those of the 'old foundation', which existed prior to the Reformation (St Paul's London, York, Hereford, Lincoln, Lichfield, Chichester, Exeter, Salisbury and Wells), those of the 'new foundation', which prior to the Reformation had been monastic in nature (Canterbury, Winchester, Worcester, Ely, Carlisle, Durham, Rochester and Norwich); those of the 'new foundation' created *de novo* at the time of the Reformation (Chester, Peterborough, Oxford, Gloucester and Bristol); most of the cathedrals of new dioceses founded between 1836 and 1877 (Ripon, Manchester and Truro); and non-parochial cathedrals of some more modern dioceses (Liverpool and Guildford).

[5] Namely those which did not have a corporate body known as the dean and chapter before the 1999 Measure.

[6] *Heritage and Renewal* (n 2 above) 65–66, 73, 179.

[7] Including some which had come within the category of dean and chapter cathedrals.

[8] However, a cathedral may voluntarily seek to end its parochial status under the Pastoral Measure 1983, section 17 of which makes provision for, among other things, the dissolution of existing benefices and parishes, altering the area of existing benefices or parishes, and the creation of extra-parochial places.

[9] Cathedrals Measure 1999 ss 12(4), (5). The functions of the PCC vest in the Chapter: s 12(2), (3).

[10] The ecclesiastical exemption, discussed in greater detail in Chapter 7, applies also to cathedral churches: Ecclesiastical Exemption (Listed Buildings and Conservation Areas) Order 1994, SI 1994/1771, art 4(b) and art 2(1).

the faculty jurisdiction.[11] The 1990 Measure was substantially amended by the Care of Cathedrals (Amendment) Measure 2005,[12] and should be read in conjunction with the Care of Cathedrals Rules 2006.[13]

Historically, the cathedral[14] housed the bishop's throne or *cathedra* and was originally the only church of his diocese or *parochia*. The continuing importance of the cathedral as the seat of the diocesan bishop is expressly written into statute,[15] although, as will be seen, his legal powers in relation to the cathedral are relatively few in number and limited in extent.[16] **8.04**

Cathedral bodies and personnel

The Cathedrals Measure 1999 provided for four bodies to be established for each cathedral: the Council, the Chapter, the College of Canons, and the corporate body.[17] The constitution of each cathedral must provide that members for the time being of the Council, the Chapter, and the College of Canons are to be a body corporate with perpetual succession and a common seal, to be known as the common seal of the cathedral.[18] Where members of a body are to be elected or chosen in a prescribed manner, the constitution of the cathedral may specify the qualifications required for membership.[19] All these bodies are under a statutory duty, in the exercise of their functions, to have due regard to the fact that the cathedral is the seat of the bishop and a centre of worship and mission.[20] **8.05**

---

[11] The power for a parish church cathedral to be subject to the alternative faculty jurisdiction of the consistory court no longer exists consequent upon the repeal of the Care of Cathedrals Measure 1990, s 18, by the Care of Cathedrals (Amendment) Measure 2005, s 16.

[12] The Care of Cathedrals Measure 1990 appears in the Materials in its amended form incorporating the changes effected by the Care of Cathedrals (Amendment) Measure 2005. It should be noted that the various provisions of the amending measure are being brought into effect incrementally. Reference should be made to the second edition of this work for the text of the 1990 Measure prior to its amendment.

[13] The Care of Cathedrals Rules 2006, SI 2006/1941 revoked in their entirety the Care of Cathedral Rules 1990, SI 1990/2335. For background to the amendments to the 1990 Measure, see the Report of the Care of Cathedrals Measure Review Group (GS 1417, 2001).

[14] Or cathedral church, properly so called.

[15] Cathedrals Measure 1999, s 1, which prescribes that persons or bodies exercising functions under the Measure are under a statutory duty to 'have due regard to the fact that the cathedral is the seat of the bishop and a centre of worship and mission'.

[16] Ibid s 6, discussed below.

[17] Ibid s 2. Pending the establishment of these bodies, provision was made for a Transitional Council for each cathedral to frame, with the consent of the bishop, instruments providing for the constitution and statutes of the cathedral: s 38(1), Sch 1.

[18] Ibid s 9(1)(a).

[19] Ibid s 35(6). Prescribed, in this context, means prescribed by the constitution of the cathedral: ibid s 35(1).

[20] Ibid s 1.

The Archbishops of Canterbury and York were jointly empowered[21] to appoint the date upon which the substantive provisions of the Cathedrals Measure 1999[22] were to come for each cathedral, once satisfied that a constitution and statutes complying with Part I of the Cathedrals Measure 1999[23] had been framed in relation to that particular cathedral.[24] The constitution and statutes for the cathedral in question came into operation on the appointed date.[25]

The Council

8.06 The constitution of each cathedral must provide for a Council[26] comprising:

(a) a lay chairman, appointed by the bishop;[27]
(b) the dean;
(c) between two and five other members of the Chapter, chosen by it;
(d) two members of the College of Canons, chosen by it;
(e) between two and four lay persons representing the interests of the cathedral community;[28]
(f) between five and ten persons having experience in connection with the work of the cathedral or the ability to reflect local, diocesan, ecumenical or national interests in that connection.[29]

The bishop is entitled to be present and speak but not to vote at meetings of the Council.[30] Members (other than the dean) hold office for a specified term of years and are eligible for further terms of office.[31] It must meet at least twice a year.[32]

---

[21] Under ibid s 38(2).
[22] Namely ibid Pt I (ss 1–27), Pt II (ss 28–32), and ss 36 and 39.
[23] The provisions of ibid Pt I (ss 1–27) are discussed below.
[24] Ibid Sch 1 para 1.
[25] Ibid s 38(2). The Transitional Council then ceased to exist: Sch 1 para 5. All cathedrals in the provinces in Canterbury and York now have constitutions and statutes in place in accordance with the 1999 Measure, the last being Canterbury on 6 October 2002. The following text describes the law based upon the provisions of the Cathedrals Measure 1999 and is applicable as from the 'relevant date' appointed by the Archbishops of Canterbury and York, which varies from one cathedral to another. For the former law, see the first edition of this work: M Hill, *Ecclesiastical Law* (London: Butterworths, 1995) 465–472.
[26] Cathedrals Measure 1999, s 3(1).
[27] Ibid s 3(3), (4)(a). The bishop must have regard to the views of the Chapter as to the appointment in general and any specific person proposed: s 3(3)(a), (b).
[28] These persons are to be elected in the prescribed manner and may not be members of the Chapter: ibid s 3(4)(e). 'Cathedral community' is defined as persons over 16 years of age who worship regularly in the cathedral or are engaged in work or service connected with the cathedral in a regular capacity: s 35(1).
[29] Ibid s 3(4)(a)–(f). It is for the constitution to provide for the precise number to be chosen where the Measure gives a range.
[30] Ibid s 3(2).
[31] Ibid s 3(5).
[32] Ibid s 3(8).

The Council's duty is to further and support the work of the cathedral, spiritual, **8.07** pastoral, evangelistic, social and ecumenical, reviewing and advising upon the direction and oversight of that work by the Chapter.[33] In so doing, it must have due regard to the fact that the cathedral is the seat of the bishop and a centre of worship and mission.[34] Particular functions include:

(a) considering proposals submitted by the Chapter in connection with the general direction and mission of the cathedral and giving advice on them to the Chapter;
(b) receiving and considering the annual budget;
(c) receiving and considering the annual report and audited accounts;
(d) considering proposals submitted by the Chapter in connection with the constitution and statutes of the cathedral with a view to their revision under the Measure.[35]

The Council may also request reports from the Chapter on any matter concerning the cathedral; discuss and declare its opinion on any such matter; and draw any matter to the attention of the visitor or the Church Commissioners.[36]

The Council may, with the consent of the bishop, by instrument under the **8.08** common seal of the cathedral revise the constitution or statutes of the cathedral.[37] Before embarking on the procedure for revision of the constitution, the Council must afford the Chapter an opportunity to express views as to the Council's proposals and must have regard to those views.[38] The Council must publish in one or more publications circulating in the diocese and display prominently in or near the cathedral, a notice of the preparation of any draft revision to the constitution, setting out its objects and specifying where it may be inspected.[39] The notice must invite written representations and allow at least four weeks within which they may be made.[40] A copy of the draft instrument must also be sent to the Secretary-General of the General Synod.[41] The Council, having considered any representations duly made, may amend the draft instrument as it considers expedient.[42] The draft is then signed by the chairman and the common

---

[33] Ibid s 3(6).
[34] Ibid s 1.
[35] Ibid s 3(6)(a)–(d). It must also perform 'such other functions as may be prescribed': s 3(6)(e).
[36] Ibid s 3(7)(a)–(c).
[37] Ibid s 28(1). This may be in the form of new documents or by way of amendment to those already in force: s 28(2).
[38] Ibid s 28(3). The Chapter has a co-extensive duty to keep the cathedral constitution and statutes under review and to submit any proposals for their revision to the Council: s 4(8)(f).
[39] Ibid s 29(1).
[40] Ibid s 29(1).
[41] Ibid s 29(2).
[42] Ibid s 29(3).

seal of the cathedral is affixed thereto.[43] A similar procedure is followed in relation to the revision of statutes, but there is no requirement to publish a notice in any local publication, nor need the draft be sent to the Secretary-General of the General Synod.[44]

The Chapter

8.09 The constitution of the cathedral must also provide for the establishment of the Chapter,[45] which comprises:

(a) the dean and all the residentiary canons;
(b) between two and seven other persons, of whom at least two-thirds are to be lay;
(c) the administrator of the cathedral (if the constitution so provides).[46]

A person may not be a member of the Chapter if he is disqualified from being a charity trustee, unless this requirement is expressly waived by the archbishop.[47] The Chapter must meet at least nine times each year.[48] The dean is the chairman of the Chapter and may exercise a second or casting vote and is a member of every committee of the Chapter.[49] The constitution of the cathedral must provide for the establishment of a finance committee of the Chapter to advise the Chapter in connection with its responsibilities in the field of financial and investment management.[50] The statutes must provide for any presentations or nominations to benefices in the patronage of the cathedral to be exercised either by the Chapter or by a patronage committee of the Chapter.[51]

8.10 No alteration to the ordering of services in the cathedral may be made nor may the budget be settled without the consent of the dean.[52] No decision taken in

---

[43] Ibid s 31. A copy of the instrument must be sent to the Secretary-General of the General Synod: s 31(2).
[44] Ibid s 30.
[45] Ibid s 4(1). Where functions of the PCC were previously exercised either by the PCC, or were transferred to the administrative body by the PCC, the constitution of the cathedral must provide for them to be exercised by or transferred to the Chapter: s 12(2), (3).
[46] Ibid s 4(2), (3). The members specified at (b) hold office for a term of years but are eligible for membership for further terms: s 4(7).
[47] Ibid s 4(4), (5). As to such disqualification, see the Charities Act 1993, s 72.
[48] Cathedrals Measure 1999, s 4(12).
[49] Ibid s 4(6).
[50] Ibid s 9(1)(h), which requires the constitution to provide for the membership to include persons who have expertise and experience in the field of financial and investment management. Note also the general provision for the establishment of committees (including non-members of Chapter) and delegation of functions to them: s 10.
[51] Ibid s 11(b).
[52] Ibid s 7(3)(a), (b). The provisions for deemed consent do not apply to these matters.

Cathedral bodies and personnel

the absence of the dean may be implemented without his consent.[53] The dean is deemed to have consented to any decision taken in his absence unless within one month he requests the Chapter to reconsider the matter at its next meeting.[54] The cathedral constitution may contain provision enabling or requiring committees to be established by the Chapter. In cathedrals where there was formerly no corporate body known as the dean and chapter, certain of the provisions of the Parochial Church Councils (Powers) Measure 1956 have effect in relation to the parish concerned, subject to necessary modifications, and all references to the PCC are deemed to refer to the Chapter.[55]

8.11 The duty of the Chapter, having due regard to the fact that the cathedral is the seat of the bishop and a centre of worship and mission,[56] is to direct and oversee the administration of the affairs of the cathedral[57] and, in particular to:

(a) order the worship and promote the mission of the cathedral;
(b) formulate, after consultation with the bishop, proposals in connection with the general direction and mission of the cathedral and submit them to the Council for its advice;
(c) prepare an annual budget for the cathedral;
(d) submit to the Council the annual report and audited accounts and such other reports on matters concerning the cathedral as may be requested by the Council;
(e) submit to the College of Canons the annual report and audited accounts;
(f) keep under review the constitution and statutes of the cathedral and submit any proposals for revision to the Council;
(g) manage all property and income and ensure that necessary repairs and maintenance are carried out to the cathedral, its contents and other buildings and monuments.[58]

8.12 The Chapter must maintain proper records of income and expenditure, assets and liabilities, and prepare an annual report and accounts in accordance with best

---

[53] Ibid s 7(3)(c).
[54] Ibid s 7(3) proviso. Such matter is duly determined by majority vote, the dean having a second or casting vote: s 7(3) proviso.
[55] Ibid s 12(4), (5), disapplying the Parochial Church Councils (Powers) Measure 1956, ss 3, 5(1), 6, 7(iii), (iv), 8 and 9. Note also the application of the Church Representation Rules, subject to similar modifications: Cathedrals Measure 1999, s 12(4). See generally the discussion of the parish in Chapter 2.
[56] Ibid s 1.
[57] The Chapter must meet on at least nine occasions in each calendar year: s 4(12); it holds the common seal of the cathedral and affixes it when required: s 4(10); and has power to acquire and dispose of property on behalf of the corporate body: s 4(9).
[58] Ibid s 4(8)(a)–(g). It must also perform 'such other functions as may be prescribed': ibid s 4(8)(h).

professional practice and standards.[59] The accounts must be audited by a person entitled to audit charity accounts.[60] A copy of the annual report and audited accounts must be sent to the Church Commissioners and to any other person who requests it, and must be displayed in a prominent position in or in the vicinity of the cathedral.[61]

The College of Canons

8.13 The College of Canons is the third body for which the constitution of the cathedral must make provision.[62] It comprises:

(a) the dean;
(b) every suffragan bishop of the diocese;
(c) every full-time stipendiary assistant bishop of the diocese;
(d) every canon of the cathedral;[63] and
(e) every archdeacon of the diocese.[64]

8.14 The functions of the College of Canons, in the exercise of which it too must have due regard to the fact that the cathedral is the seat of the bishop and a centre of worship and mission,[65] are to receive and consider the annual report and audited accounts, and to discuss such matters concerning the cathedral as may be raised by any of its members.[66] The College exercises the functions in relation to the election of bishops which were previously exercised by the dean and chapter or cathedral chapter.[67]

The bishop

8.15 The Cathedrals Measure 1999 makes express provision for the status and role of the bishop in the cathedral.[68] He has the principal seat and dignity in the

---

[59] Ibid s 27(1). The Church Commissioners have power to specify what constitutes best professional practice and standards and to inquire into any departure from them: s 27(2).
[60] Ibid s 27(1); Charities Act 1993, s 43.
[61] Cathedrals Measure 1999, s 27(3). Note also that the annual report and audited accounts must be received and considered by the cathedral Council (s 3(6)(c)) and by the College of Canons (s 5(4)(a)).
[62] Ibid s 5(1).
[63] 'Canon' includes a lay canon and a non-residentiary canon, but not a minor canon: ibid s 35(1).
[64] Ibid s 5(2)(a)–(e).
[65] Ibid s 1.
[66] Ibid s 5(4)(a), (b). It must also perform 'such other functions as may be prescribed': s 5(4)(c).
[67] Ibid s 5(3); Appointment of Bishops Act 1533. For the appointment of diocesan bishops, see Chapter 4.
[68] Cathedrals Measure 1999, s 6. This is without prejudice to the bishop's powers under the Care of Cathedrals (Supplementary Provisions) Measure 1994 and his general powers as visitor: Cathedrals Measure 1999, s 6(8).

cathedral and may officiate therein and use it in his work of teaching and mission, for ordinations and synods and for other diocesan occasions and purposes.[69] The Chapter must, from time to time, consult the bishop in respect of the general direction and mission of the cathedral, and the bishop may at any time seek the advice of the Chapter on any matter.[70] He may at any time propose for consideration by the Council amendments to the cathedral constitution and statutes.[71]

8.16 The constitution of each cathedral must provide for the bishop to be the visitor.[72] As visitor, the bishop must hear and determine any question as to the construction of the cathedral constitution and statutes,[73] and he may hold a visitation when he considers it desirable or necessary to do so or when requested by the Council or the Chapter.[74] In the course of a visitation, the bishop may give such directions to the Chapter, to the holder of any office in the cathedral or to any person employed by the cathedral as will, in the bishop's opinion, better serve the due observance of the constitution and statutes.[75] Persons or bodies on whom functions are conferred by or under the Cathedrals Measure 1999 must act in accordance with any such determination or direction.[76]

The dean

8.17 The dean is the principal dignitary of the cathedral, next after the bishop.[77] His stipend is paid out of the general fund of the Church Commissioners.[78] It is his duty, as chairman of the Chapter,[79] to govern and direct on its behalf the work of the cathedral and, particularly, to:

(a) ensure that divine service is duly performed in the cathedral;
(b) ensure that the constitution and statutes are faithfully observed;
(c) maintain good order and proper reverence in the cathedral;
(d) secure the pastoral care of all members of the cathedral community;

---

[69] Ibid s 6(1). Such right is subject to prior consultation with the Chapter and to any provision in the statutes.
[70] Ibid s 6(2).
[71] Ibid s 6(9).
[72] Ibid s 6(3).
[73] Ibid s 6(4).
[74] Ibid s 6(5). The bishop is not obliged to hold a visitation when requested to do so.
[75] Ibid s 6(6). For a discussion of visitations generally, see P Barrett, 'Episcopal Visitation of Cathedrals of the Church of England' (2006) 8 Ecc LJ 266.
[76] Ibid s 6(7).
[77] Ibid s 7(1).
[78] Ibid s 21(1). The Chapter, with the consent of the Commissioners, may pay to the dean such additional stipend or other emoluments as they may think fit: s 21(2). Removal expenses upon appointment may also be paid by the Commissioners: s 22.
[79] Ibid s 4(6)(a).

(e) take all decisions necessary to deal with any emergency affecting the cathedral, pending consideration of the matter by the Chapter.[80]

8.18 When, prior to the Cathedrals Measure 1999 coming into force, the constitution of the cathedral provided for the dean to be appointed by the Queen, the constitution must continue so to do.[81] The monarch acts upon the advice of the Prime Minister.[82] In other cases, the incumbent of the relevant benefice is *ex officio* the dean, presented by the patron.[83] It is usual for there to be widespread consultation prior to any appointment being made, including the involvement of the archbishops' secretary for appointments.[84] No person may be appointed dean unless he has been in holy orders for at least six years and is in priest's orders at the time of appointment.[85] The duties of the dean are prescribed by Canon C 21 and are the same as those for residentiary canons, as are the provisions relating to retirement and removal from office.[86] The dean is an *ex officio* member of diocesan synod.[87]

8.19 Where the office of dean is vacant or the bishop considers that the dean will be unable to discharge any or all of his functions under the Cathedrals Measure 1999 by reason of illness, absence, or any other cause, the bishop must, after consultation with the Chapter, appoint a residentiary canon to carry out such functions as the dean is unable to discharge during the period in question.[88] A dean is subject to compulsory retirement at the age of 70.[89]

---

[80] Ibid s 7(2)(a)–(e). He too must have due regard to the fact that the cathedral is the seat of the bishop and a centre of worship and mission: s 1.

[81] Ibid s 9(2)(a). In any other case, the constitution must provide that the incumbent of the benefice which comprises the parish of which the cathedral is the parish church is to be the dean: s 9(2)(b). References in enactments, instruments and other documents to the provost of a cathedral are to be construed as references to the dean: s 36(4).

[82] For a discussion of the consultation process, see *Senior Church Appointments*, a Review of the Methods of Appointment of Area and Suffragan Bishops, Deans, Provosts, Archdeacons and Residentiary Canons (GS 1019, 1992) 66–67.

[83] Such person was previously styled the provost, but is now known as the dean: Cathedrals Measure 1999, ss 7(1), 36(4). With the exception of Sheffield and Bradford, the patron is the diocesan bishop.

[84] *Senior Church Appointments* (n 82 above) 67–68. Note that in the case of the presentation by a patron of an incumbent to the benefice, who thereby becomes the dean *ex officio*, the processes under the Patronage (Benefices) Measure 1986 are followed.

[85] Canon C 21 para 1; Ecclesiastical Commissioners Act 1840, s 27, amended by the Church of England (Miscellaneous Provisions) Measure 1995, s 5. In relation to the appointment of a woman as dean, and generally in relation to the ministry of women priests in cathedrals, see para 8.34 below.

[86] See below.

[87] Church Representation Rules, r 30(4)(a)(ii).

[88] Cathedrals Measure 1999, s 7(4).

[89] Ecclesiastical Offices (Age Limit) Measure 1975, s 1(3), Schedule. The bishop may authorize him to continue in office for up to a further year if he considers that there are special circumstances which make it desirable.

Residentiary canons

8.20 The constitution of each cathedral must provide for the appointment of canons in holy orders, the manner of their appointment, and their tenure of office, whether freehold or for a term of years.[90] No person may be appointed residentiary canon unless he has been in holy orders for at least six years except in the case of a canonry annexed to any professorship, headship or other office in any university.[91] A deacon may be so appointed notwithstanding anything in section 10 of the Act of Uniformity 1662 or in the cathedral constitution or statutes.[92] No person may hold cathedral preferments in more than one cathedral,[93] nor may he hold a cathedral preferment with one or more benefices unless the cathedral statutes so provide or allow.[94] The majority of canonries are in the gift of the bishop.[95]

8.21 A maximum number of residentiary canons must be specified,[96] and the constitution must further specify that the holders of at least two residentiary canonries in the cathedral are to be engaged exclusively on cathedral duties.[97] The archbishop and the Church Commissioners acting jointly may in special circumstances direct that the holder of a residentiary canonry who is normally engaged exclusively on cathedral duties be treated as so engaged notwithstanding that he is performing duties other than cathedral duties.[98] The statutes may provide for the creation, continuance, abolition, suspension or termination of suspension of any dignity, office or body in the cathedral and for the title by which it is to be known.[99]

---

[90] Cathedrals Measure 1999, s 9(1)(b). The recommendation in *Heritage and Renewal* (n 2 above), for the abolition of freehold (at pages 93–94, 99) has not been followed. Discretion is therefore left to individual cathedrals to provide within their own constitutions for the tenure of office of their canons.

[91] Canon C 21 para 1; Ecclesiastical Commissioners Act 1840, s 27.

[92] Church of England (Miscellaneous Provisions) Measure 1992, s 15. He may not, however, celebrate holy communion or pronounce the absolution: Canon C 21 para 1A.

[93] Pastoral Measure 1983, s 85(3).

[94] Ibid s 85(2). A person accepting a cathedral preferment is deemed to vacate the office previously held: s 85(4).

[95] See *Senior Church Appointments* (n 82 above) 68–69. The Crown and the Lord Chancellor appoint to certain canonries. The Dean of St Albans appoints the abbey's sub-dean, with the concurrence of the bishop.

[96] Cathedrals Measure 1999, s 9(1)(d).

[97] Ibid s 8(1). 'Cathedral duties' means duties (whether in the cathedral or the diocese) which should, in the opinion of the Chapter after consulting the bishop, be discharged in or from the cathedral: s 8(2). Should there be any question as to whether a person is engaged exclusively on cathedral duties, it must, after consultation with the visitor and the Chapter, be determined by the Church Commissioners subject to an appeal to the archbishop: s 8(3).

[98] Ibid s 8(2) proviso.

[99] Ibid s 11(a).

The stipends of two residentiary canons engaged exclusively on cathedral activities are paid by the Church Commissioners from their general fund.[100]

8.22 The duties of residentiary canons and deans are set out in Canon C 21. They include ensuring the diligent observance of the statutes and laudable customs of their Church, the statutes of the realm concerning ecclesiastical order, and the directions of the bishop made at his visitation.[101] They must be resident in their cathedral for the time prescribed by law and by the statutes of the cathedral and must there preach the Word of God and perform all the duties of their office unless otherwise hindered by weighty and urgent cause.[102] In addition they, together with the minor canons, vicars choral and other ministers of the cathedral, must provide as far as in them lies that during the time of divine service in the cathedral all things be done with such reverence, care and solemnity as sets forth the honour and glory of Almighty God.[103] The retirement age for residentiary canons is 70.[104]

8.23 Under the Church Dignitaries (Retirement) Measure 1949, provision is made for the removal of dignitaries for mental or physical incapacity. 'Dignitary' includes a dean, canon, prebendary and archdeacon.[105] Where the bishop is satisfied that such action is proper, he may by notice in writing require that a special meeting of the Chapter of the cathedral be summoned for the purpose of considering and reporting to him whether in its opinion the dignitary is unable, through disability arising from age or infirmity (whether bodily or mental), to discharge adequately the duties of his office and, if so, whether he should retire from such office.[106] The notice must also be served on the dignitary concerned.[107]

8.24 The Chapter must consider the questions put to it and must invite the dignitary concerned[108] and the bishop's representative (if any)[109] to confer with it either

---

[100] Ibid s 21(1). The Chapter may, with the consent of the Commissioners, pay to any such residentiary canon such additional stipend or other emoluments as they may think fit: s 21(2). Removal expenses upon appointment may also be paid the Commissioners: s 22.
[101] Canon C 21 para 2.
[102] Canon C 21 para 3.
[103] Canon C 21 para 4.
[104] Ecclesiastical Offices (Age Limit) Measure 1975, s 1(3), Schedule. The bishop may authorize a residentiary canon to continue in office for up to a further year if he considers that there are special circumstances which make it desirable.
[105] Church Dignitaries (Retirement) Measure 1949, s 12.
[106] Ibid s 1(1). The Chapter should also report on what, if any, additional pension provision should be made for the dignitary: s 1(1). If the dignitary is a member of the Chapter, he may not sit or vote at the special meeting: s 13(5).
[107] Ibid s 1(1).
[108] He may be assisted by or, in his absence, represented by a friend or adviser: ibid s 1(4).
[109] The bishop may appoint a clerk in holy orders to represent him: ibid s 1(2).

together or separately, and must make its report in writing, answering the questions put to it by the bishop.[110] If the Chapter reports that it is desirable that the dignitary should retire,[111] the bishop may, within six months of the receipt of the report, petition the monarch to declare the office vacant,[112] or execute an instrument declaring the office vacant.[113] Where the dignitary is also an incumbent of a parochial benefice, a declaration of vacation of his office as dean or archdeacon has the effect also of vacating his benefice, whether the office is annexed to the benefice or vice versa.[114] A dignitary who is also the incumbent of a parochial benefice who resigns his benefice, or whose benefice is declared vacant under the Incumbents (Vacation of Benefices) Measure 1977 (as amended) following a finding of mental or physical incapacity, may be removed from his office as if the report of the provincial tribunal had been a report by the Chapter under the Cathedral Dignitaries (Retirement) Measure 1949.[115] Where an office held by a dignitary has been declared vacant, the vacancy may be filled in the same manner as if the dignitary had died.[116]

Non-residentiary canons

8.25 The constitution of the cathedral must make provision for the maximum number of non-residentiary canons.[117] They are members of the College of Canons.[118] Their appointment, function and period of office is determined by each cathedral. Often no specific duties are required of a non-residentiary canon, whose selection generally marks distinguished service within the diocese. Provision must be made in the constitution of each cathedral enabling lay canons to be appointed.[119] Lay canons are members of the College of Canons.[120]

---

[110] Ibid s 1(3).
[111] It must not report that it is desirable that the dignitary should retire unless at least two-thirds of the members present and voting at the meeting have voted in favour: ibid s 1(3) proviso.
[112] If the office is one to which the right of appointment is vested in the Crown.
[113] Church Dignitaries (Retirement) Measure 1949, s 2(1).
[114] Ibid s 14(1), substituted by the Incumbents (Vacation of Benefices) Measure 1977, s 20(1).
[115] Church Dignitaries (Retirement) Measure 1949, s 14(2). For a discussion of the Incumbents (Vacation of Benefices) Measure 1977, see Chapter 4.
[116] Church Dignitaries (Retirement) Measure 1949, s 15.
[117] Cathedrals Measure 1999, s 9(1)(d). They are sometimes styled 'prebendaries' and the term 'honorary canon' is also used. There is no uniformity of practice in the titles or status of non-residentiary canons.
[118] Ibid ss 5(2)(d), 35(1).
[119] Ibid s 9(1)(c).
[120] Ibid s 5(2)(d).

Other staff

8.26 The constitution of each cathedral must provide for the appointment of an administrator of the cathedral;[121] of an architect and an auditor for the cathedral;[122] and for a person to supervise the music in the cathedral.[123] The duty to have due regard to the fact that the cathedral is the seat of the bishop and a centre of worship and mission applies only to persons or bodies on whom functions are conferred by or under the Cathedrals Measure 1999, and only in relation to the exercise of those functions.[124] Administrators, music supervisors and the finance committee have functions conferred by or under the Measure, but the Measure is silent as to the functions of lay canons, architects and auditors.[125]

8.27 There is provision for the Church Commissioners to make grants from their general fund for the payment of the salary or other emoluments of any lay person employed in connection with the cathedral,[126] and the stipend or other emoluments of any clerk in holy orders holding office in the cathedral other than a dean or residentiary canon.[127] Such clerks in holy orders, variously styled 'minor canons', 'vicars choral' or 'priest vicars', do not have a cure of souls. They have the same obligations regarding the proper conduct of divine service as the dean and residentiary canons.[128]

Cathedral community

8.28 The constitution of each cathedral which is not a parish church cathedral must provide for the formation and maintenance of a roll containing the names of persons who are members of the cathedral community and apply to be enrolled as such.[129] In this context, 'cathedral community' means persons over the age of 16 who worship regularly in the cathedral or who are engaged in work or service

---

[121] Ibid, s 9(1)(e).
[122] Ibid s 9(1)(f). See also n 163 below.
[123] Ibid s 9(1)(g). The nature of the relationship between an organist and his employer institution (being a royal peculiar) was discussed in *Neary v Dean of Westminster* (1998) 5 Ecc LJ 303, per Lord Jauncey of Tullichettle. One feature which was absent in this case, Westminster Abbey not being a cathedral, but will be present in all cases affecting cathedral organists, is the statutory duty of the person 'having the function of supervising music in the cathedral', under the Cathedrals Measure 1999, s 1, to have due regard to the fact that the cathedral is the seat of the bishop and a centre of worship and mission.
[124] Ibid s 1.
[125] Note the differences in wording in ibid s 9(1)(c), (e), (f), (g), (h). A generous reading of the term 'under' should ensure that the spirit of the legislation prevails.
[126] Ibid s 23(b).
[127] Ibid s 23(a). Minor canons would be included in this category, they being expressly omitted from the definition of 'canon' in s 25(1).
[128] Canon C 21 para 4.
[129] Cathedrals Measure 1999, s 9(3).

connected with the cathedral in a regular capacity.[130] The constitution may provide for a Cathedral Community Committee, the membership consisting of persons whose names are on the roll of members.[131] Provision exists for the laity who worship regularly at cathedrals to participate in the wider processes of synodical government.[132]

Property and finance

Property previously vested in the dean and chapter or in the cathedral chapter automatically now vests in the cathedral,[133] and the Chapter has power to acquire and dispose of property on behalf of the corporate body.[134] In addition, the Church Commissioners may, with the consent of the Chapter, prepare a scheme providing for the transfer of property from the Commissioners to the cathedral.[135] Certain consents are required before the cathedral may acquire or dispose of land.[136] Before the disposal of a residence may be authorized, the consent of the dean or residentiary canon who normally occupies it must be obtained.[137] The Church Commissioners may make grants out of their general fund to secure the better housing of clerks in holy orders who hold office in the cathedral.[138] **8.29**

The Chapter may exercise certain powers in respect of money which forms part of the endowment of the cathedral or is otherwise vested in the cathedral or in the Church Commissioners on its behalf. Such powers permit the investment of such money in the acquisition of land, in any investment fund or deposit fund constituted under the Church Funds Investment Measure 1958, and as a trustee **8.30**

---

[130] Ibid s 35(1). This roll may include both clergy and laity, unlike a church electoral roll which is not open to those in holy orders.

[131] Ibid s 10(1)(a). The constitution may provide for the delegation of functions to such a committee: s 10(1).

[132] The normal processes apply for parish church cathedrals for representation of the laity on deanery synod: see Chapter 2. Laity of other cathedrals may be represented under a scheme made pursuant to the Church Representation Rules, r 27, amended by the Cathedrals Measure 1999, s 39(1), Sch 2 para 8. There is, however, no provision for a PCC.

[133] Cathedrals Measure 1999, s 13. 'Cathedral' here means the Chapter, Council and College of Canons, who together are a body corporate with perpetual succession and a common seal under ibid s 9(1)(a): s 35(5).

[134] Ibid s 4(9).

[135] Ibid s 14(1).

[136] See ibid s 15(1). 'Acquire' is to be construed as comprising a power to acquire property for any purpose connected with the cathedral and to acquire property by gift *inter vivos* or by will: s 35(4). 'Disposal' is taken to mean comprising a power to sell, grant a lease or licence of, exchange, mortgage or charge land and to dedicate land for the purposes of a highway: s 35(3).

[137] Ibid s 15(1)(a). Where the house is allocated for the use of the holder of a dignity the right of presentation to which is vested in the Queen, then her consent is also required: ibid s 15(1)(b).

[138] Ibid s 24.

under the Trustee Act 2000.[139] They also include a power to use such money for the improvement or development of any property vested in the cathedral.[140] Money forming part of the endowment of the cathedral[141] may not be used for the improvement or development of the cathedral or other ecclesiastical building.[142] Such may only be used for the improvement or development of other buildings with the consent of the Church Commissioners.[143] The use of such money for the repair of any property is prohibited save in the case of an emergency justifying expenditure on the repair of the cathedral or other ecclesiastical building, in which case, with the consent of the Church Commissioners, the money may be incurred and the sum expended replaced by the Chapter within such period and in such manner as may be agreed between the Commissioners and the Chapter.[144] The Commissioners may make grants out of their general fund for the repair of any chancel, other than that of the cathedral, which the cathedral is wholly or partly liable to repair.[145] The Chapter has power to borrow money for any purpose connected with the cathedral.[146]

8.31 The Chapter may allocate any house vested in the cathedral for the use as a residence of any person holding an office in connection with the cathedral.[147] The Chapter must arrange for an architect or surveyor of the fabric to carry out an inspection of all property and ancillary buildings, other than the cathedral, which the Chapter is liable to repair and maintain and to report in writing to the Chapter on any works which the architect or surveyor considers will need to be carried out in relation to that property and of the urgency with which he considers that they should be carried out.[148] The first inspection is required to be carried out within five years of the Cathedrals Measure 1999 coming into force for the cathedral,[149]

---

[139] Cathedrals Measure 1999, s 16(1)(a)–(c) (as amended by the Trustee Act 2000).
[140] Cathedrals Measure 1999, s 16(1)(d). When investing in land, the like consents should be obtained as when acquiring land: s 16(2).
[141] This includes the proceeds of disposal of property forming part of the endowment: ibid s 17.
[142] Ibid s 16(3). The 'other buildings' are those falling within the Ecclesiastical Exemption (Listed Buildings and Conservation Areas) Order 1994, SI 1994/1771, art 5(2)(a).
[143] Cathedrals Measure 1999, s 16(3).
[144] Ibid s 16(4). The Commissioners may make payments out of money held by them which forms part of the endowment of the cathedral if the Chapter so requests for this purpose: s 18.
[145] Ibid s 25. See generally the Chancel Repairs Act 1932, s 2; and *Aston Cantlow and Wilmcote with Billesley Parochial Church Council v Wallbank* [2004] 1 AC 546, [2003] 3 All ER 1213, HL (as to enforceability) and The Times, 21 February 2007, Lewison J (as to quantum).
[146] Cathedrals Measure 1999, s 26. The consent of the Church Commissioners is required if the purpose for which the money is to be borrowed is such that the use of money forming part of the endowment of the cathedral for that purpose would require such consent: s 26 proviso.
[147] Ibid s 19.
[148] Ibid s 20(1) (as amended).
[149] As to establishing the date for each cathedral see para 8.05 above.

and subsequent inspections during every five-year period thereafter.[150] The Chapter must compile and keep up to date a plan indicating the extent of the land surrounding the cathedral church of which the fee simple is vested in the corporate body.[151] The Cathedrals Fabric Commission, after consultation with the Chapter, must indicate thereon the precinct of the cathedral church, namely such land as is necessary in the opinion of the Commission, to preserve or protect the architectural, archaeological, artistic or historic character of the cathedral church and its setting.[152]

Ministry

8.32 In every cathedral, the Common Prayer must be said or sung distinctly, reverently and in an audible voice, every morning and evening, and the Litany on the appointed days, the officiating ministers and others of the clergy present in the choir being duly habited.[153] Holy communion must be celebrated at least on all Sundays and other feast days, on Ash Wednesday and on other days as often as may be convenient.[154] In every cathedral, the dean, the residentiary canons and the other ministers of the church must all receive holy communion every Sunday at the least unless they have a reasonable cause to the contrary.[155]

8.33 The Chapter may, with the approval of the bishop, invite members of another Church to which Canon B 43 (one of the 'ecumenical canons') applies to take part in joint worship with the Church of England or to use the cathedral for worship in accordance with the forms of service and practice of that other Church on such occasions as may be specified in the approval given by the bishop.[156] The cathedral may also participate in a local ecumenical project.[157]

8.34 Provision is made under the Priests (Ordination of Women) Measure 1993, for what is now the Chapter to pass either or both of resolutions A and B in

---

[150] Cathedrals Measure 1999, s 20(1). In the case of property within the precinct of the cathedral, the report must be compiled in consultation with the archaeological consultant of the cathedral (if any) and the Chapter must send a copy of the report to the fabric advisory committee of the cathedral and to the Cathedrals Fabric Commission for England: s 20(2).
[151] Care of Cathedrals Measure 1990, s 13(3) (as amended).
[152] Ibid s 13(4) (as amended). This is merely a summary of the extended statutory definition and explanation of precinct, the amended section being somewhat more detailed. Once notified of any changes to the plan, the Cathedrals Fabric Commission, again after consultation with the Chapter, may make any alterations to the precinct as delineated as it considers appropriate.
[153] Canon B 10.
[154] Canon B 13 para 1. It must be celebrated distinctly, reverently and in an audible voice.
[155] Canon B 13 para 2.
[156] See Canon B 43 para 10, and the Cathedrals Measure 1999, s 36(1).
[157] Canon B 44 para 6. Appropriate modifications are provided for.

Schedule 2 to that Measure.[158] Such resolutions remain in force until rescinded.[159] A motion for such a resolution may not be considered by the Chapter if the dean or any of the residentiary canons is a woman priest.[160] Where a resolution remains in force, no person discharging any functions in relation to the conduct of services in the cathedral or in relation to the appointment of the dean may act in contravention of it.[161]

Care and maintenance

8.35 The duty of the Chapter to arrange for an architect or surveyor of the fabric to carry out an inspection of all property, other than the cathedral,[162] has already been mentioned, as has the requirement for the constitution to provide for the appointment of an architect or surveyor of the fabric for the cathedral.[163] It is the duty of the Chapter to appoint a cathedral archaeologist, save where the Cathedrals Fabric Commission for England notifies it that, in its view, the archaeological significance of the cathedral does not justify such an appointment.[164] The Chapter is required to ensure that the cathedral architect or surveyor of the fabric, in consultation with the cathedral archaeologist (if there is one), makes a written report every five years on any works which he considers will need to be carried out in relation to the cathedral church and any ancillary building and on the urgency with which they should be carried out.[165] The cathedral architect or surveyor of the fabric must make a written report to the Chapter containing a summary of any works to the cathedral church and ancillary buildings carried out during the preceding year, and an account of progress made in giving effect

---

[158] Priests (Ordination of Women) Measure 1993, s 4(1), Sch 2.
[159] Priests (Ordination of Women) Measure 1993, s 4(2).
[160] Ibid s 4(3).
[161] Ibid s 4(5). It is an ecclesiastical offence for a bishop, priest or deacon so to do: ibid s 5(c).
[162] Cathedrals Measure 1999, ss 9: see para 8.31 above.
[163] Ibid s 9(1)(f). Before so doing, it must consult the Cathedrals Fabric Commission: Care of Cathedrals Measure 1990 (as amended), s 12(1). It may also appoint a surveyor of the fabric, and if it does so it must first consult the Cathedrals Fabric Commission: s 12(1).
[164] Care of Cathedrals Measure 1990 (as amended), s 12(2). The former requirement was for 'an archaeological consultant to the cathedral'. If a cathedral archaeologist is appointed, he must assess those matters of archaeological interest which relate to the cathedral church and its precinct and, in consultation with the cathedral architect and the architect or surveyor appointed under the Cathedrals Measure 1999, s 20 (if a different person), make a report in writing to the Chapter containing recommendations on how those matters should be managed: Care of Cathedrals Measure 1990, s 14A(1) (as amended). Thereafter he must make an annual report to the Chapter containing an account of progress made in fulfilling the recommendations: s 14A(2). Other more detailed reporting requirements, including the maintenance of records, are contained in s 14B.
[165] Ibid s 14(1) (as amended). A copy of each report must be sent to the Cathedrals Fabric Commission.

to recommendations in the quinquennial report.[166] The Chapter must compile and maintain an inventory of all objects in the possession or custody of the corporate body comprising members of the Council, Chapter and College of Canons.[167] The Chapter must make an annual report to the fabric advisory committee on the contents of the inventory, certifying its accuracy and describing any alterations.[168] It is the duty of the fabric advisory committee to designate those objects on the inventory which it considers, after consultation with the Cathedrals Fabric Commission, to be of outstanding architectural, archaeological, artistic or historic merit.[169]

8.36 The carrying out of alterations to any cathedral is governed by the provisions of the Care of Cathedrals Measure 1990. It provides a statutory framework comparable to, but different from, the faculty jurisdiction. As with the faculty jurisdiction, there is a general prohibition on the carrying out of works in the absence of specific approval. Without the necessary consents, discussed below, the Chapter may not implement or consent to the implementation of any proposal for:

(a) the carrying out of works on, above or below land vested in the corporate body which would materially affect the architectural, archaeological, artistic or historic character of the cathedral or any building within its precinct which is being used for ecclesiastical purposes or the immediate setting of the cathedral or any archaeological remains within the precinct; or

(b) the sale, loan or other disposal of any object vested in the corporate body (or which is in the possession or custody of the corporate body)[170] which is of architectural, archaeological, artistic or historic interest, or which would constitute treasure under the Treasure Act 1996;[171] or

(c) the carrying out of any work to any of the above objects which would materially affect the architectural, archaeological, artistic or historic character of the object, or

---

[166] Ibid s 14(5) (as amended). It should be in consultation with the architect or surveyor of the fabric appointed under the Cathedrals Measure 1999, s 20 (if a different person), and the cathedral archaeologist (if there is one). Ancillary building, for this purpose, excludes any residence: Care of Cathedrals Measure 1990, s 14(6) (as amended).

[167] Ibid, s 13(1) (as amended). The timescale for the completion of the inventory for each cathedral is to be determined by the Cathedrals Fabric Commission, after consultation with the Chapter and the fabric advisory committee.

[168] Ibid, s 13(1B) (as amended).

[169] Ibid s 13(2).

[170] Or one to whose possession or custody the corporate body is entitled: ibid s 2(1)(b).

[171] For specific provisions on treasure, see the Care of Cathedrals Measure 1990, s 6A (as amended).

(d) the permanent addition to the cathedral of any object which would materially affect the architectural, archaeological, artistic or historic character of the cathedral.[172]

The prohibition does not apply to anything done by the Chapter in furtherance of its duties under the constitution and statutes of the cathedral with respect to the ordering of services or furtherance of the mission of the cathedral which is of a temporary nature and does not affect the fabric of the cathedral.[173] Proposals implemented in contravention of these provisions may be the subject of retrospective approval.[174]

Fabric advisory committee

8.37 Each cathedral is required (jointly with the Cathedrals Fabric Commission, discussed below) to establish a fabric advisory committee.[175] This committee must give advice to the Chapter on the care, conservation, repair or development of the cathedral[176] and consider and determine applications made to it under the Care of Cathedrals Measure 1990.[177] In the exercise of its functions, the fabric advisory committee must 'have due regard to the fact that the cathedral church is the seat of the bishop and a centre of worship and mission'.[178]

8.38 The committee comprises between three and five members appointed by the Chapter after consultation with the Cathedrals Fabric Commission[179] and between three and five members appointed by the Cathedrals Fabric Commission after consultation with the Chapter who have special knowledge with respect to the care and maintenance of buildings of outstanding architectural or historic interest and a particular interest in the cathedral concerned.[180] The committee's legitimate

---

[172] Ibid s 2(1)(a), (b), (bb), (c) (as amended).
[173] Ibid s 2(2)(a)–(c).
[174] Ibid, s 2(3).
[175] Ibid s 4(1).
[176] This is now given a much extended definition such as to include any buildings or archaeological remains within its precinct, the landscape and environment in which it is situated and any object vested or the corporate body, as broadly defined: ibid s 4(2)(a) (as amended).
[177] Ibid s 4(2)(a), (b) (as amended).
[178] Ibid s 1. This mandatory requirement is identical to that in respect of those exercising functions under the Cathedrals Measure 1999: see s 1 of the latter Measure. Note also the general duties of approval bodies at set out in the Care of Cathedrals Measure 1990, s 11A (as amended).
[179] Ibid s 4(3), Sch 2 para 1(a) (as amended). They may not be members of the Chapter or persons who are employed or hold paid office in the cathedral; nor may they be persons who hold paid office within the Cathedrals Fabric Commission: Sch 2 para 5.
[180] Ibid Sch 2 para 1(b). The Chapter and the Cathedrals Fabric Commission have an equal number of appointees: Sch 2 para 1.

expenses are met by the Chapter.[181] The dean, the administrator of the cathedral and such other members of the Chapter as the Chapter, after consulting the fabric advisory committee, considers appropriate, are entitled to attend and speak at meetings of the committee but may not vote.[182] The cathedral architect or surveyor of the fabric and cathedral archaeologist must attend meetings of the committee unless the chairman permits or directs otherwise.[183] The committee must meet at least twice a year;[184] it must appoint a chairman from among its number,[185] and a secretary.[186]

Cathedrals Fabric Commission

The role of the Cathedrals Fabric Commission is a national one, akin to that of the Council for the Care of Churches in its expertise, but it also exercises a function which is quasi-judicial. It is required, in particular: **8.39**

(a) to give advice to the Chapter of a cathedral and the fabric advisory committee on the care, conservation, repair or development of the cathedral church, any buildings or archaeological remains within its precinct, the landscape and environment in which it is situated and any objects vested in the corporate body;[187]
(b) to give advice to bishops and to the vicar-general's court when it is sought in relation to matters of enforcement;
(c) to consider and determine applications made to it under the Care of Cathedrals Measure 1990;
(d) to promote co-operation between the Commission and relevant organizations;
(e) to assist Chapters in educational and research projects; and
(f) to maintain, jointly with the Council for the Care of Churches, a library of books, plans, drawings, photographs etc relating to cathedrals and objects in them.[188]

---

[181] Ibid Sch 2 para 8.
[182] Ibid Sch 2 para 3 (as amended).
[183] Ibid Sch 2 paras 4.
[184] Ibid Sch 2 para 12.
[185] Ibid Sch 2 para 2.
[186] Ibid Sch 2 para 7 (as amended). The secretary may be a member of the committee but if a member of Chapter or employed by or holding paid office in the cathedral, the committee must have particular regard to any possible conflict of interest which would make it inappropriate to appoint that person as secretary.
[187] Adopting the extended definition of possession or custody prescribed in ibid s 2(1)(b).
[188] Ibid s 3(2)(a), (aa), (b)–(e) (as amended). The Commission may also, upon request, give advice to the Council for the Care of Churches in relation to a church of the Church of England, and may advise in relation to a cathedral church in Wales or, exceptionally, one outside England and Wales: s 11(1).

Following an amendment introduced by the Care of Cathedrals (Amendment) Measure 2005, the Commission is now also required to promote, in consultation with Chapters, fabric advisory committees and such other persons or organizations as it thinks fit, by means of guidance or otherwise, standards of good practice to be observed in relation to matters of the care and conservation of cathedrals, the role and duties of cathedral architects or surveyors of the fabric, and cathedral archaeologists, the compilation, maintenance and dissemination of relevant information, and the form and content of mandatory records.[189]

8.40 The Cathedrals Fabric Commission comprises a chairman, vice-chairman and 22 other members.[190] The membership is designed to achieve a breadth of expert representation in the areas of care of historic buildings, archaeology, architecture, archives, art, the care and conservation of books, manuscripts and other historic objects, history (including history of art and architecture) and liturgy (including church music), as well as the way in which cathedrals are currently used and their contribution to the work of the Church of England.[191] The Cathedrals Fabric Commission must, in the exercise of its functions, 'have due regard to the fact that the cathedral church is the seat of the bishop and a centre of worship and mission'.[192]

Procedure

8.41 The fabric advisory committee has power to determine whether, under section 2(1) of the Care of Cathedrals Measure 1990, an application by the Chapter for approval to a proposal is required;[193] and, after consultation with the Chapter and subject to the agreement of the Cathedrals Fabric Commission, to determine that the prohibition on carrying out works etc without approval, under section 2(1), is not to apply to proposals of a specified class or description.[194]

8.42 Applications for the approval of any proposal are to be made in the first instance to the fabric advisory committee unless they come within certain specified

---

[189] Ibid s 3(2A) (as inserted).
[190] Ibid s 3(3), Sch 1 para 1. Its quorum is eight: Sch 1 para 14; and its business is decided by a majority of the members present and voting, with the chairman having a second and casting vote in the event of an equal division: Sch 1 para 14A (as amended).
[191] Ibid Sch 1 paras 3, 3A, 4 (as amended).
[192] Ibid s 1. This mandatory requirement is identical to that in respect of those exercising functions under the Cathedrals Measure 1999, to be found at s 1. Note also the general duties of approval bodies in the Care of Cathedrals Measure 1990, s 11A. See n 178 above.
[193] Ibid s 5(1)(a) (as amended).
[194] Ibid s 5(1)(b) (as amended). It also has power to vary or revoke such a determination: ibid. The fabric advisory committee has power to determine whether or not a proposal is one to which s 2 does not apply by virtue of s 5(1)(b): see s 5(2) (as amended).

Care and maintenance

categories, in which case they are made to the Commission.[195] These categories comprise:

(a) works (including repair or maintenance) which would permanently alter the fabric of the cathedral or any building within its precinct used for ecclesiastical purposes;
(b) the demolition of any part of the cathedral or any such building;
(c) the disturbance or destruction of archaeological remains within the precinct;
(d) the sale, loan or other disposal of, or the carrying out of any work to, objects designated[196] as being of outstanding architectural, archaeological, artistic or historic interest;
(e) where the Commission declares in writing that the proposal gives rise to considerations of such special architectural, archaeological, artistic or historic interest that the application should be determined by it;
(f) any application for the approval of any proposal which has already been implemented in contravention of section 2 of the Care of Cathedrals Measure 1990.[197]

The Commission has power to determine whether an application for approval is to be made to the fabric advisory committee or to the Commission,[198] although there is now a discretion for the Commission to declare that a proposal does not give rise to considerations of sufficient importance to require consideration by the Commission.[199] If three members of the fabric advisory committee consider that an application which has been made to it should be determined by the Commission, the secretary must refer it accordingly.[200] There are now particular provisions dealing with treasure under the Treasure Act 1996.[201]

Where an application is made by the Chapter for approval by the fabric advisory committee, the administrator[202] must display a notice in the required form stating   **8.43**

---

[195] Ibid s 6(1) (as amended).
[196] Under ibid s 13(2).
[197] Ibid s 6(1)(a)(i)–(iv), (b), (3A), amended by the Care of Cathedrals (Supplementary Provisions) Measure 1994, s 7(4).
[198] Care of Cathedrals Measure 1990, s 6(2).
[199] Ibid s 6(2A) (as amended), in which case it makes a declaration in writing to that effect and any application for approval is made instead to the fabric advisory committee. The Cathedrals Advisory Commission also has power, subject to detailed consultation, to determine that proposals which ordinarily fall to be determined by the Commission under s 6(1)(a) shall be dealt with by way of application to the fabric advisory committee, either for cathedrals generally or for particular cathedrals: s 6(2B). There is also provision in particular circumstances, in respect of a proposal which does not relate to the cathedral or a building used for ecclesiastical purposes, for the Commission to declare that no approval is required under the Measure, leaving the matter in the hands of the local planning authority: s 6(2C), (2D).
[200] Ibid s 6(3).
[201] See the Care of Cathedrals Measure 1990, s 6A.
[202] Formerly known as the chapter clerk: see Cathedrals Measure 1999, s 36(1A) (as amended).

where details of the proposal are available for inspection and that representations in writing may be sent to the secretary of the committee within a specified period.²⁰³ The administrator must also send a notice to the Cathedrals Fabric Commission and, if the proposal involves the carrying out of works, to English Heritage, the National Amenity Societies and the local planning authority.²⁰⁴ After considering any representations, the fabric advisory committee determines whether to give its approval to the proposal either conditionally or subject to conditions, or whether to refuse to give its approval.²⁰⁵ The secretary of the committee must send notice of the decision to the Chapter, the Commission and those bodies on whom notice was served.²⁰⁶ If the committee refuses to give its approval, or gives it subject to conditions, the Chapter may appeal to the Commission.²⁰⁷ On considering an appeal, the Commission may reverse, confirm or vary the decision of the committee or any part thereof.²⁰⁸

8.44 Where an application is made to the Cathedrals Fabric Commission, the administrator must display in the prescribed manner and send to the fabric advisory committee,²⁰⁹ English Heritage and the National Amenity Societies a notice in the prescribed form, stating where details of the proposal are available for inspection and that representations in writing may be sent to the secretary of the Commission within a prescribed period.²¹⁰ After considering any representations, the Commission determines whether to give its approval, either unconditionally or subject to conditions, or whether to refuse to do so.²¹¹ Notification of the Commission's decision must be sent by its secretary to the Chapter, the fabric advisory committee, English Heritage, the National Amenity Societies, and, if appropriate, the local planning authority and the Church Commissioners.²¹²

---

²⁰³ Care of Cathedrals Measure 1990, s 7(1).
²⁰⁴ Ibid s 7(1)(a), (b).
²⁰⁵ Ibid s 7(2).
²⁰⁶ Ibid s 7(3).
²⁰⁷ Ibid s 9(1). Equally, if the application is not determined by the committee within three months, the Chapter may by notice in writing request that the application be dealt with by the Commission, whose determination has effect as if it had been given by the committee: ibid s 9(2), (4). Where the Commission is considering an appeal, no member of the Commission who is also a member of the relevant fabric advisory committee may participate in the proceedings: Sch 1 para 16A.
²⁰⁸ Ibid s 9(3). See generally the Care of Cathedrals Rules 2006, SI 2006/1941, r 8.
²⁰⁹ Following receipt of the notice, the fabric advisory committee must inform the Commission in writing whether the committee has considered the proposal and, if so, of its views: Care of Cathedrals Measure 1990, a 8(1A) (as amended).
²¹⁰ Ibid s 8(1). The local planning authority should also be notified if the proposal includes the carrying out of works: s 8(1).
²¹¹ Ibid s 8(2). Before determining whether to give approval to any proposal for the sale, loan, or other disposal of an object falling within s 6(1)(a)(iv), the Commission may consult the Church Commissioners on any financial considerations which may be relevant: s 8(2A) (as amended); and may request the Chapter to consult the cathedral Council and inform the Commission of the Council's views: s 8(2B).
²¹² Ibid s 8(3) (as amended).

8.45 Where the Cathedrals Fabric Commission refuses to give its approval or gives it subject to conditions, the Chapter may, by notice within the prescribed period, request that the Commission's decision be reviewed by a Commission of Review.[213] Further, if the Cathedrals Fabric Commission fails to determine an application or appeal within three months, the Chapter may request that the matter be dealt with by a Commission of Review.[214] The Commission of Review consists of the Dean of Arches or his appointee, a person appointed by the Archbishops of Canterbury and York who is or has been a dean, provost or residentiary canon of some other cathedral, and a person appointed by the Secretary of State for Culture, Media and Sport who has special knowledge of the architecture, archaeology, art or history of cathedral churches.[215] The Commission of Review may reverse, confirm or vary the decision of the Cathedrals Fabric Commission.[216]

8.46 When exercising any function conferred by the Care of Cathedrals Measure 1990, all so-called 'approval bodies', namely fabric advisory committees, the Cathedrals Fabric Commission, and any Commission of Review, without prejudice to the general duty at section 1, must have regard to the desirability of preserving:

(a) the fabric of the cathedral and any features of architectural, archaeological, artistic or historic interest which it possesses;
(b) the immediate setting of the cathedral;
(c) any building within the precinct of the cathedral of architectural, archaeological, artistic or historic interest;
(d) any archaeological remains within the precinct of the cathedral;
(e) any object vested in the corporate body.[217]

8.47 Any approval given under the 1990 Measure lapses after ten years.[218] Notification of completion of works for which approval has been granted must be given by the administrator of the cathedral to the fabric advisory committee.[219] A register of applications must be kept by the fabric advisory committee and the Cathedrals Fabric Commission.[220]

8.48 When the Chapter of a cathedral proposes to make any application for listed building consent or scheduled monument consent in respect of any building

---

[213] Ibid s 10(1). This procedure applies in the case of refusals given by the Commission both at first instance, including those under the default power under s 9(2), and in its appellate capacity under s 9(1). A tenant of cathedral property has an independent right of appeal: s 10C (as amended).
[214] Ibid s 10(2).
[215] Ibid s 10(3)(a)–(c).
[216] Ibid s 10(4). Its decision is final: ibid s 10(7).
[217] Ibid s 11A (a)–(e) (as amended).
[218] Ibid s 10A(1) (as amended), although the body which gave approval may extend this period.
[219] Ibid s 10A(2) (as amended).
[220] Ibid s 10B (as amended).

or monument within the precinct of the cathedral, the Chapter clerk must send a notice to the Cathedrals Fabric Commission stating that representations in writing with respect to the proposed application may be sent to him before the end of the prescribed period.[221]

Enforcement

8.49 The enforcement of the foregoing provisions is dealt with in the Care of Cathedrals (Supplementary Provisions) Measure 1994, which creates a number of procedures for dealing with actual or threatened contravention of the Care of Cathedrals Measure 1990. The procedures vary in their form and legalism, depending upon the nature of the contravention and the urgency of the need to intervene.

8.50 First, the 1994 Measure provides for the members of the Chapter to be afforded the opportunity of being interviewed by the bishop in private where it appears to him that the Chapter may have committed or be intending to commit an act in contravention of section 2 of the Care of Cathedrals Measure 1990.[222] If the bishop considers that such an act has occurred or is threatened, he must order a special visitation in order to inquire into the matter and must cause a written statement of his reasons to be sent to the Chapter,[223] whereupon the Chapter has no power to act with regard to the matter under inquiry without the prior approval in writing of the bishop.[224] It is, however, unnecessary for the bishop to order a special visitation if he is satisfied that the Chapter intends to make an application for approval under the Care of Cathedrals Measure 1990; that such an application has been made and has not been refused; or if he considers that there are exceptional reasons for not doing so.[225]

8.51 The 1994 Measure is silent as to the manner in which the special visitation is to be conducted,[226] although it provides for the bishop to make directions to avoid any contravention of section 2 of the Care of Cathedrals Measure 1990 and makes it the duty of the Chapter to obey such directions.[227] The bishop has power to make interim directions where he is satisfied, having regard to the urgency of the matter, that there is insufficient time to afford the members of the Chapter

---

[221] Ibid s 15.
[222] Care of Cathedrals (Supplementary Provisions) Measure 1994, s 1. He may do so of his own motion, on the advice of the Cathedrals Fabric Commission, or on the basis of an allegation made by another person: s 1.
[223] Ibid s 2(1).
[224] Ibid s 2(1), (3).
[225] Ibid s 2(2)(a)–(c).
[226] See ibid, s 9, which provides for rules to be made by the Rules Committee under the Care of Churches and Ecclesiastical Jurisdiction Measure 1991, s 29. For visitations generally, see P Barrett, 'Episcopal Visitation of Cathedrals in the Church of England' (2006) 8 Ecc LJ 266.
[227] Care of Cathedrals (Supplementary Provisions) Measure 1994, s 3.

an opportunity of being interviewed by him in private.[228] Once a special visitation has been ordered, the bishop may give directions from time to time to the Chapter.[229]

8.52 Where a special visitation has been ordered, the bishop may authorize a person designated by him for the purposes of the 1994 Measure to institute proceedings seeking an injunction and/or restoration order if he considers it necessary or expedient in respect of any actual or intended contravention of section 2 of the Care of Cathedrals Measure 1990.[230] Proceedings are heard and determined in the vicar-general's court in each of the provinces.[231] Additional parties to the proceedings may be added by way of special citation.[232] The vicar-general's court of the relevant province[233] has power to issue an injunction restraining the Chapter from committing or continuing to commit acts in contravention of section 2 or any other party to the proceedings from committing or continuing to commit any act in furtherance of the contravention.[234]

8.53 In addition, where the court is satisfied that the Chapter has committed any act in contravention of section 2 of the Care of Cathedrals Measure 1990, it may make a restoration order requiring the Chapter or any other party to the proceedings to take specified steps within a specified time to restore the status quo.[235] No restoration order may be made more than six years after the contravention alleged.[236]

---

[228] Ibid s 3(1).

[229] Ibid s 3(2). The directions may include taking steps to avoid a contravention, refraining from steps likely to lead to a contravention, and taking steps to restore the position so far as possible to that which existed before the act was committed: s 3(3)(a)–(c); but directions to restore the *status quo* may be given only after the bishop has first sought the advice of the Cathedrals Fabric Commission: s 3(4). Any directions must be in writing unless the bishop is satisfied, having regard to the urgency of the matter, that there is insufficient time for them to be committed to writing, in which case they may be given orally but must be reduced into writing as soon as practicable: s 3(5).

[230] Care of Cathedrals (Supplementary Provisions) Measure 1994, s 4(1). He may authorize a person designated by him, either generally or in a particular case, to institute proceedings. When the bishop proposes to authorize the institution of such proceedings, he must inform the Church Commissioners who must then decide whether, and to what extent, they would be prepared to pay any costs or expenses incurred: s 4(2).

[231] Ibid s 5(1). If the vicar-general is unable to act or the cathedral church is in a diocese of which the vicar-general is chancellor, the archbishop of the province appoints a chancellor to act as deputy vicar-general: s 5(2).

[232] Ibid s 6(1). Such persons must be or have been concerned in furthering the alleged contravention of the Care of Cathedrals Measure 1990, s 2.

[233] It sits in any place which is convenient, having regard to the convenience of parties and witnesses (Ecclesiastical Jurisdiction Measure 1963, s 80) and has the same powers as to witnesses and documents as the High Court (s 81(1)). Proceedings are instituted and conducted in such manner as the vicars-general of Canterbury and York, acting jointly, direct: Care of Cathedrals (Supplementary Provisions) Measure 1994, s 5(3).

[234] Ibid s 6(3).

[235] Care of Cathedrals (Supplementary Provisions) Measure 1994, s 6(4).

[236] Ibid s 6(5). Deliberate concealment will prevent time from running: s 6(7).

Before making a restoration order, the advice of the Cathedrals Fabric Commission must first be sought.[237]

8.54 The vicar-general's court may order that the special visitation continue on such terms as it considers just or that it cease, and may make such further order in relation to the proceedings as it considers just.[238] Failure to comply with any requirement of an injunction or restoration order is a contempt of court.[239] Costs may be awarded and taxed at the discretion of the vicar-general's court.[240] An appeal from the vicar-general's court lies to the Court of Arches or the Chancery Court of York, as appropriate.[241]

---

[237] Ibid s 6(6).

[238] Ibid s 6(10). Note that in this regard, 'the proceedings' are those instituted under s 4 for an injunction or restoration order. The vicar-general's court has no power to give or refuse approval for works undertaken in contravention of the Care of Cathedrals Measure 1990, s 2. This power vests in the Cathedrals Fabric Commission under the Care of Cathedrals Measure 1990, s 6(3A), added by the Care of Cathedrals (Supplementary Provisions) Measure 1994, s 7(4). This is in marked contrast with the faculty jurisdiction where the consistory court has jurisdiction to grant injunctions and restoration orders as well as confirmatory faculties: see Chapter 7.

[239] Care of Cathedrals (Supplementary Provisions) Measure 1994, s 6(9). As to the procedure for dealing with a contemnor, see the Ecclesiastical Jurisdiction Measure 1963, s 81(2), (3) (substituted by the Care of Churches and Ecclesiastical Jurisdiction Measure 1991, s 8(1), Sch 4 para 11), discussed in Chapter 7.

[240] Ecclesiastical Jurisdiction Measure 1963, s 60(2).

[241] Ibid s 7(1A), added by the Care of Cathedrals (Supplementary Provisions) Measure 1994, s 8, Schedule para 2.

Materials

The Canons of the Church of England	311
Statutes and Measures	373
Statutory Instruments	543
Church Representation Rules	617
Cases	657

THE CANONS OF THE CHURCH OF ENGLAND

A. The Church of England	311	F. Things Appertaining to Churches	357
B. Divine Service and the Administration of the Sacraments	312	G. The Ecclesiastical Courts	360
		H. The Synods of the Church	363
C. Ministers, their Ordination, Function and Charge	335	Supplementary Material	369
		Proviso to Canon 113 of 1603	369
D. The Order of Deaconesses	349	Admission of Baptised Children to Holy Communion Regulations 2006	369
E. The Lay Officers of the Church	352		

The Church of England

A 1 OF THE CHURCH OF ENGLAND

The Church of England, established according to the laws of this realm under the Queen's Majesty, belongs to the true and apostolic Church of Christ; and, as our duty to the said Church of England requires, we do constitute and ordain that no member thereof shall be at liberty to maintain or hold the contrary.

A 2 OF THE THIRTY-NINE ARTICLES OF RELIGION

The Thirty-nine Articles are agreeable to the Word of God and may be assented unto with a good conscience by all members of the Church of England.

A 3 OF THE *BOOK OF COMMON PRAYER*

1. The doctrine contained in the *Book of Common Prayer* and Administration of the Sacraments and other Rites and Ceremonies of the Church according to the Use of the Church of England is agreeable to the Word of God.

2. The form of God's worship contained in the said Book, forasmuch as it is not repugnant to the Word of God, may be used by all members of the Church of England with a good conscience.

A 4 OF THE FORM AND MANNER OF MAKING, ORDAINING, AND CONSECRATING OF BISHOPS, PRIESTS, AND DEACONS

The Form and Manner of Making, Ordaining, and Consecrating of Bishops, Priests, and Deacons, annexed to the *Book of Common Prayer* and commonly known as the Ordinal, is not repugnant to the Word of God; and those who are so made, ordained, or consecrated bishops, priests, or deacons, according to the said Ordinal, are lawfully made, ordained, or consecrated and ought to be accounted, both by themselves and others, to be truly bishops, priests, or deacons.

A 5   OF THE DOCTRINE OF THE CHURCH OF ENGLAND

The doctrine of the Church of England is grounded in the Holy Scriptures, and in such teachings of the ancient Fathers and Councils of the Church as are agreeable to the said Scriptures.

In particular such doctrine is to be found in the Thirty-nine Articles of Religion, the *Book of Common Prayer*, and the Ordinal.

A 6   OF THE GOVERNMENT OF THE CHURCH OF ENGLAND

The government of the Church of England under the Queen's Majesty, by archbishops, bishops, deans, provosts, archdeacons, and the rest of the clergy and of the laity that bear office in the same, is not repugnant to the Word of God.

A 7   OF THE ROYAL SUPREMACY

We acknowledge that the Queen's excellent Majesty, according to the laws of the realm, is the highest power under God in this kingdom, and has supreme authority over all persons in all causes, as well ecclesiastical as civil.

A 8   OF SCHISMS

Forasmuch as the Church of Christ has for a long time past been distressed by separations and schisms among Christian men, so that the unity for which our Lord prayed is impaired and the witness to his gospel is grievously hindered, it is the duty of clergy and people to do their utmost not only to avoid occasions of strife but also to seek in penitence and brotherly charity to heal such divisions.

Divine Service and the Administration of the Sacraments

B 1   OF CONFORMITY OF WORSHIP

1. The following forms of service shall be authorised for use in the Church of England:
    (a) the forms of service contained in the *Book of Common Prayer*;
    (b) the shortened forms of Morning and Evening Prayer which were set out in the Schedule to the Act of Uniformity Amendment Act 1872;
    (c) the form of service authorised by Royal Warrant for use upon the anniversary of the day of the accession of the reigning Sovereign;
    (d) any form of service approved under Canon B 2 subject to any amendments so approved, to the extent permitted by such approval;
    (e) any form of service approved under Canon B 4 subject to any amendments so approved, to the extent permitted by such approval;
    (f) any form of service authorised by the archbishops under Canon B 5A, to the extent permitted by such authorisation.

2. Every minister shall use only the forms of service authorised by this Canon, except so far as he may exercise the discretion permitted by Canon B 5. It is the minister's responsibility to have a good

B. Divine Service and the Administration of the Sacraments

understanding of the forms of service used and he shall endeavour to ensure that the worship offered glorifies God and edifies the people.

3. In this Canon the expression 'form of service' shall be construed as including—
    (i) the prayers known as Collects;
    (ii) the lessons designated in any Table of Lessons;
    (iii) any other matter to be used as part of a service;
    (iv) any Table of Rules for regulating a service;
    (v) any Table of Holy Days which expression includes 'A Table of all the Feasts' in the *Book of Common Prayer* and such other Days as shall be included in any Table approved by the General Synod.

B 2   OF THE APPROVAL OF RORMS OF SERVICE

1. It shall be lawful for the General Synod
    (a) to approve forms of services for use in the Church of England and to amend any form of service approved by the General Synod under this paragraph;
    (b) to approve the use of any such form of service for a limited period, or without limit of period;
    (c) to extend the period of use of any such form of service and to discontinue any such form of service;

and any form of service or amendment thereof approved by the General Synod under this paragraph shall be such as in the opinion of the General Synod is neither contrary to, nor indicative of any departure from, the doctrine of the Church of England in any essential matter.

2. Any approval, amendment, continuance or discontinuance of any form of service under paragraph 1 above shall not have effect unless the form of service or the amendment, continuance or discontinuance thereof is finally approved by the General Synod with a majority in each House thereof of not less than two-thirds of those present and voting.

2A(1) It shall be lawful for the bishop of a diocese or other Ordinary of the place, on a request made in accordance with sub-paragraphs (5) and (6) below on behalf of a parish or in a place of worship of a kind specified in paragraph (5)(a) below, by notice in writing to approve the continued use in the parish or place of worship, for such period as shall be specified in the notice, of any form of service—
    (a) the use of which has ceased to be approved by the General Synod by virtue of the expiry of any limited period imposed under paragraph 1(b) above; or
    (b) the use of which has ceased to be approved by the General Synod by virtue of the expiry of any period of extension granted under paragraph 1(c) above; or
    (c) which has been discontinued under paragraph 1(c) above.

(2) Approval under sub-paragraph (1) above for the continued use of a form of service on a request made on behalf of a parish shall either—
    (a) apply to all places of worship in the parish in question; or
    (b) be limited in its application to such place or places of worship in the parish as may be specified in the notice.

(3) Where a bishop or other Ordinary has approved the continued use of a form of service under sub-paragraph (1) above he may, on a request made on behalf of the parish or place or worship concerned in accordance with sub-paragraphs (5) and (7) below, by notice in writing extend (on one occasion only) the period of continued use of the form of service for such further period as shall be specified in the notice.

(4) The period of continued use referred to in sub-paragraphs (1) and (3) above shall commence on the date on which the use of the form of service in question ceases or ceased to be

approved by the General Synod or on the expiry of the original period of continued use, as the case may be.

(5) A request for approval under sub-paragraph (1) above for the continued use of a form of service or for an extension under sub-paragraph (3) shall be made—
- (a) in the case of a place of worship which is an extra-parochial place or in respect of which a clerk in Holy Orders is licensed under section 2 of the Extra-Parochial Ministry Measure 1967, by the minister concerned; and
- (b) in any other case, by the minister and parochial church council concerned acting jointly.

(6) A request for approval under sub-paragraph (1) above for the continued use of a form of service shall not be made after the expiry of the period of twelve months following the date on which the use of the form of service has ceased to be approved by the General Synod and the period for which approval is given shall not exceed three years.

(7) A request for an extension under sub-paragraph (3) above of a period of continued use for a further period shall not be made after the expiry of the original period and the further period shall not exceed the original period or two years, whichever is the less.

2B(1) Paragraph 2A above (except sub-paragraphs (2) and (5) and with the omission from sub- paragraphs (1) and (3) of references to the Ordinary) shall apply to forms of service used in a cathedral church as it applies to forms of service used in a parish, with the following adaptations.

(2) Where Part I of the Cathedrals Measure 1999 applies in relation to the cathedral church, for references to a request on behalf of a parish or place of worship there shall be substituted references to the request of the Chapter with the consent of the dean.

(3) Where the Cathedrals Measure 1963 continues to apply in relation to a cathedral church in accordance with section 38(3) of the said Measure of 1999, for references to a request on behalf of a parish or place of worship there shall be substituted references to the request of the following bodies acting jointly, namely—
- (a) the administrative body; and
- (b) the dean or provost as the case may be; and also
- (c) in the case of a parish church cathedral for the parish of which there is a parochial church council whose functions have not been transferred to the administrative body in pursuance of section 12(1), that council.

In this sub-paragraph 'administrative body' and 'parish church cathedral' have the same meanings as in the Cathedrals Measure 1963.

(4) In relation to the cathedral church of Christ in Oxford, for references to a request on behalf of a parish or place of worship there shall be substituted references to the request of the dean and canons.

2C. In the case of a request in respect of a cathedral church or a place of worship which is an extra-parochial place, the request shall only be made after consultation with the representatives of persons over the age of sixteen years who worship regularly therein

3. In this Canon the expression 'form of service' has the same meaning as in Canon B 1 and the reference in paragraph 2A(5)(b) above to the minister shall, where there is no minister, be construed as a reference to the rural dean.

B 3 OF THE FORM OF SERVICE TO BE USED WHERE ALTERNATIVE FORMS ARE AUTHORISED

1. Decisions as to which of the forms of service authorised by Canon B 1, other than the services known as occasional offices, are to be used in any church in a parish or in any guild church shall be taken jointly by the minister and the parochial church council or, as the case may be, by the vicar of the guild church and the guild church council. In this Canon 'church' includes any building or part

B. Divine Service and the Administration of the Sacraments

of a building licensed by the bishop for public worship according to the rites and ceremonies of the Church of England.

2. If there is disagreement as to which of the said forms of service are to be used in any such church, then, so long as the disagreement continues, the forms of service to be used in that church shall be those contained in the *Book of Common Prayer* unless other forms of service authorised by Canon B 1 were in regular use therein during at least two of the four years immediately preceding the date when the disagreement arose and the parochial church council or guild church council, as the case may be, resolves that those other forms of service shall be used either to the exclusion of, or in addition to, the forms of service contained in the said Book.

3. The foregoing paragraphs of this Canon shall not apply in relation to a cathedral which is a parish church nor to any part of a cathedral which is a parish church.

4. Where more than one form of any of the services known as occasional offices, other than the Order of Confirmation, is authorised by Canon B 1 for use on any occasion the decision as to which form of service is to be used shall be made by the minister who is to conduct the service, but if any of the persons concerned objects beforehand to the use of the service selected by the minister and he and the minister cannot agree as to which form is to be used, the matter shall be referred to the bishop of the diocese for his decision.

5. Where more than one form of service of ordination of deacons or priests or of the ordination or consecration of a bishop is authorised by Canon B 1 for use, the decision as to which form of service is to be used shall be made by the bishop or archbishop, as the case may be, who is to conduct the service and, where more than one form of service of confirmation is so authorised, the decision as to which service is to be used shall be made by the bishop or archbishop, as the case may be, who is to conduct the service after consulting the minister of the church where the service is to be held.

6. In this Canon the expression 'form of service' has the same meaning as in Canon B 1.

B 4 OF FORMS OF SERVICE APPROVED BY THE CONVOCATIONS, ARCHBISHOPS OR ORDINARY FOR USE ON CERTAIN OCCASIONS

1. The Convocations of Canterbury and York may approve within their respective provinces forms of service for use in any cathedral or church or elsewhere on occasions for which no provision is made in the *Book of Common Prayer* or by the General Synod under Canon B 2, being forms of service which in both words and order are in their opinion reverent and seemly and neither contrary to, nor indicative of any departure from, the doctrine of the Church of England in any essential matter.

2. The archbishops may approve forms of service for use in any cathedral or church or elsewhere in the provinces of Canterbury and York on occasions for which no provision is made in the *Book of Common Prayer* or by the General Synod under Canon B 2 or by the Convocations under this Canon, being forms of service which in both words and order are in their opinion reverent and seemly and are neither contrary to, nor indicative of any departure from, the doctrine of the Church of England in any essential matter.

3. The Ordinary may approve forms of service for use in any cathedral or church or elsewhere in the diocese on occasions for which no provision is made in the *Book of Common Prayer* or by the General Synod under Canon B 2 or by the Convocation or archbishops under this Canon, being forms of service which in the opinion of the Ordinary in both words and order are reverent and seemly and are neither contrary to, nor indicative of any departure from, the doctrine of the Church of England in any essential matter.

4. In this Canon the expression 'form of service' has the same meaning as in Canon B 1.

B 5 OF THE DISCRETION OF MINISTERS IN CONDUCT OF PUBLIC PRAYER

1. The minister who is to conduct the service may in his discretion make and use variations which are not of substantial importance in any form of service authorised by Canon B 1 according to particular circumstances.

2. The minister having the cure of souls may on occasions for which no provision is made in the *Book of Common Prayer* or by the General Synod under Canon B 2 or by the Convocations, archbishops, or Ordinary under Canon B 4 use forms of service considered suitable by him for those occasions and may permit another minister to use the said forms of service.

3. All variations in forms of service and all forms of service used under this Canon shall be reverent and seemly and shall be neither contrary to, nor indicative of any departure from, the doctrine of the Church of England in any essential matter.

4. If any question is raised concerning the observance of the provisions of this Canon, it may be referred to the bishop in order that he may give such pastoral guidance, advice or directions as he may think fit, but such reference shall be without prejudice to the matter in question being made the subject matter of proceedings under the Ecclesiastical Jurisdiction Measure 1963.

5. In this Canon the expression 'form of service' has the same meaning as in Canon B 1.

B 5A OF AUTHORISATION OF FORMS OF SERVICE FOR EXPERIMENTAL PERIODS

1. Where a form of service has been prepared with a view to its submission to the General Synod for approval by the Synod under Canon B 2 the archbishops after consultation with the House of Bishops of the General Synod may, prior to that submission, authorise such form of service for experimental use for a period specified by them on such terms and in such places or parishes as they may designate.

2. Where any form of service has been authorised under paragraph 1 of this Canon for experimental use and it is proposed that it shall be used in any church the requirements of Canon B 3 shall apply.

3. In this Canon the expression 'form of service' has the same meaning as in Canon B 1.

B 6 OF SUNDAYS AND OTHER DAYS OF SPECIAL OBSERVANCE

1. The Lord's Day, commonly called Sunday, is ever to be celebrated as a weekly memorial of our Lord's Resurrection and kept according to God's holy will and pleasure, particularly by attendance at divine service, by deeds of charity, and by abstention from all unnecessary labour and business.

2. The principal Feasts which are to be observed in the Church of England are Christmas Day, Epiphany, the Annunciation of the Blessed Virgin Mary, Easter Day, Ascension Day, Whitsunday or Pentecost, Trinity Sunday and All Saints' Day.

3. The Days of Fasting or Abstinence and the Vigils which are to be observed in the Church of England are set out in the *Book of Common Prayer*, whereof the forty days of Lent, particularly Ash Wednesday and the Monday to Saturday before Easter, ought specially to be observed.

4. Good Friday is ever to be observed by prayer with meditation on the death and Passion of our Lord and Saviour Jesus Christ, by self-discipline, and by attendance at divine service.

5. It is lawful for the General Synod to approve Holy Days which may be observed generally or provincially, and, subject to any directions of the Convocation of the province, for the Ordinary to approve Holy Days which may be observed locally.

B. Divine Service and the Administration of the Sacraments

B 7 OF THE GIVING NOTICE OF FEAST DAYS AND FAST DAYS

The minister having the cure of souls shall give adequate public notice, in any way which is locally convenient, of the Feast Days and Fast Days to be observed and of the time and place of services on those days.

B 8 OF THE VESTURE OF ORDAINED AND AUTHORISED MINISTERS DURING THE TIME OF DIVINE SERVICE

1. The Church of England does not attach any particular doctrinal significance to the diversities of vesture permitted by this Canon, and the vesture worn by the minister in accordance with the provisions of this Canon is not to be understood as implying any doctrines other than those now contained in the formularies of the Church of England.

2. Notwithstanding the provisions of this Canon no minister shall change the form of vesture in use in the church or chapel in which he officiates unless he has ascertained by consultation with the parochial church council that such changes will be acceptable: Provided always that in case of disagreement the minister shall refer the matter to the bishop of the diocese, whose direction shall be obeyed.

3. At the Holy Communion the presiding minister shall wear either a surplice or alb with scarf or stole. When a stole is worn other customary vestments may be added. The epistoler and gospeller (if any) may wear surplice or alb to which other customary vestments may be added.

4. At Morning and Evening Prayer on Sundays the minister shall normally wear a surplice or alb with scarf or stole.

5. At the Occasional Offices the minister shall wear a surplice or alb with scarf or stole.

B 9 OF REVERENCE AND ATTENTION TO BE USED IN THE TIME OF DIVINE SERVICE

1. All persons present in the time of divine service shall audibly with the minister make the answers appointed and in due place join in such parts of the service as are appointed to be said or sung by all present.

2. They shall give reverent attention in the time of divine service, give due reverence to the name of the Lord Jesus and stand at the Creed and the reading of the Holy Gospel at the Holy Communion. When the Prayers are read and Psalms and canticles are said or sung, they shall have regard to the rubrics of the service and locally established custom in the matter of posture, whether of standing, kneeling or sitting.

B 10 OF MORNING AND EVENING PRAYER IN CATHEDRAL CHURCHES

In every cathedral church the Common Prayer shall be said or sung, distinctly, reverently, and in an audible voice, every morning and evening, and the Litany on the appointed days, the officiating ministers and others of the clergy present in choir being duly habited.

B 11 OF MORNING AND EVENING PRAYER IN PARISH CHURCHES

1. Morning and Evening Prayer shall be said or sung in every parish church at least on all Sundays and other principal Feast Days, and also on Ash Wednesday and Good Friday. Each service shall be said or sung distinctly, reverently, and in an audible voice. Readers, such other lay persons as may be authorised by the bishop of the diocese, or some other suitable lay person, may, at the invitation of the minister of the parish or, where the cure is vacant or the minister is incapacitated,

at the invitation of the churchwardens say or sing Morning and Evening Prayer (save for the Absolution).

2. On all other days the minister of the parish, together with other ministers licensed to serve in the parish, shall make such provision for Morning and Evening Prayer to be said or sung either in the parish church or, after consultation with the parochial church council, elsewhere as may best serve to sustain the corporate spiritual life of the parish and the pattern of life enjoined upon ministers by Canon C 26. Public notice shall be given in the parish, by tolling the bell or other appropriate means, of the time and place where the prayers are to be said or sung.

3. The reading of Morning and Evening Prayer in any parish church as required by this Canon may only be dispensed with in accordance with the provisions of Canon B 14A.

B 12 OF THE MINISTRY OF THE HOLY COMMUNION

1. No person shall consecrate and administer the holy sacrament of the Lord's Supper unless he shall have been ordained priest by episcopal ordination in accordance with the provisions of Canon C 1.

2. Every minister, as often as he shall celebrate the Holy Communion, shall receive that sacrament himself.

3. No person shall distribute the holy sacrament of the Lord's Supper to the people unless he shall have been ordained in accordance with the provisions of Canon C 1, or is otherwise authorised by Canon or unless he has been specially authorised to do so by the bishop acting under such regulations as the General Synod may make from time to time.

4. Subject to the general directions of the bishop, the Epistle and the Gospel and the Prayer of Intercession may at the invitation of the minister be read by a lay person at the celebration of the Holy Communion.

B 13 OF HOLY COMMUNION IN CATHEDRAL CHURCHES

1. In every cathedral church the Holy Communion shall be celebrated at least on all Sundays and other Feast Days, on Ash Wednesday and on other days as often as may be convenient, according to the statutes and customs of each church. It shall be celebrated distinctly, reverently, and in an audible voice.

2. In every cathedral church the dean or provost, the canons residentiary, and the other ministers of the church, being in holy orders, shall all receive the Holy Communion every Sunday at the least, except they have a reasonable cause to the contrary.

B 14 OF HOLY COMMUNION IN PARISH CHURCHES

1. The Holy Communion shall be celebrated in every parish church at least on all Sundays and principal Feast Days, and on Ash Wednesday and Maundy Thursday. It shall be celebrated distinctly, reverently, and in an audible voice.

2. The celebration of the Holy Communion in any parish church as required by this Canon may only be dispensed with in accordance with the provisions of Canon B 14A.

3. In churches and chapels dependent on a parish church, the Holy Communion shall be celebrated as regularly and frequently as may be convenient, subject to the direction of the Ordinary under Canon B 14A.

B. Divine Service and the Administration of the Sacraments

B 14A Of Services in Churches and Other Places of Worship

1. The reading of Morning and Evening Prayer in any parish church as required by Canon B 11 or the celebration of the Holy Communion in any parish church as required by Canon B 14 may be dispensed with as follows:
   (a) on an occasional basis, as authorised by the minister and the parochial church council acting jointly;
   (b) on a regular basis, as authorised by the bishop on the request of the minister and the parochial church council acting jointly.

In exercising the powers under this paragraph the minister and the parochial church council or the bishop as the case may be must be satisfied that there is good reason for doing so and shall—
   (i) have regard to the frequency of services of Morning and Evening Prayer or the celebration of the Holy Communion (as the case may be) in other parish churches or places of worship in the benefice; and
   (ii) ensure that no such church ceases altogether to be used for public worship.

2. Where there is more than one parish church or place of worship in a benefice or where a minister holds benefices in plurality with more than one parish church or place of worship the minister and the parochial church council acting jointly shall make proposals to the bishop as to what services of Morning and Evening Prayer or the celebration of the Holy Communion (as the case may be) are to be held in each of the parish churches or places of worship and if the bishop is satisfied with the proposals he shall authorise them accordingly. In default of the minister and parochial church council making satisfactory proposals, the bishop shall make such direction as he considers appropriate. In exercising the powers under this paragraph the bishop shall ensure that no church ceases altogether to be used for public worship.

3. The powers under paragraphs 1 and 2 of this Canon shall extend to any parish centre of worship designated under section 29(2) of the Pastoral Measure 1983.

4. The bishop of a diocese may direct what services shall be held or shall not be required to be held in any church in the diocese which is not a parish church or in any building, or part of a building, in the diocese licensed for public worship under section 29 of the Pastoral Measure 1983 but not designated as a parish centre of worship.

B 15 Of the Receiving of Holy Communion

1. It is the duty of all who have been confirmed to receive the Holy Communion regularly, and especially at the festivals of Christmas, Easter and Whitsun or Pentecost.

2. The minister shall teach the people from time to time, and especially before the festivals of Christmas, Easter and Whitsun or Pentecost, that they come to this holy sacrament with such preparation as is required by the *Book of Common Prayer*.

B 15A Of the Admission to Holy Communion

1. There shall be admitted to the Holy Communion:
   (a) members of the Church of England who have been confirmed in accordance with the rites of that Church or are ready and desirous to be so confirmed or who have been otherwise episcopally confirmed with unction or with the laying on of hands except as provided by the next following Canon;
   (b) baptised persons who are communicant members of other Churches which subscribe to the doctrine of the Holy Trinity, and who are in good standing in their own Church;
   (c) any other baptised persons authorised to be admitted under regulations of the General Synod; and
   (d) any baptised person in immediate danger of death.

2. If any person by virtue of sub-paragraph (b) above regularly receive the Holy Communion over a long period which appears likely to continue indefinitely, the minister shall set before him the normal requirements of the Church of England for communicant status in that Church.

3. Where any minister is in doubt as to the application of this Canon, he shall refer the matter to the bishop of the diocese or other Ordinary and follow his guidance thereon.

B 16 Of Notorious Offenders Not to be Admitted to Holy Communion

1. If a minister be persuaded that anyone of his cure who presents himself to be a partaker of the Holy Communion ought not to be admitted thereunto by reason of malicious and open contention and his neighbours, or other grave and open sin without repentance, he shall give an account of the same to the bishop of the diocese or other the Ordinary of the place and therein obey his order and direction, but so as not to refuse the sacrament to any until in accordance with such order and direction he shall have called him and advertised him that in any wise he presume not to come to the Lord's Table: Provided that in case of grave and immediate scandal to the congregation the minister shall not admit such person, but shall give an account of the same to the Ordinary within seven days after at the furthest and therein obey his order and direction. Provided also that before issuing his order and direction in relation to any such person the Ordinary shall afford to him an opportunity for interview.

2. The references in this Canon to 'the bishop of the diocese or other the Ordinary of the place' and to 'the Ordinary' include, in the case of the Ordinary being the bishop of the diocese and the see being vacant, the archbishop of the province or, in the case of the archbishopric being vacant or the vacant see being Canterbury or York, the archbishop of the other province.

B 17 Of Bread and Wine for the Holy Communion

1. The churchwardens of every parish, with the advice and direction of the minister, shall provide a sufficient quantity of bread and wine for the number of communicants that shall from time to time receive the same.

2. The bread, whether leavened or unleavened, shall be of the best and purest wheat flour that conveniently may be gotten, and the wine the fermented juice of the grape, good and wholesome.

3. The bread shall be brought to the communion table in a paten or convenient box and the wine in a convenient cruet or flagon.

B 17A Of the Disposition of the Alms at Holy Communion

Notwithstanding any rubric in the *Book of Common Prayer* moneys given or collected in church at Holy Communion shall form part of the general funds of the parochial church council and shall be disposed of by the parochial church council in accordance with the provisions of section 7(iv) of the Parochial Church Councils (Powers) Measure 1956.

B 18 Of Sermons in Parish Churches

1. In every parish church a sermon shall be preached at least once each Sunday, except for some reasonable cause approved by the bishop of the diocese.

2. The sermon shall be preached by a minister, deaconess, reader or lay worker duly authorised in accordance with Canon Law. At the invitation of the minister having the cure of souls another person may preach with the permission of the bishop of the diocese given either in relation to the particular occasion or in accordance with diocesan directions.

B. Divine Service and the Administration of the Sacraments

3. The preacher shall endeavour with care and sincerity to minister the word of truth, to the glory of God and to the edification of the people.

B 19 OF THE BIDDING PRAYER WHICH MAY BE USED BY A PREACHER BEFORE HIS SERMON

Before any sermon, lecture, or homily, the preacher may move the people to join with him in prayer in this form or to this effect, as briefly as is convenient, always concluding with the Lord's Prayer:

Ye shall pray for Christ's holy Catholic Church, that is, for the whole congregation of Christian people dispersed throughout the whole world, and especially for the Church of England.

And herein I require you most especially to pray for the Queen's most excellent Majesty our Sovereign Lady Elizabeth, by the grace of God of the United Kingdom of Great Britain and Northern Ireland, and of her other realms and territories, Queen, Head of the Commonwealth, Defender of the Faith, and ye shall also pray for Elizabeth the Queen Mother, Philip Duke of Edinburgh, the Prince of Wales, and all the Royal Family.

Ye shall also pray for the ministers of God's holy word and sacraments, as well archbishops and bishops, as other pastors and curates; for the Queen's most honourable Privy Council and the Ministers of the Crown, for the High Court of Parliament, for the Convocations of the Clergy, for the General Synod of the Church of England, and for civil governors and magistrates; that all and every of these, in their several callings, may serve truly and diligently, to the glory of God and the edifying and well governing of her people, remembering the strict and solemn account that they must one day make when they shall stand before the judgment seat of Christ.

And, that there may never be wanting a succession of persons duly qualified to serve God in Church and State, ye shall implore his blessing on all places of religious and useful learning, particularly the universities, colleges, and schools of this land; that in all places of education true religion and sound learning may for ever flourish and abound.

And more particularly (as in private duty bound) I ask your prayers for ...

Also ye shall pray for the whole people of this realm, that they may live in the true faith and fear of God, in dutiful obedience to the Queen, and in brotherly charity one to another.

Finally, let us praise God for all those who are departed out of this life in the faith of Christ, and pray unto God that we may have grace to direct our lives after their good example; that, this life ended, we may be made partakers with them of the glorious resurrection in the life everlasting.

B 20 OF THE MUSICIANS AND MUSIC OF THE CHURCH

1. In all churches and chapels, other than in cathedral or collegiate churches or chapels where the matter is governed by or dependent upon the statutes or customs of the same, the functions of appointing any organist, choirmaster (by whatever name called) or director of music, and of terminating the appointment of any organist, choirmaster or director of music, shall be exercisable by the minister with the agreement of the parochial church council, except that if the archdeacon of the archdeaconry in which the parish is situated, in the case of termination of an appointment, considers that the circumstances are such that the requirement as to the agreement of the parochial church council should be dispensed with, the archdeacon may direct accordingly. Where the minister is also the archdeacon of the archdeaconry concerned, the function of the archdeacon under this paragraph shall be exercisable by the bishop of the diocese.

2. Where there is an organist, choirmaster or director of music the minister shall pay due heed to his advice and assistance in the choosing of chants, hymns, anthems, and other settings, and in the ordering of the music of the church; but at all times the final responsibility and decision in these matters rests with the minister.

3. It is the duty of the minister to ensure that only such chants, hymns, anthems, and other settings are chosen as are appropriate, both the words and the music, to the solemn act of worship and prayer in the House of God as well as to the congregation assembled for that purpose; and to banish all irreverence in the practice and in the performance of the same.

B 21   Of Holy Baptism

It is desirable that every minister having a cure of souls shall normally administer the sacrament of Holy Baptism on Sundays at public worship when the most number of people come together, that the congregation there present may witness the receiving of them that be newly baptised into Christ's Church, and be put in remembrance of their own profession made to God in their baptism.

B 22   Of the Baptism of Infants

1. Due notice, normally of at least a week, shall be given before a child is brought to the church to be baptised.

2. If the minister shall refuse or unduly delay to baptise any such infant, the parents or guardians may apply to the bishop of the diocese, who shall, after consultation with the minister, give such directions as he thinks fit.

3. The minister shall instruct the parents or guardians of an infant to be admitted to Holy Baptism that the same responsibilities rest on them as are in the service of Holy Baptism required of the godparents.

4. No minister shall refuse or, save for the purpose of preparing or instructing the parents or guardians or godparents, delay to baptise any infant within his cure that is brought to the church to be baptised, provided that due notice has been given and the provisions relating to godparents in these Canons are observed.

5. A minister who intends to baptise any infant whose parents are residing outside the boundaries of his cure, unless the names of such persons or of one of them be on the church electoral roll of the same, shall not proceed to the baptism without having sought the good will of the minister of the parish in which such parents reside.

6. No minister being informed of the weakness or danger of death of any infant within his cure and therefore desired to go to baptise the same shall either refuse or delay to do so.

7. A minister so baptising a child in a hospital or nursing home, the parents of the child not being resident in his cure, nor their names on the church electoral roll of the same, shall send their names and address to the minister of the parish in which they reside.

8. If any infant which is privately baptised do afterwards live, it shall be brought to the church and there, by the minister, received into the congregation of Christ's flock according to the form and manner prescribed in and by the office for Private Baptism authorised by Canon B 1.

9. The minister of every parish shall warn the people that without grave cause and necessity they should not have their children baptised privately in their houses.

B 23   Of Godparents and Sponsors

1. For every child to be baptised there shall be not fewer than three godparents, of whom at least two shall be of the same sex as the child and of whom at least one shall be of the opposite sex; save that, when three cannot conveniently be had, one godfather and godmother shall suffice. Parents may be godparents for their own children provided that the child have at least one other godparent.

2. The godparents shall be persons who will faithfully fulfil their responsibilities both by their care for the children committed to their charge and by the example of their own godly living.

B. Divine Service and the Administration of the Sacraments

3. When one who is of riper years is to be baptised he shall choose three, or at least two, to be his sponsors, who shall be ready to present him at the font and afterwards put him in mind of his Christian profession and duties.

4. No person shall be admitted to be a sponsor or godparent who has not been baptised and confirmed. Nevertheless the minister shall have power to dispense with the requirement of confirmation in any case in which in his judgment need so requires.

B 24 OF THE BAPTISM OF SUCH AS ARE OF RIPER YEARS

1. When any such person as is of riper years and able to answer for himself is to be baptised, the minister shall instruct such person, or cause him to be instructed, in the principles of the Christian religion, and exhort him so to prepare himself with prayers and fasting that he may receive this holy sacrament with repentance and faith.

2. At least a week before any such baptism is to take place, the minister shall give notice thereof to the bishop of the diocese or whomsoever he shall appoint for the purpose.

3. Every person thus baptised shall be confirmed by the bishop so soon after his baptism as conveniently may be; that so he may be admitted to the Holy Communion.

B 25 OF THE SIGN OF THE CROSS IN BAPTISM

The Church of England has ever held and taught, and holds and teaches still, that the sign of the Cross used in baptism is no part of the substance of the sacrament: but, for the remembrance of the Cross, which is very precious to those that rightly believe in Jesus Christ, has retained the sign of it in baptism, following therein the primitive and apostolic Churches.

B 26 OF TEACHING THE YOUNG

1. Every minister shall take care that the children and young people within his cure are instructed in the doctrine, sacraments, and discipline of Christ, as the Lord has commanded and as they are set forth in the Holy Scriptures, in the *Book of Common Prayer*, and especially in the Church Catechism; and to this end he, or some godly and competent persons appointed by him, shall on Sundays or if need be at other convenient times diligently instruct and teach them in the same.

2. All parents and guardians shall take care that their children receive such instruction.

B 27 OF CONFIRMATION

1. The bishop of every diocese shall himself minister (or cause to be ministered by some other bishop lawfully deputed in his stead) the rite of confirmation throughout his diocese as often and in as many places as shall be convenient, laying his hands upon children and other persons who have been baptised and instructed in the Christian faith.

2. Every minister who has a cure of souls shall diligently seek out children and other persons whom he shall think meet to be confirmed and shall use his best endeavour to instruct them in the Christian faith and life as set forth in the Holy Scriptures, the *Book of Common Prayer*, and the Church Catechism.

3. The minister shall present none to the bishop but such as are come to years of discretion and can say the Creed, the Lord's Prayer, and the Ten Commandments, and can also render an account of their faith according to the said Catechism.

4. The minister shall satisfy himself that those whom he is to present have been validly baptised, ascertaining the date and place of such baptism, and, before or at the time assigned for the confirmation, shall give to the bishop their names, together with their age and the date of their baptism.

5. If the minister is doubtful about the baptism of a candidate for confirmation he shall conditionally baptise him in accordance with the form of service authorised by Canon B 1 before presenting him to the bishop to be confirmed.

6. If it is desired for sufficient reason that a Christian name be changed, the bishop may, under the laws of this realm, confirm a person by a new Christian name, which shall be thereafter deemed the lawful Christian name of such person.

B 28   OF RECEPTION INTO THE CHURCH OF ENGLAND

1. Any person desiring to be received into the Church of England, who has not been baptised or the validity of whose baptism can be held in question, shall be instructed and baptised or conditionally baptised, and such baptism, or conditional baptism, shall constitute the said person's reception into the Church of England.

2. If any such person has been baptised but not episcopally confirmed and desires to be formally admitted into the Church of England he shall, after appropriate instruction, be received by the rite of confirmation, or, if he be not yet ready to be presented for confirmation, he shall be received by the parish priest with appropriate prayers.

3. If any such person has been episcopally confirmed with unction or with the laying on of hands he shall be instructed, and, with the permission of the bishop, received into the Church of England according to the Form of Reception approved by the General Synod, or with other appropriate prayers, and if any such person be a priest he shall be received into the said Church only by the bishop of the diocese or by the commissary of such bishop.

B 29   OF THE MINISTRY OF ABSOLUTION[1]

1. It is the duty of baptised persons at all times to the best of their understanding to examine their lives and conversations by the rule of God's commandments, and wheresoever they perceive themselves to have offended by will, act, or omission, there to bewail their own sinfulness and to confess themselves to Almighty God with full purpose of amendment of life, that they may receive of him the forgiveness of their sins which he has promised to all who turn to him with hearty repentance and true faith; acknowledging their sins and seeking forgiveness, especially in the general Confessions of the congregation and in the Absolution pronounced by the priest in the services of the Church.

2. If there be any who by these means cannot quiet his own conscience, but requires further comfort or counsel, let him come to some discreet and learned minister of God's Word; that by the ministry of God's holy Word he may receive the benefit of absolution, together with ghostly counsel and advice, to the quieting of his conscience and avoiding of all scruple and doubtfulness.

3. In particular a sick person, if he feels his conscience troubled in any weighty matter, should make a special confession of his sins, that the priest may absolve him if he humbly and heartily desire it.

4. No priest shall exercise the ministry of absolution in any place without the permission of the minister having the cure of souls thereof, unless he is by law authorised to exercise his ministry in that place without being subject to the control of the minister having the general cure of souls of the parish or district in which it is situated: Provided always that, notwithstanding the foregoing provisions of the Canon, a priest may exercise the ministry of absolution anywhere in respect of any person who is in danger of death or if there is some urgent or weighty cause.

---

[1] See also the unrepealed proviso to Canon 113 of the Code of 1603 reproduced at the end of this section of the Materials (p 369).

B. Divine Service and the Administration of the Sacraments

B 30 OF HOLY MATRIMONY

1. The Church of England affirms, according to our Lord's teaching, that marriage is in its nature a union permanent and lifelong, for better for worse, till death them do part, of one man with one woman, to the exclusion of all others on either side, for the procreation and nurture of children, for the hallowing and right direction of the natural instincts and affections, and for the mutual society, help and comfort which the one ought to have of the other, both in prosperity and adversity.

2. The teaching of our Lord affirmed by the Church of England is expressed and maintained in the Form of Solemnisation of Matrimony contained in the *Book of Common Prayer*.

3. It shall be the duty of the minister, when application is made to him for matrimony to be solemnised in the church of which he is the minister, to explain to the two persons who desire to be married the Church's doctrine of marriage as herein set forth, and the need of God's grace in order that they may discharge aright their obligations as married persons.

B 31 OF CERTAIN IMPEDIMENTS TO MARRIAGE

1. No person who is under sixteen years of age shall marry, and all marriages purported to be made between persons either of whom is under sixteen years of age are void.

2. Subject to the provisions of the Marriage (Prohibited Degrees of Relationship) Act 1986 no person shall marry within the degrees expressed in the following Table, and all marriages purported to be made within the said degrees are void.

A Table of Kindred and Affinity

A man may not marry his	A woman may not marry her
mother	father
daughter	son
adopted daughter	adopted son
father's mother	father's father
mother's mother	mother's father
son's daughter	son's son
daughter's daughter	daughter's son
sister	brother
wife's mother	husband's father
wife's daughter	husband's son
father's wife	mother's husband
son's wife	daughter's husband
father's father's wife	father's mother's husband
mother's father's wife	mother's mother's husband
wife's daughter's daughter	husband's daughter's son
wife's son's daughter	husband's son's son
father's sister	father's brother
mother's sister	mother's brother
brother's daughter	brother's son
sister's daughter	sister's son

In this Table the term 'brother' includes a brother of the half-blood, and the term 'sister' includes a sister of the half-blood.

The Table shall be in every church publicly set up and fixed at the charge of the parish.

B 32   Of certain Impediments to the Solemnisation of Matrimony

No minister shall solemnise matrimony between two persons either of whom (not being a widow or widower) is under eighteen years of age otherwise than in accordance with the requirements of the law relating to the consent of parents or guardians in the case of the marriage of a person under eighteen years of age.

B 33   Of the Duty of the Minister to inquire as to Impediments

It shall be the duty of the minister, when application is made to him for matrimony to be solemnised in the church or chapel or which he is the minister, to inquire whether there be any impediment either to the marriage or to the solemnisation thereof.

B 34   Of Requirements Preliminary to the Solemnisation of Matrimony

1. A marriage according to the rites of the Church of England may be solemnised:
    (a) after the publication of banns of marriage;
    (b) on the authority of a special licence of marriage granted by the Archbishop of Canterbury or any other person by virtue of the Ecclesiastical Licences Act 1533 (in these Canons, and in the statute law, referred to as a 'special licence');
    (c) on the authority of a licence (other than a special licence) granted by an ecclesiastical authority having power to grant such a licence (in these Canons, and in the statute law, referred to as a 'common licence'); or
    (d) on the authority of a certificate issued by a superintendent registrar under the provisions of the statute law in that behalf.

2. The Archbishop of Canterbury may grant a special licence for the solemnisation of matrimony without the publication of banns at any convenient time or place not only within the province of Canterbury but throughout all England.

3. The archbishop of each province, the bishop of every diocese, and all others who of ancient right have been accustomed to issue a common licence may grant such a licence for the solemnisation of matrimony without the publication of banns at a lawful time and in a lawful place within the several areas of their jurisdiction as the case may be; and the Archbishop of Canterbury may grant a common licence for the same throughout all England.

B 35   Of Rules to be Observed as to the Preliminaries and to the Solemnisation of Holy Matrimony

1. In all matters pertaining to the granting of licences of marriage every ecclesiastical authority shall observe the law relating thereto.

2. In all matters pertaining to the publication of banns of marriage and to the solemnisation of matrimony every minister shall observe the law relating thereto, including, so far as they are applicable, the rules prescribed by the rubric prefixed to the office of Solemnisation of Matrimony in the *Book of Common Prayer*.

3. A marriage may not be solemnised at any unreasonable hours but only between the hours of eight in the forenoon and six in the afternoon.

4. Every marriage shall be solemnised in the presence of two or more witnesses besides the minister who shall solemnise the same.

5. When matrimony is to be solemnised in any church, it belongs to the minister of the parish to decide what music shall be played, what hymns or anthems shall be sung, or what furnishings or flowers should be placed in or about the church for the occasion.

B. Divine Service and the Administration of the Sacraments

B 36 OF A SERVICE AFTER CIVIL MARRIAGE

1. If any persons have contracted marriage before the civil registrar under the provisions of the statute law, and shall afterwards desire to add thereto a service of Solemnisation of Matrimony, a minister may, if he see fit, use such form of service, as may be approved by the General Synod under Canon B 2, in the church or chapel in which he is authorised to exercise his ministry: Provided first, that the minister be duly satisfied that the civil marriage has been contracted, and secondly that in regard to this use of the said service the minister do observe the Canons and regulations of the General Synod for the time being in force.

2. In connection with such a service there shall be no publication of banns nor any licence or certificate authorising a marriage: and no record of any such service shall be entered by the minister in the register books of marriages provided by the Registrar General.

B 37 OF THE MINISTRY TO THE SICK

1. The minister shall use his best endeavours to ensure that he be speedily informed when any person is sick or in danger of death in the parish, and shall as soon as possible resort unto him to exhort, instruct, and comfort him in his distress in such manner as he shall think most needful and convenient.

2. When any person sick or in danger of death or so impotent that he cannot go to church is desirous of receiving the most comfortable sacrament of the Body and Blood of Christ, the priest, having knowledge thereof, shall as soon as may be visit him, and unless there be any grave reason to the contrary, shall reverently minister the same to the said person at such place and time as may be convenient.

3. If any such person so desires, the priest may lay hands upon him and may anoint him with oil on the forehead with the sign of the Cross using a form of service authorised by Canon B 1 and using pure olive oil consecrated by the bishop of the diocese or otherwise by the priest himself in accordance with such form of service.

B 38 OF THE BURIAL OF THE DEAD

1. In all matters pertaining to the burial of the dead every minister shall observe the law from time to time in force in relation thereto, and, subject to this paragraph in general, the following paragraphs of this Canon shall be obeyed.

2. It shall be the duty of every minister to bury, according to the rites of the Church of England, the corpse or ashes of any person deceased within his cure or of any parishioners or persons whose names are entered on the church electoral roll of his parish whether deceased within his cure or elsewhere that is brought to a church or burial ground or cemetery under his control in which the burial or interment of such corpse or ashes may lawfully be effected, due notice being given; except the person deceased have died unbaptised, or being of sound mind have laid violent hands upon himself, or have been declared excommunicate for some grievous and notorious crime and no man to testify to his repentance; in which case and in any other case at the request of the relative, friend, or legal representative having charge of or being responsible for the burial he shall use at the burial such service as may be prescribed or approved by the Ordinary, being a service neither contrary to, nor indicative of any departure from, the doctrine of the Church of England in any essential matter: Provided that, if a form of service available for the burial of suicides is approved by the General Synod under Canon B 2, that service shall be used where applicable instead of the aforesaid service prescribed or approved by the Ordinary, unless the person having charge or being responsible for the burial otherwise requests.

3. Cremation of a dead body is lawful in connection with Christian burial.

4. (a) When a body is to be cremated, the burial service may precede, accompany or follow the cremation; and may be held either in the church or at the crematorium.
   (b) The ashes of a cremated body should be reverently disposed of by a minister in a churchyard or other burial ground in accordance with section 3 of the Church of England (Miscellaneous Provisions) Measure 1992 or on an area of land designated by the bishop for the purpose of this sub-paragraph or at sea.

5. When a body is to be buried according to the rites of the Church of England in any unconsecrated ground, the officiating minister, on coming to the grave, shall first bless the same.

6. If any doubts shall arise whether any person deceased may be buried according to the rites of the Church of England, the minister shall refer the matter to the bishop and obey his order and direction.

7. A funeral service at a crematorium or cemetery shall be performed only in accordance with directions given by the bishop.

B 39 Of the Registration of Baptisms, Confirmations, Marriages, and Burials

1. In all matters pertaining to the registration of baptisms, marriages, and burials every minister shall observe the law from time to time in force relating thereto.

2. When any person is presented for confirmation, the minister presenting the said person shall record and enter the confirmation in his register book of confirmations provided in accordance with paragraph 3 of Canon F 11, together with any change of name made under paragraph 6 of Canon B 27.

B 40 Of Holy Communion Elsewhere than in Consecrated Buildings

No minister shall celebrate the Holy Communion elsewhere than in a consecrated building within his cure or other building licensed for the purpose, except he have permission so to do from the bishop of the diocese: Provided that at all times he may celebrate the Holy Communion as provided by Canon B 37 in any private house wherein there is any person sick, or dying, or so impotent that he cannot go to church.

B 41 Of Divine Service in Private Chapels

1. No chaplain, ministering in any house where there is a chapel dedicated and allowed by the ecclesiastical laws of this realm, shall celebrate the Holy Communion in any other part of the house but in such chapel, and shall do the same seldom upon Sunday and other greater Feast Days, so that the residents in the said house may resort to their parish church and there attend divine service.

2. The bishop of a diocese within which any college, school, hospital, or public or charitable institution is situated, whether or not it possesses a chapel, may under the Extra-Parochial Ministry Measure 1967 license a minister to perform such offices and services of the Church of England as may be specified in the licence on any premises forming part of or belonging to the institution in question but, except as provided by section 2(1A) of that Measure, no such licence shall extend to the solemnisation of marriage.

3. The performance of offices and services in accordance with any such licence shall not require the consent or be subject to the control of the minister of the parish in which they are performed.

B. Divine Service and the Administration of the Sacraments

B 42 OF THE LANGUAGE OF DIVINE SERVICE

1. (1) Subject to the following provisions of this Canon, authorised forms of services shall be said or sung in English.

(2) In the provinces of Canterbury and York outside England authorised forms of service may be said or sung in the vernacular.

2. Authorised forms of service may be said or sung in Latin in the following places:
   Provincial Convocations
   Chapels and other public places in university colleges and halls
   University churches
   The colleges of Westminster, Winchester and Eton
   Such other places of religious and sound learning as custom allows or the bishop or other the Ordinary may permit

3. (1) It shall be lawful for the Standing Committee of the House of Bishops of the General Synod to approve translations of authorised forms of service for use when permitted in accordance with sub-paragraph (2) below.

(2) The bishop of a diocese may, on the written application of the minister and parochial church council of a parish in the diocese acting jointly, give written permission for the use in the church or churches of the parish (whether as a whole or as part of the service in question) of a translation approved under sub-paragraph (1) above, and any such permission shall be subject to such conditions as the bishop may specify.

(3) The bishop of a diocese may, on the written application of authorised representatives of the Deaf Church, give written permission for the use in the church or churches of a parish in the diocese (whether as the whole or as part of the service in question) of an authorised form of service performed in British Sign Language, and any such permission shall be subject to such conditions as the bishop may specify.

4. (1) Paragraph 3 above shall apply to forms of service used in a cathedral church as it applies to forms of service used in the church of a parish, with the following adaptations.

(2) Where Part 1 of the Cathedrals Measure 1999 applies in relation to the cathedral church for the reference to a written application of the minister and parochial church council there shall be substituted a reference to a written application of the Chapter with the consent of the dean.

(3) Where the Cathedrals Measure 1963 continues to apply in relation to a cathedral church in accordance with section 38(3) of the said Measure of 1999, for the reference to a written application of the minister and parochial church council there shall be substituted a reference to a written application of the following bodies acting jointly, namely—
   (a) the administrative body; and
   (b) the dean or provost as the case may be; and also
   (c) in the case of a parish church cathedral for the parish church of which there is no parochial church council whose functions have not been transferred to the administrative body in pursuance of section 12(1), that council.

In this paragraph 'administrative body' and 'parish church cathedral' have the same meanings as in the Cathedrals Measure 1963.

(4) In relation to the cathedral church of Christ in Oxford, for the reference to a written application of the minister and parochial church council there shall be substituted a reference to a written application of the dean and canons.

5. In this Canon—
   (a) 'authorised form of service' means a form of service authorised by Canon B 1 for use in the Church of England and 'form of service' shall be construed accordingly;
   (b) the reference to the minister shall, where there is no minister, be construed as a reference to the rural dean.

B 43   OF RELATIONS WITH OTHER CHURCHES

1. (1) A minister or lay person who is a member in good standing of a Church to which this Canon applies and is a baptised person may, subject to the provisions of this Canon, be invited to perform all or any of the following duties—
    (a)   to say or sing Morning or Evening Prayer or the Litany;
    (b)   to read the Holy Scriptures at any service;
    (c)   to preach at any service;
    (d)   to lead the Intercessions at the Holy Communion and to lead prayers at other services;
    (e)   to assist at Baptism or the Solemnisation of Matrimony or conduct a Funeral Service;
    (f)   to assist in the distribution of the holy sacrament of the Lord's Supper to the people at the Holy Communion;
if the minister or lay person is authorised to perform a similar duty in his or her own Church.

(2) An invitation to perform in a parish church or other place of worship in the parish any of the duties mentioned in sub-paragraph (1) above, other than duties in connection with a service of ordination or confirmation, may be given only by the incumbent and may be given only if
    (a)   in the case of
        (i)   any duty mentioned in sub-paragraph (1)(f) above or,
        (ii)   any duty mentioned in sub-paragraph (1)(a), (c) or (e) above, which is to be performed on a regular basis,
        the approval of the bishop has been obtained; and
    (b)   in the case of any duty mentioned in sub-paragraph (1)(e) above, the persons concerned have requested the incumbent to give the invitation; and
    (c)   in the case of any duty mentioned in sub-paragraph (1)(a), (c) or (f) above, the approval of the parochial church council has been obtained.

(3) An invitation to perform in a parish church or other place of worship in the parish any duty in connection with a service of ordination or confirmation may be given only by the bishop and may be given only if the approval of the incumbent and the parochial church council has been obtained.

(4) Sub-paragraphs (2) and (3) above shall apply in relation to an invitation to perform in a cathedral church any of the duties mentioned in sub-paragraph (1) above subject to the following modifications—
    (a)   for any reference to the incumbent there shall be substituted—
        (i)   in the case of a dean and chapter cathedral, the dean and chapter, and
        (ii)   in the case of a parish church cathedral, the cathedral chapter; and
    (b)   the provisions relating to the approval of the parochial church council shall not apply.

2. Notwithstanding any provision of any Canon, a bishop who receives from a person authorised by a Church to which this Canon applies an invitation to take part in a service may in the course of that service perform any duty assigned to him if—
    (a)   the duty assigned to him is or is similar to a duty which he is authorised to perform in the Church of England; and
    (b)   he has before accepting the invitation obtained
        (i)   the approval of the incumbent of the parish in which the service is to take place, and
        (ii)   in the case of an invitation to take part in a service in another diocese, the approval of the bishop of that diocese, and
        (iii) in the case of an invitation to take part in the ordination or consecration of a minister of a Church to which this Canon applies, to take part in a service of confirmation or to preside at the Holy Communion, the approval of the archbishop of the province.

B. Divine Service and the Administration of the Sacraments

3. Notwithstanding any provision of any Canon, a priest or deacon of the Church of England who receives from a person authorised by a Church to which this Canon applies an invitation to take part in a service may in the course of that service perform any duty assigned to him if—
   (a) the duty assigned to him is or is similar to a duty which he is authorised to perform in the Church of England; and
   (b) he has before accepting the invitation obtained—
       (i) the approval of the incumbent of the parish in which the service is to take place, and
       (ii) in the case of an invitation to take part in the ordination or consecration of a minister of a Church to which this Canon applies or to preside at the Holy Communion, the approval of the bishop of the diocese in which the service is to take place, and,
       (iii) in the case of an invitation to take part in any service on a regular basis, the approval of both the bishop of the diocese and the parochial church council of the parish in which the service is to take place.

4. In the case of an invitation to preside at the Holy Communion, the archbishop shall not give his approval under paragraph 2 above and the bishop shall not give his approval under paragraph 3 above unless the archbishop or the bishop, as the case may be, is satisfied that there are special circumstances which justify acceptance of the invitation and that the rite and the elements to be used are not contrary to, nor indicative of any departure from the doctrine of the Church of England in any essential matter.

5. A bishop or priest who has accepted an invitation to take part in the ordination or consecration of a minister of a Church to which this Canon applies may not, by the laying on of hands or otherwise, do any act which is a sign of the conferring of Holy Orders, unless that Church is an episcopal Church with which the Church of England has established intercommunion.

6. Notwithstanding any provision of any Canon, a deaconess, lay worker or reader of the Church of England who receives from a person authorised by a Church to which this Canon applies an invitation to take part in a service may in the course of that service perform any duty assigned to him or her if—
   (a) the duty so assigned is or is similar to a duty which he or she is authorised to perform in the Church of England; and
   (b) he or she has before accepting the invitation obtained the approval of the incumbent of the parish in which the service is to take place and also, in the case of an invitation to take part in a service on a regular basis, the approval of both the bishop of the diocese and the parochial church council of that parish.

7. Where, on an application under paragraph 3 or 6 above for the approval of an incumbent, that approval is withheld, the applicant may appeal to the bishop of the diocese in which the service is to take place and if, after considering the views of the applicant and the incumbent, the bishop determines that approval has been unreasonably withheld, the bishop may authorise the applicant to take part in the service in question and where the bishop so determines the bishop shall inform the incumbent in writing of the reasons for that determination.

8. Where the approval of the parochial church council is required for the giving or accepting of an invitation under the preceding provisions of this Canon, that approval may be given in respect of the performance of such duties as may be specified in the approval by such person or persons, or such class of persons, as may be so specified and may either be given generally for an unlimited period or given subject to such limitations, whether as to duration or occasion, as may be so specified.

9. The incumbent of a parish may, with the approval of the parochial church council and the bishop of the diocese, invite members of another Church to which this Canon applies to take part in joint worship with the Church of England or to use a church in the parish for worship in accordance with the forms of service and practice of that other Church on such occasions as may be specified in the approval given by the bishop.

10. The dean and chapter or the cathedral chapter of any cathedral church may with the approval of the bishop of the diocese invite members of another Church to which this Canon applies to take part in joint worship with the Church of England, or to use the cathedral church for worship in accordance with the forms of service and practice of that other Church, on such occasions as may be specified in the approval given by the bishop.

11. Any approval required by this Canon to be obtained from a bishop or archbishop shall be in writing and shall be given in accordance with such directions as may from time to time be given by the House of Bishops of the General Synod.

12. (1) This Canon applies to every Church to which the Church of England (Ecumenical Relations) Measure 1998 applies.

(2) In this Canon 'incumbent', in relation to a parish, includes—
   (a) in a case where the benefice concerned is vacant (and paragraph (b) below does not apply), the rural dean; and
   (b) in a case where a suspension period (within the meaning of the Pastoral Measure 1983) applies to the benefice concerned, the priest-in-charge; and
   (c) in a case where a special cure of souls in respect of the parish has been assigned to a vicar in a team ministry by a scheme under the Pastoral Measure 1983 or by his licence from the bishop, that vicar, and 'place of worship' means a building or part of a building licensed for public worship.

B 44 OF LOCAL ECUMENICAL PROJECTS

1. (1) The bishop of a diocese may enter into an agreement with the appropriate authority of each participating Church with regard to the participation of the Church of England in a local ecumenical project established or to be established for an area comprising any parish in his diocese (not being the parish of a cathedral church) or part of such a parish.

(2) Where the area of a local ecumenical project is extended so as to include a parish which was not previously included (not being the parish of a cathedral church) or to include part of such a parish, the Church of England shall not participate in the project in respect of that parish or part of a parish unless the bishop of the diocese has agreed thereto.

(3) A bishop shall not enter into any agreement under sub-paragraph (1) or (2) above as respects any parish or part of a parish unless the participation of the Church of England in the project in respect of the parish concerned has been approved—
   (a) by the incumbent of that parish; and
   (b) by 75% of those present and voting at a meeting of the parochial church council of that parish; and
   (c) by either the annual parochial church meeting or a special parochial church meeting of that parish; and
   (d) by the diocesan pastoral committee after consultation with the deanery synod concerned or the standing committee of that synod.

2. (1) Any agreement made under paragraph 1(1) above shall have effect for such period of not more than seven years as may be specified therein, but may from time to time be extended by an agreement made by the bishop of the diocese concerned for such further period of not more than seven years as may be specified in that later agreement.

(2) Where a local ecumenical project is amended so as to include a Church which was not previously participating in the project, or to include an additional congregation of a participating Church, the Church of England shall not continue to participate in that project unless the bishop of the diocese concerned has agreed to that amendment or, if the area of the project comprises parishes or part of parishes in more than one diocese, the bishops of those dioceses have so agreed.

B. Divine Service and the Administration of the Sacraments

(3) A bishop of a diocese shall not make any agreement under sub-paragraph (1) or (2) above unless he has obtained the consent of—
- (a) the incumbent of each parish concerned; and
- (b) each parochial church council concerned; and
- (c) the diocesan pastoral committee.

3. (1) A bishop may at any time revoke any agreement made under the foregoing provisions of this Canon after consultation with the appropriate authority of each participating Church, each parochial church council concerned and the diocesan pastoral committee.

(2) Any agreement made under the foregoing provisions of this Canon shall be in writing.

4. (1) A bishop who has given his agreement to participation in a local ecumenical project under the foregoing provisions of this Canon may by an instrument in writing made after consultation with the parochial church council of each parish or part of a parish in the area of the project—
- (a) make special provision as to the ministry in that area of clerks in Holy Orders, deaconesses, lay workers and readers beneficed in or licensed to any parish wholly or partly in that area;
- (b) exercise in relation to that area his powers under Canon B 14A, Canon B 40 and Canon B 43;
- (c) authorise ministers of any other participating Church with the goodwill of the persons concerned to baptise in a place of worship of the Church of England in that area in accordance with a rite authorised by any participating Church;
- (d) authorise a priest of the Church of England to preside in that area at a service of Holy Communion in accordance with a rite authorised by any other participating Church;
- (e) make provision for the holding in that area of joint services with any other participating Church, including services of baptism and confirmation;
- (f) authorise the holding, in a place of worship of the Church of England in that area, of services of Holy Communion presided over by a minister of any other participating Church.

(2) A bishop shall not by any instrument made under this paragraph authorise any rite to be used in any service mentioned in sub-paragraph (1)(d), (e) or (f) above unless he is satisfied that the rite and the elements to be used are not contrary to, nor indicative of any departure from, the doctrine of the Church of England in any essential matter.

(3) Where the holding of a service of Holy Communion is authorised under sub-paragraph (1)(f) above
- (a) notice of the holding of any such service shall, so far as practicable, be given upon the Sunday immediately preceding with an indication of the rite to be used and the Church to which the minister who is to preside thereat belongs; and
- (b) no such service, notwithstanding that the form of service used may follow a form authorised under Canon B 1 or a form substantially similar thereto, shall be held out or taken to be a celebration of the Holy Communion according to the use of the Church of England; and
- (c) no portion of the bread and wine consecrated at any such service shall be carried out of the church in accordance with the provisions of Canon B 37(2) except at the express wish of the individual sick communicant, in which case this shall be done either during or immediately after the service, or as soon as practicable on the same day.

(4) An instrument made under this paragraph with respect to any local ecumenical project may be amended or revoked by a subsequent instrument made after consultation with the parochial church council of each parish which is in, or part of which is in, the area of that project.

5. Before exercising his powers under paragraph 4 above in relation to any local ecumenical project the bishop shall consult the authorities of the other participating Churches, and he shall so exercise those powers as to ensure that public worship according to the rites of the Church of England is

maintained with reasonable frequency in a parish which is in, or part of which is in, the area of the project and in particular that a service of Holy Communion according to the rites of the Church of England and presided over by a priest of the Church of England or by an episcopally ordained priest in a Church whose Orders are recognised and accepted by the Church of England shall be celebrated at least on Christmas Day, Ash Wednesday, Easter Day, Ascension Day and Pentecost.

6. (1) Where a local ecumenical project is established or is to be established for an area in which a cathedral church is situated, the bishop of the diocese may, after consultation with the dean and chapter or cathedral chapter of that cathedral church and after such other consultation as he considers appropriate, enter into an agreement with the appropriate authority of each participating Church with regard to the participation of that cathedral church in the project.

(2) The provisions of paragraphs 2 to 4 above shall apply in relation to an agreement made or project participated in by virtue of sub-paragraph (1) above subject to the following modifications—

    (a) sub-paragraph (3) of paragraph 2 shall not apply but the bishop before making an agreement under sub-paragraph (1) or (2) of that paragraph with respect to a project in which a cathedral church is participating shall consult the dean and chapter or cathedral chapter of that cathedral church;

    (b) in paragraph 3(1) for the reference to each parochial church council concerned and the diocesan pastoral committee there shall be substituted a reference to the dean and chapter or cathedral chapter of the cathedral church concerned;

    (c) in paragraph 4 for the reference in sub-paragraphs (1) and (4) to the parochial church council of each parish or part of a parish in the area of the project there shall be substituted a reference to the dean and chapter or cathedral chapter of the cathedral church concerned and for the reference in sub-paragraph (1)(a) to clerks in Holy Orders, deaconesses, lay workers and readers beneficed or licensed to any parish wholly or partly in the area there shall be substituted a reference to clerks in Holy Orders, deaconesses, lay workers and readers ministering in or licensed to the cathedral church concerned; and

    (d) before exercising his powers under paragraph 4 in relation to a project participated in by virtue of sub-paragraph (1) above the bishop shall consult the authorities of the other participating Churches.

(3) Nothing in this paragraph shall affect the requirements of Canon B 10 or Canon B 13 regarding services in cathedral churches.

7. (1) Where a local ecumenical project is established or to be established for an institution and a clerk in Holy Orders is licensed under section 2 of the Extra-Parochial Ministry Measure 1967 in respect of that institution, the bishop of the diocese may, after such consultation as he considers appropriate, enter into an agreement with the appropriate authority of each participating Church with regard to the participation of the Church of England in that project.

(2) A bishop shall not enter into an agreement under sub-paragraph (1) above as respects any institution unless the participation of the Church of England in the project concerned has been approved by the diocesan pastoral committee.

(3) The provisions of paragraphs 2 to 5 above shall, so far as applicable, apply in relation to an agreement made or project participated in by virtue of this paragraph as they apply in relation to an agreement made or project participated in by virtue of paragraph 1 above, subject to the following modifications—

    (a) for any reference to the area of the project there shall be substituted a reference to the institution concerned;

    (b) for the reference to clerks in Holy Orders, deaconesses, lay workers and readers beneficed in or licensed to a parish there shall be substituted a reference to any clerk in Holy Orders, deaconess, lay worker or reader licensed in respect of the institution concerned; and

(c) any reference to an incumbent or to a parochial church council shall be omitted.

8. The powers of a bishop under this Canon may be exercised only in respect of a local ecumenical project in which every other Church participating in the project is a Church to which the Church of England (Ecumenical Relations) Measure 1988 applies.

9. In this Canon
'incumbent', in relation to a parish includes
    (a) in a case where the benefice concerned is vacant (and paragraph (b) below does not apply), the rural dean; and
    (b) in a case where a suspension period (within the meaning of the Pastoral Measure 1983) applies to the benefice concerned, the priest-in-charge; and
    (c) in a case where a special cure of souls in respect of the parish has been assigned to a vicar in a team ministry by a scheme under the Pastoral Measure 1983 or by his licence from the bishop, that vicar;

'local ecumenical project' has the same meaning as in the Church of England (Ecumenical Relations) Measure 1988;

'minister', in relation to any other participating church, means any person ordained to the ministry of the word and sacraments;

'participating Church', in relation to a local ecumenical project, means a Church which is participating in that project.

Ministers, their Ordination, Function and Charge

C 1   OF HOLY ORDERS IN THE CHURCH OF ENGLAND

1. The Church of England holds and teaches that from the apostles' time there have been these orders in Christ's Church: bishops, priests, and deacons; and no man shall be accounted or taken to be a lawful bishop, priest, or deacon in the Church of England, or suffered to execute any of the said offices, except that he be called, tried, examined, and admitted thereunto according to the Ordinal or any form of service alternative thereto approved by the General Synod under Canon B 2, authorised by the Archbishops of Canterbury and York under Canon C 4A or has had formerly episcopal consecration or ordination in some Church whose orders are recognised and accepted by the Church of England.

2. No person who has been admitted to the order of bishop, priest, or deacon can ever be divested of the character of his order, but a minister may either by legal process voluntarily relinquish the exercise of his orders and use himself as a layman, or may by legal and canonical process be deprived of the exercise of his orders or deposed therefrom.

3. According to the ancient law and usage of this Church and Realm of England, the priests and deacons who have received authority to minister in any diocese owe canonical obedience in all things lawful and honest to the bishop of the same, and the bishop of each diocese owes due allegiance to the archbishop of the province as his metropolitan.

4. Where any bishop, priest or deacon ceases to hold office in the Church of England or otherwise ceases to serve in any place he continues to owe canonical obedience in all things lawful and honest to the archbishop of the province or the bishop of the diocese (as the case may be) in which he resides for the time being.

C 2 Of the Consecration of Bishops

1. No person shall be consecrated to the office of bishop by fewer than three bishops present together and joining in the act of consecration, of whom one shall be the archbishop of the province or a bishop appointed to act on his behalf.

2. The consecration of a bishop shall take place upon some Sunday or Holy Day, unless the archbishop, for urgent and weighty cause, shall appoint some other day.

3. No person shall be consecrated bishop except he shall be at least thirty years of age.

4. No person shall be refused consecration as bishop on the ground that he was born out of lawful wedlock.

5. Nothing in this Canon shall make it lawful for a woman to be consecrated to the office of bishop.

C 3 Of the Ordination of Priests and Deacons

1. Ordination to the office of priest or deacon shall take place upon the Sundays immediately following the Ember Weeks, or upon St Peter's Day, Michaelmas Day or St Thomas's Day, or upon a day within the week immediately following St Peter's Day, Michaelmas Day or St Thomas's Day, or upon such other day, being a Sunday, a Holy Day or one of the Ember Days, as the bishop of the diocese on urgent occasion shall appoint.

2. Ordination of priests and deacons shall be in the cathedral church of the diocese, or other church or chapel at the discretion of the bishop.

3. One of the archdeacons, or his deputy, or such other persons as by ancient custom have the right so to do, shall present to the bishop every person who is to be ordained.

4. The priests taking part in an ordination shall together with the bishop lay their hands upon the head of every person who receives the order of priesthood.

4A. Any form of service of Holy Communion which is authorised by Canon B 1 may be used at an ordination.

5. No person shall be made deacon, except he be at least twenty-three years of age, unless he have a faculty from the Archbishop of Canterbury.

6. No person shall be ordained priest, except he be at least twenty-four years of age, unless being over the age of twenty-three he have a faculty from the Archbishop of Canterbury.

7. No person shall be ordained both deacon and priest upon one and the same day, unless he have a faculty from the Archbishop of Canterbury.

8. A deacon shall not be ordained to the priesthood for at least one year, unless the bishop shall find good cause for the contrary, so that trial may be made of his behaviour in the office of deacon before he be admitted to the order of priesthood. During a vacancy of the see, the power of the bishop under this paragraph shall be exercisable by the archbishop of the province in which the diocese is situate.

C 4 Of the Quality of Such as are to be Ordained Deacons or Priests

1. Every bishop shall take care that he admit no person into Holy Orders but such as he knows either by himself, or by sufficient testimony, to have been baptised and confirmed, to be sufficiently instructed in Holy Scripture and in the doctrine, discipline, and worship of the Church of England, and to be of virtuous conversation and good repute and such as to be a wholesome example and pattern to the flock of Christ.

C. Ministers, their Ordination, Function and Charge

2. No person shall be admitted into Holy Orders who is suffering, or who has suffered, from any physical or mental infirmity which in the opinion of the bishop will prevent him from ministering the word and sacraments or from performing the other duties of the minister's office.

3. Subject to paragraph 3A of this Canon no person shall be admitted into Holy Orders who has remarried and, the other party to that marriage being alive, has a former spouse still living; or who is married to a person who has been previously married and whose former spouse is still living.

3A. The archbishop of the province, on an application made to him by the bishop of a diocese on behalf of a person who by reason of paragraph 3 of this Canon could not otherwise be admitted into Holy Orders, may grant a faculty for the removal of the impediment imposed by that paragraph to the admission of that person into Holy Orders, and any request made to a bishop for an application to be made on his behalf under this paragraph shall be made and considered, and any application made by the bishop to the archbishop shall be made and determined, in accordance with directions given from time to time by the Archbishops of Canterbury and York acting jointly.

4. No person shall be refused ordination as deacon or priest on the ground that he was born out of lawful wedlock.

C 4A OF WOMEN DEACONS

1. A woman may be ordained to the office of deacon if she otherwise satisfies the requirements of Canon C 4 as to the persons who may be ordained as deacons.

2. A deaconess who is licensed or holds a bishop's permission to officiate, and in either case satisfies the requirements of Canon C 4 as to the persons to be ordained as deacons, may apply to a bishop for his consent to her ordination as a deacon for service in the diocese of that bishop, and the bishop may give that consent notwithstanding—
   (a) that she has not after applying to be so ordained been further examined concerning her knowledge of Holy Scripture or of the doctrine, discipline and worship of the Church of England, or
   (b) that she has not exhibited to the bishop any certificate or other document which is required to be so exhibited under Canon C 6.

3. Where a bishop is ordaining a woman according to the Order for the Making of Deacons in the Ordinal attached to the *Book of Common Prayer* the post-Communion Collect beginning 'Almighty God, giver of all good things' shall be omitted and it shall be lawful for the bishop to use the variations to that service set out in the Schedule to this Canon.

4. The Archbishops of Canterbury and York may jointly authorise forms of service for deaconesses to be ordained deacon, being forms of service which in both words and order are in their opinion reverent and seemly and are neither contrary to, nor indicative of any departure from, the doctrine of the Church of England in any essential matter.

The Schedule

1. For any relevant reference to 'he' or 'him' there may be substituted the words 'she' or 'her'.

2. For the prescribed Epistle, namely, either 1 Timothy 3. 8–13 or Acts 6. 2–7, there may be substituted either Isaiah 6. 1–8 or Romans 12. 1–12 or such other lections as may from time to time be duly authorised.

3. For the prescribed Gospel, namely Luke 12. 35–38 there may be substituted Mark 10. 35–45 or such other lection as may from time to time be duly authorised.

C 4B OF WOMEN PRIESTS

1. A woman may be ordained to the office of priest if she otherwise satisfies the requirements of Canon C 4 as to the persons who may be ordained as priests.

2. In the forms of service contained in the *Book of Common Prayer* or in the Ordinal words importing the masculine gender in relation to the priesthood shall be construed as including the feminine, except where the context otherwise requires.

C 5 OF THE TITLES OF SUCH AS ARE TO BE ORDAINED DEACONS OR PRIESTS

1. Any person to be admitted into Holy Orders shall first exhibit to the bishop of the diocese of whom he desires imposition of hands a certificate that he is provided of some ecclesiastical office within such diocese, which the bishop shall judge sufficient, wherein he may attend the cure of souls and execute his ministry.

2. A bishop may also admit into Holy Orders
    (a) any person holding office in any university, or any fellow, or any person in right as a fellow, in any college or hall in the same;
    (b) any master in a school;
    (c) any person who is to be a chaplain in any university or in any college or hall in the same or in any school;
    (d) any person who is to be a member of the staff of a theological college;
    (e) any person who is living under vows in the house of any religious order or community:

Provided that the said university, college, hall, school, or house of a religious order or community be situate within his diocese.

3. A bishop may also admit into Holy Orders persons for service overseas in accordance with the statutory provisions in that behalf in force from time to time.

4. No person shall be admitted into Holy Orders by any bishop other than the bishop of the diocese in which he is to exercise his ministry, except he shall bring with him Letters Dimissory from the bishop of such diocese.

5. Notwithstanding any provision of the preceding paragraphs of this Canon, the ancient privilege of any fellow or any person in right as a fellow in any college or hall in the University of Oxford or of Cambridge to be admitted into Holy Orders without Letters Dimissory by any bishop willing to ordain him shall be unimpaired.

C 6 OF THE CERTIFICATES AND TESTIMONY TO BE EXHIBITED TO THE BISHOP BY SUCH AS ARE TO BE ORDAINED DEACONS OR PRIESTS

1. Every person who is to be made a deacon shall exhibit to the bishop of the diocese:
    (a) a certificate or other sufficient evidence of the date and place of his birth;
    (b) testimony of his former good life and behaviour from persons specified by the bishop.

2. Every person who is to be ordained priest shall exhibit to the bishop of the diocese:
    (a) his Letters of Orders;
    (b) testimony of his former good life and behaviour from persons specified by the bishop.

C 7 OF EXAMINATION FOR HOLY ORDERS

No bishop shall admit any person into Holy Orders, except such person on careful and diligent examination, wherein the bishop shall have called to his assistance the archdeacons and other ministers appointed for this purpose, be found to possess a sufficient knowledge of Holy Scripture and of the doctrine, discipline and worship of the Church of England as set forth in the Thirty-nine Articles

C. Ministers, their Ordination, Function and Charge

of Religion, the *Book of Common Prayer*, and the Ordinal: and to fulfil the requirements as to learning and other qualities which, subject to any directions given by the General Synod, the bishop deems necessary for the office of deacon.

C 8 OF MINISTERS EXERCISING THEIR MINISTRY

1. Every minister shall exercise his ministry in accordance with the provisions of this Canon.

2. A minister duly ordained priest or deacon, and, where it is required under paragraph 5 of this Canon, holding a licence or permission from the archbishop of the province, may officiate in any place only after he has received authority to do so from the bishop of the diocese or other the Ordinary of the place.
    Save that:
    (a) The minister having the cure of souls of a church or chapel or the sequestrator when the cure is vacant or the dean or provost and the canons residentiary of any cathedral or collegiate church may allow a minister, concerning whom they are satisfied either by actual personal knowledge or by good and sufficient evidence that he is of good life and standing and otherwise qualified under this Canon, to minister within their church or chapel for a period of not more than seven days within three months without reference to the bishop or other Ordinary, and a minister so allowed shall be required to sign the services register when he officiates; but nothing in this sub-paragraph authorises
        (i) a minister or sequestrator in a parish to which a resolution in the form set out as Resolution A in Schedule 1 to the Priests (Ordination of Women) Measure 1993 applies, or
        (ii) a dean or provost or the canons residentiary of a cathedral church to which a resolution in the form set out as Resolution A in Schedule 2 to the said Measure applies to allow an act in contravention of that resolution to be committed.
    (b) No member of the chapter of a cathedral church shall be debarred from performing the duties of his office in due course and exercising his ministry within the diocese merely by lack of authority from the bishop of the diocese within which the cathedral is situate.
    (c) Any minister who has a licence to preach throughout the province from the archbishop or throughout England from the University of Oxford or of Cambridge, may preach the Word of God in any diocese within that province or throughout England, as the case may be, without any further authority from the bishop thereof.
    (d) A funeral service which may, under section 2 of the Church of England (Miscellaneous Provisions) Measure 1992, be performed in a parish without the consent of the minister of the parish may be performed without any further authority from the bishop of the diocese within which the parish is situated.

3. The bishop of a diocese confers such authority on a minister either by instituting him to a benefice, or by admitting him to serve within his diocese by licence under his hand and seal, or by giving him written permission to officiate within the same.

4. No minister who has such authority to exercise his ministry in any diocese shall do so therein in any place in which he has not the cure of souls without the permission of the minister having such cure, except at the homes of persons whose names are entered on the electoral roll of the parish which he serves and to the extent authorised by the Extra-Parochial Ministry Measure 1967, or in a university, college, school, hospital, or public or charitable institution in which he is licensed to officiate as provided by the said Measure and Canon B 41 or, in relation to funeral services, as provided by section 2 of the Church of England (Miscellaneous Provisions) Measure 1992.

5. A minister who has been ordained priest or deacon
    (a) by an overseas bishop within the meaning of the Overseas and Other Clergy (Ministry and Ordination) Measure 1967;

(b) under section 5 of that Measure for ministry overseas;
(c) by a bishop in a Church not in communion with the Church of England, whose orders are recognised or accepted by the Church of England;

may not minister in the province of Canterbury or York without the permission of the archbishop of the province in question under the said Measure: Provided that this paragraph shall not apply to any person ordained priest or deacon by any such bishop on the request and by the commission in writing of the bishop of a diocese in the province of Canterbury or York.

C 9   OF COLLATION AND PRESENTATION

1. A vacancy or impending vacancy in any benefice shall be notified by the bishop of the diocese to the patron and to the parochial church council, and the provisions of the law from time to time in force relating to the filling of such vacancy shall be complied with.

2. Every bishop shall have twenty-eight days' space to inquire and inform himself of the sufficiency and qualities of every minister, after he has been presented to him to be instituted to any benefice.

C 10   OF ADMISSION AND INSTITUTION

1. No person shall be admitted or instituted to any benefice before such time as he shall have been ordained priest by episcopal ordination in accordance with the provisions of Canon C 1.

2. No bishop shall admit or institute to a benefice any priest who has been ordained by any other bishop, except such priest first show unto him his Letters of Orders or other sufficient evidence that he has been ordained, and bring him sufficient testimony, if the bishop shall require it, of his former good life and behaviour, and lastly, shall appear on due examination to be of sufficient learning.

2A. No bishop shall admit or institute a priest who is a woman to a benefice if a resolution under section 3(1) of the Priests (Ordination of Women) Measure 1993 is in force in the parish concerned or, in the case of a benefice which comprises two or more parishes, in any of the parishes concerned.

3. A bishop may refuse to admit or institute any priest to a benefice
    (a) on the ground that at the date of presentation not more than three years have elapsed since the priest who has been presented to him was ordained deacon, or that the said priest is unfit for the discharge of the duties of a benefice by reason of physical or mental infirmity or incapacity, pecuniary embarrassment of a serious character, grave misconduct or neglect of duty in an ecclesiastical office, evil life, having by his conduct caused grave scandal concerning his moral character since his ordination; or
    (b) in the case of a presentee who has not previously held a benefice or the office of vicar in a team ministry, on the ground that he has had no experience or less than three years' experience as a full-time assistant curate or curate in charge licensed to a parish.

This ground shall not apply in the Channel Islands and the Isle of Man, but the above references to a benefice and the office of vicar in a team ministry and a parish shall be construed as applying to any benefice or any such office and any parish in the provinces of Canterbury and York and to any benefice (or corresponding office) and any parish in the Church in Wales, the Church of Ireland or the Episcopal Church of Scotland.

4. No bishop shall admit or institute any priest to a benefice until the expiration of a period of three weeks from the date on which notice in the prescribed form of his intention to do so has been served on the secretary of the parochial church council.

5. After the expiration of three weeks from the serving of that notice on the secretary of the parochial church council, the bishop shall, as speedily as may be, proceed to give institution to the priest to whom he has collated the benefice, or who has been presented to him to be instituted thereto, in

accordance with the laws and statutes in that behalf provided; which institution he shall use his best endeavour to give in the parish church of the benefice.

6. The bishop, when he gives institution, shall read the words of institution from a written instrument having the episcopal seal appended thereto; and during the reading thereof the priest who is to be instituted shall kneel before the bishop and hold the seal in his hand.

7. If the bishop for some grave and urgent cause be unable to give institution himself he shall delegate power to some commissary in Holy Orders to give the same on his behalf.

8. The provisions of this Canon are without prejudice to the right of a patron or a presentee to appeal, in accordance with the laws of this realm, against the refusal of the bishop to institute.

C 11 Of Induction

1. The bishop, after giving institution to any priest, shall issue directions for induction to the archdeacon or other the person to whom induction belongs, who shall thereupon induct the said priest into possession of the temporalities of the benefice.

2. The archdeacon or other such person, when he makes the induction, shall take the priest who is to be inducted by the hand and lay it upon the key or upon the ring of the church door, or if the key cannot be had and there is no ring on the door, or if the church be in ruins, upon any part of the wall of the church or churchyard, at the same time reading the words of induction; after which the priest who has been inducted shall toll the bell to make his induction public and known to the people.

3. The archdeacon may authorise the rural dean or any other minister beneficed or licensed in his archdeaconry to make the induction on his behalf.

C 12 Of the Licensing of Ministers under Seal

1. A licence, granted by the bishop under his hand and seal to any minister to serve within his diocese, shall be in the form either
    (a) of a general licence to preach or otherwise to minister subject to the provisions of paragraph 4 of Canon C 8 in any parish or ecclesiastical district; or
    (b) of a licence to perform some particular office,

and a licence granted to an assistant curate or to a minister to whom section 20(3B) of the Pastoral Measure 1983 applies may be in a form which specifies the term of years for which the licence shall have effect.

2. No bishop shall grant any such licence to any minister who has come from another diocese, except such minister first show unto him Letters of Orders or other sufficient evidence that he is ordained, and bring him testimony, from the bishop of the diocese whence he has come, of his honesty, ability, and conformity to the doctrine, discipline, and worship of the Church of England.

3. *[Repealed by Amending Canon No 5]*

4. *[Repealed by Amending Canon No 19]*

5. The bishop of a diocese may by notice in writing revoke summarily, and without further process, any licence granted to any minister within his diocese for any cause which appears to him to be good and subject to section 7(1A) of the Church of England (Legal Aid and Miscellaneous Provisions) Measure 1988, where a bishop has granted a licence to any minister to serve within his diocese otherwise than as a member of a team ministry, the bishop may revoke the licence summarily, and without further process, for any cause which appears to him to be good and reasonable (other than for misconduct in respect of which disciplinary proceedings may be instituted under the Clergy Discipline Measure 2003) after explaining the reasons for the revocation and having given the

minister sufficient opportunity of showing reason to the contrary; and the notice shall notify the minister that he may, within twenty-eight days from the date on which he receives the notice, appeal to the archbishop of the province in which that diocese is situated.

On such an appeal the archbishop may either hear the appeal himself or appoint a person holding the office of diocesan bishop or suffragan bishop in his province (otherwise than in the diocese concerned) to hear the appeal in his place; and, after hearing the appeal or, if he has appointed a bishop to hear the appeal in his place, after receiving a report in writing from that bishop, the archbishop may confirm, vary or cancel the revocation of the licence as he considers just and proper; and there shall be no appeal from the decision of the archbishop.

Where the see of the archbishop is vacant or the archbishop is also the bishop of the diocese concerned, any reference in the preceding provision of this paragraph to the archbishop of the province shall be construed as a reference to the archbishop of the other province, but any bishop appointed by the archbishop of the other province by virtue of this paragraph shall be a bishop serving in the province which contains the diocese concerned.

Any appeal under this paragraph shall be conducted in accordance with rules approved by the Archbishops of Canterbury and York; and any such rules may provide for the appointment of one or more persons to advise the archbishop or bishop hearing such an appeal on any question of law arising in the course thereof.

6. (1) This paragraph applies where a licence has been granted by a bishop to any minister to serve within his diocese for a term of years otherwise than as a member of a team ministry.

(2) The bishop may before the expiration of the term of years by notice in writing request the minister to vacate his office when the term expires.

(3) Where no such request has been made before the expiration of the term of years the minister may continue in office, but the bishop may by notice in writing request the minister to vacate his office at the expiration of the period of three months following the giving of the notice.

C 13 OF THE OATH OF ALLEGIANCE

1. Every person whose election to any archbishopric or bishopric is to be confirmed, or who is to be consecrated or translated to any suffragan bishopric, or to be ordained priest or deacon, or to be instituted, installed, licensed or admitted to any office in the Church of England or otherwise to serve in any place, shall first, in the presence of the archbishop or bishop by whom his election to such archbishopric or bishopric is to be confirmed, or in whose province such suffragan bishopric is situate, or by whom he is to be ordained, instituted, installed, licensed or admitted, or of the commissary of such archbishop or bishop, take the Oath of Allegiance in the form following:

> I, A B, do swear that I will be faithful and bear true allegiance to Her Majesty Queen Elizabeth II, her heirs and successors, according to law: So help me God.

2. The aforesaid Oath of Allegiance shall not be required to be taken
    (a) by any subject or citizen of a foreign state whom either archbishop, calling to assist him such bishops as he thinks fit, shall consecrate to officiate as a bishop in any foreign state; or
    (b) by any overseas clergyman to whom section 2 of the Overseas and Other Clergy (Ministry and Ordination) Measure 1967 applies or any other person ordained under section 5 of that Measure for ministry overseas,

if the bishop dispenses with the said oath.

3. Instead of taking the aforesaid Oath of Allegiance a solemn affirmation may be made in the circumstances mentioned in section 5 of the Oaths Act 1978 in the form following:

> I, AB, do solemnly, sincerely and truly declare and affirm that I will be faithful and bear true allegiance to Her Majesty Queen Elizabeth II, her heirs and successors, according to law.

C. Ministers, their Ordination, Function and Charge

C 14 OF THE OATHS OF OBEDIENCE

1. Every person whose election to any bishopric is to be confirmed, or who is to be consecrated bishop or translated to any bishopric or suffragan bishopric or who is to be licensed as an assistant bishop, shall first take the oath of due obedience to the archbishop and to the metropolitical Church of the province wherein he is to exercise the episcopal office in the form and manner prescribed in and by the Ordinal.

2. Either archbishop consecrating any person to exercise episcopal functions elsewhere than in England may dispense with the said oath.

3. Every person who is to be ordained priest or deacon shall first take the Oath of Canonical obedience to the bishop of the diocese by whom he is to be ordained, in the presence of the said bishop or his commissary, and in the form following:

> I, A B, do swear by Almighty God that I will pay true and canonical obedience to the Lord Bishop of C and his successors in all things lawful and honest: So help me God.

4. Instead of taking the aforesaid Oath of Canonical Obedience a solemn affirmation may be made in the circumstances mentioned in section 5 of the Oaths Act 1978 in the form following:

> I, A B, do solemnly, sincerely and truly declare and affirm that I will pay true and canonical obedience to the Lord Bishop of C and his successors in all things lawful and honest.

5. Every bishop, priest or deacon who is to be translated, instituted, installed, licensed or admitted to any office in the Church of England or otherwise to serve in any place shall reaffirm the Oath of Canonical Obedience or his solemn affirmation taken at his ordination or consecration to the archbishop of the province or the bishop of the diocese (as the case may be) by whom he is to be instituted, installed, licensed or admitted in the presence of the said archbishop or bishop or his commissary in the form set out in this Canon.

C 15 OF THE DECLARATION OF ASSENT

1. (1) The Declaration of Assent to be made under this Canon shall be in the form set out below:

Preface

The Church of England is part of the One, Holy, Catholic and Apostolic Church worshipping the one true God, Father, Son and Holy Spirit. It professes the faith uniquely revealed in the Holy Scriptures and set forth in the catholic creeds, which faith the Church is called upon to proclaim afresh in each generation. Led by the Holy Spirit, it has borne witness to Christian truth in its historic formularies, the Thirty-nine Articles of Religion, the *Book of Common Prayer* and the Ordering of Bishops, Priests and Deacons. In the declaration you are about to make will you affirm your loyalty to this inheritance of faith as your inspiration and guidance under God in bringing the grace and truth of Christ to this generation and making Him known to those in your care?

Declaration of Assent

I, A B, do so affirm, and accordingly declare my belief in the faith which is revealed in the Holy Scriptures and set forth in the catholic creeds and to which the historic formularies of the Church of England bear witness; and in public prayer and administration of the sacraments, I will use only the forms of service which are authorised or allowed by Canon.

(2) The preface which precedes the Declaration of Assent in the form set out above (with in each case such adaptations as are appropriate) shall be spoken by the archbishop or bishop or commissary in whose presence the Declaration is to be made in accordance with the following provisions of this paragraph and shall be spoken by him before the making of the Declaration.

(3) Every person who is to be consecrated bishop or suffragan bishop shall on the occasion of his consecration publicly and openly make the Declaration of Assent in the presence of the archbishop by whom he is to be consecrated and of the congregation there assembled.

(4) Every person who is to be ordained priest or deacon shall before ordination make the Declaration of Assent in the presence of the archbishop or bishop by whom he is to be ordained.

(5) Every clerk in Holy Orders who is to be instituted, installed, admitted or licensed to any office in the Church of England or otherwise licensed to serve in any place shall first make the Declaration of Assent in the presence of the bishop by whom he is to be instituted, installed, admitted or licensed or of the bishop's commissary unless he has been ordained the same day and has made the Declaration.

(6) Where any bishop, priest or deacon ceases to hold office in the Church of England or otherwise ceases to serve in any place the Declaration made under this Canon shall continue to have effect in so far as he continues to minister in the Church.

2. Every archbishop and bishop shall, on the occasion of his enthronement in the cathedral church of his province or diocese, as the case may be, and before he is enthroned, publicly and openly make the Declaration of Assent in the presence of the congregation there assembled.

Before the archbishop or bishop makes the Declaration the preface which precedes the Declaration in the form set out in paragraph 1(1) of this Canon (with the appropriate adaptations) shall be spoken by the dean or provost or, if the dean or provost is absent abroad or incapacitated through illness or the office of dean or provost is vacant, by such one of the residentiary canons as those canons may select.

3. A suffragan bishop who is to be invested by the archbishop of the province in which he is to serve shall on the occasion of his investiture publicly and openly make the Declaration of Assent in the presence of the congregation there assembled.

Before the bishop makes the Declaration the preface which precedes the Declaration in the form set out in paragraph 1(1) of this Canon (with the appropriate adaptations) shall be spoken by the archbishop.

4. Where any minister has been instituted, installed, licensed or admitted to office in some place other than the place where he is to serve he shall
   (a) on the first Lord's Day on which he officiates in the church or one of the churches in which he is to serve; or
   (b) in the case of a minister instituted or licensed to serve in a guild church, in that church on such weekday as the bishop may approve,

publicly and openly make the Declaration of Assent at the time of divine service in the presence of the congregation there assembled.

Before the minister makes the Declaration the preface which precedes the Declaration in the form set out in paragraph 1(1) of this Canon (with the appropriate adaptations) shall be spoken by the incumbent or another priest having a cure of souls.

5. Any person who in pursuance of a request and commission from a bishop of any diocese in England is ordained by an overseas bishop within the meaning of the Overseas and Other Clergy (Ministry and Ordination) Measure 1967, or a bishop in a church not in communion with the Church of England whose orders are recognised or accepted by the Church of England, shall be deemed to be ordained by a bishop of a diocese in England and accordingly shall make the Declaration of Assent.

C 17 OF ARCHBISHOPS

1. By virtue of their respective offices, the Archbishop of Canterbury is styled Primate of All England and Metropolitan, and the Archbishop of York Primate of England and Metropolitan.

2. The archbishop has throughout his province at all times metropolitical jurisdiction, as superintendent of all ecclesiastical matters therein, to correct and supply the defects of other bishops, and, during the time of his metropolitical visitation, jurisdiction as Ordinary, except in places and over persons exempt by law or custom.

3. Such jurisdiction is exercised by the archbishop himself, or by a vicar-general, official, or other commissary to whom authority in that behalf shall have been formally committed by the archbishop concerned.

4. The archbishop is, within his province, the principal minister, and to him belongs the right of confirming the election of every person to a bishopric, of being the chief consecrator at the consecration of every bishop, of receiving such appeals in his provincial court as may be provided by law, of holding metropolitical visitations at times or places limited by law or custom, and of presiding in the Convocation of the province either in person or by such deputy as he may lawfully appoint. In the province of Canterbury, the Bishop of London, or in his absence, the Bishop of Winchester, has the right to be so appointed; and in their absence the archbishop shall appoint some other diocesan bishop of the province. The two archbishops are joint presidents of the General Synod.

5. By ancient custom, no Act is held to be an Act of the Convocation of the province unless it shall have received the assent of the archbishop.

6. By statute law it belongs to the archbishop to give permission to officiate within his province to any minister who has been ordained priest or deacon by an overseas bishop within the meaning of the Overseas and Other Clergy (Ministry and Ordination) Measure 1967, or a bishop in a Church not in communion with the Church of England whose orders are recognised or accepted by the Church of England, and thereupon such minister shall possess all such rights and advantages and be subject to all such duties and liabilities as he would have possessed and been subject to if he had been ordained by the bishop of a diocese in the province of Canterbury or York.

7. By the laws of this realm the Archbishop of Canterbury is empowered to grant such licences or dispensations as are therein set forth and provided, and such licences or dispensations, being confirmed by the authority of the Queen's Majesty, have force and authority not only within the province of Canterbury but throughout all England.

C 18 OF DIOCESAN BISHOPS

1. Every bishop is the chief pastor of all that are within his diocese, as well laity as clergy, and their father in God; it appertains to his office to teach and to uphold sound and wholesome doctrine, and to banish and drive away all erroneous and strange opinions; and, himself an example of righteous and godly living; it is his duty to set forward and maintain quietness, love, and peace among all men.

2. Every bishop has within his diocese jurisdiction as Ordinary except in places and over persons exempt by law or custom.

3. Such jurisdiction is exercised by the bishop himself, or by a vicar-general, official, or other commissary, to whom authority in that behalf shall have been formally committed by the bishop concerned.

4. Every bishop is, within his diocese, the principal minister, and to him belongs the right, save in places and over persons exempt by law or custom, or celebrating the rites of ordination and confirmation; of conducting, ordering, controlling, and authorising all services in churches, chapels,

churchyards and consecrated burial grounds; of granting a faculty or licence for all alterations, additions, removals, or repairs to the walls, fabric, ornaments, or furniture of the same; of consecrating new churches, churchyards, and burial grounds; of instituting to all vacant benefices, whether of his own collation or of the presentation of others; of admitting by licence to all other vacant ecclesiastical offices; of holding visitations at times limited by law or custom to the end that he may get some good knowledge of the state, sufficiency, and ability of the clergy and other persons whom he is to visit; of being president of the diocesan synod.

5. Where the assent of the bishop is required to a resolution of the diocesan synod it shall not lightly nor without grave cause be withheld.

6. Every bishop shall be faithful in admitting persons into holy orders and in celebrating the rite of confirmation as often and in as many places as shall be convenient, and shall provide, as much as in him lies, that in every place within his diocese there shall be sufficient priests to minister the word and sacraments to the people that are therein.

7. Every bishop shall correct and punish all such as be unquiet, disobedient, or criminous, within his diocese, according to such authority as he has by God's Word and is committed to him by the laws and ordinances of this realm.

8. Every bishop shall reside within his diocese, saving the ancient right of any bishop, when resident in any house in London during his attendance on the Parliament, or on the Court, or for the purpose of performing any other duties of his office, to be taken and accounted as resident within his own diocese.

C 19   Of Guardians of Spiritualities

[Revoked by Amending Canon No 23]

C 20   Of Bishops Suffragan

1. Every bishop suffragan shall endeavour himself faithfully to execute such things pertaining to the episcopal office as shall be delegated to him by the bishop of the diocese to whom he shall be suffragan.

2. Every bishop suffragan shall use, have, or execute only such jurisdiction or episcopal power or authority in any diocese as shall be licensed or limited to him to use, have, or execute by the bishop of the same.

3. Every bishop suffragan shall reside within the diocese of the bishop to whom he shall be suffragan, except he have a licence from that bishop to reside elsewhere.

C 21   Of Deans or Provosts, and Canons Residentiary of Cathedral or Collegiate Churches

1. No person shall be capable of receiving the appointment of dean, provost, or canon residentiary until he has been six years complete in Holy Orders and, in the case of a dean or provost, is in priest's orders at the time of the appointment, except in the case of a canonry annexed to any professorship, headship, or other office in any university.

1A. A person who is in the deacon's orders and who has been ordained for a period exceeding six years shall be capable of receiving the appointment of canon residentiary of a cathedral church notwithstanding anything in the statutes or customs of that cathedral church to the contrary, but nothing in any such statutes or customs shall be construed as authorising or requiring a person in deacon's orders so appointed to preside at or celebrate the Holy Communion or to pronounce the Absolution.

C. Ministers, their Ordination, Function and Charge

2. The dean, or provost, of every cathedral or collegiate church, and the canons residentiary of the same, shall take care that the statutes and laudable customs of their church (not being contrary to the Word of God or prerogative royal), the statutes of this realm concerning ecclesiastical order, and all other constitutions set forth and confirmed by Her Majesty's authority, and such as shall be enjoined by the bishop of the diocese in his visitation, according to the statutes and customs of the same church, and the ecclesiastical laws of the realm, shall be diligently observed.

3. The dean, or provost, and the canons residentiary shall be resident in their cathedral or collegiate church for the time prescribed by law and by the statutes of the said cathedral or collegiate church, and shall there preach the Word of God and perform all the duties of their office, except they shall be otherwise hindered by weighty and urgent cause.

4. The dean, or provost, and the canons residentiary of every cathedral or collegiate church, together with the minor canons, vicars choral, and other ministers of the same, shall provide, as far as in them lies, that during the time of divine service in the said church all things be done with such reverence, care, and solemnity as shall set forth the honour and glory of Almighty God.

C 22   OF ARCHDEACONS

1. No person shall be capable of receiving the appointment of archdeacon until he has been six years complete in Holy Orders and is in priest's orders at the time of the appointment.

2. Every archdeacon within his archdeaconry exercises the jurisdiction which he has therein as an ordinary jurisdiction.

3. Such jurisdiction is exercised either by the archdeacon in person or by an official or commissary to whom authority in that behalf shall have been formally committed by the archdeacon concerned.

4. Every archdeacon shall within his archdeaconry carry out his duties under the bishop and shall assist the bishop in his pastoral care and office, and particularly he shall see that all such as hold any ecclesiastical office within the same perform their duties with diligence, and shall bring to the bishop's attention what calls for correction or merits praise.

5. Every archdeacon shall within his archdeaconry hold yearly visitations save when inhibited by a superior Ordinary; he shall also survey in person or by deputy all churches, chancels, and churchyards and give direction for the amendment of all defects in the walls, fabric, ornaments, and furniture of the same, and in particular shall exercise the powers conferred on him by the Inspection of Churches Measure 1955; he shall also, on receiving the directions of the bishop, induct any priest who has been instituted to a benefice into possession of the temporalities of the same.

C 23   OF RURAL DEANS

1. Every rural dean shall report to the bishop any matter in any parish within the deanery which it may be necessary or useful for the bishop to know, particularly any case of serious illness or other form of distress amongst the clergy, the vacancy of any cure of souls and the measures taken by the sequestrators to secure the ministration of the word and sacraments and other rites of the Church during the said vacancy, and any case of a minister from another diocese officiating in any place otherwise than as provided in Canon C 8.

2. In the case of any omission in any parish to prepare and maintain a church electoral roll or to form or maintain a parochial church council or to hold the annual parochial church meeting, the rural dean on such omission being brought to his notice shall ascertain and report to the bishop the cause thereof.

3. If at any time the rural dean has reason to believe that there is any serious defect in the fabric, ornaments, and furniture of any church or chapel, or that the buildings of any benefice are in a state of disrepair, he shall report the matter to the archdeacon.

4. The rural dean shall be a joint chairman (with a member of the House of Laity) of the deanery synod.

C 24 OF PRIESTS HAVING A CURE OF SOULS

1. Every priest having a cure of souls shall provide that, in the absence of reasonable hindrance, Morning and Evening Prayer daily and on appointed days the Litany shall be said in the church, or one of the churches, of which he is the minister.

2. Every priest having a cure of souls shall, except for some reasonable cause approved by the bishop of the diocese, celebrate, or cause to be celebrated, the Holy Communion on all Sundays and other greater Feast Days and on Ash Wednesday, and shall diligently administer the sacraments and other rites of the Church.

3. Every priest having a cure of souls shall, except for some reasonable cause approved by the bishop of the diocese, preach, or cause to be preached, a sermon in the church or churches of which he is the minister at least once each Sunday.

4. He shall instruct the parishioners of the benefice, or cause them to be instructed, in the Christian faith; and shall use such opportunities of teaching or visiting in the schools within his cure as are open to him.

5. He shall carefully prepare, or cause to be prepared, all such as desire to be confirmed and, if satisfied of their fitness, shall present them to the bishop for confirmation.

6. He shall be diligent in visiting the parishioners of the benefice, particularly those who are sick and infirm; and he shall provide opportunities whereby any of such parishioners may resort unto him for spiritual counsel and advice.

7. He and the parochial church council shall consult together on matters of general concern and importance to the parish.

8. If at any time he shall be unable to discharge his duties whether from non-residence or some other cause, he shall provide for his cure to be supplied by a priest licensed or otherwise approved by the bishop of the diocese.

C 25 OF THE RESIDENCE OF PRIESTS ON THEIR BENEFICES

1. Every beneficed priest shall keep residence on his benefice, or on one of them if he shall hold two or more in plurality, and in the house of residence (if any) belonging thereto.

2. No beneficed priest shall be absent from his benefice, or from the house of residence belonging thereto, for a period exceeding the space of three months together, or to be accounted at several times in any one year, except he have a licence to be so absent, granted by the bishop of the diocese subject to the statutory provisions in this behalf for the time being in force, or be otherwise legally exempt from residence.

3. Any beneficed priest, within one month after refusal of any such licence, may appeal to the archbishop of the province, who shall confirm such refusal or direct the bishop to grant a licence, as shall seem to the said archbishop just and proper.

4. In the case of any benefice in which there is no house, or no fit house of residence, the priest holding that benefice may be licensed by the bishop of the diocese to reside in some fit and convenient house, although not belonging to that benefice: Provided that such house be within three miles

D. The Order of Deaconesses

of the church or chapel of the benefice, or, if the same be in any city or borough town or market town, within two miles of such church or chapel.

C 26 OF THE MANNER OF LIFE OF MINISTERS

1. Every clerk in Holy Orders is under obligation, not being let by sickness or some urgent cause, to say daily the Morning and Evening Prayer, either privately or openly; and to celebrate the Holy Communion, or be present thereat, on all Sundays and other principal Feast Days. He is also to be diligent in daily prayer and intercession, in examination of his conscience, and in the study of the Holy Scriptures and such other studies as pertain to his ministerial duties.

2. A clerk in Holy Orders shall not give himself to such occupations, habits, or recreations as do not befit his sacred calling, or may be detrimental to the performance of the duties of his office, or tend to be a just cause of offence to others; and at all times he shall be diligent to frame and fashion his life and that of his family according to the doctrine of Christ, and to make himself and them, as much as in him lies, wholesome examples and patterns to the flock of Christ.

C 27 OF THE DRESS OF MINISTERS

The apparel of a bishop, priest, or deacon shall be suitable to his office; and, save for purposes of recreation and other justifiable reasons, shall be such as to be a sign and mark of his holy calling and ministry as well to others as to those committed to his spiritual charge.

C 28 OF THE OCCUPATIONS OF MINISTERS

1. No minister holding ecclesiastical office shall engage in trade or any other occupation in such manner as to affect the performance of the duties of his office, except so far as he be authorised so to do under the statutory provisions in this behalf for the time being in force or he have a licence so to do granted by the bishop of the diocese.

2. The bishop of the diocese shall have power to grant such a licence after consultation with the parochial church council of the parish in which the minister holds office or to refuse such a licence after consultation with that council.

3. If the bishop of the diocese shall refuse such a licence, the minister may within one month of such refusal appeal to the archbishop of the province, who shall confirm or overrule such refusal as may seem good to him.

4. During a vacancy of the see, the powers of the bishop of a diocese under paragraphs 1 and 2 of this Canon shall be exercisable by the archbishop of the province in which the diocese is situate, and paragraph 3 of this Canon shall not apply.

The Order of Deaconesses

D 1 OF THE ORDER OF DEACONESSES

1. The order of deaconesses is an order of ministry in the Church of England to which women are admitted by prayer and the laying on of hands by the bishop.

2. It belongs to the office of a deaconess, in the place where she is licensed to serve and under the direction of the minister, to lead the people in public worship, to exercise pastoral care, to instruct the people in the Christian faith, and to prepare them for the reception of the sacraments.

3. A deaconess may:
   (a) in accordance with Canon B 11, be authorised and invited to say or sing Morning or Evening Prayer (save for the Absolution);
   (b) distribute the holy sacrament of the Lord's Supper to the people and to read the Epistle and the Gospel.

4. The bishop may also authorise a deaconess to perform any of the following duties at the invitation of the minister of a parish or an extra-parochial place within the meaning of section 1 of the Deaconesses and Lay Ministry Measure 1972:
   (a) to preach at divine service;
   (b) to church women and, in the absence of the minister, to baptise;
   (c) with the goodwill of the persons responsible, to bury the dead or read the burial service before, at or after a cremation;
   (d) to publish banns of marriage at Morning and Evening Prayer (on occasions on which a lay person is permitted by the statute law so to do, and in accordance with the requirements of that law).

When a cure is vacant the first reference in this paragraph to the minister of a parish shall be construed as a reference to the rural dean.

5. Deaconesses may accept membership of any lay assembly of the Church of England.

6. Paragraph 4(b) and (c) of this Canon shall not apply to the Channel Islands.

D 2   OF ADMISSION TO THE ORDER OF DEACONESSES

1. Every woman to be admitted to the order of deaconesses shall be at least twenty-three years of age, unless she have a faculty from the Archbishop of Canterbury, shall be baptised and confirmed, and shall satisfy the bishop that she is a regular communicant of the Church of England.

2. Every woman who is to be admitted to the order of deaconesses shall first present to the bishop of the diocese:
   (a) a certificate signed by a person approved by the bishop that she has been nominated to exercise the office of deaconess within his diocese either in a cure of souls or in a wider area, or is a teacher or lecturer in a school or college or is living under vows in the house of a religious order or community; the said school, college, or house of a religious order or community being situated within such diocese;
   (b) (i) her birth certificate;
       (ii) a certificate or other evidence of her baptism and confirmation;
       (iii) testimony of her former good life and behaviour from persons specified by the bishop.

2A. No woman shall be admitted to the order of deaconesses unless she was accepted for training for admission to that order before the commencement of the Deacons (Ordination of Women) Measure 1986.

3. No woman shall be admitted to the order of deaconesses except she be found on examination, held by the bishop or by competent persons appointed by him for this purpose, to possess a sufficient knowledge of Holy Scripture and of the doctrine, discipline, and worship of the Church of England.

4. No woman shall be admitted to the order of deaconesses who is suffering or who has suffered from any physical or mental infirmity which, in the opinion of the bishop, will prevent her from exercising the office of a deaconess.

5. Every woman who is to be admitted to the order of deaconesses shall, in the presence of the bishop by whom she is to be so admitted or of the bishop's commissary, make and subscribe the

D. The Order of Deaconesses

declaration set out below, the preface which precedes the Declaration of Assent in paragraph 1(1) of Canon C 15 (with the appropriate adaptations) having first been spoken by the bishop or commissary:

> I, A B, do so affirm, and accordingly declare my belief in the faith which is revealed in the Holy Scriptures and set forth in the catholic creeds and to which the historic formularies of the Church of England bear witness; and in public prayer I will use only the forms of service which are authorised or allowed by Canon.

She shall also make the oath following:

> I, A B, will give due obedience to the Lord Bishop of C and his successors in all things lawful and honest: so help me God.

6. A woman shall be admitted to the order of deaconesses according to the form of service authorised by Canon B 1.

D 3 OF THE LICENSING OF DEACONESSES

1. No deaconess shall exercise her office in any diocese until she has been licensed so to do by the bishop thereof: Provided that, when any deaconess is to exercise her office temporarily in any diocese, the written permission of the bishop shall suffice.

1A. A licence authorising a deaconess to serve in a benefice in respect of which a team ministry is established may be in a form which specifies the term of years for which the licence shall have effect.

2. Every deaconess who is to be licensed to exercise her office in any place shall make a declaration and take an oath in the form and manner prescribed for a deaconess before her admission to the order.

3. Every bishop, before licensing a deaconess to exercise her office in any place, shall satisfy himself that adequate provision has been made for her salary, for her insurance against sickness or accident, and for a pension on her retirement.

3A. The bishop of a diocese may by notice in writing revoke summarily, and without further process, any licence granted to a deaconess within his diocese for any cause which appears to him to be good and reasonable, after having given her sufficient opportunity of showing reason to the contrary; and the notice shall notify the deaconess that she may, within twenty-eight days from the date on which she receives the notice, appeal to the archbishop of the province in which that diocese is situated.

On such an appeal the archbishop may either hear the appeal himself or appoint a person holding the office of diocesan bishop or suffragan bishop in his province (otherwise than in the diocese concerned) to hear the appeal in his place; and, after hearing the appeal or, if he has appointed a bishop to hear the appeal in his place, after receiving a report in writing from that bishop, the archbishop may confirm, vary or cancel the revocation of the licence as he considers just and proper; and there shall be no appeal from the decision of the archbishop.

Where the see of the archbishop is vacant or the archbishop is also the bishop of the diocese concerned, any reference in the preceding provisions of this paragraph to the archbishop of the province shall be construed as a reference to the archbishop of the other province, but any bishop appointed by the archbishop of the other province by virtue of this paragraph shall be a bishop serving in the province which contains the diocese concerned.

Any appeal under this paragraph shall be conducted in accordance with rules approved by the Archbishops of Canterbury and York; and any such rules may provide for the appointment of one or more persons to advise the archbishop or bishop hearing such an appeal on any question of law arising in the course thereof.

3B. Where a bishop has granted a licence to a deaconess to serve in his diocese for a term of years specified in the licence, the bishop may revoke that licence under paragraph 3A of this Canon before the expiration of that term, and where he does so that deaconess shall have the like right of appeal as any other deaconess whose licence is revoked under that paragraph.

4. The bishop of every diocese shall keep a register book wherein shall be entered the names of every person whom he has either admitted to the order of deaconesses or licensed to exercise the office of a deaconess in his diocese.

The Lay Officers of the Church

E 1   Of Churchwardens

1. The churchwardens of parishes and districts shall be chosen in accordance with the Churchwardens Measure 2001, and any other Measure, Act, or scheme affecting churchwardens.

2. (a) At a time and place to be appointed by the bishop annually, being on a date not later than 31st July in each year, each person chosen for the office of churchwarden shall appear before the bishop, or his substitute duly appointed, and be admitted to the office of churchwarden after–
   (i) making a declaration in the presence of the bishop or his substitute, that he will faithfully and diligently perform the duties of his office; and
   (ii) subscribing a declaration to that effect and also that he is not disqualified under section 2(1), (2) or (3) of the Churchwardens Measure 2001.
   (b) In relation to a filling of a casual vacancy the reference in paragraph (a) above to the 31st July shall be construed as a reference to a date three months after the person who is to fill the vacancy is chosen or the date of the next annual meeting of the parishioners to elect churchwardens, whichever is the earlier.

3. Subject to any provision of any Measure, Act, or scheme relating to the resignation or vacation of their office, the churchwardens so chosen and admitted shall continue in their office until they, or others as their successors, be admitted in like manner by the bishop or his substitute duly appointed or, if no person is so admitted by 31st July in the year in question, until that date.

4. The churchwardens when admitted are officers of the bishop. They shall discharge such duties as are by law and custom assigned to them; they shall be foremost in representing the laity and in co-operating with the incumbent; they shall use their best endeavours by example and precept to encourage the parishioners in the practice of true religion and to promote unity and peace among them. They shall also maintain order and decency in the church and churchyard, especially during the time of divine service.

5. In the churchwardens is vested the property in the place, ornaments, and other movable goods of the church, and they shall keep an inventory thereof which they shall revise from time to time as occasion may require. On going out of office they shall duly deliver to their successors any goods of the church remaining in their hands together with the said inventory, which shall be checked by their successors.

6. In this Canon 'bishop' means the bishop of the diocese concerned.

E 2   Of Sidesmen or Assistants to the Churchwardens

1. The sidesmen of the parish shall be appointed by the annual parochial church meeting or, if need arises between annual parochial church meetings, by the parochial church council.

2. No person whose name is not on the church electoral roll is eligible as a sidesman, but all persons whose names are on the roll are so eligible.

3. It shall be the duty of the sidesmen to promote the cause of true religion in the parish and to assist the churchwardens in the discharge of their duties in maintaining order and decency in the church and churchyard, especially during the time of divine service.

E 3 OF PARISH CLERKS AND OTHER OFFICERS

In any parish in which the services of a parish clerk, sexton, verger, or other officer are required the minister and the parochial church council may in accordance with the law appoint some fit and proper person to these offices to perform such services upon such terms and conditions as they may think fit.

E 4 OF READERS

1. A lay person, whether man or woman, who is baptised and confirmed and who satisfies the bishop that he is a regular communicant of the Church of England may be admitted by the bishop of the diocese to the office of reader in the Church and licensed by him to perform the duties which may lawfully be performed by a reader according to the provisions of paragraph 2 of this Canon or which may from time to time be so determined by Act of Synod.

2. It shall be lawful for a reader:
    (a) to visit the sick, to read and pray with them, to teach in Sunday school and elsewhere, and generally to undertake such pastoral and educational work and to give such assistance to any minister as the bishop may direct;
    (b) during the time of divine service to read Morning and Evening Prayer (save for the Absolution), to publish banns of marriage at Morning and Evening Prayer (on occasions on which a layman is permitted by the statute law so to do, and in accordance with the requirements of that law), to read the Word of God, to preach, to catechise the children, and to receive and present the offerings of the people;
    (c) to distribute the holy sacrament of the Lord's Supper to the people.

2A. The bishop may also authorise a reader to bury the dead or read the burial service before, at or after a cremation but only, in each case, with the goodwill of the persons responsible and at the invitation of the minister of a parish or an extra-parochial place within the meaning of section 1 of the Deaconesses and Lay Ministry Measure 1972.

When a cure is vacant the reference in this paragraph to the minister of a parish shall be construed as a reference to the rural dean.

3. The bishop of every diocese shall keep a register book wherein shall be entered the names of every person whom he has either admitted to the office of reader or licensed to exercise that office in any place.

E 5 OF THE NOMINATION AND ADMISSION OF READERS

1. A candidate for the office of reader in a parish or district shall be nominated to the bishop by the minister of that parish or district; and a candidate for the said office in a wider area by one of the rural deans or archdeacons after consultation with the minister of his parish or district.

2. The nominator in making such nomination shall also satisfy the bishop that the said person is of good life, sound in faith, a regular communicant, and well fitted for the work of a reader, and provide all such other information about the said person and the duties which it is desired that he should perform as the bishop may require.

3. No person shall be admitted to the office of reader in the Church except it be found on examination, held by the bishop or by competent persons appointed by the bishop for this purpose, that he possesses a sufficient knowledge of Holy Scripture and of the doctrine and worship of the Church of England as set forth in the *Book of Common prayer*, that he is able to read the services of the Church plainly, distinctly, audibly, and reverently, and that he is capable both of teaching and preaching.

4. Every person who is to be admitted to the office of reader shall first, in the presence of the bishop by whom he is to be so admitted or of the bishop's commissary, make the declarations set out below, the preface which precedes the Declaration of Assent in paragraph 1(1) of Canon C 15 (with the appropriate adaptations) having first been spoken by the bishop or commissary:

> I, A B, do so affirm, and accordingly declare my belief in the faith which is revealed in the Holy Scriptures and set forth in the catholic creeds and to which the historic formularies of the Church of England bear witness; and in public prayer I will use only the forms of service which are authorised or allowed by Canon.

> I, A B, will give due obedience to the Lord Bishop of C and his successors in all things lawful and honest.

5. The bishop shall admit a person to the office of reader by the delivery of the New Testament, but without imposition of hands.

6. The bishop shall give to the newly admitted reader a certificate of his admission to the office; and the admission shall not be repeated if the reader shall move to another diocese.

E 6 OF THE LICENSING OF READERS

1. No person who has been admitted to the office of reader shall exercise his office in any diocese until he has been licensed so to do by the bishop thereof: Provided that, when any reader is to exercise his office temporarily in any diocese, the written permission of the bishop shall suffice.

1A. A licence authorising a reader to serve in a benefice in respect of which a team ministry is established may be in a form which specifies the term of years for which the licence shall have effect.

2. Every reader who is to be licensed to exercise his office in any diocese shall first, in the presence of the bishop by whom he is to be licensed, or of the commissary of such bishop—
   (a) make the declarations of assent and of obedience in the form and manner prescribed by paragraph 4 of Canon E 5;
   (b) make and subscribe the declaration following:

I, A B, about to be licensed to exercise the office of reader in the parish (or diocese) of C, do hereby promise to endeavour, as far as in me lies, to promote peace and unity, and to conduct myself as becomes a worker for Christ, for the good of his Church, and for the spiritual welfare of [my][2] all people. I will give due obedience to the Bishop of C and his successors and the minister in whose cure I may serve, in all things lawful and honest.

If the declarations of assent and of obedience have been made on the same occasion in pursuance of paragraph 4 of Canon E 5 it shall not be necessary to repeat them in pursuance of this paragraph and in the declaration set out above the words 'the Bishop of C and his successors and' may be omitted.

3. The bishop of a diocese may by notice in writing revoke summarily, and without further process, any licence granted to a reader within his diocese for any cause which appears to him to be good and reasonable, after having given the reader sufficient opportunity of showing reason to the

---

[2] The word 'my' should have been removed by Amending Canon No 23. A future Amending Canon will correct this omission, in the meantime, the word should be omitted as required by the sense.

contrary; and the notice shall notify the reader that he may, within twenty-eight days from the date on which he receives the notice, appeal to the archbishop of the province in which that diocese is situated.

On such an appeal the archbishop may either hear the appeal himself or appoint a person holding the office of diocesan bishop or suffragan bishop in his province (otherwise than in the diocese concerned) to hear the appeal in his place; and, after hearing the appeal or, if he has appointed a bishop to hear the appeal in his place, after receiving a report in writing from that bishop, the archbishop may confirm, vary or cancel the revocation of the licence as he considers just and proper; and there shall be no appeal from the decision of the archbishop.

Where the see of the archbishop is vacant or the archbishop is also the bishop of the diocese concerned, any reference in the preceding provisions of this paragraph to the archbishop of the province shall be construed as a reference to the archbishop of the other province, but any bishop appointed by the archbishop of the other province by virtue of this paragraph shall be a bishop serving in the province which contains the diocese concerned.

Any appeal under this paragraph shall be conducted in accordance with rules approved by the Archbishops of Canterbury and York; and any such rules may provide for the appointment of one or more persons to advise the archbishop or bishop hearing such an appeal on any question of law arising in the course thereof.

3A. Where a bishop has granted a licence to a reader to serve in his diocese for a term of years specified in the licence, the bishop may revoke that licence under paragraph 3 of this Canon before the expiration of that term, and where he does so that reader shall have the like right of appeal as any other reader whose licence is revoked under that paragraph.

4. No bishop shall license any reader to be a stipendiary in any place until he has satisfied himself that adequate provision has been made for the stipend of the said reader, for his insurance against sickness or accident, and for a pension on his retirement.

E 7   OF LAY WORKERS

1. A lay person, whether man or woman, who satisfies the bishop that he or she
    (a)   is baptised and confirmed and a regular communicant of the Church of England;
    (b)   has the proper training; and
    (c)   possesses the other necessary qualifications,

may be admitted by the bishop as a lay worker of the Church. A lay worker may perform the duties set out in this Canon or any of them, if authorised to do so by licence or permission of the bishop of the diocese in which he or she is to serve.

2. A man or woman admitted to the office of evangelist is thereby admitted as a lay worker of the Church.

3. A lay worker may in the place where he or she is licensed to serve, and under the direction of the minister, lead the people in public worship, exercise pastoral care, evangelise, instruct the people in the Christian faith, and prepare them for the reception of the sacraments.

4. A lay worker may:
    (a)   in accordance with Canon B 11, be authorised and invited to say or sing Morning or Evening Prayer (save for the Absolution);
    (b)   distribute the holy sacrament of the Lord's Supper to the people and read the Epistle and the Gospel.

5. The bishop may also authorise a lay worker to perform any of the following duties at the invitation of the minister of a parish or an extra-parochial place within the meaning of section 1 of the Deaconesses and Lay Ministry Measure 1972:

(a) to preach at divine service;
(b) to church women;
(c) with the goodwill of the person responsible, to bury the dead or read the burial service before, at or after a cremation;
(d) to publish banns of marriage at Morning and Evening Prayer (on occasions on which a lay person is permitted by the Statute Law so to do and in accordance with the requirements of that law).

When a cure is vacant the first reference in this paragraph to the minister of a parish shall be construed as a reference to the rural deal.

6. Paragraph 5(b) and (c) of this Canon shall not apply to the Channel Islands.

E 8 OF THE ADMISSION AND LICENSING OF LAY WORKERS

1. A bishop shall give to every person admitted by him as a lay worker of the Church a certificate of admission as a lay worker, and the admission shall not be repeated if the person admitted thereby moves to another diocese.

2. No person who has been admitted as a lay worker of the Church shall serve as such in any diocese unless he or she has a licence so to do from the bishop thereof: Provided that, when any lay worker is to serve temporarily in the diocese, the written permission of the bishop shall suffice.

2A. A licence authorising a lay worker to serve in a benefice in respect of which a team ministry is established may be in a form which specifies the term of years for which the licence shall have effect.

3. Where any person is to be a stipendiary lay worker in any place in a diocese, the bishop shall not license that person as a lay worker unless he is satisfied that adequate provision has been made for his or her salary, appropriate insurance and a pension on retirement.

4. Every person who is to be admitted or licensed as a lay worker shall, in the presence of the bishop or his commissary, make and subscribe the declarations set out below, the preface which precedes the Declaration of Assent in paragraph 1(1) of Canon C 15 (with the appropriate adaptations) having first been spoken by the bishop or commissary:

> I, A B, do so affirm and accordingly declare my belief in the faith which is revealed in the Holy Scriptures and set forth in the catholic creeds and to which the historic formularies of the Church of England bear witness; and in public prayer I will use only the forms of service which are authorised or allowed by Canon.

> I, A B, will give due obedience to the Lord Bishop of C and his successors in all things lawful and honest.

5. The bishop of a diocese may by notice in writing revoke summarily, and without further process, any licence granted to a lay worker within his diocese for any cause which appears to him to be good and reasonable, after having given the lay worker sufficient opportunity of showing reason to the contrary; and the notice shall notify the lay worker that he may, within twenty-eight days from the date on which he receives the notice, appeal to the archbishop of the province in which that diocese is situated.

On such an appeal the archbishop may either hear the appeal himself or appoint a person holding the office of diocesan bishop or suffragan bishop in his province (otherwise than in the diocese concerned) to hear the appeal in his place; and, after hearing the appeal or, if he has appointed a bishop to hear the appeal in his place, after receiving a report in writing from that bishop, the archbishop may confirm, vary or cancel the revocation of the licence as he considers just and proper; and there shall be no appeal from the decision of the archbishop.

Where the see of the archbishop is vacant or the archbishop is also the bishop of the diocese concerned, any reference in the preceding provisions of this paragraph to the archbishop of the province shall be construed as a reference to the archbishop of the other province, but any bishop appointed by the archbishop of the other province by virtue of this paragraph shall be a bishop serving in the province which contains the diocese concerned.

Any appeal under this paragraph shall be conducted in accordance with rules approved by the Archbishops of Canterbury and York; and any such rules may provide for the appointment of one or more persons to advise the archbishop or bishop hearing such an appeal on any question of law arising in the course thereof.

5A. Where a bishop has granted a licence to a lay worker to serve in his diocese for a term of years specified in the licence, the bishop may revoke that licence under paragraph 5 of this Canon before the expiration of that term, and where he does so that lay worker shall have the like right of appeal as any other lay worker whose licence is revoked under that paragraph

6. The bishop of every diocese shall keep a register book wherein shall be entered the name of every person either admitted or licensed by him as a lay worker, together with the particular duties which that person has been licensed to perform.

Things Appertaining to Churches

F 1   OF THE FONT

1. In every church and chapel where baptism is to be administered, there shall be provided a decent font with a cover for the keeping clean thereof.

2. The font shall stand as near to the principal entrance as conveniently may be, except there be a custom to the contrary or the Ordinary otherwise direct; and shall be set in as spacious and well-ordered surroundings as possible.

3. The font bowl shall only be used for the water at the administration of Holy Baptism and for no other purpose whatsoever.

F 2   OF THE HOLY TABLE

1. In every church and chapel a convenient and decent table, of wood, stone, or other suitable material, shall be provided for the celebration of the Holy Communion, and shall stand in the main body of the church or in the chancel where Morning and Evening Prayer are appointed to be said. Any dispute as to the position where the table shall stand shall be determined by the Ordinary.

2. The table, as becomes the table of the Lord, shall be kept in a sufficient and seemly manner, and from time to time repaired, and shall be covered in the time of divine service with a covering of silk or other decent stuff, and with a fair white linen cloth at the time of the celebration of the Holy Communion.

F 3   OF THE COMMUNION PLATE

1. In every church and chapel there shall be provided, for the celebration of the Holy Communion, a chalice for the wine and a paten or other vessel for the bread, of gold, silver, or other suitable metal. There shall also be provided a basin for the reception of the alms and other devotions of the people, and a convenient cruet or flagon for bringing the wine to the communion table.

2. It is the duty of the minister of every church or chapel to see that the communion plate is kept washed and clean, and ready for the celebration of the Holy Communion.

F 4 OF THE COMMUNION LINEN

In every parochial church and chapel there shall be provided and maintained a sufficient number of fair white linen cloths for the covering of the communion table and of other fair linen cloths for the use of the priest during the celebration of Holy Communion.

F 5 OF SURPLICES FOR THE MINISTER

In every church and chapel surplices shall be provided and maintained in a clean condition for the use of the minister.

F 6 OF THE READING DESKS AND PULPIT

In every church and chapel there shall be provided convenient desks for the reading of Prayers and God's Word, and, unless it be not required, a decent pulpit for the sermon, to be set in a convenient place; which place, in the case of any dispute, shall be determined by the Ordinary.

F 7 OF SEATS IN CHURCH

1. In every church and chapel there shall be provided seats for the use of the parishioners and others who attend divine service.

2. In parish churches and chapels it belongs to the churchwardens, acting for this purpose as the officers of the Ordinary and subject to his directions, to allocate the seats amongst the parishioners and others in such manner as the service of God may be best celebrated in the church or chapel; saving the right of the minister to allocate seats in the chancel and the rights of any person to a seat or to allocate seats conferred by faculty, prescription, or statutory authority.

3. Such allocation of seats to non-parishioners shall not interfere with the rights of the parishioners to have seats in the main body of the church.

F 8 OF CHURCH BELLS

1. In every church and chapel there shall be provided at least one bell to ring the people to divine service.

2. No bell in any church or chapel shall be rung contrary to the direction of the minister.

F 9 OF THE BIBLE AND THE *BOOK OF COMMON PRAYER* FOR THE USE OF THE MINISTER

In every church and chapel there shall be provided for the use of the minister a Bible, including the Apocrypha, and a *Book of Common Prayer*, both of large size; a convenient Bible to be kept in the pulpit for the use of the preacher; and a service book, together with a cushion or desk, for use at the communion table.

F 10 OF THE ALMS BOX

In every parochial church and chapel there shall be provided in a convenient place a box for the alms of the people; which alms are to be applied to such uses as the minister and parochial church council shall think fit; wherein if they disagree, the Ordinary shall determine the disposal thereof.

F. Things Appertaining to Churches

F 11 OF THE REGISTER BOOKS AND THEIR CUSTODY

1. In every parish church and chapel where baptism is to be administered or matrimony solemnised there shall be provided register books of baptism, banns, and marriage respectively, and, if a churchyard or burial ground belonging to such church or chapel is used for burials, a register book of burials.

2. Register books shall be provided, maintained, and kept in accordance with the Statutes and Measures relating thereto, and the rules and regulations made thereunder and from time to time in force.

3. In every parish church and chapel there shall also be provided a register book of confirmations.

F 12 OF THE REGISTER BOOK OF SERVICES

1. A register book of services shall be provided in all churches and chapels.

2. In the said register book shall be recorded every service of public worship, together with the name of the officiating minister and of the preacher (if he be other than the officiating minister), the number of communicants, and the amount of any alms or other collection and, if desired, notes of significant events.

F 13 OF THE CARE AND REPAIR OF CHURCHES

1. The churches and chapels in every parish shall be decently kept and from time to time, as occasion may require, shall be well and sufficiently repaired and all things therein shall be maintained in such an orderly and decent fashion as best becomes the House of God.

2. The like care shall be taken that the churchyards be duly fenced, and that the said fences be maintained at the charge of those to whom by law or custom the liability belongs, and that the churchyards be kept in such an orderly and decent manner as becomes consecrated ground.

3. It shall be the duty of the minister and churchwardens, if any alterations, additions, removals, or repairs are proposed to be made in the fabric, ornaments, or furniture of the church, to obtain the faculty or licence of the Ordinary before proceeding to execute the same.

4. In the case of every parochial church and chapel, a record of all alterations, additions, removals, or repairs so executed shall be kept in a book to be provided for the purpose and the record shall indicate where specifications and plans may be inspected if not deposited with the book.

F 14 OF THE PROVISION OF THINGS APPERTAINING TO CHURCHES

The things appertaining to churches and chapels, and the obligations relating thereto, and to the care and repair of churches, chapels, and churchyards referred to in the foregoing Canons shall, so far as the law may from time to time require, be provided and performed in the case of parochial churches and chapels by and at the charge of the parochial church council.

F 15 OF CHURCHES NOT TO BE PROFANED

1. The churchwardens and their assistants shall not suffer the church or chapel to be profaned by any meeting therein for temporal objects inconsistent with the sanctity of the place, nor the bells to be rung at any time contrary to the direction of the minister.

2. They shall not suffer any person so to behave in the church, church porch, or churchyard during the time of divine service as to create disturbance. They shall also take care that nothing be done therein contrary to the law of the Church or of the Realm.

3. If any person be guilty of riotous, violent, or indecent behaviour in any church, chapel, or churchyard, whether in any time of divine service or not, or of disturbing, vexing, troubling, or misusing any minister officiating therein, the said churchwardens or their assistants shall take care to restrain the offender and if necessary proceed against him according to law.

F 16   OF PLAYS, CONCERTS, AND EXHIBITIONS OF FILMS AND PICTURES IN CHURCHES

1. When any church or chapel is to be used for a play, concert, or exhibition of films or pictures, the minister shall take care that the words, music, and pictures are such as befit the House of God, are consonant with sound doctrine, and make for the edifying of the people.

2. The minister shall obey any general directions relating to such use of a church or chapel issued from time to time by the bishop or other the Ordinary.

3. No play, concert, or exhibition of films or pictures shall be held in any church or chapel except the minister have first consulted the local or other authorities concerned with the precautions against fire and other dangers required by the law to be taken in the case of performances of plays, concerts, or exhibitions of cinematograph films, and the said authorities have signified that the proposed arrangements are a sufficient compliance with the regulations in force as to precautions against fire or other dangers.

4. If any doubt arises as to the manner in which the preceding clauses of this Canon are to be observed, the minister shall refer the matter to the bishop or other the Ordinary, and obey his directions therein.

F 17   OF KEEPING A RECORD OF THE PROPERTY OF CHURCHES

1. Every bishop within his diocese shall procure so far as he is able that a full note and terrier of all lands, goods, and other possessions of the parochial churches and chapels therein be compiled and kept by the minister and churchwardens in accordance with instructions and forms prescribed from time to time by the General Synod.

2. Every archdeacon shall at least once in three years, either in person or by the rural dean, satisfy himself that the directions of the preceding paragraph of this Canon have been carried out in all the parishes within his jurisdiction.

F 18   OF THE SURVEY OF CHURCHES

Every archdeacon shall survey the churches, chancels, and churchyards within his jurisdiction at least once in three years, either in person or by the rural dean, and shall give direction for the amendment of all defects in the fabric, ornaments, and furniture of the same. In particular he shall exercise the powers conferred upon him by the Inspection of Churches Measure 1955.

The Ecclesiastical Courts

G 1   OF ECCLESIASTICAL COURTS AND COMMISSIONS

The Ecclesiastical Courts which are or may be constituted in accordance with the provisions of the Ecclesiastical Jurisdiction Measure 1963 and the Clergy Discipline Measure 2003 are as follows:

1. For each diocese the court of the bishop thereof, called the Consistory Court of the diocese or, in the case of the diocese of Canterbury, the Commissary Court thereof, for the trial of faculty and other cases as provided in the Ecclesiastical Jurisdiction Measure.

G. The Ecclesiastical Courts

1A. A tribunal for the diocese in question (to be called the bishop's disciplinary tribunal) for the hearing of disciplinary proceedings against a priest or deacon not involving matters of doctrine, ritual or ceremonial as provided in the Clergy Discipline Measure 2003.

2. For each of the provinces of Canterbury and York
   (a) A court of the archbishop (to be called in the case of the court of the province of Canterbury the Arches Court of Canterbury, and, in the case of the court for the province of York, the Chancery Court of York) having appellate jurisdiction as provided in the Ecclesiastical Jurisdiction Measure 1963.
   (b) The Vicar-General's court constituted in accordance with the Clergy Discipline Measure 2003 for the hearing of disciplinary proceedings against a bishop or an archbishop not involving matters of doctrine, ritual or ceremonial as provided in that Measure,

3. For both of the said provinces
   (a) a court called the Court of Ecclesiastical Causes Reserved for the trial of offences against the laws ecclesiastical involving doctrine, ritual, or ceremonial and all suits of duplex querela. The court also has appellate jurisdiction in faculty causes involving doctrine, ritual, or ceremonial.

4. There may be appointed by Her Majesty a Commission of Review, to review any finding of the Court of Ecclesiastical Causes Reserved.

4A. The Arches Court of Canterbury and the Chancery Court of York have jurisdiction to hear appeals from the bishop's disciplinary tribunal referred to in paragraph 1A above and from the Vicar-General's court constituted as mentioned in paragraph 2(b) above.

5. Her Majesty in Council has jurisdiction to hear appeals from the Court of Arches or the Chancery Court in faculty causes not involving matter of doctrine, ritual, or ceremonial.

G2 OF THE CHANCELLOR OR JUDGE OF A CONSISTORY COURT

1. The judge of the Consistory Court of a diocese is styled the chancellor of the diocese or, in the case of the diocese of Canterbury, the commissary general, and is appointed by the bishop of the diocese.

2. The qualifications of a person appointed to be chancellor of a diocese are that he shall be at least thirty years old and either a person who has a 7-year general qualification within the meaning of section 71 of the Courts and Legal Services Act 1990 or a person who has held high judicial office. Before appointing a layman, the bishop must satisfy himself that the person to be appointed is a communicant.

3. The chancellor of a diocese, a person appointed to act as deputy chancellor of a diocese and a person appointed to preside over a court by virtue of section 27(1) of the Ecclesiastical Jurisdiction Measure 1963, before he enters on the execution of his office, is required to take, either before the bishop of the diocese in the presence of the diocesan registrar, or in open court in the presence of the registrar
   (a) the Oath of Allegiance, in the same form as in Canon C 13;
   (b) the following oath:

I, A B, do swear that I will, to the uttermost of my understanding, deal uprightly and justly in my office, without respect of favour or reward: So help me God.

If he is a layman, he is also required to make and subscribe, in the like circumstances, the Declaration of Assent in the following form:

I, A B, declare my belief in the faith which is revealed in the Holy Scriptures and set forth in the catholic creeds and to which the historic formularies of the Church of England bear witness.

G3 OF THE JUDGES OF THE ARCHES COURT OF CANTERBURY AND THE CHANCERY COURT OF YORK

1. The judges of the Arches Court of Canterbury and the Chancery Court of York respectively are five in number.

2. Of the judges of each of the said courts:
    (a) one, who is a judge of both courts (and, in respect of his jurisdiction in the province of Canterbury, is styled Dean of the Arches and, in respect of his jurisdiction in the province of York, is styled Auditor) is appointed by the Archbishops of Canterbury and York jointly with the approval of Her Majesty;
    (b) two are persons in Holy Orders appointed by the Prolocutor of the Lower House of the Convocation of the relevant province;
    (c) two are laymen appointed by the Chairman of the House of Laity after consultation with the Lord Chancellor and possessing such judicial experience as the Lord Chancellor thinks appropriate;
    (d) the others are all the diocesan chancellors appointed under section 2 of the Ecclesiastical Jurisdiction Measure 1963 except the chancellor of the diocese of Gibraltar in Europe.

3. The qualifications of a person appointed to the Dean of the Arches and Auditor are that he should be either a person who has a ten-year general qualification within the meaning of section 71 of the Courts and Legal Services Act 1990 or a person who has held high judicial office, and, before appointing a layman, the archbishops must satisfy themselves that he is a communicant.

4. Before the Chairman of the House of Laity appoints a person to be a judge of either of the said courts, he must satisfy himself that that person is a communicant.

5. The Dean of the Arches and Auditor and a person appointed to act as deputy Dean of the Arches and Auditor, before he enters on the execution of his office, is required to take
    (i) before the Archbishop of Canterbury in the presence of the registrar of the province of Canterbury and before the Archbishop of York in the presence of the registrar of the province of York; or
    (ii) in open court in both of these province in the presence of the registrar of the province

the oaths specified in paragraph 3 of Canon G 2, and, if he is a layman, to make and subscribe, in like circumstances, the declaration therein specified.

6. A person (other than the Dean of the Arches and Auditor) appointed to hold the office of a judge of either of the said courts is required, before he enters on the execution of his office, to take the said oaths either before the archbishop of the relevant province and in the presence of the registrar of that province, or in open court in the presence of that registrar, and, if he is a layman, to make and subscribe, in the like circumstances, the said declaration.

G4 OF REGISTRARS

1. The registrar of a province and of the provincial court is appointed by the archbishop of that province, and the registrar of a diocese and its consistory court is appointed by the bishop of the diocese.

2. The qualifications of a person appointed to be such a registrar as aforesaid are that he should be a person who has a general qualification within the meaning of section 71 of the Courts and Legal Services Act 1990 learned in the ecclesiastical laws and the laws of the realm; and the archbishop or bishop appointing him must satisfy himself that the said person is a communicant.

3. A registrar, before he enters on the execution of his office, is required to take, in the presence of the archbishop or bishop, as the case may be, the oaths specified in paragraph 3 of Canon G 2, and to make and subscribe, in the like presence, the declaration therein specified.

G 5 OF VISITATIONS

1. Every archbishop, bishop, and archdeacon has the right to visit, at times and places limited by law or custom, the province, diocese, or archdeaconry committed to his charge, in a more solemn manner, and in such visitation to perform all such acts as by law and custom are assigned to his charge in that behalf for the edifying and well-governing of Christ's flock, that means may be taken thereby for the supply of such things as are lacking and the correction of such things as are amiss.

2. During the time of such visitation the jurisdiction of all inferior Ordinaries shall be suspended save in places which by law or custom are exempt.

G 6 OF PRESENTMENTS

1. Every archbishop, bishop, and archdeacon, and every other person having ecclesiastical jurisdiction, when they summon their visitation, shall deliver or cause to be delivered to the minister and churchwardens of every parish, or to some of them, such articles of inquiry, as they, or any of them, shall require the minister and churchwardens to ground their presentments upon.

2. With the said articles shall be delivered the form of declaration which must be made immediately before any such presentment, to the intent that the minister and churchwardens having had beforehand sufficient time to consider both what their said declarations shall be, and also the articles upon which they are to ground their presentments, may frame them advisedly and truly according to their consciences.

The Synods of the Church

H 1 OF THE GENERAL SYNOD AND THE CONVOCATIONS

This is a conflated text of two parallel Canons promulged by the Convocations of Canterbury and York. Wording which appears only in the Canterbury or the York version is shown in square brackets.

1. On such day as may be appointed by the Archbishops of Canterbury and York under the Synodical Government Measure 1969, the powers to legislate by Canon and other functions of the Convocation of [Canterbury] [York], and the authority, rights and privileges of the said Convocation, shall vest in the General Synod of the Church of England, being the Church Assembly renamed and reconstituted by the said Measure.

2. Notwithstanding such vesting as aforesaid, the said Convocation may continue to meet separately, within the Province or elsewhere at such places and times as they may determine, for the purpose of considering matters concerning the Church of England and making provision by appropriate instruments for such matters in relation to their province or referring such matters to the General Synod and shall meet for the purpose of discharging their functions under section 3 of this Measure and their functions under Article 7 of the Constitution of the General Synod in respect of provisions touching doctrinal formulae or the service or ceremonies of the Church of England or the administration of the sacraments or sacred rites thereof, or to consider any other matter referred to them by the General Synod:

Provided that the power to make provision as aforesaid shall not be exercisable by Canon, and shall (without prejudice to the said Article 7) be exercisable consistently with the exercise of functions by the General Synod and, in the event of any inconsistency, the provision made by the General Synod shall prevail.

3. The said Convocation may, by their Standing Orders or otherwise, make provision for joining to their two Houses, at such sittings and for the purposes of such of their functions as they may determine, a House of Laity composed of:—
   (a) such of the members of the House of Laity of the General Synod as are elected for areas in the province;
   (b) such of the ex officio and co-opted members of the said House as may be allocated to the province for the purposes of this paragraph by the President and the Prolocutor of the Houses of the said Convocation and the Prolocutor and Pro-Prolocutor of the House of Laity of the General Synod; and
   (c) the member or members of the said House chosen by the lay members of religious communities in the said province:

Provided that the House of Laity joined as aforesaid to the two Houses of the said Convocation shall not be given any power to vote on any matter referred to the Convocation under Article 7 of the said Constitution, or any matter in respect of which powers are exercisable by the Convocation in accordance with section 3 of the said Measure.

4. The vesting of rights and privileges of the said Convocation in the General Synod by this Canon shall not affect the right of the said Convocation (which shall be exercisable also by the General Synod) to present addresses to Her Majesty, or the right of the Lower House of the said Convocation to present gravamina to the Upper House thereof.

H 2 OF THE REPRESENTATION OF THE CLERGY IN THE LOWER HOUSE OF THE CONVOCATIONS

This is a conflated text of two parallel Canons promulged by the Convocations of Canterbury and York. Wording which appears only in the Canterbury or the York version is distinguished by the paragraph heading or shown in square brackets.

Canterbury

1. Whenever the Lord Archbishop of Canterbury shall summon a Convocation of that province, the following persons, and they only, shall henceforth be cited to appear in the Lower House of the said Convocation:
   (a) three persons elected by and from among the deans of all the cathedral churches in the province, the deans of the two collegiate churches of St Peter in Westminster and of St George, Windsor, and the Dean of the Cathedral Church of the Holy Trinity in Gibraltar in such manner as may be provided by rules made under this Canon;
   (b) either the Dean of Jersey or the Dean of Guernsey as may be determined in such manner as may be provided by rules made under this Canon;
   (c) *[Repealed by Amending Canon No 26]*;
   (d) not less than three nor more than four persons in holy orders elected or chosen from among the chaplains of the armed forces in such manner as may be determined by the Forces Synodical Council as soon as practicable after any dissolution of the Convocation, provided that the total number of persons elected or chosen under this sub-paragraph, paragraph 1(bb) of Canon H 3 and Rule 35(1)(d) of the Church Representation Rules shall not exceed seven;

(dd) the Chaplain General of Prisons or, where the holder of that office is not a person in holy orders, such prison chaplain as may be nominated by the Archbishop of Canterbury;
(e) proctors of the clergy who shall be elected in accordance with the following provisions of this Canon, provided that not more than one archdeacon shall be elected for any diocese or, where a diocese is divided into electoral areas, for any such area;
(f) not more than two persons chosen by and from the priests and deacons who are members of religious communities having their mother house in the province in such manner as may be provided by rules made under this Canon;;
(g) each of the following persons, if he is a priest or deacon, the Dean of the Arches and Auditor; the Vicar-General of the province, the Third Church Estates Commissioner, the Chairman of the Church of England Pensions Board and any member of the Archbishops' Council beneficed, licensed or resident in the province;

and those persons, together with any persons co-opted under paragraph 11 hereof, shall constitute the said Lower House. For the purposes of this Canon and any rules made thereunder the diocese in Europe shall be deemed to be a diocese in the province of Canterbury and references to a diocese shall be construed accordingly.

York

1. Whenever the Lord Archbishop of York shall summon a Convocation of that province, the following persons, and they only, shall henceforth be cited to appear in the Lower House of the said Convocation:
  (a) two persons elected by and from among the deans of all the cathedral churches in the province in such manner as may be provided by rules made under this Canon;
  (b) *[Repealed by Amending Canon No 26]*;
  (c) proctors of the clergy who shall be elected in accordance with the following provisions of this Canon, provided that not more than one archdeacon shall be elected for any diocese or, where a diocese is divided into electoral areas, for any such area;
  (d) not more than two persons chosen by and from the priests and deacons who are members of religious communities having their mother house in the province in such manner as may be provided by rules made under this Canon;
  (e) each of the following persons, if he is a priest or deacon, the Vicar-General of the province and any member of the Archbishops' Council beneficed, licensed or resident in the province;

and those persons, together with any person co-opted under paragraph 11 hereof, shall constitute the said Lower House.

Both Convocations

1A. A person in episcopal orders shall not be qualified to be elected, appointed, chosen or co-opted to be a member of the Lower House and no person who is a member of the House of Bishops of a diocesan synod shall be entitled to elect or choose a member or members of the Lower House; and any member of the Lower House who is ordained or consecrated as a bishop shall be deemed to have vacated his seat.

2. Each diocese in the province shall be an electoral area, and the number of persons elected for a diocese shall be in such proportion to the number of electors in that diocese as shall be determined from time to time by the General Synod:

Provided that
  (a) The total number of proctors directly elected and specially elected from the dioceses in the province shall not exceed 136 in the case of the Province of Canterbury and 59 in the case of the Province of York, and no diocese shall have fewer than three directly elected

proctors [except the diocese in Europe which shall have two proctors (Canterbury)] [except the diocese of Sodor and Man which shall have one proctor (York)]. The priests and deacons chosen from the members of the religious communities, the chaplains mentioned in paragraph 1(d) of the provisions relating to the Convocation of Canterbury and ex officio and co-opted proctors shall be additional to the said total number.

In this paragraph 'proctors specially elected' means the deans, [the Dean of Jersey or Guernsey as the case may be, (Canterbury)] and the university proctors and they shall be included in the said total number;

'ex officio proctors' means the proctors referred to in [paragraph 1(dd) and (g) (Canterbury)] [paragraph 1(e) (York)] of this Canon; and

'co-opted proctors' means the proctors referred to in paragraph 11 of this Canon.

(b) it shall be competent for the archbishop of the province on the petition of the electors in any diocese to divide the diocese into electoral areas and to assign a number of proctors to each area from the number allowed to the whole diocese; the division and assignment to be made in such manner that no electoral area will have fewer than three proctors and the number of proctors assigned to each area will be proportionate to the number of electors within that area.

(c) in determining the number of proctors to be assigned to or elected for an electoral area such divisor method as may from time to time be specified by the Business Committee of the General Synod shall be used.

Canterbury

3. The universities in the province shall constitute four electoral areas:
   (a) the University of Oxford;
   (b) the University of Cambridge;
   (c) the University of London;
   (d) the other universities in the province acting together for this purpose;

and one proctor shall be elected for each such electoral area.

York

3. The universities in the province shall constitute two electoral areas:
   (a) the Universities of Durham and Newcastle acting together for this purpose;
   (b) the other Universities in the province acting together for this purpose;

and one proctor shall be elected for each such electoral area.

Both Convocations

4. Where a diocese or part thereof is an electoral area, the electors shall be:
   (a) all clerks in holy orders exercising the office of Assistant Bishop in the area,
   (b) all archdeacons holding office in the area,
   (c) all clerks in holy orders beneficed in the area,
   (d) all clerks in holy orders holding office in a cathedral church in the area or, in the case of the Province of Canterbury, either of the two collegiate churches referred to in paragraph 1(a) above; and
   (e) all clerks in holy orders licensed under seal by the bishop of the diocese and all clerks in holy orders who are members of a deanery synod in the area and have written permission from the bishop of the diocese to officiate within that diocese,

but excluding members of the House of Bishops of the diocesan synod, deans, in the case of the Province of Canterbury the chaplains mentioned in paragraphs 1(d) and (dd) above and members of the religious communities,

Provided that no person shall be entitled to vote in more than one electoral area.

H. The Synods of the Church

In the application of this paragraph to an electoral area consisting of the diocese in Europe the word 'archdeacons' in sub-paragraph (a) shall be omitted.

5. Subject to paragraphs 5A, 5B and 5C of this Canon the persons eligible as proctors for an electoral area shall be those who have been admitted to deacon's or priest's orders and are entitled to vote in that electoral area or would have been so entitled under paragraph 4(d) above had they been members of a deanery synod.

In the application of this paragraph to an electoral area consisting of the diocese in Europe the words from 'and shall' to 'paragraph 1' shall be omitted.

5A. Where any person, being a clergyman who
   (a) is beneficed in, or licensed to, any parish in an electoral area consisting of a diocese or part of a diocese; or
   (b) is licensed to serve as a vicar in a team ministry established for the area of any benefice in that electoral area;

would be entitled to vote in that electoral area but for the fact that he is entitled to vote in an electoral area consisting of a university or group of universities, then, subject to paragraphs 5B and 5C of this Canon, that person shall be eligible as a proctor for such one of those electoral areas as he may elect before any election.

5B. No person shall be entitled to offer himself for election in more than one electoral area.

5C. Where any person makes an election under paragraph 5A of this Canon in a general election of proctors for either of the electoral areas referred to in that paragraph, or in an election to fill a casual vacancy in the proctors elected for either of those areas, then, if he is a candidate in any subsequent election to fill such a vacancy which occurs before the next following general election of proctors for the said areas, he shall be eligible as a proctor only for the electoral area for which he was eligible by virtue of the election made by him under the said paragraph 5A.

6. Elections of proctors shall, subject to the foregoing provisions of this Canon, be conducted in accordance with rules made under this Canon.

7. Any proctor elected for a diocese or part thereof who ceases to be eligible under paragraph 5 and 5A of this Canon for that diocese or any part thereof shall, unless the clerical members of the Bishop's Council and Standing Committee of the diocese have determined before the vacancy occurs or as provided below that he is able and willing to continue to discharge to their satisfaction the duties of a member of the Lower House elected for that diocese, be deemed to have vacated his seat:

Provided that there shall be no power for the Bishop's Council to make a determination under this paragraph where the seat is vacated by virtue of the proviso to paragraph 5 hereof. And provided further that the clerical members of the Bishop's Council and Standing Committee of the diocese shall not later than one year after any such determination and annually thereafter review the proctor's membership and determine whether he is able and willing as aforesaid.

8. Where any person:
   (a) being a member of the Lower House under paragraph [1(a), (b), (dd) or (g) (Canterbury)] [1(a) or (e) (York)] of this Canon, vacates the office by virtue of which he was eligible for or entitled to such membership;
   (b) having been chosen under paragraph 1 [(f) (Canterbury)] [(d) (York)], ceases to be a member of a religious community in the province;
   [(bb) having been nominated by the Archbishop of Canterbury under paragraph 1(dd) either vacates his office or a clerk in Holy Orders is admitted to the office referred to in the said paragraph – Canterbury];
   (c) having been elected under paragraph 3, ceases to be eligible for the electoral area for which he was elected;

(d) being a member of the said Lower House has his election or choice declared void in accordance with rules made under this Canon;

he shall be deemed to have vacated his seat.

9. Subject to the provisions of this paragraph an election, appointment, or choice of a person to fill a casual vacancy shall, except as may be otherwise provided by rules made under this Canon, be conducted in the same manner as an ordinary election, appointment or choice and shall be completed, so far as possible, within six months of the occurrence of the vacancy and in the event of the vacancy not being filled within that period, the Prolocutor of the Lower House may give directions to the presiding officer as to the date by which the vacancy must be filled:

Provided that where a casual vacancy occurs less than twelve months before an ordinary election to the Lower House will be held, the vacancy shall not be filled unless the clerical members of the bishop's council and standing committee so direct.

10. The powers to make rules under this Canon shall be exercised by the General Synod in accordance with Standing Orders of the General Synod.

11. The Lower House of the Convocation shall have power to co-opt not more than [three (Canterbury)] [two (York)] persons who have been admitted to priest's orders to be members of that House. The House may, in the case of any such member, fix a period of membership shorter than the lifetime of the Convocation.

H3 OF THE CONSTITUTION OF THE UPPER HOUSES OF THE CONVOCATION

1. Whenever the Lord Archbishop of Canterbury shall summon a Convocation of that province, the following persons, and they only, shall henceforth be cited to appear in the Upper House of the said Convocation:
   (a) the diocesan bishops of the province;
   (b) the Bishop of Dover;
   (bb) the Bishop to the Forces, if chosen by the Forces Synodical Council as soon as practicable after any dissolution of the Convocation;
   (c) four persons elected in such manner as may be provided by rules made under this Canon by and from among the suffragan bishops of the province (other than the Bishop of Dover) and the other persons in episcopal orders working in a diocese in the province who are members of the House of Bishops of that diocese;
   (d) other persons in episcopal orders residing in the province who are members of the Archbishops' Council;

and those persons together with the said Archbishop shall constitute the said Upper House. Provided that, where a See is vacant during any meeting of the Upper House, and a suffragan bishop is, during the period of that meeting, exercising functions of the diocesan bishop by virtue of an instrument under section 8 of the Church of England (Miscellaneous Provisions) Measure 1983, and has not been elected to the Upper House under sub-paragraph (c) above, the suffragan bishop may attend and speak, but not vote, at that meeting in place of the bishop.

For the purposes of this Canon and any rules made thereunder the diocese in Europe shall be deemed to be a diocese in the province of Canterbury.

2. Whenever the Lord Archbishop of York shall summon a Convocation of that Province, the following persons, and they only, shall henceforth be cited to appear in the Upper House of the said Convocation:
   (a) the diocesan bishops of the province;
   (b) three persons elected in such manner as may be provided by rules made under this Canon by and from among the suffragan bishops of the province and the other persons in

episcopal orders working in a diocese in the province who are members of the House of Bishops of that diocese;

(c) other persons in episcopal orders residing in the province who are members of the Archbishops' Council;

and those persons together with the said Archbishop shall constitute the said Upper House. Provided that, where a See is vacant during any meeting of the Upper House, and a suffragan bishop is, during the period of that meeting, exercising functions of the diocesan bishop by virtue of an instrument under section 8 of the Church of England (Miscellaneous Provisions) Measure 1983, and has not been elected to the Upper House under sub-paragraph (b) above, the suffragan bishop may attend and speak, but not vote, at that meeting in place of the bishop.

3. Where any person, being a member of the Upper House of the Convocation of Canterbury or a member of the Upper House of the Convocation of York ceases to be eligible for such membership, he shall be deemed to have vacated his seat.

4. An election to fill a casual vacancy shall, except as may be otherwise provided by rules made under this Canon, be conducted in the same manner as an ordinary election.

5. The power to make rules under this Canon shall be exercised by the General Synod in accordance with Standing Orders of the General Synod.

Supplementary Material

Proviso to Canon 113 of the Code of 1603 (See Canon B 29)

Provided always, that if any man confess his secret and hidden sins to the minister, for the unburdening of his conscience, and to receive spiritual consolation and ease of mind from him; we do not in any way bind the said minister by this our Constitution, but do straitly charge and admonish him, that he do not at any time reveal and make known to any person whatsoever any crime or offence so committed to his trust and secrecy, (except they be such crimes as by the laws of this realm his own life may be called into question for concealing the same), under pain of irregularity.

Admission of Baptised Children to Holy Communion Regulations 2006 (Canon C B 15A)

The General Synod hereby makes the following Regulations under paragraph 1(c) of Canon B15A:—

1. These Regulations may be cited as the Admission of Baptised Children to Holy Communion Regulations 2006 and shall come into force on the fifteenth day of June 2006 as appointed by the Archbishops of Canterbury and York

2. Children who have been baptised but who have not yet been confirmed and who are not yet ready and desirous to be confirmed as required by paragraph 1(a) of Canon B15A may be admitted to Holy Communion provided that the conditions set out in these Regulations are satisfied.

3. Every diocesan bishop may at any time make a direction to the effect that applications from parishes under these Regulations may be made in his diocese. The bishop's discretion in this respect shall be absolute, and he may at any time revoke such a direction (without prejudice to the validity of any permissions already granted thereunder).

4. Where a direction under paragraph 3 is in force in a diocese, an incumbent may apply to the bishop for permission that children falling within the definition in paragraph 2 may be

admitted to Holy Communion in one or more of the parishes in the incumbent's charge. Such application must be made in writing and must be accompanied by a copy of a resolution in support of the application passed by the parochial church council of each parish in respect of which the application is made.

5. Before granting any permission under paragraph 4, the bishop must first satisfy himself (a) that the parish concerned has made adequate provision for preparation and continuing nurture in the Christian life and will encourage any child admitted to Holy Communion under these Regulations to be confirmed at the appropriate time and (b) where the parish concerned is within the area of a local ecumenical project established under Canon B 44, that the other participating Churches have been consulted.

6. The bishop's decision in relation to any application under paragraph 4 shall be final, but a refusal shall not prevent a further application being made on behalf of the parish concerned, provided that at least one year has elapsed since the most recent previous application was refused.

7. Any permission granted under paragraph 4 shall remain in force unless and until revoked by the bishop. The bishop must revoke such permission upon receipt of an application for the purpose made by the incumbent. Such application must be made in writing and accompanied by a copy of a resolution in support of the application passed by the parochial church council of each parish in respect of which the application is made. Otherwise, the bishop may only revoke a permission granted under paragraph 4 if he considers that the conditions specified in paragraph 5 are no longer being satisfactorily discharged. Before revoking any permission on these grounds, the bishop shall first notify the incumbent of his concerns in writing and shall afford the incumbent a reasonable time to respond and, where appropriate, to take remedial action.

8. Where a permission granted under paragraph 4 is in force, the incumbent shall not admit any child to Holy Communion unless he or she is satisfied that (a) the child has been baptised and (b) a person having parental responsibility for the child is content that the child should be so admitted. Otherwise, subject to any direction of the bishop, it is within the incumbent's absolute discretion to decide whether, and if so when, any child should first be admitted to Holy Communion.

9. The incumbent shall maintain a register of all children admitted to Holy Communion under these Regulations, and where practicable will record on the child's baptismal certificate the date and place of the child's first admission. If the baptismal certificate is not available, the incumbent shall present the child with a separate certificate recording the same details.

10. A child who presents evidence in the form stipulated in paragraph 9 that he or she has been admitted to Holy Communion under these Regulations shall be so admitted at any service of Holy Communion conducted according to the rites of the Church of England in any place, regardless of whether or not any permission under paragraph 4 is in force in that place or was in force in that place until revoked.

11. These Regulations shall apply to a cathedral as if it were a parish, with the modifications that:
   (a) any application under paragraphs 3 or 7 must be made by the dean of the cathedral concerned, accompanied by a copy of a resolution in support of the application passed by the chapter of the cathedral concerned;
   (b) the obligations imposed on the incumbent under paragraphs 8 and 9 shall be imposed on the dean of the cathedral concerned.

12. A diocesan bishop may delegate any of his functions under these Regulations (except his functions under paragraph 3) to a person appointed by him for the purpose, being a suffragan or assistant bishop or archdeacon of the diocese.

13. In these Regulations:
   (a) 'incumbent', in relation to a parish, includes:
      (i) in a case where the benefice concerned is vacant (and paragraph (ii) below does not apply), the rural dean;

(ii) in a case where a suspension period (within the meaning of the Pastoral Measure 1983) applies to the benefice concerned, the priest-in-charge; and

(iii) in a case where a special cure of souls in respect of the parish has been assigned to a vicar in a team ministry by a Scheme under the Pastoral Measure 1983 or by licence from the bishop, that vicar; and

(b) references to paragraph numbers are to the relevant paragraph or paragraphs in these Regulations.

STATUTES AND MEASURES

Church of England Assembly (Powers) Act 1919	373	Incumbents (Vacation of Benefices) Measure 1977	431
Inspection of Churches Measure 1995	375	Pastoral Measure 1983	444
Parochial Church Councils (Powers) Measure 1956	378	Patronage (Benefices) Measure 1986	447
		Care of Cathedrals Measure 1990	461
Ecclesiastical Jurisdiction Measure 1963	382	Care of Churches and Ecclesiastical Jurisdiction Measure 1991	477
Faculty Jurisdiction Measure 1964	402		
Matrimonial Causes Act 1965	405	Priests (Ordination of Women) Measure 1993	493
Synodical Government Measure 1969	405	Care of Cathedrals (Supplementary Provisions) Measure 1994	496
Sharing of Church Buildings Act 1969	412	National Institutions Measure 1998	500
Repair of Benefice Buildings Measure 1972	420	Cathedrals Measure 1999	506
		Churchwardens Measure 2001	518
Church of England (Worship and Doctrine) Measure 1974	429	Clergy Discipline Measure 2003	524

The extracts from the Statutes and Measures which follow are in their form as at 1 April 2007 and all amendments to the original texts have been incorporated herein. Space does not permit a summary of the legislative history of each section for which reference should be made to *Halsbury's Statutes*, to Her Majesty's Stationery Office or to other sources. Where sections of limited relevance or practical utility have been omitted, this is indicated by the inclusion of the heading to that section. Transitional provisions have been omitted when the time for their operation has passed. In addition, provisions relating to the short title, commencement and extent are not included.

Church of England Assembly (Powers) Act 1919

Definitions

1. In this Act—
   (1) 'The National Assembly of the Church of England' (hereinafter called 'the Church Assembly') means the Assembly constituted in accordance with the constitution set forth in the Appendix to the Addresses presented to His Majesty by the Convocations of Canterbury and York on the tenth day of May nineteen hundred and nineteen, and laid before both Houses of Parliament;

(2) 'The Constitution' means the Constitution of the Church Assembly set forth in the Appendix to the Addresses presented by the Convocations of Canterbury and York to His Majesty as aforesaid;

(3) 'The Legislative Committee' means the Legislative Committee of the Church Assembly appointed in accordance with the provisions of the Constitution;

(4) 'The Ecclesiastical Committee' means the Committee established as provided in section two of this Act;

(5) 'Measure' means a legislative measure intended to receive the Royal Assent and to have effect as an Act of Parliament in accordance with the provisions of this Act.

Establishment of an Ecclesiastical Committee

2.—(1) There shall be a Committee of members of both Houses of Parliament styled 'The Ecclesiastical Committee'.

(2) The Ecclesiastical Committee shall consist of fifteen members of the House of Lords, nominated by the Speaker of the House of Lords and fifteen members of the House of Commons nominated by the Speaker of the House of Commons, to be appointed on the passing of this Act to serve for the duration of the present Parliament and thereafter to be appointed at the commencement of each Parliament to serve for the duration of that Parliament.

Any casual vacancy occurring by the reason of the death, resignation, or incapacity of a member of the Ecclesiastical Committee shall be filled by the nomination of a member by the Speaker of the House of Lords or the Speaker of the House of Commons, as the case may be.

(3) The powers and duties of the Ecclesiastical Committee may be exercised and discharged by any twelve members thereof, and the Committee shall be entitled to sit and to transact business whether Parliament be sitting or not, and notwithstanding a vacancy in the membership of the Committee. Subject to the provisions of this Act, the Ecclesiastical Committee may regulate is own procedure.

Measures passed by Church Assembly to be submitted to Ecclesiastical Committee

3.—(1) Every measure passed by the Church Assembly shall be submitted by the Legislative Committee to the Ecclesiastical Committee, together with such comments and explanations as the Legislative Committee may deem it expedient or be directed by the Church Assembly to add.

(2) The Ecclesiastical Committee shall thereupon consider the measure so submitted to it, and may, at any time during such consideration, either of its own motion or at the request of the Legislative Committee, invite the Legislative Committee to a conference to discuss the provisions thereof, and thereupon a conference of the two committees shall be held accordingly.

(3) After considering the measure, the Ecclesiastical Committee shall draft a report thereon to Parliament stating the nature and legal effect of the measure and its views as to the expediency thereof, especially with relation to the constitutional rights of all His Majesty's subjects.

(4) The Ecclesiastical Committee shall communicate its report in draft to the Legislative Committee, but shall not present it to Parliament until the Legislative Committee signify its desire that it should be so presented.

(5) At any time before the presentation of the report to Parliament the Legislative Committee may, either on its own motion or by direction of the Church Assembly, withdraw a measure from further consideration by the Ecclesiastical Committee; but the Legislative Committee shall have no power to vary a measure of the Church Assembly either before or after conference with the Ecclesiastical Committee.

(6) A measure may relate to any matter concerning the Church of England, and may extend to the amendment or repeal in whole or in part of any Act of Parliament, including this Act:

Provided that a measure shall not make any alteration in the composition or powers or duties of the Ecclesiastical Committee, or in the procedure in Parliament prescribed by section four of this Act.

(7) No proceedings of the Church Assembly in relation to a measure shall be invalidated by any vacancy in the membership of the Church Assembly or by any defect in the qualification or election of any member thereof.

Procedure on measures reported on by the Ecclesiastical Committee

4. When the Ecclesiastical Committee shall have reported to Parliament on any measure submitted by the Legislative Committee, the report, together with the text of such measure, shall be laid before both Houses of Parliament forthwith, if Parliament be then sitting, or, if not, then immediately after the next meeting of Parliament, and thereupon, on a resolution being passed by each House of Parliament directing that such measure in the form laid before Parliament should be presented to His Majesty, such measure shall be presented to His Majesty, and shall have the force and effect of an Act of Parliament on the Royal Assent being signified thereto in the same manner as to Acts of Parliament:

Provided that, if upon a measure being laid before Parliament the Chairman of Committees of the House of Lords and the Chairman of Ways and Means in the House of Commons acting in consultation, shall be of opinion that the measure deals with two or more different subjects which might be more properly divided, they may, by joint agreement, divide the measure into two or more separate measures accordingly, and thereupon this section shall have effect as if each of the measures resulting from such division had been laid before Parliament as a separate measure.

Inspection of Churches Measure 1955

Diocesan Synods to Establish Schemes for Inspection of Churches

1.—(1) As soon as may be after the passing of this Measure and in any case not later than three years thereafter the Diocesan Synod of every diocese to which this Measure applies shall establish a scheme to provide for the inspection of every church in the diocese at least once in every five years.

(2) Every scheme:—
- (a) shall provide for the establishment of a fund by means of contributions from parochial, diocesan or other sources;
- (b) shall provide for the payment out of such fund or otherwise of the cost of the inspection of churches in the diocese;
- (c) shall provide for the appointment of a qualified person or persons approved by the advisory committee to inspect the churches in the diocese and to make a report on every church inspected;
- (d) shall provide in the case of every church inspected for a copy of the report so made to be sent to the archdeacon of the archdeaconry, to the parochial church council of the parish in which the church is situate and to the incumbent of the benefice comprising that parish and to the secretary of the advisory committee of the diocese, in which the church is situate; and
- (e) may contain such other provisions not inconsistent with this Measure as the Diocesan Synod shall think fit.

(3) The Diocesan Synod shall have power at any time or times to establish a further scheme taking the place of any prior scheme but so that every such further scheme shall be for the purpose specified in subsection (1) of this section and shall comply with the provisions of subsection (2) thereof.

(4) Any scheme made in pursuance of this section and passed at a meeting of the Diocesan Synod shall be signed by the Chairman of that meeting and shall come into operation as from the date on which it is so signed.

Inspections to Extend to Certain Valuable Articles, etc

1A. Where, in accordance with a scheme established under section 1 of this Measure, a person inspects a church the inspection shall extend to—
- (a) any movable article in the church which he is directed by the archdeacon concerned, after consultation with the advisory committee, to treat as being, and such other articles as the person inspecting the church considers to be,—
    - (i) of outstanding architectural, artistic, historical or archaeological value; or
    - (ii) of significant monetary value; or
    - (iii) at special risk of being stolen or damaged;
- (b) any ruin in the churchyard (open or closed) which is for the time being designated by the Council for British Archaeology and the Royal Commission on the Historical Monuments of England acting jointly as being of outstanding architectural, artistic, historical or archaeological value;
- (c) any tree in the churchyard (open or closed) belonging to the church in respect of which a tree preservation order under the Town and Country Planning Act 1990 is for the time being in force,

and references in this Measure to the inspection of a church shall be construed accordingly.

Duty of Bishops to Establish Schemes

1B.—(1) Where, for any diocese to which this Measure applies, a scheme has not been made in pursuance of section 1 of this Measure it shall be the duty of the bishop of the diocese to establish a scheme for the purpose specified in subsection (1) of that section complying with the provisions of subsection (2)(a) to (d) thereof and containing such other provisions not inconsistent with this Measure as the bishop shall think fit.

(2) Any scheme made in pursuance of this section shall, for the purposes of this Measure (except section 1(4)), be deemed to have been made in pursuance of section 1 of this Measure.

Power for Archdeacon to Ensure Inspection of Churches Once in Five Years

2.—(1) Where the archdeacon of any archdeaconry finds at a survey of the churches of his jurisdiction or at any other time that a church in his archdeaconry has not been inspected to his satisfaction by a qualified person for a period of at least five years, he may serve upon the parochial church council of the parish in which the church is situate a notice in writing requiring the council to cause the church to be inspected in accordance with the scheme made in pursuance of section one of this Measure for the diocese in which the church is situate.

(2) At any time after the expiration of three months from the date when the said notice was served, the archdeacon, with the consent of the bishop, may, if the church has not been so inspected in the meantime, himself make arrangements for the required inspection and report.

(3) For the purposes of this section any reference to a church shall be construed as including a reference to any movable article in a church which the archdeacon concerned, after consultation with the advisory committee, considers to be—
- (a) of outstanding architectural, artistic, historic or archaeological value; or
- (b) of significant monetary value; or
- (c) at special risk of being stolen or damaged.

Cost of Inspection Arranged by Archdeacon

3. In any case where a church has been inspected pursuant to a notice served, or to arrangements made by the archdeacon under section two of this Measure, the cost of such inspection as certified by the archdeacon shall be paid out of the fund established by the scheme mentioned in that section.

Parishes without Parochial Church Councils

4.—(1) Where at any material time a parish has no parochial church council, the provisions of this Measure (and of any scheme made under section one thereof) with respect to notices to be sent to, and other acts and things to be done to or by, a parochial church council shall, as regards that parish, if there are churchwardens thereof, have effect as if the churchwardens were the parochial church council.

(2) For the purpose of this section, a certificate by the bishop of a diocese stating that at any time specified in the certificate a particular parish in the diocese had no parochial church council shall be conclusive.

Service of Notices

5. Any notice required or authorised by this Measure to be served on a parochial church council or churchwardens may be served:—

   (a) in the case of a parochial church council, by sending it by post in a registered letter addressed to the secretary of the council by his name at his usual, or last known, residence, or, if his name or residence is unknown, then in such a letter addressed to him by the title of secretary of the council in question at the usual, or last known, residence of the incumbent of the parish;

   (b) in the case of the churchwardens of a parish, by sending it by post in registered letters addressed to any two of them at their usual, or last known, residences, or, if there is only one churchwarden, by sending it by post in such a letter addressed to him at his usual, or last known, residence.

Interpretation

6. In this Measure the following expressions have the meanings hereby respectively assigned to them:—

'advisory committee' means the advisory committee for the care of churches of the diocese in question appointed under the Faculty Jurisdiction Measure 1938;

'the bishop' when used with reference to a church means the bishop of the diocese in which the church is situate (including during a vacancy in the see the guardian of the spiritualities thereof);

'church' means—

   (a) any parish church other than one to which the Care of Cathedrals Measure 1990 applies;

   (b) any other church or chapel (not being a cathedral church to which the Care of Cathedrals Measure 1990 applies or a church or chapel which is not subject to the jurisdiction of the bishop of a diocese or the Cathedral Church of Christ in Oxford) which has been consecrated for the purpose of public worship according to the rites and ceremonies of the Church of England; and

   (c) any building licensed for public worship according to the rites and ceremonies of the Church of England other than—

      (i) a building which is in a university, college, school, hospital or public or charitable institution but which has not been designated under section 29(2) of the 1983 Measure as a parish centre of worship;

      (ii) a building which has been excluded from the provisions of this Measure by direction of the bishop with the approval of the advisory committee; and

      (iii) a building used solely for the purpose of religious services relating to burial or cremation;

'diocese' in the case of the diocese of Winchester does not include the Channel Islands;

'qualified person' means a person registered under the Architects Act 1997 or a member of the Royal Institution of Chartered Surveyors qualified as a chartered building surveyor;

'ruin' means any site comprising the remains of any building above the surface of the land, not being—
  (a) a monument (within the meaning of section 3 of the Faculty Jurisdiction Measure 1964); or
  (b) a site which is for the time being used for the purpose of public worship according to the rites and ceremonies of the Church of England.

Parochial Church Councils (Powers) Measure 1956

Definitions

1. In this Measure—

'Council' means a parochial church council;

'Diocesan Authority' means the Diocesan Board of Finance or any existing or future body appointed by the Diocesan Synod to act as trustees of diocesan trust property;

'Minister' and 'Parish' have the meanings respectively assigned to them in the Rules for the Representation of the Laity;

'Relevant date' means the first day of July 1921.

General Functions of Council

2.—(1) It shall be the duty of the minister and the parochial church council to consult together on matters of general concern and importance to the parish.

(2) The functions of parochial church councils shall include—
  (a) co-operation with the minister in promoting in the parish the whole mission of the Church, pastoral, evangelistic, social and ecumenical;
  (b) the consideration and discussions of matters concerning the Church of England or any other matters of religious or public interest, but not the declaration of the doctrine of the Church on any question;
  (c) making known and putting into effect any provisions made by the diocesan synod or the deanery synod, but without prejudice to the powers of the council on any particular matter;
  (d) giving advice to the diocesan synod and the deanery synod on any matter referred to the council;
  (e) raising such matters as the council consider appropriate with the diocesan synod or deanery synod.

(3) In the exercise of its functions the parochial church council shall take into consideration any expression of opinion by any parochial church meeting.

Council to be Body Corporate

3. Every council shall be a body corporate by the name of the parochial church council of the parish for which it is appointed and shall have perpetual succession. Any act of the council may be signified by an instrument executed pursuant to a resolution of the council and under the hands or if an instrument under seal is required under the hands and seals of the chairman presiding and two other members of the council present at the meeting at which such resolution is passed.

Powers Vested in Council as Successor to Certain Other Bodies

4.—(1) Subject to the provisions of any Act or Measure passed after the relevant date and to anything lawfully done under such provisions, the council of every parish shall have—

(i) The like powers duties and liabilities as, immediately before the relevant date, the vestry of such parish had with respect to the affairs of the church except as regards the election of churchwardens and sidesmen and as regards the administration of ecclesiastical charities but including the power of presentation to the benefice of such parish if the right to present thereto was vested in or in trust for the parishioners and the power of making any voluntary church rate.

(ii) The like powers duties and liabilities as, immediately before the relevant date, the churchwardens of such parish had with respect to—

  (a) The financial affairs of the church including the collection and administration of all moneys raised for church purposes and the keeping of accounts in relation to such affairs and moneys;

  (b) The care maintenance preservation and insurance of the fabric of the church and the goods and ornaments thereof;

  (c) The care and maintenance of any churchyard (open or closed), and the power of giving a certificate under the provisions of section eighteen of the Burial Act 1855, with the like powers as, immediately before the relevant date, were possessed by the churchwardens to recover the cost of maintaining a closed churchyard:

Provided that nothing herein contained shall affect the property of the churchwardens in the goods and ornaments of the church or their powers duties and liabilities with respect to visitations.

(iii) The like powers duties and liabilities as, immediately before the relevant date, were possessed by the church trustees (if any) for the parish appointed under the Compulsory Church Rate Abolition Act 1868.

(2) All enactments in any Act whether general or local or personal relating to any powers duties or liabilities transferred to the council from the vestry churchwardens or church trustees as the case may be shall subject to the provisions of this Measure and so far as circumstances admit be construed as if any reference therein to the vestry or the churchwardens or church trustees referred to the council to which such powers duties or liabilities have been transferred and the said enactments shall be construed with such modifications as may be necessary for carrying this Measure into effect.

(3) Where any property is applicable to purposes connected with any such powers duties or liabilities as aforesaid, any deed or instrument which could be or could have been made or executed in relation to such property by a vestry, or by churchwardens or church trustees, may be made or executed by the council of the parish concerned.

(4) This Measure shall not affect any enactment in any private or local Act of Parliament under the authority of which church rates may be made or levied in lieu of or in consideration of the extinguishment or of the appropriation to any other purpose of any tithes customary payments or other property or charge upon property which tithes payments property or charge previously to the passing of such Act had been appropriated by law to ecclesiastical purposes or in consideration of the abolition of tithes in any place or upon any contract made or for good or valuable consideration given and every such enactment shall continue in force in the same manner as if this Measure had not been passed.

For the purposes of this subsection 'ecclesiastical purposes' shall mean the building rebuilding enlargement and repair of any church and any purpose to which by common or ecclesiastical law a church rate is applicable or any of such purposes.

Holding of Property for Ecclesiastical Purposes: Educational Schemes

5.—(1) Subject to the provisions of this Measure, the council of every parish shall have power to acquire (whether by way of gift or otherwise) any property real or personal—
- (a) for any ecclesiastical purpose affecting the parish or any part thereof;
- (b) for any purpose in connection with schemes (hereinafter called 'educational schemes') for providing facilities for the spiritual moral and physical training of persons residing in or near the parish.

(2) Subject to the provisions of this Measure and of the general law and to the provisions of any trusts affecting any such property, the council shall have power to manage, administer and dispose of any property acquired under this section.

(3) A council shall have power, in connection with any educational scheme, to constitute or participate in the constitution of a body of managers or trustees or a managing committee consisting either wholly or partly of persons appointed by the council, and may confer on any such body or committee such functions in regard to the implementation of the scheme, and such functions relating to property held for the purposes of the scheme, as the council thinks expedient.

(4) The powers of a council with respect to educational schemes shall be exercised subject to and in accordance with the terms of any undertaking which may have been given by the council to the Minister of Education or to any local authority in connection with any financial or other assistance given by the Minister or the authority in relation to the scheme.

(5) A council shall not exercise any of its powers in relation to educational schemes without the consent of the diocesan board of education for the diocese, and any such consent, may be given upon such terms and conditions as the committee considers appropriate in all the circumstances of the case.

Supplementary Provisions Relating to Certain Property

6.—(1) After the commencement of this Measure, a council shall not acquire any interest in land (other than a short lease as hereinafter defined) or in any personal property to be held on permanent trusts, without the consent of the diocesan authority.

(2) Where, at or after the commencement of this Measure, a council holds or acquires an interest in land (other than a short lease as hereinafter defined) or any interest in personal property to be held on permanent trusts, such interest shall be vested in the diocesan authority subject to all trusts, debts and liabilities affecting the same, and all persons concerned shall make or concur in making such transfers (if any) as are requisite for giving effect to the provisions of this subsection.

(3) Where any property is vested in the diocesan authority pursuant to subsection (2) of this section, the council shall not sell, lease, let, exchange, charge or take any legal proceedings with respect to the property without the consent of the authority; but save as aforesaid, nothing in this section shall affect the powers of the council in relation to the management, administration or disposition of any such property.

(3A) Where any property which is occupied by a member of the team in a team ministry is vested in the diocesan authority pursuant to subsection (2) of this section and the council proposes to alter or dispose of the property or any part thereof, the council shall—
- (a) keep that member informed of matters arising from the proposal;
- (b) afford that member an opportunity to express views thereon before taking any action to implement the proposal; and
- (c) have regard to those views before taking any such action.

(4) Where any property is vested in the diocesan authority pursuant to subsection (2) of this section, the council shall keep the authority indemnified in respect of:
- (a) all liabilities subject to which the property is vested in the authority or which may thereafter be incident to the property;

(b) all rates, taxes, insurance premiums and other outgoings of whatever nature which may from time to time be payable in respect of the property;

(c) all costs, charges and expenses incurred by the authority in relation to the acquisition or insurance of the property or as trustee thereof;

(d) all costs, proceedings, claims and demands in respect of any of the matters hereinbefore mentioned.

(5) The consents required by subsection (3) of this section are additional to any other consents required by law, either from the Charity Commission or the Minister of Education or otherwise.

(6) In this section the expression 'short lease' means a lease for a term not exceeding one year, and includes any tenancy from week to week, from month to month, from quarter to quarter, or from year to year.

(7) Any question as to whether personal property is to be held on permanent trusts shall be determined for the purposes of this section by a person appointed by the bishop.

Miscellaneous Powers of the Council

7. The council of every parish shall have the following powers in addition to any powers conferred by the Constitution or otherwise by this Measure:—

(i) power to frame an annual budget of moneys required for the maintenance of the work of the Church in the parish and otherwise and to take such steps as they think necessary for the raising collecting and allocating of such moneys;

(ii) power to make levy and collect a voluntary church rate for any purpose connected with the affairs of the church including the administrative expenses of the council and the costs of any legal proceedings;

(iii) power jointly with the minister to appoint and dismiss the parish clerk and sexton or any persons performing or assisting to perform the duties of parish clerk or sexton and to determine their salaries and the conditions of the tenure of their offices or of their employment but subject to the rights of any persons holding the said offices at the appointed day;

(iv) power jointly with the minister to determine the objects to which all moneys to be given or collected in church shall be allocated;

(v) power to make representations to the bishop with regard to any matter affecting the welfare of the church in the parish.

Accounts of the Council

8.—(1) Every council shall furnish to the annual parochial church meeting for discussion the financial statements of the council for the financial year immediately preceding the meeting.

(2) The financial year referred to in subsection (1) above shall be such period as may be prescribed and the financial statements referred to in that subsection shall be prepared in the prescribed form, audited or independently examined as prescribed and published and displayed in the prescribed manner.

(3) In subsection (2) above 'prescribed' means prescribed by the Church Representation Rules or by regulations made under those Rules.

Powers of Bishop

9.—(1) The bishop may subject to the provisions of this Measure and the Constitution make rules for carrying this Measure into effect within the diocese.

(2) If any act required by this Measure to be done by any person is not done within such time as the bishop may consider reasonable it may be done by or under the authority of the bishop.

(3) In the event of a council and a minister being unable to agree as to any matter in which their agreement or joint action is required under the provisions of this Measure, such matter shall be dealt with or determined in such manner as the bishop may direct.

(4) During a vacancy in a diocesan see the powers conferred upon the bishop by this section may be exercised by the guardian of the spiritualities.

Ecclesiastical Jurisdiction Measure 1963

Part I
The Ecclesiastical Judicial System

The courts

The ecclesiastical courts

1.—(1) For each diocese there shall be a court of the bishop thereof (to be called the consistory court of the diocese or, in the case of the court for the diocese of Canterbury, the commissary court thereof) which shall have the original jurisdiction in non-disciplinary matters conferred on it by this Measure.

(2) For each of the provinces of Canterbury and York—
  (a) there shall be a court of the archbishop thereof (to be called, in the case of the court for the province of Canterbury, the Arches Court of Canterbury, and, in the case of the court for the province of York, the Chancery Court of York) which shall have the appellate jurisdiction conferred on it by this measure; and
  (b) *Repealed.*

(3) For both of the said provinces—
  (a) *Repealed*;
  (b) there shall be a court (to be called the Court of Ecclesiastical Causes Reserved) which shall have the original and appellate jurisdiction conferred on it by this Measure;
  (c) there may, in accordance with the provisions in that behalf of this Measure, be appointed by Her Majesty commissioners who shall have such jurisdiction as is conferred on them by this Measure with respect to the review of findings of the Court of Ecclesiastical Causes Reserved; and
  (d) Her Majesty in Council shall have such appellate jurisdiction as is conferred on Her by this Measure.

The Judges of the Courts constituted by this Measure

Judge of consistory court

2.—(1) Subject to the following provisions of this Measure, the consistory court of a diocese shall be presided over by a single judge who shall be styled the chancellor of the diocese or, in the case of the diocese of Canterbury, the commissary general, and appointed by the bishop thereof by letters patent.

(1A) Before appointing a person to be chancellor of a diocese the bishop shall consult the Lord Chancellor and the Dean of the Arches and Auditor.

(2) A person appointed to be chancellor of a diocese shall be at least thirty years old and either a person who has a 7 year general qualification, within the meaning of section 71 of the Courts and Legal Services Act 1990, or a person holds or has held high judicial office or the office of circuit judge, and, before appointing a layman, the bishop shall satisfy himself that the person to be appointed is a communicant.

(3) *Repealed.*

(4) Subject to the provisions of subsections (3) and (4A) of this section, the appointment of a person to be chancellor of a diocese shall be for the period beginning with the date of the appointment and ending with the date on which he attains the age at which a circuit judge is obliged to vacate that office, but he—

- (a) may resign his office by instrument in writing under his hand addressed to, and served on, the bishop of the diocese;
- (b) may be removed by that bishop if the Upper House of the Convocation of the relevant province resolves that he is incapable of acting or unfit to act.
- (c) may continue to act as chancellor for the purpose of any proceedings or cause of faculty in the consistory court of the diocese during the course of which he attains the age at which a circuit judge is obliged to vacate that office as if the date of the conclusion in that court of those proceedings or that cause, as the case may be, were the date on which he attains that age.

(4A) Where the bishop of a diocese considers it desirable in the interests of the diocese to retain the chancellor of the diocese in office after the time at which he would otherwise retire in accordance with subsection (4) above, he may from time to time authorise the continuance in office of the chancellor until such date, not being later than the date on which the chancellor attains the age at which a puisne judge of the High Court is obliged to vacate that office, as he thinks fit.

(5) The chancellor of a diocese shall, before he enters on the execution of his office,—

- (a) take, either before the bishop of the diocese in the presence of the diocesan registrar, or in open court in the presence of that registrar, the oaths set out in Part I of the First Schedule to this Measure;

and the diocesan registrar shall record the taking of the said oaths.

Number of chancellorships to be held by one person may be limited

2A.—(1) Regulations made by the House of Bishops of the General Synod may make provision with respect to the maximum number of chancellorships or deputy chancellorships of dioceses which any one person may hold.

(2) Nothing in any regulation made under this section shall be taken as prohibiting any person who at the date on which the regulation comes into force holds more than the maximum number of chancellorships or deputy chancellorships prescribed by the regulation from continuing to hold such offices.

(3) Regulations made under this section shall be laid before the General Synod and shall not come into operation until they have been approved by the General Synod.

(4) The Statutory Instruments Act 1946 shall apply to any regulations approved under subsection (3) of this section as if they were a statutory instrument and were made when so approved, as if this Measure were an Act providing that any such regulations should be subject to annulment in pursuance of a resolution of either House of Parliament.

Judges of the Arches and Chancery Courts

3.—(1) The judges of the Arches Court of Canterbury and the Chancery Court of York respectively shall be as set out in subsection (2) of this section, but proceedings which, by virtue of the following provisions of this Measure, are cognisable by either of those Courts shall be heard and disposed of by such of the judges thereof as may be determined in accordance with those provisions.

(2) Of the judges of each of the said Courts—

- (a) one, who shall be a judge of both Courts (and, in respect of his jurisdiction in the province of Canterbury shall be styled Dean of the Arches and, in respect of his jurisdiction in the province of York, shall be styled Auditor, and is hereinafter referred to in this Measure as the Dean of the Arches and Auditor), shall be appointed by the archbishops of Canterbury and York jointly with the approval of Her Majesty signified by warrant under the sign manual;

(b) two shall be persons in holy orders appointed by the president of tribunals from among the persons serving on the provincial panel of the relevant province.
(c) two shall be laymen appointed by the president of tribunals from among the persons serving on the provincial panel of the relevant province;
(d) the others shall be all the diocesan chancellors appointed under section 2 of this Measure (in whichever province), except the chancellor of the diocese in Europe.

(3) A person appointed to be Dean of the Arches and Auditor shall be either a person who holds or has a 10 year High Court qualification, within the meaning of section 71 of the Courts and Legal Services Act 1990, or a person who holds or has held high judicial office, and, before appointing a layman, the archbishops of Canterbury and York shall satisfy themselves that he is a communicant.

(4) Before the president of tribunals appoints a person to be a judge of either of the said Courts under paragraph (c) of subsection (2) of this section, he shall satisfy himself that that person is a communicant.

(5) The appointment of any person under paragraph (a), (b) or (c) of subsection (2) of this section to be a judge of either of the said Courts shall be for a period beginning with the date of the appointment and ending with the date on which that person attains the age of seventy-five years, but—
(a) the Dean of the Arches and Auditor—
  (i) may resign his office by instrument in writing under his hand addressed to, and served on, the archbishops of Canterbury and York;
  (ii) may be removed by the archbishops of Canterbury and York jointly if the Upper Houses of the Convocations of the provinces of Canterbury and York each resolve that he is incapable of acting or unfit to act;
(b) any other judge of either of the said Courts—
  (i) may resign his office by instrument in writing under his hand addressed to, and served on, the archbishop of the relevant province;
  (ii) may be removed by the archbishop of that province if the president of tribunals determines that he is incapable of acting or unfit to act;
(c) any judge of either of the said Courts may continue to act as a judge thereof for the purpose of any proceedings in that Court during the course of which he attains the age of seventy-five years as if the date of the conclusion in that Court of those proceedings were the date on which he attains that age.

(6) The Dean of the Arches and Auditor and every chancellor of a diocese shall, before he enters on the execution of his office as a judge of the said Courts,—
(a) take,—
  (i) before the archbishop of Canterbury in the presence of the registrar of the province of Canterbury and before the archbishop of York in the presence of the registrar of the province of York; or
  (ii) in open court in both of those provinces in the presence of the registrar of the province;
  the oaths set out in Part I of the First Schedule to this Measure;

(7) A person appointed under paragraph (b) or (c) of subsection (2) of this section to hold the office of judge of either of the said Courts shall, before he enters on the execution of his office,—
(a) take the said oaths either before the archbishop of the relevant province and in the presence of the registrar of that province or in open court in the presence of that registrar.

(8) A provincial registrar shall record the taking of an oath in his presence in pursuance of either of the two last foregoing subsections.

Appointment of deputy judges

4.—(1) Where the Dean of the Arches and Auditor or any chancellor is for any reason unable to act as such, or the office of the Dean or any chancellor is vacant, the archbishops of Canterbury and York in the former case, and the bishop of the diocese concerned in the latter, may appoint a fit and proper person to act as deputy Dean of the Arches and Auditor or deputy chancellor of such diocese as the case may be during the period of inability or vacancy, and every person so appointed shall have all the powers and perform all the duties of the office in respect of which he is appointed to act as deputy.

(1A) The Dean of the Arches and Auditor may, with the consent of the Archbishops of Canterbury and York appoint a fit and proper person to act as deputy Dean of the Arches and Auditor for such period not exceeding twelve months or for such purpose as may be specified in the instrument of appointment, and during that period or for that purpose every person so appointed shall have all the powers and perform all the duties of the office of Dean of the Arches and Auditor.

(1B) Any chancellor may, with the consent of the bishop of the diocese, appoint, in writing, a fit and proper person to act as deputy chancellor of the diocese and any person so appointed shall have all the powers and perform all the duties of the office of chancellor.

(1C) The appointment of a deputy chancellor appointed under subsection (1B) of this section shall continue so long as the chancellor who appointed the deputy chancellor continues in office and, thereafter, for the period of three months beginning with the date on which the chancellor ceases to hold office or until the deputy chancellor attains the age at which the chancellor would be required to vacate the office of chancellor under section 2(4) of this Measure, whichever is sooner, but a deputy chancellor—
- (a) may resign the office of deputy chancellor by notice in writing addressed to the chancellor,
- (b) may be removed by the chancellor, after consultation with the bishop, if the chancellor considers that the deputy is incapable of acting or unfit to act, and
- (c) may continue to act as chancellor for the purpose of any proceedings or cause of faculty in the consistory court of the diocese during the course of which the deputy chancellor attains the said age or, as the case may be, the three months period referred to above expires, as if the date of the conclusion in the court of those proceedings or that cause, as the case may be, were the date on which that age is attained or, as the case may be, that period has expired.

(2) Every deputy judge appointed to act pursuant to the provisions of the foregoing subsections shall be qualified as hereinbefore provided with respect to the person whose functions he is appointed to perform and, before he enters on the execution of his office, such deputy shall take and subscribe such oaths as are required to be taken, and subscribed by the Dean of the Arches and Auditor or by a chancellor of a diocese, as the case may be, under the preceding provisions of this Measure in manner thereby appointed, and such oaths shall be recorded in the like manner.

Judges of the Court of Ecclesiastical Causes Reserved

5. The Court of Ecclesiastical Causes Reserved shall be constituted of five judges appointed by Her Majesty, and of them two shall be persons who hold, or have held, high judicial office and who make a declaration that they are communicants and three shall be persons who are, or have been, diocesan bishops.

Jurisdiction of the courts

Jurisdiction of the consistory court

6.—(1) Subject to the provisions of the following subsection the consistory court of a diocese has original jurisdiction to hear and determine—
- (a) *Repealed*;
- (b) a cause of faculty for authorising—
  - (i) any act relating to land within the diocese, or to anything on or in such land, being an act for the doing of which the decree of a faculty is requisite;
  - (ii) the sale of books comprised in a library within the diocese, being a library to which the Parochial Libraries Act 1708, applies;

(bb) proceedings for an injunction or restoration order under section 13 of the Care of Churches and Ecclesiastical Jurisdiction Measure 1991;
(c) proceedings upon any *jus patronatus* awarded by the bishop of the diocese;
(d) proceedings for the recovery of any penalty or forfeiture incurred under section thirty-two of the Pluralities Act 1838, in relation to a benefice in the diocese and any proceedings consequent upon the return into the court of a monition in pursuance of section 112 of that Act;
(e) any proceedings (other than as aforesaid) which, immediately before the passing of this Measure, it had power to hear and determine, not being proceedings jurisdiction to hear and determine which is expressly abolished by this Measure.

(2) Nothing contained in the foregoing subsection shall extend, or be construed as extending, the jurisdiction of the consistory court in faculty matters to any land or to anything on or in such land in respect of which such court had no jurisdiction immediately before the passing of this Measure.

Jurisdiction of Arches and Chancery Courts

7.—(1) The Arches Court of Canterbury and the Chancery Court of York each have jurisdiction to hear and determine appeals from judgments, orders or decrees of consistory courts of dioceses within the provinces for which they are constituted respectively, being judgments, orders or decrees given, made or pronounced—
(a) in such proceedings as are mentioned in paragraphs (d) and (e) of subsection (1) of the last foregoing section, or
(b) in causes of faculty not involving matter of doctrine, ritual or ceremonial, or
(c) in proceedings for an injunction under section 13(4) of the Care of Churches and Ecclesiastical Jurisdiction Measure 1991 or for a restoration order under section 13(5) of that Measure,

and from interlocutory orders of those consistory courts in causes of faculty involving doctrine, ritual or ceremonial.

(1A) Each of the said Courts shall also have jurisdiction to hear and determine appeals from judgments, orders or decrees of the Vicar-General's court of the province of Canterbury or York (including that Court as constituted in accordance with the Clergy Discipline Measure 2003), as the case may be.

(1B) Each of the said Courts shall also have jurisdiction to hear and determine appeals from judgments, orders or decrees of disciplinary tribunals within the provinces for which they are constituted respectively.

(2) An appeal which, by virtue of this section, either of the said Courts has jurisdiction to entertain lies—
(a) in a disciplinary case, at the instance of any party to the proceedings on a question of law and the defendant on a question of fact;
(b) in any other case, at the instance of any party to the proceedings but only with the leave of the consistory court or the Vicar-General's Court as the case may be or, if leave is refused by that court, of the Dean of the Arches and Auditor.

(3) Appeals under this section shall be lodged and conducted in such manner as may be prescribed.

Appellate jurisdiction of Her Majesty in Council

8.—(1) Her Majesty in Council has jurisdiction to hear and determine appeals from judgments of the Arches Court of Canterbury and the Chancery Court of York in proceedings which, by virtue of paragraph (b) of subsection (1) of the last foregoing section, those Courts have jurisdiction to entertain.

(2) An appeal which, by virtue of this section, Her Majesty in Council has jurisdiction to entertain lies at the instance of any party to the proceedings with the leave of Her Majesty in Council.

Jurisdiction of commissions of convocation

9. *Repealed.*

Jurisdiction of Court of Ecclesiastical Causes Reserved

10.—(1) The Court of Ecclesiastical Causes Reserved has original jurisdiction to hear and determine—
- (a) proceedings upon articles charging an offence against the laws ecclesiastical involving matter of doctrine ritual or ceremonial committed by—
    - (i) a priest or deacon who when the offence was alleged to have been committed or when the proceedings were instituted, held preferment in a diocese or resided therein;
    - (ii) an archbishop or a bishop who, at one of those times, was a diocesan or a suffragan commissioned by a diocesan or (not being either a diocesan or a suffragan) held preferment in a diocese or resided therein;
- (b) all suits of *duplex querela*;

and also has jurisdiction to hear and determine appeals from judgments, orders or decrees of consistory courts of dioceses given, made or pronounced in causes of faculty involving matter of doctrine, ritual or ceremonial.

(2) An appeal which, by virtue of this section, the Court of Ecclesiastical Causes Reserved has jurisdiction to entertain lies at the instance of any party to the proceedings.

(3) For the purpose of determining whether an appeal from a judgment, order or decree of a consistory court in a cause of faculty lies to the Arches Court of Canterbury or the Chancery Court of York under paragraph (b) of subsection (1) of section seven of this Measure or to the Court of Ecclesiastical Causes Reserved by virtue of this section, it shall be the duty of the chancellor to certify upon the application of the party desiring to appeal whether or not a question of doctrine, ritual or ceremonial is involved.

(4) In any proceedings in the Court of Ecclesiastical Causes Reserved on an appeal from a judgment, order or decree of a consistory court of a diocese given, made or pronounced in a cause of faculty, the court—
- (a) if it considers that it has heard and determined the appeal in so far as it relates to matter involving doctrine, ritual or ceremonial but that the appeal relates also to other matter, may, if it considers it expedient to do so, deal with the other matter, but otherwise shall refer it, and
- (b) if it considers that no matter of doctrine, ritual or ceremonial is involved, shall refer the appeal (notwithstanding any certificate to the contrary issued under subsection (3) of this section),

to the Arches Court of Canterbury or the Chancery Court of York, as appropriate, to be heard and determined by that court.

(5) In any proceedings in the Arches Court of Canterbury or the Chancery Court of York on an appeal from a judgment, order or decree of a consistory court of a diocese given, made or pronounced in a cause of faculty, the court may, if it considers that the appeal relates to matter involving doctrine, ritual or ceremonial, refer the appeal (notwithstanding any certificate to the contrary issued under subsection (3) of this section) to the Court of Ecclesiastical Causes Reserved to be heard and determined by that court.

(6) Subject to any rules made under section 26 of the Care of Churches and Ecclesiastical Jurisdiction Measure 1991, any reference of an appeal under subsection (4) or (5) of this section shall be in accordance with such practice directions as may be issued jointly by the Dean of the Arches and Auditor and the two judges of the Court of Ecclesiastical Causes Reserved appointed in accordance with section 5 of this Measure by virtue of their holding, or having held, high judicial office.

Jurisdiction of Her Majesty with respect to review of findings of commissions of convocation or of Court of Ecclesiastical Causes Reserved

11.—(1) *Repealed.*

(2) A petition addressed to Her Majesty praying that She will be pleased to cause a finding of the Court of Ecclesiastical Causes Reserved to be reviewed may be lodged with the Clerk of the Crown in Chancery—

    (a)   in a case where the finding of the Court was in exercise of the jurisdiction it has by virtue of paragraph (a) of subsection (1) of the last foregoing section, by any party to the proceedings on a question of law and the defendant on a question of fact;

    (b)   in any other case, by any party to the proceedings.

(3) Any such petition must be in the prescribed form and must be lodged as aforesaid within the prescribed period after the finding to which it relates.

(4) Upon a petition being duly lodged under this section, a commission shall be directed under the Great Seal to such five persons as Her Majesty may be pleased to nominate, of whom three shall be judges of the Supreme Court, or members of the supplementary panel under section 39 of the Constitutional Reform Act 2005, who make a declaration that they are communicants and two shall be lords spiritual sitting as Lords of Parliament, to review the finding to which the petition relates.

(5) A commission appointed under this section shall be called a Commission of Review.

Miscellaneous provisions relating to the courts and the judges

Consistory, Arches and Chancery Courts to be unaffected by vacation of sees

12. The vacation of the see of Canterbury or of the see of York shall not render the Arches Court of Canterbury or the Chancery Court of York unable to exercise their respective jurisdictions nor shall the vacation of those sees or the see of the bishop of any other diocese render any consistory court, Vicar-General's court or disciplinary tribunal unable to exercise its jurisdiction, and subject to the provisions of subsection (3) of section two of this Measure no such vacancy shall affect the discharge by the judges, members or officers of any such court or tribunal as aforesaid of their functions.

Certain judges to be *ex officio* officials principal

13.—(1) The Dean of the Arches and Auditor shall, by virtue of his office, be the Official Principal of the archbishop of Canterbury and the Official Principal of the archbishop of York in their respective capacities of Metropolitans and shall also be Master of the Faculties to the archbishop of Canterbury.

(2) The chancellor of a diocese shall by virtue of his office be the Official Principal of the bishop of that diocese.

Part II
Offences Cognisable under the Measure and Provisions as to Persons Chargeable Herewith

Offences under the Measure

14.—(1) Proceedings may be instituted under this Measure against any of the persons specified in section seventeen thereof charging—

    (a)   an offence against the laws ecclesiastical involving matters of doctrine, ritual or ceremonial.

    (b)   *Repealed.*

(2) The repeal by this Measure of any statutory provision under which proceedings could have been taken for an offence against the law ecclesiastical shall not prevent the taking of any proceedings under this Measure in respect of any such offence.

Place where offence committed

15. Proceedings under this Measure for an offence involving matters of doctrine, ritual or ceremonial shall only be instituted if the offence was committed within the province of Canterbury or York.

Limitation of time for institution of proceedings under this Measure

16. No proceedings under this Measure shall be instituted unless the act or omission constituting the offence, or the last of them if the offence consists of a series of acts or omissions, occurred within the period of three years ending with the day on which proceedings are instituted.

Persons against whom proceedings may be instituted

17. Proceedings under this Measure may be instituted against an archbishop, any diocesan bishop or any suffragan bishop commissioned by a diocesan bishop or any other bishop or a priest or deacon who, when the offence was alleged to have been committed or when the proceedings are instituted, held or holds preferment in any diocese or resided therein as the case may be.

PART III
INSTITUTION OF PROCEEDINGS IN RESPECT OF OFFENCES UNDER THE MEASURE

Mode of instituting proceedings

18.—(1) Proceedings charging an offence under this Measure shall be instituted in the case of an archbishop or a bishop by way of complaint laid before the registrar of the relevant province and in the case of a priest or deacon by way of complaint laid before the registrar of any diocese in which the accused held or holds preferment or in which he resides at the date when the alleged offence was committed or at the date of such complaint.

(2) A complaint laid in accordance with the provisions of the preceding subsection shall be in writing in the prescribed form, contain the prescribed particulars of the offence the commission of which is alleged therein and be verified on oath.

(3) A copy of the complaint duly laid and verified shall be served on the accused forthwith after it is laid.

Persons by whom proceedings against a priest or deacon may be instituted

19. Proceedings against a priest or deacon may be instituted by the following persons, that is to say—
   (a) in all cases by an authorised complainant; or
   (b) in the case of any priest or deacon who is an incumbent of a parochial benefice, a stipendiary curate licensed to a benefice or a curate in charge of a conventional district, by six or more persons of full age whose names are on the electoral roll either of the parish of that benefice or of the district as the case may be; or
   (c) in the case of a stipendiary curate licensed to a benefice, by the incumbent of that benefice.

Persons by whom proceedings against an archbishop or bishop may be instituted

20. Proceedings against an archbishop or bishop may be instituted by the following persons, that is to say:—
   (a) in the case of an archbishop:—
      (i) save in respect of any act or omission in relation to his duties as diocesan by not less than two of his comprovincial diocesan bishops; or
      (ii) save in respect of any act or omission in relation to his duties as metropolitan by not less than ten persons of whom not less than five are incumbents in the diocese of the accused and not less than five are lay members of the diocesan conference of such diocese; or

(b) in the case of a diocesan bishop other than an archbishop:—
  (i) by an authorised complainant; or
  (ii) by not less than ten persons of whom not less than five are incumbents in the diocese of the accused and not less than five are lay members of the diocesan conference of such diocese; or
(c) in the case of a suffragan bishop:
  (i) by the bishop who commissioned him; or
  (ii) by an authorised complainant; or
  (iii) by not less than ten persons of whom not less than five are incumbents in the diocese of the bishop by whom the accused is commissioned and not less than five are lay members of the diocesan conference of such diocese; or
  (iv) if he is the incumbent of a parochial benefice by six or more persons of full age whose names are on the electoral roll of that parish; or
(d) in the case of any other bishop:—
  (i) by the bishop of the diocese in which the accused holds preferment or resides; or
  (ii) by an authorised complainant; or
  (iii) if he is the incumbent of a parochial benefice by six or more persons of full age whose names are on the electoral roll of that parish.

Supplementary provisions in special cases

21.—(1) For the purposes of the last two preceding sections of this Measure:—
  (a) where a bishop, priest or deacon is an incumbent of or licensed to more than one parochial benefice or a parochial benefice which comprises more than one parish, each of the six or more persons empowered to institute proceedings under paragraph (b) of section nineteen or subparagraph (iv) of paragraph (c) and subparagraph (iii) of paragraph (d) of section twenty of this Measure may be on the electoral roll of any of the parishes comprised in those benefices or that benefice; and
  (b) a church designated and established as a guild church under the City of London (Guild Churches) Acts 1952 and 1960, shall be deemed to be a parochial benefice and, accordingly, references in the said sections to the incumbent of a parochial benefice, to the electoral roll of a parish and to a stipendiary curate licensed to a benefice (whether parochial or not) shall, in the case of a guild church, be construed as references to the vicar of such church, to the church electoral roll thereof and to a curate licensed to assist the vicar thereof respectively.

(2) The provisions of paragraph (a) of the foregoing subsection shall apply in any case where a bishop or priest, as well as being licensed to a benefice, is licensed also to a conventional district, or to any such person as is licensed to more than one conventional district.

Part IV

Conduct of Proceedings against Priests or Deacons for Offences under the Measure not involving Matter of Doctrine, Ritual or Ceremonial

[Repealed]

Part V
Conduct of Proceedings against Bishops for Offences under the Measure not involving Matter of Doctrine, Ritual or Ceremonial

[Repealed]

Part VI
Conduct of Proceedings against Deacons, Priests or Bishops for Offences under the Measure involving Matter of Doctrine, Ritual or Ceremonial

Scope of Part VI

Scope of Part VI

38. The provisions of this Part of this Measure shall have effect for the purpose of regulating proceedings against a deacon, priest, bishop or archbishop against whom a complaint has been made in accordance with the provisions of Part III of this Measure alleging the commission of an offence against the laws ecclesiastical involving matter of doctrine, ritual or ceremonial.

Procedure under Part VI after laying of complaint

Duty of diocesan upon the making of a complaint against a deacon or priest

39.—(1) Upon a complaint under this Part of this Measure against a priest or deacon being only laid and verified the bishop of the diocese before whose registrar it is laid shall take it into consideration and as soon as may be after a copy thereof has been served on the accused, shall afford to the accused and the complainant an opportunity of being interviewed in private by him either separately or together as the bishop thinks fit with respect to the matter of the complaint, and thereafter shall either—
   (a) decide that no further step be taken under this Part of this Measure in the matter of the complaint; or
   (b) refer the complaint for inquiry under the following provisions of this Part of this Measure.

(2) Where, in pursuance of the foregoing subsection, the bishop decides that no further step be taken in the matter of the complaint he shall forthwith give notice of his decision to the complainant and to the accused and thereafter no further action shall be taken by any person in regard thereto.

Duty of archbishop upon the making of a complaint against a bishop

40. Upon a complaint under this Part of this Measure against a bishop being laid and verified the archbishop of the relevant province shall have the same powers and duties in relation thereto as are conferred and imposed upon a diocesan bishop by the last preceding section in regard to a complaint against a priest or deacon and, according to his decision, the like consequences shall ensure as are referred to in such section.

Complaint against an archbishop to stand referred for inquiry

41. A complaint against an archbishop of the nature referred to in section 38 of this Measure duly laid and verified under this Part of this Measure shall thereupon stand referred for inquiry under the following provisions of this Part of this Measure.

Inquiry into complaint by committee of convocation

42.—(1) Where, by virtue of the foregoing provisions of this Part of this Measure, a complaint is referred, or stands referred, for inquiry, the following provisions shall have effect.

(2) The reference shall be to a committee whose duty it shall be to inquire into the complaint for the purpose of deciding whether there is a case to answer in respect of which the accused should be put on trial upon articles by the Court of Ecclesiastical Causes Reserved, for any offence under this Measure involving matter of doctrine, ritual or ceremonial.

(3) The committee shall—
- (a) where the accused is a priest or deacon, consist of—
    - (i) one member of the Upper House of the Convocation of the relevant province, appointed by the archbishop;
    - (ii) two members of the Lower House of that Convocation, appointed by the prolocutor of that House; and
    - (iii) two chancellors of dioceses in that province, appointed by the Dean of the Arches and Auditor;
- (b) where the accused is an archbishop or a bishop, consist of—
    - (i) such even number of persons, to be appointed by the Upper House of the Convocation of the relevant province, as that House shall determine; and
    - (ii) the Dean of the Arches and Auditor or a deputy who is nominated by him and who shall make a declaration that he is a communicant being a person holding or having held high judicial office, or a person who has a 10 year High Court qualification, within the meaning of section 71 of the Courts and Legal Services Act 1990;

and the determination of any matter before the committee shall be according to the opinion of the majority of the members thereof.

(4) Either the accused or the complainant may, if he so desires, be assisted or represented by a friend or adviser at any meeting of such a committee at which he is invited to be present.

(5) The complainant and the accused may lay before the committee such evidence as they shall think fit and such evidence shall be given by affidavit but the committee shall on the application of either party and may on its own motion request the person making such affidavit to attend the inquiry for the purpose of answering such questions on oath as may be put to him by the committee or by or on behalf of any party, and unless such person shall attend the inquiry for that purpose his affidavit shall be disregarded:

Provided that the evidence of any person who is incapable of giving evidence on oath shall be given orally at the inquiry.

(6) If the committee, after making due inquiry into the complaint, decide that there is a case for the accused to answer in respect of Ecclesiastical Causes Reserved for any such offence as aforesaid, they shall declare their decision, specifying the offence.

(7) Where the committee decide as mentioned in the last foregoing subsection, but are of opinion on consideration of the evidence, of any statement made to them by the accused and of any representations made to them by the bishop of the diocese where the accused is a deacon or a priest—
- (a) that the offence charged by the complaint is too trivial to warrant further proceedings thereon; or
- (b) that the offence was committed under extenuating circumstances; or
- (c) that further proceedings on the complaint would not be in the interests of the Church of England;

they may dismiss the complaint and report to the Convocation of the relevant province that they have dismissed it and the ground on which they have taken that course.

(8) If the committee, after making due inquiry into the complaint, decide that there is no case for the accused to answer, they shall declare their decision.

(9) The committee shall reduce their decision, or decisions, to writing and shall send a copy thereof to the accused and to the Upper House of the Convocation of the relevant province and in the case of an accused archbishop, to the archbishop of the other province.

(10) Where the committee dismiss a complaint and report their dismissal of it under subsection (7) of this section or declare that there is no case for the accused to answer under subsection (8) of this section, no further step shall be taken in the matter of the complaint.

Appointment of person to promote complaint

43. Where a committee inquiring into a complaint declare, in pursuance of subsection (6) of the last foregoing section, their decision that there is a case for the accused to answer and do not dismiss the same under subsection (7) of that section, the Upper House of the Convocation of the relevant province shall nominate a fit person to promote a complaint against the accused in the Court of Ecclesiastical Causes Reserved.

Provided that when the accused is an archbishop the Upper House of the Convocation of the relevant province shall for this purpose meet under the presidency of the senior diocesan bishop of that province and the accused archbishop shall take no part in the proceedings of the said meeting.

Contents of articles

44. Where a person is prosecuted by virtue of the foregoing provisions of this Part of this Measure, the articles may with the leave of the committee who inquired into the complaint or of the Court of Ecclesiastical Causes Reserved include, either in substitution for or in addition to, particulars of the offence or offences specified by that committee, particulars of any other offence founded on evidence disclosed in the course of the committee's inquiry, being particulars of an offence involving matter of doctrine, ritual or ceremonial.

Conduct of trial under Part VI

45.—(1) The following provisions shall have effect with respect to the trial of a person by the Court of Ecclesiastical Causes Reserved under this Part of this Measure, namely:—

    (a) the procedure at the trial shall, so far as circumstances admit and subject to any rules which may be prescribed, be the same as at the trial of a person by a court of assize exercising criminal jurisdiction;

    (b) the accused shall be entitled to be supplied with a copy of the articles;

    (c) the rules as to the admissibility of evidence and as to whether a witness is competent or compellable to give evidence shall be the same as those observed at the trial of a person by such a court of assize;

    (d) the registrar before whom the complaint was laid shall give not less than fourteen clear days' notice of the sittings of the court to the promoter thereof and to the accused and at any sitting the court may proceed in the absence of the accused if satisfied that he was given proper notice of the sitting;

    (e) the court, if satisfied that it is in the interests of justice so to do, may give directions that during any part of the proceedings such person or persons as the court may determine shall be excluded;

    (f) the determination of any matter before the court shall be according to the opinion of the majority of the members thereof;

    (g) if the accused shall be found guilty of an offence charged, the court shall decide such censure therefor as is warranted by the following provisions of this Measure;

    (h) the censure shall be reduced to writing by the court, shall be pronounced in open court by the person presiding over the court and shall not be invalid by reason only that it is not pronounced in the presence of the accused.

(2) For the purposes of this section it shall be the duty of the Upper Houses of the Convocations of Canterbury and York jointly to draw up, the approval of the Lower Houses of those Convocations,

and from time to time to revise, with like approval, a panel of persons each of whom shall be an eminent theologian or an eminent liturgiologist, and the Court of Ecclesiastical Causes Reserved shall, when trying a person sit with not less than three nor more than five advisers selected by the Dean of the Arches and Auditor from amongst the members of the panel.

(3) In the exercise of its jurisdiction under this Measure the court of Ecclesiastical Causes Reserved shall not be bound by any decision of the Judicial Committee of the Privy council in relation to matter of doctrine ritual or ceremonial.

Part VII
Other Proceedings

Proceedings in consistory court not falling within Part IV

46.—(1) Proceedings in the consistory court of a diocese shall be heard and disposed of by the chancellor of the diocese:

Provided that proceedings in a cause of faculty may be heard and disposed of by the bishop of the diocese alone or with the chancellor if, and in so far as, provision in that behalf is made in the letters patent by which the chancellor of the diocese is appointed.

(2) Proceedings to which this section applies other than those falling within paragraph (b) of subsection (1) of section six of this Measure shall be instituted and conducted in such manner as may be prescribed.

Proceedings in Arches and Chancery Courts

47.—(1) Proceedings in the Arches Court of Canterbury or the Chancery Court of York under this Measure shall be heard and disposed of by the Dean of the Arches and Auditor and two diocesan chancellors designated by him for the purposes of the case.

(2) Proceedings under this Measure in the said Courts shall be instituted and conducted in such manner as may be prescribed.

Proceedings before Commissions of Review

48.—(1) Subject to the following provisions of this section all proceedings before a Commission of Review shall be instituted and conducted in such manner as may be prescribed.

(2) In order to give assistance to any Commission of Review in reviewing any decision of the Court of Ecclesiastical Causes Reserved involving a question of doctrine the Upper Houses of the Convocations of the Provinces of Canterbury and of York shall jointly appoint a panel of persons consisting of members of either of the Upper Houses and also if thought fit of theologians who are not members of either of the Upper Houses in such numbers as the Upper Houses may jointly determine.

(3) When any review by a Commission of Review involves a question of doctrine the Commission shall request five persons selected by it from the panel appointed under subsection (2) of this section to sit with it as advisers and to give such assistance on the matters of doctrine involved in the review as the Commission may require.

(4) The judgment of the Commission shall be according to the opinion of the majority of the members thereof and each member of the Commission shall state his own opinion on the question under review.

(5) In the exercise of its jurisdiction under this Measure a Commission of Review shall not be bound by any decision of the Judicial Committee of the Privy council in relation to matter of doctrine, ritual or ceremonial.

(6) A decision of a previous commission of Review shall be binding on a Commission subsequently appointed in any matter which shall, by virtue of this Measure, be within the jurisdiction of such Commission except in regard to a matter on which new information or evidence is adduced which was not before the Commission on the previous occasion.

Part VIII
Censures

Censures

49.—(1) The censures to which a person found guilty of an offence under this Measure renders himself liable are the following, namely,—

(a) deprivation, that is to say, removal from any preferment which he then holds and disqualification from holding any other preferment except as hereinafter provided, and if he holds no preferment at the time the censure is pronounced, disqualification from holding any preferment in the future except as hereinafter provided;

(b) inhibition, that is to say, disqualification for a specified time from exercising any of the functions of his Order;

(c) suspension, that is to say, disqualification for a specified time from exercising or performing without leave of the bishop any right or duty of or incidental to his preferment or from residing in the house of residence of his preferment or within such distance thereof as shall be specified in the censure;

(d) monition that is to say an order to do or refrain from doing a specified act;

(e) rebuke.

(2) Where a censure of suspension or inhibition has been pronounced against any person, he shall not be readmitted to his benefice or permitted to exercise the functions of his order unless he satisfies the bishop (or, where the person is himself a bishop, the Upper House of the Convocation of the relevant province) of his good conduct during the term of his suspension or inhibition.

(3) In proceedings under this Measure no censure more severe than monition shall be imposed unless the Court is satisfied that the accused has already been admonished on a previous occasion in respect of another offence of the same or substantially the same nature.

(4) No censure of deprivation on any archbishop or bishop or on any person in respect of any preferment the right to appoint to which is vested in Her Majesty (not being a parochial benefice) shall have effect unless and until Her Majesty by order in Council shall confirm the same.

(5) Where by virtue of any censure of deprivation a bishop, priest or deacon is disqualified from holding any preferment, the disqualification shall not extend to a preferment to which the bishop of a diocese, with the consent of the archbishop of the relevant province and in the case of a priest or deacon of the bishop of the diocese in which the proceedings were instituted, shall appoint him, and shall cease upon the occasion of any such appointment if the archbishop when consenting thereto shall so direct.

(6) Not more than one censure shall be imposed in respect of any one offence save that when a censure of suspension is pronounced a censure of inhibition may be pronounced for the same period.

Power of bishop to depose priest or deacon from Holy Orders

50. When a censure of deprivation is pronounced in pursuance of proceedings under this Measure on any priest or deacon the bishop of the diocese may by sentence without any further legal proceedings depose him from Holy Orders and the sentence of deposition shall be recorded in the registry of the diocese:

Provided that before deposing him from Holy Orders the bishop shall serve on the priest or deacon concerned and on the provincial registrar of the relevant province a written notice in the prescribed form of his intention so to depose him and within the period of one month from the date of such notice the said priest or deacon may appeal to the archbishop of the relevant province or, if the diocesan be the archbishop, to the archbishop of the other province in such manner as may be prescribed and the diocesan shall not proceed so to depose him until the time for the making of such appeal has passed or, in the event of an appeal being made, unless or until it shall have been dismissed.

Power to depose archbishop or bishop from Holy Orders

51. Where a censure of deprivation is pronounced in pursuance of proceedings under this Measure on an archbishop or bishop the Upper House of Convocation of the relevant province may by resolution depose him from Holy Orders:

Provided that before any motion for such a resolution is put to the Upper House a notice in the prescribed form shall be served on the archbishop or bishop concerned and the House shall consider any written representations made to it by such archbishop or bishop within one month of the service of such notice and afford him an opportunity of being heard before it personally.

Effect of deposition

52. When a person is deposed under this Measure from Holy Orders the like consequences shall ensue as by paragraph (3) of section four of the Clerical Disabilities Act 1870 would ensue, if, more than six months before the day on which such disqualification takes effect, he had executed a deed of relinquishment in the form set out in the Second Schedule to that Act and done the things prescribed by section three thereof and the bishop had on that day caused the deed to be registered in the registry of his diocese.

Restoration on pardon

53. Where by virtue of anything done under this Measure an archbishop, bishop or other clergyman is deprived or deposed his incapacities shall cease if he receives a free pardon from the Crown, and he shall be restored to any preferment he previously held if it has not in the meantime been filled.

Disobedience to censure

54. *Repealed*

Part IX
Deprivation Consequent upon certain Judgments, Orders or Decrees of Secular Courts

Deprivation of priest or deacon following certain proceedings in secular courts

55. *Repealed*

Deprivation of bishop or archbishop following certain proceedings in secular courts

56. *Repealed*

Consequences of declarations under this Part of this Measure

57. *Repealed*

Part X
Costs

Payment of costs of bishop and promoter by Commissioners

58. The Commissioners may at their absolute discretion pay out of their general fund the whole or contribute any part of costs and expenses which have been incurred by—
   (a) any archbishop or bishop (other than an archbishop or bishop himself accused of an offence cognisable under section fourteen of this Measure in relation to the costs and expenses incurred as a result of such accusation)—
      (i) in or in relation to or directly or indirectly arising out of legal proceedings authorised, taken or contemplated in any court or before any commission, committee or examiner (and notwithstanding that proceedings are not eventually taken) by any person in respect of any offence cognisable under section fourteen of this Measure, or

(ii) in relation to any declaration made or to be made in accordance with the provisions of Part IX of this Measure; and
(b) any person nominated under the provisions of this Measure to promote proceedings in respect of any such offence as is mentioned in the foregoing section; and
(c) any bishop or person designated by a bishop to act on his behalf for the purposes of the Care of Cathedrals (Supplementary Provisions) Measure 1994 in or in relation to or directly or indirectly arising out of legal proceedings authorised, taken or contemplated in the Vicar-General's court under section 4 of that Measure:

Provided that the Commissioners before paying the whole or any part of any costs and expenses in pursuance of this section shall first be satisfied that they are reasonable in amount.

Powers of courts and commissions in regard to costs

60.—(1) Subject, in the case of any party to whom legal aid is granted under the Church of England (Legal Aid) Measure 1994, to rules made under section 4 of that Measure any court or commission having jurisdiction under this Measure and the Vicar-General's court of each of the provinces of Canterbury and York in proceedings instituted under section four of the Care of Cathedrals (Supplementary Provisions) Measure 1994 shall have power at any stage of the proceedings to order any party to give security for costs.

(2) Any court (including a Vicar-General's court), commission, committee or examiner shall have power at its discretion to make an order for payment of taxed costs against any party and may take into account the fact that the whole or part of the costs of a complainant or accused person are being or have been met out of the Fund maintained under the Church of England (Legal Aid) Measure 1994.

(3) An award of costs to any person under the last foregoing subsection may direct that, instead of taxed costs, that person shall be entitled—
(a) to a proportion specified in the direction of the taxed costs or to the taxed costs from or up to a stage of the proceedings so specified; or
(b) to a gross sum so specified in lieu of taxed costs.

(4) In this section the expression 'costs' includes fees, charges, disbursements, expenses and remuneration and the expression 'taxed costs' in relation to costs incurred by any person to whom legal aid is granted under the Church of England (Legal Aid) Measure 1994, means costs taxed or assessed in accordance with rules made under section 4 of that Measure and in relation to costs incurred by any other person means costs taxed by a registrar in the prescribed manner.

(5) Where an order for payment of taxed costs has been made under subsection (2) of this section any party to the proceedings may appeal to the chancellor of the diocese in which the proceedings took place against the registrar's taxation, and on any such appeal the chancellor may confirm or vary the registrar's taxation.

(6) An appeal under subsection (5) of this section shall be lodged and conducted in such manner as may be prescribed.

Recovery of costs

61.—(1) Where an order or direction for the payment of costs is made against any person under the last foregoing section such costs may be recovered by the person in whose favour the order for payment of costs is made by proceedings in the county court of the district in which the award or direction was made or, if the sum recoverable exceeds the amount which under any enactment for the time being in force is recoverable in the county court in respect of a contract debt, then by proceedings in the High Court of Justice, in either case in all respects as if the said sum was a contract debt payable by the person against whom the order was made.

(2) In any proceedings in a civil court for recovery of costs a certificate purporting to be signed by the registrar of the diocese or province within which the relevant award or direction for payment of costs was made, stating that the sum specified in the certificate is the sum due to be paid by the

Payments of expenses of courts, &c by Central Board

62.—(1) Save in so far as the same shall be payable by any other person under this Measure or any order or rule for the time being in force, the Central Board shall pay the costs and expenses of all courts, commissions, committees and examiners constituted or appointed under this Measure for the purpose of proceedings in respect of offences cognisable under section fourteen thereof and of the Vicar-General's court for the purpose of proceedings instituted under section four of the Care of Cathedrals (Supplementary Provisions) Measure 1994:

Provided that the Central Board before paying the whole or any part of any costs and expenses in pursuance of this section shall first be satisfied that they are reasonable in amount.

(2) The Commissioners shall have power from time to time at their absolute discretion to contribute out of their general fund such sums as they shall think fit in relief of the liability of the Central Board under the foregoing subsection.

Fees payable in or in connection with proceedings under this Measure or the Care of Cathedrals (Supplementary Provisions) Measure 1994

63. The fees to be demanded, taken and received by any legal officer as remuneration for the performance by him of the duties of his office in or in connection with any proceedings or contemplated proceedings or otherwise under or arising out of the provisions of this Measure shall be fixed in manner provided by the Ecclesiastical Fees Measure 1986.

Part XII
Miscellaneous and General

Interpretation

66.—(1) In this Measure unless the context otherwise requires the following expressions have the meanings hereby assigned to them respectively, namely:—

'authorised complainant' means a person authorised by a bishop to lay a complaint under Part III of this Measure or, in the case of proceedings against a bishop, a person authorised by the archbishop of the province;

'benefice' includes all rectories with cure of souls vicarages perpetual curacies endowed public chapels and parochial chapelries and chapelries or districts belonging or reputed to belong or annexed or reputed to be annexed to any church or chapel or districts formed for ecclesiastical purposes by virtue of statutory authority and includes benefices in the patronage of the Crown or of the Duchy of Cornwall but does not extend to any Royal peculiar nor to any cathedral or capitular preferment or dignity, nor to any chapel belonging to any college school hospital inn of court asylum or public or charitable institution nor to any private chapel;

'the Central Board' means the Central Board of Finance of the Church of England;

'the Commissioners' means the Church Commissioners for England;

'communicant' means a person who has received communion according to the use of the Church of England or of a church in communion therewith at least once within the twelve months preceding the date of his declaration that he fulfils that requirement, or if a declaration is not required of him, at least once within the twelve months preceding the date upon which he is offered the appointment or requested to act in a capacity for which that qualification is required;

'diocese' means a diocese in the province of Canterbury or a diocese ... in the province of York and 'diocesan' shall be construed accordingly;

'high judicial office' means such office within the meaning of Part 3 of the Constitutional Reform Act 2005 or membership of the Judicial Committee of the Privy Council;

'preferment' includes an archbishopric, a bishopric, archdeaconry, dignity or office in a cathedral or collegiate church, and a benefice, and every curacy, lectureship, readership, chaplaincy, office or place which requires the discharge of any spiritual duty;

'prescribed' means prescribed by rules made under section 26 of the Care of Churches and Ecclesiastical Jurisdiction Measure 1991;

'relevant province' in relation to—
(a) a House of Convocation;
(b) a diocese comprised in a province;
(c) a court having jurisdiction in a province; and
(d) a person holding any office or preferment or residing in any such diocese or province at any time;

means, according to the context, the province of Canterbury or the province of York as the case may be;

'disciplinary tribunal', 'president of tribunals' and 'provincial panel' have the same meanings as in the Clergy Discipline Measure 2003.

(2) In this Measure, except and where the context otherwise requires, references to the consistory court of a diocese and to the chancellor of a diocese shall, in their application to the diocese of Canterbury, be construed as references to the commissary court thereof and to the commissary general of such court respectively.

(3) For the purposes of this Measure an extra-diocesan place (including any place exempt or peculiar other than a Royal Peculiar) which is surrounded by one diocese shall be deemed to be situate within that diocese, and an extra-diocesan place which is surrounded by two or more dioceses shall be deemed to be situate within such one of them as the archbishop of the relevant province may direct.

(4) Nothing in this section shall prejudice or affect the provisions of subsection (2) of section six of this Measure.

Rules for determining seniority of diocesan bishops

67. For the purposes of this Measure the seniority of diocesan bishops (other than archbishops) shall be determined by reference to the length of time that each of them has held office as diocesan in either province without interruption from any cause.

Exercise of powers of diocesans during vacation of sees

68. *Repealed.*

Criminal proceedings in ecclesiastical courts to be taken only in accordance with this Measure

69. No proceedings by way of a criminal suit, other than those authorised by Part VI of this Measure, shall be instituted against a person in the consistory court of a diocese or in the Court of Ecclesiastical Causes Reserved, and no proceedings so authorised shall be instituted except in accordance with those Parts of this Measure.

Nominated persons to have exclusive right to promote complaint

70. A person nominated under Part VI of this Measure to promote a complaint against an accused person shall have the right to do so to the exclusion of all others.

Performance of ecclesiastical duties during suspension or inhibition

71.—(1) Where a censure of suspension or inhibition is pronounced against an archbishop the archbishop of the other province shall perform the functions which the archbishop against whom the censure of suspension or inhibition has been pronounced is unable to perform on account of such censure.

(2) Where a censure of suspension or inhibition is pronounced against a diocesan bishop, the archbishop of the relevant province may appoint another bishop to perform during the period of suspension or inhibition the functions the performance of which the diocesan bishop against whom

the censure of suspension or inhibition has been pronounced is unable to perform on account of such censure.

(3) Where a censure of suspension or inhibition is pronounced against a suffragan bishop, the diocesan bishop by whom he is commissioned may appoint another bishop to perform during the period of suspension or inhibition the functions which the suffragan bishop against whom the censure or suspension or inhibition has been pronounced is unable to perform on account of such censure.

(4) When a censure of suspension or inhibition is pronounced against any priest or deacon, it shall be lawful for the bishop in whose diocese such person holds preferment to appoint some person or persons to perform the duties of the preferment; and in all such cases the bishop may assign such part of and one or more of the following, that is to say, the guaranteed annuity payable in respect of the benefice under section 1 of the Endowments and Glebe Measure 1976, the personal grant, if any, to which such person is entitled under section 2 of that Measure and the profits of the benefice, as he thinks fit and may, if necessary, sequester the said profits for the payment of the part thereof so assigned.

Occupation of parsonage house by person appointed by bishop

72.—(1) A bishop who has appointed a person to perform the duties of any benefice under subsection (4) of section 71 of this Measure may require such person to reside in the parsonage house belonging thereto, and may assign to him the use of such parsonage house, together with the offices, gardens and appurtenances thereto belonging, or any part or parts thereof, without payment of any rent.

(2) A person residing in the parsonage house under the provisions of this section shall be liable to pay the rates payable in respect of such house, and any sequestrator appointed during any suspension or inhibition under this Measure shall have power to deduct from the stipend of such person any payments for which he shall be liable under this subsection.

(3) The bishop shall have power in any case in which possession of the premises allocated to any person under the provisions of this section is not given up to him, and until such possession shall be given up, to direct that the profits of the benefice arising from the sequestration thereof under this Measure be applied subject to the provisions thereof as if the same arose under a sequestration for non-residence.

(4) A right of residence and any other right vested in a person under the provisions of this section shall determine upon the determination of his appointment.

Suspension of censure pending appeal

73. In any case in which pursuant to the provisions of this Measure, an appeal is lodged against a judgment order or decree of any court or commission constituted under this Measure in proceedings charging an offence or claiming a penalty or forfeiture against a clergyman, the censure or award of the court or commission from whose judgment order or decree the appeal is made shall be suspended until the appeal is determined, but an appeal shall not affect an inhibition *pendente lite* under section 77 of this Measure.

Restrictions during a period of suspension or inhibition

74.—(1) In any case in which by reason of a censure pronounced against him a person is suspended or inhibited under this Measure for a specified time from discharging all or any of the duties attached to any office held by him:—
  (a) he shall not interfere with any other person who may be appointed to discharge any of the said duties;
  (b) subject to the provisions of the following subsection he shall not reside in or occupy any house of residence belonging to his office; and
  (c) he shall not be liable under any penalty or forfeiture for non-residence

(2) In the case of an incumbent of a parochial benefice the bishop may for special reasons permit him non-residence to reside in or occupy such house of residence or some part thereof.

(3) In the case of such an incumbent, subject to any direction to the contrary given by the bishop, he shall not receive any part of the income of the benefice while he remains resident within a distance of ten miles from the parish or other principal church of the parish or other area in which, prior to the commencement of the period of inhibition, he had the cure of souls.

Provisions as to lapse on avoidance of preferment

75. Where by virtue of anything in or done under this Measure any preferment is vacant the time for lapse shall run from the date on which the notice of the vacancy is given.

Rights of patronage during suspension or inhibition

76.—(1) In any case in which by virtue of a censure pronounced against him a person is suspended or inhibited under this Measure for a specified time from discharging all or any of the duties attaching to his preferment, any right of patronage vested in him by virtue of his preferment shall, during the period of suspension or inhibition, and subject to the provisions of the following subsection, vest in the person entitled to appoint to such preferment and so that in the case of a diocesan bishop, any such right of patronage shall vest in the archbishop of the relevant province, and, in the case of an archbishop, shall vest in the archbishop of the other province.

(2) In any case in which an incumbent is himself the patron of his benefice, the right of patronage of such benefice shall, so long as the period of suspension or inhibition remains in force, vest in the archbishop of the relevant province.

Inhibition pendente lite

77. *Repealed.*

Recording of declarations, resolutions and censures

78. Any declaration or resolution made by a bishop, or by an archbishop, or by an Upper House of Convocation or any censure pronounced by any court, pursuant to the provisions of this Measure shall be recorded in the diocesan registry concerned or in the provincial registry of the relevant province as the case may be.

When convictions, orders or findings are to be deemed conclusive

79. *Repealed.*

Place where courts, &c, are to sit

80. Any court, commission, committee or inquiry established or held by or under the provisions of this Measure and the Vicar-General's court of each of the provinces of Canterbury and York may be held in any place convenient to the court, commission, committee or person holding the inquiry, due regard being paid to the convenience of parties and witnesses.

Evidence and general powers and rights of courts and commissions

81.—(1) Any court or commission established under this Measure and the Vicar-General's Court of each of the provinces of Canterbury and York shall have the same powers as the High Court in relation to the attendance and examination of witnesses and the production and inspection of documents.

(2) If any person does or omits to do anything in connection with proceedings before, or with an order made by, such court or commission or Vicar-General's court which is in contempt of that court or commission by virtue of any enactment or which would, if the court or commission had been a court of law having power to commit for contempt, have been in contempt of that court, the judge or presiding judge of the court or the presiding member of the commission, as the case may be, may certify the act or omission under his hand to the High Court.

(3) On receiving a certificate under subsection (2) above the High Court may thereupon inquire into the alleged act or omission and after hearing any witnesses who may be produced against or on behalf of the person who is the subject of the allegation, and after hearing any statement that may be offered in defence, exercise the same jurisdiction and powers as if that person had been guilty of contempt of the High Court.

(4) In this section 'order' includes a special citation under section 13(2) of the Care of Churches and Ecclesiastical Jurisdiction Measure 1991 or section 6(1) of the Care of Cathedrals (Supplementary Provisions) Measure 1994 and an injunction under section 13(4) of the former Measure or section 6(3) of the latter Measure.

Abolition of obsolete jurisdictions, courts, &c

82. *Repealed.*

Savings

83.—(1) Any judge or registrar of an ecclesiastical court appointed to office before the commencement of this Measure shall continue in his office as if he had been appointed under this Measure and nothing contained in this Measure shall affect the terms and conditions on and subject to which his appointment was made.

(2) Nothing in this Measure affects—
- (a) any prerogative of Her Majesty the Queen; or
- (b) the existing procedure relating to the confirmation of the election of bishops; or
- (c) any power of the High Court to control the proper exercise by ecclesiastical courts of their functions; or
- (d) the mode of appointment, office, and duties of vicars-general of provinces or dioceses; or
- (e) the visitatorial powers of archdeacons; or
- (f) the mode of appointment, office and duties of the official principal or an archdeacon; or
- (g) the jurisdiction of the Master of the Faculties.

(3) Subject to the provisions of section twenty-nine of the Ecclesiastical Commissioners Act 1840, nothing in this Measure shall authorise proceedings against a holder of an office in a Royal Peculiar.

SCHEDULE 1
OATHS TO BE TAKEN BY JUDGES OF CONSISTORY, ARCHES AND CHANCERY COURTS

[Omitted]

Faculty Jurisdiction Measure 1964

Jurisdiction in faculty cases

Vesting of privately owned parts of churches in the persons in whom the churches are vested

1.—(1) In this section 'building' means any building or structure forming part of and physically connected with a church and 'incumbent' means the incumbent of the benefice comprising the parish in which the church is situated.

(2) A court may in proceedings taken by an incumbent or parochial church council grant a faculty vesting any building in the person or body in whom the church is vested where the incumbent or parochial church council satisfies the court that:—
- (i) the person in whom the church is vested is not the owner entitled to possession of the building or that there is reasonable doubt as to the ownership or right to possession thereof; and
- (ii) the incumbent or parochial church council or some other person has taken all reasonable steps since, or shortly before, the commencement of the proceedings to communicate

with all persons who may reasonably be supposed to have any rights of ownership or possession, whether absolute or limited, over the building; and

(iii) notwithstanding such reasonable steps there has been no communication with such person or persons or that all persons with whom communication has been made and who, on reasonable grounds, claim rights of ownership or possession over the building consent to the grant of a faculty under this section; and

(iv) no works of repair, redecoration or reconstruction have been executed upon the building by or on behalf of any person claiming any title thereto adverse to the title of the person in whom the church is vested during the seven years immediately preceding the commencement of the proceedings.

(3) In any proceedings for obtaining a faculty under this section the court may appoint a person being a solicitor to represent all persons other than those represented, known or unknown, who may have rights of ownership or possession over the building in question, and all proper costs of such solicitor in the proceedings shall be paid by the persons bringing the proceedings, unless otherwise ordered by the court.

(4) Where a faculty under this section is granted the buildings specified therein shall, by virtue of such faculty and without any further or other assurance or conveyance, vest in the person in whom the church is vested as part of the church for all purposes and any rights of property of any other person therein shall thereupon determine.

Faculties affecting monuments owned by persons withholding consent thereto

3.—(1) This section shall apply to faculties for the moving, demolition, alteration or execution of other work to any monument erected, whether before or after the passing of this Measure, in or upon any church or other consecrated building or the curtilage thereof or upon consecrated ground other than consecrated burial grounds to which section 11 of the Open Spaces Act 1906, applies or has been applied.

(2) Subject to the provisions of the succeeding sub-section a court may grant a faculty to which this section applies:—

(i) although the owner of the monument withholds his consent thereto or cannot be found after reasonable efforts to find him have been made; and

(ii) in respect of a monument erected under a faculty or affecting which any faculty has been granted, whatever the date of such faculty.

(3) No faculty to which this section applies shall be granted if the owner of the monument in question withholds his consent thereto but satisfies the court that he is, within a reasonable time, willing and able to remove the monument (or so much thereof as may be proved to be his property) and to execute such works as the court may require to repair any damage to the fabric of any building or to any land caused by such removal. The court may, upon a petition for a faculty to which this section applies, grant a faculty authorising such removal and for all purposes connected therewith and may make such orders as may be just as to the execution and cost of all necessary works.

(4) For the purposes of this section 'monument' includes a tomb, gravestone or other memorial and any kerb or setting forming part thereof, and 'owner' means the person who erected the monument in question and, after his death, the heir or heirs at law of the person or persons in whose memory the monument was erected and 'property' shall be construed accordingly.

Sale of books in parochial libraries under a faculty

4.—(1) Notwithstanding anything to the contrary contained in section 10 of the Parochial Libraries Act 1708, any book in a parochial library within the operation of that Act may be sold under the authority of a faculty, and in the case of every sale so authorised the proceeds of sale shall be applied for such of the ecclesiastical purposes of the parish as in such faculty may be directed. Before granting such a faculty the judge shall require the advisory committee to advise him thereon and shall consider such advice as the committee may tender to the court.

(2) Any question whether a library is within the said Act shall be finally determined by the Charity Commission.

Licensed chapels may be made subject to faculty jurisdiction

6.—(1) Where the bishop has, before the coming into force of section 11 of the Care of Churches and Ecclesiastical Jurisdiction Measure 1991 licensed a building for public worship and he considers that circumstances have arisen which make it desirable that such building should be subject to the faculty jurisdiction he may by order direct that such building shall be subject to the jurisdiction of the court of the diocese during such period as may be specified in the order.

(2) Any building in respect of which an order is made under this section shall, during the period specified in the order, be subject, together with its furnishings and contents, to the jurisdiction of the court specified in the order as though it were a consecrated church; but an order shall not require the issue of faculties confirming such acts.

(3) The bishop shall send every order made under this section to the registrar of the diocese and the registrar shall register any order so made in the diocesan registry. There shall be payable to the diocesan registrar for registering such order, for permitting searches for and giving inspection and furnishing copies of any such order such fees as may from time to time be authorised by an order made under the Ecclesiastical Fees Measure 1986.

(4) An order made under this section shall be revocable by the bishop at any time.

Curtilages of churches

7.—(1) For the avoidance of doubt it is hereby declared that where unconsecrated land forms, or is part of, the curtilage of a church within the jurisdiction of a court that court has the same jurisdiction over such land as over the church.

(2) This section shall not render unlawful any act done or proceedings taken in good faith before the passing of this Measure nor shall require the issue of faculties confirming such acts.

Rights of sepulture

Exclusive right to burial places

8.—(1) Any right to the exclusive use of any particular part of a churchyard, burial ground or other consecrated land for the purposes of sepulture, whether absolute or limited and however granted or acquired, shall cease one hundred years after the passing of this Measure, unless granted, enlarged or continued by a faculty issued after the passing of this Measure:

Provided that the court shall not issue a faculty granting enlarging or continuing any such right for any period longer than one hundred years from the date of the faculty.

(2) This section shall not apply to burial grounds and cemeteries provided under the Burial Acts 1852 to 1906, or the Public Health (Interments) Act 1879.

Parties and procedure in faculty cases

Mode of enforcing orders as to costs and expenses

11. Any sum payable by virtue of an order of the court in or consequent upon any proceeding for a faculty shall, if the county court so orders, be recoverable by execution issued from the county court or otherwise as if payable under an order of that court.

Miscellaneous

Interpretation

15. In this Measure unless the context otherwise requires:—
  'advisory committee' means the advisory committee for the care of churches of a diocese appointed under section thirteen of this Measure;
  'bishop' means the bishop of the diocese concerned;
  'church' includes any building or part of a building which is licensed for public worship according to the rites and ceremonies of the Church of England and is subject to the faculty jurisdiction;

'council' means the Central Council of Diocesan Advisory Committees for the Care of Churches, as constituted in accordance with the resolution of the Church Assembly passed on the 18th June, 1958, or any body subsequently constituted to exercise the functions of the Council as so constituted;

'court' means the ecclesiastical court of any province or diocese;

'judge' means the judge of any such court;

'prescribed' means prescribed by rules made under section twenty-six of the Care of Churches and Ecclesiastical Jurisdiction Measure 1991.

Matrimonial Causes Act 1965

Part I
Divorce, Nullity and other Matrimonial Suits

Divorce

Remarriage of divorced persons

8.—(1) *Repealed*.

(2) No clergyman of the Church of England or the Church in Wales shall be compelled—
  (a) to solemnise the marriage of any person whose former marriage has been dissolved and whose former spouse is still living; or
  (b) to permit the marriage of such a person to be solemnised in the church or chapel of which he is the minister.

Synodical Government Measure 1969

Vesting of functions and authority of Convocations in a General Synod

1.—(1) It shall be lawful for the Convocations of Canterbury and York to submit for Her Majesty's Licence and Assent Canons in the form set out in Schedule 1 to this Measure providing—
  (a) for vesting in the General Synod of the Church of England, being the Church Assembly renamed and reconstituted in accordance with this Measure, the functions, authority, rights and privileges of the said Convocations;
  (b) for modifying the functions of the said Convocations when sitting separately for their provinces;

and, if Her Majesty is pleased to grant Her Licence and Assent it shall be lawful for the said Convocations to make, promulge and execute the said Canons, which shall have full force and effect.

(2) The function so vested shall be exercisable in accordance with the Constitution of the General Synod set out in Schedule 2 to this Measure and shall be exercisable for the Church of England as a whole, instead of being exercisable provincially, but without prejudice to the making of different provision, where appropriate, for the two provinces.

(3) The provisions of sections 1 and 3 of the Submission of the Clergy Act 1533—
  (a) requiring the Queen's Assent and Licence to the making, promulging and executing of Canons by the said Convocations, and

(b) providing that no Canons shall be made or put in execution by the said Convocations which are contrary or repugnant to the Royal prerogative or the customs, laws or statutes of this realm,

shall apply in like manner to the making, promulging and executing of Canons by the General Synod.

(4) The dissolution and calling together of the said Convocations in pursuance of the Royal Writ (or otherwise under the Church of England Convocations Act 1966) shall have the effect, in accordance with the said Constitution, of dissolving and bringing into being the General Synod.

(5) The functions vested in the General Synod by the said Canons—
- (a) shall include the power of the said Convocations as declared by the Convocations of the Clergy Measure 1920, to make, promulge and execute Canons for the amendment of the Constitution of the Lower Houses thereof;
- (b) shall not include the functions of the said Convocations under the Measures mentioned in section 3 of this Measure, which shall be exercisable in accordance with that section.

Renaming and reconstitution of the Church Assembly as the General Synod

2.—(1) As from the appointed day, the Church Assembly shall be renamed the General Synod of the Church of England (and may be referred to as 'the General Synod') and shall be reconstituted in accordance with the Constitution of the General Synod set out in Schedule 2 to this Measure.

(2) References in sections 3 and 4 of the Church of England Assembly (Powers) Act 1919 and in other Measures, enactments and instruments to the Church Assembly and to its Constitution and Legislative Committee shall, as from the appointed day, be construed as references or, where the contexts so require, as including references to the General Synod and its Constitution and the Legislative Committee appointed thereunder, respectively, and any definitions of the said expressions and of 'the National Assembly of the Church of England' in section 1 of the said Act and in the Interpretation Measure 1925 shall cease to apply or be limited to the said contexts.

Functions under the Prayer Book Measures and the Ecclesiastical Jurisdiction Measure

3.— (1)–(3) *Repealed.*

(4) The powers exercisable by the said Convocations with the concurrence of the House of Laity under the Prayer Book (Versions of the Bible) Measure 1965 shall be exercisable by the General Synod.

(5) *Repealed.*

(6) The powers exercisable by the said Convocations or the Houses thereof under the Ecclesiastical Jurisdiction Measure 1963 shall continue to be exercisable by them for their respective provinces.

(7) Section 1(2) of this Measure shall apply to the functions exercisable by the General Synod under this section, and accordingly the exercise of those functions shall be subject, in particular, to Article 7 of the Constitution of the General Synod.

(8) *Repealed.*

Constitution and functions of diocesan synods

4.—(1) Diocesan synods shall be constituted for all dioceses in accordance with Part IV of the Church Representation Rules contained in Schedule 3 to this Measure and the transitional provisions contained in Schedule 4.

(2) The function of the diocesan synod shall be—
- (a) to consider matters concerning the Church of England and to make provision for such matters in relation to their diocese, and to consider and express their opinion on any other matters of religious or public interest;
- (b) to advise the bishop on any matters on which he may consult the synod;

(c) to consider and express their opinion on any matters referred to them by the General Synod, and in particular to approve or disapprove provisions referred to them by the General Synod under Article 8 of the Constitution;

(d) to consider proposals for the annual budget for the diocese and to approve or disapprove them;

(e) to consider the annual accounts of the diocesan board of finance of the diocese:

Provided that the functions referred to in paragraph (a) hereof shall not include the issue of any statement purporting to declare the doctrine of the Church on any question.

(3) It shall be the duty of the bishop to consult with the diocesan synod on matters of general concern and importance to the diocese.

(4) Except as may be provided by standing orders or directions of the diocesan synod, the advisory and consultative functions of the synod under subsections (2)(b) and (3) of this section may be discharged on behalf of the synod by the bishops council and standing committee appointed in accordance with rule 28 of the Church Representation Rules contained in Schedule 3 to this Measure, but either the bishop or the body so appointed may require any matter to be referred to the synod.

(5) The diocesan synod shall keep the deanery synods of the diocese informed of the policies and problems of the diocese and of the business which is to come before meetings of the diocesan synod, and may delegate executive functions to deanery synods; and shall keep themselves informed, through the deanery synods, of events and opinion in the parishes, and shall give opportunities for discussing at meetings of the diocesan synod matters raised by deanery synods and parochial church councils.

(6) The General Synod may by Canon or Regulation extend, amend or further define functions of diocesan synods, and if any question arises as to whether any matter falls within the functions of a diocesan synod as laid down by subsection (2) of this section or any such Canon or Regulation relating to that subsection, it shall be decided by the bishop.

(7) As soon as a diocesan synod has been constituted, the diocesan conference shall be dissolved and all functions exercisable by the diocesan conference shall be transferred to the diocesan synod, and any reference in any Measure or instrument to diocesan conferences shall be construed as references to diocesan synods:

Provided that nothing herein shall prevent the bishop from summoning a conference of persons appearing to him to be representative of the clergy and laity of the diocese, on such occasions and for such purposes as he thinks fit.

Constitution and functions of deanery synods

5.—(1) Deanery synods shall be constituted for all deaneries in accordance with Part III of the Church Representation Rules contained in Schedule 3 to this Measure and the transitional provisions contained in Schedule 4.

(2) Deanery synods shall, as soon as they are constituted, take the place of ruri-decanal conferences where they exist, and those conferences shall thereupon be dissolved, and any references in any Measure to ruri-decanal conferences shall be construed as references to deanery synods.

(3) The functions of a deanery synod shall be:

(a) to consider matters concerning the Church of England and to make provision for such matters in relation to their deanery, and to consider and express their opinion on any other matters of religious or public interest;

(b) to bring together the views of the parishes of the deanery on common problems, to discuss and formulate common policies on those problems, to foster a sense of community and interdependence among those parishes, and generally to promote in the deanery the whole mission of the Church, pastoral, evangelistic, social and ecumenical;

(c) to make known, and so far as appropriate put into effect any provision made by the diocesan synod;

(d) to consider the business of the diocesan synod, and particularly any matters referred to that synod by the General Synod, and to sound parochial opinion whenever they are required or consider it appropriate to do so;

(e) to raise such matters as the deanery synod consider appropriate with the diocesan synod:

Provided that the functions referred to in paragraph (a) hereof shall not include the issue of any statement purporting to declare the doctrine of the Church on any question.

(4) If the diocesan synod delegate to deanery synods functions in relation to the parishes of their deaneries, and in particular the determination of parochial shares in quotas allocated to the deaneries, the deanery synod shall exercise those functions.

In this subsection 'quota' means an amount to be subscribed to the expenditure authorised by diocesan synods.

(5) The General Synod may by Canon or Regulation extend, amend or further define the functions of deanery synods.

Church Representation Rules

7.—(1) The rules contained in Schedule 3 to this Measure, which may be cited as the Church Representation Rules,[1] shall have effect for the purpose of providing for the constitution and proceedings of diocesan and deanery synods and making further provision for the synodical government of the Church, including the matters hitherto provided for by the Rules for the Representation of the Laity:

Provided that the said rules may at any time be amended by a resolution of the General Synod passed by a majority in each House of not less than two-thirds of those present and voting.

(2) The Statutory Instruments Act 1946 shall apply to any such resolution as if it were a statutory instrument and as if this Measure were an Act providing that it should be subject to annulment in pursuance of a resolution of either House of Parliament.

(3) *Repealed.*

SCHEDULE 1
FORM OF PROPOSED CANON

[Omitted]

SCHEDULE 2
CONSTITUTION OF THE GENERAL SYNOD

Section 2

1. The General Synod shall consist of the Convocations of Canterbury and York joined together in a House of Bishops and a House of Clergy and having added to them a House of Laity.

2. The House of Bishops and the House of Clergy shall accordingly comprise the Upper and the Lower Houses respectively of the said Convocation, and the House of Laity shall be elected and otherwise constituted in accordance with the Church Representation Rules.

3.—(1) The General Synod shall meet in session at least twice a year, and at such times and places as it may provide, or, in the absence of such provision, as the Joint Presidents of the Synod may direct.

(2) The General Synod shall, on the dissolution of the Convocations, itself be automatically dissolved, and shall come into being on the calling together of the new Convocations.

---

[1] For convenience these are reproduced in a separate section of the Materials at pp 617 ff.

(3) Business pending at the dissolution of the General Synod shall not abate, but may be resumed by the new Synod at the stage reached before the dissolution, and any Boards, Commissions, Committees or other bodies of the Synod may, so far as may be appropriate and subject to any Standing Orders of any directions of the Synod or of the Archbishops of Canterbury and York, continue their proceedings during the period of the dissolution, and all things may be done by the Archbishops or any such bodies or any officers of the General Synod as may be necessary or expedient for conducting the affairs of the Synod during the period of dissolution and for making arrangements for the resumption of business by the new Synod.

(4) A member of the General Synod may continue to act during the period of the dissolution as a member of any such Board, Commission, Committee or body:

Provided that, if a member of the Synod who is an elected proctor of the clergy or an elected member of the House of Laity does not stand for re-election or is not re-elected, this paragraph shall cease to apply to him with effect from the date on which the election of this successor is announced by the presiding officer.

4.—(1) The Archbishops of Canterbury and York shall be joint Presidents of the General Synod, and they shall determine the occasions on which it is desirable that one of the Presidents shall be the chairman of a meeting of the General Synod, and shall arrange between them which of them is to take the chair on any such occasion:

Provided that one of the Presidents shall be the Chairman when any motion is taken for the final approval of a provision to which Article 7 of this Constitution applies and in such order cases as may be provided in Standing Orders.

(2) The Presidents shall, after consultation with the Appointments Committee of the Church of England, appoint from among the members of any House of the Synod a panel of such number of persons as the Presidents may determine, who shall be available to take the chair at meetings of the Synod, being persons who shall be chosen for their experience of chairing and ability to chair meetings; and it shall be the duty of one of the persons on the panel, in accordance with arrangements approved by the Presidents and subject to any special directions of the Presidents, to take the chair at meetings of the Synod at which neither of the Presidents take the chair.

(3) The Provincial Registrars shall be Joint Registrars of the General Synod.

5.—(1) A motion for the final approval of any Measure or Canon shall not be deemed to be carried unless, on a division by Houses, it receives the assent of the majority of the members of each House present and voting:

Provided that by permission of the chairman and with the leave of the General Synod given in accordance with Standing Orders this requirement may be dispensed with.

(2) All other motions of the General Synod shall, subject as hereinafter provided, be determined by a majority of the members of the Synod present and voting, and the vote may be taken by a show of hands or a division:

Provided that, except in the case of a motion relating solely to the course of business or procedure, any 25 members present may demand a division by Houses and in that case the motion shall not be deemed to be carried unless, on such a division, it receives the assent of the majority of the members of each House present and voting.

(3) The Article shall be subject to any provision of this Constitution or of any Measure with respect to special majorities of the Synod or of each House thereof, and where a special majority of each House is required the vote shall be taken on a division by Houses, and where a special majority of the whole Synod is required, the motion shall, for the purposes of this Article, be one relating solely to procedure.

(4) Without prejudice to Article 11(1) below, where a vote is to be taken by a division either of the whole Synod or by Houses, Standing Orders may provide for the vote to be taken either by physical separation of the members voting or by other means including such electronic method of voting as may from time to time be determined by the Business Committee.

6. The functions of the General Synod shall be as follows:—
   (a) to consider matters concerning the Church of England and to make provision in respect thereof—
      (i) by Measure intended to be given, in the manner prescribed by the Church of England Assembly (Powers) Act 1919, the force and effect of an Act of Parliament, or
      (ii) by Canon made, promulged and executed in accordance with the like provisions and subject to the like restrictions and having the like legislative force as Canons heretofore made, promulged and executed by the Convocations of Canterbury and York, or
      (iii) by such order, regulation or other subordinate instrument as may be authorised by Measure or Canon; or
      (iv) by such Act of Synod, regulation or other instrument or proceeding as may be appropriate in cases where provision by or under a Measure or Canon is not required;
   (b) to consider and express their opinion on any other matters of religious or public interest.

7.—(1) A provision touching doctrinal formulae or the services or ceremonies of the Church of England or the administration of the Sacraments or sacred rites thereof shall, before it is finally approved by the General Synod, be referred to the House of Bishops, and shall be submitted for such final approval in terms proposed by the House of Bishops and not otherwise.

(2) A provision touching any of the matters aforesaid shall, if the Convocations or either of them or the House of Laity so require, be referred, in the terms proposed by the House of Bishops for final approval by the General Synod, to the two Convocations sitting separately for their provinces and to the House of Laity; and no provision so referred shall be submitted for final approval by the General Synod unless it has been approved, in the terms so proposed, by each House of the two Convocations sitting as aforesaid and by the House of Laity.

(3) The question whether such a reference is required by a Convocation shall be decided by the President and Prolocutor of the Houses of that Convocation, and the Prolocutor shall consult the Standing Committee of the Lower House of Canterbury or, as the case may be, the Assessors of the Lower House of York, and the decision of the President and Prolocutor shall be conclusive:

Provided that if, before such a decision is taken, either House of a Convocation resolves that the provision concerned shall be so referred or both Houses resolve that it shall not be so referred, the resolution or resolutions shall be a conclusive decision that the reference is or is not required by that Convocation.

(4) The question whether such a reference is required by the House of Laity shall be decided by the Prolocutor and Pro-Prolocutor of that House who shall consult the Standing Committee of that House, and the decision of the Prolocutor and the Pro-Prolocutor shall be conclusive:

Provided that if, before such a decision is taken, the House of Laity resolves that the reference is or is not required, the resolution shall be a conclusive decision of that question.

(5) Standing Orders of the General Synod shall provide for ensuring that a provision which fails to secure approval on a reference under this Article by each of the four Houses of the Convocations or by the House of Laity of the General Synod is not proposed again in the same or a similar form until a new General Synod comes into being, except that, in the case of objection by one House or one Convocation only, provision may be made for a second reference to the Convocations and, in the case of a second objection by one House only, for reference to the Houses of Bishops and Clergy of the General Synod for approval by a two-thirds majority of the members of each House present and voting, in lieu of such approval by the four Houses aforesaid.

(6) If any question arises whether the requirements of this Article or Standing Orders made thereunder apply to any provision, or whether those requirements have been complied with, it shall be conclusively determined by the Presidents and Prolocutors of the Houses of the Convocations and the Prolocutor and Pro-Prolocutor of the House of Laity of the General Synod.

8.—(1) A Measure or Canon providing for permanent changes in the Services of Baptism or Holy Communion or in the Ordinal, or a scheme for a constitutional union or a permanent and substantial change of a relationship between the Church of England and another Christian body being a body a substantial number of whose members reside in Great Britain, shall not be finally approved by the General Synod unless, at a stage determined by the Archbishops, the Measure or Canon or scheme, or the substance of the proposals embodied therein, has been approved by a majority of the dioceses at meetings of their Diocesan Synods or, in the case of the diocese in Europe, of the bishop's council and standing committee of that diocese.

(1A) If the Archbishops consider that this Article should apply to a scheme which affects the Church of England and another Christian body but does not fall within paragraph (1) of this Article, they may direct that this Article shall apply to that scheme, and where such a direction is given this Article shall apply accordingly.

(1B) The General Synod may by resolution provide that final approval of any such scheme as aforesaid, being a scheme specified in the resolution, shall require the assent of such special majorities of the members present and voting as may be specified in the resolution, and the resolution may specify a special majority of each House or of the whole Synod or of both, and in the latter case the majorities may be different.

(1C) A motion for the final approval of a Measure providing for permanent changes in any such Service or in the Ordinal shall not be deemed to be carried unless it receives the assent of a majority in each House of the General Synod of not less than two-thirds of those present and voting.

(2) Any question whether this Article applies to any Measure or Canon or scheme, or whether its requirements have been complied with, shall be conclusively determined by the Archbishops, the Prolocutors of the Lower Houses of the Convocations and the Prolocutor and Pro-Prolocutor of the House of Laity of the General Synod.

9.—(1) Standing Orders of the General Synod may provide for separate sittings of any of the three Houses or joint sittings of any two Houses, and as to who is to take the chair at any such separate or joint sitting.

(2) The House of Laity shall elect a Chairman and Vice-Chairman of that House who shall also discharge the functions assigned by this Constitution and the Standing Orders and by or under any Measure or Canon to the Prolocutor and Pro-Prolocutor of that House.

10.—(1) The General Synod shall appoint a Legislative Committee from members of all three Houses, to whom shall be referred all Measures passed by the General Synod which it is desired should be given, in accordance with the procedure prescribed by the Church of England Assembly (Powers) Act 1919, the force of an Act of Parliament; and it shall be the duty of the Legislative Committee to take such steps with respect to any such Measure as may be so prescribed.

(2) The General Synod may appoint or provide by their Standing Orders for the appointment of such Committees, Commissions and other bodies (in addition to the Committees mentioned in section 10 of the National Institutions Measure 1998), which may include persons who are not members of the Synod, and such officers as they think fit.

(3) Each House may appoint or provide by their Standing Orders for the appointment of such Committees of their members as they think fit.

11.—(1) The General Synod may make, amend and revoke Standing Orders providing for any of the matters for which such provision is required or authorised by this Constitution to be made, and consistently with this Constitution, for the meetings, business and procedure of the General Synod.

(1A) Provision may be made by Standing Order that the exercise of any power of the General Synod to suspend the Standing Orders or any of them shall require the assent of such a majority of the members of the whole Synod present and voting as may be specified in the Standing Order.

(2) Each House may make, amend and revoke Standing Orders for the matter referred to in Article 10(3) hereof and consistently with this Constitution and with any Standing Orders of the General Synod, for the separate sittings, business and procedure of that House.

(3) Subject to this Constitution and to any Standing Orders, the business and procedure at any meeting of the General Synod or any House or Houses thereof shall be regulated by the chairman of the meeting.

12.—(1) References to final approval shall, in relation to a Canon or Act of Synod be construed as referring to the final approval by the General Synod of the contents of the Canon or Act, and not to the formal promulgation thereof:

Provided that the proviso to Article 4(1) shall apply both to the final approval and to the formal promulgation of a Canon or Act of Synod.

(2) Any question concerning the interpretation of this Constitution, other than questions for the determination of which express provision is otherwise made, shall be referred to and determined by the Archbishops of Canterbury and York.

(3) No proceedings of the General Synod or any House or Houses thereof, or any Board, Commission, Committee or body thereof shall be invalidated by any vacancy in the membership of the body concerned or by any defect in the qualification, election or appointment of any member thereof.

13. Any functions exercisable under this Constitution by the Archbishops of Canterbury and York, whether described as such or as Presidents of the General Synod, may, during the absence abroad or incapacity through illness of one Archbishop or a vacancy in one of the Sees, be exercised by the other Archbishop alone.

Sharing of Church Buildings Act 1969

Agreements for sharing church buildings

1.—(1) It shall be lawful, notwithstanding any statutory or other legal provision, for any two or more Churches to which this Act applies to make agreements, through the parties mentioned in this section and in accordance with the provisions thereof, for the sharing by them of church buildings, and to carry such agreements into effect, and such agreements are in this Act referred to as 'sharing agreement'.

(2) A sharing agreement may be made in respect of a single church building or two or more church buildings in the same locality, and in respect of any existing or proposed church building, and, subject to the following provisions of this Act relating to consecrated churches of the Church of England and the sharing of residential buildings, may provide for the shared building or any of the shared buildings to be owned or continue to be owned by one only of the sharing Churches or to be jointly owned by all or some of the sharing Churches.

(3) The parties to a sharing agreement shall—
(a) as respects the Church of England, be the Diocesan Board of Finance of the diocese and the incumbent and parochial church council of the parish in which the building or buildings is or are or will be situated and, where a team ministry is established for the benefice comprising that parish,—
    (i) any vicar in the team ministry to whom a special cure of souls in respect of the parish has been assigned by a scheme under the Pastoral Measure 1983 or by his licence from the bishop; or
    (ii) any member of the team to whom a special responsibility for pastoral care in respect of the parish has been assigned under section 20(8A) of that Measure, the parish not being one in respect of which a special cure of souls has been assigned as mentioned in paragraph (i) above
(b) as respects any other Church, be such persons as may be determined by the appropriate authority of that Church;

and shall also include, in the case of an existing building, the person (if not otherwise a party) in whom the building is vested and any managing trustees thereof, and may also include, in the case of a proposed building, any person in whom it is to be vested or who is to be a managing trustee thereof.

(4) A sharing agreement shall not be made on behalf of the Church of England without the consent of the bishop and the Pastoral Committee of the diocese concerned, and the appropriate authority of any other Church to which this Act applies may require the consent of any body or person specified by the authority to be given to sharing agreements made on behalf of that Church.

(5) Where a church building is held on trust for educational purposes which include instruction in religious knowledge according to the faith and practice of the Church of England, the consent of the Diocesan Education Committee of the diocese concerned to a sharing agreement in respect of that building shall be required in lieu of the consent of the Pastoral Committee thereof, and the agreement shall be subject to the approval of the Secretary of State.

(6) Where a benefice is vacant and a suspension period is current under section 67 of the Pastoral Measure 1968, subsection (3)(a) of this section shall have effect with the substitution for the reference to the incumbent of a reference to the minister in charge of the parish, but otherwise a sharing agreement shall not be made on behalf of the Church of England during a vacancy in the benefice concerned.

(7) Where a see is vacant, or the bishop of the diocese is unable because of illness or absence to give his consent under subsection (4) of this section, the archbishop of the province may appoint by an instrument under his hand a suffragan or assistant bishop or an archdeacon of the diocese to act in place of the bishop under the said subsection for a period specified in the instrument; and in the event of a vacancy in the see of an archbishop or his illness or absence, and appointment under this subsection, either in respect of the see of the archbishop or another see in the province, may be made by the other archbishop.

(8) A sharing agreement shall be under seal and shall be registered, in the case of the Church of England, in the registries of the province and diocese, and, in the case of other Churches, in the registry or office of the appropriate authority, and the consent required as aforesaid shall be signified in writing by the secretary or clerk of the body concerned or by the person concerned and shall be registered with the deed.

(9) A sharing agreement shall be binding on the successors to the parties thereto, that is to say, on the persons who would at any subsequent time be required to be parties if the agreement were then being made, and any reference in this Act to the parties to a sharing agreement shall be construed, as respects anything done at a subsequent time, as referring to the said persons.

(10) A sharing agreement may be amended by agreement of the parties thereto and with the consents that would then be required to a new sharing agreement.

Trusts of shared church buildings

2.—(1) Where a sharing agreement is made with respect to an existing or proposed church building which is to be owned or continue to be owned by one only of the sharing Churches, the trusts or purposes on or for which the building is held or to be held shall include the purposes and provisions of the agreement, as for the time being in force, and any instrument declaring those trusts and purposes shall be deemed to have effect, or (in the case of a proposed building) shall provide, accordingly.

(2) Where a sharing agreement is made with respect to an existing or proposed church building which is to be owned jointly by all or some of the sharing Churches, that ownership shall be effected by vesting the building in trustees representing those Churches, or in a custodian trustee with managing trustees representing those Churches, to be held on trust to be used for the purposes of the sharing agreement and in accordance with its terms and, subject thereto, for such other charitable purposes of the sharing Churches as may be appropriate, and the trust instrument relating to the building shall provide accordingly.

(3) The body or person in whom an existing church building is vested shall have power, notwithstanding any statutory or other legal provision, to convey the building to the managing trustees or custodian trustee aforesaid, for such consideration (if any) as may be provided in the sharing agreement or determined thereunder.

(4) The references in this section to a custodian trustee shall, subject to the making of such an order as is required by the Charities Act 1993 for the vesting of property in the official custodian for charities, include references to the said custodian.

(5) The purposes of a sharing agreement shall be limited to purposes which are exclusively charitable according to the law of England and Wales.

Financial and management provisions

3.—(1) A sharing agreement shall make provision with respect to the financial and other obligations of the parties thereto in respect of the provision, improvement and management of the church building or buildings shared or to be shared under the agreement, and the powers of any body or person under any statutory or other legal provision to apply money, whether by grant or loan, in respect of the provision, improvement or management of church buildings of a Church to which this Act applies shall be applicable in like manner in respect of any church building shared or to be shared by that Church under a sharing agreement.

(2) The powers of any body or person under any statutory or other legal provision—
  (a) to acquire, hold, improve or manage church buildings of a Church to which this Act applies, or any property to be used for or in connection with the provision of such church buildings, or
  (b) to grant property for or in connection with the provision of such church buildings, whether for a full consideration or for less than a full consideration,

shall be applicable in like manner in respect of any church building to which a sharing agreement relates and which, under the agreement, is or is to be owned by that Church or jointly owned by that Church and any other Church or Churches, and any such power to hold church buildings shall include a power to be a trustee (representing that Church) of such a jointly owned church building or, in the case of a corporation aggregate, to be the custodian trustee thereof.

(3) The powers of the Church Commissioners under the New Housing Areas (Church Buildings) Measure 1954, and the powers of the said Commissioners and certain other bodies and persons under sections 13 and 14 of the New Parishes Measure 1943 (which relate to the provision and improvement of church buildings), shall not be applicable for the purposes mentioned in the foregoing provisions of this section except as may be provided by a Measure of the Church Assembly extending the said Measures.

(4) The responsibility for the management of a church building owned by one only of the sharing Churches under a sharing agreement and of its contents shall remain with the authorities of or trustees representing that Church, but that responsibility shall be discharged in accordance with the provisions of the agreement and any arrangements made thereunder, including provisions or arrangements for consultation with any other sharing Church and for the payment of contributions by any other sharing Church towards the expenses of management.

(5) Where a sharing agreement provides for the joint ownership of the shared building by all or some of the sharing Churches, the responsibility of the trustees for the management of the building shall be in place of any responsibility of the authorities of the sharing Churches as respects that building, including responsibility under any statutory or other legal provision:
Provided that—
  (a) the trustees shall discharge that responsibility in accordance with the provisions of the sharing agreement and any arrangements made thereunder, including provisions or arrangements for consultation with any sharing Church which is not a joint owner and for the payment of contributions by the sharing Churches towards the expenses of management;
  (b) the agreement may provide that any moveables required for the worship of any sharing Church shall be the responsibility of the authorities of that Church.

(6) In this section 'management', in relation to a church building, includes the repair and furnishing of the building.

Sharing of church buildings for purposes of worship

4.—(1) A sharing agreement shall make provision, in the case of a building used as a place of worship, for determining the extent to which it is to be available for worship in accordance with the forms of service and practice of the sharing Churches respectively, and may provide for the holding of such joint services on such occasions as may be approved by those Churches, and may dispense, to such extent as may be necessary, with the requirement to hold certain services of the Church of England on Sundays and other days.

(2) Notwithstanding any statutory or other legal provision, a minister, reader or lay preacher of one of the Churches sharing a church building under a sharing agreement may, by invitation of a minister, reader or lay preacher of another such Church, take part in conducting worship in that building in accordance with the forms of service and practice of that other Church; but the rights given by this subsection shall be exercised in accordance with any rules or directions given by either Church and to any limitation imposed by or under the sharing agreement.

(3) Subject to the foregoing provisions of this section, the participation of the communities of the sharing Churches in each other's worship shall be governed by the practices and disciplines of those Churches in like manner as if they worshipped in separate buildings.

Consecrated churches and parish churches of Church of England

5.—(1) A sharing agreement shall not be made with respect to an existing consecrated church of the Church of England unless—
  (a) the church will under the agreement remain in the sole ownership of the Church of England; or
  (b) authority to make the agreement on behalf of the Church of England is given by a pastoral scheme under the Pastoral Measure 1968 as extended for the purpose by a subsequent Measure of the Church Assembly, and the Church will under the agreement be in the joint ownership of the Church of England and another Church or Churches.

(2) Where a sharing agreement is made on behalf of the Church of England with respect to a church building used or to be used as a place of worship, but not an existing consecrated church, the building shall not be consecrated unless it will under the agreement be in the sole ownership of the Church of England.

(3) Where a sharing agreement relates to a consecrated church, the faculty jurisdiction shall not apply in respect of movables required for the worship of any sharing Church other than the Church of England.

(4) Where a church building being a place of worship is shared by the Church of England under a sharing agreement:—
  (a) if the agreement provides for the sole ownership of the building by the Church of England, but not otherwise, the building may become or remain a parish church;
  (b) in any case the agreement shall not prevent or affect the designation of the building as a parish centre of worship under section 29 of the Pastoral Measure 1968.

Solemnization of marriages in shared or other inter-denominational buildings

6.—(1) A church building to which a sharing agreement relates (including a building in the sole ownership of the Church of England) may be certified under the Places of Worship Registration Act 1855 as a place of religious worship of any Church sharing the building other than the Church of England, and the provisions of the Marriage Act 1949 relating to the registration of buildings shall apply for and in relation to the registration of any such church building certified as aforesaid, subject to the modifications specified in Schedule 1 to this Act.

(2) The provisions of the Marriage Act 1949 relating to the publication of banns and the solemnization of marriages according to the rites of the Church of England shall apply to a church

building shared by the Church of England under a sharing agreement, and shall so apply notwithstanding that the building is registered under Part III of the Act, and accordingly—
  (a) if the building is a parish church or parish centre of worship, the said provisions shall apply as they apply to other parish churches and parish centres of worship: and
  (b) in any other case, section 20 of the said Act (which provides for the licensing of chapels for such publication and solemnization) shall apply.

(3) The proviso to section 26(2) of the said Act shall not apply to a church building to which a sharing agreement relates, except in respect of marriages to be solemnized according to the rites of the Church of England.

(4) Where a chapel of any university, college, school, hospital or other public or charitable institution, or a building held on trust for purposes of public worship but not a church building to which a sharing agreement relates, is used for the purposes of public worship in accordance with the forms of service and practice of two or more Churches to which this Act applies, the foregoing provisions of this section shall apply thereto in like manner as they apply to church buildings to which a sharing agreement relates, except that—
  (a) the provisions of Schedule 1 shall not apply;
  (b) in subsection (2)(b) of this section the reference to section 20 of the Marriage Act 1949 shall include a reference to section 21 of that Act.

(5) This section (except where it refers to parish centres of worship) shall apply to the Church in Wales in like manner as it applies to the Church of England.

Sharing of residential buildings

7.—(1) Where a sharing agreement is made with respect to a church building or buildings proposed to be used under the agreement as a residence or residences for ministers or lay workers, the purpose of the agreement shall be to provide residential accommodation, whether in the form of separate residences or otherwise, available for occupation by the ministers or lay workers of the sharing Churches in accordance with arrangements made under the agreement.

(2) Where under any such agreement a separate residence is let to an incumbent of the Church of England in his corporate capacity, it shall be the residence house of the benefice during the term of the lease.

(3) A sharing agreement shall not be made with respect to an existing residence house of a benefice of the Church of England, unless authority to make the agreement on behalf of that Church is given by a pastoral scheme under the Pastoral Measure 1968 as extended for the purpose by a subsequent Measure of the Church Assembly.

(4) No right of pre-emption, or provision for the property to revert to previous ownership, shall be exercisable or operate on the conveyance, vesting or disposal of such an existing residence house under section 2 or section 9 of this Act (except section 9(4)).

Application to shared buildings of certain provisions of Charities Act 1960

8.—(1) A sharing agreement with respect to any church building shall not affect any exception or exemption for the building from any provisions of the Charities Act 1993.

(2) A sharing agreement with respect to any church building which under the agreement is owned by the Church of England shall not affect the application to the building of section 96(2) of the Charities Act 1993 (which excludes from the definition of 'charity' certain corporations of the Church of England in respect of their corporate property and certain trusts of consecrated property).

(3) Section 36 of the Charities Act 1993 (restrictions on dispositions of charity land) shall not apply to the conveyance, vesting or disposal of church buildings under section 2 or section 9 of this Act.

Termination of sharing

9.—(1) A sharing agreement shall contain provisions for terminating the sharing of the church building or buildings, and such provisions may—
 (a) if the agreement relates to two or more buildings, provide for terminating the sharing of any building before the others; and
 (b) if there are two or more sharing Churches, provide for the withdrawal of any Church from the sharing of any church building, not being a Church which is the sole owner or previous owner of the building;

and the sharing agreement may make provision for financial adjustments as between the Churches, on such termination or withdrawal, by payments out of moneys held for the purposes of the sharing agreement or of any shared building or by other payments by one Church to another.

(2) On the termination of the sharing of a church building owned by one only of the sharing Churches, the building shall be held on the trusts or for the purposes on or for which it was held before the sharing agreement or would be held but for the sharing agreement.

(3) On the termination of the sharing of a church building jointly owned by all or some of the sharing Churches, being a building which before the sharing agreement was owned by one only of those Churches, the building shall, without any conveyance or other assurance, vest as follows:—
 (a) if the building was previously a consecrated church of the Church of England or a building (other than a consecrated church) vested in the incumbent of a Church of England parish, it shall vest in the incumbent of the parish in which the building is then situated, for the same purposes as before, as nearly as may be;
 (b) in any other case, it shall vest in such of the trustees in whom the building is vested as represent the Church who previously owned the building or, if the building is vested in a custodian trustee, it shall remain so vested but be managed by such of the managing trustees as represent that Church, and it shall be held and managed on the trusts or for the same purposes as before, as nearly as may be.

(4) Where the sharing of a church building jointly owned as aforesaid but not previously owned by one only of the sharing Churches is terminated, the sharing agreement and the trust instrument may provide for the disposal of the building (including disposal to one of the sharing Churches) and for the application of the proceeds to charitable purposes of the sharing Churches.

Cathedrals, peculiars, extra-diocesan and extra-parochial churches of the Church of England

10.—(1) No sharing agreement shall be made with respect to a cathedral church or peculiar of the Church of England or any church building of that Church situated in an extra-diocesan or extra-parochial place.

(2) The dean or provost and chapter of such a cathedral church may, notwithstanding any statutory or other legal provision, authorise a chapel or other part of the cathedral church to be used for the purposes of public worship in accordance with the forms of service and practice of two or more Churches to which this Act applies, and section 6 of this Act shall apply to any such chapel or part of a cathedral church in like manner as it applies to a chapel of any such institution as is mentioned in subsection (4) of that section.

(3) Nothing in this section shall be taken as preventing a church building in an extra-diocesan or extra-parochial place being used, otherwise than in pursuance of a sharing agreement, by two or more Churches to which this Act applies, or as preventing the application of section 6(4) of this Act to such a church building.

Churches to which this Act applies, and appropriate authorities thereof

11.—(1) The Churches to which this Act applies are the Churches specified in the first column of Schedule 2 to this Act, the Church of England and all other Churches who give notice under subsection (3) of this section.

(2) The expression 'appropriate authority', in relation to each of the Churches specified in the first column of Schedule 2 to this Act, means the authority specified in the second column of the

Schedule in respect of that Church, and if different authorities are specified in relation to different provisions of this Act, means in each such provision the authority specified in relation thereto.

(3) Any Church for the time being represented on the General Council of the British Council of Churches or on the governing body of the Evangelical Alliance or the British Evangelical Council may give notice in writing to the General Secretary of the British Council of Churches or as the case may be of the governing body concerned, that it desires that this Act should apply to the Church, and the notice shall specify the appropriate authority or authorities of that Church for the purposes of this Act, and the General Secretary concerned shall publish in the London Gazette a notice signed by him—

    (a) stating that the Church concerned is represented on the said General Council or governing body and has expressed its desire that this Act should apply to that Church;

    (b) stating that this Act will apply to that Church as from the date of publication of the notice; and

    (c) specifying the appropriate authority or authorities of that Church for the purposes of this Act;

and thereupon this Act shall apply to that Church as from that date and shall have effect as if an entry in respect of that Church and the appropriate authority or authorities so specified were made in Schedule 2 thereto.

Interpretation

12.—(1) In this Act, unless the context otherwise requires,—

'building' includes a part of a building;

'church building' means a building used or proposed to be used by a Church or Churches to which this Act applies—

    (a) as a place of worship;

    (b) as a church hall or centre available wholly or mainly for activities other than worship;

    (c) as a youth club or centre or youth hostel;

    (d) as a residence or residences for ministers or lay workers:

Provided that—

    (i) a sharing agreement may provide for including any land (other than land used or appropriated for use for burials) or out-buildings held or to be held with a church building, and any easements or rights enjoyed or to be enjoyed with a church building, and references to a church building shall in relation to that agreement, be construed accordingly;

    (ii) the said expression shall not include any school;

'consecrated' means consecrated for the purpose of public worship according to the rites and ceremonies of the Church of England;

'Diocesan Board of Finance' means the Board of that name constituted under the Diocesan Board of Finance Measure 1925 for that diocese:

Provided that, if the bishop certifies that a board of finance not so constituted or a body constituted for the holding on trust of diocesan property is to be treated for the purposes of this Measure as the Diocesan Board of Finance for that diocese, the board or body so certified shall be so treated;

'Diocesan Education Committee' means a committee constituted in accordance with the Schedule to the Diocesan Education Committees Measure 1955 or in accordance with an order made by the Secretary of State under that Measure;

'statutory or other legal provision' means any Act or Measure, any instrument or document made or having effect under or by virtue of any Act or Measure, any other instrument or document affecting legal rights or obligations, any trust (whether arising under a trust instrument or otherwise), and any rule of law, being an Act, Measure, instrument, document, trust, or rule in force at the passing of this Act:

Provided that the said expression shall not include a lease or tenancy of a church building or any mortgage, charge, covenant or rights affecting a church building and operating for the benefit of persons other than a Church to which this Act applies, or any general Act of Parliament regulating or affecting the use of land.

(2) For the purposes of this Act, a church building shall be deemed to be owned by a Church if the building is held by any body or person, whether for a freehold or leasehold estate, for purposes of that Church or on behalf of that Church, and, in the case of a leasehold building, any reference to the conveyance or vesting of the building shall be construed as a reference to the conveyance or vesting of the leasehold estate.

(3) If it is certified by the Church Commissioners that the ownership of a consecrated Church of the Church of England cannot be ascertained with certainty, and that the Church ought to be treated as vested in the incumbent of the parish in which it is situated, the Church shall be deemed for the purposes of this Act to be so vested.

(4) Any reference in this Act to any Act or Measure shall be construed as a reference to that Act or Measure as amended by any subsequent Act or Measure.

Saving for temporary loans of church buildings

13. Nothing in this Act shall be taken as affecting any practice of a Church to which this Act applies of lending church buildings temporarily for particular occasions to other religious bodies.

SCHEDULE 1
MODIFICATIONS OF PROVISIONS OF THE MARRIAGE ACT 1949 RELATING TO THE REGISTRATION OF BUILDINGS, IN THEIR APPLICATION TO SHARED CHURCH BUILDINGS

[Omitted]

SCHEDULE 2
CHURCHES AND THEIR APPROPRIATE AUTHORITIES

Section 11

Name of Church	Appropriate Authority or Authorities
Any Church of the Baptist Denomination	As respects section 1(3) and (4), the Baptist Trust Corporation as hereinafter defined, acting with the concurrence of the Church meeting. As respects section 1(8), the Baptist Trust Corporation.
Any Church of the Congregational Denomination	As respects section 1(3) and (4), the Congregational Trust Corporation as hereinafter defined, acting with the concurrence of the Church meeting. As respects section 1(8), the Congregational Trust Corporation.
Any Congregation of the Association of Churches of Christ in Great Britain and Ireland	As respects section 1(3) and (4), the Annual Conference of the Association of Churches of Christ acting with the concurrence of the duly constituted Church meeting. As respects section 1(8), the Annual Conference of the Association of Churches of Christ.
The Methodist Church	The Annual Conference of the Methodist Church.
The Presbyterian Church of England	The Presbytery in whose bounds the church building or buildings is or are or will be situated.
The United Reformed Church	The Synod of the province of the United Reformed Church, in which the church building or buildings is, or are, or will be situated.
The Roman Catholic Church	The Bishop of the diocese in which the church building or buildings is or are or will be situated.
The Church in Wales	The Governing Body of the Church in Wales.

For the purposes of this Schedule, 'the Baptist Trust Corporation' and 'the Congregational Trust Corporation' have the following meanings:—
- (a) if the church building or buildings to which the sharing agreement concerned relates is or are or will be vested in a Baptist or Congregational Trust Corporation within the meaning of the Baptist and Congregational Trusts Act 1951, it means that Corporation;
- (b) otherwise it means the Baptist or Congregational Trust Corporation (within the meaning of the said Act) in whose area of operations the church building or buildings is or are or will be situated, or if there is more than one such Corporation, the one determined by the Church meeting.

Repair of Benefice Buildings Measure 1972

Diocesan Parsonages Boards

Appointment or designation and constitution of Parsonages Boards

1.—(1) As soon as possible after the passing of this Measure every diocesan synod shall provide by scheme either—
- (a) for the appointment of a Board for the purposes of this Measure, which shall be known as the Parsonages Board for the diocese concerned; or
- (b) for designating the Diocesan Board of Finance as the Board for the purposes of this Measure;

and references in this Measure to 'the Board' shall be construed as referring to the Parsonages Board or, as the case may be, the Diocesan Board of Finance for the diocese concerned.

(2) Every such scheme shall provide for the appointment of fit persons to be surveyors for the purposes of this Measure (hereinafter referred to as 'diocesan surveyors') and for determining their remuneration and terms of service.

Provided that no person appointed as a surveyor after the coming into force of section 6 of the Church of England (Miscellaneous Provisions) Measure 2005 shall be considered to be a fit person for the purposes of this subsection unless that person is registered under the Architects Act 1997 or is a corporate member of the Chartered Institute of Building or the Royal Institution of Chartered Surveyors or a member of such other body as the Commissioners may determine and appearing to them to be suitably qualified.

(3) If the scheme provides for the appointment of a Parsonages Board, it shall also provide for the appointment of a secretary of the Board, and for determining his remuneration and terms of service.

(4) All archdeacons of a diocese for which a Parsonages Board is appointed shall be ex officio members of the Board, and of the remaining members not less than one third shall be clergymen elected by the beneficed and, if the scheme so provides, the licensed clergy of the diocese, and not less than one third shall be lay persons; but subject as aforesaid the membership of the Board and the method of election or appointment and term of office of its members other than ex-officio members shall be prescribed by the scheme.

(5) A Parsonages Board shall be a body corporate, with perpetual succession and a common seal, and the purposes of the Board shall be the furtherance of the work of the Church of England by the exercise of their functions under this Measure, and they shall in the exercise of those functions have power to enter into contracts, hold property, borrow money, execute works (whether by entering into contracts or by the employment of direct labour) and have such other ancillary powers as may be provided by scheme of the diocesan synod.

(6) Subject to the preceding provisions of this section, the constitution and procedure of a Parsonages Board shall be prescribed by scheme of the diocesan synod, and provision may be made

for the appointment of committees and the exercise of functions by them, and for the appointment of officers and other staff of a Parsonages Board and for determining their remuneration and terms of service.

(7) A Parsonages Board shall present an annual report and annual accounts to the diocesan synod, and within one month of such presentation the secretary of the synod shall send a copy of the report and accounts to the Commissioners together with a copy of any resolutions passed thereon by the synod.

(8) The Board shall comply with any such directions as may be given to them by resolution of the diocesan synod.

(9) If the Diocesan Board of Finance is designated by a scheme under subsection (1),—
- (a) the scheme shall provide for the delegation of the Board's functions under this Measure to a committee or committees of the Board constituted in accordance with the scheme, and regard shall be had in prescribing the membership of the committee or committees (which may include persons other than members of the Board) to the need for adequate representation of the clergy and laity, and the scheme may contain provisions as to the procedure of any such committee;
- (b) the Memorandum and Articles of Association of the Board or (if they are not a registered company) the constitution thereof shall be deemed to include the furtherance of the work of the Church of England by the exercise of functions under this Measure and such ancillary powers as are necessary for the exercise of those functions and to give effect to any provisions of the said scheme;
- (c) subsection (7) shall apply to the Board with the modification that the annual report and annual accounts there mentioned may be presented as a separate part of the Board's annual report and annual accounts.

Repair of benefice buildings

Meaning of repairs

2.—(1) In this Measure 'repairs', in relation to a parsonage house, means such works of repair and replacement as are needed—
- (a) to keep in repair the structure and exterior of the buildings of the parsonage house, including doors, windows, drains, gutters and external pipes; and
- (b) to keep in repair all walls, fences, gates, drives and drains of the parsonage house, other than those which some person other than the incumbent is wholly liable to repair;
- (c) to keep in repair and proper working order—
  - (i) the installations in the parsonage house for the supply of water, gas and electricity, and for sanitation, including basins, sinks, baths and sanitary conveniences, and
  - (ii) the installations in the parsonage house for space heating or heating water, and
  - (iii) any fixtures fittings and appliances in the parsonage house (other than those mentioned in the preceding sub-paragraphs), if they belong to the benefice but not otherwise;

and includes works of interior decoration necessitated in consequence of such works as aforesaid.

(2) *Repealed.*

(3) In determining for the purposes of this Measure the standard of repair appropriate to any building of a benefice, regard shall be had to the age, character and prospective life of the building, and, in particular, in the case of a building included in a list under section 1 of the Planning (Listed Buildings and Conservation Areas) Act 1990, the special architectural or historic interest of the building.

Periodic inspections by diocesan surveyors

3.—(1) It shall be the duty of the Board to cause an inspection to be made by a diocesan surveyor of all the buildings of each benefice in the diocese within an initial period of five years from the commencement of this Measure, and for subsequent such inspections to be made periodically at intervals not exceeding, in the case of any benefice, five years from the last such inspection thereof.

(2) Where a new building of a benefice is provided and is not inspected within the initial period, the Board shall cause it to be inspected by a diocesan surveyor as soon as possible after it is provided and thereafter at intervals not exceeding five years.

Reports by diocesan surveyors

4.—(1) On every such inspection as aforesaid of the buildings of a benefice, the diocesan surveyor shall make a report to the Board—

    (a)   stating what repairs are required, specifying them in detail and estimating their cost, and stating whether they should be executed immediately or otherwise;

    (b)   specifying any repairs to a parsonage house which are in his opinion necessary by reason of damage caused or aggravated by any deliberate act of the incumbent or a previous incumbent or any default in his duties under section 13 of this Measure, and estimating the cost of executing those repairs or, in the case of aggravation, the additional cost attributable to the act or default;

    (c)   stating whether any improvements to a parsonage house appear to him expedient and, if an estimate appears to him practicable and useful, estimating their cost;

    (d)   stating whether in his opinion a parsonage house should be replaced;

    (e)   *Repealed.*

    (f)   commenting on the state of the interior decoration of any parsonage house and the state of fixtures and things in any building of the benefice which belong to the benefice;

    (g)   advising on the respective amounts for which the buildings of the benefice should be insured under this Measure, and specifying any special risks to which they are liable.

(2) Where a diocesan surveyor reports that any outbuilding of a parsonage house appears to him to be superfluous, it shall not be necessary for him to specify what repairs to the building are required.

(3) On the first inspection of the buildings of a benefice under this Measure, the diocesan surveyor shall attach to his report a list of the fixtures and things in any such building which belong to the benefice, and a list of the trees of a parsonage house which in his opinion (after taking such expert advice, if any, as he thinks fit) ought to be preserved, and on subsequent inspections he shall make such additions to and amendments of the lists as may be necessary.

(4) The Board shall cause a copy of the report to be sent to the incumbent together with a notice stating his right to make representations and the date by which the representations must be made, which shall not be less than one month from the date on which the notice is sent.

(5) The Board shall consider any representations duly made by the incumbent and, if the incumbent so desires, give him an opportunity of meeting the Board or (at the discretion of the Board) a committee or representative of the Board, and the Board may make by their members such inspections as they think fit and may obtain such professional or other advice as they may require.

(6) If no representations are made within the period allowed by the notice, then on the expiration of that period, or if representations are made, after the consideration thereof, the Board shall confirm the report of the diocesan surveyor without variation or with such variation as the Board may in its discretion decide, and the Board shall thereupon notify the incumbent of any such variation, and references in the following provisions of this Measure to the report of the diocesan surveyor shall be construed as references to the report as confirmed:

Provided that, if the Board propose to vary the report otherwise than for the purpose of giving effect to representations of the incumbent, they shall give him an opportunity of making representations with respect to the proposal and the last preceding subsection shall apply to any such representations.

(7) Where the report specifies any repairs under subsection (1)(b) in respect of the act or default of a previous incumbent, the last three subsections shall have effect as if the references to the incumbent included references to that previous incumbent or his personal representative.

Duty of Board to carry out repairs in report relating to parsonage house

5.—(1) It shall be the duty of the Board—
- (a) to commence within a period of 12 months from the date when the diocesan surveyor's report is confirmed all repairs specified in the report and relating to a parsonage house the execution of which is therein stated to be immediately necessary, and to complete them as soon as possible;
- (b) to execute all other repairs so specified and relating to a parsonage house within such period as may be recommended in the report or, if no period is recommended, as the Board think expedient:

Provided that, if it appears to the Board and the bishop of the diocese that a parsonage house or a part thereof should be sold, exchanged or demolished, and for that reason it is not necessary or desirable to execute the repairs, or all the repairs, specified in relation thereto in the report of the diocesan surveyor, the Board may at any time within a period of six months from the date of the confirmation of the report, notify the incumbent that such repairs as are specified in the notice are not to be executed and giving the reasons therefor.

(2) A notice under the preceding subsection shall state the incumbent's right to make representations and the date by which the representations must be made, which shall not be less than one month from the date on which the notice is sent; and the Board shall consider any representations duly made by the incumbent, which shall be limited to the question of what repairs are not to be executed, and subsection (5) of the last preceding section shall apply to their consideration of such representations.

(3) The Board shall notify the incumbent of their decision, and the incumbent may, if not satisfied with the decision, appeal therefrom within one month from the notification thereof to the Commissioners, who shall decide the matter after consultation with the Board and the incumbent.

(4) If the report of the diocesan surveyor states that any outbuilding of the parsonage house appears to be superfluous, the Board may at any time after the confirmation of the report, notify the incumbent that they intend to demolish the outbuilding, and the last preceding subsection shall apply to any such notice, and if there is no appeal or the notice is upheld, the Board may demolish the outbuilding.

Interim inspectors and repairs

8.—(1) In addition to the periodic inspections required by the preceding provisions of this Measure, the Board may at any time cause an inspection of any building of a benefice or any part thereof to be made by a diocesan surveyor and a report made thereon.

(2) If it appears to the Board, whether as a result of such inspection and report or otherwise, that any repairs to a parsonage house are necessary, they may execute those repairs:

Provided that repairs which are not specified in such a report shall not be executed without the consent of the incumbent.

(3) A report under this section relating to a parsonage house may specify such repairs and make such estimates as are mentioned in section 4(1)(b) of this Measure, and in that case subsections (4) to (7) of that section shall apply to that report.

(4) *Repealed.*

Repairs to party walls etc

9. Where any party wall or fence of a parsonage house or any drive, drain or other appurtenance of a parsonage house is maintainable by the incumbent in common with other persons, and any works of repair or replacement are needed in respect thereof, the Board shall have power to act in place of the incumbent in making agreements with those other persons for the execution and financing of such repairs and for enforcing the liability of those persons in respect of such repairs.

Regulation of inspections, reports and repairs

10. A diocesan synod may by scheme provide for regulating—
- (a) inspections of buildings of a benefice by diocesan surveyors and the making of reports following on such inspections;

(b) the execution of repairs to buildings of a benefice, including the supervision thereof by diocesan surveyors and otherwise, and any other matters required for securing efficiency and economy in such execution.

Powers of entry

11. For the purpose of carrying out any inspection or executing any repairs to a building of a benefice which the Board are required or authorised to carry out or execute under this Measure, it shall be lawful for a diocesan surveyor or any workmen or other persons employed by him or the Board or any person authorised by him or the Board to enter the building at all reasonable hours during the daytime:

Provided that, except where repairs are suddenly and urgently needed, the Board or the diocesan surveyor shall before exercising their powers under this section use their best endeavours to reach agreement with the incumbent as to the times at which the inspection is to be carried out or the repairs executed, and shall in default of such agreement give not less than fourteen days notice to the incumbent.

Insurance

12.—(1) It shall be the duty of the Board—
(a) to insure all the parsonage houses in their diocese against all such risks as are included in the usual form of houseowner's policy relating to buildings;

and such insurance shall be effected with the Ecclesiastical Insurance Office Ltd. or such other insurance office as may be selected by the Board.

(2) The Board shall make and prosecute all claims arising under any insurance policy effected under this section, and all moneys payable under any such policy shall be paid to the Board.

(3) If a liability in respect of damage to a parsonage house arises under any such policy, and the insurance office elects to pay the insurance money instead of making good the damage at the expense of the office, the Board shall, make good the damage:

Provided that—
(a) the damages may be made good with such alterations as the Board may with the consent of the incumbent and after consulting the registered patron determine;
(b) the whole or part of the damage may, if the Board so determine with such consent and after such consultation as aforesaid, be not made good.

(4) *Repealed.*

(5) In this section, references to damage and the making good thereof shall include references to the destruction of the building in whole or in part and to the reinstatement thereof.

Obligations and powers of incumbent in relation to parsonage house

13.—(1) The incumbent shall have a duty to take proper care of a parsonage house, being a duty equivalent to that of a tenant to use premises in a tenant-like manner.

(2) The duties of the Board under this Measure in respect of repairs to parsonage houses shall not affect any liability of an incumbent, as owner, tenant or occupier of a parsonage house, to persons other than the Board, but the Board shall indemnify the incumbent in respect of any claim by any such person or any expense reasonably incurred by reason of any such liability, if and so far as the claim or expense arises out of the execution of repairs or a failure to execute repairs to the parsonage house and is not covered by an insurance policy effected under the last preceding section:

Provided that an incumbent shall not be under any liability to his successor in respect of any repairs or failure to execute repairs to a parsonage house.

(3) The incumbent shall notify the Board of any repairs to a parsonage house appearing to him to be necessary and, in the case of repairs urgently required for reasons of safety or to prevent further damage or deterioration or to meet a liability to other persons, shall do so without delay.

(4) Where the report of a diocesan surveyor, whether under section 4 or section 8 of this Measure, specifies any repairs to a parsonage house as necessary by reason of damage caused or aggravated by any deliberate act of the incumbent or a previous incumbent or any default in his duties under this section, the Board may, on completion of the repairs, by notice require the incumbent concerned or his personal representative to pay to them the whole or part of the cost certified by the diocesan surveyor to be attributable to the said act or default and, if the notice is not complied with, the Board may take proceedings for the enforcement thereof:

Provided that in any such proceedings it shall be open to the defendant to show that the cost so certified is not attributable to such act or default as aforesaid, or that the amount required to be paid exceeds the cost so attributable, and judgment may be given accordingly.

(5) The incumbent may carry out as agent of the Board such repairs to a parsonage house, whether following an inspection by a diocesan surveyor or otherwise, as the Board may generally or specially authorise.

Parsonage house ceasing to be such

14.—(1) Where the Board is satisfied that a parsonage house may be sold or exchanged without the consent of the Commissioners under the Parsonages Measure 1938 or is notified by the Commissioners that they have consented to the sale or exchange of a parsonage house, or that the Commissioners are satisfied that any objection raised under section 3(1) of the Parsonages Measure 1938 ought not to prevent any such sale or exchange, the duties of the Board under the preceding provisions of this Measure shall apply to that parsonage house to the following extent only:—

    (a) the Board shall keep the insurance of the parsonage house in force until the sale or exchange is effected; and

    (b) the Board shall carry out such repairs thereto as they think necessary or desirable to facilitate the sale or exchange thereof; and

    (c) so long as the parsonage house remains in occupation, the Board shall carry out such repairs as they think necessary for such occupation.

(2) Where a parsonage house ceases, otherwise than in consequence of a sale or exchange or proposals therefor, to be a parsonage house, the preceding provisions of this Measure so far as they relate to parsonage houses shall cease to apply thereto.

(3) Nothing in this section shall affect any liability of the Board under subsection (2) of the last preceding section, or any liability of the incumbent or his personal representative under subsection (4) of that section or section 20(2) or this Measure, being a liability accrued before the preceding provisions of this section took effect in relation to the parsonage house.

(4) References in this section to the sale and the exchange of a parsonage house shall, if it is held on lease, be construed as references to the sale and the exchange of the leasehold interest therein.

Other functions of Parsonage Boards

Extension by scheme of functions of Parsonages

15.—(1) The diocesan synod may by scheme authorise the Board to execute—

    (a) works of interior decoration of parsonage houses, by agreement with the incumbent;

    (b) works of improvement, demolition or erection of parsonage houses in pursuance of the powers conferred by sections 1, 2 and 2A of the Parsonages Measure 1938, by agreement with the persons on whom those powers are conferred.

(2) The diocesan synod may by scheme provide for the inspection by a diocesan surveyor of buildings in the diocese (other than parsonage houses used as residences by clergy or lay workers of the Church of England, and for the making of reports to the Board on such inspections.

(3) The diocesan synod may by scheme provide for authorising the Board to execute works of repair, interior decoration, improvement, demolition of erection of any buildings in the diocese held for charitable purposes connected with the Church of England, by agreement with the persons having the management or control of such buildings.

(4) A scheme made under this section shall make provision for securing that the cost of any such works as are mentioned in this section and the cost of inspections and reports mentioned in subsection (2) thereof, including any administrative cost attributable to such works, inspections and reports, shall be met by any fund or funds capable of being used for the purposes in question, and may contain other provisions relating to the administration of the scheme.

(5) In this section references to parsonage houses and to buildings used or held for certain purposes shall include references, where appropriate, to buildings intended to be used as parsonage houses or to be used or held for those purposes.

Powers of Board to pay rates, rent and other outgoings

16.—(1) The Board shall, in respect of any parsonage house or other residence of an incumbent in the diocese, have power to make good to the incumbent or defray on his behalf—

    (a)   any general rate, water rate or drainage rate;
    (b)   any payments for the maintenance of a private road, common drive, party fence or wall, or other thing maintainable in common;
    (c)   any payment in respect of a rent charge or other charge;
    (d)   any rent or other payment under a lease or tenancy.

(2) The Board shall have power to defray the cost of repairs to any such residence not being a parsonage house, or any repairs to a parsonage house held on lease being repairs for which the incumbent is liable.

(3) The Board shall in respect of any parsonage house in the diocese have power to defray on behalf of the Diocesan Board of Finance for the diocese any periodical payment in respect of a loan made by the Commissioners to that Board for the provision, improvement, division or demolition of that house or the safeguarding of the amenities thereof and any accrued interest thereon.

(4) The Board shall in respect of any building in the diocese (other than a parsonage house or other residence of an incumbent in the diocese) used as a residence by any person declared by the bishop to be engaged in the cure of souls within the diocese have power to defray on behalf of the Diocesan Board of Finance for the diocese the cost of any such payments as are referred to in paragraphs (a) to (d) of subsection (1) above and the costs, charges and expenses of any sale.

Financial provisions

Expenditure of the Board

17. All expenditure of the Board, except expenditure defrayed out of a specific trust fund, shall be defrayed out of any fund or funds capable of being applied for the purposes in question.

Other Financial Provisions

19. *Text omitted.*

Felling of trees

20.—(1) Any trees included in the current list scheduled to the report of the diocesan surveyor under section 4(3) of this Measure in respect of a parsonage house shall not be felled, chopped or topped without the consent of the Board:

Provided that this subsection shall not apply if the felling, lopping or topping is necessary to avoid immediate danger to the occupants of the parsonage house or any other building or to the general public.

(2) If any such trees are felled, lopped or topped in contravention of this section or any such timber is felled in contravention thereof, the Board may by notice require the incumbent or his personal representative to pay to the Board the amount of any resulting depreciation, as estimated by a diocesan surveyor, of the parsonage house or, as the case may be, the net value of the timber, or such part of that amount or value as the Board think fit, and, if the notice is not complied with, the Board may take proceedings for the enforcement thereof:

Provided that in any such proceedings it shall be open to the defendant to show that the contravention did not cause any depreciation of the parsonage house or that the timber had no net value or that the amount required to be paid exceeds the amount of the depreciation or value, and judgment may be given accordingly.

(3), (4) *Repealed.*

(5) The consent of the registered patron or ordinary shall not be necessary for any felling in accordance with this section.

(6) The net proceeds of any such felling and any moneys recovered by the Board under subsection (2) of this section may be applied for the purpose of planting new trees, and so far as they are not so applied, shall be treated in the same way as the net proceeds of the demolition of outbuildings of a parsonage house, under section 19(4) of this Measure.

(7) Where the expense to the incumbent of felling, lopping or topping any trees in accordance with this section exceeds the proceeds thereof, the Board may defray the amount of the excess.

Additions and alterations to parsonage houses and glebe buildings

21.—(1) An incumbent shall not make any additions or alterations to the buildings of a parsonage house until after he has obtained the consent of the Board, and if he does so, the Board may by notice require him or his personal representative to restore the buildings to the condition in which they were before, and, on receipt of the notice, the incumbent or his personal representative shall restore the buildings as directed by the notice.

(2) If the incumbent or his personal representative refuses or neglects to comply with the notice, the Board may, if they think fit, execute such works as may be necessary to restore the buildings as aforesaid, and the powers of entry conferred by section 11 of this Measure shall apply for that purpose and the cost of the works shall be recoverable as a debt due to the Board from the incumbent or his personal representative.

(3) Before refusing their consent under this section, the Board shall give notice to the incumbent of their intention to do so.

(4) Before making additions or alterations to the buildings of a parsonage house the incumbent shall consult the registered patron (as defined in section 39(1) of the Patronage (Benefices) Measure 1986), if any, of the benefice and, in the case of a parsonage house which is occupied by a person who is a member of the team in a team ministry established by a pastoral scheme under the Pastoral Measure 1983 and not by the incumbent, that person also.

(5) Any notice under this section shall inform the incumbent or the person or representative as the case may be, of the right to make representations and the date by which the representations must be made, which shall be not less than one month from the date on which the notice is sent, and section 4(5) above shall apply to the consideration of any representations duly made and the Board shall then decide whether or not to proceed with the notice.

Board to be informed and to advise and negotiate on matters affecting benefice property

23. The incumbent of a benefice shall keep the Board informed of matters affecting buildings and land belonging to the benefice, other than churches, and in particular of matters arising from any notice given to him by a Government department, local or public authority, public utility undertakers or in the case of property held on a lease or tenancy the landlord of the property; and the Board shall, at the request of the incumbent, advise on or undertake negotiations in respect of any such matters.

Guidance by Commissioners

24. *Text omitted.*

Charities

25. *Text omitted.*

Application of Measure during vacancies

26. *Text omitted.*

Notices and other documents

27. *Text omitted.*

Transfer to Board of functions of Diocesan Dilapidations Board

29. As soon as the Board is appointed or designated under section 1 of this Measure, the functions of the Diocesan Dilapidations Board for that diocese shall be exercisable by the Board, and the Diocesan Dilapidations Board (if a separate body) shall thereupon be dissolved, and for references in any Measure to a Diocesan Dilapidations Board and to surveyors appointed by them there shall be substituted, as respects that diocese, references to the Board and surveyors appointed by the Board.

Schemes of diocesan synods

30.—(1) A copy of any scheme made by a diocesan synod under this Measure shall be sent to the Commissioners and filed in the diocesan registry.

(2) The duties and powers of diocesan synods to provide by scheme for the matters specified in this Measure may be exercised by a single scheme or by separate schemes, and any scheme may be varied, revoked or replaced by a subsequent scheme made and approved in like manner.

(3) Any such scheme may contain such supplementary and incidental provisions as may be necessary or expedient for the purposes of the scheme, and may provide that the scheme shall come into operation on a specified date, and may specify different dates for different provisions or different areas.

Interpretation

31.—(1) In this Measure, unless the context otherwise requires, the following expressions have the meanings hereby respectively assigned to them, that is to say:—

'benefice' means the office of a rector or vicar of a parish or parishes, with cure of souls, but not including the office of a vicar in a team ministry;

'building' includes part of a building;

'buildings of a benefice' means any parsonage house;

'the commencement of this Measure' means, in relation to a diocese, the coming into operation of this Measure on the day appointed for that diocese under the next following section;

'the Commissioners' means the Church Commissioners;

'Diocesan Board of Finance' means in relation to a diocese the Board of that name constituted under the Diocesan Board of Finance Measure 1925 for that diocese;

'Diocesan Dilapidations Board' means, in relation to a diocese, the Board constituted under the Ecclesiastical Dilapidations Measure 1923 for that diocese;

'diocesan glebe land' has the same meaning as in the Endowments and Glebe Measure 1976;

'improvement', in relation to any building, includes enlargement and reduction in size (whether by division or otherwise);

'parsonage house' means a residence vested in the incumbent of a benefice (when the benefice is full), being his official residence, except a residence held under a lease which makes the landlord wholly or mainly responsible for the repairs, and includes the buildings, gardens, orchards, paddock, walls, fences, and appurtenances necessary for the convenient occupation of the residence and for the purposes of this definition the separate letting of a part of the residence shall not be deemed to exclude it from the residence unless it is excluded by a certificate of the bishop under section II of the Paronages Measure 1938;

'registered patron' has the same meaning as in the Patronage (Benefices) Measure 1986

'repairs' has the meaning assigned to it by section 2 of this Measure

'team vicar's house' means a residence vested in a Diocesan Board of Finance, being the designated residence of a vicar in a team ministry established for a benefice under section 19 of the Pastoral Measure 1968, except a residence held under a lease which makes the landlord wholly or mainly responsible for the repairs, and includes the buildings, gardens, orchards, paddocks, walls, fences and appurtenances necessary for the convenient occupation of the residence.

(2) This Measure shall, so far as applicable, apply to a team vicar's house as it applies to a parsonage house with the omission of references to the registered patron and to a previous incumbent, and with the substitution, for references to the incumbent, of references to the Diocesan Board of Finance in which the house is vested and the vicar, except that—

(a) in sections 9, 12(3), 13(5), 15(1)(a) and 16(2), the references shall be to that Board only;

(b) in sections 4(1)(b), 11 and 13(1) and (4), the references shall be to the vicar only; and

(c) in sections 20(2) and 21(2), the references shall be to such one of them as is responsible for the contravention in question.

(3) Any reference in this Measure to any Act or Measure shall be construed as a reference to that Act or Measure as amended by any subsequent Measure.

Church of England (Worship and Doctrine) Measure 1974

Provision by Canon for worship in the Church of England

1.—(1) It shall be lawful for the General Synod—

(a) to make provision by Canon with respect to worship in the Church of England, including provision for empowering the General Synod to approve, amend, continue or discontinue forms of service;

(b) to make provision by Canon or regulations made thereunder for any matter, except the publications of banns of matrimony, to which any of the rubrics contained in the Book of Common Prayer relate;

but the powers of the General Synod under this subsection shall be so exercised as to ensure that the forms of service contained in the Book of Common Prayer continue to be available for use in the Church of England.

(2) Any Canon making any such provision as is mentioned in subsection (1) of this section, and any regulations made under any such Canon, shall have effect notwithstanding anything inconsistent therewith contained in any of the rubrics in the Book of Common Prayer.

(3) The General Synod shall provide by Canon—

(a) that decisions as to which of the forms of service authorised by or approved under Canon are to be used in any church in a parish or in any guild church shall be taken jointly by the incumbent and the parochial church council or, as the case may be, by the vicar of the guild church and the guild church council; and

(b) that in case of disagreement, and so long as the disagreement continues, the forms of service to be used in that church shall be those contained in the Book of Common Prayer unless other forms of service so approved were in regular use therein during at least two of the four years immediately preceding the date when the disagreement arose and the said council resolves that those other forms of service shall be used either to the exclusion of, or in addition to, the forms of service contained in the said Book.

This subsection shall not apply in relation to a cathedral which is a parish church nor to any part of a cathedral which is a parish church.

(4) Subsection (3) of this section shall not apply in relation to any of the services known as occasional offices, but, in the case of those services, other than the Order of Confirmation, the General Synod shall provide by Canon that where more than one form of service is authorised by or approved under Canon for use on any occasion, the decision as to which form of service is to be used shall be

made by the minister who is to conduct the service, but that if any of the persons concerned objects beforehand to the use of the service selected by the minister and he and the minister cannot agree as to which form is to be used, the matter shall be referred to the bishop of the diocese for his decision.

(5) Without prejudice to the generality of subsection (1) of this section, the General Synod may make provision by Canon—
  (a) for empowering the Convocations, the archbishops and the bishops of dioceses to approve forms of service for use on occasions for which no provision is made by forms of service contained in the Book of Common Prayer or approved by the General Synod or the Convocations under Canon;
  (b) for empowering any minister to make and use minor variations in the forms of service contained in the said Book or approved by the General Synod, Convocation, archbishops or bishop under Canon and to use forms of service considered suitable by him on occasions for which no provision is made by any such form of service.

(6) The General Synod may provide by Canon that where a form of service is in course of preparation with a view to its submission to the General Synod for approval by the Synod under Canon, the archbishops may authorise that service in draft form to be conducted by a minister in the presence of a congregation consisting of such persons only as the archbishops may designate.

(7) In the prayers for or referring to the Sovereign or other members of the Royal Family contained in any form of service authorised for use in the Church of England, the names may be altered, and any other necessary alterations made, from time to time as the circumstances require by Royal Warrant, and those prayers as so altered shall be used thereafter.

Assent or subscription to doctrine

2.—(1) It shall be lawful for the General Synod to make provision by Canon with respect to the obligations of the clergy, deaconesses and lay officers of the Church of England to assent or subscribe to the doctrine of that church and the forms of that assent or subscription which may include an explanatory preface.

(2) In this section 'lay officers' means licensed lay workers, readers, lay judges or consistory or provincial courts, and lay holders of other offices admission to which is for the time being regulated by Canon.

Majorities required for final approval of Canons under section 1 or 2 and things done thereunder

3. No Canon making any such provision as is mentioned in section 1(1) or 2(1) of this Measure shall be submitted for Her Majesty's Licence and Assent unless it has been finally approved by the General Synod with a majority in each House thereof of not less than two-thirds of those present and voting; and no regulation under any Canon made under the said section 1(1) nor any approval, amendment, continuance or discontinuance of a form of service by the General Synod under any such Canon shall have effect unless the regulation, the form of service or the amendment, continuance or discontinuance of a form of service, as the case may be, has been finally approved by the General Synod with such a majority as aforesaid in each House thereof.

Safeguarding of doctrine

4.—(1) Every Canon or regulation making any such provision as is mentioned in section 1(1) of this Measure, every form of service or amendment thereof approved by the General Synod under any such Canon and every Canon making any such provision as is mentioned in section 2(1) of this Measure shall be such as in the opinion of the General Synod is neither contrary to, nor indicative of any departure from, the doctrine of the Church of England in any essential matter.

(2) The final approval by the General Synod of any such Canon or regulation or form of service or amendment thereof shall conclusively determine that the Synod is of such opinion as aforesaid with respect to the matter so approved.

(3) Where provision is made by Canon by virtue of section 1(5) of this Measure, the Canon shall provide for requiring the forms of service and variations approved, made or used thereunder to be neither contrary to, nor indicative of any departure from, the doctrine of the Church of England in any essential matter.

Interpretation

5.—(1) References in this Measure to the doctrine of the Church of England shall be construed in accordance with the statement concerning that doctrine contained in the Canons of the Church of England, which statement is in the following terms: 'The doctrine of the Church of England is grounded in the holy Scriptures, and in such teachings of the ancient Fathers and Councils of the Church as are agreeable to the said Scriptures. In particular such doctrine is to be found in the Thirty-nine Articles of Religion, the Book of Common Prayer, and the Ordinal.'.

(2) In this Measure the following expressions have the meanings hereby assigned to them:—

'the appointed day' means the day appointed under section 7(2) of this Measure;

'Book of Common Prayer' means the Book annexed to the Act of Uniformity 1662 and entitled 'The Book of Common Prayer and Administration of the Sacraments and other Rites and Ceremonies of the Church according to the use of the Church of England together with the Psalter or Psalms of David appointed as they are to be sung or said in Churches and the Form and Manner of Making, Ordaining and Consecrating Bishops, Priests and Deacons', as altered or amended by any Act or Measure or in accordance with section 1(7) of this Measure;

'church' includes any building or part of a building licensed by the bishop for public worship according to the rites and ceremonies of the church of England;

'form of service' means any order, service, prayer, rite or ceremony whatsoever, including the services for the ordination of priests and deacons and the consecration of bishops and the catechism or form of instruction before confirmation;

'guild church' means a church in the City of London designated and established as a guild church under the City of London (Guild Churches) Acts 1952 and 1960;

'incumbent' includes—

(a) a curate licensed to the charge of a parish or a minister acting as priest-in-charge of a parish in respect of which rights of presentation are suspended; and

(b) a vicar in a team ministry to the extent that the duties of an incumbent are assigned to him by a scheme under the Pastoral Measure 1968 or his licence from the bishop;

'rubrics' of the Book of Common Prayer include all directions and instructions contained in the said Book, and all tables, prefaces, rules, calendars and other contents thereof.

Amendments, repeals, transitional provisions and savings

6.—(1) Section 3 of the Submission of the Clergy Act 1533 (which provides that no Canons shall be contrary to the Royal Prerogative or the customs, laws or statutes of this realm) shall not apply to any rule of ecclesiastical law relating to any matter for which provision may be made by Canon in pursuance of this Measure.

Incumbents (Vacation of Benefices) Measure 1977

Part I
Institution of Enquiry into Pastoral Situation in a Parish

Code of Practice as to reconciliation

1.—(1) It shall be the duty of the House of Bishops to draw up rules of guidance for the purposes of this Measure generally and, in particular, as to the steps which that House considers should be

taken, where the bishop of a diocese receives notice of intention to make a request under section 1A of this Measure, to—
  (a) promote better relations between the incumbent and the parishioners; and
  (b) remove the causes of their estrangement,

and to promulgate the rules of guidance in a Code of Practice.

(2) The House of Bishops may at any time amend or replace a Code of Practice issued under subsection (1) above by a further Code of Practice issued under that subsection.

Request for enquiry into pastoral situation in a parish

1A.—(1) A request for an enquiry under this Part of this Measure into the pastoral situation in a parish on the ground that there has been a serious breakdown of the pastoral relationship between the incumbent and the parishioners to which the conduct of the incumbent or of the parishioners or of both has contributed over a substantial period may, subject to subsection (1A) below be made by—
  (a) the incumbent of the benefice to which the parish belongs; or
  (b) the archdeacon in whose archdeaconry the parish is; or
  (c) a majority of not less than two-thirds of the lay members of the parochial church council of the parish present and voting at a duly convened meeting of that council on a resolution that the request be made; or
  (d) where the incumbent mentioned in paragraph (a) above is the archdeacon mentioned in paragraph (b) above, a majority of the members of the bishop's council and standing committee of the diocesan synod of the diocese in which the parish is.

(1A) An enquiry under this Part of this Measure shall only be undertaken after the persons concerned have had an opportunity to resolve the pastoral situation in the parish in question; and, accordingly, a request for such an enquiry shall not be made unless notice of intention to make the request has been given by the person or persons concerned to the bishop of the diocese in which the parish in question is at least six months, and not more than twelve months, before the request is made.

(2) A request for such an enquiry, and a notice of intention to make it, shall be made or given in writing to the bishop of the diocese in which the parish in question is and the secretary of the diocesan synod of that diocese and, in the case of a request, shall contain particulars of the facts which appear to the person or persons making the request to justify an enquiry.

(3) A request for such an enquiry, and a notice of intention to make it, made or given by the persons mentioned in subsection (1)(c) or (d) above must—
  (a) be signed by all of those persons and include the address of each of them; and
  (b) specify two persons from among those signing the request or notice who are willing to act as representatives of those persons in connection with the enquiry or notice and indicate which of those two is willing to conduct and receive correspondence relating to the enquiry or notice (in this Measure referred to as 'the designated representative').

(4) A request for such an enquiry, and a notice of intention to make it, made or given by the persons mentioned in subsection (1)(c) above must also contain a statement that the persons who have signed the request or notice constitute a majority of two-thirds or more of those lay members of the parochial church council of the parish in question who were present at a duly convened meeting of that council and voted thereat on a resolution that the request be made or the notice be given.

(5) A request for such an enquiry, and a notice of intention to make it, made or given by the persons mentioned in subsection (1)(d) above must also contain a statement that the persons who have signed the request or notice constitute a majority of the members of the bishop's council and standing committee of the diocesan synod of the diocese in which the parish in question is.

(6) Where a request or notice made or given under this section is received by the secretary of the diocesan synod, he shall notify—
  (a) the incumbent of the benefice to which the parish in question belongs, unless it was he who made the request or gave the notice;
  (b) the archdeacon in whose archdeaconry that parish is, unless it was he who made the request or gave the notice; and
  (c) the secretary of the parochial church of that parish, unless it was the persons mentioned in subsection (1)(c) above who made the request or gave the notice.

(7) A request made under this section may be withdrawn by notice in writing given to the bishop of the diocese in which the parish in question is and the secretary of the diocesan synod of that diocese by—
  (a) in the case of a request made by the person mentioned in subsection (1)(a) or (b) above, that person;
  (b) in the case of a request made by the persons mentioned in subsection (1)(c) above, a majority of the lay members of the parochial church council of the parish present and voting at a duly convened meeting of that council on a resolution that the request be withdrawn;
  (c) in the case of a request made by the persons mentioned in subsection (1)(d) above, by a majority of the members of the bishop's council and standing committee of the diocesan synod of the diocese in which the parish is,

and where a request is withdrawn under this subsection no further steps shall be taken under this Part of this Measure in connection with the request.

Action to be taken by archdeacon in certain cases before institution of enquiry

2.—(1) Where the bishop of a diocese receives a request under section 1A of this Measure, then, unless—
  (a) the request was made by the archdeacon in whose archdeaconry the parish in question is, or
  (b) that archdeacon is the incumbent of the benefice to which the parish in question belongs,

the bishop shall direct the first mentioned archdeacon to report in accordance with subsection (5) below.

(2) Where the archdeaconry in which the parish in question is situated is vacant, the bishop shall appoint some other archdeacon holding office in the diocese to act in the case and shall inform the secretary of the diocesan synod accordingly.

(3) Where the archdeacon in whose archdeaconry the parish in question is situated is of opinion that it would not be right or expedient for him to act in the case, he shall so inform the bishop and the bishop shall appoint some other archdeacon holding office in the diocese to act in his place and shall inform the secretary of the diocesan synod accordingly.

(4) *Repealed.*

(5) Not more than six weeks after receiving the directions of the bishop the archdeacon shall report to the bishop whether in his opinion an enquiry into the pastoral situation in the parish to which the request relates would be in the best interest of the incumbent and the parishioners and should accordingly be instituted; and the archdeacon, in making his report to the bishop, shall have regard to the extent to which the current Code of Practice issued under section 1 of this Measure has been complied with.

(6) On receiving the archdeacon's report the bishop shall inform the secretary of the diocesan synod of the archdeacon's opinion as stated in his report and direct him to inform the incumbent, the secretary of the parochial church council and the designated representative, if any, of it.

Institution of enquiry

3.—(1) Where—
  (a) the request for an enquiry under this Part of this Measure was made by the archdeacon in whose archdeaconry the parish in question is or that archdeacon is the incumbent of the benefice to which the parish in question belongs; or

(b) the archdeacon appointed to act under section 2 of this Measure reports that in his opinion such an enquiry should be instituted; or

(c) within six months after the making of his report the archdeacon informs the bishop that notwithstanding that he did not report as aforesaid he considers that the circumstances are such that an enquiry is nevertheless required; or

(d) within six months after the making of the archdeacon's report the incumbent, the secretary of the parochial church council or the designated representative, if any, informs the bishop that notwithstanding that the archdeacon did not report as aforesaid such an enquiry is nevertheless required,

then, the bishop may, if he thinks fit, direct the secretary of the diocesan synod to institute such enquiry.

(1A) If, within the period of six months after the relevant date, the bishop neither gives a direction under subsection (1) above nor notifies the secretary of the diocesan synod that he has decided not to give such a direction, such a direction shall be deemed to have been given.

(1B) In this section 'relevant date' means—

(a) in either of the cases described in subsection (1)(a) above, the date on which the request was made;

(b) in the case described in subsection (1)(b) above, the date on which the report was made;

(c) in the case described in subsection (1)(c) or (d) above, the date on which the bishop is informed that, notwithstanding that the archdeacon did not report that in his opinion an enquiry under this Part of this Measure should be instituted, such an enquiry is nevertheless required.

(2), (3) *Repealed.*

Provisions with respect to resignation of benefice by incumbent

4.—(1) Where a request for an enquiry under this Part of this Measure is made in accordance with section 1 thereof, the incumbent concerned may when, or at any time before, he receives a notification from the bishop of the diocese under section 12(1) of this Measure may request the bishop to accept his resignation of his benefice, and the bishop may, if he thinks it would be in the interest of the Church to do so, accept the resignation.

(2) An incumbent who has been informed that the bishop has accepted his resignation of his benefice under subsection (1) above shall execute a deed resigning his benefice as from such date as may be specified in the deed, being a date not later than three months after the date on which he was informed as aforesaid, and shall vacate the parsonage house or other his official residence not later than three months after the date on which the benefice became vacant by virtue of that deed.

(3) Where the bishop accepts the resignation of an incumbent under this section, he shall notify the secretary of the diocesan synod that no further steps are to be taken in connection with the enquiry and direct him to inform the secretary of the parochial church council of the parish in question, the designated representative, if any, and, if necessary, the archdeacon in whose archdeaconry that parish is and the members of the body by which the enquiry was to have been, or is being, conducted of that fact.

Enquiry to be conducted by provincial tribunal

5. An enquiry into the pastoral situation in a parish shall be conducted by a provincial tribunal for the province in which the parish in question is situated.

Part II
Institution of Enquiry into Disability of Incumbent

Enquiry whether incumbent is unable to discharge duties by reason or age or infirmity

6.—(1) Subject to subsection (2) below, in any case where the bishop of a diocese is satisfied that it is proper to do so he may by notice in writing instruct the secretary of the diocesan synod to institute an enquiry as to whether the incumbent of a benefice in the diocese is unable by reason of age or infirmity of mind or body to discharge adequately the duties attaching to his benefice and, if so, whether it is desirable that he should resign his benefice or be given assistance in discharging those duties.

(1A) An enquiry under this section shall be conducted by a provincial tribunal for the province in which the benefice in question is situated.

(2) This section shall not apply to an incumbent who is also—
  (a) a suffragan bishop to whom the Bishops (Retirement) Measure 1986 applies; or
  (b) a dean, provost or archdeacon to whom the Church Dignitaries (Retirement) Measure 1949 applies.

Part III
Enquiries and Subsequent Proceedings

Constitution and procedure of committees and tribunals

7.—(1) Provincial tribunals for the purposes of this Measure shall be constituted in accordance with the provisions of Schedule 1 to this Measure:

Provided that where, in the course of an enquiry conducted by a provincial tribunal, a member of the tribunal other than the chairman dies or becomes unable to act as a member by reason or illness or other incapacity, the tribunal may, with the consent of the parties, continue to conduct the enquiry in the absence of that member.

(2), (3) *Repealed.*

(4) Without prejudice to subsection (5) below, at any meeting of any such tribunal to which the incumbent concerned is invited, or at which he is entitled to be present, he may, if he so desires, be assisted, or in his absence represented, by some other person whether having professional qualifications or not.

(5) At an enquiry under this Measure the parties may be represented by a barrister or solicitor.

(6) For the purposes of this section the parties, in relation to an enquiry, are—
  (a) the incumbent concerned;
  (b) the archdeacon in whose archdeaconry the benefice of the incumbent concerned is;
  (c) the parochial church council of the parish concerned or, in the case of an enquiry under Part I of this Measure requested by the persons mentioned in section 1A(1)(c), the persons specified in the request as being willing to act as the representatives of the first-mentioned persons;
  (d) in the case of such an enquiry requested by the persons mentioned in section 1A(1)(d), the persons specified in the request as being willing to act as the representatives of the first-mentioned persons.

Medical examinations

7A.—(1) The tribunal by which an enquiry under Part I or II of this Measure is being conducted may direct that the incumbent concerned should undergo a medical examination in accordance with rules made under section 18 of this Measure for the purpose of obtaining a report on his mental or physical condition; and the tribunal may at any time revoke or vary a direction given under this subsection.

(2) Where a tribunal gives a direction under subsection (1) above and the incumbent concerned fails to take any step required of him for the purpose of giving effect to the direction, the tribunal may draw such inferences (if any) from that fact as appear proper in the circumstances, without prejudice to the drawing of any other inferences that may properly be drawn by the tribunal in the course of the enquiry.

Ancillary provisions with respect to enquiry under Part I

8.—(1) In the case of an enquiry under Part I of this Measure, the secretary of the diocesan synod shall notify—
- (a) the secretary of the parochial church council of the parish to which the enquiry relates, and
- (b) the secretary of the parochial church council of any other parish belonging to the benefice of which the incumbent concerned is the incumbent,

of the institution of the enquiry and ask him whether that council wishes to make representations to the tribunal which is to conduct the enquiry.

(2) In the case of an enquiry under the said Part I, the secretary of the diocesan synod shall supply each member of the tribunal by which the enquiry is to be conducted with a copy of the request for such enquiry and, in the case of an enquiry to which subsection (1) above applies, shall inform the tribunal whether or not any parochial church council wishes to make representations to it.

Report to be made to the bishop

9.—(1) Subject to subsection (2) below, the tribunal by which an enquiry under Part I of this Measure was conducted shall report to the bishop whether in its opinion there has been a serious breakdown of the pastoral relationship between the incumbent concerned and the parishioners and whether in its opinion the breakdown is one to which the conduct of the incumbent or of the parishioners or of both has contributed over a substantial period.

(2) Where the tribunal by which such enquiry was conducted is of opinion that the incumbent concerned is unable by reason of age or infirmity of mind or body to discharge adequately the duties attaching to his benefice it may so report to the bishop instead of reporting in accordance with subsection (1) above.

(3) The tribunal by which an enquiry under Part II of this Measure was conducted shall report to the bishop whether in its opinion the incumbent to which the enquiry related is unable by reason of age or infirmity of mind or body to discharge adequately the duties attaching to his benefice.

(4) Where the tribunal is of opinion that there has been such a breakdown as is mentioned in subsection (1) above, or, as the case may be, is of opinion that the incumbent in question is unable by reason of age or infirmity of mind or body to discharge adequately the duties attaching to his benefice, then, subject to subsection (5) below, it shall include in its report its recommendations as to the action to be taken by the bishop.

(5) A report to the bishop under this Measure shall not include a recommendation—
- (a) in a case to which section 10 of this Measure applies, that the bishop should execute a declaration of avoidance in relation to the benefice of the incumbent concerned, or
- (b) in a case to which section 11 of this Measure applies, that it is desirable that the incumbent concerned should resign his benefice,

unless four or more members of the tribunal were in favour of making that recommendation.

(7) Without prejudice to the preceding provisions of this section, the bishop may give such pastoral advice and guidance to the incumbent concerned and his parishioners as he thinks appropriate having regard to the findings and recommendations of the committee or tribunal.

(8) Where the bishop disqualifies an incumbent under subsection (4) or (5) above, he shall make such provision for the discharge of the duties attaching to the benefice of the incumbent during the period of disqualification as he thinks fit, and the incumbent shall not interfere with any person who may be appointed to discharge any of those duties.

Inhibition in disability cases

9A.—(1) Subject to the following provisions of this section, where—
- (a) the bishop of a diocese has instructed the secretary of the diocesan synod to institute an enquiry under Part II of this Measure; or
- (b) the tribunal by which an enquiry under Part I of this Measure was conducted has reported to the bishop in accordance with section 9(2) of this Measure,

and it appears to the bishop that it is desirable in the interests of the Church of England that he should take action under this section, it shall be lawful for the bishop to cause a notice to be served on the incumbent who is the subject of the enquiry inhibiting him from executing or performing without the consent of the bishop any such right or duty of or incidental to his office as the bishop may specify.

(2) A notice of inhibition shall not be served under subsection (1) above in the circumstances mentioned in paragraph (a) of that subsection after the tribunal by which the enquiry was conducted has made its report to the bishop unless it reports that in its opinion the incumbent concerned is unable by reason of age or infirmity of mind or body to discharge adequately the duties attaching to his benefice.

(3) Where the tribunal has reported to the bishop that in its opinion the incumbent concerned is unable by reason of age or infirmity of mind or body to discharge adequately the duties attaching to his benefice, a notice of inhibition shall not be served under subsection (1) above after the expiry of the period of three months following the making of the report unless—

(a) the bishop has notified the incumbent under section 11(2)(a) of this Measure that it is desirable that he should resign his benefice, in which case such a notice may be served at any time before he ceases to be the incumbent; or

(b) the bishop has given the incumbent leave of absence under section 11(2)(c) of this Measure, in which case such a notice may be served at any time during the leave of absence.

(4) A notice of inhibition served under subsection (1) above shall cease to have effect—

(a) if it is served before the tribunal makes its report to the bishop, on the making of the report unless it reports that the incumbent concerned is unable by reason of age or infirmity of mind or body to discharge adequately the duties attaching to his benefice; or

(b) on the expiry of the period of three months following the making of the report to the bishop unless the bishop has taken action under section 11(2)(a) or (c) of this Measure; or

(c) if the bishop gives the incumbent leave of absence under section 11(2)(c) of this Measure, on the expiry of the leave of absence; or

(d) on the benefice of the incumbent becoming vacant.

(5) The bishop may at any time revoke a notice of inhibition served under this section.

Powers of bishop in cases of breakdown of pastoral relationship

10.—(1) The provisions of this section shall have effect where the tribunal by which an enquiry under Part I of this Measure was conducted reports to the bishop that in its opinion there has been such a breakdown as is mentioned in section 9(1) of this Measure.

(2) If, but only if, the tribunal so recommends, the bishop may execute a declaration of avoidance declaring the benefice of the incumbent concerned vacant as from a date specified in the declaration, being a date not less than three or more than six months after the date on which the declaration is made.

(3) Where the incumbent concerned holds two or more benefices in plurality, the bishop may include both or all of those benefices in such a declaration notwithstanding that the recommendation of the tribunal related to one only of them.

(4) Where the bishop executes a declaration under subsection (2) above, he shall disqualify the incumbent concerned from executing or performing without the consent of the bishop any right or duty of or incidental to his office during the period beginning with the date on which the declaration is executed and ending with the date on which the benefice or benefices of the incumbent will become vacant in accordance with the declaration.

(5) Where the tribunal reports to the bishop that in its opinion the serious breakdown of the pastoral relationship between the incumbent concerned and the parishioners is one to which the conduct of the incumbent has contributed over a substantial period, the bishop may rebuke the incumbent and may, if he thinks fit, disqualify him from executing or performing without the

consent of the bishop any such right or duty of or incidental to his office, and during such period, as the bishop may specify.

(6) Where the tribunal reports to the bishop that in its opinion such a breakdown as is mentioned in subsection (5) above is one to which the conduct of the parishioners has contributed over a substantial period, the bishop may rebuke such of them as he thinks fit and may, if he thinks fit, disqualify such of them as he thinks fit from being a churchwarden or member or officer of the parochial church council of the parish in question and of such other parishes in his diocese as he may specify during such period not exceeding five years as he may specify.

(6A) Where the bishop disqualifies a person who is or who becomes a lay member of a deanery synod, a diocesan synod, or the General Synod from being a member of a parochial church council during any period under subsection (6) above, that person shall not be a member of that council by virtue of that lay membership during that period, notwithstanding rule 12(1)(e) [now rule 14(1)(f)] of the Church Representation Rules.

(7) Without prejudice to the preceding provisions of this section, the bishop may give such pastoral advice and guidance to the incumbent concerned and the parishioners as he thinks appropriate having regard to the findings and recommendations of the tribunal.

(8) Where the bishop disqualifies an incumbent under subsection (4) or (5) above, he shall make such provision for the discharge of the duties attaching to the benefice of the incumbent during the period of disqualification as he thinks fit, and the incumbent shall not interfere with any person who may be appointed to discharge any of those duties.

(9) The bishop may revoke any disqualification effected under subsection (5) or (6) above.

Powers of bishop in cases of disability of incumbent

11.—(1) The provisions of this section shall have effect where the tribunal by which an enquiry under Part I or II of this Measure was conducted reports to the bishop that in its opinion the incumbent concerned is unable by reason of age or infirmity of mind or body to discharge adequately the duties attaching to his benefice.

(2) Subject to subsection (3) below, the bishop may—
- (a) notify the incumbent concerned that it is desirable that he should resign his benefice; or
- (b) with the consent of the incumbent concerned, appoint and license an assistant curate to assist the incumbent; or
- (c) give the incumbent concerned leave of absence for a period not exceeding two years and make provision for the discharge of the duties attaching to the benefice during that period; or
- (d) make such other temporary provision for the discharge of those duties as the bishop thinks fit.

(3) The bishop shall not exercise the power conferred on him by subsection (2)(a) above unless the tribunal recommended that it was desirable that the incumbent concerned should resign his benefice.

(4) Where the incumbent concerned holds two or more benefices in plurality, then, without prejudice to section 17(4) of the Pastoral Measure 1968 (which makes provision with respect to the resignation of benefices held in plurality), the bishop may, if he thinks fit, include both or all of those benefices in a notification given by him to the incumbent under subsection (2)(a) above notwithstanding that the recommendation of the tribunal related to one only of them.

(5) An incumbent who is notified by the bishop under this section that it is desirable that he should resign his benefice or benefices shall execute a deed resigning it or them as from such date as may be specified in the deed, being a date not later than three months after the date on which the deed is executed.

(6) Where the bishop notifies an incumbent under this section that it is desirable that he should resign his benefice or benefices, and the incumbent refuses or fails within one month after the notification is given to resign it or them in accordance with subsection (5) above, the bishop shall

Incumbents (Vacation of Benefices) Measure 1977

execute a declaration of avoidance declaring the benefice or benefices, as the case may be, vacant as from a date specified in the declaration, being a date not less than three or more than six months after the date on which the declaration is made.

(7) Where the bishop requests an incumbent under this section to consent to the appointment of an assistant curate and the incumbent refuses or fails within one month after the request is made to comply with it, the bishop shall execute a declaration of avoidance declaring the benefice vacant as from the date mentioned in subsection (6) above.

(8) Where the incumbent concerned holds two or more benefices in plurality, the bishop may, if he thinks fit, include both or all of those benefices in a declaration executed by him under subsection (7) above.

Provisos supplementary to ss 10 and 11

12.—(1) As soon as practicable after the report of an enquiry under this Measure has been received by the bishop he shall notify the incumbent concerned of the action he is required or proposes to take under section 10 or 11 of this Measure, as the case may be, or, if no such action is required of, or proposes to be taken by, him, of that fact and shall send a similar notification to—
    (a) the archdeacon in whose archdeaconry the parish concerned is, unless he is the incumbent concerned;
    (b) the secretary of the parochial church council of that parish; and
    (c) the designated representative, if any.

(2) The incumbent of any benefice which has been declared vacant under the said section 10 or 11 or which he has resigned in accordance with section 11(5) shall vacate the parsonage house or other his official residence not later than three months after the date on which the benefice became vacant by virtue of the declaration of avoidance or deed of resignation, as the case may be.

(3) The bishop shall cause any declaration executed by him under the said section 10 or 11 to be filed in the registry of the diocese and a copy thereof to be sent to the incumbent concerned, to the patron of the benefice and to the Church of England Pensions Board.

Compensation

13.—(1) Subject to the provisions of this Measure, where—
    (a) after obtaining the agreement of the bishop under subsection (1) of section 4 of this Measure, an incumbent resigns his benefice in accordance with subsection (2) of that section; or
    (b) after an enquiry under Part I thereof, the bishop has declared the benefice of an incumbent vacant under section 10 of this Measure,
the incumbent shall, on application in writing made to the diocesan board of finance, be entitled to compensation for any loss suffered by him in consequence of his resignation or the vacation of his benefice.

(2) Schedule 2 to this Measure shall have effect for the purpose of determining the form and amount of compensation under this section and of prescribing the circumstances in which payments of compensation thereunder may be altered, terminated, suspended or refused and of providing for other matters relating thereto.

(3) Regulations approved by the General Synod under section 6 of the Clergy Pensions (Amendment) Measure 1972 may make such amendments to Schedule 2 to this Measure as the Synod considers necessary or expedient in consequence of any regulations made under subsection (1)(a) of that section.

Provision with respect to pension of incumbent found to be unable to perform duties attaching to benefice

14.—(1) Where—
    (a) after an enquiry under Part I of this Measure in which the tribunal reported to the bishop in accordance with section 9(2) thereof; or
    (b) after an enquiry under Part II thereof,

the incumbent concerned resigns his benefice consequent upon a notification from the bishop under section 11(2)(a) of this Measure or the bishop has declared the benefice of the incumbent vacant under that section, the incumbent shall be deemed for the purposes of the Church of England (Pensions) Measures 1961 to 1988 and any regulations approved by the General Synod under section 6 of the Clergy Pensions (Amendment) Measure 1972 to have become incapable through infirmity of performing the duties of his office on the date on which his resignation took effect or the date on which by virtue of the declaration his benefice became vacant, as the case may be, and to have satisfied the Church of England Pensions Board that he was so incapable and that the infirmity was likely to be permanent.

(2) Subsection (1) above shall not apply to an incumbent who at whichever of the dates mentioned in that subsection applies in his case has attained the retiring age within the meaning of the said Measures and regulations.

Part IV
Supplemental

Certain expenses to be paid by Diocesan Board of Finance

16.—(1) The following expenses, that is to say—
- (a) any expenses incurred for the purpose of enabling a provincial tribunal to discharge its functions under this Measure;
- (b) any travelling or other personal expenses reasonably incurred by the members of such a tribunal for the purpose of or in connection with the exercise of the functions of the tribunal under this Measure;
- (c) any such expenses reasonably incurred by an incumbent in connection with an enquiry under this Measure which concerns him;
- (d) any such expenses reasonably incurred by an archdeacon under section 2 of this Measure;
- (e) any such expenses reasonably incurred by a person in connection with his attendance at a meeting of a tribunal conducting an enquiry under this Measure, being a meeting which he was entitled, or invited by the tribunal to attend or which he attended as a witness; and
- (f) any fee payable to the chairman of the tribunal which conducted the enquiry,

shall be paid by the Diocesan Board of Finance.

(2) Any question whether any such expenses as are referred to in paragraph (b), (c), (d) or (e) of subsection (1) above were reasonably incurred or as to the amount thereof shall be determined by the bishop of the diocese.

Exercise of powers of bishop during absence abroad, etc

17. During the absence abroad or incapacity through illness of the bishop of a diocese or a vacancy in the see anything required or authorised by this Measure to be done by, to or before him shall be done or, as the case may be, may be done, by to or before the archbishop of the province to which the diocese belongs or a person, being a person in episcopal orders, appointed by that archbishop for that purpose.

Procedural rules

18.—(1) There shall be a committee, to be known as the Vacation of Benefices Rule Committee, which shall consist of a chairman and four other members appointed by the Appointments Committee of the General Synod.

(2) The Vacation of Benefices Rule Committee shall have power to make rules for carrying into effect the provisions of this Measure and, in particular, for—
- (a) regulating the procedure and practice (including the mode and burden of proof and admissibility of evidence) of provincial tribunals in connection with enquiries under this Measure;

(b) obtaining medical evidence in connection with enquiries under this Measure.

(3) Any three members of the Vacation of Benefices Rule Committee may exercise all the powers of the committee.

(4) Any rules made under this section shall be laid before the General Synod and shall not come into force until approved by the General Synod, whether with or without amendment.

(5) Where the Business Committee determines that the rules do not need to be debated by the General Synod then, unless—
- (a) notice is given by a member of the General Synod in accordance with its Standing Orders that he wishes the rules to be debated, or
- (b) notice is so given by any such member that he wishes to move an amendment to the rules

the rules shall for the purposes of subsection (4) above be deemed to have been approved by the General Synod without amendment.

(6) The Statutory Instruments Act 1946 shall apply to any rules approved by the General Synod under subsection (4) above as if they were statutory instruments and were made when so approved, and as if this Measure were an Act providing that any such rules should be subject to annulment in pursuance of a resolution of either House of Parliament.

Meaning of 'benefice'

19. Without prejudice to section 6(2) of this Measure, in this Measure 'benefice' means the office of rector or vicar, with cure of souls, including the office of vicar in a team ministry established under the Pastoral Measure 1968 or the Pastoral Measure 1983 but does not include any office in a Royal Peculiar nor the office of dean or provost of a parish church cathedral within the meaning of the Cathedrals Measure 1963.

Meaning of references to pastoral situation

19A. In this Measure any reference to a serious breakdown of the pastoral relationship between an incumbent and the parishioners shall be construed as a reference to a situation where the relationship between an incumbent and the parishioners of the parish in question is such as to impede the promotion in the parish of the whole mission of the Church of England, pastoral, evangelistic, social and ecumenical.

Schedule 1
Constitution of Provincial Tribunals

Section 7

1.—(1) A provincial tribunal shall consist of five persons appointed by the Vicar-General of the province in which the parish in question is situated.

(2) Of the five persons to be so appointed—
- (a) one, who shall be the chairman, shall be either the chancellor of a diocese in the province for which the tribunal is to be appointed, other than the diocese in which the parish in question is situated, or a Queen's Counsel who is a communicant member of the Church of England;
- (b) two shall be clerks in Holy Orders from the panel appointed from the members of the Lower House of the Convocation of the province concerned under paragraph 15(1)(b) of Schedule 4 to the Pastoral Measure 1983 (Appeal Tribunal for compensation of clergy); and
- (c) two shall be lay persons from the panel appointed from the members of the House of Laity of the General Synod under paragraph 15(1)(c) of the said Schedule 4:

Provided that no person who is ordinarily resident in the diocese in which the parish in question is or whose name is entered on the electoral roll of any parish in that diocese or who is a clerk in Holy Orders authorised to exercise his ministry in any such parish, shall be appointed.

2.—(1) Where the secretary of the diocesan synod is required to institute an enquiry under this Measure, the said secretary shall request the Vicar-General of the province to constitute a provincial tribunal in accordance with paragraph 1 above and to send him a list of the names and addresses of the proposed members.

(2) Any person appointed to serve as a member of the tribunal from a panel mentioned in sub-paragraph 1(2)(b) or (c) above may refuse to accept the appointment if in his opinion it would not be right for him to serve as a member of the tribunal.

(3) On receiving such list the said secretary shall send a copy of it to the incumbent concerned and shall inform him of his right of objection under paragraph 3 below and of the period within which the right must be exercised.

3.—(1) The incumbent concerned may, within three weeks after a list of the proposed members is sent to him, object to any one or more of them by sending to the said secretary a written notice specifying the member or members to whom he objects and stating, in relation to that member or each of those members, as the case may be, the grounds of his objection.

(2) If notice of objection is duly given under sub-paragraph (1) above, the said secretary shall refer the matter to the Vicar-General of the province, other than the province for which the tribunal is to be appointed, for him to determine whether the objection is reasonable and should accordingly be allowed, and his decision shall be final.

(3) For the purpose of enabling him to decide whether the objection is reasonable, the Vicar-General may require the incumbent to supply him with such information as he may specify.

(4) Where, in the case of any member objected to by the incumbent, the Vicar-General decides that the objection should be allowed, the said secretary shall request the Vicar-General mentioned in paragraph 1(1) above to appoint another person having the appropriate qualifications to serve in place of that member and to inform him of the name and address of the person appointed, and on receiving that information the said secretary shall inform the incumbent of the name and address of that person.

(5) Subject to sub-paragraph (6) below, the incumbent may within three weeks after he is informed of the name of the proposed member appointed under sub-paragraph (4) above object to that member by sending to the said secretary a written notice stating the grounds of his objection, and sub-paragraphs (2) to (4) above shall have effect where a notice of objection is duly given under this sub-paragraph as they have effect where such a notice is so given under sub-paragraph (1) above.

(6) The incumbent shall not be entitled to object to a person appointed under sub-paragraph (4) above from a panel mentioned in paragraph 1(2)(b) or (c) above if, were the objection to be allowed, the result would be that the tribunal could not be constituted, there being no other person on the appropriate panel available for appointment as a member of the tribunal.

4. As soon as the provincial tribunal which is to conduct an enquiry has been constituted the said secretary shall send a list of the members to the incumbent concerned, the archdeacon concerned, the designated representative (if any), the secretary of the parochial church council of the parish to which the enquiry relates and the person who is to act as secretary of the tribunal.

5. The Synodical Secretary of the Convocation of Canterbury or some other person nominated by him shall act as secretary of any tribunal constituted under this Schedule to conduct an enquiry in relation to a parish in the province of Canterbury, and the Synodal Secretary of the Convocation of York or some other person nominated by him shall act as secretary of any tribunal so constituted to conduct an enquiry in relation to a parish in the province of York.

Schedule 2
Compensation under Section 13

Section 13

1.—(1) If agreement as to the form, amount and conditions of provision of compensation is reached between the person concerned and the diocesan board of finance, it shall be provided in accordance with the terms of the agreement.

(2) If no agreement is reached as aforesaid, the compensation shall consist of—

(a) in respect of loss of stipend, a basic award in accordance with paragraph 2 below; and

(b) in respect of loss of housing and removal expenses, a housing allowance and a resettlement allowance in accordance with paragraphs 3 and 4 below.

2.—(1) The basic award shall be in the form of periodical payments which shall be paid monthly to the person concerned during a period commencing on the date when he ceases to be the incumbent of the benefice concerned ('the material date') and expiring at the end of—

(a) such number of months immediately following the material date as results from adding together—

(i) one month for each year or part of a year during which the person concerned has served in whole-time stipendiary ecclesiastical service; and

(ii) one month for each year or part of a year which has passed before the material date since the person concerned attained the age of forty years; or

(b) thirty-six months immediately following the material date,

whichever is the greater:

Provided that where the person concerned has at the material date attained the age of fifty years the payments shall continue, if they would otherwise cease, until he attains an age within five years of the retiring age.

(2) Such payments shall cease to be payable in respect of the person concerned—

(a) when he attains the retiring age; or

(b) if he receives a pension under the pensions regulations before attaining that age, on the date on which the pension is first paid; or

(c) if he re-enters whole-time stipendiary ecclesiastical service (being service which is pensionable service for the purposes of the pensions regulations) within the Province of Canterbury (including the Diocese in Europe) or the Province of York, on the date of re-entry.

(3) Subject to paragraph (5) below, each monthly payment shall be of an amount equal to one-twelfth of the following—

(a) in the first period of twelve months, the national minimum stipend for the year in which the payment falls to be made;

(b) in the second period of twelve months, three-quarters of the national minimum stipend for the year in which the payment falls to be made;

(c) thereafter, two-thirds of the national minimum stipend for the year in which the payment falls to be made.

(4) Where a pension is payable under the pensions regulations to a person who has received periodical payments under this paragraph, the Church of England Pensions Board shall augment the pension so as to ensure that it is at the same rate as it would have been had the period during which the periodical payments were made been one of pensionable service for the purpose of the regulations.

3.—(1) The housing allowance shall be in the form of periodical payments which shall be paid monthly to the person concerned during the period in which the basic award is paid under paragraph 2 above.

(2) Each monthly payment shall be of such amount as may be determined by the diocesan board of finance, and in determining the amount the diocesan board of finance shall consult the Church of England Pensions Board as to its practice where a person retires on grounds of ill-health, and shall have regard to its advice.

4. The resettlement allowance shall be a single payment of an amount equal to three-tenths of the national minimum stipend for the year in which application for compensation was made or such greater amount as the Central Board of Finance of the Church of England may determine.

5.—(1) Subject to paragraph (2) below, if a person who is applying for or receiving payments under paragraph 2(1) or 3(1) above accepts any office or employment, the diocesan board of finance may refuse the application or, as the case may be, may suspend the periodical payments or reduce the amount thereof so as to take account of the emoluments of or other benefits which arise from the office or employment.

(2) The diocesan board of finance shall not exercise its powers under paragraph (1) above in a manner whereby the total annual amount of the emoluments in question and the periodical payments (if any) would be less than the national minimum stipend.

(3) It shall be the duty of every person who applies for or receives periodical payments under paragraph 2(1) or 3(1) above to disclose to the diocesan board of finance any office or employment which has been accepted by him and the terms thereof; and if he fails to do so and it appears to the board that in consequence it has made periodical payments which otherwise it would not have made or periodical payments in excess of those it would otherwise have made, it may, without prejudice to its powers under paragraph (1) above, direct the repayment of the amount of the payments or excess or such part thereof as it thinks just, and that amount shall be recoverable as a debt due to the board.

6.—An application for compensation shall be made to the diocesan board of finance in such manner as that board may determine; and where a person is incapacitated from making such an application himself that board may authorise some other person to make it on his behalf.

7.—The cost of compensation shall be borne by the diocesan board of finance and charged either on the capital or the income amount of the diocesan stipends fund, as may be determined by the diocesan board of finance.

8.—(1) In this Schedule—
'compensation' means compensation under section 13 of this Measure;
'diocesan board of finance' has the same meaning as in the Pastoral Measure 1983;
'national minimum stipend', in relation to any year, means the national minimum stipend recommended for the stipends of clergymen of incumbent status for that year in the Annual Report of the Central Stipends Authority;
'pensions regulations' means regulations for the time being in force under section 6 of the Clergy Pensions (Amendment) Measure 1972.

(2) In this Schedule the following expressions have the same meanings as in the pensions regulations—
 'retiring age';
 'stipendiary ecclesiastical service'.

Pastoral Measure 1983

It is anticipated that during the lifetime of the current edition of this text substantial changes will be effected to the provisions of the Pastoral Measure 1983 by virtue of the Dioceses, Pastoral and Mission Measure which received the approval of the General Synod of the Church of England at its February 2007 group of sessions. Accordingly the provisions of this Measure are not reproduced and reference should be made to pages 419-447 of the Second Edition of this work. However, for convenience, section 56 of the Pastoral Measure 1983 is reproduced below in its amended form following the enactment of the Pastoral (Amendment) Measure 2006, s 1, pursuant to which leases of a part of a church may now be created.

56.—Churches not to be closed or disposed of otherwise than under this Measure

(1) It shall not be lawful to make any order or give any direction for closing a church on the ground that it is no longer required for use as a church, and the only procedure for closing a church on that ground shall be by way of a declaration of redundancy or the exercise of powers under section 55.

(2) Subject to subsections (2A) and (2B), it shall not be lawful to sell, lease or otherwise dispose of any church or part of a church or the site or part of the site of any church or any consecrated land belonging or annexed to a church except in pursuance of powers under this Part or section 30.

(2A) Without prejudice to subsection (3)(a), on an application by the incumbent of the benefice comprising or including the parish in which the church is situated or, where the benefice is vacant, the bishop in the name and on behalf of the incumbent in the corporate capacity of the incumbent, the court may grant a faculty for a lease to be granted by the incumbent or, as the case may be, the bishop, of part of a church, provided that the court shall ensure that the premises remaining unlet, together with the premises let, under any lease or leases granted under this subsection, are, taken as a whole, used primarily as a place of worship.

(2B) On an application by any person referred to in subsection (2A) the court may, whether or not it grants a faculty under that subsection, grant a faculty for the lease of any land belonging to or annexed to a church.

(2C) The parochial church council for the parish in which the church or land is situated shall be a party to any lease granted under subsection (2A) or (2B) and, without prejudice to the rights and obligations of the lessor, shall have the same rights as the lessor to enforce any term of the lease which may be binding on the lessee, including any rights to forfeit the lease or to distrain on the property of the lessee.

(2D) Subject to any directions of the court, any rent or other payment payable under any lease granted under subsection (2A) or (2B) shall be paid to the parochial church council.

(2E) Subject to subsections (2D) and (2F), any such lease shall be for such period, and may contain such terms, as the court may determine and the lease or any terms contained therein may be varied at any time by the court on application by any party to the lease or otherwise as authorised by the court.

(2F) Any such lease shall be deemed to contain the following terms—
  (a) in the case of a lease of part of a church granted under subsection (2A), the premises which are the subject of the lease shall not be used for purposes which are, or in a way which is, inconsistent with the use specified in that subsection, and
  (b) in the case of a lease granted under subsection (2A) or (2B), no use shall be permitted for residential purposes except by a person who, as an employee of the lessor or otherwise, is required, as a condition of the employment or contract, to reside in the premises or part thereof,

and the lease shall be deemed to contain a covenant on the part of the lessee to perform the said terms.

(2G) Where any lease is granted under subsection (2A) or (2B)—
  (a) in the case of a lease of premises to trustees to be held on trust to be used for the purposes of a place of worship, the trustees shall not be entitled to exercise the right conferred by the Places of Worship (Enfranchisement) Act 1920 (10 & 11 Geo 5 c 56) to enlarge the leasehold interest by acquiring the freehold;

(b) in the case of a lease consisting of a tenancy of premises occupied or to be occupied wholly or partly for the purposes of a business, the tenancy shall not be subject to any provision of Part II of the Landlord and Tenant Act 1954 (2 & 3 Eliz 2 c 56) under which the lease is continued until determined, or under which the tenant is entitled to apply to the court for the grant of a new tenancy, in accordance with the provisions of that Part; and

(c) in the case of a lease of land consisting of a tenancy which would, but for this subsection, be a farm business tenancy to which the Agricultural Tenancies Act 1995 (1995 c 8) applied, that Act shall not apply to the tenancy and, accordingly, the tenant shall not be entitled to exercise any of the rights conferred by Part I, II or III of that Act

(2H) Without prejudice to section 84, where at any time, there is no parochial church council, the foregoing provisions of this section shall have effect and any lease granted under subsection (2A) or (2B) shall be construed as if, for any reference therein to the council, there were substituted a reference to the churchwardens.

(2I) Where a lease has been granted under subsection (2A) or (2B) and, at any time, the benefice is vacant, the bishop in the name and on behalf of the incumbent in the incumbent's corporate capacity may exercise the power conferred on the lessor by subsection (2E) to apply to the court for a variation of the lease or any terms therein and the lease shall be construed as if any reference therein to the incumbent were a reference to the bishop acting in the name and on behalf of the incumbent as aforesaid.

(2J) Any question relating to the interpretation or enforcement of any term of any lease granted under subsection (2A) or (2B) shall be determined by the court and section 11 of the Faculty Jurisdiction Measure 1964 (1964 No 5) shall apply in relation to proceedings under subsection (2E) and this subsection as it applies to the proceedings mentioned in that section.

(2K) Section 16(2), so far only as it applies to the archdeacon, (3) and (4) of the Care of Churches and Ecclesiastical Jurisdiction Measure 1991 (1991 No 1), shall apply to proceedings under subsections (2A), (2B), (2E) and (2J) as they apply to other proceedings for a faculty.

(2L) In this section, except subsection (2G)(b), 'the court' means the consistory court of the diocese in which the building is situated or, in the case of the diocese of Canterbury, the commissary court thereof and section 14 of the Care of Churches and Ecclesiastical Jurisdiction Measure 1991 (1991 No 1) shall not apply to the jurisdiction of the court conferred by the foregoing provisions of this section.

(3) The foregoing provisions of this section shall not—
(a) prevent the grant of a faculty authorising a suitable use of part of a church or the grant of any faculty in respect of any such land as aforesaid; or
(b) affect any powers under any Act of Parliament;
(c) affect the power of the bishop of a diocese under section 22 of the Care of Churches and Ecclesiastical Jurisdiction Measure 1991 to make an order directing that a building or land shall not be subject to the legal effects of consecration.

(4) Where any church other than a church which has been declared redundant is purchased compulsorily or is purchased by agreement under an enactment conferring powers of compulsory purchase, then for the purposes of any enactment applying to the disposal of sums paid to the Commissioners in respect of the purchase of the church or any land annexed or belonging thereto, or in respect of compensation for damage to other ecclesiastical property arising in connection with the purchase, the provisions of this Part relating to the disposal of the proceeds of sale of a redundant building or any land annexed or belonging to a redundant church shall be deemed not to be applicable.

Patronage (Benefices) Measure 1986

Part I
Registration and Transfer of Rights of Patronage

Registration of patrons

1.—(1) Subject to the provisions of this Measure, the registrar of each diocese shall compile and maintain a register indicating in relation to every benefice in the diocese the person who is the patron of the benefice and containing such other information as may be prescribed.

(2) Except as provided by this Measure, no person shall be entitled, after the expiration of the period of fifteen months beginning with the date on which this section comes into force, to exercise any of the functions of a patron of a benefice unless he is registered as patron of that benefice, and the said period is in this Measure referred to as the 'registration period'.

(3) The provisions of Schedule 1 to this Measure shall have effect with respect to the registration of patrons of benefices and other matters relating thereto.

(4) The registration under this Measure of any person as a patron of a benefice shall be conclusive evidence of the matters registered.

(5) Any register maintained under this Measure shall be open to inspection by the public at all reasonable times.

Registration of patronage belonging to an office

2. In the case of a right of patronage of a benefice which belongs to an office, the duty of the registrar of the diocese under section 1(1) of this Measure to register in relation to that benefice the person who is the patron thereof shall be construed as a duty to register that office as a patron of that benefice; and section 1(4) shall apply in relation to an office which is registered as a patron as it applies in relation to a person who is so registered.

Transfer of rights of patronage

3.—(1) No right of patronage of a benefice shall be capable of sale and any transfer thereof for valuable consideration shall be void.

(2) Subject to the provisions of this section, a right of patronage vested in an ecclesiastical corporation shall not be transferred to any body or person unless—
  (a) the consent of the bishop or, if the bishop is the proposed transferor, the consent of the archbishop has been obtained; or
  (b) the transfer is made by a pastoral scheme or order.

(3) Where a right of patronage of a benefice is proposed to be transferred otherwise than by a pastoral scheme or order, the proposed transferor shall sent to the bishop (or, if the bishop is the proposed transferor, to the archbishop) and to the registrar of the diocese a notice stating—
  (a) his intention to transfer that right;
  (b) the name and address of the proposed transferee; and
  (c) particulars of the terms of the proposed transfer.

(4) On receiving a notice under subsection (3) above, the registrar shall send to the secretary of the parochial church council of the parish concerned a notice informing him of the proposed transfer and stating that before the expiration of the period of one month beginning with the date on which the notice is sent to him representations with respect to the proposed transfer may be made to the registrar by the parochial church council; and the registrar shall notify the bishop and the proposed transferor, or, if the bishop is the proposed transferor, the bishop and the archbishop, of any representations made to him within that period.

(5) After the expiration of the period of one month mentioned in subsection (4) above, the bishop or, if the bishop is the proposed transferor, the archbishop shall consider any representations

made under that subsection and, whether or not any such representations have been made, the bishop or archbishop may request the proposed transferor (either personally or through some person appointed by the proposed transferor) to confer with him (or with some person appointed by the bishop or, as the case may be, the archbishop) as to the proposed transfer; and the bishop or, as the case may be, the archbishop shall not give any consent required under this section until after any such representations have been considered and any such request has been complied with.

(6) Any transfer of a right of patronage otherwise than by a pastoral scheme or order shall be in the prescribed form.

(7) Where a right of patronage of a benefice is transferred otherwise than by a pastoral scheme or order, the registrar shall not register the transferee as a patron of that benefice unless—
- (a) he is satisfied that the requirements of this section have been complied with; and
- (b) an application for registration is made in accordance with Schedule 1 to this Measure before the expiration of the period of twelve months from the date of the execution of the transfer;

and if no such application for registration is made before the expiration of that period of twelve months the transfer shall be of no effect.

(8) No transfer of a right of patronage of a benefice shall take effect during the period of a vacancy in that benefice unless the benefice is one to which a suspension period (within the meaning of section 67 of the Pastoral Measure 1983) applies and a person holds office as priest in charge for the benefice.

(9) In this section 'transfer' means a transfer inter vivos including a transfer by way of exchange; but except in subsection (6) it does not include a transfer by operation of law, a transfer upon the appointment of a new trustee or a transfer by the personal representatives of a deceased person.

Rectification of register

4.—(1) The registrar of a diocese may rectify an entry in the register of patrons in any case—
- (a) where all the persons interested agree to the rectification of the entry; or
- (b) where the registrar decides that the entry should be rectified—
  - (i) because a person is, or is not, entitled to be registered as patron of a benefice, or
  - (ii) because information registered as to the exercise of a right of presentation to a benefice is incorrect,

  and in either case, no appeal against the registrar's decision has been brought within the period specified in paragraph 8 of Schedule 1 to this Measure or the appeal has been dismissed; or
- (c) where any rectification of the entry is required by reason of a decision of the chancellor of the diocese under that Schedule.

(2) Where in the case of an entry in the register relating to any benefice—
- (a) the entry has been adverse to the claim of any person for a period of more than thirty years, or
- (b) if the period of thirty years from the end of the registration period has not expired, the benefice has been held adversely to the claim of any person for a period of more than thirty years,

then, notwithstanding anything in subsection (1) above or in paragraph 5 of Schedule 1 to this Measure, no rectification of that entry may be made in favour of that person unless all the persons interested agree to that rectification.

(3) Section 25 of the Limitation Act 1980 (time limits for actions to enforce advowsons) shall cease to have effect at the end of the registration period.

Rights of patronage exercisable otherwise than by registered patron

5.—(1) Where an office is registered as a patron of a benefice, the person who is for the time being the holder of that office shall, subject to the provisions of Part II of this Measure, be entitled to discharge all the functions of a patron of that benefice.

(2) Where a registered patron of a benefice dies then, until the person to whom the right of patronage is to be transferred is registered as a patron of that benefice, the personal representatives of the deceased patron shall, subject to the provisions of Part II of this Measure, be entitled to discharge all the functions of a patron of that benefice.

(3) A registered patron of a benefice may by an instrument creating a power of attorney confer on the donee of the power authority to discharge on his behalf all the functions of a patron of that benefice, and where such a power is created the donee shall, subject to the provisions of Part II of this Measure, be entitled to discharge those functions until the power is revoked.

(3A) The reference in subsection (3) to a power of attorney does not include an enduring power of attorney or lasting power of attorney (within the meaning of the Mental Capacity Act 2005).

(4) Any person entitled to discharge any functions in relation to a benefice by virtue of this section shall be entitled to discharge those functions notwithstanding that he is not registered in the register of patrons in relation to that benefice.

Abolition of registration of advowsons at Land Registry

6. *Repealed.*

Part II
Exercise of Rights of Presentation

General provisions as to filling of vacancies

Notification of vacancies

7.—(1) Subject to section 70 of the Pastoral Measure 1983, where a benefice becomes vacant by reason of the death of the incumbent, the bishop shall, as soon as practicable after he becomes aware of the vacancy, give notice of that fact to the designated officer of the diocese.

(2) Subject to section 70 of the Pastoral Measure 1983, where the bishop is aware that a benefice is shortly to become vacant by reason of resignation or cession, the bishop shall give such notice of that fact as he considers reasonable in all the circumstances to the designated officer of the diocese.

(3) Any notice required to be given to the designated officer under subsection (1) or (2) above shall also be given to the registrar of the diocese, unless he is the designated officer.

(4) As soon as practicable after receiving a notice under subsection (1) or (2) above the designated officer shall send notice of the vacancy to the registered patron of the benefice and to the secretary of the parochial church council of the parish belonging to the benefice; and any such notice shall include such information as may be prescribed.

(5) In this Measure 'the designated officer', in relation to a diocese, means such person as the bishop, after consulting the bishop's council, may designate or, if no person is designated, the secretary of the pastoral committee of the diocese.

Provisions as to declarations of membership

8.—(1) Where the registered patron of a benefice is an individual and is not a clerk in Holy Orders, he shall on receiving notice of a vacancy in the benefice under section 7(4) of this Measure—
 (a) if able to do so, make a written declaration (in this Measure referred to as 'the declaration of membership') declaring that he is an actual communicant member of the Church of England or of a Church in communion with that Church; or
 (b) if unable to make the declaration himself, appoint some other person, being an individual who is able and willing to make it or is a clerk in Holy Orders or one of the bodies mentioned in subsection (7) below, to act as his representative to discharge in his place the functions of a registered patron.

(2) Where the registered patron of a benefice is a body of persons corporate or unincorporate then, on receiving notice of a vacancy in the benefice under section 7(4) of this Measure, that body shall appoint an individual who is able and willing to make the declaration of membership or is a

clerk in Holy Orders to act as its representative to discharge in its place the functions of a registered patron.

(3) Notwithstanding anything in subsection (1) above, where the registered patron of a benefice who is an individual and is not the bishop of a diocese is of the opinion, on receiving notice of a vacancy in the benefice under section 7(4) of this Measure, that he will be unable for any reason to discharge his functions as a patron of that benefice he may, notwithstanding that he is able to make the declaration of membership, appoint such a representative as is mentioned in subsection (1)(b) above to discharge those functions in his place.

(4) Where a benefice the right of presentation to which belongs to an office (other than an ecclesiastical office) becomes vacant, the person who holds that office on the date on which the benefice becomes vacant shall be entitled to present on that vacancy and shall as soon as practicable after that date—
- (a) if able to do so, make the declaration of membership, or
- (b) if unable to make the declaration himself, appoint some other person, being a person who may be appointed as a representative under subsection (1)(b) above, to act as his representative to discharge in his place the functions of a registered patron.

(5) Where the right of presentation to a benefice is exercisable by the donee of a power of attorney, the donee shall as soon as practicable after receiving notice of the vacancy in the benefice (or, if the power is created during the vacancy, as soon as practicable after it is created)—
- (a) if able to do so, make the declaration of membership, or
- (b) if unable to make the declaration himself, appoint some other person, being a person who may be appointed as a representative under subsection (1)(b) above, to act as his representative to discharge in his place the functions of a registered patron.

(6) Where under the preceding provisions of this section a body mentioned in subsection (7) below is appointed to discharge the functions of a registered patron, that body shall as soon as practicable after being so appointed appoint as its representative an individual who is able and willing to make the declaration of membership or is a clerk in Holy Orders.

(7) The bodies referred to in subsection (1)(b) above are—
- (a) the dean and chapter or the cathedral chapter of the cathedral church of the diocese;
- (b) the dean and chapter of the collegiate church of St Peter in Westminster;
- (c) the dean and canons of the collegiate church of St George, Windsor;
- (d) any diocesan board of patronage;
- (e) any patronage board constituted by a pastoral scheme;
- (f) any university in England or any college or hall in such a university; and
- (g) the college of Eton and Winchester.

Information to be sent to designated officer

9.—(1) Before the expiration of the period of two months beginning with the date on which a benefice becomes vacant or the expiration of three weeks after receiving notice of the vacancy from the designated officer under section 7(4) of this Measure, whichever is later, a registered patron who is an individual shall send to the designated officer of the diocese—
- (a) the declaration of membership made by him, or
- (b) the name and address of his representative and the declaration of membership made by that representative.

(2) Before the expiration of the said period of two months or three weeks, as the case may be, a registered patron which is a body of persons corporate or unincorporate shall send to the designated officer of the diocese the name and address of the individual who is to act as its representative and the declaration of membership made by that representative.

(3) Where the functions of a registered patron are to be discharged by the holder of an office, subsection (1) above shall apply to the person who holds that office on the date on which the benefice becomes vacant as it applies to the registered patron.

(4) Where the functions of a registered patron are to be discharged by the donee of a power of attorney, subsection (1) above shall apply to the donee as it applies to the registered patron except that, if the power is created during the vacancy concerned, there shall be substituted for the period of two months mentioned in that subsection the period of two months beginning with the date on which the power is created, and the information required to be sent under that subsection shall include information as to that date.

(5) Where the registered patron or his representative is a clerk in Holy Orders, the registered patron shall, before the expiration of the period during which the declaration of membership is required to be sent to the designated officer under the preceding provisions of this section, notify the designated officer of that fact, and a declaration of membership made by that clerk shall not be required to be sent to the designated officer under this section.

(5A) Subsections (5B) and (5C) apply where the functions of a registered patron are, as a result of paragraph 10 of Schedule 2 to the Mental Capacity Act 2005 (patron's loss of capacity to discharge functions), to be discharged by an individual appointed by the Court of Protection.

(5B) If the individual is a clerk in Holy Orders, subsection (5) applies to him as it applies to the registered patron.

(5C) If the individual is not a clerk in Holy Orders, subsection (1) (other than paragraph (b)) applies to him as it applies to the registered patron.

(6) As soon as practicable after receiving information under this section as to the appointment of a representative, the designated officer shall send to the secretary of the parochial church council the name and address of that representative.

Disqualification for presentation

10. Where the registered patron of a benefice or the representative of that patron, is a clerk in Holy Orders or is the wife of such a clerk, that clerk shall be disqualified for presentation to that benefice.

Requirements as to meetings of parochial church council

11.—(1) Before the expiration of the period of four weeks beginning with the date on which the notice under section 7(4) of this Measure is sent to the secretary of the parochial church council, one or more meetings of that council shall be held for the purposes of—

(a) preparing a statement describing the conditions, needs and traditions of the parish;
(b) appointing two lay members of the council to act as representatives of the council in connection with the selection of an incumbent;
(c) deciding whether to request the registered patron to consider advertising the vacancy;
(d) deciding whether to request a meeting under section 12 of this Measure;
(e) deciding whether to request a statement in writing from the bishop describing in relation to the benefice the needs of the diocese and the wider interests of the Church; and
(f) deciding whether to pass a resolution under section 3(1) or (2) of the Priests (Ordination of Women) Measure 1993.

(2) A meeting of the parochial church council for which subsection (1) above provides shall be convened by the secretary thereof, and no member of that council who is—

(a) the outgoing incumbent or the spouse or civil partner of the outgoing incumbent, or
(b) the registered patron, or
(c) the representative of the registered patron,

shall attend that meeting.

(3) None of the following members of the parochial church council, that is to say—

(a) any person mentioned in subsection (2) above, and
(b) any deaconess or lay worker licensed to the parish, shall be qualified for appointment under subsection (1)(b) above.

(4) If before the vacancy in the benefice is filled any person appointed under subsection (1)(b) above dies or becomes unable for any reason to act as the representative of, or ceases to be a member

of, the council by which he was appointed, then, except where he ceases to be such a member and the council decides that he shall continue to act as its representative, his appointment shall be deemed to have been revoked and the council shall appoint another lay member of the council (not being a member disqualified under subsection (3) above) to act in his place for the remainder of the proceedings under this Part of this Measure.

(5) If a parochial church council holds a meeting under subsection (1) above but does not appoint any representatives at that meeting, then, subject to subsection (6) below, two churchwardens who are members of that council (or, if there are more than two churchwardens who are members of the council, two churchwardens chosen by all the churchwardens who are members) shall act as representatives of the council in connection with the selection of an incumbent.

(6) A churchwarden who is the registered patron of a benefice shall not be qualified under subsection (5) above to act as a representative of the parochial church council or to choose any other churchwarden so to act, and in any case where there is only one churchwarden qualified to act as such a representative that churchwarden may act as the sole representative of that council in connection with the selection of the incumbent.

(7) Any representative of the parochial church council appointed under subsection (1) or (4) above and any churchwarden acting as such a representative by virtue of subsection (5) or (6) above is in this Part of this Measure referred to as a 'parish representative', and where a churchwarden is entitled to act as the sole parish representative any reference in this Part to the parish representatives shall be construed as a reference to that churchwarden.

(8) A copy of the statement prepared under subsection (1)(a) above together with the names and addresses of the parish representatives shall, as soon as practicable after the holding of the meeting under that subsection, be sent by the secretary of the parochial church council to the registered patron and, unless the bishop is the registered patron, to the bishop.

Joint meeting of parochial church council with bishop and patron

12.—(1) Where a request for a meeting under this section is made—
   (a)   by a notice sent by the registered patron or the bishop to the secretary of the parochial church council, or
   (b)   by a resolution of the parochial church council, passed at a meeting held under section 11 of this Measure,

a joint meeting of the parochial church council with the registered patron and (if the bishop is not the registered patron) the bishop shall be held for the purpose of enabling those present at the meeting to exchange views on the statement prepared under section 11(1)(a) of this Measure (needs of the parish) and the statement presented under subsection (2) below (needs of the diocese).

(2) At any meeting held under this section the bishop shall present either orally or, if a request for a statement in writing has been made by the registered patron or the parochial church council, in writing a statement describing in relation to the benefice the needs of the diocese and the wider interests of the Church.

(3) Any notice given under subsection (1)(a) above shall be of no effect unless it is sent to the secretary of the parochial church council not later than ten days after a copy of the statement prepared under subsection (1)(a) of section 11 of this Measure is received by the persons mentioned in subsection (8) of that section.

(4) The outgoing incumbent and the spouse or civil partner of the outgoing incumbent shall not be entitled to attend a meeting held under this section.

(5) A meeting requested under this section shall be held before the expiration of the period of six weeks beginning with the date on which the request for the meeting was first made (whether by the sending of a notice as mentioned in subsection (1)(a) above or by the passing of a resolution as mentioned in subsection (1)(b) above), and at least fourteen days' notice (unless a shorter period is agreed by all the persons concerned) of the time and place at which the meeting is to be held shall be given by the secretary of the parochial church council to the registered patron, the bishop (if he is not the registered patron) and the members of the parochial church council.

(6) If either the registered patron or the bishop is unable to attend a meeting held under this section, he shall appoint some other person to attend on his behalf.

(7) The chairman of any meeting held under this section shall be such person as the persons who are entitled to attend and are present at the meeting may determine.

(8) No meeting requested under this section shall be treated for the purposes of this Measure as having been held unless there were present at the meeting—
- (a) the bishop or the person appointed by the bishop to attend on his behalf, and
- (b) the registered patron or the person appointed by the patron to attend on his behalf, and
- (c) at least one third of the members of the parochial church council who were entitled to attend.

(9) The secretary of the parochial church council shall invite both the rural dean of the deanery in which the parish is (unless he is the outgoing incumbent) and the lay chairman of the deanery synod of that deanery to attend a meeting held under this section.

Provisions with respect to the selection of incumbent

13.—(1) The registered patron of a vacant benefice shall not make to any priest an offer to present him to a benefice until—
- (a) if a request for a meeting under section 12 of this Measure has been made, either—
  - (i) that meeting has been held, or
  - (ii) all the parties concerned have agreed that no such meeting should be held, or
  - (iii) the period of six weeks mentioned in section 12(5) has expired; and
- (b) (whether or not such a request has been made) the making of the offer to the priest in question has been approved—
  - (i) by the parish representatives, and
  - (ii) if the registered patron is a person other than the bishop of the diocese in which the benefice is, by that bishop.

(2) If, before the expiration of the period of four weeks beginning with the date on which the registered patron sent to the bishop a request for him to approve under paragraph (b) of subsection (1) above the making of the offer to the priest named in the request, no notice is received from the bishop of his refusal to approve the making of the offer, the bishop shall be deemed to have given his approval under that paragraph.

(3) If, before the expiration of the period of two weeks beginning with the date on which the registered patron sent to the parish representatives a request for them to approve under paragraph (b) of subsection (1) above the making of the offer to the priest named in the request, no notice is received from any representative of his refusal to approve the making of the offer, the representatives shall be deemed to have given their approval under that paragraph.

(4) If—
- (a) the bishop refuses to approve under paragraph (b) of subsection (1) above the making of the offer to the priest named in the request, or
- (b) any parish representative refuses to approve under that paragraph the making of that offer,

the bishop or the representative, as the case may be, shall notify the registered patron in writing of the grounds on which the refusal is made.

(5) Where approval of an offer is refused under subsection (4) above, the registered patron may request the archbishop to review the matter and if, after review, the archbishop authorises the registered patron to make the offer in question, the patron may make that offer accordingly

Provided that this subsection shall not apply in respect of—
- (a) a parish in a diocese to which a declaration under section 2(1)(b) of the Priests (Ordination of Women) Measure 1993 applies; or

(b) a benefice comprising a parish to which a resolution under section 3(1) of that Measure applies,

where the refusal is made solely on grounds of gender.

(6) Where a priest accepts an offer made in accordance with the provisions of this section to present him to a benefice and the registered patron is a person other than the bishop, the patron shall send the bishop a notice presenting the priest to him for admission to the benefice.

Failure of registered patron to comply with section 9

14.—(1) Where any declaration of membership or other information required to be sent to the designated officer under section 9 of this Measure is not sent to that officer before the expiration of the period during which it is required to be so sent and the registered patron is a person other than the bishop then, after the expiration of that period—
- (a) no meeting shall be held under section 12 of this Measure by reason of any request made by the registered patron and subsections (2), (5), (6) and (8) of that section shall not apply in relation to that patron; and
- (b) no offer shall be made to any priest under section 13 of this Measure;

but the bishop may, subject to subsection (2) below, make to such priest as he thinks fit an offer to collate him to the benefice.

(2) The bishop shall not make an offer under subsection (1) above unless the making of the offer has been approved by the parish representatives, and subsections (3), (4)(b) and (5) of section 13 of this Measure shall apply in relation to a request sent by the bishop to those representatives by virtue of this subsection as if for any reference to the registered patron there were substituted a reference to the bishop.

(3) Where under subsection (1) above the bishop makes to a priest an offer to collate him to a benefice in respect of which there is more than one person registered under this Measure, the registered patron whose turn it was to present to the benefice shall be treated for the purposes of this Measure as having exercised that turn.

Failure of council to comply with section 11 or 12

15. If a copy of the statement prepared under section 11(1)(a) of this Measure is not sent under subsection (8) of that section to the persons mentioned in that subsection or if notice is not given under section 12(5) of this Measure of any joint meeting requested under subsection (1)(a) of the said section 12 then—
- (a) if the bishop is the registered patron, he may, without making any request for the approval of the parish representatives, make to such priest as he thinks fit an offer to collate him to the benefice; and
- (b) if the bishop is not the registered patron, that patron shall be entitled to proceed under section 13 of this Measure as if paragraphs (a) and (b)(i) of subsection (1), subsection (3) and paragraph (b) of subsection (4) thereof had not been enacted.

Provisions which apply where benefice remains vacant for nine months

Presentation to benefices remaining vacant for nine months

16.—(1) If at the expiration of the period of nine months beginning with the date on which a benefice becomes vacant—
- (a) no notice of presentation under section 13(6) of this Measure has been received by the bishop, or
- (b) where the bishop is the registered patron, he has not received an acceptance of any offer made by him to collate a priest to the benefice,

the right of presentation to that benefice shall be exercisable by the archbishop in accordance with the provision of this section; and a notice to that effect shall be sent by the bishop to the archbishop.

(2) In calculating the period of nine months mentioned in subsection (1) above, no account shall be taken of any of the following periods, that is to say—
  (a) a period during which the decision of the bishop to refuse to approve the making to a priest of an offer to present him to a benefice is under review by an archbishop,
  (b) a suspension period within the meaning of the Pastoral Measure 1983, and
  (c) a period during which the exercise of rights of presentation is restricted under section 24 or 69 of that Measure.

(3) As soon as practicable after a right of presentation becomes exercisable by an archbishop under this section, the archbishop shall send to the secretary of the parochial church council of the parish concerned a notice requiring him within three weeks after receiving the notice to send to the archbishop copies of the statement describing the conditions, needs and traditions of the parish prepared in accordance with section 11 of this Measure together with copies of any additional observations which the council wishes the archbishop to consider.

(4) The bishop may, and if the archbishop so requests shall, send to the archbishop a statement describing in relation to the benefice the needs of the diocese and the wider interests of the Church.

(5) Before the archbishop decides on the priest to whom an offer to present him to the benefice is to be made he shall consult the bishop, the parish representatives and such other persons as he thinks fit, including other persons who in his opinion can also represent the views of the parishioners and, if during the period of nine months mentioned in subsection (1) above the approval of the bishop or the parish representatives to the making of an offer to a priest by the registered patron of the vacant benefice has been refused under section 13 of this Measure, the archbishop shall not make any offer to that priest under this section unless the consent of the bishop or, as the case may be, the parish representatives has been obtained.

(6) Where a priest accepts an offer to present him to a benefice made in accordance with the provisions of this section, the archbishop shall send to the bishop a notice presenting the priest to him for admission to the benefice.

Institution and collation

Provisions to have effect where bishop refuses to institute presentee

17.—(1) Nothing in the preceding provisions of this Measure shall be taken as affecting the power of a bishop under section 2(1)(b) of the Benefices Act 1898 or section 1 of the Benefices Measure 1972 or any rule of law to refuse to institute or admit a presentee to the benefice.

(2) Where in exercise of any such power a bishop refuses to institute or admit a presentee to a benefice, and either no legal proceedings in respect of the refusal are brought or the refusal of the bishop is upheld in such proceedings, the presentation to the benefice affected shall be made by the registered patron whose turn it was to present when the vacancy first occurred; and for the purposes of sections 7, 9, 11 and 12 of this Measure a new vacancy shall not be treated as having occurred by virtue of this section.

Amendment of Benefices Act 1898

18. *Text omitted.*

Notice of intention of bishop to institute or collate person to benefice

19.—(1) Subject to subsection (3) below, a bishop shall not on a vacancy in a benefice institute or collate any person to the benefice unless after the occurrence of the vacancy a notice in the prescribed form, signed by or on behalf of the bishop, is served on the secretary of the parochial church council of the parish concerned informing him of the bishop's intention to institute or collate that person to the benefice specified in the notice and a period of three weeks has expired since the date of the service of the notice.

(2) As soon as practicable after receiving a notice under subsection (1) above the secretary shall cause the notice or a copy thereof to be fixed on or near the principal door of every church in

the parish and every building licensed for public worship in the parish and to remain affixed thereon for two weeks.

(3) Subsection (1) above shall not apply in relation to a person designated by or selected under a pastoral scheme or order as the incumbent of any benefice.

Provisions relating to benefice of which an incumbent is patron

Bishop to act in place of incumbent patron in certain cases

20. Where a benefice ('the ancillary benefice') becomes vacant and it is the turn of the incumbent of another benefice ('the principal benefice'), being the registered patron of the ancillary benefice, to present to that benefice, then if, when the ancillary benefice becomes vacant or at any time during the vacancy thereof and before a notice of presentation under section 13(6) of this Measure is sent to the bishop by the incumbent of the principal benefice—
  (a) the principal benefice is or becomes vacant, or
  (b) the principal benefice is under sequestration, or
  (c) the incumbent of the principal benefice is suspended or inhibited from discharging all or any of the duties attached to his preferment,

the bishop shall discharge in his place the functions of a registered patron.

Exercise of patronage by personal representatives

Exercise of patronage by personal representatives

21. Where a benefice becomes vacant and either—
  (a) the registered patron who would have been entitled to present upon the vacancy is dead and the person to whom the right of patronage is to be transferred has not before the vacancy occurs been registered as a patron of that benefice, or
  (b) the registered patron dies during the vacancy,

then, notwithstanding anything in section 3(8) of this Measure the right of presentation to that benefice upon that vacancy shall be exercisable by that patron's personal representatives; but, before they exercise that right, they shall comply with the requirements of sections 8 and 9 of this Measure as if they were the registered patron.

Exchange of benefices

Exchange of benefices

22.—(1) Two incumbents may by instrument in writing agree to exchange their benefices if the agreement of the following persons has been obtained—
  (a) the bishop of the diocese in which each benefice is,
  (b) any registered patron whose turn it is to present to either of the benefices, and
  (c) the parochial church council of the parish of each benefice, the agreement having in each case been given by resolution of the council.

(2) Where a registered patron whose turn it is to present to a benefice has given his agreement under subsection (1) above to an exchange by the incumbent of that benefice, he shall be treated for the purposes of this Measure as having exercised that turn.

Special provisions as to certain benefices

Special provisions applicable to certain benefices

23. The provisions of this Part of this Measure shall in their application to—
  (a) a benefice which comprises two or more parishes,
  (b) a benefice of which the parochial church council of the parish belonging to the benefice is the registered patron, and
  (c) benefices held in plurality,

have effect subject to the provisions of Schedule 2 to this Measure.

Interpretation of Part II

Interpretation of Part II

24.—(1) Subject to subsections (2) and (3) below, in this Part of this Measure, except in sections 7(4) and 10, any reference to a registered patron, in relation to any vacancy in a benefice in respect of which there is more than one patron registered under this Measure, shall be construed as a reference to the registered patron whose turn it is, according to the information in the register of patrons on the date on which the vacancy occurs, to present on that vacancy.

(2) In a case where the functions of the registered patron of a benefice in relation to a vacancy in the benefice are to be discharged by the holder of an office or the donee of a power of attorney, any reference in this Part of this Measure (except in sections 8, 9(1) to (4) and 21) to the registered patron shall (subject to subsection (3) below) be construed as a reference to that office-holder or donee as the case may be.

(3) In sections 11 and 12 of this Measure any reference to the registered patron of a benefice (except the reference in section 11(2)(b)) shall in a case where the functions of the patron in relation to a vacancy in the benefice are to be discharged by a representative be construed as a reference to that representative, and in section 13 of this Measure any reference to the registered patron of a benefice shall, in a case where the registered patron, being an individual, has appointed a body mentioned in section 8(7) of this Measure or another individual to discharge those functions, be construed as a reference to that body or that other individual, as the case may be.

(4) In this Part of this Measure, except in section 8, 'representative', in relation to a registered patron, means—
- (a) in the case of a registered patron who is an individual, the individual appointed under section 8(1)(b), (3) or (6);
- (b) in the case of a registered patron which is a body of persons, the individual appointed under section 8(2);
- (c) in the case of a registered patron which is an office, the individual appointed under section 8(4) or (6);
- (d) in a case where the functions of a registered patron are to be discharged by the donee of a power of attorney, the individual appointed under section 8(5) or (6).

(5) In this Part of this Measure 'parish representative' has the meaning assigned to it by section 11(7) of this Measure.

Part III

Miscellaneous Provisions as to Patronage

Appointment of patron of benefice which has no registered patron

Appointment of patron of benefice which has no registered patron

25. Where at the expiration of the registration period or at any subsequent time no person is registered as the patron of a benefice, then unless in relation to that benefice—
- (a) a notice under paragraph 7 of Schedule 1 to this Measure has been served on any person by the registrar of the diocese in which the benefice is and either the period mentioned in paragraph 8 of that Schedule has not expired or an appeal under paragraph 9 thereof has not been determined; or
- (b) the right of presentation to the benefice is exercisable by the personal representatives of a deceased patron,

the Diocesan Board of Patronage for the diocese shall become the patron of that benefice, and the registrar of the diocese shall register that Board as patron accordingly.

Diocesan Boards of Patronage

Diocesan Boards of Patronage

26.—(1) There shall continue to be a body corporate in every diocese called the Diocesan Board of Patronage.

(2) The constitution and rules of procedure of Diocesan Boards of Patronage shall be those set out in Schedule 3 to this Measure.

Powers of Diocesan Boards of Patronage

27.—(1) Subject to subsection (2) below, a Diocesan Board of Patronage shall have power to acquire, hold and transfer any right of patronage and to exercise any right of presentation or other right incident to a right of patronage held by the Board.

(2) Subject to subsection (3) below, a Diocesan Board of Patronage shall not transfer any right of patronage held by it to any other person without the consent of the parochial church council of the parish or each of the parishes belonging to the benefice concerned unless the transfer is authorised by or under any enactment.

(3) If a parish is transferred from a benefice in one diocese to a benefice in another diocese, the Diocesan Board of Patronage for the first-mentioned diocese may transfer its right of patronage to the Diocesan Board of Patronage of that other diocese without the consent of the parochial church council of that parish.

(4) Where the transfer of a right of patronage requires the consent of a parochial church council under this section, any transfer of the right effected without that consent shall be void.

Presentation by Diocesan Board of Patronage in case of void benefice

28. Where a benefice becomes void under section 4 of the Simony Act 1588 (simoniacal presentation etc to a benefice declared void and the presentation to be made by the Crown for that turn) the presentation to that benefice upon that vacancy shall be made by the Diocesan Board of Patronage.

Benefices affected by pastoral re-organisation

Provisions as to patronage affected by pastoral schemes

29.—(1) *Text omitted.*

(2) Where any right of patronage of a benefice is transferred to or becomes vested in any person by virtue of a pastoral scheme the registrar of the diocese in which that benefice is shall, on receiving a copy of the Order in Council confirming the scheme, register him as the patron of that benefice.

(3) Subject to any provision for the designation or selection of the first incumbent of a new benefice created by a pastoral scheme, sections 7 to 16 of this Measure shall apply to the making of the first presentation to the benefice as if the coming into operation of the scheme were the occurrence of a vacancy in the benefice.

Other amendments of the law relating to rights of patronage etc

Removal of certain disabilities

30. *Text omitted.*

Abrogation of rules as to lapse

31. *Text omitted.*

Advowsons appendant to become advowsons in gross

32. *Text omitted.*

Transfer of advowson held on trust for sale or comprised in settled land

33. *Text omitted.*

Abolition of certain rights etc of patronage

34. *Text omitted.*

Part IV
General and Supplementary Provisions

Benefices in the patronage of the Crown, Duke of Cornwall or Lord Chancellor

Provisions with respect to benefices in the patronage of the Crown or Duke of Cornwall

35. *Text omitted.*

Provisions with respect to benefices in patronage of Lord Chancellor

36. *Text omitted.*

Supplementary provisions

Provisions as to notices and other documents

37.—(1) All notices, agreements, approvals, consents and requests required or authorised by this Measure to be served, sent, given or made shall be in writing, and all such notices, other than notices under paragraphs 7 and 8 of Schedule 1 to this Measure shall be in the prescribed form.

(2) Any notice or other document required or authorised by this Measure to be served on or sent or given to any person may be served, sent or given by delivering it to him, or by leaving it at his proper address, or by post.

(3) Any notice or other document required or authorised to be served, sent or given to a corporation or to an unincorporated body having a secretary or clerk or to a firm, shall be duly served, sent or given if it is served on or sent or given to, as the case may be, the secretary or clerk of the corporation or body or a partner of the firm.

(4) Subject to subsection (5) below, for the purposes of this section and of section 7 of the Interpretation Act 1978 in its application to this section, the proper address of the person on or to whom any such notice or other document is required or authorised to be served, sent or given shall be his last known address, except that in the case of the secretary or clerk of a corporation, it shall be that of the registered or principal office of the corporation, and in the case of the secretary or clerk of an unincorporated body or a partner of a firm, it shall be that of the principal office of the body or firm.

(5) If the person on or to whom any such notice or other document is to be served, sent or given has specified an address within the United Kingdom for the serving, sending or giving of the notice or other document, his proper address for the said purposes shall be that address.

Patronage (Procedure) Committee

38.—(1) There shall be a committee, to be known as the Patronage (Procedure) Committee, which shall consist of a chairman and four other members appointed by the Appointments Committee.

(2) The Patronage (Procedure) Committee shall have power to make rules with regard to any matter of procedure arising under this Measure and in particular with regard to any matter to be prescribed thereunder, except that no rules may be made under this subsection with regard to any matter in respect of which rules may be made by the Patronage (Appeals) Committee under paragraph 11 of Schedule 1 to this Measure.

(3) Any three members of the Patronage (Procedure) Committee may exercise all the powers of the Committee.

(4) Any rules made by the Patronage (Procedure) Committee shall be laid before the General Synod and shall not come into force until approved by the General Synod, whether with or without amendment.

(5) Where the Business Committee determines that the rules do not need to be debated by the General Synod, then, unless—
   (a) notice is given by a member of the General Synod in accordance with its Standing Orders that he wishes the rules to be debated, or
   (b) notice is so given by any such member that he wishes to move an amendment to the rules

the rules shall for the purposes of subsection (4) above be deemed to have been approved by the General Synod without amendment.

(6) The Statutory Instruments Act 1946 shall apply to rules approved by the General Synod under this section as if they were statutory instruments and were made when so approved, and as if this Measure were an Act providing that any such rules shall be subject to annulment in pursuance of a resolution of either House of Parliament.

Interpretation

39.—(1) In this Measure, unless the context otherwise requires—

'actual communicant member of the Church of England' means a member of the Church of England who is confirmed or ready and desirous of being confirmed and has received Communion according to the use of the Church of England or of a Church in communion with the Church of England at least three times during the twelve months preceding the date on which he makes the declaration of membership;

'actual communicant member of a Church in communion with the Church of England' means a communicant member of a Church in communion with the Church of England who has received Communion according to the use of the Church of England or of a Church in communion with the Church of England at least three times during the twelve months preceding the date on which he makes the declaration of membership;

'archbishop' means the archbishop of the province in which the benefice is or, where the benefice is in the diocese of the archbishop of that province or the archbishopric of that province is vacant or the archbishop is the patron of that benefice, the archbishop of the other province;

'benefice' means the office of rector or vicar of a parish or parishes with cure of souls, but not including the office of vicar in a team ministry or any office in a cathedral church;

'the bishop' means the bishop of the diocese concerned;

'clerk in Holy Orders' means a priest or deacon of the Church of England and 'priest' includes a bishop;

'the declaration of membership' has the meaning assigned to it by section 8(1);

'the designated officer' has the meaning assigned to it by section 7(5);

'parish' means a parish constituted for ecclesiastical purposes and does not include a conventional district;

'pastoral committee', 'pastoral order' and 'pastoral scheme' have the same meanings respectively as in the Pastoral Measure 1983;

'patron', in relation to any benefice, means the person or persons entitled, otherwise than by virtue of section 16, to present to that benefice upon a vacancy, including—

(a) in any case where the right to present is vested in different persons jointly, every person whose concurrence would be required for the exercise of the joint right, and

(b) in any case where the patronage is vested in different persons by way of alternate or successive rights of presentation, every person who would be entitled to present on the next or any subsequent turn;

'register of patrons' means a register compiled and maintained under section 1;

'registered' means registered under this Measure in a register of patrons;

'registered patron', in relation to a benefice, means any person who or office which is for the time being registered as a patron of that benefice;

'registration period' has the meaning assigned to it by section 1(2);

'the Standing Committee' means the Standing Committee of the General Synod.

(2) Where a pastoral scheme or pastoral order provides for the holding of benefices in plurality any reference in this Measure to a benefice shall be construed as including a reference to benefices held in plurality.

(3) If any question arises whether a Church is a Church in communion with the Church of England, it shall be conclusively determined for the purposes of this Measure by the Archbishops of Canterbury and York.

Temporary provision with respect to filling of certain vacancies

40. *Text omitted.*

SCHEDULE 1

REGISTRATION OF PATRONS

[Omitted]

SCHEDULE 2

MODIFICATION OF PART II IN ITS APPLICATION TO CERTAIN BENEFICES

[Omitted]

SCHEDULE 3

CONSTITUTION AND PROCEDURE OF A DIOCESAN BOARD OF PATRONAGE

[Omitted]

Care of Cathedrals Measure 1990

General principle

Duty to have regard to cathedral's purpose

1. Any body on which functions of care and conservation are conferred by this Measure shall in exercising those functions have due regard to the fact that the cathedral church is the seat of the bishop and a centre of worship and mission.

Approval required for alterations to cathedrals

Approval required for alterations to cathedrals

2.—(1) Subject to subsection (2) below and to sections 5 and 6 of this Measure, the Chapter of a cathedral shall not implement or consent to the implementation of any proposal—
  (a) for the carrying out of works, including works of repair or maintenance, on, above or below land the fee simple in which is vested in the corporate body, being works which would materially affect—
    (i) the architectural, archaeological, artistic or historic character of the cathedral church or any building within the precinct of the cathedral church which is for the time being used for ecclesiastical purposes, or
    (ii) the immediate setting of the cathedral church, or
    (iii) any archaeological remains within the precinct of the cathedral church, or
  (b) for the sale, loan or other disposal of any object the property in which is vested in the corporate body or which is in the possession or custody of the corporate body or to whose possession or custody the corporate body is entitled, being an object of architectural, archaeological, artistic or historic interest, including any object to which section 6A below applies, or
  (bb) for the carrying out of any work to any such object as is referred to in paragraph (b) above which would materially affect the architectural, archaeological, artistic or historic character of the object, or

(c) for the permanent addition to the cathedral church of any object which would materially affect the architectural, archaeological, artistic or historic character of the cathedral church,

unless the proposal has been approved under this Measure.

(2) Subsection (1) above shall not apply in relation to anything which—
- (a) is done by the Chapter in furtherance of its duties under the constitution and statutes of the cathedral church with respect to the ordering of services or otherwise in furtherance of the mission of the cathedral church,
- (b) is of a temporary nature, and
- (c) does not materially affect the fabric of the cathedral church.

(3) Where a proposal has been implemented in contravention of this section, anything done in connection with such implementation may be approved under this Measure and, in that event, shall be deemed to have been done in compliance with this section.

Establishment and functions of the Cathedrals Fabric Commission and fabric advisory committee

The Cathedrals Fabric Commission for England

3.—(1) There shall be established a body to be called the Cathedrals Fabric Commission for England (in this Measure referred to as 'the Commission') which shall have the functions assigned to it by this Measure.

(2) It shall be the duty of the Commission—
- (a) to give advice to the Chapter of a cathedral, and to the fabric advisory committee, on the care, conservation, repair or development of the cathedral church, any buildings or archaeological remains within its precinct, the landscape and environment in which the cathedral church is situated and any objects referred to in section 2(1)(b) above;
- (aa) to give advice to bishops and to the Vicar-General's court when it is sought under the Care of Cathedrals (Supplementary Provisions) Measure 1994;
- (b) to consider and determine any application made to it in accordance with the provisions of this Measure by the Chapter of a cathedral;
- (c) to promote co-operation between the Commission and organisations concerned with the care and study of buildings of architectural, archaeological, artistic or historic interest in England;
- (d) to assist the Chapters of cathedrals by participating in educational and research projects which in the view of the Commission will promote the care, conservation, repair or development of cathedral churches and their ancillary buildings; and
- (e) to maintain jointly with the Council for the Care of Churches, a library of books, plans, drawings, photographs and other material relating to cathedral churches and the objects in them.

(2A) It shall also be the duty of the Commission to promote, in consultation with Chapters, fabric advisory committees and such other persons or organisations as it thinks fit, by means of guidance or otherwise, standards of good practice to be observed in relation to—
- (a) the matters referred to in subsection (2)(a) above;
- (b) the role and duties of cathedral architects or surveyors of the fabric and cathedral archaeologists;
- (c) the compilation, maintenance and dissemination of information of architectural, archaeological, artistic and historic interest concerning cathedral churches, buildings and archaeological remains within their precincts and any objects referred to in section 2(1)(b) above; and
- (d) the form and content of the records required to be kept by the Chapter under section 14B(a) below.

(3) The provisions of Schedule 1 to this Measure shall have effect with respect to the Commission.

Establishment of fabric advisory committees

4.—(1) The Chapter of every cathedral and the Commission shall jointly establish a committee, to be called the fabric advisory committee, which shall have the functions assigned to it by this Measure.

(2) It shall be the duty of the fabric advisory committee—
  (a) to give advice to the Chapter of the cathedral on the care, conservation, repair or development of the cathedral church, any buildings or archaeological remains within its precinct, the landscape and environment in which the cathedral church is situated and any objects referred to in section 2(1)(b) above; and
  (b) to consider and determine any application made to it in accordance with the provisions of this Measure by the Chapter of the cathedral.

(3) The provisions of Schedule 2 to this Measure shall have effect with respect to fabric advisory committees.

Powers of fabric advisory committee in relation to application of section 2

5.—(1) The fabric advisory committee shall have power—
  (a) if requested to do so by the Chapter, to determine whether, under section 2(1) above, an application for approval of a proposal by the Chapter is required to be made; and
  (b) after consultation with the Chapter and subject to the agreement of the Commission, to determine that section 2 above is not to apply to proposals of any class or description specified by the committee, and to vary or revoke any determination made under this paragraph.

(2) If the Chapter wishes to have it determined whether a proposal is one to which section 2 above does not apply by virtue of subsection (1)(b) above the fabric advisory committee shall have power to determine that question.

(3) Where the Commission has made a determination under section 6(2) below in relation to any matter, the fabric advisory committee shall not make a determination under subsection (1)(a) above in relation to the same matter.

Applications for Approval

Body to which application for approval to be made

6.—(1) Any application for approval for a proposal shall be made to the Commission where—
  (a) the proposal would involve—
    (i) the carrying out of works, including works of repair or maintenance, which would permanently alter the fabric of the cathedral church or any building within the precinct of the cathedral church which is for the time being used for ecclesiastical purposes, or
    (ii) the demolition of any part of the cathedral church or any such building, or
    (iii) the disturbance or destruction of any archaeological remains within the precinct of the cathedral church, or
    (iv) the sale, loan or other disposal of or the carrying out of any work to any object for the time being designated under section 13(2) of this Measure in relation to the cathedral church as being of outstanding architectural, archaeological, artistic or historic interest, or
  (b) the Commission declares in writing that the proposal gives rise to considerations of such special architectural, archaeological, artistic or historic interest that the application should be determined by it;

and any application for approval for any other proposal other than an application under section 6A(4)(a) below shall be made to the fabric advisory committee.

(2) If the Chapter or the fabric advisory committee wishes to have it determined whether under subsection (1) above an application for approval is required to be made to the committee or to the Commission, the Commission shall have power to determine that question.

(2A) If the Commission considers that a proposal falls within subsection (1)(a) above, but that the proposal does not give rise to considerations of sufficient importance to require an application to be considered by it, it may make a declaration in writing to that effect and any application for approval of the proposal shall be made instead to the fabric advisory committee.

(2B) The Commission shall also have power, after consultation with any relevant Chapter and any relevant fabric advisory committee, English Heritage, the national amenity societies (or such person as the societies shall jointly appoint for the purposes of this section) and, in the case of a proposal of a kind described in section 2(1)(a) above, any relevant local planning authority, to determine that subsection (1)(a) above shall not apply to proposals of any class or description specified by the Commission in relation either to cathedrals generally or to such cathedrals as may be specified and to vary or revoke any determination made under this subsection and any application for approval of any such proposal shall be made instead to the fabric advisory committee.

(2C) If, following a request in writing from the Chapter of a cathedral, the Commission is satisfied—

(a) that a proposal or intended proposal falls within section 2(1)(a)(ii) or (iii) above;

(b) that the proposal does not relate to the cathedral church or a building within the precinct of the cathedral church for the time being used for ecclesiastical purposes;

(c) that planning permission, listed building consent or scheduled monument consent is required for the carrying out of all the works to which the proposal relates; and

(d) that any considerations relevant to preserving the immediate setting of the cathedral church or any archaeological remains within the precinct of the cathedral church will be or have been adequately taken into account by the person or body responsible for granting the permission or consent;

the Commission may, after consulting the local planning authority, the fabric advisory committee and English Heritage, make a declaration in writing that no approval is required under this Measure for the proposal.

(2D) In subsection (2C) above 'planning permission', 'listed building consent' and 'scheduled monument consent' have the meanings respectively assigned to them by section 336(1) of the Town and Country Planning Act 1990 (c 8), section 8(7) of the Planning (Listed Buildings and Conservation Areas) Act 1990 (c 9) and section 2(3)(a) of the Ancient Monuments and Archaeological Areas Act 1979 (c 46).

(3) Where, on an application made to the fabric advisory committee by virtue of subsection (1) above (not being an application in respect of which a determination has been made under subsection (2) above), at least three members of the committee present and voting determine that the proposal in question gives rise to considerations of such special architectural, archaeological, artistic or historic interest that the application should be determined by the Commission, the secretary of the committee shall refer the application to the Commission and shall notify the Chapter accordingly; and section 8 of this Measure shall apply in relation to that application.

(3A) Any application for approval in pursuance of section 2(3) above shall be made to the Commission.

(4) Any application under this section shall be made in accordance with rules made under this Measure.

Treasure

6A.—(1) This section applies to any object which would, but for an order under section 2(2) of the Treasure Act 1996 (c 24), be treasure within the meaning of that Act and which is found within the precinct of a cathedral.

(2) Where the administrator of the cathedral becomes aware that an object has been discovered which appears to be an object to which this section applies the administrator—
(a) shall within fourteen days notify the Commission in writing of the discovery; and
(b) shall arrange for the object to be recorded in the inventory required to be compiled and maintained under section 13 below and designated as treasure in that inventory in accordance with directions issued by the Commission.

(3) On receipt of a notification under subsection (2) above the secretary of the Commission shall report the discovery, in writing, to the Secretary of State or to such person or body as may be designated by the Secretary of State.

(4) The Chapter of the cathedral shall—
(a) before implementing any proposal for the sale, loan or other disposal of an object to which this section applies, apply to the Commission for approval, unless the Commission's approval is required under section 6 above; and
(b) before implementing any proposal for the sale or other disposal (other than a loan) of such an object, afford the British Museum or another registered museum nominated by the British Museum an opportunity of purchasing the object.

(5) Rules made under section 26 of the Care of Churches and Ecclesiastical Jurisdiction Measure 1991 (1991 No 1) may prescribe the procedure to be followed in connection with any matters arising under this section and in particular shall make provision for determining the purchase price to be paid under subsection (4)(b) above and for the procedure for and the matters to be taken into account in arriving at the purchase price.

(6) In subsection (4)(b) above 'registered museum' has the meaning ascribed to it in the Code of Practice issued under section 11 of the Treasure Act 1996 or such other meaning as may be specified by the Secretary of State.

Applications for approval of fabric advisory committee

7.—(1) Where any application is made by the Chapter of a cathedral for the approval of the fabric advisory committee, the administrator shall display in the prescribed manner a notice in the prescribed form specifying the place where details of the proposal are available for inspection and stating that representations in writing with respect to the proposal may be sent to the secretary of the committee before the end of the prescribed period; and he shall also send such a notice—
(a) to the Commission, and
(b) if the application relates to a proposal of a kind described in section 2(1)(a) above—
  (i) to English Heritage,
  (ii) to the national amenity societies (or such person as those societies shall jointly appoint for the purposes of this section), and
  (iii) to the local planning authority.

(2) After considering any representations made to it under this section, the fabric advisory committee shall determine whether to give its approval to the proposal, either unconditionally or subject to such conditions as it may specify, or whether to refuse to give its approval.

(3) The secretary of the fabric advisory committee shall send a notice of the committee's decision—
(a) to the Chapter of the cathedral,
(b) to the Commission, and
(c) to any body or person to whom notice of the application is required to be sent by virtue of subsection (1)(b) above,

and the administration of the cathedral shall display in the prescribed manner a copy of the notice sent to the Chapter under this subsection.

Applications for approval of Cathedrals Fabric Commission

8.—(1) Where any application is made by the Chapter of a cathedral for the approval of the Commission, the administrator shall—
- (a) display in the prescribed manner, and
- (b) send to the fabric advisory committee, English Heritage and the national amenity societies (or such person as those societies may jointly appoint for the purposes of this section),

a notice in the prescribed form specifying the place where details of the proposal are available for inspection and stating that representations in writing with respect to the proposal may be sent to the secretary of the Commission before the end of the prescribed period; and, if the application relates to a proposal of a kind described in section 2(1)(a) of this Measure, the administrator shall also send such a notice to the local planning authority.

(1A) Following receipt of the notice referred to in subsection (1) above, the secretary of the fabric advisory committee shall inform the Commission in writing whether the committee has considered the proposal and, if so, of its views.

(2) After considering any representations made to it under this section, the Commission shall determine whether to give its approval to the proposal, either unconditionally or subject to such conditions as it may specify, or whether to refuse to give its approval.

(2A) Before determining whether to give approval to any proposal for the sale, loan or other disposal of an object falling within section 6(1)(a)(iv) above the Commission may consult the Church Commissioners on any financial considerations (other than any which relate to the valuation of the object in question) which may be relevant to the proposal and on which the Commission considers it appropriate to receive the advice of the Commissioners and the Commissioners shall give such advice as they consider appropriate.

(2B) Before determining whether to give approval to any proposal for the sale, loan or other disposal of an object falling within section 6(1)(a)(iv) above the Commission may request the Chapter of the cathedral to—
- (a) consult the Council of the cathedral if it has not already done so; and
- (b) inform the Commission of the Council's views on the proposal.

(2C) If a meeting is arranged between the Commission and the Chapter of the cathedral to discuss the proposal the administrator shall notify the secretary of the fabric advisory committee of the meeting and the committee's representatives shall be entitled to be present at the meeting.

(3) The secretary of the Commission shall send notice of the Commission's decision—
- (a) to the Chapter of the cathedral,
- (b) to the fabric advisory committee,
- (c) to the English Heritage,
- (d) to the national amenity societies (or such person as those societies may jointly appoint for the purposes of this section), and
- (e) if the decision relates to a proposal of a kind described in section 2(1)(a) above, to the local planning authority,
- (f) if the Commission has consulted the Church Commissioners on the proposal under subsection (2A) above, to the Church Commissioners,

and the administrator shall display in the prescribed manner a copy of the notice sent to the Chapter under this subsection.

(4) This section shall apply in relation to an application for approval in pursuance of section 2(3) above as it applies in relation to an application for approval of a proposal.

Appeals

Appeals to Cathedrals Fabric Commission

9.—(1) Where, on an application made by the Chapter for the approval of the fabric advisory committee, approval is refused or is given subject to conditions, the Chapter may within the prescribed period appeal to the Commission.

(2) Where, on an application made by the Chapter for the approval of the fabric advisory committee, the application is not determined by the fabric advisory committee within the period of three months immediately following the making of the application, the Chapter may, by notice given within the prescribed period to the Commission, request that the application be dealt with by the Commission.

(3) The Commission, on considering an appeal under subsection (1) above may reverse, confirm or vary the decision of the fabric advisory committee or any part thereof.

(4) The Commission, on dealing with an application for approval under subsection (2) above, shall, after considering any representations made to the fabric advisory committee under section 7 of this Measure, determine whether to give its approval to the proposal, either unconditionally or subject to such conditions as it may specify, or whether to refuse to give its approval; and any such determination shall have effect as if it had been given by the fabric advisory committee.

Commission of Review

10.—Where—
   (a) on an application for approval made to the Commission (including an application being dealt with by the Commission under section 9(2) of this Measure), the Commission refuses to give its approval or gives approval subject to conditions, or
   (b) on an appeal to the Commission under section 9(1) of this Measure, the Commission refuses to give its approval or refuses to reverse or vary conditions subject to which approval was given by the fabric advisory committee,

the Chapter may, by notice given within the prescribed period to the registrar of the province in which the cathedral church is situated, request that the decision of the Commission be reviewed by a Commission of Review constituted under this section.

(2) Where, on an application for approval made to the Commission (including an application being dealt with by the Commission under section 9(2) of this measure) or on an appeal to the Commission under section 9(1) of this Measure, the application or appeal is not determined by the Commission within the period of three months immediately following the end of the period prescribed for the purposes of section 8 or section 9(1) or (2), as the case may be, the Chapter may, by notice given within the prescribed period to the registrar of the province in which the cathedral church is situated, request that the application or appeal be dealt with by a Commission of Review constituted under this section.

(3) A Commission of Review shall be constituted of—
   (a) the Dean of Arches and Auditor or a person appointed by him, being a person who is qualified under section 3(3) of the Ecclesiastical Jurisdiction Measure 1963 to be appointed Dean of the Arches and Auditor;
   (b) one person appointed by the Archbishops of Canterbury and York, being a person who is or has been a dean, provost or residentiary canon of a cathedral church other than the cathedral church to which the application or appeal relates; and
   (c) one person appointed by the Secretary of State, being a person who has special knowledge of the architecture, archaeology, art (including history of art) or history of cathedral churches;

but no person who has been a member of the Cathedrals Fabric Commission at any time during the preceding five years shall be appointed under paragraph (b) or (c) above.

(4) A Commission of Review, on reviewing a decision of the Cathedrals Fabric Commission, may reverse, confirm or vary that decision or any part thereof.

(5) A Commission of Review, on dealing with an application for approval under subsection (2) above, shall, after considering any representations made to the Commission under section 8 of this Measure, determine whether to give its approval, either unconditionally or subject to such conditions as it may specify, or whether to refuse to give its approval; and any such determination shall have effect as if it had been given by the Commission.

(6) A Commission of Review, on dealing with an appeal under subsection (2) above, may reverse, confirm or vary the decision of the fabric advisory committee or any part thereof.

(7) The decision of a Commission of Review shall be final.

Conditions applying to approval

10A.—(1) Any approval given to an application under this Measure shall lapse at the expiry of the period of ten years from the date on which notice of the decision is given to the Chapter, provided that the body which gave the approval may extend that period by such period as it may specify.

(2) As soon as possible after the completion of any work for which approval has been given, the administrator of the cathedral shall notify the fabric advisory committee or the Commission, as the case may be, of the date of the completion.

(3) In subsection (1) above, the reference to the date on which notice of the decision is given shall, in the case of an appeal to the Commission under section 9(1) above or an application for review by a Commission of Review under section 10(1) above, be construed as a reference to the date on which notice of the decision of the Commission or, as the case may be, of the Commission of Review, is given to the Chapter.

(4) Subsection (1) above shall apply to approvals given before the date of the coming into force of section 9 of the Care of Cathedrals (Amendment) Measure 2005 as if for the reference to ten years from the date referred to therein there were substituted a reference to ten years from the date of the coming into force of the said section 9.

Registers of applications

10B.—(1) The Commission and any fabric advisory committee shall each keep a register, in the prescribed form, of applications for approval dealt with by them and shall make such arrangements as are prescribed—
   (a)   for inspection of the registers by any person;
   (b)   for the supply, on application by any person, of extracts of that part of the register which relates to an application for approval specified by that person;
   (c)   for enabling the Commission or a fabric advisory committee to supply, if it thinks fit, copies of the whole register or further parts of it, on application by any person.

(2) The Commission or any fabric advisory committee may impose a fee of a reasonable amount for the supply of copies of or extracts from the register under subsection (1) above and the amount charged may vary according to the circumstances.

Right of appeal by tenant

10C.—(1) Where the Commission or a fabric advisory committee has refused approval for a proposal from a Chapter of a cathedral for the carrying out of works by a tenant for which the Chapter's consent is required or given approval subject to conditions, the tenant may, whether or not the Chapter has appealed against the refusal or the imposition of conditions, or requested that the decision be reviewed by a Commission of Review, as the case may be, within the prescribed period, appeal to the Commission (against a decision of a fabric advisory committee) or request that a decision of the Commission be reviewed by a Commission of Review constituted under section 10 above.

(2) A tenant who appeals or requests a review under subsection (1) above shall give written notice of the appeal or review to the Chapter.

(3) The Chapter shall be entitled to appear at the proceedings on any appeal or review under subsection (1) above.

(4) Sections 9(3) and 10(4) above shall apply to an appeal or review under subsection (1) above as they apply to an appeal or review under those sections.

Miscellaneous and general

Further powers of the Cathedrals Fabric Commission

11.—(1) The Commission may, on receiving a request from the Council for the Care of Churches, give advice to the Council with respect to works which are proposed to be carried out in relation to a church of the Church of England which is not a cathedral church.

(2) The Commission—
  (a) may, on receiving a request made with the approval of the Representative Body of the Church in Wales, give advice with respect to works which are proposed to be carried out in relation to a cathedral church in Wales; and
  (b) may in exceptional circumstances, with the agreement of the governing body of the Church concerned and of the Archbishops' Council, give advice in relation to works which are proposed to be carried out in relation to a cathedral church other than a cathedral church of the Church of England or the Church in Wales;

but it shall be a condition of giving any advice by virtue of this subsection that any expenses incurred by the Commission in giving that advice are reimbursed.

(3) The Commission shall have power to exercise any functions in relation to moneys held by any other body or person for the benefit of cathedral churches generally, being functions delegated to it by that body or person.

(4) For the purpose of exercising its functions under this Measure the Commission—
  (a) may acquire books, plans, drawings, photographs and other material relating to cathedral churches; and
  (b) may from time to time hold conferences for cathedral clergy and staff, cathedral architects or surveyors of the fabric, cathedral archaeologists and others concerned with the care, conservation and maintenance of cathedral churches.

General duties of approval bodies

11A. The Commission, any fabric advisory committee and any Commission of Review shall, without prejudice to the duty conferred upon them by section 1 above, in exercising any function conferred upon them by the preceding sections of this Measure, have due regard to the desirability of preserving—
  (a) the fabric of the cathedral church and any features of architectural, archaeological, artistic or historic interest which it possesses;
  (b) the immediate setting of the cathedral church;
  (c) any building within the precinct of the cathedral church of architectural, archaeological, artistic or historic interest;
  (d) any archaeological remains within the precinct of the cathedral church; and
  (e) any objects referred to in section 2(1)(b) above.

Provisions as to cathedral architects or surveyors of the fabric and cathedral archaeologists

12.—(1) It shall be the duty of the Chapter of a cathedral to consult the Commission before appointing a cathedral architect or surveyor of the fabric.

(2) It shall be the duty of the Chapter of a cathedral after consulting the Commission to appoint a cathedral archaeologist, except in any case in which the Commission notifies the Chapter that in the view of the Commission the archaeological significance of that cathedral church does not justify such an appointment.

Inventories, etc

13.—(1) It shall be the duty of the Chapter of a cathedral to compile and maintain an inventory of all objects the property in which is vested in the corporate body or which are in the possession or custody of the corporate body or to whose possession or custody the corporate body is entitled which the fabric advisory committee considers to be of architectural, archaeological, artistic or historic interest in accordance with rules made under section 26 of the Care of Churches and Ecclesiastical Jurisdiction Measure 1991 (1991 No 1).

(1A) The compilation of the inventory under subsection (1) above shall be completed within such period as the Commission, after consultation with the Chapter and the fabric advisory committee, determines, being such period as it considers reasonable, having regard to the particular circumstances of each case, and different periods may be specified by the Commission for different parts of the inventory.

(1B) The Chapter shall make an annual report to the fabric advisory committee on the contents of the inventory or on progress made in compiling the inventory, which shall, in particular, certify the accuracy of the inventory or any part of it which has been compiled and describe any alterations which have been made to the inventory during the twelve months preceding the report.

(1C) The first annual report required by subsection (1B) above shall be made within the period of twelve months beginning with the date of the coming into force of section 13 of the Care of Cathedrals (Amendment) Measure 2005.

(2) It shall be the duty of the fabric advisory committee of a cathedral church to designate those objects included in the inventory compiled and maintained for the cathedral church under subsection (1) above which the committee considers, after consultation with the Commission, to be of outstanding architectural, archaeological, artistic or historic interest.

(3) It shall be the duty of the Chapter of a cathedral to prepare a plan indicating the extent of the land surrounding the cathedral church of which the fee simple is vested in the corporate body and to complete the preparation of that plan before the expiration of the period of two years beginning with the date on which this section comes into force, and the administrator shall send the plan to the Commission.

(4) On receiving a plan prepared by the Chapter under subsection (3) above, the Commission shall, after consultation with the Chapter, indicate thereon the precinct of the cathedral church for the purposes of this Measure which shall consist of so much of the land referred to in subsection (3) above as, in the opinion of the Commission, is necessary to preserve or protect the architectural, archaeological, artistic or historic character of the cathedral church and of any buildings of architectural, archaeological, artistic or historic interest associated with it and of any archaeological remains associated with or situated in, under or near to the cathedral church or any such buildings and the setting of the cathedral church and any such buildings and remains; and in implementing the requirements of this subsection the Commission shall have regard to the context in which the cathedral church and any such buildings have developed over time.

(5) The Chapter shall keep the plan prepared under subsection (3) above up to date and shall notify the Commission of any changes made to it, whereupon the Commission shall, after consultation with the Chapter, make any alterations to the precinct indicated on the plan which it considers appropriate, having regard to subsection (4) above.

(6) The Commission may, after consultation with the Chapter, make such alterations to the precinct indicated on the plan prepared under subsection (3) above as it considers appropriate, having regard to subsection (4) above.

Reports and inspections by cathedral architects or surveyors of the fabric

14.—(1) Subject to subsection (3) below, it shall be the duty of the Chapter of a cathedral to arrange during the period of five years beginning with the date on which this section comes into force and during every subsequent period of five years, for the cathedral architect or surveyor of the fabric, in consultation with the cathedral archaeologist (if any), to make a report in writing to the Chapter on any works which the architect or surveyor of the fabric considers will need to be carried out in relation to the cathedral church and any ancillary building and on the urgency with which the architect or surveyor of the fabric considers that they should be carried out; and a copy of that report shall be sent to the Commission.

(2) Subject to subsection (3) below, the reports referred to in subsection (1) above shall be based upon such inspection or inspections of the fabric of the cathedral church and any ancillary building

as the cathedral architect or surveyor of the fabric considers necessary to enable the architect or surveyor of the fabric to fulfil the requirements of subsection (1) above.

(3) The first report referred to in subsection (1) above made by a cathedral architect or surveyor of the fabric appointed after the date of the coming into force of section 14 of the Care of Cathedrals (Amendment) Measure 2005 shall be based on a full and detailed inspection of the cathedral church and any ancillary building and shall be made within the period of two years beginning with the date of the appointment.

(4) In its application to a cathedral architect or surveyor of the fabric appointed after the first date referred to in subsection (3) above, subsection (1) above shall have effect so that the second and subsequent reports of the architect or surveyor of the fabric shall be made during the period of five years beginning with the date of the first report and every subsequent period of five years.

(5) The cathedral architect or surveyor of the fabric shall, within the period of twelve months beginning with the date of the coming into force of section 14 of the Care of Cathedrals (Amendment) Measure 2005 and annually thereafter make, in consultation with the architect or surveyor appointed under section 20 of the Cathedrals Measure 1999 (if a different person) and the cathedral archaeologist (if any), a report in writing to the Chapter containing a summary of any works to the cathedral church and any ancillary building carried out during the preceding year, an account of progress made in giving effect to the recommendations made in the reports referred to in subsection (1) above and any other matters which the cathedral architect or surveyor of the fabric considers to be relevant to the care and conservation of the cathedral church.

(6) In this section 'ancillary building' means any building which the Chapter may from time to time specify, being a building attached to or adjacent to the cathedral church and used for purposes ancillary to the use of the cathedral church, but excluding any building used wholly or mainly for residential purposes.

Reports by cathedral archaeologists

14A.—(1) It shall be the duty of the Chapter of a cathedral which has appointed a cathedral archaeologist to arrange, within the period of two years beginning with the date of the coming into force of section 15 of the Care of Cathedrals (Amendment) Measure 2005 for the cathedral archaeologist to assess those matters of archaeological interest which relate to the cathedral church and its precinct, including buildings and remains within the precinct and, in consultation with the cathedral architect or surveyor of the fabric and the architect or surveyor appointed under section 20 of the Cathedrals Measure 1999 (if a different person), to make a report in writing to the Chapter containing recommendations on how those matters should be managed, and on the compilation and maintenance of archaeological records relating thereto; and a copy of the report shall be sent to the Commission.

(2) The cathedral archaeologist shall, within the period of twelve months beginning with the date of the coming into force of section 15 of the Care of Cathedrals (Amendment) Measure 2005 and annually thereafter, make in consultation with the persons referred to in subsection (1) above a report to the Chapter containing an account of progress made in fulfilling the recommendations of the report (if made) referred to in subsection (1) above and any other matters which the archaeologist considers to be relevant to the archaeological interest of the cathedral church and its precinct.

Maintenance of records

14B. The cathedral architect or surveyor of the fabric and the cathedral archaeologist (if any) shall each, in consultation with the architect or surveyor appointed under section 20 of the Cathedrals Measure 1999 (if a person other than the cathedral architect or surveyor of the fabric) include in the annual report required to be made to the Chapter under section 14(5) or 14A(2) above advice as to those works carried out in the previous year of which a permanent record should in the opinion of the cathedral architect or surveyor of the fabric or cathedral archaeologist be maintained and it shall be the duty of the Chapter—

    (a)   to have regard to that advice and, pursuant thereto, to make and maintain appropriate permanent records of any such works; and

(b) during the period of five years beginning with the date of the coming into force of section 15 of the Care of Cathedrals (Amendment) Measure 2005 and during every subsequent period of five years, to make a report in writing to the fabric advisory committee of the records made under paragraph (a) above and on the arrangements for maintaining those records and to send a copy of the report to the Commission.

Applications for listed building or scheduled monument consent

15. Where the Chapter of a cathedral church proposes to make any application for—
(a) listed building consent under section 55 of the Town and Country Planning Act 1971, or
(b) scheduled monument consent under section 2 of the Ancient Monuments and Archaeological Areas Act 1979,

in respect of any building or monument within the precinct of the cathedral church, the administrator shall send to the Commission a notice stating that representations in writing with respect to the proposed application may be sent to him before the end of the prescribed period.

Saving

17. Nothing in this Measure shall dispense with any consent or approval which is required by or under the constitution and statutes of a cathedral church for anything done by the Chapter of that cathedral church.

Power to exclude parish church cathedrals

18. *Repealed.*

Notices

19. All notices required to be given under this Measure shall be in writing and shall be in the prescribed form.

Interpretation

20.—(1) In this Measure, unless the context otherwise requires—
'administrator of the cathedral' means the person, by whatever name called, appointed under section 9(1)(e) of the Cathedrals Measure 1999;
'archaeological remains' means the remains of any building, work or artefact, including any trace or sign of the previous existence of the building, work or artefact in question;
'architect' means a person registered under the Architects Act 1997;
'building' includes any monument or other structure or erection and any part of a building as so defined and 'fabric' shall be construed accordingly;
'cathedral archaeologist' means the person appointed under section 12(2) above, by whatever name called, being a person who possesses such qualifications and expertise in archaeological matters as the Commission may recognise as appropriate;
'cathedral architect or surveyor of the fabric' means any architect or surveyor appointed by virtue of section 9(1)(f) of the Cathedrals Measure 1999 by whatever name called;
'cathedral church' means any cathedral church in the provinces of Canterbury and York, except—
(a) the Cathedral Church of Christ in Oxford,
(b) any cathedral church in the diocese of Sodor and Man or in the diocese in Europe,

'Chapter' means the body of that name established by section 2 of the Cathedrals Measure 1999;
'chartered building surveyor' means a member of the Royal Institution of Chartered Surveyors qualified as a chartered building surveyor;
'corporate body' means the body established under section 9(1)(a) of the Cathedrals Measure 1999;
'Council for the Care of Churches' means the body so named at the passing of this Measure or any body subsequently exercising the functions of that body under a different name or with a different constitution;

'English Heritage' means the Historic Buildings and Monuments Commission for England, known as English Heritage;

'Liturgical Commission' means the body so named at the passing of this Measure or any body subsequently exercising the functions of that body under a different name or with a different constitution;

'local planning authority' in relation to any area means the body exercising the functions of a local planning authority under section 55 of the Town and Country Planning Act 1971 in that area;

'national amenity societies' means the Ancient Monuments Society, the Council for British Archaeology, the Georgian Group, the Society for the Protection of Ancient Buildings and the Victorian Society and such other body as may from time to time be designated by the Dean of the Arches and Auditor as a national amenity society for the purpose of this Measure;

'precinct' in relation to a cathedral church means the precinct for the time being indicated on the plan required for that cathedral church by section 13 of this Measure;

'prescribed' means prescribed by rules made under section 26 of the Care of Churches and Ecclesiastical Jurisdiction Measure 1991.

(2) For the purposes of this Measure any object or structure permanently situated in or affixed to a cathedral church or any building within the precinct of a cathedral church shall be treated as part of that cathedral church or building or of its fabric, as the case may be.

(3) For the purposes of this Measure a building shall be treated as being used for ecclesiastical purposes if it would be so used but for any works proposed to be carried out in relation to it.

Schedule 1
The Cathedrals Fabric Commission for England

Section 3

Membership

1. The Commission shall consist of a chairman, a vice-chairman and twenty-two other members.

2. The chairman shall be a lay person appointed by the Archbishops of Canterbury and York after consultation with the Secretary of State, and the vice-chairman shall be appointed by the Archbishops after consultation with the Archbishops' Council and with such organisation as appears to the Archbishops to be representative of the deans of cathedral churches.

3. Seventeen members of the Commission shall be appointed by the Archbishops of Canterbury and York as follows—

(a) one member shall be appointed on the nomination of the House of Bishops from among the members of that House;

(b) two members shall be appointed on the nomination of such organisation as appears to the Archbishops to be representative of the deans ... of cathedral churches and at least one of those two members shall be a dean ... of a cathedral church;

(c) three members shall be appointed on the nomination of the Council for the Care of Churches, of whom two shall be selected from among the members of the Council or a committee thereof;

(d) two members shall be persons holding office as cathedral architects or surveyors of the fabric one of whom shall be appointed after consultation with the President of the Royal Institute of British Architects and the other shall be appointed after consultation with that President and the President of the Royal Institution of Chartered Surveyors;

(e) one member shall be an architect or chartered building surveyor appointed after consultation with the President of the Ecclesiastical Architects and Surveyors Association and one member shall be a chartered engineer appointed after consultation with the President of the Institution of Structural Engineers and the President of the Institution of Civil Engineers, being persons with experience of the care of historic buildings;

(f) one member shall be a painter, sculptor or other artist, with experience of work for cathedral or other churches, who shall be appointed after consultation with the President of the Royal Academy of Art;

(g) six members shall be appointed as follows—
  (i) one shall be appointed after consultation with the Secretary of State;
  (ii) one shall be appointed after consultation with the Chairman of English Heritage;
  (iii) one shall be appointed after consultation with the President of the Council for British Archaeology and the President of the Society of Antiquaries of London;
  (iv) two shall be appointed after consultation with the Chairman of the Liturgical Commission; and
  (v) one shall be appointed after consultation with the Director of the Royal School of Church Music.

3A. All the members of the Commission appointed in pursuance of paragraph 3(b) to (g) above shall be persons who between them have special knowledge of archaeology, architecture, archives, art, the care and conservation of books, manuscripts and other historic objects, history (including history of art and architecture) and liturgy (including church music).

4. Five members of the Commission, of whom at least one shall be a member of the Chapter of a cathedral, shall be elected by the General Synod from among its members, each person so elected having knowledge of the ways in which cathedral churches are currently used and of their contribution to the work of the Church of England.

5. No person who is a member of the Chapter or fabric advisory committee of any cathedral church or a member or officer of a relevant committee of any designated organisation shall be eligible for appointment as the chairman or vice-chairman of the Commission.

6. The chairman and other members of the Commission shall hold office for five years beginning on the first day of May in the year next following the year in which the General Synod is dissolved and a new Synod comes into being.

7. Any member of the Commission shall on ceasing to hold office be eligible for re-appointment or re-election unless he became such a member by virtue of re-appointment or re-election under this paragraph or appointment under paragraph 7A below following re-election under this paragraph.

7A. Where a member of the Commission elected by the General Synod under paragraph 4 above has, following the dissolution of the Synod, not been re-elected to the new Synod, that person may be appointed by the Appointments Committee of the Church of England as a member and shall hold office until the thirtieth day of April following the year in which the new Synod comes into being.

Casual vacancies

8. Where a casual vacancy occurs among the members of the Commission appointed by the Archbishops of Canterbury and York, the Archbishops, after such consultation as appears to them to be appropriate having regard to the knowledge or experience of the person whose place is to be filled, may appoint a person to fill the vacancy.

9. Where a casual vacancy occurs among the members of the Commission elected by the General Synod, the General Synod may elect one of its members to fill the vacancy, the person so elected having knowledge of the matters mentioned in paragraph 4 above.

10. Any person appointed or elected to fill a casual vacancy shall hold office only for the unexpired portion of the term of office of the person in whose place he is appointed or elected, but shall be eligible for re-appointment or re-election for one further term of office in accordance with paragraph 7 above, and if the Archbishops of Canterbury and York so direct, shall be eligible for re-appointment or re-election for a second further term.

Secretary

11. The Commission shall appoint a secretary to the Commission but no person shall be appointed who is a member or officer of the Chapter or fabric advisory committee of any cathedral church or a member of a relevant committee of any designated organisation.

Committees

12. The Commission shall have power to appoint such committees as it considers expedient.

13. Persons who are not members of the Commission may be appointed to any committee thereof, but the number of such persons appointed to a committee shall be less than half the total number of members of the committee.

Proceedings

14. The quorum of the Commission shall be eight members.

14A. The business of the Commission shall be decided by a majority of the members present and voting thereon and, in the event of an equal division of votes, the Chairman shall have a second or casting vote.

15. Subject to paragraph 14 above, the Commission may act notwithstanding any vacancy in its membership.

16. The Commission shall have power to hold public hearings in connection with any matter to be considered by it for the purpose of receiving oral representations from members of the public and may appoint a panel of not less than three members for the purpose of holding a public hearing on any matter specified by the Commission and reporting thereon to the Commission.

16A. Where the Commission is considering an appeal under section 9 or 10C above no member of the Commission who is also a member of the fabric advisory committee against whose decision the appeal is brought shall participate in the proceedings.

17. Subject to the preceding provision of this Schedule and to any directions as to procedure given by the General Synod, the Commission shall have power to regulate its own procedure.

Designated organisations

18. The Archbishops of Canterbury and York acting jointly may designate the organisations which are to be 'designated organisations' for the purposes of paragraphs 5 and 11 above and may specify the committees of those organisations which are to be 'relevant committees' for the purposes of those paragraphs.

SCHEDULE 2
FABRIC ADVISORY COMMITTEES

Section 4

Membership

1. The fabric advisory committee shall consist of—
    (a) not less than three nor more than five members appointed by the Chapter after consultation with the Cathedrals Fabric Commission not being members of the Chapter or persons who are employed or hold paid office in the cathedral; and
    (b) not less than three nor more than five members appointed by the Commission after consultation with the Chapter, being persons having special knowledge with respect to the care and maintenance of buildings of outstanding architectural or historic interest and a particular interest in the cathedral church concerned.

The number of members to be appointed by the Chapter and by the Commission shall be the same in each case and shall be determined, on each occasion when the committee is appointed, by the Chapter after consultation with the Commission.

2. The committee shall appoint a chairman from among its members.

3. The dean of the cathedral, the administrator of the cathedral and such other members of the Chapter as the Chapter, after consulting the fabric advisory committee, considers appropriate, shall be entitled to attend, and to speak, at meetings of the committee or such meetings of the committee as may be specified by the Chapter, but no such person shall be entitled to vote.

4. It shall be the duty of the cathedral architect or surveyor of the fabric and the person (if any) holding office as cathedral archaeologist to attend meetings of the committee unless the chairman permits or directs otherwise.

5. No person who holds any paid office in the Commission shall be eligible for appointment as a member of the committee.

6. The members of the committee shall hold office for a period of five years but shall be eligible for reappointment.

7. The committee shall appoint some person, whether or not a member of the committee, to be secretary of the committee, provided that, in the case of a member of the Chapter or a person who is employed or holds paid office in the cathedral, the committee shall have particular regard to the question whether there is any conflict of interests which would make it inappropriate to appoint that person as the secretary.

8. Any expenses properly incurred by a member of the committee for the purposes of this Measure shall be reimbursed by the Chapter of the cathedral.

Casual vacancies

9. Where a casual vacancy occurs among the members of the committee, the body which appointed the person whose place is to be filled may after carrying out the like consultation as was required when the appointment was made appoint a person to fill the vacancy, and any person so appointed shall hold office for the unexpired portion of the term of office of the person in whose place he is appointed.

Procedure

10. The quorum of the committee shall be—
    (a) six members, if the membership of the committee is ten;
    (b) five members, if the membership of the committee is eight;
    (c) four members, if the membership of the committee is six.

11. Subject to paragraph 10 above, the committee may act notwithstanding any vacancy in its membership.

11A. The business of the committee shall be decided by a majority of the members present and voting thereon and, in the event of an equal division of votes, the chairman shall have a second or casting vote.

12. The committee shall hold not less than two meetings each year, and if three or more members, by notice sent to the secretary of the committee, request that a special meeting be held, such a meeting shall be held within four weeks of the sending of that notice.

13. The secretary of the committee shall place on the agenda for the next meeting any matter requested by any member of the committee.

14. The secretary of the committee shall before each meeting send to the Chapter and to the Commission a copy of the agenda for that meeting and shall after each meeting send to the Chapter and to the Commission a copy of the minutes of that meeting.

15. Subject to the preceding provisions of this Schedule, the committee shall have power to regulate its own procedure.

Care of Churches and Ecclesiastical Jurisdiction Measure 1991

Part I
General Principle

Duty to have regard to church's purpose

1. Any person or body carrying out functions of care and conservation under this Measure or under any other enactment or rule of law relating to churches shall have due regard to the role of a church as a local centre of worship and mission.

Part II
Care, Inspection and Accountability

Diocesan advisory committees

2.—(1) In every diocese there shall continue to be an advisory committee for the care of churches, to be known as 'the Diocesan Advisory Committee'.

(2) For each advisory committee there shall be a written constitution provided by the diocesan synod of the diocese concerned, containing the provisions set out in Schedule 1 to this Measure or provisions to the like effect.

(3) The written constitution required by subsection (2) above may include such further provisions consistent with those set out in Schedule 1 to this Measure as the diocesan synod considers appropriate—
  (a) in connection with its procedure; or
  (b) for the establishment of sub-committees and the delegation thereto of any of its functions.

(4) The written constitution required by subsection (2) above shall be provided as soon as practicable and in any event not later than the expiration of the period of three years immediately following the coming into operation of this section.

(5) The advisory committee shall have the functions specified in Schedule 2 to this Measure and such other functions as may be determined by the diocesan synod of the diocese concerned by resolution; and in carrying out its functions the committee and sub-committees (if any) shall have regard to the rites and ceremonies of the Church of England.

(6) Any expenses incurred for the purpose of giving the advisory committee a written constitution under this section and for enabling it to discharge its functions properly and effectively shall be paid by the Diocesan Board of Finance for the diocese concerned:

Provided that a Diocesan Board of Finance shall not be liable for any expenses by virtue of this subsection unless the expenses were approved by the Board before they were incurred.

(7) As soon as practicable after the end of each year the advisory committee shall prepare a report of its work and proceedings during that year and cause it to be laid before the diocesan synod of the diocese concerned; and the secretary to the committee shall send a copy of the report to the Council for the Care of Churches.

(8) *Text omitted.*

Amendment of Inspection of Churches Measure 1955

3. *Text omitted.*

Duties of churchwardens as to recording of information about churches

4.—(1) In every parish it shall be the duty of the churchwardens—
  (a) to compile and maintain—
    (i) a full terrier of all lands appertaining to the church;
    (ii) a full inventory of all articles appertaining to the church;
  (b) to insert in a log-book maintained for the purpose a full note of all alterations, additions and repairs to, and other events affecting, the church and the lands and articles appertaining thereto and of the location of any other documents relating to such alterations, additions, repairs and events which are not kept with the log-book.

(2) In carrying out their duty under subsection (1) above the churchwardens shall act in consultation with the minister.

(3) The form of the terrier, inventory and log-book shall accord with such recommendations as the Council for the Care of Churches may make.

(4) The churchwardens shall send a copy of the inventory to such person as the bishop of the diocese concerned may designate from time to time for the purpose of this subsection as soon as practicable after it is compiled and shall notify that person of any alterations at such intervals as the bishop may direct from time to time.

(5) This section applies in relation to each church in a parish containing more than one church.

Duties of churchwardens as to fabric etc of churches

5.—(1) In every parish it shall be the duty of the churchwardens—
  (a) at least once in every year, to inspect or cause an inspection to be made of the fabric of the church and all articles appertaining to the church;
  (b) in every year, to deliver to the parochial church council and on behalf of that council to the annual parochial church meeting a report (referred to below as 'the annual fabric report') on the fabric of the church and all articles appertaining to the church, having regard to the inspection or inspections carried out under paragraph (a) above, including an account of all actions taken or proposed during the previous year for their protection and maintenance and, in particular, for the implementation of any recommendation contained in a report under a scheme made in pursuance of section 1 of the Inspection of Churches Measure 1955.

(2) In carrying out their duty under subsection (1) above the churchwardens shall act in consultation with the minister.

(3) The annual fabric report shall be delivered to the parochial church council at its meeting next before the annual parochial church meeting and, with such amendments as that council may make, to the ensuing annual parochial church meeting.

(4) The churchwardens shall, as soon as practicable after the beginning of each year, produce to the parochial church council the terrier, the inventory and the log-book relating to events occurring in the previous year and such other records as they consider likely to assist the council in discharging its functions in relation to the fabric of the church and articles appertaining to the church.

(5) Any terrier, inventory or log-book produced to the parochial church council in accordance with subsection (4) above shall be accompanied by a statement, signed by the churchwardens, to the effect that the contents thereof are accurate.

(6) This section applies in relation to each church in a parish containing more than one church.

(7) In this section 'year' means calendar year.

Provisions relating to trees in churchyards

6.—(1) The powers, duties and liabilities of a parochial church council with respect to the care and maintenance of a churchyard which the council is liable to maintain shall extend to trees therein, including those proposed to be planted.

(2) Where a tree in a churchyard which a parochial church council is liable to maintain is felled, lopped or topped the council may sell or otherwise dispose of the timber and the net proceeds of any sale thereof shall be paid to the council and applied for the maintenance of any church or churchyard which the council is liable to maintain.

(3) The chancellor of a diocese shall, after consultation with the advisory committee, give written guidance to all parochial church councils in the diocese as to the planting, felling, lopping and topping of trees in churchyards.

(4) The provisions of section 20 of the Repair of Benefice Buildings Measure 1972 (which relates to the felling etc of trees) in so far as they relate to trees in churchyards shall cease to have effect.

(5) In this section 'churchyard' includes a closed churchyard.

Payment of expenses in connection with ruins

7. Any expenses properly incurred by a parochial church council, with the prior approval in writing of the Diocesan Board of Finance for the diocese concerned, for the purpose of implementing a recommendation contained in a report made in respect of a ruin in pursuance of section 1A(b) of the Inspection of Churches Measure 1955 shall be paid by that Board.

Part III
Ecclesiastical Jurisdiction

Amendment of Ecclesiastical Jurisdiction Measure 1963

8. *Text omitted.*

Amendment of Ecclesiastical Judges and Legal Officers Measure 1976

9. *Text omitted.*

Amendment of Ecclesiastical Fees Measure 1986

10. *Text omitted.*

General provisions as to faculty jurisdiction

11.—(1) For the avoidance of doubt and without prejudice to the jurisdiction of consistory courts under any enactment or rule of law, it is hereby declared that the jurisdiction of the consistory court of a diocese applies to all parish churches in the diocese and the churchyards and articles appertaining thereto.

(2) Except as provided by subsection (3) below, a building licensed by the bishop of a diocese after the coming into operation of this section for public worship according to the rites and ceremonies of the Church of England and all articles appertaining thereto shall be subject to the jurisdiction of the consistory court of the diocese as though the building were a consecrated church.

(3) Where the bishop of a diocese, after consultation with the advisory committee, considers that any building in the diocese so licensed should not be subject to the faculty jurisdiction he may by order direct that subsection (2) above shall not apply to the building.

(4) Where the bishop of a diocese, after consultation with the advisory committee, considers that any article appertaining to a building in the diocese so licensed in respect of which an order under subsection (3) above is in force should be subject to the faculty jurisdiction by reason of its being—

(a) of outstanding architectural, artistic, historical or archaeological value; or
(b) of significant monetary value; or
(c) at special risk of being stolen or damaged,

he may by order direct that the article shall be subject to the jurisdiction of the consistory court of the diocese during such period as may be specified in the order.

(5) Any article in respect of which an order under subsection (4) above is in force shall, during the period specified in the order, be subject to the jurisdiction of the court specified in the order as though it were an article appertaining to a consecrated church.

(6) An order under subsection (3) or (4) above may be varied or revoked by an order made by the bishop of the diocese concerned after consultation with the advisory committee.

(7) An order under this section which has the effect of subjecting an article to the faculty jurisdiction shall not render unlawful any act done before the making of the order nor shall require the issue of faculties confirming such acts.

(8) The chancellor of a diocese shall give written guidance to all parochial church councils, ministers and churchwardens in the diocese as to those matters within the jurisdiction of the consistory court which he for the time being considers, after consultation with the advisory committee, to be of such a minor nature that they may be undertaken without a faculty.

Grant of faculties, etc

12.—(1) In any proceedings for obtaining a faculty, the court may grant the faculty subject to conditions, including in particular—
- (a) a condition requiring the work authorised thereby or any part thereof to be carried out under the supervision of the archdeacon concerned or of any other person nominated by the court in that behalf;
- (b) in the case of a faculty authorising the disposal of an article, a condition requiring a specified period to elapse before the disposal takes place.

(2) Where the court grants a faculty to a person other than an archdeacon and considers that the work authorised thereby should be carried out (whether or not by that person), it may also order that, in default of that person carrying out the work, a faculty shall issue to the archdeacon concerned authorising him to carry out the work and, in that event, that the expenses incurred by the archdeacon in carrying out the work be paid by that person.

Orders against persons responsible for defaults

13.—(1) Subject to subsection (7) below, if in any proceedings by any person for obtaining a faculty it appears to the court that any other person being a party to the proceedings was responsible wholly or in part for any act or default in consequence of which the proceedings were instituted the court may order the whole or any part of the costs and expenses of the proceedings or consequent thereon, including expenses incurred in carrying out any work authorised by the faculty (so far as such costs and expenses have been occasioned by that act or default), to be paid by the person responsible.

(2) Subject to subsection (7) below, in any such proceedings the court may by way of special citation add as a further party to the proceedings any person alleged to be so responsible or partly responsible and not already a party and notwithstanding that such person resides outside the diocese concerned.

(3) A special citation under subsection (2) above may require the person to whom it is issued to attend the court concerned at such time and place as may be specified in the citation.

(4) Where at any time (whether before or after faculty proceedings have been instituted) it appears to the consistory court of a diocese that a person intends to commit or continue to commit, or cause or permit the commission or continuance of, any act in relation to a church or churchyard in the diocese or any article appertaining to a church in the diocese, being an act which would be unlawful under ecclesiastical law, the court may issue an injunction restraining the first-mentioned person from committing or continuing to commit that act or from causing or permitting the commission or continuance of that act, as the case may be.

(5) Where at any time (whether before or after faculty proceedings have been instituted) it appears to the consistory court of a diocese that a person has committed, or caused or permitted the commission of any act in relation to a church or churchyard in the diocese or any article appertaining to a church in the diocese which was unlawful under ecclesiastical law, the court may make an

order (a 'restoration order') requiring that person to take such steps as the court may consider necessary, within such time as the court may specify, for the purpose of restoring the position so far as possible to that which existed immediately before the act was committed.

(6) An injunction under subsection (4) above may be issued and a restoration order under subsection (5) above may be made on an application made by the archdeacon concerned or any other person appearing to the court to have a sufficient interest in the matter or on its own motion.

(7) In any proceedings for obtaining a faculty the court shall not make an order under subsection (1) above or issue a special citation under subsection (2) above in respect of any act unless the court is satisfied that the proceedings were instituted less than six years after the act was committed.

(8) The court shall not make a restoration order under subsection (5) above in respect of any act unless the court is satisfied that less than six years have elapsed since the act was committed.

(9) Where proceedings for obtaining a faculty are instituted by an archdeacon or an application for a restoration order under subsection (5) above is made by an archdeacon and any fact relevant to the institution of such proceedings or the making of such an application has been deliberately concealed from him the period of six years mentioned in subsection (7) above or, as the case may be, subsection (8) above, shall not begin to run until the archdeacon has discovered the concealment or could with reasonable diligence have discovered it.

(10) For the purpose of subsection (9) above, deliberate commission of a breach of duty in circumstances in which it is unlikely to be discovered for some time amounts to deliberate concealment of the facts involved in that breach of duty.

(11) Failure to comply without reasonable excuse with any requirement of a special citation or injunction issued, or a restoration order made, under this section by any court shall be a contempt of the court.

Delegation to archdeacons of power to grant faculties

14.—(1) Subject to the following provisions of this section the chancellor of a diocese shall confer upon the archdeacon of every archdeaconry in the diocese the jurisdiction of the consistory court of the diocese in such faculty matters relating to the archdeaconry, to such extent and in such manner as may be prescribed.

(2) An archdeacon upon whom such jurisdiction is conferred shall have power to grant a faculty in any cause of faculty falling to be considered by him which is unopposed.

(3) Where, in any cause of faculty falling to be considered by an archdeacon—
   (a) he declines to grant a faculty; or
   (b) he considers that the matter should be dealt with as a matter of urgency without reference to the advisory committee for advice in accordance with section 15(2) below; or
   (c) the grant of a faculty is opposed by any person,

he shall cause the matter to be referred to the chancellor of the diocese concerned to be dealt with by him.

(4) A faculty granted by an archdeacon under subsection (2) above shall have effect as if it had been granted by the chancellor of the diocese concerned.

(5) Nothing in this section shall be construed as enabling an archdeacon to—
   (a) order any costs or expenses to be paid by any person; or
   (b) issue an injunction or make a restoration order against any person; or
   (c) grant an interim faculty pending the final determination of the matter;

and where an archdeacon considers that any question arises as to the payment of costs or expenses, the issue of an injunction, the making of a restoration order or the grant of an interim faculty, he shall cause the matter to be referred to the chancellor of the diocese concerned to be dealt with by him.

(6) A certificate issued by an archdeacon under section 12 of the 1964 Measure before the coming into operation of this section shall continue in force and have effect as if it were a faculty granted under subsection (2) above.

Consultation with diocesan advisory committees

15.—(1) The chancellor of a diocese shall seek the advice of the advisory committee before making a final determination in any cause of faculty or issuing a permanent injunction under section 13(4) above or making a restoration order under section 13(5) above, unless the action proposed relates exclusively to exhumation or the reservation of a grave space or he is satisfied that the matter is sufficiently urgent to justify the grant of a faculty or issue of an injunction without obtaining the committee's advice.

(2) An archdeacon shall seek the advice of the advisory committee before making a final determination in any cause of faculty, unless the action proposed relates exclusively to exhumation or the reservation of a grave space.

(3) In every diocese the Secretary to the advisory committee shall compile and maintain a register of all petitions for a faculty referred to the committee for advice under this section, and shall ensure that the register is available for inspection by the public by prior appointment at such place in the diocese as the bishop of the diocese may designate for the purposes of this subsection.

Parties

16.—(1) Proceedings for obtaining a faculty may be instituted by—
   (a) the archdeacon of the archdeaconry in which the parish concerned is situated; or
   (b) the minister and churchwardens of the parish concerned; or
   (c) any other person appearing to the court to have a sufficient interest in the matter.

(2) For the purposes of any proceedings for obtaining a faculty the archdeacon shall be deemed to have an interest as such, and any person whose name is entered on the church electoral roll of the parish concerned but who does not reside therein shall be deemed to have an interest as though he were a parishioner of that parish.

(3) If—
   (a) the archdeaconry is vacant; or
   (b) the archdeacon is incapacitated by absence or illness from acting; or
   (c) in the opinion of the bishop
      (i) the archdeacon is for any other reason unable or unwilling to act; or
      (ii) it would be inappropriate for the archdeacon to act,

such other person as the bishop shall appoint in that behalf in writing (either generally or in a particular case) shall have power to act in the place of the archdeacon for the purposes of this Measure or of any other enactment relating to the institution of, or participation in, proceedings in the court.

(4) If the archdeacon or such other person as may be appointed under subsection (3) above institutes or intervenes in any proceedings for obtaining a faculty all costs and expenses properly incurred by him or which he is ordered by the court to pay shall be paid by the Diocesan Board of Finance for the diocese concerned:

Provided that a Diocesan Board of Finance shall not be liable for any sum by virtue of this subsection unless the institution of proceedings or intervention is approved by the bishop of the diocese concerned in writing after consultation with the Board and, if such approval is duly given, any order in the proceedings that the costs or expenses of the archdeacon or other appointed person be paid by any other party may be enforced by the Board in the name of the archdeacon or other appointed person.

(5) Anything done under or for the purposes of section 9 of the 1964 Measure and having effect immediately before the coming into force of this section shall continue to have effect and be deemed to have been done under or for the purposes of this section.

Faculties for demolition of churches

17.—(1) A court shall not grant a faculty for the demolition or partial demolition of a church except on the grounds specified in this section.

(2) Subject to the following provisions of this section, a court may grant a faculty for the demolition of the whole or part of a church if it is satisfied that another church or part of a church will be erected on the site or curtilage of the church or part of a church in question or part thereof to take the place of that church or part of a church.

(3) Subject to the following provisions of this section, a court may grant a faculty for the demolition of part of a church if it is satisfied that—
- (a) the part of the church left standing will be used for the public worship of the Church of England for a substantial period after such demolition; or
- (b) such demolition is necessary for the purpose of the repair or alteration of the church or the reconstruction of the part to be demolished.

(4) The court shall not grant a faculty under subsection (2) or (3)(a) above unless—
- (a) the person bringing proceedings for the faculty has—
  - (i) obtained the written consent of the bishop of the diocese concerned to the proceedings being brought; and
  - (ii) within the prescribed time, caused to be published in 'The London Gazette' and in such other newspapers as the court may direct a notice stating the substance of the petition for the faculty;
- (b) the registrar has given notice in writing to the Council for the Care of Churches and the advisory committee of the diocese concerned of the petition;
- (c) the judge of the court has thereafter considered such advice as the advisory committee has tendered to the court; and
- (d) the judge has heard evidence in open court, after application for the purpose has been made to the court in the prescribed manner, from—
  - (i) a member of the said Council or some person duly authorised by the Council; and
  - (ii) any other person, unless in the opinion of the judge his application or the evidence which he gives is frivolous or vexatious.

(5) Without prejudice to the requirements of subsection (4) above, the court shall not grant a faculty under subsection (2) or (3)(a) above in the case of a church which is a listed building or in a conservation area unless—
- (a) the registrar has given notice in writing to—
  - (i) the Secretary of State;
  - (ii) the local planning authority concerned;
  - (iii) the Historic Buildings and Monuments Commission for England; and
  - (iv) the national amenity societies;
- (b) the judge of the court has thereafter considered such advice as any of those bodies may have tendered to the court;
- (c) the registrar has given notice in writing to the Royal Commission on the Historical Monuments of England and thereafter either—
  - (i) for a period of at least one month following the giving of the notice reasonable access to the church has been made available to members or officers of the said Royal Commission for the purpose of recording it; or
  - (ii) the said Royal Commission have, by their Secretary or other officer of theirs with authority to act on their behalf for the purposes of this section, stated in writing that they have completed their recording of the church or that they do not wish to record it.

(6) A court shall not grant a faculty under subsection (3)(b) above unless—
- (a) the court is satisfied, after consultation with the advisory committee, that when the proposed repair, alteration or reconstruction is completed the demolition will not materially affect the external or internal appearance of the church or the architectural, archaeological, artistic or historic character of the church; or

(b) the requirements of subsection (4) above and also, in the case of a church which is a listed building or in a conservation area, the requirements of subsection (5) above have been complied with.

(7) Anything done under or for the purposes of section 2 of the 1964 Measure and having effect immediately before the coming into force of this section shall continue to have effect and be deemed to have been done under or for the purposes of this section.

Emergency demolition of churches

18.—(1) Without prejudice to the powers exercisable under any rule of law by diocesan chancellors at the coming into operation of this section, where the chancellor of a diocese is satisfied—
- (a) that the demolition of the whole or part of a church in the diocese is necessary in the interests of safety or health or for the preservation of the church and, having regard to the urgency of the matter, there is insufficient time to obtain a faculty in respect of it; and
- (b) in the case of a church which is a listed building or is in a conservation area—
    - (i) that it is not practicable to secure safety or health or, as the case may be, the preservation of the building by works of repair or works for affording temporary support or shelter; and
    - (ii) that the works to be carried out are limited to the minimum measures immediately necessary,

he may by an instrument under his hand authorise the carrying out of the demolition without a faculty.

(2) An instrument under subsection (1) above—
- (a) may require the person to whom it is issued (subject to his obtaining any necessary faculty) to carry out such works for the restoration of the church following its demolition or partial demolition as may be specified in the instrument;
- (b) in the case of partial demolition of a church which is a listed building or is in a conservation area, shall require the person to whom it is issued, as soon as practicable after the works have been carried out, to give to the local planning authority notice in writing describing the works carried out.

(3) Where the chancellor of a diocese issues an instrument under subsection (1) above he shall send a copy of the instrument to the Council for the Care of Churches and the local planning authority.

Meaning of 'church'

19. In this Part, unless the context otherwise requires, 'church' includes any building which is licensed for public worship according to the rites and ceremonies of the Church of England and is subject to the faculty jurisdiction.

Part IV
Miscellaneous and General

Discussion and reporting of defaults

20. If it appears to an archdeacon that—
- (a) anything has been done in a parish in his archdeaconry which ought not to have been done without a faculty; or
- (b) anything which ought to have been done in connection with the care of any church in his archdeaconry or any article appertaining to any such church has not been done,

he may convene an extraordinary meeting of the parochial church council, or an extraordinary parochial church meeting, of the parish concerned for the purpose of discussing the matter, and shall either take the chair himself or shall appoint a chairman to preside. The chairman, not being otherwise entitled to attend such meeting, shall not be entitled to vote upon any resolution before the meeting.

Deposit of articles in places of safety

21.—(1) If it appears to an archdeacon that any article appertaining to a church in his archdeaconry, being an article which he considers to be of architectural, artistic, historical or archaeological value, is exposed to danger of loss or damage and ought to be removed to a place of safety, he may subject to subsection (2) below order that the article in question shall be removed from the church and deposited in such place of safety as may be specified in the order.

(2) Unless the archdeacon is of the opinion that the article in question should be removed to a place of safety immediately, he shall notify the churchwardens and any other person having custody of the article and the parochial church council and advisory committee of the facts as they appear to the archdeacon and inform them that he will consider any written representations made to him by any of them before a date specified in the notice being a date not less than twenty-eight days after service of the notice; and in that event the archdeacon shall not make an order under this section before that date and shall before making such an order consider any representations duly made to him under this subsection.

(3) Where the archdeacon makes an order under this section without giving the advisory committee an opportunity to make representations to him in connection with the making of the order, he shall, as soon as practicable after the removal of the article in question to a place of safety, notify the committee of the removal.

(4) An order under this section shall be in such form as may be prescribed and shall be directed to, and served on, the churchwardens and any other person having custody of the article in question.

(5) If any person on whom an order made by an archdeacon under this section is served refuses or fails to comply with the order, the archdeacon may apply to the consistory court of the diocese in which the article in question is for an order that that person shall deliver the article to the place of safety specified in the order made by the archdeacon, and the court, if satisfied that that order was made in accordance with the provisions of this section, may make an order accordingly.

(6) Where an order is made by an archdeacon under this section the archdeacon shall, within twenty-eight days after the removal of the article in question to a place of safety, apply to the consistory court of the diocese concerned for a faculty authorising the retention of the article in the place of safety.

(7) In this section 'article' does not include a record or register to which section 10(1) of the Parochial Registers and Records Measure 1978 applies.

Power of bishop to remove legal effects of consecration

22.—(1) Where the bishop of a diocese, on the application of the archdeacon of an archdeaconry in the diocese in respect of any building or land in the archdeaconry which is subject to the legal effects of consecration, is satisfied that—
   (a) the building or land is not held or controlled by any ecclesiastical corporation (that is to say, any corporation in the Church of England, whether sole or aggregate, which is established for spiritual purposes) or by any Diocesan Board of Finance; and
   (b) no purpose will be served by its remaining subject to the legal effects of consecration,

he may by order direct that the building or land or part of the building or land shall not be subject to the legal effects of consecration.

(2) Subject to subsection (3) below, an order under subsection (1) above may impose such conditions and requirements as the bishop thinks fit as to—
   (a) the preservation or disposal of any human remains believed to be buried in or beneath any building affected by the order or in any land so affected and of any tombstones, monuments or memorials commemorating the deceased persons; and
   (b) the maintenance of orderly behaviour in or on the building or land so affected;

and for the purposes of paragraph (a) above such an order may apply to the building or land such provisions of section 65 of and Schedule 6 to the 1983 Measure as may be specified in the order subject to such modifications and adaptations as may be so specified.

(3) A condition or requirement as to a matter falling within paragraph (a) of subsection (2) above shall not be imposed by an order under subsection (1) above except with the consent of the Secretary of State.

(4) Where an order is made under subsection (1) above in respect of any building or land then—
- (a) the building or land shall not be subject to the legal effects of consecration; and
- (b) in particular, the jurisdiction of any court or person with respect to the granting of faculties shall cease to extend to the building or land.

(5) Any conditions or requirements imposed under subsection (2) above shall be enforceable as if the archdeacon of the archdeaconry in which the building or land affected is situated was the owner of adjacent land and the conditions or requirements were negative covenants expressed to be entered into for the benefit of that adjacent land.

(6) For the purposes of subsection (5) above the enforcement of a condition or requirement shall be deemed to be for the benefit of the archdeacon concerned.

(7) Section 84 (except subsection (2)) of the Law of Property Act 1925 (which enables the Lands Tribunal to discharge or modify restrictions affecting land) shall not apply in relation to conditions and requirements imposed under subsection (2) above.

(8) A condition or requirement imposed by an order under subsection (1) above shall be a local land charge, and for the purposes of the Local Land Charges Act 1975 the bishop by whom the order was made shall be treated as the originating authority as respects the charge constituted by the condition or requirement.

Application of section 22 in relation to Crown land

23.—(1) Subject to subsection (2) below, section 22 above shall apply in relation to Crown land and to buildings situated on Crown land as it applies to other land and buildings.

(2) A condition or requirement as to a matter falling within paragraph (b) of subsection (2) of section 22 above shall not be imposed by an order under subsection (1) of that section relating to Crown land or a building situated on Crown land except with the consent of the appropriate authority.

(3) For the purposes of subsection (2) above any land which is used for the purposes of the Church of England and which will become Crown land on ceasing to be so used or on the exercise of a right of re-entry shall be treated as Crown land.

(4) In this section 'Crown land' and 'the appropriate authority' have the same meanings as in section 293 of the Town and Country Planning Act 1990; and, if any question arises as to what authority is the appropriate authority in relation to any land or building, that question shall be referred to the Treasury, whose decision shall be final.

Repeal of s 4 of Parish Notices Act 1837

24. *Text omitted.*

Rule Committee

25.—(1) There shall be a Rule Committee which shall consist of the following persons, namely—
- (a) a diocesan bishop nominated by the Archbishops of Canterbury and York;
- (b) the Dean of the Arches and Auditor;
- (c) one archdeacon nominated by the Archbishops of Canterbury and York;
- (d) two diocesan chancellors nominated by the Archbishops of Canterbury and York;
- (e) two diocesan registrars nominated by the Archbishops of Canterbury and York;
- (f) one person nominated by the Council for the Care of Churches;

(g) two persons nominated by the Standing Committee of the House of Laity from among the members of that House,

together with eleven other persons nominated for particular purposes in accordance with subsection (2) below.

(2) The members of the committee to be nominated for particular purposes shall be as follows—
- (a) for the purpose of making rules relating to proceedings in the Court of Ecclesiastical Causes Reserved or a Commission of Review appointed under section 11 of the 1963 Measure, one person nominated by the Lord Chancellor, being a person who holds or has held high judicial office;
- (b) for the purpose of making rules relating to cathedral churches—
  - (i) one person nominated by the Appointments Committee of the General Synod, being a person who is a member of the administrative body of a cathedral church;
  - (ii) three persons nominated by the Cathedrals Fabric Commission from among the members of that Commission, being persons having special knowledge of the conservation of cathedrals;
  - (iii) three persons nominated by the Association of English Cathedrals;
- (c) for the purpose of making rules relating to proceedings in respect of offences cognisable under section 14 of the 1963 Measure or disciplinary proceedings under the Clergy Discipline Measure 2003—
  - (i) a diocesan bishop nominated by the Archbishops of Canterbury and York (in addition to the bishop nominated under subsection (1)(a) above);
  - (ii) the Prolocutor of the Lower House of the Convocation of Canterbury or a member of that House nominated by him;
  - (iii) the Prolocutor of the Lower House of the Convocation of York or a member of that House nominated by him.

(3) The quorum of the committee shall be five members, but a member nominated for a particular purpose under subsection (2) above shall not be included in a quorum for any other purpose.

(4) The chairman of the committee shall be the Dean of the Arches and Auditor, unless he declines or is unable to act as such in which case the chairman shall be such other member of the committee as may be nominated by the Dean of the Arches and Auditor after consultation with the Archbishops of Canterbury and York.

(5) Subject to subsection (3) above, the committee may act notwithstanding any vacancy in its membership and may regulate its own procedure.

Functions of Rule Committee

26.—(1) The Rule Committee may make rules for carrying into effect the provisions of—
- (a) this Measure;
- (b) the 1963 Measure;
- (c) the 1964 Measure;
- (d) the Care of Cathedrals Measures 1990 and 1994;
- (e) the Care of Places of Worship Measure 1999;
- (f) the Clergy Discipline Measure 2003;

(hereafter referred to in this section as 'the relevant provisions').

(2) Rules made under subsection (1) above may in particular (so far as the same are not regulated by the relevant provisions or by rules made under section 4 of the Church of England (Legal Aid) Measure 1994 make provision for—
- (a) regulating the procedure and practice (including the mode and burden of proof and admissibility of evidence) of all courts, disciplinary tribunals, commissions, committees and examiners provided for in the 1963 Measure, the Care of Cathedrals Measures 1990

and 1994 or the Clergy Discipline Measure 2003, including courts of appellate jurisdiction (so far as rules made by the Judicial Committee of the Privy Council do not extend);
- (b) the procedure and practice where archdeacons have jurisdiction in faculty matters under section 14 above;
- (c) the appointment and duties of officers of the said courts, disciplinary tribunals, commissions and committees;
- (cc) the procedure and practice where complaints are referred to registrars under section 11 of the Clergy Discipline Measure 2003;
- (d) the time within which any act required or permitted to be performed by the relevant provisions is to be performed;
- (e) matters relating to the appointment of authorised complainants and prosecutors in connection with proceedings or contemplated proceedings under the relevant provisions;
- (f) the forms of complaint instituting proceedings under the relevant provisions and of any answers to be made thereto;
- (g) all other forms and notices required in connection with the relevant provisions;
- (h) the mode of effecting service of complaints, articles or other documents including provision for substituted service;
- (i) the fixing of the time and place of any hearing or trial and for notifying the parties thereof;
- (j) the passing of censures and the forms of certificates of findings;
- (k) matters relating to costs, fees and expenses in respect of any proceedings under the relevant provisions;
- (l) enabling evidence to be obtained of compliance with the relevant provisions; and
- (m) any matter which may be prescribed by virtue of the relevant provisions.

(3) The Rule Committee may also make rules containing provision—
- (a) for enabling a parochial church council, after consultation with the advisory committee of the diocese concerned, to deposit (without a faculty) moveable articles appertaining to a church in the parish concerned for safekeeping in places approved for the purpose by such persons as may be specified in the rules, subject to such requirements, terms and conditions as may be so specified or as may be determined by persons so specified;
- (b) for requiring parochial church councils to keep records of the location of burials carried out in churchyards in their parish and of reserved grave-spaces in respect of which a faculty has been granted;
- (c) for the safekeeping, care, inspection and preservation of books and other documents (not being register books or records within the meaning of section 25 of the Parochial Registers and Records Measure 1978) which, in the opinion of such person as may be specified in the rules, are of historic interest to the Church of England, including provision for the appointment of persons with duties in that respect.

Supplementary provisions as to rules

27.—(1) Any rule made under—
- (a) section 65 of the 1963 Measure; or
- (b) section 14 of the 1964 Measure; or
- (c) section 16 of the Care of Cathedrals Measure 1990,

being a rule in force immediately before the coming into force of this section, shall continue in force and be deemed to have been made under section 26 above.

(2) Any rules made under section 26 above shall be laid before the General Synod and shall not come into force until approved by the General Synod, whether with or without amendment.

(3) Where the Standing Committee determines that the rules do not need to be debated by the General Synod then, unless—
- (a) notice is given by a member of the General Synod in accordance with its Standing Orders that he wishes the rules to be debated, or

(b) notice is so given by any such member that he wishes to move an amendment to the rules

the rules shall for the purposes of subsection (2) above be deemed to have been approved by the General Synod without amendment.

(4) The Statutory Instruments Act 1946 shall apply to any rules approved by the General Synod under subsection (2) above as if they were statutory instruments and were made when so approved, and as if this Measure were an Act providing that any such rules should be subject to annulment in pursuance of a resolution of either House of Parliament.

General provisions as to orders by bishops

28. The bishop of a diocese shall send every order made by him under this Measure to the registrar of the diocese and the registrar shall register any order so made in the diocesan registry.

Diocesan registrars' fees

29. There shall be payable to a diocesan registrar for registering any order under section 28 above and for permitting searches for and inspection and furnishing copies of any such order such fees as may from time to time be authorised by an order made under Part II of the Ecclesiastical Fees Measure 1986.

Service of notices and orders

30.—(1) Any notice, order or other document required or authorised by this Measure to be served on or sent or given to any person may be served, sent or given by delivering it to him, or by leaving it at his proper address, or by post.

(2) For the purposes of this section and of section 7 of the Interpretation Act 1978 the proper address of the person on or to whom any such notice, order or other document is required or authorised to be served, sent or given shall be the last known address of that person.

Interpretation

31.—(1) In this Measure, unless the context otherwise requires—

'the 1963 Measure' means the Ecclesiastical Jurisdiction Measure 1963;

'the 1964 Measure' means the Faculty Jurisdiction Measure 1964;

'the 1983 Measure' means the Pastoral Measure 1983;

'administrative body'—
  (a) in relation to a cathedral church in respect of which there is a corporate body known as the dean and chapter, means the body by which administrative functions in relation to the cathedral church are performed by virtue of paragraph (b) of section 7 of the Cathedrals Measure 1963;
  (b) in relation to any other cathedral church, means the body by which administrative functions in relation to the cathedral church are performed by virtue of paragraph (b) of section 8 of that Measure;

'advisory committee' in relation to a diocese or archdeaconry means the Diocesan Advisory Committee of the diocese or of the diocese in which the archdeaconry is situated, as the case may be;

'article' includes part of an article and any thing affixed to land or a building;

'building' includes any structure or erection, and any part of a building as so defined;

'Cathedrals Fabric Commission' means the Cathedrals Fabric Commission for England;

'conservation area' has the same meaning as in the Planning (Listed Buildings and Conservation Areas) Act 1990;

'Council for the Care of Churches' means the body so named at the passing of this Measure or any body subsequently exercising the functions of that body under a different name or with a different constitution;

'Diocesan Board of Finance' has the same meaning as in the Endowments and Glebe Measure 1976; 'high judicial office' means such office within the meaning of Part 3 of the Constitutional Reform Act 2005 or membership of the Judicial Committee of the Privy Council;

'inventory' means the inventory maintained under section 4(1) above;

'land' includes buildings;

'listed building' has the same meaning as in the Planning (Listed Buildings and Conservation Areas) Act 1990;

'local planning authority' in relation to any area means the body exercising the functions of a local planning authority under section 8 of the Planning (Listed Buildings and Conservation Areas) Act 1990 in that area;

'log-book' means the log-book maintained under section 4(1) above;

'minister', in relation to a parish, means—
- (a) in a case where a special cure of souls in respect of the parish has been assigned to a vicar in a team ministry by a scheme under the 1983 Measure or by his licence from the bishop, that vicar;
- (aa) in a case where a special responsibility for pastoral care in respect of the parish has been assigned to a member of the team in a team ministry under section 20(8A) of that Measure but a special cure of souls in respect of the parish has not been assigned as mentioned in paragraph (a) above, that member;
- (b) in any other case
  - (i) the incumbent of the benefice comprising the parish; or
  - (ii) a curate licensed to the charge of the parish or a minister acting as priest-in-charge of the parish, where rights of presentation are suspended;

'national amenity society' means any of the following, the Ancient Monuments Society, the Council for British Archaeology, the Georgian Group, the Society for the Protection of Ancient Buildings, the Victorian Society and such other body as may from time to time be designated by the Dean of the Arches and Auditor as a national amenity society for the purpose of this Measure;

'parish' means—
- (a) an ecclesiastical parish; and
- (b) a district which is constituted a 'conventional district' for the cure of souls;

'parish church' does not include a parish church cathedral to which the Care of Cathedrals Measure 1990 applies;

'place of worship' includes the curtilage of a place of worship;

'prescribed' means prescribed by rules made under section 26 above;

'Rule Committee' means the Rule Committee established under section 25 above;

'terrier' means the terrier maintained under section 4(1) above.

(2) In Parts I, II and IV of this Measure 'church' means—
- (a) any parish church;
- (b) any other church or chapel (not being a cathedral church to which the Care of Cathedrals Measure 1990 applies or chapel which is not subject to the jurisdiction of the bishop of a diocese or the Cathedral Church of Christ in Oxford) which has been consecrated for the purpose of public worship according to the rites and ceremonies of the Church of England; and
- (c) any building licensed for public worship according to the rites and ceremonies of the Church of England other than—
  - (i) a building which is in a university, college, school, hospital or public or charitable institution but which has not been designated under section 29(2) of the 1983 Measure as a parish centre of worship;
  - (ii) a building which has been excluded from the provisions of Parts II and IV of this Measure by direction of the bishop of the diocese concerned with the approval of the advisory committee; and

(iii) a building used solely for the purpose of religious services relating to burial or cremation.

(3) In this Measure references to work authorised by a faculty shall be construed as including a reference to work ordered by a faculty.

(4) In this Measure references to the consistory court of a diocese and to the chancellor of a diocese shall, in their application to the diocese of Canterbury, be construed as references to the commissary court thereof and to the commissary general of such court respectively.

(5) Any reference in any enactment to an advisory committee for the care of churches appointed under section 13 of the 1964 Measure shall be construed as including a committee constituted under section 2 above.

(6) Nothing in this Measure shall be construed as prejudicing or affecting the provisions of the Ancient Monuments and Archaeological Areas Act 1979, the Town and Country Planning Act 1990 or the Planning (Listed Buildings and Conservation Areas) Act 1990 or any instrument made thereunder.

Schedule 1
Provisions to be Included in Diocesan Advisory Committee Constitutions

Section 2(2)

Name

1. The committee shall be known as the (name of diocese concerned) Diocesan Advisory Committee.

Membership

2. The committee shall consist of a chairman, the archdeacons of the diocese and not less than twelve other members.

3. The chairman shall be appointed by the bishop of the diocese after consultation with the bishop's council, the chancellor and the Council for the Care of Churches.

4. The other members shall be—
   (a) two persons appointed by the bishop's council of the diocese from among the elected members of the diocesan synod of the diocese;
   (b) not less than ten other persons appointed by the bishop's council of the diocese, of whom one shall be appointed after consultation with the Historic Buildings and Monuments Commission for England, one shall be appointed after consultation with the relevant associations of local authorities and one shall be appointed after consultation with the national amenity societies;
   (c) such other persons as may be co-opted under paragraph 12 below.

5. In making appointments under paragraph 4(b) above, the bishop's council shall ensure that the persons appointed have, between them,—
   (a) knowledge of the history, development and use of church buildings;
   (b) knowledge of Church of England liturgy and worship;
   (c) knowledge of architecture, archaeology, art and history; and
   (d) experience of the care of historic buildings and their contents.

6. The first appointment of the chairman and other members of the committee under paragraph 4(a) and (b) above shall take place as soon as practicable, and subsequent new appointments of the chairman and those members shall be made within the period of one year following the formation of the second new diocesan synod after the latest appointments.

7. The term of office of the chairman and any other member of the committee appointed under paragraph 4(a) or (b) above shall be the period from his appointment to the making of new appointments in accordance with paragraph 6 above.

8. A member of the committee who ceases to hold a qualification by virtue of which he became a member shall thereupon cease to be a member.

9. A member of the committee who ceases to hold office otherwise than by virtue of paragraph 8 above shall be eligible for reappointment.

10. Where a casual vacancy occurs among the chairman and other members of the committee appointed under paragraph 4(a) or (b) above, the bishop shall appoint a person to fill the vacancy, and if the person whose place is to be filled was a member of the committee by virtue of his membership of the diocesan synod of the diocese the person so appointed shall also be a member of that diocesan synod.

11. Any person appointed to fill a casual vacancy shall hold office only for the unexpired portion of the term of office of the person in whose place he is appointed.

12. With the consent of the bishop of the diocese, the committee may from time to time co-opt such persons (of a number not exceeding one third of the total number of the other members) as it thinks fit to be additional members of the committee, but any person so co-opted shall cease to be a member of the committee on the making of new appointments of members in accordance with paragraph 6 above.

Miscellaneous

13. The bishop of the diocese may appoint suitably qualified persons to act as consultants to the committee if the committee request him to do so.

14. The secretary to the committee shall be appointed by the bishop of the diocese after consultation with the chairman of the committee and the chief administrative officer of the diocese.

15. In this constitution 'national amenity society' has the same meaning as in the Care of Churches and Ecclesiastical Jurisdiction Measure 1991.

In paragraph 4(b) above 'relevant associations of local authorities' means such associations as may from time to time be designated by the Dean of the Arches and Auditor as the relevant associations of local authorities for the purposes of this Schedule in relation to the diocese concerned.

SCHEDULE 2
FUNCTIONS OF DIOCESAN ADVISORY COMMITTEE

Section 2(5)

1. The functions of a Diocesan Advisory Committee shall be—
    (a) to act as an advisory body on matters affecting places of worship in the diocese and, in particular, to give advice when requested by any of the persons specified in paragraph 2 below on matters relating to—
        (i) the grant of faculties;
        (ii) the architecture, archaeology, art and history of places of worship;
        (iii) the use, care, planning, design and redundancy of places of worship;
        (iv) the use and care of the contents of such places;
        (v) the use and care of churchyards and burial grounds;
    (b) to review and assess the degree of risk to materials, or of loss to archaeological or historic remains or records, arising from any proposals relating to the conservation, repair or alteration of places of worship, churchyards and burial grounds and the contents of such places;

(c) to develop and maintain a repository of records relating to the conservation, repair and alteration of places of worship, churchyards and burial grounds and other material (including inspection reports, inventories, technical information and photographs) relating to the work of the committee;
(d) to issue guidance for the preparation and storage of such records;
(e) to make recommendations as to the circumstances when the preparation of such a record should be made a condition of a faculty;
(f) to take action to encourage the care and appreciation of places of worship, churchyards and burial grounds and the contents of such places, and for that purpose to publicise methods of conservation, repair, construction, adaptation and redevelopment;
(g) to perform such other functions as may be assigned to the committee by any enactment, by any Canon of the Church of England or by resolution of the diocesan synod or as the committee may be requested to perform by the bishop or chancellor of the diocese.

2. The persons referred to in paragraph 1(a) above are—
(a) the bishop of the diocese;
(b) the chancellor of the diocese;
(c) the archdeacons of the diocese;
(d) the parochial church councils in the diocese;
(e) intending applicants for faculties in the diocese;
(f) the pastoral committee of the diocese;
(g) persons engaged in the planning, design or building of new places of worship in the diocese, not being places within the jurisdiction of the consistory court;
(h) such other persons as the committee may consider appropriate.

Priests (Ordination of Women) Measure 1993

Part I
Power to Legislate by Canon

Provision for ordination of women as priests

1.—(1) It shall be lawful for the General Synod to make provision by Canon for enabling a woman to be ordained to the office of priest if she otherwise satisfies the requirements of Canon Law as to the persons who may be ordained as priests.

(2) Nothing in this Measure shall make it lawful for a woman to be consecrated to the office of bishop.

Part II
Discharge of Functions

Bishops

2.—(1) A bishop of a diocese in office at the relevant date may make any one or more of the following declarations—
(a) that a woman is not to be ordained within the diocese to the office of priest; or
(b) that a woman is not to be instituted or licensed to the office of incumbent or priest-in-charge of a benefice, or of team vicar for a benefice, within the diocese; or
(c) that a woman is not to be given a licence or permission to officiate as a priest within the diocese.

(2)–(8) *Text omitted.*

Parishes

3.—(1) Subject to the following provisions of this section the parochial church council of a parish may pass either or both of the resolutions set out as Resolution A and Resolution B in Schedule 1 to this Measure.

(2) Subject to the following provisions of this section a parochial church council which has passed a resolution under subsection (1) above may by resolution rescind it, and the first-mentioned resolution shall continue in force until rescinded.

(3) A motion for a resolution in the form set out as Resolution A in Schedule 1 to this Measure shall not be considered by a parochial church council if the incumbent or priest-in-charge of the benefice concerned, or any team vicar or assistant curate for that benefice, is a woman ordained to the office of priest.

(4) A resolution shall not be passed by a parochial church council under subsection (1) or (2) above unless—

(a) except where notice of a vacancy has been sent to the secretary of the council under section 7(4) of the Patronage (Benefices) Measure 1986, the secretary of the council has given to the members of the council at least four weeks' notice of the time and place of the meeting at which the motion proposing the resolution is to be considered; and

(b) the meeting is attended by at least one half of the members of the council entitled to attend.

(5) A copy of any resolution passed by a parochial church council under subsection (1) or (2) above shall be sent to the following—

(a) the bishop of the diocese concerned;
(b) the rural dean of the deanery concerned;
(c) the lay chairman of the deanery synod concerned;
(d) the registrar of the diocese concerned;
(e) the designated officer for the diocese concerned, within the meaning of section 7(5) of the Patronage (Benefices) Measure 1986;
(f) the registered patron of the benefice concerned, within the meaning of section 39(1) of that Measure.

(6) Where a resolution under subsection (1) above is in force a person discharging any function in relation to the parish or benefice concerned shall not act in contravention of the resolution:

Provided that this subsection shall not apply in relation to a service held in a parish church cathedral on the direction of the bishop of the diocese.

(7) *Text omitted.*

(8) Subsections (1) to (6) above and Schedule 1 to this Measure shall apply in relation to a guild church designated and established under section 4 of the City of London (Guild Churches) Act 1952 as they apply in relation to a parish, but as if the references to the parochial church council of the parish were references to the guild church council of the guild church.

(9) In the case of a parish in which there is a parish church cathedral and in respect of which functions of the parochial church council have been transferred to the administrative body of the cathedral in pursuance of section 12 of the Cathedrals Measure 1963 or section 12 of the Cathedrals Measure 1999, this section shall have effect as if the references to the parochial church council of the parish were references to the administrative body of the cathedral.

(10) In this section 'parish' means—

(a) an ecclesiastical parish; and
(b) a district which is constituted a conventional district for the cure of souls.

Cathedrals

4.—(1) The administrative body of a cathedral church other than a parish church cathedral may pass either or both of the resolutions set out as Resolution A and Resolution B in Schedule 2 to this Measure.

(2) An administrative body which has passed a resolution under subsection (1) above may by resolution rescind it, and the first-mentioned resolution shall continue in force until rescinded.

(3) A motion for a resolution under subsection (1) above in respect of a cathedral church shall not be considered by an administrative body if the dean or any of the residentiary canons of the cathedral church is a woman ordained to the office of priest.

(4) A copy of any resolution passed under subsections (1) or (2) above shall be sent to the following—
  (a) Her Majesty;
  (b) the bishop of the diocese concerned;
  (c) the secretary of the diocesan synod of the diocese concerned;
  (d) the registrar of the diocese concerned.

(5) Where a resolution under subsection (1) above is in force in respect of a cathedral church a person discharging any function in relation to the conduct of services in the cathedral church or in relation to the appointment of the dean shall not act in contravention of the resolution.

Ecclesiastical offences

5. It shall be an offence against the laws ecclesiastical, for which proceedings may be taken under the Ecclesiastical Jurisdiction Measure 1963—
  (a) for any bishop to act in contravention of a declaration under section 2(1) above; or
  (b) for any bishop, priest or deacon to act in contravention of a resolution under section 3(1) above or to permit any act in contravention of such a resolution to be committed in any church or any building licensed for public worship according to the rites and ceremonies of the Church of England; or
  (c) for any bishop, priest or deacon to act in contravention of a resolution under section 4(1) above or to permit any act in contravention of such a resolution to be committed in any cathedral church.

Discriminatory discharge of certain functions

6. *Repealed.*

Benefices in the patronage of the Crown etc

7.—(1) Sections 2 and 3 above shall apply in relation to a Crown benefice and to a benefice the patronage or a share of the patronage of which is vested in the Lord Chancellor as they apply in relation to any other benefice.

(2) Section 4(5) above, in so far as it relates to the appointment of the dean of a cathedral church, shall apply in respect of the appointment of any dean by Her Majesty.

(3) In this section 'Crown benefice' has the same meaning as in the Patronage (Benefices) Measure 1986.

Interpretation of Part II

8. In this Part—
'administrative body' has the same meaning as in the Cathedrals Measure 1963;
'benefice' includes—
  (a) the office of incumbent of a parish church cathedral but does not include any other office in a cathedral church; and
  (b) the office of priest-in-charge of a district which is constituted a conventional district for the cure of souls;
'cathedral church' means any cathedral church in England except the cathedral church of Christ in Oxford;
'parish church cathedral' means any cathedral church other than a cathedral church in respect of which there is a corporate body known as the dean and chapter.

Part III
General

General interpretation

9. In any Canon, order, rule or regulation relating to priests, words importing the masculine gender include the feminine unless the contrary intention appears.

Minor and consequential amendments

10. *Text omitted.*

Amendment etc of Measure or Canon

11. A motion for the final approval of a Measure or Canon of the Church of England which amends or repeals any provision of this Measure or of any Canon promulged under section 1 above shall not be deemed to be carried unless it receives the assent of a majority in each House of the General Synod of not less than two-thirds of those present and voting.

Schedule 1
Forms of Parish Resolution

Section 3(1)

Resolution A

That this parochial church council would not accept a woman as the minister who presides at or celebrates the Holy Communion or pronounces the Absolution in the parish.

Resolution B

That this parochial church council would not accept a woman as the incumbent or priest-in-charge of the benefice or as a team vicar for the benefice.

Schedule 2
Forms of Dean and Chapter Cathedral Resolution

Section 4(1)

Resolution A

That the administrative body would not accept a woman as the minister who presides at or celebrates the Holy Communion or pronounces the Absolution in the cathedral church at any service other than a service held on the direction of the bishop of the diocese.

Resolution B

That the administrative body would not accept a woman as the dean of this cathedral church.

Care of Cathedrals (Supplementary Provisions) Measure 1994

Preliminary interview re contravention of s 2 of 1990 Measure

1. Subject to section 3(1) below, where it appears to the bishop of a diocese, whether of his own motion or on the advice of the Cathedrals Fabric Commission or on the basis of an allegation made by another person, that the administrative body of the cathedral church of the diocese may have committed or be intending to commit an act in contravention of section 2 of the 1990 Measure, he

shall, as soon as practicable and before taking any further action, afford to the members of the administrative body an opportunity of being interviewed in private by him with respect to the matter in question.

Power of bishop to order special visitation

2.—(1) Subject to subsection (2) below, where it appears to a bishop, after complying with section 1 above with respect to the members of an Chapter, that the Chapter has committed or is intending to commit an act as mentioned in that section, he shall within such period as may be prescribed order a special visitation under this section in respect of the cathedral church concerned for the purpose of inquiring into the matter in question; and, if he does so, he shall cause a written statement of his reasons for ordering the visitation to be sent to the Chapter.

(2) It shall not be necessary for a bishop to order a special visitation under this section in respect of any act if—
  (a) he is satisfied that the Chapter concerned intends to make an application for approval of that act under the 1990 Measure; or
  (b) the Chapter concerned has made such an application and the application has not been refused; or
  (c) he considers that there are exceptional reasons for not doing so.

(3) Without prejudice to any rule of law as to the effect of episcopal visitations, where a special visitation under this section is ordered by a bishop in respect of a cathedral church, the Chapter of the cathedral shall have no power to act as such with regard to the matter under inquiry without the prior approval in writing of the bishop.

(4) A special visitation under this section shall not be treated as an episcopal visitation for the purposes of any provision contained in the constitution and statutes of the cathedral church concerned restricting the ordering of such visitations.

Power of bishop to give directions

3.—(1) Where it appears to a bishop that a Chapter may have committed or be intending to commit an act in contravention of section 2 of the 1990 Measure and he is satisfied, having regard to the urgency of the matter, that there is insufficient time to comply with section 1 above he may from time to time give such interim directions with respect to the matter in question as he thinks fit to the Chapter before complying with that section.

(2) Where a bishop has ordered a special visitation he may from time to time give such directions with respect to the matter in question as he thinks fit to the Chapter concerned.

(3) Without prejudice to the generality of the powers to give directions under this section, such directions may require the Chapter—
  (a) to take such steps as the bishop may consider necessary for the purpose of avoiding a contravention of section 2 of the 1990 Measure;
  (b) to refrain from taking such steps as the bishop may consider likely to lead to such a contravention;
  (c) to take such steps as the bishop may consider necessary for the purpose of restoring the position so far as possible to that which existed before the act was committed.

(4) Before a bishop gives directions under this section which include a requirement of the kind mentioned in subsection (3)(c) above he shall seek the advice of the Cathedrals Fabric Commission.

(5) Directions given by a bishop under this section shall be in writing unless he is satisfied, having regard to the urgency of the matter, that there is insufficient time for them to be committed to writing; but if they are given orally he shall as soon as practicable commit them to writing.

(6) It shall be the duty of a Chapter to which directions are given under this section to comply with them.

Statutes and Measures

Institution of proceedings for injunction or restoration order

4.—(1) Where a bishop has ordered a special visitation and he considers it necessary or expedient to take further steps in respect of any actual or intended contravention of section 2 of the 1990 Measure, he may authorise a person designated by him for the purposes of this Measure, either generally or in a particular case, to institute proceedings on his behalf against the Chapter of the cathedral concerned for the purpose of obtaining an injunction or restoration order or both against the Chapter.

(2) Where a bishop proposes to authorise the institution of proceedings under subsection (1) above, he shall inform the Commissioners of the course he proposes to take and the Commissioners shall, as soon as practicable—
  (a) decide whether or not they would be prepared to pay, under section 58 of the Ecclesiastical Jurisdiction Measure 1963, any costs or expenses incurred in respect of the proceedings and, if so, to what extent; and
  (b) notify the bishop of their decision.

Jurisdiction and composition of Vicar-General's court

5.—(1) The Vicar-General's court of each of the provinces of Canterbury and York shall, in respect of every cathedral church in the province, have original jurisdiction to hear and determine proceedings instituted under section 4 above.

(2) Where, in any such proceedings—
  (a) the Vicar-General is for any reason unable to act; or
  (b) the cathedral church concerned is in a diocese of which the Vicar-General is the chancellor,

the court shall be presided over by a chancellor appointed by the Archbishop of the province of Canterbury or York, as the case may be, to act as deputy Vicar-General; and a chancellor so appointed shall have all the powers and perform all the duties of the Vicar-General.

(3) Any such proceedings shall be instituted and conducted in such manner as the Vicars-General of Canterbury and York, acting jointly, may direct.

Powers of court

6.—(1) In any proceedings instituted under section 4 above against an Chapter the court may by way of special citation add as a further party to the proceedings any person who appears to the court to be or to have been concerned in furthering the alleged contravention of section 2 of the 1990 Measure.

(2) A special citation under subsection (1) above may require the person to whom it is issued to attend the court concerned at such time and place as may be specified in the citation.

(3) Where, in any such proceedings, it appears to the court that the Chapter concerned intends to commit or continue to commit any act in contravention of section 2 of the 1990 Measure, the court may issue an injunction restraining—
  (a) the Chapter from committing or continuing to commit that act; or
  (b) any other party to the proceedings from committing or continuing to commit any act in furtherance of the contravention.

(4) Where, in any such proceedings, it appears to the court that the Chapter against which the proceedings were instituted, has committed any act in contravention of the said section 2, the court may make an order (a 'restoration order') requiring the Chapter or any other party to the proceedings to take such steps as the court may consider necessary, within such time as the court may specify, for the purpose of restoring the position so far as possible to that which existed before the act was committed.

(5) The court shall not make a restoration order in respect of any act unless the court is satisfied that less than six years have elapsed since the act was committed.

(6) The court shall seek the advice of the Cathedrals Fabric Commission before making a restoration order.

(7) Where proceedings for obtaining a restoration order are instituted on behalf of a bishop under section 4 above and any fact relevant to the institution of such proceedings has been deliberately concealed from him the period of six years mentioned in subsection (5) above shall not begin to run until the bishop has discovered the concealment or could with reasonable diligence have discovered it.

(8) For the purpose of subsection (7) above, deliberate commission of a breach of duty in circumstances in which it is unlikely to be discovered for some time amounts to deliberate concealment of the facts involved in that breach of duty.

(9) Failure to comply without reasonable excuse with any requirement of an injunction or restoration order shall be a contempt of the court.

(10) In any such proceedings the court may order that the special visitation from which the proceedings ensued shall continue on such terms as it considers just or shall cease and may make such further order in relation to the proceedings as it considers just.

Amendment of 1990 Measure

7. *Text omitted.*

Amendment of Ecclesiastical Jurisdiction Measure 1963

8. *Text omitted.*

Rules

9. *Text omitted.*

Interpretation

10. In this Measure—

'the 1990 Measure' means the Care of Cathedrals Measure 1990;

'Chapter'—
- (a) in relation to a cathedral church in respect of which there is a corporate body known as the dean and chapter, means the body by which administrative functions in relation to the cathedral church are performed by virtue of paragraph (b) of section 7 of the Cathedrals Measure 1963;
- (b) in relation to any other cathedral church, means the body by which administrative functions in relation to the cathedral church are performed by virtue of paragraph (b) of section 8 of that Measure;

'cathedral church' means any cathedral church in the provinces of Canterbury and York, except—
- (a) the Cathedral Church of Christ in Oxford;
- (b) any cathedral church in the diocese of Sodor and Man or in the diocese in Europe; and
- (c) any cathedral church to which the 1990 Measure does not, for the time being, apply by virtue of an order under section 18(1) of that Measure;

'Cathedrals Fabric Commission' means the Cathedrals Fabric Commission for England established under section 3 of the 1990 Measure;

'Commissioners' means the Church Commissioners;

'the court', in relation to proceedings instituted under section 4 above in respect of a cathedral church, means the Vicar-General's court of the province in which the cathedral church is situated;

'injunction' means an injunction under section 6(3) above;

'prescribed' means prescribed by rules made under section 26 of the Care of Churches and Ecclesiastical Jurisdiction Measure 1991;

'restoration order' means a restoration order under section 6(4) above;

'special visitation' means a special visitation under section 2 above.

National Institutions Measure 1998

Archbishops' Council

Establishment of the Archbishops' Council

1.—(1) There shall be a body to be known as 'the Archbishops' Council' whose objects shall be to co-ordinate, promote, aid and further the work and mission of the Church of England.

(2) It is hereby declared that the Council is established for charitable purposes.

(3) The provisions of Schedule 1 to this Measure shall have effect with respect to the Council and its members, to the appointment of its staff and to its proceedings and incidental powers.

(4) Part I of Schedule 1 to this Measure may at any time be amended by resolution of the General Synod.

(5) The Statutory Instruments Act 1946 shall apply to any resolution of the General Synod under subsection (4) above as if it were a statutory instrument and as if this Measure were an Act providing that any such resolution shall be subject to annulment in pursuance of a resolution of either House of Parliament.

Application of funds

2.—(1) It shall be the duty of the Church Commissioners—
  (a) from time to time in general meeting to determine the amount of income from their assets which is to be made available to the Council for application or distribution under subsection (3) below in the course of such period as may be specified in the determination, and
  (b) to the extent that the Church Commissioners are satisfied that it is available for application or distribution, to pay that amount to the Council in equal monthly instalments or as otherwise agreed by them and the Council.

(2) Before determining the amount mentioned in subsection (1)(a) above the Church Commissioners shall consult the Council and in making the determination they shall have regard to any proposals made by the Council.

(3) The Council shall consider and determine how to apply or distribute such sums as have been made available by the Church Commissioners under subsection (1) above, but those sums shall not be applied or distributed by the Council for any purpose other than one for which the balance in the Church Commissioners' general fund was available immediately before the coming into force of this section and in applying or distributing those sums the Council shall have particular regard to the requirements of section 67 of the Ecclesiastical Commissioners Act 1840 relating to the making of additional provision for the cure of souls in parishes where such assistance is most required.

(4) Where a decision is taken by the Council or the Church Commissioners to the effect that a plan should be produced under this subsection, those bodies acting jointly shall after consultation with any body appearing to them to be significantly affected, produce a plan which—
  (a) contains an estimate by the Church Commissioners, having regard to any recommendation made by the Assets Committee under section 6(3)(b) of the Church Commissioners Measure 1947, of the amount of income from their assets available for application or distribution under subsection (3) above during a period not exceeding three years, and
  (b) identifies the purposes for which the sums mentioned in subsection (3) above are to be applied or distributed in the course of that period or part thereof and the proportion of those sums appropriate for each purpose.

Any such plan may be amended or replaced in the same manner.

(5) Where a plan is produced under subsection (4) above—
  (a) the Church Commissioners, in complying with the requirements of subsection (2) above, shall have regard to the plan, and

(b) the Council, in complying with the requirements of subsection (3) above, shall act in accordance with the plan,

in so far as the plan relates to the period in question.

(6) As soon as practicable after the end of each year the Council shall cause a certificate to be issued to the Church Commissioners to the effect that the application and distribution of the sums made available by them as aforesaid has been in accordance with subsection (3) above.

Accounts and audit

3.—(1) The following provisions of this section shall have effect without prejudice to the provisions of Part VI of the Charities Act 1993.

(2) The accounts of the Council for each year shall be audited by a person appointed by the Council with the approval of the General Synod, being a person eligible under subsection (2) of section 43 of that Act to carry out an audit under that subsection.

(3) The person so appointed shall be deemed, for the purposes of the said Part VI, to have been appointed in pursuance of the said section 43.

(4) The auditor's report for any year, together with the accounts for that year, shall be laid before the General Synod before the end of June in the following year.

Reports and budgets

4.—(1) The Council shall cause a report of its work and proceedings during the year in question, including any decisions taken as to its future work, to be laid before the General Synod before the end of June in the following year.

(2) The Council shall also, at each group of sessions of the General Synod, cause an account of the matters discussed and the decisions taken by it at its meetings held since the previous group of sessions to be laid before the General Synod for its approval.

(3) In each year the Council shall prepare a budget indicating its expected income and expenditure for the following year and, before the end of June, cause it to be laid before the General Synod for its approval.

(4) In considering the annual budget it shall not be open to the General Synod to alter the amount of the sums to be made available to the Council by the Church Commissioners under section 2 above or the proposed application or distribution of those sums.

(5) The General Synod may request reports from the Council on any matter relating to the functions of the Council.

Transfer of functions and officers

Transfer of functions

5.—(1) Subject to the following provisions of this section the Archbishops of Canterbury and York acting jointly may, after consultation with any body appearing to them to be significantly affected, by order transfer to the Council or such other body as may be specified in the order any function previously exercisable by—

(a) the Church Commissioners other than—
   (i) a function relating to the management or ownership of the Commissioners' assets,
   (ii) a function relating to bishops under any enactment specified in Part I of Schedule 2 to this Measure,
   (iii) a function relating to cathedrals under any enactment specified in Part II of that Schedule, and
   (iv) a function under the Church of England (Pensions) Measures 1961 to 1997, or
(b) the Central Board of Finance, or
(c) the Standing Committee of the General Synod or any of its sub-committees.

(2) Any such order may contain such incidental, consequential and supplemental provisions as may be necessary or expedient for the purpose of giving full effect to the order, including provisions—
  (a) amending paragraph 1 of Schedule 1 to the Church Commissioners Measure 1947 (as substituted by section 7 below) so as to reduce the number of Commissioners;
  (b) for the carrying on and completion by or under the authority of the Council or other body so specified of anything commenced by or under the authority of the Commissioners, the Central Board of Finance or the Standing Committee before the date on which the order takes effect;
  (c) for such adaptation of the statutory provisions relating to any such function transferred as may be necessary to enable it to be exercised by or on behalf of the Council or other body so specified;
  (d) for the substitution of the Council or other body so specified for the Commissioners, the Central Board of Finance or the Standing Committee in any instrument, contract or legal proceedings made or commenced before the date on which the order takes effect.

(3) Before making any such order which relates to the functions of the Church Commissioners under the Dioceses Measure 1978 or the Pastoral Measure 1983 the Archbishops shall consult with the Prime Minister and the Church Commissioners.

(4) An order under subsection (1) above may be varied by a subsequent order made thereunder.

(5) A draft of any order proposed to be made under subsection (1) above shall be laid before the General Synod and if it is approved by the General Synod, whether with or without amendment, the draft order as so approved shall be referred to the Archbishops.

(6) Where a draft order is referred to the Archbishops under subsection (5) above then—
  (a) if it has been approved by the General Synod without any amendment, the Archbishops shall make the order;
  (b) if it has been approved by the General Synod with amendment, the Archbishops may make the order but, in the case of any order which relates to the functions of the Church Commissioners under the Dioceses Measure 1978 or the Pastoral Measure 1983, shall not do so without further consultation as required by subsection (3) above.

(7) An order under subsection (1) above which relates to the functions of the Church Commissioners under the Dioceses Measure 1978 or the Pastoral Measure 1983 shall not come into operation unless and until it has been approved by resolution of each House of Parliament.

(8) The Statutory Instruments Act 1946 shall apply to any order under subsection (1) above as if it were a statutory instrument and, in the case of an order which does not relate to a function to which subsection (7) above applies, as if this Measure were an Act providing that any such order shall be subject to annulment in pursuance of a resolution of either House of Parliament.

Transfer of officers

6.—(1) Where a person or body to whom this section applies determines that all or any of the officers of that person or body should be transferred to any body or partnership of the kind mentioned in subsection (4) below as a common employer and the last mentioned body or partnership agrees to the transfer, the provisions of Schedule 3 to this Measure shall have effect in relation to each officer transferred.

(2) This section applies to the following bodies—
the Archbishops' Council,
the Church Commissioners,
the Central Board of Finance,
the Pensions Board.

(3) This section also applies to such other bodies or persons as the Archbishops of Canterbury and York acting jointly may by order determine after consultation with the bodies specified in subsection (2) above.

(4) Where two or more of the bodies or persons to whom this section applies enter into an agreement—
  (a) which would be a partnership within the meaning of the Partnership Act 1890 if they were carrying on a business with a view to profit, and
  (b) which provides for the employment of officers,

that agreement shall be deemed to be a partnership for the purposes of that Act, notwithstanding that they are not carrying on such a business.

(5) Any partnership agreement of the kind mentioned in subsection (4) above may provide for the admission to the partnership of one or more of the bodies mentioned in subsection (2) above as general partners and of one or more of the bodies or persons to whom this section applies as limited partners.

In this subsection 'limited partner' and 'general partner' have the same meanings as in the Limited Partnerships Act 1907.

Church Commissioners

Amendment of Church Commissioners Measure 1947

7. *Text omitted.*

Management of assets

8. *Text omitted.*

General provisions

Standing Orders of the General Synod

9. The Standing Orders regulating the procedure of the General Synod shall include provision—
  (a) permitting the Archbishops' Council or the Business Committee of the General Synod to introduce to the General Synod draft legislation proposed to be passed by the General Synod;
  (b) affording the General Synod an opportunity at each group of sessions—
    (i) to consider any report or budget laid before it in pursuance of section 3 or 4 above,
    (ii) to consider such other matters as may be referred to it by the Council, and
    (iii) to question representatives of the Council in connection with any such report, budget or other matter.

Committees

10. The General Synod shall, without prejudice to paragraph 10 of Schedule 2 to the Synodical Government Measure 1969, appoint or provide by its Standing Orders for the appointment of—
  (a) a committee to be known as 'the Appointments Committee of the Church of England', the membership of which shall consist of persons who are members of the General Synod, at least one third being members of the Council;
  (b) a committee to be known as 'the Business Committee of the General Synod', the membership of which shall consist of persons who are members of the General Synod.

Restriction on elected membership of certain bodies

11.—(1) Where a person is elected by the General Synod or one of its Houses as a member of any body to whom this section applies when he is a member of any other such body, he shall cease to be a member of that other body.

(2) It shall not be open to any person to stand for election as a member of more than one such body at the same time.

(3) This section applies to—
the Archbishops' Council,
the Church Commissioners,
the Church of England Pensions Board,

the Appointments Committee of the Church of England, and
the Business Committee of the General Synod.

Interpretation

12.—(1) In this Measure, unless the context otherwise requires—
'the Council' means the Archbishops' Council established by section 1 above;
'functions' includes powers and duties;
'officer' includes servant;
'statutory provision' means any provision contained in an Act or Measure or in an instrument made under an Act or Measure;
'year' means the financial year of the Church Commissioners.

(2) References in this Measure to the House of Bishops, the House of Clergy or the House of Laity shall be construed as references to the relevant House of the General Synod.

Amendments and repeals

13. *Text omitted.*

Schedule 1
The Archbishops' Council

Section 1(3) and (4)

Part I
Constitution and Membership

1.—(1) The Council shall consist of—
  (a) the Archbishops of Canterbury and York;
  (b) the Prolocutors of the Convocations of Canterbury and York;
  (c) the chairman and vice-chairman of the House of Laity;
  (d) two bishops elected by the House of Bishops from among its members;
  (e) two clerks in Holy Orders elected by the House of Clergy from among its members;
  (f) two lay persons elected by the House of Laity from among its members;
  (g) such persons as may be appointed under sub-paragraph (2) below;
  (h) one of the Church Estates Commissioners appointed by the Archbishops of Canterbury and York acting jointly.

(2) Subject to sub-paragraph (3) below, the Archbishops of Canterbury and York, acting jointly, may appoint not more than six persons as members of the Council.

(3) No appointment under sub-paragraph (2) above shall be made without the approval of the General Synod; and in considering the making of any such appointment (except on the first occasion when the power to appoint is exercised) the Archbishops of Canterbury and York shall consult the Council and the Appointments Committee of the Church of England.

2. The Archbishops of Canterbury and York shall be joint Presidents of the Council.

3. The Archbishop of Canterbury shall preside at meetings of the Council unless he determines otherwise, in which case the Archbishop of York or one of the other members of the Council appointed by the Council after consultation with the Archbishops, either generally for the purposes of this paragraph or on a particular occasion, shall preside.

4.—(1) Subject to the following provisions of this Schedule, a member of the Council shall hold and vacate office in accordance with the terms of his appointment.

(2) Members of the Council elected under paragraph 1(1)(d), (e) or (f) above or appointed under paragraph 1(2) above shall serve for such number of years as may be determined in each case by the General Synod, being—
  (a) in the case of members so elected, not less than three and not more than five years, and

(b) in the case of members so appointed, not less than one year and not more than five years.

(3) In this paragraph 'year' means a period of twelve months.

5.—(1) A member of the Council may, by notice in writing addressed to the Archbishop of Canterbury, resign his membership.

(2) Where a member of the Council fails throughout a period of six consecutive months from his last attendance to attend any meeting of the Council he shall be deemed to have resigned his membership unless the Archbishop of Canterbury determines that he had reasonable cause for not attending.

6. A member of the Council who ceases to be a member shall be eligible for re-election or re-appointment:

Provided that a member elected under paragraph 1(1)(d), (e) or (f) above or appointed under paragraph 1(2) above shall not be eligible for re-election or reappointment as such if he has served as a member for a period amounting in the aggregate to ten years unless an interval of five years has elapsed since he last ceased to be a member.

7. The quorum of the Council shall be ten.

Part II
General Provisions

8. The Council shall be a body corporate, with perpetual succession and a common seal.

9.—(1) A member of the Council appointed under paragraph 1(2) above shall, if not otherwise a member of the General Synod, be an ex-officio member—
   (a) in the case of a bishop, of the House of Bishops,
   (b) in the case of any other clerk in Holy Orders, of the House of Clergy, and
   (c) in the case of a lay person who is an actual communicant (as defined in Rule 54(1) of the Church Representation Rules), of the House of Laity.

(2) A lay member of the Council appointed under paragraph 1(2) above who is not an actual communicant (as so defined) shall be entitled to attend at a group of sessions of the General Synod and, subject to such restrictions as may be imposed by the Standing Orders of the General Synod, to speak in any debate.

10. The arrangements relating to meetings of the Council shall be such as the Council may determine and, subject to paragraph 7 above, the Council shall have power to regulate its own procedure.

11. The validity of any proceedings of the Council shall not be affected by any vacancy among the members or by any defect in the appointment of any member.

12. The application of the seal of the Council shall be authenticated by the signature of the Secretary-General or of some other person authorised by the Council, either generally or specifically, to act for that purpose.

13. Any document purporting to be a document duly executed under the seal of the Council, or to be signed on behalf of the Council, shall be received in evidence and shall, unless the contrary is proved, be deemed to be so executed or, as the case may be, signed.

14. (1) It shall be within the capacity of the Council as a statutory corporation, in so far as its objects permit to do all such things and enter into all such transactions as are incidental or conducive to the discharge of its functions.

(2) Without prejudice to the foregoing, the powers of the Council shall include power to acquire or dispose of any property and to borrow money.

15.—(1) The Council may appoint such committees as it considers expedient and may delegate any of its functions to a committee.

(2) Persons who are not members of the Council may be appointed to a committee.

16. The Council shall appoint a chief executive, to be known as 'the Secretary General', and may appoint such other officers as it may determine.

Cathedrals Measure 1999

Part I
Governing Bodies and Financial Provisions

General provisions

Duty to have regard to cathedral's purpose

1. Any person or body on whom functions are conferred by or under this Measure shall, in exercising those functions, have due regard to the fact that the cathedral is the seat of the bishop and a centre of worship and mission.

Establishment of cathedral bodies

2. For each cathedral there shall, as from the relevant date, be a body called 'the Council', a body called 'the Chapter' and a body called 'the College of Canons' and references in this Measure to any of those bodies shall be construed as referring to that body as established for the cathedral concerned.

The Council

3.—(1) The constitution of each cathedral shall provide for the establishment of the Council in accordance with the following provisions of this section.

(2) The bishop shall be entitled to be present and speak, but not to vote, at meetings.

(3) The bishop shall appoint a lay person, not being a member of the Chapter, to be chairman, but—
  (a) before doing so he shall afford the Chapter an opportunity to express views both in general as to the appointment and as to any specific person proposed by the bishop for appointment, and
  (b) in deciding whom to appoint he shall have regard to those views.

(4) The membership shall consist of—
  (a) the chairman,
  (b) the dean,
  (c) a prescribed number (not less than two nor more than five) of other members of the Chapter chosen by it,
  (d) two members of the College of Canons appointed by it,
  (e) a prescribed number (not less than two nor more than four) of lay persons, not being members of the Chapter, representing the interests of the cathedral community elected in the prescribed manner, and
  (f) a prescribed number (not less than five nor more than ten) of persons appointed in the prescribed manner, being persons having experience in connection with the work of the cathedral or the ability to reflect local, diocesan, ecumenical or national interests in that connection.

(5) The members of the Council (other than the dean) shall hold office for a term of years to be prescribed but shall be eligible for membership for further terms of office.

(6) It shall be the duty of the Council to further and support the work of the cathedral, spiritual, pastoral, evangelistic, social and ecumenical, reviewing and advising upon the direction and

oversight of that work by the Chapter and in particular, without prejudice to the generality of the foregoing, to—
- (a) consider proposals submitted by the Chapter in connection with the general direction and mission of the cathedral and to give advice on them to the Chapter,
- (b) receive and consider the annual budget of the cathedral,
- (c) receive and consider the annual report and audited accounts,
- (d) consider proposals submitted by the Chapter in connection with the constitution and statutes of the cathedral with a view to their revision under Part II of this Measure,

and
- (e) perform such other functions as may be prescribed.

(7) The Council may—
- (a) request reports from the Chapter on any matter concerning the cathedral,
- (b) discuss and declare its opinion on any such matter, and
- (c) draw any matter to the attention of the Visitor or the Church Commissioners.

(8) The Council shall meet on at least two occasions in each calendar year.

The Chapter

4.—(1) The constitution of each cathedral shall provide for the establishment of the Chapter in accordance with the following provisions of this section.

(2) Subject to the following provisions of this section the membership shall consist of—
- (a) the dean and all the residentiary canons of the cathedral, and
- (b) a prescribed number (not less than two nor more than seven) of other persons, at least two-thirds of whom shall be lay, chosen in the prescribed manner.

(3) The constitution may provide for the administrator of the cathedral to be an additional member of the Chapter.

(4) A person shall be disqualified from being a member of the Chapter if he is disqualified from being a charity trustee under section 72(1) of the Charities Act 1993 and the disqualification is not for the time being subject to a waiver by the archbishop of the province concerned under subsection (5) below in respect of that Chapter; and a member who becomes disqualified by virtue of this subsection shall cease to be a member.

(5) The archbishop of the province concerned may, on the application of any person disqualified under subsection (4) above from being a member of the Chapter, waive his disqualification in respect of that Chapter; and any waiver under this subsection shall be notified in writing to the person concerned.

(6) The dean shall be—
- (a) the chairman and shall have a second or casting vote, and
- (b) a member of every committee of the Chapter.

(7) The members mentioned in subsection (2)(b) above shall hold office for three years but shall be eligible for membership for further terms of office.

(8) It shall be the duty of the Chapter to direct and oversee the administration of the affairs of the cathedral and in particular, without prejudice to the generality of the foregoing, to—
- (a) order the worship and promote the mission of the cathedral,
- (b) formulate, after consultation with the bishop, proposals in connection with the general direction and mission of the cathedral and submit them to the Council for its advice,
- (c) prepare an annual budget for the cathedral,
- (d) submit to the Council the annual report and audited accounts prepared by the Chapter in accordance with section 27 below and such other reports as may be requested by the Council on any matter concerning the cathedral,
- (e) submit to the College of Canons the annual report and audited accounts prepared as aforesaid,

(f) keep under review the constitution and statutes of the cathedral and submit any proposals for their revision to the Council,

(g) manage all property vested in the cathedral and the income accruing from it and, in particular, ensure that necessary repairs and maintenance in respect of the cathedral and its contents and other buildings and monuments are carried out, and

(h) perform such other functions as may be prescribed.

(9) The Chapter shall have power to acquire and dispose of property on behalf of the corporate body established in accordance with section 9(1)(a) below, subject to any consent required by section 15 below:

Provided that moneys which form part of the endowment of the cathedral shall not be invested or used except as provided by section 16 below.

(10) The Chapter shall hold the common seal of the cathedral and affix it when required.

(11) Decisions taken by the Chapter in the absence of the dean are subject to the provisions of section 7(3) below.

(12) The Chapter shall meet on at least nine occasions in each calendar year.

The College of Canons

5.—(1) The constitution of each cathedral shall provide for the establishment of the College of Canons in accordance with the following provisions of this section.

(2) The membership shall consist of—
 (a) the dean,
 (b) every suffragan bishop of the diocese in question,
 (c) every full-time stipendiary assistant bishop of the diocese in question,
 (d) every canon of the cathedral, and
 (e) every archdeacon of the diocese in question.

(3) The College of Canons shall perform the functions conferred by the Appointment of Bishops Act 1533 on the dean and chapter, and that Act shall accordingly have effect as if references to the dean and chapter were references to the College of Canons.

(4) The College of Canons shall—
 (a) receive and consider the annual report and audited accounts,
 (b) discuss such matters concerning the cathedral as may be raised by any of its members, and
 (c) perform such other functions as may be prescribed.

Provisions concerning bishops

6.—(1) The bishop shall have the principal seat and dignity in the cathedral.

After consultation with the Chapter and subject to any provisions in the statutes, he may officiate in the cathedral and use it in his work of teaching and mission, for ordinations and synods and for other diocesan occasions and purposes.

(2) The Chapter shall from time to time consult the bishop in respect of the general direction and mission of the cathedral, and the bishop may at any time seek the advice of the Chapter on any matter.

(3) The constitution of each cathedral shall provide that the bishop shall be the Visitor thereof.

(4) The bishop shall as Visitor hear and determine any question as to the construction of the constitution and statutes.

(5) The bishop may hold a visitation of the cathedral when he considers it desirable or necessary to do so or when requested by the Council or the Chapter.

(6) In the course of a visitation, the bishop may give such directions to the Chapter, to the holder of any office in the cathedral or to any person employed by the cathedral as will, in the opinion of the bishop, better serve the due observance of the constitution and statutes.

(7) It shall be the duty of any person or body on whom functions are conferred by or under this Measure to act in accordance with any determination under subsection (4) above and any direction under subsection (6) above.

(8) The provisions of subsections (4) to (7) above are without prejudice to the powers of the bishop under the Care of Cathedrals (Supplementary Provisions) Measure 1994 and his powers as Visitor generally.

(9) The bishop may at any time propose for consideration by the Council amendments to the constitution and statutes.

Provisions concerning deans

7.—(1) The principal dignitary of the cathedral, next after the bishop, shall be known as the dean.

(2) It shall be the duty of the dean as chairman of the Chapter to govern and direct on its behalf the life and work of the cathedral and in particular, without prejudice to the generality of the foregoing, to—

(a) ensure that Divine Service is duly performed in the cathedral,
(b) ensure that the constitution and statutes are faithfully observed,
(c) maintain good order and proper reverence in the cathedral,
(d) secure the pastoral care of all members of the cathedral community, and
(e) take all decisions necessary to deal with any emergency affecting the cathedral, pending consideration of the matter by the Chapter.

(3) The following steps shall not be taken without the consent of the dean—

(a) any alteration of the ordering of services in the cathedral;
(b) the settlement of the cathedral's budget;
(c) the implementation of any decision taken by the Chapter in the dean's absence:

Provided that, in the case of a decision taken by the Chapter as to any matter other than one mentioned in paragraph (a) or (b) above, his consent shall be deemed to have been given for the purposes of paragraph (c) above after the expiry of one month following the date on which the decision was taken unless, within that period, the dean requests the Chapter to reconsider the decision at the next meeting of the Chapter, in which case the matter shall be decided by a majority vote of those present and voting at the meeting, the dean having a second or casting vote.

(4) If the office of dean is vacant, or the bishop considers that the dean will be unable to discharge any or all of his functions under this Measure by reason of illness or absence or any other cause, the bishop shall, after consultation with the Chapter, appoint a residentiary canon to carry out such functions as the dean is unable to discharge during the period in question; and references in this Measure to the dean shall be construed accordingly.

(5) If any question arises whether an appointment under subsection (4) above is justified, that question shall be determined by the archbishop of the province.

Two residentiary canons to be engaged exclusively on cathedral duties

8.—(1) The constitution of each cathedral shall provide that the holders of at least two residentiary canonries in the cathedral shall be engaged exclusively on cathedral duties.

(2) In this section and section 21 below the expression 'cathedral duties' means duties (whether in the cathedral or in the diocese) which should, in the opinion of the Chapter after consultation with the bishop, be discharged in or from the cathedral:

Provided that the archbishop of the province and the Church Commissioners acting jointly may in special circumstances direct that the holder of a residentiary canonry who is normally engaged exclusively on cathedral duties shall, for such period as they may specify, be treated as so engaged for the purposes of this section notwithstanding that he is performing duties other than cathedral duties.

(3) If any question arises under this Measure whether a person is engaged exclusively on cathedral duties that question shall, after consultation with the Visitor and the Chapter, be determined by the Church Commissioners, and if any person is dissatisfied with th e decision of the Church

Commissioners he may appeal therefrom to the archbishop of the province whose decision shall be final:

Provided that during a vacancy of the see of the bishop who is the Visitor of the cathedral the provisions of this section requiring consultation with the Visitor shall not apply.

Further provisions required to be included in constitution

9.—(1) The constitution of each cathedral shall—
- (a) provide that the members for the time being of the Council, the Chapter and the College of Canons shall be a body corporate with perpetual succession and a common seal (to be known as the common seal of the cathedral),
- (b) provide for the appointment of canons in Holy Orders, the manner of their appointment and their tenure of office (whether freehold or for a term of years),
- (c) contain provision enabling lay canons to be appointed,
- (d) specify the maximum number of residentiary canons and non-residentiary canons of the cathedral,
- (e) provide for the appointment of an administrator of the cathedral, having such functions as may be prescribed,
- (f) provide for the appointment of an architect or surveyor of the fabric and an auditor for the cathedral,
- (g) provide for the appointment of a person having the function of supervising music in the cathedral, and
- (h) provide for the establishment of a finance committee of the Chapter having the function of advising the Chapter in connection with its responsibilities in the field of financial and investment management, and for the membership to include persons who have expertise and experience in that field.

(1A) The constitution of each cathedral shall provide that the architect or surveyor of the fabric appointed by virtue of subsection (1)(f) above shall be an architect or surveyor having such qualifications and expertise in matters relating to the conservation of historic buildings and other matters as the Chapter, after consultation with the Cathedrals Fabric Commission and such other persons or bodies as it thinks fit, considers appropriate to enable the role and duties of the post of architect or surveyor of the fabric to be discharged.

(2)
- (a) Where, immediately before the relevant date, the constitution of a cathedral provided for the appointment of the dean to be by Her Majesty the constitution shall continue to so provide.
- (b) In any other case, the constitution shall provide that the incumbent of the benefice which comprises the parish of which the cathedral is the parish church shall be the dean.

(3) The constitution of each cathedral which is not a parish church shall provide for the formation and maintenance of a roll containing the names of persons who are members of the cathedral community and apply to be enrolled as such.

(4) A provision of the constitution of the kind mentioned in subsection (1)(b) above shall not affect the provisions of section 4 of the Priests (Ordination of Women) Measure 1993.

Further provisions which may be included in constitution

10.—(1) In addition to the matters for which the constitution of each cathedral is required to provide under the foregoing provisions of this Measure, the constitution may contain provision—
- (a) enabling or requiring a committee, to be known as 'the Cathedral Community Committee', to be established, the membership consisting of persons whose names are for the time being on the roll maintained under section 9(3) above,
- (b) enabling or requiring committees to be established by the Chapter,

and for the delegation of functions to any committee.

(2) Any provision enabling or requiring a committee to be established by the Chapter may provide that persons who are not members of the Chapter may be members of the committee.

Statutes

11. The statutes of each cathedral shall make provision (being a provision which is consistent with the constitution) for the good government of the cathedral and may in particular, without prejudice to the generality of the foregoing—
    (a) provide for the creation, continuance, abolition, suspension or termination of suspension of any dignity, office or body in the cathedral and for the title by which any dignity or office is to be known;
    (b) provide that any presentations or nominations to benefices in the patronage of the cathedral shall be exercised by the Chapter or by a patronage committee of the Chapter;
    (c) provide, where a cathedral is a parish church, that part of that cathedral shall be the parish church or, where part of a cathedral is a parish church, that the cathedral or any other part thereof shall be the parish church;
    (d) provide for any incidental and supplementary matters.

Provisions as to cathedrals for which there was no dean and chapter

12.—(1) This section applies in the case of a cathedral in respect of which, immediately before the relevant date, there was no corporate body known as the dean and chapter.

(2) Where before the relevant date the functions previously exercisable, in relation to the parish of the cathedral, by the parochial church council were transferred to the administrative body of the cathedral in pursuance of section 12(1) of the Cathedrals Measure 1963, the constitution shall provide that those functions shall be exercisable by the Chapter.

(3) Where those functions were not transferred as aforesaid, the constitution of the cathedral shall provide for their transfer to the Chapter.

(4) The Church Representation Rules shall have effect in relation to the parish concerned subject to the following modifications—
    (a) for any reference to the parochial church council or the secretary thereof there shall be substituted, as the context requires, a reference to the Chapter or the clerk thereto;
    (b) the following provisions shall not apply—
        rule 6(3)(d), rules 4, 7(3) and 8(1) in so far as they relate to the vice-chairman of a parochial church council, rules 9(3) and (4), 9(5)(b) and (d) and (6)(a), rule 10 in so far as it relates to a parochial church council, rules 14 to 21 and 23 and Appendix II;
    (c) notwithstanding anything in rule 6(3), residentiary canons of the cathedral and other clerks in Holy Orders holding office in the cathedral shall be entitled to attend any annual or special parochial church meeting of the parish and to take part in its proceedings, whether or not they are resident in the parish.

(5) The Parochial Church Councils (Powers) Measure 1956 shall have effect in relation to the parish concerned subject to the following modifications—
    (a) for any reference to the parochial church council there shall be substituted a reference to the Chapter;
    (b) sections 3, 5(1), 6, 7(iii) and (iv), 8 and 9 shall not apply.

(6) Upon the transfer of the functions of a parochial church council in pursuance of subsection (3) above, all property held by that council and all property vested in the diocesan authority under section 6(2) of the Parochial Church Councils (Powers) Measure 1956 or vested in that authority as a custodian trustee on behalf of that council, shall by virtue of this section and without any conveyance, assignment, transfer or other assurance vest in the cathedral:

Provided that—
    (a) any stock which is only transferable in books kept by a company shall not vest in the cathedral by virtue of this subsection, but any person in whom the stock is vested shall, at

the request of the Chapter, forthwith apply to the company to transfer the stock into the name of the cathedral, and

(b) the vesting or transfer of property by virtue of this subsection shall not affect any previously existing trust or contract or any mortgage or other charge affecting the property.

(7) For the purposes of this section the functions of a parochial church council include any power to act in the administration of a charity established for ecclesiastical purposes.

Provisions as to property

Vesting of property in cathedral

13. Where immediately before the relevant date any property is vested in the dean and chapter of a cathedral or the cathedral chapter of a cathedral, that property shall by virtue of this section and without any conveyance, assignment, transfer or other assurance vest in the cathedral together with, in the case of land, any easements, rights or other privileges annexed thereto:

Provided that the vesting of any property by virtue of this section shall not affect any previously existing trust or contract or any mortgage or other charge affecting the property.

Schemes for transfer of property to cathedral

14.—(1) The Church Commissioners with the consent of the Chapter may prepare a scheme providing for the transfer of property by the Commissioners to the cathedral.

(2) A scheme under subsection (1) above may—
 (a) amend or repeal the provisions of any other scheme made under any Act or Measure relating to the property of the cathedral concerned, other than provisions forming part of the constitution and statutes of the cathedral;
 (b) contain such incidental, consequential or supplementary provisions as may be necessary or expedient for giving full effect to the scheme.

Acquisition and disposal of land

15.—(1) Before exercising any power to acquire or dispose of land the Chapter shall obtain the consent of the Church Commissioners and also in the case of the disposal of a house of residence—
 (a) the consent of the dean or residentiary canon who normally occupies the house except during a vacancy in the office of the dean or residentiary canon, as the case may be, and
 (b) where the house is allocated for the use of the holder of a dignity the right of presentation to which is vested in Her Majesty, the consent of Her Majesty:

Provided that no consent shall be required under this subsection for—
 (i) the grant of a lease to a clerk in Holy Orders holding office in the cathedral or to any person employed in connection with the cathedral, or
 (ii) the acquisition of land by a gift inter vivos or by will, or
 (iii) any transaction for which the sanction of an order is required under section 36 of the Charities Act 1993, or
 (iv) any transaction relating to land which immediately before the relevant date is held by the dean and chapter of the cathedral of St Paul in London as part of the Tillingham estate.

(2) The Church Commissioners may by order except from the provisions of subsection (1) above transactions relating to land forming part of an estate specified in the order or transactions of a class so specified or relating to property of a class so specified.

(3) The powers conferred by section 4(9) above may be exercised notwithstanding that the consideration for any transaction executed thereunder may not be the full consideration.

(4) The sealing by the Church Commissioners of any document under this section shall be conclusive evidence that all the requirements of this section with respect to the transaction to which the document relates have been complied with.

(5) A statement in a document sealed by the Chapter that the consent thereto of the Church Commissioners is not required under this section shall be sufficient evidence of that fact.

Cathedral moneys: investment powers, etc

16.—(1) Subject to the provisions of this section, the Chapter of any cathedral may exercise the following powers in respect of moneys which form part of the endowment of the cathedral or are otherwise vested in the cathedral or which are vested in the Church Commissioners on its behalf, that is to say—

(a) power to invest such moneys in the acquisition of land, including participation in any collective investment scheme operated for the purposes of this paragraph by the Church Commissioners,

(b) power to invest such moneys in any investment fund or deposit fund constituted under the Church Funds Investment Measure 1958,

(c) power to invest in any investments in which trustees may invest under the general power of investment in section 3 of the Trustee Act 2000 (as restricted by sections 4 and 5 of that Act),

(d) subject to subsection (3) below, power to use such moneys for the improvement or development of any property vested in the cathedral.

(2) The Chapter of any cathedral shall before investing any moneys in the acquisition of land obtain the like consents as are required under section 15 above for the acquisition of land.

(3) Moneys which form part of the endowment of the cathedral may not be used for the improvement or development of the cathedral or any other building falling within paragraph 5(2)(a) of the Ecclesiastical Exemption (Listed Buildings and Conservation Areas) Order 1994 and the Chapter shall before using them for the improvement or development of any other property obtain the consent of the Church Commissioners.

(4) Moneys which form part of the endowment of the cathedral may not be used for the repair of any property:

Provided that, where the Chapter is satisfied that an emergency has arisen which justifies the expenditure of such moneys on the repair of the cathedral or any other building falling within paragraph 5(2)(a) of the said Order of 1994, it may, with the consent of the Church Commissioners, incur that expenditure and the sum expended shall be replaced by the Chapter within such period and in such manner as may be agreed between the Church Commissioners and the Chapter.

Proceeds of disposal of property forming part of endowment of cathedral

17. Where any property which forms part of the endowment of a cathedral is disposed of, the proceeds of the disposal (including any moneys received by way of loan on a mortgage or charge on land or premium on the grant of a lease) shall be treated as part of the endowment of the cathedral.

Provisions as to moneys held by Church Commissioners on behalf of a cathedral

18. Where the Church Commissioners hold on behalf of any cathedral any moneys which form part of the endowment of that cathedral the Church Commissioners may, if the Chapter requests them to do so, make payments out of those moneys for the purpose of enabling the Chapter to exercise any of the powers conferred by section 16 above.

Allocation of houses for residentiary use

19. The Chapter of any cathedral may allocate for the use of any person holding an office in connection with the cathedral, as a residence from which to perform the duties of that office, any house vested in the cathedral.

Inspection of cathedral property

20.—(1) It shall be the duty of the Chapter of each cathedral to arrange, during the period of five years beginning with the relevant date and during every subsequent period of five years, for an architect or surveyor to carry out an inspection of all property (other than the cathedral) and any ancillary building within the meaning of section 14(6) of the Care of Cathedrals Measure 1990 which the Chapter is liable to repair and maintain, and to make a report in writing to the Chapter on any works which the architect or surveyor considers will need to be carried out in relation to that property and of the urgency with which the architect or surveyor considers that they should be carried out.

(2) In the case of property within the precinct of the cathedral the report required by subsection (1) above shall be compiled in consultation with the cathedral archaeologist (if any) appointed under section 12(2) of the Care of Cathedrals Measure 1990, and the Chapter shall send a copy of the report to the fabric advisory committee of the cathedral and to the Cathedrals Fabric Commission for England.

Financial provisions

Stipends of dean and residentiary canons

21.—(1) The Church Commissioners shall pay out of their general fund to the dean of each cathedral and to two residentiary canons of each cathedral who are engaged exclusively on cathedral duties such sums by way of stipend or other emoluments as the Commissioners may from time to time determine.

(2) The Chapter of a cathedral may, with the consent of the Church Commissioners, pay to the dean or to any residentiary canon to whom the Commissioners are required to make a payment under subsection (1) above such additional stipend or other emoluments as they may think fit.

Payment towards expenses incurred by newly appointed deans and canons

22. Where any person is appointed dean of a cathedral or is appointed a residentiary canon whose stipend is to be paid by the Church Commissioners in accordance with the provisions of section 21 above, the Commissioners shall have power to make out of their general fund to that person a grant towards removal expenses incurred by him.

Grants for the payment of stipends and salaries

23. The Church Commissioners shall have power to make out of their general fund such grants as they may from time to time determine for the payment of—
   (a)   the stipend or other emoluments of any clerk in Holy Orders holding office in the cathedral, other than a dean or residentiary canon;
   (b)   the salary or other emoluments of any lay person employed in connection with the cathedral.

Grants for houses to be occupied by clerks holding office in the cathedral

24. The Church Commissioners shall have power to make out of their general fund to any cathedral such grants as they may think fit for the purpose of securing the better provision of houses for clerks in Holy Orders who hold office in the cathedral.

Grants for repair of chancels

25. The Church Commissioners shall have power to make out of their general fund to any cathedral such grants as they may think fit for the repair of any chancel, other than the chancel of the cathedral, which that body is wholly or partly liable to repair.

Borrowing powers of Chapters

26. The Chapter of any cathedral shall have power to borrow money for any purpose connected with the cathedral:

Provided that if the purpose for which the money is to be borrowed is such that the use of moneys forming part of the endowment of the cathedral for that purpose would require the consent of the Church Commissioners, then the consent of the Church Commissioners shall be required for the borrowing of that money under this section.

Accounts, etc

27.—(1) The Chapter of any cathedral shall maintain proper records of income and expenditure, assets and liabilities, and shall prepare an annual report and accounts which show a true and fair view of the transactions throughout the year and of the position at the end of the year in accordance with best professional practice and standards.

Those accounts shall be audited by a person who may, under section 43 of the Charities Act 1993, audit the accounts of a charity.

(2) The Church Commissioners shall have the power to specify what constitutes best professional practice and standards relating to the report and accounts, and to enquire into any departure from those practices and standards.

(3) A copy of the annual report and audited accounts prepared by the Chapter in accordance with subsection (1) above shall be—
- (a) sent to the Church Commissioners and to any other person who requests it, and
- (b) displayed in a prominent position in or in the vicinity of the cathedral.

Part II
Revision of Constitution and Statutes

Power of Council to revise constitution and statutes

28.—(1) Subject to the following provisions of this Part the Council of any cathedral may, with the consent of the bishop, by instrument under the common seal of the cathedral revise the constitution or statutes of the cathedral.

(2) Any such instrument may either provide a new constitution or new statutes for the cathedral to which it relates or may amend the constitution or statutes in force therefor immediately before the instrument comes into force.

(3) Before taking any steps under the following provisions of this Part the Council shall afford the Chapter an opportunity to express views as to the Council's proposals for revision and shall have regard to those views.

Procedure for revision of constitution

29.—(1) In the case of a revision of the constitution, the Council shall prepare a draft of the instrument and—
- (a) publish in one or more publications circulating in the diocese to the cathedral of which the draft instrument relates, and
- (b) display in a prominent position in or in the vicinity of the cathedral,

a notice of the preparation of the draft instrument setting out its objects and specifying the place in the diocese where copies thereof may be inspected and stating that the Council will consider any written representations with respect to the draft instrument made before such date as may be so specified, being a date not less than four weeks after the date of the publication or displaying of the notice.

(2) The Council shall also send a copy of the draft instrument to the Secretary-General of the General Synod.

(3) After the expiration of the period during which representations with respect to the draft instrument may be made under subsection (1) above the Council, having considered any representations duly made to it under this section, may, whether as a result of such representations or otherwise, amend the draft instrument as it thinks expedient.

Procedure for revision of statutes

30.—(1) In the case of a revision of the statutes, the Council shall prepare a draft of the instrument and display in a prominent position in or in the vicinity of the cathedral a notice of its preparation setting out its objects and specifying the place in the diocese where copies thereof may be inspected and stating that the Council will consider any written representations with respect to the draft instrument made before such date as may be so specified, being a date not less than four weeks after the date of the displaying of the notice.

(2) After the expiration of the period during which representations with respect to the draft instrument may be made under subsection (1) above the Council, having considered any representations duly made to it under this section, may, whether as a result of such representations or otherwise, amend the draft instrument as it thinks expedient.

Signatories

31.—(1) After compliance with the requirements of section 29 or 30 above, as the case may be, a copy of the draft instrument shall be signed by the chairman of the Council on its behalf or, in the case of the absence or incapacity of its chairman, by two other members of the Council nominated by it for that purpose; and the signing of the copy of the draft instrument by the chairman or by two members nominated as aforesaid and the affixing of the common seal of the cathedral thereto shall be conclusive evidence that the provisions of this Part relating to the preparation of the instrument have been complied with.

(2) A copy of the instrument shall be sent to the Secretary-General of the General Synod.

Saving for Crown rights

32. An instrument under this Part which affects any right or interest of Her Majesty shall not be made without the consent of Her Majesty.

Part III
Miscellaneous and General

Saving for existing interests

33. No provision of this Measure or of any instrument made under Part II or Schedule 1 shall adversely affect the tenure of office or any right to pension of any person who, immediately before the relevant date or, in the case of an instrument made under Part II, the coming into operation of the instrument, holds or has held a freehold or other office conferring fixity of tenure in any cathedral unless, by an instrument in writing under his hand, he agrees to be bound by that provision.

Charities

34. The provisions of this Measure other than those of section 12 shall not apply to any charity, or to property of any charity, except to the extent to which the Charity Commission for England and Wales shall determine that the said provisions shall apply to that charity or property.

In this section the expression 'charity' has the same meaning as in the Charities Act 1993 but does not include an exempt charity within the meaning of that Act.

Interpretation

35.—(1) In this Measure, except where the context otherwise requires—
'architect' means a person registered under the Architects Act 1997;
'bishop', when used in relation to a cathedral, means the bishop of the diocese in which the cathedral is situated;
'canon' includes a lay canon and a non-residentiary canon but not a minor canon;
'cathedral community', in relation to a cathedral, means persons over the age of sixteen years who—
   (a) worship regularly in the cathedral, or
   (b) are engaged in work or service connected with the cathedral in a regular capacity,

   and includes such other persons as may be prescribed;
'cathedral duties' has the meaning assigned to it by section 8 above;
'company' includes the Bank of England and any company or person keeping books in which any stock is registered or inscribed;
'diocesan authority' means the diocesan board of finance or any existing or future body appointed by the diocesan synod to act as trustees of diocesan trust property;
'functions' includes powers and duties;

'house of residence' includes all buildings, gardens and other land held therewith;
'land' includes any corporeal or incorporeal hereditaments of any tenure;
'lease' includes a tenancy;
'moneys' includes any stock, share, or other security;
'non-residentiary canon' includes a prebendary who is not a residentiary canon;
'precinct', in relation to a cathedral, means the precinct for the time being indicated on the plan required for that cathedral by section 13(3) and (4) of the Care of Cathedrals Measure 1990;
'prescribed', in relation to a cathedral, means prescribed by the constitution of the cathedral;
'property' includes a thing in action and any interest in real or personal property;
'relevant date', in relation to any cathedral existing at the passing of this Measure, means the date appointed in respect of that cathedral under section 38(2) below;
'residentiary canon' includes a stipendiary canon;
'stock' includes any share, annuity or other security;
'surveyor' means a member of the Royal Institution of Chartered Surveyors qualified as a chartered building surveyor.

(2) Any reference in this Measure to a cathedral which is a parish church shall, in relation to a cathedral existing at the passing of this Measure, be construed as a reference to a cathedral in respect of which there was, immediately before the relevant date, no corporate body known as the dean and chapter.

It is hereby declared, for the avoidance of doubt, that the Cathedral and Abbey Church of St Alban is such a cathedral.

(3) Any reference in this Measure to a power to dispose of land shall be construed as comprising a power to sell, grant a lease or licence of, exchange, mortgage or charge land and to dedicate land for the purposes of a highway.

(4) Any reference in this Measure to a power to acquire property shall be construed as comprising a power to acquire property for any purpose connected with the cathedral and to acquire property by gift inter vivos or by will.

(5) In any provision of this Measure relating to patronage, the vesting or transfer of property or the making of grants by the Church Commissioners any reference to a cathedral shall be construed as a reference to the corporate body thereof established in accordance with section 9(1)(a) above.

(6) Where, by virtue of any provision of this Measure, members of a body are to be elected or chosen 'in the prescribed manner' that expression shall be construed as including a power for the constitution of a cathedral to specify the qualifications required for membership.

Construction of references to dean and chapter, etc

36.—(1) Any reference in an enactment, instrument or other document to any of the following bodies of a cathedral, that is to say—
the dean and chapter,
the administrative chapter,
the administrative body,
the cathedral chapter,
the capitular body,
the cathedral council,
shall, unless the context otherwise requires or this Measure otherwise provides, be construed as a reference to the Chapter of the cathedral.

(1A) *Text omitted.*

(2) Any reference in an enactment mentioned below to a chapter, cathedral chapter, dean and chapter (or the corporation thereof) or capitular body shall be construed as a reference to the corporate body of the cathedral—
Ecclesiastical Leases Act 1800 section 1
Ecclesiastical Leases Act 1836 section 1
Ecclesiastical Leases (Amendment) Act 1836 section 1

Ecclesiastical Commissioners Act 1840 sections 68 and 84
Universities and College Estates Act 1925 section 37
Leasehold Reform Act 1967 section 31
Administration of Justice Act 1982 section 41(3)
Pastoral Measure 1983 Schedule 3, paragraph 7(1)
Leasehold Reform Housing and Urban Development Act 1993 Schedule 2, paragraph 8 and Schedule 14, paragraph 11.

(3) Any reference in an enactment, instrument or other document to a parish church cathedral shall, unless the context otherwise requires or this Measure otherwise provides, be construed as a reference to a cathedral in respect of which, immediately before the relevant date, there was no corporate body known as the dean and chapter.

(4) Any reference in an enactment, instrument or other document to the provost of a cathedral shall, unless the context otherwise requires, be construed as a reference to the dean of the cathedral.

(5) Any reference in an enactment, instrument or other document to capitular revenues or capitular funds in relation to a cathedral shall be construed as a reference to the revenues or funds (respectively) of the cathedral.

(6) Nothing in this section applies in relation to Westminster Abbey, St George's Chapel, Windsor or the cathedral church of Christ in Oxford.

Application

37. This Measure shall apply to every cathedral church in England (other than the cathedral church of Christ in Oxford except where this Measure otherwise provides) and references therein to a cathedral shall be construed accordingly.

Transitional provisions and savings

38. *Text omitted.*
Amendments and repeals
39. *Text omitted.*

Schedule 1
Transitional Provisions

[Omitted]

Churchwardens Measure 2001

Number and qualifications of churchwardens

1.—(1) Subject to the provisions of this Measure there shall be two churchwardens of every parish.

(2)
 (a) Where by virtue of a designation made by a pastoral scheme or otherwise a parish has more than one parish church, two churchwardens shall be appointed for each of the parish churches, and this Measure shall apply separately to each pair of churchwardens, but all the churchwardens shall be churchwardens of the whole parish, except so far as they may arrange to perform separate duties in relation to the several parish churches.
 (b) A church building or part of a building designated as a parish centre of worship under section 29(2) of the Pastoral Measure 1983 shall, subject to subsection (4) of that section, be deemed while the designation is in force to be a parish church for the purposes of this subsection.

(3) The churchwardens of every parish shall be chosen from persons who have been baptised and—
- (a) whose names are on the church electoral roll of the parish;
- (b) who are actual communicants;
- (c) who are twenty-one years of age or upwards; and
- (d) who are not disqualified under section 2 or 3 below.

(4) If it appears to the bishop, in the case of any particular person who is not qualified by virtue of paragraph (a), (b) or (c) of subsection (3) above, that there are exceptional circumstances which justify a departure from the requirements of those paragraphs the bishop may permit that person to hold the office of churchwarden notwithstanding that those requirements are not met. Any such permission shall apply only to the period of office next following the date on which the permission is given.

(5) No person shall be chosen as churchwarden of a parish for any period of office unless he—
- (a) has signified consent to serve as such; and
- (b) has not signified consent to serve as such for the same period of office in any other parish (not being a related parish) or, if such consent has been signified and the meeting of the parishioners to elect churchwardens of that other parish has been held, was not chosen as churchwarden of that other parish.

In this subsection 'related parish' means a parish—
- (i) belonging to the benefice to which the first-mentioned parish belongs; or
- (ii) belonging to a benefice held in plurality with the benefice to which the first-mentioned parish belongs; or
- (iii) having the same minister as the first-mentioned parish.

(6) In relation to the filling of a casual vacancy among the churchwardens the reference in subsection (5)(b) above to the same period of office shall be construed as a reference to a period of office which includes the period for which the casual vacancy is to be filled.

General disqualifications

2.—(1) A person shall be disqualified from being chosen for the office of churchwarden if he is disqualified from being a charity trustee under section 72(1) of the Charities Act 1993 (c 10) and the disqualification is not for the time being subject to a general waiver by the Charity Commission under subsection (4) of that section or to a waiver by it under that subsection in respect of all ecclesiastical charities established for purposes relating to the parish concerned.

In this subsection 'ecclesiastical charity' has the same meaning as that assigned to that expression in the Local Government Act 1894 (c 73).

(2)
- (a) A person shall be disqualified from being chosen for the office of churchwarden if he has been convicted of any offence mentioned in Schedule 1 to the Children and Young Persons Act 1933 (c 12).
- (b) In paragraph (a) above the reference to any offence mentioned in Schedule 1 to the Children and Young Persons Act 1933 shall include an offence which, by virtue of any enactment, is to be treated as being included in any such reference in all or any of the provisions of that Act.

(3) A person shall be disqualified from being chosen for the office of churchwarden if he is disqualified from holding that office under section 10(6) of the Incumbents (Vacation of Benefices) Measure 1977 (No 1).

(4) All rules of law whereby certain persons are disqualified from being chosen for the office of churchwarden shall cease to have effect.

Disqualification after six periods of office

3. Without prejudice to section 2 above, a person shall be disqualified from being chosen for the office of churchwarden when that person has served as a churchwarden of the same parish for six successive periods of office until the annual meeting of the parishioners to elect churchwardens in the next year but one following the date on which that person vacated office at the end of the last such period:

Provided that a meeting of the parishioners may by resolution decide that this section shall not apply in relation to the parish concerned.

Any such resolution may be revoked by a subsequent meeting of the parishioners.

Time and manner of choosing

4.—(1) The churchwardens of a parish shall be chosen annually not later than the 30th April in each year.

(2) Subject to the provisions of this Measure the churchwardens of a parish shall be elected by a meeting of the parishioners.

(3) Candidates for election at the meeting must be nominated and seconded in writing by persons entitled to attend the meeting and each nomination paper must include a statement, signed by the person nominated, to the effect that that person is willing to serve as a churchwarden and is not disqualified under section 2(1), (2) or (3)above.

(4) A nomination shall not be valid unless—
 (a) the nomination paper is received by the minister of the parish before the commencement of the meeting; and
 (b) in the case of a person who is not qualified by virtue of section 1(3)(a), (b) or (c) above, the bishop's permission was given under section 1(4)above before the nomination paper is received by the minister of the parish.

(5) If it appears to the minister of the parish that the election of any particular person nominated might give rise to serious difficulties between the minister and that person in the carrying out of their respective functions the minister may, before the election is conducted, make a statement to the effect that only one churchwarden is to be elected by the meeting. In that event one churchwarden shall be appointed by the minister from among the persons nominated, the name of the person so appointed being announced before the election is conducted, and the other shall then be elected by the meeting.

(6) During any period when there is no minister—
 (a) subsection (4) above shall apply with the substitution for the words 'minister of the parish' of the words 'churchwarden by whom the notice convening the meeting was signed'; and
 (b) subsection (5) above shall not apply.

(7) A person may be chosen to fill a casual vacancy among the churchwardens at any time.

(8) Any person chosen to fill a casual vacancy shall be chosen in the same manner as was the churchwarden whose place he is to fill except that, where the churchwarden concerned was appointed by the minister and the minister has ceased to hold office, the new churchwarden to fill the casual vacancy shall be elected by a meeting of the parishioners.

Meeting of the parishioners

5.—(1) A joint meeting of—
 (a) the persons whose names are entered on the church electoral roll of the parish; and
 (b) the persons resident in the parish whose names are entered on a register of local government electors by reason of such residence,

shall be deemed to be a meeting of the parishioners for the purposes of this Measure.

(2) The meeting of the parishioners shall be convened by the minister or, during any period when there is no minister or when the minister is unable or unwilling to do so, the churchwardens of the parish by a notice signed by the minister or a churchwarden as the case may be.

(3) The notice shall state the place, day and hour at which the meeting of the parishioners is to be held.

(4) The notice shall be affixed on or near to the principal door of the parish church and of every other building licensed for public worship in the parish for a period including the last two Sundays before the meeting.

(5) The minister, if present, or, if he is not present, a chairman chosen by the meeting of the parishioners, shall preside thereat.

(6) In case of an equal division of votes on any question other than one to determine an election of a churchwarden the chairman of the meeting of parishioners shall not have a second or casting vote and the motion on that question shall be treated as lost.

(7) The meeting of the parishioners shall have power to adjourn, and to determine its own rules of procedure.

(8) A person appointed by the meeting of the parishioners shall act as clerk of the meeting and shall record the minutes thereof.

Admission

6.—(1) At a time and place to be appointed by the bishop annually, being on a date not later than 31st July in each year, each person chosen for the office of churchwarden shall appear before the bishop or his substitute duly appointed, and be admitted to the office of churchwarden after—

(a) making a declaration, in the presence of the bishop or his substitute, that he will faithfully and diligently perform the duties of his office; and

(b) subscribing a declaration to that effect and also that he is not disqualified under section 2(1), (2) or (3) above.

No person chosen for the office of churchwarden shall become churchwarden until such time as he shall have been admitted to office in accordance with the provisions of this section.

(2) Subject to the provisions of this Measure the term of office of the churchwardens so chosen and admitted as aforesaid shall continue until a date determined as follows, that is to say—

(a) in the case of a person who is chosen again as churchwarden at the next annual meeting of the parishioners—
   (i) if so admitted for the next term of office by 31st July in the year in question, the date of the admission; or
   (ii) if not so admitted for the next term of office by 31st July in the year in question, that date;

(b) in the case of a person who is not chosen again as churchwarden at the next annual meeting of the parishioners—
   (i) if that person's successor in office is so admitted for the next term of office by 31st July in the year in question, the date of the admission; or
   (ii) if that person's successor in office is not so admitted for the next term of office by 31st July in the year in question, that date.

In the application of paragraph (b) above to any person, where there is doubt as to which of the new churchwardens is that person's successor in office the bishop may designate one of the new churchwardens as that person's successor for the purposes of that paragraph.

(3) Where any person ceases to hold the office of churchwarden at the end of July in any year by virtue of paragraph (a)(ii) or (b)(ii) above a casual vacancy in that office shall be deemed to have arisen.

(4) In relation to the filling of a casual vacancy the reference in subsection (1) above to the 31st July shall be construed as a reference to a date three months after the person who is to fill the vacancy

is chosen or the date of the next annual meeting of the parishioners to elect churchwardens, whichever is the earlier.

Resignation

7.—(1) A person may resign the office of churchwarden in accordance with the following provisions of this section, but not otherwise.

(2) Written notice of intention to resign shall be served on the bishop by post.

(3) The resignation shall have effect and the office shall be vacated—
  (a) at the end of the period of two months following service of the notice on the bishop; or
  (b) on such earlier date as may be determined by the bishop after consultation with the minister and any other churchwarden of the parish.

Vacation of office

8.—(1) The office of churchwarden of a parish shall be vacated if—
  (a) the name of the person concerned is removed from the church electoral roll of the parish under rule 1 of the Church Representation Rules; or
  (b) the name of the person concerned is not on a new church electoral roll of the parish prepared under rule 2(4) of those Rules; or
  (c) the churchwarden becomes disqualified under section 2(1), (2) or (3) above.

(2) For the purposes of this section a person who has been chosen for the office of churchwarden but has not yet been admitted to that office shall be deemed to hold that office, and the expressions 'office' and 'churchwarden' shall be construed accordingly.

Guild Churches

9.—(1) In the case of every church in the City of London designated and established as a Guild Church under the City of London (Guild Churches) Acts 1952 and 1960 the churchwardens shall, notwithstanding anything to the contrary contained in those Acts, be actual communicant members of the Church of England except where the bishop shall otherwise permit.

(2) Subject to subsection (1) above, nothing in this Measure shall apply to the churchwardens of any church designated and established as a Guild Church under the City of London (Guild Churches) Acts 1952 and 1960.

(3) In this section 'actual communicant member of the Church of England' means a member of the Church of England who is confirmed or ready and desirous of being confirmed and has received Communion according to the use of the Church of England or of a church in communion with the Church of England at least three times during the twelve months preceding the date of his election or appointment.

Special provisions

10.—(1) In the carrying out of the provisions of this Measure the bishop shall have power—
  (a) to make provision for any matter not herein provided for;
  (b) to appoint a person to do any act in respect of which there has been any neglect or default on the part of any person or body charged with any duty under this Measure;
  (c) so far as may be necessary for the purpose of giving effect to the intentions of this Measure, to extend or alter the time for holding any meeting or election or to modify the procedure laid down by this Measure in connection therewith;
  (d) in any case in which there has been no valid choice to direct a fresh choice to be made, and to give such directions in connection therewith as he may think necessary; and
  (e) in any case in which any difficulty arises, to give any directions which he may consider expedient for the purpose of removing the difficulty.

(2) The powers of the bishop under this section shall not enable him to validate anything that was invalid at the time it was done.

Savings

11.—(1) Subject to section 9 above, nothing in this Measure shall be deemed to amend, repeal or affect any local act or any scheme made under any enactment affecting the churchwardens of a parish:

Provided that for the purposes of this Measure the Parish of Manchester Division Act 1850 shall be deemed to be a general act.

(2) Subject to section 12 below, in the case of any parish where there is an existing custom which regulates the number of churchwardens or the manner in which the churchwardens are chosen, nothing in this Measure shall affect that custom:

Provided that in the case of any parish where in accordance with that custom any churchwarden was, before the coming into force of the Churchwardens (Appointment and Resignation) Measure 1964, chosen by the vestry of that parish jointly with any other person or persons that churchwarden shall be chosen by the meeting of the parishioners jointly with the other person or persons.

Abolition of existing customs

12.—(1) A meeting of the parishioners of a parish may pass a resolution abolishing any existing custom which regulates the number of churchwardens of the parish or the manner in which the churchwardens of the parish are chosen.

(2) Where any such resolution is passed the existing custom to which it relates shall cease to have effect on the date on which the next meeting of parishioners by which the churchwardens are to be elected is held.

(3) In the case of an existing custom which involves a person other than the minister in the choice of the churchwardens, a resolution under subsection (1) above shall not be passed without the written consent of that person.

Interpretation

13.—(1) In this Measure, except in so far as the context otherwise requires—

'bishop' means the diocesan bishop concerned;

'existing custom' means a custom existing at the coming into force of this Measure which has continued for a period commencing before 1st January 1925;

'minister' has the same meaning as that assigned to that expression in rule 54(1) of the Church Representation Rules except that, where a special responsibility for pastoral care in respect of the parish in question has been assigned to a member of the team in a team ministry under section 20(8A) of the Pastoral Measure 1983 but a special cure of souls in respect of the parish has not been assigned to a vicar in the team ministry by a scheme under that Measure or by his licence from the bishop, it means that member;

'pastoral scheme' has the same meaning as that assigned to that expression in section 87(1) of the Pastoral Measure 1983;

'actual communicant', 'parish' and 'public worship' have the same meanings respectively as those assigned to those expressions in rule 54(1) of the Church Representation Rules.

(2) Where by virtue of any custom existing at the coming into force of the Churchwardens (Appointment and Resignation) Measure 1964 the choice of a churchwarden was, under section 12(2) of that Measure, required to be made by the meeting of the parishioners jointly with another person or persons that custom shall be deemed to be an existing custom for the purposes of this Measure.

Transitional provisions

14. *Text omitted.*

Consequential amendment and repeal

15. *Text omitted.*

Clergy Discipline Measure 2003

Introductory

Duty to have regard to bishop's role

1. Any body or person on whom functions in connection with the discipline of persons in Holy Orders are conferred by this Measure shall, in exercising those functions, have due regard to the role in that connection of the bishop or archbishop who, by virtue of his office and consecration, is required to administer discipline.

Disciplinary tribunals

2. Where a complaint is to be referred under this Measure to a disciplinary tribunal the tribunal (to be called the bishop's disciplinary tribunal) shall be constituted for the diocese in question in accordance with section 22 below to deal with the complaint.

Clergy Discipline Commission

3.—(1) There shall be a body (to be called the Clergy Discipline Commission) consisting of not more than twelve persons appointed by the Appointments Committee of the Church of England including at least—
  (a) two persons from each House of the General Synod;
  (b) two persons who have either a seven years general qualification within the meaning of the Courts and Legal Services Act 1990 (c. 41) or who have held or are holding high judicial office or the office of Circuit judge.

(2) The Appointments Committee shall, after consultation with the Dean of the Arches and Auditor, appoint a member of the Commission to be the chairman of the Commission and also a member to be the deputy chairman, being members who have the qualifications referred to in subsection (1)(b) above.

(3) The Commission shall exercise the functions conferred on it by this Measure and in addition shall have the following duties—
  (a) to give general advice to disciplinary tribunals, the courts of the Vicars-General, bishops and archbishops as to the penalties which are appropriate in particular circumstances;
  (b) to issue codes of practice and general policy guidance to persons exercising functions in connection with clergy discipline;
  (c) to make annually to the General Synod through the House of Bishops thereof a report on the exercise of its functions during the previous year.

President of tribunals

4.—(1) The chairman and deputy chairman of the Commission shall be the president of tribunals and the deputy president respectively for the purposes of this Measure.

(2) The president of tribunals shall exercise the functions conferred on him by this Measure and in addition shall have the following duties—
  (a) to issue practice directions;
  (b) to act as the chairman of a disciplinary tribunal where, in his opinion, important points of law or principle are involved;
  (c) to exercise such other functions as may be prescribed.

(3) The deputy president of tribunals shall act for the president when the president is absent or is unable or unwilling to act.

Registrar of tribunals

5.—(1) The archbishops of Canterbury and York shall each for his province, after consultation with the president of tribunals, appoint a person to be the registrar of tribunals for the province for the purposes of this Measure.

(2) A person so appointed shall be a person who has a general qualification within the meaning of the Courts and Legal Services Act 1990 (c. 41).

(3) The person holding the office of registrar of tribunals for a province shall vacate that office on the date on which he attains the age of seventy years or such earlier age as may be prescribed by regulations made by the House of Bishops of the General Synod under section 5 of the Ecclesiastical Judges and Legal Officers Measure 1976 (1976 No. 2).

(4) The registrar of tribunals for a province may resign his office by instrument in writing under his hand addressed to, and served on, the archbishop of the province and the instrument shall specify the date, being a date not less than twelve months after the service of the instrument or such earlier date as the archbishop may allow, on which the resignation is to take effect.

(5) The appointment of a person as registrar of tribunals for a province may be terminated by an instrument in writing under the hand of the archbishop of the province (after consultation with the president of tribunals) addressed to, and served on, that person, and the instrument shall specify the date, being a date not less than twelve months after the date of service of the instrument, on which the appointment is to terminate.

(6) The registrar of tribunals for a province shall exercise the functions conferred on him by this Measure and in addition shall have the following duties—
  (a) to direct and supervise the general administration of disciplinary tribunals in the province;
  (b) to exercise such other functions as may be prescribed.

(7) If the person holding the office of registrar of tribunals for a province is for any reason unable or unwilling to perform the duties of a registrar or it would be inappropriate for him to perform those duties, the registrar of tribunals for the other province shall perform those duties and, for that purpose, shall have all the powers and duties of the registrar of the first-mentioned province.

Jurisdiction in disciplinary proceedings

6.—(1) A disciplinary tribunal constituted for a diocese has jurisdiction to hear and determine disciplinary proceedings under this Measure against a priest or deacon—
  (a) who, when the misconduct complained of was alleged to have been committed, held preferment in the diocese or, subject to subsection (3) below, was resident therein; or
  (b) who is alleged to have officiated as a minister in the diocese without authority.

(2) The Vicar-General's court of each of the provinces of Canterbury and York constituted in accordance with the provisions of this Measure has jurisdiction to hear and determine disciplinary proceedings under this Measure—
  (a) against any bishop who, when the misconduct complained of was alleged to have been committed, held preferment in the province or, subject to subsection (3) below, was resident therein; or
  (b) against any bishop who is alleged to have officiated as a minister in the province without authority; or
  (c) against the archbishop of the other province.

(3) Where disciplinary proceedings in respect of any matter are instituted under section 10 below against—
  (a) a priest or deacon in the diocese in which he holds or held preferment or in which he is alleged to have officiated as a minister without authority, or
  (b) a bishop in the province in which he holds or held preferment or in which he is alleged to have officiated without authority,

no such proceedings in respect of the same matter shall be instituted in any other diocese or the other province, as the case may be, on the basis of residence therein and any such proceedings previously instituted on that basis shall be discontinued.

(4) Where disciplinary proceedings in respect of any matter are instituted under section 10 below against—
- (a) a priest or deacon in the diocese in which he is alleged to have officiated without authority, or
- (b) a bishop in the province in which he is alleged to have officiated without authority,

no such proceedings in respect of the same matter shall be instituted in any other diocese or the other province, as the case may be, on the basis of preferment therein and any such proceedings previously instituted on that basis shall be discontinued.

(5) In this section and elsewhere in this Measure 'preferment' has the meaning assigned to it by section 43 below.

Disciplinary proceedings concerning matters not involving doctrine, ritual or ceremonial

Application

7.—(1) The following provisions of this Measure shall have effect for the purpose of regulating proceedings against a clerk in Holy Orders who is alleged to have committed an act or omission other than one relating to matters involving doctrine, ritual or ceremonial, and references to misconduct shall be construed accordingly.

(2) Proceedings in relation to matters involving doctrine, ritual or ceremonial shall continue to be conducted in accordance with the 1963 Measure.

Misconduct

8.—(1) Disciplinary proceedings under this Measure may be instituted against any archbishop, bishop, priest or deacon alleging any of the following acts or omissions—
- (a) doing any act in contravention of the laws ecclesiastical;
- (b) failing to do any act required by the laws ecclesiastical;
- (c) neglect or inefficiency in the performance of the duties of his office;
- (d) conduct unbecoming or inappropriate to the office and work of a clerk in Holy Orders.

(2) In the case of a minister licensed to serve in a diocese by the bishop thereof, the licence shall not be terminated by reason of that person's misconduct otherwise than by way of such proceedings.

(3) No proceedings in respect of unbecoming conduct shall be taken in respect of the lawful political opinions or activities of any bishop, priest or deacon.

Limitation of time for institution of proceedings

9. No disciplinary proceedings under this Measure shall be instituted unless the misconduct in question, or the last instance of it in the case of a series of acts or omissions, occurred within the period of one year ending with the date on which proceedings are instituted:

Provided that, when the misconduct is one for which the person concerned has been convicted either on indictment or summarily, proceedings may be instituted within twelve months of the conviction becoming conclusive, notwithstanding that the aforesaid period of one year has elapsed:

And provided further that the president of tribunals may, if he considers that there was good reason why the complainant did not institute proceedings at an earlier date, after consultation with the complainant and the respondent, give his written permission for the proceedings to be instituted after the expiry of the said period of one year.

Institution of proceedings

10.—(1) Disciplinary proceedings under this Measure may be instituted against any person who is subject to the jurisdiction of a disciplinary tribunal or the Vicar-General's court by virtue of section 6 above, by way of complaint made in writing, only as follows—

(a) in the case of a priest or deacon, by—
   (i) a person nominated by the parochial church council of any parish which has a proper interest in making the complaint, if not less than two-thirds of the lay members of the council are present at a duly convened meeting of the council and not less than two-thirds of the lay members present and voting pass a resolution to the effect that the proceedings be instituted; or
   (ii) a churchwarden of any such parish; or
   (iii) any other person who has a proper interest in making the complaint;
(b) in the case of a bishop, by—
   (i) a person nominated by the bishop's council of the diocese concerned, if not less than two-thirds of the members of the council are present at a duly convened meeting of the council and not less than two-thirds of the members present and voting pass a resolution to the effect that the proceedings be instituted; or
   (ii) any other person who has a proper interest in making the complaint;
(c) in the case of an archbishop by—
   (i) a person nominated by the archbishop's council of his diocese if not less than two-thirds of the members of the council are present at a duly convened meeting of the council and not less than two thirds of the members present and voting pass a resolution to the effect that the proceedings be instituted; or
   (ii) any other person who has a proper interest in making the complaint.

(2) A complaint under this section shall be laid—
(a) in the case of a priest or deacon, before the diocesan bishop concerned,
(b) in the case of a bishop, before the archbishop concerned,
(c) in the case of an archbishop, before the other archbishop,

and references in the following provisions of this Measure to the bishop by whom a complaint is received shall, in the case of proceedings against a bishop or archbishop, be construed as references to the archbishop or other archbishop respectively.

(3) A complaint made under this section shall be accompanied by written particulars of the alleged misconduct, and written evidence in support of the complaint shall be sent to the bishop or archbishop, as the case may be, either with the complaint or at such later time as he may allow.

Preliminary scrutiny of complaint

11.—(1) When a complaint in writing has been made in accordance with section 10 above it shall be referred in the first instance to the registrar of the diocese or province concerned, as the case may be, who shall thereupon scrutinise the complaint in consultation with the complainant with a view to—
(a) forming a view as to whether or not the parochial church council or other person making the complaint has a proper interest in doing so or, if the complainant purports to be a churchwarden, establishing that he is such, and
(b) forming a view as to whether or not there is sufficient substance in the complaint to justify proceeding with it in accordance with the following provisions of this Measure,

and the registrar shall notify the respondent that the complaint has been referred to him.

(2) Having scrutinised the complaint the registrar shall, within the period of twenty-eight days following its receipt by him or such longer period as he considers to be justified in the particular circumstances of the case, send a written report to the bishop by whom the complaint was received setting out the registrar's views and thereupon the bishop shall deal with the complaint in accordance with the following provisions of this Measure, having regard to the registrar's report:

Provided that the period of twenty-eight days referred to above shall not be extended as aforesaid more than once.

(3) On receipt of the registrar's report the bishop may dismiss the complaint and, if he does so, he shall give written notice of the dismissal to the complainant and the respondent, together with a copy of the report.

(4) On receipt of a notice of dismissal the complainant may request the president of tribunals to review the dismissal, and the president may then uphold the dismissal or, if he considers the dismissal to be plainly wrong, reverse it and direct the bishop to deal with the complaint in accordance with section 12 below.

(5) Where the registrar proposes to extend the period of twenty-eight days referred to in subsection (2) above, he shall, before doing so, consult the complainant and the respondent.

(6) The registrar may delegate any or all of his functions under this section to such person as he may designate.

Courses available to bishop

12.—(1) If the complaint is not dismissed under section 11(3) above the bishop shall, within the period of twenty-eight days following the receipt by him of the registrar's report under section 11(2) above or the president of tribunal's direction under section 11(4), as the case may be, or such longer period as he considers to be justified in the particular circumstances of the case, determine which of the following courses is to be pursued—

(a) he may take no further action, in which case the provisions of section 13 below apply; or

(b) he may, if the respondent consents, direct that the matter remain on the record conditionally, in which case the provisions of section 14 below apply; or

(c) he may direct that an attempt to bring about conciliation in accordance with section 15 below is to be made; or

(d) he may impose a penalty by consent in accordance with section 16 below; or

(e) he may direct that the complaint is to be formally investigated in accordance with section 17 below.

(2) Where the bishop proposes to extend the period of twenty-eight days referred to in subsection (1) above he shall, before doing so, consult the complainant and the respondent.

No further action

13.—(1) Where the bishop determines that there is to be no further action the following provisions of this section shall apply.

(2) The bishop shall reduce his determination to writing and shall give a copy of it to the complainant and the respondent.

(3) The complainant may refer the complaint to the president of tribunals and, if the president considers that the bishop's determination was plainly wrong, he may direct the bishop to pursue such of the courses specified in section 12(1)(b) to (e) above as he considers appropriate, in which case the bishop shall proceed accordingly.

Conditional deferment

14.—(1) Where the bishop, with the consent of the respondent, determines that the matter is to be recorded conditionally the following provisions of this section shall apply.

(2) The complaint and the bishop's determination shall be notified to the archbishop concerned and remain on a record maintained by the diocesan registrar concerned for such period not exceeding five years as the bishop may determine and, subject to subsection (3) below, no further action shall be taken.

(3) Notwithstanding the provisions of section 9 above, if another complaint is made under section 10 above against the respondent and that complaint is dealt with under paragraph (c), (d) or (e) of section 12(1) above, the recorded complaint may be dealt with under any of those paragraphs together with the other complaint.

(4) The bishop shall reduce his determination to writing and give a copy of it to the complainant and the respondent. He shall also supply them with a statement explaining the effect of subsections (2) and (3) above.

Conciliation

15.—(1) Where the bishop determines that an attempt to bring about conciliation is to be made he shall afford the complainant and the respondent an opportunity to make representations and, if both of them agree to the appointment of a conciliator, an appointment shall be made under subsection (2) below.

(2) The appointment of a conciliator shall be by the bishop with the agreement of the complainant and the respondent.

(3) The bishop shall not appoint any person to be a conciliator unless he is satisfied that there is no reason to question the impartiality of that person.

(4) A conciliator appointed under this section shall use his best endeavours to bring about a conciliation between the complainant and the respondent and—

  (a) if, within the period of three months following his appointment or such further period as he may, with the agreement of the complainant and the respondent, allow a conciliation is brought about, he shall submit a report on the case to the bishop, together with such recommendations as he may wish to make;

  (b) if a conciliation is not brought about but the complainant and the respondent agree that another conciliator should be appointed, the bishop may appoint that other person as the conciliator for the purposes of this section;

  (c) if a conciliation is not brought about and the complainant and the respondent do not agree as aforesaid, he shall refer the matter back to the bishop.

(5) If—

  (a) the complainant and the respondent do not agree to the appointment of a conciliator or as to the person to be appointed, or

  (b) the matter is referred back to the bishop by the conciliator under subsection (4)(c) above,

the bishop shall proceed to deal with the complaint under paragraph (a), (b), (d) or (e) of section 12(1) above.

Penalty by consent

16.—(1) Where the bishop considers that the imposition of a penalty by consent might be appropriate, he shall afford the complainant and the respondent an opportunity to make representations and, if the respondent consents to the imposition of a penalty under this section and he and the bishop agree as to the penalty, the bishop shall, subject to subsection (2) below, proceed accordingly and thereafter no further step shall be taken in regard thereto.

(2) Where it is agreed that prohibition for life or resignation is the appropriate course the respondent or the bishop may, within the period of seven days following the date of the agreement, withdraw his agreement and the prohibition or resignation shall not be implemented in pursuance of this section.

(3) If the consent of the respondent to the imposition of a penalty under this section is not obtained or he and the bishop are unable to reach agreement as to the nature of the penalty, the bishop shall proceed to deal with the complaint under paragraph (e) of section 12(1) above.

(4) The bishop shall notify the complainant of any action taken in pursuance of this section and shall also notify the archbishop of the province concerned and the registrar of the diocese concerned of any penalty agreed in pursuance of subsection (1) above.

Formal investigation

17.—(1) Where the bishop directs that the complaint is to be formally investigated, he shall refer the matter to the designated officer and it shall then be the duty of that officer to cause inquiries to be made into the complaint.

(2) After due inquiries have been made into the complaint the designated officer shall refer the matter to the president of tribunals for the purpose of deciding whether there is a case to answer in respect of which a disciplinary tribunal or the Vicar-General's court, as the case may be, should be requested to adjudicate.

(3) If the president of tribunals decides that there is a case for the respondent to answer he shall declare that as his decision and refer the complaint to a disciplinary tribunal or the Vicar-General's court, as the case may be, for adjudication.

(4) If the president of tribunals decides that there is no case for the respondent to answer he shall declare his decision, and thereafter no further steps shall be taken in regard thereto.

(5) The president of tribunals shall reduce his decision to writing and shall give a copy of it to the complainant, the respondent, the bishop and the designated officer.

Conduct of proceedings

18.—(1) In disciplinary proceedings under this Measure it shall be the duty of the designated officer or a person duly authorised by him to conduct the case for the complainant.

(2) In any such proceedings the president of tribunals may direct—
- (a) that the complaint is to be withdrawn, whereupon no further action shall be taken in the proceedings; or
- (b) that an attempt or further attempt to bring about conciliation is to be made, whereupon the provisions of section 15 above shall apply.

(3) In any such proceedings—
- (a) the standard of proof to be applied by the tribunal or court shall be the same as in proceedings in the High Court exercising civil jurisdiction;
- (b) the determination of any matter before the tribunal or court shall be according to the opinion of the majority of the members thereof and shall be pronounced in public together with its reasons therefor;
- (c) the hearing shall be in private, except that the tribunal or court, if satisfied that it is in the interests of justice so to do or the respondent so requests, shall direct that the hearing shall be in public in which case the tribunal or court may, during any part of the proceedings, exclude such person or persons as it may determine.

Imposition of penalty

19.—(1) Upon a finding by a disciplinary tribunal or the Vicar-General's court in disciplinary proceedings that the respondent committed the misconduct complained of, the tribunal or court may—
- (a) impose on the respondent any one or more of the penalties mentioned in section 24 below; or
- (b) defer consideration of the penalty, and for that purpose may adjourn the proceedings; or
- (c) impose no penalty.

(2) Before imposing a penalty the disciplinary tribunal or court may invite—
- (a) in the case of a disciplinary tribunal, the bishop of the diocese concerned, or
- (b) in the case of the Vicar-General's court, the archbishop concerned or, if the respondent is an archbishop, the other archbishop,

to express in writing his views as to the appropriate penalty and the tribunal or court shall have regard to any such views in imposing the penalty, if any and the views of the bishop or archbishop, as the case may be, shall be conveyed in writing to the respondent:.

Provided that, if the bishop or archbishop has given evidence in the proceedings, he shall not be consulted.

(3) In this section any reference to a penalty includes a reference to an order for conditional discharge under section 25 below.

Right of appeal

20.—(1) In disciplinary proceedings under this Measure—
   (a) the respondent may appeal against any penalty imposed on him, and
   (b) the respondent on a question of law or fact, and the designated officer, on a question of law, may appeal against any finding of the disciplinary tribunal or the Vicar-General's court,

to the Arches Court of Canterbury (where the proceedings take place in the province of Canterbury) or the Chancery Court of York (where the proceedings take place in the province of York).

(2) Proceedings on an appeal under subsection (1) above shall be heard and disposed of by all the judges of the court mentioned in section 3(2) (a), (b) and (c) of the 1963 Measure.

Composition of tribunal and Vicar-General's court

Provincial panels

21.—(1) It shall be the duty of the Clergy Discipline Commission to compile and maintain for each province, in accordance with the provisions of subsection (2) below, a list (hereinafter referred to as 'the provincial panel') of persons available for appointment under the following provisions of this Measure as members of a disciplinary tribunal or of the Vicar-General's court.

(2) Each provincial panel shall contain the names of—
   (a) two lay persons from each diocese nominated by the bishop of the diocese after consultation with the bishop's council, being persons who are resident in the diocese and are on the electoral roll of a parish in the diocese or on the community roll of a cathedral which is not a parish church;
   (b) two persons in Holy Orders from each diocese nominated by the bishop of the diocese after consultation with the bishop's council, being persons who have served in Holy Orders for at least seven years and are resident in the diocese;
   (c) ten persons nominated by the archbishop of the relevant province, being persons who have a seven year general qualification within the meaning of section 71 of the Courts and Legal Services Act 1990 (c. 41) or who have held or are holding high judicial office or the office of Circuit judge;
   (d) such persons as may be nominated under subsection (3) below.

(3) The archbishop of the relevant province may also nominate for inclusion on the provincial panel—
   (a) not more than five persons who are resident in the province and are on the electoral roll of a parish in the province or on the community roll of a cathedral which is not a parish church; and
   (b) not more than five persons who have served in Holy Orders for at least seven years and reside in the province.

(4) No person who is not an actual communicant, within the meaning of rule 54(1) of the Church Representation Rules (1969 No. 2 Sch. 3), shall be nominated to serve on the provincial panel.

(5) Persons nominated to serve on the provincial panel shall so serve for a period of six years, and on retiring from the panel shall be eligible to be nominated to serve for not more than one further period of six years:

Provided that, of the persons nominated to serve on the provincial panel on the first occasion after the passing of this Measure, half of those nominated under paragraph (a) of subsection (2) above, half of those nominated under paragraph (b), half of those nominated under paragraph (c) and half of those nominated under subsection (3) above shall retire from the panel after serving for a period of three years, those retiring being determined by lot.

(6) Where the period of service of a person nominated to serve on the provincial panel expires while he is a member of a disciplinary tribunal or of the Vicar-General's court to which proceedings under this Measure are referred, he shall continue to be a member of the tribunal or court until the completion of the proceedings.

(7) Where a casual vacancy occurs on the provincial panel the Archbishop of the relevant province or the bishop of the relevant diocese, as the case may be, may nominate a person to fill the vacancy, and the provisions of subsections (2) and (4) above, relating to qualifications and consultations shall apply for the purposes of this subsection as they applied for the purposes of the nomination of the person whose place he takes on the panel.

(8) Any person nominated to fill a casual vacancy shall serve only for the unexpired term of service of the person whose place he takes on the panel.

Disciplinary tribunals

22.—(1) A disciplinary tribunal shall consist of five members as follows—
- (a) the chairman, who shall be the president of tribunals or such other person as he may appoint as chairman from those nominated under section 21(2)(c) above to serve on the relevant provincial panel;
- (b) two lay persons appointed by the president of tribunals from those nominated under section 21(2)(a) or (3)(a) above otherwise than by the bishop of the diocese concerned to serve on the relevant provincial panel; and
- (c) two persons in Holy Orders appointed by the president of tribunals from those nominated under section 21(2)(b) or (3)(b) above otherwise than by the bishop of the diocese concerned to serve on the relevant provincial panel.

(2) The president of tribunals shall not appoint any person to be a member of a disciplinary tribunal unless he is satisfied that there is no reason to question the impartiality of that person, and before doing so he shall afford an opportunity to the respondent to make representations as to the suitability of that person to be appointed.

Vicar-General's court

23.—(1) The Vicar-General's court, when exercising its jurisdiction in disciplinary proceedings under this Measure against a bishop, shall consist of five members as follows—
- (a) the chairman, who shall be the Vicar-General of the relevant province unless he declares himself to be personally acquainted with the complainant or the respondent, in which case the president of tribunals shall appoint a person to be the chairman from those nominated under section 21(2)(c) above to serve on the relevant provincial panel of the province other than that in which the bishop serves;
- (b) two persons in Holy Orders (one of whom shall be in Episcopal Orders) appointed by the president of tribunals;
- (c) two lay persons appointed by the president of tribunals from among those nominated under section 21(2)(a) or (3)(a) above to serve on the provincial panel of the province other than that in which the bishop serves.

(2) The Vicar-General's court, when exercising its jurisdiction in disciplinary proceedings under this Measure against an archbishop of a province, shall consist of five members as follows—
- (a) the chairman, who shall be the Vicar-General of the other province unless he declares himself to be personally acquainted with the complainant or the respondent, in which case the president of tribunals shall appoint a person to be chairman from those nominated under section 21(2)(c) above to serve on the provincial panel of the other province;
- (b) two persons in Holy Orders (one of whom shall be in Episcopal Orders) appointed by the president of tribunals;
- (c) two lay persons appointed by the president of tribunals from among those nominated under section 21(2)(a) or 3(a) above to serve on the provincial panel of the other province.

(3) The president of tribunals shall not appoint any person to be a member of the Vicar-General's court of a province unless he is satisfied that there is no reason to question the impartiality of that person, and before doing so he shall afford an opportunity to the respondent to make representations as to the suitability of that person to be appointed.

Penalties

Types of penalty

24.—(1) One or more of the following penalties may be imposed on a respondent upon a finding that he has committed any misconduct, namely—
  (a) prohibition for life, that is to say prohibition without limit of time from exercising any of the functions of his Orders;
  (b) limited prohibition, that is to say prohibition for a specific time from exercising any of the functions of his Orders;
  (c) removal from office, that is to say, removal from any preferment which he then holds;
  (d) in the case of a minister licensed to serve in a diocese by the bishop thereof, revocation of the licence;
  (e) injunction, that is to say, an order to do or to refrain from doing a specified act;
  (f) rebuke.

(2) No penalty of removal from office imposed on an archbishop or bishop or on any person holding any preferment the right to appoint to which is vested in Her Majesty (not being a parochial benefice) shall have effect unless and until Her Majesty by Order in Council confirms the penalty.

Conditional discharge

25.—(1) Where, upon a finding that the respondent has committed any misconduct, the disciplinary tribunal or Vicar-General's court, as the case may be, is of opinion, having regard to the circumstances including the nature of the misconduct and the character of the respondent, that it is inexpedient to impose a penalty it may make an order discharging him subject to the condition that he commits no misconduct during such period not exceeding two years from the date of the order as may be specified in the order.

(2) Before making an order under subsection (1) above the tribunal or court shall explain to the respondent in ordinary language that if he commits further misconduct during the period specified in the order a penalty may be imposed for the original misconduct.

(3) Where, under subsection (4) below, a penalty is imposed on a person conditionally discharged under subsection (1) above for the misconduct in respect of which the order for conditional discharge was made, that order shall cease to have effect.

(4) If a person in whose case an order has been made under subsection (1) above is found, in disciplinary proceedings under this Measure, to have committed misconduct during the period specified in the order, the disciplinary tribunal or the Vicar-General's court, as the case may be, may deal with him for the misconduct for which the order was made in any manner in which it could deal with him if it had just found that he had committed that misconduct.

Removal of prohibition for life and deposition

26.—(1) Where by virtue of anything done under this Measure or the 1963 Measure a priest or deacon is prohibited for life or deposed he may make an application to the archbishop concerned for the prohibition or deposition to be nullified on the grounds—
  (a) that new evidence has come to light affecting the facts on which the prohibition or deposition was based; or
  (b) that the proper legal procedure leading to the prohibition or deposition was not followed.

(2) If the archbishop, on an application made in accordance with subsection (1) above, considers that the prohibition or deposition was not justified he may, after consultation with the Dean of the Arches and Auditor, declare that the prohibition or deposition be nullified, whereupon it shall be treated for all purposes in law as never having been imposed.

(3) This section shall apply to archbishops and bishops who are prohibited for life or deposed as it applies to priests and deacons who are prohibited for life or deposed, with the following adaptations—

(a) in the case of an archbishop, the references to the archbishop concerned shall be read as references to the Dean of the Arches and Auditor and the reference to consultation with him shall be omitted;
(b) in the case of a bishop, the references to the archbishop concerned shall be read as references to the archbishop of the other province.

Removal of limited prohibition

27. Where by virtue of anything done under this Measure or the 1963 Measure an archbishop, bishop, priest or deacon is prohibited from exercising functions for a specific time he and the archbishop or bishop of the province or diocese concerned (or his successor in office) acting jointly may make an application to the Dean of the Arches and Auditor sitting with the two Vicars-General for the removal of the prohibition; and on receiving such an application they may make an order removing the prohibition, whereupon he shall be eligible for any preferment.

Restoration on pardon

28. Where by virtue of anything done under this Measure an archbishop, bishop, priest or deacon is prohibited from exercising functions or removed from office his incapacities shall cease if he receives a free pardon from the Crown and he shall be restored to any preferment he previously held if it has not in the meantime been filled.

Disobedience to penalty etc.

29. Any person (including a person deposed from Holy Orders under the 1963 Measure) who performs in the Church of England any function which, under a penalty imposed on him under this Measure or a censure imposed on him under the 1963 Measure, he is not permitted to perform commits an act of misconduct under this Measure and, in the case of a person deposed from Holy Orders, disciplinary proceedings under this Measure may be instituted against him in respect of the misconduct as if he had not been deposed.

Proceedings in secular courts

Sentences of imprisonment and matrimonial orders: priests and deacons

30.—(1) If a person who is a priest or deacon—
(a) is convicted (whether in England or elsewhere) of an offence and a sentence of imprisonment (including one which is not implemented immediately) is passed on him, or
(b) has a decree of divorce or an order of separation made against him following a finding of adultery, behaviour in such a way that the petitioner cannot reasonably be expected to live with the respondent or desertion and, in the case of divorce, the decree has been made absolute,

he shall be liable without further proceedings to a penalty of removal from office or prohibition (whether for life or limited) or both.

(2) Where a person is liable to a penalty of removal from office or prohibition or both by virtue of subsection (1) above and the bishop of the relevant diocese proposes to impose such a penalty, he shall, after consultation with the president of tribunals, inform that person in writing of the proposal, together with an invitation to send representations in writing to the bishop within the period of twenty-eight days. On the expiry of that period the bishop shall decide whether or not to impose the penalty and shall inform that person in writing of the decision. If the decision is to impose the penalty, that person may request the archbishop of the relevant province to review the decision and upon such a review the archbishop may uphold or reverse the decision after consideration of all the circumstances, including any representations made under this subsection.

(3) A penalty shall not be imposed under this section after the expiry of the period of two years beginning with the date on which the sentence becomes conclusive or, as the case may be, the decree absolute or order is made.

(4) Where a penalty is to be imposed under this section, it shall be imposed by the bishop of the relevant diocese, and before imposing it the bishop shall require the registrar of his diocese to give

(if it is practicable to do so) not less than fourteen days notice in writing to the priest or deacon concerned of the time and place at which the penalty will be imposed and if the priest or deacon appears at that time and place he shall be entitled to be present when the penalty is imposed.

(5) When imposing a penalty under this section the bishop shall be attended by the registrar of his diocese. The penalty shall be reduced to writing and a copy thereof shall be sent to the archbishop of the province concerned and to the registrar of the diocese concerned.

(6) The functions exercisable under this section by an archbishop shall, during the absence abroad or incapacity through illness of the archbishop or a vacancy in the see, be exercised by the other archbishop.

(7) In this section 'relevant diocese' means—
- (a) the diocese in which the priest or deacon, in relation to whom a penalty may be imposed under this section, holds preferment at the date on which the sentence which justifies the imposition of the penalty becomes conclusive; or
- (b) if at that date he is not holding preferment, but is residing in a diocese, the diocese in which he is residing at that date; or
- (c) if at that date he neither holds preferment nor resides in a diocese, the diocese in which he last held preferment before that date or, in the case of a priest or deacon who has not held preferment in any diocese, the diocese in which he was ordained.

Sentences of imprisonment and matrimonial orders; bishops and archbishops

31.—(1) If a person who is a bishop or archbishop—
- (a) is convicted (whether in England or elsewhere) of an offence and such a sentence as is mentioned in section 30(1) above is passed on him, or
- (b) has a decree of divorce or an order of separation made against him following a finding of adultery, behaviour in such a way that the petitioner cannot reasonably be expected to live with the respondent or desertion and, in the case of divorce, the decree has been made absolute,

he shall be liable without further proceedings to a penalty of removal from office or prohibition (whether for life or limited) or both.

(2) Where a person is liable to a penalty of removal from office or prohibition or both by virtue of subsection (1) above and the archbishop concerned proposes to impose such a penalty, he shall, after consultation with the president of tribunals, inform that person in writing of that proposal, together with an invitation to send representations in writing to the archbishop within the period of twenty-eight days. On the expiry of that period the archbishop shall decide whether or not to impose the penalty and shall inform that person in writing of the decision. If the decision is to impose a penalty, that person may—
- (a) if he is a bishop, request the other archbishop, or
- (b) if he is an archbishop, request the president of tribunals,

to review the decision and upon such a review the archbishop or the president of tribunals, as the case may be, may uphold or reverse the decision after consideration of all the circumstances, including any representations made under this subsection.

(3) A penalty shall not be imposed under this section after the expiry of the period of two years beginning with the date on which the sentence becomes conclusive or, as the case may be, the decree absolute or order is made.

(4) Where a penalty is to be imposed under this section it shall be imposed—
- (a) in the case of a person who is a bishop, by the archbishop of the relevant province after consultation with the two senior diocesan bishops of the province, and
- (b) in the case of a person who is an archbishop, by the other archbishop after consultation as aforesaid.

(5) When imposing a penalty under this section the archbishop shall be attended by the registrar of his province. The penalty shall be reduced to writing and a copy thereof shall be recorded in the registry of the province concerned and sent to the archbishop concerned.

(6) The functions exercisable under this section by the archbishop of the relevant province shall, during the absence abroad or incapacity through illness of the archbishop or a vacancy in the see, be exercisable by the other archbishop.

(7) In this section 'bishop' means any diocesan bishop, any suffragan bishop and any other bishop.

Consequences of penalties imposed under section 30 or 31

32. Where a penalty of removal from office or prohibition is imposed on any person pursuant to the provisions of section 30 or 31 above the penalty shall have effect subject to the provisions of sections 24 to 29 above, and the like consequences shall ensue in all respects as if such person had been found to have committed misconduct under this Measure and such a penalty had been imposed on him.

Duty to disclose criminal convictions and arrests

33.—(1) A person in Holy Orders who (whether in England or elsewhere) is convicted of an offence or is arrested on suspicion of committing an offence shall be under a duty, within the period of twenty-eight days following the conviction or arrest,—

(a) in the case of a priest or deacon, to inform the bishop of the diocese concerned,

(b) in the case of a bishop, to inform the archbishop concerned, and

(c) in the case of an archbishop, to inform the other archbishop,

of the conviction or arrest.

(2) Failure to comply with the requirements of subsection (1) above shall be regarded as a failure to do an act required by the laws ecclesiastical for the purposes of section 8(1) above.

Duty to disclose divorce and separation orders

34. Section 33 above shall apply to a person in Holy Orders in respect of whose marriage a decree nisi of divorce has been made absolute or an order of judicial separation has been made as it applies to a person who is convicted of an offence.

Miscellaneous

Application of 1963 Measure's provisions

35.—(1) The following provisions of the 1963 Measure shall apply for the purpose of this Measure as they apply for the purposes of that Measure, with the adaptations specified in subsection (2) below—

Section 58 (payment of costs)
Section 60 (powers re-costs)
Section 61 (recovery of cost)
Section 62 (payment of expenses)
Section 63 (fees payable)
Section 71 (performance of duties during suspension etc)
Section 72 (occupation of parsonage house)
Section 73 (suspension of penalty during appeal)
Section 74 (restrictions during suspension etc.)
Section 75 (provisions as to lapse on avoidance of preferment)
Section 76 (rights of patronage during suspension etc.)
Section 78 (recording of declarations etc.)
Section 80 (place of sitting)
Section 81 (evidence etc.)
Section 83(2) and (3) (savings).

(2) In the application of those provisions for the purposes of this Measure they shall be read with the following adaptations—

(a) subject to the following provisions of this subsection, for any reference to the 1963 Measure there shall be substituted a reference to this Measure;

(b) for any reference to an offence cognisable under section 14 of the 1963 Measure there shall be substituted a reference to misconduct;

(c) any reference to a court shall be construed as including a reference to a disciplinary tribunal;

(d) for any reference to a declaration made or to be made in accordance with the provisions of the 1963 Measure there shall be substituted a reference to a penalty imposed under section 30 or 31 above;

(e) any reference to a person nominated to promote proceedings shall be construed as a reference to a person who may, by virtue of section 10 above or section 42 below, institute disciplinary proceedings under this Measure;

(f) for any reference to suspension or inhibition there shall be substituted a reference to prohibition;

(g) for any reference to a censure there shall be substituted a reference to a penalty.

Suspension of priest or deacon during proceedings

36.—(1) Where—
   (a) a complaint in writing is made under section 10(1) above against a priest or deacon holding any preferment in a diocese, or
   (b) a priest or deacon holding any preferment in a diocese is arrested on suspicion of committing a criminal offence,

the bishop of the diocese may, by notice in writing served on him, suspend him from exercising or performing without the leave of the bishop any right or duty of or incidental to his office:

Provided that, in the case of a complaint made as aforesaid, the priest or deacon shall not be suspended under this subsection unless and until the complaint falls to be considered under section 12(1) above.

(2) The bishop may at any time, by notice in writing served on the priest or deacon concerned, revoke a notice of suspension served under subsection (1) above.

(3) Where a notice of suspension is served under subsection (1) above and it has not been revoked under subsection (2) the suspension shall continue until the expiry of the period of three months following service of the notice or until the proceedings under this Measure or for the criminal offence are concluded, whichever occurs earlier, but if the proceedings are not concluded before the expiry of that period a further notice of suspension under subsection (1) above may be served, and this subsection shall apply in relation to the further suspension as it applied to the earlier suspension or suspensions.

(4) Where a notice of suspension is served under subsection (1) above the bishop may, after consultation with the churchwardens and with the incumbent or priest in charge concerned, make such arrangements as he thinks fit for the ministrations of the church or churches concerned while the suspension remains in force.

(5) While a notice of suspension under subsection (1) above remains in force in relation to a priest or deacon he shall not interfere with any person performing the services of a church in pursuance of arrangements made under subsection (4) above, and any such interference shall be regarded as an act in contravention of the laws ecclesiastical for the purposes of section 8(1) above.

(6) A priest or deacon on whom a notice of suspension is served under subsection (1) above may appeal against the suspension to the president of tribunals and on any such appeal the president of tribunals may, within twenty-eight days following the lodging of the appeal, either confirm or revoke the suspension.

Suspension of bishop or archbishop during proceedings

37.—(1) Where—
   (a) a complaint in writing is made under section 10(1) above against a bishop or archbishop, or
   (b) a bishop or archbishop is arrested on suspicion of committing a criminal offence,

the archbishop of the province in which the bishop holds office or, in the case of an archbishop, the other archbishop, may with the consent of the two most senior diocesan bishops in that province or the province of the other archbishop, as the case may be, by notice in writing suspend him from exercising any right or duty of or incidental to his office:

Provided that, in the case of a complaint made as aforesaid, the bishop or archbishop shall not be suspended under this subsection unless and until the complaint falls to be considered under section 12(1) above.

(2) The archbishop may at any time, by notice in writing served on the bishop or archbishop concerned, revoke a notice of suspension served under subsection (1) above.

(3) Where a notice of suspension is served under subsection (1) above the archbishop may, after consultation with the two most senior diocesan bishops of his province, make such arrangements as he thinks fit for the ministrations of the diocese or province concerned while the suspension remains in force.

(4) While a notice of suspension under subsection (1) above remains in force in relation to a bishop or archbishop he shall not interfere with any person performing functions in pursuance of arrangements made under subsection (3) above.

(5) In this section 'bishop' means any diocesan bishop, any suffragan bishop or any other bishop.

(6) Subsections (3) and (6) of section 36 above shall apply for the purposes of this section as they apply for the purposes of that section.

Archbishops' list

38.—(1) Subject to the following provisions of this section, it shall be the duty of the archbishops acting jointly to compile and maintain a list of all clerks in Holy Orders—

  (a) on whom a penalty or censure (by consent or otherwise) has been imposed under this Measure or the 1963 Measure; or

  (b) who have been deposed from Holy Orders under the 1963 Measure; or

  (c) who have executed a deed of relinquishment under the Clerical Disabilities Act 1870 (c. 31); or

  (d) who have resigned preferment following the making of a complaint in writing against them under section 10(1) above or under the 1963 Measure; or

  (e) who, in the opinion of the archbishops, have acted in a manner (not amounting to misconduct) which might affect their suitability for holding preferment.

(2) Where the archbishop has included a person falling within paragraphs (a) to (d) of subsection (1) above in the list he shall take all reasonable steps to inform that person in writing that he has done so and of the particulars recorded in respect of that person. That person may request the president of tribunals to review the matter and upon such a review the president of tribunals shall direct that that person should continue to be included in the list or should be excluded therefrom and, in the former case, may also direct that the particulars relating to that person should be altered in such manner as may be specified.

(3) Where the archbishop proposes to include a person falling within paragraph (e) of subsection (1) above in the list he shall take all reasonable steps to inform that person in writing of the proposal and the particulars to be recorded, together with an invitation to send comments or representations in writing to the archbishop within the period of twenty-one days. On the expiry of that period the archbishop shall decide whether or not to include that person in the list and shall inform that person in writing of his decision. If the decision is to include that person in the list that person may request the president of tribunals to review the decision and upon such a review the president of tribunals shall uphold or reverse the decision.

(4) It shall be the duty of the archbishop to review the inclusion of a person in the list, in such manner as may be prescribed, on the expiry of the period of five years following the inclusion and also if requested to do so by that person or by the bishop of a diocese:

Provided that that person shall not be entitled to make a request under this subsection within the said period of five years nor within the period of five years following any previous review.

Code of Practice

39.—(1) It shall be the duty of the Clergy Discipline Commission to formulate guidance for the purposes of the Measure generally and, with the approval of the Dean of the Arches and Auditor, to promulgate the guidance in a Code of Practice.

(2) The Clergy Discipline Commission may at any time amend or replace a Code of Practice issued under subsection (1) above by a further Code of Practice issued in accordance with the provisions of this section.

(3) A Code of Practice shall be laid before the General Synod and shall not come into force until approved by the General Synod, whether with or without amendment.

(4) Where the Business Committee of the General Synod determines that a Code of Practice does not need to be debated by the General Synod then, unless—
   (a) notice is given by a member of the General Synod in accordance with its Standing Orders that he wishes the Code to be debated, or
   (b) notice is so given by any such member that he wishes to move an amendment to the Code,

the Code shall, for the purposes of subsection (3) above, be deemed to have been approved by the General Synod without amendment.

When convictions etc. are to be deemed conclusive

40.—(1) Proceedings under this Measure and a conviction by a secular court shall become conclusive for the purposes of this Measure—
   (a) where there has been an appeal, upon the date on which the appeal is dismissed or abandoned or the proceedings on appeal are finally concluded, but, if varied on appeal, shall be conclusive only as so varied, and so far as it is reversed on appeal shall cease to have effect;
   (b) if there is no such appeal, upon the expiration of the time limited for such appeal, or in the case of a conviction where no time is so limited, of two months from the date of the conviction; and
   (c) in the case of a conviction against which there is no right of appeal from the date of the conviction.

(2) After the conviction of a clerk in Holy Orders by a secular court becomes conclusive a certificate of such conviction shall, for the purposes of this Measure be conclusive proof that he has committed the act therein specified.

(3) In the event of any such conviction by a secular court as makes a clerk in Holy Orders subject to removal from any preferment, or renders him liable to proceedings under this Measure the court shall cause the prescribed certificate of the conviction to be sent to the bishop of the diocese in which the court sits, and such certificate shall be preserved in the registry of the diocese, or of any other diocese to which it may be sent by the direction of the bishop.

Compensation

41. Any person in respect of whom a penalty of removal from office or revocation of a licence to serve in a diocese is imposed under this Measure and subsequently revoked on appeal shall be entitled to compensation, and the provisions of Schedule 4 to the Pastoral Measure 1983 (1983 No. 1) shall apply in relation to such a person as they apply to an incumbent of a benefice deemed to be vacated by virtue of section 25 of that Measure.

Application of Measure in special cases

42.—(1) In the application of this Measure to the following—
Cathedral clergy
Chaplains of prisons, hospitals, universities, schools and institutions in an extra-parochial place
Chaplains of the armed forces of the Crown

Ministers who have a licence from the archbishop of a province to preach throughout the province

Ministers who have a licence from the University of Oxford or Cambridge to preach throughout England

it shall be read with the following adaptations.

(2) In the case of a clerk in Holy Orders serving in a cathedral church, disciplinary proceedings may be instituted only by—
- (a) a person nominated by the council of the cathedral church; or
- (b) any other person, if the diocesan bishop concerned determines that that person has a proper interest in making the complaint.

(3) In the case of a chaplain of a prison, hospital, university, school or other institution, disciplinary proceedings may be instituted only by a person duly authorised by the diocesan bishop concerned to institute such proceedings.

(4) In the case of a chaplain of one of the armed forces of the Crown—
- (a) disciplinary proceedings may be instituted only if the archbishop of Canterbury determines that the person concerned has a proper interest in making the complaint;
- (b) the complaint shall be laid before the archbishop of Canterbury and references to the diocesan bishop concerned shall be construed as references to that archbishop.

(5) In the case of a minister who has a licence from the archbishop of a province—
- (a) disciplinary proceedings may be instituted only by a person duly authorised by the archbishop to institute such proceedings;
- (b) the complaint shall be laid before that archbishop and references to the diocesan bishop concerned shall be construed accordingly.

(6) In the case of a minister who has a licence from the University of Oxford or Cambridge—
- (a) disciplinary proceedings may be instituted only by a person duly authorised by the archbishop of Canterbury to institute such proceedings;
- (b) the complaint shall be laid before that archbishop and references to the diocesan bishop concerned shall be construed accordingly.

Interpretation

43.—(1) In this Measure, unless the context otherwise requires–

'the 1963 Measure' means the Ecclesiastical Jurisdiction Measure 1963 (1963 No. 1);

'the Commission' means the Clergy Discipline Commission;

'designated officer' means an officer of the legal office of the National Institutions of the Church of England designated by the Archbishops' Council for the purposes of this Measure;

'diocese' means a diocese in the province of Canterbury or a diocese in the province of York and 'diocesan' shall be construed accordingly;

'disciplinary tribunal' means a bishop's disciplinary tribunal constituted in accordance with section 22 above;

'high judicial office' has the meaning assigned to it by section 25 of the Appellate Jurisdiction Act 1876 (c. 59);

'limited prohibition' has the meaning assigned to it by section 24(1)(b) above;

'misconduct' means any act or omission referred to in section 8(1) above.

'preferment' includes an archbishopric, a bishopric, archdeaconry, dignity or office in a cathedral or collegiate church, and a benefice, and every curacy, lectureship, readership, chaplaincy, office or place which requires the discharge of any spiritual duty;

'prescribed' means prescribed by rules made under section 26 of the Care of Churches and Ecclesiastical Jurisdiction Measure 1991 (1991 No. 1);

'prohibition for life' has the meaning assigned to it by section 24(1)(a) above and 'prohibited for life' shall be construed accordingly;

'relevant province' means, according to the context, the province of Canterbury or the Province of York;

'resident' means ordinarily resident;

'Vicar-General's court' means the Vicar-General's court constituted in accordance with section 23 above.

(2) For the purposes of this Measure an extra-diocesan place (including any place exempt or peculiar other than a Royal Peculiar) which is surrounded by one diocese shall be deemed to be situate within that diocese, and an extra-diocesan place which is surrounded by two or more dioceses shall be deemed to be situate within such one of them as the archbishop of the relevant province may direct.

(3) For the purposes of this Measure the seniority of diocesan bishops (other than archbishops) shall be determined by reference to the length of time that each of them has held office as diocesan in either province without interruption from any cause.

STATUTORY INSTRUMENTS

Patronage (Benefices) Rules 1987	543	Faculty Jurisdiction Rules 2000	559
Faculty Jurisdiction (Injunctions and Restoration Orders) Rules 1992	546	Clergy Discipline Rules 2005	577
		Clergy Discipline (Appeal) Rules 2005	607
Faculty Jurisdiction (Appeals) Rules 1998	549		

Patronage (Benefices) Rules 1987

SI 1987/773

1.—(1) In these Rules:—

'the Committee' means the Patronage (Procedure) Committee prescribed by section 38 of the Measure;

'the designated officer' means in relation to a diocese such person as the bishop, after consulting the bishop's council, may designate or, if no person is designated, the secretary of the pastoral committee of the diocese;

'a Fees Order' means an Order made under Part II of the Ecclesiastical Fees Measure 1986;

'the Measure' means the Patronage (Benefices) Measure 1986;

'the registrar' means the registrar of the diocese;

'the registration period' means the period from 1st October 1987 until 31st December 1988.

(2) The Interpretation Measure 1925 and the Interpretation Act 1978 shall apply for the interpretation of these Rules as they apply for the interpretation of Measures passed by the General Synod.

Registration and transfer of rights of patronage

Register

2. The registrar shall keep at the diocesan registry a register of rights of patronage (hereinafter called 'the register') required to be registered under the Measure.

3.—(1) The form of the register shall be in accordance with that prescribed by the Committee and shall contain in relation to each benefice in the diocese the following particulars—
   (a) the name of the benefice;
   (b) the date of registration of the interest of each registered patron;
   (c) the name, style and address, of each registered patron;
   (d) the interest of each registered patron;
   (e) the name, style and address of any transferee from a registered patron, the date of registration consequent upon that transfer and the interest registered;

(f) the name of the patron collating a priest or presenting a priest for institution, the name of that priest and the date of his collation or institution to the benefice.

(2) In this rule 'transfer' means a transfer inter vivos including a transfer by way of exchange, a transfer by operation of law, a transfer upon the appointment of a new trustee and a transfer by the personal representatives of a deceased person.

Advertising the compilation of the Register

4. Within six weeks of the coming into operation of the Measure, the registrar shall cause advertisements to be placed in such newspaper or newspapers circulating in the diocese as, after consultation with the bishop, he shall think fit. The advertisement shall state—

(a) that the registrar has prepared a list of all persons whom he considers are entitled to be registered as patron of a benefice in the diocese;
(b) that each person so listed will receive a notice concerning such registration and should acknowledge receipt of such notice;
(c) that each person will be so registered at the end of the registration period as a patron of the benefice unless before that date some other person applies to be so registered or otherwise disagrees with the information submitted;
(d) the hours during which, and the address at which the list may be inspected; and
(e) that any person who, notwithstanding the fact that he is not named in the list, claims to be entitled to be registered as patron is required to obtain an application form from the registrar and lodge such form duly completed by 31st December 1988.

Application for registration

5.—(1) Subject to paragraph 1 of Schedule 1 of the Measure every application for registration shall be signed by or on behalf of the applicant who shall furnish the particulars required to be registered in the form prescribed by the Committee.

(2) Any person (not being a person named on the list prepared by the registrar) who, before the end of the registration period, applies to the registrar to be registered as patron of a benefice shall apply in accordance with the form prescribed by the Committee. Such person shall also be responsible for the proper charges of the registrar in respect of the investigation of a claim made under paragraphs 3, 4 or 5 of Schedule 1.

(3) Any such person shall at his own expense supply the registrar with all documents and other information as the registrar may require in order to examine the claim.

Failure to apply for registration

6. If at the end of the registration period the registrar has received no acknowledgement from a prospective patron to whom he has sent a notice under rule 4(b) and no other person has claimed the right of patronage in question, the registrar shall send a second notice to the prospective patron giving him a further month within which to submit his acknowledgement of the notice and advising him that where no person is registered as the patron of a benefice the Measure provides that the Diocesan Board of Patronage for the diocese shall become the patron of that benefice and requires the registrar to register that Board as patron.

Registration of transfers

7.—(1) On a transfer inter vivos the applicant shall send to the registrar with the instrument of transfer any notice of consent required by the Measure.

(2) On a transfer by personal representatives, the applicant shall send to the registrar with the instrument of transfer an Office Copy of the Grant of Probate or of the Letters of Administration to the estate of the deceased patron.

(3) Where it is necessary for a form in connection with a transfer prescribed under these Rules to be modified to meet the circumstances of a particular case, the registrar shall have power to agree to such modification.

Duty of registrar to register

8. On being satisfied with an application made in accordance with the Measure and these Rules, the registrar shall register a transferee as patron.

Notification of registration

9. On the completion of a registration the registrar shall send the patron, without charge, a certified copy of the relevant entry in the register.

Inspection of register

10.—(1) The register shall be open to inspection at all reasonable times, and any person may make searches therein and make extracts therefrom on payment of such fees as may be prescribed in a Fees Order.

(2) The registrar shall, on request, supply a certified copy of an entry in the register on payment of such fee as may be prescribed in a Fees Order.

Exercise of rights of presentation

Review of refusal to approve offer

11.—(1) Where, on the refusal either by the bishop or by a parish representative of the making of an offer to a priest the patron has requested the archbishop of the province to review the matter, the archbishop, after making such enquiries as he deems necessary, shall give his reasons in writing for giving or withholding his authorisation to the patron to make the offer in question.

(2) The archbishop may appoint the Vicar General of the province to make the enquiries on his behalf. The Vicar General shall send a written report to the archbishop who shall then determine the matter.

(3) A copy of the determination by the archbishop shall be sent to the bishop and to the parish representatives.

(4) Where the see of the archbishop is vacant or the archbishop is also the bishop of the diocese concerned, any reference in this rule to the archbishop of the province shall be construed as a reference to the archbishop of the other province. Where under this paragraph the review is to be made by the archbishop of the other province, if he wishes to appoint the Vicar General to make enquiries under paragraph 2 of this rule, he shall appoint the Vicar General of the province in which the benefice is situated.

Notice of proposal to collate, etc

12.—(1) The notice by or on behalf of the bishop that he proposes to collate or institute a person to a benefice shall be served on the secretary of the parochial church council by the designated officer or the registrar as the bishop shall direct.

(2) The notice shall state the name of the priest in full and the ecclesiastical preferments previously held and declared by him and so far as they are known to the bishop.

Publication of notice

13.—(1) The secretary of the parochial church council shall immediately on receipt of the notice cause it to be fixed in accordance with the requirements of the Measure and shall take such other steps as he thinks expedient for giving publicity to the notice.

(2) At the expiration of the period during which the notice has been published the secretary of the council shall sign an endorsement attached to the notice that he has complied with the provisions of this rule and shall return the notice.

General and supplementary provisions

Notices and other documents

14.—(1) All notices, agreements, approvals, consents and requests required or authorised by the Measure to be served, sent, given or made shall be in writing and notices and other matters required by the Measure to be prescribed shall be in the form set out in the Appendix to these Rules.

(2) Any other matters may be in such form as may be approved from time to time by the Committee. The precedents of such matters and any amendments revocations or additions thereto shall be approved by the Standing Committee of the General Synod and shall then be communicated to the registrar and designated officer of every diocese.

15. If at the material time a parish has no parochial church council or no secretary of the council the provisions of the Measure and these Rules with respect to notices, consents and other things required or authorised to be given or done by or to such council or such secretary shall, if the parish has churchwardens, have effect as if the churchwardens were the council or the secretary thereof and, if there are no churchwardens, shall have no effect with respect to that parish.

Revocation and transitional provisions

16.—(1) Subject to paragraph (2) of this rule, the Benefices Rules 1926 and the Benefices (Purchase of Rights of Patronage) Rules 1933 are hereby revoked.

(2) Where any benefice which is vacant before the end of the registration period is to be filled in accordance with law in force before that date as provided by section 40 of the Measure, the Rules referred to in paragraph (1) of this rule shall remain in force and continue to apply in respect of the filling of that vacancy.

Citation and commencement

17.—(1) These Rules may be cited as the Patronage (Benefices) Rules 1987.

(2) Rules 1 to 10, 14, 15 and this rule shall come into force on 1st October 1987 and rules 11 to 13 and 16 shall come into force on 1st January 1989.

Faculty Jurisdiction (Injunctions and Restoration Orders) Rules 1992

SI 1992/2884

Citation and commencement

1. These Rules may be cited as the Faculty Jurisdiction (Injunctions and Restoration Orders) Rules 1992 and shall come into force on the first day of March 1993.

Interpretation

2.—(1) In these Rules
 'the Measure' means the Care of Churches and Ecclesiastical Jurisdiction Measure 1991;
 'article' includes any article appertaining to a building which is subject to the faculty jurisdiction by virtue of an order made under section 11(4) of the Measure;
 'the archdeacon' means the archdeacon of the archdeaconry in which the church or churchyard concerned is situated;
 'the chancellor' and 'the registrar' mean, in relation to any proceedings, the chancellor and the registrar respectively of the diocese in which the church or churchyard is situated, and include any person appointed to act as the deputy of the chancellor or registrar, as the case may be;
 'church' includes any building (1) which is for the time being subject to the faculty jurisdiction by an order made by the bishop under section 6 of the Faculty Jurisdiction Measure 1964, or (2) which is licensed by the bishop of a diocese after the coming into operation of section 11 of the Measure for public worship according to the rites and ceremonies of the Church of England unless such building has been excluded from the faculty jurisdiction by order made under section 11(3) of the Measure;

'court' means the consistory court of the diocese in which the church or churchyard is situated and the chancellor or registrar thereof;

'injunction' means an order constituting an injunction under section 13(4) of the Measure;

'minister' has the same meaning in these Rules as in section 31(1) of the Measure;

'restoration order' means an order made under section 13(5) of the Measure.

(2) The Interpretation Act 1978 shall apply for the interpretation of these Rules as it applies for the interpretation of Measures passed by the General Synod.

Applicant

3. An application for an injunction or for a restoration order may be made by
   (a) the archdeacon concerned
   (b) any other person appearing to the registrar or the chancellor to have a sufficient interest in the matter.

Form of application

4.—(1) Subject to rule 8(1) any application under section 13 of the Measure shall be made in writing and shall be in Form No 1 in the Appendix.

(2) An application made under rule 4(1) shall be accompanied by an affidavit of the applicant, or of a person acting on his behalf, giving details of the facts and matters relied upon in support of his application for an injunction or restoration order. An affidavit for the purposes of this rule may contain statements of information or belief with the sources and grounds thereof.

(3) An application made under rule 4(1) shall not be served on any person unless it contains details of a date of hearing which shall be provided by the registrar who issues the application.

Service

5.—(1)
   (a) subject to rule 8 an application under rule 4(1) shall be served
      (i) upon any person against whom the applicant is seeking an injunction or restoration order, and
      (ii) where faculty proceedings have been instituted in relation to or concerning the subject matter of the application, upon each of the petitioners and any other parties to the proceedings, and
      (iii) if it appears to the court that it is impracticable for any reason to serve the application on all or any of the persons described in paragraph (i) and (ii) of this rule, the court may make an order giving leave for such steps to be taken as the court directs to bring the application to the notice of any person to be served.
   (b) Unless the court otherwise directs, service shall be effected not less than 2 clear days before the date specified in rule 4(3).

(2) A copy of any application made under rule 4(1) (other than by the archdeacon) shall be sent by the applicant to the archdeacon and also to the minister (if he is not the applicant) at the same time as steps are taken to effect service under rule 5(1).

(3) Before he lays any application made under rule 4(1) before the chancellor the registrar shall satisfy himself that service has been effected and shall require by way of proof thereof either an acknowledgement of service signed by the person against whom an injunction or restoration order is sought, or his solicitor, or an affidavit that personal service or service in accordance with any order under rule 5(1)(a)(iii) has been effected.

Evidence

6.—(1) Any person upon whom an application under rule 4(1) is served shall be entitled to answer the application by way of affidavit evidence from himself and witnesses on his behalf, or, subject to the directions of the chancellor, by oral evidence at the hearing.

(2) Any affidavit in answer to an application under rule 4(1) shall be served on the applicant within fourteen days after service of the application upon the person answering the same and a copy of the affidavit shall at the same time be sent to the registrar.

Hearing

7.—(1) The evidence at the hearing of an application under rule 4(1) shall be given by affidavit, unless leave is given by the chancellor for evidence to be given orally, provided that the makers of affidavits may be required to attend the hearing for cross-examination.

(2)
- (a) The chancellor may issue an injunction or make a restoration order on such terms as appear to him to be just and such terms shall be set out in an order in Form No 2 or Form No 3 in the Appendix which shall contain a notice stating that failure to comply without reasonable excuse with any requirement of the injunction or order is a contempt of court.
- (b) Any order requiring any person to do an act, shall state the time within which the act is to be done.
- (c) The chancellor shall give such directions as to service of the order as he considers appropriate.

(3) On the hearing of an application under rule 4(1) the chancellor shall give such directions in relation to the institution of faculty proceedings as he considers appropriate.

Emergency application

8.—(1) Where an applicant considers that it is necessary to apply to the chancellor under section 13(4) of the Measure for an injunction without complying with rule 5(1) the applicant may so inform the registrar and he shall immediately refer the matter to the chancellor, who may issue an injunction on such terms as may appear to him to be just by way of an order in Form No 4 in the Appendix provided that he shall
- (a) require the applicant immediately to serve an application in Form No 1 in the Appendix on the person or persons against whom the injunction is issued,
- (b) order that the injunction shall continue in force for a specified period of time which, unless he otherwise directs, shall be not more than fourteen days from the date of the order, and
- (c) give directions for the hearing of the application.

(2) Where as the result of information brought to his attention (whether before or after faculty proceedings have been instituted) the chancellor considers it necessary to issue an injunction against any person without any application having been made under rule 4(1), he may of his own motion issue an injunction on such terms as appear to him to be just by way of an order in Form No 5 in the Appendix provided that he shall make an order in accordance with rule 8(1)(b) and shall give directions for the hearing of the application.

Restoration order without application

9. Where no application has been made under rule 4(1) but it appears to the chancellor as the result of information brought to his attention (whether before or after faculty proceedings have been instituted) that there are grounds on which he might make a restoration order he shall not make such an order of his own motion by way of an order in Form No 6 in the Appendix without first considering the desirability of
- (a) directing that a special citation be served on any person against whom such a restoration order might be made requiring the attendance of such person before the court at such time and place as is specified in the citation, and
- (b) giving that person an opportunity to be heard as to whether or not a restoration order should be made.

General provisions

10.—(1) Service of any document may be effected in the manner provided for in rule 28 of the Faculty Jurisdiction Rules 1992 and the provisions of rules 29 and 33 of the Faculty Jurisdiction Rules 1992 shall apply for the purposes of these Rules.

(2) Any injunction or restoration order made under these Rules may be varied, extended or discharged by the chancellor as he thinks fit.

(3) At any stage of any proceedings pursuant to these Rules the chancellor shall give such directions as appear to him to be necessary to enable the proceedings to be expeditiously and justly determined, and he may adjourn the hearing of any application or other proceedings from time to time on such terms as he considers just.

Costs

11. The Chancellor may make such orders for costs in respect of any application for an injunction or restoration order as he considers just.

Faculty Jurisdiction (Appeals) Rules 1998

SI 1998/1713
PART I
PRELIMINARY

Citation, commencement and revocation

1. *Text omitted.*

Transitional

2. *Text omitted.*

Interpretation

3.—(1) In these Rules—

'appellate court' means the Arches Court of Canterbury or the Chancery Court of York, or the Court of Ecclesiastical Causes Reserved, as the case may be;

'certificate' means a certification under section 10(3) of the Measure;

'Commission' means a Commission of Review;

'the Council' means the Council for the Care of Churches;

'the Dean' means the Dean of the Arches and Auditor or his duly appointed Deputy;

'faculty proceedings' means any cause of faculty within section 6(1)(b) or any proceedings for an injunction and a restoration order within section 6(1)(bb) of the Measure;

'judgment' includes an order or decree, and any reference to the giving of judgment shall include a reference to the making or pronouncing of an order or decree;

'leave to appeal' means leave to appeal to the Arches Court of Canterbury or the Chancery Court of York required by section 7(2) of the Measure;

'the Measure' means the Ecclesiastical Jurisdiction Measure 1963;

'other body' includes English Heritage and any national amenity society as defined in the Faculty Jurisdiction Rules 1992 and the local planning authority;

'party to the faculty proceedings' means any person or body who is a party as a petitioner or as an interested person as defined in the Faculty Jurisdiction Rules 1992;

'registrar of the appellate court', in relation to appeals from the consistory court of any diocese, means the registrar of the province comprising that diocese, whose duties shall accordingly include the duty of acting as a registrar of the Court of Ecclesiastical Causes Reserved in relation to any such appeals, and includes a deputy registrar or person appointed under section 3(4C) of the Ecclesiastical Judges and Legal Officers Measure 1976;

'registrar of the diocese' includes a deputy registrar or a person appointed under section 4(5C) of the Ecclesiastical Judges and Legal Officers Measure 1976.

(2) The Interpretation Measure 1925 and the Interpretation Act 1978 shall apply for the interpretation of these Rules as they apply for the interpretation of Measures of the General Synod.

Part II
Applications to Determine the Court to which a Faculty Appeal Lies and for Leave to Appeal

General

4. Any party to faculty proceedings in the consistory court who wishes to appeal against a judgment of the consistory court shall in accordance with these Rules first apply for and obtain—
    (a) a certificate from the chancellor pursuant to section 10(3) of the Measure stating whether or not a question of doctrine, ritual or ceremonial is involved in the proposed appeal; and
    (b) leave to appeal to the Arches Court of Canterbury or the Chancery Court of York either from the chancellor, or from the Dean on appeal from a refusal of leave to appeal by the chancellor, in any case where the certificate given under (a) is to the effect that no question of doctrine, ritual or ceremonial is involved.

Application to chancellor

5.—(1) Any application for a certificate pursuant to section 10(3) of the Measure shall be made to the chancellor within 21 days from the date of delivery of the judgment if given or made orally, or from the date when the judgment was delivered in writing and sent to, or served upon, the parties to the faculty proceedings.

(2) An application for a certificate shall be made by notice in writing in Form 1 in the Appendix to these Rules and shall be accompanied by—
    (a) a short and concise statement in writing in numbered paragraphs identifying those parts of the judgment to which the proposed appeal relates; and
    (b) the proposed grounds of appeal in writing.

The matters set out in (a) and (b) may be relied upon in support of an application for leave to appeal in the event of the chancellor determining that no question of doctrine, ritual or ceremonial is involved, and no separate application for leave to appeal shall be required.

(3) Two copies of the application in Form 1 together with two copies of the documents referred to in paragraph (2)(a) and (b) of this rule shall be lodged with the registrar of the diocese and a copy of the application and the said documents shall be served upon each of the other parties to the proceedings within 7 days of the lodging of the application with the registrar.

(4) The chancellor may determine the application with or without a hearing and may make such order in relation to costs on the application, including the court costs, as he deems fit.

(5) If the chancellor directs that there shall be a hearing of the application it shall take place at a time and place fixed by the registrar of the diocese who shall give not less than 7 days' notice to the parties as to the time and place of the hearing.

(6) The parties may attend a hearing themselves or by their representatives (whether or not legally qualified) to make their submissions to the chancellor in support of the application for a certificate and for leave to appeal to the Arches Court of Canterbury or the Chancery Court of York.

(7) As soon as he has determined an application under this rule the chancellor shall—
    (a) give a certificate in writing in Form No 2 in the Appendix to these rules and shall state in writing in summary form his reasons for so certifying; and

(b) state whether or not he is granting leave to appeal to the Arches Court of Canterbury or the Chancery Court of York.

(8) The registrar of the diocese shall forthwith serve copies of such certificate and notice of decision to grant or refuse leave to appeal on all the parties.

Application to Dean for leave to appeal

6.—(1) Where—
(a) a party to any faculty proceedings before a consistory court desires to appeal against a judgment of that court;
(b) the appeal lies under the Measure to the Arches Court of Canterbury or the Chancery Court of York; and
(c) the chancellor refuses leave to appeal;

that party may apply to the Dean for leave to appeal.

(2) An application under paragraph (1) of this rule shall be made by notice in writing in Form No 3 in the Appendix to these rules which shall be lodged with the registrar of the appellate court, and notice of which shall be served by the applicant on the other parties, not later than 14 days after the notice of the chancellor's refusal to grant leave to appeal is served on the applicant under paragraph (8) of rule 5.

(3) The applicant shall lodge with the registrar of the appellate court 3 copies of—
(a) the chancellor's judgment or a note thereof approved by the chancellor in the case;
(b) the application and documents referred to in rule 5(2);
(c) a short and concise statement in writing in numbered paragraphs of the reasons relied upon by the applicant in support of the application to the Dean for leave to appeal;
(d) the certificate given by the chancellor under rule 5(7)(a).

(4) The Dean may determine the application with or without a hearing and may make such order in relation to costs on the application, including the court costs, as he deems fit.

(5) Before determining the application without a hearing the Dean shall give the parties not less than 14 days within which to make representations in writing to him in relation to the application.

(6) If the Dean directs that there shall be a hearing of the application it shall take place at a time and place fixed by the registrar of the appellate court who shall give not less than 7 days' notice to the parties as to the time and place of the hearing.

(7) The parties may attend a hearing themselves or by their representatives (whether or not legally qualified) to make their submissions to the Dean in support of or in opposition to the application for leave to appeal to the Arches Court of Canterbury or the Chancery Court of York.

(8) Where an application is made under paragraph (1) of this rule any party other than the applicant may request the Dean to exercise the power to grant security for costs under rule 8, and any such request shall be by notice in writing which shall be lodged with the registrar of the appellate court, and copies of which shall be served on the other parties, not later than 10 days after a copy of the notice of the application under paragraph (1) of this rule is served on the party making the request.

(9) Leave to appeal may be granted by the Dean on such terms, including the provision of security for the costs of any other party and the payment or reimbursement of court costs, fees and expenses already incurred in relation to the proceedings in the consistory court and the application for leave to appeal or to be incurred on the appeal as he deems just.

(10) As soon as the Dean has determined any application under paragraph (1) of this rule the registrar of the appellate court shall serve notice of the Dean's decision on each of the parties.

Part III
Procedure on Faculty Appeals to Provincial Courts or the Court of Ecclesiastical Causes Reserved

Lodging of appeal

7.—(1) A party to any faculty proceedings before a consistory court who desires and is entitled under the Measure to appeal to an appellate court shall lodge his appeal in accordance with the following provisions of this rule not later than 21 days after whichever is applicable of the following dates—

    (a) in the case of an appeal to the Arches Court of Canterbury or the Chancery Court of York, the date on which notice is served on him that the chancellor or the Dean has granted leave to appeal; or

    (b) in the case of an appeal to the Court of Ecclesiastical Causes Reserved, the date on which a copy of the certificate by the chancellor is served on him

provided that the registrar of the appellate court may extend the period within which the notice of appeal must be lodged on an application made to him either within that period or after it has expired.

(2) The lodging of an appeal under paragraph (1) of this rule shall be effected—

    (a) in the case of an appeal to the Court of Ecclesiastical Causes Reserved by lodging with the registrar of the appellate court 6 copies of the notice of appeal and of the chancellor's judgment or a note thereof approved by the chancellor and of the certificate of the chancellor given under rule 5(7)(a);

    (b) in the case of an appeal to the Arches Court of Canterbury or the Chancery Court of York by lodging with the registrar of the appellate court 4 copies of—
        (i) the notice of appeal;
        (ii) the chancellor's judgment or a note thereof approved by the chancellor;
        (iii) the certificate given by the chancellor under rule 5(7)(a);
        (iv) the notice served on the appellant pursuant to rule 5(8) or 6(10) stating that the chancellor or the Dean has granted leave to appeal.

(3) If an appeal is lodged under paragraph (2)(a) or (b) of this rule then the appellant shall in either case lodge two copies of the notice of the appeal with the registrar of the diocese and shall serve a copy of the notice of appeal on each of the parties to the faculty proceedings in the consistory court within 14 days of the lodging of the appeal.

(4) The registrar of the appellate court shall inform the Council and any other body which gave evidence in the consistory court that an appeal has been lodged in the Court of Ecclesiastical Causes Reserved or in the Arches Court of Canterbury or in the Chancery Court of York as the case may be. On the direction of the Court of Ecclesiastical Causes Reserved or of the Dean the registrar of the appellate court shall notify any other body which did not participate in the faculty proceedings that an appeal has been lodged as aforesaid and such notification shall be given to such body in the manner and within the period of time so directed by the appellate court in question.

(5) Notice of an appeal under paragraph (1) of this rule—

    (a) shall be in form No 4 or 5 in the Appendix to these Rules as appropriate;

    (b) shall set out the grounds of appeal and the relief which the party appealing seeks from the appellate court; and

    (c) if the appeal relates to part only of the judgment of the consistory court, shall specify that part.

(6) Except with the leave of the appellate court, the appellant shall not be entitled at the hearing of the appeal to rely on any grounds of appeal not stated in the notice of appeal, whether as originally lodged or, if it has been amended under rule 9, as so amended.

(7) The registrar of the diocese—
(a) shall cause one of the two copies of the notice of appeal lodged with him to be displayed for a period of two weeks on a notice board outside the church or place of worship to which the faculty proceedings related or, if they related to a churchyard, on a notice board outside the church or place of worship to which the churchyard belongs; and
(b) shall send or deliver to the registrar of the appellate court the court file maintained by the registrar of the diocese relating to the proceedings in the consistory court.

(8) Any party to the proceedings and the Council and any other body shall be entitled on giving reasonable notice to the registrar of the appellate court to inspect the court file referred to in paragraph (7)(b) and the file maintained by the registrar of the appellate court relating to the appeal and to have copies of documents contained therein made at the expense of the party, the Council or body requesting them.

(9) The appellate court may, on the application of the appellant, grant a stay of proceedings on the judgment of the consistory court.

Security for costs

8.—(1) At any time on or after the lodging of an appeal under rule 7 (or, in the case of an appeal to the Arches Court of Canterbury or the Chancery Court of York, at any time on or after the granting of leave to appeal) and before the hearing of the appeal, the appellate court may, on the application of any other party, or of its own motion, order the appellant or party desiring to appeal to give such security as it thinks just for—
(a) the costs of any other party;
(b) the payment or reimbursement of court costs, fees and expenses already incurred in relation to proceedings in the consistory court and on the appeal or to be incurred on the appeal in such manner and within such period as the court may direct.

(2) A party who fails to comply with an order for security for costs under paragraph (1) of this rule shall not proceed with or take any further steps in relation to his appeal without the leave of the appellate court.

Amendment or withdrawal of appeal

9. The appellate court may at any time at or before the hearing of any such appeal, on the application of the appellant—
(a) allow the appeal to be withdrawn; or
(b) allow the notice of the appeal to be amended

on such terms as the appellate court thinks just, which may in the case of amendment include the adjournment or postponement of the hearing.

Service on additional parties

10.—(1) The appellate court may at any time at or before the hearing of any such appeal, on the application of any person who was not a party but might have been made a party to the proceedings in the consistory court, by order direct that a copy of the notice of appeal shall be served on him and that he shall be made a party to the appeal, and the appellate court may give such consequential directions and make such further orders as it thinks just.

(2) Any application under paragraph (1) of these rules shall be accompanied by a summary statement of the applicant's reasons for wishing to be a party to the appeal and it may be granted on such terms as the court thinks just, which may include the adjournment or postponement of the hearing.

Hearing for directions

11.—(1) Upon receipt of a notice of appeal under rule 7 the registrar of the appellate court shall fix a time and place for a hearing for directions to be held not later than 28 days after the lodging of the notice of appeal and he shall give not less than 7 days' notice in writing thereof to the parties and bodies which participated in the faculty proceedings in the consistory court and any other person who has become a party pursuant to rule 10.

(2) The appellant and any other party or body which participated in the faculty proceedings in the consistory court and any other party to the appeal shall specify in writing any directions to be sought at the hearing for directions and shall give notice thereof in writing to the registrar of the appellate court in Form No 6 in the Appendix to these Rules not less than 2 days before the date fixed for the hearing for directions and shall send a copy thereof to every other party or body as aforesaid.

(3) At the hearing for directions the registrar shall give such directions as he considers will facilitate the hearing of the appeal and, without prejudice to the generality thereof, may give directions as to all or any of the following—

    (a)   the identification by the parties of such parts of the statements given in evidence, exhibits or other documents material to the issues to be considered at the hearing of the appeal;

    (b)   the preparation of paginated bundles of material identified in (a) by one or more of the parties in sufficient numbers to provide for each member of the appellate court;

    (c)   the lodging and service of the outline arguments of the parties and their lists of authorities (or photocopies of them), if any;

    (d)   where an application is to be made to the appellate court to hear evidence not given in the consistory court, directions as to the preparation of a proof of evidence for the witness in question together with a short and concise written explanation as to—

        (i)   why the evidence was not called in the consistory court,

        (ii)   the relevance and importance of the further evidence in relation to the decision of the consistory court and the issues raised in the grounds of appeal;

    (e)   the time within which any direction is to be complied with or within which any other thing is to be done.

(4) The registrar may, if he thinks fit, adjourn the hearing for directions to a date which shall be not later than 14 days after the date fixed for the hearing for directions and at the time of the adjournment he shall give notice to the parties to the appeal and to any other person or body who participated in the faculty proceedings in the consistory court of the date, time and place for the adjourned hearing.

Further evidence

12.—(1) At any time before or at the hearing of an appeal the appellate court may, on the application by notice in Form No 7 in the Appendix to these Rules of a party or any other body which participated in the faculty proceedings in the consistory court, or any other party to the appeal, give leave for evidence to be placed before the appellate court which was not before the consistory court.

(2) In exercising its discretion the appellate court shall consider the proof of evidence and written explanation provided pursuant to a direction of the registrar under rule 11(3)(d), or pursuant to a direction to the same effect of the appellate court, and shall hear submissions from other parties or bodies in response to the application as it deems fit.

(3) If the appellate court decides to grant leave under paragraph (1) of this rule it shall do so on such terms, including such provision as to costs and any adjournment, as seems to it to be just in all the circumstances.

Inspection

13. The appellate court may of its own motion, or upon the application of any party, inspect any property or thing the subject of the appeal or concerning which any question arises in the appeal.

Conservation interests

14. Where the Council or any other body concerned with conservation matters (whether or not it was informed of or cited in respect of the faculty proceedings in the consistory court) applies to the

appellate court to be heard, or to call evidence at the hearing of the appeal, the appellate court may give leave to the Council or any such body to be heard or to call evidence at the hearing but this power shall only be exercised in exceptional circumstances and on such terms as the court deems just.

Fixing time and place of hearing

15.—(1) After the hearing for directions under rule 11 the registrar of the appellate court shall fix the time and place for the hearing of the appeal, and the court may at any time before the hearing, on an application by a party, or of its own motion (subject to prior notice being given to all parties), alter the time or place of the hearing or both.

(2) The appellate court may at any time, on an application by a party or of its own motion, adjourn the hearing of the appeal.

(3) Except in so far as the appellate court directs otherwise or a party consents to receive a shorter period of notice, the registrar of the appellate court shall give to all the parties not less than 21 days' notice in writing of the time and place of the hearing of the appeal and not less than 7 days' notice in writing of any sitting of the appellate court to deliver judgment.

Hearing of Appeal

16.—(1) On the hearing of any appeal the appellate court may—
 (a) draw any inference of fact which might have been drawn in the proceedings in the consistory court;
 (b) give any judgment or direction which could have been given in the consistory court or remit the matter for rehearing and determination in the consistory court by the chancellor or a deputy chancellor, as the court considers appropriate;
 (c) make such order for costs, having heard argument on the subject of costs from the parties at the conclusion of the hearing of the appeal, as the court deems fit.

(2) The judgment of the court may be delivered in writing and sent to the parties by the registrar of the appellate court, or delivered orally in the presence of not less than two members of the court as is deemed appropriate by the court.

(3) The registrar of the court shall give notice in writing to the registrar of the diocese of the judgment of the court and any directions given by it at the hearing of the appeal or upon delivering judgment.

Part IV
Procedure on Review by Commission of Review

Lodging of petition

17.—(1) Where in any cause of faculty involving matters of doctrine, ritual or ceremonial any party desires that a finding of the Court of Ecclesiastical Causes Reserved should be reviewed by a Commission of Review the petition shall be lodged within 28 days after the finding to which the petition relates.

(2) The lodging of a petition shall be effected by lodging with the Clerk of the Crown in Chancery six copies of—
 (i) the petition in Form No 8 in the Appendix to these Rules which shall state the grounds of the petition and, if the petition relates to part only of the finding of the Court of Ecclesiastical Causes Reserved, shall specify that part;
 (ii) the judgment containing the finding of the appellate court which is to be reviewed; and
 (iii) the certificate given by the chancellor under rule 5(7)(a).

(3) The petitioner shall lodge one copy of the petition with the registrar of the appellate court and two copies thereof with the registrar of the diocese and shall serve one copy thereof on every party to the proceedings.

(4) Except with the leave of the Commission of Review, the petitioner shall not be entitled on the hearing of the petition to rely on any grounds not stated in the petition whether as originally lodged or, if it is amended under rule 9 as applied by rule 18, as so amended.

(5) As soon as a petition under this rule has been lodged the Clerk of the Crown in Chancery shall appoint a person to be the registrar of the Commission of Review, and shall hand over the six copies of the petition to the registrar so appointed, who shall file one of them.

(6) The registrar of the appellate court shall send or deliver to the registrar of the Commission of Review the file relating to the proceedings in the appellate court and the court file maintained by the registrar of the diocese relating to the proceedings in the consistory court.

(7) Any party to the proceedings and the Council and any other body shall be entitled on giving reasonable notice to the registrar of the Commission of Review to inspect the files referred to in paragraph (6) and to have copies of documents contained therein made at the expense of the party, the Council or body requesting them.

(8) The registrar of the Commission of Review shall notify the parties of the names of the Commission and, if the cause involves a question of doctrine, the persons selected under section 48(3) of the Measure to sit with the Commissioners as advisers.

(9) The Commission may, on an application by the petitioner, grant a stay of proceedings on the judgment or finding of either of the courts below.

Application to Commission of rules relating to appellate courts

18.—(1) Rules 7(7)(a), 8 to 11, 15, 16 and 19 to 24 of these Rules shall apply in relation to a petition under rule 17 as they apply in relation to appeals under rule 7 subject to such modifications as may be necessary.

Part V
General Provisions

Interlocutory applications

19.—(1) This rule applies to—
(a) applications made under these rules to a registrar; and
(b) applications made under these rules, except under rules 10, 13 and 15, to an appellate court or Commission of Review otherwise than at the hearing of an appeal or petition.

(2) An application to which this rule applies shall be in writing in Form No 9 in the Appendix to these Rules and shall be lodged with the registrar to whom it is made or the registrar of the court or Commission to which it is made, and a copy of the application shall be served on each other party.

(3) A registrar may grant any application made to him (other than an application for directions under rule 11 without a hearing), if there is lodged with the application a consent in writing signed by each of the other parties or his solicitor, or if the registrar is otherwise satisfied that none of the other parties opposes the application.

(4) In the case of any application lodged with a registrar under this rule (other than an application under paragraph (3)) the registrar shall fix a time and place for the hearing of the application and shall give not less than 7 days' notice in writing of that time and place to all the parties.

(5) An application under this rule may be granted or a direction may be made on an application under this rule on such terms as the person or body granting the application may think just.

(6) Any party may appeal from a decision of a registrar of an appellate court or Commission of Review to that appellate court or Commission.

(7) Any party wishing to appeal from a decision of a registrar under paragraph (6) of this rule shall lodge with the registrar not more than 7 days after the decision in question a notice of appeal

in writing in Form No 10 in the Appendix to these Rules, setting out the grounds of the appeal, and shall serve a copy of the notice of appeal on each other party, and the registrar shall fix the time and place of the hearing of the appeal and give not less than 7 days' notice in writing of that time and place to all parties.

(8) Any application or appeal under this rule to the Arches Court of Canterbury or the Chancery Court of York may be heard and determined by the Dean.

(9) Any application or appeal under this rule to the Court of Ecclesiastical Causes Reserved may be heard and determined by such two of the judges of the Court of Ecclesiastical Causes Reserved as may be agreed between the judges of that court.

(10) Any application or appeal under these rules to a Commission of Review may be heard and determined by the presiding judge of the Commission of Review.

Service of document

20.—(1) Service of any document may be effected—
- (a) by leaving the document at the proper address of the person to be served; or
- (b) by sending it by post to that address; or
- (c) by leaving it at a document exchange as provided for in paragraph (3) of this rule; or
- (d) by FAX as provided for in paragraph (4) of this rule; or
- (e) only in such other manner as the registrar or the appellate court may direct.

(2) For the purpose of this rule and the Interpretation Act 1978 in its application to this rule, the proper address of any person on whom a document is to be served under this rule shall be—
- (a) his usual or last known address; or
- (b) the business address of the solicitor (if any) who is acting for him in the proceedings.

(3) Where—
- (a) the proper address for service includes a numbered box at a document exchange; or
- (b) there is inscribed on the writing paper of the party on whom the document is served (where such party acts in person) or on the writing paper of his solicitor (where such party acts by a solicitor) a document exchange box number, and such a party or his solicitor (as the case may be) has not indicated in writing to the party serving the document that he is unwilling to accept service through a document exchange,

service of the document may be effected by leaving the document addressed to that numbered box at that document exchange or at a document exchange which transmits documents every business day to that document exchange; and any document which is left at a document exchange in accordance with this paragraph shall, unless the contrary is proved, be deemed to have been served on the second business day following the day on which it is left.

(4) Service by FAX may be effected where—
- (a) the party serving the document acts by a solicitor;
- (b) the party on whom the document is served acts by a solicitor and service is effected by transmission to the business address of such solicitor;
- (c) the solicitor acting for the party on whom the document is served has indicated in writing to the solicitor serving the document that he is willing to accept service by FAX at a specified FAX number and the document is transmitted to that number and for this purpose the inscription of a FAX number on the writing paper of a solicitor shall be deemed to indicate that such a solicitor is willing to accept service by FAX unless he has indicated in writing that he is not prepared to do so.

(5) Any document required by these Rules to be lodged with the registrar of the appellate court may be lodged by delivering the document at the address of the registrar or by sending it by post properly addressed to the registrar.

General provisions

21.—(1) Where anything is required by these rules to be done not more than a specified number of days or weeks after a specified act or event, the day on which the act or event occurred shall not be counted.

(2) The registrar of the appellate court, or the appellate court, may on an application made by the person or body concerned extend the time within which anything is required to be done by these rules, and the application may be made notwithstanding that the time has expired.

(3) The registrar or the appellate court may exercise the power under paragraph (2) on an ex parte application or may give directions for the giving of notice thereof and for a hearing.

(4) Any such application may be granted on such terms as the registrar of the appellate court thinks just.

Non-compliance with rules

22. Non-compliance with any of these Rules shall not render any proceeding void unless the appellate court or Commission so directs but the proceedings may be set aside either wholly or in part, as irregular, or may be amended or otherwise dealt with in such manner and upon such terms as the court or Commission thinks fit.

Use of forms in Appendix

23. Where any of these Rules require a document to be in a form set out in the Appendix to these Rules, and that form is not in all respects appropriate, the Rules shall be construed as requiring a form of the like character with such variations as circumstances may require to be used.

Procedural questions

24. Where in the exercise of the appellate jurisdiction in faculty matters any procedural question or issue arises or it is expedient that any procedural direction shall be given in order that the proceedings may expeditiously and justly be disposed of, and where no provision of these Rules appears to the appellate court or Commission to be applicable, the court or Commission shall resolve such question or issue, or shall give such directions as shall appear to be just and convenient, and in doing so the appellate court or Commission shall be guided, so far as practicable, by the Rules of the Supreme Court for the time being in force.

Part VI
Appeal to Her Majesty in Council

Lodging of Appeal

25. In any cause of faculty not involving matter of doctrine, ritual or ceremonial any party to the proceedings who wishes to appeal to Her Majesty in Council against the whole or part of a judgment of the Arches Court of Canterbury or the Chancery Court of York shall—
  (a) within 28 days of the delivery of judgment in writing leave with the Registrar of the Judicial Committee of the Privy Council a petition of appeal in the form prescribed by the Rules relating to the appellate jurisdiction of Her Majesty in Council on an appeal under the Measure; and
  (b) forthwith give notice in writing to every party to the proceedings of the presentation of the petition of appeal.

26. All matters relating to the appeal shall thereafter be governed by the Rules made by or applying to proceedings in the Judicial Committee of the Privy Council in exercise of the appellate jurisdiction of Her Majesty in Council.

Faculty Jurisdiction Rules 2000

SI 2000/2047

Part I

Preliminary

Citation, commencement and revocation

1. *Text omitted.*

Interpretation

2.—(1) In these Rules

'the archdeacon' means the archdeacon of each archdeaconry in the diocese;

'advisory committee' in relation to a diocese or archdeaconry means the Diocesan Advisory Committee of the diocese or of the diocese in which the archdeaconry is situated, as the case may be;

'article' includes any article appertaining to a building which is subject to the faculty jurisdiction by virtue of an order made under section 11(4) of the Measure;

'the chancellor' and 'the registrar' mean, in relation to any proceedings, the chancellor and the registrar respectively of the diocese in which the church, churchyard or building licensed for public worship (which is for the time being subject to the faculty jurisdiction by an order made under section 6 of the Faculty Jurisdiction Measure 1964 or which is not excluded from the faculty jurisdiction by order under section 11(3) of the Measure) is situated, and include any person appointed to act as the deputy of the chancellor or registrar, as the case may be;

'church' includes the curtilage of a church unless the context otherwise requires;

'churchyard' includes a consecrated burial ground not adjacent to the church;

'confirmatory faculty' means a faculty which validates any act requiring a faculty (including any work to the fabric or fixtures of any church or any movables therein, or the introduction into or removal from the church or churchyard of any item, or any work affecting any churchyard) which has been done without prior authorisation by faculty;

'the Council' refers to the Council for the Care of Churches;

'English Heritage' means the Historic Buildings and Monuments Commission for England;

'exhumation' means the removal from the ground, catacomb, mausoleum, or columbarium of a body or cremated human remains;

'interim faculty' means any licence or order made by the chancellor in respect of any works or proposals pending the final determination by him of a petition for faculty for such works or proposals;

'listed church' or 'listed building' means a building which is listed under the Planning (Listed Buildings and Conservation Areas) Act 1990;

'the Measure' means the Care of Churches and Ecclesiastical Jurisdiction Measure 1991;

'minister' has the same meaning in these Rules as in the Measure;

'national amenity society' means any of the following, the Ancient Monuments Society, the Council for British Archaeology, the Georgian Group, the Society for the Protection of Ancient Buildings, the Victorian Society, the Twentieth Century Society and such other body as may from time to time be designated by the Dean of the Arches and Auditor as a national amenity society for the purpose of the Measure;

'Statement of Needs' means a document which sets out the reasons why it is considered that the needs of the parish cannot be met without making changes to the church building and the reasons why the changes are regarded as necessary to assist the church in its worship and mission;

'Statement of Significance' means a document which summarises the historical development of the church and identifies the important features that make major contributions to the character of the church.

(2) The Interpretation Act 1978 shall apply for the interpretation of these Rules as it applies for the interpretation of Measures passed by the General Synod.

Part II
Petition and Public Notice

Seeking advisory committee advice

3.—(1) Before submitting a petition for a faculty in the consistory court intending applicants should seek the advice of the advisory committee in respect of the works or other proposals for which a faculty is required (except where the action proposed relates exclusively to exhumation or the reservation of a grave space).

(2) Except in a case within paragraph (4) intending applicants should submit to the advisory committee designs, plans, photographs and other documents giving particulars of the works or other proposals together with a summary list of the works or proposals.

(3) Where significant changes to a listed church are proposed the intending applicant should
   (a) provide the advisory committee (in addition to the particulars required by paragraph (2) of this rule) with a Statement of Significance and a Statement of Needs, and
   (b) if the works fall within paragraph 1 of Appendix B consult English Heritage, such of the national amenity societies as appears likely to have an interest in the church or the works, and the local planning authority in accordance with Appendix B.

(4) Where the intending applicants are proposing to carry out works to a tree or trees in a churchyard or in a consecrated burial ground for which a faculty is required they shall complete Form No 16 in Appendix C and send it to the advisory committee at the time of seeking the advice of the advisory committee in respect of the proposed works.

(5) If the advisory committee decides to recommend the works or proposals or to raise no objection to them its decision together with any provisos shall be set out in a certificate in Form No 1 in Appendix C and shall be sent to the intending applicants together with the designs, plans, photographs and other documents which were submitted to the advisory committee under paragraph (2) of this rule and are the subject of the certificate.

(6) If the advisory committee decides not to recommend the works or proposals it shall inform the intending applicants by way of a certificate in Form No 1 in Appendix C and shall advise them that they are entitled to petition for a faculty from the chancellor, if they so wish, notwithstanding the committee's decision.

(7) When the advisory committee issues a certificate under paragraph (5) or (6) the certificate may include a recommendation to the intending applicants that they should consult English Heritage, or the local planning authority, or one or more of the national amenity societies, or the Council for the Care of Churches or any other body or person about some or all of the works or other proposals for which a certificate is sought if they have not already done so, and the advisory committee shall consider including such a recommendation in any case where it appears to the committee that the works
   (a) involve alteration to or extension of a listed church to such an extent as is likely to affect its character as a building of special architectural or historic interest, or
   (b) are likely to affect the archaeological importance of the church or archaeological remains existing within the church or its curtilage, or
   (c) in the case of an unlisted church in a conservation area, will involve demolition affecting the exterior of the church.

Submission of petition

4.—(1) As soon as they have received the advice of the advisory committee under paragraph (5) or (6) of rule 3 the applicants may submit to the diocesan registry a petition for a faculty in Form No 2 in Appendix C in respect of the works or other proposals and

(a) the works or other proposals shall be fully and accurately stated in the petition and shall be the same as those in respect of which the advisory committee has supplied a certificate in Form No 1 in Appendix C under paragraph (5) or (6) of rule 3, and

(b) any designs, plans, photographs and other documents giving particulars of the works or proposals for which the faculty is required, together with the certificate of the advisory committee relating to those documents, shall be submitted with the petition.

(2) Where significant changes to a church are proposed a copy of the designs, plans, photographs and other documents submitted with the petition shall be displayed in the church to which the works or other proposals relate and shall remain on display until the petition for a faculty has been determined.

(3) As soon as they have received the advice of the advisory committee under rule 3(5) or (6) in respect of works within rule 3(4) the applicants may send or deliver to the diocesan registry the petition for a faculty in Form No 16 in Appendix C which was considered by the advisory committee.

(4) Notwithstanding that any of the requirements of rule 3 have not been complied with a petition may at any time be submitted to the diocesan registry and every petition shall (subject to rule 36) be in Form No 2 or in Form No 16 in Appendix C.

Petition for partial demolition or demolition

5. A Petition for a faculty for the partial demolition or demolition of a church shall include all such statements and information, so far as relevant, as are required by Form No 2 in Appendix C.

Public notice of petition for a faculty

6.—(1) As soon as a petitioner is ready to submit a petition for a faculty the petitioner shall fill in the public notice in Form No 3 in Appendix C (except where the petitioner is not the minister or a churchwarden or where the petition relates to exhumation or reservation of a grave space) and shall describe the works or proposals in the public notice in the same manner as they are described in the schedule to the petition.

(2) Notwithstanding paragraph (1) above any petitioner may, if he so wishes, consult the registrar for advice prior to completing any petition or public notice, and he should do so in respect of a public notice where the petition relates to a matter which is not within Appendix A.

(3) As soon as a petitioner has filled in the public notice he shall immediately
   (a) send or deliver to the registry the petition and the documents required by rule 4(1)(b) and a copy of the completed public notice; and
   (b) display the public notice in accordance with paragraph (4) below save that if he is not the minister or a churchwarden he shall send the public notice to the registrar for directions about display; and
   (c) send a copy of the public notice to English Heritage or other grant making body in accordance with the terms of any previous grant.

(4) Subject to paragraph (3)(b) of this rule and rule 13(10) a copy of the public notice shall be displayed for a continuous period of not less than 28 days in accordance with paragraphs (a) to (d) of this paragraph.
   (a) Display of the public notice shall take place as follows:
      (i) in the case of a petition relating to a parish church or its churchyard, display of the notice shall be at that parish church
      (ii) in the case of a petition relating to a church or place of worship (or any churchyard belonging to it) which is not a parish church, display of the notice shall be at that church or place of worship and also at the parish church or parish churches of the parish
      (iii) in the case of a petition relating to any other churchyard or consecrated burial ground, display of the notice shall be at the parish church (if any) and the churchyard or consecrated burial ground concerned.

(b) Display of the notice shall take place under paragraph (a)(i) and (ii)
  (i) inside the church on a notice board or in some other prominent position, and
  (ii) on a notice board outside that church or in some other prominent position (whether on the outside of the church door or elsewhere) so that it is readily visible to the public.
(c) Display of the notice shall take place in accordance with paragraph (b)(i) and (ii) in respect of each church or place of worship where display is required under paragraph (a)(i) and (ii).
(d) Display of the notice in accordance with paragraph (a)(iii) shall take place on a notice board outside the parish church (if any) and on a notice board or other suitable place at the churchyard or consecrated burial ground concerned so that it is readily visible to the public.

(5) If on receipt of the petition and copy public notice the registrar considers that
  (a) the works or proposals are not adequately described in the public notice, or
  (b) a copy of the public notice should be displayed inside or outside any other church or place of worship in the parish concerned, or
  (c) a copy of the public notice should be displayed in some prominent position elsewhere in the parish concerned (whether inside or outside a building) where it will be clearly visible to the public, or
  (d) the public notice should be displayed for a longer period than is provided for in paragraph (4) of this rule

then the registrar may give such directions to the petitioners as are appropriate in the circumstances of the case.

(6) Upon the expiry of the period of 28 days required under paragraph (4) or such longer period as may be directed under paragraph (5)(d) of this rule the public notice or a copy thereof shall be returned to the registrar by the petitioners with the certificate of publication duly completed in accordance with Form No 3 in Appendix C.

Part III
Matters Within the Archdeacon's Jurisdiction

Allocation to the archdeacon

7.—(1) Where a petition for a faculty for any of the works or other proposals specified in Appendix A to these Rules (not being works falling within rule 13(3)) is unopposed and the advisory committee recommends the works or proposals in question or raises no objection to them, the archdeacon may exercise the jurisdiction of the consistory court of the diocese in respect of every petition for faculty arising in that archdeaconry to the extent provided in that Appendix.

(2) Subject to rule 8, if the registrar is satisfied that the subject matter of the petition falls within the jurisdiction conferred upon an archdeacon under paragraph (1) of this rule the registrar shall endorse the petition accordingly and send it to the archdeacon for consideration.

(3) An archdeacon with jurisdiction under paragraph (1) shall not make a final determination in relation to any petition for faculty without first seeking the advice of the advisory committee in respect of the works or proposals the subject of the petition, provided that where the advisory committee supplied a certificate in Form No 1 under rule 3(5) above in respect of the same works or proposals not more than 12 months prior to the submitting of the petition the advisory committee may, if appropriate, confirm that they do not wish to alter that certificate.

(4) Having decided to grant a faculty the archdeacon shall endorse the petition accordingly and shall return it to the registrar whereupon the registrar on the expiry of the period for objection specified in rule 16 and provided the petition is unopposed shall issue
  (a) the faculty in Form No 5 in Appendix C, and

(b) a certificate in Form No 6 in Appendix C to be completed in accordance with the requirement in the faculty.

(5) If any person objects to the grant of a faculty before the archdeacon has determined the matter the registrar shall notify the archdeacon who shall immediately return the petition to the registrar and if an objection is received after the archdeacon has endorsed the petition under paragraph (4) above the archdeacon's decision shall be of no effect and the petition shall be referred to the chancellor by the registrar and be dealt with by the chancellor.

Referral from the archdeacon to the chancellor

8.—(1) An archdeacon who
  (a) is the minister of the parish to which the petition relates, or
  (b) has been personally involved with the petitioners in relation to the subject matter of the petition or otherwise to such an extent that the archdeacon deems it inappropriate to act in the matter

shall decline to exercise jurisdiction in relation to the petition for a faculty and shall so inform the registrar prior to the allocation of the petition, or if this is not practicable shall as soon as possible return the petition and accompanying papers to the registrar who shall immediately endorse the petition as one to be dealt with by the chancellor.

(2) An archdeacon may for any reason decline in advance to exercise jurisdiction in relation to any petition for faculty within Appendix A and may after referral of a petition falling within the archdeacon's jurisdiction, return the petition to the registrar with a request that the petition or any matter raised in it be referred to the chancellor for decision or advice.

(3) If an archdeacon becomes aware of any matter for which a faculty is required and considers that the matter
  (a) needs to be dealt with as a matter of urgency without reference to the advisory committee for advice in accordance with section 15(2) of the Measure, or
  (b) may necessitate the issue of an injunction, the making of a restoration order or the grant of any interim faculty pending the final determination of the matter, or
  (c) gives rise to any question as to the payment of costs or expenses,

then whether or not a petition has been submitted the archdeacon shall inform the registrar who shall immediately refer the matter to the chancellor who may give such licence or other directions in respect of the matter on such terms or conditions as are appropriate in the circumstances of the case.

Temporary re-ordering

9.—(1) On the application of a minister and the majority of the parochial church council an archdeacon may give a licence in writing in accordance with Form No 7 in Appendix C for a temporary period not exceeding 15 months for a scheme of minor re-ordering provided the archdeacon is satisfied that
  (a) the scheme does not involve any interference with the fabric of the church and
  (b) it does not involve the fixing of any item to the fabric of the church nor the disposal of any fixture and
  (c) if the scheme involves the moving of any item, the same is to be done by suitably competent or qualified persons and such item will be safeguarded and stored in the church or in such other place as is approved by the archdeacon, and can easily be reinstated.

(2) The archdeacon may add such other conditions to the licence as may be considered necessary.

(3) A copy of any such licence shall be submitted to the registrar and the secretary to the advisory committee.

(4) The period specified in the licence shall not be extended by the archdeacon provided that where a petition for a chancellor's faculty in respect of the scheme is submitted to the registry not

later than two months before the expiry of the period the scheme shall be deemed to be authorised until the determination of the petition by the chancellor.

(5) An archdeacon may for any reason decline to grant such a licence in which event the archdeacon shall advise the minister to apply to the chancellor for an interim faculty authorising the scheme.

Referral by the registrar to the chancellor

10.—(1) Notwithstanding anything in rule 7(1) the registrar shall refer the petition to the chancellor when it appears that
- (a) a confirmatory faculty is required, or
- (b) the proposed works or proposals raise a question of law or as to the doctrine, ritual or ceremonial of the Church of England or affect the legal rights of any person or body, or
- (c) any person or body may need to be specially notified, or
- (d) there is uncertainty whether the subject matter of the petition falls within the jurisdiction conferred on the archdeacon by rule 7(1), or
- (e) the advisory committee has not recommended the works or proposals and has so certified by paragraph 4 of Form No 1 in Appendix C, or
- (f) the petition raises matters which may justify the issue of any injunction, or
- (g) for any other reason it is desirable to refer the petition to the chancellor.

(2) Where a matter is being dealt with by the archdeacon if at any stage in the proceedings the registrar becomes aware that information supplied in the petition is incorrect, or that information has been omitted from the petition, so that the matter falls outside the jurisdiction conferred on the archdeacon under rule 7(1) the registrar shall in writing immediately cancel the allocation of the petition to the archdeacon, give written notice thereof to the archdeacon and refer the matter to the chancellor, and the archdeacon shall immediately return the petition and accompanying documents to the registrar.

(3) If any petition is referred to the chancellor pursuant to rules 8(1) or (2), or 10(1) or (2) above then, unless the chancellor orders otherwise, the matter shall proceed from the stage reached in the proceedings immediately before the petition was sent to the archdeacon under rule 7(2) as if the petition had been presented to the chancellor from the commencement of proceedings.

Register of petitions

11. On receipt of any petition for a faculty for which the advice of the advisory committee is required to be sought under the Measure or these Rules the registrar shall notify the secretary to the advisory committee of the details of the petition in Form No 8 in Appendix C and the secretary shall enter the details in the register of petitions maintained on behalf of the advisory committee.

Part IV
Matters Within the Chancellor's Jurisdiction

Matters for chancellor

12.—(1) Unless otherwise provided in these Rules all faculty matters shall be dealt with by the chancellor.

(2) Any faculty granted by the chancellor in unopposed proceedings shall (subject to rule 36) be issued by the registrar in Form No 5 in Appendix C together with a certificate in Form No 6 in Appendix C to be completed in accordance with the requirement in the faculty.

Requirements as to notice of petition

13.—(1) If the chancellor directs or the law otherwise requires any person to be specially notified the registrar shall serve on him a copy of the public notice.

(2) The chancellor may order that relevant details from the public notice be published in such newspapers or other publications and within such period of time as the chancellor directs.

(3) Subject to the generality of rule 13(1), where it appears to the chancellor on preliminary consideration of the petition that the works for which a faculty is sought
   (a) involve alteration to or extension of a listed church to such an extent as is likely to affect its character as a building of special architectural or historic interest, or
   (b) are likely to affect the archaeological importance of the church or archaeological remains existing within the church or its curtilage, or
   (c) involve demolition affecting the exterior of an unlisted church in a conservation area

then, unless it appears to the chancellor from the available information that each of the following bodies has previously been consulted about those works and has indicated that it has no objection or comment to make the chancellor shall direct that English Heritage, the local planning authority and such of the national amenity societies as appears to be likely to have an interest in the church or the works shall be specially notified in accordance with the criteria applicable to consultation set out in paragraphs 2, 3 or 4 of Appendix B as appropriate.

(4) In any case falling within
   (i) paragraph (3)(a) of this rule which affects a grade I or grade II* listed church or the exterior of a grade II listed church, or
   (ii) paragraph 3(c) of this rule,

the chancellor shall direct that a notice stating the substance of the petition and giving a date by which any objection is to reach the registrar shall be published by the petitioners in a newspaper circulating in the locality and publication shall take place within 14 days of the giving of the direction, or within such other period as the chancellor may direct.

(5) If the chancellor considers that the works or proposals intended to be carried out in a churchyard will or may affect a grave or memorial maintained by the Commonwealth War Graves Commission the chancellor shall direct that the Commonwealth War Graves Commission be specially notified and the registrar shall pursuant to such direction serve on the said Commission a copy of the public notice.

(6) Where a body has been specially notified pursuant to paragraph (3) or (5) of this rule that body shall have a period of 28 days from the date of service of special notice within which to send to the registry and the petitioners a written notice of objection containing the information required by Form No 4 in Appendix C or to send comments to the registrar in respect of the proposed works.

(7) Where the petition is for a faculty for the partial demolition or demolition of a church and falls within section 17(2) or (3)(a) of the Measure
   (a) the registrar shall give notice in writing to the bodies specified in section 17(4)(b) and, if relevant, to the bodies specified in section 17(5)(a) of the Measure and the bodies concerned shall have a period of 28 days from the date of the notice within which to give advice or to send to the registry and the petitioners a written notice of objection containing the information required by Form No 4 in Appendix C in respect of the proposed partial demolition or demolition,
   (b) the notice stating the substance of the petition (which is required by section 17(4)(a)(ii) of the Measure to be published by the petitioners in the London Gazette and in such other newspaper as the chancellor may direct) shall be published:
      (i) in the case of the London Gazette not more than 28 days after the petition was submitted to the registry,
      (ii) in the case of such other newspaper (including a newspaper circulating in the locality) within such period as the chancellor shall direct or, if no period is directed, within 14 days of the giving of the direction.

(8) Where a petition relates exclusively to exhumation or reservation of a grave space or in any case where the chancellor gives directions in relation to a public notice or an amended public notice then subject to paragraph (9) below the registrar shall complete the public notice and give such directions for display of the public notice under rule 6(5)(b) to (d) as the registrar considers appropriate or as the chancellor has directed.

(9) In the case of a petition for a faculty for exhumation, the chancellor shall have the following powers that is to say:
  (a) if the chancellor is satisfied that any near relatives of the deceased person still living and any other persons who in the opinion of the chancellor it is reasonable to regard as being concerned with the matter are the petitioners or that they consent to the proposed faculty being granted, then the chancellor may dispense with the issue of a public notice and decree the issue of the faculty immediately;
  (b) in any other case the chancellor may dispense with public notice and may direct that any of the persons referred to in sub-paragraph (a) above who are not the petitioners shall be specially notified.

(10) In any case where the chancellor is satisfied that a matter is an emergency that involves interests of safety or health, or the preservation of a church or part of it, and is of sufficient urgency to justify the grant of a faculty without obtaining the advice of the advisory committee, the chancellor
  (a) may dispense with the display of a notice under rule 6, and
  (b) having regard to all the circumstances may direct that a short period of notice be given to the persons or bodies identified in the directions,

and thereafter the chancellor may order the issue of a faculty immediately.

Advice of advisory committee

14. Save where a petition relates exclusively to exhumation or reservation of a grave space or the chancellor is satisfied that the matter is sufficiently urgent to justify the grant of a faculty without obtaining the advisory committee's advice the chancellor shall not make a final determination in any cause of faculty without first seeking the advice of the advisory committee in respect of the works or proposals the subject of the petition, provided that where the advisory committee supplied a certificate in Form No 1 under rule 3(5) in respect of the same works or proposals not more than 12 months prior to the submission of the petition the advisory committee may, if appropriate, confirm that they do not wish to alter that certificate.

Consultation with the Council for the Care of Churches

15.—(1) Paragraph (2) of this rule applies where a petition for a faculty—
  (a) concerns an article of particular historic, architectural, archaeological or artistic interest, and involves the introduction, conservation, alteration or disposal of that article,
  (b) involves the alteration to or extension of a listed church or re-ordering of any church, which is likely in the opinion of the chancellor significantly to affect (when completed) the setting of any such article as is described in sub-paragraph (a), or
  (c) involves the movement or removal of any such article, which in the opinion of the advisory committee may be adversely affected thereby unless specific precautions are taken.

(2) Where paragraph (1) applies then, unless the chancellor is satisfied that there has already been consultation with the Council for the Care of Churches in respect of the proposals the subject of the petition, insofar as they relate to the article in question, the chancellor shall direct the registrar to serve on the Council notice in Form No 9 in Appendix C.

(3) In any case not within paragraph 1 of this rule where the chancellor considers that advice from the Council would be of assistance in relation to a petition for a faculty, the chancellor may direct the registrar to serve on the Council notice in Form No 9.

(4) Where notice in Form No 9 is served under this rule, the registrar shall also serve on the Council a copy of the petition and such plans and other relevant documents which were submitted to the Registry under rule 4(1) as the registrar considers appropriate.

(5) The written advice of the Council in response to such a notice shall be sent to the registrar as soon as practicable but in any event no later than six weeks from the date of receipt of the notice;

if no such advice is received within six weeks (or such longer period as may be granted on request from the Council), the chancellor may proceed to determine the petition without such advice.

(6) For the purposes of this rule, 'article' includes not only an ornament or moveable object but also an object fixed to land or a building, and a part of any such object.

Objections to petition

16.—(1) Any interested person who wishes to object to a proposed faculty being granted for all or some of the works or other proposals shall at any time during the period of 28 days display of public notice of the petition required by rule 6(4) of such longer period as may be directed under rule 6(5)(d) write to the registrar and to the petitioners a letter of objection so as to arrive within the period of 28 days.

(2) In this rule 'interested person', in relation to a petition for a faculty, means—
  (a) any person who is resident in the ecclesiastical parish concerned and any person whose name is entered on the church electoral roll of the ecclesiastical parish concerned but who does not reside therein;
  (b) the archdeacon of the archdeaconry in which the parish concerned is situated;
  (c) the parochial church council;
  (d) the local planning authority for the area in which the church or place of worship is situated;
  (e) any national amenity society;
  (f) any other body designated by the chancellor for the purpose of the petition; and
  (g) any other person or body appearing to the chancellor to have a sufficient interest in the subject matter of the petition.

(3) Following receipt of a letter of objection from an interested person (whether as to all or some of the works or proposals) the registrar shall after the end of the period of display of the public notice inform the objector in writing that he may:
  (a) leave the chancellor to take the letter of objection into account in reaching a decision without the objector becoming a party in the proceedings, in which case a copy of the letter of objection will be sent to the petitioners to allow them to comment on it before the chancellor reaches a decision, or
  (b) send or deliver to the registrar formal written particulars of objection in Form No 4 in Appendix C and thereupon become a party in the proceedings.

(4) The registrar shall in addition
  (i) inform the interested person that unless he chooses alternative (b) in paragraph (3) above, he will not be entitled to be heard at any hearing of the matter in open court in the consistory court which the chancellor may decide to hold, nor to make written representations if the proceedings are to be dealt with under rule 26, nor will he be a party to the proceedings for the purpose of any order for costs which may be made by the chancellor under section 60 of the Ecclesiastical Jurisdiction Measure 1963;
  (ii) inform the interested person that if he chooses alternative (b) in paragraph (3) above he will be entitled to participate in the proceedings at a hearing in the consistory court or in any disposal of the proceedings under rule 26 and that he will be a party to the proceedings for the purpose of any order for costs which may be made by the chancellor under section 60 of the Ecclesiastical Jurisdiction Measure 1963, and shall send him a brief statement in terms approved by the chancellor as to the principles which apply to costs in the consistory court; and
  (iii) provide the interested person with a copy of Form No 4 notifying him that if he chooses alternative (b) in paragraph 3 above he must send or deliver his completed Form No 4 to arrive at the registry within 21 days of receipt of the letter of notification and form from the registrar and also serve a copy of his completed Form No 4 on the petitioners within the same period of 21 days at such address as the registrar may direct, and

(iv) further inform the interested person that if no response and no Form No 4 is received by the registrar within the period of 21 days as required by sub-paragraph (iii) above, he will be treated as having chosen the alternative course of action in paragraph (3)(a) and the matter will proceed accordingly.

(5) Where any person has taken the course of action in paragraph (3)(a), or is to be treated as having done so under paragraph (4)(iv), then the registrar shall, after the expiry of the period of 21 days
- (a) forward a copy of any letter of objection to the petitioners for comment by them within 7 days, and
- (b) not later than 7 days after expiry of the last date for comment, forward to the chancellor a copy of any letter of objection received under paragraph (1) above, together with any comments received from the petitioners.

(6) On receipt of any letters or comments forwarded by the registrar under paragraph (5), the chancellor shall take them into account in reaching a decision on the petition, or in giving any directions in the proceedings.

Unopposed petition

17. In a case where either no letter of objection has been received under rule 16 or, if such letter of objection has been received, no particulars of objection have been submitted within the time allowed by rule 16(4)(iii), or where the chancellor is satisfied that all the parties concerned consent to the grant of a faculty, the chancellor may, subject to the production of any relevant evidence, and subject to the requirements of section 17 of the Measure, grant the faculty.

Further pleadings

18. Where particulars of objection have been submitted to the registry the petitioners may, and if ordered to do so shall, submit to the registry a written answer thereto within 21 days of the submitting of those particulars and shall serve a copy of the answer on each of the other parties.

Directions

19.—(1) In any case the chancellor may give directions in writing without a hearing or may hold a hearing for directions which the parties or their representatives (whether or not legally qualified) and such other persons as the chancellor deems fit will be requested to attend. The chancellor or the registrar (if authorised by the chancellor) shall preside at any hearing for directions.

(2) The purposes of the giving of directions are:
- (i) to encourage the parties to co-operate with each other in the exchange of information and documents in preparation for a hearing;
- (ii) to fix timetables or otherwise control the progress of the proceedings;
- (iii) to identify the issues which will need to be resolved at a hearing;
- (iv) to deal with as many aspects of the matter as possible on the same occasion;
- (v) to give directions to ensure that the petition is considered and determined as quickly and efficiently as possible.

(3) Having regard to paragraph (2) above the chancellor or the registrar shall direct as appropriate
- (i) how any evidence may be presented, whether by written statement or report followed by oral evidence at the hearing, or otherwise;
- (ii) where there is a large number of objections making a similar point or points in the written objections that a specified number of them shall represent the interest of all those objectors at the hearing and may appear by themselves or by representatives (whether or not legally qualified);
- (iii) that there be an exchange of the reports of expert witnesses to be called by the parties and that they be requested to identify matters upon which they agree and those upon which they disagree;

(iv) that the number of expert witnesses to be called on behalf of any party be limited to such number as the chancellor or registrar deems appropriate in the case in question;

(v) that any reports provided to the chancellor by the advisory committee, the Council for the Care of Churches, English Heritage, any national amenity society or any local planning authority or other body shall be copied to the parties not less than 21 days before the date of the hearing.

(4) In deciding whether and how to exercise the powers under this rule, the chancellor or registrar shall have regard to all the circumstances including:
   (a) the justice of the case;
   (b) the desirability of minimising dispute;
   (c) saving unnecessary expense;
   (d) avoiding delay;
   (e) the number of objectors and the grounds of objection to the proposals.

Time and place of hearing

20.—(1) Within the period of 28 days after the expiry of the last date of compliance with any directions given under rule 19 above or, where the case is one to which section 17(4)(d) of the Measure applies, the registrar shall lay all the documents submitted to the registry before the chancellor who shall give directions as to a time and place for the hearing of the case.

(2) In addition to notifying the parties the registrar shall send to the archdeacon, the Council, the advisory committee, and any other body which has given advice to the chancellor, written notice of the time and place of the hearing.

Evidence

21.—(1) The evidence at the hearing of any proceedings for a faculty shall be given orally save that the chancellor upon application by a party or the court of its own motion may by order direct
   (a) that all or any part of the evidence may be given before an examiner appointed by the chancellor or by affidavit, or
   (b) subject to paragraphs (2) and (3) below, that a written statement may be given in evidence without the attendance of the maker of the statement.

(2) An application to submit a written statement in evidence at the hearing may be made by or on behalf of any person who is not a party to the proceedings and the chancellor may give leave for a written statement to be admitted in evidence without the attendance of the maker of the statement provided that a copy of the written statement is submitted to the registry and that a copy is delivered by that person to the parties not less than 21 days before the date of the hearing.

(3) Notwithstanding anything in paragraph (1) above, the chancellor shall be entitled on receiving a copy of a written statement to require the attendance at the hearing of the maker of the statement for cross-examination by the parties, and if any party on receiving a copy of the statement applies to the chancellor for an order requiring the attendance of the maker of the statement at the hearing for cross-examination, the chancellor may make an order accordingly, and in the event of the failure of the maker of the statement to attend the hearing when required to do so under this paragraph, his written statement shall not be admitted in evidence save in exceptional circumstances with the leave of the chancellor.

Petition for partial demolition or demolition

22. An application to give evidence made by a member of the Council for the Care of Churches or other person by virtue of section 17(4)(d) of the Measure shall be made to the registrar and shall
   (a) if made by a member of the Council or a person authorised by the Council, be in Form No 10 in Appendix C and be submitted to the diocesan registry not more than six weeks after the Council has received notice in writing of the petition under section 17(4)(b) of the Measure;

(b) if made by any other persons, be in Form No 11 in Appendix C and be submitted to the registry not more than four weeks after the date of the last publication in accordance with rule 13(7) of the notice stating the substance of the petition;

(c) be accompanied in either case (a) or (b) with a statement of the evidence to be relied upon.

Evidence of Council for the Care of Churches

23. In any case not falling under rule 22 an application to give evidence may be made by a member of the Council for the Care of Churches or other person authorised by the Council to the registrar in Form No 10 in Appendix C and be submitted to the diocesan registry not less than 21 days before the hearing and shall be accompanied by a statement of the evidence to be relied upon.

English Heritage

24. In any case where English Heritage has been specially notified pursuant to rule 13(3) or in any other case an application to give evidence may be made by English Heritage to the registrar in Form No 10 in Appendix C and be submitted to the diocesan registry not less than 21 days before the hearing and shall be accompanied by a statement of the evidence to be relied upon.

Judge's witness

25.—(1) The chancellor may direct the attendance of a member of the advisory committee, the Council for the Care of Churches or any other person to give evidence at the hearing of any petition for a faculty, if it appears to the chancellor that the person directed to attend may be able to give relevant evidence and is willing to give it.

(2) Where any person has applied in accordance with rule 22, 23 or 24 or has been directed under paragraph (1) to give evidence in proceedings for a faculty, the registrar shall give to the parties to the proceedings not less than 14 days' notice in writing that the evidence is to be given and of the name and address of the proposed witness and, in the case of a witness directed under paragraph (1) of this rule, of the nature of the evidence required of him.

(3) Evidence given by any such person as is referred to in paragraph (2) of this rule shall be subject to cross-examination by the party or parties to the proceedings and any such witness may be permitted to ask questions of the party or parties with the leave of the chancellor.

Disposal of proceedings by written representation

26.—(1) If the chancellor considers it expedient to do so and is satisfied that all the parties to the proceedings have agreed in writing, then the chancellor may order that the proceedings shall be determined upon consideration of written representations instead of by a hearing in court provided that no such order may be made in any case in which the chancellor is required to hear evidence in open court for the purposes of section 17(2) or 3(a) by virtue of section 17(4) of the Measure.

(2) Where an order has been made by the chancellor under paragraph (1) above the registrar shall give notice

(a) that the petitioners shall submit to the registry and serve on each of the other parties within 21 days of the direction a written statement in support of their case including the documentary or other evidence upon which they wish to rely;

(b) that each of the other parties shall not more than 21 days after the submitting of the petitioners' statement submit to the registry and serve on the petitioners a written statement in reply to the petitioners' statement and in support of his case including any documentary or other evidence upon which he wishes to rely;

(c) that the petitioners may not more than 14 days after the submitting of the statement of an opposing party submit to the registry and service on such opposing party a written statement in response.

(3) If any party does not comply with any such direction, the chancellor may declare him to be in default and may proceed to dispose of the case without any further reference to such party.

(4) Any party against whom an order declaring him to be in default is made may at any time apply to the court to revoke that order, and the chancellor may as a matter of discretion revoke the order on such terms as to costs or otherwise as may be just.

(5) Notwithstanding the existence of an order that the proceedings shall be dealt with by written representations, the chancellor may at any stage revoke the order and direct that the proceedings shall be determined at an oral hearing and the chancellor shall thereupon give directions for the future conduct of the proceedings.

(6) The chancellor may, whether or not an application is made to the court by any party, inspect the church or any article or thing the subject of the petition or concerning which any question arises in the proceedings.

(7) If no order has been made under paragraph (5), the chancellor shall determine the proceedings upon the pleadings and the written statements and evidence submitted under this rule, and the chancellor's decision shall be as valid and binding on all parties as if it had been made after an oral hearing.

(8) The chancellor or the registrar (if so authorised by the chancellor) may give such other directions as appear just and convenient for the expeditious dispatch of proceedings under this rule.

Issue of faculty after opposed proceedings

27. If the chancellor decides to grant a faculty allowing either an oral hearing or a determination on the basis of written representations under rule 26 the registrar shall issue a faculty in Form No 5 in Appendix C adapted to meet the circumstances of the case and shall issue a certificate in Form No 6 in Appendix C to be completed in accordance with the requirement in the faculty.

PART V
MISCELLANEOUS AND GENERAL

Appointment of person to act for archdeacon

28.—(1) In making an appointment under section 16(3) of the Measure of a person to act in place of an archdeacon on the ground of incapacity, the bishop may act on such evidence of the incapacity of the archdeacon as he shall think sufficient, and a statement of the fact of the incapacity in the instrument of appointment shall be conclusive.

(2) An instrument of appointment under section 16(3) shall be in Form No 12 in Appendix C.

Removal of article to place of safety

29.—(1) In any case where an archdeacon is of the opinion that an article falling within section 21(1) of the Measure should be removed to a place of safety immediately the archdeacon may make an order in Form No 13 in Appendix C.

(2) In any case not requiring an immediate order under paragraph (1) of this rule, an archdeacon shall not make an order under section 21 of the Measure unless and until
    (a) the churchwardens and any other person having custody of the article and the parochial church council and the advisory committee have been notified by Form No 14 in Appendix C of the facts as they appear to the archdeacon and that written representations made by any of them will be considered if made before the date specified in the notice being not less than 28 days after the service of the notice, and
    (b) any representations duly made under sub-paragraph (a) have been considered.

(3) Subject to fulfilling the requirements of paragraph (2) of this rule in any case falling within that paragraph the archdeacon may make an order in Form No 15 in Appendix C.

Appointment of person to sit as clerk of the court in place of registrar

30. If the chancellor by whom any proceedings for a faculty are to be heard is of opinion that by reason of the fact that the registrar has acted for any of the parties or has otherwise been personally connected with the proceedings the registrar ought not to sit as clerk of the court at the hearing, another

practising solicitor or diocesan registrar shall be appointed by the chancellor to sit as such clerk in place of the registrar.

Service of document

31.—(1) Service of any document may be effected—
- (a) by leaving the document at the proper address of the person to be served, or
- (b) by sending it by post to that address, or
- (c) by leaving it at a document exchange as provided for in paragraph (3) of this rule; or
- (d) by FAX as provided for in paragraph (4) of this rule; or
- (e) in such other manner (including electronic means) as the chancellor or registrar may direct.

(2) For the purpose of this rule, and of the Interpretation Act 1978 in its application to this rule, the proper address of any person on whom a document is to be served under this rule shall be—
- (a) his usual or last known address, or
- (b) the business address of the solicitor (if any) who is acting for him in the proceedings.

(3) Where—
- (a) the proper address for service includes a numbered box at a document exchange; or
- (b) there is inscribed on the writing paper of the party on whom the document is served (where such party acts in person) or on the writing paper of his solicitor (where such party acts by solicitor) a document exchange box number, and such a party or his solicitor (as the case may be) has not indicated in writing to the party serving the document that he is unwilling to accept service through a document exchange,

service of the document may be effected by leaving the document addressed to that numbered box at that document exchange or at a document exchange which transmits documents every business day to that document exchange; and any document which is left at a document exchange in accordance with this paragraph shall, unless the contrary is proved, be deemed to have been served on the second business day following the day on which it is left.

(4) Service by FAX may be effected where
- (a) the party serving the document acts by a solicitor;
- (b) the party on whom the document is served acts by a solicitor and service is effected by transmission to the business address of such a solicitor; and
- (c) the solicitor acting for the party on whom the document is served has indicated in writing to the solicitor serving the document that he is willing to accept service by FAX at a specified FAX number and the document is transmitted to that number and for this purpose the inscription of a FAX number on the writing paper of a solicitor shall be deemed to indicate that such a solicitor is willing to accept service by FAX unless he has indicated in writing that he is not prepared to do so.

(5) Any document required by these Rules to be submitted to the diocesan registry may be delivered at the registry, or sent by post properly addressed to the registrar at the registry.

General provisions

32.—(1) Where anything is required by these Rules to be done not more than a specified number of days or weeks after a specified act or event, the day on which the act or event occurred shall not be counted.

(2) The registrar or chancellor, on an application made by the person concerned, or the court of its own motion, may extend the time within which anything is required to be done by these Rules and the application may be made although the time has expired.

(3) The registrar or chancellor may exercise the power under paragraph (2) on an application made without notice to any other party, or may give directions for the giving of notice of the application and for a hearing.

(4) Any such application may be granted on such terms as the registrar or chancellor thinks just.

Non-compliance and setting aside

33.—(1) Non-compliance with any of these Rules shall not render any proceeding void unless the chancellor so directs, but the proceedings may be set aside, either wholly or in part, as irregular, or may be amended or otherwise dealt with in such manner and upon such terms as the chancellor thinks fit.

(2) Whenever it appears to the chancellor that it is just and expedient to do so the chancellor may order that a faculty be
- (a) set aside, or
- (b) amended, provided that the amendment will not constitute a substantial change in the works or proposals already authorised by the faculty.

Procedural questions

34. Where, in the exercise of the faculty jurisdiction, any procedural question or issue arises, or it is expedient that any procedural direction shall be given in order that the proceedings may expeditiously and justly be disposed of, and where no provision of these Rules appears to the chancellor to be applicable, the chancellor shall resolve such question or issue, or shall give such directions as shall appear to be just and convenient, and in doing so shall be guided, so far as practicable, by the Civil Procedure Rules for the time being in force.

Adjournment of hearing

35. The chancellor may adjourn the hearing of any proceedings or application from time to time on such terms as the chancellor considers just.

Departure from forms in Appendix C

36.—(1) Where any of these Rules (other than Rules 3(4) and (5), 4(1) and (4) and 6(1) and (6)) require a document to be in a form set out in Appendix C, and that form is not in all respects appropriate, the Rules shall be construed as requiring a form of the like character, with such variations as circumstances may require, to be used.

(2) The chancellor may approve and direct forms to be used where a faculty is sought for exhumation or reservation of a grave space or in relation to any memorial in a churchyard or consecrated burial ground or in any other appropriate case except where any of these Rules (other than rule 4(1)) require a document to be in a form set out in Appendix C.

Application

37. These Rules shall not apply to any building, curtilage, object or structure which is subject to the faculty jurisdiction by virtue of section 3(2) of the Care of Places of Worship Measure 1999 and to which the Faculty Jurisdiction (Care of Places of Worship) Rules 2000 apply.

Transitional provisions

38. *Text omitted.*

Appendix A

(Rule 7(1))

(A) In addition to any authority conferred on the archdeacon by the chancellor's guidance under section 11(8) of the Measure, the archdeacon has jurisdiction in faculty matters in respect of any of the matters set out below which affect any parish church, licensed building, consecrated chapel, curtilage of such building or churchyard (whether consecrated or not), which is within the jurisdiction of the consistory court.

(B) In any case where a church has been in receipt of grant aid from English Heritage or other publicly funded grant making body, a faculty shall not be granted until the archdeacon is satisfied that the specification for the works to the fabric under items 1(i) and (ii) or works involving additions to the fabric under item 2(b) has been agreed with English Heritage or other publicly funded grant making body as is required by the terms of the relevant grant.

1. **Work to the fabric**
    (i) Minor structural alterations not involving demolition or partial demolition;
    (ii) external or internal decoration or redecoration except where in the opinion of the advisory committee the work proposed is likely to affect the character of the church as a building of special architectural or historic interest;
    (iii) repairs (using matching materials);
    (iv) treatment of timber against beetle or fungal activity.

2. **Work affecting fixtures**
    (a) Repairs
        (i) repairs and alterations to an existing heating system;
        (ii) repairs to and redecoration of fixtures (with matching materials);
        (iii) repairs to broken or cracked quarries in clear glazed windows;
        (iv) repairs, rewiring and minor alterations to an existing electrical system;
        (v) repairs to lightning conductors;
        (vi) repairs to organs or harmoniums using matching materials;
        (vii) repairs using matching materials to bells and bell frames and replacement of parts not requiring the removal of the bells from their frames;
        (viii) repairs using matching materials to and redecoration of clocks and clock faces;
        (ix) treatment of fixtures against beetle or fungal activity;
        (x) repair of flagpole fixed to the fabric of the building;
        (xi) repair of wire mesh window guards with non-ferrous fittings.
    (b) New work

The following items of new work (except where the advisory committee has certified that the work proposed is likely to affect
    (a) the character of the church as a building of special architectural or historic interest, or
    (b) the archaeological importance of the church or
    (c) archaeological remains existing within the church or its curtilage):
        (i) installation of a new heating system including laying of electrical cables, gas pipes or water mains through the churchyard;
        (ii) installation of a sound reinforcement system or loop system or alteration to an existing system;
        (iii) installation of a new electrical system or lighting or floodlighting including laying of electrical cables through the churchyard;
        (iv) installation of a wall offertory box;
        (v) installation of a wall safe in a vestry;
        (vi) installation of a lightning conductor;
        (vii) installation of security cameras and alarms or closed circuit television security systems;
        (viii) installation of wire mesh window guards with non-ferrous fittings.

3. **Work affecting movables**
    (i) Introduction of any article which may lawfully be used in the performance of divine service or the rites of the Church (other than an aumbry);
    (ii) repairs to movables (using matching materials) not including Royal Coats of Arms, unfixed hatchments, heraldic achievements, paintings, historic textiles, historic silver and base metal work;

    (iii) installation of minor items of furniture or minor fixtures in the church;
    (iv) provision of new or replacement carpets and curtains;
    (v) introduction of altar frontals and falls;
    (vi) a scheme for replacement of all or a substantial number of hassocks;
    (vii) laying up of banners;
    (viii) introduction of a Book of Remembrance and a stand for it; and
    (ix) removal or disposal of any items (iii)–(vii) above.

4. **Work affecting churchyards**
    (i) Re-surfacing of paths in the same material resulting in the same appearance;
    (ii) repairs to walls, fences, gates and lych gates where matching materials are to be used;
    (iii) introduction of a garden seat (including any memorial inscription);
    (iv) provision or replacement or repainting in a new colour scheme of a noticeboard;
    (v) introduction of a free standing flagpole.

Appendix B

(Rule 3)

Consultation with English Heritage, any national amenity society and the local planning authority

1. Where the works for which a faculty is to be sought
    (a) involve alteration to or extension of a church which is listed under the Planning (Listed Buildings and Conservation Areas) Act 1990 to such an extent as is likely to affect its character as a building of special architectural or historic interest, or
    (b) are likely to affect the archaeological importance of the church or archaeological remains existing within the church or its curtilage or,
    (c) involve demolition affecting the exterior of an unlisted church in a conservation area

then, at the same time as advice is being sought from the advisory committee consultation should take place with English Heritage, any national amenity society likely to have an interest in the church or works, and the local planning authority so far as provided by and in accordance with the criteria set out in the following paragraphs.

2. **Consultation with English Heritage**

2.1 The likely effect of the works for which a faculty is sought will determine whether or not English Heritage should be consulted.
    (i) Grade I or II*. Even small alterations to the structure of a church listed Grade I or II* can affect the character of the building. These include the introduction of different materials or features, the covering over or removal of parts of the structure, changing the composition of existing elements such as stained glass windows, sub-division or additions to the fabric as well as removal of elements or piercing through historic fabric. Consultation should take place in respect of any alteration or extension within paragraph 1(a);
    (ii) Grade II. Consultation should take place for a Grade II church in respect of alteration within paragraph (1)(a) which comprises the demolition or removal of all or a substantial part of the structure of the interior. For this purpose the structure of the interior includes principal internal elements such as a staircase, gallery, load-bearing wall, floor structure or roof structure and major internal fixtures such as fixed pews, a rood screen or an organ;
    (iii) Archaeology. Consultation should take place in respect of works within paragraph 1(b) affecting any church or its curtilage.

3. The national amenity societies

The age of the church and the nature and likely effect of the works for which a faculty is to be sought will determine which one or more of the national amenity societies should be consulted.

    3.1. Any society likely to have an interest in the church or works should be consulted in respect of works within paragraph 1(a), (b) or (c).

    3.2. Consultation in respect of alteration or extension within paragraph 1(a) should take place to a church of any grade (I, II* or II). Alteration for this purpose has the meaning given in paragraph 5.

4. The local planning authority

Although listed building consent is not required in addition to a faculty, except where there is an external object or structure listed separately from the church building, consultation should take place with the local planning authority in any case falling within paragraph 1(a) or (b) above. Consultation should also take place for works within paragraph 1(c).

    4.1. Consultation in respect of an alteration within paragraph 1(a) should take place whatever the grade (I, II* or II). Alteration for this purpose has the meaning given in paragraph 5.

5. Meaning of alteration for the purpose of consultation with the national amenity societies and the local planning authority

For the purpose of consultation under paragraphs 3.2 and 4.1 alteration of a church includes

    (a) the demolition of a significant part of the structure of the interior, which includes principal internal elements such as a staircase, gallery, floor structure or roof structure;

    (b) the removal of major internal fixtures such as a fixed pews, a rood screen or an organ;

    (c) the addition of any significant new element such as the creation of new spaces through subdivision.

6. Documents to accompany consultation

The documents which the intending applicants for a faculty should submit to each of the bodies being consulted under paragraphs 2, 3 or 4 above should be

    (a) designs, plans or other documents (including photographs) giving particulars of the works together with a summary list of the works;

    (b) a Statement of Significance and a Statement of Needs.

    6.1. The particulars given under paragraph 6(a) above should be sufficiently clear for a comparison to be made between the church in its existing state and in its future state if the works are permitted to be carried out so as to enable an assessment to be made of the likely impact of the works on the listed church.

7. Period for response to consultation

At the same time as submitting the particulars referred to in paragraph 6 to any body consulted under paragraphs 2, 3, or 4 the intending applicants should write to that body stating that a response to consultation will be taken into account provided that it is received within 28 days from the date of the letter.

8. Diocesan advisory committee

Intending applicants should inform the secretary of the advisory committee which of the bodies in paragraphs 2 to 4 above has been consulted and the date when the 28 day period referred to in paragraph 6 is due to expire. On receipt of a response within the 28 day period from any of the bodies consulted, the intending applicants should provide a copy of the response to the secretary of the advisory committee. The advisory committee is not obliged to await a response which is not received within the 28 day period before reaching a decision and issuing a certificate in Form No 1 in Appendix C.

Clergy Discipline Rules 2005

SI 2005/2022

PART I

Introductory

Overriding Objective

1. The overriding objective of these rules is to enable formal disciplinary proceedings brought under the Measure to be dealt with justly, in a way that is both fair to all relevant interested persons and proportionate to the nature and seriousness of the issues raised. The rules are, so far as is reasonably practicable, to be applied in accordance with the following principles —
    (a) The complainant and the respondent shall be treated on an equal footing procedurally.
    (b) The complainant and the respondent shall be kept informed of the procedural progress of the complaint.
    (c) Undue delay is to be avoided.
    (d) Undue expense is to be avoided.

Duty to co-operate

2.—(1) All parties shall co-operate with any person, tribunal or court exercising any function under the Measure in order to further the overriding objective.

(2) Any failure to co-operate by a party may result in adverse inferences being made against that party at any stage of the proceedings.

Application of rules

3. These rules apply to proceedings under the Clergy Discipline Measure 2003 alleging misconduct against a clerk in Holy Orders, other than in relation to matters involving doctrine, ritual or ceremonial.

PART II

Institution of proceedings

Institution of proceedings against priests or deacons

4.—(1) No disciplinary proceedings under section 10(1)(a) of the Measure may be instituted against priests or deacons except by way of a written complaint made in form 1a in the Schedule, or in a document which is substantially to the like effect containing the information required by sub-rule (2).

(2) A complaint in writing made under section 10(1)(a) of the Measure shall—
    (a) state—
        (i) the bishop to whom the complaint is being made,
        (ii) the full name and contact address, including postcode, of the complainant,
        (iii) the name and position held of the priest or deacon about whom the complaint is made,
        (iv) why the complainant claims to have a proper interest or is otherwise entitled to make the complaint,
        (v) in summary form the nature and details of the acts or omissions alleged to be misconduct under section 8 of the Measure,
        (vi) the date or dates of the alleged misconduct,
        (vii) the evidence in support that the complainant relies upon, which shall be in writing signed and dated by the maker of the statement in each case.

(b) where the complainant has been nominated by a Parochial Church Council, have attached to it a certified copy of the resolution passed by the Parochial Church Council in accordance with section 10(1)(a)(i) of the Measure,

(c) contain a declaration that the complainant believes the facts of the complaint to be true, and

(d) be signed and dated by the complainant, and be sent or delivered to the bishop.

Joint complainants

5. Where a complaint is signed by two or more persons jointly, they shall nominate one of them to be the correspondent for the purposes of these rules.

Form of statements in support

6.—(1) The maker of any statement submitted as evidence in support of a complaint shall indicate which matters in it are within the maker's own knowledge and which are matters of information and belief, and shall identify the source of any matters of information and belief.

(2) Any such statement in support shall be made in form 3 in the Schedule or in a document which is substantially to the like effect, and shall contain a declaration that the maker of the statement believes the facts in it are true.

Submission of statements in support

7.—(1) All written evidence relied upon in support of the complaint shall be sent to the bishop at the same time as the complaint, save as provided for in sub-rules (2) and (3).

(2) Any request to the bishop for permission to send written evidence in support of the complaint after the date of the complaint shall be in writing and shall state the reasons relied upon.

(3) A reasonable period of time for written evidence in support of the complaint to be sent may be allowed by the bishop but this should not exceed 28 days from the date of the complaint.

(4) The complainant shall be notified promptly in writing of any permission or refusal by the bishop to allow written evidence to be sent after the date of the complaint.

Complaint out of time

8.—(1) Any application to the President to permit a complaint instituting disciplinary proceedings outside the period prescribed in section 9 of the Measure shall be made in writing in form 1c in the Schedule or in a document which is substantially to the like effect containing the information required for completion of form 1c, and shall set out the reasons why proceedings were not instituted within time.

(2) Within 7 days of receipt of the application the President shall start consultation by providing the respondent with a copy of the complainant's application, and shall invite the respondent to make written comments within 21 days about the reasons given by the complainant for not instituting proceedings in time.

(3) A copy of any comments received from the respondent shall be supplied by the President to the complainant within 7 days of receipt.

(4) The President shall inform the complainant that within 21 days of receiving a copy of any comments from the respondent the complainant may send written comments in reply to the President.

(5) Having considered any comments of the complainant and the respondent, and if satisfied that there was good reason why the complainant did not institute proceedings at an earlier date, the President may give permission in writing to the complainant for a complaint to be made under section 10(1)(a) of the Measure, and if so, shall specify the time within which the complaint in writing shall be made in accordance with rule 4. The President shall send a copy of the written permission to the respondent and the relevant bishop.

(6) If, having considered any comments of the complainant and the respondent, the President does not give permission for a complaint to be made outside the period prescribed in section 9 of the Measure, the President shall in writing so notify the complainant, the respondent and the relevant bishop.

Part III

Preliminary scrutiny

Receipt of complaint

9.—(1) On receipt of a complaint the bishop, or a person authorised by the bishop, shall send the complainant an acknowledgment of the complaint, which states—
- (a) the date when proceedings were instituted, which is the date the complaint was received, and
- (b) subject to paragraph (c), that the complaint together with the written evidence in support of the complaint, if any, will be referred to the registrar for a written report to be prepared setting out the registrar's views on—
  - (i) whether at the date when proceedings were instituted the complainant was entitled under section 10 of the Measure to make the complaint, and
  - (ii) whether there is sufficient substance in the complaint to justify proceeding with it in accordance with the provisions of the Measure.

Where a complaint alleges misconduct which might constitute a criminal offence, the acknowledgment shall state that resolution of the complaint under the Measure may be postponed to await the outcome of police or other investigations.

(2) The bishop, or a person authorised by the bishop, shall refer the complaint and written evidence in support of the complaint to the registrar within 7 days of receipt.

Notifying the respondent about the complaint

10.—(1) Subject to sub-rule (2), within 7 days of receiving the complaint from the bishop, the registrar shall notify the respondent in writing—
- (a) that a complaint has been made,
- (b) that the registrar's function is limited to scrutinising the complaint in order to produce a written report for the bishop setting out the registrar's views on—
  - (i) whether, at the date when proceedings were instituted, the complainant was entitled under section 10 of the Measure to make the complaint, and
  - (ii) whether there is sufficient substance in the complaint to justify proceeding with it,
- (c) that no formal response or detailed evidence is required from the respondent at this preliminary stage as the registrar's function is limited to the matters in paragraph (b) above,
- (d) that the respondent will be requested by the bishop to respond to the complaint in detail with evidence in support if it proceeds beyond preliminary scrutiny,
- (e) of the date when the registrar expects to submit the written report to the bishop.

(2) For the protection of the interests of a child, the registrar may in exceptional circumstances delay notifying the respondent that a complaint has been made until no later than 42 days after receipt of the complaint.

(3) When notifying the respondent under sub-rule (1), the registrar shall send the respondent a copy or, where sub-rule (4) applies, an edited transcript of the complaint and the written evidence in support.

(4) The registrar may delete from the respondent's copy of the complaint form and written evidence in support any details which would or may reveal the identity of the complainant, a child or a witness, provided that—
- (a) the registrar is satisfied there are exceptional circumstances and that to do so would be in the interests of justice, and
- (b) the bishop is immediately notified in writing with an explanation of the registrar's reasons.

Thereafter, details which would or may reveal the identity of the complainant, a child or a witness as the case may be, shall be withheld from the respondent and shall be erased from any papers sent to the respondent unless and until the bishop has decided not to dismiss the complaint under section 11(3) of the Measure or the President has reversed such a dismissal under section 11(4).

Consulting the complainant for clarification

11. During the course of the preliminary scrutiny of the complaint the registrar shall consult the complainant only for the purpose of clarification of any matter directly related to the complaint. Such consultation should be conducted in writing, but if oral, it shall be recorded by the registrar in written memoranda, and a copy of any correspondence and memoranda shall be sent by the registrar to the respondent and the complainant.

Registrar's written report

12.—(1) Subject to rule 19(1), having scrutinised the complaint, within 28 days of receiving it or within any extended period under rule 13, the registrar shall send a written report to the bishop setting out the registrar's views as to—
  (a) whether at the date the proceedings were instituted, the complainant had a proper interest to make the complaint, and
  (b) whether there is sufficient substance in the complaint to justify proceeding with it under the Measure.

(2) When the report is sent to the bishop, the registrar shall attach to it the complaint and the evidence in support.

Registrar extends time for sending the written report

13.—(1) Where the registrar proposes under section 11(2) of the Measure to extend the period of 28 days for the submission of the written report to the bishop, the registrar shall, not later than 21 days after receipt of the complaint, notify the complainant and the respondent of the reasons why an extension is required and the period of extension proposed, and shall invite their views about whether there should be an extension.

(2) Any comments by the complainant and the respondent shall be made within 7 days of notification by the registrar.

(3) If, having consulted the complainant and the respondent, the registrar decides to extend the period of 28 days, they and the bishop must be notified of the new date by which the written report is to be submitted to the bishop.

Multiple complaints and the written report

14.—(1) Where the complainant makes more than one complaint against the same respondent, the registrar may prepare one written report dealing with all the complaints referred to the registrar by the bishop.

(2) Where the complainant makes a complaint against two or more respondents, the registrar shall prepare separate written reports in respect of each respondent.

(3) Where two or more complainants make separate complaints against the same respondent in respect of the same alleged misconduct, the registrar may prepare one written report dealing with all the complaints.

Dismissal of the complaint by the bishop under section 11(3) of the Measure

15.—(1) If the bishop, after considering the registrar's report, dismisses a complaint under section 11(3) of the Measure, the bishop shall within 28 days of receiving the registrar's written report send to the complainant and the respondent written notice of dismissal together with reasons for the dismissal and a copy of the registrar's report.

(2) The written notice shall explain the complainant's right to request the President to review the dismissal.

President's review of a dismissal

16.—(1) A request by the complainant to the President for a review of the dismissal shall be made within 14 days of receipt of the notice of dismissal, and shall—
  (a) be in writing in form 4 in the Schedule, or in a document which is substantially to the like effect,
  (b) set out the reasons for seeking a review of the bishop's decision, and
  (c) be accompanied by a copy of the complaint and the written evidence in support, the registrar's report, and the bishop's notice of dismissal.

(2) No new or further evidence may be submitted by the complainant with the request for a review.

(3) The President shall notify the bishop and the respondent that the review has been requested.

(4) Within 28 days of receiving the complainant's request the President shall notify the complainant, the respondent and the bishop in writing as to whether the President is upholding the dismissal or reversing it, and directing the bishop to deal with the complaint in accordance with section 12 of the Measure.

Part IV

Consideration of the courses available to the bishop

Respondent's answer

17.—(1) If the complaint is not dismissed under section 11(3) of the Measure, or if the President reverses such a dismissal, the bishop shall—
  (a) notify the complainant and the respondent in writing that the complaint has not been dismissed,
  (b) provide the complainant and the respondent with a copy of the registrar's written report unless previously provided under rule 15(1),
  (c) send to the respondent a copy of form 2 in the Schedule, and
  (d) request the respondent to submit a written answer to the complaint within 21 days using form 2.

(2) The respondent's answer shall be in form 2 in the Schedule, or in a document which is substantially to the like effect containing the information required for completion of form 2, and shall—
  (a) provide the full name, contact address including postcode, and telephone number of the respondent,
  (b) state which, if any, matters are admitted and which are contested,
  (c) subject to sub-rule (5), be accompanied by any written evidence in support upon which the respondent wishes to rely, plus a copy of any such evidence,
  (d) where the respondent admits any misconduct, give details of any matters relied upon by way of mitigation,
  (e) contain a declaration that the respondent believes the facts of the answer to be true, and
  (f) be signed and dated by the respondent, and be sent or delivered to the bishop, together with a copy.

(3) The maker of any statement submitted as evidence in support of an answer shall indicate which matters in it are within the maker's own knowledge and which are matters of information and belief, and shall identify the source of any matters of information and belief.

(4) Any such statement in support shall be made in form 3 in the Schedule or in a document which is substantially to the like effect, and shall contain a declaration that the maker of the statement believes the facts in it are true.

(5) The respondent may be granted a further 7 days by the bishop within which to submit any evidence in support.

(6) The bishop on receipt shall by way of notification send to the complainant a copy of the respondent's answer and evidence in support.

(7) Whether or not an answer is received in accordance with this rule the bishop may proceed to make a determination under section 12(1) of the Measure.

Extension of period for bishop to consider complaint under section 12 of the Measure

18.—(1) Where the bishop proposes to extend by such longer period as the bishop considers to be justified in the particular circumstances of the case the period of 28 days for determining which course under section 12 of the Measure to pursue, the bishop shall consult the complainant and the respondent, stating the reasons for the proposed extension and the period of time proposed.

(2) The bishop may from time to time extend the period for determining which course to pursue for such period as appears necessary in the interests of justice, provided the complainant and the respondent are consulted as required by sub-rule (1) each time the bishop proposes to extend the period.

(3) Where the bishop decides to extend the period for determining which course to pursue the bishop shall notify the complainant and the respondent promptly in writing of the extension.

Other proceedings

19.—(1) Where a respondent against whom a complaint is made in accordance with rule 4—
    (a) is, or is likely to be, subject to disciplinary proceedings in respect of any alleged misconduct during the course of any employment, or
    (b) serves in Her Majesty's armed forces and is, or is likely to be, subject to any proceedings in respect of any alleged misconduct during his or her service in the armed forces, or
    (c) has been arrested on suspicion of committing a criminal offence, and is, or is likely to be, subject to criminal proceedings in connection with the arrest, or
    (d) is respondent to proceedings for divorce or judicial separation alleging adultery, behaviour such that the petitioner cannot reasonably be expected to live with the respondent, or desertion, the registrar may, in accordance with rule 13, extend the period for submission of the written report until 28 days after being notified of the final outcome of those other proceedings or that such other proceedings will not be pursued.

(2) Where the registrar does not extend the period of 28 days under rule 13, the bishop may, in accordance with rule 18, extend the period for determining which course to pursue until 28 days after being notified of the final outcome of those other proceedings or that such other proceedings will not be pursued.

No further action

20. Where the bishop under section 13(1) of the Measure determines there is to be no further action, the determination shall be in writing, and the bishop shall—
    (a) state reasons for taking no further action,
    (b) notify the complainant and the respondent that the complainant may refer the complaint to the President for consideration of the bishop's determination,
    (c) send a copy of the determination to the complainant and the respondent.

No further action: referral by complainant to the President

21.—(1) The complainant may refer the complaint to the President within 14 days of receiving the bishop's determination that there is to be no further action.

(2) Any such referral by the complainant to the President shall—
    (a) be in writing in form 5 in the Schedule or in a document which is substantially to the like effect,
    (b) state the grounds for requesting the President to consider the bishop's determination, and
    (c) be accompanied by a copy of the complaint and of the respondent's answer with the written evidence in support of each, the registrar's report, and the bishop's determination.

(3) Within 7 days the President shall notify the bishop and the respondent that the written referral has been received and send each of them a copy.

(4) No new or further evidence may be submitted to the President for the purposes of consideration of the bishop's determination.

No further action: President's decision

22. Within 28 days of receipt of the complainant's referral, the President's decision shall be given in writing with reasons and sent to the complainant, the respondent and the bishop, and if the President decides that the bishop's determination was plainly wrong the President may direct the bishop to pursue such of the courses specified in section 12(1)(b) to (e) as the President considers appropriate.

Consent to conditional deferment

23. Consent by the respondent, given under section 14(1) of the Measure, to a conditional deferment of the complaint shall—
    (a) be in writing and be given in form 6 in the Schedule or in a document which is substantially to the like effect, and
    (b) be signed and dated by the respondent.

Written determination imposing conditional deferment

24. The written determination to impose a conditional deferment shall contain the bishop's reasons and set out—
    (a) the period of deferment, and
    (b) that the complaint and the conditional deferment will be notified to the archbishop and remain on a record maintained by the diocesan registrar for the period of deferment, and
    (c) that, if during the period of deferment another complaint in accordance with rule 4 is made against the respondent and is dealt with by attempting to bring about conciliation, or by the imposition of a penalty by consent, or by means of a formal investigation, the recorded complaint may likewise be so dealt with together with the later complaint.

Record of conditional deferment

25.—(1) Within 21 days of obtaining the respondent's written consent to a conditional deferment the bishop must send—
    (a) to the complainant and the respondent a copy of the bishop's written determination, and
    (b) to the archbishop a copy of the bishop's written determination, the complaint, and the respondent's answer, if any, whereupon the provincial registrar shall note the conditional deferment, and
    (c) to the diocesan registrar a copy of the bishop's written determination, the complaint with evidence in support, and the respondent's answer, if any, with evidence in support, and the diocesan registrar shall maintain a record of the conditional deferment for such period not exceeding five years as the bishop may determine.

(2) The registrar's record of the conditional deferment shall not be open to public inspection but shall be made available to diocesan bishops and registrars.

Conciliation

26.—(1) Where the bishop directs under section 15 of the Measure that an attempt at conciliation should be made, the bishop shall notify the complainant and the respondent accordingly and invite them to agree to the appointment of the conciliator within 21 days.

(2) Subject to the agreement of the complainant and the respondent under sub-rule (1), the bishop shall propose in writing the name or names of potential conciliators with details of their suitability, experience and qualifications for appointment, and shall invite the complainant

and the respondent to indicate within 14 days which names, if any, they would each agree to be appointed.

Provided the complainant and the respondent agree on a person to be appointed and the bishop has no reason to question that person's impartiality, the bishop shall appoint that person as conciliator.

(3) At the time of appointment of the conciliator the bishop shall supply the conciliator with a copy of the complaint and the respondent's answer, together with the evidence in support of each.

(4) The conciliator may use such conciliation procedures as he or she thinks fit.

(5) The conciliator shall use his or her best endeavours to bring about a conciliation within 3 months, or within any further period he or she allows with the agreement of the complainant and the respondent.

Where the period for bringing about a conciliation is extended, the conciliator shall notify the bishop.

(6) Where a conciliation has been brought about—
  (a) The conciliator shall—
      (i) reduce the agreed points into writing and obtain the signatures of the complainant and the respondent, and
      (ii) submit to the bishop the signed points of agreement and a written report signed by the complainant and the respondent with such recommendations as the conciliator may wish to make.
  (b) Within 21 days of receipt the bishop shall notify the complainant and the respondent in writing that the bishop—
      (i) accepts the signed points of agreement, and
      (ii) that the bishop will pursue any agreed course, provided the bishop could have pursued that course under section 12 of the Measure had the bishop not instead directed an attempt be made to bring about conciliation.

(7) If a conciliation is not brought about but the complainant and the respondent agree that another conciliator should be appointed, the bishop may appoint that other conciliator.

(8) If a conciliation is not brought about, and the complainant and the respondent do not agree to a further period of time under sub-rule (5) or to the appointment of another conciliator under subrule (7), the matter shall be referred back to the bishop.

(9) If the complainant and the respondent do not agree to the appointment of a conciliator or to any of the proposed names to be appointed, or if the matter is referred back to the bishop by the conciliator under sub-rule (8), the bishop shall deal with the complaint under section 12(1)(a), (b), (d) or (e) of the Measure.

Penalty by consent

27.—(1) A penalty by consent under section 16 of the Measure may only be imposed in respect of such misconduct alleged in the complaint as the respondent admits.

(2) In addition to resignation by consent under section 16 of the Measure, any of the penalties that may be imposed under section 24 of the Measure upon a finding of misconduct may be imposed by consent under section 16 of the Measure.

(3) Where the bishop considers that the imposition of a penalty might be appropriate, the bishop shall invite the complainant and the respondent to make written representations if they so wish upon the proposed penalty within 14 days.

(4) The respondent's consent to the proposed penalty must be given in writing in form 7 in the Schedule or in a document which is substantially to the like effect. Subject to sub-rule (5) below, the bishop shall send the respondent written confirmation of the agreed penalty within 7 days of receiving the respondent's consent.

(5) Where the bishop and the respondent agree that prohibition for life or resignation is appropriate and agree upon a date for it to take effect—
- (a) The bishop shall give the respondent written notice that either of them may withdraw from the agreement by notifying the other in writing of the withdrawal within 7 days following the date of the agreement.
- (b) At the end of the 7 day period, if neither the bishop nor the respondent has given written notice withdrawing from the agreement the bishop shall send the respondent written confirmation of the penalty of prohibition for life or resignation, as the case may be.
- (c) In the case of resignation, no deed or letter of resignation from the respondent shall be required to implement the penalty.
- (d) The agreed date for the prohibition or resignation to take effect shall be not later than 3 months after the bishop's written confirmation.

(6) The bishop shall notify the complainant in writing of any penalty by consent within 14 days of sending the written confirmation to the respondent.

(7) The bishop shall notify the archbishop and the registrar of the diocese in writing of the penalty imposed by consent within 14 days of sending the written confirmation to the respondent.

(8) If the respondent does not consent to the imposition of a penalty or does not agree with the bishop as to the nature of the penalty, the bishop shall direct that the complaint is to be formally investigated in accordance with rule 28.

Reference to the Designated Officer for formal investigation

28.—(1) Where the bishop directs under section 12(1)(e) of the Measure that the complaint is to be formally investigated, the bishop shall refer it to the Designated Officer, and shall supply the Designated Officer with a copy of the complaint and the respondent's answer together with all written evidence in support of each of them, and the registrar's written report.

(2) Within 14 days of referring the complaint to the Designated Officer the bishop shall give written notice of the referral to the complainant and the respondent.

(3) The complainant and the respondent shall co-operate with the Designated Officer during the investigation, in particular by responding in writing within 14 days (or such extended period as the Designated Officer may allow) to any questions asked by the Designated Officer for the purpose of clarification of the complaint or the respondent's answer or of the evidence in support of each.

(4) If any new material information is disclosed to the Designated Officer by or on behalf of the complainant or the respondent in the course of the investigation, the Designated Officer shall pass it on to the party who did not disclose it and invite that party to comment within a stated period of time.

(5) The Designated Officer shall investigate the complaint and shall send or deliver a written report to the President within 3 months of the date of the receipt of the documents specified in sub-rule (1).

The time within which the Designated Officer is required to report to the President may be extended for such period as the President deems to be justified in the particular circumstances of the case. Any application for an extension of time shall be made by the Designated Officer in writing to the President.

PART V

Referring the complaint to the tribunal

The President's decision

29.—(1) Within 28 days of receipt of the Designated Officer's report the President shall decide if there is a case for the respondent to answer and shall send a written copy of the decision to the complainant, the respondent, the bishop and the Designated Officer.

(2) Where there is a case to answer, the President shall refer the case to the tribunal and shall specify in the written decision which allegation or allegations of misconduct are to be determined.

(3) If the President decides that there is no case for the respondent to answer then copies of the President's written decision with reasons shall be sent to the complainant, the respondent, the bishop and the Designated Officer, and thereafter no further action shall be taken with regard thereto.

Part VI

Directions preparatory to a hearing before the tribunal

General

30.—(1) Where a complaint is referred to a tribunal for adjudication, the Registrar of Tribunals—
   (a) may hold one or more preliminary hearings to identify the issues and give directions, and shall give notice to the parties of such hearings, and
   (b) shall give directions for the just disposal of the proceedings in accordance with the overriding objective.

(2) The Registrar of Tribunals may at any stage refer any matter of difficulty or dispute to the Chair.

(3) Directions may be given or varied at any stage—
   (a) at a hearing,
   (b) where sub-rule (6) below applies, during a telephone hearing, or
   (c) in writing.

(4) At any hearing or telephone hearing the respondent may be legally represented, and the complainant's case shall be conducted by the Designated Officer or someone duly authorised by the Designated Officer.

(5) Directions may be given or varied—
   (a) on the application of the Designated Officer or the respondent, or
   (b) on the initiative of the Registrar of Tribunals or the Chair without a hearing.

(6) Where a hearing for directions is likely to last no longer than 30 minutes the Registrar of Tribunals or the Chair, as the case may be, may direct that—
   (a) it be conducted by telephone, and
   (b) that the Designated Officer and the respondent send in advance of the hearing for directions a written summary of their respective submissions, and send or deliver copies of their submissions to each other.

(7) Any direction given by the Registrar of Tribunals or the Chair under this rule shall be given or confirmed in writing, and a copy sent or delivered to the Designated Officer and the respondent.

Form of application

31.—(1) Applications by the respondent for directions on any matter shall be made in writing—
   (a) to the Registrar of Tribunals using form 8 in the Schedule, and
   (b) a copy shall be sent or delivered to the Designated Officer at the same time as it is sent or delivered to the Registrar of Tribunals.

(2) The respondent shall respond in writing using form 9 in the Schedule to any application made by the Designated Officer, and shall send such response to the Registrar of Tribunals and a copy of it to the Designated Officer.

(3) The Designated Officer shall adapt forms 8 and 9 as appropriate, and shall send or deliver a copy to the respondent at the same as the application or response, as the case may be, is sent or delivered to the Registrar of Tribunals.

Setting aside or varying directions given without a hearing

32. Where an order has been made without a hearing giving or varying directions under rule 30(5) on the initiative of the Registrar of Tribunals or the Chair, a party may apply within 14 days to the Registrar of Tribunals or the Chair, as the case may be, to have it set aside or varied, and the order shall notify the parties that they may make such an application.

Matters which may be covered in directions

33.—(1) Directions may be given in respect of all procedural matters and in particular—
- (a) for the exchange of witness statements (notwithstanding that the complainant and the respondent may already have respectively supplied statements in support of the complaint form and the respondent's answer),
- (b) for the exchange of copies of documents intended to be relied upon at the final hearing,
- (c) to direct the complainant and the respondent to disclose and produce at or before the hearing of the complaint any specified documents in their possession or control which may reasonably be required by another party,
- (d) to permit written questions to be put by one party to the other, and to require those questions to be answered by the other party,
- (e) in relation to any expert evidence, including the number of expert witnesses,
- (f) to exclude evidence that would be irrelevant or unnecessary, or which should otherwise be excluded in the interests of justice in accordance with the overriding objective,
- (g) to direct any party to prepare a written outline argument and to send or deliver a copy of it to the Registrar of Tribunals, the Chair, and to the other party, together with photocopies of any authorities relied upon,
- (h) to provide for the preparation of bundles of documents for a hearing, and for them to be sent or delivered to the tribunal and each party,
- (i) to require the attendance of any person at the hearing of the complaint for the purpose of—
  - (i) giving evidence, or
  - (ii) producing documents for inspection,
- (j) to order two or more complaints against the same respondent to be heard on the same occasion,
- (k) to order complaints against more than one respondent to be heard on the same occasion,
- (l) to order any part of any proceedings to be dealt with separately.

(2) A direction may be given that if a document has not been disclosed to the other party, that document may not be relied upon at the hearing of the complaint unless the Chair gives permission.

Production appointment

34.—(1) The Registrar of Tribunals or the Chair may give notice to a person to attend a production appointment to provide reasons as to why that person should not be ordered to produce any documents specified or described.

(2) Any notice under sub-rule (1) shall be in form 10 in the Schedule or in a form which is substantially to the like effect, and—
- (a) shall be given only where—
  - (i) the production of the documents specified or described in the notice appears to the Registrar of Tribunals or the Chair to be relevant and necessary for dealing fairly with the complaint, and
  - (ii) the person to whom the notice is given has been sent in writing a request by a party to produce the documents and has failed to do so within a reasonable time, and

(b) shall state that the person to whom the notice is directed need not attend the appointment if that person does not object to producing the documents specified or described or if that person sends any objections in writing to the Registrar of Tribunals or Chair no later than a stated time before the appointment.

(3) A person attending a production appointment pursuant to a notice under sub-rule (1) shall be permitted to be represented at the appointment, and to make representations objecting to the production of any documents in question.

(4) A person who received notice under sub-rule (1) may be ordered at the production appointment to produce for inspection by a party within a stated time any documents specified or described.

(5) Any order under sub-rule (4) shall be in form 11 in the Schedule or in a form which is substantially to the like effect, and—
- (a) shall be made only where the production of the documents specified or described in the order appears to the Registrar of Tribunals or the Chair to be necessary for dealing fairly with the complaint, and where it appears just in all the circumstances to make such an order,
- (b) shall state—
   - (i) that the person to whom the order is directed must obey the order, and
   - (ii) failure to do so may be a contempt of the tribunal, and
   - (iii) that the person to whom the order is directed may be sent to prison or fined, or both, if the order is not obeyed.

Part VII

Evidence

Witness statements for use at a hearing before a tribunal

35.—(1) A witness statement is a written statement signed by a person and containing evidence which that person would be allowed to give orally.

(2) A witness statement must indicate—
- (a) which matters in it come from the witness's own knowledge, and which are matters of information or belief, and
- (b) the source of any matters of information or belief.

(3) A witness statement intended for use before a tribunal must contain at the end a declaration of truth in the following form—'I believe that the contents of this witness statement are true', and shall be dated and signed by the witness.

(4) A party wishing to rely on a witness statement at the hearing of the complaint shall call the witness to give oral evidence unless—
- (a) the parties agree that the witness statement may be put in evidence, or
- (b) the witness has died, is too ill to attend or is overseas, or
- (c) the Registrar of Tribunals or the Chair directs otherwise.

(5) Where a witness is called to give oral evidence the witness statement of the witness shall stand as the witness's evidence in chief unless the Chair directs otherwise.

(6) A witness giving oral evidence at a hearing may with the permission of the Chair—
- (a) amplify the witness statement, and
- (b) give evidence in relation to new matters which have arisen since the witness statement was made.

(7) Any witness who gives oral evidence may be cross-examined.

(8) If a party exchanges a witness statement with another party but does not—
- (a) call the witness to give evidence at the hearing, or
- (b) put the statement in evidence without calling the witness, the other party may put the witness statement in evidence without calling the witness to give oral evidence.

Expert evidence

36.—(1) No party may rely upon expert evidence without the permission of the Registrar of Tribunals or the Chair.

(2) If permission is given for expert evidence to be relied upon,
(a) the permission must be in respect of a named expert or a specific subject, and
(b) the evidence must be reasonably required for the purposes of the proceedings.

(3) An expert witness must be independent from the complainant and respondent, and at all times is under an overriding duty to help the tribunal on the matters within that person's expertise.

(4) Expert evidence is to be set out in a written report, and the report shall contain—
(a) details of the expert's qualifications and experience,
(b) details of the information provided and the questions asked of the expert for the preparation of the report,
(c) where there is a range of opinion on the matter dealt with in the report,
  (i) a summary of the range of opinion,
  (ii) reasons for the expert's own opinion,
(d) a statement that the expert understands his or her duty to the tribunal, and has complied with that duty.

(5) Expert evidence cannot be relied upon without permission from the Chair, unless a copy of the report has been sent or delivered to the other party in accordance with directions given under rule 33.

(6) Where both parties wish to submit expert evidence on a particular issue, the Registrar of Tribunals or the Chair shall, save in exceptional circumstances, direct that the evidence on that issue is to be given by a single joint expert only.

(7) If the parties cannot agree who should be the single joint expert, the Registrar of Tribunals or the Chair may—
(a) nominate the expert from a list presented by the parties, or
(b) direct that the expert be nominated in another specified manner.

(8) Where a single joint expert is to be used, the parties should try to agree joint instructions, failing which each party may give instructions to the expert provided that at the same time a copy of those instructions is sent to the other party.

(9) A party may put written questions to any expert for the purpose of clarifying the expert's report. An expert's answers to written questions are to be treated as part of the expert's report. Where an expert does not answer a written question the Registrar of Tribunals or the Chair may direct that part or all of the expert's evidence may not be relied upon.

(10) An expert may not give oral evidence at a hearing unless permission has previously been given by the Registrar of Tribunals or the Chair.

Part VIII

The tribunal

Appointment of members of the tribunal

37.—(1) Within 14 days of being notified under section 22(2) of the Measure of their identity, the respondent may make written representations to the President about the suitability of any of the proposed members of the tribunal which will hear the complaint, and the President shall not appoint any of the members until such representations, if any, have been received and considered.

(2) If the President is not satisfied that a proposed appointee is impartial, the President shall propose an alternative person, and shall afford an opportunity to the respondent to make representations about that person within 14 days of being notified of that person's identity.

Fixing the date and place of the hearing of the complaint

38.—(1) The Registrar of Tribunals may direct the parties to provide time estimates of the likely length of the hearing of the complaint.

(2) Thereafter, as soon as may be expedient, in consultation with the Chair and with due regard being paid to the convenience of the complainant, the respondent, the Designated Officer and the witnesses, the Registrar of Tribunals shall fix the date, time and place for the hearing of the complaint, and shall give not less than 14 days written notice of the same to the complainant, the respondent and the Designated Officer.

(3) The Registrar of Tribunals or the Chair may vary the date, time and place of any hearing, and written notice of the variation shall be given by the Registrar of Tribunals to the complainant, the respondent and the Designated Officer.

The tribunal and the overriding objective

39. The tribunal shall in accordance with the overriding objective in rule 1—
    (a) conduct the hearing in the manner it considers most appropriate to the issues before it and to the just handling of the complaint generally,
    (b) set a suitable timetable for the hearing.

Tribunal hearing normally to be in private

40. The hearing shall be in private except where—
    (a) the tribunal is satisfied that it is in the interests of justice to have a hearing in public, or
    (b) the respondent so requests, in which case the tribunal shall direct that the hearing shall be in public, but during any part of the proceedings the tribunal may exclude such person or persons as it may determine.

Power to adjourn

41. The hearing may be adjourned from time to time if necessary.

Absence from a hearing

42. The Registrar of Tribunals or the Chair may proceed with a hearing notwithstanding the absence of the complainant or the respondent, provided the Registrar of Tribunals or the Chair is satisfied that the absent person has had notice of the hearing.

Admissions by the respondent

43. If, after referral of the complaint under rule 29, the respondent makes an admission before or at the hearing, the tribunal may make a finding of misconduct on the basis of that admission without considering any or any further evidence, and the tribunal may then proceed under section 19 of the Measure.

Entitlement to call evidence

44. At the hearing, subject to rules 35, 36 and 39, the complainant and the respondent are entitled to give evidence, and the Designated Officer and the respondent are entitled to call witnesses, to question any witnesses who give oral evidence, and to address the tribunal on evidence, the law and on the issues generally.

Oral evidence

45. Oral evidence shall be given on oath or solemn affirmation, and shall be recorded.

Tribunal may require personal attendance of witness

46. The tribunal may at any stage of the proceedings require the personal attendance at the hearing of the author of a witness statement or an expert who has produced a report.

Attendance at a hearing in private

47. Where the hearing is held in private, in addition to members and staff of the tribunal, the following may attend—
    (a) the complainant and the respondent,
    (b) the legal representatives of the respondent,
    (c) the Designated Officer, any supporting staff, and any person authorised by the Designated Officer to conduct the case for the complainant,

(d) the bishop,
(e) the relevant archdeacon,
(f) any other person with the tribunal's permission.

Power to exclude from hearing

48. The tribunal may exclude from the hearing any person who threatens to disrupt or has disrupted the hearing or has otherwise interfered with the administration of justice.

Tribunal may order identity not to be published

49. The tribunal may order that the name and any other identifying details of any person involved or referred to in the proceedings must not be published or otherwise made public, if satisfied that such an order—
    (a) is desirable to protect the private life of any person, or
    (b) is desirable to protect the interests of any child, or
    (c) is otherwise in the interests of the administration of justice.

Pronouncement of the tribunal's determination of the complaint

50.—(1) The determination of the complaint shall be according to the opinion of the majority of the members of the tribunal.

(2) The Chair shall pronounce the tribunal's determination of the complaint in public—
    (a) at the end of the hearing, or
    (b) at a later date when the Chair may sit alone for that purpose.

(3) The tribunal's determination shall be recorded in writing with reasons, and shall set out the opinion of the majority of its members together with the minority opinions if any, and shall be signed by each member.

(4) The tribunal may omit from the written determination the name and any other identifying details of any person, if satisfied that such an order—
    (a) is desirable to protect the private life of that person, or
    (b) is desirable to protect the interests of any child, or
    (c) is otherwise in the interests of the administration of justice.

(5) A copy of the tribunal's written determination shall be sent to the complainant, the respondent, the Designated Officer, the bishop, the registrar, and the provincial registrar.

Tribunal may invite the bishop to give views about the penalty

51. Before imposing a penalty the tribunal may invite the bishop of the diocese concerned to express in writing the bishop's views as to the appropriate penalty, save where the bishop has given evidence to the tribunal. If the tribunal decides to do so—
    (a) the bishop shall be invited to express any views in writing to the tribunal within 14 days of being requested to do so, and
    (b) a copy of the bishop's views shall be provided by the tribunal to the respondent and to the Designated Officer.

Pronouncement of penalty

52.—(1) The Chair shall pronounce in public the penalty or penalties imposed by the tribunal and may sit alone for that purpose.

(2) The pronouncement of the penalty or penalties may be on the same occasion as the pronouncement of the determination under rule 50, or at a later date.

(3) The decision to impose a penalty or penalties shall be recorded in writing, and a copy of the written decision shall be sent to the respondent, the Designated Officer, the bishop, the registrar and the provincial registrar.

Record of conditional discharges

53.—(1) The provincial registrar shall maintain a record of conditional discharges.

(2) The record shall not be open to public inspection but shall be made available to diocesan bishops and registrars.

(3) A conditional discharge shall be removed from the record at the end of the period specified in the order of the tribunal which imposed it.

Part IX

Termination, substitution, and withdrawal

Death of the respondent

54. Any disciplinary proceedings are automatically terminated on the death of the respondent.

Death, serious illness or incapacity of complainant nominated by the Parochial Church Council

55.—(1) In the event of the death or serious illness or incapacity of the complainant who has been nominated by the parochial church council, that council may, on its own initiative or at the invitation of the bishop, nominate another person as complainant in the proceedings, and shall send or deliver notice in writing of any such nomination to—

    (a)   the bishop,

    (b)   the respondent, and

    (c)   where the complaint has been referred by the bishop under section 17 of the Measure for a formal investigation, the Registrar of Tribunals and the Designated Officer.

(2) If the parochial church council does not nominate another person within 28 days of being invited by the bishop to do so, any person claiming to have a proper interest in making the complaint may apply in writing to be substituted as the complainant. The application shall set out the grounds for the claim, and shall be made to the bishop unless the complaint has already been referred to the Designated Officer for a formal investigation, in which case it shall be made to the President.

Death, serious illness or incapacity of complainant not nominated by the Parochial Church Council

56.—(1) In the event of the death, serious illness or incapacity of the complainant other than a person nominated by a parochial church council, any other person claiming to have a proper interest in making the complaint may apply in writing to be substituted as the complainant. The application shall set out the grounds for the claim, and shall be made to the bishop unless the complaint has already been referred to the Designated Officer for a formal investigation, in which case it shall be made to the President.

(2) Where an application to be substituted as the complainant is made to the bishop, the bishop may seek advice from the registrar as to whether the applicant has a proper interest in the complaint.

(3) The bishop or the President, as the case may be, may substitute an applicant as the complainant if satisfied that the applicant has a proper interest in the complaint, and that it is in the interests of justice to do so, and shall notify the respondent accordingly.

President may direct withdrawal if no person is nominated or substituted

57. In the event of the death, serious illness or incapacity of the complainant, if no other person is duly nominated or substituted as complainant in the proceedings, the President may direct under rule 58 that the complaint is to be withdrawn, whereupon no further action shall be taken in the proceedings.

President's powers under section 18 of the Measure

58.—(1) At any stage of proceedings after the bishop has directed they are to be formally investigated, the President may—

    (a)   on the President's own initiative, or

    (b)   on application by letter by the respondent or the Designated Officer setting out the reasons why the relevant direction should be made, direct that a complaint is to be withdrawn (whereupon no further action shall be taken in the proceedings) or that an attempt or further attempt is to be made to bring about conciliation.

(2) The President's direction shall be made in writing and a copy shall be given to the complainant, the respondent, the Designated Officer, the bishop, the Registrar of Tribunals and the diocesan registrar.

Complainant wishes to withdraw

59.—(1) Where a complainant wishes to withdraw a complaint at any stage before the bishop determines which course to pursue under section 12 of the Measure, the bishop, after consulting the respondent in writing, shall direct—
  (a) that the complaint shall be withdrawn, whereupon no further action shall be taken upon it, or
  (b) that the complaint shall proceed, and a nominated person with a proper interest, who has agreed to act as the complainant, shall be substituted in place of the complainant who wishes to withdraw.

(2) The bishop may seek advice from the registrar as to whether the person to be substituted as complainant has a proper interest in making the complaint.

(3) The bishop's direction shall be made in writing and a copy shall be given to the respondent, the complainant, the person to be substituted as complainant, and the registrar.

(4) Where a complainant wishes to withdraw a complaint after the bishop has directed that it is to be formally investigated, the President, after consulting the respondent, the bishop, and the Designated Officer in writing, may direct that—
  (a) the complaint shall proceed, and
  (b) a nominated person with a proper interest, who has agreed to act as the complainant, shall be substituted in place of the complainant who wishes to withdraw.

(5) The President's direction shall be made in writing and a copy shall be given to the respondent, the complainant, the person to be substituted as complainant, the Designated Officer, the bishop, the Registrar of Tribunals and the registrar.

Part X

Suspension

Suspension of a priest or deacon during proceedings

60.—(1) Where a complaint against a priest or deacon falls to be considered under section 12(1) of the Measure, the bishop may suspend the priest or deacon from exercising or performing without leave of the bishop any right or duty of or incidental to the office of priest or deacon, as the case may be.

(2) A notice suspending a priest or deacon under sub-rule (1) shall be in form 12a in the Schedule or in a form which is substantially to the like effect and may specify any rights or duties which by leave of the bishop are not suspended.

Suspension of a priest following arrest

61.—(1) Where a priest or deacon holding any preferment in a diocese is arrested on suspicion of committing a criminal offence the bishop may suspend the priest or deacon from exercising or performing without the leave of the bishop any right or duty of or incidental to the office of priest or deacon, as the case may be.

(2) A notice suspending a priest or deacon under sub-rule (1) shall be in form 13a in the Schedule or in a form which is substantially to the like effect, and may specify any rights or duties which by leave of the bishop are not suspended.

Contents of notice of suspension

62. A notice of suspension given under rule 60(2) or 61(2) shall be signed by the bishop and shall—
  (a) state the date from when the suspension takes effect,

(b) explain that the suspension, unless revoked by the bishop, will continue until the expiry of the period of 3 months following the date of service of the notice on the priest or deacon, or until—
   (i) the proceedings under the Measure have been concluded, or
   (ii) the proceedings for the criminal offence have been concluded, whichever is the earlier in either case,
(c) explain—
   (i) that where the proceedings under the Measure have not been concluded, or the proceedings for the criminal offence have not been concluded before the expiry of the period of three months from the date of service of the notice of suspension, as the case may be, then the bishop may cause a further notice of suspension to be served on the priest or deacon, and that this will continue for the same period as is specified in paragraph (b), and
   (ii) that a further notice or notices of suspension, which may be in different terms from any previous notice, may be served on the priest or deacon if the circumstances in paragraph (i) of this sub-rule apply, until the proceedings under the Measure or the proceedings for the criminal offence have been concluded, as the case may be;
(d) state that the effect of the suspension is that the priest or deacon is forbidden to exercise or perform without the leave of the bishop any right or duty of or incidental to the office of priest or deacon, as the case may be,
(e) explain that within a period of 14 days from the date when the suspension takes effect the priest or deacon may appeal against the suspension to the President, who may within days following the lodging of the appeal either confirm or revoke the suspension.

Notification to others of suspension

63. A copy of the notice of suspension of a priest or deacon under rule 60(2) or 61(2) shall be sent or delivered by the bishop to—
   (a) the archdeacon of the archdeaconry in which the priest or deacon holds office,
   (b) the rural dean or area dean of the deanery in which the priest or deacon holds office,
   (c) other clergy who hold office in the parish or parishes where the priest or deacon holds office,
   (d) the churchwardens for each parish where the priest or deacon holds office,
   (e) the registrar.

Revocation of suspension

64.—(1) The bishop may at any time during any period of suspension under rule 60 or rule 61 revoke a notice of suspension, and on so doing the bishop shall serve a notice in writing on the priest or deacon concerned stating that the notice of suspension has been revoked and that the period of suspension has been terminated.

(2) A copy of any notice revoking a notice of suspension shall be sent or delivered by the bishop to the persons specified in rule 63.

Notification of cessation of suspension

65. Where—
   (a) a suspension expires and no further notice of suspension is given by the bishop to the priest or deacon, or
   (b) the proceedings under the Measure, or the proceedings for the criminal offence, are concluded without the imposition of any penalty of prohibition or removal from office or revocation of licence, the bishop shall notify in writing the priest or deacon concerned and the persons specified in rule 63 that the suspension has ended.

Appeals by priest or deacon against notice of suspension

66.—(1) An appeal to the President by a priest or deacon shall be made in writing within 14 days of receipt of the notice of suspension, and—
 (a) a copy of the notice of suspension shall be attached to the written appeal,
 (b) the written appeal shall set out the grounds of the appeal,
 (c) a copy of the written appeal shall be sent or delivered to the bishop by the appellant at the same time as the appeal is sent or delivered to the President.

(2) Within 14 days of the date of the lodging of the appeal with the President the bishop may send or deliver to the President written comments in answer to the appeal against suspension, and a copy of those comments shall be sent or delivered by the bishop to the appellant at the same time as they are sent or delivered to the President.

(3) The President may confirm or revoke the suspension and shall do so in writing within 28 days of the appeal being lodged, and a copy of the confirmation or revocation shall be sent or delivered to the appellant and the bishop.

(4) Where the suspension is revoked by the President on appeal, the bishop shall notify the persons specified in rule 63 that the suspension has been revoked.

(5) There shall be no stay of the suspension pending the determination of an appeal to the President against the suspension.

Part XI

Penalties imposed under section 30 of the Measure

Certificate of conviction

67. Where a priest or deacon is liable to a penalty of prohibition or removal from office, or both, by virtue of section 30(1)(a) of the Measure, the bishop shall not propose to impose any penalty until the conviction has become conclusive under section 40(1) of the Measure and the court has sent to the bishop the certificate of conviction in the form used by the court for that purpose.

Bishop proposes a penalty after sentence of imprisonment or matrimonial order

68. Where the bishop proposes to impose a penalty of prohibition or removal from office, or both, upon a priest or deacon falling within section 30(1)(a) or (b) of the Measure, the bishop, after consultation with the President, shall—
 (a) inform the priest or deacon in writing of the details of the proposed penalty, and
 (b) invite the priest or deacon to send to the bishop any representations in writing about the proposal within 28 days of the date of that invitation.

Bishop makes decision on imposition of penalty

69. After expiry of the 28 days specified in rule 68 the bishop shall decide whether or not to impose the proposed penalty under section 30 of the Measure and shall—
 (a) give the priest or deacon written notification of the decision, and
 (b) if the decision is to impose the penalty, inform the priest or deacon that an application may be made to the archbishop of the relevant province to review the decision, and that the penalty will not be imposed unless and until the time for making an application for a review has expired or the bishop's decision has been upheld by the archbishop following a review.

Application to review decision to impose penalty

70.—(1) An application by a priest or deacon for the review of a bishop's decision under section 30(2) of the Measure shall—
 (a) be sent or delivered in writing to the archbishop of the relevant province within 21 days from the date of the bishop's decision, and
 (b) contain details of the facts and matters which the priest or deacon wishes the archbishop to consider in conducting the review, and the archbishop shall arrange for it to be copied and sent or delivered to the bishop who made the decision.

(2) The priest or deacon shall send or deliver to the archbishop with the application under subrule (1) a copy of—
  (a) the notification of the bishop's intention to impose the penalty,
  (b) the representations made by the priest or deacon to the bishop, and
  (c) the bishop's notification of the decision to impose the penalty.

Bishop may respond to application for review

71. Within 21 days of receiving from the archbishop a copy of the application for a review under rule 70, the bishop may send or deliver to the archbishop written comments in response to the application, together with copies of any documents taken into account by the bishop when deciding to impose the penalty, and a copy of the comments and any such documents shall be sent or delivered by the bishop to the priest or deacon.

Archbishop reviews imposition of penalty

72.—(1) The archbishop shall conduct the review with or without a hearing and, after considering the application and the documents supplied under rules 70(2) and 71 and all the circumstances, the archbishop shall decide whether to uphold or reverse the bishop's decision to impose the penalty and shall put that decision in writing and send or deliver copies to the priest or deacon and to the bishop.

(2) Where the review is conducted without a hearing the archbishop shall send or deliver the written decision within 3 months of receiving the application for review. Where a hearing is held for the purposes of the review the archbishop shall send or deliver the written decision within 28 days after the hearing.

Imposition of penalty by bishop under section 30 of the Measure

73. When the time for making an application for review under rule 70 has expired, or the archbishop has decided following a review to uphold the bishop's decision, then the bishop shall impose the penalty in accordance with section 30(4) and section 30(5) of the Measure.

Part XII

The Archbishops' list

Access to the list

74.—(1) There shall be a single list compiled and maintained jointly by the archbishops for the purposes specified in section 38(1) of the Measure, and the list shall be in the custody of the Archbishop of Canterbury.

(2) A copy of the list shall be in the custody of the Archbishop of York. (3) Subject to the provisions of section 38(2) and section 38(3) of the Measure, the list shall not be open to public inspection but shall be made available to the President, diocesan bishops of the Church of England, and registrars.

Inclusion of name in list under section 38(1)(a) to (d) of the Measure

75.—(1) Within 21 days of including in the list with the agreement of the other archbishop the details of a person falling within paragraphs (a) to (d) of section 38(1) of the Measure, the archbishop of the relevant province shall take all reasonable steps to inform that person in writing of—
  (a) the inclusion,
  (b) the particulars recorded,
  (c) the person's right to request the President in writing to review the matter.

(2) Within 21 days of being so informed, that person may in writing request the President to review the matter, and the President upon receipt of the request shall send a copy of it to the archbishop of the relevant province.

(3) The archbishop of the relevant province may, within 21 days of receiving the copy of the request, make written representations to the President and shall send a copy of those representations to the person requesting the review.

(4) Within 42 days of receiving the request for a review the President shall in writing direct whether the person requesting the review is to continue to be included or is to be excluded from the list. If the person requesting the review is to continue to be included in the list, the President may direct that the particulars relating to that person shall be altered in such manner as are specified in the direction.

(5) A copy of the President's direction under sub-rule (4) shall be sent to the person requesting the review and to the archbishop of the relevant province.

Inclusion of name in list under section 38(1)(e) of the measure

76.—(1) Where the archbishops propose to include in the list a person falling within paragraph (e) of section 38(1) of the Measure, the archbishop of the relevant province shall take all reasonable steps to inform that person in writing of the proposal and the particulars to be recorded, and shall invite that person to send comments or representations in writing within 21 days from the date of the written invitation.

(2) On expiry of the period of 21 days the archbishop of the relevant province, after considering any comments or representations received, shall—

(a) with the agreement of the other archbishop give a decision whether or not to include that person in the list, and

(b) inform the person in writing of the decision.

(3) If the decision under sub-rule (2) is that the person is to be included in the list then the archbishop of the relevant province shall notify the person in writing of—

(a) the particulars to be recorded, and

(b) the person's right to request the President in writing to review the decision.

(4) Within 21 days of being so informed under sub-rule (3), the person may request the President in writing to review the decision and shall give reasons for seeking a review, and the President upon receiving the request shall send a copy to the archbishop of the relevant province.

(5) The archbishop of the relevant province may, within 21 days of receiving a copy of the request for a review of the decision, make written representations to the President and shall send a copy of those representations to the person requesting the review.

(6) Within 42 days of receiving the request for a review of the decision, and after considering the request and any representations from the archbishop of the relevant province, the President shall in writing uphold or reverse the archbishops' decision to include the person in the list, and if the decision is upheld the President may also direct that the particulars relating to that person should be altered in such manner as are specified in the direction.

(7) The President's written decision on a review under sub-rule (4) shall be sent by the President to the person requesting the review and to the archbishop of the relevant province.

Review of an entry in the list – (a), (b) & (c)

77.—(1) Where a person has been included in the list under section 38(1)(a) or (b) of the Measure the archbishop of the relevant province shall, with the agreement of the other archbishop, direct that the name of that person together with the particulars recorded be removed from the list on being satisfied that—

(a) a declaration has been made under section 26 of the Measure that the penalty of prohibition for life or deposition, by reason of which the person was included in the list, be nullified, or

(b) an order has been made under section 27 of the Measure that the penalty of limited prohibition, by reason of which the person was included in the list, be removed, or

(c) a free pardon from the Crown has been received by the person included in the list in respect of the matters recorded in the list.

(2) Where a person has been included in the list under section 38(1)(c) of the Measure and the archbishop of the relevant province makes a request under section 1 of the Clerical Disabilities Act 1870 (Amendment) Measure 1934 for the vacation of the enrolment of the deed of relinquishment

executed by that person, the archbishop shall with the agreement of the other archbishop remove that person from the list.

Review of an entry in the list – (d) & (e)

78.—(1) On the expiry of the period of five years following the inclusion of a person in the list under section 38(1)(d) or (e), the archbishop of the relevant province shall—
   (a) inform the person in writing that a review is to be carried out,
   (b) send to the person a transcript of the relevant entry in the list,
   (c) for the purposes of the review invite the person to send written comments or representations within 28 days of the date of the invitation to do so,
   (d) consult the bishop of the diocese in which the person resides or holds office at the time of review and the bishop of any diocese which was concerned at the date of inclusion.

(2) After the 28 day period specified in sub-rule 1(c) has expired, and after considering any comments and representations received, the archbishop of the relevant province shall—
   (a) with the agreement of the other archbishop, decide—
       (i) whether or not the person shall remain in the list, and
       (ii) where the person is to remain in the list, whether or not the particulars recorded in respect of that person shall be altered, and if so, how they shall be altered,
   (b) in writing, notify the decision to—
       (i) the person included in the list,
       (ii) the bishop of the diocese where that person resides or holds office, and
       (iii) any other bishop who was consulted in the course of the review.

BISHOP MAY REQUEST REVIEW OF INCLUSION IN THE LIST

79. A bishop of a diocese may, at any time following the inclusion of a person in the list under section 38(1)(d) or (e), request a review of the inclusion, and the archbishop of the relevant province shall follow the same procedure as set out in rule 78.

Person named in the list may request review of inclusion after 5 years

80. A person included in the list under section 38(1)(d) or (e) may request a review under section 38(4) of the Measure only after the expiry of a period of 5 years from the inclusion or after the expiry of a period of 5 years from the date of a previous review. Where such a request is made the archbishop of the relevant province shall follow the same procedure as set out in rule 78.

PART XIII

Proceedings against bishops and archbishops

Application of rules to bishops and archbishops

81.—(1) Subject to rules 82 to 90 these rules apply to proceedings against bishops and archbishops under the Measure as they apply to priests and deacons, and are to be construed accordingly for the purposes of such proceedings.

(2) Unless the context otherwise requires, in proceedings against a bishop references in the rules to the bishop to whom a complaint is made shall be construed as references to the archbishop of the relevant province, and in proceedings against an archbishop such references to the bishop shall be construed as references to the other archbishop.

Institution of proceedings against bishops or archbishops

82.—(1) No disciplinary proceedings under section 10 of the Measure against a bishop or archbishop may be instituted except by way of a written complaint made in form 1b in the Schedule, or in a document which is substantially to the like effect containing the information required for the completion of form 1b.

(2) Where the complainant has been nominated by the bishop's council or the archbishop's council of the relevant diocese the complaint in writing shall have attached to it a certified copy of the council's resolution passed in accordance with section 10(1)(b)(i) or (c)(i) as the case may be.

(3) A complaint shall be referred for preliminary scrutiny in accordance with rule 9 to the provincial registrar in the case of a bishop, and in the case of an archbishop to the provincial registrar of the other province.

Conditional Deferment of a Complaint Against a Bishop or Archbishop

83.—(1) Where the respondent is a bishop or archbishop and has consented in writing to a conditional deferment, the archbishop or the other archbishop, as the case may be, shall within 21 days send—
  (a) to the complainant and the respondent a copy of the determination to impose a conditional deferment, and
  (b) to the registrar of the province of the respondent a copy of the determination, the complaint with evidence in support, and the respondent's answer, if any, with evidence in support, and the provincial registrar shall maintain a record of the conditional deferment for such period not exceeding five years as the archbishop or other archbishop may determine;

and form 6 and rule 24(b) shall be adapted accordingly by omitting reference to notification to the archbishop.

(2) The provincial registrar's record of the conditional deferment shall not be open to public inspection but shall be made available to diocesan bishops, and registrars.

Death or serious illness or incapacity of the complainant

84. Rules 55 and 56 shall be read as if the words 'the parochial church council' wherever they appear are replaced by 'the bishop's council' or 'the archbishop's council', as the case may be.

Notice of suspension of a bishop or archbishop during proceedings

85. For the purposes of rule 60 a notice of suspension on a bishop or archbishop shall be—
  (a) in form 12b in the Schedule or in a form which is substantially to the same effect,
  (b) signed by the archbishop of the province in which the bishop to be suspended holds office, or, in the case of an archbishop to be suspended, signed by the other archbishop,
  (c) countersigned by the two most senior diocesan bishops in that province or the province of the other archbishop, as the case may be, and rule 62 shall be construed accordingly.

Notice of suspension of a bishop or archbishop following arrest

86. For the purposes of rule 61 a notice of suspension on a bishop or archbishop shall be—
  (a) in form 13b in the Schedule or in a form which is substantially to the like effect, (b) signed by the archbishop of the province in which the bishop to be suspended holds office, or, in the case of an archbishop to be suspended, signed by the other archbishop, and
  (c) countersigned by the two most senior diocesan bishops in that province or the province of the other archbishop, as the case may be. and rule 62 shall be construed accordingly.

Notification to others of suspension of bishop

87. For the purposes of rule 63 a copy of the notice of suspension of a bishop shall be sent or delivered to—
  (a) the other archbishop,
  (b) other bishops of the diocese of the suspended bishop, including assistant bishops,
  (c) the secretary of the bishop's council of the diocese of the suspended bishop,
  (d) the diocesan registrar,
  (e) the provincial registrar,

and rules 64(2), 65 & 66(4) shall be construed accordingly.

Notification to others of suspension of archbishop

88. For the purposes of rule 63 a copy of the notice of suspension of an archbishop shall be sent or delivered by the other archbishop to—
    (a) each diocesan bishop of the province of the suspended archbishop,
    (b) the secretary of the archbishop's council of the diocese of the suspended archbishop,
    (c) the provincial registrars,

and rules 64(2), 65 and 66(4) shall be construed accordingly.

Sentences of imprisonment & matrimonial orders: bishops & archbishops

89. In rules 67 to 73 references to provisions in section 30 of the Measure shall be read as references to the corresponding provisions in section 31 of the Measure.

Application by bishop or archbishop for review of penalty

90. An application under rule 70 for a review of a penalty imposed under section 31(2) of the Measure shall be made by a bishop to the other archbishop, and by an archbishop to the President, and rules 70 to 73 shall be construed accordingly.

Part XIV

Application of rules to special cases

Special cases under section 42 of the Measure

91. In the application of these rules to—
    (a) Cathedral clergy,
    (b) Chaplains of prisons, hospitals, universities, schools and institutions in an extra-parochial place,
    (c) Chaplains of the armed forces of the Crown,
    (d) Ministers who have a licence from the archbishop of a province to preach throughout the province,
    (e) Ministers who have a licence from the University of Oxford or Cambridge to preach throughout England, the rules shall apply and be read with the following adaptations.

Clerk in holy orders serving in a cathedral church

92. In the case of a clerk in holy orders serving in a cathedral church—
    (a) No disciplinary proceedings under section 10 of the Measure may be instituted except by way of a written complaint made in form 1d in the Schedule, or in a document which is substantially to the like effect containing the information required for completion of form 1d.
    (b) A person shall be duly nominated to institute proceedings for the purposes of section 42(2)(a) of the Measure if there has been a duly convened meeting of the council of the cathedral church, at which not less than two-thirds of the lay members of the council are present, and not less than two-thirds of the lay members present and voting pass a resolution to the effect that proceedings be instituted.
    (c) An application to the bishop for a determination that a person has a proper interest in making a complaint under section 42(2) of the Measure shall be made in writing and shall et out the grounds for making the application. The bishop may seek advice from the registrar as to whether the applicant has a proper interest in making the complaint.

    The bishop's determination that a person has a proper interest in making a complaint shall be in writing signed by the bishop, and the bishop shall send or deliver it to that person and provide a copy for the registrar.
    (d) A complaint in writing shall have attached to it either a certified copy of the resolutions in favour of the institution of proceedings and of the nomination of the complainant, or the bishop's written determination under paragraph (c) above, as the case may be.

(e) Rules 55 and 56 shall be read as if the words 'the parochial church council' wherever they appear read as 'the council of the cathedral church'.
(f) For the purposes of rule 63 a copy of a notice of suspension shall be sent or delivered by the bishop to—
  (i) other clergy who serve in the relevant cathedral church,
  (ii) the secretary of the relevant cathedral council,
  (iii) the registrar,
  and rules 64(2), 65 and 66(4) shall be construed accordingly.

Chaplains of prisons, hospitals, universities, schools and other institutions

93. In the case of a chaplain of a prison, hospital, university, school or other institution—
  (a) No disciplinary proceedings under section 10 of the Measure may be instituted except by way of a written complaint made in form 1e in the Schedule, or in a document which is substantially to the like effect containing the information required for completion of form 1e.
  (b) A request to the bishop for authorisation to institute disciplinary proceedings under the Measure shall be made in writing and shall set out the grounds for making the request.
  The bishop's authorisation to institute proceedings shall be in writing signed by the bishop, and the bishop shall send or deliver it to the person who is to act as complainant, and shall send or deliver a copy to the registrar.
  (c) A complaint in writing shall have attached to it the bishop's written authorisation under paragraph (b) above.
  (d) For the purposes of rule 63 a copy of a notice of suspension shall be sent or delivered by the bishop—
   (i) to the employer of the chaplain,
   (ii) where the chaplain also holds office in a parish, to each person referred to in paragraphs (a) to (d) of rule 63, and
   (iii) to the registrar and rules 64(2), 65 and 66(4) shall be construed accordingly.

Chaplain of the armed forces of the Crown

94. In the case of a chaplain of one of the armed forces of the Crown—
  (a) No disciplinary proceedings under section 10 of the Measure may be instituted except by way of a written complaint made in form 1f in the Schedule, or in a document which is substantially to the like effect containing the information required for completion of form 1f.
  (b) An application to the Archbishop of Canterbury for a determination that a person has a proper interest in making a complaint under the Measure shall be made in writing and shall set out the grounds for making the application.
  The Archbishop of Canterbury may seek advice from the provincial registrar as to whether the applicant has a proper interest in making the complaint. The Archbishop of Canterbury's determination that a person has a proper interest in making a complaint shall be in writing signed by the Archbishop, and the Archbishop shall send or deliver it to that person and provide a copy for the provincial registrar.
  (c) A complaint in writing shall have attached to it the Archbishop of Canterbury's written determination under paragraph (b) above.
  (d) Any reference in these rules to the bishop shall be construed as references to the Archbishop of Canterbury, and any reference to the registrar shall be construed as references to the provincial registrar.
  (e) Where the respondent has consented in writing to a conditional deferment the Archbishop of Canterbury shall within 21 days send—
   (i) to the complainant and the respondent a copy of the determination to impose a conditional deferment, and

(ii) to the provincial registrar a copy of the determination, the complaint with evidence in support, and the respondent's answer, if any, with evidence in support, and the provincial registrar shall maintain a record of the conditional deferment for such period not exceeding five years as the Archbishop may determine;

and form 6 and rule 24(b) shall be adapted accordingly by omitting reference to notification to the archbishop.

(f) For the purposes of rule 27(7) any penalty by consent is to be notified by the Archbishop of Canterbury to the provincial registrar.

(g) For the purposes of rule 63 a copy of a notice of suspension shall be sent or delivered by the Archbishop—
  (i) to the Secretary of State for Defence,
  (ii) to the provincial registrar,
and rules 64(2), 65 and 66(4) shall be construed accordingly.

(h) An application for a review of a decision of the Archbishop of Canterbury under section 30(2) of the Measure shall be made to the Archbishop of York, and rules 70 to 73 shall be construed accordingly.

(i) An application for a prohibition for life or deposition to be nullified under section 26(1) of the Measure shall be made to the Archbishop of York and rule 97 shall be construed accordingly.

(j) For the purposes of an application for the removal of a limited prohibition, reference in section 27 of the Measure to the archbishop of the province concerned shall be construed as meaning the Archbishop of Canterbury.

Ministers with a licence from the Archbishop of the province

95. In the case of a minister who has a licence from the archbishop of a province to preach throughout the province—

(a) No disciplinary proceedings under section 10 of the Measure may be instituted except by way of a written complaint made in form 1g in the Schedule, or in a document which is substantially to the like effect containing the information required for completion of form 1g.

(b) A request to the archbishop of the province for authorisation to institute disciplinary proceedings under the Measure shall be made in writing and shall set out the grounds for making the request.

The authorisation by the archbishop of the province for the institution of proceedings shall be in writing signed by the archbishop, and the archbishop shall send or deliver it to the person who is to act as complainant and provide a copy for the provincial registrar.

(c) A complaint in writing shall have attached to it the written authorisation of the archbishop of the province under paragraph (b) above.

(d) Any reference in these rules to the bishop shall be construed as references to the archbishop of the province, and any reference to the registrar shall be construed as references to the provincial registrar.

(e) Where the respondent has consented in writing to a conditional deferment the archbishops of the province shall within 21 days send—
  (i) to the complainant and the respondent a copy of the determination to impose a conditional deferment, and
  (ii) to the provincial registrar a copy of the determination, the complaint with evidence in support, and the respondent's answer, if any, with evidence in support, and the provincial registrar shall maintain a record of the conditional deferment for such period not exceeding five years as the archbishop may determine; and form 6 and rule 24(b) shall be adapted accordingly by omitting reference to notification to the archbishop.

(f) For the purposes of rule 27(7) any penalty by consent is to be notified by the archbishop of the province to the provincial registrar.
(g) For the purposes of rule 63 a copy of a notice of suspension shall be sent or delivered by the archbishop of the province—
  (i) to the employer, if any, of the minister,
  (ii) to the provincial registrar, and
  (iii) to such other persons as the archbishop deems appropriate,
  and rules 64(2), 65 and 66(4) shall be construed accordingly.
(h) An application for a review of a decision of the archbishop of a province under section 30(2) of the Measure shall be made to the other archbishop, and rules 70 to 73 shall be construed accordingly.
(i) An application for a prohibition for life or deposition to be nullified under section 26(1) of the Measure shall be made to the other archbishop and rule 97 shall be construed accordingly.

Ministers with a Licence from the University of Oxford or Cambridge

96. In the case of a minister who has a licence from the University of Oxford or Cambridge—
  (a) No disciplinary proceedings under section 10 of the Measure may be instituted except by way of a written complaint made in form 1g in the Schedule, or in a document which is substantially to the like effect containing the information required for completion of form 1g.
  (b) A request to the Archbishop of Canterbury for authorisation to institute disciplinary proceedings under the Measure shall be made in writing and shall set out the grounds for making the request.
     The authorisation by the Archbishop of Canterbury for the institution of proceedings shall be in writing signed by the Archbishop, and the Archbishop shall send or deliver it to the prospective complainant and provide a copy for the provincial registrar.
  (c) A complaint in writing shall have attached to it the written authorisation of the Archbishop of Canterbury under paragraph (b) above.
  (d) Any reference in these rules to the bishop shall be construed as references to the Archbishop of Canterbury, and any reference to the registrar shall be construed as references to the provincial registrar.
  (e) Where the respondent has consented in writing to a conditional deferment the Archbishop of Canterbury shall within 21 days send—
    (i) to the complainant and the respondent a copy of the determination to impose a conditional deferment, and
    (ii) to the provincial registrar a copy of the determination, the complaint with evidence in support, and the respondent's answer, if any, with evidence in support, and the provincial registrar shall maintain a record of the conditional deferment for such period not exceeding five years as the Archbishop may determine; and form 6 and rule 24(b) shall be adapted accordingly by omitting reference to notification to the archbishop.
  (f) For the purposes of rule 27(7) any penalty by consent is to be notified by the Archbishop of Canterbury to the provincial registrar.
  (g) For the purposes of rule 63 a copy of a notice of suspension shall be sent or delivered by the Archbishop of Canterbury—
    (i) to the employer, if any, of the minister,
    (ii) to the provincial registrar, and
    (iii) to such other persons as the Archbishop deems appropriate, and rules 64(2), 65 and 66(4) shall be construed accordingly.

(h) An application for a review of a decision of the Archbishop of Canterbury under section 30(2) of the Measure shall be made to the Archbishop of York, and rules 70 to 73 shall be construed accordingly.

(i) An application for a prohibition for life or deposition to be nullified under section 26(1) of the Measure shall be made to the Archbishop of York and rule 97 shall be construed accordingly.

(j) For the purposes of an application for the removal of a limited prohibition, reference in section 27 of the Measure to the archbishop of the province concerned shall be construed as meaning the Archbishop of Canterbury.

Part XV

Removal of prohibitions

Removal of prohibition for life and deposition: priests and deacons

97.—(1) An application for a prohibition for life or deposition to be nullified shall—
   (a) be made in writing,
   (b) set out the reasons upon which it is made,
   (c) be accompanied by any written evidence upon which the applicant seeks to rely.

(2) The archbishop may invite any person involved in the proceedings leading to the prohibition or deposition to make written representations within 21 days of being invited to do so, and a copy of any such representations shall be sent or delivered by the archbishop to the applicant.

(3) The archbishop shall consider the application with or without a hearing.

(4) Having considered the application and after consultation with the Dean of the Arches and Auditor, the archbishop shall declare in writing whether the prohibition for life or deposition was justified, and a copy of the declaration shall be sent or delivered to the applicant and the provincial registrar. Where the application is considered without a hearing the archbishop shall send or deliver the written decision within 3 months of receiving the application. Where a hearing is held for the purposes of the application the archbishop shall send or deliver the written decision within 28 days after the hearing.

Removal of limited prohibition: priests and deacons

98.—(1) An application for the removal of a limited prohibition shall—
   (a) be made in writing jointly by the bishop and the priest or deacon,
   (b) set out the grounds upon which it is made.
   (c) be accompanied by any written evidence upon which the joint applicants seek to rely.

(2) The Dean of the Arches and Auditor and the two Vicars-General shall consider the application with or without a hearing.

(3) The Dean of the Arches and Auditor and the two Vicars-General shall make their order in writing and a copy shall be sent or delivered to the joint applicants and the provincial registrar. Where the application is considered without a hearing the order shall be sent or delivered within 3 months of receiving the application. Where a hearing is held for the purposes of the application the order shall be sent or delivered within 28 days after the hearing.

Removal of prohibition for life and deposition: bishops and archbishops

99. For the purposes of rule 97 an application for a prohibition or deposition to be nullified under section 26(3) of the Measure shall be made—
   (a) by a bishop to the archbishop of the other province,
   (b) by an archbishop to the Dean of the Arches and Auditor, and in the case of an application by an archbishop rule 97(4) shall be read as if reference to any consultation were omitted.

Removal of limited prohibition: bishops and archbishops

100. For the purposes of rule 98 an application to the Dean of the Arches and Auditor sitting with the two Vicars-General for the removal of a limited prohibition under section 27 of the Measure shall be made—
    (a) by a bishop jointly with the archbishop of the relevant province,
    (b) by an archbishop jointly with the other archbishop.

Part XVI

Miscellaneous

Sending or delivering documents

101.—(1) Any document required by these rules to be sent or delivered to any person shall be sent or delivered by any of the following means—
    (a) by first class post to the proper address of that person,
    (b) by leaving it at the proper address of that person,
    (c) by document exchange by leaving it addressed to that person's numbered box—
        (i) at the DX of that person, or
        (ii) at a DX which sends documents to that person's DX every business day,
    (d) in such other manner (including electronic means) as the President, Registrar of Tribunals or Chair may direct.

(2) The proper address shall be the usual or last known address of a person, except as follows—
    (a) where proceedings have been referred by the President to the tribunal, the proper address for the respondent, if legally represented, shall be the business address of any solicitor acting for the respondent in the proceedings,
    (b) the proper address for the President shall be care of The Legal Office of the National Institutions of the Church of England,
    (c) the proper address for the Dean of the Arches and Auditor shall be the address of the Provincial Registry of the province concerned,
    (d) the proper address for the Designated Officer shall be The Legal Office of the National Institutions of the Church of England.

Time

102.—(1) Save where these rules provide that the time for doing an act may be extended by another person, the President may extend any time limit specified under the rules for doing an act even if the time so specified has expired, unless an extension would be inconsistent with any provision of the Measure.

(2) Where proceedings have been referred by the President to the tribunal, the Registrar of Tribunals or the Chair may extend any time limit specified under these rules for doing an act even if the time so specified has expired, unless an extension would be inconsistent with the provisions of the Measure.

(3) Where an order or direction imposes a time limit for doing an act the last date for compliance shall wherever practicable be expressed as a calendar date and include the time by which the act must be done.

Irregularities

103. Where there has been an irregularity or error of procedure—
    (a) such irregularity or error does not invalidate any step taken in the proceedings unless the President, Registrar of Tribunals, Chair or tribunal so orders, or unless on appeal the Arches Court of Canterbury or the Chancery Court of York so holds,
    (b) the President, Registrar of Tribunals, Chair or tribunal may give directions to cure or waive the irregularity.

Revision of forms

104. Any forms in the Schedule may from time to time be revised or amended by direction of the Dean of the Arches and Auditor if deemed appropriate.

Contempt

105.—(1) If any person does or omits to do anything which is a contempt in connection with proceedings before, or in connection with an order made by, the Registrar of Tribunals, the Chair or the tribunal, the Chair may certify the act or omission as a contempt and refer the matter to the High Court under section 81(3) of the Ecclesiastical Jurisdiction Measure 1963(a).

(2) Failure to comply with an order shall not be deemed to be a contempt unless the order provides that the person to whom it is directed may be sent to prison, or fined, or both, if the order is not obeyed.

Interpretation

106. In these rules, unless the context otherwise requires—

'Schedule' means the Schedule to these rules;

'bishop' includes the suffragan or area bishop where disciplinary functions under the Measure have been delegated in a diocese or where there is a relevant area scheme covering disciplinary functions under section 10 & section 11 respectively of the Dioceses Measure 1978(b);

'Chair' means the chairman (within the meaning of section 22(1)(a), section 23(1)(a) and section 23(2)(a) of the Measure) of the tribunal or Vicar-General's court which is hearing, or will in due course be hearing, the complaint;

'child' means a person under the age of 18 years old;

'complainant' means the person or persons making or intending to make a complaint under section 10 of the Measure, or the person duly nominated to do so whether under section 10, section 42 or rule 55 or the person authorised or determined to have a proper interest under section 42, or the person substituted as complainant under rules 55, 56 or 59, as the case may be;

'conciliator' includes joint-conciliators;

'Designated Officer' means the officer of the Legal Office of the National Institutions of the Church of England designated by the Archbishops' Council for the purposes of the Measure, who conducts the case on behalf of the complainant when the complaint is referred to the tribunal or the Vicar-General's court, and who acts independently from the complainant, the respondent, the bishop, the archbishop, or any other person or body; 'party' and 'parties' refer to the complainant and the respondent, except in Parts VI, VII, and VIII where they refer to the Designated Officer and the respondent.

'President' means the President of Tribunals;

'provincial registrar' means the provincial registrar of the relevant province, or in the case of a complaint against an archbishop, the provincial registrar of the other province;

'registrar' means the diocesan registrar, or in the case of a complaint made against a bishop the provincial registrar, or in the case of a complaint made against an archbishop the provincial registrar of the other province;

'Registrar of Tribunals' means the registrar of tribunals for the relevant province;

'respondent' means the person in respect of whom disciplinary proceedings are instituted or intended to be instituted;

'the list' means the archbishops' list compiled and maintained by the archbishops under section 38 of the Measure;

'the Measure' means the Clergy Discipline Measure 2003;

'tribunal' means a bishop's disciplinary tribunal or a Vicar-General's Court exercising its jurisdiction in disciplinary proceedings, as the case may be.

Clergy Discipline (Appeal) Rules 2005

SI 2005/3201

Overriding objective

1. The overriding objective of these appeal rules is to enable appeals in disciplinary proceedings under the Measure to be dealt with justly, in a way that is both fair to all relevant interested persons and proportionate to the nature and seriousness of the issues raised. These appeal rules are, so far as is reasonably practicable, to be applied in accordance with the principle that undue delay and undue expense are to be avoided.

Duty to co-operate

2. —(1) In order to further the overriding objective the parties shall co-operate with any person or court exercising any function in connection with an appeal under the Measure.

(2) Any failure to co-operate by an appellant may result in that party's appeal being struck out.

Right of appeal under section 20 of the Measure

3. In disciplinary proceedings under the Measure, subject to rules 5 to 8—
   (a) the respondent may appeal—
       (i) on a question of law or fact against any finding of the tribunal, and
       (ii) against any penalty imposed by the tribunal,
   (b) the Designated Officer may appeal on a question of law against any finding of the tribunal.

The appellate court

4. Any appeal under rule 3 shall be heard by the Arches Court of Canterbury for disciplinary proceedings in the province of Canterbury, and by the Chancery Court of York for disciplinary proceedings in the province of York.

Notice of appeal from respondent

5. —(1) An appeal by a respondent shall be made by sending or delivering to the Provincial Registrar a written notice of appeal in form A1 in the Schedule or a document which is substantially to the like effect containing the information required by sub-rule (2).

(2) A notice of appeal under sub-rule (1) shall—
   (a) state the full name, contact address including postcode, and telephone number of the respondent,
   (b) where the respondent is legally represented, state the name, contact address and telephone number of the solicitor acting for the respondent,
   (c) identify the tribunal which heard the complaint, and state the complaint reference number and the date of the pronouncement of the decision in public,
   (d) state whether the appeal is against—
       (i) findings of law or fact, or both, or
       (ii) findings of law or fact or both, and also the penalty, or
       (iii) the penalty only,
   (e) set out briefly any findings of the tribunal on matters of law or fact against which the respondent wishes to appeal, and in respect of those findings set out briefly the reasons for appealing,
   (f) if the respondent is appealing against a penalty, state what the penalty is, and set out the reasons for contending that a different penalty should be imposed,
   (g) be signed and dated by the respondent or the representative of the respondent.

Notice of appeal from the Designated Officer

6.—(1) An appeal by the Designated Officer shall be made by sending or delivering to the Provincial Registrar a written notice of appeal in form A2 in the Schedule or a document which is substantially to the like effect containing the information required by sub-rule (2) below.

(2) A notice of appeal under sub-rule (1) shall—
- (a) state the full name and contact details of the Designated Officer,
- (b) state the full name and contact address including postcode of the respondent,
- (c) if the Designated Officer believes the respondent to be legally represented, state the name, contact address and telephone number of the solicitor acting for the respondent,
- (d) identify the tribunal which heard the complaint, and state the complaint reference number and the date of the pronouncement of the decision in public,
- (e) set out briefly the matters of law arising from the tribunal's decision in respect of which the Designated Officer wishes to appeal, and briefly the reasons for appealing,
- (f) be signed and dated by the Designated Officer or a person duly authorised by the Designated Officer.

Documents to be attached to the notice of appeal

7. The following documents shall be attached by an appellant to the notice of appeal—
- (a) a copy of the tribunal's decision,
- (b) if a penalty was imposed by the tribunal, a copy of the written decision imposing the penalty.

Time for appealing and for sending or delivering the notice of appeal

8.—(1) Subject to rule 9 no appeal may be made unless the appropriate notice of appeal with the attached documents referred to in rule 7 are sent or delivered to the Provincial Registrar together with five additional copies, so as to be received within 28 days of the date of the pronouncement in public of—
- (a) the tribunal's decision, or
- (b) any penalty imposed by the tribunal,

whichever is the later to occur.

(2) A copy of the notice of appeal and attached documents shall at the same time be sent or delivered by the appellant to the Designated Officer or the respondent as the case may be.

Application to the Dean for permission to appeal out of time

9.—(1) The respondent and the Designated Officer may apply for permission to appeal out of time. An application by the respondent shall be made in writing in form A3 in the Schedule or in a document which is substantially to the like effect containing the information required by sub-rule (2) below. The Designated Officer shall adapt form A3 as appropriate when making such an application.

(2) An application for permission to appeal out of time shall—
- (a) set out the reasons why the appeal was not made within time,
- (b) contain a declaration that the party making the application believes the facts of the application to be true, and
- (c) be signed and dated.

(3) The party making the application shall attach the following documents to an application for permission to appeal out of time—
- (a) a completed draft notice of appeal in form A1 or A2, as the case may be,
- (b) a copy of the tribunal's decision,
- (c) if a penalty was imposed by the tribunal, a copy of the written decision imposing the penalty.

(4) The party making the application shall send or deliver the application and attached documents to the Provincial Registrar, and shall at the same time send or deliver a copy to the Designated Officer or respondent, as the case may be.

(5) The application shall be determined by the Dean without a hearing.

(6) Before determining the application the Dean shall give the other party 14 days within which to make written representations in response to the application, and the other party shall send or deliver to the party making the application a copy of any such representations.

(7) The Dean may give permission to appeal out of time if satisfied that—
  (a) there was good reason why the party making the application did not appeal within the time allowed,
  (b) there would be a good arguable case on appeal, and
  (c) the other party would not suffer significant prejudice as a result of the delay.

(8) The Dean's determination of the application shall be put into writing, and shall be sent or delivered to the parties by the Provincial Registrar within 21 days of the expiry of the time allowed for the written representations referred to in sub-rule (6) above.

(9) If the Dean gives permission to appeal out of time the draft notice of appeal attached to the application shall be treated as the notice of appeal, and within 7 days of receiving the Dean's determination, the appellant shall send or deliver to the Provincial Registrar five additional copies of the notice of appeal with the documents referred to in rule 7 attached to it.

Postponement of penalty

10.—(1) The implementation of a penalty under section 24 which has been imposed by the tribunal shall be postponed pending the disposal of an appeal made under rules 5 or 6 above.

(2) Until proceedings on an appeal have been disposed of, a respondent may be suspended under sections 36 or 37 of the Measure, as the case may be.

(3) Until proceedings on an appeal have been disposed of, no further steps shall be taken under section 38 of the Measure to record the penalty in the archbishops' list.

Interim directions

11.—(1) Upon receipt of a notice of appeal the Provincial Registrar shall give directions for the just disposal of the proceedings in accordance with the overriding objective in rule 1.

(2) The Provincial Registrar may at any stage refer any matter of difficulty or dispute to the Dean.

(3) Directions may be given or varied at any stage—
  (a) at a hearing,
  (b) where sub-rule (5) applies, during a telephone hearing, or
  (c) in writing.

(4) At any hearing or telephone hearing the respondent may be represented by another person, and the Designated Officer may appear in person or authorise another person to act on his or her behalf.

(5) Where a hearing for directions is likely to last no longer than 30 minutes the Dean or Provincial Registrar, as the case may be, may direct that—
  (a) it be conducted by telephone, and
  (b) that the parties send in advance of the hearing for directions a written summary of their respective submissions, and send or deliver copies of their submissions to each other.

(6) Where the respondent appeals solely against the penalty imposed, the Dean or Provincial Registrar may at any stage direct that the Designated Officer need not appear.

Matters on which directions may be given

12.—(1) Directions may be given in respect of all procedural matters and in particular may—
  (a) identify the written and oral witness evidence, exhibits and other documents put before the tribunal which are relevant to the issues to be considered at the hearing of the appeal,
  (b) provide for the preparation by one or more of the parties, in sufficient numbers for the appellate court, of bundles of documents containing—
    (i) material identified in (a), including if available a transcript of the relevant oral evidence,

        (ii) the notice of appeal, together with the attached documents referred to in rule 7,
    (c) give directions about the attendance of any witness who gave evidence to the tribunal, when permission to re-call that witness before the appellate court is given under rule 16 below,
    (d) require any party to prepare a written outline argument, and to send or deliver such number of copies of it as may be directed, together with photocopies of any authorities to be relied upon.

(2) Where an order has been made giving or varying directions without a hearing, a party may apply within 14 days to have it set aside or varied, and the order shall notify the parties that they may make such an application.

(3) Any directions given by the Dean or the Provincial Registrar shall be given or confirmed in writing, and a copy sent or delivered to the parties.

Striking out an appeal

13. The Dean or the appellate court may on application or on their own initiative strike out an appeal if satisfied that the appeal is not being pursued with due expedition.

Absence of a party

14. The Provincial Registrar, Dean or the appellate court may proceed with a hearing notwithstanding the absence of a party, provided they are satisfied that the absent party has had notice of the hearing.

Fixing the date and place of the appeal hearing

15. —(1) The Provincial Registrar may direct the parties to provide time estimates of the likely length of the hearing of the appeal.

(2) Thereafter, as soon as may be expedient, in consultation with the Dean, and with due regard being paid to the convenience of the parties and any witnesses, the Provincial Registrar shall fix the date, time and place for the hearing of the appeal, and shall give at least 14 days written notice of it to the parties.

(3) On an application by a party or at the request of the Dean, the Provincial Registrar may vary the date, time or place of any appeal hearing, and written notice of the variation shall be given to the parties by the Provincial Registrar.

Re-calling witnesses to give evidence before the appellate court

16. —(1) No witness who gave evidence before the tribunal may be called to give oral evidence to the appellate court without permission from the Provincial Registrar, the Dean or the appellate court.

(2) Where a respondent is appealing against a finding of fact and proposes that any witness who gave evidence to the tribunal should give oral evidence to the appellate court, at least 14 days before the directions hearing he or she shall give to the Designated Officer and to the Provincial Registrar (or the Dean where the matter has been referred to the Dean under rule 11(2)) notice in writing of the intention to ask for permission.

(3) The notice in sub-rule (2) shall set out—
    (a) the name of any witness the respondent proposes should give evidence to the appellate court,
    (b) the reasons why it is considered necessary for the witness to give evidence to the appellate court.

(4) The appellate court may at any stage give permission under sub-rule (1).

(5) Permission under sub-rule (1) shall not be granted unless the Provincial Registrar, the Dean or the appellate court, as the case may be, is satisfied that the evidence is necessary for the just disposal of the appeal.

New evidence

17. Without the permission of the Dean or the appellate court, no evidence may be put before the appellate court which was not before the tribunal.

Application for new evidence to be admitted

18. —(1) An application by the respondent to the Dean for permission to put evidence before the appellate court which was not before the tribunal shall be made in writing in form A4 in the Schedule, or in a document which is substantially to the like effect, and shall—

    (a) identify the new evidence,
    (b) explain why the evidence was not before the tribunal,
    (c) explain the relevance and importance of the new evidence in relation to the matters determined by the tribunal and the issues raised in the appeal, and
    (d) contain a declaration that the party making the application believes the facts of the application to be true.

(2) The Designated Officer shall adapt form A4 as appropriate when making such an application.

(3) Where the application relates to evidence from a new witness, the party making the application shall attach to the application a copy of a statement from the witness setting out the proposed evidence, and the witness statement shall—

    (a) indicate which matters in it come from the witness's own knowledge, and which are matters of information or belief,
    (b) indicate the source of any matters of information or belief,
    (c) contain a declaration of truth in the following form—
        'I believe that the contents of this witness statement are true', and
    (d) be signed and dated by the author.

(4) The party making the application shall send or deliver to the other party a copy of the application and any attached witness statement.

(5) Before determining the application the Dean shall give the other party at least 14 days within which to make written representations in response to the application, and the other party shall send or deliver to the party making the application a copy of any such representations.

(6) The Dean may determine the application with or without a hearing. Subject to sub-rule (7) the Dean may grant or refuse the application or in exceptional circumstances may refer it to the appellate court for determination.

(7) The Dean or the appellate court may permit evidence that was not before the tribunal to be put before the appellate court, provided the Dean or the appellate court, as the case may be, is satisfied that—

    (a) the evidence was not available and could not reasonably have been obtained for the tribunal hearing,
    (b) the evidence, if it had been before the tribunal, could have had an important bearing on the determination of the matters before it, and
    (c) the evidence appears to be credible.

Amendment or withdrawal of the appeal

19. The appellate court may at the hearing, or the Dean may at any time before the hearing, on an application by the appellant after giving the other party an opportunity to respond to the application—

    (a) allow the appeal to be withdrawn, or
    (b) allow the notice of appeal to be amended,

on such terms as may be just, which in the case of amendment may include adjourning or postponing the hearing.

Hearing of the appeal

20. The appellant shall not, without permission from the Dean or the appellate court, be entitled on the hearing of the appeal to challenge any findings of the tribunal not set out in the notice of

appeal under rules 5(2) or 6(2), as the case may be (whether as originally submitted to the Provincial Registrar or as amended under rule 19).

Power to adjourn

21. The hearing may be adjourned from time to time if necessary.

Oral evidence

22. If oral evidence is permitted by the appellate court, it shall be given on oath or solemn affirmation.

Appellate court may require personal attendance of witness

23. The appellate court may, if satisfied that special circumstances exist, require the personal attendance at the hearing of the author of a witness statement or an expert who has produced a report.

Power to exclude from hearing

24. The appellate court may exclude from the hearing any person who threatens to disrupt or has disrupted the hearing or has otherwise interfered with the administration of justice.

Appeal normally to be heard in public

25. The hearing shall be in public, but at any stage the appellate court may sit in private and may exclude any person or persons if satisfied that to do so—
- (a) is desirable to protect the private life of any person, or
- (b) is desirable to protect the interests of any child, or
- (c) is otherwise in the interests of the administration of justice.

Court may order identity not to be published

26. The appellate court may order that the name and any other identifying details of any person involved or referred to in the proceedings must not be published or otherwise made public, if satisfied that such an order—
- (a) is desirable to protect the private life of any person, or
- (b) is desirable to protect the interests of any child, or
- (c) is otherwise in the interests of the administration of justice.

The powers of the appellate court

27. On any appeal the appellate court may—
- (a) confirm, reverse or vary any finding of the tribunal,
- (b) refer a particular issue back to the tribunal for hearing and determination in accordance with any direction that may be given by the appellate court,
- (c) order the complaint to be reheard by the same or a differently constituted tribunal,
- (d) confirm or set aside a penalty imposed by the tribunal, or substitute a greater or lesser penalty,
- (e) impose one or more of the penalties under section 24 of the Measure where the tribunal has not imposed any penalty or when upholding an appeal on a question of law by the Designated Officer.

Court may invite bishop to express a view on penalty

28. —(1) Where the appellate court proposes to exercise its powers under rule 27(d) or (e), subject to sub-rule (3), the court may invite—
- (a) in the case of an appeal from the decision of a bishop's disciplinary tribunal, the bishop of the diocese concerned, or
- (b) in the case of an appeal from the decision of a Vicar-General's court, the archbishop concerned, or if the respondent is an archbishop, the other archbishop,

to express in writing within 14 days views as to the appropriate penalty, and the appellate court shall have regard to any such views.

(2) A copy of the bishop's or archbishop's views shall be provided by the Provincial Registrar forthwith to the respondent and to the Designated Officer.

(3) The bishop or archbishop shall not be invited to express any such views if the bishop or archbishop has given evidence in the proceedings at any stage.

(4) The Dean shall pronounce in public any penalty imposed by the appellate court, and may sit alone for that purpose.

Determination of the appeal to be by a majority

29. The determination of the appeal shall be according to the opinion of the majority of the members of the appellate court and shall be recorded in writing.

Pronouncement of the determination

30. The Dean shall pronounce the appellate court's determination of the appeal in public—
    (a) at the end of the hearing, or
    (b) at a later date when the Dean may sit alone for that purpose.

Determination may omit identifying details

31. The appellate court may omit from the written determination the name and any other identifying details of any person, if satisfied that such an order—
    (a) is desirable to protect the private life of that person, or
    (b) is desirable to protect the interests of any child, or
    (c) is otherwise in the interests of the administration of justice.

Provincial Registrar to distribute the written determination

32. A copy of the appellate court's written determination shall be sent by the Provincial Registrar to the complainant, the respondent, the Designated Officer, the bishop, and the diocesan registrar.

Applications

33. —(1) Unless otherwise provided for in these appeal rules, applications by a respondent shall be made in writing to the Provincial Registrar in form A5 in the Schedule, and the respondent shall send or deliver a copy at the same time to the Designated Officer.

(2) The Designated Officer shall adapt form A5 as appropriate when making an application, and shall send or deliver a copy to the respondent.

(3) Any response by a respondent to an application made by the Designated Officer shall be in writing using form A6 in the Schedule, and shall be sent or delivered to the Provincial Registrar within 14 days of the date when the notice of application was sent or delivered by the Designated Officer. The respondent shall at the same time send or deliver a copy of the response to the Designated Officer.

(4) The Designated Officer shall adapt form A6 as appropriate when responding to an application, and shall send or deliver a copy of the response at the same time to the respondent.

Costs

34. —(1) Where a respondent's conduct in the course of appeal proceedings has been unreasonable, the Provincial Registrar, the Dean or the appellate court may make at any stage an order for the payment of costs by the respondent to the Central Board of Finance of the Church of England.

(2) Any such order for the payment of costs may be in respect of—
    (a) costs paid, or authorised by the Legal Aid Commission to be paid, out of the Legal Aid Fund in respect of the respondent's legal costs incurred in the appeal proceedings,
    (b) costs incurred by the Central Board of Finance of the Church of England arising out of or in connection with the appeal proceedings,

and shall require the respondent to pay such gross sum as is deemed appropriate in all the circumstances.

Designated Officer

35. For the purposes of these appeal rules the Designated Officer may act through another person duly authorised by the Designated Officer.

Death of complainant

36.—(1) An appeal, whether made by the respondent or the Designated Officer, shall continue despite the death of a complainant.

(2) The parties may apply for further directions, where necessary, following the death of the complainant.

Death of respondent

37.—(1) Following the death of a respondent the Dean may give permission for an appeal to be heard, whether the appeal is made by the respondent or the Designated Officer, provided the Dean is satisfied that—
- (a) a point of law of general importance is in issue, or
- (b) it is in the interests of justice.

(2) The Dean shall appoint a representative to stand in the place of the deceased respondent for the purposes of the appeal.

Sending or delivering documents

38.—(1) Any document required by these appeal rules to be sent or delivered to any person shall be sent or delivered by any of the following means—
- (a) by first class post to the proper address of that person,
- (b) by leaving it at the proper address of that person,
- (c) by document exchange by leaving it addressed to that person's numbered box—
  - (i) at the DX of that person, or
  - (ii) at a DX which sends documents to that person's DX every business day,
- (d) in such other manner (including electronic means) as the Dean or the Provincial Registrar may direct.

(2) The proper address shall be the usual or last known address of a person, except as follows —
- (a) the proper address for the respondent, if legally represented, shall be the business address of the solicitor acting for the respondent,
- (b) the proper address for the Provincial Registrar shall be the address of the Provincial Registry of the province concerned,
- (c) the proper address for the Dean shall be care of the Provincial Registrar at the Provincial Registry of the province concerned,
- (d) the proper address for the Designated Officer shall be The Legal Office of the National Institutions of the Church of England.

Extension of time

39. Except where rule 9(1) applies, the Dean or the Provincial Registrar may extend any time limit specified under these appeal rules for doing an act even if the time so specified has expired.

Date for compliance

40. Where an order or direction imposes a time limit for doing an act the last date for compliance shall wherever practicable be expressed as a calendar date and include the time of day by which the act must be done.

Irregularities

41. Where there has been an irregularity or error of procedure—
- (a) such irregularity or error does not invalidate any step taken in the appeal proceedings unless the appellate court, Dean or Provincial Registrar so holds, and
- (b) the appellate court, Dean or Provincial Registrar may give directions to cure or waive the irregularity.

Revision of forms

42. Any form in the Schedule may from time to time be revised or amended by direction of the Dean if deemed appropriate.

Interpretation

43. In these appeal rules, unless the context otherwise requires—

'appellant' means the respondent or the Designated Officer, as the case may be, who appeals under rule 3, and, for the avoidance of doubt, does not include a complainant;

'appellate court' means the Arches Court of Canterbury when the proceedings take place in the province of Canterbury, and the Chancery Court of York when the proceedings take place in the province of York;

'complainant' means the person who made the complaint under section 10 of the Measure, or the person duly nominated to do so whether under section 10 or section 42 of the Measure, or rule 55 of the Clergy Discipline Rules 2005[3], or the person authorised or determined to have had a proper interest under section 42 of the Measure in making the complaint, or the person substituted as complainant under rules 55, 56 or 59 of the Clergy Discipline Rules 2005, as the case may be;

'Dean' means the Dean of the Arches and Auditor;

'decision' means a determination by a tribunal or Vicar-General's court within the meaning of section 18(3)(b) of the Measure;

'Designated Officer' means the officer of the Legal Office of the National Institutions of the Church of England designated by the Archbishops' Council for the purposes of the Measure, and who acts independently from the complainant, the respondent, the bishop, the archbishop or any other person or body;

'Legal Aid Fund' and 'Legal Aid Commission' shall mean the fund and the commission referred to in section 1 of the Church of England (Legal Aid) Measure 1994[4];

'parties' means the respondent and the Designated Officer, and 'other party' shall mean either the respondent or the Designated Officer, as the case may be according to the context;

'Provincial Registrar' in the case of an appeal from a bishop's disciplinary tribunal means the provincial registrar for the relevant province, and in the case of an appeal from the Vicar-General's court means the provincial registrar for the other province;

'respondent' means the person against whom disciplinary proceedings were instituted;

'Schedule' means the Schedule to these appeal rules;

'the Measure' means the Clergy Discipline Measure 2003;

'tribunal' means a bishop's disciplinary tribunal or a Vicar-General's court exercising its jurisdiction in disciplinary proceedings, as the case may be.

Citation and commencement

44. —(1) These appeal rules shall be known as the Clergy Discipline Appeal Rules 2005.

(2) These appeal rules shall come into operation on the day appointed under section 48(2) of the Measure for the coming into operation of section 8 of the Measure.

CHURCH REPRESENTATION RULES

Part I: Church Electoral Roll	617	Part VI: Appeals and Disqualifications	643
Part II: Parochial Church Meetings and Councils	620	Part VII: Supplementary and Interpretation	647
Part III: Deanery Synods	631	Appendix II: General Provisions Relating to Parochial Church Councils	652
Part IV: Diocesan Synods	634		
Part V: House of Laity of General Synod	638		

These Rules constitute Schedule 3 to the Synodical Government Measure 1969

Part I
Church Electoral Roll

Formation of Roll

1.—(1) There shall be a church electoral roll (in these rules referred to as 'the roll') in every parish, on which the names of lay persons shall be entered as hereinafter provided. The roll shall be available for inspection by bona-fide inquirers.

(2) A lay person shall be entitled to have his name entered on the roll of a parish if he is baptised, of sixteen years or upwards, has signed an application form for enrolment set out in Appendix I of these rules and declares himself either—

(a) to be a member of the Church of England or of a Church in communion therewith resident in the parish; or

(b) to be such a member and, not being resident in the parish, to have habitually attended public worship in the parish during a period of six months prior to enrolment; or

(c) to be a member in good standing of a Church which subscribes to the doctrine of the Holy Trinity (not being a Church in communion with the Church of England) and also prepared to declare himself to be a member of the Church of England having habitually attended public worship in the parish during a period of six months prior to enrolment.

Provided that where a lay person will have his sixteenth birthday after the intended revision of the electoral roll or the preparation of a new roll but on or before the date of the annual parochial church meeting, he may complete a form of application for enrolment and his name shall be enrolled but with effect from the date of his birthday.

(3) Where a person resides in an extra-parochial place he shall be deemed for the purposes of these rules to reside in the parish which it abuts, and if there is any doubt in the matter a determination shall be made by the bishop's council and standing committee.

(4) A person shall be entitled to have his name on the roll of each of any number of parishes if he is entitled by virtue of paragraphs (2) and (3) of this rule to have his name entered on each roll; but a person whose name is entered on the roll of each of two or more parishes must choose one of those parishes for the purposes of the provisions of these rules which prescribe the qualifications for election to a deanery synod, a diocesan synod or the General Synod or for membership of a parochial church council under rule 14(1)(f) or of a deanery synod under rule 24(6)(b).

(5) The roll shall, until a parochial church council has been constituted in a parish, be formed and revised by the minister and churchwardens (if any), and shall, after such council has been constituted, be kept and revised by or under the direction of the council. Reference in this rule to a parochial church council shall, so far as may be necessary for giving effect to these rules, be construed as including references to the minister and churchwardens (if any).

(6) Where a new parish is created by a pastoral scheme, the roll of that parish shall in the first instance consist—

    (a)   in the case of a parish created by the union of two or more former parishes, of the rolls of those parishes combined to form one roll;

    (b)   in any other case, of the names of the persons whose names are at the date of the coming into existence of the new parish entered on the roll of a parish the whole or any part of which forms part of the new parish and who are either resident in the new parish or have habitually attended public worship therein.

(7) The parochial church council shall appoint a church electoral roll officer to act under its directions for the purpose of carrying out its functions with regard to the electoral roll.

(8) The names of persons who are entitled to have their names entered upon the roll of the parish shall, subject to the provisions of these rules, be from time to time added to the roll. It shall be the duty of the electoral roll officer to keep the roll constantly up to date by the addition and removal of names as from time to time required by these rules and to report such additions and removals at the next meeting of the parochial church council. When additions and removals have been made by the electoral roll officer a list of such amendments shall be published by being exhibited continuously for not less than fourteen days on or near the principal door of every church in the parish and every building in the parish licensed for public worship in such manner as the Council may appoint and the list shall contain notification of the right of appeal referred to in rule 43.

(9) Subject to the provisions of this rule, a person's name shall, as the occasion arises, be removed from the roll, if he:—

    (a)   has died; or

    (b)   becomes a clerk in Holy Orders; or

    (c)   signifies in writing his desire that his name should be removed; or

    (d)   ceases to reside in the parish, unless after so ceasing he continues, in any period of six months, habitually to attend public worship in the parish, unless prevented from doing so by illness or other sufficient cause; or

    (e)   is not resident in the parish and has not attended public worship in the parish during the preceding six months, not habitually having been prevented from doing so by illness or other sufficient causes; or

    (f)   was not entitled to have his name entered on the roll at the time when it was entered.

(10) The removal of a person's name from the roll under any of the provisions of these rules shall be without prejudice to his right to have his name entered again, if he has or acquires that right.

(11) The roll shall where practicable contain a record of the address of every person whose name is entered on the roll, but a failure to comply with this requirement shall not prejudice the validity of any entry on the roll.

Revision of roll and preparation of new roll

2.—(1) Except in a year in which a new roll is prepared, the roll of a parish shall be revised annually by or under the direction of the council. Notice of the intended revision in the form set out in section 2 of Appendix I to these rules shall be affixed by the minister or under his direction on or near the principal door of every church in the parish and every building in the parish licensed for public worship and remain so affixed for a period of not less than fourteen days before the commencement of the revision. The revision shall be completed not less than fifteen days or more than twenty-eight days before the annual parochial church meeting.

(2) Upon every revision all enrolments or removals from the roll which have been effected since the date of the last revision (or since the formation of the roll, if there has been no previous revision) shall be reviewed, and such further enrolments or removals from the rolls as may be required shall be effected.

(3) After the completion of the revision, a copy of the roll as revised shall, together with a list of the names removed from the roll since the last revision (of since the formation of the roll, if there has been no previous revision), be published by being exhibited continuously for not less than fourteen days before the annual parochial church meeting on or near the principal door of the parish church in such manner as the council shall appoint. During the period while the copy is so exhibited any errors and omissions in the roll may be corrected but subject thereto and to the provisions of rule 1(2), no names may be added to or removed from the roll during the period in any year between the completion of the revision and the close of the annual parochial church meeting.

(4) Not less than two months before the annual parochial church meeting in the year 2007 and every succeeding sixth year notice in the form set out in section 3 of Appendix I to these rules shall be affixed by the minister or under his direction on or near the principal door of every church in the parish and every building in the parish licensed for public worship and remain so affixed for a period of not less than fourteen days. On the affixing of the notice a new roll shall be prepared.

At every service held on each of the two Sundays within the period of fourteen days beginning with the date of the affixing of the notice or, in the case of a church in which no service is held on either of those Sundays, at every service held in that church on the first Sunday after that date the person conducting the service shall inform the congregation of the preparation of the new roll.

(5) The parochial church council shall take reasonable steps to inform every person whose name is entered on the pervious roll that a new roll is being prepared and that if he wishes to have his name entered on the new roll he must apply for enrolment. No such steps need be taken with respect to any person whose name could be removed from the previous roll under rule 1(9).

(6) The new roll shall be prepared by entering upon it the names of persons entitled to entry under rule 1(2), and a fresh application shall be required from persons whose names were entered on the previous roll. A person whose name was so entered shall not be disqualified for entry on the new roll by reason only of his failure to comply with the conditions specified in rule 1(2)(b) and (c), if he was prevented from doing so by illness or other sufficient cause, and the circumstances shall be stated on the application form. The preparation of the new roll shall be completed not less than fifteen days or more than twenty-eight days before the annual parochial church meeting.

(7) After the completion of the new roll, a copy shall be published by being exhibited continuously for not less than fourteen days before the annual parochial church meeting on or near the principal door of the parish church in such manner as the council shall appoint. During the period while the copy is so exhibited any errors and omissions in the roll may be corrected but subject thereto and to the provisions of rule 1(2) no names may be added to or removed from the roll during the period in any year between the completion of the new roll and the close of the annual parochial church meeting. On the publication of the new roll it shall come into effect and the previous roll shall cease to have effect.

(8) Upon the alteration of the boundaries of any parishes the parochial church council of the parish from which any area is transferred shall enquire from the persons resident in that area whose names are entered on the roll of the parish, whether they wish to have their names transferred to the roll of the other parish. The parochial church council shall remove the names of persons answering in the affirmative from its own roll and shall inform the parochial church council of the parish in which such persons now reside, which shall enter the names on its roll without any application for enrolment being required.

Procedural provisions relating to entry and removal of names

3.—(1) When a person applying for enrolment on the roll of any parish signifies his desire that his name should be removed from the roll of any other parish, notice of that fact shall be sent by the parochial church council receiving the application to the parochial church council of that other parish.

(2) When the name of any person is removed from the roll of the parish owing to his having become resident in another parish, notice of that fact shall, whenever possible, be sent by the parochial church council of the first mentioned parish to the parochial church council of the last mentioned parish.

Certification of numbers on rolls

4. Not later than the 1st June the chairman, vice-chairman, secretary or church electoral roll officer of the parochial church council shall notify in writing the secretary of the diocesan synod of the number of names on the roll of each parish as at the date of the annual meeting and a copy of such notification shall be affixed at or near to the principal door of every church in the parish and every building licensed for public worship in the parish when notification is sent to the secretary of the diocesan synod, and shall remain so affixed for a period of not less than fourteen days.

5.—(1) A person whose name is entered on the roll of a guild church shall for the purpose of the provisions of these rules which prescribe the qualifications for election to a deanery synod, a diocesan synod or the House of Laity of the General Synod, or for membership of a deanery synod under rule 26(6)(b), be deemed to be a person whose name is on the roll of the parish in which the guild church is, and references in those provisions or in rule 1(4) to a person whose name is on the roll of a parish or on the roll of each of two or more parishes, and in rule 46 to entry on the roll of a parish, shall be construed accordingly.

(2) In this rule 'guild church' means a church in the City of London designated and established as a guild church under the City of London (Guild Churches) Acts 1952 and 1960.

PART II
PAROCHIAL CHURCH MEETINGS AND COUNCILS

Annual meetings

6.—(1) In every parish there shall be held not later than the 30th April in each year the annual parochial church meeting (hereafter in these rules referred to as 'the annual meeting').

(2) All lay persons whose names are entered on the roll of the parish shall be entitled to attend the annual meeting and to take part in its proceedings, and no other lay person shall be so entitled.

(3) A clerk in Holy Orders shall be entitled to attend the annual meeting of a parish and take part in its proceedings—
  (a) if he is either beneficed in or licensed to the parish or any other parish in the area of the benefice to which the parish belongs; or
  (b) if he is resident in the parish and is not beneficed in or licensed to any other parish; or
  (c) if he is not resident in the parish and is not beneficed or licensed to any other parish, the parochial church council with the concurrence of the minister has declared him to be a habitual worshipper in the parish, such declaration being effective until the conclusion of the annual meeting in the year in which a new roll is prepared under rule 2 or his ceasing to be a habitual worshipper in the parish whichever is the earlier, but without prejudice to a renewal of such declaration; or
  (d) if he is a co-opted member of the parochial church council in accordance with rule 14(1)(h).

(4) Without prejudice to paragraphs (2) and (3) of this rule—
  (a) all the members of the team of a team ministry shall be entitled to attend, and take part in the proceedings of, the annual meeting of the parish or each of the parishes in the area

of the benefice for which the team ministry is established, and where the area of a group ministry includes the area of a benefice for which a team ministry is established, all the vicars in that ministry shall be entitled to attend, and take part in the proceedings of, the annual meeting of each of the other parishes in the area for which the group ministry is established;

(b) all the incumbents and priests in charge in a group ministry shall be entitled to attend, and take part in the proceedings of, the annual meeting of each of the parishes in the area for which the group ministry is established.

(5) Where two or more benefices are held in plurality and a team ministry is, or is to be, established for the area of one of those benefices, then, if a pastoral scheme provides for extending the operation of the team ministry, so long as the plurality continues, to the area of any other benefice so held, paragraph (4) of this rule shall have effect as if the references to the area of the benefice were references to the combined area of the benefices concerned.

Convening of meeting

7.—(1) The annual meeting shall be convened by the minister of the parish by a notice in the form set out in section 4 of Appendix I to these rules affixed on or near to the principal door of every church in the parish and every building licensed for public worship in the parish, for a period including the last two Sundays before the day of the meeting.

(2) The annual meeting shall be held at such place on such date and at such hour as shall be directed by the previous annual meeting, or by the parochial church council (which may vary any direction given by a previous annual meeting) or in the absence of any such direction as shall be appointed by the minister.

(3) During the vacancy of the benefice or curacy or when the minister is absent or incapacitated by illness or any other cause, the vice-chairman of the parochial church council, or if there is no vice-chairman, or if he is unable or unwilling to act, the secretary of or some other person appointed by that council shall have all the powers vested in the minister under this rule.

(4) The annual meeting shall be held at a place within the parish unless the parochial church council decide otherwise.

(5) The minister of a new parish created by a pastoral scheme, or, in the absence of the minister, a person appointed by the bishop, shall as soon as possible after the scheme comes into operation convene a special parochial church meeting, and, subject to paragraph (6) of this rule, the provisions of these rules relating to the convening and conduct of the annual meeting shall apply to a special meeting convened under this paragraph.

(6) A special meeting so convened and held in the month of November or the month of December may, if the meeting so resolves, be for all purposes under these rules the annual meeting for the succeeding year, and a special meeting so convened shall in any event be for all such purposes the annual meeting for the year in which it is so convened and held.

Chairman

8.—(1) The minister, if present, or, if he is not present, the vice-chairman of the parochial church council, or, subject to paragraph (2) of this rule, if he also is not present, a chairman chosen by the annual meeting shall preside thereat.

(2) Where a parish is in the area of a benefice for which a team ministry is established, and a vicar in that ministry is entitled to preside at an annual meeting of that parish by virtue of a provision in a pastoral scheme or the bishop's licence assigning to the vicar the duties, or a share in the duties, of the chairmanship of the annual meeting of that parish, then, if both he and the vice-chairman of the parochial church council are not present at that meeting, but the rector in that ministry is present, the rector shall preside thereat.

(3) In case of an equal division of votes, the chairman of the meeting shall have a second or casting vote unless it is a case where rule 11(8) applies but no clerical chairman shall have a vote in the election of the parochial representatives of the laity.

Business

9.—(1) The annual meeting shall receive from the parochial church council and shall be free to discuss:—
    (a) a report on changes in the roll since the last annual parochial church meeting or, in a year in which a new roll is prepared, a report on the numbers entered on the new roll;
    (b) an annual report on the proceedings of the parochial church council and the activities of the parish generally;
    (c) the financial statements of the parochial church council for the year ending on the 31st December immediately preceding the meeting, independently examined or audited as provided by paragraph (3) hereof;
    (d) a report upon the fabric, goods and ornaments of the church or churches of the parish, under section 5 of the Care of Churches and Ecclesiastical Jurisdiction Measure 1991; and
    (e) a report on the proceedings of the deanery synod.

(2) The council shall cause a copy of the said roll to be available for inspection at the meeting.

(3) The said financial statements shall—
    (a) be independently examined or audited in such manner as shall be prescribed in accordance with rule 54(8);
    (b) be considered and, if thought fit, approved by the parochial church council and signed by the chairman presiding at the meeting of the council; and
    (c) be displayed for a continuous period of at least seven days before the annual meeting, including at least one Sunday when the church is used for worship, on a notice-board either inside or outside the church.

(4) The annual report referred to in paragraph (1)(b) above and the said financial statements shall be prepared in such form as shall be prescribed in accordance with rule 54(8) hereof for consideration by the annual meeting. Following such meeting the council shall cause copies of the annual report and statements to be sent within twenty eight days of the annual meeting to the secretary of the diocesan board of finance for retention by the board.

(5) The annual meeting shall in the manner provided by rule 11—
    (a) elect in every third year parochial representatives of the laity to the deanery synod;
    (b) elect parochial representatives of the laity to the parochial church council;
    (c) appoint sidesmen;
    (d) appoint the independent examiner or auditor to the council for a term of office ending at the close of the next annual meeting, provided that such person shall not be a member of the council.

and the elections and appointments shall be carried out in the above order.

(6) Without prejudice to the foregoing provisions and rule 7(6), a special parochial church meeting convened under rule 7(5) shall, in addition to other business,—
    (a) decide on the number of members of the parochial church council who are to be elected representatives of the laity;
    (b) elect in the manner provided by rule 11 parochial representatives of the laity to the deanery synod, if such representatives are required to be elected in the year for which that meeting is the annual meeting by virtue of rule 7(6).

(7) Any person entitled to attend the annual meeting may ask any question about parochial church matters, or bring about a discussion of any matter of parochial or general church interest, by moving a general resolution or by moving to give any particular recommendation to the council in relation to its duties.

(8) The annual meeting shall have power to adjourn and to determine its own rules of procedure.

(9) The secretary of the parochial church council (or another person appointed by the meeting in his place) shall act as a clerk of the annual meeting, and shall record the minutes thereof.

Part II: Parochial Church Meetings and Councils

Qualifications of persons to be chosen or elected by annual meetings

10.—(1) Subject to the provisions of rule 1(4) and paragraph (3) of this rule, the qualifications of a person to be elected a parochial representative of the laity to either the parochial church council or the deanery synod are that—

(a) his name is entered on the roll of the parish and, unless he is under the age of eighteen years at the date of the election, has been so entered for at least the preceding period of six months;

(b) he is an actual communicant as defined in rule 54(1); and

(c) he is of sixteen years or upwards.

(2) The qualification of a person to be appointed a sidesman is that his name is entered on the roll of the parish.

(3) No person shall be nominated for election under rule 9—

(a) to serve on either the parochial church council, or the deanery synod unless he has signified his consent to serve, or there is in the opinion of the meeting sufficient evidence of his willingness to serve;

(b) to serve on the parochial church council, if he has been disqualified under rule 46A;

Conduct of Elections at Annual Meetings

11.—(1) Subject to the provisions of any resolution under rule 12 and for the time being in force This rule shall apply to all elections at annual meetings.

(2) All candidates for election at an annual meeting must be nominated and seconded by persons entitled to attend the annual meeting, and in the case of parochial representatives of the laity, by persons whose names are entered on the roll of the parish. A candidate shall be nominated or seconded either before the meeting in writing or at the meeting.

(3) If the number of candidates nominated is not greater than the number of seats to be filled, the candidates nominated shall forthwith be declared elected.

(4) If more candidates are nominated than there are seats to be filled, the election shall take place at the annual meeting.

(5) No clerk in Holy Orders shall be entitled to vote in the election of any parochial representatives of the laity.

(6) Each person entitled to vote shall have as many votes as there are seats to be filled but may not give more than one vote to any one candidate.

(7) Votes may be given—

(a) by show of hands, or

(b) if one or more persons object—

(i) on voting papers signed by the voter on the reverse thereof; or

(ii) if at least one tenth of the persons present and voting at the meeting so request, on numbered voting papers.

(8)

(a) Where owing to an equality of votes an election is not decided, the decision between the persons for whom the equal numbers of votes have been cast shall be taken by lot.

(b) When an election or any stage of an election is recounted, either on appeal or at the request of the presiding officer or of a candidate, if the original count and the re-count are identical at the point when a lot must be drawn to resolve a tie, the original lot shall be used to make the determination.

(9) The result of any election by an annual meeting shall be announced as soon as practicable by the person presiding over the election, and a notice of the result shall in every case be affixed on or near the principal door of every church in the parish and every building licensed for public worship in the parish, and shall bear the date on which the result in declared. The notice shall remain affixed for not less than fourteen days. Thereafter the secretary of the parochial church council shall hold a

list of the names and addresses of the members of the council which shall be available for inspection on reasonable notice being given by any person who either is resident in the parish or has his name on the electoral roll, but the secretary shall not be bound to provide a copy of such list.

(10) Names and addresses, of parochial representatives of the laity elected to the deanery synod shall be sent by the secretary of the parochial church council to the diocesan electoral registration officer appointed in accordance with rule 29 and to the secretary of the deanery synod.

(11) Where a vote is conducted in accordance with paragraph (7)(b)(ii) above, a record shall be made of the identity of each person to whom a numbered voting paper is issued and any such record, so long as it is retained, shall be kept separate from the voting papers.

Variation of method of election by scheme

12.—(1) The annual meeting may pass a resolution which provides that the election of parochial representatives of the laity to the parochial church council or to the deanery synod or to both that council and that synod shall be conducted by the method of the single transferable vote under rules, with the necessary modifications, made by the General Synod under rule 39(7) and for the time being in force, except that where the vote is conducted in accordance with Rule 11(7)(b)(ii), those rules shall have effect with the omission of any requirement that the voting paper be signed by the voter.

(2) The annual meeting may pass a resolution which provides that any person entitled to attend the annual meeting and vote in the elections of parochial representatives of the laity to the parochial church council or to the deanery synod or to both that council and that synod may make application in the form set out in section 4A of Appendix I for a postal vote.

(3) Where applications for postal votes have been received by the date specified in the notice convening the annual meeting and where the number of candidates nominated for an election referred to in paragraph (2) of this rule is greater than the number of seats to be filled, the annual meeting shall appoint a presiding officer who shall not be a candidate in the election. Voting papers shall be distributed to each person present at the meeting entitled to vote and completed papers shall be returned into the custody of the presiding officer before the close of the meeting. The presiding officer shall ensure that persons who have made application for a postal vote shall be sent or have delivered a voting paper within 48 hours of the close of the meeting such paper to be returned to the presiding officer within such period of not less than 7 days nor more than 14 days from the date of the meeting as the presiding officer shall specify.

(4) A resolution passed under this rule shall be invalid unless approved by at least two thirds of the persons present and voting at the annual meeting nor shall it be operative until the next ensuing annual meeting. Such resolution may be rescinded by a subsequent resolution passed in the same manner.

CONDUCT OF ELECTIONS OF CHURCHWARDENS

13.—(1) Elections of churchwardens under the Churchwardens Measure 2001 shall be conducted, announced and notified in the same manner as elections under rule 11 except that all persons entitled to attend the meeting of parishioners other than the minister shall be entitled to nominate and vote at such elections of churchwardens.

PAROCHIAL CHURCH COUNCIL

Members

14.—(1) Subject to the provisions of rule 1(4) and paragraph (3) of this rule, the parochial church council shall consist of:—
    (a)   all clerks in Holy Orders beneficed in or licensed to the parish;
    (aa) any clerk in Holy Orders who is duly authorised to act as chairman of meetings of the council by the bishop in accordance with paragraph 5(b) of Appendix II to these rules;

Part II: Parochial Church Meetings and Councils

(b) any deaconess or lay worker licensed to the parish;

(c) in the case of a parish in the area of a benefice for which a team ministry is established, all the members of the team of that ministry;

(d) the churchwardens and any deputy churchwardens who are ex officio members of the parochial church council by virtue of a scheme made under rule 18(4) of these rules, being actual communicants whose names are on the roll of the parish;

(e) such, if any, of the readers who are licensed to that parish or licensed to an area which includes that parish and whose names are on the roll of the parish as the annual meeting may determine;

(f) all persons whose names are on the roll of the parish and who are lay members of any deanery synod, diocesan synod or the General Synod;

(g) six representatives of the laity where there are not more than fifty names on the electoral roll, nine such representatives where there are not more than one hundred names on the roll and, where there are more than one hundred names on the roll, a further three such representatives for every one hundred (or part thereof) names on the roll up to a maximum of fifteen such members, and so that the aforesaid numbers 'six', 'nine', 'three' and 'fifteen' may be altered from time to time by a resolution passed at any annual meeting, but such resolution shall not take effect before the next ensuing annual meeting; and

(h) co-opted members, if the parochial church council so decides, not exceeding in number one-fifth of the representatives the laity elected under the last preceding sub-paragraph of this paragraph, or two persons whichever shall be the greater, and being either clerks in Holy Orders or actual lay communicants of sixteen years of age or upwards. The term of office of a co-opted member shall be until the conclusion of the next annual meeting; but without prejudice to his being co-opted on subsequent occasions for a similar term, subject to and in accordance with the provisions of these rules.

(2) Any person chosen, appointed or elected as a churchwarden of a parish, being an actual communicant whose name is on the roll of the parish, shall as from the date on which the choice, appointment or election, as the case may be, is made be a member of the parochial church council of the parish by virtue of this paragraph until he is admitted to the office of churchwarden, and he shall thereafter continue to be a member of that council by virtue of paragraph (1)(d) of this rule unless and until he ceases to be qualified for membership by virtue of that sub-paragraph.

(3) A person shall cease to be a member of a parochial church council—

(a) if his name is removed from the roll of the parish under rule 1, on the date on which his name is removed;

(b) if he refuses or fails to apply for enrolment when a new roll is being prepared, on the date on which the new roll is completed;

(c) if he is or becomes disqualified under rule 46A, from the date on which the disqualification takes effect;

but, so far as the provisions of (a) and (b) above are concerned, shall be without prejudice to any right which that council may have to make that person a co-opted member.

(4) Where a group ministry is established the incumbents of all benefices in the group every priest in charge of any benefice therein and where the area of the group ministry includes the area of a benefice for which a team ministry is established, all the vicars in that ministry shall be entitled to attend meetings of the parochial church councils of all the parishes in the area for which the group ministry is established. They shall be entitled to receive documents circulated to members of councils of which they are not themselves members and to speak but not to vote at meetings of such councils.

(5) Where two or more benefices are held in plurality and a team ministry is, or is to be, established for the area of one of those benefices, then, if a pastoral scheme provides for extending the operation of the team ministry, so long as the plurality continues, to the area of any other benefice so held, paragraphs (1)(c) and (4) of this rule shall have effect as if the references to the area of the benefice were references to the combined area of the benefices concerned.

General provisions relating to parochial church councils

15. The provisions in Appendix II to these rules shall have effect with respect to parochial church councils, and with respect to the officers, the meetings and the proceedings thereof:

Provided that a parochial church council may, with the consent of the diocesan synod, vary the said provisions, in their application to the council.

Term of office

16.—(1) Subject to the following provisions of these rules, representatives of the laity serving on the parochial church council by virtue of rule 14(1)(g) shall hold office from the conclusion of the annual meeting at which they were elected until the conclusion of the third annual meeting thereafter, one third retiring and being elected each year, but, subject to rule 17, shall on retirement be eligible for re-election.

(2) Where a representative of the laity resigns or otherwise fails to serve for his full term of office the casual vacancy shall be filled for the remainder of his term of office in accordance with rule 48(1).

(3) Notwithstanding the preceding provisions of this rule an annual meeting may decide that the representatives of the laity serving by virtue of rule 14(1)(g) shall retire from office at the conclusion of the annual meeting next following their election, but any such decision shall not affect the terms of office as members of the parochial church council of those due to retire from office at the conclusion of an annual meeting held after that at which the decision was taken.

(4) A decision taken under paragraph (3) above shall be reviewed by the annual meeting at least once every six years; and on any such review the annual meeting may revoke the decision, in which case paragraph (1) above shall apply unless and until a further decision is taken under paragraph (3).

(5) Persons who are members of a parochial church council by virtue of their election as lay members of a deanery synod shall hold office as members of the council for a term beginning with the date of their election and ending with the 31st May next following the election of their successors.

(6) At an annual meeting at which all the representatives of the laity serving by virtue of rule 14(1)(g) are elected to hold office in accordance with paragraph (1) above, lots shall be drawn to decide which third of the representatives is to retire in the first year following that in which the meeting is held, which third is to retire in the second year and which third is to retire in the third year.

Limitation on years of service

17. The annual meeting may decide that no representative of the laity being a member of the parochial church council by virtue of rule 14(1)(g) may hold office after the date of that meeting for more than a specified number of years continuously and may also decide that after a specified interval a person who has ceased to be eligible by reason of such decision may again stand for election as a representative of the laity on the council.

Parishes with more than one place of worship

18.—(1) In any parish where there are two or more churches or places of worship the annual meeting may make a scheme, which makes provision for either or both of the following purposes, that is to say:—
    (a) for the election of representatives of the laity to the parochial church council in such manner as to ensure due representation of the congregation of each such church or place; and
    (b) for the election by the annual meeting for any district in the parish in which a church or place of worship is situated of a district church council for that district.

(2) A scheme for the election of any district church council or councils under the preceding paragraph shall provide for the election of representatives of the laity on to such council, for ex-officio members and for the chairmanship of such council and shall contain such other provisions as to membership and procedure as shall be considered appropriate by the annual meeting.

(3) Such a scheme may also provide for the delegation by the parochial church council to a district church council of such functions as may be specified in the scheme and, subject to the provisions of the scheme, the parochial church council may by resolution also delegate to a district church council such of its functions as it shall think fit but not including (in either case) the functions of the parochial church council—

  (i) in respect of producing the financial statement of the parish;
  (ii) as an interested party under Part I of the Pastoral Measure 1983;
  (iii) under Part II of the Patronage (Benefices) Measure 1986;
  (iv) under section 3 of the Priests (Ordination of Women) Measure 1993.

(4) A scheme may provide for the election or choice of one or two deputy churchwardens, and for the delegation to him or them of such functions of the churchwardens relating to any church or place as the scheme may specify, and the churchwardens may, subject to the scheme, delegate such of their said functions as they think fit to the deputy churchwarden or churchwardens. The scheme may also provide for the deputy churchwardens to be ex officio members of the parochial church council.

(5) No scheme under this rule shall be valid unless approved by at least two-thirds of the persons present and voting at the annual meeting nor shall the scheme provide for it to come into operation until such date as the bishop's council and standing committee may determine being a date not later than the next ensuing annual meeting. Every such scheme shall on its approval be communicated to the bishop's council and standing committee of the diocesan synod which may determine—

  (a) that the scheme shall come into operation; or
  (b) that the scheme shall not come into operation; or
  (c) that the scheme shall come into operation with specified amendments, if such amendments are approved by an annual or special parochial church meeting and the scheme as amended is approved by at least two-thirds of the persons present and voting at that meeting.

(5A) *Repealed.*

(6) A special parochial church meeting of a parish to which this rule applies may be convened for the purpose of deciding whether to make such a scheme, and where such a meeting is convened the foregoing provisions shall have effect with the substitution for references to the annual meeting of references to the special meeting.

(7) Where a pastoral scheme establishing a team ministry, or an instrument of the bishop made by virtue of that scheme, makes, in relation to a parish in the area of the benefice for which the team ministry is established, any provision which may be made by a scheme under this rule, no scheme under this ruling relating to that parish shall provide for the scheme to come into operation until on or after the date on which the provisions in question of the pastoral scheme or of the instrument, as the case may be, cease to have effect.

(8) A scheme under this rule may be amended or revoked by a subsequent scheme passed in accordance with the provisions of paragraph (4) of this rule.

(9) Every member of the team of a team ministry shall have a right to attend the meetings of any district church council elected for any district in a parish in the area of the benefice for which the team ministry is established.

(10) This rule shall be without prejudice to the appointment, in parishes with more than one parish church, of two church-wardens for each church under section 27(5) of the Pastoral Measure 1983.

(11) In this rule 'place of worship' means a building or part of a building licensed for public worship.

Joint parochial church councils

19.—(1) Where there are two or more parishes within the area of a single benefice or two or more benefices are held in plurality, the annual meetings of all or some of the parishes in the benefice or benefices may make a joint scheme to provide:—

    (a) for establishing a joint parochial church council (hereinafter referred to as 'the joint council') comprising the ministers of the parishes and such numbers of representatives of each of those parishes elected by and from among the other members of the parochial church council of the parish as may be specified in the scheme;

    (b) for the chairmanship, meetings and procedure of the joint council;

    (c) subject to paragraph 20 of Schedule 2 to the Patronage (Benefices) Measure 1986 for the delegation by the parochial church council of each such parish to the joint council of such of its functions, other than its functions as an interested party under Part I of the Pastoral Measure 1983 and its functions under section 3 of the Priests (Ordination of Women) Measure 1993, as may be so specified.

(2) Subject to the scheme and to any pastoral scheme or order made under paragraph 13 of Schedule 3 to the said Measure and to paragraph 20 of Schedule 2 to the Patronage (Benefices) Measure 1986, the parochial church council of any such parish may delegate to the joint council such of its functions, other than its functions as an interested party under the said Part I and its functions under section 3 of the Priests (Ordination of Women) Measure 1993, as it thinks fit.

(3) The joint council shall meet from time to time for the purpose of consulting together on matters of common concern.

(4) No scheme under this rule shall be valid unless approved by at least two-thirds of the persons present and voting at the annual meeting nor shall the scheme provide for it to come into operation until such date as the bishop's council and standing committee may determine being a date not later than the next ensuing annual meeting. Every such scheme shall on its approval be communicated to the bishop's council and standing committee of the diocesan synod which may determine—

    (a) that the scheme shall come into operation; or

    (b) that the scheme shall not come into operation; or

    (c) that the scheme shall come into operation with specified amendments, if such amendments are approved by an annual or special parochial church meeting and the scheme as amended is approved by at least two-thirds of the persons present and voting at the meeting.

(5) A special parochial church meeting of a parish to which this rule applies may be convened for the purpose of deciding whether to join in making such a scheme, and where such a meeting is convened the foregoing provisions shall have effect with the substitution for references to the annual meeting of references to the special meeting.

(6) Where a pastoral scheme or order, or any instrument of the bishop made by virtue of such a scheme or order, establishes a joint parochial church council for two or more of the parishes in a single benefice or two or more of the parishes in benefices held in plurality, no scheme under this rule relating to those parishes shall provide for the scheme to come into operation until on or after the date on which the provisions of the pastoral scheme, pastoral order or instrument, as the case may be, establishing the joint parochial church council cease to have effect.

(7) Where the provisions of a pastoral scheme or order for the holding of benefices in plurality are terminated under section 18(2) of the Pastoral Measure 1983, any provision of a scheme under this establishing a joint parochial church council for all or some of the parishes of those benefices and the other provisions thereof affecting that council shall cease to have effect on the date on which the first mentioned provisions cease to have effect.

(8) A scheme under this rule may be amended or revoked by a subsequent scheme passed in accordance with the provisions of paragraph (4) of this rule to be.

Part II: Parochial Church Meetings and Councils

Team councils

20.—(1) Where a team ministry is established for the area of a benefice which comprises more than one parish the annual meetings of the parishes in that area may make a joint scheme to provide—

    (a) for establishing a team council comprising—
- (i) the team rector;
- (ii) the members of the team other than the team rector;
- (iii) every assistant curate, deaconess and lay worker licensed to a parish within the team who are not members of the team;
- (iv) such number of lay representatives elected by and from among the lay representatives of the parochial church council of each parish in the area as may be specified in the scheme.

Provided that where the total number of persons in sub-paragraphs (ii) and (iii) above would otherwise number more than one quarter of the total membership of the team council they may, and where those persons number more than one third they shall select among themselves which members shall be members of the team council so that the total number of those persons shall not exceed more than one third of the council.

    (b) for the chairmanship, meetings and procedure of the team council; and

    (c) subject to paragraph 19 of Schedule 2 to the Patronage (Benefices) Measure 1986 for the delegation by the parochial church council of each such parish to the team council of such functions, other than its functions as an interested party under Part I of the Pastoral Measure 1983 as may be so specified and its functions under section 3 of the Priests (Ordination of Women) Measure 1993, as may be so specified.

(2) Subject to the scheme and to any pastoral scheme relating to the team council made under paragraph 4(3) of Schedule 3 to the said Measure and to paragraph 19 of Schedule 2 to the Patronage (Benefices) Measure 1986, the parochial church council of any such parish may delegate to the team council such of its functions, other than its functions as an interested party under the said Part I and its functions under section 3 of the Priests (Ordination of Women) Measure 1993, as it thinks fit.

(3) The team council shall meet from time to time for the purpose of consulting together on matters of common concern.

(4) No scheme under this rule shall be valid unless approved by at least two-thirds of the persons present and voting at the annual meeting nor shall the scheme provide for it to come into operation until such date as the bishop's council and standing committee may determine being a date not later than the next ensuing annual meeting. Every such scheme shall on its approval be communicated to the bishop's council and standing committee of the diocesan synod which may determine—

    (a) that the scheme shall come into operation; or

    (b) that the scheme shall not come into operation; or

    (c) that the scheme shall come into operation with specified amendments, if such amendments are approved by an annual or special parochial church meeting and the scheme as amended is approved by at least two-thirds of the persons present and voting at that meeting.

(5) A special parochial church meeting of a parish to which this rule applies may be convened for the purpose of deciding whether to join in making such a scheme, and where such a meeting is convened the foregoing provisions shall have effect with the substitution for references to the annual meeting of references to the special meeting.

(6) Where a pastoral scheme establishing a team ministry, or an instrument of the bishop made by virtue of that scheme, establishes a team council for that ministry, no scheme under this rule relating to that ministry shall provide for the scheme to come into operation until on or after the date on which the provisions of the pastoral scheme or of the instrument, as the case may be, establishing the team council cease to have effect.

(7) A scheme under this rule may be amended or revoked by a subsequent scheme passed in accordance with the provisions of paragraph (4) of this rule to be.

Group councils

21.—(1) Where a pastoral scheme establishes a group ministry, the annual meetings of the parishes in the area for which the group ministry is established may make a joint scheme to provide—
- (a) for establishing a group comprising—
  - (i) all the members of the group ministry,
  - (ii) every assistant curate, deaconess, and lay worker licensed to any such parish, and
  - (iii) such number of lay representatives elected by and from among the lay members of the parochial church council of each such parish, as may be specified in the scheme;
- (b) for the chairmanship, meetings and procedure of the group council; and
- (c) for the delegation by the parochial church council of each such parish to the group council of such functions, other than its functions as an interested party under Part I of the Pastoral Measure 1983 and its functions under Part II of the Patronage (Benefices) Measure 1986 and section 3 of the Priests (Ordination of Women) Measure 1993, as may be so specified.

(2) If the area of a group ministry includes the area of a benefice for which a team ministry is established, a scheme under this rule shall provide for the vicars in that ministry, as well as the rector, and all the other members of the team to be members of the group council.

(3) Paragraphs (2) to (7) of rule 20 shall apply in relation to a scheme under this rule as they apply in relation to a scheme under that rule with the modification that for the references to a team ministry and a team council there shall be substituted references to a group ministry and a group council respectively except that the functions of a parochial church council under Part II of the Patronage (Benefices) Measure 1986 and section 3 of the Priests (Ordination of Women) Measure 1993 may not be delegated to a group council.

Special Meetings

22.—(1) In addition to the annual meeting the minister of a parish may convene a special parochial church meeting, and he shall do so on a written representation by not less than one-third of the lay members of the parochial church council; and the provisions of these rules relating to the convening and conduct of the annual meeting shall, with the necessary modifications, apply to a special parochial church meeting.

(2) All lay persons whose names are entered on the roll of the parish on the day which is twenty-one clear days before the date on which any special parochial church meeting is to be held shall be entitled to attend the meeting and to take part in its proceedings, and no other lay person shall be so entitled.

(3) A clerk in Holy Orders shall be entitled to attend any such meeting and to take part in its proceedings if by virtue of rule 6(3), (4) or (5) he would have been entitled to attend the annual meeting of the parish had it been held on the same date, and no other such clerk shall be so entitled.

Extraordinary Meetings

23.—(1) On a written representation made to the archdeacon by not less than one-third of the lay members of the parochial church council, or by one tenth of the persons whose names are on the roll of the parish, and deemed by the archdeacon to have been made with sufficient cause, the archdeacon shall convene an extraordinary meeting of the parochial church council or an extraordinary parochial church meeting, and shall either take the chair himself or shall appoint a chairman to preside. The chairman, not being otherwise entitled to attend such meeting, shall not be entitled to vote upon any resolution before the meeting.

(2) In any case where the archdeacon is himself the minister, any representation under paragraph (1) of this rule shall be made to the bishop, and in any such case the references to the archdeacon in

paragraph (1) of this rule shall be construed as references to the bishop, or to a person appointed by him to act on his behalf.

(3) Paragraphs (2) and (3) of rule 22 shall apply in relation to an extraordinary parochial church meeting under this rule as they apply in relation to a special parochial church meeting under that rule with the modification that for the word 'special' in paragraph (2) of that rule there shall be substituted the word 'extraordinary'.

Part III
Deanery Synods

Membership

24.—(1) A Deanery synod shall consist of a house of clergy and a house of laity.

(2) The members of the house of clergy of a deanery synod shall consist of—
  (a) the clerks in Holy Orders beneficed in or licensed to any parish in the deanery;
  (b) any clerks in Holy Orders licensed to institutions in the deanery under the Extra-Parochial Ministry Measure 1967;
  (c) any clerical members of the General Synod or diocesan synod resident in the deanery;
  (d) such other clerks in Holy Orders holding the bishop's licence to work throughout the diocese or in more than one deanery and resident in the deanery subject to any direction which may be given by the members of the House of Clergy of the bishop's council that, having regard to the number of parochial and non-parochial clergy in the deanery, such clerk shall have membership of a specified deanery synod other than the deanery where he resides provided that no person shall thereby be a member of more than one deanery synod in the diocese.
  (e) one or more clerks in Holy Orders holding permission to officiate in the diocese who are resident in the deanery or who have habitually attended public worship in a parish in the deanery during the preceding six months. One clerk may be elected or chosen for every ten such clerks or part thereof, elected or chosen in such manner as may be approved by the bishop by and from such clerks.

(3) Where an extra parochial place is not in a deanery it shall be deemed for the purposes of these rules to belong to the deanery which it abuts and if there is any doubt in the matter a determination shall be made by the bishop's council and standing committee.

(4) For the purposes of paragraph (2)(e) of this rule the relevant date shall be the 31st December in the year immediately preceding any election of the parochial representatives of the laity, and as soon as possible after that date the rural dean of the deanery shall inform the bishop of the number of clerks in Holy Orders who are qualified for membership of the deanery synod by virtue of that sub-paragraph.

(5) Not later than 1st July following the election of parochial representatives of the laity to the deanery synod the secretary of the said synod shall send to the diocesan electoral registration officer appointed in accordance with rule 29 a list of the names and addresses of the members of the house of clergy, specifying the class of membership, and shall keep the said officer informed of subsequent changes in membership.

(6) Subject to the provisions of rule 1(4) the members of the house of laity of a deanery synod shall consist of the following persons, that is to say
  (a) the parochial representatives elected to the synod by the annual meetings of the parishes of the deanery;
  (b) any lay members of the General Synod a diocesan synod or an area synod constituted in accordance with section 17 of the Diocese Measure 1978 whose names are entered on the roll of any parish in the deanery;
  (c) if in the opinion of the bishop of the diocese any community of persons in the deanery who are in the spiritual care of a chaplain licensed by the bishop should be represented in

that house, one lay person, being an actual communicant member of the Church of England of sixteen years or upwards, chosen in such manner as may be approved by the bishop by and from among the members of that community;

(d) the deaconesses and lay workers licensed by the bishop to work in any part of the deanery;

(e) such other deaconesses or lay workers holding the bishop's licence to work throughout the diocese or in more than one deanery and resident in the deanery subject to any direction which may be given by the members of the House of Laity of the bishop's council that, having regard to the number of deaconesses or lay workers in the deanery, such person shall have membership of a specified deanery synod other than the deanery where they reside provided that no person shall thereby be a member of more than one deanery synod in the diocese.

(7) The house of clergy and house of laity of a deanery synod may co-opt additional members of their respective houses, being clerks in Holy Orders or, as the case may be, lay persons who shall be actual communicant members of the Church of England of sixteen years or upwards:

Provided that the number of members co-opted by either house shall not exceed five per cent of the total number of members of that house or three, whichever is the greater.

The names and addresses of co-opted members shall be sent by the secretary of the deanery synod to the diocesan electoral registration officer appointed in accordance with rule 29.

Election and choice of members

25.—(1) The parochial representatives of the laity elected by annual meetings shall be so elected every three years, and shall hold office for a term of three years beginning with the 1st June next following their election.

(2) The numbers to be so elected from the several parishes shall be determined by resolution of the diocesan synod not later than the 31st December in the year preceding any such elections, and those numbers shall be calculated by reference to the numbers of names on the rolls of the parishes as certified under 4 or the number of parish churches or districts in each parish or a combination of both such methods, in each case in such manner as the diocesan synod shall determine provided that such resolution shall not make it possible for a parish with fewer than 26 names on the roll to have more than one representative.

(3) Not later than the 31st December in the year preceding any such elections, the secretary of the diocesan synod shall certify to the secretary of each parochial church council the number of such representatives to be elected at the annual meeting of the parish and shall send to the secretary of each deanery synod copies of the certificates and information relating to the parishes of the deanery.

(4) Any person to be chosen as mentioned in rule 24(2)(e) or 24(6)(c) shall be so chosen every three years and shall hold office for a term of three years beginning with the 1st June next following the date on which he is so chosen.

(5) A direction by the appropriate members of the Bishop's Council making provision under rule 24(2)(d) or 24(6)(e) for the membership of the clerks in Holy Orders or the deaconesses or lay workers therein mentioned may provide for the choice by a class of such persons of some of their number to be members, and for the term of office of persons so chosen.

(6) The diocesan synod shall exercise their powers under this and the last preceding rule so as to secure that the total number of members of any deanery synod in the diocese shall not be more than 150 and, so far as practicable, shall not be less than 50:

Provided that the maximum number of 150 may be exceeded for the purpose of securing that the house of laity is not less in number than the house of clergy.

For the avoidance of doubt it is hereby declared that the number 150 specified in this paragraph includes the maximum number of members who may be co-opted by each house.

Part III: Deanery Synods

Variation of membership of deanery synod by scheme

26.—(1) If it appears to the diocesan synod that the preceding rules in this Part relating to the membership of deanery synods ought to be varied to meet the special circumstances of the diocese or the deaneries and to secure better representation of clergy or laity or both on the deanery synods, they may make a scheme for such variation, and, if the scheme comes into operation under this rule, the said rules shall have effect subject to the scheme:

(2) Copies of every such scheme must be sent to members of the diocesan synod at least fourteen days before the session at which they are considered, and every such scheme shall require the assent of the house of bishops and a two-thirds majority of the members of each of the other houses of the synod present and voting.

(3) A scheme approved by the diocesan synod as aforesaid shall be laid before the General Synod.

(4) If a member of the General Synod gives notice in accordance with the standing Orders of that Synod that he wishes such a scheme to be debated, the scheme shall not come into operation unless it is approved by the General Synod.

(5) If no notice is given under paragraph (4) of this rule with respect to any such scheme, or such notice having been given, the scheme is approved by the General Synod, it shall come into operation on the day after the end of the group of sessions during which it was laid before, or approved by, the General Synod or on such later date as may be specified in the scheme.

Representation of cathedral clergy and laity

27.—(1) Any diocesan synod may provide by scheme for the representation on such deanery synod as may be determined by or under the scheme—
   (a) of the dean or provost, the residentiary canons and other ministers of the cathedral church of the diocese, or any of them; and
   (b) in the case of a cathedral church which is not a parish church, of lay persons who are on the roll of members of the cathedral community (hereinafter in these rules referred to as 'the community roll') required to be kept under section 9 of the Cathedrals Measure 1999 or, in the case of Westminster Abbey, St George's Chapel, Windsor and the cathedral church of Christ in Oxford, who are declared by the dean to be habitual worshippers at the cathedral church and whose names are not entered on the roll of any parish.

(2) The provisions of rule 21(2) shall apply to schemes made under this rule.

Procedure

28.—(1) The diocesan synod shall make rules for deanery synods which shall provide—
   (a) that the rural dean and a member of the house of laity elected by that house shall be joint chairmen of the deanery synod and that they shall agree between them who shall chair each meeting of the synod as particular items of business or the agenda of the synod;
   (b) that there shall be a secretary of the deanery synod;
   (c) that a specified minimum number of meetings shall be held by the deanery synod in each year;
   (d) that on such matters and in such circumstances as may be specified in the rules, voting shall be by houses, but that otherwise decisions shall be taken by a majority of the members of the synod present and voting;
   (e) that there shall be a standing committee of the synod with such membership and functions as the rules may provide;
   (f) that the synod shall prepare and circulate to all parochial church councils in the deanery a report of its proceedings;

and may provide for such other matters consistent with these rules as the diocesan synod think fit.

(2) Subject to any such rules, the deanery synod shall have power to determine its own procedure.

Diocesan electoral registration officer

29.—(1) In every diocese, there shall be a diocesan electoral registration officer who shall be appointed by the bishop's council and standing committee of the diocesan synod and who shall record the names and addresses of all members of the House of Clergy and House of Laity of the deanery synods in the diocese in two registers (in these rules respectively referred to as 'the register of clerical electors' and 'the register of lay electors'); the members co-opted to the house shall be listed separately in the appropriate register.

(2) The diocesan electoral registration officer shall not later than twenty one days before the nomination papers are circulated send a copy of the names and addresses of clerical electors and lay electors as recorded by him to the secretary of the deanery synod of which those electors are members and the secretary of the deanery synod shall within seven days of receipt certify in writing to the electoral registration officer that the names and addresses are correct or notify him in writing of any necessary corrections.

(3) The diocesan electoral registration officer shall, not later than seven days before nomination papers are circulated, send a copy of the corrected names and addresses of electors to the appropriate presiding officer in the election.

Part IV
Diocesan Synods

Membership of Diocesan Synods

30.—(1) A diocesan synod shall consist of a house of bishops, a house of clergy and a house of laity.

(2) The members of the house of bishops shall consist of the bishop of the diocese, every suffragan bishop of the diocese and such other person or persons, being a person or persons in episcopal orders working in the diocese, as the bishop of the diocese, with the concurrence of the archbishop of the province, may nominate.

(3) The bishop of the diocese shall be the president of the diocesan synod.

(4) The members of the house of clergy shall consist of—
 (a) the following ex-officio members, that is to say:—
   (i) any person or persons in episcopal orders nominated by the bishop of the diocese, other than a suffragan bishop or a person nominated under paragraph (2) of this rule;
   (ii) the dean or provost of the cathedral (including in appropriate dioceses, the Dean of Westminster, the Dean of Windsor and the Deans of Jersey and Guernsey);
   (iii) the archdeacons;
   (iv) the proctors elected from the diocese or from any university in the diocese (the University of London being treated for this purpose as being wholly in the diocese of London) to the Lower House of the Convocation of the Province;
   (v) any other member of that House, being the person chosen by and from among the clerical members of the religious communities in the Province, who resides in the diocese;
   (vi) the chancellor of the diocese (if in Holy Orders); and
   (vii) the chairman of the diocesan board of finance and the chairman of the diocesan advisory committee (if in Holy Orders);
 (b) members elected by the houses of clergy of the deanery synods in the diocese in accordance with the next following rules; and
 (c) not more than five members (being clerks in Holy Orders) co-opted by the house of clergy of the diocesan synod.

Part IV: Diocesan Synods

(5) The members of the house of laity shall consist of:—
  (a) the following ex-officio members, that is to say:—
    (i) the chancellor of the diocese (if not in Holy Orders);
    (ii) the chairman of the diocesan board of finance and the chairman of the diocesan advisory committee (if not in Holy Orders);
    (iii) the members elected from the diocese to the House of Laity of the General Synod;
    (iv) any other member of that House, being an ex-officio or co-opted member of the House of Laity of the General Synod or a person chosen by and from among the lay members of religious communities in the Province, who resides in the diocese;
  (b) members elected by the houses of laity of the deanery synods in the diocese in accordance with the next following rules; and
  (c) not more than five members co-opted by the house of laity of the diocesan synod, who shall be actual communicants of age to vote at a Parliamentary election.

(6) The bishop of the diocese may nominate ten additional members of the diocesan synod, who may be of the clergy or the laity and shall be members of the appropriate house.

Except in regard to their appointment the nominated members shall have the same rights and be subject to the same rules as elected members. Where necessary the bishop's council and standing committee shall designate the deanery synod of which the nominated member shall be a member and, where a nominated lay person is on more than one electoral roll, he shall choose the parochial church council of which he is to be a member.

(7) No person shall be entitled to be a member of more than one diocesan synod at the same time except—
  (a) the chancellor of the diocese;
  (b) a suffragan bishop appointed to act as a provincial episcopal visitor for the purposes of the Episcopal Ministry Act of Synod 1993 who, in addition to membership of the diocesan synod of the diocese of which he is suffragan, may be invited by the bishop of the diocese where he resides to be a member of that diocesan synod in accordance with paragraph (2) or paragraph (4)(a)(i) of this rule provided that he shall exercise his vote on a matter referred by the General Synod under Article 8 of the Constitution only in the diocesan synod of the diocese of which he is suffragan.

(8) The registrar of the diocese and any deputy registrar of the diocesan synod shall be disqualified from standing for election to the diocesan synod or from being nominated, co-opted or ex-officio member of that synod.

Elections of members of diocesan synods by deanery synods

31.—(1) The elections of members of the diocesan synod by the houses of clergy and laity of the deanery synods in the diocese shall take place every three years, and the members so elected shall hold office for a term of three years beginning with the 1st August next following their election.

(2) Any clerk in Holy Orders who is a member of the deanery synod shall be qualified to be so elected by the house of clergy of a deanery synod, and the electors shall be those whose names and addresses are recorded in the register of clerical electors being the persons referred to in rule 24(2) and not including the persons co-opted to the deanery synod under rule 24(7):

Provided that no clerk shall stand for election by more than one deanery synod.

(3) Subject to the provisions of rule 1(4) any lay person who is an actual communicant as defined in rule 54(1) of sixteen years or upwards and whose name is entered on the roll of any parish in the deanery or who is on the community roll or, in the case of Westminster Abbey, St George's Chapel, Windsor and the cathedral church of Christ in Oxford declared by the dean to be an habitual worshipper at the cathedral church, shall be qualified to be so elected by the house of laity of a deanery synod, and the electors shall be those whose names and addresses are recorded in the register of lay electors persons co-opted to the deanery synod under rule 24(7).

(4) The qualifying date for electors under paragraphs (2) and (3) of this rule and when a casual vacancy is being filled shall be 6.00 a.m. on the date on which the nomination papers are issued in accordance with rule 32(4).

(5) The register of clerical electors and the register of lay electors shall be open to inspection at the diocesan office and any errors and omissions in the list may be corrected until the close of nominations. Thereafter no names may be added or removed until the declaration of the result of the election and those persons whose names are entered in the register shall be the qualified electors entitled to vote in that election.

(6) The diocesan synod shall, not later than the 31st December in the year preceding any such election determine the numbers of members to be so elected by the houses of the several deanery synods in the diocese, and the numbers shall—

    (a)   in the case of elections by the houses of clergy, be related to the numbers of members of those houses in the respective deanery synods;

    (b)   in the case of elections by the houses of laity, be related to the total numbers of names on the rolls of the parishes in the respective deaneries as certified under rule 4:

Provided that at least two members shall be elected by each house of every deanery synod.

(7) For the purpose of such determination by the diocesan synod, the secretary of every deanery synod shall, not later that the 1st June, certify to the secretary of the diocesan synod the number of members of the house of clergy of the synod as at the 30th April.

(8) The diocesan synod shall so exercise their powers under this rule as to secure that the number of members of the synod is not less than 120 and not more than 270 and that the numbers of the houses of clergy and laity are approximately equal.

For the avoidance of doubt it is hereby declared that the number 270 specified in this paragraph includes the maximum number of members who may be co-opted by each house or nominated by the bishop.

(9) Not late than the 31st December in each year preceding any such elections, the secretary of the diocesan synod shall certify to the secretary of every deanery synod the numbers determined under this rule for that deanery synod.

32.—(1) Elections of members of the diocesan synod by the houses of the deanery synods shall be completed by the 15th day of July, the period and dates of the election being fixed by the bishop of the diocese and communicated to the secretaries of the deanery synods.

(2) The bishop shall appoint the presiding officers for the elections by the houses of the deanery synods, provided that no person shall be appointed as a presiding officer for an election by a house of which he is a member. The expenses of elections shall be paid out of diocesan funds.

(3) The diocesan electoral registration officer shall furnish the presiding officer with the names and addresses of the qualified electors and the presiding officer shall ensure that the persons qualified to nominate and vote in elections to the diocesan synod, and only such persons, shall be sent or given nomination and voting papers in respect of the said election at the address entered against their names in the register of electors.

(4) Every candidate must be nominated and seconded by a qualified elector. A notice in the form set out in section 5 of Appendix I indicating the number of seats to be filled and inviting nominations shall be dispatched to every elector together with a form of nomination in the form set out in section 6 of Appendix I shall be delivered either by post, by facsimile transmission or in person to the presiding officer of the area within such period, being a period of not less than fourteen days ending on a date specified by the presiding officer, provided that where a nomination paper has been sent by facsimile transmission the name of the candidate shall not appear on the voting paper unless the original nomination paper has been received by the presiding officer within three days of the closing date for nominations. The nomination form shall be accompanied by a statement signed by the candidate stating his willingness to serve if elected and, if he so desires, setting out in not more than 100 words a factual statement for circulation with the voting papers of the candidate's professional qualifications, present office and any relevant past experience.

Part IV: Diocesan Synods

(5) It shall be the duty of the presiding officer—
  (a) to scrutinise nomination papers as soon as they have been lodged and shall, without delay, inform the candidate concerned whether the nomination is valid. Where the nomination is invalid the presiding officer shall give his reasons for so ruling and if, by the close of the nomination period, no valid nomination is received, the candidate shall be excluded from the election;
  (b) to supply free of charge to a duly nominated candidate in the election one copy of the names and addresses of the qualified electors within seven days of receiving his written request.

(6) If more candidates are nominated than there are seats to be filled the names of the candidates nominated shall be circulated on a voting paper in the form set out either in section 7 or in section 8 of Appendix I to every qualified elector. The diocesan synod shall, not later than the 31st December in each year preceding any such election as is referred to in rule 31, make a determination as to which form of voting paper is to be used by the deaneries in that election, and that determination shall apply to any election to fill a casual vacancy which occurs during the next ensuing three years.

(7) The voting paper marked and, on the reverse thereof, signed by the elector and with his full name written shall be returnable to the presiding officer within such period not being less than 14 days as he shall specify. No vote shall be counted if given on a voting paper not in accordance with this paragraph.

(8) Where voting papers in the form set out in section 7 of Appendix I have been used and owing to an equality of votes an election is not decided, the decision between the persons for whom the equal numbers of votes have been cast shall be taken by lot by the presiding officer.

(9) Where voting papers in the form set out in section 8 of Appendix I are used, the election shall be conducted under rules, with the necessary modifications, made by the General Synod under rule 39(7) and for the time being in force.

(10) A return of the result of the election shall be sent by the presiding officer to the secretary of the diocesan synod and a statement of the result shall be sent by the presiding officer to every candidate not later than the 1st August in each election year.

Variation of membership of diocesan synods by scheme

33.—(1) If it appears to the diocesan synod that the preceding rules in this Part relating to the membership of diocesan synods ought to be varied to meet the special circumstances of the diocese and to secure better representation of the clergy or laity or both on the diocesan synod, they may make a scheme for such variation, and if the scheme comes into operation in accordance with the provisions hereinafter applies, the said rules shall have effect subject to the scheme.

(2) Paragraphs (2) to (5) of rule 26 shall apply to schemes under this rule as it applies to schemes under that rule.

Procedure of diocesan synods

34.—(1) The diocesan synod shall make standing orders which shall provide—
  (a) that the bishop need not be chairman of its meetings if and to the extent that standing orders otherwise provide;
  (b) that there shall be a secretary of the diocesan synod;
  (c) that a specified minimum number of meetings being in the case of a diocese in which area synods have been constituted in accordance with section 17 of the Dioceses Measure 1978, not less than one, and in the case of any diocese not less than two shall be held in each year;
  (d) that a meeting of the diocesan synod shall be held if not less than a specified number of members of the synod so request;
  (e) that subject to the three next following sub-paragraphs, nothing shall be deemed to have the assent of the diocesan synod unless the three houses which constitute the synod have

assented thereto but that if in the case of a particular question (except a matter referred to the diocesan synod by the General Synod under the provisions of Article 8 of the Constitution) the diocesan bishop (if present) so directs, that question shall be deemed to have the assent of the house of bishops only if the majority of the members of that house who assent thereto includes the diocesan bishop;

(f) that questions relating only to the conduct of business shall be decided by the votes of all the members of the diocesan synod present and voting;

(g) that every other question shall be decided by the votes of all the members of the diocesan synod present and voting, the assent of the three Houses being presumed, unless the diocesan bishop (if present) requires or any ten members require that a separate vote of each House be taken;

(h) that if the votes of the houses of clergy and laity are in favour of any matter referred to the diocesan synod by the General Synod under the provisions of Article 8 of Schedule 2 of this Measure, that matter shall be deemed to have been approved for the purposes of the said Article;

(i) that where there is an equal division of votes in the house of bishops, the diocesan bishop shall have a second or casting vote;

(j) that the diocesan bishop shall have a right to require that his opinion on any question shall be recorded in the minutes;

(k) that there shall be a bishop's council and standing committee of the diocesan synod with such membership as may be provided by standing orders and with the functions exercisable by it under section 4(4) of the Measure and such other functions as may be provided by the standing orders or by these rules or by any Measure or Canon;

and may contain such further provisions consistent with these rules as the diocesan synod shall consider appropriate.

(2) No person shall be entitled to serve as a member of more than one bishop's council and standing committee at the same time.

(3) The registrar of the diocese shall be the registrar of the diocesan synod, and may appoint a deputy.

Part V
House of Laity of General Synod

35.—(1) The House of Laity of the General Synod shall consist of—
  (a) the members elected by the diocesan electors of each diocese as hereinafter provided;
  (b) two members chosen by and from the members of religious communities having their mother house in either province in such manner as may be provided by a resolution of the General Synod;
  (c) such ex-officio and co-opted members as are hereinafter provided;
  (d) not less than three nor more than four members elected or chosen in such manner as may be determined by the Forces Synodical Council as soon as practicable after any dissolution of the General Synod, being actual communicants, provided that the total number of persons elected or chosen to serve on the General Synod by virtue of this sub-paragraph, paragraph 1(d) of the provisions relating to the Convocation of Canterbury of Canon H 2 and paragraph 1(bb) of Canon H 3 shall not exceed seven.

(2) For the purposes of this Part of these rules the diocese in Europe shall be deemed to be a diocese in the province of Canterbury.

(3) For the purposes of this Part of these rules, the diocesan electors of a diocese other than the diocese in Europe shall be the members of the houses of laity of all the deanery synods in the diocese other than—
  (a) persons co-opted to the deanery synod under rule 24(7); or

Part V: House of Laity of General Synod

(b) persons who are lay members of a religious community with separate representation in the General Synod under paragraph (1)(b) of this rule.

(4) The diocesan electors of the diocese in Europe shall be such number of persons elected by the annual meetings of the chaplaincies in the said diocese as may be determined by the bishop's council and standing committee of the said diocese, and any lay person who is:
  (a) an actual communicant as defined in rule 54(1),
  (b) of eighteen years or upwards, and
  (c) a person whose name is entered on the electoral roll of such a chaplaincy,

shall be qualified for election as a diocesan elector by the annual meeting of that chaplaincy.

(5) The qualifying date for lay members of religious communities under paragraph (1)(b) of this rule and for diocesan electors under paragraphs (3) and (4) of this rule shall be 6.00 a.m. on the date of the dissolution of the General Synod, save that when a casual vacancy is being filled, the qualifying date shall be 6.00 a.m. on the date on which the nomination papers are issued.

(6) The register of lay electors shall be open to inspection at the diocesan office and any errors and omissions in the list may be corrected until the close of nominations. Thereafter no names may be added or removed until the declaration of the result of the election and those persons whose names are entered in the register shall be the qualified electors entitled to vote in that election.

ELECTIONS OF MEMBERS

Number of Elected Members

36.—(1) The total number of members directly elected and specially elected from the dioceses in the Province shall not exceed 136 for Canterbury and 59 for York and no diocese shall have fewer than three directly elected members (except the diocese in Europe which shall elect two members, and the diocese of Sodor and Man which shall elect one member). The representatives of the religious communities referred to in rule 35(1)(b), the elected or chosen persons referred to in rule 35(1)(d), ex officio and co-opted members (as defined in rule 42) shall be additional to the said total number.

In this rule the term 'specially elected' means the representatives of the Channel Islands elected in accordance with the provisions of the Channel Islands (Representation) Measure 1931 and such persons shall be included in the said total number.

(2) The total number of members to be elected by the diocesan electors of all the dioceses shall be fixed by resolution of the General Synod not later than the last day of February in the fifth year after the last preceding election of the house of Laity (but subject as hereinafter provided), and the resolution shall apportion the number so fixed to the Provinces of Canterbury and York in a proportion of 70 to 30 or as nearly as possible thereto and shall divide the number among the dioceses (using such divisor method as may from time to time be specified for the purpose by the Business Committee of the General Synod) so that the number of members to be elected by the several dioceses are as nearly as possible proportionate to the total number of names on the rolls of the parishes of the diocese in question.

(3) *Repealed.*

(4) The number of members of the House of Laity to be elected by each diocese, when fixed by the General Synod as aforesaid, shall forthwith be certified to the secretaries of the diocesan synods.

(5) If the General Synod is at any time dissolved before the fixing of numbers under this rule by the General Synod, the General Synod or the Presidents thereof may give directions with respect to the fixing and certifying of the numbers of members to be elected to the House of Laity by each diocese, and the directions may provide that the numbers so fixed and certified on the last previous occasion shall be deemed to have been fixed and certified for the purpose of the election following the dissolution, and the directions may, if the dissolution is known to be impending, be given before it occurs.

37.—(1) Subject to the provisions of rule 1(4) and of rule 46A, a lay person shall be qualified for election for any diocese by the diocesan electors of the diocese if—
   (a) he is an actual communicant as defined in rule 54(1) but as if, in that definition, for the words 'whose name is on the roll of a parish and' there were substituted the word 'who';
   (b) he is of eighteen years of age on the date of the dissolution of the General Synod or, when a casual vacancy is being filled on the date on which the nomination papers are issued in accordance with rule 39(3);
   (c) his name is at 6.00 am on the date of dissolution of the General Synod or, when a casual vacancy is being filled, on the date on which the nomination papers are issued in accordance with rule 39(3) entered on the roll of any parish in the diocese or, in the case of a cathedral which is not a parish church, on the community roll or, in the case of Westminster Abbey, St George's Chapel, Windsor and the cathedral church of Christ in Oxford is a person who at any time within the period of two months beginning one month immediately before that date is declared by the dean of the cathedral church to be a habitual worshipper at that cathedral church.

(1A) *Repealed.*
(2) *Repealed.*
(3) Where a diocese is divided into two or more areas in accordance with rule 38(2), any person who under this rule is qualified for election for the diocese shall be qualified for election for any such area whether or not the parish on whose roll his name is entered, or the cathedral church on whose community roll his name is entered, is situated in that area, but no person shall be nominated for more than one such area at the same time.

Electoral Areas

38.—(1) Subject to any division of a diocese under this rule every diocese shall be an electoral area for the purposes of elections to the House of Laity.
(2) So far as is consistent with any rule made under the Standing Orders of the General Synod under rule 39(8) and subject to paragraph (3) of this rule a diocesan synod may, for the purposes of any election, divide a diocese into two or more areas, and apportion the number of members of the House of Laity to be elected for the diocese among such areas, and the election shall be conducted in each area as if such area were a separate diocese. Where a diocese is so divided, a diocesan elector who is a representative of the laity shall vote in the area to which the body by which he was elected belongs, and a diocesan elector who is not a representative of the laity shall vote in such area as the diocesan synod may decide. Any such division shall remain in force until it is revoked by the diocesan synod.
(3) If a diocesan synod decides to divide the diocese into two or more areas in pursuance of this rule the division shall be made in such manner that the number of members to be elected in any such area will be not less than three.

Conduct of Elections

39.—(1) Subject to any directions by the General Synod or the President thereof, elections to the House of Laity shall be carried out during the three months immediately following any dissolution of the General Synod and shall be so carried out in each diocese during such period within the said three months as shall be fixed by the archbishops of Canterbury and York.
(2) The presiding officer in each diocese or each area of a diocese shall be the registrar of the diocese or a person appointed by him with the approval of the registrar of the province, except that, if the said registrar is a candidate in the election, the presiding officer shall be a person appointed by the registrar of the province. The expenses of the elections shall be paid out of diocesan funds.

(3) On receipt of the names and addresses of the qualified electors from the diocesan electoral registration officer the presiding officer shall ensure that in respect of the election—
  (i) those persons are sent or given nomination papers; and
  (ii) only such persons are sent or given voting papers at the address entered against their names in the register of electors.

The presiding officer shall also send nomination papers to any other person who requests them.

(4) Every candidate must be nominated and seconded by diocesan electors qualified to vote in the area in which the candidate is seeking to be elected. All nominations shall be in writing, shall include the year of the candidate's birth and a statement as to whether the candidate is seeking re-election and, if so, as to the dates of the candidate's previous service and shall be delivered either by post, by facsimile transmission or in person to the presiding officer of the area, together with evidence of the candidate's consent to serve, within such period, being a period of not less than twenty-eight days ending on such date as may be specified by the presiding officer, provided that where a nomination paper has been sent by facsimile transmission the name of the candidate shall not appear on the voting paper unless the original nomination paper has been received by the presiding officer within three days of the closing date for nominations.

(5) It shall be the duty of the presiding officer—
  (a) to scrutinise nomination papers as soon as they have been lodged and he shall, without delay, inform the candidate concerned whether the nomination is valid. Where the nomination is invalid the presiding officer shall give his reasons for so ruling and if, by the close of the nomination period, no valid nomination is received, the candidate shall be excluded from the election;
  (b) to supply free of charge to a duly nominated candidate in the election one copy of the names and addresses of the qualified electors (including, if an elector has authorised the use of an electronic mail address, that address) within seven days of receiving his written request.

(6) If any of the candidates so request the presiding officer shall despatch to every elector election addresses from those candidates being not more than one sheet of A4 paper. One copy of the address shall be provided by the candidates at their own expense and be delivered or sent by electronic mail to the presiding officer by such date as he shall determine being not less than seven days after the close of nominations. The presiding officer shall be under no obligation to despatch to electors election addresses which are received after the due date or which are not in the prescribed form.

(7) It shall be the duty of the presiding officer in any election under these rules to seek to ensure that during the period beginning with the date on which nominations are invited and ending on the last date for the return of voting papers, no papers or other literature except election addresses prepared by the candidates under paragraph 6 of this rule shall be circulated to the electors by him or by or under authority of the diocesan synod or the deanery synod or distributed at a synod meeting which in his opinion are likely to prejudice the election. The rural dean and the lay chairman and secretary of the deanery synod shall also be under a duty to seek to ensure that during the election period no papers or other literature form part of an official circulation or are distributed at a synod meeting which in the opinion of any of them are likely to prejudice the election.

(8) Subject to rule 51, if more candidates are nominated for any area than there are seats to be filled, the election shall be conducted by voting papers by the method of the single transferable vote under rules to be made from time to time as provided by the Standing Orders of the General Synod. Every voting paper, which shall include the year of birth of each candidate and a statement as to whether the candidate is seeking re-election and, if so, as to the dates of the candidate's previous service, shall be marked and signed on the reverse thereof by the elector and shall be returnable to the presiding officer within such period, being a period of not less than twenty-one days after the date on which the voting paper is issued, as that officer may specify, provided that a voting paper sent by facsimile transmission shall not be counted as a valid vote.

(9) A candidate or a person nominated by him has the right to be present at the counting of the votes in order to scrutinise the count but shall take no part in it. The presiding officer shall give not

less than seven days notice in writing to each candidate of the time and place at which the votes are to be counted.

(10) Where within seven days of a count being completed the presiding officer is of the opinion that a recount should take place because of a possible irregularity or inaccuracy in the count, he may, with the concurrence of the registrar of the province, order such a recount and shall give notice in writing to each candidate of the time and place at which the votes are to be recounted.

(11) A full return of the result of any election and of the result sheet shall be sent by the presiding officer within four working days of the declaration of the result to every candidate in the election, the Clerk to the General Synod and an election scrutineer appointed by the Business Committee of the General Synod. The scrutineer shall have power within ten days of the declaration of the result to order a recount of the voting papers if in his opinion this might be material to the result of the election.

(12) The result sheet shall be publicly displayed in the diocesan office in such manner as the bishop may approve and at the General Synod office until the end of the first group of sessions of the new Synod as the Clerk to the General Synod may direct.

(13) The presiding officer in each area shall ensure that the valid voting papers received by him for the purposes of any election to the House of Laity are preserved for a period of not less than two years beginning with the date of the election.

Conduct of elections

40.—(1) Rules defining the duties to be undertaken by the presiding officers in connection with elections to the House of Laity shall be prepared by the provincial registrars acting jointly, but no such rules shall have effect unless approved by the Business Committee of the General Synod.

(2) A presiding officer shall be entitled to such fees for the performance by him of the duties aforesaid as may be specified in any order for the time being in force made under the Ecclesiastical Fees Measure 1986; and where with the prior agreement in writing of the bishop's council and standing committee the presiding officer or any other person performs any other duties in connection with elections to the House of Laity he shall be entitled to such fees as may be specified in the agreement.

Term of office of membership of General Synod and other bodies

41. The term of office of elected members of the House of Laity, of the members elected or chosen under rule 35(1)(d) above and of members chosen by the lay members of religious communities shall be for the lifetime of the General Synod for which they are elected or chosen, but without prejudice to their acting under Article 3(4) of the Constitution during the period of the dissolution of the General Synod or to their continuing to be ex-officio members of other bodies constituted under these rules during that period.

Ex-officio and co-opted members of the House of Laity

42.—(1) The following persons, if they are not in Holy Orders, shall be ex-officio members of the House of Laity:—
    (a)   the Dean of the Arches and Auditor;
    (b)   the Vicar-General of the Province of Canterbury;
    (c)   the Vicar-General of the Province of York;
    (d)   the three Church Estates Commissioners;
    (e)   the Chairman of the Central Board of Finance;
    (f)   the Chairman of the Church of England Pensions Board;
    (g)   the members of the Archbishops' Council who are actual communicants.

(2) The House of Laity shall have power to co-opt persons who are actual lay communicants of eighteen years or upwards to be members of the House of Laity:
Provided that:—
    (a)   the co-opted members shall not at any time exceed five in number; and,
    (b)   no person shall be qualified to become a co-opted member unless not less than two-thirds of the members of the Standing Committee of the House of Laity shall have first

consented to his being co-opted, either at a meeting of the Standing Committee or in writing.

(3) Except in regard to their appointment, the ex-officio and co-opted members shall have the same rights and be subject to the same rules and regulations as elected members:

Where such members are on more than one electoral roll, they shall choose the parochial church council of which they are to be a member.

(4) Co-opted members shall continue to be members of the House of Laity until the next dissolution of the General Synod, but without prejudice to their acting under Article 3(4) of the Constitution during the period of the dissolution: or to their continuing to be ex-officio members of other bodies constituted under these rules during that period:

Provided that the House of Laity may, in the case of co-opted member, fix a shorter period of membership.

(5) The House of Laity may make standing orders for regulating the procedure of and incidental to the appointment of co-opted members and otherwise for carrying this rule into effect.

PART VI
APPEALS AND DISQUALIFICATIONS

Enrolment appeals

43.—(1) There shall be a right of appeal with regard to—
  (a) any enrolment, or refusal of enrolment, on the roll of a parish or the registers of lay or clerical electors;
  (b) the removal of any name, or the refusal to remove any name, from the roll of a parish or the registers of lay or clerical electors.

(2) The following persons shall have a right of appeal under this rule—
  (a) a person who is refused enrolment on the roll or register;
  (b) a person whose name is removed from the roll or register; or
  (c) any person whose name is entered on the roll or register who wishes to object to the enrolment or removal of the name of any other person on that roll or register.

(3) In an appeal concerning the roll of a parish, notice of the appeal shall be given in writing to the lay chairman of the deanery synod and in an appeal concerning the register of lay or clerical electors notice of the appeal shall be given in writing to the Chairman of the House of Laity or the Chairman of the House of Clergy of the diocesan synod as the case may be.

(4) Notice of appeal shall be given not later than fourteen days after the date of notification of the enrolment, removal or refusal or not later than fourteen days after the last day of the publication (as provided by rule 2(3)) of a new roll or register or of a list of additions or removals from such roll or register.

(5) In any appeal arising under this rule the chairman of the House concerned of the Diocesan Synod or the lay chairman of the deanery synod, as the case may be, shall within fourteen days refer any appeal to the bishop's council and standing committee of the diocese unless within that period the appellant withdraws the appeal in writing. The said bishop's council shall appoint three or a greater number being an odd number of their lay members or clerical members as the case may be to consider and decide the appeal.

Election appeals

44.—(1) There shall be a right of appeal with regard to—
  (a) the allowance or disallowance of any vote given or tendered in an election of a churchwarden or in an election under these rules or to a body constituted under or in accordance with these rules;

(b) the result of any election of a churchwarden or of any election or choice held or made or purporting to be held or made under these rules, or any election or choice of members of a body constituted under or in accordance with these rules.

(2) The following persons shall have a right of appeal under this rule—
   (a) an elector in the said election;
   (b) a candidate in the said election; or
   (c) the chairman of the House of Laity or of the House of Clergy of the diocesan synod or, in an election to the House of Laity of the General Synod, the chairman and vice-chairman of that House of Laity as specified in paragraph (5) of this rule.

(3) The provisions of this rule (except paragraph (6) of this rule), insofar as they confer a right of appeal by any person referred to in paragraph (2) above against the result of an election and provide for notice of an appeal and the determination thereof, shall apply in relation to an election to the House of Laity of the General Synod by the diocesan electors of the diocese in Europe.

(4) Subject to paragraph (6) of this rule in the case of an appeal arising out of an election to the House of Laity of the General Synod or the diocesan synod notice of the appeal shall be given in writing to the chairman of the House of Laity of the diocesan synod. In any other case concerning the laity, notice of the appeal shall be given in writing to the lay chairman of the deanery synod. Notices under this paragraph shall be given:
   (a) in the case of an appeal against the allowance or disallowance of a vote, not later than fourteen days after such allowance or disallowance;
   (b) in the case of an appeal against the result of an election or choice, not later than fourteen days after the day on which the result is declared by the presiding officer.

(5) The Chairman and Vice-Chairman of the House of Laity of the General Synod shall each have a right of appeal under this rule in accordance with paragraph (1) of this rule in respect of any election to the House of Laity of the General Synod in either of the Provinces of Canterbury and York and he shall give notice in writing of such appeal to the presiding officer concerned not later than three months after the result of the election has been declared by the said presiding officer. Provided that if the office of Chairman or Vice-Chairman is vacant when the result of the election is published the person who last held office shall be deemed to hold that office for the purposes of this rule.

(6) An error in the electoral roll or the registers of clerical or lay electors shall not be a ground of appeal against the result of any election unless—
   (a) either it has been determined under this rule that there has been such an error or the question is awaiting determination under rule 43; and
   (b) the error would or might be material to the result of the election;

and the allowance or disallowance of a vote shall not be a ground of appeal against the result of an election unless the allowance or disallowance would or might be material to the result of the election.

(7) An error in the electoral roll of a chaplaincy or in the register of lay electors in the diocese in Europe shall not be a ground of appeal against the result of an election to the House of Laity of the General Synod by the diocesan electors of that diocese unless—
   (a) either it has been determined under the rule which applies in that diocese and corresponds with rule 43 that there has been such an error or the question is awaiting determination under that rule; and
   (b) the error would or might be material to the result of that election;

and the allowance or disallowance of a vote shall not be a ground of appeal against the result of such an election unless the allowance or disallowance would or might be material to the result of the election.

(8) An appeal arising out of an election or choice of members of the House of Laity of the General Synod shall, within the period of fourteen days of the appeal being lodged, be referred to

Part VI: Appeals and Disqualifications

the Chairman and Vice-Chairman of that House unless, within that period, the appellant withdraws the appeal in writing. Subject to paragraph (9) of this rule, the Chairman and Vice-Chairman acting jointly shall appoint three persons (one of whom shall be a qualified lawyer) from an appeal panel consisting of the Dean of the Arches and Auditor, the Vicar General of the Province of Canterbury, the Vicar General of the Province of York and twelve members of the House of Laity of the General Synod nominated by the Appointments Committee of the Church of England to consider and decide the appeal.

(9)
- (a) Where the Chairman or Vice-Chairman of the House of Laity has given notice of appeal under paragraph (5) above, or where he comes from the diocese to which the appeal relates he shall take no part in the appointing of the three persons to hear the appeal and he shall not be appointed to hear the appeal.
- (b) Where a member of the appeal panel comes from the diocese to which the appeal relates, or might otherwise have a benefit from the outcome of the election, he shall not be appointed to hear the appeal.

(10) In any appeal arising under this rule except an appeal arising out of an election to the House of Laity of the General Synod, the Chairman of the House of Laity of the diocesan synod or the lay chairman or the deanery synod, as the case may be, shall refer any appeal to the bishop's council and standing committee of the diocese who shall appoint three or a greater number, being an odd number, of their lay members to consider and decide the appeal.

(11) In any appeal arising under this rule to the House of Clergy of the diocesan synod the Chairman of the House of Clergy of the said synod shall refer any appeal to the bishop's council and standing committee of the diocese who shall appoint three or a greater number, being an odd number, of their clerical members to consider and decide the appeal.

(12) Where an appeal is pending under this rule in respect of an election to any synod any person who was declared elected in accordance with rule 33 but whose election is or may be affected by the appeal shall for all purposes be deemed to be a member of that Synod until the appeal is heard and disposed of.

45.—(1) For the purpose of the consideration and decision of any appeal under rules 43 and 44, the persons appointed to consider and decide the appeal—
- (a) shall consider all the relevant circumstances and shall be entitled to inspect all documents and papers relating to the subject matter of the appeal and be furnished with all information respecting the same which they may require;
- (b) shall give to the parties to the appeal an opportunity of appearing before them in person or through a legal or other representative;
- (c) shall have power at any time to extend the time within which a notice of appeal is given;
- (d) shall, unless by consent of the persons appointed the appeal is withdrawn, determine the matter at issue and, in an election appeal shall determine whether—
  - (i) the person or persons whose election is complained or was or were duly elected;
  - (ii) the facts complained of amount to a minor infringement of the rules which did not affect the outcome of the election in which event the appeal shall be dismissed; or
  - (iii) the facts complained of amount to a procedural irregularity in the conduct of the election, but that in all the relevant circumstances the appeal shall be dismissed; or
  - (iv) the election was void. The determination so certified shall be final as to the matters at issue and, in any case in which there has been no valid election, the members shall direct a fresh election to be held and shall give such directions in connection therewith as they may think necessary;
- (e) shall have power at any time to consent to the withdrawal of the appeal by an appellant subject to a determination in respect of costs in accordance with paragraph (f) of this rule;

(f) shall have power to direct that any party to an appeal shall be entitled to payment of costs by any other party or by the diocesan board of finance and to direct that a party shall be responsible for the reasonable expenses of the persons appointed to hear the appeal; save that in so far as the same have not been paid by any other person, the diocesan board of finance shall pay all expenses of the persons appointed to hear the appeal provided that the said board shall first be satisfied that they are reasonable in amount.

Vacation of seat by members ceasing to be qualified for election

46.—(1) Where—
- (a) any lay member of a deanery synod, being a parochial representative or a representative under rule 27, ceases to be entered on the roll of the parish by which he was elected or, as the case may be, on the community roll of the cathedral church of the diocese or to be declared under the said rule to be a habitual worshipper at the cathedral church;
- (b) any member of a diocesan synod elected by the house of clergy of a deanery synod ceases to be qualified for election by that house;
- (c) any lay member of a diocesan synod elected by the house of laity of a deanery synod ceases to have the qualification of entry on the roll of any parish in that deanery or (in appropriate cases) of being on the community roll of the cathedral church of the diocese or of being declared a habitual worshipper at the cathedral church of the diocese under rule 27;
- (d) any elected member of the House of Laity of the General Synod ceases to have the qualification of entry on the roll of any parish in the diocese for which he was elected or of being, as the case may be, on the community roll of the cathedral church of the diocese or declared a habitual worshipper as aforesaid;
- (e) any elected member of the House of Laity of the General Synod takes any paid office or employment as provided by rule 46A(c);
- (f) any member of a deanery synod, a diocesan synod or of the House of Laity of the General Synod has his election declared void in accordance with the provision of rule 45 or becomes disqualified in accordance with the provisions of rule 46A(a) hereof,

his seat shall subject to the following provisions of this rule forthwith be vacated.

(2) If the name of a person to whom paragraph 1(a) of this rule applies is entered on the roll of any parish in the diocese other than that of the parish referred to in that paragraph or, as the case may be, on the community roll of the cathedral church of the diocese or if he is declared under rule 27 to be a habitual worshipper at the cathedral church of the diocese, his seat shall not be vacated under this rule if, before the vacancy occurs, the parochial church council so resolve.

(3) If a person to whom paragraph (1)(b) of this rule applies continues to work or reside in the diocese, his seat shall not be vacated under this rule if, before the vacancy occurs, the clerical members of the standing committee of the deanery synod so resolve.

(4) If the name of a person to whom paragraph (1)(c) of this rule applies is entered on the roll of any parish in the diocese other than that of the parish referred to in that paragraph or, as the case may be, on the community roll of the cathedral church of the diocese or if he is declared under rule 27 to be a habitual worshipper at the cathedral church of the diocese, neither his seat as a member of that House nor his seat as a lay member of the diocesan synod shall be vacated under this rule if, before the vacancy occurs, the lay members of the standing committee of the deanery synod so resolve.

(5) If the lay members of the bishop's council and standing committee has determined before the vacancy occurs that a person to whom paragraph (1)(d) of this rule applies is able and willing to continue to discharge to their satisfaction the duties of a member of the House of Laity elected for that diocese, neither his seat as a member of that House nor his seat as a lay member of the diocesan synod shall be vacated under this rule.

(5A) The lay members of the bishop's council and standing committee shall not later than one year after the determination referred to in paragraph (5) above and annually thereafter review the

Part VII: Supplementary and Interpretation

membership of a member to whom paragraph (1)(d) above applies and determine whether he is able and willing as mentioned in paragraph (5) above.

(6) This rule shall apply in relation to a member of the House of Laity of the General Synod elected for the diocese in Europe with the substitution for the words in paragraph (1)(d) from 'roll' to 'aforesaid' of the words 'electoral roll of any chaplaincy in that diocese'.

46A.
   (a) A person shall be disqualified from being nominated, chosen or elected or from serving as a churchwarden, a member of a parochial church council, a district church council or any synod under these rules if he is disqualified from being a charity trustee under section 72(1) of the Charities Act 1993 and the disqualification is not for the time being subject to a general waiver by the Charity Commission under subsection (4) of that section or to a waiver by it under that subsection in respect of all ecclesiastical charities established for purposes relating to the parish concerned.
   In this paragraph 'ecclesiastical charity' has the same meaning as that assigned to that expression in the Local Government Act 1894;
   (b) A person shall also be disqualified from being nominated, chosen or elected or from serving as a churchwarden or member of a parochial church council if he has been so disqualified from holding office under section 10(6) of the Incumbents (Vacation of Benefices) Measure 1997;
   (c) A person shall be disqualified from being nominated for election or from continuing to serve as a member of the General Synod if he holds or takes any paid office or employment appointment to which is or may be made or confirmed by the General Synod, the Convocations, the Archbishops' Council, the Central Board of Finance, the Church Commissioners for England (except that such disqualification shall not apply to any Commissioner so appointed in receipt of a salary or other emoluments), the Church of England Pensions Board or the Corporation of the Church House.

Ex-officio membership not to disqualify for election

47. No person shall be disqualified from being elected or chosen a member of any body under these rules by the fact that he is also a member ex-officio of that body; and no person shall be deemed to vacate his seat as such an elected or chosen member of any body by reason only of the fact that subsequently to his election or choice he has become a member of that body ex-officio.

PART VII
SUPPLEMENTARY AND INTERPRETATION

Casual vacancies

48.—(1) Casual vacancies among the parochial representatives elected to the parochial church council or deanery synod shall be filled as soon as practicable after the vacancy has occurred. Where the annual parochial church meeting is not due to be held within the next two months following the occurrence of the vacancy, a vacancy among the parochial representatives elected to the parochial church council may be filled, and a vacancy among the parochial representatives elected to the deanery synod shall be filled, by the election by the parochial church council of a person qualified to be so elected. Returns of parochial representatives of the laity elected to fill one or more casual vacancies on the deanery synod shall be sent by the secretary of the parochial church council to the diocesan electoral registration officer and to the secretary of the deanery synod.

(2) Where a casual vacancy among the members of a diocesan synod elected by either house of a deanery synod occurs, the vacancy may be filled by the election by that house of a person qualified to be so elected, and a meeting of the members of that house who are electors may be held for that purpose.

(3) Subject to paragraphs (1), (2) and (6) of this rule, casual vacancies among persons elected under these rules shall be filled and elections to fill such casual vacancies shall be conducted in the same manner as ordinary elections. The qualifying date for diocesan electors shall be determined in accordance with rule 35(5).

(4) Elections to fill casual vacancies shall, where possible, be held at such times as will enable all casual vacancies among representatives of the laity who are electors to be filled at the time of every election to the House of Laity of the General Synod, but no such election shall be invalid by reason of any casual vacancies not having been so filled.

(5)
- (a) Subject to the provisions of this rule, an election to fill a casual vacancy in the House of Laity shall be completed, so far as possible, within six months from the occurrence of the vacancy and, in the event of the vacancy not being filled within that period, the Chairman of the House of Laity of the General Synod may give directions to the presiding officer as to the date by which the vacancy must be filled.
- (b) Where a casual vacancy occurs in the House of Laity of the General Synod and the period for holding a general election to that House is due to begin within twelve months of the vacancy, the vacancy shall not be filled unless the lay members of the bishop's council and standing committee, acting in accordance with any directions of the diocesan synod, otherwise direct.
- (c) Where a casual vacancy in the House of Laity of the General Synod occurs within the period of two years—
  - (i) beginning with 1st August in the year of the last general election to that House, or
  - (ii) beginning with the date of the declaration of the result of an election to fill a casual vacancy where the election was conducted by voting papers in the same manner as a general election;

  the election to fill the casual vacancy shall be conducted by those papers in accordance with paragraph (6) of this rule

(6)
- (a) Where the election is to be conducted by the voting papers of a general election, the number of persons to be elected shall be the same as in the general election, provided that no continuing candidate elected during the original count shall be excluded.
- (b) Where the election is to be conducted by the voting papers of an election other than the general election, the number of persons elected shall be calculated by adding together the number of persons previously elected using these voting papers who are still continuing as elected persons, and the number of casual vacancies to be filled, provided that no continuing candidate elected during the original count shall be excluded.
- (c) The presiding officer for the area in question shall ask every candidate not elected in the previous election who is still qualified for election for the diocese in question if he consents to serve.
- (d) If the number of candidates is the same as the places to be filled and he or they so consent or only one of those candidates so consents he shall be elected to fill the casual vacancy.
- (e) If more candidates than places to be filled so consent the votes validly cast in the preceding election shall be recounted from the beginning in accordance with the rules mentioned in rule 39(8), the presiding officer having first withdrawn those candidates who did not consent or are no longer eligible for election.

(7) An election to fill a casual vacancy in either house of the diocesan synod shall be completed so far as possible within six months from the occurrence of the vacancy, provided that where a casual vacancy occurs in either house and the period for holding a general election to that house is due to begin within nine months of the vacancy, the vacancy shall not be filled unless the members of the bishop's council and standing committee who are from the same house otherwise direct.

Part VII: Supplementary and Interpretation

(8) The preceding provisions of this rule shall apply, so far as applicable and with the necessary modifications, to the choosing of persons under these rules as it applies to the election of persons thereunder, and shall also apply to the election or choosing of members of any body constituted under or in accordance with these rules.

(9) Any person elected or chosen to fill a casual vacancy shall hold office only for the unexpired portion of the term of office of the person in whose place he is elected or chosen.

(10) In calculating the period of six months referred to in paragraphs (5) and (7) of this rule—
  (a) where during the course of an election irregularities are found which are of such a kind that the presiding officer is of the opinion that he should declare the proceedings null and void, he shall so declare and shall notify all electors of the declaration and shall cause a fresh election to be held which shall be completed within the period of six months from the date of the notice to the electors of the fresh election;
  (b) where in an appeal a determination is made that there has been no valid election and the presiding officer is directed to hold a fresh election, the period of six months shall run from the date of such direction.

(11) In this rule the expression 'casual vacancy' includes the case where insufficient candidates have been nominated to fill the places available.

Resignations

49. Any person holding any office under these rules or being a member of any body constituted by or under these rules may resign his office or membership by notice in writing signed by him and sent or given to the secretary of the body of which he is an officer or member, as the case may be; and his resignation shall take effect on the date specified in the notice or, if no date is so specified, on the receipt of the notice by the secretary of that body.

Notices

50. Any notice or other document required or authorised to be sent or given under these rules shall be deemed to have been duly sent or given if sent through the post addressed to the person to whom it is required or authorised to be sent or given at that person's last known address.

Constraints in elections

51.—(1) If in any election conducted in accordance with these rules it is a requirement that a given number or not less than a given number of places of those elected shall be filled by candidates of a named category, the presiding officer shall follow the procedure set out in paragraphs (2) to (4) of this rule.

(2) The presiding officer shall examine the nomination papers to ascertain if the number of candidates nominated in any named category is less than or equal to the required given number.

(3) If the number of candidates nominated in any named category is less than or equal to the required given number, those candidates shall be declared to be elected and their names shall not be included on the voting paper and thereafter the requirement shall be disregarded and the election shall proceed with the number of seats to be filled being reduced by the number of persons declared elected.

(4) The presiding officer shall circulate with the voting papers a separate notice giving the names of any who have been declared elected in accordance with paragraph (3) of this rule.

Revocation and variation of rules, etc

52. Subject to the provisions of these rules any power conferred by these rules to make, approve, frame, pass or adopt any rule, order, resolution, determination, decision, appointment or scheme, or to give any consent or settle any constitution, or to prescribe the manner of doing anything, shall be construed as including a power, exercisable in a like manner and subject to the like conditions, to

revoke or vary any such rule, order, resolution, determination, decision, appointment, scheme, consent or constitution, or anything so prescribed.

Special provisions

53.—(1) In the carrying out of these rules in any diocese the bishop of such diocese shall have power:—
  (a) to make provision for any matter not herein provided for;
  (b) to appoint a person to do any act in respect of which there has been any neglect or default on the part of any person or body charged with any duty under these rules;
  (c) so far as may be necessary for the purpose of giving effect to the intention of these rules, to extend or alter the time for holding any meeting or election or to modify the procedure laid down by these rules in connection therewith provided that such power shall not be exercised in relation to the conduct of the elections referred to in rules 39 and 48 of these Rules;
  (d) subject to paragraph (1)(c) of this rule, in any case in which difficulties arise, to give any directions which he may consider expedient for the purpose of removing the difficulties.

(2) The powers of the bishop under this rule shall not enable him:—
  (a) to validate anything that was invalid at the time when it was done;
  (b) to give any direction that is contrary to any resolution of the General Synod.

(3) No proceedings of any body constituted under these rules shall be invalidated by any vacancy in the membership of that body or by any defect in the qualification, election or appointment of any members thereof.

(4) No proceedings shall be invalidated by the use of a form which differs from that prescribed by these rules if the form which has in fact been used is to a substantially similar effect. Any question as to whether the form which has been used is to a substantially similar effect shall be determined by the bishop.

(5) In the case of an omission in any parish to prepare or maintain a roll or form or maintain a council or to hold the annual meeting, the rural dean upon such omission being brought to his notice shall ascertain and report to the bishop the cause thereof.

(6) During a vacancy in an archbishopric or where by reason of illness an archbishop is unable to exercise his functions under these rules or to appoint a commissary under paragraph (10) of this rule the functions of an archbishop under these rules shall be exercisable by the other archbishop.

(7) During a vacancy in a diocesan bishopric the functions of a diocesan bishop under these rules, including his functions as president of the diocesan synod, shall be exercisable by such person, being a person in episcopal orders, as the archbishop of the province may appoint.

(8) Where by reason of illness a diocesan bishop is unable to exercise his functions under these rules or to appoint a commissary under paragraph (10) of this rule, the archbishop of the province may, if he thinks it necessary or expedient to do so, appoint a person in episcopal orders to exercise the functions mentioned in paragraph (7) of this rule during the period of the bishop's illness.

(9) If a person appointed in pursuance of paragraph (7) or (8) of this rule becomes unable by reason of illness to act under the appointment, the archbishop may revoke the appointment and make a fresh one.

(10) An archbishop or diocesan bishop may appoint a commissary and delegate to him all or any of the functions of the archbishop under these rules but if a bishop proposes to delegate to a commissary his functions as president of the diocesan synod he shall appoint a person in episcopal orders as commissary.

(11) If a person appointed in pursuance of paragraph (7) or (8) of this rule, or a person to whom the functions of a bishop as president of the diocesan synod are delegated under paragraph (10) of this rule, is a member of the House of Clergy of the diocesan synod, his membership of that house shall be suspended during the period for which the appointment or delegation has effect.

(12) The preceding provisions of this rule shall have effect in the diocese in Europe as if the references therein to these rules were references to such of these rules as apply in that diocese, and subject

Part VII: Supplementary and Interpretation

to paragraph (6) of this rule, the powers of an archbishop under this rule shall, as respects that diocese, be exercisable by the Archbishop of Canterbury.

Meaning of minister, parish and other words and phrases

54.—(1) In these rules:—

'actual communicant' means a person who has received Communion according to the use of the church of England or of a Church in communion with the Church of England at least three times during the twelve months preceding the date of his election or appointment being a person whose name is on the roll of a parish and is either—
  (a) confirmed or ready and desirous of being confirmed; or
  (b) receiving the Holy Communion in accordance with the provisions of Canon B 15A paragraph 1(b);

'auditor' shall mean a person eligible as the auditor of a charity under section 43(2) of the Charities Act 1993;

'independent examiner' shall mean a person as defined in Section 43(3)(a) of the Charities Act 1993;

'the Measure' means the Synodical Government Measure 1969;

'minister' means:—
  (a) the incumbent of a parish;
  (b) a curate licensed to the charge of a parish or a minister acting as priest-in-charge of a parish in respect of which rights of presentation are suspended; and
  (c) a vicar in a team ministry to the extent that the duties of a minister are assigned to him by a pastoral scheme or order or his license from the bishop;

'parish' means:—
  (a) an ecclesiastical parish; and
  (b) a district which is constituted a 'conventional district' for the cure of souls;
  (c) in relation to the Diocese in Europe, a chaplaincy which is constituted as part of the diocese.

'public worship' means public worship according to the rites and ceremonies of the Church of England.

(2) Any reference in these rules to the laity shall be construed as a reference to persons other than Clerks in Holy Orders, and the expression 'lay' in these rules shall be construed accordingly.

(3) Where a person has executed a deed of relinquishment under the Clerical Disabilities Act 1870 and the deed has been enrolled in the High Court and recorded in the registry of a diocese under that Act then, unless and until the vacation of the enrolment of the deed is recorded in such a registry under the Clerical Disabilities Act 1870 (Amendment) Measure 1934, that person (2) of this rule or of any other provision of these rules which refers to such a clerk.

(4) References in these rules to the cathedral church of the diocese shall include, in the case of the dioceses of London and Oxford, references to Westminster Abbey and St. George's Chapel, Windsor, respectively.

(5) If any question arises whether a Church is a Church in communion with the Church of England, it shall be conclusively determined for the purposes of these rules by the Archbishops of Canterbury and York.

(6) In these rules words importing residence include residence of a regular nature but do not include residence of a casual nature.

(7) Any reference herein to 'these rules' shall be construed as including a reference to the Appendices hereto.

(8)
  (a) In these rules any matters or regulations to be prescribed shall be prescribed by the Business Committee of the General Synod of the General Synod in accordance with the following procedure.

(b) Any matters or regulations made under this rule shall be laid before the General Synod and shall not come into force until they have been approved by the General Synod, whether with or without amendment.

(c) Where the Business Committee of the General Synod determines that matters or regulations made under this rule do not need to be debated by the General Synod then, unless—
   (i) notice is given by a member of the General Synod in accordance with Standing Orders that he wishes the business to be debated, or
   (ii) notice is so given by any such member that he wishes to move an amendment to the business,
the matters or regulations shall for the purposes of sub-paragraph (b) above be deemed to have been approved by the General Synod without amendment.

Appendix I

[This Appendix comprises forms and is omitted]

Appendix II: General Provisions Relating to Parochial Church Councils

Rule 13

Officers of the council

1.—(a) The minister of the parish shall be chairman of the parochial church council (hereinafter referred to as 'the council').

(b) A lay member of the council shall be elected as Vice-Chairman of the council.

(c) During the vacancy of the benefice or when the chairman is incapacitated by absence or illness or any other cause or when the minister invited him to do so the vice-chairman of the council shall act as chairman and have all the powers vested in the chairman.

(d)
   (i) The Council may appoint one of their number to act as secretary of the Council. Failing such appointment the office of secretary shall be discharged by some other fit person who shall not thereby become a member of the Council, provided that such person may be co-opted to the Council in accordance with the provisions of rule 14(1)(h);
   (ii) where a person other than a member of the Council is appointed to act as secretary, that person may be paid such remuneration (if any) as the council deems appropriate provided that such person shall not be eligible to be a member of the council;
   (iii) the secretary shall have charge of all documents relating to the current business of the council except that, unless he is the electoral roll officer, he shall not have charge of the roll. He shall be responsible for keeping the minutes, shall record all resolutions passed by the council and shall keep the secretary of the diocesan synod and deanery synod informed as to his name and address.

(e)
   (i) The council may appoint one or more of their number to act as treasurer solely or jointly. Failing such appointment, the office of treasurer shall be discharged either—
      by such of the churchwardens as are members of the council, or if there is only one such churchwarden, by that churchwarden solely; or
      by some other fit person who shall not thereby become a member of the council, provided that such person may be co-opted to the council in accordance with the provisions of rule 14(1)(h).

(ii) where a person other than a member of the Council is appointed to act as treasurer that person may be paid such remuneration (if any) as the Council deems appropriate provided that such person shall not be eligible to be a member of the Council.

(f) The council shall appoint an electoral roll officer, who may but need not be a member of the council and may be the secretary, and if he is not a member may pay to him such remuneration as it shall think fit. He shall have charge of the roll.

(g) If an independent examiner or auditor to the Council is not appointed by the annual meeting or if an independent examiner or auditor appointed by the annual meeting is unable or unwilling to act, an independent examiner or auditor (who shall not be a member of the council) shall be appointed by the council for a term of office ending at the close of the next annual meeting. The remuneration (if any) of the independent examiner or auditor shall be paid by the council.

(h) For the purposes of this paragraph, where a special cure of souls in respect of a parish has been assigned to a vicar in a team ministry, or where there has been no such assignment but a special responsibility for pastoral care in respect of the parish has been assigned to a member of the team under section 20(8A) of the Pastoral Measure 1983, that vicar or that member, as the case may be, shall be deemed to be the minister unless incapacitated by absence or illness or any other cause, in which case the rector in the team ministry shall be deemed to be the minister.

Meetings of Council

2. The council shall hold not less than four meetings in each year. Meetings shall be convened by the chairman and if not more than four meetings are held they shall be quarterly intervals so far as possible.

Power to call meetings

3. The chairman may at any time convene a meeting of the council. If he refuses or neglects to do so within seven days after a requisition for that purpose signed by not less than one-third of the members of the council has been presented to him those members may forthwith convene a meeting.

Notices relating to meetings

4.—(a) Except as provided in paragraph 8 of this Appendix, at least ten clear days before any meeting of the council notice thereof specifying the time and place of the intended meeting and signed by or on behalf of the chairman of the council or the persons convening the meeting shall be posted at or near the principal door of every church, or building licensed for public worship in the parish.

(b) Not less than seven days before the meeting a notice thereof specifying the time and place of the meeting signed by or on behalf of the secretary shall be posted or delivered to every member of the council or, if the member has authorised the use of an electronic mail address, to that address. Such notice shall contain the agenda of the meeting including any motion or other business proposed by any member of the council of which notice has been received by the secretary. The notice required by this sub-paragraph shall not be required for a council meeting immediately following the annual parochial church meeting being a council meeting which has been called solely for the purpose of appointing or electing any officers of the Council or the members of the standing committee thereof provided that the notice required by sub-paragraph (a) hereof has been given.

(c) If for some good and sufficient reason the chairman, vice-chairman and secretary, or any two of them, consider that a convened meeting should be postponed, notice shall be given to every member of the council specifying a reconvened time and place within fourteen days of the postponed meeting.

Chairman at meetings

5. Subject to the provisions of rules 22 and 23 the chair at a meeting of the council shall be taken:—
   (a) by the chairman of the council if he is present;

(b) if the chairman is not present, by the clerk in Holy Orders, licensed to or with permission to officiate in the parish duly authorised by the bishop with the clerk's agreement, following a joint application by the minister of the parish and the council or, if the benefice is vacant, by the council for the purposes of this sub-paragraph;

(c) if neither the chairman of the council nor the clerk mentioned in sub-paragraph (b) above is present, by the vice-chairman of the council:

Provided that at any meeting the chairman presiding shall, if he thinks it expedient to do so or the meeting so resolves, vacate the chair either generally or for the purposes of any business in which he has a personal interest or for any other particular business.

Should none of the persons mentioned above be available to take the chair for any meeting or for any particular item on the agenda during a meeting then a chairman shall be chosen by those members present from among their number and the person so chosen shall preside for that meeting or for that particular item.

Quorum and agenda

6. No business shall be transacted at any meeting of the council unless at least one-third of the members are present thereat and no business which is not specified in the agenda shall be transacted at any meeting except by the consent of three-quarters of the members present at the meeting.

Order of business

7. The business of a meeting of the council shall be transacted in the order set forth in the agenda unless the council by resolution otherwise determine.

Short notice for emergency meetings

8. In case of sudden emergency or other special circumstances requiring immediate action by the council a meeting may be convened by the chairman of the council at not less than three clear days' notice in writing to the members of the council but the quorum for the transaction of any business at such meetings shall be a majority of the then existing members of the council and no business shall be transacted at such meeting except as is specified in the notice convening the meeting.

Place of meetings

9. The meeting of the council shall be held at such place as the council may direct or in the absence of such direction as the chairman may direct.

Vote of majority to decide

10. The business of the Council shall be decided by a majority of the members present and voting thereon.

Casting vote

11. In the case of an equal division of votes the chairman of the meeting shall have a second casting vote.

Minutes

12.—(a) The names of the members present at any meeting of the council shall be recorded in the minutes.

(b) If one-fifth of the members present and voting on any resolution so require, the minutes shall record the names of the members voting for and against that resolution.

(c) Any member of the council shall be entitled to require that the minutes shall contain a record of the manner in which his vote was cast on any resolution.

(d) Minutes of meetings of the council shall be available to all members of the Council. The members shall also have access to past minutes which the Chairman and Vice-Chairman jointly determine to be relevant to current Council business.

(e) The independent examiner or auditor of the council's financial statements, the bishop, the archdeacon and any person authorised by one of them in writing shall have access to the approved minutes of council meetings without the authority of the Council.

(f) Other persons whose names are on the church electoral roll may have access to the approved minutes of Council meetings held after the annual parochial church meeting in 1995 except any minutes deemed by the Council to be confidential.

(g) Other persons may have access to the minutes of Council meetings only in accordance with a specific authorisation of the Council provided that, where minutes have been deposited in the diocesan record office pursuant to the Parochial Registers and Records Measure 1978, the authorisation of the council may be dispensed with.

Adjournments

13. Any meeting of the council may adjourn its proceedings to such time and place as may be determined at such meeting.

Standing committee

14.—(a) The council shall have a standing committee consisting of not less than five persons. The minister and such of the churchwardens as are members of the council shall be ex-officio members of the standing committee, and the council shall by resolution appoint at least two other members of the standing committee from among its own members and may remove any person so appointed. Unless removed from office, the appointed members shall hold office from the date of their appointment until the conclusion of the next annual meeting of the parish.

(b) The standing committee shall have power to transact the business of the council between the meetings thereof subject to any directions given by the council.

Other committees

15. The Council may appoint other committees for the purpose of the various branches of church work in the parish and may include therein persons who are not members of the Council. The minister shall be a member of all committees ex-officio.

16. An independent examiner or auditor of the Council's financial statements shall—
   (a) have a right of access with respect to books, documents or other records (however kept) which relate to the said financial statements;
   (b) have a right to require information and explanations from past or present treasurers or members of the council and, in case of default, the independent examiner or auditor may apply to the Charity Commission for an order for directions pursuant to section 44(2) of the Charities Act 1993 or any statutory modification thereof for the time being in force.

Validity of proceedings

17. No proceedings of the council shall be invalidated by any vacancy in the membership of the council or by any defect in the qualification or election of any member thereof.

Interpretation

18. Any question arising on the interpretation of this Appendix shall be referred to the bishop of the diocese and any decision given by him or by any person appointed by him on his behalf shall be final.

CASES

Re Blagdon Cemetery	657	Re Welford Road Cemetery, Leicester	686
Blake v Associated Newspapers Limited	665	Aston Cantlow and Wilmcote with Billesley Parochial Church Council v Wallbank	702
Re Emmanuel Church, Bentley	672		

Re Blagdon Cemetery[1]

ARCHES COURT OF CANTERBURY
CAMERON QC, DEAN; CLARK QC AND GEORGE QC CHS
16 APRIL 2002

1. This is an appeal from the decision of Briden Ch given on 16 February 2000 in the Consistory Court of the Diocese of Bath and Wells, by which he refused to grant a faculty for the exhumation of the remains of Steven Whittle from Blagdon Cemetery, Somerset with a view to their reinterment in Stowmarket Cemetery, Suffolk. The appeal is brought following the grant of leave to appeal under rule 6 of the Faculty Jurisdiction (Appeals) Rules 1998 (SI 1998/1713).

The facts

2. The petitioners had three children, two sons and a daughter, until the untimely death of their son Steven, aged 21, on 25 September 1978.

3. Mr Whittle spent his working life as a publican and moved every few years from one public house to another in different parts of the country. In August 1978 he and his wife left a public house in Ellesmere Port, Wirral to move to another one at Blagdon, Bristol. Steven and their daughter remained in Ellesmere Port. Only a few weeks after their move Mr and Mrs Whittle heard on 25 September 1978 that Steven had tragically died in an industrial accident at his work. His employers assumed responsibility for the funeral arrangements and Steven's body was brought from Ellesmere Port to Blagdon. A funeral service was held in Blagdon Church and Steven was buried in the consecrated part of Blagdon Cemetery.

4. Mr and Mrs Whittle left Blagdon just over a year later, in October 1979. They then moved around both in Wales and in England every few years, ending up in 1995 in Long Melford, Suffolk, Mr Whittle's last position before his retirement. Their daughter had lived in Suffolk since her

---

[1] [2002] Fam 299, [2002] 4 All ER 482.

marriage in the early 1980s, and Mr and Mrs Whittle decided to retire to Suffolk to be near to her and their granddaughter.

5. These facts were before Briden Ch and he referred to them in his judgment of 16 February 2000. In addition, he recorded the difficulties encountered by Mr and Mrs Whittle in visiting Steven's grave in Blagdon following upon Mr Whittle's deteriorating health and his impaired vision, which made it impossible for him to drive from Suffolk. Mrs Whittle does not drive.

6. As the result of additional evidence admitted with leave in this court we know that Mr and Mrs Whittle raised with their solicitor in about 1982 the question of moving Steven's remains away from Blagdon to somewhere near their intended permanent home. Not surprisingly, they were advised that until they had established such a permanent home it was premature and inappropriate to consider exhumation and reburial.

7. Briden Ch was told that the burial plot which Mr and Mrs Whittle had acquired in Stowmarket cemetery was a triple depth plot in the consecrated section of the cemetery. However, some time after the hearing of this appeal we were provided with a letter from Stowmarket Town Council saying that the plot is 'in the unconsecrated section of the cemetery as there are no consecrated plots remaining'.

8. It is to this plot that Mr and Mrs Whittle wish to move Steven's remains. They intend to have a minister present at the reinterment, if allowed, to bless the grave before the coffin is placed in it. Their permanent home is in Stowmarket and they have purchased the plot with the intention that they will both be buried in it in due course.

9. This appeal necessitates the consideration of a number of different matters, both as to the principles in relation to faculties for exhumation and reburial and the practical application of those principles. The court has received great assistance from the arguments put forward with skill and sensitivity by Mr Hill and Mr Petchey. Mr Petchey's article 'Exhumation Reconsidered' (2001) 6 Ecc LJ 122 was helpfully cited to us, and we express our appreciation of their contributions.

Consecrated land

10. The difference between consecrated and unconsecrated land is not widely known or understood. It is appropriate to differentiate between them in this case, which is concerned with a petition for a faculty to exhume remains from a consecrated part of one local authority cemetery so as to transport them for reburial in the unconsecrated part of another local authority cemetery.

11. Land becomes consecrated when the bishop of a diocese signs a document, called a sentence, by which he separates and sets apart an area of land and dedicates the land to the service of Almighty God. The effect of this sentence where the land is to be used for the interment of the remains of the dead, whether the land consists of churchyard around a church or an identified area of land in a cemetery, is to set apart the land as being held for sacred uses and to bring it within the jurisdiction of the consistory court.

12. Unconsecrated burial land is not set apart as sacred and is not usually within the jurisdiction of the consistory court. There is, therefore, a difference between the consecrated and the unconsecrated parts of local authority cemeteries. This does not mean that a local authority has different management responsibilities for the unconsecrated part of the cemetery as compared with the consecrated part. The management has to be carried out in accordance with the rules laid down under the Local Authorities' Cemeteries Order 1977 (SI 1977/204), for the whole cemetery, but any question of exhumation is determined by the consistory court in relation to the consecrated part of the cemetery, whereas in the unconsecrated part it is a matter for the local authority, in terms of policy, and for the Secretary of State as a matter of law.

13. Prior to the Burial Act 1857 consistory courts, as a matter of practice, declined to grant a faculty authorising remains buried in consecrated ground to be reinterred in unconsecrated ground. The reason was that, per Dr Tristram QC Ch, in *In re Talbot* [1901] P 1, 5: 'by so doing they would be sanctioning the removal of remains from a place of burial under the special protection of the ecclesiastical courts to a place of interment under the protection of no court.'

14. That particular objection was removed when unconsecrated land became subject to statutory control on the introduction of a licensing system under section 25 of the Burial Act 1857. This was a new system of protection for remains buried in unconsecrated ground, which provided that remains could not be removed without permission from the Secretary of State. Thus remains in unconsecrated ground became protected just as remains in consecrated ground had been, and continue to be, under the protection of the consistory court and removable only under faculty, that is by permission of the court.

15. Apart from this legal protection afforded to remains in the unconsecrated part of a cemetery, it can generally be assumed that local authorities carry out their legal responsibilities for care and maintenance of their cemeteries. Thus, if remains are to be removed from the consecrated ground of a churchyard, or the consecrated part of a cemetery, and to be reinterred in the unconsecrated part of the same or another cemetery it is reasonable for the consistory court to conclude, certainly in the absence of evidence to the contrary, that the new grave will be cared for in a seemly manner and will be protected in this sense.

16. Reinterment in unconsecrated ground which is not in a local authority cemetery is a different matter. No general inference of the suitability for reinterment in such land can properly be drawn by the consistory court. Questions about proper care of the new grave in the future and the prospects for visiting access by future generations would need to be addressed by those involved in such cases, and in turn examined with care by the consistory court in deciding whether or not to exercise its discretion to grant a faculty for exhumation.

17. In the present case the principle of suitability of reinterment in unconsecrated ground, in the absence of any available consecrated ground, is not an issue for the reasons we have already given. However, because of the two different systems of legal control, if a faculty is granted permitting the exhumation of Steven's remains from Blagdon Cemetery it will also be necessary for a Home Office licence to be obtained to permit the transfer of his remains to the new grave in Stowmarket Cemetery. This is because a faculty alone is sufficient to authorise exhumation from consecrated land, but a Home Office licence as well as a faculty is required where an exhumation is proposed from consecrated land but reinterment is proposed into unconsecrated land.

Exhumation: general principles

18. During the period of human history respect for the dead and the recognition of the inevitable process of decay have led to different cultural practices and laws about disposal of the dead. Whether such disposal has been by way of burial or cremation it has been a feature of such cultures that the disposal has had an aura of permanence about it.

19. In English common law there is a duty to dispose of a dead body: *Halsbury's Laws of England*, 4th ed, vol 10 (1975), para 1017. The general concept of permanence is reflected in the fact that it is a criminal offence to disturb a dead body without lawful permission: *Halsbury's Law of England*, 4th ed, vol 10, para 1196. Moreover, the fact that there is no ownership of a dead body according to English law, and the absence of any legal right in English law or under the Convention for the Protection of Human Rights and Fundamental Freedoms to exhume a body or cremated remains, reflects a culture in which the norm is that the remains of a dead person should not be disturbed once they have undergone the initial act of interment.

20. Lawful permission can be given for exhumation from consecrated ground as we have already explained. However, that permission is not, and has never been, given on demand by the consistory court. The disturbance of remains which have been placed at rest in consecrated land has only been allowed as an exception to the general presumption of permanence arising from the initial act of interment.

21. This presumption originates in the Christian theology of burial. This theology underlies the consecration of land especially for burials, and it is present in every funeral service and burial of a body or interment of cremated remains according to the rites of the Church of England.

22. Many chancellors have emphasised the finality of Christian burial in their judgments, and the recent judgment of the Chancery Court of York in *In re Christ Church, Alsager* [1999] Fam 142 refers

to the evidence of the archdeacon about the theology of burial. We agree with that court that exhumation cases do not 'involve a question of doctrine, ritual or ceremonial'. Briden Ch correctly so certified in this case as did the chancellor in *In re Christ Church, Alsager*. However, we consider that a summary of the theological principles can be usefully stated here so as to promote a better understanding of the theological reason for the approach taken by the consistory courts to applications for exhumation from consecrated land.

Exhumation: theology of burial

23. We have been greatly assisted by a paper on the 'Theology of Burial', September 2001, from the Right Reverend Christopher Hill, Bishop of Stafford. He drew attention to the fact that

> 'The funeral itself articulates very clearly that its purpose is to remember before God the departed; to give thanks for their life; to commend them to God the merciful redeemer and judge; to commit their body to burial/cremation and finally to comfort one another.'

He went on to explain more generally that:

> 'The permanent burial of the physical body/the burial of cremated remains should be seen as a symbol of our entrusting the person to God for resurrection. We are commending the person to God, saying farewell to them (for their "journey"), entrusting them in peace for their ultimate destination, with us, the heavenly Jerusalem. This commending, entrusting, resting in peace does not sit easily with "portable remains", which suggests the opposite: reclaiming, possession, and restlessness; a holding onto the "symbol" of a human life rather than a giving back to God.'

24. In the light of his restatement of these theological principles the bishop expressed the opinion that a reluctance by the consistory court to grant faculties for exhumation is well grounded in Christian theology.

25. In this case Steven Whittle was a baptised and confirmed member of the Church of England and his parents chose to have a funeral service in Blagdon Church conducted by a minister of the Church of England. The purpose of the funeral, as described by the Bishop of Stafford, will, therefore, have been made known to Mr and Mrs Whittle at the service. At the time when he was buried in the consecrated part of Blagdon Cemetery they entrusted Steven to God for resurrection. They, therefore, come to this court seeking to persuade us that there are special circumstances in their case which should be treated as an exception to the principle that as Steven was laid finally at peace in 1978 his remains should not be disturbed.

26. Many people choosing to have their relatives or friends buried in a churchyard or in the consecrated part of a local authority cemetery may have little or no understanding of the Christian theology of burial as outlined in the passages we have quoted above from the Bishop of Stafford. It is, therefore, very important that cemetery managers and funeral directors give a simple explanation to the bereaved about the difference between consecrated land, to which the theology of burial has application, and unconsecrated land. Members of the public do have choices nowadays in relation to burial and cremation and places of disposal of the dead, and they need to be informed in making their choices. We hope that the principles we have stated above will be noted and used for the purpose of providing such information.

27. It is important that any guidance issued by cemetery managers or funeral directors should make it clear that permanence of burial is the norm in relation to consecrated land, so that remains are not to be regarded as 'portable' at a later date, because relatives move elsewhere and have difficulty in visiting the grave.

Exhumation: general approach

28. We have explained that the norm is permanence in relation to Christian burial. The question then arises as to how to determine the exceptional circumstances which would justify departure from the norm. The Chancery Court of York formulated the question in *In re Christ Church, Alsager*

[1999] Fam 142, 149 as 'Is there a good and proper reason for exhumation that reason being likely to be regarded as acceptable by right thinking members of the Church at large?'

29. Whilst we understand the Chancery Court's intention to set some objective standard within a Christian context, we note that the court in *In re Christ Church, Alsager* did not have the advantage of any argument from counsel. The appeal was dealt with on written representations alone at the specific request of the petitioner appellant, who was seeking a faculty for exhumation of the cremated remains of his father.

30. Both Mr Hill and Mr Petchey have argued in this court that the reference to right thinking members of the Church at large is an extremely difficult test to apply in practice. The chancellor may consider that evidence ought to be taken on the matter. It could then transpire that there are various different views which are honestly and rationally held upon the subject of exhumation. If the chancellor does not take evidence, then an assumption has to be made as to the notional views of right thinking members of the Church at large: George QC Ch in *In re Kingston Cemetery* (unreported) 3 July 2000. For a petitioner the test may give the impression that mustering support for the petition is the way to persuade the court that exhumation would be acceptable within the notional body of right thinking members of the Church at large for the reason relied upon in the petition.

31. The difficulty of applying the test formulated by the Chancery Court of York is exemplified in this case. Briden Ch set out the question early in his judgment, then considered the various factors recommended as guidance in *In re Christ Church, Alsager* [1999] Fam 142 and concluded:

> 'Bearing in mind that the judgment in *In re Christ Church, Alsager* sets out guidelines as opposed to rules of law, and that it is necessary to evaluate all the circumstances placed before me, the critical question which has already been quoted from that judgment must be answered in the negative.'

The chancellor made no assessment of the notional views of 'right thinking members of the Church at large' in respect of 'all the circumstances before him'. He confined himself to determining whether 'a good and proper reason for exhumation' had been established to his satisfaction on the evidence before him.

32. Having regard to the practical difficulties associated with the test, as formulated by the Chancery Court of York, we do not consider that Briden Ch can be criticised for not seeking to justify his conclusion by reference to the notional views of 'right thinking members of the Church at large'.

33. We have concluded that there is much to be said for reverting to the straightforward principle that a faculty for exhumation will only be exceptionally granted. Exceptional means 'forming an exception' (Concise Oxford Dictionary, 8th ed (1990)) and guidelines can assist in identifying various categories of exception. Whether the facts in a particular case warrant a finding that the case is to be treated as an exception is for the chancellor to determine on the balance of probabilities.

34. The Chancery Court of York in *In re Christ Church, Alsager* [1999] Fam 142, 148 quoted part of the judgment of Edwards QC Ch in *In re Church Norton Churchyard* [1989] Fam 37 on the subject of the discretion of the consistory court. In that passage Edwards QC Ch said: 'there should be no disturbance of that ground except for good reason.' In a later decision, *In re St Mary Magdalene, Lyminster* (1990) 9 Consistory and Commissary Court Cases 1, the same chancellor used somewhat different language in saying: 'the question may be thus stated: has this petitioner shown that there are sufficient special and exceptional grounds for the disturbance of two churchyards?'

35. The variety of wording which has been used in judgments demonstrates the difficulty in identifying appropriate wording for a general test in what is essentially a matter of discretion. We consider that it should always be made clear that it is for the petitioner to satisfy the consistory court that there are special circumstances in his/her case which justify the making of an exception from the norm that Christian burial, that is burial of a body or cremated remains in a consecrated churchyard or consecrated part of a local authority cemetery, is final. It will then be for the chancellor to decide whether the petitioner has so satisfied him/her.

Relevant factors

36. The Chancery Court of York in *In re Christ Church, Alsager* [1999] Fam 142 considered various factors which can arise in connection with a petition for a faculty for exhumation. Many of these have arisen in this appeal and we have had the benefit of argument upon them. We consider them in turn.

(i) Medical reasons

We were shown a medical certificate relating to Mr Whittle's health in the context of his inability to drive from Stowmarket to Blagdon so that he and his wife might visit Steven's grave. Mr Whittle is receiving appropriate medication and, as a senior citizen, he is in no different a predicament than many thousands of his age group who find that advancing years have an effect on certain aspects of life, including travelling. In so far as Briden Ch treated the petition of Mr and Mrs Whittle as one seeking exhumation of Steven simply in order to visit his grave more easily, we cannot fault his conclusion that this was not a sufficient reason for exhumation. Mr Hill wisely abandoned any reliance upon Mr Whittle's state of health in the course of his argument at the hearing of this appeal. If advancing years and deteriorating health, and change of place of residence due to this, were to be accepted as a reason for permitting exhumation then it would encourage applications on this basis. As George QC Ch pointed out in *In re South London Crematorium* (unreported) 27 September 1999:

> 'Most people change place of residence several times during their lives. If such petitions were regularly to be allowed, there would be a flood of similar applications, and the likelihood of some remains, and ashes, being the subject of multiple moves.'

Such a practice would make unacceptable inroads into the principle of permanence of Christian burial and needs to be firmly resisted. We agree with the Chancery Court of York that moving to a new area is not an adequate reason by itself for removing remains as well. Any medical reasons relied upon by a petitioner would have to be very powerful indeed to create an exception to the norm of permanence, for example, serious psychiatric or psychological problems where medical evidence demonstrates a link between that medical condition and the question of location of the grave of a deceased person to whom the petitioner had a special attachment.

(ii) Lapse of time

Briden Ch treated the lapse of time of a period in excess of 20 years since Steven's death as determinative: 'Despite the particular circumstances of Steven Whittle's death and burial, and the inability of his parents to take any active steps for so long, I am forced to conclude that it is now simply too late for a disturbance of his remains to be permitted.' The chancellor was probably influenced by the statement of the Chancery Court of York *In re Christ Church, Alsager* [1999] Fam 142, 149H that 'the passage of a substantial period of time will argue against the grant of a faculty'. However, we do not read this statement as signifying that time alone will be determinative. It may well be a factor in relation to assessing the genuineness of the petitioner's case. Long delay with no credible explanation for it may well tip the balance against the grant of a faculty but lapse of time alone is not the test. Mr Hill pointed to a period of 110 years *In re Talbot* [1901] P 1 and examples of up to 20 years since the date of burial in other reported cases. Having found that Mr and Mrs Whittle had been unable to take any active steps earlier to apply for a faculty for exhumation of Steven's remains because of their peripatetic existence, we consider that the chancellor erred in treating the lapse of time as determinative instead of concluding that there was a credible explanation for the delay. Having so concluded, he should then have proceeded to consider what other factors operated for or against the grant of a faculty

(iii) Mistake

We agree with the Chancery Court of York that a mistake as to the location of a grave can be a ground upon which a faculty for exhumation may be granted. We also agree that a change of mind as to the place of burial on the part of relatives or others responsible in the first place for the interment should not be treated as an acceptable ground for authorising exhumation. Mr and Mrs Whittle very properly did not attempt to justify their petition on the basis that they had made a mistake in burying Steven at Blagdon. The evidence showed clearly that, however traumatic the experience of his sudden death was for them, their unequivocal decision was that he should be buried in Blagdon Cemetery. Sometimes genuine mistakes do occur, for example, a burial may take place in the wrong burial plot in a cemetery or in a space reserved for someone else in a churchyard. In such cases it may be those responsible for the cemetery or churchyard who apply for a faculty to exhume the remains from the wrong burial plot or grave.

Faculties can in these circumstances readily be granted, because they amount to correction of an error in administration rather than being an exception to the presumption of permanence, which is predicated upon disposal of remains in the intended not an unintended plot or grave. A mistake may also occur due to a lack of knowledge at the time of burial that it was taking place in consecrated ground with its significance as a Christian place of burial. For those without Christian beliefs it may be said that a fundamental mistake had been made in agreeing to a burial in consecrated ground. This could have been a sufficient ground for the grant of a faculty to a humanist *In re Crawley Green Road Cemetery, Luton* [2001] Fam 308 and to orthodox Jews in *In re Durrington Cemetery* [2001] Fam 33, without the need for recourse to the Human Rights Act 1998. The need for greater clarity about the significance of consecrated ground in cemeteries, in particular, is demonstrated by these examples and we reiterate our plea for more readily available information so as to reduce the chances of such mistakes occurring again in the future

(iv) Local support

Mr Hill argued that this court should take account of the fact that Mr and Mrs Whittle's petition is supported by Steven's closest relatives and also by the Rural Dean of Stowmarket. In so arguing he was relying upon *In re Christ Church, Alsager* [1999] Fam 142, 149, where it was suggested that persuasive matters may be 'that all close relatives are in agreement; and the fact that the incumbent, the parochial church council and any nearby residents agree'. We differ from the Chancery Court of York in this respect. We consider that the views of close relatives are very significant and come in a different category from the other categories mentioned by the Chancery Court. We do not regard it as persuasive that there is particular support for an unopposed petition any more than support for a contested petition of this nature would affect the decision on the merits of the petition. It is the duty of the consistory court to determine whether the evidence reveals special circumstances which justify the making of an exception from the norm of the finality of Christian burial, as we have already said earlier in this judgment. The amount of local support, whether clerical or lay, should not operate as a determining factor in this exercise and will normally be irrelevant.

(v) Precedent

Mr Hill made some limited criticism of Briden Ch's reference to the fact that there was nothing, in his view, to distinguish the motivation of Mr and Mrs Whittle 'from that of many other petitioners whose similar objective has been held an inadequate reason for granting a faculty'. The suggestion was that precedent was taking priority over consideration of the merits of the case. We do not accept that criticism of the chancellor, or the implication that precedent should play no part in the decision making process in the consistory court. We are aware that the common law doctrine of precedent was not historically part of canon law, and that on the facts of *In re Christ Church, Alsager* the Chancery Court of York considered the possibility of creating a precedent as irrelevant. However, we consider that Edwards QC Ch was right in *In re St Mary Magdalene, Lyminster* (1990) 9 Consistory and Commissary Court Cases 1, to have regard to the effect of setting a precedent. More recently George QC Ch in *In re West Norwood Cemetery* (unreported) 6 July 2000 was right in saying: 'Whilst the focus must be on the particular circumstances of the individual petition, the court's approach has to take account also of the impact its decision is likely to have on other similar petitions.' In our view, precedent has practical application at the present day because of the desirability of securing equality of treatment, so far as circumstances permit it, as between petitioners.

(vi) Family grave

Both Mr Hill and Mr Petchey invited us to regard the death of Steven at such early age, and the circumstances of his sudden death and burial, as unnatural and thus creating special circumstances in themselves. The intention of Mr and Mrs Whittle, they said, is essentially to bring Steven's remains to a family grave. In the normal course of events, they would have expected to predecease him and be the first occupants. The concept of a family grave is, of course, of long standing. In a less mobile society in the past, when generations of a family continued to live in the same community, it was accepted practice for several members of a family to be buried in one grave. Headstones give a vivid picture of family relationships and there are frequent examples of one or more children predeceasing their parents due to childhood illnesses, which were incurable. Burials in double or treble depth graves continue to take place at the present time. They are to be encouraged. They express family unity and they are environmentally friendly in demonstrating an economical use of land for burials. Normally the burial of family members in the family grave occurs immediately following the death of the particular member of the family, whereas in this case Steven's remains will have to be disturbed after many years in order to inter them in a new family grave.

37. Notwithstanding this, we have concluded that there are special factors in this case which make it an exception to the norm of permanence which we have explained earlier in this judgment. These factors are: (1) the sudden and unnatural death of Steven at an age when he had expressed no view about where he would like to be buried; (2) the absence of any link between him and the community in which he was buried; (3) his parents' lack of a permanent home at the time of his unexpected death; (4) his parents' inquiries of their solicitor shortly after Steven's death about the possibility of moving his remains once they had acquired a permanent home; (5) having lived in Stowmarket for several years as their permanent home and having become part of the local community, their purchase of a triple depth burial plot in Stowmarket Cemetery.

38. Our decision is not a novel one. Faculties have been granted in the past for the bringing together, or accumulation, of family members in a single grave after many years provided special reasons were put forward for the lapse of time since the date of burial. Mr Hill drew our attention to a decision of Newsom QC Ch in *In re St James's Churchyard, Hampton Hill* (1982) 4 Consistory and Commissary Court Cases 25, where he granted a faculty over 50 years after the death for remains to be exhumed and transported to Canada to be reburied in a family plot in Woodstock, Ontario.

39. Briden Ch did not address this petition specifically in terms of the bringing together of parents and child in a family grave. We are satisfied that the exercise of his discretion was flawed in so far as it was based on an erroneous evaluation of the facts in this respect and, as we have already said, in the way he treated the lapse of time as being determinative.

40. We, therefore, allow this appeal. In doing so it should not be assumed that whenever the possibility of a family grave is raised a petition for a faculty for exhumation will automatically be granted. As in this case it is to be expected that a husband and wife will make provision in advance by way of acquisition of a double grave space if they wish to be buried together. Where special circumstances are relied upon in respect of a child who has predeceased his or her parents, it will be insufficient if there is simply a possibility of establishing a family grave. As in this case there would have to be clear evidence as to the existence of the legal right to such a grave if no family member was already buried in it.

41. Finally, we record that although article 8 of the European Convention for the Protection of Human Rights and Fundamental Freedoms was mentioned in argument greater emphasis was rightly placed on other factors to be taken into account in the exercise of the discretion of the consistory court. We are not persuaded that the judgment of Briden Ch constituted an interference with any article 8 right. In the absence of any right to exhumation petitioners can expect fairness and equality of treatment in the exercise of the discretion of the consistory court. Those safeguards have been and will continue to be present as courts exercise their discretion on a proper evaluation of the facts in the light of the principles set out above.

42. This court directs that a faculty be issued out of the Consistory Court of the Diocese of Bath and Wells, on the usual terms, for the exhumation of the remains of Steven Whittle from plot 100

in Blagdon Cemetery and for their transportation to, and reinterment in, plot E148 in Stowmarket Cemetery on condition that the exhumation does not take place unless and until a Home Office licence has been obtained authorising the reinterment as proposed in Stowmarket Cemetery.

43. No order as to costs save that the petitioners will pay the prescribed fee and also correspondence fees of the registrar and the expenses incurred by the court.

Appeal allowed.

Blake v Associated Newspapers Limited

HIGH COURT OF JUSTICE, QUEEN'S BENCH DIVISION
GRAY J
31 JULY 2003

The issue

1. The question which I have to decide at the present hearing is whether, given that it is common ground that the defence advanced in this libel action by the Defendant raises issues which are non-justiciable, it is necessary that the action as a whole be stayed with the consequences that the Claimant would be denied the opportunity to vindicate his reputation.

2. That question arises procedurally in the form of two preliminary issues directed by me on 22 November 2002. Those issues are:

   (i) Whether, and, if so, to what extent, in order to determine the issues in this action, it is necessary to determine matters which are non-justiciable; and
   (ii) If the answer to question (i) is 'yes', whether the action should be stayed.

The parties

3. The Claimant, who has represented himself at this hearing in a dignified and persuasive manner, describes himself in the title to the action as 'The Right Reverend Jonathan Clive Blake'. His history is in summary that was ordained into the Anglican Church in 1981 and in due course became vicar of a parish in southeast London. He resigned his incumbency in 1993 following the breakdown of his marriage involving adultery on his part. In 1994 he relinquished his status as a priest within the Church of England. Thereafter he continued to describe himself as 'Reverend Jonathan Blake' and to wear clerical robes similar to those worn by clergymen in the Church of England. The Claimant asserts that he remained a clergyman and that his robes were not designed to imitate those worn within the Church of England.

4. In January 2000 the Claimant and Richard Palmer co-founded 'The Society for Independent Christian Ministry' ('SICM'). The documents in the case do not reveal how many others were involved. Subsequently 'The Province for Open Episcopal Ministry and Jurisdiction' ('POEM') was brought into existence following lengthy discussions between the Claimant and Richard Palmer. The Claimant told me that the impetus for the foundation of POEM was the wish of a particular clergyman to be ordained by the laying on of hands by a bishop which SICM was unable to provide. I was further told that, being a 'province' within the one Church of God, POEM was in a position through Richard Palmer, himself a former bishop of the Liberal Catholic Church, to consecrate bishops.

5. On 9 December 2000 the Claimant was ordained a priest by Richard Palmer. The following day, 10 December 2000, the Claimant was consecrated a bishop, again by Richard Palmer. An announcement of the forthcoming consecration of the Claimant had been placed in the issue of *The Times* for 11 October 2000. Included in the papers is an Order of Service; there are also a video and still photographs of the ceremony. At the time of the consecration of the Claimant POEM

Cases

was not, as I understand it, part of or attached to any particular church or denomination. But the Claimant informed me that POEM was a diocese or province within the Open Episcopal Church, whose canons were promulgated on 18 November 2001.

6. The defendant is the publisher of the *Daily Mail*.

The newspaper articles

7. The articles published in the *Daily Mail* which are the subject of the Claimant's complaint followed an appearance by the Claimant on a nationwide daytime television programme in the course of which the Claimant officiated in a ceremony which was described as the marriage of two homosexual men. The Claimant was dressed throughout in robes similar to those worn by bishops of the Church of England or the Roman Catholic Church. He was described by the presenters as 'a real bishop'. Reference was made in an interview with the Claimant before the ceremony to the fact that he had been ordained a priest and had 'worked traditionally in the Church of England for 12 years'. No reference was made to SICM or POEM.

8. On the following day, 15 February 2001, the first article complained of appeared in the *Daily Mail*. It was headed:

> 'A gay "wedding" conducted by a self-styled bishop, with Richard and Judy as witnesses. How daytime TV celebrated Valentine's Day.'

9. The relevant part of the text of the article read:

> '... Jonathan Blake, a self-styled bishop in costume mitre and cloak, led the ten-minute segment in which he gave the union his blessing.
>
> The divorced father-of-two and former vicar left the Church of England after question over his private life in September 1994. He was embroiled in an acrimonious divorce battle after confessing to his wife that the he had an affair with a parishioner.
>
> He now practises with The Society for Independent Christian Ministry, an organisation he helped to establish. It operates outside the conventional church. His previous wedding "blessings" have been conducted on a speed boat and the Internet'.

Two days later, on 17 February 2001, there appeared in a comment column the second article of which the Claimant complains:

> 'Rites and wrongs
>
> This week's most repulsive stunt—shown on TV when elderly ladies and small children were almost certainly watching—was the Valentine Day "marriage" of two particularly cheesy homosexuals on the Richard and Judy show. Officiating was an imitation bishop who was a once-divorced former clergyman. The only thing that surprised me about this disgusting event was that the producers couldn't find a real bishop to do it. Given the appalling moral confusion of the Church of England these days, I'd have thought its bishops would have been queuing up. It's at times like this I thank God I'm an atheist.'

10. In his letter and e-mail of complaint about these two articles, the Claimant stressed that he was a validly consecrated bishop of the Christian church. He insisted that his proper title is the Right Reverend Jonathan Blake or Bishop Jonathan Blake.

The parties' statements of case

11. In due course these proceedings were commenced. It is important to note how at the outset the Claimant put his case. The defamatory meanings attributed to the two articles in the Particulars of Claim, as foreshadowed in the letter before action, are:

> (i) that the first article meant that the Claimant, though not a validly consecrated bishop and not entitled to be called a bishop, publicly styles himself as a bishop and publicly masquerades as a bishop in bishop's costume.

(ii) That the second article meant that the Claimant, though not even a clergyman, publicly and dishonestly imitates a bishop, an office for which he has no qualification whatsoever, and thereby sets out to deceive the public.

12. The Amended Defence puts in issue the claim of the Claimant to have been consecrated a bishop within the Province for Open Episcopal Ministry and Jurisdiction and his claim to apostolic succession going back to Vatican Records. There are pleas of justification and fair comment. The primary meaning sought to be justified as true is:

> 'that the Claimant is a self-styled bishop in that he calls himself a bishop and presents himself as such in the costume of a bishop, in circumstances where he has created himself, or caused himself to be created a bishop of an organisation created by him, and of a diocese also created by him; and in circumstances where, by ordinary standards of this society, he is not a bishop and would not merit appointment as one'.

13. In the alternative the newspaper contends that the articles were true in the meanings put upon them by the Claimant which I have set out at paragraph 11 above. In the further alternative the Defendant pleads that it is true that the Claimant is in all the circumstances an imitation bishop. This last meaning is also sought to be defended as being a fair comment on a matter of public interest.

14. The supporting particulars set out in some detail from paragraph 6.41 to 6.54 the events leading up to the ceremony which took place on 10 December 2000. It is asserted that, having left the Liberal Catholic Church, Richard Palmer had no authority to ordain the Claimant as a priest beyond the authority he assumed upon the founding of SICM which was founded by Palmer and the Claimant. As to the consecration of the Claimant as a bishop within POEM, the Defendant alleges that Richard Palmer purported by self-appointment to be a bishop within POEM. It is further alleged that the consecration did not take place within, or in conformity with the rules of, any established Christian denomination or according to any rules or criteria established independently of SICM and POEM. Accordingly it is the Defendant's case that the Claimant's claim to the status of a bishop was without any validity, save as accorded to it by the Claimant and Palmer by agreement between themselves.

15. The Defendant alleges that the Claimant caused and/or instigated his own appointment as a bishop in an organisation founded by him and in circumstances where he did not have the seniority or good standing required for such an appointment. So, it is alleged, the Claimant is rightly described as a 'self-styled' bishop: by publicly styling himself a bishop and dressing up in the costume of a bishop of the Church of England and the Roman Catholic Church, he is masquerading as an independently appointed religious leader of high rank who attained such status as the product of appropriate and established procedures. By this means, it is contended the Claimant has been dishonestly imitating a bishop, an office for which his history and record show him to be unsuited.

16. In the Reply the Claimant asserts that Bishop Palmer, following the Augustinian principle maintained in the Western church, retained the power to ordain him as a priest. As to his own consecration, the Claimant relies on the fundamental principle, enshrined in all the codes of canon law of catholic apostolic churches, that only a bishop can confer orders to a bishop, thereby by logical process securing the succession. The Claimant contends that there was a Mandate for his consecration which had nothing to do with him. He denies masquerading as or imitating a bishop.

The evidence

17. Witness statements have been exchanged. Unsurprisingly in the light of the contents of the Defence, the statements of the Claimant and his witnesses Richard Palmer and Professor Elizabeth Stewart are redolent with doctrinal, procedural, jurisdictional and historical arguments in support of the validity of his consecration.

18. Each side has also retained an expert. Mr Mark Hill, a barrister specialising in ecclesiastical law, prepared a report for the Defendant. He alone gave oral evidence which consisted entirely in cross-examination by the Claimant. For the Claimant the Reverend Dr Kenneth Leech, an Anglican

priest and community theologian, prepared two briefer reports. Since it is common ground between the parties that issues do arise in the present case which are non-justiciable, it is unnecessary for me to say more at this stage about the experts' reports. I shall, however, have to return to the conclusion expressed at the end of the second report of Dr Leech.

The area of non-justiciability

19. There is, as I have said, a measure of agreement between the parties on the question whether the court can or should adjudicate upon the claim of the Claimant to validity as a bishop. In his skeleton argument the Claimant states:

> 'It is a fact … that there is no forum or expert anywhere worldwide that can make an objective doctrinal determination as to who is or who is not a validly consecrated bishop.'

20. In his report for the Defendant Mr Hill agrees with that proposition. He does not consider that the Claimant's claim to validity can be adjudicated upon by the court. It would involve a detailed and painstaking examination of questions of doctrine, theology and ecclesiology combining an assessment of history and a full understanding of contemporary and emergent theology and ecumenism. Mr Hill accepts that legitimate yet differing views may be held with integrity. Dr Leech concurs.

21. It seems to me that Mr Hill is right to say that the area of non-justiciability is somewhat wider than those formulations suggest. It is well-established by such cases as *General Assembly of Free Church of Scotland v Lord Overtoun* [1904] AC 515; *R v Archbishops of Canterbury and York ex parte Williamson* (transcript from M Hill, *Ecclesiastical Law* (2nd edn, Oxford: Oxford University Press, 2001) 672–676) and *Varsani v Jesani* [1999] Ch 219 that the court will not venture into doctrinal disputes or differences. But there is authority that the court will not regulate issues as to the procedures adopted by religious bodies or the customs and practices of a particular religious community or questions as to the moral and religious fitness of a person to carry out the spiritual and pastoral duties of his office. The topic is addressed in M Hill 'Judicial Approaches to Religious Disputes' in R O'Dair & A Lewis *Current Legal Issues 4: Law and Religion* (Oxford: Oxford University Press, 2001) 409.

22. In *R v Chief Rabbi ex parte Wachmann* [1992] 1 WLR 1036, where a local rabbi sought judicial review of the declaration of the Chief Rabbi, following an investigation into allegations of adultery with members of his congregation, that he was religiously and morally unfit to occupy his position, Simon Brown J said at p1042:

> 'As Mr Beloff points out, the court would never be prepared to rule on questions of Jewish Law. Mr Carus, recognising this prospective difficulty, says that in advancing his challenge here, the applicant would be prepared to rely solely upon the common law concept of natural justice. But it would not always be easy to separate out procedural complaints from consideration of substantive principles of Jewish law which may underlie them…
>
> That consideration apart, this court is hardly in a position to regulate what is essentially a religious function—the determination whether someone is morally and religiously fit to carry out the spiritual and pastoral duties of his office. The Court must inevitably be wary of entering so self-evidently sensitive an area, straying across the well-recognised divide between church and state. One cannot, therefore, escape the conclusion that if judicial review lies here, then one way or another this secular court must inevitably be drawn into adjudicating upon matters intimate to a religious community.'

23. That reasoning was applied by Auld J (whose judgment was upheld by the Court of Appeal) in *R v the Imam of Bury Park Jame Masjid Luton and others ex parte Suliman Ali* (The Independent, 13 September 1991; The Times 12 May 1993), where the court had been asked to intervene in an internal dispute as to the role of Imam in a mosque community. Auld J said:

> 'In short, the issues raised involve an examination of religious law and the custom and traditions of a particular local religious community which the court is not competent to undertake.'

24. My conclusion is that many of the issues raised by the prefatory averments in paragraph 1 of the Particulars of Claim and by the particulars relied on in support of the defences of justification and fair comment fall within the territory which the courts, by self-denying ordinance, will not enter.

Should the action be stayed?

25. If it be right that the court will decline to determine those issues, the next question which arises is whether the action can nevertheless proceed to trial, perhaps with some adaptation of the issues as they stand at present on the pleadings, or whether the action must be stayed. This is the essential question which I have to decide. In approaching it, I must and do bear in mind the extreme reluctance of the court to stay proceedings in circumstances where, as here, the consequence of doing so would be to prevent the claimant achieving the vindication which is the avowed object of the proceedings.

26. *Prebble v Television New Zealand Limited* [1995] 1 AC 321 was a libel action brought by a government minister, where the defence of justification relied on by the defendant included particulars charging the claimant and other ministers with making misleading statements in parliament and introducing legislation for dishonest and improper motives. Giving the reasons of the Privy Council for reversing the decision of the New Zealand Court of Appeal to impose a stay, Lord Browne-Wilkinson said at 337:

> '... The stay effectively prevents the Plaintiff from establishing, if he can, that he has been most seriously defamed. Their Lordships were told that it was not part of the Defendant's case before the Court of Appeal that there should be such a stay: the suggestion of a stay originated from the court itself. Before their Lordships, the Plaintiff's counsel suggested that he had not been allowed sufficient opportunity to address the Court of Appeal on the point and that as a result they had fallen into error as to the importance of the allegations struck out relative to the main issues in the case.'

The majority of the Court of Appeal took the view that the allegations struck out were 'very close to the core of this political case' ... and without regard to such allegations the court could not adequately 'consider a substantial plea of justification or ... properly quantify damages' ... Therefore the dispute was, in their view, incapable of being fairly tried and should be stayed. McKay J took the view that the allegations struck out would not be determinative of the defence of justification and would have refused a stay.

Their Lordships are of the opinion that there may be cases in which the exclusion of material on the grounds of parliamentary privilege makes it quite impossible fairly to determine the issues between the parties. In such a case the interests of justice may demand a stay of proceedings. But such a stay should only be granted in the most extreme circumstances. The effect of a stay is to deny justice to the plaintiff by preventing him from establishing his good name in the courts. There may be cases, such as *Wright and Advertiser Newspapers Ltd v Lewis* (1990) 53 SASR 416, S Australia SC, where the whole subject matter of the alleged libel relates to the Plaintiff's conduct in the house, so that the effect of parliamentary privilege is to exclude virtually all the evidence necessary to justify the libel. If such an action were to be allowed to proceed, not only would there be an injustice to the defendant but also there would be a real danger that the media would be forced to abstain from the truthful disclosure of a member's misbehaviour in parliament, since justification would be impossible. That would constitute a most serious inroad into freedom of speech'.

The Privy Council held that the allegations which had to be excluded on the ground of parliamentary privilege were comparatively marginal so that the case could proceed, albeit deprived of the full evidence.

27. Realistically recognising the existence of a problem of non-justiciability, the Claimant, basing himself on the second report of Dr Leech, maintains that underlying the doctrinal issue as to the

validity of his consecration there is what is described as a secular issue which may appropriately be determined by the court. Dr Leech formulates the secular issue as follows:

> 'The (secular) legal issue is whether Jonathan Blake was, in historical fact, consecrated as a bishop'.

28. The Claimant in his skeleton argument elaborates: he asserts that his claim is (or could be) based on the 'self-evident historical facts' that he was ordained a priest and consecrated a bishop within POEM in a ceremony officiated by Bishop Palmer. He adds that both he and those in attendance at his consecration and those to whom he has ministered since believe him to be a validly consecrated bishop.

29. Dr Leech supports this approach. He expresses the opinion that on the historical evidence the Claimant was clearly consecrated as a bishop. Dr Leech adds that, if the question is then asked whether the Claimant was consecrated within a valid historical succession, the answer is also Yes. Dr Leech concedes that other churches may not recognise this. But this has been the case for hundreds of years. Other churches may reject him, but there is no doubt that the Claimant was consecrated a bishop 'within an actual church'.

30. The Claimant makes the point that readers of the *Daily Mail* were kept in ignorance of these 'historical' facts with the result that the impression was given that 'one day I had decided to pop in to Wippel's (ecclesiastical outfitters) and purchase a purple cassock to con the public into believing I was one when the fact was I was not a bishop, because no one had appointed me a bishop other than myself, that I was imitating a bishop, was masquerading as a bishop and was an impostor'. The essence of the Claimant's complaint is that the *Daily Mail* articles, which came after 20 years of trying to help people through his ministry, attacked his integrity. If the action were to be stayed, he would be prevented from demonstrating that he is no mere imitation bishop, with the result that his integrity would be further undermined.

31. For the Defendant Miss Adrienne Page QC argues that the issues which are accepted by the Claimant to be non-justiciable are so fundamental that the action cannot fairly be tried. The defences of justification and fair comment are properly pleaded being directed at meanings which the newspaper articles are capable of bearing or in the alternative at the meanings of which the Claimant complains. She suggests that the European Convention on Human Rights is engaged. Citing *Serif v Greece* [2001] 31 EHRR 561, *Manoussakis v Greece* [1996] 23 EHRR 387 and section 13(1) of the Human Rights Act 1998, she submits that for the court to reject the claim of the Claimant to have been validly appointed a bishop might contravene the rights of the Claimant under Article 9 (the right to freedom of religion). At the same time she contends that, if the right of the newspaper to deploy material in support of the defences of justification and fair comment were to be circumscribed by the court, its right to freedom of expression under Article 10 might be infringed: see *Otto-Preminger-Institut v Austria* [1994] 19 EHRR 34 and section 12(4) of the 1998 Act. This is one of those exceptional cases where justice requires that the action be stayed.

Conclusion

32. I start by considering the question whether, on the pleadings as they stand at present, the Defendant can establish its case for the imposition of a stay by reason of the existence of issues which are non-justiciable.

33. I have already expressed my conclusion at paragraph 24 above as to the range of issues which the court will decline to determine in this field. It seems plain to me that there are numerous questions raised on the parties' statements of case which, according to the authorities already cited, are non-justiciable. Such questions include, by way of example only, substantive doctrinal questions including the canon law of catholic apostolic churches; questions of ecclesiastic procedure such as the authority and entitlement of Richard Palmer to consecrate the Claimant and the validity (in the absence at the time of any denomination or established church) of the consecration of the Claimant; questions whether the consecration of the Claimant was in conformity with the

customs and practices of any established Christian denomination or criteria independently of POEM and finally questions as to the moral standing and fitness of both Richard Palmer and the Claimant for episcopal office. I emphasise that these are no more than examples of the questions arising on the pleadings which appear to me to come within the forbidden territory of non-justiciability.

34. On the existing statements of case it is impossible for me to say, as was said in *Prebble*, that the non-justiciable issues are so marginal that the action can proceed to trial.

35. Bearing in mind, however, that a stay will only be granted in the most extreme circumstances because the effect would be to deny the Claimant the opportunity of establishing his good name in the courts, I must consider whether the issues which at present arise on the pleadings can be so adapted or tailored as to permit the action to proceed albeit with some limitation imposed as to the nature of the material which may be deployed. This was the solution proposed on behalf of the plaintiffs in *Hamilton and Greer v Hencke* (May J, 21 July 1995, unreported (the 'cash for questions' case)). Lord Williams of Mostyn QC for the plaintiffs proposed that there might be excised from the case all reference to the motive which Mr Hamilton may have had for asking certain parliamentary questions.

36. I suggested to the Claimant in the course of argument possible ways out of the impasse, for instance that he might withdraw his claim to have been validly consecrated as a bishop and complain instead that the *Daily Mail* articles defamed him by suggesting that his claim to be a bishop was dishonest because he had not taken part in any consecration ceremony. This suggestion is a modified version of the secular issue which Dr Leech maintains could be decided by the court (see paragraph 27 above). The Claimant was understandably somewhat reluctant to abandon his claim to have been validly consecrated. Even if he had been more enthusiastic, I think that the objection to the suggested course which was taken by Miss Page is well-founded: she argued that the newspaper would still wish to advance the case that the consecration service had no religious or ecclesiastic validity, so that it was in effect a charade, and that to prevent the newspaper from advancing this case would be manifestly unfair and a serious invasion of its Article 10 right.

37. I note that in the passage from *Prebble* quoted in paragraph 26 above Lord Browne-Wilkinson made reference to the risk of an inroad into the right of the defendant to freedom of speech. That was the reason why May J rejected the course proposed by counsel for the plaintiffs in *Hamilton and Greer v Hencke*. He pointed out that:

> 'it has to invite the court to prevent the defendants from attributing to the publication the wider meaning for which they contend, a meaning which … the publication plainly bears and which the plaintiffs themselves have in substance attributed to it in their pleading … it would be both unfair to the defendants and quite impractical to confine their justification so as to omit the alleged link between the alleged payments and the admitted asking of the questions …'.

38. It appears to me that the issues in the present action cannot be adapted so as to circumvent the insuperable obstacle placed in the way of a fair trial of this action by the fact that the court must abstain from determining questions which lie at the heart of the case. I am of course well aware that a stay will deprive the Claimant of the opportunity to obtain vindication. But I am driven to the conclusion that in the present case, as in *Buttes Gas v Hammer* [1982] AC 888, *Allason v Haines*, The Times, 25 July 1995, Owen J and *Hamilton and Greer*, there is no alternative but to stay the action.

Order accordingly.

Re Emmanuel Church, Bentley[2]

ARCHES COURT OF CANTERBURY
CAMERON QC, DEAN; BURSELL QC AND BRIDEN CHS
29 NOVEMBER 2005

Introduction

1. This is an appeal from the decision of Judge Shand Ch given on 18 January 2005 in the consistory court of the diocese of Lichfield by which he refused to grant a faculty. The chancellor did not hold a hearing but determined the matter upon written representations from the parties. The faculty was sought by the churchwardens as first petitioners (there being no incumbent) and Quintel S4 Ltd ('QS4') as second petitioner. The work for which a faculty was sought was the installation of mobile telephone aerials both on the outside and the inside of the tower of the church of Bentley, Emmanuel in the parish of Bentley. A formal objection using Form No 4, as prescribed by the Faculty Jurisdiction Rules 2000 (SI 2000/2047), was made jointly by Mrs Ince, the chair of governors of King Charles Primary School, and Ms Machin, the head teacher, although throughout the proceedings Ms Machin has acted on behalf of both objectors. QS4 lodged the notice of appeal against the chancellor's decision but is supported on the appeal by both churchwardens. Leave to appeal was granted by Judge Shand Ch on 28 February 2005.

Procedure on appeal

2. The procedure to be followed on appeal to the Arches Court of Canterbury or the Chancery Court of York is contained in the Faculty Jurisdiction (Appeals) Rules 1998 (SI 1998/1713). QS4 complied with the requirements of rule 7 in respect of lodging their appeal, and they served copies of the notice of appeal on the registrar of the diocese and upon the objectors as required by rule 7(3).

3. The diocesan registrar was then required to arrange for the display of a copy of the notice of appeal for a period of two weeks on a notice board outside the church. This was done. Next the registrar was required by rule 7(7)(b) to 'send or deliver to the registrar of the appellate court the court file maintained by the registrar of the diocese relating to the proceedings in the consistory court'. For reasons that we do not understand the file sent to the provincial registrar was incomplete. Some of the documentation came to light piecemeal and at a late stage in the hearing of the appeal: other documentation came to our notice only after the hearing had been completed (necessitating distribution to the parties so that they were made aware of it and had an opportunity to comment on it if they wished to do so).

4. We consider this piecemeal approach to the provision of documents relating to a petition for a faculty as wholly unsatisfactory. In the interests of justice it is important on every appeal that the appellate court has the opportunity to consider the whole file relating to the progress of a petition. It is doubly important where, as in this case, the chancellor has not held a hearing but has determined the matter on the basis of written representations alone.

5. If there is any general uncertainty about the meaning in rule 7(7)(b) of the Faculty Jurisdiction (Appeals) Rules 1998 of the words 'the court file ... relating to the proceedings in the consistory court' we wish to make it clear that they mean the totality of the documentation relating to a petition notwithstanding that for practical reasons some of the items may be kept in separate folders; for example, correspondence with the Diocesan Advisory Committee may be kept separate in the registry from correspondence with the parties. All folders form part of the 'court file' generated by

---

[2] [2006] Fam 39.

the petition in question and all should be sent to comply with rule 7(7)(b). It has to be remembered that a petition for a faculty is addressed 'To the Consistory Court of the Diocese of …' The registrar is the officer of the court with responsibility for maintaining, on behalf of the consistory court of the diocese, a full and complete file relating to the petition. This includes all documentation placed before the chancellor.

6. We are confident that registrars, in general, do in fact maintain files properly marked with the name of the parish and the petition so that documents can be readily identified if there is an appeal. It is this court file that has to be sent to the appellate court under rule 7(7)(b). Finally on this subject, we point out that rule 7(8) gives the parties to an appeal the right to inspect the court file and to copy documents from it. This demonstrates that transparency is a feature of faculty cases. There is a corresponding expectation of orderliness in court files.

The appellant, QS4

7. In June 2002 the Archbishops' Council of the Church of England ('The Archbishops' Council') announced that it had entered into an agreement with QS4 giving the company approved status for telecommunication installations in churches. QS4 was described as a specialist installer of aerials and associated infrastructure and a subsidiary of Quintel Group Ltd, which is a joint venture between the Government's Defence Evaluation and Research Agency and Rotch Property Group, one of Britain's leading property and investment companies.

8. The Archbishops' Council approved a model form of licence for use between a parish and QS4 but the obtaining of a faculty remains a prerequisite to any installation in a church. 'Best Practice Commitments' were built into the agreement and in summary these require QS4: (1) to take a precautionary approach. (In line with the recommendations of the Stewart Report on Mobile Phones and Health (2000), the report of the Independent Expert Group on Mobile Phones, the standard licence will require the regular monitoring of emission levels in and around the church. A periodic report will be made to the incumbent and parochial church council.) (2) To proceed only through rigorous controls. (Each installation will require permission from the chancellor of the diocese who will be advised by the diocesan advisory committee. Aerials will be required to be out of sight or otherwise unobtrusive.) (3) To hold meaningful consultation. (Consultation material will be provided and consultation that embraces the local community and is based on up to date information will be encouraged.) QS4's argument is that the requirements of best practice, as so summarised, have been or will be complied with in this case and that a faculty should be granted for their scheme.

Telecommunication installations in churches: general principles

9. The judgment under appeal has to be considered in the context of increasingly frequent applications for parts of churches to be put to secular use by the introduction of telecommunication equipment. Since the first reported case of this kind, *In re All Saints', Harborough Magna* [1992] 1 WLR 1235, 12 judgments on the topic (helpfully brought to our attention by Mr George) have been given by consistory courts. This figure has doubtless to be increased significantly to reflect the volume of unopposed cases in which no full judgment was delivered.

10. The proper approach to such petitions is illustrated by Judge Grenfell Ch in *In re St Margaret's, Hawes* [2003] 1 WLR 2568, para 12:

> 'In my judgment, there is no reason as a matter of ecclesiastical law why a faculty should not be granted for wholly secular and commercial use of part of a church building. Each case must be considered on its own merits. It is for the petitioners to show that there is good reason why a faculty should be granted and, once the issue of whether it involves risk to human health has been raised, it is for the petitioners to satisfy the court that the grant of a faculty will not give rise to a real, as opposed to a fanciful, risk to human health. In my judgment a real risk is properly described as being measurable or, put another way, significant.'

Nothing in the Canons of the Church of England conflicts with this statement of the law. Canons of the Church of England, 6th ed (2000), Canon F15, 'Of churches not to be profaned' and Canon

F16 'Of plays, concerts, and exhibitions of films and pictures in churches', both deal with instances of secular use. The principle underlying these canons is that a church building must be treated in a reverent manner, which is consistent with its sacred character. The primary consideration is that the secular use is not unseemly. Thus the public has been allowed to benefit from public clocks on church towers, and in parts of the country a light may be fixed to the church to act as a navigational aid in the interests of safety for sections of the public. The presence of telecommunication equipment in a church can bring benefit to the public and, providing it is subject to appropriate controls, does not violate the principle in these canons.

11. Ms Machin brought to our attention a news report by Philip Willan, in Networkworld, www.networkworld.com/edge/news/2001/0302masts.html, dated 3 February 2001, summarising a circular issued to the Roman Catholic Church in Italy in January 2001 and prohibiting the presence of mobile telephone masts in church buildings. The circular, signed by Bishop Ennio Antonelli, secretary general of the Italian Bishops' Conference, is reported as stating:

> 'Use of church buildings for purposes unconnected with worship would violate church law and could jeopardise the fiscal exemptions and other privileges currently granted to churches by the Italian Government ...'

This pronouncement, assuming it to have been summarised correctly, was however made in relation to the national fiscal laws in Italy, and the principles of a system of canon law which do not apply to the Church of England.

12. The arrival on the scene of QS4 as approved installers has not brought about any change in the law. Their approved status does not prevent a parish from dealing with other telecommunication providers in the free market. Whoever the provider may be, the chancellor has to decide in each case (whether opposed or not) if a faculty ought on the merits to be granted. Where a faculty is to issue, the chancellor must also consider what conditions, if any, need to be attached to it. QS4 produced the model licence (referred to in para 8 above) and wish to use it at Bentley Emmanuel Church, Bentley. This licence addresses many of the issues which previously caused concern such as the duration of the agreement, rights of access to the building, and the provision of insurance. Although chancellors are not bound by the model licence, consistory courts are likely to find its existence helpful in dealing fairly and appropriately with cases in which QS4 are petitioners. Particular circumstances relating to a church or its location may require some modification of the model licence, or the imposition of a faculty condition. Moreover, as a general rule faculties should be granted subject to a condition that the parties to the licence, together with any assignees or sub-licensees, comply with the terms of the licence. A condition of this nature will ensure that the court retains control over all aspects of the installation.

'Out of sight or otherwise unobtrusive'

13. We turn next to the aesthetic considerations, which were before the chancellor. The church of Bentley Emmanuel, Bentley was built in 1956 and is unlisted. None the less it is a good example of the work of the architects Lavender Twentyman & Percy. It is clear from the diocesan advisory committee's deliberations that the church is regarded by English Heritage, and others, as being of considerable architectural merit. However, it has to be recognised that the church is not in fact listed. We agree with the chancellor that the burden rests on the petitioners 'to establish a case for the granting of a faculty on the balance of probabilities'. That the burden of proof is upon those proposing change has been accepted in faculty cases since the statement to this effect by Lord Penzance, Dean of the Arches, in *Peek v Trower* (1881) 7 PD 21, 27–28. The chancellor went on to say 'considerations closely analogous to the establishment of a case for necessity inevitably arise'. If this was intended to be a reference to the approach to be adopted in relation to listed buildings, as explained in *In re St Luke the Evangelist, Maidstone* [1995] Fam 1, 8–9, then we would have to disagree with him. We issue a note of caution because it is important to recognise the distinction between listed and unlisted churches in dealing with them under the faculty jurisdiction. The rigorous system

applied by the Church of England to all its churches results in the diocesan advisory committee looking carefully at proposals for change to unlisted as well as to listed churches. But having received the views and recommendation of the diocesan advisory committee in respect of proposed work to an unlisted church, there is no requirement to consult external bodies, such as English Heritage, nor to do the kind of analysis explained in In re St Luke the Evangelist, Maidstone, which is required in relation to listed churches. In this case the diocesan advisory committee took commendable care to arrive at an appropriate solution for the installation of the aerials within louvre openings and on the brickwork on the north side of the church. In the light of the diocesan advisory committee's recommendation the chancellor found the proposal aesthetically acceptable. Ms Machin told us that no objection had been or was taken on aesthetic grounds. It is clear that QS4 has satisfied the 'Best Practice Commitment' of making the proposed aerials unobtrusive, and we find that the chancellor was correct in his conclusion on this issue.

'Local consultation'

14. The church is situated on top of a prominent hill; save for the vicarage there are no houses in its immediate vicinity, although the surrounding area is fairly densely populated. King Charles Primary School is at the bottom of this hill and across one road. Children from the school join the church for Harvest Festival and Christmas celebrations. Ms Machin told us that the previous vicar had been one of the school governors. A similar type of aerial had been situated on a block of flats a few streets away to the west of the church but that block of flats is due to be, or has recently been, demolished. Close to this block of flats is the Bentley West Primary School. In the general vicinity there are other schools, namely, County Bridge Primary School, Jane Lane Special School and the Alan Well Nursery, Infant, Junior and Secondary School. There are apparently other schools nearby, but Ms Machin informed us that it is believed that those schools will not be affected by the proposed work.

15. The chancellor had before him the petitioners' 'Summary of Public Consultation' dated 13 October 2004. It reads:

> 'A key stakeholders meeting was held on Thursday, 27 May 2004. Leaders of groups at the church, local councillors and the heads of local schools were invited. The heads of the schools attended as well as some members of the PCC. A drop-in session was held on 10 June 2004. Two church members and three local residents attended. As the drop-in session had been held on election day and the school was closed, an additional meeting for parents was held at the school on Monday, 14 June. This was attended by members of staff and up to a dozen parents. Letters of objection and a petition were received. The letters were responded to. These are enclosed. The head teacher of the school also wrote to the Bishop of Wolverhampton. His reply is enclosed.'

It was presumably in the light of that information that the chancellor described the consultation process as commendable.

16. However, at the hearing of the appeal we were told by Ms Machin that, although QS4 sent letters addressed to the relevant heads of each of the schools that we have named, those letters were incorrectly addressed. This was accepted by QS4. Apparently, the only head teacher to receive a copy was that of Bentley West Primary School. She rang Ms Machin and Ms Machin contacted the two others. The Jane Lane School was already aware of the proposals because the school secretary is a member of the Bentley Emmanuel Church congregation. It was felt that the Alan Well School was too far away to be affected.

17. Letters were apparently also sent to houses in the parish giving notice of the consultative presentation but some roads were not included in this posting and the exact location of the meeting was not given. The meeting was held at the church and the presentation was well made. However, Ms Machin informed us that, when the question of inadequate posting was raised, the response on behalf of QS4 was merely: 'You're here now. Does it matter?' If this was indeed the reply, we regard it as very unsatisfactory. In our view, 'meaningful consultation', as described in the best practice

commitments given to the Archbishops' Council, means the giving of proper notice of the date, time and place of a public meeting so that local people are sufficiently informed to decide whether or not they wish to attend. Many of those who attended did so as the result of the efforts of Ms Machin and her colleague, but others, kept in the dark due to the lack of notification, were not given the appropriate opportunity to attend and may consequently have been disadvantaged.

18. Ms Machin remained concerned and therefore arranged a meeting at her school between interested local parties and Mrs Noble from QS4 and a representative of T-Mobile (UK) Ltd ('T4 Mobile' will be a user of the aerial if a faculty is granted). A number of older school children also attended the meeting. Unfortunately the T4 Mobile representative arrived three-quarters of an hour late and the meeting was therefore delayed. We do not know if some people had to leave but, not surprisingly, those kept waiting were disgruntled and gave the representatives a hard time. Ms Machin told us that the T4 Mobile representative was asked what would happen if the aerial was not placed on the church and that his reply was to the effect: 'You'll get four or five others and you won't know where they are, so you may as well accept these.' The petitioners are not directly responsible for the employees of T4 Mobile, but if that which Ms Machin told us is accurate (and it was not disputed by Mr George on behalf of QS4), the consultation process was far from commendable. Indeed, we are not at all surprised if local feeling was thereby inflamed rather than allayed.

19. It was argued that any deficiency in the consultation process had been cured by the presence of local people at the two meetings, one organised by Ms Machin. The local consultation was not required by law, so that the question of 'curing a deficiency' in a technical sense is not strictly relevant. It was 'best practice' which was not complied with, although we consider that thanks to Ms Machin those directly interested were in fact given a fair opportunity to hear about the proposal and to express their views. We hope that lessons will have been learnt in this case and that rigorous steps will be taken by QS4 to ensure that such communication errors do not occur again elsewhere. We consider that the deficiencies we have identified here underline the advisability of publishing details of meetings by way of notices in local newspapers in addition to properly addressed individual notification to those living in the close vicinity of the church. If such advertisements are not placed voluntarily by petitioners in cases such as this, which may give rise particular concerns in the locality, the petitioners should be ordered to do so by the chancellor under rule 13(2) of the Faculty Jurisdiction Rules 2000.

Public notice under the Faculty Jurisdiction Rules 2000

20. The Faculty Jurisdiction Rules 2000 prescribe the procedure to be followed in faculty cases. Many of the requirements are mandatory and have been devised to protect the interests of petitioners and objectors and to ensure that the consistory court operates under a procedure which is fair to all. We have concerns about aspects of the procedure followed in this case.

21. The public notice required by law was apparently displayed from 1 to 29 August 2004 (although the certificate of publication is dated 1 August, this is presumably an error for 1 September). However, the public notice is required by rule 6(1) of the Faculty Jurisdiction Rules 2000 to be displayed 'as soon as the petitioner is ready to submit a petition'. The petitioners were not ready to do this in August because the diocesan advisory committee did not give its certificate until 17 September 2004 (see rule 4) and the parochial church council did not vote in favour of the application until 14 October 2004. Moreover, in spite of the provisions of rule 6(3)(a), the petition (which is dated 19 October 2004) was not 'immediately' sent or delivered to the registry once the public notice was filled in. Mr George told us that this latter error arose because Form C (the public notice) was sent to the petitioners by the diocesan advisory committee with instructions to go ahead and display it, in spite of the fact that the matter was still under consideration by the diocesan advisory committee. The letter from the diocesan advisory committee is dated 21 July 2004. Having set out various possibilities as to the siting of the aerial still under consideration it continued:

> 'While the architect and Quintel talk, I think there is mileage in you displaying the public notices for the aerial so that we can move forward if and when there is a green light. Would you display these as the instructions and then return the certificate you will find on the back…?'

22. Those directions from the diocesan advisory committee were no doubt well intentioned but, regrettably, what was recommended was entirely contrary to law. The whole purpose of such public notice is to enable a member of the public to know what proposals are being made and then to consider whether or not to object. If the proposals are not finalised, that is impossible. No notice should, therefore, be given until a final decision has been reached as to what works are to be sought by way of faculty. In the present case the public notice merely described the proposed works as: 'Installation of a mobile phone aerial and associated machinery within the tower.' It is true that any inquiries would have been likely to have elicited the fact that no plans had yet been finalised, but that can in no way excuse the failure properly to follow the Faculty Jurisdiction Rules 2000.

23. Our remarks are directed to the diocesan advisory committee and to the registrar and not to the petitioners, who understandably assumed they were given the correct advice as to procedure. Rule 3 of the Faculty Jurisdiction Rules 2000 sets out the duties of the diocesan advisory committee, which are limited to the provision of a certificate. Rule 4 enables a petitioner to submit a petition for a faculty describing the works referred to in the diocesan advisory committee certificate. Rule 6 requires the public notice to describe the works in the same manner as they are described in the petition. This sequence is essential to ensure that parishioners who are interested members of the public are accurately informed of the proposed works. In this case the chronology should have made it obvious to the registrar that the petitioners had published their notice too soon, and he should have directed that a new public notice be displayed following the submission of the petition to the registry on 19 October 2004.

24. The registrar appears to have overlooked the fact that the only public notice (that displayed prior to submission of the petition) gave the address for inspection of plans as that of QS4 in Malvern. This was possibly understandable on a literal reading of the public notice by QS4, because a note on the form requires plans to be 'available for inspection at either an address of a petitioner or in the parish and/or on display inside the church'. Common sense might have indicated that the note envisages that plans should be available locally, in this case possibly at the address of one of the churchwardens who were co-petitioners. In any event, a registrar can in such circumstances rely upon rule 4(2) which requires a copy of the designs, plans, photographs and other documents to be 'displayed in the church to which the works or other proposals relate and shall remain on display until the petition for a faculty has been determined'. We trust that in future the rules will be observed by this diocesan advisory committee and this registry (as well as by all other diocesan advisory committees and registries) and that QS4 will familiarise themselves with them for any other scheme of theirs in a church.

25. It is, of course, for all petitioners to ensure that the Rules are followed and this duty cannot be delegated to others. Although some petitioners may find them difficult to follow they may, none the less, always 'consult the registrar for advice prior to completing any petition or public notice': see rule 6(2).

Objections prior to petition

26. At the school meeting Ms Machin inquired how to raise objection to the proposal and was told by Mrs Noble that a form of petition of objection would be the normal way to proceed. Ms Machin was aware of the pitfalls of such petitions. Therefore, after consultation with those present, she herself drafted the heading to the petition presently before us. Its heading states that it is from the parents of children at King Charles Primary School and reads:

> 'We, the undersigned, wish to object to the installation of telecommunications equipment in the tower of Bentley Emmanuel Church. As there is contradictory evidence in the public domain, with regards to health issues connected with the frequency of emissions from this type of equipment, we do not wish to expose our children (or other members of the local community) to any potential hazards or risks. We therefore feel this equipment should not be installed in the church tower.'

27. Ms Machin was concerned that no fictitious names or names of persons who were not parents of children at the school, or (in spite of the heading) not local residents, should appear on

their petition. She therefore checked each name and signed the bottom of each page. There are 172 signatories. A Mrs Hakesley also wished for another 12 to be added; this list too is signed by Ms Machin. Mrs Hakesley also wrote a separate strongly worded letter of objection to Mrs Noble of QS4 16 June 2004. The signed petition and Mrs Hakesley's letter were quite properly forwarded in due course by QS4 to the registry.

28. As to general petitions of objection or memorials, the law is set out in footnote 3 to para 1324 in *Halsbury's Laws of England*, 4th ed, vol 14 (1975), p 744:

> 'Supporting or opposing memorials purporting to be signed by petitioners as to which there is no proof of the signatures or evidence of the representations made to those who sign are inadmissible: *Rector and Churchwardens of Capel St Mary, Suffolk v Packard* [1927] P 289; *In re Christ Church, Chislehurst* [1973] 1 WLR 1317, 1321.'

Such proof will often be provided by way of affidavits. In this case Ms Machin authenticated the petition by checking the names and signing each page. Here the petitioners accept the admissibility of the memorial. We consider that they are right to do so. Without ourselves hearing any detailed argument about their admissibility we accept that such memorials or petitions of objection are admissible in any case (contested or uncontested) as long as they are properly proved.

29. After the meetings Ms Machin wrote to the Bishop of Wolverhampton on 9 July 2004 expressing her concerns about the quality of consultation and the unfortunate consequence that the church was being blamed for the deficiencies of QS4:

> 'As a governing body of a local school, which has always had a good working relationship with Emmanuel Church, we were concerned that you needed to be made aware of the local situation. We do not want to see the local church placed in a difficult position due to no fault of its own and hope that you can offer them some support.'

In reply on 29 July 2004 the Bishop of Wolverhampton referred to the misaddressed letters for which he said Mrs Noble had apologised and he went on to explain his understanding of the church's position. He stated:

> 'Under the licence which QS4 issues when equipment is sited in a church, the operators are obliged to measure the level of emissions if requested by the parochial church council, which is not the case with mobile phone base stations at other sites. I shall certainly recommend to Bentley PCC that they do request these measurements every three months if and when the mast is installed. I understand that T-Mobile have a legal obligation to provide cover for 80% of the population by 2007, and Bentley is sure to be included in this figure. So the question is not whether, but how, this coverage is achieved. It is my understanding that, because the church is so well above the residential area of Bentley, it is a much better site from the point of view of both coverage and health risks than antennae being placed on much lower buildings or lamp posts, which would be the case if the church tower project does not go through. The antennae in the church will be hidden, and some 30 metres above the ground, and apparently the congregations within the church will be in the safest possible place. Given these considerations, I do not think that the PCC of Bentley can justifiably be accused of being irresponsible in the matter, and I will support their decision, if it is positive, with the strong request that they require quarterly measurements of the emissions.'

We can see no reason, if a faculty is granted, why the provision of such measurements both to the parochial church council and interested parishioners should not be made a condition of the faculty.

30. The correspondence between Ms Machin and the Bishop of Wolverhampton took place shortly before the erroneous display of the public notice by QS4 from 1–29 August 2004 upon which we have already commented. When a petition was eventually submitted on 19 October 2004 both the registrar's assistant and the chancellor noted that the public notice had been displayed during the school holidays. The chancellor decided to give an extension of time for objections, but apparently

did not consider ordering a fresh display of the public notice despite the premature display of the notice in breach of the Faculty Jurisdiction Rules 2000. The registrar was aware of the possibility of local objections because of the signed petition and letter from Ms Machin, plus the letter from Mrs Hakesley, which had all been forwarded by QS4. Following the chancellor's direction the registrar's assistant wrote to Ms Machin on 21 October 2004 asking whether she was 'still opposed to the installation of these aerials'. There is no suggestion that a similar letter was sent to Mrs Hakesley; it was certainly not Ms Machin's duty to co-ordinate all opposition to the proposed works. Ms Machin replied to the diocesan registrar's assistant on 1 November stating that the governors of her school wished to object and enclosing a copy of her letter to the Bishop of Wolverhampton dated 9 July 2004.

31. On 8 November 2004 the registrar's assistant wrote to Ms Machin setting out in detail the relevant procedures in the consistory court and including an outline of the possible procedure for a decision based upon written representations. On 25 November Ms Machin phoned the registry stating that the school governors wished formally to object and that they were willing to proceed by way of written representations. Only then was a copy of Form 4 (particulars of objection) e-mailed to Ms Machin.

32. Mrs Ince and Ms Machin entered formal objection on 25 November 2004. The particulars of objection stated:

> 'We are concerned that there is still no conclusive evidence that mobile phone masts are not a potential health risk. This mast is going to be located extremely close to our school, with 170 3–11 year olds on site every school day. The site is also used in school holidays to provide holiday play schemes for local children. We feel while there is no conclusive evidence that there is no risk we should not be putting our children's future health at risk and would wish the diocese to exercise caution, as advised in the Stewart Report. I refer specifically to the summary para 1.18 and 1.19 and would like to see the diocese to [sic] adopt the precautionary approach as recommended in this report.'

This was acknowledged by the registrar's assistant on 29 November 2004.

Procedure in respect of determination of petition for faculty

33. It is clear that Ms Machin was asked for, and gave, her agreement to proceeding by way of written representations before she had formally become a party to the proceedings; it is also clear that at no time did she give her agreement in writing. These were both breaches of rule 26(1) of the Faculty Jurisdiction Rules 2000.

34. For the avoidance of doubt we consider it necessary to draw attention to the procedural alternatives available to a chancellor under the Faculty Jurisdiction Rules 2000. First, the chancellor as the judge of the consistory court has to be satisfied that it is appropriate to determine a petition without a hearing. This discretion exists even when a petition is not the subject of an objection: rule 17. The chancellor may consider that the petition raises issues of law or fact, which need to be examined publicly notwithstanding that the petition is unopposed. Secondly, where formal written particulars of objection have been provided in Form 4 (rule 16(4)(iii)) and an opportunity has been given to the petitioners to submit a written answer to the objection (rule 18) the registrar should submit the pleadings to the chancellor for directions. At this stage rule 26(1) provides that:

> 'If the chancellor considers it expedient to do so and is satisfied that all parties to the proceedings have agreed in writing, then the chancellor may order that the proceedings shall be determined upon consideration of written representations instead of by a hearing in court …'

This is subject to the proviso that a hearing in open court is not required by law: rule 26(1). The reason why the chancellor should consider whether it is a suitable case to be determined on written representations before asking the parties whether they agree is that the chancellor will have no opportunity to obtain any additional information, save that which is presented on paper, and the parties could be prejudiced because they will be agreeing to forgo their right to a hearing where questions could be asked of them. The written representation procedure was introduced by the Faculty

Jurisdiction Rules 1992 (SI 1992/2882) to provide an alternative procedure in a suitable case where the issues are clear-cut. We believe that the procedure has been found to be useful. However, if after making an order under rule 26(1) of the 2000 Rules the chancellor concludes that a hearing is desirable after all, then the order may be revoked and an oral hearing ordered: rule 26(5).

35. Thirdly, an additional form of procedure for objectors was introduced by the Faculty Jurisdiction Rules 2000 to deal with the situation where persons wish to have their letters of objection taken into account but do not wish to become parties to the proceedings with the prospect of having to give evidence in the consistory court and becoming potentially liable to pay some of the costs. Such persons have to be informed that they will not be entitled to be heard in open court at any hearing which the chancellor may decide to hold: rule 16(4)(i) of the 2000 Rules. Here again the overriding discretion vested in the chancellor to hold a hearing is affirmed.

36. We infer that in this case the chancellor did order a determination on written representations after the objectors became parties, although no written direction from the chancellor to the registrar was among the papers forwarded to this court. On 9 December 2004 letters were sent by the registrar's assistant both to the churchwardens and to QS4 requiring them to 'submit to the court and serve upon the party opponent within 21 days a written statement of any representations you may wish to make in support of the petition'. (This, however, was only in partial compliance with rule 26(2)(a) as no mention is made of evidence to be relied upon by the petitioners.)

37. On 15 December 2004 QS4 wrote to the registrar with a response to the particulars of objection; this was countersigned by one of the churchwardens and copied to Ms Machin. In this letter they set out how QS4 intended to comply with the precautionary approach recommended by the Stewart Report and stated that the beam of greatest intensity would not fall on the school grounds. Ms Machin responded on 5 January 2005 stating:

> 'QS4 make reference to para 6.37 of the Stewart Report. The phrase "The balance of evidence to date suggests" does not give us surety in our minds that the health of our children may not be being put at risk by placing the mast at Bentley Emmanuel Church. This is reinforced by the penultimate sentence in that paragraph which states that "continued research is needed". If the Stewart Report felt it was safe to install these items of equipment it would not be recommending further research. While further research is undertaken to remove any queries of risk to our children's health and future, the location of these masts near to schools should not be allowed to occur, whatever the intensity of output. We therefore ask the diocese to withhold permission for the mast to be installed at Emmanuel Church, Bentley until we can be given positive reassurance that our children's health will not be affected rather than the balance of evidence suggesting that our children's health may not be affected.'

There is no suggestion in the documents before us that Mrs Hakesley herself was ever asked whether she wished to 'leave the chancellor to take the letter of objection into account in reaching a decision without [her] becoming a party in the proceedings' (see rule 16(3)(a) of the 2000 Rules), although the chancellor directed that her letter was 'acceptable' despite the fact that it was not written within the prescribed timescale (registrar's letter to Ms Machin dated 8 November 2004). We regard it as doubtful whether that letter should have been taken into consideration by the chancellor at all.

The judgment

38. In his judgment the chancellor found that QS4 had established a commercial case for placing an aerial on the church and that the parish had made out a case of need, although he said it 'has not been properly articulated' (which we would attribute, certainly in part, to the deficiency in the procedural steps followed in this case). These findings are of importance when considering the matters which influenced his decision.

39. The chancellor proceeded to identify three 'potential objections'. He decided in favour of the petitioners on the first and second but against them on the third. The first was an aesthetic and

architectural issue upon which he accepted the recommendation of the diocesan advisory committee, and which we have already found complied with the best practice commitment given to the Archbishops' Council: para 8 above. The second potential objection was the issue of 'objective health and safety risks'. Here again the chancellor found in favour of the petitioners. He recorded that the objectors were arguing that there is 'no conclusive evidence that mobile phone masts are not a potential health risk' and quoted the request contained in Ms Machin's letter of 5 January 2005 for 'positive reassurance'. Having pointed out that QS4 installations use the precautionary approach, that the beam of greatest radio frequency intensity would not fall on the school grounds and that 'concerns can be met by an insistence on quarterly measurements of emissions' he concluded that 'all else being equal' he would have 'felt obliged to grant a faculty'. We observe that his finding is consistent with QS4 having complied with the best practice commitment given to the Archbishops' Council in relation to the precautionary approach: para 8 above.

40. The third potential objection related:

'to a more subjective perception of hazard and its relation to the duty of the parish church (as opposed to QS4) to give primacy under the Faculty Jurisdiction Measure to mission (coupled with worship). This is a factor of great weight also for this consistory court.'

It was on the basis of this factor that he decided to refuse a faculty, having concluded:

'that for a parish, in the face of strong local opposition, to permit the installation of an aerial in close proximity to a school raised pastoral issues which go far beyond the commercial consideration of this case. I have already commended the parties opponent for their moderate and reasoned arguments. This cannot conceal, however, the depth of feeling locally against this proposal. As one lady put it, "Why not do us a favour and demolish the church, as very few people make use of it." To provoke this sort of response can only undermine the prime objective of the mission and worship of a church which, I fully understand, is already facing huge and demoralising problems.'

41. Before proceeding to consider the substantive grounds of appeal we think it necessary to comment in general on this third issue on which the chancellor based his decision. It was in fact a matter that had never been raised by Ms Machin and which, therefore, had never been addressed by any party. The chancellor had made findings in favour of the petitioners but then decided against them on this new issue. The petitioners might well have wished to challenge the statement of Mrs Hakesley that 'few people use [the church]'. In our view, if the chancellor intended to consider such a new argument based upon matters not addressed by the parties, it was incumbent upon him at the very least to warn the parties and to ask if they wished to make further representations. Indeed, in the interests of natural justice in this case the better procedure would have been a hearing in open court: see rule 26(5) of the 2000 Rules.

Grounds of appeal

42. In his outline submissions Mr George refined QS4's grounds of appeal into three propositions. His first criticism was that, in referring to 'the duty of the parish church to give primacy under the Faculty Jurisdiction Measure to mission (coupled with worship)', the chancellor misdirected himself in law. This criticism is well founded. Although the chancellor referred to the 'Faculty Jurisdiction Measure', we read this as a reference to section 1 of the Care of Churches and Ecclesiastical Jurisdiction Measure 1991, which provides:

'Any person or body carrying out functions of care and conservation under this Measure or under any other enactment or rule of law relating to churches shall have due regard to the role of a church as a local centre of worship and mission.'

This section does not impose a legal 'duty' upon a church. Further, it is a misconception to treat the section as applying to the jurisdiction of the chancellor in the consistory court (as Judge Grenfell Ch suggested in *In re St Margaret's, Hawes* [2003] 1 WLR 2568, para 4). The section applies to those discharging a function of 'care and conservation', such as diocesan advisory committees and the

Council for the Care of Churches, as this court made clear in *In re St Luke the Evangelist, Maidstone* [1995] Fam 1, 7. So far as chancellors are concerned, this court said in that case, at p 7:

> 'in the absence of words expressly limiting the wide jurisdiction long enjoyed by chancellors section 1 cannot be said to apply to chancellors since they are not persons carrying out functions of care and conservation. Rather, in carrying out their functions under the faculty jurisdiction, the chancellors are to "hear and determine … a cause of faculty": see section 6 of the Ecclesiastical Jurisdiction Measure.'

This means looking at all aspects of a 'cause' and exercising the court's discretion in a fair way.

43. It is, of course true that the primary purpose of a church is for the worship of Almighty God, and that the Church as a whole, and thence the local church, has a missionary role but this does not arise from a legal duty imposed by any Measure. The wording used by Judge Shand Ch gives the impression that he was testing a 'subjective perception of hazard' against a legal duty and this was unfortunate and incorrect. A chancellor is required to consider the arguments for and against a proposal assessing the weight of the case for the petitioners and the objectors. In well known terms this necessitates a 'balance of opposing considerations which are involved in the exercise of a judicial discretion': see Lord Penzance in *Nickalls v Briscoe* [1892] P 269, 283. Because he apparently started from the wrong premise we have concluded that this led the chancellor to attach disproportionate weight to the 'subjective perception of hazard' on the part of the objectors and this resulted in an erroneous evaluation of the evidence, as we shall point out shortly.

44. Mr George's second criticism is that the chancellor took into account a factor, namely the scientifically unproven concerns of local residents about health risks, which he should have treated as irrelevant. He argued that the description of the objections as 'reasoned and moderately presented' did not alter the fact that the chancellor had already found that there was no 'objectively established risk'. This then left the question of 'public concern', and Mr George took us by way of illustration to a number of cases in planning law where the courts have considered the question of whether unjustified public concern can be a material planning consideration.

45. Because of conflicting views expressed in the Court of Appeal by differently constituted courts (see *Gateshead Metropolitan Borough Council v Secretary of State for the Environment* [1994] 1 PLR 85 as contrasted with *Newport Borough Council v Secretary of State for Wales* [1998] Env LR 178 and *West Midlands Probation Committee v Secretary of State for the Environment* (1997) 76 P & CR 589 where the conflict of these authorities was recognised but not resolved), Mr George had some difficulty in extracting any definitive principle from the various decisions cited to us. However, he later cited *Smith v First Secretary of State* [2005] EWCA Civ 859 where the Court of Appeal, on the subject of 'material consideration', drew from the *West Midlands Probation Committee* case 76 P & CR 589, per Buxton LJ at para 9, the conclusion that:

> 'fear and concern must be real, by which I would assume to be required that the fear and concern must have some reasonable basis, though falling short of requiring the feared outcome to be proved as inevitable or highly likely.'

Mr George relied upon this passage in support of his argument that the objectors' concern in the present case was not a material consideration or, alternatively, it was given undue weight by the chancellor.

46. Whilst we note this latest dictum on fear and concern as a 'material consideration', we do not consider that it would be appropriate to incorporate a concept of 'material consideration' into the deliberations of the consistory court, since that terminology has a special function in planning law and the two jurisdictions should not become confused. The wide-ranging role of the consistory court, which we have referred to above, enables a chancellor to take account of concerns expressed by objectors. Provided they have some relevance to the issues before the court and are not merely fanciful, it is for the chancellor to make an assessment of their weight in each case.

47. Mr George properly drew our attention to the Government's policy on telecommunications as contained in PPG8. It was the Government which instigated the production of the Stewart Report

into the health effects from the use of mobile phones, base stations and transmitters. Consequently The Government's Planning Policy Guidance Note 8. (Revised) 'Telecommunications' August 2001, encapsulating the Government's approach to telecommunications and health, is relevant when the subject of possible health implications is raised in the consistory court in relation to a petition for a faculty involving telecommunication apparatus. the Appendix of Supporting Guidance in PPG8, para 1, reminds us that:

> 'Modern telecommunications are an essential and beneficial element in the life of the local community and in the national economy. Much of the telephone network is, of course, long established. However, the growth in the UK mobile communications sector over the past 15 years has been remarkable. New communications technology has spread rapidly to meet the growing demand for better communications at work and at home, in business, in public services and in support of electronic commerce.'

The appendix goes on, at para 5, to explain that the Government's policy is: 'to facilitate the growth of new and existing telecommunications systems whilst keeping the environmental impact to a minimum. The Government also has responsibility for protecting public health.' In relation to health and public concern about mobile phone base stations the Planning Policy Guidance Note 8 explains, at para 98, that:

> 'In the Government's view, if a proposed mobile phone base station meets the ICNIRP guidelines for public exposure it should not be necessary for a local planning authority, in processing an application for planning permission or prior approval, to consider further the health aspects and concerns about them.'

48. Judge Shand Ch did not refer to PPG8 nor to *In re St Margaret's, Hawes* [2003] 1 WLR 2568 where Judge Grenfell Ch heard expert evidence in relation to risk to health from radio waves from the three cross-polar antennae to be installed behind louvres in the church tower. Importantly, the two experts representing the petitioners and the objectors agreed that 'there is no risk to health from thermal effects of radiowaves transmitted from a telecommunications antenna'. Whereas one expert adopted the Government guidelines, the other argued that there should be lower levels 'unless and until it can be shown that there is no risk of non-thermal effects from radiowaves'. As Judge Grenfell Ch noted, at para 52, this meant that 'if Dr Hyland's theories are right, then nothing short of a complete ban on the use of mobile telephones would suffice'.

49. The objectors in this case are effectively asking for a ban on any installation at Bentley Emmanuel Church until it can be shown that there is no prospect of any risk from radiowaves at all. Whilst the concern of parents to protect their children is natural, we cannot overlook the fact that it is not possible to eradicate every element of risk before introducing some new feature into modern life. Technological advances have resulted, for example, in high performance cars, aeroplanes and sophisticated forms of medical or surgical treatments, which all carry an element of risk, but their advantages are generally regarded as outweighing any risk of injury or death which can come from their use. Here, as Judge Shand Ch recorded in his judgment, QS4 complied with the Stewart Report's recommendation. The evidence before him in Mrs Noble's letter, dated 9 November 2004, was that 'the beams of greatest intensity do not fall on the school grounds and that radio frequency levels are all well below the ICNIRP standard'.

50. We agree with Judge Grenfell Ch in *In re St Margaret's, Hawes* [2003] 1 WLR 2568, para 84 that:

> 'in the absence of compelling evidence of a real risk to human health as a result of transmitting radiowaves up to the levels set by the United Kingdom Government in their adoption of the ICNIRP guidelines, it would be wrong to adopt lower guidelines for a base station just because it happens to come under the jurisdiction of the consistory court in addition to planning requirements.'

This applies with equal force to the suggestion that a faculty should be refused because of concern (however genuine) about the possibility of a health risk, which cannot be substantiated in any way by evidence. Judge Shand Ch referred to the use of mobile phones by children, which is a different point from the location of aerials, as he made clear. This topic was not of assistance on the issue before him. The question which he should have considered was whether in view of his findings in favour of the petitioners there was any reasonable ground demonstrated by evidence for refusing to let them have a faculty. We can find none and we consider that he misdirected himself in attaching so much weight to 'depth of feeling locally'.

51. Although the chancellor mentioned the point, drawn to his attention by QS4, that 'concerns can be met by an insistence on quarterly measurements of emissions', he apparently did not attach weight to this in his judgment. He did not mention any of the provisions to this effect in the model licence agreed with the Archbishops' Council and to be used by QS4 if a faculty is granted. We consider that clause 6 of the licence is sufficiently important to justify quoting it in full:

> 'Direct monitoring of emissions
>
> '6.1.2. The grantee shall: (a) without prejudice to clause 6.1.1 comply with and oblige its authorised licensees to comply with all legal obligations and recognised industry standards regarding the notification and measurement of electromagnetic emission levels in the vicinity of telecommunications apparatus; (b) (if requested by the incumbent and council but not more than once in any period of three months) carry out direct radio frequency emission measurements in the vicinity of the equipment and the building and report to the incumbent and the council the results of such measurements; and (c) co-operate with any body appointed by or on behalf of the incumbent and the council to monitor such emissions, and comment on the results of any such monitoring to the incumbent and the council.
>
> '6.2 The grantee shall immediately notify the incumbent and the council if it becomes aware that radio frequency emissions from the equipment are (or for any period during the term of this licence have been): 6.2.1 in excess of the manufacturer's recommended level; or 6.2.2 at a level that would cause the grantee to be in breach of its obligations in clause 5.1.6.'

52. Clause 5.1.6 of the licence calls for compliance both with current safety standards and, for the future, with any more stringent requirements, which may be imposed in the light of further research. These obligations are of importance. The arrangements for direct monitoring in clause 6.1.2 enable the parochial church council to maintain an independent check on the level of radio emissions. Mr George confirmed, on instructions from QS4, that once the relevant information had been passed to the parochial church council it would be in the public domain and might be shared with other interested parties.

53. Although they fall short of the virtual guarantee of safety sought by Mrs Ince and Ms Machin, these safeguards offer reassurance that a close check will be kept on the use of the QS4 aerials on the church to ensure that they comply with standards set from time to time by the bodies which are expert in these matters.

54. We now turn to the third ground of appeal, which was that the chancellor attached undue weight to the level of local opposition, the existence of which in his view was likely to undermine the mission and worship of the church. We have already stated earlier in this judgment that in this respect we consider that the chancellor made an erroneous evaluation of the evidence. He did not explain how he weighed the case for the petitioners against that of the objectors at the last stage in his judgment. For the petitioners he had evidence that: there would be a beneficial and steady income stream, of at least £6,250 per annum for a period of 20 years, which would be derived from the licence. For a church facing financial problems, and struggling to pay off its arrears of diocesan quota, such an additional source of income would inevitably be welcome. Weight should have been attached to the fact that improved financial health in relation to the substantial costs of maintaining the church would enable its role of worship and mission to be enhanced. There would be benefit to the local community in (a) providing the means of improving the quality of transmission, and (b) in positioning the aerials on the church tower rather than on much lower buildings or lamp posts (as was pointed out by the Bishop of Wolverhampton in his letter of 29 July 2004 to Ms Machin).

There was substantial support for the proposal as demonstrated by the supportive resolution of the 18-strong parochial church council and the absence of opposition from the parishioners, some 90 in number, who were registered on the electoral roll. The chancellor had before him an e-mail dated 16 December 2004 from the Archdeacon of Lichfield, who was also acting as Archdeacon of Walsall, in which he said that 'many of the congregation live very close to the church and expressed no concerns themselves for the siting of this equipment'. Regrettably this e-mail was not disclosed to the parties as it should have been in accordance with the principles of natural justice: see *Owners of the Ship Bow Spring v Owners of the Ship Manzanillo II (Practice Note)* [2005] 1 WLR 144, paras 57–58 where the Court of Appeal stressed 'the need for the court to know, before it reaches a conclusion, what the parties have to say about the issues and the evidence which goes to them'. However, we directed disclosure of this e-mail and invited the parties to comment on it if they wished to do so, and we believe that this cured any injustice that might otherwise have been done. In response to the chancellor's request for information regarding the pastoral implications of the proposal and whether the parish had taken full account of these, the archdeacon in the same e-mail gave a supportive answer saying:

> 'My inquiries seem to reveal that the parish honestly believes that it is not only finding a source of income, but also providing a service to the community by taking the mast away from most of the population! In saying that, because the church is in a relatively isolated position, it is further away from people's homes, albeit somewhat nearer to the school than the radio masts formerly were, on top of the block of flats. The frustrating part for the parish is to witness members of the school coming in and using the facilities and yet also feeling free to use their own mobile phones on the church premises.'

55. The grounds of objection, even though expressed in moderate terms, did not receive the close analysis which the circumstances demanded once the chancellor had concluded that the objectors' case was not made out on scientific grounds. It became clear from Ms Machin's submissions to us that the flawed consultation process had engendered a lack of trust in the proposals and provoked much of the opposition to them. The opposition was thus directed as much, if not more so, to QS4 and T Mobile than to the church. The chancellor would have heard this if he had asked for further submissions from the parties.

56. As to the letter from Mrs Hakesley (even if procedurally he could properly take it into account) he did not assess it in context. She expressed concern that the introduction of the aerials would affect the value of her property and then went on to make the comment quoted by the chancellor about demolition of the church 'as very few people make use of it'. Viewed objectively, Mrs Hakesley's reaction, borne of personal grief arising from the recent loss of relatives, did not carry matters further. Neither is there evidence that Mrs Hakesley's isolated letter was representative of local feeling generally.

57. We are satisfied that when weighing the opposing arguments the balance comes down firmly in favour of QS4.

Conclusion

58. For the reasons we have already given we have concluded that on a proper evaluation of the evidence the chancellor should have exercised his discretion in favour of the petitioners and granted a faculty. Consequently, as his decision was based on an erroneous evaluation of the facts taken as a whole this court is justified in setting it aside in accordance with the well known principles in *In re St Edburga's, Abberton* [1962] P 10.

59. Accordingly, the appeal is allowed and we direct that a faculty be issued out of the Consistory Court of the Diocese of Lichfield, authorising the minister (if in post) and the parochial church council to enter into the licence agreement, as amended in one respect, and permitting QS4 thereafter to proceed with the installation and use of the apparatus. The proposed terms of the licence are appropriate to the requirements of the parish, save that in clause 3.1.3(a), which concerns QS4 rights of access to the church, Ascension Day should be added to the list of holy days excluded from

the usual ambit of those rights. The licence must be amended accordingly. Subject to this amendment of the licence the faculty will be subject to the following conditions: (i) all parties to the licence and any assignee or sub-licensee thereof shall observe and perform its requirements as if they were conditions of the faculty; (ii) the parochial church council shall exercise their right under clause 6.1.2(b) of the licence to receive reports at three-monthly intervals of direct radio frequency measurements, and shall communicate the contents of such reports to the parties opponent and any other person in the parish requesting them.

60. Finally, we express our appreciation to Ms Machin for the clear and helpful way she presented the case for the objectors, who could not have been better represented, and to Mr George for his helpful presentation for QS4, including his assistance on matters of law and procedure.

61. QS4 will pay the court costs including correspondence fees for the registrar and the expenses incurred by the court.

Appeal allowed. Faculty granted.

Re Welford Road Cemetery, Leicester[3]

ARCHES COURT OF CANTERBURY
CAMERON QC, DEAN; TURNER QC AND HILL CHS
13 OCTOBER 2006

Introduction

1. This is an appeal from the decision of Chancellor Behrens given on 23 January 2006 in the Consistory Court of the diocese of Leicester. By his judgment of that date the Chancellor

  (i) refused to grant a confirmatory faculty to Leicester City Council ('the Council') in respect of work already carried out to memorials in Welford Road Cemetery, Leicester;

  (ii) ordered the Council 'to reinstate and repair to a safe condition all memorials which had been laid flat (save where the owner wished to carry out such repairs himself, or had already done so)';

  (iii) on condition that the Council complied with the above order, granted a faculty for the future testing and making safe of memorials in the cemetery and the giving of notice to owners or other persons interested in the particular memorial, when known. The petition by the Rural Dean and the Bereavement Services Manager on behalf of the Council was dated 25 March 2004 and sought a faculty 'To carry out memorial safety assessments to all memorials in Welford Road Cemetery. Any memorial found to be a potential hazard will be temporarily made safe by laying the memorial on the grave space with the inscription facing up.' This wording did not include any reference to the fact that work had already been done without a faculty, but this was drawn to the Chancellor's attention in a covering letter.

2. This was a contested petition for a faculty and the Chancellor heard evidence and legal submissions over a period of three days in December 2005. The Council and the parties opponent ('the opponents'), a number of relatives of Polish persons commemorated by memorials affected by the work done by the Council, were represented by counsel at the hearing.

---

[3] [2007] 2 WLR 506, [2007] 1 All ER 426.

3. At the conclusion of the hearing the Chancellor heard argument about the costs of the proceedings. Mr Stanley Best, on behalf of the opponents, sought an order for costs against the Council on an indemnity basis. Mr Andrew Sharland, on behalf of the Council, accepted that the Court costs should be paid by the Council, as petitioner, but contended that there should be no order for costs between the parties. The Chancellor rejected the opponents' application, ordered the Council to pay the Court costs, and left the parties to bear their own costs by making no order as to costs between them.

4. On 16 February 2006 the Chancellor granted the Council leave to appeal against his judgment, and granted the opponents leave to cross-appeal on the issue of costs on condition that if the Council abandoned its appeal the opponents could only proceed with the cross-appeal with the permission of this Court. In the event, the Council has proceeded with the appeal. In this Court the opponents resisted that part of the appeal relating to the Chancellor's order for reinstatement and repair of memorials commemorating their relatives, and also pursued their cross-appeal against the Chancellor's refusal to make an order for costs in their favour.

5. Both counsel who appeared before the Chancellor also represented the parties in this Court, and they have assisted us greatly by presenting their arguments succinctly and expeditiously.

Welford Road Cemetery

6. This cemetery was opened in 1849 and is listed Grade 2 in English Heritage's register of parks and gardens of historic importance. It is extremely extensive, covering a total of 30 acres. Part of the cemetery is consecrated and there are 10,000 memorials in this area. About 1,000 of those memorials have been laid flat after being tested for stability by, or on behalf of, the Council in the period between 2002 and 2004. Of these some 119 relate to members of families within the Polish community in Leicester.

7. Although the Chancellor was under the impression that Edwards, solicitors, acted 'for numerous members of the Polish community of Leicester whose forbears lie in the consecrated part of the cemetery' (paragraph 2 of judgment) Mr Best clarified the position for us. A letter, dated 8 July 2004, had been sent to the Registrar by Edwards, solicitors, saying 'We represent over 100 families whose relatives' graves have been laid down at the above cemetery without prior notice to them'. However, Mr Best explained that Edwards had ultimately received formal instructions only from those who had provided written statements of evidence, some 35 in all. It is they who are the opponents in these faculty proceedings, and not the firm of solicitors as might appear from the Chancellor's judgment.

Need for a faculty

8. Although the parties to the appeal accepted that the jurisdiction of the consistory court applies in this case, we consider it appropriate to say something generally on the subject of the faculty jurisdiction in relation to consecrated parts of local authority cemeteries.

9. It is necessary to bear in mind that it was in the mid-nineteenth century that the Church of England ceased to be the principal provider of land for burials. Up until then burials took place in consecrated ground, usually in a churchyard adjacent to the church. Parliamentary intervention enabled burial grounds to be provided and maintained by cemetery companies and burial boards. Legislation, such as the Cemeteries Clauses Act 1847 and various Burial Acts, established the framework and contained the powers necessary to enable new land to be set out for burials. From the beginning it was recognised that it should be possible for such land to accommodate the burial of those who wished to be buried in consecrated ground, as well as those who had no such desire, possibly because they were adherents of religious denominations other than the Church of England or had no particular religious affiliation. Consecration was no longer automatic, but by section 23 of the Cemeteries Clauses Act 1847 a cemetery company was empowered to apply to the bishop of the diocese in which the cemetery was situated to 'consecrate any portion of the cemetery set apart for the burial of the dead according to the rites of the Established Church'.

10. The effect of the consecration of land by a bishop has always been to give the land a sacred character. Whether the land consists of a churchyard belonging to the Church of England, or a part of a cemetery or a burial ground maintained by a local authority, the legal effect of consecration is to subject it to the faculty jurisdiction See *Re St John's Chelsea* [1962] 2 All ER 850; [1962] 1 WLR 706 at 708. As this Court explained in *Re Blagdon Cemetery* [2002] 4 All ER 482 at para 11:

> 'Land becomes consecrated when the bishop of a diocese signs a document called a sentence by which he separates and sets apart an area of land and dedicates the land to the service of Almighty God. The effect of this sentence where the land is to be used for the interment of the remains of the dead, whether the land consists of churchyard around a church or an identified area of land in a cemetery, is to set apart the land as being held for sacred uses and to bring it within the jurisdiction of the Consistory Court'.

11. In view of the age of Welford Road Cemetery the consecration of part of it will undoubtedly have taken place under earlier legislation now replaced by the Local Authorities Cemeteries Order 1977 ('the 1977 Order').[4] The power to apply to the bishop of the diocese for consecration of part of a cemetery provided and maintained by a burial authority, which was conferred by the earlier legislation, is preserved in article 5 of the 1977 Order. Article 5 (2) requires a burial authority to satisfy itself that 'a sufficient part of the cemetery remains unconsecrated.' This ensures that there is a proper balance: an appropriate degree of choice is offered to members of the public, catering for those who do, as well as those who do not, have religious beliefs influencing their choice of where they wish to be buried.

12. The 1977 Order rightly confers extensive powers on a burial authority to manage and improve the cemetery (articles 3 & 4) as well as to grant burial rights and rights to erect memorials (article 10). The burial authority has a discretionary power to 'put and keep in order any grave or vault, or any tombstone or other memorial in a cemetery' (article 16 (1) (a)) and to remove or reposition any memorial (article 16 (2)). These powers are undoubtedly necessary. However, it is because consecrated land has special significance as a place for Christian burial that the faculty jurisdiction comes into play when works are proposed which may interfere with respectful treatment of the dead interred within consecrated land. This applies in the case of proposed exhumation[5] and in respect of proposed disturbance of memorials. The rationale was well summarised in *Re West Norwood Cemetery* [1994] Fam 210, [1995] 1 All ER 387 where the late Chancellor Gray said (at p 398)

> 'One of the ways in which respect is shown to the dead by the bereaved is by ensuring their decent and undisturbed interment, and, particularly in those cases where the bereaved or a wider public have been moved to do so, to protect the monuments which have been erected to recall to future generations the achievements of those interred during their earthly life, and a legitimate way of proclaiming and perpetuating those achievements to future generations.'

13. Whenever a burial authority wishes to use any of the powers in article 16 (2) to interfere with a memorial, either by removing it or re-positioning it, or part of it, the power has to be exercised in accordance with a prescribed procedure of notification and publicity set out in Schedule 3 to the Order. In respect of consecrated land this includes notification of a rural dean or other person 'representative of the particular denomination or religious body.' The procedure is clearly designed to ensure that not only individuals but also those concerned with the protection of consecrated land are alerted to any proposed interference with memorials in that area. It is noticeable that memorials in a dangerous condition are not mentioned in article 16 but in article 3.

---

[4] SI 1977 No. 204. The Cemeteries Clauses Act 1847 ceased to apply to cemeteries provided by local authorities on 10 March 1977, the date the 1977 Order came into force. See Sch 24 para 14(a) to the Local Government Act 1972.

[5] Specific provision is made in s 25 Burial Act 1857.

14. Article 3 excludes from the general power of management 'any action in relation to any vault, or any tombstone or other memorial other than action which is necessary to remove a danger which arises by reason of the condition of the vault, or the tombstone or other memorial itself' (emphasis added). The article contains no procedural guidance as in article 16 (2). The word 'danger' is not defined and thus leaves open what can reasonably be treated as 'danger' in a particular case.

15. Article 3 was formulated many years ago, long before burial authorities were faced with the present day task of dealing with substantial numbers of potentially dangerous memorials. The Institute of Cemetery & Crematorium Management (ICCM) points out in the 'Management of Memorials' that

> 'It is evident from the research that many of the less serious accidents have been caused by memorials that have been installed relatively recently within the last 30 years' (para. 2.3.2. vol.1 court file p.187).

16. Taking 'action which is necessary to remove a danger' must inevitably result in some interference with a memorial, which has been lawfully placed in the cemetery under the terms of a grant. The consistory court is able to offer protection to the burial authority by granting a faculty in advance of action being taken under article 3. The owners' interests will then have been taken into account, and there will not subsequently be grounds for the owners to object to the authorised action being taken.

17. The Council rightly applied for a faculty as soon as the requirement was drawn to the Council's attention. It is by no means the only burial authority which has been unaware of the fact that consecration of part of a cemetery brings that part within the jurisdiction of the consistory court of the diocese in which the cemetery is situated. The Chancellor found it necessary to make certain criticisms of the way in which the presentation of the petition was handled on behalf of the Council, but this Court does not consider that this matter has any bearing on the merits of the petition for the purpose of this appeal.

Safety of memorials generally

18. The Chancellor recorded in paragraph 22 of his judgment that late in 2001 the Council became aware of an increasing number of safety issues relating to memorials nationally. The evidence before the Chancellor revealed that this subject was highlighted by a press release issued by the Health and Safety Executive ('the HSE') on 17 October 2001, which referred to serious injury and death caused to children by gravestones toppling on them.

19. Chancellor Behrens, in paragraphs 6 and 7 of his judgment, summarised the legal responsibilities placed on burial authorities by the Health and Safety legislation. These cannot be treated lightly. This was made clear in the expert evidence of Elaine Sherlock, the Council's Health and Safety Adviser, who told the Chancellor that 'authorities are being served with improvement orders by the Health and Safety Executive' and that 'failure to remove dangers in the shape of unstable memorials could result in legal action, including prosecutions being taken against authorities corporately, and individually against responsible officers.'

20. From the documents which were before the Chancellor, including the report of the decision in *Re Keynsham Cemetery*,[6] it is noticeable that the HSE did not give any specific guidance to burial authorities after initiating its safety campaign in the autumn of 2001. In the Annex to a letter, dated 1 June 2004, from the chair of the Health and Safety Commission to every local authority Chief Executive and to HSE's Regional Directors, the HSE expressly said that it had not published any guidance. It went on to say 'It has issued information to HSE inspectors (and their [Local Authority] equivalents in their role as enforcers in respect of churchyards and private cemeteries

---

[6] [2003] 1 WLR 66 at para 4 at p 69. Keynsham Town Council said that it 'was disappointed that there was no nationally agreed procedure for inspecting memorials and that the Health and Safety Executive had not issued any guidance on this subject'.

[Local Authorities Circular 23/18)]). This is not guidance to [Local Authorities] as [Burial Authorities], although it has been misinterpreted as such.'

21. We have no doubt that burial authorities, including this Council, either experienced pressure, or perceived that they were under pressure, from the HSE to take immediate action over memorials found to be unstable. This is apparent, for example, in the Final Report of a Special Scrutiny Committee set up by Stockport Council in response to public concern about the laying flat of memorials in a number of that Council's cemeteries. In its conclusions the Special Scrutiny Committee recorded

> '4.6 Although the Committee has heard from the Principal Inspector that the HSE was very concerned about memorial safety and that events in late 2002 gave the HSE cause to revive earlier enquiries in relation to local authority memorial testing programmes, we have also heard from the Director of Community Services that his colleagues in other local authorities received different requests from the HSE and were given different deadlines. Evidence from other local authorities confirms this. We also know from what the principal Inspector told us that earlier enquiries from the HSE about memorial safety testing (those made in 1997) were not followed up. We are not, therefore, satisfied that the HSE has been consistent in its approach to this issue across different local authorities, or over time, nor are we satisfied that the time scale for accelerated testing imposed on Stockport Council was reasonable. 4.7 The Committee calls on the HSE to carry out a thorough investigation into the consistency of the advice it has given; its requirements of local authorities; and deadlines it has imposed upon local authorities throughout the country in relation to memorial safety testing in cemeteries.'

22. Stockport Council's report was published in December 2003, but it was not until 1 June 2004 that the chair of the Health and Safety Commission wrote the circular letter already referred to. Although it was not described as guidance, the Annex attached to that letter was in effect a form of guidance. Part of the HSE's introductory statement in the Annex said

> 'HSE recognises the social and emotional impact the laying down of headstones can have on the community. It urges all [Burial Authorities] to check they are following their industry guidance diligently so that the issue is handled with the utmost sensitivity.'

23. The industry guidance referred to by the HSE was that contained in 'The Management of Memorials' published in 2000 by the Institute of Burial and Cremation Administration, now the ICCM. It is from the ICCM that advice was sought by the Council in September 2003. Elaine Sherlock's evidence was that the system of risk assessment used by the Council's staff, after training by ICCM, was approved by the HSE Inspector overseeing the Council. By this system of risk assessment, advocated by ICCM, those memorials which were identified as creating high risk of possible death were to be carefully laid down, and those which were identified as medium risk, namely capable of causing disabling injury, were to be staked and securely tied and a warning sign was to be displayed on the memorial. The evidence given in the consistory court was that this system was followed by the Council in 2004.

24. It is important to look at the Council's actions in relation to the stability of memorials in Welford Road Cemetery in the context of the HSE's campaign in 2001 and the lack of any general guidance from the HSE at that time, whether presented as such or in the form of answers to questions as eventually published in 2004. It would be wrong to judge the Council on the basis of hindsight and the views expressed by the HSE in 2004. The relevant period of action for the Council was from 2002 until the spring of 2004 and the Chancellor found that the Council had 'acted throughout in good faith' (paragraph 34 of judgment). This applied to their engagement of a firm reputedly expert in safety testing of memorials in the period 2002–2003 and their subsequent safety work in 2004 carried out by the Council's own trained employees. We consider the Chancellor's conclusion to have been amply justified.

25. Although some of the opponents said that their relatives' memorials had been damaged by the Council in the course of laying them flat, it was not contended that the Council acted inappropriately

in testing the large number of memorials in the consecrated part of the cemetery and then laying flat a proportion of them. In fact, after his inspection of the cemetery, the Chancellor concluded that whilst 'most of the memorials belonging to the Polish community were about 3 feet high' they were still dangerous and a potential source of injury to a child or any other person leaning on the memorial to get up from the ground (paragraph 1 of judgment).

26. Chancellor Behrens was aware of the dilemma facing the Council in view of the risk of accident in their cemetery and the campaign by HSE. He quoted the answer given by the Under Secretary of State for Work and Pensions to a Parliamentary question referring to the lack of good guidance for burial authorities on the subject of safety testing of memorials. We repeat the Parliamentary answer quoted in paragraph 67 of the judgment 'Any over reaction has the potential to cause distress, but it is often far from easy for burial authorities to deal with the issue. On the one hand, they must consider the feelings of the bereaved who want the graves of their loved ones treated with dignity and respect. On the other hand, if someone is injured or even killed, there is an outcry. It is necessary to strike a sensible balance.'

27. We agree with this statement by Mrs Anne McGuire, but it was not made until 29 June 2005, long after the events in Welford Road Cemetery which gave rise to opposition in the consistory court in Leicester, and it was not guidance given at the material time to the Council and other burial authorities. Accordingly, it was of no assistance to the Chancellor in assessing the reasonableness of the Council's actions in respect of unstable memorials in the period 2002 to 2004.

28. In the light of the evidence of careful testing which took place in accordance with the industry guidelines, as approved by the HSE Inspector, we are unable to find the Council at fault in laying down memorials. In considering the totality of the memorials which had been laid down (some 1,000 out of 10,000) in the consecrated part of the cemetery, the Chancellor concluded that the laying flat had been 'an over-reaction to health and safety concerns and should only be allowed if there is no sensible alternative.' If the Council had acted precipitately or without advice and support from the HSE, then this conclusion might have been justified. However, in the absence of any evidence of any alternative proposal in respect of the majority of the memorials found to be unstable, because no one claiming any interest in those memorials had come forward with a proposal for repair, we can find no basis for this conclusion and regard it as erroneous.

Responsibility for memorials

29. Appendix 1 to the ICCM Code of Practice for the Management of Memorials refers to the responsibility for memorials and points out that 'the responsibility for ongoing maintenance of individual memorials rests with the grave owner, (owner of the Exclusive Right of Burial) or other person granted the right to place and maintain a memorial on a grave space. Many burial authorities, however, experience great difficulty in tracing owners, either due to their relocation or death.' These remarks are correct as to the law and, in this Court's experience, also factually correct in respect of the difficulty of tracing 'owners' in respect of memorials which have been in position for some time.

30. The responsibility of owners of memorials is not discussed in detail in the Chancellor's judgment, although it is mentioned in paragraph 23 where he records Mr Watson's evidence that 'he had received advice that repairs to memorials is the responsibility of the memorials' owners rather then the Council'. It is however, an important factor when considering the relationship between the Council and the owners of memorials identified as being unsafe.

31. In general terms the legal responsibility for a memorial is the same whether the memorial is placed in a churchyard or a local authority cemetery, and whether that churchyard or cemetery is open or closed for burials. Members of the public do not always understand who is responsible. The legal principle is derived from a different source for churchyards as compared with cemeteries. In *Re Keynsham Cemetery* at page 71 Briden Ch explained the position at common law which applies to churchyards, namely that the memorial initially belongs to the person who sets it up and then to the heir at law of the person commemorated. For memorials in cemeteries the legal position is derived from the 1977 Order. Article 10 (1) (b) provides that a burial authority

'may grant on such terms and subject to such conditions as they think proper…

(b) to the owner of a right [of burial] (or to any person who satisfies them that he is a relative of a person buried in the grave or vault or is acting at the request of such a relative and that it is impractical for him or such relative to trace the owner of the [burial] right) the right to place and maintain or to put any additional inscription on, a tombstone or other memorial on the grave space, grave or vault in respect of which the [burial] right subsists.'

32. This Court endorses the statement made by Briden Ch in *Re Keynsham Cemetery* that 'the ownership of the monument is separate and distinct from the ownership of the underlying land' (at para. 17). The cases cited on this point by Gray Ch in *Re West Norwood Cemetery* (at 218 C–D) deal with the principles which apply to the fixing of items in houses. We do not regard them as having any relevance to the subject of ownership of memorials in cemeteries or churchyards. If Gray Ch. were right and the memorial became the property of the owner of the soil, then it could theoretically be altered or removed at the whim of that owner. This is neither the legal position at common law nor in respect of a cemetery. The fact that burial authorities need to point to express powers in the 1977 Order to enable them to interfere with memorials demonstrates that they remain the personal property of the grantee and his or her successors.

33. The right to keep a memorial on a grave in a cemetery lasts for the period specified in the grant and must not exceed 100 years (article 10 (2)). Mr Sharland told this Court that the Council makes grants for a period of 99 years. It follows that at the end of that period the legal right comes to an end and the memorial should be removed from the cemetery. A burial authority is given a discretionary power to move a memorial to another place in the cemetery or to remove it from the cemetery 'for preservation elsewhere or for destruction' at the end of the period of the grant (article 10 (5)). This power of removal in article 10 (5) applies to memorials placed under a grant made under 'any enactment' replaced by the 1977 Order, so it affects pre-1977 memorials authorised under earlier legislation where the period of the grant has since expired.

34. It is abundantly clear that the words 'the right to place and maintain' in article 10 (1) (b) mean that the grantee and his/her successor during the period of 99 years has responsibility for the maintenance of the memorial in a safe condition. This interpretation is reinforced by the fact that article 10 (7) provides a burial authority with the power 'to agree with any person, on such terms and subject to such conditions as they think proper, to maintain any…memorial for a period not exceeding 100 years from the date of the agreement.' In other words, the person with responsibility for maintaining a particular memorial could pass that responsibility to the Council, as burial authority, but only on terms set by the Council in an agreement, which would almost certainly involve paying the Council to take over the maintenance. None of the opponents said in their evidence that any such agreement with the Council existed in respect of their relatives' memorials. In fact all the written statements of evidence emphasised that if the writer had been informed that the memorial in question was unstable he or she would have had this rectified. So the witnesses accepted the liability for maintenance arising from the grants permitting them, or their predecessors, to erect memorials to their relatives.

35. The main weaknesses identified in memorials in the consecrated part of the cemetery, including those of the opponents, were described in evidence by Elaine Sherlock as 'inadequate dowelling of the headstone into the base', or instances where the cement holding the headstone onto the base had deteriorated. We were told that photographs demonstrating these matters were shown to the Chancellor and, of course, he was able to see examples on his visit to the cemetery. Mr Linsell, an expert witness from ICCM, confirmed in his evidence that these were the weaknesses which were the primary problem. He went on to comment 'The main reasons for these problems are due to poor workmanship from the memorial masons responsible for erecting the memorials.'

36. It is desirable for this Court to repeat what Briden Ch said in *Re Keynsham* on the subject of the liability of a stonemason for an unstable memorial, namely

'A mason is liable in tort for injury caused by a negligently constructed monument: *Brown v Cotterill* (1934) 51 TLR 21. Apart from this duty of care, he is likely depending on the terms of the agreement, to owe contractual obligations to the purchaser of the monument.' (at p. 71). We would only add that the contractual obligation applies for the statutory limitation period of six years in respect of the erection or re-erection of any monument (for example after removal to add an inscription). This Court does not know how many of the opponents are within this category.

Communications in relation to safety testing

37. In paragraph 55 of his judgment Chancellor Behrens recorded that the 'Polish community considered the Council's actions both outrageous and disrespectful.' Whilst this Court understands that the witnesses were undoubtedly distressed to find their relatives' memorials laid flat or tied to a stake, that is not the primary or sole consideration. The subject of safety raises a number of issues about the respective responsibilities of (a) those maintaining the cemetery, (b) the owners of burial and memorial rights, and (c) the stonemasons installing memorials in the cemetery, as we have pointed out above.

38. The Council's safety programme between 2002 and 2003, when Welters were acting for the Council, and between 2003 and 2004 when the Council acted directly through its own employees, is described in paragraphs 22 to 24 and 36 to 38 of Chancellor Behrens' judgment. Although Welters were expected by the Council to notify owners as part of their contractual duties, the evidence given on behalf of the Council was that this had not been done, certainly not as effectively as the Council had anticipated. The thrust of the argument on behalf of the opponents has been directed to the Council's role in the second period 2003-2004. The Chancellor rightly did not make any finding against the Council in respect of the handling of the notification process in the first period 2002–2003. It would indeed have been wrong to do so, as Welters were engaged as a firm which offered specialist skills, and the Council was entitled to assume that the contract would be properly executed.

39. When he considered the evidence about communication of information in relation to the safety testing programme the Chancellor properly took account of the various steps which had been taken to publicise it on site and through the local media. In paragraph 51 he said

> 'The Council cannot be blamed for the fact that the Polish witnesses do not read the Leicester Mercury or listen to Leicester Radio. If the Council had applied for a faculty, this court would probably have directed the Council to place the advertisements which the Council did in fact place. If the witnesses are correct that the Council's telephone line was not answered when it should have been, that at least shows that the witnesses saw something which caused them to contact the Council.'

40. The chronology helpfully prepared by counsel reveals the extent of the publicity given to the work during both periods. In summary this consisted of

31 October 2002: Press release about safety inspection;

November 2002: Article in the Leicester Mercury stating that monuments found to be unstable would be propped up or laid down;

11 November 2002: Radio interview about safety work needed at the cemetery;

21 December 2002: Newspaper article about memorial safety: this supplied a telephone number to call if a reader had concerns;

8 February 2003: Notice in Leicester Mercury urging all owners to carry out repairs and saying that the Council in order to remove immediate danger may have to lay the memorial down;

5 March 2003: Press release and article in the Leicester Mercury about temporary closure of the cemetery following concerns about the safety of visitors;

Between June 2003 and June 2004 there was only limited access to the cemetery by prior arrangement. A large notice was placed on the main gate saying

NOTICE TO ALL CEMETERY VISITORS
THE MEMORIALS IN THIS CEMETERY ARE BEING ASSESSED FOR URGENT HEALTH AND SAFETY REASONS
THIS GATE WILL REMAIN LOCKED UNTIL FURTHER NOTICE
SORRY FOR ANY INCONVENIENCE
IF YOU REQUIRE ANY FURTHER INFORMATION PLEASE CONTACT
BURIAL AND CREMATION OFFICE
LEICESTER CITY COUNCIL
NEW WALK CENTRE TEL: 0116 252 7382

41. It is true that it was not until 26 February 2004 that a letter was written to Father Kordys, the parish priest for the Polish community, in relation to the temporary making safe of memorials, but if any of the parties opponent had visited the cemetery during the period June 2003 to February 2004 they would certainly have discovered that there was something unusual occurring there, because admission to the cemetery was closely regulated. The inference, as the Chancellor concluded (paragraph 39 above), was that some of them were aware of events, although they may have assumed that they would not be affected. The notice quoted above gave them an opportunity to find out whether their own memorials were to be tested. The Council cannot be blamed if no-one took advantage of this opportunity.

42. The Council gave widespread publicity to what they were doing in the cemetery. In view of the fact that, like many cemeteries and churchyards (as the Chancellor noted in paragraph 54), there were not up to date records of owners or their successors, we do not regard the Council as having acted 'outrageously' as alleged by the opponents. However, if a faculty had been applied for in advance of the work then appropriate directions could have been given about notification, and the Council would have had these as protection against any such charge.

The case of the opponents

43. In paragraph 12 of his skeleton argument in this Court Mr Best adopted what the Chancellor had said 'as to the law and facts and his reasons for finding as he does, and say that the judgment herein should be upheld.' He asked us to treat his written submissions to the Chancellor of 28 December 2005 as if they were incorporated with his skeleton argument in this Court and we have done so. Those earlier submissions dealt with the Stockport report and used it to support his criticism of the way in which the Council in this case had dealt with the problem of safety of memorials at Welford Road.

44. Implicit in Mr Best's argument was support for the Chancellor's emphasis on article 16(1)(a) of the 1977 Order (paragraphs 10 and 31 of judgment) empowering a burial authority to 'put and keep in order ... any tombstone or other memorial.' However, we consider that it is misplaced to regard this power as properly exercisable to deal with rectification of a safety deficiency in memorials where the grantee, or his or her successors, are identifiable and can be required to carry out the work of stabilisation as part of the obligation to maintain the memorial.

45. In his supplementary skeleton argument in this Court Mr Best argued that Chancellor Behrens was correct procedurally in making a restoration order, and was right to take into account changes post-*Keynsham* 'which he was entitled/obliged to take into account and it is submitted that he was in any event not bound to follow the judgement in *Re Keynsham Cemetery*'. However, he helpfully made it clear that he was not seeking to uphold that part of the Chancellor's order relating to other memorials because 'the concern of the Polish relatives was to seek relief for themselves' (paragraph 11).

Grounds of appeal

46. Bearing in mind the opponents' case we turn to consider the grounds on which the appellant Council challenges the Chancellor's judgment.

Restoration order

47. Several of the grounds of appeal relied upon by the Council relate to the restoration order made by the Chancellor. The validity of the order is challenged in terms of procedure and jurisdiction.

48. First, it is said that the Chancellor was wrong to state, as he did in paragraph 3 of his judgment, that the opponents sought a 'restoration order'. It is undisputed that no formal application for such an order had been made by anyone using rule 4 of the Faculty Jurisdiction (Injunctions and Restoration Orders) Rules 1992, SI (1992) No. 2884, ('the 1992 Rules').

49. It is correct that the Chancellor used the term 'restoration order' and that nowhere in his judgment did he refer to the 1992 Rules. Insofar as he was using the term without regard to the procedural requirements laid down by the Rules he was in error.

50. That is not the end of the procedural matters because rule 9 of the 1992 Rules implements section 13 (6) of the Care of Churches and Ecclesiastical Jurisdiction Measure 1991 ('the 1991 Measure'), which empowers the chancellor in the consistory court to make a restoration order in certain circumstances of his or her own motion, that is without any prior application. The power is a wide one. The form of order prescribed by the 1992 Rules (Form No.6) contains a notice stating that 'if without reasonable excuse you fail to comply with the directions contained in this order you will be guilty of contempt of court and could be committed to prison if proceedings are brought against you for contempt of court.' This is the same notice as is contained in any restoration order made after the hearing of a formal application (rule 7) and puts into effect section 13 (11) of the 1991 Measure.

51. Mr Sharland contended that because the Chancellor was mistakenly proceeding on the basis that a restoration order was being sought he cannot have applied his mind properly to the requirements of rule 9 before deciding to make such an order of his own motion. Alternatively, he argued that the Chancellor failed to give the Council any notice or warning of his intention to make a restoration order at all, let alone one which extended to the totality of memorials in the consecrated area which had been laid flat. That was said to be fundamentally unfair and we were referred to a dictum of Lord Diplock in *Hadmor Productions v Hamilton* [1983] 1 AC 191 at 233 B–C in which he identifies 'one of the most fundamental rules of natural justice; the right of each party to be informed of any point adverse to him that is going to be relied upon by the judge and to be given an opportunity of stating what his answer to it is.'

52. There are two possibilities: either Chancellor Behrens did not believe he was making a 'restoration order,' or he concluded that both parties were present and represented before him and the issues relating to restoration had been sufficiently canvassed at the hearing. If the former were the case, he was mistaken in his approach because his 'direction' was in effect a mandatory order and not a condition attached to a confirmatory faculty because he refused to grant one. If the second alternative were the case, and this was argued by Mr Best, then he was in error because procedural fairness demanded that the Council should be forewarned and given a proper opportunity to address the court about such an order and its proposed extent, and this was not done.

53. Mr Sharland's next ground was that section 13 (5) of the 1991 Measure does not allow an order to be made which requires improvement of memorials rather than simply returning them to the position they were in before they were laid down. Mr Best argued that the Chancellor was right to order the Council to reinstate and make safe his clients' memorials, because it would be 'a nonsense' to restore memorials to a potentially dangerous state.

54. Section 13 (5) enables an order to be made requiring a person 'to take such steps as the court may consider necessary within such time as the court may specify for the purpose of restoring the position so far as possible to that which existed immediately before the act was committed.'

55. In paragraph 61 of his judgment the Chancellor gave four reasons for rejecting Mr Sharland's argument as to the scope of the section. First, he considered the words 'so far as possible' indicated that there could be flexibility in the court's approach. We do not agree that there is any flexibility allowing a court to direct improvement. 'So far as possible' merely recognises that subsequent events may have rendered only partial or incomplete restoration possible. Those words cannot trump the plain requirement of the section that restoration must be to 'that which existed immediately before the act was committed.' The Chancellor's second reason was that 'I do not consider the court has to be blind to changes in building techniques and standards.' But this proposition is irrelevant to the

interpretation of section 13 (5), however pertinent it might be in assessing evidence about current techniques and standards. His third reason that the insertion of dowels would restore memorials as far as possible to what they were like before repeats the erroneous interpretation used in the first reason to justify ordering improvement and flies in the face of the clear evidence about the absence of dowels from memorials which had been laid flat. Finally, his fourth reason that 're-erecting and restabilising memorials…is more a repair than an improvement' is his personal gloss on the section which we regard as unsustainable in the light of its wording.

56. However, there is a more fundamental matter which neither the Chancellor nor counsel for the parties identified when considering the scope of section 13 (5). It is probable that they accepted the view of the late Chancellor Gray in *Re West Norwood Cemetery* about the scope of the word 'churchyard' used in section 13 (5), namely, 'I do not consider that the word 'churchyard' in its ordinary use means anything other than a burial ground or a cemetery' (page 404). We disagree with this interpretation because, in the absence of any definition extending the meaning to a cemetery, the word 'churchyard' should be given its ordinary meaning. According to the Shorter Oxford English Dictionary[7] this is 'an enclosed ground in which a church stands, esp. as used for burials'.

57. We point out that section 5 (now repealed) of the Faculty Jurisdiction Measure 1964 conferred a specific power on the consistory court to make an order for costs against a party found responsible for executing work in 'a churchyard or other consecrated ground,' thus distinguishing between two types of burial ground. The words 'or other consecrated ground' are singularly absent from section 13 (5). The reason why it is appropriate to compare the two sections is that they demonstrate that where legislation is intended to apply to land which is consecrated, but not a churchyard, it will specifically say so.

58. For the reasons we have given we do not consider that section 13 (5), which confers on the Chancellor an enforcement power in relation to churches and churchyards similar to that available to local planning authorities in respect of listed buildings, is applicable to the consecrated part of a cemetery. In an appropriate case it is a useful power, but one which must always be exercised in accordance with the 1992 Rules and with care in order to achieve procedural fairness, particularly when an order is to be made of the court's own motion. A restoration order is likely to be useful, for example, to secure the timely return of an item illegally removed from a church or churchyard, or to reverse some relatively simple work illegally undertaken. It has to be kept in mind that the item, or the work, must be capable of being defined with clarity and specificity, as contempt proceedings can follow for non-compliance with a restoration order (See paragraph 50 above).

59. In paragraphs 63 and 64 of his judgment Chancellor Behrens went on to consider an alternative scenario if he were wrong on his interpretation of section 13 (5). We agree with him that the general power in section 12 of the 1991 Measure is widely drawn and enables the court to require work to be done as a condition of a faculty. The question to be determined is what work it is reasonable to order the Council to do if a faculty subject to conditions is to be granted. This is addressed later in this judgment.

Discrimination and irrationality

60. The Council's fourth ground of appeal was that 'the Chancellor erred in law in concluding that the risk of unlawful 'discrimination' meant that any orders had to apply to all gravestones laid flat in consecrated land rather than just the 119 Polish graves'.

61. The basis for the Chancellor taking this view appears to have been the submissions made to him by Mr Sharland, who argued in his written closing submissions, augmented in oral argument, that 'It is not open to the Council to decide to pay only for the repair of Polish graves, such a decision would, it is submitted, amount to unlawful discrimination on the grounds of race in relation to the

---

[7] 5th ed, Oxford University Press.

provision of services and further would be open to challenge by way of judicial review on the grounds of irrationality.' (quoted in paragraph 58 of the judgment).

62. We consider that the Chancellor may have misunderstood the scope of this submission. Before this Court, where he was subjected to some robust questioning, Mr Sharland's argument was more carefully nuanced. He contended that there were two occasions to be taken into account: first when the Council had completed the laying flat of the memorials, and secondly when the consistory court was considering what (if any) order to make on the petition for a faculty. It was in relation solely to the first matter which Mr Sharland ran his argument on discrimination. His contention was that

(i) the Council had no legal power to spend taxpayers' money on repairing private memorials;
(ii) the cost of such repair throughout the cemetery would have been tens of thousands of pounds;
(iii) if the Council decided to pay only for the repair of the Polish memorials that decision would have amounted to unlawful discrimination on the grounds of race in relation to the provision of services.

63. There are several reasons why we regard that argument as unsustainable. First, the events with which we are concerned pre-date the anti-discriminatory provisions embodied in the Equality Act 2006. The Poles are not a racial group as Mr Sharland conceded in argument (see *Mandla v Dowell Lee* [1983] 2 AC 548 HL). He invited us to substitute 'ethnicity' for race but this does not alter our view.

64. Secondly, we do not consider that he is assisted by the Human Rights Act 1998. Contrary to popular misconception Article 14 is not a free-standing right. It is headed 'Prohibition of discrimination' and reads

'The *enjoyment of the rights and freedoms set forth in this Convention* shall be secured without discrimination on any ground such as sex, race, colour, language, religion, political or other opinion, national or social origin, association with a national minority, property, birth or other status.' (emphasis added)

It is necessary to demonstrate that one or other Convention right is engaged before the question of Article 14 discrimination arises (See *Abdulaziz Cabales and Balkandali v United Kingdom* (1985) 7 EHRR 471). We use the word 'engaged' advisedly because, as was accepted by Mr Sharland in argument, it is unnecessary to demonstrate a breach, merely an act or omission impinging to some degree on the right.

65. The only Convention right raised for consideration was Article 1 of the First Protocol. This deals with peaceful enjoyment of possessions and contains a prohibition on deprivation of possessions save in the public interest and in accordance with the law. In this case there is no question of memorials having been disposed of by the Council thus depriving the owners of possession. In *Re Keynsham Cemetery Briden Ch* was careful to make clear that the faculties he was granting were concerned with protection for private property and did not, and could not, interfere with rights of ownership recognised by Article 1. Similar considerations apply to the memorials which are the subject of the petition for a faculty in this case.

66. Mr Sharland mentioned Article 8, which states that 'Everyone has the right to respect for his private and family life, his home and his correspondence'. However, there is an important limitation in Article 8 which recognises that there can be interference by a public authority with this right where action is taken in accordance with the law in the interests of 'public safety' and in other specific instances. Although Mr Best mentioned Article 8 in paragraph 3 of his skeleton argument he did not develop the point or present any oral argument upon it to this Court. We do not consider that Article 8 is engaged here in respect of the Council's dealings with unsafe memorials in accordance with the statutory framework.

67. Even if our interpretation of Article 1 of the First Protocol and Article 8 could be said to be too narrow, we nonetheless consider that there would have been no discrimination by the Council

under Article 14 were it to have decided to reinstate the Polish memorials. It would not have constituted discrimination on the ground of national origin but would simply have reflected the fact that those with relatives in some 119 graves sought reinstatement whereas others did not. Different treatment does not amount to discrimination where it can be objectively justified.

68. In paragraph 58 of his judgment Chancellor Behrens referred to Mr Sharland's argument that a decision by the Council to pay for the repair of just the Polish memorials might well be open to challenge by judicial review on the grounds of irrationality but he did not comment further on this point. Mr Sharland repeated the submission in this Court. The substance of the argument is that such a decision by the Council would have given rise to a legitimate expectation that other memorials would likewise be reinstated upon application by the owner. Any refusal to reinstate could well give rise to a successful judicial review claim, either on the basis of legitimate expectation or upon the irrationality of a decision by the Council to limit the works of reinstatement to a finite group, which happened to apply at a certain time. We regard this as a sound argument in support of the stance which was taken at the time by the Council. We have no criticism of the Council for waiting until its position in relation to the subject of reinstatement, as well as in relation to its actions prior to the petition for a faculty, had been clarified and determined by the consistory court.

69. For the reasons given above we consider that the Chancellor was in error in concluding that a risk of unlawful discrimination meant that his order had to apply to all memorials laid flat in the consecrated part of the cemetery rather than being confined to those belonging to the parties to the proceedings. It would be highly unusual for a consistory court to afford specific relief to someone who had not sought it. The effect of the Chancellor's order would be to compel the Council to expend a significant sum of money on the betterment of privately owned property. This would be particularly inappropriate when the property had become a danger to public safety through ignorance, indifference, or a failure to maintain it in breach of the obligation imposed by the grant made by the cemetery authority and a disregard for third party interests. Mr Best informed this Court that, so far as his instructing solicitor was aware, the individuals whom he represented had not taken out public liability insurance cover in respect of their memorials.

Temporary stakes

70. Mr Sharland argued that the Chancellor had failed to attach sufficient weight to the evidence that the Council had followed the recommended practice of staking some of the dangerous memorials in the first instance, and had only laid them flat after the stakes had been removed without any remedial action by the 'owners' to make the memorials safe. The undisputed evidence given by Mr Watson was that some 24 memorials out of the 119 memorials belonging to those members of the Polish community, who had raised any objection, had been staked and had warning notices attached to them. In two cases repairs had subsequently been carried out with the approval of the Council.

71. In paragraph 55 of his judgment the Chancellor said

'There was evidence that a number of the warning notices which had been placed round some memorials had been deliberately removed and I consider it unlikely that this was entirely the work of vandals'. Chancellor Behrens made no finding of fact as to which, if any, of the opponents' memorials had been dealt with in this way and Mr Best had no instructions on the subject. The action by the Council should certainly be taken into account in its favour when consideration is given to a confirmatory faculty, and similarly it is appropriate to note the lack of co-operation on the part of some unidentified "owners" within the Polish community.'

Re Keynsham Cemetery

72. In paragraph 65 of his judgment Chancellor Behrens recognised that in essence two faculties were being sought, a confirmatory faculty in respect of what the Council had already done in the cemetery and a faculty permitting it to carry out similar works in the future in the remainder of the cemetery. However, he became diverted from the principles laid down in *Re Keynsham*, possibly by Mr Best's emphasis upon the need for the Council to restore his clients memorials 'safely secured in

the ground,' and by his argument that later events such as the Stockport report could properly be taken into account in relation to any decision. Thus an element of confusion arose when he came to his conclusion, because a line was not clearly drawn between past events and authority for the future.

73. Even where there is only one petition before the court it is essential for a chancellor to consider past events, in respect of which a confirmatory faculty may or may not be granted, separately from any facts relating to a faculty for the future. The process was simplified in cases such as *Re St Mary's Balham* [1978] 1 All ER 993 where the Chancellor gave leave to amend the petition to seek a confirmatory faculty and there was a counter petition from the archdeacon, and in *Re West Norwood Cemetery* where there were similarly two petitions before the court.

74. If Chancellor Behrens had adopted the 'reasonableness' approach used in *Re Keynsham Cemetery*, when assessing the past actions of the Council, he could only have come to one conclusion namely that a confirmatory faculty, albeit subject to conditions should be granted. His findings in paragraph 34 were clear and unequivocal

'I agree entirely that the Council has acted throughout in good faith. I also consider that the Council has acted reasonably in following what it thought was the right procedures in the light of its understanding of the law.'

75. Unfortunately he quoted from *Re West Norwood Cemetery* a short passage which in turn was a quotation from *Re St Mary's Balham*. In *Re St Mary's Balham* [1978] 1 All ER 993 at 996 Garth Moore Ch made certain general comments in his judgment which should be read in the context of a petition in respect of unlawful work to an organ in a church. In the relevant passage he said

'I am concerned to uphold the law and I am concerned to see that justice is done to everybody. I must remind the petitioners that they are the temporary custodians of the property which comes into their hands and are in the nature of trustees for both the past, the present and for the future. What I am concerned with mostly now is the present and the future.'

The word 'mostly' is significant in this passage because Garth Moore Ch rightly went on to consider past facts in mitigation of the unlawful work carried out by the petitioners before deciding against granting a confirmatory faculty.

76. We consider that in reaching his conclusions Chancellor Behrens was undoubtedly distracted by his acceptance of the argument that he should take the Stockport report into account overall (this could only be relevant to the future and not the past because of its date); his misinterpretation of his power to make a restoration order; and his misunderstanding of the possibility of discrimination. In relation to the undoubted distress caused to the opponents by the failure to notify them individually the Chancellor failed to consider at that stage in his judgment the mitigating factor of the amount of publicity given to the Council's actions. He was therefore erroneous in the order which he made as well as in his refusal of a confirmatory faculty. Consequently, the appeal is allowed and this Court sets aside that part of the order refusing a confirmatory faculty and ordering the Council to reinstate and make safe all the memorials laid down on the consecrated section of the Welford Road cemetery.

Confirmatory faculty

77. A confirmatory faculty is always a matter of discretion because it is an indulgence when there has been a failure to observe the requirement to obtain a faculty before undertaking work. However, where there has been genuine ignorance on the part of the petitioner about the need to obtain a faculty, as in this case, and the action for which a confirmatory faculty is sought was done in good faith (as the Chancellor found), then it is necessary to proceed to the next stage of identifying appropriate conditions to be attached to the faculty which are fair and just in all the circumstances.

78. For the reasons of law and fact already given above, this Court rejects Mr Best's argument that the Council should make safe, as well as reinstate, his clients' memorials because of the Council's behaviour. It is essential to take account of the legal responsibilities placed respectively on the Council and on the opponents. If the opponents (or their stonemasons) had kept their memorials

in a safe condition then the Council would not have needed to interfere with them by staking them or laying them flat on safety grounds. Conversely, if the Council had alerted the opponents earlier through their priest, then the opponents would have been given an opportunity to put their memorials in a safe condition. We therefore consider that the just solution in this case is for the cost of reinstating them and making them safe to be shared between the Council and the opponents.

79. Some limited evidence was given to the Chancellor about the cost of reinstating memorials and making them safe. Mr Watson in cross-examination said the average cost in Stockport had been £100. Mr Jan Jarowicki said that it had cost him £100 plus VAT and Mr Andrzej Lipinski said that to reinstate and instal ground anchors on the memorial of his parents-in-law had cost him £151 including VAT. These figures are a helpful indicator of what should reasonably be spent on reinstating and making safe other memorials in the consecrated part of the cemetery.

80. In respect of the 119 memorials belonging to members of the Polish community there are two categories of person: (i) the opponents who are concerned with many of the memorials, and (ii) those who did not instruct Edwards, solicitors, formally but who accept responsibility for the remainder of the memorials listed by Mr E S Hryniewiecki in attachment 1 to his witness statement. He was the Chairman of the Federation of Poles in Leicester at the time of making his statement and in paragraph 8 he said 'I attach a list of gravestones of the Polish community to which I refer and on behalf of which families I am making this statement and objection against the action taken by the Leicester City Council.'

81. As to those who are not formally opponents, we consider that they could well have regarded representation by the chairman of the Federation as sufficient to protect their interests, so rather than giving them leave to apply to be joined as opponents (which would be granted) and in order to save time and expense we will treat them as if they were indeed parties to the proceedings.

82. It follows that the opponents, together with those whom we treat as opponents, will all fall within the ambit of the condition attached to the confirmatory faculty, which is to be issued out of the consistory court of the diocese of Leicester.

83. Having established the order of magnitude of the cost of reinstating and making safe individual memorials, we have formulated a process whereby the cost is to be shared between the Council and any opponent who applies to the Council within three months from the date of this judgment for reinstatement of a memorial included amongst the 119 memorials referred to above. The apportionment of cost should be capable of agreement, given goodwill on both sides, but in default of agreement we have provided for the reasonable cost of reinstatement to be determined by the consistory court.

84. We therefore direct that a confirmatory faculty be issued out of the consistory court of the diocese of Leicester subject to a condition incorporating the detailed terms set out in the Appendix to this judgment.

Faculty for the Future

85. It is in relation to the future that the comments in the Stockport report and the Special Report on Memorial Safety in Cemeteries published by the Local Government Ombudsmen and the Public Services Ombudsman for Wales (March 2006) contain helpful advice for burial authorities generally. Much of what the Council did complies with that advice, but there are useful matters in these reports which they will no doubt note for the future.

86. In the light of those reports we consider that a faculty for the future to be issued out of the consistory court of Leicester should contain the following conditions:

Area of consecrated land still to be tested and retesting of memorials in the consecrated part of the cemetery in the future

(1) Memorials may be tested by hand or to a 35 kilogram standard by a topple tester or similar device used strictly in accordance with the manufacturer's directions;
(2) Before commencing any safety testing the Council should conduct a public awareness campaign to include placing a notice at the entrances to the cemetery and in one or more

conspicuous positions within or adjoining the area where the testing is to take place giving the date (which shall be no sooner than 6 weeks from the date of the notice) when safety testing is to commence and supplying contact details of the Council;

(3) Before commencing testing the Council shall give written notice of the date of the proposed testing to the person named in the cemetery record maintained by the Council as the person with responsibility for the memorial;

(4) If any memorial fails a test under (1) the Council may secure it and make it safe temporarily by a metal or other appropriate stake with a warning notice placed on it identifying it as dangerous and giving contact details of the Council;

(5) If any memorial fails a test and has been made safe temporarily under (4) the Council shall notify in writing the person referred to in (3) above that the memorial should be made safe so as to conform with NAMM guidance, or the British standard, within a period of 4 months from the date of the letter to that person;

(6) Where there is no response from the person referred to in (3), or the owner of the burial right and/or the memorial is unknown the Council should display a list of the names of the memorials required to be made safe in two or more conspicuous places in or adjoining the relevant part of the consecrated area(s) and should publish the list on the Council's website;

(7) Failing any response under (5) or (6) above the Council may, if it considers it necessary or desirable to do so, lay the memorial in question flat after the expiry of the period of 4 months specified in (5) above, or may leave the stake in place for such further period as it deems fit pending implementation of a plan for improvement of the area.

Areas where memorials have been laid down

87. Whilst it is clear that the Council here acted in good faith, advertised the testing regime, and acted reasonably in laying down memorials, we share the concern of the Chancellor about the effect of the programme. To this Court the result appears unseemly (because it seems to show lack of respect for the dead); unsightly (because it seems to show lack of respect for the dead); unsightly (because memorials should be upright, not tipped over and creating visual disharmony in an important cemetery); unsafe (because they are potentially a hazard from tripping, and an attraction to vandals, who usually have scant respect for anything which appears to be broken). Consequently, we attach a further condition to the faculty requiring the Council, within a period no later than 18 months from the date of this judgment, to prepare and lodge with the consistory court of Leicester a plan for the following 5 year period setting out the actions which the Council is proposing to take in respect of memorials which have been laid down in the consecrated areas and in respect of which the owners are untraced. The plan should be prepared after consultation with all relevant bodies including the Friends of Welford Road Cemetery.

Costs

88. In support of the cross-appeal Mr Best argued vigorously that the opponents should have been granted their costs against the Council and that the Chancellor was in error in refusing their application. He relied upon a number of decisions in different consistory courts over the years. However, such cases turn on their own facts and they all precede in *Re St Mary Sherborne* [1996] Fam 63 in which the principles applicable in the consistory court, and on appeal, were set out.

89. He referred first to in *Re St John's Chelsea* [1962] 1 WLR 706 at 722, a lengthy decision dealing with the legality of various uses of consecrated land. The order that the parties opponent, who had cross-petitioned, should recover part of their costs depended upon the facts and Mr Best was unable to point to any comparison with the facts in the case before us. His next authority was in *Re Woldingham Churchyard* [1971] 1 WLR 811 in which a stonemason had illegally entered the churchyard and erected a memorial after the incumbent had refused him permission. Mr Best suggested that the Council's conduct was like that of the stonemason, but it was not comparable at all. Chancellor Behrens found that the Council had acted in good faith whereas the stonemason

clearly had not. The order for costs made against the latter was because of his flagrant illegal action. Neither of Mr Best's next authorities (*Re St Mark's Haydock* [1981] 1 WLR 1104 and in *Re All Saints, Leamington Priors* [1963] 1 WLR 206 afforded him any more help, and in his last authority, *Re St Mary's Luton* [1968] P. 47, the Chancellor ordered the parties opponent to pay the costs of the petitioners, quite the opposite of Mr Best's request in the present case.

90. Both in the Grounds of Appeal and in Mr Best's skeleton argument there was reference to the opponents being poor but this assertion, even if true, cannot affect the merits of an order in respect of costs. Grounds 4 and 5 argue that it is wrong that by their action the opponents should have brought benefit to 'a very large number of people outwith the Polish community' and, conversely, that the refusal of costs was unjust and could deter others from pursuing objections in Leicester and elsewhere. These matters do not have a bearing on the appropriate order for costs between the parties to the proceedings.

91. We find nothing perverse or unreasonable in the refusal of costs by the Chancellor, and the cross-appeal is dismissed.

92. As to the costs of this appeal the Council, as appellant, will pay the court costs in accordance with the principles in *Re St Mary, Sherborne*. These will include correspondence fees for the Registrar and the expenses incurred by the Court. Mr Sharland submitted that if the Council succeeded on the appeal, which it has done to a substantial degree, then costs should be awarded in the appellant's favour. Mr Best, on the other hand, argued that his clients should have their costs irrespective of the outcome. We have to take account of the fact that the opponents did not need to participate in the appeal by arguing on the merits, but they decided to do so and to argue for a restoration order on which they failed. It is open to this Court to make an order for costs against the opponents on the basis of their failure. We are only departing from the principle which normally applies, because (a) the appeal would still have had to be pursued to a full hearing in any event even in the absence of resistance from the opponents; (b) the cross-appeal occupied this Court for relatively little time; and (c) we recognise the genuine distress occasioned to the opponents by the events in question. There will, therefore, be no order as to costs between the parties to the appeal and the cross-appeal.

Appeal allowed.

Aston Cantlow and Wilmcote with Billesley Parochial Church Council v Wallbank[8]

High Court of Justice, Chancery Division
Lewison J
5 February 2007

1. Mr and Mrs Wallbank are the owners of Glebe Farm in Aston Cantlow. They are the lay rectors or among the lay rectors of that Parish. This means that they own property that once belonged to the rector of that Parish. Their case has already been to the House of Lords. The House of Lords decided

---

[8] HC/95/03710; The Times, 21 February 2007. This judgment deals solely with the inquiry into the amount due by the lay rectors pursuant to the Chancel Repairs Act 1932. For the decision in the House of Lords, see *Aston Cantlow and Wilmcote with Billesley Parochial Church Council v Wallbank* [2004] 1 AC 546; [2003] 3 All ER 1213, HL; in the Court of Appeal, see *Aston Cantlow and Wilmcote with Billesley Parochial Church Council v Wallbank* [2001] 2 All ER 363; and at first instance, see *Aston Cantlow and Wilmcote with Billesley Parochial Church Council v Wallbank* (2001) 81 P & CR 14; [2000] EGLR 149, Ferris J.

that the imposition of a liability on a lay rector to pay for the repair of a chancel of the parish church was not incompatible with the Human Rights Act, 1998.

2. In *Wickhambrook PCC v Croxford* [1935] 2KB 417 the Court of Appeal decided that the liability of a lay rector is a personal liability and is not limited to the value of the glebe land and its profits. That decision is binding upon me and indeed the Court of Appeal, although what it decided may still be open to argument in the House of Lords. In the course of giving judgement in *Wickhambrook PCC v Croxford*, Lord Justice Romer said this:

> 'The Act does not impose as a condition precedent to the court giving judgement for the responsible authority that it should find that the defendant would, but for the provisions of the Act, had been in fact admonished, but whether the defendant would, but for those provisions, have been liable to be admonished. The word liable shows, in my opinion, the question to be considered by the court is whether the defendant could consistently with the law have been admonished, and not the question whether the defendant would, in fact, have been admonished in this particular case. The only question, therefore, to be determined upon this appeal is whether the defendant could, but for the Act, have been admonished to repair the chancel. If so then the court was obliged by the Act to give judgement for the plaintiffs for the full sum of £123, 12s 6d. This may in certain cases lead to considerable hardship. It is not a matter which we are entitled to take into consideration because the words of the Act itself are unambiguous.'

3. Following the decision of the House of Lords it is my task to assess the amount for which Mr and Mrs Wallbank are liable. Mr Wallbank has himself presented the case for himself and his wife, and has marshalled his arguments and presented his points with cogency and clarity. His principal argument is that the liability of a lay rector is limited to keeping the chancel wind and watertight. The main source for this argument is a website maintained at www.churchlaw.co.uk. In answer to the question; what is the extent of the liability? The website states:

> 'The liability is not unlimited. It is regarded as extending to ensuring the chancel is kept wind and watertight and that essential fixtures are maintained.'

4. Unfortunately, however, in my judgement that is not the law. The common law is laid down in two cases of the Court of the King's Bench. The first of those is *Wise v Metcalfe* (1829) 10 B&C 299. In that case three possible standards of repair were placed before the court as the basis for the rector's liability. At page 312 Mr Justice Bayley delivering the judgement for the court described the three possibilities as follows:

> 'First, that the predecessor ought to have left the premises in good and substantial repair with painting, papering, and whitewashing being in proper and decent condition for the immediate occupation and use of his successor, and that such repairs were to be ascertained with reference to the state and character of the buildings which were to be restored, where necessary, according to their original form without addition or modern improvement. The estimate according to this rule came to £399, 18s 6d.
>
> The second rule proposed was that they were to be left as an out-going lay tenant ought to leave his buildings where he is under covenants to leave them in good and sufficient repair, order and condition. The estimate in that rule was £310; the papering, painting and whitewashing not being included.
>
> The third rule was that they were left to be wind and watertight only or as the case expresses it in such conditions as an out-going lay tenant, not obliged by covenant to do any repairs ought to leave them, and by that rule the estimate would be £75, 11s. We are not prepared to say that any of these rules are precisely correct, although the second approaches the most nearly to that which we consider as the proper rule.'

It follows, therefore, that the third rule, namely, that the liability was limited to keeping the chancel wind and watertight was expressly rejected by the court.

5. At page 313 Mr Justice Bayley having quoted from earlier treatises said this,

> 'From this statement of the common law two propositions may be deduced. First, that the incumbent is bound not only to repair the buildings belonging to his benefice but also to restore and rebuild them if necessary. Secondly, that he is bound only to repair and to sustain and rebuild when necessary.'

6. At page 314 Mr Justice Bayley expressly rejected the third mode of computation which he said,

> '... cannot be the right one, because a tenant not obliged by covenant to do repairs is not bound to rebuild or replace.'

7. A gloss was placed upon that statement of the law in the latter case of *Pell v Addison* (1862) F & F 291, In that case Mr Justice Willes said that *Wise v Metcalfe*,

> '... does no more than decide that the repairs are to be more than such as a tenant not under covenant to repair is bound to do, and less than what a tenant under such a covenant is bound to do. The reasonable rule is perhaps to put the edifice into substantial repair without ornament.'

That gloss on the case of *Wise v Metcalfe* has been taken to the law thenceforth. It is in my judgement not consistent with the statement of the law in the website at www.churchlaw.co.uk.

8. The matter is in my judgement put beyond doubt by the terms of the Chancel Repairs Act 1932. Section 2 of that Act describes the nature of proceedings to enforce liability to repair chancels. Section 2 subsection (1) provides for the service of a notice to repair which states in general terms the grounds upon which a person is alleged to be liable to repair the chancel and the extent of the disrepair. Subsection (2) goes on to provide for the bringing of proceedings,

> '... to recover the sum required to put the chancel is proper repair.'

Section 2 subsection (3) goes on to provide,

> 'In any proceedings brought as aforesaid the court, if it finds that the defendant would, but for the provisions of the Act, have been liable to be admonished to repair the chancel by the appropriate Ecclesiastical court in a cause of office promoted against him in that court on the date when the notice to repair was served shall give judgement for the responsible authority for such sum as appears to the court to represent the cost of putting the chancel in proper repair.'

9. My task, therefore, is to determine the sum that appears to me to represent the costs of putting the chancel in proper repair. Proper repair, in my judgement, necessarily means more than simply wind and watertight and must be assessed in accordance with the tests laid down in *Wise v Metcalfe* and *Pell v Addison*.

10. Acting on the joint instructions of parties Mr John Jones, RIBA, reported on the condition of the chancel. He summarised his opinion in paragraph 2.01 of his report as follows:

> 'The extent and nature of the repairs are considered to be as listed in the description of works section of my specification dated November 2003, which are generally; investigations of repair of walls and foundations. Replacement of stone tracery to windows. Repair of roof and ceiling. Repair of glazing. Repair of decoration of rainwater goods. Internal plaster repair. Redecoration of internal walls. It is my professional opinion that all of the items of work listed above are necessary to put the chancel into substantive repair without ornament, except internal decoration of walls and ceiling.'

In paragraph 2.03 he said,

> 'I do not believe that temporary repair is a satisfactory solution and from past experience I think that if English Heritage are to be involved in the project they will agree.'

11. Mr Jones disclaimed expertise himself in estimating costs, but by agreement between the parties the costs were estimated by Mr John Griffin, a qualified quantity surveyor. Some of the items

which Mr Griffin costed have now been abandoned by the claimant and the revised cost of the items now claimed, exclusive of VAT, now come to £215,496.50.

12. Mr Wallbank has made it clear that he does not in principle dispute Mr Jones' report or the assessed costs. His primary argument is based on the contention that the liability of a lay rector is limited to keeping the chancel wind and watertight. That, as I have said, is an argument which in my judgement is incorrect in law. Mr Wallbank has also submitted that in effect Mr Jones has recommended a Rolls-Royce job when a more limited programme of works would have sufficed. There are, it seems to me, at least three difficulties with that argument. The first is that as I have quoted Mr Jones gave it as his opinion that a temporary repair would not have been a satisfactory solution and he has not been questioned or cross-examined on that opinion. The second is that no alternative scheme has been put forward. The third is that as a matter of general principle where an obligation to repair can be performed in a number of different ways it is for the person undertaking the repairs to choose how to carry them out, providing that his choices are reasonable ones. Mr Wallbank also submits that the Church ought to act in accordance with its own teaching and temper the wind to the shorn lamb. This court is a court of law only and must apply the law as it finds it. Mr Wallbank also says that the liability for chancel repairs is anachronistic, unfair and has been made even more unfair by changes in relativity between the values of land on the one hand and the cost of works on the other. What was a liability once intended to keep the chancel in a state in which the incumbent could celebrate the Holy Office has become a means of keeping up parts of the national heritage to the high standards expected by English Heritage at the expense of a few landowners. In this submission he has the support of the Law Commission, the Law Society and many distinguished academic commentators. But again reform of the law is not a matter for the courts which must take the law as they find it.

13. Turning to the detail of the schedule of works Items 1 and 2 relate to survey work. In his comments on the Scott schedule Mr Wallbank has said that this is survey work and not the responsibility of the lay rector. Mr Jones was asked about this work in clarification of the expert report and he described it in his letter of 23 January 2007, as follows:

'(a) Item 1 relates to trial holes and these are necessary to check ground conditions, determine an allowable ground bearing pressure and assess, if possible, the adequacy of underpinning work carried out to the chancel walls in the past following substantial movements of the walls. It is thought and hoped that the underpinning is satisfactory, but it needs to be checked otherwise the chancel cannot be said to be in a state of good repair. If ground conditions and foundations are not checked then the only other way to be certain of stability would be to include for new underpinning work. A report on existing ground conditions is a necessary first stage.

(b) Item 2 relates to existing storm water drainage. Again the adequacy of drains and outfall is not known or whether any defects may be causing or contributing to the movement. If the drains are not inspected then the only way to be certain that they are satisfactory is to replace them. It is unfortunate that no records are available of existing construction.'

The upshot of this description in my judgement is that it is not known whether repairs are needed or not. The purpose of the survey is to determine that question. I cannot, therefore, be satisfied that the costs of these surveys are costs required to put the chancel into proper repair. These costs amount in aggregate to £3,500.00.

14. The second item on which I wish to comment is that of the contingency. This amounts to £25,000.00. The nature of the contingency is that it is for works that are unforeseen. Since the works for which the contingency is allowed are themselves unidentified again I cannot be satisfied that this sum represents any part of the costs of putting the chancel into repair. The preliminaries appear to be individually costed items rather than conventionally arrived at as a percentage of the primary works. The reduction in the primary works, therefore, gives no ground for interfering with the preliminaries.

15. The upshot is that I disallow costs of £28,500.00, but otherwise I am required to give judgment for the sums claimed in the Scott schedule which amount to £186,969.50. In principle VAT is part of the costs of the repair to the extent that the claimant is liable to pay it. Some works may be zero rated if they count as alterations to a listed building, but I will give judgement for each sum as represents VAT properly payable on the costs of repairs.

Judgment for the PCC accordingly.

INDEX

absolution, ministry of 5.61
access audit 7.102
Acts of Convocation 1.35
Acts of Parliament affecting Church 1.23
Acts of Synod 1.35n, 2.21
administrator, cathedral
   appointment of 8.26
   Chapter member, as 8.09
allegiance, oath of
   chancellor, by 2.48
   ordinand, by 4.07
alms box, provision of 7.123
altar
   nature of 7.91
   provision of 7.91
alterations, minor
   archdeacon's jurisdiction 7.43
Alternative Service Book 1980 502n
amicus curiae, archdeacon as 7.10, 7.81
Ancient Monuments Society
   national amenity society, as 7.18
Anglican Communion
   Archbishop of Canterbury's role in 2.01n
   Churches within 2.01
   nature of 2.01
Anglican Consultative Council 2.01n
annual parochial church meeting
   chairman and clerk 3.07
   business at 3.08
   date for 3.07
   elections at 3.10
   entitlement to attend 3.07
   financial statements 3.09, 3.29
   questions to 3.09
   voting at 3.07
archaeological importance
   special notification of faculty petition 7.47
archaeological interest
   article of: notice to Council for the Care of Churches 7.51
   consultation 7.27, 7.33
   special notification 7.47
Archbishop of Canterbury
   Anglican Communion, role in 2.01n
   appointment 4.66
   Church Commissioner, as 2.39
   diocesan responsibilities 2.10n
   disciplinary proceedings against
      conduct case 6.10, 6.12, 6.20
      doctrine case 6.74, 6.78, 6.79
   dispensations granted by 4.66
   General Synod joint President 2.20
   House of Lords, in 4.61
   incapacity 4.67
   jurisdiction 4.66
   licences granted by 4.66, 5.41
   Primate of All England, as 2.10n
   qualifications 4.66
   resignation 4.67
   retirement age 4.67
   service, may approve forms of 5.07, 5.08
Archbishop of York
   appointment 4.66
   Church Commissioner, as 2.39
   diocesan responsibilities 2.10n
   disciplinary proceedings against
      conduct case 6.10, 6.12, 6.20
      doctrine case 6.74, 6.78, 6.79
   General Synod joint President 2.20
   House of Lords, in 4.61
   incapacity 4.66
   licences granted by 5.41
   Primate of England, as 2.10n
   qualifications 4.66
   resignation 4.67
   retirement age 4.67
   service, may approve forms of 5.07, 5.08
Archbishops' Commission on Canon Law (1947) 1.06
Archbishops' Council
   boards and councils 2.14
   composition 2.12
   establishment 2.11
   functions and objects 2.13
   Ministry Division 4.04
   Vocations, Recruitment and Selection Committee 4.04

archbishops' list
  maintenance of 6.69
  notice to person named 6.70, 6.71
  review of 6.70–6.72
  who is included 6.69
  who may see 6.69n
archdeacon
  alterations, minor: jurisdiction 7.43
  appointment 4.54
  benefice
    report on vacancy in 4.44
    vacation of, inquiry 4.45
  churchwarden, admission to office 3.40
  churchyard, and minor works in 7.43
  College of Canons, on 8.13
  court of 2.57
  diocesan advisory committee
    advice from 7.17
    on 7.09, 7.16
  decoration: jurisdiction 7.43
  expenses of 7.81
  faculty
    amicus curiae, as 7.10, 7.81
    appearing in proceedings 7.10
    costs 7.10, 7.79
    declining jurisdiction 7.46
    expenses 7.81
    granted or supervised by 7.09, 7.46
    interested person, as 7.09
    jurisdiction 7.43–7.46
    objection to, by 7.53
    petition referred by registrar to 7.44
    role in proceedings 7.09–7.15
    urgent matter 7.14
  functions 4.55
  incapacity of 8.23, 8.24
  induction of incumbent, and 4.28
  injunction, applying for 7.85
  movables, and introduction etc of 7.43
  ordination, presents persons for 4.07
  PCC, calling meeting of 7.11
  parochial church meeting, calling 7.11
  qualifications 4.54
  re-ordering, licensing temporary 7.13, 7.127
  repairs: jurisdiction 7.43
  restoration order, applying for 7.85
  retirement 4.54
  safe place, ordering removal to 7.12
  visitation 2.57, 3.49, 7.15
architect
  cathedral
    appointment of 8.26
    fabric advisory committee meeting,
      at 8.38

  inspection by 8.31, 8.55
  parish
    appointment of 3.82
    works under faculty, supervision
      of 7.74
area bishop 4.65
area dean
  rural dean, same as 4.53
arrest, clergy privilege from 4.14
article
  historic etc interest of: notice to Council for
    the Care of Churches 7.51
  meaning 7.51n
articles of inquiry on visitation 3.49, 4.37
ashes, burial of
  conduct of 5.56
  consecration of ground for 5.51
  right to 5.51
aspergill, legality of 7.124
assent, declaration of
  chancellor, by 2.48
  ordinand, by 4.07
Auditor
  same person as Dean of the Arches 2.59
auditor, cathedral 8.26
aumbry, legality of 7.124
avoidance, declaration of
  pastoral breakdown, on 4.46

Bancroft, Richard: collection of
  Canons (1603) 1.16
banns *see* **marriage**
baptism
  age for 5.12
  certificate of 5.12n
  conditional 5.12, 5.16
  deacon, by 4.11, 5.13
  death, of child in danger of 5.12
  delay in 5.12
  fee for, no 5.12
  font for *see* font
  godparents 5.13
  instruction before 5.12
  lay person, by 5.13
  procedure 5.14
  public worship, in 5.13
  refusal of 5.12
  registration 5.14
  repeated, cannot be 5.1
  service, voting on changes to 2.25
  Sunday, on 5.13
Baptist Union
  ecclesiastical exemption applies to 7.06
  sharing of church buildings 3.95

Index

bells
  church
    nuisance, as 3.51n
    provision of 7.123
    ringing of 3.51
  sanctuary, legality of 7.124
benefice
  area of, alteration of 3.89
  incumbent is holder of 4.17
  meaning 4.17
  name of 3.89
  nature of 3.02
  patrons, register of 4.18
  plurality, held in 4.48
  suspension of presentation
    bishop, by 4.23
    notice of 4.23, 4.24
    period of 4.24
    priest-in-charge 4.32
    reason for 4.23
    sequestrators during 4.26
  vacancy in
    acceptance of offer 4.21
    advertisement of 4.20
    archdeacon's report 4.44
    bishop's decision 4.45, 4.46
    cause of 4.19
    churchwardens and rural dean and 3.56
    declaration of avoidance 4.46
    inhibition 4.45
    inquiry concerning 4.43–4.45
    notice of 4.19
    PCC consultation 3.29, 4.19, 4.20
    pastoral breakdown, on 4.43
    presentee
      refusal to institute 4.22
      selection of 4.21
    procedure 443–446
    rural dean and 4.53
    tribunal conducting inquiry 4.45
Bible, version of: PCC's views 3.29
bishop
  age 4.56
  appointment 4.57
  archdeacon
    appoints 4.54
    assisted by 4.55
  area 4.65
  benefice, selection of presentee to 4.21, 4.22
  cathedral
    canons, appointing residentiary 8.20
    Council meetings, at 8.06
    seat of, as 8.04
    visitor, as 8.16

chancellor, appoints 2.47
character 4.56
churchwardens, powers respecting 3.46
confirmation
  by 4.60
  form of service, decides 505n
consecration
  by 4.60, 7.02
  of 4.59
delegation to suffragan 4.61
diocesan synod, presides over 4.61
disciplinary proceedings against
  conduct cases 6.10, 6.12, 6.19, 6.20
  doctrine cases 6.74, 6.77–6.79
election of 4.58
enthronement service 5.60
extended episcopal oversight 4.63
faculty cases, hearing 2.51
flying 4.63
functions 4.60
General Synod, on 2.15
House of Lords, in 1.21, 4.61
incapacity 4.64
incumbent, institution of 4.19, 4.27
jurisdiction 4.60
Ordinary, as 4.60
ordination by 4.60
PCC representations to 3.28
residence 4.61
retirement age 4.64
service, may approve forms of 5.07, 5.08
suffragan
  appointment 4.65
  area of 4.65
  College of Canons, member of 8.13
  delegation of powers to 4.61
  diocesan pastoral committee, member of 4.65
  diocesan synod, member of 4.65
  functions 4.65
  General Synod, on 2.14
  residence 4.65
  retirement 4.65
translation of 4.59
vacancy in see committee 4.57
vacation of office 4.64
visitation by 4.37, 4.62
woman 4.02, 4.03
bishopric, vacation of 4.64
bishop's council of diocesan synod 2.28
Bishops, House of *see* General Synod
Bishopsgate questions
  addition to? 7.71
  adoption of 7.70
  catechism, not a 7.71n

Bishopsgate questions (*cont.*)
  nature of 7.70
  order in which questions asked 7.71
  re-ordering, in 7.126
Book of Common Prayer
  alternatives to 5.02, 5.04
  authority for 1.04, 5.02
  Canons and 1.28
  continued use of 5.04, 5.05
  rubrics in, elasticity of 7.124
British Sign Language
  services in 5.03
Building Faith in Our Future (2004) 7.118
burial
  church, in, not allowed 5.51
  churchyard, in
    conditional on space available 5.51
    particular spot, no right to 5.51
  consent to 7.113
  cremated remains, of
    conduct of 5.56
    consecration of ground for 5.51
    right to 5.51
  ground *see* burial ground
  permanence of 7.106
  right of parishioner to 5.51, 7.113
  theology of 7.106
  unconsecrated ground, in 5.51
  See also cemetery; exhumation; funeral; grave; headstone
burial ground
  closure of 7.95
  disused
    building on 7.93
    open space, as 7.94
    transfer to local authority 7.94, 7.95
  maintenance of closed 7.95

Cambridge canon law faculty
  abolished 1.14
candles: legality 7.124
canon (cathedral)
  College of Canons, member of 8.13
  lay 8.25
  honorary 8.25n
  meaning 8.13n
  minor 8.27
  non-residentiary
    appointment 8.25
    functions 8.25
  prebendary 8.25n
  residentiary
    appointment 8.20
    cathedral duties, engaged in 8.21

duties 8.22
incapacity 8.23, 8.24
number of 8.21
residence 8.22
retirement age 8.22
stipend 8.21
Canon (legislation)
  1603 collection 1.16–1.18
  1640 collection 1.17
  1964 and 1969 collection 1.18
  Bancroft's collection (1603) 1.16
  doctrine, concerning: reference to House of Bishops 2.24
  early collections 1.07–1.09
  ecumenical 3.99
  General Synod legislation by 1.28, 2.04
  Hertford, adopted at 1.08
  human rights and 1.29
  Measure, made under 1.28
  origins 1.107
  Royal Assent to 1.28
  subordinate legislation, as 1.29
  vires of unpromulged, questioning 1.31
canon law
  1533 Commission 1.12, 1.13, 1.16
  custom abrogating,
    pre-Reformation 1.15n
  dispensation 1.41
  meaning 1.02
  origins, pre-Reformation 1.11
  sources 1.11
canonical obedience
  duty of 4.37
  oath of 4.07
care of places of worship 7.130–7.132
case law and precedent 1.33, 1.34
catechism 5.15
cathedra 8.04
cathedral
  administrator
    appointment of 8.26
    Chapter, as member of 8.09
  alteration to
    application for approval 8.42
    categories reserved for Commission approval 8.42
    Cathedrals Fabric Commission approval 8.42, 8.44, 8.45
    Commission of Review powers 8.45
    enforcement of provisions 8.49–8.54
    fabric advisory committee approval 8.41–8.43
    legislation 8.03
    principles governing 8.46

Index

cathedral (cont.)
  alteration to (cont.)
    register of applications 8.47
    restrictions on 8.36
  architect
    appointment of 8.26
    inspections and reports by 8.31, 8.35
  auditor, appointment of 8.26
  bishop
    as seat of 8.04
    visitation by 8.16
    visitor, as 8.15
  budget
    Chapter's functions 8.11
    Council's functions 8.07
    dean's functions 8.10
  canon see canon (cathedral)
  Cathedrals Measure 1999 commencement 8.05
  Chapter see Chapter (cathedral)
  Church Representation Rules, application of 8.02
  College of Canons
    composition 8.13
    constitutional requirements 8.05
    functions 8.14
    provision for 8.05
  community
    meaning 8.28
    roll 8.28
  constitution
    amendment 8.15
    drawing up 8.01
    revising 8.08, 8.11
  corporate body, provision for 8.05
  Council
    composition 8.06
    constitution, revision of 8.08
    constitutional requirements 8.05, 8.06
    duties and functions 8.07
    meetings 8.06
    provision for 8.05
    statutes, revision of 8.08
    term of office 8.06
    transitional 8.05n
  dean and chapter 8.02
  dignitaries
    incapacity of 8.23, 8.24
    meaning 8.23
  dignity in, creation etc of 8.21
  disciplinary proceedings against clergy 6.17
  duties: meaning 8.21n
  evening prayer in 5.09
  fabric advisory committee see fabric advisory committee

  funds, restrictions on use of 8.30
  Gibraltar in Europe, in diocese of 8.01n
  holy communion in 8.32
  inspections and reports by architect 8.31, 8.35
  Isle of Man, in 8.01n
  land surrounding, plan of 8.31
  legislation 8.01
  maintenance of 8.11
  ministry in 8.32–8.34
  morning prayer in 5.09
  music, supervision of 8.26
  new foundation, of 8.02n
  old foundation, of 8.02n
  organist 8.26
  parish church 8.02
  parochial status, ending 8.02n
  plan of land surrounding 8.31
  precinct, delineation of 8.31
  property vested in 8.29
  provost 8.18n
  residence
    allocation of 8.31
    disposal of 8.29
  sale of object vested in 8.36
  services
    daily offices 5.09, 8.32
    dean's consent to alterations 8.10
    ecumenical 8.33
  staff
    appointment 8.26
    payment 8.27
  statutes
    amendment 8.15
    drawing up 8.01
    revising 8.08, 8.11
  visitation of 8.16, 8.50–8.52, 8.54
  women priests in 8.34
  worship and mission, as centre of 8.05
Cathedral Community Committee 8.28
Cathedrals Commission 8.01n
Cathedrals Fabric Commission
  composition 8.40
  functions 8.40
  precinct, duty to identify 8.31
cemetery
  consecrated, and faculty jurisdiction 7.02
  restoration order over 7.02n
chancel repairs 3.78–3.81
chancellor, diocesan
  appointment 2.47
  bishop
    independent of 2.50
    official principal of, as 2.47
  Commissary-General ranks as 2.47

711

Index

chancellor, diocesan (*cont.*)
  communicant, must be 2.47
  consistory court, presides over 2.47
  deputy 2.49
  dual offices 2.48
  faculty
    jurisdiction 7.01, 7.47–7.55
    minor works, guidance as to 7.03
    urgent cases 7.14
  judicial oath 2.48
  oath of allegiance 2.48
  qualifications 2.47
  vacancy in see does not affect 2.48
  vacation of office 2.48
  vicar-general, as 2.52
Chancery Court of York
  appeal from consistory court 2.59
  binding effect of decisions 1.34
Channel Islands
  Church legislation in 2.09
  General Synod representation 2.16, 2.18n
  Winchester, in Diocese of 2.09
chapel
  forces 3.107
  hospital 3.106
  private
    chaplain in 3.105
    holy communion in 3.105, 5.23
  school 3.106
chaplain
  disciplinary proceedings against 6.17
  forces 2.16, 3.107
  private chapel, in 3.105
Chaplain General of Prisons
  General Synod, on 2.16
Chapter (cathedral)
  accounts 8.12
  architects, arranging inspection
    by 8.31, 8.35
  bishop, consulting 8.15
  borrowing powers 8.30
  chairman 8.09
  committees 8.10
  composition 8.09
  constitutional requirements 8.05
  contraventions by 8.50
  duties 8.11
  fabric advisory committee, report to 8.35
  finance committee 8.09
  housing, allocation of 8.31
  injunction against 8.52
  inspection of buildings 8.31, 8.35
  investment powers 8.30
  listed building consent application 8.48

  meetings 8.09, 8.11n
  patronage, exercise of 8.09
  property, acquiring etc 8.11, 8.29
  provision for 8.05
  reports 8.12
  restoration order against 8.52, 8.53
  women priests, resolution as to 8.34
chippings, removal from grave 7.115n
choirmaster, appointment of 3.65
Christ Church, Oxford, is *sui generis* 8.01n
church
  alteration to
    advice, preliminary 7.22
    consultation 7.22n
    information as to 7.20
    opinions as to, differing 7.19
    plans and drawings 7.21, 7.24
    why? how? and when? 7.20
  bells
    nuisance, as 3.51n
    provision of 7.123
    ringing of 3.51
  collections in 3.28
  consecrated, faculty jurisdiction applies 7.02
  demolition of *see* **demolition of church**
  disturbance in 3.51
  electoral roll *see* **church electoral roll**
  fabric
    annual report on 3.54
    inspection 3.54
    PCC responsibility 3.27
  freehold vests in incumbent 3.55, 7.118
  inspection
    fabric, of 3.54
    qualified person, by 7/17
    quinquennial 3.82
  insurance 3.55
  keys, incumbent as custodian of 3.55
  lease of 7.120
  licence for secular use of 7.118, 7.119
  listed *see* **listed building**
  mission, as local centre of 7.04
  movables, faculty relating to 7.123, 7.124
  order and decency in 3.49
  quinquennial inspection 3.82
  rate, power to raise voluntary 3.28
  re-ordering *see* **re-ordering**
  riotous etc behaviour in 3.52
  seating in 3.50, 7.125
  secular use of
    licence for 7.118, 7.119
    principles 7.118
  sharing of buildings 3.95–3.98
  worship, as local centre of 7.04

Index

Church and State, Archbishops' Committee
  on (1916) 2.02
Church Commissioners
  annual general meeting 2.41
  Archbishops' Council, payments to 2.42
  Assets Committee 2.43
  Audit Committee 2.43
  Board of Governors 2.41
  body corporate, as 2.38
  cathedral
    staff, paying 8.27
    transfer of property 8.29
  composition 2.39
  functions 2.40
  general fund 2.44
  investment policy 2.45
  pastoral schemes and orders 3.87,
    3.91–3.93, 4.25
church electoral roll
  appeal 3.06
  application for entry of name on 3.04
  new roll every six years 3.06
  officer 3.05
  qualification for inclusion 3.04
  removal of name from 3.05
  revision, annual 3.06
  self-certification? 3.04n
Church Estates Commissioner
  appointment 2.38n
  Church Commissioners, as 2.39
  General Synod, on 2.16, 2.19
  Second, as MP 1.21, 2.39n
Church in Wales
  Anglican Communion, within 2.01
  deposition, reversibility of 6.80
  ecclesiastical exemption applies to 7.06
  sharing of church buildings 3.95
Church of England
  Anglican Communion, and 2.01
  Church Assembly of (1919) 2.04
  deanery synod *see* **deanery synod**
  dioceses 2.10
  diocesan synod *see* **diocesan synod**
  doctrine *see* **doctrine**
  early Church 1.07
  ecclesiastical exemption applies to 7.06
  entity, not a legal 1.01
  establishment 1.19–1.21, 2.02
  General Synod of *see* **General Synod**
  historical development 1.06–1.18
  law *see* **ecclesiastical law**
  legislation 1.22–1.32, 2.02, 2.03
  mission of 1.19
  National Assembly of (1919) 2.04

orders of bishops, priests and deacons 4.01
  papal authority, abolition of 1.19
  provinces of 2.01, 2.10
  religious organisation, essentially a 1.19
  State, relationship with 1.01, 1.19
  Supreme Governor of 1.19
  Supreme Head of 1.12
  status 1.01, 1.19, 2.38
  synodical government 2.10
churchwarden
  access to church 3.55
  admission to office 3.40
  appointed by minister 3.36
  bishop
    powers of 3.46
    relations with 3.49
  casual vacancy 3.39, 3.41
  consent to serve 3.35
  customs as to 3.44, 3.45
  deputy 3.57, 3.58
  disciplinary complaint by 6.17
  election 3.35, 3.38
  fabric, annual inspection of 3.54
  faculty, duty to obtain 3.55, 7.01, 7.02
  furnishings, owner of church 3.53, 3.82, 7.103
  holy communion, provides bread and wine
    for 3.53, 5.23
  inventory, compiles 3.54
  laity, represents 3.49, 7.68
  meeting to choose 3.35, 3.37, 3.38
  minister's say in choice of 3.36
  minor works not requiring faculty, advice as
    to 7.03
  misconduct of 3.47
  mission, participation in 3.49
  modern role 3.32
  number of 3.35, 3.44
  order and decency, maintaining 3.49, 3.51, 3.52
  ornaments, owner of church 3.53, 3.82, 7.103
  parishioners' views, evidence as to 7.68
  parochial church council
    inherited churchwardens' old
      powers 3.27, 3.48
    member of 3.12, 3.13, 3.48
  pews, allocation of 7.125
  powers and duties 3.48–3.56
  qualifications 3.34
  quasi-corporation, as 3.48, 3.53
  resignation 3.42
  riotous etc behaviour, curbing 3.52
  seating in church, and 3.50, 7.125
  sequestrator, as 3.56, 4.26
  sidesmen assist 3.51
  statement of needs, preparing 7.23

713

Index

churchwarden (*cont.*)
  term of office 3.41
  terrier, compiles 3.54
  vacancy in benefice, during 3.56
  vacation of office 3.43
  visitation, and 3.49, 4.37

churchyard
  closed, no right to burial in 5.51n
  consecrated: faculty jurisdiction 7.02
  consecration, effect of 7.92
  disturbance in 3.51
  easement over 7.94
  maintained by PCC 3.27, 7.96
  minor works in: archdeacon's jurisdiction 7.43
  open, effect of 7.93
  order and decency in 3.49
  PCC responsibility for 3.27, 7.96
  regulations 7.115
  re-ordering 7.96
  right of way over 7.94
  riotous etc behaviour in 3.52
  transferred to local authority 7.94, 7.95
  unconsecrated, subject to faculty jurisdiction 7.92
  See also **burial ground**

Churchyards Handbook 7.96

City of London guild churches 3.108

civil partnership
  clergy in 4.05
  undermining marriage? 5.49n

Clementines of Clement V (1317) 1.09n

clergy
  absence from benefice 4.16
  arrest, privilege from 4.14
  beneficed 4.17–4.28
  civil partnership, in 4.05
  collation 4.19n, 4.27
  deacon
    functions 4.11, 4.12
    ordination 4.06
  devotion to service of God 4.13
  disabilities 4.05
  discipline *see* **clergy discipline**
  divorced 4.05
  dress 4.15, 5.22
  employees, as 4.42
  evening prayer, reading 4.15, 4.16
  holy communion, celebrating 4.15, 4.16, 5.22
  Houses of Parliament, in 4.14
  illegitimacy 4.05
  illness 4.53
  induction 4.28
  institution into spiritualities 4.19, 4.27
  jury service 4.14
  morning prayer, reading 4.15, 4.16
  occupations, other 4.13
  ordination *see* **ordination**
  overseas
    for service 4.09
    ordained 4.10
  permission to officiate 4.36
  political activities 4.14, 6.15
  priest
    functions 4.13–4.16
    ordination 4.06
  prohibition of exercise of orders 4.38
  qualification 4.04
  relinquishment of exercise of orders 4.38
  residence 4.16
  sick, visiting the 5.58
  trade, engaged in 4.13
  unbeneficed
    licence to officiate 4.29
    who are 4.29
  visitation of 4.37
  voting at elections 4.14
  widow etc, residence of 4.16
  See also **bishop; deacon; incumbent; minister**

clergy discipline
  conduct cases
    appeal
      adjournment 6.63
      bishop's views on penalty 6.64
      Court of Arches, to 6.58
      death of parties 6.64
      determination of 6.64, 6.65
      directions 6.62
      general 6.58
      evidence 6.62
      hearing 6.63
      notice of
        amendment 6.63
        contents 6.60
        delivery 6.60, 6.61
      rules for 6.59
      striking out 6.62
      time limits 6.61
      withdrawal of 6.63
    archbishop, proceedings against
      to whom complaint is made 6.20
    Vicar-General's court
      composition 6.10
      jurisdiction 6.12
    arrest, failure to disclose 6.14
    bishop, proceedings against
      to whom complaint is made 6.20

clergy discipline (*cont.*)
  conduct cases (*cont.*)
    bishop, proceedings against (*cont.*)
      Vicar-General's court
        composition 6.10
        jurisdiction 6.12
        who may institute 6.19
    cathedral clergy, against 7.17
    chaplains, against 6.17
    Clergy Discipline Commission
      chairman 6.04
      composition 6.04
      functions 6.05
    Code of Practice 6.02
    commencement of new system 6.02
    complaint
      answer by respondent 6.25
      bishop
        dismissal by 6.24
        options of 6.25, 6.27
        report to 6.24
      conditional deferment 6.27, 6.29, 6.30
      contents 6.18
      form 6.18
      no further action on 6.27, 6.28
      president of tribunals, reference to 6.28n
      reconciliation 6.31, 6.32
      registrar
        reference to 6.23
        scrutiny by 6.23
      to whom made 6.20
      who may make 6.17, 6.19, 6.20
      withdrawal of 6.21
    conduct unbecoming 6.14
    conviction, failure to disclose 6.14
    costs 6.67, 6.68
    criminal proceedings contemplated
      6.26, 6.37
    designated officer 6.11
    inefficiency 6.13
    investigation, formal
      contempt 6.46
      death of respondent 6.46
      designated officer, reference to 6.35
      directions for 6.34
      disciplinary tribunal
        conduct of 6.39
        composition 6.09
        evidence 6.41, 6.42
        reference to 6.36
        witnesses 6.41
      documents, delivery of 6.45
      hearing
        adjournment 6.42
        admission before or at 6.44
        directions, for 6.40
        date and place 6.42
        private or public 6.43
        timetable 6.42
      majority decision 6.45
      president of tribunals, reference to 6.36
      proof, standard of 6.45
      time, extension of 6.46
    laws ecclesiastical
      act contravening 6.13
      failure to obey 6.13
      meaning 6.13n
    legal aid, ecclesiastical 6.67
    legislation 6.01, 6.02
    matrimonial proceedings contemplated 6.26
    ministers with provincial licences,
      against 6.17
    minor complaints 6.13n
    misconduct
      allegation of 6.13
      what amounts to 6.13, 6.13n, 6.14
    neglect of duties 6.13
    new system 6.01
    other disciplinary proceedings
      contemplated 6.26
    penalty
      bishop's views on appropriate 6.47
      conditional discharge 6.49, 6.53
      consent, by 6.33, 6.34, 6.51
      Guidance on 6.50, 6.53
      injunction 6.48, 6.51–6.53
      licence, revocation of 6.48, 6.52
      nullification of 6.55
      office, removal from 6.48, 6.52–6.54
      pardon 6.57
      prohibition 6.48, 6.51–6.54
      public pronouncement of 6.47
      range of 6.48
      rebuke 6.48, 6.51–6.53
      removal of prohibition 6.56
      secular court proceedings, after 6.54
    political acts, lawful, not misconduct
      4.14, 6.15
    principle, statement of 6.01
    purpose of discipline 6.02
    rules 6.02, 6.03
    suspended priest interfering 6.14
    suspension during proceedings
      appeal against 6.37
      arrangements for ministry during 6.38
      imposition of 6.37
      revocation of 6.37, 6.38
    time limits 6.16

Index

clergy discipline (cont.)
  conduct cases (cont.)
    tribunals
      disciplinary
        composition 6.09
        constitution 6.09
        jurisdiction 6.12
        representations as to membership 609n
      president of 6.06
      provincial panels 6.08
      registrar of 2.56, 6.07
      unauthorised function, performing 6.14
      Under Authority 6.01
      Vicar-General's court
        composition 6.10
        jurisdiction 6.12
  doctrinal question, what is 6.15
  doctrine, ritual or ceremonial, offences involving
    archbishop, by 6.74, 6.78, 6.79
    bishop, by 6.74, 6.77–6.69
    censure
      deposition, reversibility of 6.80
      deprivation 6.77–6.79
      inhibition 6.77, 6.78
      monition 6.76, 6.77
      readmission after suspension etc 6.78
      rebuke 6.77
      suspension 6.77, 6.78
      unfrocking 6.79
    Commission of Review
      appeal to 6.76
      composition of 6.76
    complaint trivial, determination that 6.75
    Court of Ecclesiastical Causes Reserved
      appeal to Commission of Review 6.76
      censure imposed by 6.76, 6.77
      composition 6.76
      Privy Council decisions don't bind 6.76
      reference to 6.75
    extenuating circumstances, finding of 6.75
    further proceedings undesirable, finding
      that 6.75
    inquiry
      committee conducting 6.75
      reference for 6.74, 6.75
    investigation 6.74
    new system, proposed 6.73
    no case to answer, finding that 6.75
    pardon 6.80
code of practice
  clergy discipline 6.02
  patronage 4.21
  quasi-legislation, as 1.35
collation 419n, 427

collections, church 3.28, 5.23
college, holy communion in 5.23, 5.24
College of Canons *see* cathedral
Commissary Court
  Canterbury, for 2.47
  consistory court, ranks as 2.47
Commissary-General
  Canterbury, for 2.47
  chancellor, ranks as 2.47
Commission of Review
  cathedral alterations, considering 8.48
  discipline appeal to 6.76
Common Worship, approval of 5.03
Commonwealth War Graves Commission
  notice to, of works affecting war grave 7.47, 7.96
communion *see* holy communion
conduct cases *see* clergy discipline
confession
  disclosure of 5.62
  private 5.61
confirmation
  bishop
    by 4.60, 5.16
    decides form of service 5.05n
  name, change of 5.17
  origin of rite 5.16
  preparation 4.16, 5.16
  procedure 5.16
  register 5.16, 5.17
  seeking out candidates 5.16
consecration
  bishop, by 7.02
  cremated remains, of ground for 5.51
  dedication contrasted 7.02
  effect of 7.92
  meaning 7.02
  removal of legal effects of 7.02n
  validity of 5.01
consistory court
  appeal from 2.59
  binding effect of decisions 1.34
  bishop, as court of 2.47
  chancellor *see* chancellor, diocesan
  Commissary Court ranks as 2.47
  contempt of 7.76
  criminal jurisdiction abolished 2.58
  faculty jurisdiction, exercises 7.01
  injunction to restrain illegal acts 7.84
  judgment collection in Middle Temple
    library 7.90n
  planning issues, will not re-litigate 7.66
  registrar 2.54, 2.55
  restoration order to restore status quo 7.84
  trees, jurisdiction over 7.128

Index

contempt of consistory court 7.76
continuing Episcopal oversight 1.34n
conventional district 3.02n
Convocations
    Canons made by 1.28, 2.04
    powers 1.28n
    service, may approve forms of 5.07, 5.08
coronation service 5.60
corporal punishment, ban on 1.48
corpus juris canonici 1.09
costs in faculty proceedings
    amount of 7.82
    archdeacon
        costs of 7.10
        expenses of 7.81
        may not award 7.79
    court fees 7.80
    injunction, of 7.89
    legal expenses 7.80
    objection unreasonable, where 7.80
    recovery of 7.82
    restoration order, of 7.89
    security for 7.79
Council for British Archaeology
    national amenity society, as 7.18
Council for the Care of Churches
    advice desirable, notice of petition
        where 7.52
    consultation with 7.51
    demolition of church
        must be heard on 7.97, 7.99
        notice of petition to 7.50, 7.98
    hearing, direction to appear at 7.65
    historic articles etc, notice of petition
        concerning 7.51
    list of places of worship
        application for inclusion in 7.08
        faculty jurisdiction applies 7.08, 7.130
        modification to procedure 7.131, 7.132
Court of Arches
    binding effect of decisions 1.34
    consistory court, appeal from 2.59
    disciplinary appeal to 2.60, 6.58
    faculty appeal to
        evidence on, further 7.78
        right of appeal 2.59, 7.77
        leave for 7.78
        rules 7.77, 7.78
        written representations, on 7.78
    judgment, usually gives one 1.34n
Court of Ecclesiastical Causes Reserved
    appellate jurisdiction 2.59
    censure imposed by 6.76, 6.77
    Commission of Review, appeal to 6.76

    composition on discipline appeal 6.76
    faculty appeals to 2.59, 7.77
    Privy Council decisions don't bind 6.76
    reference to, as to discipline 6.75
Court of Faculties
    functions 2.61
    nature of 2.61
creed
    ability to say 5.16
    standing to say 5.11
cremation *see* **funeral**
curate, assistant 4.30, 4.31
cure of souls 3.02, 4.07, 4.17
custom as source of law 1.38, 1.39

DAC *see* **diocesan advisory committee**
deacon
    baptism by 4.11, 5.13
    functions 4.11, 4.12
    marriage by 5.44
    ordination 4.06
    See also **clergy**
deaconess 3.71
dean
    Arches, of *see* **Dean of the Arches**
    area: the same as rural dean 4.53
    cathedral, of *see* **dean of cathedral**
    rural *see* **rural dean**
dean of cathedral
    absence of, decisions taken in 8.10
    appointment 8.18
    budget functions 8.10
    Chapter, member and chairman of 8.09
    College of Canons, member of 8.13
    Council, member of 8.06
    diocesan synod, member of 8.18
    duties 8.17, 8.18
    incapacity of 8.19, 8.23, 8.24
    retirement age 8.19
    services, consent to alterations 8.10
    status 8.17
    stipend 8.17
    vacancy in office 8.19
Dean of the Arches
    appellate jurisdiction 2.59
    Auditor: same person 2.59
    Court of Arches, presides over 2.59
    General Synod, on 2.16, 2.19
deanery
    meaning 2.33
    pastoral order affecting 3.89
deanery synod
    composition 2.34
    doctrine, may not declare 5.01

Index

deanery synod (*cont.*)
  election
    diocesan synod, to 2.36
    General Synod, to 2.36
    to 3.10
  electoral college, as 2.36
  establishment 2.33
  functions 2.35
  meetings 2.37
  member on PCC 3.12
  officers 2.37
  procedure 2.37
  purpose 2.35
  standing committee 2.37
decoration of fabric
  archdeacon's jurisdiction 7.43
decretals 1.07–1.09
Decretals of Gregory IX (1234) 1.09n
Decretum of Gratian (c 1140) 1.09
dedication
  consecration, contrasted with 7.02
defamation
  jurisdiction moved to secular courts 2.46n
demolition of church
  conservation area, in 7.47
  emergency, in 7.101
  faculty
    bishop's consent 7.100
    evidence 7.99, 7.100
    grounds for 7.97
    listed building 7.100, 7.101
    notice of application 7.98, 7.100
    petition for
      newspaper advertisement of 7.49
    other notices of 7.50
      special notification 7.47
    objections 7.98
    procedure 7.98–7.100
    requires 7.97
  recording before 7.100
diocesan advisory committee (DAC)
  advice by 7.17, 7.22, 7.25, 7.25n
  archdeacon on 7.09, 7.16
  certificate of 7.32, 7.33
  chairman and secretary 7.16
  composition 7.16
  constitution 7.16n
  consultation with 7.24
  exhumation, not concerned with 7.104
  expenses 7.16
  functions 2.32, 7.17
  hearing, direction to appear at 7.65
  meetings 7.17
  name 7.16n
  plans etc submitted to 7.25
  works, not recommending 7.32, 7.45
diocesan board of education
  functions 2.32
diocesan board of finance
  functions 2.32
  incumbent's fees paid to 3.84
  sharing agreement, party to 3.96
diocesan board of patronage
  functions 2.32
diocesan parsonages board
  functions 2.32
  parsonage, consent to parting with 3.83
diocesan pastoral committee
  functions 2.32
  pastoral schemes and orders, and 3.86, 3.87
  sharing agreement, and 3.96
  suspension of presentation, consent to 4.23
diocesan redundant churches uses committee
  functions 2.32
diocesan synod
  bishop's council 2.28
  boards and committees 2.32
  composition 2.26
  dean of cathedral as member 8.18
  doctrine, may not declare 5.01
  functions 2.2.7, 2.28, 2.30
  member on PCC 3.12
  president 4.61
  procedure 2.31
  purpose 2.27
  standing committee 2.28
  voting 2.31
diocese
  areas, divided into 4.65
Dionysiana 1.08
disability discrimination
  access audit 7.102
  re-ordering, effect on 7.102
district church council 3.16, 3.17
divorce, marriage after 5.35, 5.49, 5.50
Doctors' Commons 1.14
doctrine
  cases involving *see* **clergy discipline**
  deanery synod may not declare 5.01
  diocesan synod may not declare 5.01
  faculty petition invoking 7.45, 7.77
  House of Bishops, referred to 2.24
  marriage, of, minister explaining 5.33
  Measure may change 2.05
  PCC may not declare 5.01
  safeguarding sound 7.123
  secular courts may not declare 1.44, 5.01

Index

doctrine (*cont.*)
  where found 5.01
  young people to be instructed in 5.15
dress
  communion celebrant, of 5.22
  wearing of religious 1.48–1.50

easement over churchyard 7.94
Easter offerings 3.84
ecclesiastical building
  listed building consent, exempt from 7.05
Ecclesiastical Commissioners
  functions transferred to Church Commissioners 2.38
Ecclesiastical Committee of Parliament 2.07, 2.08
ecclesiastical court
  archdeacon's court 2.57
  Commissary Court 2.47
  Court of Faculties 2.61
  See also Chancery Court of York; Commission of Review; consistory court; Court of Arches; Court of Ecclesiastical Causes Reserved; vicar-general
ecclesiastical exemption
  cathedral, applies to 7.02n, 8.03n
  Churches benefiting from 7.06
  extent of 7.06–7.08
  nature of 7.05
  peculiar, applies to 7.08
  planning permission still needed 7.66
  religious community, applies to 7.08
ecclesiastical law
  assists people to follow Christ 1.04
  Canon *see* **Canon (legislation)**
  case law 1.33
  Church of England, applicable to 1.02
  codes of practice 1.35
  custom 1.38, 1.39
  law of England, part of 1.02
  meaning 1.02
  medieval period, in 1.08–1.11
  Measure *see* **Measure**
  post-Reformation 1.16–1.18
  purpose of 1.03
  quasi-legislation 1.35
  Reformation, at 1.12–1.15
  Scripture, in 1.07
  secondary legislation 1.32
  sources of 1.22
ecclesiastical purposes
  buildings used for: exempt from listed building consent 7.05

ecumenical
  Canons 3.99
  cathedral services 8.33
  relations
    local ecumenical project 3.101, 3.102
    services shared with other Churches 3.99, 3.100
electoral roll *see* church electoral roll
Enabling Act (1919) 2.04
English Heritage
  consultation with 7.27, 7.28, 7.31
  demolition, notice of petition for 7.50
  national amenity society, as 7.18
  special notification of faculty petition 7.47
establishment of Church of England 1.19–1.21, 2.02
eucharist *see* holy communion
Europe, Diocese of *see* Gibraltar in Europe, Diocese of
evening prayer
  cathedral, in 5.09
  clergy to read daily 4.15, 4.16, 5.09, 5.57
  dispensing with 5.10
  lay worker may read 3.73
  reader may read 3.70
excommunicated person's funeral 5.52
excommunication, lesser 5.26
exhumation
  faculty for
    delay in seeking 7.107
    grave, difficulty in visiting 7.107
    guidelines 7.105–7.107
    mistake 7.107
    necessity for 7.104
    notice of petition for 7.40
  Home Office licence for 7.104
  human rights implications 7.111
  research, for purposes of 7.108–7.110
  unlawful 7.104
exorcism 5.59
extended episcopal oversight 4.63
Extravagantes Communes (by 1484) 1.09n
Extravagantes of John XXII (1325) 1.09n

fabric advisory committee
  approval to proposal 8.41–8.43
  composition 8.38
  duties 8.37
  establishment of 8.37
  expenses 8.38
  meetings 8.38
  report by Chapter to 8.35
faculty
  advice on proposals
    formal 7.25
    preliminary 7.22

Index

faculty (*cont.*)
  amendment of 7.75
  appeal
    Court of Arches, to 2.59, 7.77
    Court of Ecclesiastical Causes Reserved, to 2.59, 7.77
    doctrine, on matters of 2.59, 7.77
    rules for 7.77
  archdeacon
    appearing in proceedings 7.10
    costs
      may not award 7.79
      of 7.10, 7.81
    granted by 7.09, 7.46
    interested person, as 7.09
    jurisdiction 7.43–7.46
    minor works, powers as to, repealed 7.13
    role of 7.09–7.15
    supervision of works by 7.09
    unopposed petition 7.43
  bishop hearing case 2.51
  burial ground transfer to local authority, for 7.94
  chancellor
    addresses to 7.73
    advice from DAC to 7.25n
    confirmatory faculty referred to 7.45
    jurisdiction 7.47–7.55
    petition referred to 7.45
  church, addition etc to 7.122
  churchwardens' duties 3.55, 7.01, 7.02
  churchyard re-ordering, for 7.96
  conditions attached to 7.74
  confirmatory 7.01, 7.45, 7.83
  consultation 7.22n, 7.24, 7.27–7.31
  costs *see* **costs in faculty proceedings**
  diocesan advisory committee
    advice
      applicants, to 7.22, 7.25
      chancellor, to 7.25n
    certificate of 7.32, 7.33
    consultation with 7.24
    failure to recommend 7.32, 7.45
    plans etc submitted to 7.25
    statements of needs etc submitted to 7.26
  directions
    evidence, as to 7.61
    hearing, for 7.63
    making of 7.60, 7.62
    nature of 7.61
    notice of petition, as to 7.39
    service of documents, as to 7.67
    witness, for attendance of 7.65
  doctrine, petition invoking 7.45
  duty to obtain 7.01, 7.02

evidence
  affidavit 7.64
  cross-examination 7.64
  directions as to 7.61
  examiner, before 7.64
  oral 7.64
  written statements 7.64
exhumation, for *see* **exhumation**
experts
  exchange of reports 7.61
  number of 7.61
  form 7.73
gravespace, for reservation of 7.114
headstone, relating to 7.115
hearing
  adjournment 7.63
  addresses to chancellor 7.73
  clerk of the court 7.63
  directions for 7.63
  notice of 7.63
  photographing or sketching at 7.63
  place for 7.63
information as to proposals 7.20
interest, who has sufficient 7.34, 7.53
judgment: *ex tempore* or reserved 7.73
jurisdiction
  archdeacon's 7.43–7.46
  cemetery, over consecrated 7.02, 7.92
  chancellor's 7.01, 7.47–7.55
  churchyard, over 7.02, 7.92
  consistory court exercises 7.01
  ecclesiastical exemption, over buildings within 7.08
  places of worship, over 7.08, 7.130
  unconsecrated land surrounding church, over 7.02
lease of church, for 7.120
licence for use of church, for 7.118, 7.119
meaning 7.01
memorial in church, for 7.121
minister's duty to obtain 7.01, 7.02
minor works
  archdeacon's powers repealed 7.13
  not requiring 7.03
movables, relating to 7.123, 7.124
national amenity societies, interest of 7.18
notice of petition
  certificate of publication 7.42
  directions as to 7.39
  dispensing with 7.40, 7.41
  display of 7.38
  exhumation, in case of 7.40
  form 7.37
  newspaper, in 7.49

Index

faculty (*cont.*)
  objection
    answer to, petitioner's 7.57
    form for written particulars 7.55
    interested person, by 7.53
    letter of 7.53
    notice of 7.48
    procedure 7.54, 7.55
    representative parties 7.61
    time for 7.54
    unreasonable: costs liability 7.80
    who may make 7.53
  opinions on, differing 7.19
  parishioners' views 7.19, 7.68
  petition
    chancellor, referred to 7.45
    contents 7.35
    DAC not recommending 7.32, 7.45
    doctrine, invoking 7.45
    form 7.35
    notice of *see* notice of petition *above*
    register of 7.17
    special notification 7.47
    submission of 7.35
    unopposed
      archdeacon's jurisdiction 7.43
      grant of faculty 7.56
    who may submit 7.34
  pews, to remove 7.125
  plans and drawings 7.21, 7.24, 7.36
  proof
    Bishopsgate questions 7.70, 7.71
    burden lies on petitioner 7.68
    listed building, in case of 7.70
    standard of 7.69
  registrar
    directions to petitioner by 7.39
    issues faculty 7.73
    petition submitted to 7.35
  re-ordering
    church, of 7.126, 7.127
    churchyard, of 7.96
  reports
    copied to parties 7.61
    experts', exchange of 7.61
    representative objectors 7.61
  safe place, for article's retention in 7.12
  sale of church property, for 7.103
  security for costs 7.79
  service of documents 7.67
  statement
    needs, of 7.23, 7.26
    significance, of 7.23, 7.26
  trees, relating to 7.129

  urgent matter 7.14
  why? how? and when? 7.20
  windows, for stained glass 7.122
  works
    carried out without 7.01, 7.83
    certificate of completion of 7.73
    supervised by archdeacon 7.09
    time limit for completion 7.74
  written representations, disposal by
    determination of case 7.59
    inspection of church 7.59
    order for 7.58
    revocation of order 7.59
    statements by parties 7.58
Faith in the Countryside (1990) 7.118
family services discouraged 5.57
flying bishop 4.63
font
  baptism in 5.14
  number of 7.112
  position of 5.14, 7.112
  provision of 5.14, 7.112
Foxe, code by John (1571) 1.13n
funeral
  another parish, in 4.17
  authorized rite to be used 5.52
  certificate, after registrar's 5.54
  coroner's order, after 5.54
  cremation
    ashes, disposal of 5.56
    lawful 5.55
    who may conduct service 5.55
  deacon, by 4.12
  excommunicated person, of 5.52
  lay worker, by 3.73, 5.53
  minister's duty 5.52
  reader, by 3.70, 5.53
  suicide, after 5.52
  who may conduct 5.52, 5.53
  See also **burial**

General Synod
  baptism service, changes to 2.25
  bishops in 2.15
  Canons promulged by 1.28, 2.04, 2.23
  chairman 2.22
  Church Assembly, reconstituted from 2.04
  Common Worship approved by 5.03
  constitution 2.20–2.22
  deliberative body, as 2.15
  doctrine, consideration of 2.24
  executive functions, no 2.21
  Gibraltar in Europe representation 2.18
  holy communion services, changes to 2.25

Index

General Synod (*cont.*)
  House of Bishops
    matters referred to 2.24
    membership 2.15
    statements by 1.35
  House of Clergy membership
    Canterbury 2.16
    York 2.17
  House of Laity
    elections 2.18
    membership 2.18, 2.19
  judicial functions, no 2.21
  Legislative Committee 2.07
  legislative functions 2.15, 2.21
  Measures passed by 1.25, 2.23
  meetings 2.22
  Ordinal, changes to 2.25
  PCC, synod member on 3.12
  President 2.20
  service, approval of forms of 5.03, 5.04
  Sodor and Man representation 2.18
  standing committee functions passed to Archbishops' Council 2.21
  standing orders 2.22
  voting 2.23
Georgian Group
  national amenity society, as 7.18
Gibraltar in Europe, Diocese of
  Canterbury, in Province of 2.01n, 2.10n
  cathedrals in 8.01n
  General Synod representation 2.18
  statute, a creature of 2.09
glebe land vests in diocese 3.84
godparents 5.13
government ministers
  legislating for the Church 1.24, 2.06
Gratian's *Decretum* (c 1140) 1.09
grave
  chippings, removal of 7.115n
  headstone *see* **headstone**
  kerbs, removal of 7.115n
  mistake as to: exhumation? 7.107
  visiting, difficulty in: exhumation? 7.107
  war: special notification of petition 7.47
gravespace, reservation of: faculty 7.114
gravestone *see* **headstone**
group council 3.20
group ministry 4.47, 4.50, 4.51
guild church 3.108

headstone
  churchyard regulations 7.115
  faculty relating to 7.115
  guidelines 7.115

  inscription on 7.116
  ownership 7.96, 7.96n
  permission for 7.115
  photograph on 7.115
  relocation of 7.96
Henry VIII: Supreme Head of Church 1.12
Hertford, council of (673) 1.08
high judicial office: meaning 2.47n
historic etc interest, article in church of
  consultation on 7.27, 7.33
  newspaper notice of petition 7.49
  notice to Council for the Care of Churches 7.51
  special notification of petition 7.47
holy communion
  baptism a condition precedent 5.18
  bread and wine
    both to be taken 5.20
    churchwardens provide 3.53, 5.23
    nature of 5.23
  cathedral, in 5.24, 8.32
  central to Anglican worship 5.18
  chapel, in private 5.23
  children admitted to 5.18n
  conditions precedent to 5.18
  confirmation a condition precedent 5.18
  deacon distributing 5.22
  dress of celebrant 5.22
  gospel at, standing for 5.11
  hospital, in 5.23
  lay worker distributing 3.73
  nature of 5.24
  notorious offenders and 5.25
  number of communicants 5.20
  offertory at 5.23
  parishioner's duty to communicate 5.24
  reader distributing 3.70
  reservation of *see* **reservation of the sacrament**
  school, in 5.23
  service, voting on changes to 2.25
  sick, to 5.27, 5.28
  sin, for those in grave and open 5.26
  transubstantiation and 5.19
  where celebrated 5.23
  who may be admitted to 5.18n
  who may celebrate 4.15, 4.16, 5.22
  who may distribute 3.70, 3.73, 522
  withholding 5.25, 5.26
holy matrimony *see* **marriage**
hospital, holy communion in 5.23
House of Bishops *see* **General Synod**
House of Clergy *see* **General Synod**
House of Commons
  clergy sitting in 4.14
  Measure, and passing of 2.08

Index

House of Commons (cont.)
  Second Church Estates Commissioner
    sitting in 1.21
House of Laity *see* General Synod
House of Lords
  bishops sitting in 1.21, 4.61
  clergy sitting in 4.14
  Measure, and passing of 2.08
human rights
  Canons and 1.29
  compatibility of Church legislation
    with 1.26, 1.27
  conscience, freedom of 1.46–1.49
  corporal punishment 1.48
  courts as public authorities 2.62
  dress, religious customs as to 1.48–1.50
  PCC, whether a public authority 1.19, 3.01n,
    3.22, 3.23
  relevant 1.26n
  religion, freedom of 1.43, 1.45–1.49
  secondary legislation and 1.32
  thought, freedom of 1.46–1.49

icon, legality of 7.124
incense, legality of 7.124n
incumbent
  benefice
    absence from 4.16, 4.41
    holder of, as 4.17
  carved likeness of, faculty for 7.122
  collation of 4.19n, 4.27
  corporation sole, as 4.17
  cure of souls, has 4.17
  expenses paid by PCC 3.84
  fees go to diocesan board of finance 3.84
  freehold vests in 3.76, 4.17, 7.118
  headstone, does not own 7.96
  incapacity
    inquiry into possible 4.40, 4.41
    leave of absence during 4.41
  induction of 4.28
  institution of 4.19, 4.27
  keys, as custodian of 3.55
  pastoral breakdown 3.26, 4.43–4.46
  retirement age 4.39
  See also clergy; minister
induction of incumbent 4.28
inhibition on vacation of benefice 4.45
injunction
  answer to application for 7.86
  application for 7.85
  cathedral Chapter, against 2.52, 8.52
  chancellor, by, of his own motion 7.88
  costs 7.89

  evidence 7.86
  faculty petition justifying issue of 7.45
  illegal acts, to restrain, 7.84
  order, making of 7.86
  rules for 7.84
  service of application for 7.85
  urgent cases 7.87
  variation etc 7.89
inquiry, articles of, on visitation 3.49, 4.37
insurance of church 3.27, 3.55
interregnum *see* benefice, vacancy in
inventory
  cathedral 8.35
  church 3.54
  churchwardens' duties 3.54
Isle of Man *see* Sodor and Man, Diocese of

Jerusalem, Synod of (c 48) 1.05n
Jew as patron 4.19n
judicial oath by chancellor 2.48
judicial review, courts subject to 2.62
jury service by clergy 4.14
jus commune 1.09, 1.10
jus divinum 1.03, 1.36
jus humanum 1.03
jus liturgicum 1.40, 5.07

kerbs, removal of 7.96, 7.115n
keys in custody of incumbent 3.55

laity
  involvement of 3.03
  meaning 4.01n
Lambeth
  Conference 2.01
  degree, grant of 2.61
laos, nature of 4.01
lawful authority: meaning 5.07n
lay worker
  admission of 3.72, 3.74
  functions 3.73
  funeral by 3.73, 5.53
  holy communion, distributing 3.73
  licensing 3.74
  PCC, on 3.12, 3.74
  sermon by 3.73, 5.11n
  services, at 3.73
lease over consecrated land 7.02n
Liber Extra of Gregory IX (1234) 1.09n
library, parish: sale of books 7.117
licence
  marriage *see* marriage
  use of church etc, for
    faculty for 7.118

licence *(cont.)*
  grant of 7.119
  principles 7.118
light, right to, over churchyard 7.94
listed building
  alteration to, petition for
    advice before works 7.23
    Bishopsgate questions 7.70, 7.71
      consultation 7.24, 7.27, 7.28, 7.31
    guidelines 7.23
      necessity
        meaning 7.71
        standard of 7.70
      newspaper notice of 7.49
    guidelines *(cont.)*
      plans and drawings 7.24
      special notification 7.47
      standard of proof 7.70
      statement of needs 7.23
      statement of significance 7.23
  consent
    cathedral Chapter application for 8.48
    ecclesiastical building exempt from 7.05
liturgy
  1928 Prayer Book 5.02
  Alternative Service Book 1980 5.02n
  alternatives to *Book of Common Prayer* 5.02
  Book of Common Prayer 5.02
  Common Worship 5.03
  experimental 5.07n
  uniformity of 5.02
  variation in 5.06–5.08
  See also **service, forms of**
local authority
  transfer of disused burial ground to 7.94, 7.95
local ecumenical project 3.101, 3.102
local planning authority
  advice on church alterations from 7.22
  consultation with 7.24, 7.30, 7.31
  demolition of church: notice to 7.50
  faculty petition
    objection by 7.53
    special notification to 7.47
log book of church events 3.54
London Gazette
  notice of petition to demolish church 7.50
Lord's Supper *see* **holy communion**
Lords Spiritual, roll of 1.21
Lyndwood's *Provinciale* (1430) 1.10

marriage
  age for 5.32
  banns
    publication of
      certificate of 5.38
      England and Wales, outside 5.39
      forces chapel, in 5.48
      form of 5.38
      lay worker, by 3.73
      place for 5.36
      reader, by 3.70
      ship, on 5.39
      time for 5.38
      who may publish 3.70, 3.73, 5.37
    register 5.37
    residence qualification 5.36
  blessing of, following civil marriage 5.31
  Church's support for 5.31
  civil, blessing following 5.31
  civil partnership undermining? 5.49n
  consent to, if under eighteen 5.32
  deacon, by 4.12
  divorced person, of 5.35, 5.49, 5.50
  gender, of person with acquired 5.35
  kindred and affinity, within prohibited degrees of 5.32
  licence
    common
      church or chapel, solemnised in 5.40
      discretionary 5.41
      duration of 5.42
      objection to 5.42
      procedure for obtaining 5.42
      residence qualification 5.40, 5.52
      who may grant 5.41
    special
      grant of 2.61, 5.41
      place of marriage under 5.40
  parishioner's right to 5.34
  permanence of 5.31, 5.50
  preliminaries to 5.32–5.35
  refusal of right to 5.34
  registers 5.46, 5.47
  Registrar-General, quarterly returns to 5.47
  registrar's certificate, on 5.43
  shared church building, in 3.98
  solemnisation of
    forces chapel, in 5.48
    impediment raised 5.33, 5.45
    music at 5.44
    registration of 5.46
    time for 5.44
    who may conduct 5.44
    witnesses 5.44
  unlawful: minister's liability 5.32
mass *see* **holy communion**
matrimonial jurisdiction
  transferred to secular courts 2.46n

Index

Measure
  Act of Parliament
    Measure has force of 1.25, 2.05
    Measure may amend or repeal 2.05
  Canon made under 1.28
  division of, into two 2.07
  doctrine, concerning, referred to House of Bishops 2,24
  draft, questioning *vires* of 1.30
  Ecclesiastical Committee of Parliament's report on 2.07, 2.08
  human rights compatibility 1.26, 1.27, 2.05
  legislation by 1.25
  Parliament cannot amend or vary 2.08
  primary legislation, as 1.26n, 1.30
  procedure for passing 2.07, 2.08
  Royal Assent 1.25, 2.08
  subject matter 2.05
  vires cannot be challenged 1.30, 2.05
memorial
  faculty for 7.121
  ownership of 7.121
  See also headstone
Methodist Church
  ecclesiastical exemption applies to 7.06
  sharing of church buildings 3.98
Middle Temple Library
  consistory court judgments collection 7.90n
minister
  burial, consent to 7.113
  faculty
    duty to obtain 7.01, 7.02
    minor works not requiring, advice as to 7.03
    statement of needs, preparing 7.23
  funeral, duty to conduct 5.52
  licence, revocation of
    appeal 4.34
    notice of 4.34
    reason for 4.33, 4.35
  music, and choice of 3.66
  organist, and appointment of 3.65
  service, forms of
    choosing 5.05
    varying 5.07, 5.08
  See also clergy; incumbent
misconduct
  meaning 4.33
  revocation of licence for 4.33
mission, church as local centre of 7.04
morning prayer
  clergy to read daily 4.15, 4.16, 5.09, 5.57
  dispensing with 5.10
  lay worker may read 3.73
  reader may read 3.70

movable, introduction or repair of 7.43
music
  cathedral, in 8.26
  choice of 3.66
  marriage, at 5.44

name, change of 5.17
national amenity society
  advice from 7.22
  consultation with 7.24, 7.27, 7.29, 7.31
  demolition of church, notice to 7.50
  functions 7.18
  interested party in faculty proceedings 7.18
  list 7.18
  objection to faculty by 7.53
  special notification of faculty petition 7.47
  what is 7.18
necessity
  circumstance, of 5.07
  meaning 7.72
  standard of proof, in 7.70
  test of 7.126
newspaper notice of faculty petition 7.49
Nicaea, Council of (325) 1.07
non-parochial units 3.103–3.108
notary public
  registration and regulation of 2.61
nuisance, bells as 3.51n

office
  certificate of provision of 4.07
  daily 5.57
  meaning 5.57
open space, disused burial ground as 7.94
Ordinal, voting on changes to 2.25
Ordinary
  bishop's jurisdiction as 4.60
  Sovereign as supreme 1.20
ordination
  age for 4.06
  bishop, by 4.09, 4.60
  certificate of provision of office 4.07
  deacon, as 4.06
  declaration of assent 4.07
  oath
    allegiance, of 4.07
    canonical obedience, of 4.07
  objection to 4.08
  overseas
    for service 4.09
    minister here, to 4.10
  place for 4.06
  priest, as 4.06
  religious order, member of 4.07

Index

ordination *(cont.)*
  time for 4.06
  university fellow etc 4.07
organist
  appointment of 3.65
  music, and choice of 3.66
  PCC agreement to appointment 3.29, 3.65
  written agreement with 3.66

papal authority, abolition of 1.19
parish
  church, role of 1.03n
  clerk, employment of 3.28, 3.61
  community of the faithful, as 1.04n
  nature of 3.01, 3.02
  origins 3.02
  property 3.76, 3.77
  share ('quota') 2.35, 3.85
  structure 3.01, 3.02
parishioner
  buried, right to be 5.51, 7.113
  churchwardens, at meeting to choose 3.37
  holy communion, duty to take 5.24
  marry, right to 5.34
  pastoral breakdown with clergy 4.43–4.46
  seat in church, right to 3.50
  views of 7.68
parochial church council (PCC)
  annual report 3.08
  auditor, appointment of 3.10
  Bible, views on version to be used 3.29
  bishop, representations to 3.28
  body corporate, as 3.21, 3.27
  budget, annual 3.28
  burial ground, closed: maintenance liability transferred to local authority 7.95
  burials, guidance as to 7.113
  chairman 3.15
  churches, and sharing of 3.29, 3.96
  churchmanship, view of 7.124n
  churchwardens' former powers devolved on 3.27, 3.48
  churchyard maintenance 3.27, 7.96
  collections, and church 3.28, 5.23
  composition 3.12
  consulted by clergy 4.16
  co-option to 3.12
  diocesan and deanery synods
    members on 3.12
    relations with 3.24
  disciplinary complaint by nominee 6.17
  doctrine, may not declare 5.01
  elections 3.10
  expenses, meeting incumbent's 3.84
  fabric of church, care of 3.27
  faculty
    decision as to 7.20
    objection by 7.53
  financial
    affairs, control of 3.27
    statement by 3.08, 3.09, 3.28
  functions 3.21–3.31
  general provisions as to 3.15
  General Synod members on 3.12
  headstone, does not own 7.96
  insurance responsibilities 3.27, 3.55
  joint 3.18, 4.48
  meetings
    archdeacon calling 7.11
    number of 3.15
  membership
    composition 3.12
    co-option 3.12
    number 3.12n
    term 3.13
  minister
    co-operation with 3.21
    disagreement with 3.25, 3.26
  minor works, faculty advice to 7.03
  minutes 3.15
  nature of 3.11
  organist, and appointment of 3.29, 3.65
  parish clerk, appoints 3.28, 3.61
  pastoral scheme consultation 3.29, 3.86
  property, acquiring interest in 3.82
  public authority, a? 1.19, 3.01n, 3.22, 3.23
  quorum 3.15
  resignation from 3.14
  sale of articles, consent to 7.103
  secretary 3.15, 3.64
  service, decision as to forms of 3.29, 5.05
  sexton, appoints 3.28, 3.61
  standing committee 3.15
  statement of needs, preparing 7.23
  status of 3.01n
  treasurer 3.15, 3.63
  trees, maintenance of 7.128n
  vacancy of benefice
    consultation 3.29, 4.19, 4.20
    notice of, to 4.19
    representatives, appointment of 4.20
  vestry, exercises former powers of 3.27
  vestures, consultation on 3.29
  voting 3.15
  women priests, resolutions as to 3.30, 3.31
parsonage
  incumbent, vests in 3.83
  upkeep by diocese 3.83

Index

pastoral breakdown 3.26, 4.43–4.46
pastoral order
   Church Commissioners' powers 3.87, 3.91, 3.93
   making of 3.93
   powers exercisable by 3,89
pastoral scheme
   appeal against 3.92
   Church Commissioners' powers 3.87, 3.91, 3.92
   consultations 3.29, 3.86
   contents 3.88
   making of 3.92
   proposals 3.87
patron
   Jew as 4.19n
   presentation of incumbent to bishop 4.19
   register 4.18
   Roman Catholic as 4.19n
   vacancy, notice of, to 4.19
patronage
   cathedral Chapter's exercise of 8.09
   code of practice 4.21
   meaning 4.18
   Sovereign's rights of 1.20
   transfer of right of 3.29, 4.18
peculiar
   bishop does not control 3.104
   ecclesiastical exemption applies to 7.08
   faculty jurisdiction and 3.104
   meaning 3.104
penance 5.61
penitentials 1.08
permission to officiate 4.36
pews
   allocation of 7.125
   provision of 7.125
   removal of 7.125
   right to 7.125
planning permission
   chancellor will not re-litigate issues of 7.66
   faculty petition, prior to 7.66
   necessity for 7.66
prebendary
   incapacity of 8.23, 8.24
   non-residentiary canon, as 8.25n
priest-in-charge 4.32
priest vicar 8.27
Privy Council
   binding force of decisions 1.34
   pastoral scheme appeal to 3.92
probate jurisdiction
   transferred to secular courts 2.46n
procession, legality of 7.124n
proctors of the clergy on General Synod 2.16, 2.17
provincial episcopal visitor 4.63

Provinciale of Lyndwood (1430) 1.10
provost of cathedral 8.18n
pulpit, provision of 7.123
pyx, legality of 7.124

quasi-corporation, churchwardens as 3.48, 3.53
quasi-legislation 1.35
Queen Anne's Bounty Governors
   Church Commissioners exercise functions of 2.38
quinquennial inspection 3.82
quota (parish share) 2.35, 3.85

rate, voluntary church 3.28
reader
   admission to office 3.67, 3.68
   banns, reading 3.70
   candidate 3.67
   functions 3.70
   funeral, conducting 3.70, 5.53
   holy communion, distributing 3.70
   licensing 3.68
   morning prayer etc, reading 3.70
   office of 3.67
   PCC, on 3.12, 3.68
   register 3.68
   revocation of licence 3.69
   sermon by 5.11n
   written agreement with 3.68
reading desk, provision of 7.123
rector: style 4.17
redundancy, declaration of 3.86
registrar
   diocesan
      appointment 2.54
      deputy 2.54
      functions 2.54, 2.55
   provincial
      appointment 2.53
      deputy 2.53
      functions 2.53, 2.55
      qualifications 2.53
   tribunals, of (clergy discipline) 2.56, 6.07
religious community
   ecclesiastical exemption applies to 7.08
   member of 3.75
religious liberty
   common law, recognised by 1.43
   human rights, and 1.43, 1.45
re-ordering
   Bishopsgate questions 7.70, 7.71, 7.126
   change should be reversible 7.126
   churchyard, of 7.96
   necessity, test of 7.126
   temporary, licence for 7.13, 7.127

Index

reservation of the sacrament
  bishop's sanction to 5.28
  legality of 5.27, 5.29, 5.30
  nature of 5.27
  reason for 5.27, 5.28
  superstition surrounding 5.28
restoration order
  answer to application for 7.86
  application for 7.85
  cathedral Chapter, against 2.52, 8.52, 8.53
  cemetery, over 7.02n
  chancellor, by, of his own motion 7.88
  costs 7.89
  evidence 7.86
  making of order 7.86
  rules for 7.84
  service of application for 7.85
  status quo, to restore 7.84
  time limit 7.86
  variation etc of 7.89
rights, faculty petition affecting legal 7.45
riotous behaviour, churchwarden and 3.52
Roman Catholic
  Church
    ecclesiastical exemption applies to 7.06
    sharing of church buildings 3.95
  patron, as 4.19n
Royal Assent
  Canon, to 1.28
  Measure, to 1.25, 2.08
Royal Commission on Historic Monuments
  recording church before demolition 7.100
rural dean
  appointment of 2.33, 4.53
  area dean, known as 2.33
  deanery synod chairman, as 2.37
  functions 4.53
  sequestrator, as 3.56, 4.26
  vacancy in benefice, and 3.56
ruri-decanal conference, dissolution of 2.33

sacrament house, legality of 7.124
safe place, removal of article to 7.12
sale
  books in parish library, of 7.117
  cathedral, of objects vested in 8.36
  church
    of: unlawful 7.118
    property, of 7.103
  consecrated land, of: unlawful 7.118
  timber, of, proceeds of 7.128
sanctuary bells, legality of 7.124
scheduled monument consent for cathedral 8.48

school, holy communion in 5.23
seats
  allocation of 3.50
  churchwardens' duties 3.50
  provision of 7.123
security for costs in faculty case 7.79
sequestrator
  suspension of presentation, on 4.26
  vacation of benefice, on 3.56
sermon
  deacon, by 4.11
  lay worker, by 3.73, 5.11n
  minister, by 4.13, 4.16
  reader, by 3.70, 5.11n
  Sunday, to be preached every 5.11
  who may preach 5.11n
service, form of
  1928 Prayer Book 5.02
  Alternative Service Book 1980 5.02n
  authorize, who may 5.07, 5.08
  Book of Common Prayer 5.02
  British Sign Language, in 5.03
  Common Worship 5.03
  departure from authorized 5.07
  family services 5.57
  General Synod approval 5.04
  minister's choice 5.05
  PCC consultation 3.29, 5.05
  translations 5.03
  variations not of substantial importance 5.07, 5.08
services
  baptism 5.12–5.15
  confession 5.61, 5.62
  confirmation 5.16, 5.17
  daily offices 5.57
  evening prayer 5.09
  exorcism 5.59
  funeral 5.51–5.56
  holy communion 5.09, 5.18–5.30
  litany 5.09
  marriage 5.31–5.50
  morning prayer 5.09
  music in, choice of 3.66
  posture at 5.11
  regular 5.09–5.11
  sick visiting 5.58
  special 5.60
Sext of Boniface VIII (1298) 1.09n
sexton, employment of 3.28, 3.61
sharing of church buildings
  agreement for
    consecrated building, for 3.98
    obligations under 3.97

Index

sharing of church buildings *(cont.)*
  agreement for *(cont.)*
    parties 3.96
    purpose 3.95
  Churches included 3.95
  ecclesiastical exemption applies to shared buildings 7.08
  faculty jurisdiction and 3.98
  marriage in shared building 3.98
  PCC involvement 3.29, 3.96
sick visiting 5.58
sidesman
  appointment 3.10, 3.60
  churchwarden, assists 3.51, 3.60
  duties 3.60
Society for the Protection of Ancient Buildings
  national amenity society, as 7.18
Sodor and Man, Diocese of
  cathedrals in 8.01n
  General Synod representation 2.18
  legislation in 2.09
Sovereign
  communicant, must be 1.20
  Ordinary, as supreme 1.20
  patronage rights 1.20
  Supreme Governor of Church of England 1.19
stained glass window, faculty for 7.122
stare decisis, doctrine of 1.33
statement of needs 7.23, 7.26
statement of significance 7.23, 7.26
stations of the cross, legality of 7.124
suffragan bishop
  appointment 4.65
  area of 4.65
  College of Canons, member of 8.13
  delegation of powers to 4.61
  diocesan pastoral committee member 4.65
  diocesan synod member 4.65
  functions 4.65
  General Synod member 2.14
  residence 4.65
  retirement 4.65
suicide, funeral after 5.52
surveyor, parish building 3.82
suspension of presentation
  bishop, by 4.23
  notice of 4.23, 4.24
  period of 4.24
  priest-in-charge during 4.32
  reason for 4.32
  sequestrators during 4.26
synodical government 2.10

tabernacle, legality of 7.124
team
  council 3.19
  ministry 4.47, 4.49, 4.51
telecommunications equipment licence 7.119
terrier: churchwardens' duties 3.54
thurible, legality of 7.124
timber, proceeds from sale of 7.128
tithe, effective abolition of system 3.84
tombstone *see* headstone
transferred episcopal arrangements 4.02
transubstantiation 5.19
tree
  faculty relating to 7.129
  guidance by chancellor 7.128
  jurisdiction over 7.128
  PCC maintains 7.128n
  preservation order 3.82
  timber, proceeds from sale of 7.128
tribunal
  disciplinary (clergy discipline)
    conduct of 6.39
    composition 6.09
    evidence 6.41, 6.42
    reference to 6.36
    witnesses 6.41
  vacancy in benefice inquiry, and 4.45
Trullo, Council of (692) 1.07
Twentieth Century Society
  national amenity society, as

unbaptised person: funeral 5.52
United Reformed Church
  ecclesiastical exemption applies to 7.06
  sharing of church buildings 3.95

vacancy in benefice *see* benefice
vacancy in see committee 4.57
verger
  appointment of 3.62
  employee, as 3.62
vesture
  holy communion, at 5.22
  PCC consultation on 3.29
vicar: style 4.17
vicar choral 8.27
vicar-general
  chancellor as 2.52
  court of
    disciplinary proceedings against bishop 2.52, 6.10, 6.12
    generally 2.52
    injunction against cathedral 2.52, 8.52

vicar-general (*cont.*)
  court of (*cont.*)
    restoration order against cathedral 2.52, 8.52, 8.53
    functions 2.52
    General Synod, on 2.16, 2.17, 2.19
    marriage licence, issues 2.52
    office of 2.52

Victorian Society
  national amenity society, as 7.18

visitation
  archdeacon's annual 2.57, 3.49, 7.15
  articles of inquiry on 3.49, 4.37
  bishop, by 4.37, 4.62, 8.16
  cathedral, of 8.16, 8.50–8.52, 8.54
  sick, of the 5.58

water stoup, holy, legality of 7.124
way, right of, over churchyard 7.94
window, stained glass, faculty for 7.122
women
  bishops 4.02, 4.03
  priests
    cathedral, in 8.34
    church, in 3.30, 3.31
    introduction of 4.01
    resolutions as to
      cathedral Chapter, by 8.34
      PCC, by 3.30, 3.31

worship
  care of places of 7.130–7.132
  church as local centre of 7.04